Geometric Formulas

Rectangle

Area: $A = \ell w$
Perimeter: $P = 2\ell + 2w$

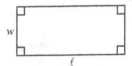

Square

Area: $A = s^2$
Perimeter: $P = 4s$

Parallelogram

Area: $A = bh$

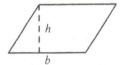

Trapezoid

Area: $A = \dfrac{1}{2}h(a + b)$

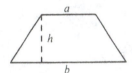

Triangle

Area: $A = \dfrac{1}{2}bh$

 or

Area: $A = \sqrt{s(s - a)(s - b)(s - c)}$,
where $s = \dfrac{1}{2}(a + b + c)$
Angle sum: $A + B + C = 180°$

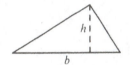

Right Triangle

Pythagorean theorem: $a^2 + b^2 = c^2$,

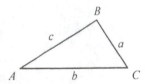

Circle

Area: $A = \pi r^2$
Circumference: $C = \pi d = 2\pi r$

SECOND EDITION

ALGEBRA & TRIGONOMETRY

FOR COLLEGE STUDENTS

DENNIS CHRISTY
Nassau Community College

ROBERT ROSENFELD

ELLEN BOTKIN
Nassau Community College

Custom Publishing

New York   Boston   San Francisco
London   Toronto   Sydney   Tokyo   Singapore   Madrid
Mexico City   Munich   Paris   Cape Town   Hong Kong   Montreal

2008360962

MH/JW

Pearson
Custom Publishing
is a division of

www.pearsonhighered.com

ISBN 10: 0-558-05803-5
ISBN 13: 978-0-558-05803-6

49 2020

Contents

Chapter 6
Radicals and Complex Numbers

Chapter 7
Second-Degree Equations in One and Two Variables

Chapter 8
Exponential and Logarithmic Functions

Chapter 9
Topics in Trigonometry

Chapter 10
Sequences, Series, and the Binomial Theorem

Chapter 11
Polynomial and Rational Functions

Preface

Audience

This book is intended for a college algebra and trigonometry course that incorporates a review of intermediate algebra, or for an extended intermediate algebra course that adds topics in college algebra and trigonometry. Throughout the text, two key principles are applied to make the material less abstract to the student.

1. Topics are developed in the context of meaningful problems by first illustrating an application for a topic before exploring the specifics of the mathematics that is involved.
2. Topics are reinforced with graphical and numerical examples so that the student will understand a topic from algebraic, geometric, and numeric viewpoints.

The presentation assumes that the student has completed a course in beginning algebra. However, a detailed review of all necessary ideas is given early in the text so that students whose basic skills need improvement have a wealth of helpful material.

Unique Goal

Texts published previously under a variety of titles in algebra and trigonometry are the basis for this book. The unique goal is to provide expanded coverage of the introductory topics in algebra and trigonometry while reducing or omitting coverage of some of the advanced topics. For instance, operations on fractional expressions receive three sections of coverage, but mathematical induction and polar coordinates are not covered at all. This approach should help to ensure proficiency in the essentials that are needed to advance to higher level mathematics.

Spiral Organization

This text is not a standard algebra text with trigonometry chapters tacked onto the end. Instead, a spiral organization is used to provide a truly integrated approach to algebra and trigonometry. After Chapter 1 reviews basic algebra, the text provides an introduction to functions, graphs, systems of equations, and trigonometry in Chapters 2, 3, and 4. The early introduction of these topics allows the student to take advantage of modern technology and develop multiple problem-solving strategies. Now, when Chapter 5 develops further algebraic techniques it is possible to show that algebraic and trigonometric expressions are factored and combined in analogous ways, and this insight is especially helpful in preparation for trigonometric identities. When a variety of equations and inequalities are solved algebraically in Chapters 5 to 7, a solution can now be pictured as an intersection of two graphs and confirmed with a Solver feature.

At Chapter 7 the text spirals back to a relations theme and considers second degree equations in one and two variables (Chapter 7), exponential and logarithmic functions (Chapter 8), more advanced topics concerning the trigonometric functions (Chapter 9), sequence functions (Chapter 10), and polynomial and rational functions (Chapter 11).

General Changes in the New Edition

- The title of the text is changed from *Essentials of Algebra and Trigonometry* to *Algebra and Trigonometry for College Students*. The new title is more consistent with the classifications used by publishers in their precalculus and developmental mathematics lists for a bridge text between college algebra and intermediate algebra.
- A complete chapter has been added on topics associated with polynomial and rational functions.
- The design of the text has been changed in many significant ways to make the text more readable.
- The text-specific website for students has been expanded to include additional exercises and quiz questions.

Features

This book is written with the belief that current textbooks must provide a balanced approach to learning algebra and trigonometry, which incorporates many of the changes recommended by various reform programs, while maintaining the sound pedagogical features that have proven to be effective in traditional texts. The former is needed so that students can make the transition in higher level math to a "conceptual approach", while the latter is needed so that students can develop basic skills. Following are a description of some feature highlights that are used to achieve the desired balance between concepts and skills.

- **Section Openers** In the spirit of problem-solving each section opens with a motivational problem that is later solved as an example problem.
- **Section Objectives** The specific objectives of each section are listed to help students focus on the basic goals of the section.
- **Titled Examples** Each example problem is titled so that students can quickly see the point of the example.
- **Progress Check Exercises** Each example problem has an associated Progress Check exercise, so that students can obtain immediate feedback of their understanding of the concept being discussed.
- **Applications** Application problems are included in the examples and exercise sets of every section. The text contains many varied and realistic applications, including numerous problems that are based on real data.
- **Calculator Use** The text encourages the use of graphing calculators and discusses how they can be used effectively throughout the examples and the exercises. In many instances, a Technology Link segment is used to enhance an example problem and show a solution from a different viewpoint.
- **"THINK ABOUT IT" EXERCISES** Each exercise set is followed immediately by a set of "Think About It" exercises. Although some of these problems are challenging, this section is not intended as a set of "mind bogglers." Instead, the goal is to help students develop critical-thinking skills by asking them to create their own examples, express concepts in their own words, extend ideas covered in the section, and analyze topics slightly out of the mainstream. These exercises are an excellent source of nontemplate problems and problems that can be assigned for group work.

For the Instructor

Instructor's Manual This manual contains the answers to the even-numbered problems in the text, as well as answers to all of the Think About It problems.

Computerized Test Generator Contact your Pearson representative for a detailed description.

Course Management and Testing System Contact your Pearson representative for a detailed description.

Acknowledgments

A project of this magnitude is a team effort that develops over many years with the input of many talented people. We are indebted to all who contributed. In particular, we wish to thank Stephen Majewicz, Kingsborough Community College; Sandra Peskin, Queensborough Community College; David Rothchild, Lehman College; Marisa Raffaele, Kimberly Yuster, Kelly Forsberg, Jessica McCarty, Marika Horstik, Pearson Publishing. Finally, but most important, we thank our spouses, Margaret, Leda, and Dave. They have given that special help and understanding only they could provide.

Dennis Christy
Robert Rosenfeld
Ellen Botkin

CHAPTER 1

Basic Algebra

TIAA-CREF is one of the nation's largest pension programs for college educators. Each participant receives a yearly benefits report that shows the total accumulation in his or her account, with various illustrations of first-year retirement income at age 65. One set of illustrations assumes that no additional premiums are paid and shows hypothetical rates of return until retirement of 3 percent, 6 percent, 9 percent, and 12 percent. Use these assumptions and find the hypothetical retirement accumulations at age 65 for a teacher whose accumulation at age 55 is \$312,573, by evaluating

$$312{,}573(1 + r)^{10}$$

where r equals 0.03, 0.06, 0.09, and 0.12. If your calculator has a Last Entry button, then use this feature to simplify the computation. (See Example 15 of Section 1.1).
Source: TIAA-CREF Annuity Benefits Report, January 2009

A common student lament goes something like, "I understand the new concepts, but the algebra is killing me!" In this chapter, we hope to remedy this problem by reviewing *in detail* some basic rules in algebra about real numbers, exponents, and first-degree equations and inequalities. We then expand the algebra review in Chapters 5 to 7 to include factoring, fractions, radicals, and a wide variety of equations and inequalities. Success in these algebra chapters will go a long way toward ensuring success in this course and in higher mathematics.

In this text we take a problem-solving approach which emphasizes that one learns mathematics by *doing* mathematics, while *thinking* mathematically. That is, you need to actively work through the problems (with pencil and paper), while *focusing on the definitions, relationships, and procedures* that link together all steps in the solution. In this spirit of problem solving we open each section with a problem. Most are applications, some are puzzles, and a few are proofs. Taken together, they illustrate the varied nature of problem solving. Since none of them requires a lot of sophisticated mathematics, we hope you will take a stab at an answer either initially or after covering the relevant section in the text.

Courtesy of PhotoDisc/Getty Images

1.1 Real Numbers

OBJECTIVES

1 Graph real numbers.

2 Identify integers, rational numbers, irrational numbers, and real numbers.

3 Identify the properties of real numbers.

4 Order real numbers and use inequality symbols.

5 Find the absolute value of a real number and operate on real numbers.

6 Evaluate numeric expressions on a graphing calculator.

In algebra numerical relations are studied in a more general way by using symbols (such as x) that may be replaced by a number from some collection of numbers. Unless stated otherwise, it is assumed that a symbol like x may be replaced by any real number. Consequently, the rules that govern real numbers determine the procedures in algebra. A good way to describe real numbers is to interpret them geometrically by considering the number line in Figure 1.1. Every point on this line corresponds to a real number, and every real number corresponds to a point on this line. Therefore, this line is called the **real number line,** or simply the number line, and may be used to define a real number.

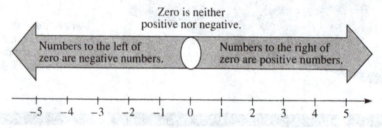

Figure 1.1

Real Number

A real number is a number that can be represented as a point on the number line.

The point on the number line corresponding to a number is called the **graph** of the number. A type of real number that is easy to graph is called an **integer.** The set* of integers is given by

$$\{\dots, -4, -3, -2, -1, 0, 1, 2, 3, 4, \dots\},$$

$$\underbrace{}_{\text{negative integers}} \quad \underbrace{}_{\text{positive integers}}$$

where the three dots ... called an **ellipsis** mean "and so on." As with all positive numbers, note that we customarily omit the sign on positive integers, so $+1 = 1$, $+2 = 2$, and so on.

*A **set** is simply a collection of objects, and we may describe a set by listing the objects or elements of the collection within braces.

EXAMPLE 1   Graphing Integers

Graph the integers 5, 0, and −3 on the number line.

Solution   Place dots on the number line at 5, 0, and −3, as shown in Figure 1.2, to graph the given integers.

Figure 1.2

PROGRESS CHECK 1   Graph the integers −2, 7, and 0 on the number line.   ■

Rational numbers and irrational numbers fill in the gaps on the number line between the integers. A number that can be written as a fraction with an integer in the numerator and a *nonzero* integer in the denominator is called a **rational number.** Using set-builder notation,* the set of rational numbers is given by

$$\left\{ \frac{p}{q} \colon p \text{ and } q \text{ are integers, } q \text{ not equal to } 0 \right\}.$$

Some examples of rational numbers are

$$\frac{4}{5}, \quad \frac{-2}{3}, \quad \frac{2}{-7}, \quad \frac{0}{6}, \quad 2.7 \left(\text{or } \frac{27}{10} \right), \quad \text{and} \quad 5 \left(\text{or } \frac{5}{1} \right).$$

Note that all integers are rational numbers, because each integer can be written with a denominator of 1. For instance,

$$5 = \frac{5}{1}, \quad -3 = \frac{-3}{1}, \quad \text{and} \quad 0 = \frac{0}{1}.$$

Also, when a rational number is written in decimal form, it can be shown that the decimal must either terminate or be a repeating decimal. In the examples that follow, a bar is placed above the portion of any decimals that repeat.

Rational Number	Decimal Form	Classification
$\dfrac{1}{2}$	0.5	Terminating decimal
$\dfrac{9}{8}$	1.125	Terminating decimal
$\dfrac{1}{3}$	$0.3333\ldots = 0.\overline{3}$	Repeating decimal
$\dfrac{200}{99}$	$2.0202\ldots = 2.\overline{02}$	Repeating decimal

Real numbers that are not rational numbers are called **irrational numbers.** Such numbers in decimal form are neither terminating nor repeating decimals. Some examples of irrational numbers with their approximate decimal forms are

$$\sqrt{2} = 1.41421\ldots, \quad \sqrt{3} = 1.73205\ldots, \quad \text{and} \quad \pi = 3.14159\ldots.$$

*__Set-builder notation__ writes sets in the form $\{x : x \text{ has property } P\}$, which is read, "the set of all elements x such that x has property P." The colon: is read "such that."

For many purposes, an irrational number like π (pi) may be approximated by rational numbers. Two well-known approximations for π are 3.14 and $\frac{22}{7}$. Example 2 shows how to graph rational numbers and irrational numbers.

EXAMPLE 2   Graphing Rational and Irrational Numbers

Graph the following numbers on the number line.

a. $-\frac{3}{4}$ **b.** $\sqrt{3}$

Solution   See Figure 1.3.

Figure 1.3

a. To graph the rational number $-\frac{3}{4}$, divide the line segment from 0 to -1 into four equal parts, and then place a dot on the third slash mark to the left of 0.
b. We approximate the graphs of irrational numbers like $\sqrt{3}$. By calculator, obtain an approximate value for $\sqrt{3}$. The symbol $\approx$ means "approximately equal."

$$\sqrt{3} \approx 1.732050808$$

Because $\sqrt{3}$ is slightly more than 1.7, divide the segment from 1 to 2 into ten equal parts, and then place a dot slightly to the right of the seventh slash mark.

Note   In practice it is usually sufficient to give a rough estimate of the graph of the types of numbers in this example.

PROGRESS CHECK 2   Graph the following numbers on the number line.

a. $-\frac{5}{3}$ **b.** $\sqrt{2}$ ▪

Real numbers, integers, rational numbers, and irrational numbers have been defined in this section. Depending on the use of the number, the distinction between these types of numbers may be important. Figure 1.4 summarizes these definitions and shows the relationships among the various sets of numbers. In set theory, when every element in set A is an element in set B, then A is called a **subset** of B. Note that all of the sets that have been discussed are subsets of the real numbers.

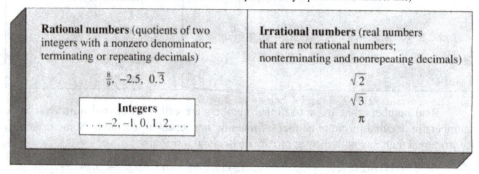

Figure 1.4

EXAMPLE 3   Classifying Numbers

For each number, select all correct classifications from the following categories: real number, irrational number, rational number, integer, or none of these.

a. $\sqrt{225}$ **b.** $\sqrt{-4}$ **c.** $0.505005\ldots$ **d.** $\dfrac{22}{7}$

Solution

a. Since $\sqrt{225} = 15$, the number $\sqrt{225}$ is an integer, a rational number, and a real number. Note from the diagram in Figure 1.4 that any integer is automatically a rational number and a real number.

b. No real number is the square root of a negative number, such as -4, because the product of two equal real numbers is never negative. Thus, $\sqrt{-4}$ belongs to none of the listed categories of numbers.

c. The number $0.505005\ldots$ is a nonrepeating decimal. Therefore, it is an irrational number and a real number.

d. The number 22/7 is a ratio of two integers (not involving division by zero), so it is a rational number and a real number. Because 22/7 is a common approximation for π, some students mistakenly think that 22/7 is irrational. It is often useful to write rational number approximations for irrational numbers, but it is important to keep in mind the difference between them.

Technology Link

In part **a** of Example 3, a calculator can be used to determine that $\sqrt{225}$ equals 15, to help classify $\sqrt{225}$, but there are limitations to this calculator method. For instance, $\sqrt{3.6101520016}$ is rational, but $\sqrt{3.6101520017}$ is not, and many calculators cannot distinguish them. In part **b** try computing $\sqrt{-4}$ on your calculator to see if an error message results. In Section 6.6 we will extend the number system beyond real numbers to complex numbers, which will enable us to work with square roots of negative numbers. If your calculator returns (0, 2) or $2i$ for $\sqrt{-4}$, then it is programmed to output complex number results.

PROGRESS CHECK 3   For each number select all correct classifications from the following categories: real number, irrational number, rational number, integer, or none of these.

a. $\sqrt{-7}$ **b.** $-\sqrt{7}$ **c.** 3.14   **d.** 5   ■

We now list the most important properties of the real numbers with respect to addition and multiplication. These properties are the basis for the justification of many algebraic manipulations.

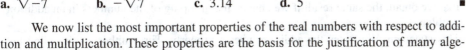

Properties of the Real Numbers

Let a, b, and c be real numbers.

	Addition	**Multiplication**
Closure Properties	$a + b$ is a unique real number	ab is a unique real number
Commutative Properties	$a + b = b + a$	$ab = ba$
Associative Properties	$(a + b) + c = a + (b + c)$	$(ab)c = a(bc)$
Identity Properties	There exists a unique real number 0 such that $a + 0 = 0 + a = a$	There exists a unique real number 1 such that $a \cdot 1 = 1 \cdot a = a$
Inverse Properties	For every real number a, there is a unique real number, denoted by $-a$, such that $a + (-a) = (-a) + a = 0$	For every real number a except zero, there is a unique real number, denoted by $1/a$, such that $a \cdot 1/a = 1/a \cdot a = 1$
Distributive Properties	$a(b + c) = ab + ac$ $(a + b)c = ac + bc$	

EXAMPLE 4   Naming Properties of Real Numbers

Name the property of real numbers illustrated in each statement.

a. $(2 + 3) + 4 = 2 + (3 + 4)$ **b.** $5 + (-5) = 0$
c. $2(x + 4) = 2 \cdot x + 2 \cdot 4$ **d.** $0 \cdot x = x \cdot 0$

Solution

a. This statement illustrates the associative property of addition. This property indicates that we obtain the same result if we change the grouping of the numbers in an addition problem.
b. This statement illustrates the addition inverse property. The number $-a$ is called the **opposite** or **additive inverse** of a. Note that there is a difference between a negative number and the opposite of a number. Although -5 is a negative number, the opposite of -5 is 5.
c. This statement illustrates the distributive property (or more technically, the distributive property of multiplication over addition).
d. This statement illustrates the commutative property of multiplication. This property indicates that the order in which we write numbers in a multiplication problem does not affect their product.

PROGRESS CHECK 4   Name the property of real numbers illustrated in each statement.

a. $5\left(\dfrac{1}{5}\right) = 1$ **b.** $(a + b)(a - b) = (a - b)(a + b)$

c. $-1(2x) = (-1 \cdot 2)x$ **d.** $-1(x + 2) = (-1)(x) + (-1)(2)$ ■

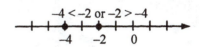

Figure 1.5

An important property of real numbers is that they can be put in numerical order. The **trichotomy property** states that if a and b are real numbers, then either a is less than b, a is greater than b, or a equals b. By definition, a is **less than** b, written $a < b$, if and only if $b - a$ is positive; a is **greater than** b, written $a > b$, if and only if $a - b$ is positive. We also define $a \leq b$ (read "a is **less than or equal to** b") to mean $a < b$ or $a = b$. Alternately, we can write $b \geq a$ and say that b is **greater than or equal to** a. Relations of "less than" and "greater than" can be seen very easily on the number line, as shown in Figure 1.5. The point representing the larger number will be to the right of the point representing the smaller number. (*Note:* The definitions use the phrase "if and only if." This phrase is commonly used in mathematical definitions and theorems, and the statement "*p* **if and only if** *q*" means "if p then q, and conversely, if q then p.")

EXAMPLE 5   Graphing and Ordering Real Numbers

Insert the property symbol ($<$, $>$, or $=$) to indicate the correct order.

a. -1 ____ -3 **b.** -3 ____ $\sqrt{2}$ **c.** $-\sqrt{9}$ ____ -3

Solution   The given numbers are graphed in Figure 1.6

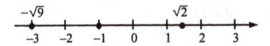

Figure 1.6

a. -1 is greater than -3, written $-1 > -3$, because -1 is to the right of -3 on the number line.

b. $-3 < \sqrt{2}$ because -3 is graphed to the left of $\sqrt{2}$. In general, any negative number is less than any positive number.

c. $-\sqrt{9} = -3$ since both numerals represent the same number.

PROGRESS CHECK 5   Insert the proper symbol ($<$, $>$, $=$) to indicate the correct order.

a. -2 ____ 0 **b.** $\dfrac{2}{3}$ ____ $\dfrac{6}{9}$ **c.** $-\sqrt{2}$ ____ $-\sqrt{5}$ ■

The **absolute value** of a real number a, denoted $|a|$, is the distance between a and 0 on the number line. For instance, $|2| = 2$, and $|-2| = 2$, as shown in Figure 1.7. The geometric interpretation of absolute value may be translated to the following algebraic rule.

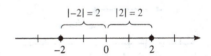

Figure 1.7

Absolute Value

For any real number a,

$$|a| = a, \quad \text{if } a \geq 0,$$

$$|a| = -a, \quad \text{if } a < 0.$$

To illustrate this definition, note from Figure 1.7 that $|-2| = 2$. This result is obtained using the algebraic rule as follows: Because -2 is less than 0, use the formula $|a| = -a$; replacing a by -2 gives $|-2| = -(-2) = 2$. From both a geometric and an algebraic perspective, note that the absolute value of a number is never negative.

EXAMPLE 6   Evaluating Absolute Value Expressions

Evaluate each expression.

a. $|2.4|$ **b.** $\left|-\frac{1}{2}\right|$ **c.** $-\left|-\frac{1}{2}\right|$

Solution

a. Figure 1.8 shows $|2.4| = 2.4$. Algebraically, 2.4 is greater than 0, so $|a| = a$ yields $|2.4| = 2.4$.

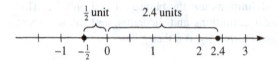

Figure 1.8

b. Figure 1.8 shows $\left|-\frac{1}{2}\right| = \frac{1}{2}$. Algebraically, $-\frac{1}{2}$ is less than 0, so $|a| = -a$ yields $\left|-\frac{1}{2}\right| = -\left(-\frac{1}{2}\right) = \frac{1}{2}$.

c. Because $\left|-\frac{1}{2}\right| = \frac{1}{2}$,

$$-\left|-\frac{1}{2}\right| = -\left(\frac{1}{2}\right) = -\frac{1}{2}.$$

PROGRESS CHECK 6   Evaluate each expression.

a. $|-\sqrt{2}|$ **b.** $-|-5|$ **c.** $|0|$ ■

Addition

Addition of two real numbers may be interpreted as movement on the number line. The initial starting point is zero. To add a positive number, we draw an arrow to the right the desired distance. To add a negative number, we draw an arrow to the left. Consider Figure 1.9, which illustrates the procedure. The sum $2 + (-4)$ is shown on the real number line by drawing an arrow with a length of 2 units, starting at zero and pointing to the right. From the tip of the arrow at 2 we draw an arrow pointing to the left with a length of 4 units. Since the tip of the second arrow is at -2, we conclude that $2 + (-4) = -2$. As another example, the diagram in Figure 1.10 may be used to show geometrically that $-2 + (-4) = -6$.

    The number line method will help you to envision the addition of real numbers, but it is not an efficient computational method. Instead, the concept of absolute value may be used to add real numbers, as described next. Observe that the two methods are in agreement with the number line procedure, since the lengths of the arrows are given by the absolute values of the numbers.

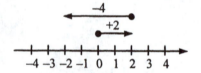

Figure 1.9

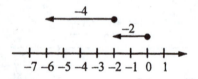

Figure 1.10

Adding Real Numbers

Like Signs To add two real numbers with the same sign, add their absolute values and attach the common sign.

Unlike Signs To add two real numbers with different signs, subtract the smaller absolute value from the larger and attach the sign of the number with the larger absolute value.

EXAMPLE 7   Adding Real Numbers

Find each sum.

a. $-9 + (-18)$

b. $-7 + 52$

c. $-\dfrac{5}{7} + \dfrac{1}{7}$

Solution

a. $-9 + (-18) = -27$ *Think:* $|-9| = 9, |-18| = 18, 9 + 18 = 27$, and the common sign is negative.

b. $-7 + 52 = 45$ *Think:* $|-7| = 7, |52| = 52, 52 - 7 = 45$, and the positive number 52 has the larger absolute value.

c. $-\dfrac{5}{7} + \dfrac{1}{7} = -\dfrac{4}{7}$ *Think:* $\left|-\dfrac{5}{7}\right| = \dfrac{5}{7}, \left|\dfrac{1}{7}\right| = \dfrac{1}{7}, \dfrac{5}{7} - \dfrac{1}{7} = \dfrac{4}{7}$, and the negative number $-\dfrac{5}{7}$ has the larger absolute value.

PROGRESS CHECK 7   Find each sum.

a. $-25 + (-19)$ **b.** $\dfrac{7}{9} + \left(-\dfrac{2}{9}\right)$ **c.** $-18 + 10$ ■

Subtraction

We define subtraction in terms of addition. If a and b are any real numbers, then

$$a - b = a + (-b)$$

To subtract b from a, we add to a the negative of b.

EXAMPLE 8   Subtracting Real Numbers

Find each difference.

a. $-5 - 2$ **b.** $5 - \left(-\dfrac{1}{2}\right)$ **c.** $-4.4 - (-1.5)$

Solution   Subtract by converting to addition.

a. $-5 - 2 = -5 + (-2) = -7$ **b.** $5 - \left(-\dfrac{1}{2}\right) = 5 + \dfrac{1}{2} = \dfrac{10}{2} + \dfrac{1}{2} = \dfrac{11}{2}$

c. $-4.4 - (-1.5) = -4.4 + 1.5 = -2.9$

PROGRESS CHECK 8   Find each difference.

a. $3 - 7$ **b.** $-9 - \left(-\dfrac{5}{9}\right)$ **c.** $1.8 - (-1.8)$ ■

Multiplication

It seems natural to define the product of two positive numbers as positive. Thus, $4 \cdot 3 = 12$. To determine what sign to use for the product of a positive number and a negative number, we use the distributive property.

$$5[2 + (-2)] = 5 \cdot 2 + 5(-2)$$
$$5 \cdot 0 = 10 + 5(-2)$$
$$0 = 10 + ?$$

We must define $5(-2)$ so that $10 + 5(-2) = 0$. Therefore, $5(-2)$ must equal -10. In every case the product of a positive number and a negative number is negative.

To determine the sign of the product of two negative numbers, consider this problem.

$$-5[2 + (-2)] = (-5)2 + (-5)(-2)$$

$$(-5)0 = -10 + (-5)(-2)$$

$$0 = -10 + ?$$

We must define $(-5)(-2)$ so that $-10 + (-5)(-2) = 0$. Therefore, $(-5)(-2)$ must equal 10. In every case the product of two negative numbers is positive.

Since multiplication and division of real numbers are related in that

$$(-5)(-2) = 10 \text{ implies } \frac{10}{-5} = -2 \text{ or } \frac{10}{-2} = -5$$

the sign rules just determined also apply to quotients. The above examples suggest the following procedures:

Products and Quotients of Nonzero Real Numbers

Same Sign: To multiply (or divide) two real numbers with the same sign, multiply (or divide) their absolute values, and make the sign of the product (or quotient) positive.

Different Signs: To multiply (or divide) two real numbers with different signs, multiply (or divide) their absolute values, and make the sign of the product (or quotient) negative.

EXAMPLE 9   Multiplying and Dividing Real Numbers

Find each product or quotient.

a. $(-6)(-9)$ **b.** $\dfrac{-12.6}{3}$ **c.** $(-4)(-4)(-4)$

Solution

a. $(-6)(-9) = 54$ *Think:* $6 \cdot 9 = 54$ and the sign of the product is positive.

b. $\dfrac{-12.6}{3} = -4.2$ *Think:* $\dfrac{12.6}{3} = 4.2$ and the sign of the quotient is negative.

c. $(-4)(-4)(-4) = -64$ *Think:* $4 \cdot 4 \cdot 4 = 64$ and the sign of the product is negative.

PROGRESS CHECK 9   Find each product or quotient.

a. $(-8)(7)$ **b.** $\dfrac{-70.5}{-5}$ **c.** $(-3)(-3)(-3)(-3)$ ■

If two or more numbers are multiplied together, each number is a **factor** of the product. In Example 9c the factor -4 is used three times. An alternate way of writing $(-4)(-4)(-4)$ is $(-4)^3$. The number $(-4)^3$, or -64, is called the third **power** of -4. In general, by a^n, where n is a positive integer, we mean to use a as a factor n times.

$$a^n = \underbrace{a \cdot a \cdot a \ldots a}_{n \text{ factors}}$$

In the expression a^n, n is called the **exponent,** and a is called the **base.** When a product contains many factors the following sign rule is helpful.

Sign Rule

A product of nonzero factors is positive if the number of negative factors is even. The product is negative if the number of negative factors is odd.

EXAMPLE 10   Evaluating a Power

Multiply

a. $(-3)^5$ b. $(-2)^4$ c. -2^4

Solution

a. $(-3)^5 = -243$ *Think:* $3^5 = 243$ and the sign of the product is negative because there are an odd number of negative factors.

b. $(-2)^4 = 16$ *Think:* $2^4 = 16$ and the sign of the product is positive because there are an even number of negative factors.

c. $-2^4 = -16$ *Think:* $2^4 = 16$ and the negative of 2^4 is -16.

Caution   In this example, note the difference in meaning of $(-2)^4$ and -2^4. The expression $(-2)^4$ denotes the fourth power of -2, while -2^4 denotes the negative of 2^4.

PROGRESS CHECK 10   Multiply

a. $(-5)^3$ b. -2^6 c. $(-2)^6$ ■

Multiplication and division involving the number 0 merit special consideration. First, the product of any number and zero is zero, so

$$a \cdot 0 = 0 \cdot a = 0$$

for any real number a. To illustrate the possible outcomes for a quotient involving zero, consider the cases of 0/2, 2/0, and 0/0.

$\dfrac{0}{2} = 0$ because $0 = 2 \cdot 0$.

$\dfrac{2}{0}$ is undefined because no number times 0 is 2.

$\dfrac{0}{0}$ is undefined because any number times 0 is 0.

These examples illustrate the two rules we will use for a division involving 0.

Division Involving 0

1. 0 divided by any nonzero number is 0.
2. Division by 0 is undefined.

EXAMPLE 11   Multiplying or Dividing with 0

Find each product or quotient.

a. $0(-2)$ b. $\dfrac{0}{-2}$ c. $\dfrac{-2}{0}$ d. $\dfrac{-2(0)}{-2 + 2}$

Solution

a. $0(-2) = 0$ *Think:* The product of 0 and any nonzero number is 0.

b. $\dfrac{0}{-2} = 0$ *Think:* 0 divided by any nonzero number is 0.

c. $\dfrac{-2}{0}$ is undefined.   *Think:* Division by 0 is undefined.

d. $\dfrac{-2(0)}{-2+2} = \dfrac{0}{0}$, which is undefined because division by 0 is undefined.

PROGRESS CHECK 11   Find each product or quotient.

a. $0 \div 0$ **b.** $0(0)$ **c.** $5/0$ **d.** $\dfrac{5 + (-5)}{-5}$ ■

When the product of two numbers is 1, then the numbers are called **reciprocals** of each other. The reciprocal of the nonzero number a is $1/a$, and the reciprocal of the nonzero fraction a/b is b/a. Using the concept of a reciprocal, division may be defined in terms of multiplication as follows.

> **Definition of Division**
>
> If a and b are real numbers with $b \neq 0$, then
> $$a \div b = a \cdot \frac{1}{b}$$

To divide a by b, we multiply a by the reciprocal of b.

EXAMPLE 12   Dividing by Using Reciprocals

Divide using the reciprocal definition of division.

a. $35 \div (-5)$ **b.** $\left(-\dfrac{7}{18}\right) \div \left(-\dfrac{4}{3}\right)$

Solution

a. $35 \div (-5) = 35\left(-\dfrac{1}{5}\right) = -7$ *Think:* Product of 35 and the reciprocal of -5.

b. $\left(-\dfrac{7}{18}\right) \div \left(-\dfrac{4}{3}\right) = \left(-\dfrac{7}{18}\right) \cdot \left(-\dfrac{3}{4}\right) = \dfrac{7}{24}$ *Think:* Product of $-\dfrac{7}{18}$ and the reciprocal of $-\dfrac{4}{3}$.

PROGRESS CHECK 12   Divide using the reciprocal definition of division.

a. $(-54) \div (-9)$ **b.** $\left(-\dfrac{7}{3}\right) \div \left(\dfrac{11}{9}\right)$ ■

Without a priority for performing operations, different values may be possible for an expression involving more than one operation. To avoid this uncertainty, use this agreed-upon order of operations.

Order of Operations

1. Perform all operations within grouping symbols, such as parentheses, first. If there is more than one symbol of grouping, simplify the innermost symbol of grouping first, and simplify the numerator and denominator of a fraction separately.
2. Evaluate powers of a number.
3. Multiply or divide working from left to right.
4. Add or subtract working from left to right.

EXAMPLE 13   Using the Order of Operations

Evaluate $1 + 7(2 - 5)^2$.

Solution   Follow the order of operations given above.

$$1 + 7(2 - 5)^2 = 1 + 7(-3)^2 \quad \textit{Think: Operate within parentheses.}$$
$$= 1 + 7(9) \quad \textit{Think: Evaluate powers.}$$
$$= 1 + 63 \quad \textit{Think: Multiply.}$$
$$= 64 \quad \textit{Think: Add.}$$

PROGRESS CHECK 13   Evaluate $8 - 5(6 - 10)^2$.   ■

Calculator Computation

A graphing calculator has three distinct capabilities useful in this course.

1. It can do numeric calculations.
2. It can display graphs.
3. It is programmable.

At this time we focus on some of the more frequently used features for numeric calculations. You should learn to use these features on your own calculator.

a. The subtraction key is different from the key for making a negative sign.

b. There is a special key, usually marked $\boxed{\wedge}$, for raising numbers to powers. For example, 3^5 is entered as 3 $\boxed{\wedge}$ 5. Special keys may be used for squaring $[x^2]$, finding square roots $\left[\boxed{\sqrt{}}\right]$, and computing reciprocals $[x^{-1}]$.

c. There is usually a menu choice called **abs** for finding the absolute value of a number.

d. There is usually a key marked $\boxed{\text{ANS}}$, which will reproduce the last answer.

e. There is usually a feature for converting decimal results (within certain limits) to fractions.

f. In some expressions multiplication is implied, which means that it is not always necessary to enter a multiplication symbol.

g. There are special keys for parentheses. Proper use of parentheses is crucial for correct evaluation of expressions.

h. There is a way to reproduce and edit the last line that was entered. This allows you to make slight changes easily without having to enter the entire expression again. In this editing procedure, you will often use keys marked $\boxed{\text{DEL}}$ (for delete) and $\boxed{\text{INS}}$ (for insert).

EXAMPLE 14   Using Parentheses to Evaluate Expressions

Evaluate on a graphing calculator.

a. $\dfrac{3 - (-5)}{-1 - 2}$

b. $\sqrt{8^2 + 15^2}$

Solution   A calculator display for these evaluations is shown in Figure 1.11.

a. Group the numerator and denominator in parentheses because the given problem may be expressed as $[3 - (-5)]/(-1 - 2)$. Note that parentheses are not needed around -5, and note that the subtraction sign and the negative sign look different from one another on your calculator. The resulting decimal display is an approximate answer. The next line on the screen shows the result of converting the answer to fractional form. Thus, the exact value of the expression is $-8/3$.

b. Use the square root key and group the sum in parentheses. The resulting display shows $\sqrt{8^2 + 15^2} = 17$.

PROGRESS CHECK 14   Evaluate on a graphing calculator.

a. $\dfrac{3 - (-1)}{-5 - 2}$

b. $|4 - 3^2|$ ■

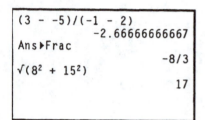

Figure 1.11

```
(3 - -5)/(-1 - 2)
            -2.66666666667
Ans▶Frac
                      -8/3
√(8² + 15²)
                        17
```

EXAMPLE 15   Using Varying Return Rates in an Annuity Benefits Report

Solve the problem in the Chapter introduction on page 1.

Solution   In the given expression, replace r with 0.03 and determine

$$312{,}573(1 + 0.03)^{10} \approx 420{,}071.97$$

as shown in the first two lines of Figure 1.12. Note that a tenth power was determined by using the power key $\boxed{\wedge}$ and that the multiplication symbol is not needed in front of the left parenthesis.

For the next calculation, since only the value of r changes, you can reproduce the original entry and edit it to change the .03 to .06. Then you press ENTER to get the new answer. You can repeat this procedure for $r = 0.09$ and $r = 0.12$ also. These steps give

$$312{,}573(1 + 0.06)^{10} \approx 559{,}770.64$$

$$312{,}573(1 + 0.09)^{10} \approx 739{,}973.97$$

$$312{,}573(1 + 0.12)^{10} \approx 970{,}804.29.$$

Observe that the total accumulation varies significantly as the rate of return increases in increments of 3 percent, and that the difference associated with each 3 percent increase is getting larger.

PROGRESS CHECK 15   Redo the problem in Example 15 assuming that the teacher has accumulated \$97,018 at age 35. You must evaluate $97{,}018(1 + r)^{30}$ where r equals 0.03, 0.06, 0.09, and 0.12.   ■

```
312573(1+.03)^10
           420071.974441
312573(1+.06)^10
           559770.637052
312573(1+.09)^10
           739973.965858
312573(1+.12)^10
```

Figure 1.12

EXERCISES 1.1

In Exercises 1–10, graph the given numbers on the real number line. To indicate scale, label slash marks at 0 and 1 in each example, and draw other slashes as needed.

1. $4, 0, -2$

2. $-5, 0, 1$

3. $1, -2, 3$

4. $-2, 3, -4$

5. $\frac{1}{2}, \frac{1}{4}, 0$

6. $-\frac{1}{3}, -\frac{2}{3}, 0$

7. $\sqrt{2}, \sqrt{4}, \sqrt{8}$

8. $-\sqrt{5}, -\sqrt{10}, -\sqrt{15}$

9. $\pi, 2\pi, \frac{\pi}{2}$

10. $\sqrt{3}, \frac{\sqrt{3}}{2}, \frac{\sqrt{3}}{3}$

In Exercises 11–22 select all correct classifications from the following categories: real number, irrational number, rational number, integer, or none of these.

11. 0

12. $\frac{0}{3}$

13. $\frac{3}{0}$

14. $\frac{3}{4}$

15. -9

16. $\sqrt{9}$

17. $-\sqrt{9}$

18. $\sqrt{-9}$

19. $\sqrt{7}$

20. π

21. $0.\overline{01}$

22. $0.101001\ldots$

In Exercises 23–26, list all numbers in the given set that are in the following sets.

a. Integers

b. Rational numbers

c. Irrational numbers

d. Real numbers

23. $\left\{\frac{1}{2}, 3\frac{3}{4}, -0.1, \sqrt{9}\right\}$

24. $\left\{\frac{10}{2}, \frac{2}{10}, -\frac{4}{5}, -\frac{5}{4}, \frac{6}{6}\right\}$

25. $\left\{\sqrt{1}, \sqrt{2}, \sqrt{3}, \sqrt{4}, \sqrt{5}\right\}$

26. $\left\{-\frac{1}{2}, -\frac{2}{1}, \frac{\pi}{1}, 0\right\}$

In Exercises 27–30 answer true or false. If false, give a specific counterexample.

27. All rational numbers are integers.

28. All rational numbers are real numbers.

29. All real numbers are irrational numbers.

30. All integers are irrational numbers.

In Exercises 31–50 name the property illustrated in the statement.

31. $2 + 7 = 7 + 2$

32. $11 + 0 = 11$

33. $4(5 \cdot 11) = (4 \cdot 5)11$

34. $6(4 + 3) = 6 \cdot 4 + 6 \cdot 3$

35. $\sqrt{2} \cdot 1 = \sqrt{2}$

36. $-7.3 + 7.3 = 0$

37. $(2.5)3 = 3(2.5)$

38. $17\left(\frac{1}{17}\right) = 1$

39. $\pi \cdot 3 + \pi \cdot 8 = \pi(3 + 8)$

40. $(5 + 3) + (2 + 1) = [(5 + 3) + 2] + 1$

41. $z(xy) = (zx)y$

42. $(xy)z = z(xy)$

43. $x + 0 = 0 + x$

44. $(-z) + z = 0$

45. $y(z + x) = (z + x)y$

46. $y \cdot 1 = 1 \cdot y$

47. $x\left(\frac{1}{x}\right) = 1$ if $x \neq 0$

48. $ax + ay = a(x + y)$

49. $y + (x + z) = (x + z) + y$

50. $(x + z) + y = x + (z + y)$

In Exercises 51–60 use the proper symbol ($<$, $>$, or $=$) between the pairs of numbers to indicate their correct order.

51. -7 ____ 1

52. 42.8 ____ -91

53. $|14|$ ____ $|-16|$

54. $|1.46|$ ____ $|-1.46|$

55. -0.0001 ____ -0.00001

56. 0.0001 ____ 0.00001

57. $\sqrt{5}$ ____ $\sqrt{7}$

58. $-\sqrt{5}$ ____ $-\sqrt{7}$

59. π ____ 3.14

60. $\frac{1}{9}$ ____ $0.\overline{1}$

In Exercises 61–106, evaluate the given expression.

61. $|1.7|$

62. $|-2|$

63. $-|4|$

64. $-|-4|$

65. $(-4) + (-3)$

66. $43 + (-21)$

67. $(-6) - (-4)$

68. $(-12) - 5$

69. $\left(-\frac{1}{5}\right) + 3$

70. $7 - \left(-\frac{3}{8}\right)$

71. $(-0.87) + 0.33$

72. $0.17 - (-0.48)$

73. $(-0.1) - 4$

74. $(-3.3) + (-0.67)$

75. $(-11)6$

76. $(-8)(-3)$

77. $(-14) \div (-7)$

78. $89 \div (-89)$

79. $-\frac{1}{8} \div 4$

80. $\left(-\frac{2}{3}\right) \div \left(-\frac{4}{15}\right)$

81. $(-5)\left(-\frac{4}{9}\right)$

82. $\left(\frac{3}{16}\right)(-2)$

83. $0 \div (-4)$

84. $(-4) \div 0$

85. $0.2(-0.2)$

86. $(-0.64) \div (-0.16)$

87. $(-32.4) \div (-3)$

88. $10.1(-11)$

89. $(-2) \div (6 - 5)$

90. $(5 - 3)(5 + 2)$

91. $-4 + 2(3 - 8)$

92. $(-4 + 2)(3 - 8)$

93. $(2 - 4)(3 - 6)$

94. $2 - 4(3 - 6)$

95. $(-3)^3$

96. $(-2)^4$

97. -2^4

98. $-4 \cdot 5^2$

99. $2\left(-\frac{1}{2}\right)^5$

100. $1 + 2 \cdot 3^4$

101. $2 - 8(3 - 7)^2$

102. $(-5 + 2)^2 + (-2 - 6)^2$

103. $-5(11 - 6) - [7 - (11 - 19)]$

104. $7 - 3[2(13 - 5) - (5 - 13)]$

105. $3(2)(-1) + (-1)(-3)(2) + (6)(1)(-3)$ $- 6(2)(2) - 3(-3)(-3) - (-1)(1)(-1)$

106. $3[2(-1) - (-3)(-3)] - (-1)[1(-1) - (-3)(2)]$ $+ 6[1(-3) - 2(2)]$

In Exercises 107 and 108 use a calculator to evaluate the given expression. If your calculator can convert decimals to fractions, express any rational answers in fractional form.

107. a. $\frac{2 + 3}{5 - 1}$

b. $\sqrt{3^2 + 5}$

c. $\frac{-2 - (-8)}{1 + 3^2}$

d. $|5 - 4^2|$

108. a. $\frac{-3 - 1}{4 + 5}$

b. $\sqrt{5^2 - 4^2}$

c. $\frac{22 - 8}{(1 + 3)^2}$

d. $|5| - |-4|^2$

109. Evaluate $\left(1 + \frac{1}{n}\right)^n$ for $n = 1, 10, 100, 1{,}000,$ and $10{,}000$.

110. Evaluate $\left(1 + \frac{2}{t}\right)^t$ for $t = 2, 20, 200, 2{,}000,$ and $20{,}000$.

111. If \$2000 is deposited in a bank account when a baby is born, then its value 21 years later is given by $2000(1 + r)^{21}$ where r is the annual interest rate. Evaluate the expression for $r = 0.03, 0.06,$ and 0.09.

112. If \$100 is deposited at the end of every month in a savings account that pays monthly interest, then the value of the account after 240 deposits (20 years) is given by $100\left[\dfrac{(1 + (r/12))^{240} - 1}{r/12}\right]$. Evaluate this expression for $r = 0.03, 0.06,$ and 0.09.

113. A glass vase has a temperature of 2,000 degrees Fahrenheit when it is removed from the glassblower's furnace. As it cools to room temperature (80 degrees), its temperature at any time x is given by the formula $T = 80 + 2000(0.942)^x$ where x is the number of minutes elapsed since removal from the furnace. Find the temperature of this vase after 15, 30, 60 and 90 minutes have elapsed.

114. A researcher worked out a formula that gives the area A in square centimeters of a growing colony of bacteria to be

$$A = \frac{0.252}{0.0051 + 0.119^x}$$

where x is the number of days elapsed from the initial measurement. Find the area after 1 and 2 days have elapsed.

THINK ABOUT IT 1.1

1. A common student error is to assume that $-a$ must represent a negative number. Explain why this assumption is incorrect.

2. Give an example in which the sum of two irrational numbers is a rational number.

3. The expression $-(-8) - 3$ illustrates three uses of the $-$ symbol. Describe the three uses.

4. Find the set of all replacements for a that make the statement true.
   a. $|a| = 2$ **b.** $|a| = -3$ **c.** $|a| = a$
   d. $|a| = -a$ **e.** $|a| = |-a|$

5. Use a dictionary to find meanings for the words *commute, associate,* and *distribute* that are consistent with the concepts expressed by the commutative, associative, and distributive properties discussed in this section.

1.2 Algebraic Expressions and Geometric Formulas

A rope is wrapped tightly around the equator of the earth. A second rope is suspended in the air 1 ft directly above the first all the way around the earth. Is the difference between the rope lengths about 6 ft, 600 ft, 60,000 ft, or 6 million ft? Justify your answer. (See Example 6.)

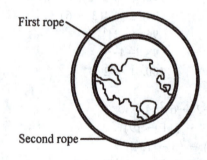

First rope

Second rope

OBJECTIVES

1. Evaluate algebraic expressions.

2. Simplify algebraic expressions by combining like terms.

3. Apply geometric formulas.

4. Translate between verbal expressions and algebraic expressions.

In algebra, two types of symbols are used to represent numbers: variables and constants. A **variable** is a symbol that may be replaced by different numbers in a particular problem, while a **constant** is a symbol that represents the same number throughout a particular problem. An expression that combines variables and constants using the operations of arithmetic is called an **algebraic expression.** For example,

$$3x^2 - 5x + 7, \qquad \frac{-b + \sqrt{b^2 - 4ac}}{2a}, \text{ and } \frac{1}{2}gt^2$$

are algebraic expressions.

   If we are given numerical values for the symbols, we can evaluate the expression by substituting the given values and performing the indicated operations. Such substitutions are based on the **substitution property** that states that if a and b are real numbers and $a = b$, then either may replace the other without affecting the truth value of the statement.

EXAMPLE 1   Evaluating an Algebraic Expression
Evaluate each expression, given that $x = -2$, $y = 3$, and $z = -4$.

a. $5y - x$
b. $-x^2 + 5yz^2$

Solution

a. $5y - x = 5(3) - (-2)$ Replace y by 3 and x by -2.
$\qquad\qquad = 15 + 2$
$\qquad\qquad = 17$
b. $-x^2 + 5yz^2 = -(-2)^2 + 5(3)(-4)^2$ Replace x by -2, y by 3 and z by -4.
$\qquad\qquad\quad = -(4) + 5(3)(16)$
$\qquad\qquad\quad = -4 + 240$
$\qquad\qquad\quad = 236$

Caution Pay close attention to how the expression $-x^2$ was evaluated in part **b.** Because powers precede multiplication in the order of operations, $-x^2$ means that you must first square x and then take the negative of your result. In general, $-a^n$ denotes the negative of a^n.

Technology Link
On some calculators, variable names may be used to name memory cells in which you can save numbers or expressions. Figure 1.13 shows a calculator display for the evaluation considered in Example 1a.

   To obtain this type of display, you should understand the Store and Alphabetic features of your calculator.

PROGRESS CHECK 1   Evaluate each expression, given that $x = -2$, $y = 3$, and $z = -4$.

a. $4x - 3y$ **b.** $-y^2 + 2xz^3$ ■

EXAMPLE 2   Evaluating an Expression Involving Subscripts
If $m = (y_2 - y_1)/(x_2 - x_1)$ evaluate m when $x_1 = 2$, $y_1 = -5$, $x_2 = -1$, and $y_2 = 3$. (*Note:* In the symbols, x_1, y_1, x_2 and y_2 the numbers 1 and 2 are called **subscripts.** In this case x_1 and x_2 are used to denote various x values.)

Solution

$$m = \frac{y_2 - y_1}{x_2 - x_1}$$

so when $x_1 = 2$, $y_1 = -5$, $x_2 = -1$, and $y_2 = 3$, we have

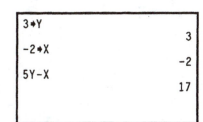

3→Y	
	3
-2→X	
	-2
5Y-X	
	17

Figure 1.13

$$m = \frac{(3) - (-5)}{(-1) - (2)} = \frac{8}{-3} = -\frac{8}{3}.$$

PROGRESS CHECK 2   Let m be defined as in Example 2, and evaluate m when $x_1 = 3$, $y_1 = -4$, $x_2 = 7$, and $y_2 = -10$.   ■

We often need to combine algebraic expressions that are added or subtracted. Those parts of an algebraic expression separated by plus ($+$) signs are called **terms** of the expression. The following example will help you recognize terms.

EXAMPLE 3   Recognizing Terms of an Algebraic Expression

Identify the term(s) in the following expressions.

a. $3x^2 - 5x + 7$ **b.** $\pi r^2 h$

Solution

a. $3x^2 - 5x + 7$ may be written as $3x^2 + (-5x) + 7$ and is an algebraic expression with three terms, $3x^2$, $-5x$, and 7.

b. Because $\pi r^2 h$ is a product (instead of a sum or difference), it is an algebraic expression with one term, $\pi r^2 h$.

PROGRESS CHECK 3   Identify the terms in the following expressions.

a. $-4x^3 + x^2 - 3x + 7$ **b.** $\dfrac{-7x}{2}$ ■

If a term is the product of some constants and variables, the constant factor is called the **(numerical) coefficient** of the term. For example, the coefficient of the term $2x$ is 2, and the coefficient of $-7x^2$ is -7. Every term has a coefficient. If the term is x, the coefficient is 1, since $x = 1 \cdot x$. Similarly, if the term is $-x$, the coefficient is -1, since $-x = -1 \cdot x$. If two terms have identical variable factors (such as $3x^2y$ and $-2x^2y$), they are called **like terms.** The distributive property indicates that we combine like terms by combining their coefficients.

EXAMPLE 4   Combining Like Terms

Simplify by combining like terms if possible.

a. $3x + 7x$ **b.** $yz^2 - 10yz^2$ **c.** $8x - y + 2y - 3x$ **d.** $-3x^2y + xy^2 - 7xy$

Solution

a. $3x + 7x = (3 + 7)x = 10x$
b. $yz^2 - 10yz^2 = (1 - 10)yz^2 = -9yz^2$
c. $8x - y + 2y - 3x = (8 - 3)x + (-1 + 2)y = 5x + y$
d. There are no like terms in $-3x^2y + xy^2 - 7xy$, so we cannot simplify the expression.

PROGRESS CHECK 4   Simplify by combining like terms if possible.

a. $x - 8x$ **b.** $3 - 8x$ **c.** $2p - 3p + 4p$ **d.** $-x^2 + 6x + 6x^2 - x$ ■

To combine algebraic expressions, it is sometimes necessary to remove the parentheses or brackets that group certain terms together. Parentheses are removed by applying the distributive property; that is, we multiply each term inside the parentheses by the factor in front of the parentheses. If the grouping is preceded by a minus sign, the factor is -1, so the sign of each term inside the parentheses must be changed. If the grouping is preceded by a plus sign, the factor is 1, so the sign of each term inside the parentheses remains the same. If there is more than one symbol of grouping, it is usually better to remove the innermost symbol of grouping first.

EXAMPLE 5   Removing Grouping Symbols and Simplifying

Remove the symbols of grouping and combine like terms.

a. $-(x - y) - 2(3x - y)$ **b.** $7 - 2[4x - (1 - 3x)]$

Solution

a. $-(x - y) - 2(3x - y)$
    $= -1(x - y) - 2(3x - y)$ Use $-(x - y) = -1(x - y)$
    $= -x + y - 6x + 2y$
    $= -7x + 3y$

b. $7 - 2[4x - (1 - 3x)]$
    $= 7 - 2[4x - 1 + 3x]$ Distributive property (remove parentheses).
    $= 7 - 2[7x - 1]$
    $= 7 - 14x + 2$ Distributive property (remove brackets).
    $= -14x + 9$

PROGRESS CHECK 5   Remove the symbols of grouping and combine like terms.

a. $-(x + y) + 3(x - y)$ **b.** $5x - 4[x - (1 + x)]$ ■

An application of combining or evaluating algebraic expressions often occurs when we apply formulas. A **formula** is an equality statement that expresses the relationship between two or more variables. For this course, a useful category of formulas is found in geometry, and Figures 1.14 and 1.15 provide some of these formulas for reference purposes.

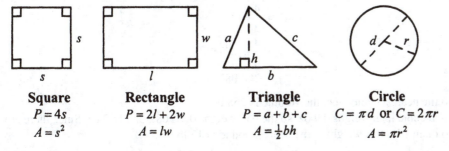

Square	**Rectangle**	**Triangle**	**Circle**
$P = 4s$	$P = 2l + 2w$	$P = a + b + c$	$C = \pi d$ or $C = 2\pi r$
$A = s^2$	$A = lw$	$A = \frac{1}{2}bh$	$A = \pi r^2$

Figure 1.14
Two-dimensional figures: Formulas for perimeter P, circumference C, and area A.

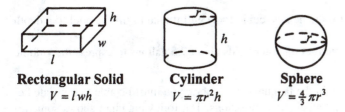

Rectangular Solid	**Cylinder**	**Sphere**
$V = lwh$	$V = \pi r^2 h$	$V = \frac{4}{3}\pi r^3$

Figure 1.15
Three-dimensional figures: Formulas for volume V.

EXAMPLE 6   A Popular Geometric Puzzle

Solve the problem in the section introduction on page 16.

Solution   Although you might expect the difference between the rope lengths to be very large, they only differ by about 6 ft. Since the equator of the earth may be approximated by a circle with diameter d, the circumference formula, $C = \pi d$, tells us that the length of the first rope is πd, while the length of the second rope is $\pi(d + 2)$. Then

$$\text{difference} = \pi(d + 2) - \pi d$$
$$= \pi d + 2\pi - \pi d$$
$$= 2\pi \text{ ft.}$$

Since $\pi \approx 3.14$, the difference is about 6 ft. Note that *any* two circles that differ by 2 ft in diameter differ by 2π ft in circumference.

PROGRESS CHECK 6   Circle A has a radius of x ft and circle B has a radius of $x + 3$ ft, as shown in Figure 1.16. How much larger is circumference B than circumference A?   ■

Figure 1.16

EXAMPLE 7   Finding the Volume and Weight of a Bowling Ball

A bowling ball has an 8-in. diameter.

a. Find its volume to the nearest cubic inch. Disregard any holes in the ball.
b. If the material weights 0.9 oz/in.^{3}, find the weight of the ball to the nearest pound. (There are 16 oz. in 1 lb.)

Solution

a. Since the shape of the ball is a sphere, the formula to use is $V = (4/3)\pi r^3$. Because $d = 8$ in. and $r = (1/2)d$, we replace r by 4. If available, use the calculator key labeled π in the computation. Otherwise, replace π by 3.14159.

$$V = \frac{4}{3}\pi r^3$$
$$= \frac{4}{3}\pi(4^3)$$
$$= 268.08257\ldots$$

To the nearest cubic inch, the volume is 268 in.^{3}.

b. Each cubic inch weighs 0.9 oz, so the ball weighs 0.9(268), or 241.2 oz. Since there are 16 oz in 1 lb, this weight to the nearest pound is 15 lb.

PROGRESS CHECK 7   A circular backyard aboveground pool has a diameter of 20 ft.

a. What volume of water (to the nearest cubic foot) will it take to fill the pool to a depth of 4.3 ft?
b. Use the fact that one cubic foot of water holds about 7.5 gallons to express the volume in gallons of water.   ■

To develop proficiency in the language of algebra, you must be able to translate between verbal expressions and algebraic expressions. The following chart shows some algebraic expressions that may be used to translate typical verbal expressions that involve arithmetic operations.

EXAMPLE 8   Translating to an Algebraic Expression

Translate each statement to an algebraic expression.

a. $3 less than the list price p.   **b.** 6 percent of the sum of x and y.

Operations	Verbal Expression	Algebraic Expression
Addition	The sum of a number x and 1	$x + 1$, or $1 + x$
	A number y plus 2	$y + 2$, or $2 + y$
	A number w increased by 3	$w + 3$, or $3 + w$
	4 more than a number b	$b + 4$, or $4 + b$
	Add 5 and a number d	$d + 5$ or $5 + d$
Subtraction	The difference of a number x and 6	$x - 6$
	A number y minus 5	$y - 5$
	A number w decreased by 4	$w - 4$
	3 less than a number b	$b - 3$
	Subtract 11 from a number d	$d - 11$
	Subtract a number d from 11	$11 - d$
Multiplication	The product of a number x and 5	$5x$
	4 times a number t	$4t$
	A number y multiplied by 7	$7y$
	Twice a number w	$2w$
	1/3 of a number n	$(1/3)n$
	25 percent of a number P	$0.25P$
Division	The quotient of a number x and 8	$x \div 8$, or $x/8$
	A number y divided by 2	$y \div 2$, or $y/2$
	The ratio of a number a to a number b	$a \div b$, or a/b, or $a{:}b$

Solution

a. \$3 less than p is expressed as $p - 3$ dollars. Note that $3 - p$ dollars is not correct here.

b. 6 percent is written as 0.06, the sum of x and y is written as $x + y$, and in this context the word *of* implies multiplication. Thus, the given expression translates to $0.06(x + y)$.

PROGRESS CHECK 8   Translate each statement to an algebraic expression.

a. \$5 more than the retail price p.   **b.** 8 percent of the product of a and b.   ■

EXAMPLE 9   Translating to a Verbal Expression

Translate each algebraic expression to a verbal expression.

a. $ab + ac$ **b.** $a(b + c)$

Solution

a. The sum $ab + ac$ may be read as "the sum of a times b and a times c."

b. The product $a(b + c)$ may be stated as "a times the sum of b and c."

Note In this type of example, other translations are possible. For instance, $a(b + c)$ may be read as "the product of a and the sum of b and c." However, care must be taken to avoid ambiguous statements like "a times b plus c" where it is not clear whether $ab + c$ or $a(b + c)$ is intended.

PROGRESS CHECK 9   Translate each algebraic expression to a verbal expression

a. $ab + c$ **b.** $\dfrac{a}{a + 5}$ ■

EXERCISES 1.2

In Exercise 1–20 evaluate each expression, given that $x = -2$, $y = 3$, and $z = -4$.

1. $x + y + z$
2. $4x - z$
3. x^3x^2
4. $\frac{y^3}{y^2}$
5. $5z - xy^2$
6. $20 - xyz^3$
7. $(-x)^2 + 2y$
8. $-x^2 + 2y$
9. $3y^3 - 2y^2 + y - 2$
10. $2x^3 + 3x^2 - x + 1$
11. $x - 2(3y - 4z)$
12. $(x - 2)(3y - 4z)$
13. $(z - x)(y - 3z)$
14. $z - x(y - 3z)$
15. $(2y - x)x - z$
16. $(2y - x)(x - z)$
17. $(x + y + z)(x + y - z)$
18. $x + y + z(x + y - z)$
19. $(x + 2)(y - 3) + (3 - z)(4 + x)$
20. $(5 - y)(z + 1) - (y - 2)(3 + x)$

In Exercises 21–26 $m = \dfrac{y_2 - y_1}{x_2 - x_1}$. Evaluate m for the following values of x_1, y_1, x_2, and y_2.

	x_1	y_1	x_2	y_2
21.	5	4	1	2
22.	1	6	4	8
23.	-3	-1	-6	-4
24.	-5	-3	-2	-6
25.	2	-1	-6	3
26.	0	3	-2	-4

In Exercises 27–32 identify the term(s) in the given expressions.

27. $2n + 4w$
28. $-m + 4x$
29. $x^2 - 3x - 2$
30. $2y^2 + 3y - 4$
31. $\frac{1}{2}bh$
32. $(2a)(3b)$

In Exercises 33–56 simplify each expression by combining like terms. Remove symbols of grouping when necessary.

33. $6a + 4a + 9a$
34. $-3b - b + 7b$
35. $8a - 3b + 6a - 5b$
36. $5k - 6m - 7 + 3k - 4m + 2$
37. $5xy - 4cd - 2xy + 9cd$
38. $4p - 5q + 4p + q + 4p - 2q$
39. $2x^3 + 6y^2 - 5x^3 + 2y^2$
40. $2a^2b + 3ab - 4ab^2$
41. $x - 2(x + y) + 3(x - y)$
42. $k + (m - k) - (m - 2k)$
43. $-2(a - 2b) - 7(2a - b)$
44. $2a - (7a + 3) + (4a - 6)$
45. $-(x + y) + 4(x - y) + 7x - 2y$
46. $a(b - c) - b(a + c)$
47. $(2x^3 + 7x^2y^2 + 9xy^3) + (6x^2y^2 - 3x^3y)$
48. $(3c^2d + 2cd - 5d^3) - (9d^3 - 6c^2d - 2cd)$
49. $(3y^3 - 2y^2 + 7y - 1) + (4y^3 - y^2 - 3y + 7)$
50. $(2n - 4n^3 + 3n^2 + 4) - (6 - 2n^2 + 7n - n^3)$
51. $(b^3 - 2b^2 + 3b + 4) - (b^2 + 2b - 1)$
52. $(4x^3 + 7x^2y^2 - 2y^3) + (-7x^3 + 2x^2y^2 + 2y^3)$
53. $2[a + 5(a + 2)] - 6$
54. $10 - 4[3x - (1 - x)]$
55. $3a - [3(a - b) - 2(a + b)]$
56. $-[x - (x + y) - (x - y) - (y - x)]$
57. The side of the inside square is x; the side of the outside square is $x + 2$. How much larger is the perimeter of the outside square than the perimeter of the inside square?

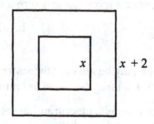

58. One solid ball with an 8-inch diameter is made of material weighing 0.8 oz./in.^{3}. A second ball is the same size, but made of material weighing 0.7 oz./in.^{3}. How much heavier is the first ball?

59. Find and simplify an expression for the perimeter of the figure shown. Use 3.14 for π. The curve is a semicircle.

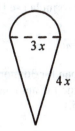

60. Find and simplify an expression for the perimeter of the figure shown. Use 3.14 for π. The curves are semicircles that have the same diameter.

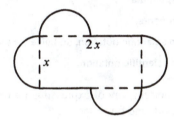

61. Find and simplify an expression for the area of the figure shown. The curves are semicircles. Use 3.14 for π.

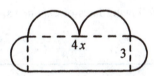

62. Find and simplify an expression for the area of the figure shown.

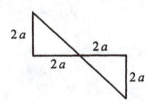

63. A cylindrical storage vat has a diameter of 8 feet and a depth of 7 feet.
   a. If it is filled with liquid to within 1 ft of the top, how much liquid does it hold? Give the answer to the nearest cubic foot.
   b. Express the volume in gallons if 1 ft^3 of liquid holds about 7.5 gallons. Give the answer to the nearest 10 gallons.

64. Redo Exercise 63, but now assume that the vat is filled to within 2 ft of the top.

In Exercise 65–72 translate the given statement to an algebraic expression.

65. 4.5 percent of the amount of sales t.
66. 10 percent of the rental fee f.
67. \$1 more than the cost of the ticket c.
68. \$9.95 less than the list price l.
69. The sum of the price p and the sales tax, which is 4 percent of the price.
70. The list price l minus the 30 percent discount on the list price.
71. The sum of a and the product of m and n.
72. The quotient of x and the sum of 2 and x.

In Exercise 73–76 translate each algebraic expression into a verbal expression

73. $4y + x$ **74.** $4(y + x)$
75. $\frac{a}{bc}$ **76.** $\frac{a}{b} \cdot c$

THINK ABOUT IT 1.2

1. Explain the difference in meaning between $-a^2$ and $(-a)^2$.
2. a. Use the distributive property to show that $2x - 2x$ equals 0 for all values of x.
   b. Use the distributive property to show that $2 - 2x$ does not equal 0 unless $x = 1$.
3. If $xy = x$, what are the possible values for x and y?
4. a. Make up two terms that are like terms with respect to $3xy^2$. Why are they like terms?
   b. Give two terms that are unlike terms with respect to $3xy^2$. Explain why they are unlike terms.
5. In parts **a** and **b** try the number trick with at least one number. Then show algebraically why the trick works.
   a. Choose a number.
   Add three.
   Multiply by two.
   Add six.
   Divide by two.
   Subtract your original number.
   Your result is six.
   b. Choose a number.
   Triple it.
   Add the number that is one larger than your original number.
   Add seven.
   Divide by four.
   Subtract two.
   The result is your original number.

Courtesy of PhotoDisc/Getty Images.

1.3 Integer Exponents

The equal-monthly-payment formula is used by banks when they finance many common loans. The problem is to find the equal monthly installment E that will pay off a loan of P dollars with interest in n months. The monthly interest rate is r and interest is charged at each payment period only on the unpaid balance. The formula used by the bank is

$$E = \frac{Pr}{1 - (1 + r)^{-n}}.$$

Suppose you obtain an $11,000 home improvement loan for 36 months with 9 percent annual interest charged on the unpaid balance. Determine the amount of the equal monthly installment that will pay off this debt. (See Example 5.)

OBJECTIVES

1 Evaluate expressions containing integer exponents.

2 Simplify expressions involving integer exponents.

3 Simplify expressions involving literal exponents.

4 Convert numbers from normal notation to scientific notation, and vice versa.

5 Solve problems by calculator that involve scientific notation.

Recall that a positive integer exponent is a shortcut way of expressing a repeating factor. That is, a^n, where n is a positive integer, is shorthand for

$$\underbrace{a \cdot a \cdot a \cdots a}_{n \text{ factors}}.$$

From this definition it is easy to obtain the following laws of exponents, which we will illustrate in specific terms in Example 1.

Laws of Positive Integer Exponents

Let a and b be any real numbers and m and n be any positive integers.

1. $a^m \cdot a^n = a^{m+n}$ **2.** $(a^m)^n = a^{mn}$ **3.** $(ab)^n = a^n b^n$

4. $\left(\dfrac{a}{b}\right)^n = \dfrac{a^n}{b^n}$ $(b \neq 0)$ **5.** $\dfrac{a^m}{a^n} = \begin{cases} a^{m-n} & \text{if } m > n \\[2mm] \dfrac{1}{a^{n-m}} & \text{if } n > m \end{cases}$ $(a \neq 0)$

EXAMPLE 1   Using the Laws of Positive Integer Exponents

Simplify by the laws of exponents and check your result.

a. $2^2 \cdot 2^3$ **b.** $(2^3)^2$ **c.** $(2 \cdot 3)^2$ **d.** $\dfrac{2^5}{2^2}$ **e.** $\dfrac{2^2}{2^5}$

Solution

a. $2^2 \cdot 2^3 = 2^{2+3} = 2^5 = 32$

b. $(2^3)^2 = 2^{3 \cdot 2} = 2^6 = 64$

c. $(2 \cdot 3)^2 = 2^2 \cdot 3^2 = 4 \cdot 9 = 36$

d. $\dfrac{2^5}{2^2} = 2^{5-2} = 2^3 = 8$

e. $\dfrac{2^2}{2^5} = \dfrac{1}{2^{5-2}} = \dfrac{1}{2^3} = \dfrac{1}{8}$

Check

$2^2 \cdot 2^3 = 4 \cdot 8 = 32$

$(2^3)^2 = 8^2 = 64$

$(2 \cdot 3)^2 = 6^2 = 36$

$\dfrac{2^5}{2^2} = \dfrac{32}{4} = 8$

$\dfrac{2^2}{2^5} = \dfrac{4}{32} = \dfrac{1}{8}$

PROGRESS CHECK 1   Simplify by the laws of exponents and check your result.

a. $3^4 \cdot 3$ **b.** $(3^4)^2$ **c.** $(4 \cdot 2)^3$ **d.** $\dfrac{3^4}{3^2}$ **e.** $\dfrac{3^2}{3^4}$ ■

EXAMPLE 2   Using the Laws of Positive Integer Exponents

Simplify by the laws of exponents

a. $(6x^5y^3)(-2xy^7)$ **b.** $\dfrac{18a^3b^2c^2}{12ab^4c}$

Solution

a. $(6x^5y^3)(-2xy^7) = 6(-2)x^{5+1}y^{3+7} = -12x^6y^{10}$

b. $\dfrac{18a^3b^2c^2}{12ab^4c} = \dfrac{18a^{3-1}c^{2-1}}{12b^{4-2}} = \dfrac{3a^2c}{2b^2}$

PROGRESS CHECK 2   Simplify by the laws of exponents.

a. $(-4x)^2(9x^5)$ **b.** $\dfrac{14xy^5}{21x^4y^4}$ ■

We now wish to extend our definition of exponents to zero and negative integers. Note that it is meaningless to use x as a factor either zero times or a negative number of times, so we must define these exponents in a different manner. However, our guideline in these new definitions is to retain the laws of exponents developed for positive integers.

We start by considering the first law of exponents.

$$a^m \cdot a^n = a^{m+n}$$

If $n = 0$, we have

$$a^m \cdot a^0 = a^{m+0} = a^m.$$

When we multiply a^m by a^0, our result is a^m. Thus, a^0 must equal 1, and we make the following definition.

Zero Exponent

If a is a nonzero real number, then

$$a^0 = 1.$$

EXAMPLE 3   Evaluating an Expression with a Zero Exponent
Evaluate each expression. Assume $x \neq 0$.

a. 9.64×10^0 **b.** $3x^0$ **c.** -4^0

Solution   Apply the zero exponent definition.
a. Because $10^0 = 1$, $9.64 \times 10^0 = 9.64(1) = 9.64$
b. $3x^0$ is equivalent to $3^1 \cdot x^0$, so $3x^0 = 3(1) = 3$.
c. Recall that the form $-a^n$ denotes the negative of a^n. Thus, $-4^0 = -(4^0) = -1$.

PROGRESS CHECK 3   Evaluate each expression. Assume $x \neq 0$.

a. $-5x^0$ **b.** -5^0 **c.** 4.72×10^0 ■

To obtain a definition for exponents that are negative integers, we will again consider the first law of exponents.

$$a^m \cdot a^n = a^{m+n}$$

If $m = 5$ and $n = -5$, we have

$$a^5 \cdot a^{-5} = a^{5+(-5)} = a^0 = 1.$$

When we multiply a^5 by a^{-5}, the result is 1. Thus, a^{-5} is the reciprocal of a^5, or $a^{-5} = 1/a^5$. In general, our previous laws of exponents may be extended by making the following definition.

Negative Exponent

If a is a nonzero real number and n is an integer, then

$$a^{-n} = \frac{1}{a^n}.$$

EXAMPLE 4   Evaluating an Expression with a Negative Exponent
Evaluate each expression.
a. 5^{-2} **b.** $(-4)^{-3}$ **c.** $\left(\dfrac{3}{2}\right)^{-4}$

Solution   Use the negative exponent definition.

a. $5^{-2} = \dfrac{1}{5^2} = \dfrac{1}{25}$ **b.** $(-4)^{-3} = \dfrac{1}{(-4)^3} = \dfrac{1}{-64} = -\dfrac{1}{64}$

c. $\left(\dfrac{3}{2}\right)^{-4} = \dfrac{1}{(3/2)^4} = \dfrac{1}{81/16} = 1 \cdot \dfrac{16}{81} = \dfrac{16}{81}$

Note   Part **c** shows the evaluation of a fraction raised to a negative power. This type of evaluation may also be done by using

$$\left(\frac{a}{b}\right)^{-n} = \left(\frac{b}{a}\right)^n \qquad a, b \neq 0.$$

For instance,

$$\left(\frac{3}{2}\right)^{-4} = \left(\frac{2}{3}\right)^4 = \frac{2^4}{3^4} = \frac{16}{81}.$$

Technology Link

Integer exponents are generally evaluated on a calculator with the Power key in the usual way. For example, Figure 1.17 displays the computation for $(-4)^{-3}$ in which we also used the feature for converting a rational number to fraction form. When entering such expressions, be careful to use the key $\boxed{(-)}$ for making a negative sign instead of the subtraction key $\boxed{-}$.

An exponent of -1 is best computed with the Reciprocal key, which is labeled x^{-1} on some calculators, and $1/x$ on others.

PROGRESS CHECK 4   Evaluate each expression.

a. 7^{-1} **b.** $(-3)^{-4}$ **c.** $\left(\dfrac{2}{5}\right)^{-3}$ ■

```
(-4)^-3
                   -.015625
Ans▶Frac
                    -1/64
```

Figure 1.17

EXAMPLE 5   Calculating Monthly Installment Payments

Solve the problem in the section introduction on page 24.

Solution   The annual interest rate is 9 percent, so the monthly interest rate is 0.09/12, or 0.0075. We substitute $r = 0.0075$, $P = 11{,}000$ and $n = 36$ in the given formula, and then simplify with the aid of a calculator.

$$E = \frac{Pr}{1 - (1 + r)^{-n}} \qquad \text{Equal monthly payment formula.}$$

$$= \frac{11{,}000(0.0075)}{1 - (1 + 0.0075)^{-36}} \qquad \text{Substitution.}$$

$$= 349.80 \qquad \text{By calculator to the nearest cent.}$$

The monthly payment will be $349.80. Note that this schedule gives a total of $12,592.80, of which $1,592.80 is interest.

PROGRESS CHECK 5   Redo Example 5, but assume that the annual interest rate is 12 percent.   ■

Integer exponents have been defined so that all previous properties of exponents continue to apply. We will therefore restate the laws of exponents as they apply to all integers. In particular, note that property 5 (the quotient property) can now be stated simply as $a^m/a^n = a^{m-n}$ because negative integer and zero exponents are now sensible.

Laws of Integer Exponents

Let a and b be any nonzero real numbers, and m and n be any integers.

1. $a^m \cdot a^n = a^{m+n}$ **2.** $(a^m)^n = a^{mn}$

3. $(ab)^n = a^n b^n$ **4.** $\left(\dfrac{a}{b}\right)^n = \dfrac{a^n}{b^n}$

5. $\dfrac{a^m}{a^n} = a^{m-n}$ **6.** $\left(\dfrac{a}{b}\right)^{-n} = \left(\dfrac{b}{a}\right)^n$

EXAMPLE 6 Using the Laws of Integer Exponents

Simplify and write the result using only positive exponents. Assume $x \neq 0$ and $y \neq 0$.

a. $2^{-5} \cdot 2^3$ **b.** $5x \cdot x^{-4}$ **c.** $\left(\dfrac{9}{y}\right)^{-2}$ **d.** $(3x^{-2})^{-3}$ **e.** $\dfrac{3^{-2}x^2y^{-3}}{3x^{-5}y}$

Solution

a. $2^{-5} \cdot 2^3 = 2^{-5+3} = 2^{-2} = \dfrac{1}{2^2} = \dfrac{1}{4}$

b. $5x \cdot x^{-4} = 5x^{1+(-4)} = 5x^{-3} = 5 \cdot \dfrac{1}{x^3} = \dfrac{5}{x^3}$

c. $\left(\dfrac{9}{y}\right)^{-2} = \left(\dfrac{y}{9}\right)^2 = \dfrac{y^2}{9^2} = \dfrac{y^2}{81}$

d. $(3x^{-2})^{-3} = 3^{-3}(x^{-2})^{-3} = \dfrac{1}{3^3} \cdot x^6 = \dfrac{x^6}{27}$

e. $\dfrac{3^{-2}x^2y^{-3}}{3x^{-5}y} = 3^{-2-1}x^{2-(-5)}y^{-3-1} = 3^{-3}x^7y^{-4} = \dfrac{1}{3^3} \cdot x^7 \cdot \dfrac{1}{y^4} = \dfrac{x^7}{27y^4}$

Technology Link

A calculator may be used to support the results in this example by evaluating both the original expression and the simplified version for at least one value of x or y. For instance, Figure 1.18 shows that when $x = 2$, both $5x \cdot x^{-4}$ and $5/x^3$ are equal to .625.

PROGRESS CHECK 6 Simplify and write the result using only positive exponents. Assume $x \neq 0$ and $y \neq 0$.

a. $2^{-5} \div 2^3$ **b.** $3y^{-5} \cdot y^4$ **c.** $\left(\dfrac{2x}{5}\right)^{-3}$ **d.** $(6y^{-4})^{-1}$ **e.** $\dfrac{3^2x^{-4}y^{-5}}{3^{-1}x^4y^{-3}}$ ■

```
2→X
                    2
5X*X^-4
                 .625
5/X^3
                 .625
```

Figure 1.18

When working with negative exponents, keep in mind the important principle that any *factor* of the numerator may be made a factor of the denominator (and vice versa) by changing the sign of the exponent. For example,

$$\frac{3^{-2}}{3^{-4}} = \frac{3^4}{3^2} \quad \text{and} \quad \frac{3^{-2}x^2y^{-3}}{3x^{-5}y} = \frac{x^2x^5}{3 \cdot 3^2y^3y}.$$

Such transformations may then be easier to simplify, as shown in the next example. When this method is used, it is important to note that this principle applies only to factors.

EXAMPLE 7 Simplifying by Rewriting Without Negative Exponents

Simplify and write the result using only positive exponents. Assume $x \neq 0$ and $y \neq 0$.

a. $\dfrac{3^{-2}}{3^{-4}}$ **b.** $\dfrac{3^{-2}x^2y^{-3}}{3x^{-5}y}$

Solution Begin by rewriting the expressions without negative exponents, as discussed above.

a. $\dfrac{3^{-2}}{3^{-4}} = \dfrac{3^4}{3^2} = 3^{4-2} = 3^2 = 9$

b. $\dfrac{3^{-2}x^2y^{-3}}{3x^{-5}y} = \dfrac{x^2x^5}{3 \cdot 3^2y^3y} = \dfrac{x^{2+5}}{3^{1+2}y^{3+1}} = \dfrac{x^7}{3^3y^4} = \dfrac{x^7}{27y^4}$

Note   Observe that Examples 6e and 7b show alternate methods for simplifying the same expression. Check that the simplified results for Progress Check 6e and 7b are the same also.

PROGRESS CHECK 7   Simplify and write the result using only positive exponents. Assume $x \neq 0$ and $y \neq 0$.

a. $\dfrac{2}{2^{-3}}$

b. $\dfrac{3^2 x^{-4} y^{-5}}{3^{-1} x^4 y^{-3}}$ ■

In algebra it is also common for variables to appear as exponents. We can apply the exponent properties of this section if we assume that the variables in the exponents represent integers. Letters used as exponents are called **literal exponents.**

EXAMPLE 8   Simplifying an Expression Involving Literal Exponents

Simplify the given expression. Assume $x \neq 0$, $b \neq 0$, and variables as exponents denote integers.

a. $\dfrac{2x^{n+3}}{-4x^n}$

b. $b^x \cdot b^{-x}$

c. $\dfrac{b^x}{b^{2x}}$

Solution

a. $\dfrac{2x^{n+3}}{-4x^n} = \dfrac{2x^{(n+3)-n}}{-4} = -\dfrac{x^3}{2}$

b. $b^x \cdot b^{-x} = b^{x+(-x)} = b^0 = 1$

c. $\dfrac{b^x}{b^{2x}} = \dfrac{1}{b^{2x-x}} = \dfrac{1}{b^x}$

PROGRESS CHECK 8   Simplify the given expression. Assume $x \neq 0$, $a \neq 0$, and variables as exponents denote integers.

a. $a^x \div a^{-x}$

b. $3^n \cdot 3^n$

c. $\dfrac{x^{3n}}{x^{2n}}$ ■

Scientific Notation

Many numbers that appear in scientific work are either very large or very small. For example, the average distance from the earth to the sun is approximately 93,000,000 mi, and the mass of an atom by hydrogen is approximately

$$0.000000000000000000000000017 \text{ g}.$$

To work conveniently with these numbers, we often write them in a form called **scientific notation.**

A number is expressed in scientific notation when it is written in the form

$$N = m \times 10^k, \text{ where } 1 \leq |m| < 10 \text{ and } k \text{ is an integer.}$$

For example,

$$93,000,000 = 9.3(10,000,000) = 9.3 \times 10^7$$

$$0.00103 = 1.03\frac{1}{1,000} = 1.03 \times 10^{-3}.$$

To convert a positive number from normal notation to scientific notation, use the following procedure.

> ### To Convert Positive Numbers to Scientific Notation
>
> 1. Immediately after the first nonzero digit of the number, place an apostrophe (').
> 2. Starting at the apostrophe, count the number of places to the decimal point. If you move to the right, your count is expressed as a positive number, if you move to the left, the count is negative.
> 3. The apostrophe indicates the position of the decimal in the factor between 1 and 10; the count represents the exponent to be used in the factor, which is a power of 10.

The following examples illustrate how this procedure is used for positive numbers. (*Note:* The arrow indicates the direction of the counting.)

Number	=	Number from 1 to 10	×	Power of 10
9'3000000.	=	9.3	×	10^7
0.0001'36	=	1.36	×	10^{-4}
6'.2	=	6.2	×	10^0

To express a negative number in scientific notation, you simply use the procedure above and write a negative sign before the number.

EXAMPLE 9   Converting to Scientific Notation

Write each number in scientific notation.

a. 27 billion   **b.** −0.00000031

Solution   Use the procedure outlined above.

a. $27,000,000,000 = 2.7 \times 10^{10}$ *Think:* 2'7,000,000,000.

b. $-0.00000031 = -3.1 \times 10^{-7}$ *Think:* −0.0000003'1.

PROGRESS CHECK 9   Write each number in scientific notation.

a. 615 million   **b.** −0.09   ■

To convert a number from scientific notation to normal notation, just carry out the indicated multiplication. When the power of 10 has a positive exponent, move the decimal point to the right and insert zeros, as needed, to indicate the final position of the decimal point. When the power of 10 has a negative exponent, the decimal point is moved to the left instead.

EXAMPLE 10   Converting to Normal Notation

Express each number in normal notation.

a. 8.07×10^6 **b.** 4.3×10^{-3}

Solution

a. To multiply by 10^6, move the decimal point 6 places to the right.

$8.07 \times 10^6 = 8,070,000$ *Think:* 8.070000

6 places

b. To multiply by 10^{-3}, move the decimal point 3 places to the left.

$4.3 \times 10^{-3} = 0.0043$ *Think:* 0.004.3

3 places

PROGRESS CHECK 10   Express each number in normal notation.

a. 9.2×10^9 **b.** -2.7×10^{-6} ■

Graphing calculators are programmed to work with scientific notation, and this feature is useful for many applied problems. To enter a positive number in scientific notation, first enter the significant digits of the number from 1 to 10, press $\boxed{\text{EE}}$ or $\boxed{\text{EXP}}$, and finally, enter the exponent of the power of 10. For example, to enter 7.3×10^{-6} on a Texas Instruments model, press

$$7.3\;\boxed{\text{EE}}\;\boxed{(-)}\;6.$$

The display looks like

$$\boxed{7.3\text{E} - 6}.$$

You should consult the owner's manual to your calculator to learn its scientific notation capabilities. In particular, here are two common features you need to check for.

1. If a calculation results in an answer that either exceeds the display range or is less than a certain number (0.001 on Texas Instruments models) in absolute value, then the calculator automatically displays the answer in scientific notation. The computations of 40^8 and $3/10,000$ on a Texas Instruments model are shown in Figure 1.19 to illustrate this feature.
2. By use of the Mode button, the calculator can be put in scientific notation display format, which forces all numeric results to appear in scientific notation.

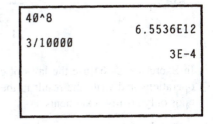

Figure 1.19

EXAMPLE 11   Number of Hemoglobin Molecules

If one red blood cell contains about 270 million hemoglobin molecules, about how many molecules of hemoglobin are there in 30 trillion red blood cells (which is the approximate number of red blood cells in a typical adult)?

Solution   270 million $= 2.7 \times 10^8$, and 30 trillion $= 3 \times 10^{13}$. Find the product of these numbers (with these keystrokes on a Texas Instruments model).

$$2.7\;\boxed{\text{EE}}\;8\;\boxed{\times}\;3\;\boxed{\text{EE}}\;13\;\boxed{\text{ENTER}}$$

The answer in the display reads 8.1E21, which means there are about 8.1×10^{21} hemoglobin molecules in the total supply of red blood cells in a typical adult.

Note   In order to interpret large numbers, it is useful to know the following names.

$$1 \text{ million} = 10^6 = 1{,}000{,}000$$

$$1 \text{ billion} = 10^9 = 1{,}000{,}000{,}000$$

$$1 \text{ trillion} = 10^{12} = 1{,}000{,}000{,}000{,}000$$

$$1 \text{ quadrillion} = 10^{15} = 1{,}000{,}000{,}000{,}000{,}000$$

Caution In this type of problem, students sometimes answer that there are 8.1E21 molecules. You should convert 8.1E21 to 8.1×10^{21} when expressing the final result.

PROGRESS CHECK 11 In a certain year the U.S. government spent about $298 billion for national defense, out of a total budget of $1.14 trillion. To the nearest tenth of a percent, what percent of the total budget was spent on national defense? ■

EXERCISES 1.3

In Exercise 1–24 evaluate each expression and check your result with a calculator.

1. $3^2 \cdot 3^3$
2. $(3^2)^3$
3. 7^0
4. -7^0
5. 3^{-2}
6. $(-2)^{-3}$
7. 2.04×10^{-3}
8. 4.12×10^0
9. $(2^3 \cdot 3)^2$
10. $(3^2 \cdot 4)^3$
11. $(4/3)^{-1}$
12. $(2/5)^{-3}$
13. $4^5 \cdot 4^{-2}$
14. $5^{-4} \cdot 5$
15. $(-3)^2 \cdot (-3)^3$
16. $(-2)^{-1} \cdot (-2)^{-3}$
17. $\dfrac{2}{2^4}$
18. $\dfrac{3^6}{3^2}$
19. $\dfrac{1}{2^{-3}}$
20. $\dfrac{2}{2^{-2}}$
21. $\dfrac{3^{-1}}{3}$
22. $\dfrac{5^{-2}}{5^{-4}}$
23. $\dfrac{6^{-1} \cdot 2^{-4}}{3^{-2} \cdot 2^{-3}}$
24. $\dfrac{2^{-3} \cdot 7^0}{4^{-1}}$

In Exercises 25–64 use the laws of exponents to perform the operations and write the result in the simplest form that contains only positive exponents.

25. $x^4 \cdot x^3$
26. $x \cdot x^5$
27. $(x^3)^4$
28. $(t^5)^2$
29. $(-2p)^2$
30. $(-y)^3$
31. $(-5y^5z)^3$
32. $(3x^3y^2)^4$
33. $c^9 \div c^3$
34. $8k^8 \div 2k^2$
35. $9x^2 \div x^3$
36. $a \div a^7$
37. $(x + y) \div (x + y)^4$
38. $(a + b)^2(a + b)^6$
39. $(-3x^2)(-3x)^2$
40. $(-4s^2c)^3(3sc^2)^5$
41. $x^5 \cdot x^{-3}$
42. $3y \cdot y^{-4}$
43. $t^{-1} \div t$
44. $a^{-2} \div a^{-3}$

45. $\left(\dfrac{y}{5}\right)^{-2}$
46. $\left(\dfrac{3}{x}\right)^{-1}$
47. $\left(\dfrac{1}{x^{-1}}\right)^{-1}$
48. $(2x^{-3})(-3x^{-2})$
49. $(4x^0)(-2x^{-3})$
50. $(2a^{-3})^{-2}$
51. $[3(x + h)^{-1}]^2$
52. $(1 - n)^{-1}(1 - n)$
53. $\left(\dfrac{2a^{-1}}{x}\right)^{-2}$
54. $\left(\dfrac{3x^{-2}}{y}\right)^{-1}$
55. $\dfrac{2a^{-1}}{a}$
56. $\dfrac{-x^{-2}}{x^{-3}}$
57. $\dfrac{(-x^3)^2(4yz)}{(-2x^2)(2y^2z^3)^3}$
58. $\dfrac{(4x^2yz^3)^4}{(-20x^6yz^2)^2}$
59. $\dfrac{3^{-1}x^2y^{-3}}{9x^{-2}y^{-3}}$
60. $\dfrac{2^2x^{-3}y^{-4}}{2^{-1}x^3y^{-2}}$
61. $\dfrac{(xyz)^{-1}}{x^{-2}yz^{-3}}$
62. $\dfrac{x^0y^{-2}z^3}{(xy^{-1}z^{-3})^{-1}}$
63. $\dfrac{(2ax^2)^{-2}(a^3x^{-1})^2}{2(ax)^{-1}(ax^5)}$
64. $\dfrac{[a^2(a + y)^3]^{-1}}{a(a + y)^2}$

In Exercise 65–88 use the laws of exponents to simplify each expression. Variables as exponents denote integers.

65. $2^x \cdot 2^y$
66. $5^a \cdot 5$
67. $\dfrac{2}{2^n}$
68. $\dfrac{5^{2x}}{5^x}$
69. $(5^x)^{2x}$
70. $3^a \cdot 3^{-a}$
71. $y^{2a} \cdot y^{5a}$
72. $x^{b+2} \cdot x^{2b}$
73. $(a - b)^x(a - b)^y$
74. $[(b - a)^x]^y$
75. $a^x \cdot a^{-x}$
76. $2x^{1-a} \cdot x^{a-1}$
77. $x \div x^{-x}$
78. $a^{-x} \div a^0$
79. $[(y^x)^{2x}]^3$
80. $(2x^a)^c(3x^c)^b$
81. $\dfrac{y^x}{y^{x+1}}$
82. $\dfrac{x^{2n+2}}{x^2}$
83. $(x^a)^{p-1} \cdot x^{a-1}$
84. $(b^x)^{1-a} \div b^x$

85. $\dfrac{x^{2a}y^{a+1}}{x^a y^{a+2}}$

86. $\dfrac{x^{a+b}y^b}{x^{a-b}y^{b-1}}$

87. $\dfrac{(1-x)^{2a}(1-x)^2}{(1-x)^a}$

88. $\dfrac{(y+2)^{1+m}}{(y+2)^m(y+2)}$

89. Use the equal-monthly-payment formula in Example 5 to determine the monthly installment that will pay off a $10,000 car loan in 48 months with a 10.8 percent annual interest rate charged on the unpaid balance.

90. Redo Exercise 89, but assume that the annual interest rate is 8.4 percent.

In Exercises 91–100 express each number in scientific notation.

91. 42   **92.** 0.6   **93.** 34,251   **94.** 7.21

95. A light-year (that is, the distance light travels in 1 year) is about 5,900,000,000,000 mi.

96. A human body contains about 10 quadrillion cells.

97. A certain radio station broadcasts at a frequency of about 1,260,000 hertz (cycles per second).

98. A certain computer can perform an addition in about 0.000014 second.

99. The weight of an oxygen molecule is approximately 0.000000000000000000000053 g.

100. The wavelength of yellow light is about 0.000023 in.

In Exercises 101–110 express each number in normal notation.

101. 9.2×10^4

102. 3×10^{-1}

103. 4.21×10^1

104. 6.3×10^0

105. The earth travels about 5.8×10^8 mi in its trip around the sun each year.

106. The number of atoms in 1 oz of gold is approximately 8.65×10^{21}.

107. One coulomb is equal to about 6.28×10^{18} electrons.

108. An atom is about 5×10^{-9} in. in diameter.

109. The mass of a molecule of water is about 3×10^{-23} g.

110. The wavelength of red light is approximately 6.6×10^{-5} cm.

111. If light travels about 186,000 mi/second, about how far will it travel in 50 minutes?

112. If one red blood cell contains about 270,000,000 hemoglobin molecules, about how many molecules of hemoglobin are there in 2 million red cells?

113. If the mass of one electron is about 0.00000000000000000000000000009 g, what is approximately the mass of 400 electrons?

114. If a certain computer can process an instruction in a nanosecond (a billionth of a second), then how long will it take this computer to process 25,000 instructions?

115. The annual budget of the U.S. government is currently between $1 trillion and $2 trillion. Represent 1 trillion and 1 million as powers of 10, and then determine how many times the government has to spend a million dollars in order to spend a trillion dollars.

116. The U.S. federal deficit in 1992 was about $4 trillion. If you spent $1,000 per second, how long would it take to spend $4 trillion? Express the answer in seconds in scientific notation. Then express the answer in years.

117. One liter of water is made up of 55.6 moles of water molecules, where 1 mole means 6.02×10^{23} things (just as 1 dozen means 12 things).

a. How many water molecules are in one liter of water?

b. One liter of distilled water contains 10^{-7} moles of hydrogen ions. What percent of the water is made up of hydrogen ions?

THINK ABOUT IT 1.3

1. Why is a^{-n} the multiplicative inverse of a^n if $a \neq 0$?

2. If $2^a = b$, then 2^{a+3} equals

  a. $b + 3$ **b.** b^3 **c.** $6b$ **d.** $8b$

3. A student reasoned that $2^3 \cdot 5^2$ must equal 10^5, because "when you multiply, you add the exponents." What crucial idea did the student forget?

4. The Greek mathematician Archimedes (c. 250 B.C.) is usually considered one of the greatest mathematicians of all time. Archimedes considered his most important achievement to be the discovery that whenever a sphere is circumscribed by a cylinder, the ratio of their volume is 3:2. He even asked that this figure and ratio be engraved on his tombstone. If the volume of a cylinder is $\pi r^2 h$, and the volume of a sphere is $(4/3)\pi r^3$, verify Archimedes' discovery.

5. a. The correct measurement in an experiment is 3.2×10^3. Which is a more serious error, to record it as 4.2×10^3 or as 3.2×10^4?

  b. When using scientific notation, why might a scientist be more concerned about the power of 10 than about the other part of the number?

Courtesy of PhotoDisc/Getty Images

1.4   Products of Algebraic Expressions

An airline offers a charter flight at a fare of $250 per person, if 120 passengers sign up. For each passenger above 120, the fare for each passenger is reduced by $2. Explain why the total revenue for the flight is given by $(120 + x)(250 - 2x)$, where x represents the number of passengers above 120. Then rewrite the expression for the total revenue by performing the indicated multiplication. (See Example 6.)

OBJECTIVES

1   Use the distributive property to multiply algebraic expressions.

2   Use the FOIL method to multiply two expressions that each contain two terms.

3   Use special product formulas to find certain products.

To multiply algebraic expressions, we use the laws of exponents and the distributive property in the forms

$$a(b + c) = ab + ac \text{ and } (a + b)c = ac + bc$$

or in an extended form such as

$$a(b + c + \ldots + n) = ab + ac + \ldots + an.$$

Example 1 shows the basic procedure.

EXAMPLE 1   Using the Distributive Property

Find each product.

a. $3x(x^2 - 2x + 1)$ **b.** $(2c^2 + t)ct$

Solution

a. $3x(x^2 - 2x + 1) = (3x)(x^2) + (3x)(-2x) + (3x)(1) = 3x^3 - 6x^2 + 3x$
b. $(2c^2 + t)ct = (2c^2)(ct) + (t)(ct) = 2c^3t + ct^2$

PROGRESS CHECK 1   Find each product.

a. $-2x^2(3x^2 - x + 9)$ **b.** $(7y - x)3y$ ■

Since division is defined in terms of multiplication, a similar procedure is used to simplify division problems in which the divisor is a single term. For example, we may divide $a + b$ by c as follows:

$$(a + b) \div c = (a + b) \cdot \frac{1}{c} = \frac{a}{c} + \frac{b}{c}.$$

This result shows that

$$\boxed{\frac{a + b}{c} = \frac{a}{c} + \frac{b}{c}}$$

EXAMPLE 2   Dividing by a Single Term Divisor

Divide $\dfrac{2xh + h^2 + 2h}{h}$.

Solution $\dfrac{2xh + h^2 + 2h}{h} = \dfrac{2xh}{h} + \dfrac{h^2}{h} + \dfrac{2h}{h} = 2x + h + 2$

PROGRESS CHECK 2   Divide $-12n^2x^2 + 2nx^2$ by $4nx$.   ■

If both factors in the multiplication contain more than one term, the distributive property must be used more than once. For example, no matter what expression is inside the parentheses

$$(\blacksquare)(x + 2) \text{ means } (\blacksquare)x + (\blacksquare)2.$$

Thus,

$$(x + 3)(x + 2) \text{ means } (x + 3)x + (x + 3)2.$$

Using the distributive property the second time, we get

$$(x + 3)x + (x + 3)2 = x^2 + 3x + 2x + 6 = x^2 + 5x + 6$$

Therefore,

$$(x + 3)(x + 2) = x^2 + 5x + 6$$

EXAMPLE 3   Using the Distributive Property Twice
Find each product.

a. $(2t + 3)(5t - 1)$ **b.** $(x^n - 2)(x^n - 1)$

Solution

a. $(2t + 3)(5t - 1) = (2t + 3)(5t) + (2t + 3)(-1)$
$$= 10t^2 + 15t - 2t - 3 = 10t^2 + 13t - 3$$

b. $(x^n - 2)(x^n - 1) = (x^n - 2)(x^n) + (x^n - 2)(-1)$
$$= x^{2n} - 2x^n - x^n + 2 = x^{2n} - 3x^n + 2$$

PROGRESS CHECK 3   Find each product.

a. $(3y - 4)(7y - 2)$ **b.** $(a^x + 3)(a^x - 5)$ ■

Notice that this method of multiplication is equivalent to multiplying each term of the first factor by each term of the second factor, and then combining like terms. This observation leads to the arrangement in Example 4, which is good for multiplying longer expressions since like terms are placed under each other.

EXAMPLE 4   Multiplying in a Vertical Format
Multiply $(c^2 - 5c + 25)(c + 3)$.

Solution   Multiply each term of $c^2 - 5c + 25$ by each term of $c + 3$. Arrange like terms in the products under each other; then add.

$$
\begin{array}{r}
c^2 - 5c + 25 \\
c + 3 \\
\hline
c^3 - 5c^2 + 25c \\
3c^2 - 15c + 75 \\
\hline
c^3 - 2c^2 + 10c + 75
\end{array}
$$

This line equals $c(c^2 - 5c + 25)$.
add   This line equals $3(c^2 - 5c + 25)$.

The product is $c^3 - 2c^2 + 10c + 75$.

PROGRESS CHECK 4   Multiply $(4x^2 + 3x - 2)(x + 3)$.   ■

When you multiply expressions that contain two terms, a mental shortcut may be used, as shown in Examples 5–7. This method is called the FOIL method, and the letters, F, O, I, and L denote the products of the **first, outer, inner,** and **last** terms, respectively.

EXAMPLE 5 Using the FOIL Method

Multiply using the FOIL method: $(2x - 1)(3x + 4)$.

Solution Note that the outer and inner pairs are like terms in this example.

$$(2x - 1)(3x + 4) = 2x(3x) + 2x(4) + (-1)(3x) + (-1)(4)$$
$$= 6x^2 + 8x - 3x - 4$$
$$= 6x^2 + 5x - 4$$

Thus, $(2x - 1)(3x + 4) = 6x^2 + 5x - 4$.

Technology Link

As in the previous section, a calculator may be used to support the results here by evaluating both the original expression and the expanded product for at least one set of values for the variables. For instance, Figure 1.20 shows that when $x = 5$, both $(2x - 1)(3x + 4)$ and $6x^2 + 5x - 4$ are equal to 171.

PROGRESS CHECK 5 Multiply using the FOIL method: $(5y - 4)(4y - 3)$. ▪

EXAMPLE 6 Revenue for a Charter Flight

Solve the problem in the section introduction on page 34.

Solution Because revenue = (number of passengers) · (fare per passenger), we first write algebraic expressions for these two factors. The variable x represents the number of passengers above 120 so

$$\text{number of passengers} = 120 + x.$$

For each passenger above 120, the fare for each passenger is reduced by \$2, so

$$\text{fare per passenger} = 250 - 2x.$$

Thus,

$$\text{revenue} = (120 + x)(250 - 2x)$$

Now multiply using the FOIL method.

$$(120 + x)(250 - 2x) = 120(250) + 120(-2x) + x(250) + x(-2x)$$
$$= 30,000 - 240x + 250x - 2x^2$$
$$= 30,000 + 10x - 2x^2$$

The revenue for the flight is given by $30,000 + 10x - 2x^2$ dollars.

PROGRESS CHECK 6 A manufacturer plans to introduce a new model of computer at a list price of \$3,000 and expects to sell 20,000 units. The sales department forecasts that for each \$100 the price is cut, sales will go up by 700 units. Explain why the formula

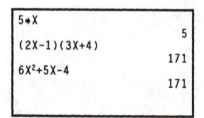

```
5→X
                          5
(2X-1)(3X+4)
                        171
6X²+5X-4
                        171
```

Figure 1.20

for estimated revenue is then $(20{,}000 + 700x)(3{,}000 - 100x)$, where x represents the number of \$100 price cuts. Then rewrite the expression for the estimated revenue by performing the indicated multiplication. ▪

EXAMPLE 7   Using the FOIL Method

Multiply using the FOIL method.

a. $(a + b)(a - b)$ **b.** $(a + b)^2$ **c.** $(a - b)^2$

Solution

a.

$$\overset{\text{F} + \text{O} + \text{I} + \text{L}}{(a + b)(a - b) = a(a) + a(-b) + b(a) + b(-b)}$$
$$= a^2 - ab + ab - b^2$$
$$= a^2 - b^2$$

Thus $(a + b)(a - b) = a^2 - b^2$.

b. $(a + b)^2 = (a + b)(a + b)$. Then,

$$\overset{\text{F} + \text{O} + \text{I} + \text{L}}{(a + b)(a + b) = a(a) + a(b) + b(a) + b(b)}$$
$$= a^2 + 2ab + b^2$$

Thus $(a + b)^2 = a^2 + 2ab + b^2$

c. $(a - b)^2 = (a - b)(a - b)$. Then,

$$\overset{\text{F} + \text{O} + \text{I} + \text{L}}{(a - b)(a - b) = a(a) + a(-b) + (-b)(a) + (-b)(-b)}$$
$$= a^2 - 2ab + b^2$$

Thus $(a - b)^2 = a^2 - 2ab + b^2$

PROGRESS CHECK 7   Multiply using the FOIL method.

a. $(k - 8)^2$ **b.** $(x + h)^2$ **c.** $(3y + 5)(3y - 5)$ ▪

Example 7 illustrates products that occur so frequently that you should memorize and use these results as special product formulas.

Special Product Formulas

		Comment
1.	$(a + b)(a - b) = a^2 - b^2$	The product of the sum and the difference of two terms is the square of the first term minus the square of the second term.
2.	$(a + b)^2 = a^2 + 2ab + b^2$	The square of the sum of two terms is the square of the first term, plus twice the product of the two terms, plus the square of the second term.
3.	$(a - b)^2 = a^2 - 2ab + b^2$	The square of the difference of two terms is the square of the first term, minus twice the product of the two terms, plus the square of the second term.

EXAMPLE 8   Using Special Product Formulas

Use a special product formula to find each product.

a. $(4x + 5)(4x - 5)$ **b.** $(3x + 4)^2$ **c.** $(x^3 - y^3)^2$

Solution

a. Replace a by $4x$ and b by 5 in the formula for the product of the sum and difference of two terms.

$$(a + b)(a - b) = a^2 \quad - b^2$$

$$\downarrow \qquad \cdot\downarrow$$

$$(4x + 5)(4x - 5) = (4x)^2 - 5^2 = 16x^2 - 25$$

b. Use the formula for $(a + b)^2$ with $a = 3x$ and $b = 4$.

$$(a + b)^2 = a^2 \quad + 2 \quad a \quad b + \quad b^2$$

$$\downarrow \qquad \downarrow \quad \downarrow \qquad \downarrow$$

$$(3x + 4)^2 = (3x)^2 + 2(\,3x)(4) + (4)^2 = 9x^2 + 24x + 16$$

c. Use the formula for $(a - b)^2$ with $a = x^3$ and $b = y^3$.

$$(a - b)^2 = a^2 - 2 \quad a \quad b + \quad b^2$$

$$\downarrow \qquad \downarrow \quad \downarrow \qquad \downarrow$$

$$(x^3 - y^3)^2 = (x^3)^2 - 2(x^3)(y^3) + (y^3)^2 = x^6 - 2x^3y^3 + y^6$$

Note   It should be your goal to become so proficient with these special products that the work displayed above is done *mentally*, and you can just write down the answer.

PROGRESS CHECK 8   Use a special product formula to find each product.

a. $(2x + 7)^2$ **b.** $(2x + 7)(2x - 7)$ **c.** $(3m - 5n)^2$ ■

EXAMPLE 9   Combining Multiplication and Division Methods

Show that $\dfrac{2(x + h)^3 - 1 - (2x^3 - 1)}{h}$ simplifies to $6x^2 + 6xh + 2h^2$.

Solution   First, we determine that

$$(x + h)^3 = (x + h)(x + h)(x + h)$$
$$= (x^2 + 2xh + h^2)(x + h)$$
$$= x^3 + 3x^2h + 3xh^2 + h^3$$

Then,

$$\frac{2(x + h)^3 - 1 - (2x^3 - 1)}{h} = \frac{2x^3 + 6x^2h + 6xh^2 + 2h^3 - 1 - 2x^3 + 1}{h}$$

$$= \frac{6x^2h + 6xh^2 + 2h^3}{h}$$

$$= 6x^2 + 6xh + 2h^2$$

PROGRESS CHECK 9   Simplify $\dfrac{3(x + h)^2 + 7 - (3x^2 + 7)}{h}$ ■

EXERCISES 1.4

In Exercise 1–40 perform the multiplication or division and combine like terms.

1. $2(x - y)$

2. $-6(z + y)$

3. $-5x(x^3 - x^2 - x)$

4. $y(3y^2 + 5y - 6)$

5. $-2xyz(4x - y + 7z)$

6. $4x^2yz^3(3x^3 - 2yz + 5xz^4)$

7. $(p^2 + q^2)p^2q^2$

8. $(a^2 - b^2)ab$

9. $(24n^2x + 18nx^2) \div 6nx$

10. $(6dt^2 - 12d^2t) \div 2dt$

11. $\dfrac{2hx + h^2}{h}$

12. $\dfrac{6xh + 3h^2}{h}$

13. $2x^4\left(\dfrac{3}{x} + \dfrac{4}{x^2} - \dfrac{5}{x^3}\right)$

14. $-12x^2\left(3x^2 - \dfrac{1}{3} + \dfrac{3}{4x} - \dfrac{1}{x^2}\right)$

15. $(a + 3)(a + 4)$

16. $(z - 2)(z - 6)$

17. $(x + 7)(x - 5)$

18. $(y - 8)(y - 2)$

19. $(x + 4)(x - 4)$

20. $(3 - t)(3 + t)$

21. $(3x - 4)(2x - 1)$

22. $(7h + 6)(5h - 3)$

23. $(2t + 5c)(6t - c)$

24. $(5y - 4x)(3y + x)$

25. $(k - 2)^2$

26. $(x + 7)^2$

27. $(2x + 3y)^2$

28. $(4c - a)^2$

29. $(x - 1)^3$

30. $(x + h)^3$

31. $(y - 4)(y^2 + 5y - 1)$

32. $(2a - 1)(a^3 + a + 1)$

33. $(x - y)(x^2 + xy + y^2)$

34. $(2y + 3z)(y^2 - 2yz + z^2)$

35. $(2y - 1)(3y + 2)(1 - y)$

36. $(x + 1)^2(2 - x)$

37. $[(x - y) - 1]^2$

38. $[3 + (4a - b)]^2$

39. $(x^2 - 2xy + y^2)(x^2 + 2xy + y^2)$

40. $(x^2 - x - 1)(x^2 + x + 1)$

In Exercises 41–60 use a special product formula to find each product.

41. $(y + 3)(y - 3)$

42. $(x - 8)(x + 8)$

43. $(5n - 7)(5n + 7)$

44. $(3t + 4)(3t - 4)$

45. $(6x + y)(6x - y)$

46. $(4a - 10b)(4a + 10b)$

47. $(a + 1)^2$

48. $(y + 9)^2$

49. $(x - 7)^2$

50. $(1 - k)^2$

51. $(3c + 5)^2$

52. $(4n + 8)^2$

53. $(2 - 7x)^2$

54. $(7x - 2)^2$

55. $(5x + 4y)^2$

56. $(6r + 2h)^2$

57. $(10a - 5b)^2$

58. $(3s - 11t)^2$

59. $[(x - y) - 1]^2$

60. $[(x + h) + 1]^2$

In Exercises 61–70 find each product. Assume that variables as exponents denote integers.

61. $(x^n + 5)(x^n + 2)$

62. $(3x^n - 2)(x^n - 1)$

63. $(z^a + 3)^2$

64. $(t^b - 7)^2$

65. $(x^a - y^b)(x^a + y^b)$

66. $(x^a + y^b)^2$

67. $(a^{bx} + a^{-bx})^2$

68. $(a^{bx} + a^{-bx})(a^{bx} - a^{-bx})$

69. $(x^n + y^n)(x^{2n} - x^ny^n + y^{2n})$

70. $(x^n - y^k)(x^{2n} + x^ny^k + y^{2k})$

71. Show that $\dfrac{(x + h)^2 + 1 - (x^2 + 1)}{h}$ simplifies to $2x + h$.

72. Show that $\dfrac{[1 - (-3 + h)^2] - [1 - (-3)^2]}{h}$ simplifies to $6 - h$.

73. Simplify $\dfrac{(x + h)^3 - x^3}{h}$.

74. Simplify $\dfrac{(2 + h)^3 - 2^3}{h}$.

75. Simplify $\dfrac{[(x + h) + 1]^2 - (x + 1)^2}{h}$.

76. Simplify $\dfrac{[128(t + h) - 16(t + h)^2] - [128t - 16t^2]}{h}$.

77. A manufacturer has been selling about 900 Model X notebook computers every month at the price of $900 each, for a gross monthly income of $810,000. The sales department estimates that for each $50 the price is cut, sales will rise by 50 units per month, so the formula

$$r = (900 - 50x)(900 + 50x)$$

gives the estimated revenue, where x represents the number of $50 price cuts. Multiply the two factors on the right side, and rewrite the result as a polynomial expression. Explain, according to this expression, why cutting the price is not a good idea.

78. For the company described in Exercise 77, if each $50 cut results in 100 new sales, the formula for expected revenue becomes

$$r = (900 - 50x)(900 + 100x).$$

Find a polynomial expression for the right-hand side, and explain why raising the price is a good idea in this case. [Hint: show that there are some values of x that will yield higher revenue than $810,000.]

79. a. Write a polynomial expression for the area of the rectangle.

b. For what value of x will the area be maximum?

80. a. Write a polynomial expression for the area of the rectangle.

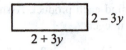

$2 - 3y$

$2 + 3y$

b. For what value of y will the area be a maximum?

81. Find a formula for the shaded area.

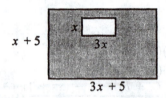

$x + 5$

x

$3x$

$3x + 5$

82. Find a formula for the shaded area.

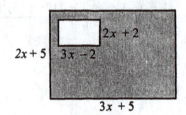

$2x + 5$

$3x - 2$

$2x + 2$

$3x + 5$

THINK ABOUT IT 1.4

1. A common student error is to expand $(a + b)^2$ as $a^2 + b^2$. Explain how the square in the diagram with side length $a + b$ may be used to illustrate geometrically the correct expansion of $(a + b)^2$.

	a	b
a	1	2
b	3	4

2. Show that for any three consecutive integers the square of the middle one is always one more than the product of the smallest and the largest.

3. a. What do the letters FOIL stand for?
 b. Would the FILO method give the same answer?
 c. How many different ways can you arrange the letters {F, O, I, L}?

4. Find these products.
 a. $(x - 1)(x + 1)$
 b. $(x - 1)(x^2 + x + 1)$
 c. $(x - 1)(x^3 + x^2 + x + 1)$

d. Assume that the pattern above holds, and find $(x - 1)(x^{20} + x^{19} + x^{18} + \cdots + x + 1)$.

e. This product can be found the hard way or the easy way. Do the calculation both ways. Find $(d^4 + e^4)(d^2 + e^2)(d + e)(d - e)$.

5. The Pythagorean relation is one of the most famous ideas in mathematics. Several hundred different proofs of this theorem have been recorded, and the National Council of Teachers of Mathematics published a book, *The Pythagorean Proposition* (1968), that presents 370 demonstrations of this statement. Early proofs, which were geometric in nature, gradually gave way to analytical proofs that used algebra to verify geometric ideas. Two well-known proofs of this variety follow.

a. Consider the square with side length $a + b$. Calculate the area of the square in two ways and establish the Pythagorean relation $c^2 = a^2 + b^2$. (**Note:** It must be shown that $\theta = 90°$.)

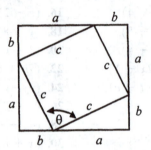

b. The trapezoid in the diagram was used by James Garfield (the twentieth president of the United States) to prove the Pythagorean theorem. Once again the idea is to find the area in two ways and establish $c^2 = a^2 + b^2$. Try it.

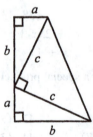

1.5   Linear Equations and Literal Equations

A hydrogen bomb is exploded that releases 6.7×10^{16} joules of energy, the equivalent of 16 million tons of TNT. Use Einstein's formula $E = mc^2$ to find m and determine how much matter was used to create this energy. If we take c, the speed of light, to be 3.0×10^8 m/second, then the units for mass will be kilograms. Use 1 kg $\approx$ 2.2 lb to also find the answer in pounds. (See Example 6.)

Courtesy of National Archives and Records Administration.

OBJECTIVES

1 Solve linear equations.

2 Find the value of a variable in a formula when given values for the other variables.

3 Solve a given formula or literal equation for a specified variable.

If you can solve equations, you can answer the section-opening problem in a straightforward manner. To solve an equation means to find the set of *all* values for the variable that make the equation a true statement. This set is called the **solution set** of the equation. Equations may be always true or always false, or their truth may depend on the value substituted for the variable. If the equation is a true statement for all admissible values of the variable, as is $2x + x = 3x$, then it is called an **identity.** A **conditional equation** is an equation in which some replacements for the variable make the statement true, while others make it false. For example, the conditional equation $x + 5 = 21$ is true if $x = 16$ and false otherwise. We call 16 the **solution** or **root** of the equation. The concept of solving equations is usually associated with conditional equations.

One of the simplest equations to solve is a linear equation. By definition, a **linear equation in one variable** is an equation that can be written in the form

$$ax + b = 0,$$

where a and b are real numbers with $a \neq 0$. This type of equation is called **linear** because (as shown in Section 2.2) it is associated with a graph that is a straight line. We solve a linear equation by isolating the variable on one side of the equation, as described next.

Solution of Linear Equations

Two equations are **equivalent** when they have the same solution set. We may change a linear equation to an equivalent equation of the form $x = $ number, by performing any combination of the following steps:

1. Adding or subtracting the same expression to (from) both sides of the equation.
2. Multiplying or dividing both sides of the equation by the same (nonzero) number.

EXAMPLE 1   Solving a Linear Equation

Solve the equation $5x + 3 = 33$.

Solution   We first isolate the term involving the variable by subtracting 3 from both sides of the equation.

$$5x + 3 = 33$$
$$5x + 3 - 3 = 33 - 3$$
$$5x = 30$$

Next we want the coefficient of x to be 1. Therefore, divide both sides of the equation by 5:

$$\frac{5x}{5} = \frac{30}{5}$$
$$x = 6$$

Thus, 6 is the solution of the equation, and the solution set is $\{6\}$. We can check the solution by replacing x by 6 in the original equation.

$$5x + 3 = 33$$
$$5(6) + 3 \stackrel{?}{=} 33$$
$$33 \stackrel{\checkmark}{=} 33$$

PROGRESS CHECK 1   Solve the equation $-5x + 9 = 64$ ■

EXAMPLE 2   Solving a Linear Equation

Solve the equation $6(x + 1) = 14x + 2$.

Solution   The form $x = $ number may be obtained as follows.

$$6(x + 1) = 14x + 2$$
$$6x + 6 = 14x + 2$$
$$6x + 6 - 6 = 14x + 2 - 6 \qquad \text{Subtract 6 from both sides.}$$
$$6x = 14x - 4$$
$$6x - 14x = 14x - 14x - 4 \qquad \text{Subtract } 14x \text{ from both sides.}$$
$$-8x = -4$$
$$\frac{-8x}{-8} = \frac{-4}{-8} \qquad \text{Divide both sides by } -8.$$
$$x = \frac{1}{2}$$

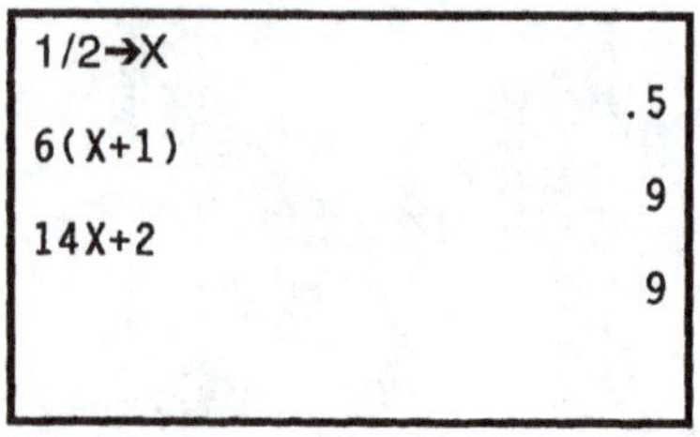

We verify that 1/2 is a solution next.

$$6\left(\frac{1}{2} + 1\right) \stackrel{?}{=} 14\left(\frac{1}{2}\right) + 2$$
$$9 \stackrel{\checkmark}{=} 9$$

Thus, the solution set is $\{1/2\}$.

Technology Link

A calculator check that both sides in this equation equal 9 when $x = 1/2$ is shown in Figure 1.21.

PROGRESS CHECK 2   Solve the equation $2(5 - 3y) = 1 - 8y$.   ■

```
1/2→X
                    .5
6(X+1)
                     9
14X+2
                     9
```

Figure 1.21

EXAMPLE 3   Solving a Linear Equation Involving Fractions

Solve $\dfrac{x-1}{2} = \dfrac{2x}{5}$.

Solution   Although equations that contain fractions are discussed in detail in Section 5.8, it is useful to solve some simple examples of these equations now. Here we can simplify by multiplying both sides of the equation by the least common denominator of the denominators, which is 10.

$$\frac{x-1}{2} = \frac{2x}{5}$$

$$10\left(\frac{x-1}{2}\right) = 10\left(\frac{2x}{5}\right) \qquad \text{Multiply both sides by 10.}$$

$$5x - 5 = 4x$$

$$x - 5 = 0 \qquad \text{Subtract } 4x \text{ from each side.}$$

$$x = 5 \qquad \text{Add 5 to both sides.}$$

Thus, the solution set is $\{5\}$.

Now check by replacing x by 5 in the original equation.

$$\frac{5-1}{2} \overset{?}{=} \frac{2(5)}{5}$$

$$2 \overset{\checkmark}{=} 2$$

Thus, the solution set is $\{5\}$.

PROGRESS CHECK 3   Solve $\dfrac{2x-5}{6} = \dfrac{x-6}{9}$.   ■

The examples shown so far illustrate the general approach to solving linear equations. The method is summarized below.

Solution of Linear Equations

1. Simplify each side of the equation if necessary. This step involves mainly combining like terms, sometimes preceded by using the distributive property to remove parentheses. If necessary, clear the equation of fractions.
2. Use the addition or subtraction properties of equality, if necessary, to write an equivalent equation of the form $cx = n$. To accomplish this, write equivalent equations with all terms involving the unknown on one side of the equation and all constant terms on the other side.
3. Use the multiplication or division properties of equality to solve $cx = n$ if $c \neq 1$. The result of this step will read $x = $ number.
4. Check the solution by substituting it in the original equation.

The next example shows what happens when the steps for solving a linear equation are applied to a false linear equation.

EXAMPLE 4 Identifying a False Equation

Solve the equation $4(x - 3) + 1 = 3(x - 2) + x$.

Solution The first step in solving this equation is to simplify both sides by using the distributive property and combining like terms.

$$
\begin{array}{ll}
4(x - 3) + 1 = 3(x - 2) + x & \text{Given equation.} \\
4x - 12 + 1 = 3x - 6 + x & \text{Distributive property.} \\
4x - 11 = 4x - 6 & \text{Combine like terms.}
\end{array}
$$

At this point we can recognize that this is a false equation, because it says that 11 less than some number is the same as 6 less than that same number, which is impossible. But if we do not spot this contradiction, we would continue. A reasonable next step is to subtract $4x$ from both sides.

$$
\begin{array}{ll}
4x - 11 - 4x = 4x - 6 - 4x & \text{Subtract } 4x \text{ from both sides.} \\
-11 = -6 &
\end{array}
$$

This result is certainly a false statement, which means that the original equation was also false, and so there are no numbers in the solution set. Thus, the solution set is $\emptyset$.

Note If a linear equation is an *identity*, then applying the usual steps will eventually lead to an equation where both sides are exactly the same, such as $2x + 3 = 2x + 3$. When you reach such an equation, you can conclude that the original equation is an identity.

PROGRESS CHECK 4 Solve $2(x + 1) = 3(x + 2) - x$. ■

To analyze relationships, we often use **literal equations,** which are equations that contain two or more letters. The letters may represent any mix of variables and constants. Common examples of literal equations are formulas, such as the perimeter formula $P = 4s$, and general forms of equations such as $ax + b = 0$. Because literal equations and formulas are types of equations we may use the equation-solving techniques developed in this section to analyze them.

EXAMPLE 5 Finding the Time in a Simple Interest Investment

When an original principal P is invested at simple interest for t years at annual interest rate r, then the amount A of the investment is given by $A = P(1 + rt)$. Find the value of t when $A = \$5,920$, $P = \$4,000$, and $r = 0.06$.

Solution Substitute the given values into the formula and then solve for t.

$$
\begin{array}{ll}
A = P(1 + rt) & \text{Given formula.} \\
5,920 = 4,000(1 + 0.06t) & \text{Substitute the given values.} \\
5,920 = 4,000 + 240t & \text{Distributive property.} \\
1,920 = 240t & \text{Subtract 4,000 from both sides.} \\
8 = t & \text{Divide both sides by 240.}
\end{array}
$$

Check the solution by replacing each letter by its value. You will get the identity $5,920 = 5,920$, proving that $t = 8$ years is correct.

Caution In this example a common student error is to replace $1 + 0.06t$ with $1.06t$. Recall that 1 and $0.06t$ are not like terms and cannot be combined. The expression $1.06t$ would result from $t + 0.06t$.

Technology Link

Some calculators have an equation-solving feature that you will find useful when working with formulas, in a wide variety of math-dependent disciplines. For instance, Figure 1.22 displays the solution to the problem in Example 5 on a particular calculator with such a feature.

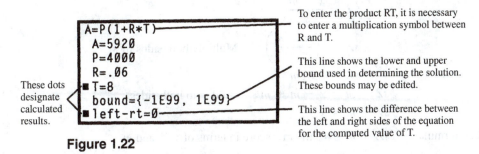

These dots designate calculated results.

To enter the product RT, it is necessary to enter a multiplication symbol between R and T.

This line shows the lower and upper bound used in determining the solution. These bounds may be edited.

This line shows the difference between the left and right sides of the equation for the computed value of T.

Figure 1.22

A nice benefit of an equation-solving feature is that it allows you to investigate quickly how a change in one variable affects another variable.

PROGRESS CHECK 5   Find the value of r in the formula $A = P(1 + rt)$ if $A = \$6,240$, $P = \$4,000$, and $t = 7$ years.   ■

EXAMPLE 6   Finding the Mass in a Hydrogen Bomb Explosion

Solve the problem in the section introduction on page 41.

Solution   First, solve for m using the given information.

$$E = mc^2 \qquad\qquad \text{Given formula.}$$

$$6.7 \times 10^{16} = m(3 \times 10^8)^2 \qquad \text{Substitute the given values.}$$

$$\frac{6.7 \times 10^{16}}{(3 \times 10^8)^2} = m \qquad\qquad \text{Divide both sides by } (3 \times 10^8)^2.$$

Now compute the quotient on a calculator. One possible sequence of keystrokes is

$$6.7 \;\boxed{\text{EE}}\; 16 \;\boxed{\div}\; 3 \;\boxed{\text{EE}}\; 8 \;\boxed{x^2}\; \boxed{\text{ENTER}}\;.$$

To the nearest hundredth, the computed result in the display rounds off to 0.74, so about 0.74 kg of matter were used. Since 1 kg is about 2.2 lb, this explosion was generated from about 1.6 lb of matter!

PROGRESS CHECK 6   The largest hydrogen bomb ever exploded (the former Soviet Union, 1961) released 2.4×10^{17} joules of energy, the equivalent of 57 million tons of TNT. Use the information in Example 6 and determine how much matter was used to create this energy. Express the answer in both kilograms and pounds.   ■

In Example 6 you may find it convenient to first rewrite

$$E = mc^2 \text{ as } m = \frac{E}{c^2}$$

before substituting the values given for E and c. This rearrangement is permitted because $E = mc^2$ may be "solved for m" by dividing both sides by c^2. It is often useful to solve a literal equation for a specified variable to obtain a more helpful version of the equation, and Examples 7–9 illustrate a few such conversions.

EXAMPLE 7   Rearranging a Statistics Formula

The Z-score formula in statistics is $Z = (x - m)/s$, where x is a raw score, m is the mean, and s is the standard deviation. Solve the formula for the raw score (x).

Solution   To solve for x, we need to isolate x on one side of the equation.

$$Z = \frac{x - m}{s}$$

$$sZ = s\left(\frac{x - m}{s}\right) \qquad \text{Multiply both sides by } s.$$

$$sZ = x - m$$

$$sZ + m = x - m + m \qquad \text{Add } m \text{ to both sides.}$$

$$sZ + m = x$$

The formula $x = sZ + m$ gives the raw score in terms of s, Z, and m.

PROGRESS CHECK 7   Solve $m = \dfrac{y - b}{x}$ for y.   ■

EXAMPLE 8   Rearranging a Temperature Conversion Formula

The formula $C = (5/9)(F - 32)$ is usually used to convert from degrees Fahrenheit to degrees Celsius. Solve this formula for F.

Solution   We will solve for F so that the result is the common formula for converting from degrees Celsius to degrees Fahrenheit.

$$C = \tfrac{5}{9}(F - 32)$$

$$\tfrac{9}{5}C = \tfrac{9}{5} \cdot \tfrac{5}{9}(F - 32) \qquad \text{Multiply both sides by } \tfrac{9}{5}.$$

$$\tfrac{9}{5}C = F - 32$$

$$\tfrac{9}{5}C + 32 = F - 32 + 32 \qquad \text{Add 32 to both sides.}$$

$$\tfrac{9}{5}C + 32 = F$$

The result, $F = (9/5)C + 32$, gives a formula for F in terms of C.

Note   In this example it is also logical to clear fractions as a first step by multiplying both sides by 9. This approach leads to the result

$$F = \frac{9C + 160}{5}.$$

When you rearrange formulas, there may be several acceptable answer forms, and you may need to consult with your instructor to see if your answer is correct.

PROGRESS CHECK 8   Solve $S = t - \tfrac{1}{2}gt^2$ for g.   ■

In Chapter 2 we will sometimes find it useful to solve equations of the form $ax + by = C$ for either x or y. Example 9 illustrates this type of problem.

EXAMPLE 9   Solving for a Specified Variable

Solve the equation $2x - 3y = 9$ for the indicated letter.

a. For x **b.** For y

Solution

a. The equation may be solved for x as follows.

$$2x - 3y = 9$$
$$2x = 3y + 9 \quad \text{Add } 3y \text{ to both sides.}$$
$$x = \frac{3y + 9}{2} \quad \text{Divide both sides by 2.}$$

b. The equation may be solved for y as follows.

$$2x - 3y = 9$$
$$-3y = 9 - 2x \quad \text{Subtract } 2x \text{ from both sides.}$$
$$y = \frac{9 - 2x}{-3} \quad \text{Divide both sides by } -3.$$
$$y = \frac{2x - 9}{3} \quad \text{Multiply numerator and denominator by } -1.$$

Note In Example 9b we choose as a last step to multiply numerator and denominator by -1 to avoid an answer with a negative number in the denominator. However, this conversion is optional, and all of the following equations are acceptable answers here.

$$y = \frac{2x - 9}{3}; y = \frac{2}{3}x - 3; y = \frac{9 - 2x}{-3}; y = \frac{-9 + 2x}{3}; y = -3 + \frac{2}{3}x$$

PROGRESS CHECK 9   Solve $5x - 2y = 30$ for the indicated letter.

a. For x **b.** For y ■

EXERCISES 1.5

In Exercises 1–30 solve each question and check your answer.

1. $6x = 18$
2. $-3x + 3 = 0$
3. $3x + 2 = 2x + 8$
4. $7y - 9 = 6y - 10$
5. $2z + 12 = 5z + 15$
6. $-6x + 7 = 5x - 4$
7. $3y - 14 = -4y + 7$
8. $3z - 8 = 13z - 9$
9. $8x - 10 = 3x$
10. $15 - 6y = 0$
11. $9 - 2y = 27 + y$
12. $15x + 5 = 2x + 14$
13. $4x - x = 3x$
14. $x - 1 = x + 3$
15. $2(x + 4) = 2(x - 1) + 3$
16. $2(x + 3) - 1 = 2x + 5$
17. $7x = 2x$
18. $3y - 7 = 2y - 7$
19. $4 - 3y = 5(4 - y)$
20. $7x - 2(x - 7) = 14 - 5x$
21. $5(x - 6) = -2(15 - 2x)$
22. $18(z + 1) = 9z + 10$
23. $3[2x - (x - 2)] = -3(3 - 2x)$
24. $2y - (3y - 4) = 4\left(y + \frac{3}{4}\right)$
25. $\frac{x - 2}{7} = -1$
26. $\frac{2y - 7}{9} = 5$
27. $\frac{x - 9}{3} = 3x - 11$
28. $\frac{-14y - 17}{-5} = 2 + 3y$
29. $\frac{9x}{4} = \frac{18 + x}{2}$
30. $\frac{7x - 5}{6} = \frac{x - 44}{9}$

In Exercises 31–40 find the value of the indicated variable in each formula.

31. $d = \frac{1}{2}at^2$; $d = 144, t = 3$. Find a.
32. $C = \frac{5}{9}(F - 32)$; $C = -25$. Find F.
33. $S = \frac{1}{2}gt^2 + vt$; $g = 32, t = 2, S = 144$. Find v.
34. $F = \frac{9}{5}C + 32$; $F = 212$. Find C.
35. $R = \frac{kL}{d^2}$; $R = 32, L = 100, d = 5$. Find k.
36. $a = p(1 + rt)$; $a = 3{,}000, p = 2{,}000, r = 0.05$. Find t.
37. $P = 2(l + w)$; $P = 76, l = 27$. Find w.
38. $V = \frac{1}{3}\pi r^2 h$; $V = 51\pi, r = 3$. Find h.
39. $T = mg - mf$; $T = 80, m = 10, g = 14$. Find f.
40. $S = \frac{1}{2}n(a + L)$; $S = 85, n = 17, a = -7$. Find L.

In Exercises 41–60 solve each formula for the variable indicated.

41. $F = ma$ for m
42. $D = r \cdot t$ for r
43. $d = \frac{1}{2}at^2$ for a
44. $V = \frac{1}{3}\pi r^2 h$ for h
45. $P = mgh$ for m
46. $i = p \cdot r \cdot t$ for r
47. $A = \frac{a + b + c}{3}$ for b
48. $T = mg - mf$ for f
49. $S = \frac{1}{2}n(a + L)$ for L
50. $A = \frac{1}{2}h(b + c)$ for b
51. $a = p(1 + rt)$ for t
52. $a = p + prt$ for t
53. $A = \pi(R^2 - r^2)$ for R^2
54. $R = \frac{kL}{d^2}$ for d^2
55. $S = \frac{a}{1 - r}$ for r
56. $C = \frac{E}{R + S}$ for R
57. $n = \frac{A + D}{A}$ for D
58. $\frac{I_1}{I_2} = \frac{r_1^2}{r_2^2}$ for I_2
59. $I = \frac{2E}{R + 2r}$ for r
60. $C = \frac{nE}{1 + nr}$ for E

In Exercises 61–68 solve each equation for x.

61. $2x = a$
62. $x - 7 = b$
63. $3az - x = 1 + t$
64. $2t - 2x = 3c$
65. $3x + b = c - x$
66. $5x - a = 2x + a$
67. $\frac{2x - a}{b} = 5$
68. $\frac{4 - 3x}{c} = 1$

In Exercises 69–76 solve for the indicated letter.

   a. For x   **b.** For y

69. $x + 2y = 4$
70. $7x - y = 2$
71. $-x - y = 2$
72. $-4x + 2y = 5$
73. $3x + 4y = 6$
74. $3x - 2y = -6$
75. $-\frac{3}{5}x + \frac{2}{5}y = 10$
76. $\frac{4}{3}x - \frac{1}{3}y = 1$

77. The formula $h = \frac{w + 200}{5}$ shows the approximate relationships of "normal" weight to height for adult females, where h is height in inches and w is weight in pounds.
   a. Solve this formula for w.
   b. How many pounds should a 5-ft. 6-in. woman "normally" weigh?

78. The formula for converting centimeters (c) to inches (i) is $i = 0.3937c$.
   a. Solve the formula for c.
   b. A yardstick is 36 in. long. Find this length to the nearest centimeter.

79. Radio waves travel at the speed of light, which is about 299,800 km/second. How long does it take for a radio message from an astronaut to travel from the moon to the earth, which is about 3.844×10^8 m away? Use the distance formula, $d = rt$.

80. Use the formula $E = mc^2$ to find m (in kilograms) if c, the speed of light, is 3×10^8 m/second and E is 4.2×10^{16} joules. This will give you the amount of matter used to create the explosive force of the first hydrogen bomb ever exploded. (This force is equivalent to 10 million tons of TNT and was released by the U.S. in 1952 at Eniwetok.)

81. The shaded area equals 55 in.^{2}. Find the area of the larger rectangle.

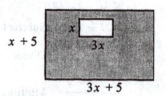

82. The shaded area equals 98 cm^2. Find the area of the smaller rectangle.

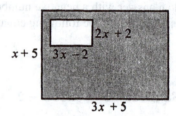

THINK ABOUT IT 1.5

1. **a.** Write in words what this equation says, and then explain why it must be an identity: $x + x = 2x$.
   b. Write in words what this equation says. Is it an identity or a false equation? $x - 1 = x + 1$.

2. The formula $S = (1/2)n(n + 1)$ gives the sum of the integers from 1 to n.
   a. To see that the formula is reasonable, let $n = 3$ and use the formula to show that $1 + 2 + 3$ is equal to 6.
   b. Find the sum of the integers from 1 to 999.
   c. Explain why these three versions of the formula are equivalent. Then use each version to find the sum of the numbers from 1 to 100.
     i. $S = [(n + 1)/2] \cdot n$
     ii. $S = (n + 1) \cdot (n/2)$
     iii. $S = [(n + 1)(n)] \div 2$

3. Assume $a \neq 0$ and solve each equation for x.
   a. $ax + a^2 = 4a^2$
   b. $4ax - 3a^{-2} = 9a^{-2}$

4. In the equation $ax = b$, a and b are constants. What combination of values for a and b results in an equation with exactly one solution? No solution? Infinitely many solutions?

5. Consider this illustration of a piece of a broken chariot wheel found by a group of archaeologists. What is the radius of the wheel?

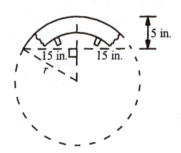

1.6 Applications of Linear Equations

In a vacation community the real estate salespeople get a 12 percent commission on rentals. An owner wants to rent out a vacation house for the summer and end up with $10,000 income. Find the required rental price for the house. (See Example 1.)

Courtesy of John Serafin/SBG.

OBJECTIVES

1 Solve word problems by translating phrases and setting up and solving equations.

2 Solve problems involving geometric figures, annual interest, uniform motion, liquid mixtures, and proportions.

Many problems that are analyzed by mathematics begin with writing an equation to express some key relationship. Then the solution to the equation is used to solve the problem. In this section we discuss how to solve several basic types of word problems that require us to write and solve linear equations. Consider carefully the following steps, which are recommended by both mathematicians and reading specialists as a general approach to solving word problems.

To Solve a Word Problem

1. **Read the problem several times.** The first reading is a preview and is done quickly to obtain a general idea of the problem. The objective of the second reading is to determine exactly what you are asked to find. Write this down. Finally, read the problem carefully and note what information is given. If possible, display the given information in a sketch or chart.

2. **Let a variable represent an unknown quantity** (which is usually the quantity you are asked to find). Write down precisely what the variable represents. If there is more than one unknown, represent these unknowns in terms of the original variable, when possible.

3. **Set up an equation** that expresses the relationship between the quantities in the problem.

4. **Solve the equation.**

5. **Answer the question.**

6. **Check the answer** by interpreting the solution in the context of the word problem.

EXAMPLE 1   Finding the Rental Price for a Vacation House

Solve the problem in the section introduction on page 49.

Solution   We need to find the required rental price for the house. If x = rental price, then the sales commission is 12 percent of x, or $0.12x$, so

rental price   minus   sales commission   equals   amount for owner.

x $-$ $0.12x$ $=$ $10{,}000$

Solve the Equation:

$$0.88x = 10{,}000 \qquad \text{Combine like terms.}$$
$$x = \frac{10{,}000}{0.88} \qquad \text{Divide both sides by } 0.88.$$
$$x = 11{,}363.64 \qquad \text{Simplify.}$$

Answer the Question: The rental price should be $11,363.64. Of course, in practice the owner usually rounds the number up a little, to say $11,400.

Check the Answer: If the rental price is $11,363.64, then

$$\text{sales commission} = 0.12(\$11{,}363.64) = \$1{,}363.64$$
$$\text{income from rental} = \$11{,}363.64 - \$1{,}363.64 = \$10{,}000$$

The solution checks.

PROGRESS CHECK 1   The total cost (including tax) of a new car is $14,256. If the sales tax rate is 8 percent, how much is paid in taxes?   ▪

     Historically, the study of algebra has always been connected with problems about number relations and properties. The next example illustrates a type of number problem that traditionally is used to build proficiency in writing and solving equations.

EXAMPLE 2   Translating Phrases to Solve a Problem

The sum of two consecutive even integers is 238. Find the integers.

Solution   If x represents the first even integer, then $x + 2$ represents the next even integer. Now **set up an equation.**

The sum of two consecutive even integers   is   238.

$x + (x + 2)$ $=$ 238

Solve the Equation:

$$2x + 2 = 238 \qquad \text{Combine like terms.}$$
$$2x = 236 \qquad \text{Subtract 2 from both sides.}$$
$$x = 118 \qquad \text{Divide both sides by 2.}$$

Answer the Question: The smaller integer is 118, and the next consecutive even integer is 120.

Check the Answer: The sum of 118 and 120 is 238, and they are consecutive even integers, so the solution checks.

PROGRESS CHECK 2   The sum of two consecutive integers is 147. Find the integers.   ■

To develop skill in problem solving, it is useful to build a supply of model problems that you understand. Then, when a new situation arises, you may find that it is similar to a problem you already know how to solve, and you will quickly know some approaches that might work. To build this base, we now consider word problems that involve geometric figures, annual interest, uniform motion, liquid mixtures, and proportions.

Geometric Problems

To solve problems about geometric figures, we often need perimeter, area, and volume formulas, and Section 1.2 contains the formulas you need for now. When triangles and angle measures are involved, then you should know that any two angles whose measures add up to 90° are called **complementary,** and any two angles whose measures add up to 180° are called **supplementary.** Also, the sum of the angle measures in a triangle is 180°, and a **right triangle** is a triangle that contains a 90° angle.

EXAMPLE 3   Solving a Geometric Problem

The length of a rectangular solar panel is three times its width. If the perimeter is 224 in., determine the area of the solar panel.

Solution   To find the dimensions of the solar panel, let

$$x = \text{width}$$

so

$$3x = \text{length.}$$

Now illustrate the given information as in Figure 1.23.

The perimeter is 224 in., and we can **set up an equation** by using $P = 2l + 2w$, the formula for the perimeter of a rectangle.

$$P = 2l + 2w$$
$$224 = 2(3x) + 2x \quad \text{Replace } P \text{ by 224, } l \text{ by } 3x, \text{ and } w \text{ by } x.$$

Solve the Equation:

$$224 = 8x \quad \text{Combine like terms.}$$
$$28 = x \quad \text{Divide both sides by 8.}$$

Figure 1.23

Answer the Question: The area is given by $A = lw$ where $w = 28$ in., and $l = 3(28) = 84$ in. So the area is 2,352 in.^{2}.

Check the Answer: The perimeter is $2(28) + 2(84) = 224$ in., while 84 in. is three times as long as 28 in. The area is $28(84) = 2,352$ in.^{2}, so the solution checks.

PROGRESS CHECK 3   In a right triangle the measure of one of the acute angles is 36° greater than the other. What is the measure of the larger acute angle?   ■

Annual Interest Problems

When a problem involves annual interest, use $I = Pr$, where P represents principal, r represents the annual interest rate, and I represents the amount of interest earned in one year. This formula is a special case of $I = Prt$ where $t = 1$.

EXAMPLE 4   Solving an Annual Interest Problem

How should a $160,000 investment be split so that the total annual earnings are $14,000, if one portion is invested at 6 percent annual interest and the rest at 11 percent?

Solution   To find the amount invested at each rate, let

$$x = \text{amount invested at 6 percent}$$

so

$$160,000 - x = \text{amount at 11 percent.}$$

In general, note that if the sum of two numbers is n, then one number can be called x and the other $n - x$. Now, use $I = Pr$ and analyze the investment in a chart format.

Investment	Principal	·	Rate	=	Interest
1st account	x		0.06		$0.06x$
2nd account	$160,000 - x$		0.11		$0.11(160,000 - x)$

Set up an equation using 14,000 as the desired amount of total interest.

Interest from 1st account	plus	interest from 2nd account	equals	total interest.
⎵	↓	⎵	↓	⎵
$0.06x$	$+$	$0.11(160,000 - x)$	$=$	$14,000$

Solve the Equation:

$$
\begin{aligned}
0.06x + 17,600 - 0.11x &= 14,000 &&\text{Distributive property.} \\
-0.05x + 17,600 &= 14,000 &&\text{Combine like terms.} \\
-0.05x &= -3,600 &&\text{Subtract 17,600 from each side.} \\
x &= 72,000 &&\text{Divide both sides by } -0.05.
\end{aligned}
$$

Answer the Question: Invest $72,000 at 6 percent and $160,000 − $72,000, or $88,000, at 11 percent.

Check the Answer: $72,000 + $88,000 = $160,000 and the first account earns 6 percent of $72,000, or $4,320, while the second account earns 11 percent of $88,000, or $9,680, for a total of $14,000 interest. The solution checks.

PROGRESS CHECK 4   How should a $200,000 investment be split so that the total annual earnings are $18,000, if one portion is invested at 10 percent annual interest and the rest at 6 percent?
■

Uniform Motion Problems

To solve uniform motion problems you need the formula $d = rt$, where d represents the distance traveled in time t by an object moving at a constant rate r. This formula applies to objects moving at a **constant** (or uniform) speed and to objects whose **average** speed is involved. A chart format is recommended for this type of problem, and a sketch of the situation may also be helpful.

EXAMPLE 5   Solving a Uniform Motion Problem

One jet takes 1 hour 15 minutes for a certain flight between two airports. Under the same conditions another jet makes the trip in 1 hour by going 100 mi/hour faster. What is the distance between airports?

Solution   The key here is to find the rate for one of the jets. If

$$x = \text{rate for slower jet},$$

then

$$x + 100 = \text{rate for faster jet}.$$

Now analyze the problem in a chart format using $d = rt$. Note that 1 hour 15 minutes is equivalent to $1 + 15/60$, or 1.25 hours.

Plane	Rate (mi/hour) ·	Time (hours) =	Distance (mi)
Slower jet	x	1.25	$1.25x$
Faster jet	$x + 100$	1	$1(x + 100)$

To **set up an equation,** sketch the situation as in Figure 1.24. From the sketch observe that both jets travel the same distance.

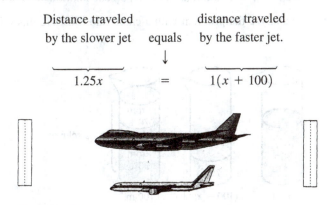

Distance traveled by the slower jet	equals	distance traveled by the faster jet.
↓	↓	↓
$1.25x$	$=$	$1(x + 100)$

Figure 1.24

Solve the Equation:

$$
\begin{aligned}
1.25x &= x + 100 && \text{Distributive property.} \\
0.25x &= 100 && \text{Subtract } x \text{ from both sides.} \\
x &= 400 && \text{Divide both sides by 0.25.}
\end{aligned}
$$

Answer the Question: The slower jet travels at 400 mi/hour for 1.25 hours, so the distance between airports is 400(1.25) mi, or 500 mi.

Check the Answer: If the distance between airports is 500 mi, then a rate of 400 mi/hour is required to complete the trip in 1.25 hours, and a rate of 500 mi/hour is required to complete the trip in 1 hour. Since 500 is 100 more than 400, the solution checks.

PROGRESS CHECK 5 On a video display, an air traffic controller notices two planes 120 mi apart and flying toward each other on a collision course. One plane is flying at 500 mi/hour; the other is flying at 300 mi/hour. How much time is there for the controller to prevent a crash? ■

Liquid Mixture Problems

To solve problems about liquid mixtures, you need to apply the concept of percentage in the following context.

$$\left(\begin{array}{c}\text{percent of}\\\text{an ingredient}\end{array}\right) \cdot \left(\begin{array}{c}\text{amount of}\\\text{solution}\end{array}\right) = \left(\begin{array}{c}\text{amount of}\\\text{the ingredient}\end{array}\right).$$

For example, the amount of acid in 10 liters of a solution that is 30 percent acid is 0.30(10), or 3 liters. Once again a chart is recommended for this type of problem.

EXAMPLE 6 Solving a Liquid Mixture Problem

A chemist has two acid solutions, one 30 percent acid and the other 70 percent acid. How much of each solution must be used to obtain 100 ml of a solution that is 41 percent acid?

Solution To find the correct mixture, let

$$x = \text{amount used of 30 percent solution,}$$

so

$$100 - x = \text{amount used of 70 percent solution.}$$

As recommended, we analyze the problem with a chart, and illustrate this information as in Figure 1.25.

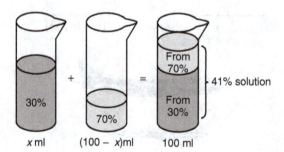

Figure 1.25

Solution	Percent Acid	·	Amount of Solution (ml)	=	Amount of Acid (ml)
1st solution	30		x		$0.3x$
2nd solution	70		$100 - x$		$0.7(100 - x)$
New solution	41		100		$0.41(100)$

To **set up an equation,** we reason that the amount of acid in the new solution is the sum of the amounts contributed by the 1st and 2nd solutions.

Amount of acid in 1st solution	plus	amount of acid in 2nd solution	equals	amount of acid in new solution.
↓		↓		
$0.3x$	$+$	$0.7(100 - x)$	$=$	$0.41(100)$

Solve the Equation:

$$0.3x + 70 - 0.7x = 41 \qquad \text{Distributive property.}$$
$$-0.4x + 70 = 41 \qquad \text{Combine like terms.}$$
$$-0.4x = -29 \qquad \text{Subtract 70 from both sides.}$$
$$x = 72.5 \qquad \text{Divide both sides by } -0.4.$$

Answer the Question: Mix 72.5 ml of the 30 percent solution with $100 - 72.5$, or 27.5, ml of the 70 percent solution.

Check the Answer: The new solution contains $72.5 + 27.5$, or 100 ml. Also, 72.5 ml from the 1st solution contains $0.3(72.5) = 21.75$ ml of acid, while 27.5 ml from the 2nd solution contains $0.7(27.5) = 19.25$ ml of acid. Thus, the new mixture contains 41 ml of acid in 100 ml of solution. Because $41/100 = 0.41 = 41$ percent, the new mixture does contain 41 percent acid, and the solution checks.

PROGRESS CHECK 6   One metal contains 30 percent gold by weight and the rest silver. Another contains 50 percent gold by weight and the rest silver. They will be melted down and mixed together to form a new alloy that is 35 percent gold. How much of each should be used to form 5 lb of the new alloy?   ■

Proportion Problems

A **ratio** is a comparison of two quantities by division, and a **proportion** is a statement that two ratios are equal. For example, the ratios 2/3 and 6/9 are equal and form a proportion that may be written as $2/3 = 6/9$ (read: 2 is to 3 as 6 is to 9) or as $2:3 = 6:9$. When we work with proportions, it is easier to write the ratios as fractions and then use the techniques we have developed for solving an equation.

EXAMPLE 7   Solving a Proportion Problem

A cylindrical tank holds 480 gal when it is filled to its full height of 8 ft. When the gauge shows that it contains water at a height of 3 ft 1 in., how many gallons are in the tank?

Solution   If we let x gal represent the unknown amount of water in the tank and *set up two equal ratios* that compare like measurements, we have the proportion

$$\frac{x \text{ gal}}{480 \text{ gal}} = \frac{37 \text{ in.}}{96 \text{ in.}} \qquad \textit{Note:} \ 3 \text{ ft } 1 \text{ in.} = 37 \text{ in. and } 8 \text{ ft} = 96 \text{ in.}$$

Solve the Equation:

$$x = \left(\frac{37}{96}\right) \cdot 480 \qquad \text{Multiply both sides by 480.}$$
$$x = 185 \qquad \text{Simplify.}$$

Answer the Question: There are 185 gal of water in the tank when the water is at a height of 3 ft 1 in.

Check the Answer: In the context of the problem, 185 gal at 37 inches is a rate of 5 gal/inch, and 480 gal at 96 inches is also a rate of 5 gal/inch. The solution checks.

Note: It is possible to set up the proportion in other ways, as long as both sides of the equation express similar ratios. For instance, as suggested in the Check, a logical proportion in this example would be

$$\frac{x \text{ gal}}{37 \text{ in.}} = \frac{480 \text{ gal}}{96 \text{ in.}}.$$

PROGRESS CHECK 7 If an idling car uses 35 oz of gasoline in 50 minutes, how long to the nearest minute must it idle to use 1 gal of gas? One gallon is 128 oz. ■

EXERCISES 1.6

Solve each problem by first setting up an appropriate equation.

1. During a test run, machine A produced x cans; machine B turned out three times as many; machine C produced 10 more cans than A. The total production during the run was 5,510. How many cans did each machine produce?

2. A magazine and a newsletter cost $1.10. If the magazine cost $1.00 more than the newsletter, how much did each cost?

3. A stockbroker, after deducting a commission, gives a client $7,650. If the commission is 10 percent of the selling price of the stock, how much was the customer's stock worth?

4. Suppose that 5 percent of your salary is deducted for a retirement fund. If your total deduction for one year is $1,725, what is your annual salary?

5. A car dealer offers a used car at a price of $6,104. This selling price represents a profit of 12 percent on the amount paid for the car. How much did the car cost the dealer?

6. If the total cost (including tax) of a new car is $13,054, how much do you pay in taxes if the sales tax rate is 7 percent?

7. The final bill for the sofa you purchased totaled $1,349. If this included 8.25 percent sales tax plus a $50 delivery fee, what was the original price of the sofa? The delivery fee was not taxed.

8. The population of a city increased 2 percent in one year to reach about 3 million people. To the nearest thousand people, about what was the population at the beginning of the year?

9. Multiplying a number by 4 gives the same result as adding 6 to the number. What is the number?

10. Taking one-half of a number gives the same result as adding 3 to the number. What is the number?

11. If a number is decreased by 5, the result is twice the original number. What is the number?

12. Multiplying a number by 4 and adding 2 to the product gives the same result as dividing the number by -2. What is the number?

13. The sum of two consecutive integers is 89. Find the larger integer.

14. The sum of two integers is 35. One of the integers is four times the other. Find the integers.

15. The sum of the three angles in a triangle is 180°. The second angle is 20° more than the first, and the third angle is twice the first. What is the measure of each of the angles in the triangle?

16. The length of a rectangle is three times its width. If the perimeter is 160 in., determine the area of the rectangle.

17. In a right triangle the measure of one of the acute angles is 3 times the measure of the other. What is the measure of the larger acute angle?

18. The sum of the angles of a quadrilateral is 360°. If the measures of the angles of a quadrilateral are four consecutive odd integers, find them.

19. Two angles are supplementary. If the measure of one of them is 5 more than 4 times the other, what are the measures of the angles?

20. If the measure of two complementary angles is represented by $2x + 3$ and $3x - 8$, what are the measures of these angles?

21. A certain amount of money is invested at 12 percent interest per year, and twice that amount is invested at 9 percent annual interest. Together, the two accounts earned annual interest of $5,400. How much is invested in each account?

22. Money in one account is earning 7 percent annually, and another account with $2,000 more earns 11 percent annually. Altogether, the two accounts earn $2,700 a year. How much money is invested in each account?

23. The trustees of a $375,000 fund that provides scholarship monies need to generate $26,000 worth of income each year. Their advisors recommend investing in two different financial instruments, one very safe but yielding only 5 percent annually, and another yielding 12 percent annually but more risky.
    a. To the nearest thousand dollars, how much should be allocated to each investment?
    b. What should be the split if they also want to generate an additional $10,000 for investment?

24. An accountant recommends two investments to a client: one earning 10 percent annually and one earning 15 percent annually. These investments should cover the cost of the client's rent ($900 per month) for a year. If there is $86,000 to invest, how should the money be split between the two investments?

25. Two fishing boats leave the harbor at the same time and using the same float plan. One averages 17 knots (nautical miles per hour), and the other averages 14.5 knots. How long will it take for the boats to be 10 nautical miles apart?

26. A moving van makes the trip along the total length of Highway 4 in about 6 hours. Another, newer moving van makes the same trip in 5.5 hours by traveling 4 mi/hour faster. How fast does each van travel? How long is Highway 4?

27. Two bicyclists make the same trip. The first takes about 3.5 hours, and the second, traveling about 1 mi/hour faster, only takes 3 hours. How many miles is the trip?

28. One plane takes 2 hours and 45 minutes for a particular flight. With a headwind, the same plane goes 20 mi/hour slower and requires 3 hours to reach its destination. How far apart are the airports?

29. A spacecraft moves through intergalactic space at a rate of 15,000 mi/hour. Unknown to the crew, a huge asteroid traveling at 7,000 mi/hour is hurtling in line directly toward the spacecraft. The craft and the asteroid are presently 165,000 mi/apart. How long will it take for them to be within scanning range (22,000 mi) of each other, at which time the crew can can make a course correction to avoid impact?

30. On a video display an air traffic controller notices two planes 120 mi apart and flying toward each other on a collision course. One plane is flying at 500 mi/hour; the other is flying at 300 mi/hour. How much time is there for the controller to prevent a crash?

31. A machine shop has two large containers that are each filled with a mixture of oil and gasoline. Container A contains 2 percent oil (and 98 percent gasoline). Container B contains 6 percent oil (and 94 percent gasoline). How much of each should be used to obtain 18 quarts (qt) of a new mixture that contains 5 percent oil?

32. A chemist has 5 liters of a 25 percent sulfuric acid solution. She wishes to obtain a solution that is 35 percent acid by adding a solution of 75 percent acid to her original solution. How much of the more concentrated acid must be added to achieve the desired concentration?

33. One bar of tin alloy is 35 percent pure tin, and another bar is 10 percent pure tin. How many pounds of each must be used to make 95 lb of a new alloy that is 20 percent pure tin?

34. An alloy of copper and silver weighs 40 lb and is 20 percent silver. How much silver must be added to produce a metal that is 50 percent silver?

35. A 20 percent antifreeze solution is a solution that consists of 20 percent antifreeze and 80 percent water. If we have 20 qt of such a solution, how much water should be added to obtain a solution that contains 10 percent antifreeze?

36. One cup of vinegar is mixed with 3 cups of a solution that is 15 percent vinegar and 85 percent oil. What is the percentage of vinegar in the final mixture?

37. In a certain concrete mix the ratio of sand to cement is 4:1. At this ratio, how many pounds of cement are needed to be mixed with 50 lb of sand?

38. A spring is stretched 6 in. by a weight of 2 lb. How much weight is needed to stretch the spring 15 in.?

39. A car travels 225 mi in 5 hours. At the same rate, how long will it take the car to travel 405 mi?

40. An object that weighs 48 lb on earth weighs 8 lb on the moon. How much will a person who weighs 174 lb on earth weigh on the moon?

41. A stake 12 ft high casts a shadow 9 ft long at the same time that a tree casts a shadow of 33 ft. What is the height of the tree?

42. The gable end of a building has the dimensions illustrated in the drawing on the left. If a carpenter wishes to keep the same proportions, what would be the vertical height of the structure illustrated in the drawing on the right?

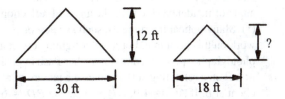

43. On a test, you received a grade of 114 on a scale of 0–120. Convert your score to a scale of 0–100.

44. A cylindrical tank holds 370 gal when it is filled to its full height of 9 ft. When the gauge shows that it contains oil at a height of 6 ft 7 in., how many gallons (to the nearest gallon) are in the tank?

45. If 72 gal of water flow through a feeder pipe in 40 minutes, how many gallons of water will flow through the pipe in 3 hours?

46. A map has a scale of 1.5 in. = 7 mi. To the nearest tenth of a mile, what distance is represented by 20 in. on the map?

47. A bus will travel 67 mi on 8 gal of gas. To the nearest mile, how far will the bus travel on 11 gal of gas?

48. If 2 g of hydrogen unite with 16 g of oxygen to form water, how many grams of oxygen are needed to produce 162 g of water? (Assume that no loss takes place during the reaction.)

49. A certain antifreeze mixture calls for 5 qt of antifreeze to be mixed with 2 gal of water. How many quarts of antifreeze are needed for a total mixture of 65 qt?

50. A team of sociologists wishes to do a survey in a city where the census report indicates that the ratio of Protestants to Catholics is 5:2. They also determine that a suitable sample size is 420 people. How many people of each religion should they interview if the sample is to have the same religious distribution as the city's population?

51. The power and beauty of mathematics is that one problem analyzed abstractly and mathematically can be applied to many different physical situations. For example, consider the following applications, all of which refer to the drawing shown.

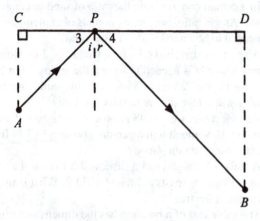

a. One of the most important phenomena in our physical world is light. The simplest principle in the mathematical approach to the theory of this subject is the **law of reflection.** This law states that a ray of light that strikes a reflecting surface is reflected so the angle of incidence (i) equals the angle of reflection (r). Many optical instruments, such as telescopes, work on this principle. For a better lighting effect a photographer positioned at A aims her flash at position P on a reflecting surface to take a picture of a client at B. If $\overline{AC} = 4$ ft, $\overline{CP} = 3$ ft, and $\overline{PD} = 6$ ft, determine $\overline{AP} + \overline{PB}$, which is the distance the light travels from the flash to the client.

b. The same principle applies to a hard body that bounces off an elastic surface. That is, it rebounds at the same angle at which it strikes. A billiards player wishes to make a ball at A strike the cushion at P to hit another ball at B. If $\overline{AC} = 2$ ft, $\overline{CD} = 6$ ft, and $\overline{DB} = 3$ ft, determine $\overline{CP}$ so that point P may be found.

c. Suppose that a company owns two plants located at A and B, and that line segment CD represents a railroad track. The company wishes to build a station at P to ship its merchandise. Naturally it wants the total trucking distance $\overline{AP} + \overline{BP}$ to be minimal. Mathematically, it can be shown that $\overline{AP} + \overline{BP}$ is minimal when angle 3 equals angle 4. If $\overline{AC} = 3$ mi, $\overline{CD} = 10$ mi, and $\overline{DB} = 5$ mi, determine $\overline{DP}$ so that the most desirable spot for the station may be found.

52. One of the classic problems from the history of mathematics is the ingenious method used by the Greek mathematician Eratosthenes to estimate the circumference of the earth in about 200 B.C. Eratosthenes obtained his estimate by noting the following information, which is illustrated here. Alexandria (where Eratosthenes was librarian) was 500 mi due north of the city of Syene. At noon on June 21 he knew from records that the sun cast no shadow at Syene, which meant that the sun was directly overhead. At the same time in Alexandria he measured from a shadow that the sun was 7.5° south from the vertical. By assuming that the sun was sufficiently far away for the light rays to be parallel to the earth, he then determined that angle AOB measured 7.5°. Why? Complete the line of reasoning and obtain Eratosthenes' estimate for the circumference. You will find the result remarkably close to the modern estimate of 24,900 mi, which is obtained with the same basic procedure but with more accurate measurements.

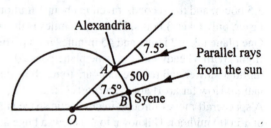

THINK ABOUT IT 1.6

1. Create a word problem that may be solved by the equation
$$1000 - x = 4x$$
where x represents the unknown requested in the problem.

2. Give two reasons why we check the answer in a word problem by interpreting the solution in the context of the word problem, instead of checking in the equation that has been set up to solve the problem.

3. The following question is a favorite of problem solvers because it makes an important point. A car leaves Washington and heads for New York at 55 mi/hour. Two hours later a bus leaves New York and heads for Washington at 60 mi/hour. When the car and the bus meet, which is closer to New York? What is the point made by this problem?

4. A chemist has two mixtures, 30 percent acid and 20 percent acid. Can they be mixed to form 6 liters of a 40 percent solution? Set up the equation for this and see what the solution tells you. What is the difficulty?

5. You have 60 in. of string to shape into a rectangle with a perimeter equal to 60 in. Make a chart that shows various possibilities for the length and width. Do they all have the same area? What dimensions appear to give the maximum area? The minimum area?

1.7   Linear Inequalities in One Variable

A recording company plans to produce and sell x compact discs of a particular album. The production cost includes a one-time, "up-front" recording cost of \$150,000 followed by a duplicating cost of \$2 per CD. The company receives \$8 on the sale of each CD. For what number of CDs sold is the revenue greater than the cost? (See Example 6.)

OBJECTIVES

1   Specify solution sets of linear inequalities by using graphs and interval notation.

2   Solve linear inequalities by applying properties of inequalities.

In applications it is often an inequality which is the key relationship to be described. For instance, the recording company in the opening problem wants revenue to be *greater than* cost so that the CD is profitable. Writing such inequalities demands the use of the symbols reviewed in the following table.

Courtesy of Silver Burdett Ginn.

Symbol	Meaning
$<$	Less than
$\leq$	Less than or equal to
$>$	Greater than
$\geq$	Greater than or equal to

An **inequality** is a statement that relates expressions by using the inequality symbols above. For example,

$$x + 2 \geq -4, \qquad x > 2, \qquad \text{and} \qquad 0 \leq x < 8$$

are inequalities. As with equations, a **solution** of an inequality is a value for the variable, that makes the inequality a true statement, and the set of all such solutions is called the **solution set.** Thus, the solution set of the inequality $x < 3$ is the set of all real numbers less than 3, and this set is written in set-builder notation as $\{x: x < 3\}$. Another way to describe this infinite set of numbers is to graph it on the number line, as shown in Figure 1.26(a). The parenthesis at 3 in this figure means that 3 is not included in the solution set, and the arrow specifies all real numbers less than 3. To graph a set like $\{x: x \leq 3\}$, we show that 3 is included in the solution set by putting a bracket at this point, as shown in Figure 1.26(b).

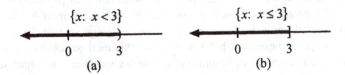

Figure 1.26

Sets of real numbers that may be represented graphically as half lines or the entire number line are examples of **intervals** that may be expressed conveniently by using **interval notation,** as outlined in the following chart.

Set Notation	Graph	Interval Notation
$\{x:\ x > a\}$	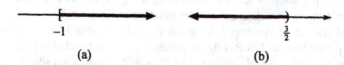	(a, ∞)
$\{x:\ x \geq a\}$		$[a, \infty)$
$\{x:\ x < a\}$		$(-\infty, a)$
$\{x:\ x \leq a\}$		$(-\infty, a]$
$\{x:\ x \text{ is a real number}\}$		$(-\infty, \infty)$

Note that the symbols ∞, read "infinity," and $-\infty$ are not real numbers but are convenient symbols that help us designate intervals that are unbounded in a positive or negative direction.

EXAMPLE 1   Using Interval Notation and Graphs to Specify Solution Sets
Write the solution set to each inequality in interval notation, and graph the interval.

a. $x \geq -1$

b. $x < \dfrac{3}{2}$

Solution

a. Draw a number line. Place a bracket at -1, and then draw an arrow from the bracket to the right, as in Figure 1.27(a). The bracket means that the number -1 is a member of the solution set, and the arrow specifies all real numbers greater than -1. In interval notation $[-1, \infty)$ represents this set of numbers.

b. Figure 1.27(b) shows the graph of $\{x:\ x < 3/2\}$, which is written as $(-\infty, 3/2)$ in interval notation. Note that in both the graph and the interval notation, the parenthesis indicates that $3/2$ is not a member of the solution set.

(a)   **(b)**

Figure 1.27

Note   As shown in Figure 1.28, it is also common notation to use an open circle in a graph instead of a parenthesis to indicate an endpoint that is not included in the solution set, and to use a solid dot instead of a bracket when the endpoint is included. In this text we choose to use parentheses and brackets because this method reinforces writing intervals in interval notation and is also more common in higher-level mathematics.

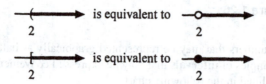

Figure 1.28

PROGRESS CHECK 1   Write the solution set of each inequality in interval notation, and graph the interval.

a. $x \leq -\frac{1}{2}$

b. $x > 0$

By analogy to equations, a **linear inequality** results if the equal sign in a linear equation is replaced by one of the inequality symbols. For example,

$$-5x + 1 < 16, \quad x \geq 2, \quad \text{and} \quad \frac{5}{9}(F - 32) \geq 100$$

are linear inequalities. The procedures for solving linear equalities are similar to the procedures for solving linear equations. The key idea is to create equivalent but simpler inequalities at each step until the solution set is clear. However, to create equivalent inequalities, we apply the following properties of inequalities. Although these properties are given only for $<$, similar properties may be stated for the other inequality symbols.

Properties of Inequalities

Let a, b, and c be real numbers.

	Comment
1. If $a < b$, then $a + c < b + c$ and $a - c < b - c$.	The sense of the inequality is preserved when the same number is added to (or subtracted from) both sides of an inequality.
2. If $a < b$ and $c > 0$, then $ac < bc$ and $a/c < b/c$.	The sense of the inequality is preserved when both sides of an inequality are multiplied (or divided) by the same positive number.
3. If $a < b$ and $c < 0$, then $ac > bc$ and $a/c > b/c$.	The sense of the inequality is reversed when both sides of an inequality are multiplied (or divided) by the same negative number.
4. If $a < b$ and $b < c$, then $a < c$.	This property is called the **transitive property.**

Note that multiplying or dividing on both sides of an inequality demands special care because there are two cases; one for positive multipliers and one for negative multipliers. To see why, notice that the true inequality $-5 < 2$ leads to a true inequality if both sides are multiplied by *positive* 3.

$$-5(3) < 2(3) \qquad \text{Multiply both sides by 3.}$$
$$-15 < 6 \qquad \text{True inequality.}$$

But $-5 < 2$ leads to a false inequality when both sides are multiplied by *negative* 3.

$$-5(-3) < 2(-3) \qquad \text{Multiply both sides by } -3.$$
$$15 < -6 \qquad \text{False inequality.}$$

To obtain a true statement when multiplying both sides by -3, the direction of the inequality must be reversed.

$$-5 < 2 \qquad \text{Original inequality.}$$
$$-5(-3) > 2(-3) \qquad \text{Multiply both sides by } -3 \text{ and } reverse \text{ the inequality symbol.}$$
$$15 > -6 \qquad \text{True inequality.}$$

Always remember to reverse the direction of the inequality when multiplying or dividing by a negative number on both sides of an inequality. This step is also called reversing the *sense* of the inequality. A formal proof for this property is discussed in "Think About It" Exercise 5.

EXAMPLE 2   Solving a Linear Inequality

Solve $2x + 1 < 5x - 8$. Express the solution set graphically and in interval notation.

Solution   We isolate x on one side of the inequality in the following sequence of equivalent (same solution set) inequalities.

$$2x + 1 < 5x - 8$$

$$2x < 5x - 9 \qquad \text{Subtract 1 from both sides.}$$

$$-3x < -9 \qquad \text{Subtract } 5x \text{ from both sides.}$$

$$\frac{-3x}{-3} > \frac{-9}{-3} \qquad \text{Divide both sides by } -3 \text{ and change the sense of the inequality.}$$

$$x > 3$$

Thus, all real numbers greater than 3 make the original inequality a true statement. The solution set is written as $(3, \infty)$ and is graphed as shown in Figure 1.29.

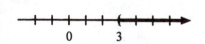

0   3

Figure 1.29

PROGRESS CHECK 2   Solve $-3x - 7 > 5$. Express the solution set graphically and in interval notation.

■

The next example contrasts the steps for solving linear inequalities with the four-step procedure for solving linear equations given in Section 1.5.

EXAMPLE 3   Contrasting Procedures

Solve $-5(x - 1) > 4x - 13$, and graph the solution set.

Solution   We follow similar steps to the general procedure for solving linear equations.

1. Simplify the left side of the inequality by removing parentheses.

$$-5(x - 1) > 4x - 13$$

$$-5x + 5 > 4x - 13 \qquad \text{Distributive property.}$$

2. Write an inequality of the form $cx > n$ by adding or subtracting on both sides of the inequality.

$$-9x + 5 > -13 \qquad \text{Subtract } 4x \text{ from both sides.}$$

$$-9x > -18 \qquad \text{Subtract 5 from both sides.}$$

3. Isolate x by multiplying or dividing on both sides of the inequality.

$$\frac{-9x}{-9} < \frac{-18}{-9} \qquad \text{Divide both sides by } -9 \text{ and reverse the inequality.}$$

$$x < 2$$

4. Although we cannot check the entire solution set because it is an infinite set of numbers, we can at least select one number less than 2 and check that our result is reasonable. Picking 1 yields

$$-5(x - 1) > 4x - 13 \qquad \text{Original inequality.}$$

$$-5(1 - 1) > 4(1) - 13 \qquad \text{Replace } x \text{ with 1.}$$

$$0 > -9. \qquad \text{True inequality.}$$

The check confirms that 1 is a solution, so $x < 2$ is reasonable. The solution set is $(-\infty, 2)$, as shown in Figure 1.30.

2

Figure 1.30

PROGRESS CHECK 3   Solve $5(x - 1) > 2x + 1$, and graph the solution set.   ■

The two inequalities $3 < 8$ and $8 > 3$ have the same meaning, and in general, the inequality

$$\boxed{a < b \text{ is equivalent to } b > a.}$$

This equivalence means that the left and right sides of an inequality are interchangeable, provided that the sense of the inequality is reversed. As illustrated in Example 4, sometimes one version is preferable because it is easier to visualize.

EXAMPLE 4   Solving a Linear Inequality

Solve $8 - 2x < 5x$, and graph the solution set.

Solution   For this inequality an efficient method is to isolate x on the right side of the inequality.

$$8 - 2x < 5x$$

$$8 < 7x \qquad \text{Add } 2x \text{ to both sides.}$$

$$\frac{8}{7} < x \qquad \text{Divide both sides by 7.}$$

Then, the answer is easier to visualize if we interchange sides and reverse the inequality symbol to get

$$x > \frac{8}{7}.$$

Substituting any number greater than 8/7 will show that our answer is reasonable. The solution set $(8/7, \infty)$ is graphed in Figure 1.31.

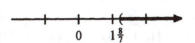

PROGRESS CHECK 4   Solve $6 - 2x \geq x$, and graph the solution set.   ■

Figure 1.31

Some inequalities are true for all real numbers, while others can never be true. The next example illustrates one of the latter cases.

EXAMPLE 5   An Inequality That is Always False

Solve $x > x + 1$.

Solution   Because no number is greater than the number that is 1 bigger than it, this inequality is never true, and the solution set is $\varnothing$. If this result is not apparent when $x > x + 1$ is examined, then a useful next step is to subtract x from both sides.

$$x > x + 1$$

$$0 > 1 \qquad \text{Subtract } x \text{ from both sides.}$$

Because $0 > 1$ is never true, it follows that $x > x + 1$ is never true.

PROGRESS CHECK 5   Solve $x < x - 3$.   ■

The section-opening problem illustrates a business application of linear inequalities.

EXAMPLE 6   Finding an Interval That Produces Profit

Solve the problem that opens the section on page 59.

Solution   If we let x represent the number of compact discs produced and sold, then $150,000 + 2x$ represents the production cost and $8x$ represents the revenue. We need to find values of x for which

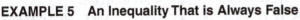

revenue	is greater than	cost.
$8x$	$>$	$150,000 + 2x$

Solve the Inequality $6x > 150,000 \qquad$ Subtract $2x$ from both sides.

$x > 25,000 \qquad$ Divide both sides by 6.

Answer the Question   Revenue is greater than cost when the company produces and sells more than 25,000 CDs.

Check the Answer   The revenue from the sale of 25,000 CDs is $\$8(25,000) = \$200,000$, while the cost of producing 25,000 CDs is $\$150,000 + \$2(25,000) = \$200,000$. Therefore, 25,000 CDs is the break-even point, and revenue is greater than cost after this point.

PROGRESS CHECK 6 Redo Example 6, but assume that the producer's cost is given by 168,000 + 3x and the revenue is given by 10x. ■

EXERCISES 1.7

In Exercises 1–8, write the solution set to each inequality in interval notation and then graph the interval.

1. $x \leq 4$ 2. $x > 2$
3. $x \geq -1$ 4. $x < -4$
5. $x < 0$ 6. $x \geq 0$
7. $x \geq \frac{1}{2}$ 8. $x \leq -\frac{2}{3}$

For Exercises 9–50, solve the given inequality. Express the solution set graphically and in interval notation.

9. $2x + 1 < 7$ 10. $4x - 3 < 13$
11. $4 - 4x \leq -3x$ 12. $5 + 3y \leq 9y + 5$
13. $x + \frac{3}{8} \geq \frac{7}{8}$ 14. $y - \frac{1}{2} \geq \frac{3}{4}$
15. $84 > -6y$ 16. $-6x - 4 < 26$
17. $3x + 4 \leq -29 - \frac{2}{3}x$
18. $8x + 6 - 2x \leq 7 + 2x - 10$
19. $5x + 5 < 6 + x - 4$
20. $7 + 6x < 14x + 35 - 6x$
21. $-2x + 1 < 7$ 22. $-4x - 3 < 13$
23. $-5x + 7 > -8$ 24. $-6x - 3 > 15$
25. $7 - x \leq 3$ 26. $4 - x \leq -3$
27. $12 - x \geq 16$ 28. $20 - x \geq 18$
29. $10 - 4x < -6$ 30. $-3x + 8 > -19$
31. $2(x + 1) > x - 3$ 32. $7(x + 2) > 4x + 2$
33. $4(x - 2) < 3x + 1$ 34. $5(x - 3) \leq 3x + 1$
35. $-7(x - 1) \geq 11x - 29$ 36. $-2(x - 3) < 2x + 18$
37. $-10(x + 7) < 50 + 2x$ 38. $-3(x + 3) > 5x + 7$
39. $-7(x - 3) \leq 33 - x$ 40. $-4(x - 4) \geq 7x - 6$
41. $5 - 3x \geq 2x$ 42. $2(3 - x) \geq x$
43. $10 - 7x \leq 3x$ 44. $-5 - x \leq 4x$
45. $x > x - 1$ 46. $x > x + 1$
47. $2(x + 1) \geq 3 + 2x$ 48. $2(x + 1) \geq -3 + 2x$
49. $2x + x < 4x + 4 - x$
50. $-5x - 3 - x < 4x - 5 - 10x$
51. Sally calculates her business overhead (rent, phone, electricity, etc.) to be $2,600 per month. The materials for each floral piece she creates cost $20. If she can sell each arrangement for $150, how many arrangements must she sell each month in order to show a profit?
52. Sally's overhead increases to $3,000 per month, and the raw materials cost rises to $25 per arrangement. If she is still only getting $150 per arrangement sold, how many such arrangements must she sell to show a profit now?

53. To qualify for a sports program, a child must weigh more than 60 lb. This is expressed as $p > 60$. Use the formula $p = 2.205k$ to express this requirement in kilograms. Round to the nearest hundredth of a kilogram.
54. For a chemistry experiment to work, the temperature of a solid must be kept below 200 in the Kelvin scale. This is expressed as $K < 200$. Use the formula $K = 273.15 + \frac{5}{9}(F - 32)$ to express this requirement in Fahrenheit. Round to the nearest hundredth of a degree.
55. A publishing company plans to produce and sell x textbooks. The cost of producing x books is given by $161,000 + 9x$, which represents a setup cost of $161,000 plus a variable cost of $9 per book. The publisher receives $23 on the sale of each book, so the revenue for selling x books is given by $23x$. For what values of x is revenue greater than cost?
56. A recording company plans to produce and sell x compact discs of a particular album. The production cost includes a one-time "up-front" recording cost of $150,000 followed by a duplicating cost of $2 per CD. The company receives $8 on the sale of each CD. For what number of CDs sold is the revenue greater than the cost?

THINK ABOUT IT 1.7

1. **a.** A student multiplied both sides of the inequality $-\frac{1}{2}x < 5$ by negative 2 and forgot to reverse the inequality. What is the relation between the solution set he got and the correct solution set? Is there any number that is in both solution sets?

   b. If you multiply both sides of $3x - 4 \leq 8$ by negative 3 and forget to reverse the direction of the inequality, you get $-9x + 12 \leq -24$. What is the relation between the solution sets of the two inequalities? Is there any number that is in both solution sets?

2. Why do you reverse the inequality when you multiply both sides of an inequality by a negative number?

3. If you purchase a discount card for $20 from a video store that entitles you to 15 percent off on all purchases, how much must you purchase for the card to save you over $25?

4. Give examples that show that these statements can be *false*.

a. If $a > b$, then $ac > bc$.

b. If $a > b$, then $a/c > b/c$.

c. If $a > b$, then $a^2 > b^2$.

5. By definition, $a < b$ if and only if $b - a$ is positive. Use the definition to prove that if $a < b$ and $c < 0$, then $ac > bc$.

(Hint: Convert all inequalities to differences and use that two positive numbers have a positive product.)

1.8   Compound Inequalities

In a philosophy class an average from 84.5 up to but not including 89.5 results in a grade of B^+. A student has grades of 93, 76, and 90 for the first three tests. With one test left, find all possible grades on the last test that result in a grade of B^+. (See Example 5.)

Courtesy of PhotoDisc/Getty Images.

OBJECTIVES

1 Solve compound inequalities involving *and* statements.

2 Solve compound inequalities involving *or* statements.

In the section-opening problem the average (a) of the student's test results leads to a grade of B^+ when a satisfies the pair of inequalities

$$84.5 \leq a \quad \text{and} \quad a < 89.5.$$

When two inequalities are joined by the word *and* or *or,* the result is called a **compound inequality.** For an *and* statement to be true, both inequalities must be true *simultaneously,* whereas an *or* statement is true when *at least one* of the inequalities is true.

The ideas of solution overlap and solution merger can be expressed clearly using the ideas of set intersection and set union, respectively. So we first expand our list of basic set definitions, and then illustrate these definitions in Example 1.

Set Definitions

1. Equality of Sets Two sets A and B are equal, written $A = B$, if and only if A and B have exactly the same elements.

2. Union of Sets The union of sets A and B, written $A \cup B$, is the set of elements that belong to A or to B or to both.

3. Intersection of Sets The intersection of sets A and B, written $A \cap B$, is the set of elements that belong to both A and B.

EXAMPLE 1   Finding Set Intersection and Set Union

If $A = \{1, 2, 3, 4\}$, $B = \{0, 2, 4\}$, and $C = \{1, 3, 5\}$, find each set.

a. $A \cup B$ **b.** $A \cap B$ **c.** $B \cap C$

Solution

a. The elements 0, 1, 2, 3, and 4 belong to A or B or both, so

$$A \cup B = \{1, 2, 3, 4\} \cup \{0, 2, 4\}$$
$$= \{0, 1, 2, 3, 4\}.$$

b. The elements 2 and 4 belong to both A and B, so

$$A \cap B = \{1, 2, 3, 4\} \cap \{0, 2, 4\}$$
$$= \{2, 4\}.$$

c. No element is common to both B and C, so the intersection of B and C is the empty set.

$$B \cap C = \{0, 2, 4\} \cap \{1, 3, 5\}$$
$$= \emptyset$$

PROGRESS CHECK 1   If $A = \{0, 1, 2\}$, $B = \{3, 4, 5\}$, and $C = \{-1, 0, 1\}$, find each set.

a. $A \cup B$ **b.** $A \cap B$ **c.** $A \cap C$ ■

To see which numbers satisfy

$$84.5 \leq a \quad \text{and} \quad a < 89.5$$

we first graph, in Figure 1.32, each inequality separately. Then, we find the set of numbers common to these two graphs, which are the real numbers between 84.5 and 89.5, including 84.5 and excluding 89.5.

The statement "$84.5 \leq a$ and $a < 89.5$" is usually expressed in compact form and written as $84.5 \leq a < 89.5$. As suggested by Figure 1.32, this set is written as $[84.5, 89.5)$ in interval notation. The following chart shows the different methods for expressing intervals that may be represented graphically as line segments.

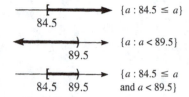

Figure 1.32

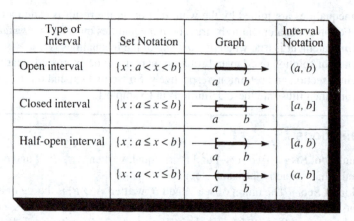

Type of Interval	Set Notation	Graph	Interval Notation
Open interval	$\{x : a < x < b\}$		(a, b)
Closed interval	$\{x : a \leq x \leq b\}$		$[a, b]$
Half-open interval	$\{x : a \leq x < b\}$		$[a, b)$
	$\{x : a < x \leq b\}$		$(a, b]$

EXAMPLE 2   Finding the Intersection of Two Solution Sets
Find the solution set to each inequality in interval notation, and graph the interval.

a. $x < 2$ and $x > 0$ **b.** $x > 2$ and $x \geq 0$
c. $x > 2$ and $x < 0$ **d.** $0 < x < 2$

Solution

a. The set of numbers that satisfies both $x < 2$ and $x > 0$ simultaneously is the set of numbers between 0 and 2, as shown in Figure 1.33 (a). In interval notation this set of numbers is written as $(0, 2)$.
b. Figure 1.33 (b) shows that the numbers common to the solution set of $x > 2$ and the solution set of $x \geq 0$ are the numbers that are greater than 2. Therefore, $(2, \infty)$ is the solution set.

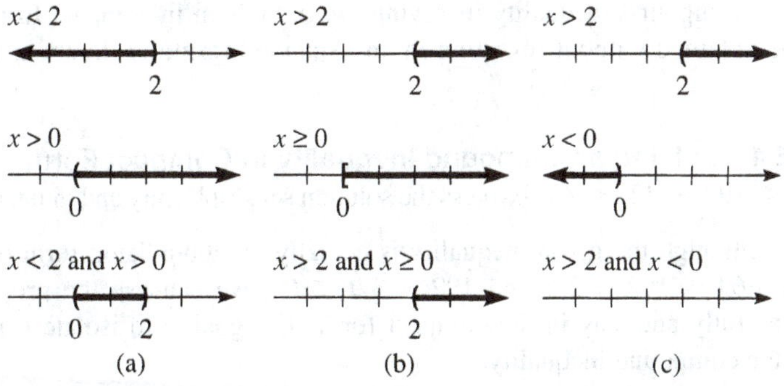

$x < 2$ $x > 2$ $x > 2$

$x > 0$ $x \geq 0$ $x < 0$

$x < 2$ and $x > 0$ $x > 2$ and $x \geq 0$ $x > 2$ and $x < 0$

     (a)   (b)   (c)

Figure 1.33

c. No number is both greater than 2 and less than 0, as can be seen in Figure 1.33 (c). So the solution set is ∅.

d. $0 < x < 2$ may be read "x is between 0 and 2," and this compound inequality is compact form for "$0 < x$ and $x < 2$." This interval is graphed as in Figure 1.34 and is written as $(0,2)$ in interval notation. Note that the inequalities in parts **a** and **d** in this example are equivalent.

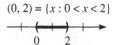

$(0, 2) = \{x : 0 < x < 2\}$

Figure 1.34

PROGRESS CHECK 2 Find the solution set to each inequality in interval notation, and graph the interval.

a. $x > 1$ and $x \geq 3$ **b.** $x < 1$ and $x \geq 3$
c. $x \geq 1$ and $x \leq 3$ **d.** $1 \leq x \leq 3$ ■

The methods used in Example 2 suggest the following general procedure for solving a compound inequality involving *and*.

Solution of *And* Inequalities

To solve a compound inequality involving *and*:

1. Solve separately each inequality in the compound inequality.
2. Find the intersection of the solution sets of the separate inequalities.

EXAMPLE 3 Solving Compound Inequalities Involving *And*

Solve $x - 4 > 0$ and $2x \leq 3x - 12$. Express the solution set graphically and in interval notation.

Solution First, solve each inequality separately.

$$x - 4 > 0 \quad \text{and} \quad 2x \leq 3x - 12$$
$$x > 4 \qquad\qquad -x \leq -12$$
$$x \geq 12$$

The intersection of the solution sets of these two inequalities is then $\{x : x \geq 12\}$, as illustrated in Figure 1.35. In interval notation, $[12, \infty)$ is the solution set.

PROGRESS CHECK 3 Solve $x - 4 < 0$ and $2x \geq 3x - 12$. Express the solution set graphically and in interval notation.   ■

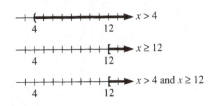

Figure 1.35

When a compound inequality involving *and* is written in compact form, a solution can often be obtained without rewriting in an expanded form, as shown in the next two examples.

EXAMPLE 4   Solving a Compound Inequality in Compact Form

Solve $-64 < 192 - 32t < 64$. Express the solution set graphically and in interval notation.

Solution   Although the given inequality is actually an abbreviated form of the pair of inequalities $-64 < 192 - 32t$ and $192 - 32t < 64$, we can use the properties of inequalities carefully and stay in the compact form. The goal is to isolate t in the middle member of the compound inequality.

$$-64 < 192 - 32t < 64$$

$-64 - 192 < 192 - 192 - 32t < 64 - 192$ Subtract 192 from each member.

$$-256 < -32t < -128$$

$\dfrac{-256}{-32} > t > \dfrac{-128}{-32}$ Divide each member by −32 and reverse the inequality signs.

$$8 > t > 4$$

$$4 < t < 8$$ $a > b$ is equivalent to $b < a$.

Thus, t is between 4 and 8, so the solution set is the interval $(4,8)$, which is graphed in Figure 1.36.

Note   In obtaining the solution set in this example, observe that an inequality like

$$8 > t > 4 \qquad \text{is equivalent to} \qquad 4 < t < 8,$$

but that we do *not* write $(8,4)$ for the solution set, because in interval notation a must be less than b when writing (a,b).

PROGRESS CHECK 4   Solve $-128 \leq 160 - 32t \leq 128$. Express the solution set graphically and in interval notation. ▪

Figure 1.36

EXAMPLE 5   Finding Test Results that Lead to Certain Grades

Solve the problem in the section introduction on page 65.

Solution   A grade of B^+ results if the average (a) satisfies $84.5 \leq a < 89.5$. Since the average is the sum of the four test grades divided by 4, letting x represent the grade on the last test yields

$$84.5 \leq \frac{93 + 76 + 90 + x}{4} < 89.5$$

$$84.5 \leq \frac{259 + x}{4} < 89.5$$

$338 \leq 259 + x < 358$ Multiply each member by 4.

$79 \leq x < 99.$ Subtract 259 from each member.

Answer the Question   Any grade in the last test from 79 up to but not including 99 results in a grade of B^+. In interval notation, the answer is $[79,99)$.

Check the Answer   If the last grade is 79, then the average of the test grades is $(93 + 76 + 90 + 79)/4 = 84.5$, the lowest average that produces B^+. If the last test grade is 99, the average is $(93 + 76 + 90 + 99)/4 = 89.5$, the excluded endpoint of the B^+ interval. The solution checks.

PROGRESS CHECK 5   An average from 74.5 up to but not including 79.5 earns a C^+. If your first three grades are 68, 83, and 75, find all possible grades on the fourth exam that result in a grade of C^+.   ▪

Because an *or* statement is true when at least one of the statements is true, we find the solution set to a compound inequality involving *or* by finding the union of the solution sets of its component inequalities.

Solution of *Or* Inequalities

To solve a compound inequality involving *or:*

1. Solve separately each inequality in the compound inequality.
2. Find the union of the solution sets of the separate inequalities.

EXAMPLE 6   Solving Compound Inequalities Involving *Or*

Solve $x - 3 < -2$ or $x - 3 > 2$. Express the solution set graphically and in interval notation.

Solution   First, solve each inequality separately.

$$x - 3 < -2 \quad \text{or} \quad x - 3 > 2$$
$$x < 1 \qquad\qquad x > 5$$

The union of the solution sets of these two inequalities is graphed in Figure 1.37. In interval notation this solution set is written as $(-\infty, 1) \cup (5, \infty)$.

Caution   Only an *and* compound inequality can be written in compact form. Common student errors occur when statements like "$x < 1$ or $x > 5$" are shortened to

Wrong		**Wrong**
$1 > x > 5$	or	$5 < x < 1.$

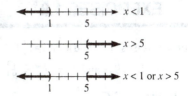

Figure 1.37

PROGRESS CHECK 6   Solve $2x - 1 < -3$ or $2x - 1 > 3$. Express the solution set graphically and in interval notation.   ▪

The next example considers the types of solutions that result when we find the union of two half lines. Solving compound inequalities involving linear inequalities and the word *or* requires this type of analysis in the second step of the general solution procedure.

EXAMPLE 7   Finding the Union of Two Solution Sets

Find the solution set to each inequality in interval notation, and graph the interval.

a. $x < 0$ or $x > 2$ **b.** $x > 0$ or $x < 2$ **c.** $x \geq 0$ or $x > 2$

Solution

a. The solution set is the union of the numbers to the left of 0 with the numbers to the right of 2, as shown in Figure 1.38(a). In interval notation, we write this interval as $(-\infty, 0) \cup (2, \infty)$. Linear inequalities joined by *or* are usually graphed as two distinct half lines on a number line, as in this example.

b. Every number is either greater than 0 or less than 2, as can be seen in Figure 1.38 (b). Thus, the solution set graphs as the entire number line, which is written as $(-\infty, \infty)$ in interval notation.

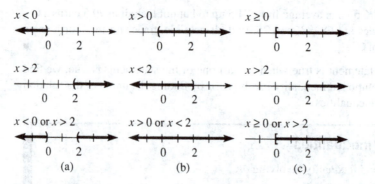

Figure 1.38

c. Figure 1.38(c) shows that the numbers in the union of $\{x: x \geq 0\}$ with $\{x: x > 2\}$ are the numbers that are greater than or equal to 0. Write $[0, \infty)$ to specify this solution set in interval notation.

PROGRESS CHECK 7 Find the solution set to each inequality in interval notation, and graph the interval.

a. $x > -1$ or $x < 1$ b. $x \leq -1$ or $x \geq 1$ c. $x \leq 0$ or $x < 1$ ■

EXERCISES 1.8

For Exercises 1–10, use $A = \left\{1, \frac{1}{2}, \frac{1}{4}, \frac{1}{8}\right\}$, $B = \{0, 2, 4, 8\}$, $C = \{0, 1, 3, 9\}$, and $D = \left\{1, \frac{1}{3}, \frac{1}{9}\right\}$.

1. Find $B \cap C$.
2. Find $A \cap B$.
3. Find $C \cap D$.
4. Find $A \cap D$.
5. True or false? $B \cap C = A \cap B$.
6. True or false? $C \cap D = A \cap D$.
7. Find $B \cup C$.
8. Find $A \cup D$.
9. Find $B \cap \emptyset$.
10. Find $B \cup \emptyset$.

In Exercises 11–44, find the solution set for each inequality. Express your answer in interval notation, and graph the interval.

11. $x < 3$ and $x > 1$
12. $x > 1$ and $x \geq 3$
13. $x > 3$ and $x < 1$
14. $1 < x < 3$
15. $-2 \leq x \leq 5$
16. $x > 0$ and $x \geq 1$
17. $x > -1$ and $x \leq 4$
18. $x \leq 7$ and $x \geq 3$
19. $x \leq -1$ and $x \leq -5$
20. $x < -2$ and $x > 3$
21. $x - 3 < 0$ and $3x \geq 2x - 5$
22. $5x - 2 > 8$ and $x - 3 > 0$
23. $x - 4 > 1$ and $x > 2x - 3$
24. $x + 2 > -1$ and $-2x \geq 6$
25. $-2x + 1 < 7$ and $4x + 5 \leq 2$
26. $-x < 2$ and $-6x - 4 > 26$

27. $3x - 6 \geq 2x - 14$ and $-6x \geq 12$
28. $-2x + 1 < 7$ and $-x < 0$
29. $8 - 3x > -19$ and $3x - 1 \leq 4x$
30. $2(x + 1) \geq x - 3$ and $5(x - 3) < 3x + 1$
31. $x + 5 < 0$ and $x < -5$
32. $5x - 2 < 28$ and $4x + 2 > 5x$
33. $-12 \leq 4 - 8x < 12$
34. $-36 \leq 4 - 8x \leq 36$
35. $-6 \leq 4x + 10 < 6$
36. $-5 < -25 + 10t < 5$
37. $-6 < 6 - 4t < -2$
38. $-16 < 48 - 64x \leq 16$
39. $-240 < 256 - 16x < 176$
40. $-112 < 168 - 56x \leq 112$
41. $-24 \leq 32 - 4t < 24$
42. $-154 \leq -63 - 21t < 154$
43. $-15 \leq -7 - 2t \leq 21$
44. $-400 < 500 + 20t \leq 100$
45. In a typical school, an average from 80 up to but not including 90 earns a B. If your first two grades are 87 and 73, find all possible grades in the third exam which result in a grade of B. Assume that 100 is the highest possible score.

46. At the Royal Rover Obedience School, dogs are rated as "well behaved" if they achieve an average score of 93 up to but not including 107 in a series of obedience tests. If your dog has already received grades of 91 and 72, what is the range of possible scores on the last exam for a "well-behaved" rating? Assume that the possible scores are 1 to 200.

47. For a laboratory experiment to work, the temperature of a solution must be kept between 37° and 39° F. Thus $37 < F < 39$. Use the formula $F = \frac{9}{5}C + 32$ to find an equivalent range of values in the Celsius scale by solving $37 < \frac{9}{5}C + 32 < 39$. Round values to the nearest hundredth.

48. The element mercury is a liquid between $-38.87°$ and $356.58°$ C. This range of temperature values is therefore given by $-38.87 < C < 356.58$. Express this in degrees Fahrenheit by using the formula $C = \frac{5}{9}(F - 32)$ and solving the resulting compound inequality. Round values to the nearest hundredth.

In Exercises 49–72, express the solution set graphically and in interval notation.

49. $x > 7$ or $x < 5$
50. $x \geq 5$ or $x > 7$
51. $x < 0$ or $x \geq -2$
52. $x > 0$ or $x < -3$
53. $x \leq 5$ or $x < 7$
54. $x < -2$ or $x \geq -5$
55. $x + 2 < -3$ or $x + 2 > 3$
56. $x - 4 > 5$ or $x - 4 < -5$
57. $x + 2 \geq -3$ or $x + 2 \leq 3$

58. $x - 4 < 5$ or $x - 4 \geq -5$
59. $x + 1 < 7$ or $x - 2 \leq 6$
60. $x - 5 > -4$ or $x - 8 \geq -1$
61. $x - 3 < -2$ or $x + 4 \leq -3$
62. $x + 5 \geq 3$ or $x + 2 > 8$
63. $x + 1 < 0$ or $x - 2 \geq 0$
64. $x - 3 \leq 4$ or $x - 1 \geq -1$
65. $x + 1 \geq 0$ or $x - 2 \leq 0$
66. $x - 3 \leq -4$ or $x - 1 \geq 1$
67. $x - 3 \leq -4$ and $x - 1 \geq 1$
68. $x - 3 \leq 4$ and $x - 1 \geq -1$
69. $x + 1 \geq 0$ and $x - 2 \leq 0$
70. $x + 1 < 0$ and $x - 2 \geq 0$
71. $x \leq 7$ or $x + 5 \geq 17$ **72.** $x - 3 \geq -4$ or $x \leq 7$

THINK ABOUT IT 1.8

1. Why is $-3 < x < 5$ called a "compound" inequality?
2. Solve $x < 3x - 12 < 2x$.
3. Solve $m - 2ts < x < m + 2ts$ for m. Assume $s > 0$. This is an inequality used in statistics to estimate the mean of a large group of people based on data from a survey of part of that group.
4. Explain why $5 < x < 1$ is a statement which contradicts itself.
5. In solving $a < bx < c$ for x, explain why you should not divide by b unless some other information is given. What is the needed information?

CHAPTER 1 OVERVIEW

Section	Key Concepts and Procedures to Review
1.1	■ Definitions of integers, rational numbers, irrational numbers, real numbers, $a < b$, $a > b$, $a \leq b$, absolute value, subtraction, factor, power, exponent and division ■ Relationships among the various sets of numbers ■ Statements of basic properties of real numbers ■ Methods to graph and order real numbers ■ Methods to add, subtract, multiply, and divide real numbers ■ Order of operations ■ Methods for performing numeric calculations on a graphing calculator

1.2
- Definitions of variable, constant, algebraic expression, terms, (numerical) coefficient, and like terms
- Methods to evaluate an algebraic expression
- Methods to add or subtract algebraic expressions

1.3
- Laws of exponents (m and n denote integers)

  1. $a^m \cdot a^n = a^{m+n}$ **2.** $(a^m)^n = a^{mn}$ **3.** $(ab)^n = a^n b^n$

  4. $\left(\dfrac{a}{b}\right)^n = \dfrac{a^n}{b^n}$ $(b \neq 0)$ **5.** $\dfrac{a^m}{a^n} = a^{m-n} = \dfrac{1}{a^{n-m}}$ $(a \neq 0)$

  6. $a^0 = 1$ $(a \neq 0)$ **7.** $a^{-n} = \dfrac{1}{a^n}$ $(a \neq 0)$

- Methods to convert a number from normal notation to scientific notation, and vice versa
- Guidelines for working with scientific notation on a graphing calculator

1.4
- Methods to multiply various types of algebraic expressions
- FOIL multiplication method
- Special product formulas:

  1. $(a + b)(a - b) = a^2 - b^2$

  2. $(a + b)^2 = a^2 + 2ab + b^2$

  3. $(a - b)^2 = a^2 - 2ab + b^2$

1.5
- Definitions of equation, conditional equation, identity, false equation, equivalent equation, solution set, linear equation, and literal equation
- Methods to obtain an equivalent equation
- Methods to solve formulas and literal equations for a given variable

1.6
- Guidelines to setting up and solving word problems
- Methods for solving problems involving geometric figures, annual interest, uniform motion, liquid mixtures, and proportions

1.7
- Definition of solution of an inequality, and representation by graphs and interval notation
- Properties of inequalities
- Methods to solve linear inequalities

1.8
- Definitions of equality of sets, union of sets, and intersection of sets
- Methods to solve compound inequalities involving <u>and</u> statements and linear inequalities
- Methods to solve compound inequalities involving <u>or</u> statements and linear inequalities

CHAPTER 1 REVIEW EXERCISES

1. Evaluate these expressions both with and without the use of a calculator.

  a. $1 - 3(2 - 4)$ **b.** $1 + \dfrac{3 - 11}{(4 - 8)^2}$

2. Is -3 a solution of the equation $\dfrac{2}{2 - c} + \dfrac{c}{c - 2} = 1$?

3. If $m = \dfrac{y_2 - y_1}{x_2 - x_1}$, evaluate m for $x_1 = 2$, $x_2 = -5$, $y_1 = -1$, and $y_2 = 4$.

4. Find the value of the expression $-x^2 + 2xy^3$ when $x = -1$ and $y = 3$.

5. If $x = -2$ and $y = 5$, then evaluate $|2x| + |y|$.

6. Find the value of t in the formula $a = p(1 + rt)$ if $a = 3{,}000$, $p = 1{,}500$, and $r = 0.05$.

7. Combine like terms: $2(x - y) + (x + y) - (3 - y)$.

8. Solve for y' (read "y prime"): $2x + 2y' = 0$.

9. Express the rational number $\frac{13}{11}$ as a repeating decimal.

10. Use inequalities and interval notation to describe the sets of numbers illustrated.

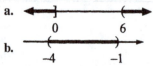

11. Simplify $x - [-x - (x - 1)]$.

12. Simplify $(5x^2 - 3x + 1) - (2x^2 - 2x + 7)$.

13. Name the property of real numbers illustrated in the given statements.

  a. $(x + y) + z = z + (x + y)$

  b. $\frac{1}{9} \cdot 8 + \frac{1}{9} \cdot 2 = \frac{1}{9}(8 + 2)$

14. Use the correct symbol ($<$, $>$, or $=$) between the following pairs of expressions.
    a. -0.1 ____ -0.01
    b. 2% ____ 0.2
    c. $|-3 + 7|$ ____ $|-3| + |7|$
    d. $|-2a|$ ____ $|-2| \cdot |a|$
15. The number 3.14 is a member of which of the following sets of numbers; reals, rationals, irrationals, integers?
16. If $x = -3$, find
    a. the absolute value of x,
    b. the reciprocal of x, and
    c. the negative of x.
17. Evaluate $2x^0 + x^{-1}$ when $x = -\frac{1}{4}$.
18. A mutual fund company manages \$28 billion in assets. Express this number in scientific notation.
19. The wavelength of violet light is about 4.0×10^{-5} cm. Express this number in normal notation.
20. Rewrite $\dfrac{2^{-3}x^2}{4y^{-2}}$ with only positive exponents.

In Exercises 21–32 use the laws of exponents to perform the operations, and write the answer in the simplest form that contains only positive exponents

21. $(-3x^3) \cdot (-3x)^3$
22. $(2st)^2 \cdot (3tc)^3$
23. $2 \cdot 2^x$
24. $2^x \cdot 2^{-x}$
25. $(3^x)^{2x}$
26. $x^{2n+2} \cdot x^2$
27. $(-3)^{-1} \cdot (-3)^{-3}$
28. $5 \div 5^{-1}$
29. $\dfrac{3}{3^n}$
30. $\dfrac{(3x)^2}{y} \cdot \left(\dfrac{2zy}{x^2}\right)^3$
31. $\dfrac{3^2 x^{-4} y^{-3}}{3^{-1} x^4 y^{-2}}$
32. $\dfrac{(2ax^2)^2}{2(ax)^{-1}}$

In Exercises 33–42 perform the multiplication or division and combine like terms.

33. $x^2 y(2x - 3y + 4)$
34. $(a - 4b)a^3 b^2$
35. $\dfrac{cs^2 - 2c^3 s}{cs}$
36. $\dfrac{2xh + h^2 + 2h}{h}$
37. $(1 - k)^2$
38. $(4x - y)^2$
39. $(x^a - y^b)^2$
40. $(x - 3)(x + 2)(x - 4)$
41. $(a + b)(a^2 - ab + b^2)$
42. $[(x + h) - 2]^2$

In Exercises 43–54 solve each equation or inequality.

43. $3(x - 6) = -2(12 - 3x)$
44. $1 - x = 1 + x$
45. $1 - x \le 1 + x$
46. $-x + 1 > 3$
47. $6{,}000 = 1{,}000(1 + 0.05t)$
48. $5 - 2(a - 2) = 2 - 3a$
49. $6x < 7x - 1$
50. $-2(x + 4) \le -2x + 4$
51. $2(x + 4) = 2x + 4$
52. $\dfrac{20 - x}{3} = \dfrac{x}{5}$
53. $-3 < 4 - 2x < 3$
54. $x + 5 \le -1$ or $x + 5 \ge 1$

In Exercises 55–60 solve each equation for the letter indicated.

55. $C = 2\pi r$ (for r)
56. $5x + 3y = 6$ (for y)
57. $ax + b = n$ (for x)
58. $2x + 2y' = 5$ (for y')
59. $P = \dfrac{x - y - z}{10}$ (for y)
60. $\dfrac{a_1}{c_1} = \dfrac{a_2}{c_2}$ (for c_2)

In Exercises 61–70 answer true or false. If false, give a specific counterexample.

61. All real numbers are rational numbers.
62. All integers are rational numbers.
63. There is no number equal to $\frac{0}{4}$.
64. If $ab = ac$, then $b = c$.
65. If $a < b$, then $a + c < b + c$.
66. If $a < b$, then $ac < bc$.
67. $|-a| = a$
68. $|a + b| = |a| + |b|$
69. $|ab| = |a| \cdot |b|$
70. $|a - b| = |b - a|$
71. Find the volume of a cylinder whose radius and height are each 6 inches.
72. A part of a microchip is a cube with side 0.001 mm. Calculate its surface area.
73. On a test you received a grade of 123 on a scale of 0–150. Convert your score to a scale of 0–100.
74. A brick weights 6 lb plus half a brick. What does one brick weigh?
75. The total cost (including tax) of a new car is \$9,222. If the sales tax is 6 percent, how much do you pay in taxes?
76. To the nearest inch, the height of a woman is 64 in. Use interval notation to write an interval that contains the woman's exact height. If we use a more accurate measuring device and record her height as 63.9 in., which interval now contains the woman's exact height?
77. Ohm's law states that the current in a circuit (I) is equal to the voltage (E) divided by the resistance (R). Write a formula for the resistance in terms of the current and the voltage.
78. You have 20 qt of a solution that is 10 percent antifreeze. How much pure antifreeze must be added to obtain a solution that is 30 percent antifreeze?
79. A map has a scale of 1.5 in. = 11 mi. To the nearest tenth of a mile, what distance is represented by 7 in. on the map?
80. A student needs an average of 90.0 or better to get an A in a course. Her first four test grades were 94, 91, 88, and 97. What possible grades on her fifth test will result in an A grade?

81. A real estate broker's commission for selling a lot is 6 percent of the selling price. If you want to sell your lot and receive $80,000, then what must be the selling price of the lot?

82. Triangle, ABC is similar to triangle EDC. If $\overline{BD} = 25$ ft, $\overline{AB} = 9$ ft, and $\overline{DE} = 11$ ft, then find $\overline{BC}$ to the nearest foot.

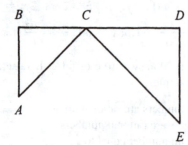

In Exercises 83–92 select the choice that answers the question or completes the statement.

83. Which statement illustrates the commutative property of multiplication?
a. $a(b + c) = (b + c)a$ b. $a(b + c) = ab + ac$
c. $(ab)c = a(bc)$ d. $a \cdot 1 = a$

84. Which number is a rational number?
a. $\sqrt{2}$ b. $\sqrt{-9}$
c. $-\sqrt{9}$ d. π

85. If $2^a = x$, then 2^{a+3} equals
a. $x + 3$ b. x^3
c. $6x$ d. $8x$

86. The side of a square is given by $4x^3$. The area of the square is given by
a. $12x^3$ b. $16x^5$
c. $16x^6$ d. $4x^9$

87. The side of a square is given by $4 + x^3$. The area of the square is given by
a. $x^6 + 8x^3 + 16$ b. $x^9 + 8x^6 + 16$
c. $x^9 + 16$ d. $x^6 + 16$

88. Pick the statement that describes the set of numbers illustrated.

a. $\{x: -1 < x < 3\}$ b. $\{x: 3 < x < -1\}$
c. $\{x: x < -1 \text{ and } x > 3\}$ d. $\{x: x < -1 \text{ or } x > 3\}$

89. If $a < 0$, then $|a|$ equals
a. a b. a^2
c. $-a$ d. $\dfrac{1}{a}$

90. If the width of a rectangle is one-fourth the length, and the perimeter is 70 cm, what is the area?
a. 140 cm^2 b. 196 cm^2
c. 392 cm^2 d. 784 cm^2

91. Which expression is undefined when $x = -1$?
a. $\dfrac{x}{x + 1}$ b. $\dfrac{x + 1}{x}$
c. x^0 d. x^{-1}

92. The inequality $-x < 1$ is equivalent to
a. $x < 1$ b. $x < -1$
c. $x > 1$ d. $x > -1$

CHAPTER 1 TEST

1. List all correct classifications of the number -5 from the following categories: real number, irrational number, rational number, integer.

2. Number the property of real numbers illustrated by $8x + 2x = (8 + 2)x$.

In Questions 3 and 4 evaluate each expression.

3. $5 - 9(2 - 7)^2$ **4.** $(-3)^{-1} \cdot (-3)^{-3}$

In Questions 5 and 6 simplify each expression and write the result using only positive exponents.

5. $\left(\dfrac{10x^{-2}}{a}\right)^{-3}$ **6.** $\dfrac{x^n}{x^{n+2}}$

In Questions 7–10 solve each equation or inequality.

7. $2(4 - y) = 26 + y$ **8.** $4 - 5x \geq x$

9. $-3(x + 2) < -3x + 1$ **10.** $\dfrac{x}{4} = \dfrac{10 - x}{8}$

11. Multiply $(5x + 7)(3x - 1)$.

12. Simplify $x - 2[5x - (1 - x)]$.

13. Evaluate $\dfrac{y_2 - y_1}{x_2 - x_1}$ if $x_1 = 4$, $y_1 = -2$, $x_2 = -6$, and $y_2 = 3$.

14. Find the value of F in the formula $C = \dfrac{5}{9}(F - 32)$ if $C = -15$.

15. Solve $0 \leq 2x - 6 < 10$ and express the answer graphically and in interval notation.

16. Solve for x: $3x + 2y = 5$.

17. Solve for c: $A = \dfrac{1}{2}h(b + c)$.

18. Simplify $\dfrac{(x + h)^2 + 5 - (x^2 + 5)}{h}$.

19. During a certain day about 172 million shares of stock were sold on the New York Stock Exchange. Express this number in scientific notation.

20. The total cost (including tax) of a new car is $13,482. If the sale tax rate is 7 percent, how much is paid in taxes?

Functions and Graphs

A designer makes and sells round tablecloths for $3 per square foot.
a. Express the cost *C* of such a tablecloth as a function of its diameter *d*.
b. What is the cost of a tablecloth that is 6 ft in diameter?
c. Specify the domain of the cost function. (See Example 2 of Section 2.1.)

We now introduce the idea of a function and its graph. This concept will then become a central theme in the text as we investigate the behavior of the trigonometric functions in Chapters 4 and 9 and the behavior of linear, quadratic, polynomial, rational, exponential, and logarithmic functions in other chapters. In addition, graphical analysis will be used to reinforce further algebraic techniques and to provide a picture of the solutions to equations and inequalities. This chapter starts us on the road to analyzing relationships with formulas, tables, and graphs, and this three-point approach will help you to understand topics from algebraic, numeric, and geometric view-points.

2.1   Functions, Relations, and Ordered Pairs

OBJECTIVES

1. Find a formula that defines a function and determine its domain and range.
2. Determine ordered pairs that are solutions of an equation.
3. Find the domain and range given an equation.
4. Find the domain and range given a set of ordered pairs.
5. Determine if a set of ordered pairs is a function.

One of the most important considerations in mathematics is determining the relationship between two variables. For example:

- The postage required to mail a package is a function of the weight of the package.
- The bill from an electric company is a function of the number of kilowatt-hours of electricity that are purchased.
- The current in a circuit with a fixed voltage is a function of the resistance in the circuit.
- The demand for a product is a function of the price charged for the product.
- The perimeter of a square is a function of the length of the side of the square.

In each of these examples we determine the relationship between the two variables by finding a rule that establishes a correspondence between values of each variable. For example, if we know the length of the side of a square, we can determine the perimeter by the formula $P = 4s$. In this case the rule is a formula or equation. Sometimes the rule is given in tabular form. For example, consider the formula table below. This rule assigns to each final average (a) a final grade for the course.

$$\text{Final grade} = \begin{cases} A & \text{if} \quad 90 \le a \le 100 \\ B & \text{if} \quad 80 \le a < 90 \\ C & \text{if} \quad 70 \le a < 80 \\ D & \text{if} \quad 60 \le a < 70 \\ F & \text{if} \quad 0 \le a < 60 \end{cases}$$

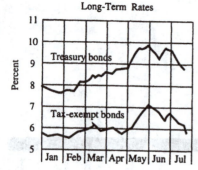

Figure 2.1

Since formulas and tables are not always applicable, it is sometimes best to give the rule verbally or to make a list that shows the correspondence. The relationship between students and their Social Security numbers is such a case. Finally, you are undoubtedly familiar with the type of graph shown in Figure 2.1, which is commonly used to specify relationships in a quick and vivid way.

Whether the rule is given by formula or table, graphically, or by a list, the rule is most useful if we obtain *exactly one* answer whenever we use it. For example, the rule in the formula table above assigns to each final average exactly one final grade. Once we compute the final average, the rule tells us exactly what grade to assign for the course. Some typical assignments are shown in Figure 2.2. Assignments are represented as arrows from the points that represent final averages to the points that represent final grades. However, some correspondences do not always give us exactly one answer. For example, if we reverse the assignments in Figure 2.2, then we cannot determine a unique final average when the final grade is A, as shown in Figure 2.3. We wish to define a function so that the correspondence in Figure 2.2 is a function, while the correspondence in Figure 2.3 is not a function. We do this as follows:

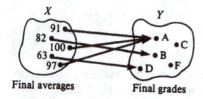

Figure 2.2
Function

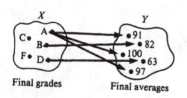

Figure 2.3
Not a Function

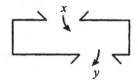

Figure 2.4

Definition of a Function

A **function** is a rule that assigns to each element x in a set X exactly one element y in a set Y. In this definition, set X is called the **domain** of the function, and the set of all elements of Y that correspond to elements in the domain is called the **range** of the function.

The analogy between a function and a computing machine may help to clarify the concept. Consider Figure 2.4, which shows a machine processing domain elements (x values) into range elements (y values). In goes an x value, out comes exactly one y value. With this in mind, you should have a clear image of the three features of a function: (1) the domain (the input), (2) the range (the output), and (3) the rule (the machine). When y is a function of x, as just described, the value of y depends on the choice for x, so we call x the **independent variable** and y the **dependent variable**.

It is common practice to refer to a function by stating only the rule, no domain or range is specified. Thus we say, "Consider the circumference function $C = \pi d$." The domain is then assumed to be the collection of values for d that are interpretable in the problem. Since the length of the diameter of a circle must be positive in this case, the domain is the set of positive real numbers. Other illustrations of context restrictions in the domain are discussed in Examples 1 to 3.

EXAMPLE 1   Writing Functions in Equation Form

Write a rule in equation form that describes the given function. In each case, specify the domain of the function.

a. Express the distance y that a car going 55 mi/hour will travel as a function of t, the hours spent traveling.

b. Express the width w of a rectangle with length 8 units as a function of its area A.

Solution

a. Using $d = rt$, the equation $y = 55t$ expresses the distance y as a function of the time t when $r = 55$. Because t cannot be negative, the domain is the interval $[0, \infty)$.

b. $A = \ell w$ implies $w = A/\ell$. When ℓ equals 8, the formula for w in terms of A is $w = A/8$. Since the area of a rectangle must be positive, the domain is the interval $(0, \infty)$.

PROGRESS CHECK 1   Use the directions given in Example 1.

a. Express the cost C of x gal of bottled water if the water costs $1.35/gal.

b. Express the side length s of a square as a function of the area A of the square.   ■

EXAMPLE 2   Creating a Cost Function

Solve the problem in the chapter introduction on page 75.

Solution

a. The tablecloth is round, so its area is given by $A = \pi r^2$. To express A as a function of the diameter d, replace r by $d/2$, to obtain

$$A = \pi\left(\frac{d}{2}\right)^2 = \frac{\pi d^2}{4}.$$

Since the cost C is the product of the area and the price per square foot (which is $3), the cost equation is

$$C = \frac{3\pi d^2}{4}.$$

b. When $d = 6$,

$$C = \frac{3\pi(6)^2}{4} = \$84.82 \text{ (to the nearest cent)}.$$

c. The domain of the function is the set of numbers that are sensible replacements for the diameter of the tablecloth. From the mathematical viewpoint, the diameter of a circle must be positive, so the domain is the interval $(0, \infty)$. Practically speaking, other limits may need to be imposed on how large or how small the tablecloth can measure.

PROGRESS CHECK 2   A designer makes and sells square tablecloths for \$4 per square foot.

a. Express the cost C of such a tablecloth as a function of its perimeter P.
b. What is the cost of a tablecloth whose perimeter is 12 ft?
c. Specify the domain of the cost function.   ■

EXAMPLE 3   Describing a Function for Bank Charges

Express the monthly cost (c) for a checking account as a function of the number (n) of checks serviced that month if the bank charges 10 cents per check plus a \$3.50 maintenance charge. Describe the domain and range of this function.

Solution   To help us see a pattern, we will first analyze the problem numerically and determine the cost of writing a specific number of checks, say 20. If the bank charges 10 cents per check plus a \$3.50 charge, then the cost of 20 checks is given by

$$c = 0.10(20) + 3.50 = \$5.50.$$

To generalize and obtain a formula for the function, let the variable n replace the specific number 20 to obtain

$$c = 0.10n + 3.50.$$

Since the cost depends on the number of checks written, c is the dependent variable, and n is the independent variable. Thus, the domain is the set of values for n that are meaningful in this context, and the range is the corresponding set of costs. Using set notation we specify these sets as follows.

$$\text{Domain} = \{0, 1, 2, 3, \ldots\}$$

$$\text{Range} = \{\$3.50, \$3.60, \$3.70, \$3.80, \ldots\}$$

Note that 0 is included in the domain because there is a monthly charge even when no checks are serviced.

PROGRESS CHECK 3   Express the cost (c) of a shipment of CDs as a function of the number (n) of CDs ordered if the charge is \$9 per CD plus \$2.95 for shipping and handling. Describe the domain and range of this function.   ■

When a relation is defined by an algebraic equation like $y = 1/x$, then the domain is the set of all real numbers for which a real number exists in the range. Thus, we exclude from the domain values for the independent variable (x) that result in division by zero or in an even root of a negative number, as considered in Example 4.

EXAMPLE 4   Finding Domain and Range from Equations

Determine the domain and range of each function.

a. $y = \dfrac{1}{x - 2}$
b. $y = \sqrt{x + 4}$

Solution

a. When $x = 2$, $y = 1/0$, which is undefined. Otherwise, the assignment of any real number for x results in a real number output for y. Thus, the domain is the set of all real numbers except 2, which may be written $\{x : x \neq 2\}$. The corresponding y values are all numbers except zero, so the range is $\{y : y \neq 0\}$. Note that y can never be zero because the numerator of the fraction can never be zero.

b. For the output of $y = \sqrt{x + 4}$ to be a real number, x must satisfy

$$x + 4 \geq 0$$
$$x \geq -4.$$

Thus, the domain is $\{x : x \geq -4\}$, or $[-4, \infty)$ in interval notation. The radical sign $\sqrt{}$ denotes the principal square root, so if $x \geq -4$, then $\sqrt{x + 4}$ is greater than or equal to zero. Therefore, the range is $\{y : y \geq 0\}$, or alternatively, $[0, \infty)$.

PROGRESS CHECK 4   Determine the domain and range of each function.

a. $y = \dfrac{1}{x + 3}$
b. $y = \sqrt{x - 2}$ ■

Functions as Ordered Pairs

In mathematical notation we use **ordered pairs** to show the correspondence in a function. For example, consider the equation $y = 2x + 1$.

If x Equals	Then $y = 2x + 1$	Thus, the Ordered Pairs Are
2	$2(2) + 1 = 5$	$(2, 5)$
1	$2(1) + 1 = 3$	$(1, 3)$
0	$2(0) + 1 = 1$	$(0, 1)$
-1	$2(-1) + 1 = -1$	$(-1, -1)$
-2	$2(-2) + 1 = -3$	$(-2, -3)$

In the pairs that represent the correspondence, we list the values of the independent variable first and the values of the dependent variable second. Thus the order of the numbers in the pair is significant. The pairing $(2, 5)$ indicates that when $x = 2$, $y = 5$; $(5, 2)$ means when $x = 5$, $y = 2$. In the equation $y = 2x + 1$, $(2, 5)$ is an ordered pair that makes the equation a true statement; so $(2, 5)$ is said to be a solution of the equation; $(5, 2)$ is not a solution of this equation.

EXAMPLE 5   Ordered Pair Solutions

Determine if the ordered pair is a solution of the equation.

a. $2x + y = 5$; $(1, 3)$
b. $y = 2x - 3$; $(-1, 1)$

Solution   Replace x and y by the appropriate components of the given ordered pair.

a. $(1,3)$ means $x = 1$, $y = 3$. Then,

$$2x + y = 5 \qquad \text{Given equation.}$$

$$2(1) + (3) \stackrel{?}{=} 5 \qquad \text{Replace } x \text{ by 1 and } y \text{ by 3.}$$

$$5 \stackrel{\checkmark}{=} 5. \qquad \text{Simplify.}$$

Since $5 = 5$ is a true statement, $(1,3)$ *is* a solution of $2x + y = 5$.

b. $(-1, 1)$ means $x = -1$, $y = 1$.

$$y = 2x - 3$$

$$1 \stackrel{?}{=} 2(-1) - 3$$

$$1 \stackrel{?}{=} -5$$

Since $1 = -5$ is a false statement, $(-1, 1)$ is *not* a solution of $y = 2x - 3$.

PROGRESS CHECK 5   Determine if the ordered pair is a solution of the equation.

a. $x - 5y = 5$; $(0, -1)$ \qquad\qquad **b.** $y = -2x + 5$; $(1, 2)$ ■

The representation of a correspondence as a set of ordered pairs gives us a different perspective on the function concept. We call any set of ordered pairs a relation, and we will see that a function is a special type of relation.

Relation Definition

A **relation** is a set of ordered pairs. The set of all first components of the ordered pairs is called the **domain** of the relation. The set of all second components is called the **range** of the relation.

EXAMPLE 6   Finding Domain and Range from Ordered Pairs

In a certain class the correspondence between the final averages and final grades for four students is given by $\{(88, B), (92, A), (71, C), (87, B)\}$. Find the domain and range of this relation.

Solution   The domain, which is the set of all first components, is $\{88, 92, 71, 87\}$. The range, which is the set of all second components, is $\{A, B, C\}$.

PROGRESS CHECK 6   Find the domain and the range of the relation $\{(65, D), (100, A), (43, F), (94, A)\}$. ■

EXAMPLE 7   Finding Domain and Range from Ordered Pairs

The relation "less than" in the set $\{2, 3, 5\}$ is defined by $\{(2, 3), (2, 5), (3, 5)\}$. Find the domain and range of this relation.

Solution   The domain of this relation is $\{2, 3\}$, and the range is $\{3, 5\}$. Note that an ordered pair like $(2,5)$ belongs to this relation because 2 is less than 5.

PROGRESS CHECK 7   The relation "greater than" in the set $\{1, 4, 9\}$ is defined by $\{(4, 1), (9, 1), (9, 4)\}$. Find the domain and range of this relation. ■

Compare the relations in the last two examples and observe that in Example 6 none of the pairs have the same first component (which customarily represents x). But in

Example 7 the pairs (2,3) and (2,5) do have the same first component. Relations in which there is no duplication in the x values are particularly convenient to work with, because each x value leads to only one y value. In other words, the rule for determining y for a specific x always produces exactly one answer. We have seen that this convenient type of relation is called a function.

Function

A **function** is a relation in which no two different ordered pairs have the same first component.

In this section we have defined a function in terms of (1) a rule and (2) ordered pairs. Since the function concept is so important, you should consider both definitions and satisfy yourself that these definitions are equivalent.

EXAMPLE 8 Determining Functions
Determine if the given relation is a function.

a. $\{(5, 3), (6, 3), (7, 3)\}$ **b.** $\{(4, 2), (0, 0), (4, -2)\}$

Solution

a. This relation is a function because the first component in the ordered pairs is always different. Note that the definition of a function does not require the second components to be different.
b. This relation is not a function because the number 4 is the first component in more than one ordered pair.

PROGRESS CHECK 8   Determine if the given relation is a function.

a. $\{(-1, 1), (0, 0), (1, 1)\}$ **b.** $\{(-1, 5), (-1, 6), (-1, 7)\}$ ■

EXERCISES 2.1

In Exercises 1–10 find five ordered pairs that are solutions of each formula or equation.

1. $y = x$ **2.** $y = -x$ **3.** $y = \sqrt{4 - x}$ **4.** $y = |2x - 7|$
5. $y = x^2 + 2x - 1$ **6.** $y = x^3 - 1$ **7.** $d = 60t$
8. $c = \pi d$ **9.** $C = \frac{5}{9}(F - 32)$ **10.** $F = \frac{9}{5}C + 32$

In Exercises 11–14 determine which of the ordered pairs are solutions of the equation.

Equation	Ordered Pairs
11. $y = 3x + 1$	$(4, 1), (-2, -5), (1, 4), (-5, -2)$
12. $y = |x|$	$(-1, -1), (1, 1), (-1, 1), (1, -1)$
13. $y = x^2$	$(-1, -1), (1, 1), (-1, 1), (1, -1)$
14. $y = 1/x$	$(2, 0.5), (0.5, 2), (-1, -1), (0, 0)$

In Exercises 15-20, determine if the ordered pair is a solution of the equation.

15. $3x - y = 1; (1, 2)$ **16.** $3y - x = 1; (1, 2)$

17. $\dfrac{1 + x}{3x} = y; (0, 1)$ **18.** $y = \dfrac{x - 1}{2x}; (1, 0)$

19. $4x + 3y + 1 = 0; \left(-\frac{1}{2}, \frac{1}{3}\right)$
20. $x^2 + y^2 = 25; (3, -4)$
21. Fill in the missing component in each of the following ordered pairs so they are solutions of the equation $y = -3x + 7: (0, \ \ ), (\ \ , 0), (-5, \ \ ), (\ \ , 5)$.

22. Fill in the missing component in each of the following ordered pairs so they are solutions of the equation $y = \dfrac{5x - 3}{6}: (0, \ \ ), (\ \ , 0), (\ \ , -2), (-3, \ \ )$.

23. If $(a, -1)$ is a solution of the equation $y = -2x + 9$, find the value of a.

24. If $(-2, b)$ is a solution of the equation $y = 7x + 5$, then find the value of b.

In Exercises 25-30, find the domain and range for the given set of ordered pairs.

25. Final course averages and course grades for five students: $\{(80, B), (89, B), (85, B), (79, C), (78, C)\}$

26. Scores on a quality control checklist and final rating for four appliances: $\{(9.2, E), (8.7, G), (8.2, G), (9.4, E)\}$

27. Four points which make a graph: $\{(1, 2), (1, 3), (1, 4), (2, 2)\}$

28. Heights (inches) and weights (pounds) for four children: $\{(36, 50), (48, 75), (48, 80), (35, 50)\}$

29. The relation "is less than" in the set $\{-1, 0, 1\}$ is defined by $\{(-1, 0), (-1, 1), (0, 1)\}$.

30. The relation "is less than or equal to" in the set $\{-1, 0, 1\}$ is defined by $\{(-1, -1), (-1, 0), (-1, 1), (0, 0), (0, 1), (1, 1)\}$.

In Exercises 31-36, determine whether the given relation is a function.

31. $\{(1, 1), (2, 2), (3, 3), (4, 4), (5, 5)\}$
32. $\{(-1, -1), (-2, -2), (-3, -3)\}$
33. $\{(2, 0), (2, 2), (2, 4), (2, 5)\}$
34. $\{(1, 3), (1, 5), (1, 7), (1, 9)\}$
35. $\{(-1, -1), (0, -1), (1, -1)\}$
36. $\left\{\left(-2, -\frac{1}{2}\right), \left(-\frac{1}{2}, 2\right), \left(-3, -\frac{1}{3}\right)\right\}$

In Exercises 37-40 determine whether the given correspondence is a function

37.

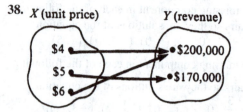

38. X (unit price) Y (revenue)

39.

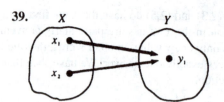

40.

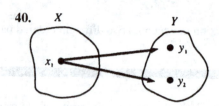

In Exercises 41-50 find the domain and range of the function.

41. $y = -2x + 3$ **42.** $y = \dfrac{x^2}{5}$

43. $y = \dfrac{1}{x + 4}$ **44.** $y = \dfrac{-2}{x - 1}$

45. $y = \dfrac{3}{x^2}$ **46.** $y = \dfrac{-4}{x^2}$

47. $y = \sqrt{x - 2}$ **48.** $y = \sqrt{x + 2}$

49. $y = \sqrt{2 - x}$ **50.** $y = 1/\sqrt{3 - x}$

In Exercise 51-60, find a formula that defines the functional relationship between the two variables; in each case indicate the domain of the function.

51. Express the area (A) of a square in terms of the length of its side (s).

52. Express the area (A) of a circle as a function of its radius (r).

53. Express the length of the side (s) of a square in terms of its perimeter (P)

54. Express the area (A) of a square as a function of the perimeter (P) of the square.

55. Express the earnings (e) of an electrician in terms of the number (n) of hours worked if the electrician makes $48 per hour.

56. Express the earnings (*e*) of a real estate agent who receives a 6 percent commission as a function of the sale price (*p*) of a house.

57. Express the weekly earnings (*e*) of a salesperson in terms of the cash amount (*a*) of merchandise sold if the salesperson earns $600 per week plus 8 percent commission on sales.

58. Express the monthly cost (*c*) for a checking account as a function of the number (*n*) of checks serviced that month if the bank charges 10 cents per check plus a 75-cent maintenance charge.

59. The total cost of producing a certain product consists of paying $400 per month rent plus $5 per unit for material. Express the company's monthly total costs (*c*) as a function of the number of units (*x*) it produces that month.

60. Express the monthly cost of renting a computer as a function of the number (*n*) of hours the computer is used if the company charges $200 plus $100 for every hour the computer is used during the month.

61. A reservoir contains 10,000 gal. of water. If water is being pumped from the reservoir at a rate of 50 gal/minute, write a formula expressing the amount (*a*) of water remaining in the reservoir as a function of the number (*n*) of minutes the water is being pumped. Describe the domain and range.

62. Oil is leaking from a tanker at the rate of 40,000 gallons per hour. Originally, the tanker was carrying 2 million gallons. Write a function that expresses the amount (*a*) of oil that remains in the tanker as a function of the number of hours (*h*) elapsed since the spill began. Describe the domain and range.

63. Express the federal income tax (*t*) for a single person as a function of taxable income (*i*) if the person's taxable income is between $115,000 and $250,000 inclusive, and the tax rate is $31,172 plus 36 percent of the excess over $115,000. Describe the domain and range.

64. A rule in a certain state income tax form says that if a person's federal tax is between $3,400 and $13,100, then the state tax is $952 plus 31 percent of the excess over $3,400. Express this state tax (*s*) as a function of the federal tax (*t*). Describe the domain and range.

65. For the given figure find a formula that expresses the area (*A*) of the shaded triangle as a function of the distance labeled as *x*. The outer figure is a rectangle. Describe the domain and range of the function.

66. A long strip of galvanized sheet metal 12 in. wide is to be formed into an open gutter by bending up the edges to form a gutter with a rectangular cross-section. Write the cross-sectional area of the gutter as a function of the depth (*x*). Describe the domain and range of the function.

THINK ABOUT IT 2.1

1. Explain the difference between a relation and a function.

2. The relation "is west of" on the set {Denver, San Diego, Boston} is given by what set of ordered pairs? Is this set a function?

3. Write a different function which has the same domain and the same range as the function {(1, 5),(2, 6)}.

4. For homework a student is assigned *every other odd-numbered* section exercise (starting with 1) in a set of 100 problems.

  a. Is Exercise 67 assigned? What about Exercise 93? Write a formula that shows the student the numbers of the exercises that are assigned. State the domain of the function. Give a verbal description of the rule.

  b. What formula will assign every other *even* exercise starting with 2?

5. A function can be described numerically by a table of ordered pairs. There need not be a formula to show how one variable depends on another, but often a table is derived from some formula. Try to find a formula that expresses *y* as a function of *x* that would give the ordered pairs in these tables. There may be more than one correct formula.

a.

x	−2	−1	0	1	2
y	4	1	0	1	4

b.

x	−2	−1	0	1	2
y	−1	1	3	5	7

c.

x	−2	−1	0	1	2
y	3	2	1	2	3

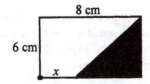

8 cm

6 cm

x

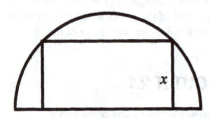

2.2 Functions and Graphs

A rectangular insert of clear glass is placed in a colored semicircular glass window of radius 1 m to improve the lighting near a stairway. To find the dimensions of the rectangular insert of greatest area that most improves the lighting, it is necessary to first find a formula for the area of the insert in terms of side dimension x, as shown. What is this formula? Find the domain and range of this function. (See Example 14.)

OBJECTIVES

1 Graph an ordered pair and determine the coordinates of a point.

2 Graph a function by the point-plotting method or by using a grapher.

3 Graph linear equations including $x = a$ and $y = b$.

4 Use the vertical line test to identify functions.

One of the sources of information and insight about a relationship is a picture that describes the particular situation. Pictures or graphs are often used in business reports, laboratory reports, and newspapers to present data quickly and vividly. Similarly, it is useful to have a graph that describes the behavior of a particular function, for this picture helps us see the essential characteristics of the relationship.

We can pictorially represent a function by using the **Cartesian coordinate system**. This system was devised by the French mathematician and philosopher René Descartes and is formed from the intersection of two real number lines at right angles. The values for the independent variable (usually x) are represented on a horizontal number line, and values for the dependent variable (usually y) on a vertical number line. These two lines are called **axes**, and they intersect at their common zero point, which is called the **origin** [see Figure 2.5 (a)].

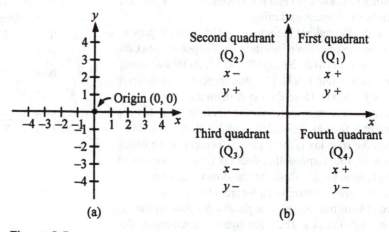

Figure 2.5

This coordinate system divides the plane into four regions called **quadrants**. The quadrant in which both x and y are positive is designated the first quadrant. The remaining quadrants are labeled in a counterclockwise direction. Figure 2.5(b) shows the name of each quadrant as well as the sign of x and y in that quadrant.

Any ordered pair can be represented as a point in this coordinate system. The first component indicates the distance of the point to the right or left of the vertical axis. The second component indicates the distance of the point above or below the horizontal axis. These components are called the **coordinates** of the point.

EXAMPLE 1   Plotting Points

Represent the ordered pairs $(0, -3)$, $(-4, -2)$, $(\pi, -5/2)$ and $\left(-4/3, \sqrt{2}\right)$ as points in the Cartesian coordinate system.

Solution   See Figure 2.6.

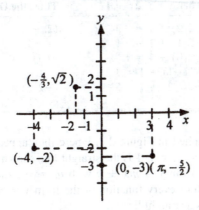

Figure 2.6

PROGRESS CHECK 1   Represent the ordered pairs $(-2, 0)$, $(-2, -4)$, $(3/2, \pi)$ and $\left(-5/3, \sqrt{5}\right)$ as points in the Cartesian coordinate system.   ■

We now consider one of the most useful ideas in mathematics. With the Cartesian coordinate system we can represent any ordered pair of real numbers by a particular point in the system. This enables us to draw a geometric picture (graph) of a relation.

Graph

The graph of a relation is the set of all points in a coordinate system that correspond to ordered pairs in the relation.

There are many techniques associated with determining the graph of a relation. One technique is simply to assign values to the independent variable and obtain a list of ordered-pair solutions. By plotting enough of these solutions, we can establish a trend and then complete the graph by following the established pattern. However, we cannot possibly list all the solutions of most equations, because they are an infinite set of ordered pairs. Determining how many and which points to plot is a difficult decision. Therefore, as we proceed in this section and succeeding chapters, we develop the more efficient method of determining the essential characteristics of the graph from the form of the equation. We may also use a graphing calculator or computer software to quickly obtain the graph of a relation. In Example 2, we begin our development of graphing techniques by considering the point-plotting method for obtaining a graph.

Example 2 Graphing a Line by Plotting Points
Graph the function $y = -2x + 1$.

Solution Make a list of ordered-pair solutions by replacing x with integer values from, say, 2 to -2.

If x Equals	Then $y = -2x + 1$	Thus, the Ordered Pairs Are
2	$-2(2) + 1 = -3$	$(2, -3)$
1	$-2(1) + 1 = -1$	$(1, -1)$
0	$-2(0) + 1 = 1$	$(0, 1)$
-1	$-2(-1) + 1 = 3$	$(-1, 3)$
-2	$-2(-2) + 1 = 5$	$(-2, 5)$

These ordered pairs are graphed in Figure 2.7, where they appear to all lie in a straight line. In fact, the graph of $y = -2x + 1$ is the straight line shown in Figure 2.8. Note that the given equation is of the form $y = mx + b$ with $m = -2$ and $b = 1$. In Section 2.8 we will prove that the graph of every function of the form $y = mx + b$, where m and b are real number constants, is a straight line.

PROGRESS CHECK 2 Graph the equation $y = 2x - 1$. ■

In Example 2 the graph of the function was a straight line so the equation $y = -2x + 1$ is called a linear equation in two variables. The next box focuses on the general form of this type of equation.

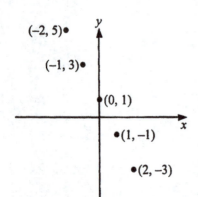

Figure 2.7

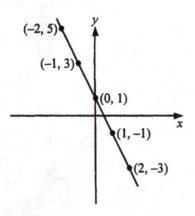

Figure 2.8

> ### Linear Equations in Two Variables
>
> A **linear equation in two variables** is an equation that can be written in the general form
>
> $$Ax + By = C,$$
>
> where A, B, and C are real numbers with A and B not both zero. The graph of a linear equation in two variables is a straight line.

In a linear equation any variable which has a nonzero coefficient must appear only to the *first power*. Thus, we see that the equation in Example 2, $y = -2x + 1$, is linear, and therefore its graph is a straight line. Rewritten in general form, this equation becomes $2x + y = 1$. Other examples of linear equations are

$$4x - 3y = 0, \qquad y = 2, \qquad \text{and} \qquad x = -3.$$

In order to draw the graph of a *linear* equation, it is sufficient to find any two distinct points in the graph and draw a line through them. But in practice, it is recommended that a third point be determined as a check. If you plot three points for a linear equation and they are not in a straight line, then there is an error in your work.

EXAMPLE 3   Graphing a Linear Equation

Graph $y = -x - 2$.

Solution   The equation $y = -x - 2$ is a linear equation (because the variables x and y appear to the first power), and therefore its graph is a straight line. We draw the line by first finding three distinct points in its graph. We will find these points by letting x equal 2, 0, and -2, but we could have chosen any three values.

If $x =$	Then $y = -x - 2$	Thus, the Ordered-Pair Solutions Are
2	$-(2) - 2 = -4$	$(2, -4)$
0	$-(0) - 2 = -2$	$(0, -2)$
-2	$-(-2) - 2 = 0$	$(-2, 0)$

These three points are plotted in Figure 2.9, and the line is drawn through them.

PROGRESS CHECK 3   Graph $y = -x - 1$.   ■

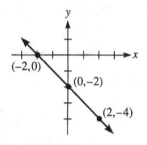

Figure 2.9

Graphing linear equations using intercepts

The point where a graph crosses the x-axis (if it does cross the x-axis) is called the **x-intercept**. Because this point is *on* the x-axis, its *second component must be zero*. Similarly, the point where a graph crosses the y-axis is called the **y-intercept**, and its *first component must be zero*. This leads to a simple way to find the intercepts.

To Find Intercepts

To find the x-intercept $(a, 0)$, let $y = 0$ and solve for x.
To find the y-intercept $(0, b)$, let $x = 0$ and solve for y.

Graphing linear equations by drawing a line through the intercepts is especially useful when the linear equation is given in general form, not solved for y or x.

EXAMPLE 4   Using Intercepts in a Graph

Graph $2x + 3y = -6$ by using the x- and y-intercepts.

Solution   To find the x-intercept, let $y = 0$ and solve for x.

$$2x + 3y = -6 \qquad \text{Given equation.}$$
$$2x + 3(0) = -6 \qquad \text{Replace } y \text{ by 0.}$$
$$2x = -6 \qquad \text{Simplify.}$$
$$x = -3 \qquad \text{Divide both sides by 2.}$$

Thus, the x-intercept is $(-3, 0)$.

To find the y-intercept, let $x = 0$ and solve for y.

$$2x + 3y = -6 \qquad \text{Given equation.}$$
$$2(0) + 3y = -6 \qquad \text{Replace } x \text{ by 0.}$$
$$3y = -6 \qquad \text{Simplify.}$$
$$y = -2 \qquad \text{Divide both sides by 3.}$$

The y-intercept is $(0, -2)$.

For a checking point we arbitrarily let $x = 3$, which leads to the solution $(3, -4)$. The two intercepts and the checking point are plotted and a line is drawn through them to get the graph in Figure 2.10.

Note Because the x-coordinate of the y-intercept is always zero, it is also conventional to define the y-intercept as just the value of y where the graph intersects the y-axis. With this definition, the y-intercept of the graph in Figure 2.10 is simply -2, rather than $(0, -2)$. In this text we choose to always write both coordinates as a reminder that an intercept is a point on the graph. Similar remarks hold for the x-intercept.

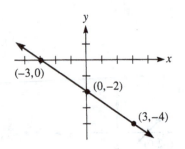

Figure 2.10

PROGRESS CHECK 4 Graph $x - 2y = 4$ by using the x- and y-intercepts. ■

Graphing horizontal and vertical lines

Linear equations which correspond to vertical and horizontal lines have particularly simple forms; they may be written in the form $x = a$ or $y = b$, as shown next.

EXAMPLE 5 Graphing a Horizontal Line

Graph the line $y = 3$.

Solution The linear equation $y = 3$ is equivalent to $0x + y = 3$, which implies that any ordered pair of the form $(a, 3)$ is a solution. Thus, a few of the solutions are $(1, 3)$, $(0, 3)$, and $(-3, 3)$. Since all these points have the *same second component*, they are all at the same height; and therefore the graph is a *horizontal* line, as shown in Figure 2.11.

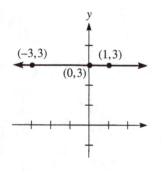

Figure 2.11

PROGRESS CHECK 5 Graph $y = -1$. ■

EXAMPLE 6 Graphing a Vertical Line

Graph $x = -1$.

Solution The linear equation $x = -1$ is equivalent to $x + 0y = -1$, which means that x equals -1 for all values of y. Thus, all points of the graph have the *same x-coordinate*, implying that the graph will be a *vertical* line. Using $(-1, 1)$, $(-1, 2)$, and $(-1, 3)$ as three arbitrary points in the graph leads to the line in Figure 2.12.

PROGRESS CHECK 6 Graph $x = 3$. ■

Examples 5 and 6 lead to the general principles described in the box below.

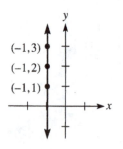

Figure 2.12

> ### To Graph $x = a$ and $y = b$
>
> 1. The graph of the linear equation $x = a$ is a vertical line that contains the point $(a, 0)$. If $a = 0$, then the equation is $x = 0$, and the line is the y-axis.
> 2. The graph of the linear equation $y = b$ is a horizontal line that contains the point $(0, b)$. If $b = 0$, then the equation is $y = 0$, and the line is the x-axis.

Examples 2 to 6 showed relations whose graphs require only lines. Graphs are in no way limited to lines, however, and the next example considers the parabola.

EXAMPLE 7   Graphing a Parabola by Plotting Points

Graph $y = 4 - x^2$.

Solution   Begin by substituting integer values for x from, say, 3 to -3 and make a list of ordered-pair solutions.

If $x =$	Then $y = 4 - x^2$	Thus, the Ordered Pairs Are
3	$4 - (3)^2 = -5$	$(3, -5)$
2	$4 - (2)^2 = 0$	$(2, 0)$
1	$4 - (1)^2 = 3$	$(1, 3)$
0	$4 - (0)^2 = 4$	$(0, 4)$
-1	$4 - (-1)^2 = 3$	$(-1, 3)$
-2	$4 - (-2)^2 = 0$	$(-2, 0)$
-3	$4 - (-3)^2 = -5$	$(-3, -5)$

Now graph these ordered pairs and draw a smooth curve through them. The resulting graph of $y = 4 - x^2$ is shown in Figure 2.13. Note that the cuplike curve in Figure 2.13 is called a **parabola**. In every case, the graph of a function that may be written in the form $y = ax^2 + bx + c$, where a, b, and c are real numbers with $a \neq 0$, is a parabola. We discuss these functions in detail in Section 7.5.

PROGRESS CHECK 7   Graph $y = x^2 - 4$.   ■

Obtaining Graphs by Graphing Calculator

A great strength of a graphing calculator is its ability to plot many points accurately in a few seconds. These points are then usually connected by line segments to obtain a better visual image of the relation. To obtain the graph of a function by calculator two important steps are necessary.

1. Enter an expression to define a function in the equation list.
2. Establish lower and upper bounds for x and y for the calculator display, and then activate the graphing routine.

The limits set in step 2 define a **viewing window**, and this procedure is often called setting the window or range for x and for y. Note that this use of the word "range" is different from the range of a function. For some graphing calculators, the **Standard Viewing Window** is obtained by letting both x and y vary from -10 to 10, where scale markers are 1 unit apart, and we will adopt this convention for this text. In the next example we use the ideas just discussed to redraw the graph of $y = 4 - x^2$ with the aid of a graphing calculator.

EXAMPLE 8   Obtaining a Graph by Calculator

Graph $y = 4 - x^2$ using a graphing calculator.

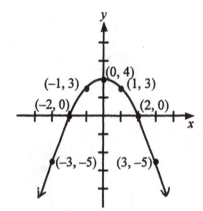

Figure 2.13

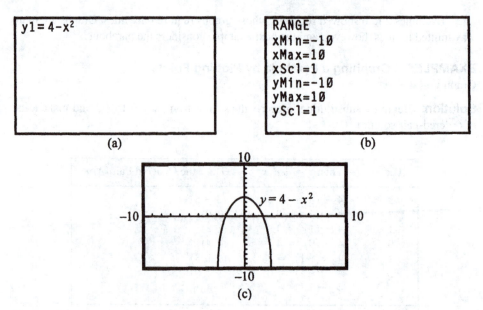

Figure 2.14

Solution   Figures 2.14(a), (b), and (c) show typical calculator screens that result from entering this function in the equation list, setting the standard window, and then obtaining the graph, respectively. Observe that the resulting graph of $y = 4 - x^2$ is in agreement with the parabola we obtained by plotting points in Example 7.

Caution   If the display is entirely blank when you expect to see a graph, the most likely cause is that the window settings are not suitable. Another possible cause is that the function to be graphed has been inadvertently turned off. For instance, on Texas Instruments models the equal sign is highlighted for a selected function, and not highlighted for an unselected function. You should learn how to turn a function "on" or "off" on your calculator.

PROGRESS CHECK 8   Graph $y = (x - 2)^2$ using a graphing calculator.   ■

When graphing functions we usually do not want to think of a function in terms of a single picture. Instead, many pictures are possible depending on how the viewing window is defined. It is assumed that when we are directed to graph a function, a complete graph is requested. A **complete graph** is a graph that shows all the significant features of a function. The next two examples involve adjusting viewing windows to obtain a complete graph.

EXAMPLE 9   Adjusting Viewing Windows to Find a Complete Graph
Graph $y = (x - 10)^2 - 15$ using the following viewing windows. Which picture shows a complete graph?

a. xMin $= -10$ **b.** xMin $= -5$
    xMax $= 10$ xMax $= 20$
    xScl $= 1$ xScl $= 5$
    yMin $= -10$ yMin $= -50$
    yMax $= 10$ yMax $= 100$
    yScl $= 1$ yScl $= 10$

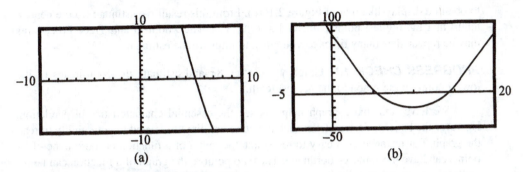

Figure 2.15

Solution: The function is graphed using the two viewing windows in Figure 2.15(a) and Figure 2.15(b), respectively. Because $y = (x - 10)^2 - 15$ may be expressed in the form $y = ax^2 + bx + c$ with $a \neq 0$, the graph is a parabola. Observe that Figure 2.15(b) shows a complete graph of the function, while Figure 2.15(a) does not illustrate all the significant features of the graph.

PROGRESS CHECK 9   Graph $y = 60 - x$ using the following viewing windows. Which picture shows a complete graph?

a. $x\text{Min} = -10$
   $x\text{Max} = 70$
   $x\text{Scl} = 10$
   $y\text{Min} = -10$
   $y\text{Max} = 70$
   $y\text{Scl} = 10$

b. $x\text{Min} = -70$
   $x\text{Max} = 10$
   $x\text{Scl} = 10$
   $y\text{Min} = -70$
   $y\text{Max} = 10$
   $y\text{Scl} = 10$ ■

The Zoom-in feature and Trace feature on a graphing calculator are particularly useful graphing operations, as shown next.

EXAMPLE 10   Using Zoom and Trace Features
Graph $y = -3x^2 + 10x - 5$ and estimate the coordinates of the highest point on the graph to the nearest tenth.

Solution   First, graph $y = -3x^2 + 10x - 5$ in the standard viewing window, as shown in Figure 2.16(a). Next, zoom in on the part of the picture that displays the highest point. Figure 2.16(b) shows a typical calculator screen that results when the cursor is located near the highest point, and the Zoom-In feature (set to zoom factors of 4) is applied twice. Finally, we activate the Trace feature and try to stop the cursor on the highest point,

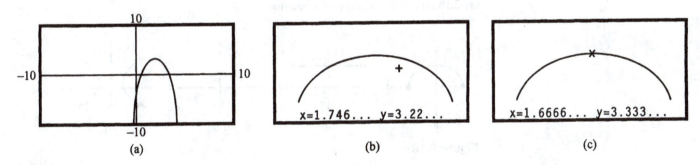

Figure 2.16

to obtain a display like that in Figure 2.16(c). From this result we estimate (to the nearest tenth) that the highest point is located at (1.7, 3.3). The Zoom-In and Trace Procedures may be repeated as many times as you wish, to improve the estimate.

PROGRESS CHECK 10 Graph $y = 3x^2 + 8x$ and estimate the coordinates of the lowest point on the graph to the nearest tenth. ■

We have said that a graph helps us see the essential characteristics of a relation. However the benefits derived from such a picture are directly related to your ability to read the graph. For instance, it is easy to recognize the graph of a function because none of its points can have the same x-coordinate. Thus, no point in the graph of a function can be directly above any other point. This feature is often summarized in the vertical line test.

Vertical Line Test

Imagine a vertical line sweeping across a graph. If the vertical line at any position intersects the graph in more than one point, then the graph is not the graph of a function.

EXAMPLE 11 Using the Vertical Line Test

Use the vertical line test to determine which graphs in Figure 2.17 represent the graph of a function.

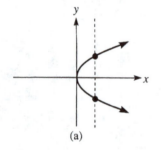
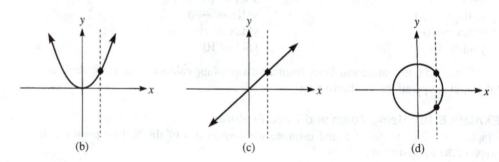

Figure 2.17

Solution By the vertical line test graphs (b) and (c) represent functions, whereas (a) and (d) do not.

PROGRESS CHECK 11 Use the vertical line test to determine which graphs in Figure 2.18 represent the graph of a function. ■

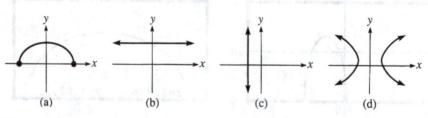

Figure 2.18

Combining algebraic and geometric methods is useful for finding the domain and range of a relation. Beginning from the geometric viewpoint, the domain is given by the variation of the graph in a horizontal direction, because the domain is the set of all first components in the ordered pairs. The range (which is the set of all second components) is given by the variation of the graph in the vertical direction.

EXAMPLE 12   Finding Domain and Range Graphically

Find the domain and range of the relation in Figure 2.19. Is this relation a function?

Solution   The x values in the semicircle start at -5, and the graph extends to the right and ends when x equals 5. Thus, the domain is

$$\{x: -5 \leq x \leq 5\} \qquad \text{or} \qquad [-5, 5] \text{ in interval notation.}$$

The minimum y value is 0, and the graph extends up to a maximum y value of 5. Thus, the range is

$$\{y: 0 \leq y \leq 5\} \qquad \text{or} \qquad [0, 5] \text{ in interval notation.}$$

Figure 2.20 specifies these results and also indicates that this relation is a function according to the vertical line test.

PROGRESS CHECK 12   Find the domain and range of the relation in Figure 2.21. Is this relation a function?   ■

EXAMPLE 13   Finding Domain and Range Algebraically and Graphically

Determine the domain and range of $y = \sqrt{x + 12}$. Use both algebraic and geometric methods.

Solution   **Algebraic Analysis:** For the output of $\sqrt{x + 12}$ to be a real number, x must satisfy

$$x + 12 \geq 0$$

$$x \geq -12.$$

Thus, the domain is $\{x: x \geq -12\}$, or $[-12, \infty)$, in interval notation. The radical sign $\sqrt{}$ denotes the nonnegative square root, so if $x \geq -12$, then $\sqrt{x + 12}$ is greater than or equal to 0. Therefore, the range is $\{y: y \geq 0\}$, or alternatively $[0, \infty)$.

Geometric Analysis

First, set $y1 = \sqrt{x + 12}$. Then we use $[-15, 15]$ by $[-10, 10]$ to define a viewing window and graph the function, as shown in Figure 2.22. This graph suggests that the domain is $[-12, \infty)$ and the range is $[0, \infty)$. With this graphical approach, analysis of the equation $y = \sqrt{x + 12}$ is required to determine that $(-12, 0)$ is a left end point of this graph, and that this graph is unbounded to the right.

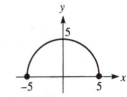

Figure 2.19

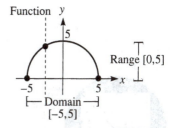

Figure 2.20

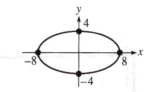

Figure 2.21

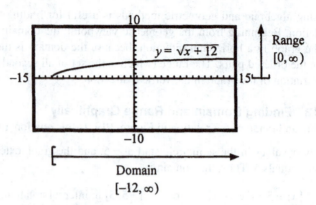

Figure 2.22

PROGRESS CHECK 13 Determine the domain and range of $y = -\sqrt{18 - x}$. Use both algebraic and geometric methods.   ■

EXAMPLE 14   Finding a Formula for a Function

Solve the problem in the section introduction on page 84.

Solution   First, consider the sketch of the situation in Figure 2.23 and note that we strategically placed the radius of the semicircle so as to form a right triangle inside the rectangle. We may then use the Pythagorean theorem to write z in terms of x as follows:

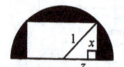

$$x^2 + z^2 = 1^2$$
$$z^2 = 1 - x^2$$
$$z = \sqrt{1 - x^2} \quad \text{(since z is positive)}.$$

Then the area formula in terms of x is

$$A = 2xz$$
$$= 2x\sqrt{1 - x^2}.$$

In the context of this problem, the meaningful replacements for x are the real numbers between 0 and 1, so the domain is the interval $(0, 1)$.

To determine the range, use $[0, 1]$ by $[0, 2]$ to define a viewing window, and then graph the function as shown in Figure 2.24. In this graph, note that the y-axis represents values of the area A. Using the Zoom and Trace features you should determine that $y \approx 1$ at the highest point in the graph. (In fact, check by calculator that when $x = \sqrt{1/2}$, then $y = 1$.) The lowest y value is 0, but $y > 0$ because of context. Thus, the range is the interval $(0, 1]$.

PROGRESS CHECK 14 Suppose the radius of the semicircle in Example 14 is 2 ft. Find a formula for the area of the rectangular insert as a function of the side dimension x, and determine the domain and the range.   ■

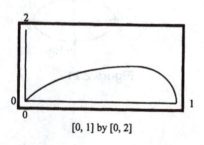

[0, 1] by [0, 2]

Figure 2.24

EXERCISES 2.2

1. Graph the following ordered pairs.
   a. $(3, 1)$ **b.** $(-3, 4)$
   c. $(0, 2)$ **d.** $(-3, 0)$
   e. $(-1, -2)$ **f.** $(2, -3)$
   g. $(-2, -3)$ **h.** $(-1, 2)$
   i. $\left(\sqrt{2}, 3\right)$ **j.** $(1, -\pi)$

2. Approximate (use integers) the ordered pairs corresponding to the points shown in the graph.

3. Three vertices of a square are $(3, 3)$, $(3, -1)$, and $(-1, 3)$. Find the ordered pair corresponding to the fourth vertex.

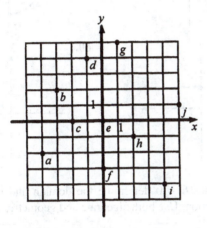

4. Three vertices of a rectangle are $(4, 2)$, $(-5, 2)$, and $(-5, -4)$. Find the ordered pair corresponding to the fourth vertex.

5. The points $(0, 0)$, $(-2, -4)$, and $(1, 2)$ lie on a straight line. Find the coordinates of three other points on this line.

6. If we designate the horizontal axis as the x axis and the vertical axis as the y axis:
   a. What is the x value of all the points on the y axis?
   b. What is the y value of all the points on the x axis?

In Exercises 7–18, graph the given equation.
   7. $y = x + 3$ **8.** $y = x - 2$
   9. $y = -x - 3$ **10.** $y = -x + 1$
   11. $2x + 5y = -10$ **12.** $3x - 4y = -12$
   13. $2x - 4y = 9$ **14.** $3x + y = 10$
   15. $y = 3$ **16.** $y = -2$
   17. $x = 2$ **18.** $x = -1$

In Exercises 19–24 graph these essential functions, and make note of their names. They will be referred to by name later in the text.

19. The squaring function: $y = x^2$
20. The square root function: $y = \sqrt{x}$
21. The cubing function: $y = x^3$
22. The identity function: $y = x$
23. The constant function: $y = c$, where c is some constant.
24. The absolute value function: $y = |x|$. Note: On many graphing calculators there is a key or menu choice labeled "abs" for absolute value. So $|x|$ is entered as abs x.

In Exercises 25–32 draw the graph by the point-plotting method. Confirm your answer with a grapher.

   25. $y = -\sqrt{3}$ **26.** $y = \pi$
   27. $y = x^2 + 1$ **28.** $y = x^2 + x$
   29. $y = (x - 1)^2$ **30.** $y = 5 - x^2$
   31. $y = 3x - x^2$ **32.** $y = x^2 - 2x + 1$

In Exercises 33–40 use a grapher to graph the function with the given viewing window, shown as [xMin, xMax]; [yMin, yMax].

33. $y = 3x + 1$ $[-10, 10]$; $[-10, 10]$
34. $y = 3x^2 - 2$ $[-5, 5]$; $[-5, 5]$
35. $y = x^2 + x + 10$ $[-10, 10]$; $[-5, 25]$
36. $y = x^2 - 10x - 10$ $[-5, 15]$; $[-40, 15]$
37. $y = \sqrt{x + 5}$ $[-10, 10]$; $[-5, 5]$
38. $y = \sqrt{x - 5}$ $[-1, 15]$; $[-2, 5]$
39. $y = |x + 5|$ $[-15, 5]$; $[-5, 15]$
40. $y = |x - 5|$ $[-5, 15]$; $[-5, 15]$

In Exercises 41–44 decide which viewing window shows a complete graph.

41. $y = (x + 12)^2 - 9$
   a. $[-10, 10]$; $[-10, 10]$
   b. $[-20, 10]$; $[-20, 10]$
42. $y = 20 + (x - 12)^2$
   a. $[-10, 10]$; $[-10, 10]$
   b. $[-5, 20]$; $[-5, 40]$
43. $y = x - 20$
   a. $[-10, 40]$; $[-40, 10]$
   b. $[-40, 10]$; $[-10, 40]$
44. $y = 3x + 20$
   a. $[-5, 50]$; $[-20, 10]$
   b. $[-20, 10]$; $[-50, 50]$

In Exercises 45–52, determine if the given graph or equation determines y as a function of x.

45.

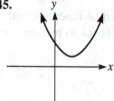

46.

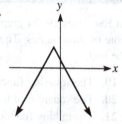

47.

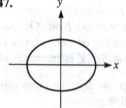

48.

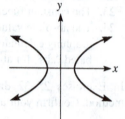

49.

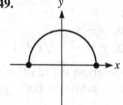

50.

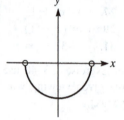

51.

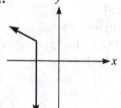

52.

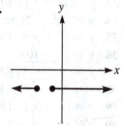

In Exercises 53–60, determine the domain and the range of the given relation.

53.

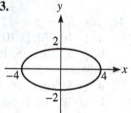

54.

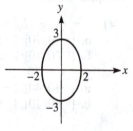

55.

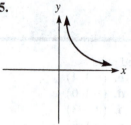

56.

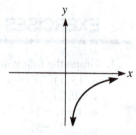

57.

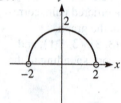

58.

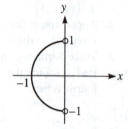

59.

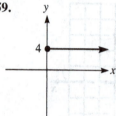

60.

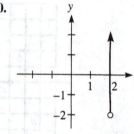

In Exercises 61–70 determine the domain and range of the given function. Use both algebraic and geometric methods.

61. $y = \sqrt{x + 6}$ **62.** $y = -\sqrt{10 - x}$

63. $y = 5 + \sqrt{3x - 9}$ **64.** $y = 4 - \sqrt{2x + 10}$

65. $y = |x - 4| + 2$ **66.** $y = |x + 4| - 1$

67. $y = 7$ **68.** $y = -8$

69. $y = \dfrac{1}{x + 1}$ **70.** $y = \dfrac{1}{\sqrt{x + 5}}$

In Exercises 71–74 use the Zoom and Trace features of a grapher to estimate the coordinates of the desired point to the nearest tenth.

71. $y = -x^2 + 5x - 3$; highest point

72. $y = -x^2 - 3x + 5$; highest point

73. $y = 5x^2 + 2x - 2$; lowest point

74. $y = 5x^2 - 3x + 2$; lowest point

75. A car rents for $60 a week plus 20¢ per mile.
   a. Write an equation for the weekly cost C. Let m represent the weekly mileage.
   b. Graph the equation with m as the horizontal axis.

76. The daily pay (P) for a carpenter is $20 per hour for labor plus $10 for lunch and travel.
   a. Write an equation for daily pay, where h represents the number of hours worked.
   b. Graph the equation with h as the horizontal axis.

77. A projectile fired vertically upward from the ground with an initial velocity of 128 ft/second will hit the ground 8 seconds later, and the speed of the projectile in terms of the elapsed time t equals $|128 - 32t|$. Graph the function $s = |128 - 32t|$. Describe the domain and range.

78. The height (y) above water of a diver t seconds after the diver steps off a platform 100 ft high is given by the formula $y = 100 - 16t^2$. Graph this function. Describe the domain and range.

79. For the given figure find a formula that expresses the area (A) of the rectangle as a function of the height (x). The outer figure is a semicircle with radius 3 inches. Describe the domain and range of the function.

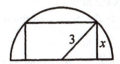

THINK ABOUT IT 2.2

1. Because $y = \dfrac{(2x + 1)(x - 2)}{(x - 2)}$ is not defined for $x = 2$, its graph has a hole in it when $x = 2$. Draw the graph.

2. The second equation below has the same form as the first, but x and y have been switched.

$$y = 3x + 2$$
$$x = 3y + 2$$

   a. Are they both linear equations?
   b. Solve the second equation for y.

c. Complete these charts, and describe the relationships between the two sets of ordered pairs.

For $y = 3x + 2$ For $y = \dfrac{x - 2}{3}$

x	y
0	
1	
2	

x	y
2	
5	
8	

   d. Find any ordered pair which is a solution in *both* equations by solving $3x + 2 = \dfrac{x - 2}{3}$. Show that it satisfies both equations.

3. a. Graph $y = x^2 + 2$ and $y = x^2 - 2$ on the same coordinate system. How do the graphs relate to $y = x^2$? In general, what is the effect of adding a constant *after* applying the squaring function?
   b. Graph $y = (x + 2)^2$ and $y = (x - 2)^2$ on the same coordinate system. How do these graphs relate to $y = x^2$? In general, what is the effect of adding a constant *before* applying the squaring function?

4. Describe a realistic situation that would produce the graph.

5. The area (A) of a square depends on its perimeter (p).
   a. Construct a table that shows corresponding values for p and A. Let p vary from 12 to 40 in increments of 4.
   b. Write a formula that expresses A as a function of p.
   c. Use a grapher to graph the formula from part **b** and describe what happens to the area as p increases. What are the domain and range of this function?

Courtesy of Digital Vision, Ltd.

2.3   Variation

The time T it takes to cook a turkey varies directly with its weight w. If it takes 3 hours and 36 minutes to cook a 12-lb turkey, how long will it take to cook a 20-lb turkey? (See Example 3.)

OBJECTIVES

1   Solve problems involving direct variation.

2   Solve problems involving inverse variation.

3   Solve problems involving combined variation or variation of powers of variables.

In many scientific laws the functional relationship between variables is stated in the language of variation. The statement "y varies *directly* as x" means that there is some nonzero number k such that $y = kx$. The constant k is called the **variation constant**. In some applications the relationship $y = kx$ is also described by saying that y is **proportional** to x, and that k is the **constant of proportionality**.

EXAMPLE 1   Expressing Direct Variation by an Equation

Write a variation equation for the given relation and determine the value of the variation constant if it is known.

a. The perimeter P of a square varies directly as the side s.
b. The sales tax T on a purchase varies directly as the price p of the item.

Solution

a. P varies directly as s means that $P = ks$. In this case we know that $k = 4$.
b. T varies directly as p means that $T = kp$. The value of k depends on the sales tax rate in a given location.

PROGRESS CHECK 1   Write a variation equation for the given relation and determine the value of the variation constant if it is known.

a. The circumference C of a circle varies directly as the diameter d.
b. The property tax T on a house varies directly as the assessed value v of the house.   ■

Figure 2.25 shows the graph of the variation equation $y = kx$, $k > 0$. Note that the graph is a straight line through the origin, and that as x increases, y increases. We may determine the value of k if one ordered pair in the relation, other than $(0, 0)$, is known. This value of k may then be used to find other corresponding values of the variables.

EXAMPLE 2   Finding and Using *k* in a Direct Variation Relation

If y varies directly as x and $y = 21$ when $x = 3$, write y as a function of x. Determine the value of y when $x = 10$.

Solution   Since y varies directly as x, we have

$$y = kx.$$

To find k, replace y by 21 and x by 3.

$$21 = k \cdot 3$$
$$7 = k$$

$y = kx, k > 0$

Figure 2.25

Thus, $y = 7x$. When $x = 10$, $y = 7(10) = 70$.

PROGRESS CHECK 2   If y varies directly as x, and $y = 3$ when $x = 4$, write y as a function of x. Find y when $x = 12$.   ■

EXAMPLE 3   Determining Cooking Time

Solve the problem in the section introduction on page 98.

Solution   Since cooking time T varies directly as weight w,

$$T = kw.$$

To find k, replace T by 3 hours and 36 minutes (216 minutes) and w by 12 lb.

$$216 = k(12)$$

$$\tfrac{216}{12} = k, \quad \text{or} \quad k = 18.$$

Thus, $T = 18w$, which means the cooking time is 18 minutes per pound of turkey.
    Next, replace w by 20 to find the cooking time for a 20-lb turkey.

$$T = 18(20) = 360$$

The cooking time is 360 minutes, or 6 hours.

PROGRESS CHECK 3   The weekly earnings of a part-time employee vary directly as the number of hours worked. For an employee who makes \$111.60 for 18 hours of work, what are the earnings for 20 hours of work?   ■

EXAMPLE 4   Hooke's Law

Hooke's law states that the distance (d) a spring is stretched varies directly as the force (F) applied to the spring (see Figure 2.26). The value of the constant of variation depends on the particular spring. Suppose that for one such spring a force of 20 lb stretches the spring 6 in.

a. Express Hooke's law using an equation of variation that gives d as a function of F, and find the value of k.
b. Graph the function from part **a** and give its domain.
c. Using the equation from part **a** or the graph from part **b**, determine how far the spring will be stretched by a force of 13 lb.

Solution

a. Since d varies directly as F, we can write

$$d = kF.$$

To find k, replace d by 6 and F by 20.

$$6 = k \cdot 20$$

$$0.3 = k$$

Thus, the desired equation is $d = 0.3F$.

b. Note that in this application there is a natural restriction of the domain of the function, which represents the force on the spring, to nonnegative values. So we take the domain to be all nonnegative real numbers. This interval is clearly an oversimplification, because in reality tiny weights may not make any observable stretch, and extremely heavy weights will stretch the spring to its full length. The graph is shown in Figure 2.27.

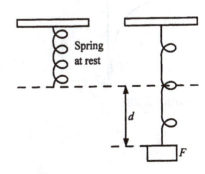

Figure 2.26

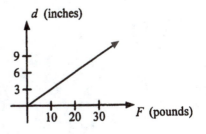

Figure 2.27

c. When $F = 13$, we get $d = 0.3(13) = 3.9$. A 13-lb force will stretch this spring 3.9 inches.

PROGRESS CHECK 4   The weight of an object on the moon w_m is proportional to its weight on Earth w_e. An object that weights 204 pounds on the Earth weighs 34 pounds on the moon.

a. Express the moon weight as a function of the Earth weight using an equation of variation, and find the value of the constant of proportionality.
b. Graph the function from part **a** and give its domain.
c. Using the equation from part **a** or the graph from part **b**, determine what a person who weighs 138 pounds on the Earth will weigh on the moon.   ■

In some relationships one variable decreases as another increases. If this happens in such a way that the product of the two variables is constant, then we say that the variables **vary inversely**, or that one is **inversely proportional** to the other. The statement "y varies inversely as x" means that there is some nonzero number k (the variation constant) such that

$$xy = k \text{ or } y = \frac{k}{x}.$$

Figure 2.28 shows the graph of the variation equation $y = k/x$ for $k > 0$. The graph in this figure, which is called a **hyperbola**, consists of two disconnected curves, known as **branches**. The graph shows that the variation equation $y = k/x$ is meaningless if $x = 0$ or $y = 0$, and that on each branch as x increases, y decreases.

EXAMPLE 5   Finding and Using *k* in an Inverse Variation Relation
If y varies inversely with x and $y = 27$ when $x = 2$, write y as a function of x. Find y when $x = 9$.

Solution   Since y varies inversely as x, we have

$$y = \frac{k}{x}.$$

To find k, replace y by 27 and x by 2.

$$27 = \frac{k}{2}$$

$$54 = k$$

Thus, $y = 54/x$. When $x = 9$, $y = 54/9 = 6$.

PROGRESS CHECK 5   If y varies inversely with x and $y = 13$ when $x = 5$, write y as a function of x. Find y when $x = 1$.   ■

EXAMPLE 6   Speed of a Gear
The speed (S) of a gear varies inversely as the number (n) of teeth. Gear A, which has 12 teeth, makes 400 rpm. How many revolutions per minute are made by a gear with 32 teeth that is connected to gear A?

Solution   Since S varies inversely with n, we have

$$S = \frac{k}{n}.$$

To find k, replace S by 400 and n by 12.

$$400 = \frac{k}{12}$$

$$4,800 = k$$

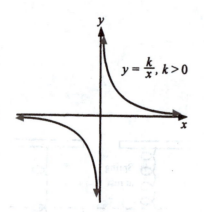

$y = \dfrac{k}{x}, \; k > 0$

Figure 2.28

Thus, $S = 4{,}800/n$. When $n = 32$, $S = 4{,}800/32 = 150$ rpm.

PROGRESS CHECK 6   The speed of a pulley is inversely proportional to the radius of the pulley. The speed of the larger of two pulleys, which has a 2-inch radius, is 45 rpm. What is the speed of a 1/2-inch pulley connected to it. ■

   We may extend the concept of variation to include direct and inverse variation of variables raised to specified powers and relationships that involve more than two variables.

EXAMPLE 7   Finding and Using *k* in a Combined Variation Relation

If y varies directly as x^2 and inversely as z^3, and $y = 18$ when $x = 3$ and $z = 2$, determine the value of y when $x = 1$ and $z = 5$.

Solution   Since y varies directly as x^2 and inversely as z^3, we have

$$y = \frac{kx^2}{z^3}.$$

To find k, replace y by 18, x by 3, and z by 2.

$$18 = \frac{k(3)^2}{(2)^3}$$

$$18 = \frac{9k}{8}$$

$$16 = k$$

Thus, $y = 16x^2/z^3$. When $x = 1$ and $z = 5$,

$$y = \frac{16(1)^2}{(5)^3} = \frac{16}{125}.$$

PROGRESS CHECK 7   If y varies directly as x^3 and inversely as z^2, and $y = 10$ when $x = 2$ and $z = 5$, determine the value of y when $x = 5$ and $z = 2$. ■

EXAMPLE 8   Gravitational Attraction Between Two Objects

Newton's law of gravitation states that the gravitational attraction between two objects varies directly as the product of their masses, and inversely as the square of the distance between their centers of mass. What will be the change in attraction between the two objects if both masses are doubled and the distance between their centers is cut in half?

Solution   If F represents the gravitational attraction, m_1 and m_2 represent the masses of the objects, and d represents the distance between the centers of mass, then algebraically, we write Newton's law as

$$F = \frac{km_1m_2}{d^2}.$$

If the masses are doubled and the distance is cut in half, we have

$$F = \frac{k(2m_1)(2m_2)}{[(1/2)d]^2}$$

$$= \frac{4km_1m_2}{(1/4)d^2}$$

$$= \frac{16km_1m_2}{d^2}.$$

Thus, the gravitational attraction becomes 16 times as great.

Note: If y varies directly as the product of other variables, say x and w, we write $y = kxw$, and we say that y **varies jointly as** x and w. In this example an alternative way to say that F varies directly as the product $m_1 m_2$ is to say that F varies jointly as m_1 and m_2.

PROGRESS CHECK 8   Using Newton's law of gravitation from Example 8, what will be the change in attraction between two objects if both masses are cut in half and the distance between them is doubled?   ■

Finally, we point out that any variation problem may also be solved by using a proportion. For example, if y varies directly as x, we know that $y = kx$. Thus, $y/x = k$ and there is a constant ratio between any corresponding values of x and y. This means that

$$\frac{y_1}{x_1} = \frac{y_2}{x_2} \text{ and } \frac{y_1}{y_2} = \frac{x_1}{x_2}.$$

The equation $y_1/y_2 = x_1/x_2$ is called a **proportion** and may be used to solve the problem. It is for this reason that the variation constant k is often called the constant of proportionality, and the expression "varies directly as" is often replaced by "is proportional to." However, the language of variation usually provides a more convenient and informative statement of a relationship.

EXERCISES 2.3

In Exercises 1–6 write a variation equation for the given relation and determine the value of the variation constant if it is known.

1. The perimeter P of an equilateral triangle varies directly as the side s.
2. The circumference C of a circle varies directly as the radius r.
3. The sales tax T on a car varies directly as the price of the car.
4. The air resistance R on a falling object varies directly as its velocity v.
5. According to Boyle's law, the volume V of a given mass of gas at a constant temperature varies inversely as the pressure P exerted on it.
6. In a manufacturing process the cost per unit c varies inversely as the number n of units produced.
7. If y varies directly as x, and $y = 14$ when $x = 6$, write y as a function of x. Determine the value of y when $x = 10$.
8. If y varies directly as x, and $y = 2$, when $x = 5$, write y as a function of x. Determine the value of y when $x = 11$.
9. If y varies directly as the square of x, and $y = 3$ when $x = 2$, write y as a function of x. Find y when $x = 4$.
10. If y varies directly as x^3, and $y = 5$ when $x = 3$, write y as a function of x. Find y when $x = 2$.
11. If y varies inversely as x, and $y = 9$ when $x = 8$, write y as a function of x. Find y when $x = 24$.
12. If y varies inversely as x, and $y = 3$ when $x = 7$, write y as a function of x. Find y when $x = 21$.

13. If y varies inversely as x^3, and $y = 3$ when $x = 2$, write y as a function of x. Find y when $x = 3$.
14. If y varies inversely as the square of x, and $y = 2$ when $x = 4$, write y as a function of x. Find y when $x = 8$.
15. If y varies directly as x and z, and $y = 105$ when $x = 7$ and $z = 5$, find y when $x = 10$ and $z = 2$.
16. If y varies directly as x and inversely as z, and $y = 10$ when $x = 4$ and $z = 3$, find y when $x = 7$ and $z = 15$.
17. If y varies directly as x and inversely as z^2, and $y = 36$ when $x = 4$ and $z = 7$, find y when $x = 9$ and $z = 9$.
18. If y varies inversely as x^2 and z^3 and $y = 0.5$ when $x = 3$ and $z = 2$, find y when $x = 2$ and $z = 3$.
19. In a spring to which Hooke's law applies (see Example 4), a force of 15 lb stretches the spring 10 in. How far will the spring be stretched by a force of 6 lb?
20. The weight of an object on the moon varies directly with the weight of the object on Earth. An object that weighs 114 lb on Earth weighs 19 lb on the moon. How much will a person who weighs 174 lb on Earth weigh on the moon?
21. The amount of garbage produced in a given location varies directly with the number of people living in the area. It is known that 25 tons of garbage are produced by 100 people in 1 year. If there are 8 million people in New York City, how much garbage is produced by New York City in 1 year?

22. Property tax varies directly as assessed valuation. The tax on property assessed at $12,000 is $400. What is the tax on property assessed at $40,000?

23. If the area of a rectangle remains constant, the length varies inversely as the width. The length of a rectangle is 9 in. when the width is 8 in. If the area of the rectangle remains constant, find the width when the length is 24 in.

24. The speed of a gear varies inversely as the number of teeth. Gear A with 48 teeth makes 40 rpm. How many revolutions per minute are made by a gear with 120 teeth that is connected to gear A?

25. The speed of a pulley varies inversely as the diameter of the pulley. The speed of pulley A, which has an 8-in. diameter, is 450 rpm. What is the speed of a 6-in. diameter pulley connected to pulley A?

26. The time required to complete a certain job varies inversely as the number of machines that work on the job (assuming each machine does the same amount of work). It takes five machines 55 hours to complete an order. How long will it take 11 machines to complete the same job?

27. The volume of a sphere varies directly as the cube of its radius. The volume is 36π cubic units when the radius is 3 units. What is the volume when the radius is 5 units?

28. The distance an object falls due to gravity varies directly as the square of the length of time of the fall. If an object falls 144 ft in 3 seconds, how far did it fall the first second?

29. The weight of an object varies inversely as the square of the distance from the object to the center of the Earth. At sea level (4,000 mi from the center of the Earth) a man weighs 200 lb. Find his weight when he is 200 mi above the surface of the Earth.

30. The intensity of light on a plane surface varies inversely as the square of the distance from the source of light. If we double the distance from the source to the plane, what happens to the intensity?

31. The exposure time for photographing an object varies inversely as the square of the lens diameter. What will happen to the exposure time if the lens diameter is cut in half?

32. The resistance of a wire to an electrical current varies directly as its length and inversely as the square of its diameter. If a wire 100 ft long with a diameter of 0.01 in. has a resistance of 10 ohms (Ω), what is the resistance of a wire of the same length and material but 0.03 in. in diameter?

33. The general gas law states that the pressure of an ideal gas varies directly as the absolute temperature and inversely as the volume. If $P = 4$ atmospheres (atms) when $V = 10 \text{ cm}^3$ and $T = 200°$ Kelvin, find P when $V = 30 \text{ cm}^3$ and $T = 250°$ Kelvin.

34. The safe load of a beam (the amount it supports without breaking) that is supported at both ends varies directly as the width and the square of the height, and inversely as the distance between supports. If the width and height are doubled and the distance between supports remains the same, what is the effect on the safe load?

35. Coulomb's law states that the magnitude of the force that acts on two charges q_1 and q_2 varies directly as the product of the magnitude of q_1 and q_2 and inversely as the square of the distance between them. If the magnitude of q_1 is doubled, the magnitude of q_2 is tripled, and the distance between the charges is cut in half, what happens to the force?

36. Newton's law of gravitation states that the gravitational attraction between two objects varies directly as the product of their masses, and inversely as the square of the distance between their centers of mass. What will be the change in attraction between the two objects if both masses are cut in half and the distance between their centers is cut in half?

37. Three people invest in a business venture. A puts in $1000, B invests $1800, and C invests $2400. They agree to split the profits each year in proportion to their original investment.
   a. Complete this chart:

Year	Profit	A share	B share	C share
1.	$2,000			
2.	$3,600			

   b. Find formulas for each person's share if the profit is x dollars.

38. Four people invest in a business venture. A puts in $1000, B invests $1800, C invests $2000, and D invests $2400. They agree to split the profits each year in proportion to their original investment.
   a. Complete this chart:

Year	Profit	A share	B share	C share	D share
1.	$24,000				
2.	$60,000				

   b. Find formulas for each person's share if the profit is x dollars.

39. The graph of an inverse variation relation goes through the point (2, 4). Find an equation for this relation, and give two other points on the graph.

40. The graph of a direct variation relation goes through the point (2, 4). Find an equation for this relation, and give two other points on the graph.

THINK ABOUT IT 2.3

1. a. If y varies directly as x, does x vary directly as y?
   b. In an example, y varies directly as x, with variation constant equal to 10. Write this as an equation; then rewrite the equation to show that x varies directly as y. What is the new variation constant?

2. a. If y varies inversely as x, does x vary inversely as y?
   b. In an example, y varies inversely as x, with variation constant equal to 5. Write this as an equation; then rewrite the equation to show that x varies inversely as y. What is the new variation constant?

3. a. What happens to the *circumference* of a circle when you triple the radius? Explain this in terms of direct variation.

   b. What happens to the *area* of a circle when you triple the radius? Explain this in terms of direct variation.

   c. The area of a circle varies directly as the square of the diameter. What is the variation constant in this relation?

4. a. Solve the problem in Exercise 20 by setting up a *proportion*.

   b. Solve the problem in Exercise 23 by setting up a *proportion*.

5. a. Describe two instances not discussed in this section in which one variable varies *directly* as another variable.

   b. Describe two instances not discussed in this section in which one variable varies *inversely* as another variable.

Courtesy of AP/Wide World Photos.

2.4   Functional Notation and Piecewise Functions

If the value V of a particular work of art is given by the function

$$V = f(x) = 50{,}000(1.07)^x,$$

where x is the number of years since its purchase at \$50,000, then find and interpret $f(9)$. (See Example 2.)

OBJECTIVES

1   Evaluate functions using functional notation.

2   Write the difference quotient for a function in simplest form.

3   Find function values and graphs for piecewise functions.

4   Read from a graph of function f the domain, range, function values, and values of x for which $f(x) = 0$, $f(x) < 0$, or $f(x) > 0$.

A useful notation commonly used with functions allows us to represent more conveniently the value of the dependent variable for a particular value of the independent variable. In this notation a letter such as f is used to name a function, and then an equation such as

$$y = 2x + 5 \text{ is written as } f(x) = 2x + 5.$$

The dependent variable y is replaced by $f(x)$, with the independent variable x appearing in parentheses. The expression $f(x)$ is read "f of x" or "f at x" and means the value of the function (the y value) corresponding to the value of x. Similarly, $f(7)$ is read "f of 7" or "f at 7" and means the function value when $x = 7$. To find $f(7)$ in this example, we substitute 7 for x in the equation $f(x) = 2x + 5$.

$$
\begin{aligned}
f(x) &= 2x + 5 &&\text{Given equation.}\\
f(7) &= 2(7) + 5 &&\text{Replace x by 7.}\\
&= 19 &&\text{Simplify.}
\end{aligned}
$$

The result $f(7) = 19$ says that when $x = 7$, $y = 19$. The notation $f(x)$ originated with the Swiss mathematician Leonhard Euler (1734), and in this context note that $f(x)$ does not mean f times x.

EXAMPLE 1   Using Functional Notation

If $y = f(x) = 2x^2 - x + 4$, find $f(2), f(15)$, and $f(-3)$.

Solution In each case replace all occurrences of x by the number inside the parentheses and then simplify.

$$y_{\text{when } x=2} = f(2) = 2(2)^2 - 2 + 4 = 10$$

$$y_{\text{when } x=15} = f(15) = 2(15)^2 - 15 + 4 = 439$$

$$y_{\text{when } x=-3} = f(-3) = 2(-3)^2 - (-3) + 4 = 25$$

Thus, $f(2) = 10$, $f(15) = 439$, and $f(-3) = 25$.

Technology Link

Most graphing calculators have special features to find many function values quickly. These features may include a functional notation capability, an Evaluate function, a Table feature, or a List feature. If your calculator has such features, then you should use them to redo the problem in Example 1 and compare your result to the text's answers.

PROGRESS CHECK 1   If $y = f(x) = 5x - x^2$, find $f(4), f(20)$, and $f(-5)$.   ▪

EXAMPLE 2   Interpreting Functional Notation

Solve the problem in the section introduction on page 104.

Solution $f(9)$ gives V when $x = 9$. Using $V = f(x) = 50,000(1.07)^x$ gives

$$V_{\text{when } x=9} = f(9) = 50,000(1.07)^9 = 91,922.96$$

Thus, the value of this particular work of art in 9 years is about $92,000 (to the nearest thousand dollars).

PROGRESS CHECK 2   Use $V = 50,000(1.07)^x$ and find $f(6)$. Interpret the meaning of $f(6)$ in the context of Example 2.   ▪

EXAMPLE 3   Evaluating Two Functions

If $f(x) = x - 1$ and $g(x) = x^2 + 1$, find $3f(-1) - 4g(2)$.

Solution   The expression given above means that you are to find the difference of 3 times "f of -1" and 4 times "g of 2." First, determine $f(-1)$ and $g(2)$.

$$f(x) = x - 1 \qquad g(x) = x^2 + 1$$
$$f(-1) = (-1) - 1 \qquad g(2) = (2)^2 + 1$$
$$f(-1) = -2 \qquad g(2) = 5$$

Then

$$3f(-1) - 4g(2) = 3(-2) - 4(5)$$
$$= -26$$

PROGRESS CHECK 3   If $f(x) = 1 - x$ and $g(x) = x^2 + 2$, find $4f(-1) - 2g(3)$.   ▪

EXAMPLE 4   Testing for Function Properties

If $f(x) = x^2$, show that $f(a + b)$ does not equal $f(a) + f(b)$ for all a and b.

Solution: To determine $f(a + b)$, $f(a)$, and $f(b)$, replace x in the function $f(x) = x^2$ by $a + b$, a, and b, respectively.

$$f(a + b) = (a + b)^2 = a^2 + 2ab + b^2$$
$$f(a) = a^2$$
$$f(b) = b^2$$

Since $a^2 + 2ab + b^2 \neq a^2 + b^2$, $f(a + b) \neq f(a) + f(b)$.

PROGRESS CHECK 4   If $f(x) = 3x$, show that $f(a + b)$ *does* equal $f(a) + f(b)$ for all a and b.   ▪

EXAMPLE 5   Finding a Difference Quotient

The difference quotient of a function $y = f(x)$ is defined as

$$\frac{f(x + h) - f(x)}{h}, h \neq 0.$$

Computing this ratio is an important consideration when you are analyzing the rate of change of a function. Find the difference quotient for $f(x) = x^2 + 2x$ in simplest form.

Solution   If $f(x) = x^2 + 2x$, we have

$$f(x + h) = (x + h)^2 + 2(x + h) = x^2 + 2xh + h^2 + 2x + 2h.$$

Then

$$\frac{f(x + h) - f(x)}{h} = \frac{(x^2 + 2xh + h^2 + 2x + 2h) - (x^2 + 2x)}{h}$$

$$= \frac{x^2 + 2xh + h^2 + 2x + 2h - x^2 - 2x}{h}$$

$$= \frac{2xh + h^2 + 2h}{h}$$

$$= \frac{2xh}{h} + \frac{h^2}{h} + \frac{2h}{h}$$

$$= 2x + h + 2.$$

PROGRESS CHECK 5   Find the difference quotient for $f(x) = x^2 + 3x$ in simplest form.   ▪

Piecewise Functions

A **piecewise function** is a function in which different rules apply for different intervals of domain values. An example of an everyday situation that leads to a piecewise function is considered next.

EXAMPLE 6   A Piecewise Function

Each week a salesperson earns $500 plus 7 percent commission on sales above $2,000. Find a rule that expresses the weekly earnings (e) of the salesperson in terms of the amount (a) of merchandise sold during the week.

Solution   If the salesperson sells less than or equal to $2,000 worth of merchandise for the week, the earnings are $500. Thus,

$$e = \$500 \text{ if } \$0 \leq a \leq \$2,000.$$

If the salesperson sells above $2,000, then e is $500 plus 7 percent of the amount above $2,000. Thus

$$e = \$500 + 0.07(a - \$2,000) \text{ if } a > \$2,000.$$

The following rule may then be used to determine the weekly earnings of the salesperson when we know the amount of merchandise sold:

$$e = \begin{cases} \$500 & \text{if } \$0 \leq a \leq \$2,000 \\ \$500 + 0.07(a - \$2,000) & \text{if } a > \$2,000. \end{cases}$$

The domain of the function is $\{a: a \geq \$0\}$, and the range is $\{e: e \geq \$500\}$.

PROGRESS CHECK 6   Express the weekly earnings (e) of a salesperson in terms of the cash amount (a) of merchandise sold if the salesperson earns $600 per week plus 8 percent commission on sales above $10,000.   ■

Examples 7 and 8 consider how to evaluate and how to graph a piecewise function.

EXAMPLE 7   Evaluating a Piecewise Function

If $f(x) = \begin{cases} 2 & \text{if } x < 0 \\ x+1 & \text{if } 0 \leq x < 3 \end{cases}$ find

a. $f(2)$ **b.** $f(-2)$ **c.** $f(3)$

Solution

a. Since 2 is in the interval $0 \leq x < 3$, use $f(x) = x + 1$, so $f(2) = 2 + 1 = 3$.
b. Since -2 is less than 0, use $f(x) = 2$, so $f(-2) = 2$.
c. Since 3 is not in the domain of the function, $f(3)$ is undefined.

PROGRESS CHECK 7   If $f(x) = \begin{cases} x - 1 & \text{if } 0 \leq x < 5 \\ 0 & \text{if } x \geq 5 \end{cases}$ find

a. $f(3)$ **b.** $f(-3)$ **c.** $f(5)$ ■

EXAMPLE 8   Graphing a Piecewise Function
Graph the function defined as follows:

$$f(x) = \begin{cases} -1 & \text{if } x < 1 \\ x + 2 & \text{if } x \geq 1 \end{cases}$$

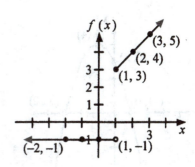

Figure 2.29

Solution   If $x < 1$, $f(x) = -1$, which is a constant function whose graph is a horizontal line with such ordered pairs as $(0, -1), (-1, -1), (-2, -1)$, and so on. If $x \geq 1$, $f(x) = x + 2$, which graphs as a line with ordered pairs $(1,3), (2,4), (3,5)$, and so on. The graph is given in Figure 2.29. Note that we draw a solid circle at $(1,3)$ and an open circle at $(1, -1)$ to show that $(1,3)$ is part of the graph, while $(1, -1)$ is not.

Technology Link

It is possible to use some graphing calculators to graph a piecewise function. For example, to graph the function in Example 8 on Texas Instruments models, it is first recommended that the calculator be switched from connected mode to dot mode. The dot mode prevents the calculator from connecting points that are in separate pieces of the graph. Then enter the following expression for this piecewise function in the equation list and obtain the graph in the usual way. In this expression the symbols $<$ and $\geq$ may be entered through a key or menu marked TEST.

$$y1 = -1(x < 1) + (x + 2)(x \geq 1)$$

The rationale for entering this expression is that the calculator returns a 1 when an expression containing a relational operation (such as $<$) is true, and a 0 when it is false. Thus, if you enter the expression $(x + 2)(x \geq 1)$, then the value of the expression in the right-hand parentheses is 1 when x is greater than or equal to one and 0 otherwise. So the graph of $y = (x + 2)(x \geq 1)$ is the line $y = x + 2$ when x is greater than or equal to one and the line $y = 0$ otherwise. Note that the line $y = 0$ graphs as the x-axis, so it cannot be seen in the display.

PROGRESS CHECK 8   Graph the function defined as follows:

$$f(x) = \begin{cases} -2x & \text{if } x \leq 0 \\ 1 & \text{if } x > 0 \end{cases}$$ ■

Reading Graphs

From a graph of a function f it is important to be able to read not only the domain and range (as considered in Section 2.2) but also function values and values of x for which $f(x) = 0, f(x) < 0,$ and $f(x) > 0.$

EXAMPLE 9   Reading a Graph

Consider the graph of $y = f(x)$ in Figure 2.30

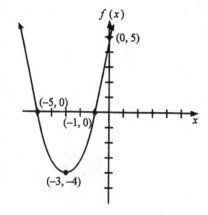

Figure 2.30

a. What is the domain of f?
b. What is the range of f?
c. Determine $f(0)$.

d. For what values of x does $f(x) = 0$?
e. For what values of x is $f(x) < 0$?
f. Solve $f(x) > 0$.

Solution

a. The graph is unbounded to the left and to the right, so the domain is the set of all real numbers, or $(-\infty, \infty)$ in interval notation.
b. The minimum y value is -4, and the graph extends indefinitely in the positive y direction, so there is no maximum value. Thus, the range is $\{y: y \geq -4\}$, or $[-4, \infty)$ in interval notation.
c. To determine $f(0)$ requires finding the y value where $x = 0$. Using the ordered pair $(0,5)$ gives $f(0) = 5$.
d. From the ordered pairs $(-5, 0)$ and $(-1, 0)$, we know $f(x)$ or y equals 0 when $x = -5$ or $x = -1$. The solution set is therefore $\{-5, -1\}$.
e. The y values are less than zero when the graph is below the x-axis. Therefore we see $f(x) < 0$ for $-5 < x < -1$, so the solution set is the interval $(-5, -1)$.
f. The y values are greater than zero when the graph is above the x-axis. Thus, $f(x) > 0$ when $x < -5$ or $x > -1$, so the solution set in interval notation is $(-\infty, -5) \cup (-1, \infty)$.

PROGRESS CHECK 9   Answer the questions in Example 9 for the graph of $y = f(x)$ in Figure 2.31.   ■

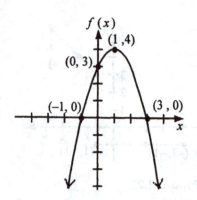

Figure 2.31

Functional Notation Concepts

In conclusion, here are some important ideas to keep in mind about functional notation.

1. If $y = f(x)$ and a is in the domain of f, then $f(a)$ means the value of y when $x = a$. Thus, evaluating $f(a)$ often requires nothing more than a *substitution* of the value a for x.

2. $f(a)$ is a y value, a is an x value. Hence, ordered pairs for the function defined by $y = f(x)$ all have the form $(a, f(a))$.

3. In functional notation we use the symbols f and x more out of custom than necessity, and other symbols work just as well. The notations $f(x) = 2x$, $f(t) = 2t$, $g(y) = 2y$, and $h(z) = 2z$ all define exactly the same function if x, t, y, and z may be replaced by the same numbers.

EXERCISES 2.4

1. If $y = f(x) = 3x + 2$, find $f(0)$ and $f(-2)$.
2. If $y = f(x) = -2x + 5$, find $f(-1)$ and $f(3)$.
3. If $y = f(x) = 3x^2 - 5x + 1$, find $f(1)$ and $f(-1)$.
4. If $y = f(x) = 7x^2 - 4$, find $f(4)$ and $f(0)$.
5. If $f(x) = x - 2$, find $f(0)$, $f(-1)$, and $f(4)$.
6. If $g(t) = t - 2$, find $g(0)$, $g(-1)$, and $g(4)$.
7. If $h(x) = -2x + 7$, find $h(-2)$, $h(1)$, and $h(5)$.
8. If $f(t) = t^2 + 1$, find $f(-1)$, $f(0)$, and $f(1)$.
9. If $g(x) = 2x^2 - x + 4$, find $g(3)$, $g(0)$, and $g(-1)$.
10. If $h(t) = -t^2$, find $h(5)$, $h(1)$, and $h(-5)$.
11. If $f(x) = \dfrac{x + 1}{x - 2}$, find $f(-3)$, $f(1)$, and $f(2)$.
12. If $h(r) = \dfrac{r}{r + 1}$, find $h(1)$, $h(0)$, and $h(-1)$.
13. If $f(x) = 5$, find $f(1)$, $f(0)$, and $f(a)$.
14. If $g(x) = 2x - 5$, find $g(a)$ and $g(m)$.
15. If $f(x) = 3x$, find $f(a + 1)$.
16. If $f(x) = x^2 - x$, find $f(a + 3)$.
17. If $f(x) = x + 1$, find
    a. $f(2)$
    b. $f(-2)$
    c. Does $f(-2) = -f(2)$?
18. If $g(x) = x^2$, find
    a. $g(2)$
    b. $g(-2)$
    c. Does $g(x) = g(-x)$ for all values of x?
19. A function which approximates the value V of a machine purchased for \$20,000 and which decreases in value 10 percent per year is $V = f(x) = 20{,}000(0.90)^x$, where x is the number of years since the machine was purchased. Find $f(4)$ and $f(7)$ and interpret their meaning.
20. If a machine that costs \$17,000 initially depreciates 6 percent per year thereafter, then its value V after x years is approximated by the function $V =$

$f(x) = 17{,}000(0.94)^x$, where x is the number of years since the original purchase. Find $f(5)$ and $f(10)$ and interpret their meaning.

21. You are about to throw out an old lamp when a friend tells you it is now "highly collectible." An appraiser says the value of the lamp has increased about 15 percent per year and gives you the function $V = f(x) = (\text{original cost})(1.15)^x$ for its value, where x is the number of years since it was purchased. If your grandmother originally paid \$45 for it, what is it worth today (50 years later)? That is, find and interpret $f(50)$.

22. If the value of a particular work of art is given by the function $V = f(x) = 40{,}000(1.08)^x$, where x is the number of years since its purchase at \$40,000, find and interpret $f(12)$.

23. The height y above the water in meters of a diver t seconds after stepping off a diving tower 10 m high is given by the function $y = f(t) = -4.9t^2 + 10$. Find and interpret $f(1)$ and $f(1.42)$.

24. The height y above the water in meters of a diver t seconds after stepping off a diving tower 20 m high is given by the function $y = f(t) = -4.9t^2 + 20$. Find and interpret $f(1)$ and $f(2.02)$.

25. During exercise a person's maximum target heart rate is a function of age. The recommended number of beats per minute is given by $y = f(x) = -0.85x + 187$, where x represents age in years and y represents the recommended number of beats per minute. Find and interpret $f(20)$ and $f(40)$.

26. During exercise a person's minimum target heart rate to have a training effect is a function of age. The recommended number of beats per minute is given by $y = f(x) = -0.7x + 154$, where x represents age in years and y represents the recommended number of beats per minute. Find and interpret $f(20)$ and $f(40)$.

27. If $f(x) = x + 3$ and $g(x) = x^2$, find $2f(-4) + 3g(2)$.

28. If $f(x) = x + 3$ and $g(x) = x^2$, find
$3f(5) + 4g(-3)$.

29. If $f(x) = x - 6$ and $g(x) = x^2 - 3$, find
$4f(7) - 3g(-5)$.

30. If $f(x) = x - 6$ and $g(x) = x^2 - 3$, find
$8f(-8) + 5g(-6)$.

31. If $f(x) = 2x + 3$ and $g(x) = 3x^2 - 2$, find
$5f(-4) + 2g(3)$.

32. If $f(x) = 3x + 2$ and $g(x) = 2x^2 - 3$, find
$6f(-2) + 7g(1)$.

33. If $f(x) = 3x^2 - 7$ and $g(x) = 5x + 9$, find
$5f(4) - 8g(3)$.

34. If $f(x) = 3x^2 - 7$ and $g(x) = 5x + 9$, find
$-2f(-6) - 9g(-6)$.

35. If $f(x) = x^2 - 2x + 10$ and $g(x) = x^2 + 1$, find
$3f(-4) - 2g(3)$.

36. If $f(x) = x^2 - 2x + 10$ and $g(x) = x^2 + 1$, find
$7f(5) - 5g(7)$.

37. If $f(x) = x - 3$, show that
$f(a - b) \neq f(a) - f(b)$ for all values of a and b.

38. If $f(x) = x + 4$, show that
$f(a + b) \neq f(a) + f(b)$ for all values of a and b.

39. If $f(x) = 3x$, show that $f(a - b) = f(a) - f(b)$ for
all values of a and b.

40. If $f(x) = -12x$, show that $f(a + b) = f(a) + f(b)$
for all values of a and b.

41. If $f(x) = x^2$, show that $f(a + b) \neq f(a) + f(b)$ for
all values of a and b, except $a = 0$ or $b = 0$.

42. If $f(x) = x^2$, show that $f\left(\dfrac{a}{b}\right) = \dfrac{f(a)}{f(b)}$ for all values
of a and b except $b = 0$.

43. If $f(x) = 2x^2 - 1$, find
 a. $f(x + h)$
 b. $f(x + h) - f(x)$
 c. $\dfrac{f(x + h) - f(x)}{h}$, if $h \neq 0$

44. If $f(x) = 1 - x$, find
 a. $f(1 + h)$
 b. $f(1 + h) - f(1)$
 c. $\dfrac{f(1 + h) - f(1)}{h}$, if $h \neq 0$

In Exercises 45–52 write the difference quotient for each
function in simplest form (see Example 5)

45. $f(x) = x^2 + x$ **46.** $f(x) = x^2 + 4x$
47. $f(x) = 7x - 5$ **48.** $f(x) = 2x + 3$
49. $g(x) = 2$ **50.** $g(x) = 7$
51. $f(x) = 1 - x^2$ **52.** $f(x) = 3 - 2x^2$

53. Express the weekly earnings (e) of a salesperson in
terms of the cash amount (a) of merchandise sold if the
salesperson earns $400 per week plus 10 percent com-
mission on sales above $5,000.

54. Express the weekly earnings (e) of a salesperson in
terms of the cash amount (a) of merchandise sold if the
salesperson earns $500 per week plus 9 percent com-
mission on sales above $3,600.

55. Express the monthly cost (c) of an electric bill in terms
of the number (n) of electrical units purchased (the unit
of measure is the kilowatt-hour) if the customer used no
more than 48 units and the electric company has the
following rate schedule:

Amount	Charge
First 12 units or less	$5.25
Next 36 units at	12.82 cents/unit

56. Express the cost (c) of a phone call in terms of the
length (m) of the call in minutes according to this table.

Length	Charge
First minute	$0.58
Each additional minute	$0.29

57. If $y = f(x) = \begin{cases} -1 \text{ if } x < 2 \\ 3x \text{ if } x \geq 2, \end{cases}$ find the following.
 a. $f(-2)$
 b. $f(2)$
 c. $f(3)$
 d. Graph the function.

58. If $y = f(x) = \begin{cases} 2 \text{ if } x \geq 3 \\ -x \text{ if } x < 3, \end{cases}$ find the following.
 a. $f(1)$
 b. $f(3)$
 c. $f(4)$
 d. Graph the function.

59. If $y = f(x) = \begin{cases} 3 \text{ if } x \geq 0 \\ 4x \text{ if } x < 0, \end{cases}$ find the following.
 a. $f(2)$
 b. $f(0)$
 c. $f(-2)$
 d. Graph the function.

60. If $y = f(x) = \begin{cases} \frac{1}{2}x \text{ if } x \geq 0 \\ 0 \text{ if } x < 0, \end{cases}$ find the following.
 a. $f\left(\frac{1}{2}\right)$
 b. $f(0)$
 c. $f\left(-\frac{1}{2}\right)$
 d. Graph the function.

61. If $y = f(x) = \begin{cases} x \text{ if } x \geq 2 \\ 1 \text{ if } x < 2, \end{cases}$ find the following.
 a. $f(1)$
 b. $f(2)$
 c. $f(3)$
 d. Graph the function.

62. If $y = f(x) = \begin{cases} -\frac{1}{2}x \text{ if } x \leq -2 \\ 4 \text{ if } x > -2, \end{cases}$ find the following.
 a. $f(-3)$
 b. $f(-2)$
 c. $f(-1)$
 d. Graph the function.

63. If $y = f(x) = \begin{cases} -\frac{1}{2}x \text{ if } x \leq -2 \\ 1 \text{ if } x > -2, \end{cases}$ find the following.
 a. $f(-4)$
 b. $f(-2)$
 c. $f(1)$
 d. Graph the function.

64. If $y = f(x) = \begin{cases} -x + 3 & \text{if } x \geq 3 \\ -x & \text{if } x < 3, \end{cases}$ find the following.

   a. $f(2)$

   b. $f(3)$

   c. $f(4)$

   d. Graph the function.

65. If $y = f(x) = \begin{cases} -x & \text{if } x < -3 \\ x & \text{if } x \geq 3, \end{cases}$ find the following.

   a. $f(-4)$

   b. $f(0)$

   c. $f(3)$

   d. $f(4)$

   e. Graph the function.

66. If $y = f(x) = \begin{cases} 2x & \text{if } x > 3 \\ 2 & \text{if } x \leq 2, \end{cases}$ find the following.

   a. $f(1)$

   b. $f(2.5)$

   c. $f(3)$

   d. $f(4)$

   e. Graph the function.

For each graph given in Exercises 67–74, answer questions **a** through **f**.

   a. What is the domain of f?

   b. What is the range of f?

   c. Determine $f(0)$.

   d. For what values of x does $f(x) = 0$?

   e. For what values of x is $f(x) < 0$?

   f. Solve $f(x) > 0$.

67.

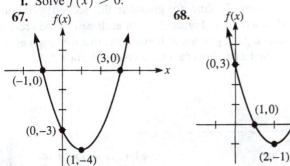

68.

69.

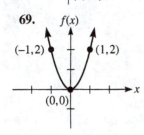

70.

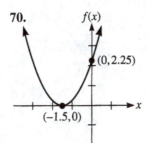

71.

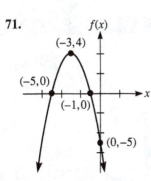

72.

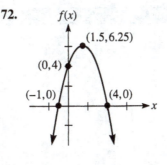

73.

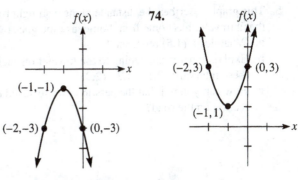

74.

THINK ABOUT IT 2.4

1. Graph $y = |x|$ and $y = -|x|$ on the same coordinate system. How are the graphs related? In general, what is the relationship between the graphs of $y = f(x)$ and $y = -f(x)$?

2. Give two examples of a function for which $f(-x) = f(x)$ for all real numbers x. In each case, graph f and describe how the graph of f is related to the y-axis.

3. The bracket notation $[x]$ means the greatest integer less than or equal to x. For example $[4.3] = 4$, $[\pi] = 3$, $\left[-\frac{1}{2}\right] = -1$ and $[2] = 2$. If $f(x) = [x]$, which is called the **greatest integer function**, find

   a. $f\left(\frac{1}{2}\right)$ **b.** $f\left(\sqrt{2}\right)$ **c.** $f(-1.4)$ **d.** $f(-\pi)$

   e. the graph of this function for $-2 \leq x < 3$

Note Some calculators have this function built in where $[x]$ is entered as $\text{int}(x)$.

   4. Consider the given graph of $y = f(x)$.

   a. What is the domain of f?

   b. What is the range of f?

   c. Determine $f(c)$.

   d. Solve $f(x) = 0$.

   e. Solve $f(x) < 0$.

   f. Solve $f(x) \geq 0$.

   g. Solve $f(x) = b$.

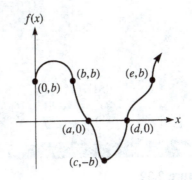

5. This graph describes the distance along a straight road that a traveler has come from home, as time goes by.
   a. What does $f(1.5)$ represent?
   b. Explain what is happening to the traveler on each of these intervals: $(0,1); (1,2); (2,3)$.
   c. How can you tell that the person never reversed direction on the road?

d. How can you tell that the traveler was slowing down during the last half-hour?

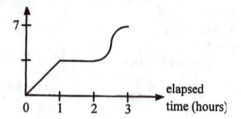

2.5   Graphing Techniques

The height y above water in meters of a diver t seconds after stepping off a diving tower 10 m high is given by

$$y = -4.9t^2 + 10.$$

Graph this function. Use a grapher only to determine when the diver hits the water to the nearest hundredth of a second. What is the domain of the function? (See Example 8)

Courtesy of Digital Vision, Ltd.

OBJECTIVES

1 Graph a function using translations.

2 Graph a function using reflecting, stretching, or flattening.

3 Graph a function using combinations of the above methods.

Many graphs may be sketched quickly if you learn to graph variations of familiar functions by properly adjusting a known curve. To draw the graphs in this section, you must memorize the graphs of the special functions in Figure 2.32. In each case some ordered pairs that were plotted as aids for drawing the graph are shown. Note that the graph of the squaring function is a curve that is called a parabola (as considered in Section 2.2).

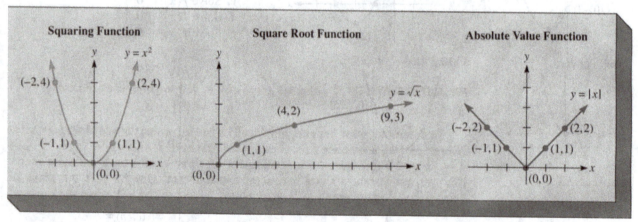

Figure 2.32

Consider Figure 2.33, which shows the graphs of $y = x^2$, $y = x^2 + 2$, and $y = x^2 - 2$ on the same coordinate system. Observe that the graph of $y = x^2 + 2$ is the graph of $y = x^2$ translated 2 units up, while the graph of $y = x^2 - 2$ is the graph of $y = x^2$ translated 2 units down. In other words, the curve that characterizes the squaring functions is used in all three graphs, and graphing each equation amounts to just positioning this parabola correctly. In Figure 2.33 we see that when 2 is added or subtracted *after* applying the squaring rule, the effect is to shift the parabola up (if adding) or down (if subtracting) a distance of 2 units. These results extend to give a general procedure for graphing $y = f(x) + c$ and $y = f(x) - c$ using the graph of $y = f(x)$.

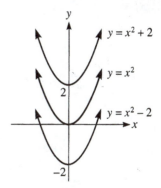

Figure 2.33

Vertical Translations

Let c be a positive constant.

1. The graph of $y = f(x) + c$ is the graph of f shifted c units up.
2. The graph of $y = f(x) - c$ is the graph of f shifted c units down.

EXAMPLE 1   Using Vertical Translations
Use the graph of $y = |x|$ to graph each function.
a. $y = |x| - 3$ **b.** $y = |x| + 1$

Solution   The graph of the absolute value function has a V shape, as shown in Figure 2.32. Translate this basic shape as follows.

a. The constant 3 is subtracted *after* the absolute value rule, so the graph of $y = |x| - 3$ is the graph of $y = |x|$ shifted 3 units down, as shown in Figure 2.34(a).
b. Shift the graph of $y = |x|$ up 1 unit to graph $y = |x| + 1$. See Figure 2.34(b).

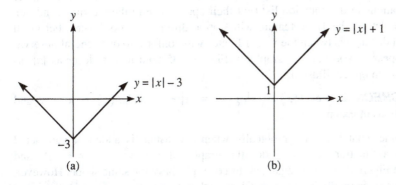

Figure 2.34

PROGRESS CHECK 1   Use the graph of $y = |x|$ to graph each function.

a. $y = |x| + 2$ **b.** $y = |x| - 4$ ■

EXAMPLE 2   Using Trace to Explore Translations
Let $f(x) = x^2$, $g(x) = x^2 + 3$, and $h(x) = x^2 - 5$.
a. Graph f, g, and h in the standard viewing window without erasing.

b. Describe how to obtain the graph of g and the graph of h from the graph of f.

c. Use the Trace feature to check that your descriptions are accurate.

Solution

a. The requested graphs are shown in Figure 2.35.

b. The graph of g is the graph of f shifted 3 units up, while the graph of h is the graph of f shifted 5 units down.

c. To check these descriptions, use the Trace feature to display the coordinates of a point in the graph of f, possibly (0,0). If you move the cursor up to the graph of g, the display reads $x = 0$, $y = 3$, so this point in g is 3 units higher than the corresponding point in f. Similarly, if you move the cursor down to the graph of h, the display reads $x = 0$, $y = -5$, so this point in h is 5 units lower then the corresponding point in f. These types of results will occur if the cursor initially starts at any point in the graph of f, so the descriptions appear to be accurate.

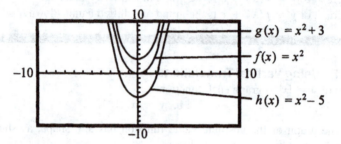

Figure 2.35

Note On many calculators the up-down arrow keys are used to move from one graph to another when more than one graph is displayed, and the cursor movement is based on the order of the equations in the equation list (not their appearance in the viewing window). On different calculators, the Trace feature will stop at different x-coordinates, but in all cases the vertical distance between the y-coordinates will conform to our general observations. It may appear to you that the graphs in Figure 2.35 tend to get closer as $|x|$ increases, but this is an optical illusion.

PROGRESS CHECK 2 Let $f(x) = |x|$, $g(x) = |x| - 7$, and $h(x) = |x| + 2$ and answer the questions in Example 2. ▪

To determine what happens graphically when a constant is added or subtracted *before* applying a function rule, consider the graphs of $y = x^2$, $y = (x + 2)^2$, and $y = (x - 2)^2$ in Figure 2.36. Once again, all three graphs have the same shape. However, the parabola shifts horizontally in this case. Observe that the graph of $y = (x + 2)^2$ is the graph of $y = x^2$ shifted 2 units to the left, while the graph of $y = (x - 2)^2$ is the graph of $y = x^2$ shifted 2 units to the right.

For horizontal shifts the direction of the translation is not supported by intuition, so be careful here. The graph of $y = (x - 2)^2$ is 2 units to the *right* (not the left) of $y = x^2$, because x must be 2 units more in $y = (x - 2)^2$ than in $y = x^2$ to produce the same y value. For instance, $y = 0$ when $x = 0$ in $y = x^2$, while $y = 0$ when $x = 2$ in $y = (x - 2)^2$. Similar reasoning applies for any function f and any constant, and the following statements summarize the rules for graphing using horizontal shifts.

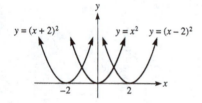

Figure 2.36

Horizontal Translations

Let c be a positive constant.

1. The graph of $y = f(x + c)$ is the graph of f shifted c units to the left.
2. The graph of $y = f(x - c)$ is the graph of f shifted c units to the right.

EXAMPLE 3   Using Horizontal Translations

Use the graph of $y = \sqrt{x}$ to graph each function.

a. $y = \sqrt{x + 4}$ **b.** $y = \sqrt{x - 1}$

Solution

a. The constant 4 is added *before* the square root rule. Therefore, the graph of $y = \sqrt{x + 4}$ is the graph of $y = \sqrt{x}$ (see Figure 2.32) shifted 4 units horizontally. Because a positive constant is added, the graph of $y = \sqrt{x}$ is shifted to the left to obtain the graph in Figure 2.37(a).

b. To graph $y = \sqrt{x - 1}$, start with the graph of $y = \sqrt{x}$ and shift this graph 1 unit to the right, as shown in Figure 2.37(b).

PROGRESS CHECK 3   Use the graph of $y = |x|$ to graph each function.

a. $y = |x - 3|$ **b.** $y = |x + 1|$ ■

The graph of the function in the next example uses both a horizontal translation and a vertical translation.

EXAMPLE 4   Combining Translations

Graph $y = (x + 2)^2 - 3$. Identify the vertex and the y-intercept of the graph.

Solution   To graph this function, first shift the graph of $y = x^2$ in Figure 2.38(a) to the left 2 units, to obtain the graph of $y = (x + 2)^2$ in Figure 2.38(b). Then shift this graph down 3 units, since the constant 3 is subtracted after the squared term. The completed graph is shown in Figure 2.38(c). The vertex in this graph is at $(-2, -3)$. When $x = 0$,

$$y = (0 + 2)^2 - 3 = 1,$$

so the y-intercept is $(0,1)$.

PROGRESS CHECK 4   Graph $y = (x - 2)^2 + 1$. Identify the vertex and the y-intercept of the graph.   ■

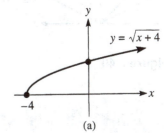

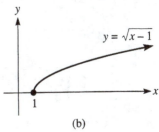

Figure 2.37

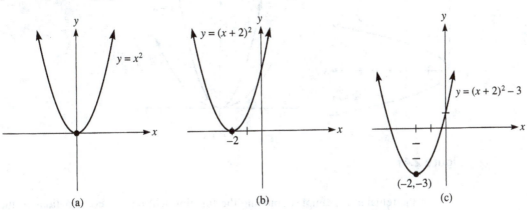

Figure 2.38

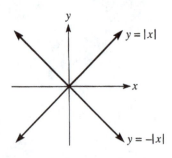

Figure 2.39

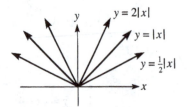

Figure 2.40

To see how to graph $y = cf(x)$ using the graph of $y = f(x)$, first consider the graphs of $y = |x|$ and $y = -|x|$ shown in Figure 2.39. Each graph is the reflection of the other about the x-axis, and the graphs of $y = f(x)$ and $y = -f(x)$ are always related in this way.

Next consider Figure 2.40, which shows the graphs of $y = |x|$, $y = 2|x|$, and $y = \frac{1}{2}|x|$. To graph $y = 2|x|$, we double each y value in $y = |x|$, which causes the graph of $y = |x|$ to stretch by a factor of 2. Likewise, we graph $y = \frac{1}{2}|x|$ by halving the y values in $y = |x|$, and we say the graph of $y = \frac{1}{2}|x|$ is the graph of $y = |x|$ flattened out by a factor of $\frac{1}{2}$. These observations generalize to the following rules for graphing $y = cf(x)$.

To Graph $y = cf(x)$

Reflecting The graph of $y = -f(x)$ is the graph of f reflected about the x-axis.
Stretching If $c > 1$, the graph of $y = cf(x)$ is the graph of f stretched by a factor of c.
Flattening If $0 < c < 1$, the graph of $y = cf(x)$ is the graph of f flattened out by a factor of c.

EXAMPLE 5   Using Reflecting or Flattening
Graph each function.

a. $y = -\sqrt{x}$ **b.** $y = \frac{1}{4}x^2$

Solution

a. Start with the graph of $y = \sqrt{x}$. Then reflect this graph about the x-axis to obtain the graph of $y = -\sqrt{x}$, as shown in Figure 2.41(a).

b. The y values in $y = \frac{1}{4}x^2$ are one-fourth the y values in $y = x^2$. Thus, the graph of $y = \frac{1}{4}x^2$ is the graph of $y = x^2$ flattened out by a factor of $\frac{1}{4}$, as shown in Figure 2.41(b).

PROGRESS CHECK 5   Graph each function.

a. $y = 3\sqrt{x}$ **b.** $y = -x^2$ ■

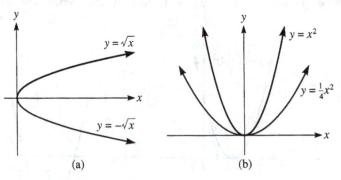

(a)   (b)

Figure 2.41

In the remaining examples graphing the function will require combinations of the graphing methods developed in this section.

EXAMPLE 6   Combining Reflection and Translation

Graph $y = 4 - x^2$ using the graph of $y = x^2$.

Solution   The equation of $y = 4 - x^2$ is equivalent to $y = -x^2 + 4$. To graph this function, first reflect the graph of $y = x^2$ about the x-axis to obtain the graph of $y = -x^2$ in Figure 2.42(a). Raising the graph of $y = -x^2$ up 4 units gives the graph of $y = -x^2 + 4$, shown in Figure 2.42(b).

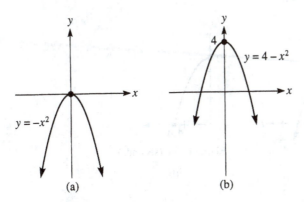

(a)   (b)

Figure 2.42

PROGRESS CHECK 6   Graph $y = 2 - |x|$ using the graph of $y = |x|$.   ■

EXAMPLE 7   Combining Reflection and Translation

Graph $y = -|x - 4| + 5$ using the graph of $y = |x|$.

Solution   Follow this sequence of graphing steps.

Step 1   Shift the graph of $y = |x|$ to the right 4 units to graph $y = |x - 4|$, as shown in Figure 2.43(a).

Step 2   Reflect the graph from the previous step about the x-axis to graph $y = -|x - 4|$, as shown in Figure 2.43(b).

Step 3   Shift the graph from the previous step up 5 units to graph $y = -|x - 4| + 5$, as shown in Figure 2.43(c).

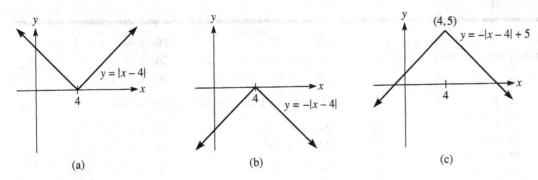

(a)   (b)   (c)

Figure 2.43

Note   In practice, it is usually possible to draw the completed graph in Figure 2.43(c) without actually sketching the other preliminary graphs. The graphs in Figures 2.43(a) and 2.43(b) are just part of the thought process that leads to the answer.

PROGRESS CHECK 7 Graph $y = 2 - |x - 1|$ using the graph of $y = |x|$. ∎

EXAMPLE 8 Graphing Techniques and Context Restrictions
Solve the problem in the section introduction on page 112.

Solution To graph this function, stretch the graph of $y = t^2$ by a factor of 4.9, reflect this graph about the t-axis, and then shift the resulting graph 10 units up. This parabola is shown in Figure 2.44(a)

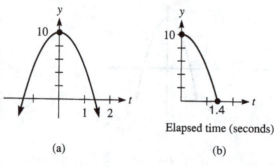

(a)   (b)

Figure 2.44

The given formula is meaningful starting at $t = 0$ seconds and ending when the diver hits the water so that the height y above water is 0. By using Zoom and Trace features you should determine that $y = 0$ when $t \approx 1.4$ seconds. (In fact, check by calculator that when $t = \sqrt{10/4.9}$, then $y = 0$.) Thus, the domain of the function is

$$0 \text{ seconds} \leq t \leq 1.4 \text{ seconds},$$

and Figure 2.44(b) shows the segment of the parabola that gives a picture of this relation.

PROGRESS CHECK 8 If a stone is dropped from a bridge at a point that is 200 ft above water, then $y = -16t^2 + 200$ gives the height y above water in feet after t seconds have elapsed. Graph this function. Use a grapher only to determine when the stone hits the water to the nearest hundredth of a second. What is the domain of the function? ∎

EXERCISES 2.5

In all exercises, use the graphs of $y = |x|$, $y = x^2$, or $y = \sqrt{x}$ as appropriate to graph each of the given functions.

1. $y = |x| - 1$
2. $y = |x| + 3$
3. $y = x^2 + 3$
4. $y = x^2 - 5$
5. $y = \sqrt{x} + 2$
6. $y = \sqrt{x} - 2$
7. $y = |x| - 5$
8. $y = x^2 + 5$
9. $y = \sqrt{x} - 1$
10. $y = \sqrt{x} + 3$
11. $y = |x - 1|$
12. $y = |x + 3|$
13. $y = (x + 3)^2$
14. $y = (x - 5)^2$
15. $y = \sqrt{x + 2}$
16. $y = \sqrt{x - 2}$
17. $y = |x + 5|$
18. $y = (x + 5)^2$
19. $y = \sqrt{x + 1}$
20. $y = \sqrt{x - 3}$

In Exercises 21–30, graph each function. Identify the minimum point and the y-intercept of the graph.

21. $y = (x - 1)^2 + 2$
22. $y = (x + 1)^2 - 2$
23. $y = |x + 1| - 1$
24. $y = |x - 1| + 2$
25. $y = \sqrt{x - 3} + 2$
26. $y = \sqrt{x + 1} - 3$
27. $y = (x - 3)^2 - 2$
28. $y = (x - 1)^2 - 1$
29. $y = |x + 4| + 1$
30. $y = |x - 4| - 1$

In Exercises 31–60, graph the given function.

31. $y = -|x|$
32. $y = \frac{1}{2}|x|$
33. $y = 2x^2$
34. $y = \frac{1}{3}x^2$
35. $y = \frac{1}{2}\sqrt{x}$
36. $y = 2\sqrt{x}$
37. $y = 5|x|$
38. $y = -\frac{1}{4}|x|$
39. $y = -3x^2$
40. $y = -\frac{1}{2}x^2$
41. $y = 2 + |x|$
42. $y = 3 - |x|$
43. $y = 4 + \sqrt{x}$
44. $y = 3 - \sqrt{x}$
45. $y = -x^2 + 1$
46. $y = 4 - x^2$
47. $y = -\sqrt{x} - 2$
48. $y = -|x| - 1$
49. $y = -x^2 - 1$
50. $y = -\sqrt{x} + 4$
51. $y = -|x + 1|$
52. $y = -(x - 2)^2$
53. $y = -\sqrt{x} - 1$
54. $y = -|x - 3|$

55. $y = -2 - (x + 3)^2$ **56.** $y = -1 + (x - 3)^2$
57. $y = 3 - |x - 1|$ **58.** $y = 2 - |x + 1|$
59. $y = -\sqrt{x + 1} - 5$ **60.** $y = -\sqrt{x - 1} + 2$
61. The height y in meters of a tightrope walker above a safety net t seconds after falling from the tightrope 40 m above the net is given by $y = -4.9t^2 + 40$. Graph this function. Use a grapher only to determine when the performer hits the safety net to the nearest hundredth of a second. What is the domain of the function?
62. The conditions of Exercise 61 remain essentially the same, but the tightrope is lowered to 30 m above the safety net. Answer the same questions. Note that in this case, the function becomes $y = -4.9t^2 + 30$.
63. A lifeboat on a certain freighter can be lowered to the surface of the water by a cable system extending from the top deck. The height of the top deck above the waterline is 75 ft, and the height of the lifeboat t seconds after the lowering process begins is given by $h = -0.005t^2 + 75$. Graph this function. Use a grapher only to determine how many seconds it takes (to the nearest second) to lower the lifeboat to the water. What is the domain of the function?
64. The conditions in Exercise 63 remain essentially the same, but the top deck is 100 ft above the waterline and the height function is accordingly $h = -0.005t^2 + 100$. Answer the same questions.

THINK ABOUT IT 2.5

1. Draw the graph of $y = x^3$ by constructing a table of ordered-pair solutions. Then use this graph and the methods of this section to graph the following functions.
a. $y = -x^3$ **b.** $y = (x - 1)^3$
c. $y = x^3 + 1$ **d.** $y = (x + 1)^3 - 2$
2. Graph $y = \sqrt{x}$ and $y = \sqrt{-x}$ on the same coordinate system. (*Note:* They have different domains.) How do the graphs relate to each other?

3. Write an equation for the graph shown, which was determined by translating the graph of $y = x^2$

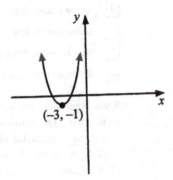

$(-3, -1)$

4. Use the given graph of $y = f(x)$ to graph each of these functions.
a. $y = 3f(x)$ **b.** $y = -f(x)$
c. $y = f(x) + 1$ **d.** $y = f(x + 1)$

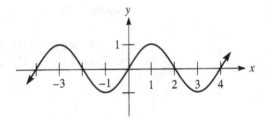

5. In translating a graph, the shape does not change, so it is reasonable to talk about points in the translated graph corresponding to points in the original graph.
a. What point on the graph of $y = x^2 + 3$ corresponds to the point (a, b) on the graph of $y = x^2$?
b. What point on the graph of $y = x^2 - 5$ corresponds to the point (a, b) on the graph of $y = x^2$?
c. What point on the graph of $y = (x - 2)^2$ corresponds to the point (a, b) on the graph of $y = x^2$?
d. What point on the graph of $y = (x + 7)^2$ corresponds to the point (a, b) on the graph of $y = x^2$?
e. What point on the graph of $y = -(x - 1)^2$ corresponds to the point (a, b) on the graph of $y = x^2$?

2.6 Absolute Value Equations and Inequalities

A projectile fired vertically up from the ground with an initial velocity of 160 ft/second will hit the ground 10 seconds later, and the speed y of the projectile in terms of the elapsed time t is given by

$$y = |160 - 32t|.$$

a. Graph this equation and describe what happens to the speed as t increases.
b. For what values of t is the projectile's speed 48 ft/second?
c. For what values of t is the projectile's speed at least 48 ft/second?

   (See Example 8.)

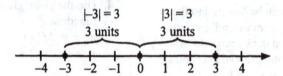

OBJECTIVES

1 Solve equations involving absolute value.

2 Solve inequalities of the form $|ax + b| < c$.

3 Solve inequalities of the form $|ax + b| > c$.

4 Write a number interval using inequalities and absolute value.

Both algebraic and geometric perspectives of the absolute value concept are useful for formulating procedures to solve equations or inequalities that involve absolute value. Recall from Section 1.1 that the absolute value of a number a is denoted by $|a|$ and is interpreted geometrically as the distance on the number line between a and zero. For instance $|3| = 3$ and $|-3| = 3$, as shown in Figure 2.45.

$$|-3| = 3 \qquad |3| = 3$$
$$\text{3 units} \qquad \text{3 units}$$

Figure 2.45

We see that if a is a positive number or 0, then $|a| = a$, while if a is a negative number then $|a| = -a$. Thus, the algebraic definition of $|a|$ is

$$|a| = \begin{cases} a, & \text{if } a \geq 0, \\ -a, & \text{if } a < 0. \end{cases}$$

In Example 1 we can now illustrate three main approaches to solving absolute value equations with respect to a simple equation like $|x| = 5$.

EXAMPLE 1   Solving Equations of the Form $|x| = c$

Solve $|x| = 5$ using (a) a number line approach, (b) a graphing approach, and (c) an algebraic approach.

Solution

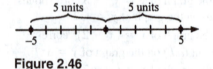

Figure 2.46

a. To solve $|x| = 5$ using a number line approach, look for two numbers that are 5 units from 0 on the number line. The required numbers are 5 and -5, as shown in Figure 2.46.

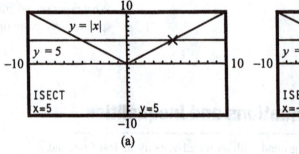
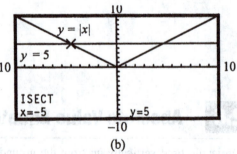

(a)   (b)

Figure 2.47

b. The x coordinates of the intersection points of the graphs of $y = |x|$ and $y = 5$ give the roots of the equation $|x| = 5$. From Figure 2.47 we can read that these roots are 5 and -5.

c. By the algebraic definition $|x|$ equals either x or $-x$. Setting these two expressions equal to 5 gives

$$x = 5 \text{ or } -x = 5$$

$$\text{so } x = 5 \text{ or } x = -5.$$

Both solutions check and the solution set is $\{5, -5\}$.

PROGRESS CHECK 1   Solve $|x| = 8$ using (a) a number line approach, (b) a graphing approach, and (c) an algebraic approach.   ■

Example 1 illustrates that for $c > 0$,

$$|x| = c \text{ implies } x = c \text{ or } x = -c.$$

Other first-degree expressions may replace x in this result to provide a general procedure for solving absolute value equations of the form $|ax + b| = c$.

Solution of $|ax + b| = c$

If $|ax + b| = c$ and $c > 0$, then

$$ax + b = c \text{ or } ax + b = -c.$$

To solve $|ax + b| = c$ when $c = 0$, note that it is only necessary to solve $ax + b = 0$, because 0 is the only number whose absolute value is 0. Also, equations such as $|x| = -3$ have no solution, since the absolute value of a number is never negative; so in general, $|ax + b| = c$ has no solution if $c < 0$.

EXAMPLE 2   Solving Equations of the Form $|ax + b| = c$
Solve $|10x + 5| = 45$.

Solution $|10x + 5| = 45$ is equivalent to

$$10x + 5 = 45 \quad \text{or} \quad 10x + 5 = -45$$

$$10x = 40 \quad \text{or} \quad 10x = -50$$

$$x = 4 \quad \text{or} \quad x = -5$$

Both solutions check (verify this), and the solution set is $\{4, -5\}$. The intersection of the graphs of $y = |10x + 5|$ and $y = 45$, which is shown in Figure 2.48, is in agreement with this solution.

PROGRESS CHECK 2   Solve $|14x - 21| = 63$.   ■

The next example shows how to solve absolute value equations of the form $|ax + b| = |cx + d|$.

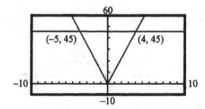

Figure 2.48

EXAMPLE 3 Solving Equations of the Form $|ax + b| = |cx + d|$
Solve $|2x + 1| = |3 - x|$.

Solution By definition, $|2x + 1| = \pm(2x + 1)$ and $|3 - x| = \pm(3 - x)$. Setting these expressions equal to each other produces two distinct cases:

$$2x + 1 = 3 - x \text{ or } 2x + 1 = -(3 - x).$$

Finally, solving each of these equations separately gives

$$
\begin{aligned}
2x + 1 &= 3 - x &\text{or}\quad 2x + 1 &= -(3 - x) \\
3x &= 2 &\text{or}\quad 2x + 1 &= -3 + x \\
x &= \frac{2}{3} &\text{or}\quad x &= -4.
\end{aligned}
$$

Thus, the solution set is $\{2/3, -4\}$. A graphical check that supports this solution is shown in Figure 2.49.

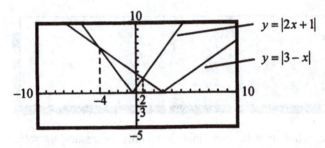

Figure 2.49

[**Note:** The given equation is also satisfied when $-(2x + 1) = -(3 - x)$ or when $-(2x + 1) = 3 - x$. However, these equations are equivalent to the two we solved and need not be considered.]

PROGRESS CHECK 3 Solve $|7x - 8| = |9x + 12|$. ■

The idea that absolute value can define a distance on the number line may be extended and used to interpret expressions of the form $|x - a|$, which occur often in higher mathematics. Given any two points a and b, the distance between them on the number line is $|a - b|$, as illustrated in Figure 2.50. Note that $|a - b| = |b - a|$, so the order in the subtraction is not significant. This geometric perspective may be used to analyze equations of the form $|x - \text{constant}| = \text{constant}$, as discussed in Example 4.

EXAMPLE 4 Solving Equations of the Form $|x - a| = c$.
Solve $|x - 2| = 5$ using

a. a number line approach
b. a graphing approach and
c. an algebraic approach.

Solution

a. Using a number line approach, $|x - 2|$ represents the distance between 2 and some number x on the number line. So when solving $|x - 2| = 5$, we are looking for two numbers that are 5 units from 2 on the number line. As shown in Figure 2.51, the required numbers are 7 and -3.
b. The graphs of $y = |x - 2|$ and $y = 5$ intersect when $x = 7$ and $x = -3$, as illustrated in Figure 2.52. Thus, the solution set is $\{7, -3\}$.

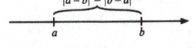

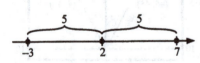

Figure 2.50

Figure 2.51

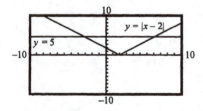

Figure 2.52

c. Algebraically, $|x - 2| = 5$ implies

$$x - 2 = 5 \quad \text{or} \quad x - 2 = -5$$

$$x = 7 \quad \text{or} \quad x = -3$$

Both solutions check and the solution set is $\{7, -3\}$.

PROGRESS CHECK 4   Solve $|x - 5| = 7$ using

a. a number line approach,
b. a graphing approach, and,
c. an algebraic approach.
                                                                    ■

   In many applications involving absolute value, the inequality signs $(<, \leq, >, \geq)$ express the required relation in a problem. For instance, we can determine when the speed of the projectile described in the section-opening problem is *less than* 48 ft/second by solving.

$$|160 - 32t| < 48$$

To solve such inequalities, first consider that

$$|x| < 3$$

can be solved from a geometric viewpoint by finding all numbers that are less than 3 units from 0 on the number line. This set of numbers is graphed in Figure 2.53 and is expressed in set-builder notation by $\{x: -3 < x < 3\}$, and in interval notation by $(-3, 3)$. This example illustrates that for $c > 0$

$$|x| < c \text{ implies } -c < x < c,$$

which gives a general procedure for solving inequalities of the form $|ax + b| < c$.

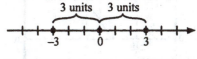

Figure 2.53

> **Solution of $|ax + b| < c$**
>
> If $|ax + b| < c$ and $c > 0$, then
>
> $$-c < ax + b < c.$$

Note that the inequality symbol $\leq$ may replace $<$ in our discussion to this point, so by similar reasoning, an inequality such as $|x| \leq 3$ implies $-3 \leq x \leq 3$.

EXAMPLE 5   Solving Inequalities of the Form $|x - a| < c$

Solve $|x - 4| < 3$ using

a. a number line approach,
b. a graphing approach, and,
c. an algebraic approach.

Solution

a. Using a number line approach, $|x - 4| < 3$ requires that the distance on the number line between 4 and some number x be less than 3 units. Figure 2.54 shows that such an interval starts at 1, ends at 7, and excludes both end points.

$$|x - 4| < 3 \text{ means } x \text{ is between 1 and 7.}$$

b. Figure 2.55 illustrates that the graph of $y = |x - 4|$ is *below* the graph of $y = 3$ for $1 < x < 7$, which confirms that the solution set is $(1, 7)$.
c. $|x - 4| < 3$ implies

$$-3 < x - 4 < 3.$$

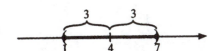

Figure 2.54

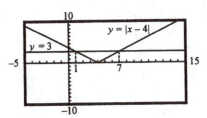

Figure 2.55

Now we proceed by obtaining equivalent inequalities using any of the properties given in Section 1.7.

$$-3 < x - 4 < 3$$

$$1 < x < 7 \qquad \text{Add 4 to each member.}$$

Thus, any number between 1 and 7 satisfies the given inequality, and the solution set is $(1, 7)$.

PROGRESS CHECK 5   Solve $|x - 2| \leq 8$ using

a. a number line approach,
b. a graphing approach, and,
c. an algebraic approach.   ■

EXAMPLE 6   Solving Inequalities of the Form $|ax + b| < c$
Solve $|3x + 5| < 11$.

Solution   We rewrite $|3x + 5| < 11$ as $-11 < 3x + 5 < 11$ and proceed as follows:

$$-11 < 3x + 5 < 11$$

$$-16 < 3x < 6 \qquad \text{Subtract 5 from each member.}$$

$$\frac{-16}{3} < x < 2. \qquad \text{Divide each member by 3.}$$

Thus, any number between $-16/3$ and 2 satisfies the inequality, and the solution set is $(-16/3, 2)$.

To check this solution graphically, observe in Figure 2.56 that the graph of $y = |3x + 5|$ is below the graph of $y = 11$ when x is between $-16/3$ and 2.

PROGRESS CHECK 6   Solve $|5x + 7| < 12$.   ■

To solve absolute value inequalities of the form $|ax + b| > c$, consider that an inequality like

$$|x| > 3$$

can be solved by finding all numbers greater than 3 units from 0 on the number line. Figure 2.57 specifies this set of numbers graphically, in set-builder notation, and in interval notation. As suggested by this example, if $c > 0$,

$$|x| > c \text{ implies } x < -c \text{ or } x > c.$$

So inequalities of the form $|ax + b| > c$ may be solved as follows.

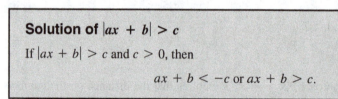

Solution of $|ax + b| > c$

If $|ax + b| > c$ and $c > 0$, then

$$ax + b < -c \text{ or } ax + b > c.$$

EXAMPLE 7   Solving Inequalities of the Form $|x - a| > c$
Solve $|x - 4| > 3$ using

a. a number line approach,
b. a graphing approach, and,
c. an algebraic approach.

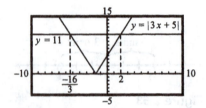

Figure 2.56

More than 3 units from 0

Solution set: $\{x: x < -3 \text{ or } x > 3\}$
Solution set: $(-\infty, -3) \cup (3, \infty)$

Figure 2.57

Solution

a. Figure 2.58 illustrates that the numbers located more than 3 units from 4 on the number line are either to the left of 1 or the right of 7, which confirms that the solution set is $(-\infty, 1) \cup (7, \infty)$.

b. The graph of $y = |x - 4|$ is *above* the graph of $y = 3$ when $x < 1$ or $x > 7$, as can be seen in Figure 2.59. So from this graph we can read that the solution set is $(-\infty, 1) \cup (7, \infty)$.

c. Algebraically, the given inequality translates to the compound statement

$$x - 4 < -3 \text{ or } x - 4 > 3.$$

We then add 4 to both sides in both inequalities to get

$$x < 1 \text{ or } x > 7$$

So the solution set in interval notation is $(-\infty, 1) \cup (7, \infty)$.

PROGRESS CHECK 7   Solve $|x - 75| > 5$ using

a. a number line approach,
b. a graphing approach and,
c. an algebraic approach.

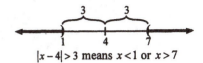

$|x - 4| > 3$ means $x < 1$ or $x > 7$

Figure 2.58

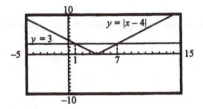

Figure 2.59

 ■

EXAMPLE 8   An Application Involving Absolute Value

Solve the problem in the section introduction on page 119.

Solution

a. Figure 2.60 shows a graph of $y = |160 - 32t|$ where the variable x is used on a grapher to represent the elapsed time t. The graph shows that the speed of the projectile decreases uniformly from an initial speed of 160 ft/second until it stops momentarily when $t = 5$; then the projectile increases in speed uniformly until it travels at 160 ft/second again, when it hits the ground after 10 seconds have elapsed.

b. Replacing y by 48 in the formula $y = |160 - 32t|$ gives $48 = |160 - 32t|$, which implies

$$
\begin{aligned}
160 - 32t = 48 \quad &\text{or} \quad 160 - 32t = -48 \\
-32t = -112 \quad &\text{or} \quad -32t = -208 \\
t = 3.5 \quad &\text{or} \quad t = 6.5.
\end{aligned}
$$

Thus, the projectile attains a speed of 48 ft/second after 3.5 seconds (on its way up) and again (on its way down) when 6.5 seconds have elapsed. The intersection of the graphs of $y = |160 - 32t|$ and $y = 48$ that is shown in Figure 2.61 reaffirms this solution.

c. To find when the speed of the projectile is at least 48 ft/second, we first need to solve $|160 - 32t| \geq 48$, which is equivalent to

$$160 - 32t \leq -48 \text{ or } 160 - 32t \geq 48.$$

Then solving each of these inequalities gives

$$
\begin{array}{lll}
160 - 32t \leq -48 \quad \text{or} \quad & 160 - 32t \geq 48 & \\
-32t \leq -208 & -32t \geq -112 & \text{Subtract 160 from both sides.} \\
t \geq 6.5 & t \leq 3.5 & \text{Divide by } -32 \text{ and reverse} \\
& & \text{the inequality symbols.}
\end{array}
$$

In the context of the problem, only values for t from 0 to 10 seconds are meaningful so the solution set is

$$[0 \text{ seconds}, 3.5 \text{ seconds}] \cup [6.5 \text{ seconds}, 10 \text{ seconds}].$$

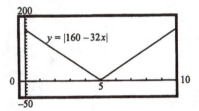

Figure 2.60

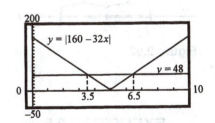

Figure 2.61

To check this solution graphically, observe in Figure 2.61 that the graph of $y = |160 - 32x|$ intersects or is above the graph of $y = 48$ when $0 \le x \le 3.5$ or when $6.5 \le x \le 10$.

PROGRESS CHECK 8 A projectile fired vertically up from the ground with an initial velocity of 256 ft/second will hit the ground 16 seconds later, and the speed y of the projectile in terms of the elapsed time t is given by $y = |256 - 32t|$. Redo the questions in Example 8 with respect to this projectile. ■

Inequalities involving absolute value are commonly seen in applications in which an interval of numbers is centered around a target number, and all numbers in the interval must be within (or must exceed) a specified distance from this target. The next two examples discuss how to translate such situations to an algebraic model.

EXAMPLE 9   Translating to an Absolute Value Inequality

The specifications for a component in a solar panel require that the length of this component part be 7.25 cm. When manufacturing this part, a sample is judged acceptable when the length l is not more than 0.04 cm from this specification. Write an inequality involving absolute value that gives all values of l for an acceptable part, and then solve this inequality.

Solution The expression $|l - 7.25|$ represents the distance between 7.25 and the length of the part. Since this distance must be less than or equal to 0.04, the requested algebraic model is

$$|l - 7.25| \le 0.04.$$

By the methods of this section, this inequality is equivalent to $7.21 \le l \le 7.29$. So the length of an acceptable part measures from 7.21 cm to 7.29 cm.

PROGRESS CHECK 9 An investor buys a certain stock at \$30 per share and wishes to hold onto this stock as long as the stock price p stays within 20 percent of the original purchase price. Write an inequality involving absolute value that gives all values of p for which the investor will continue to own the stock, and then solve this inequality. ■

Example 10   Translating to an Absolute Value Inequality

Write the interval $\{x: -3 < x < 7\}$ using inequalities and absolute value.

Solution: The interval between -3 and 7 is 10 units long and centered at 2. As shown in Figure 2.62, we are describing numbers that are within 5 units of 2. This condition means that $-3 < x < 7$ is equivalent to $|x - 2| < 5$.

PROGRESS CHECK 10 Write the interval $\{x: -2 < x < 3\}$ using inequalities and absolute value. ■

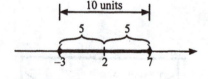

Figure 2.62

EXERCISES 2.6

In Exercises 1–8 solve the given equation using
  a. a number line approach,
  b. a graphing approach, and,
  c. an algebraic approach.
  1. $|x| = 2$
  2. $|x| = 1.6$
  3. $|x - 1| = 2$
  4. $|x - 3| = 1.6$
  5. $|x - (-2)| = 1$
  6. $|x - (-4)| = 2$
  7. $|x + 8| = 3.1$
  8. $|x + 1.2| = 8.5$

In Exercises 9–26 solve each equation.
  9. $|5x + 10| = 30$
  10. $|3x - 12| = 24$
  11. $\left|\frac{1}{2}x - 9\right| = 8$
  12. $|3x + 7| = 0$
  13. $2|x| + 7 = 10$
  14. $3|x - 1| + 2 = 11$
  15. $|x - 3| = -2$
  16. $|x + 2| = -5$
  17. $|3x - 4| = 1 + x$
  18. $|-2x + 1| = 7x$
  19. $|2x - 1| = x$
  20. $|-x + 2| = x + 1$
  21. $|x - 3| = |x + 1|$
  22. $|1 - x| = |3x - 1|$

23. $|2x + 1| = |3 + x|$ **24.** $|6x - 4| = |2x - 7|$
25. $|5 - 2x| = |2 - 5x|$ **26.** $|-3x| = |2 - 3x|$

In Exercises 27–34 solve the inequality using
  a. a number line approach,
  b. a graphing approach, and
  c. an algebraic approach.

27. $|x| < 4$ **28.** $|x| \le \dfrac{1}{2}$

29. $|x - 5| \le 3$ **30.** $|x - 3| < 0.01$
31. $|x + 1| < 2$ **32.** $|x + 2| < 1$
33. $|x - 5| \ge 3$ **34.** $|x - 0.1| > 0.8$

In Exercises 35–42 solve the given inequality.

35. $|x| > 2$ **36.** $|x| > 0$
37. $|3x + 5| < 8$ **38.** $|6x - 7| \le 10$
39. $|1 - 2x| \le 13$ **40.** $|3 - 4x| < 5$
41. $|2x - 1| > 3$ **42.** $|1 - x| + 2 \ge 4$

In Exercises 43–56 write the given interval using inequalities and absolute value.

43. $(-2, 2)$ **44.** $[-7, 7]$
45. $\{x: 1.1 < x < 1.2\}$ **46.** $\{x: -0.6 < x < -0.5\}$
47. $(-\infty, -2) \cup (2, \infty)$
48. $(-\infty, -0.1) \cup (0.1, \infty)$
49. $\{x: x < 0 \text{ or } x > 6\}$ **50.** $\{x: x \le -4 \text{ or } x \ge 0\}$

51.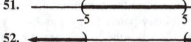

52.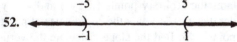

53. x is between 2 and 4.
54. x is between -8 and -1.
55. x is within one-half unit of 3.
56. x is within d units of a.
57. The speed of a projectile fired vertically from the ground in terms of time elapsed (t) is given by $s = |240 - 32t|$. For what values of t is the projectile's speed 80 ft/second?
58. The speed of a projectile fired vertically from the ground is given by $s = |49 - 32t|$, where $t = $ time elapsed. For what values of t is the projectile's speed 25 ft/second?
59. Find all values for which the absolute value of $8 - 3x$ is 100.
60. Find all values for which the absolute value of $8 + 3x$ is 100.
61. A projectile is fired vertically from the ground. Find when the speed of the projectile is less than 80 ft/second if speed s is given by $|240 - 32t|$. Express your answer graphically and in interval notation.
62. A projectile is fired vertically from the ground. If speed $s = |49 - 32t|$, when is the speed of the projectile less than 25 ft/second? Express your answer graphically and in interval notation.

63. Find all values for which the absolute value of $25 - 4x$ is greater than 100. Express your answer graphically and in interval notation.
64. Find all values for which the absolute value of $25 + 5x$ is less than 100. Express your answer graphically and in interval notation.
65. A projectile fired vertically up from the ground with an initial velocity of 128 ft/second will hit the ground 8 seconds later, and the speed of the projectile in terms of the elapsed time t is given by $y = |128 - 32t|$.
  a. Graph this equation and describe what happens to the speed as t increases.
  b. For what values of t is the speed 140 ft/sec?
  c. For what values of t is the speed less than 80 ft/sec?
  d. What is the maximum speed the projectile attains?
66. Redo Exercise 65, but assume that speed is given by $y = |153.6 - 32t|$.
67. A bulb is useful if its brightness b does not differ from 1170 lumens by more than 12.5 lumens. Write an inequality involving absolute value that gives all values of b for an acceptable bulb, and then solve the inequality.
68. In manufacturing a metal square with side 1 mm, the error in the side must be less than 0.05 mm.
  a. Let x be the actual length of the manufactured side and express this requirement using absolute value.
  b. Find an inequality that describes the area of the manufactured square.
  c. What is the maximum error in the area?
69. From a grapher you see that the root r of an equation is between 1.8940 and 1.9048.
  a. Express this interval using an absolute value inequality.
  b. What does the answer in part **a** reveal about the maximum error, E, that can be made when the midpoint, M, of the interval is used as an estimate for the root?

THINK ABOUT IT 2.6

1. Explain how the inequality $|x + 2| < 1$ may be solved geometrically. (*Hint:* Rewrite $x + 2$ in the form $a - b$.)
2. A property of absolute value is $|a/b| = |a|/|b|$. Use this property to solve each inequality. Assume $x \ne 0$.

  a. $\left|\dfrac{1}{x}\right| < 3$

  b. $\left|\dfrac{2}{x}\right| \ge 1$

3. A famous inequality with wide application in advanced mathematics is called the absolute value inequality. It states that for any real values of a and b, $|a + b|$ can never be greater than $|a| + |b|$.
  a. Find values for a and b so that the two expressions are equal. There are many correct choices.
  b. Find values for a and b so that $|a + b|$ is less than $|a| + |b|$. There are many correct choices.

4. a. Compare the graphs of and Is it true that for all x?
    b. Compare the graphs of $y = |x + (-5)|$ and $y = |x| + |-5|$. Is it true that $|x + (-5)| \leq |x| + |-5|$ for all x?
    c. Explain by referring to graphs why $|x + a| \leq |x| + |a|$ is true for all values of x and a.
5. On a math test there was an equation that looked much too difficult to solve, so a student guessed that there

was some kind of special case involved. Can you find the solution set of this equation just by looking at it?

$$\frac{4}{3}\pi|\sqrt{2.3}x - 100| + 5 = 0$$

2.7 The Slope of a Line and the Distance Formula

A certain olympic ski jump drops 60 m over a distance of 86 m. Measure the steepness of this jump by finding its slope. (See Example 3.)

OBJECTIVES

1 Find and interpret the slope of a line.

2 Determine if lines are parallel, perpendicular, or neither by using slope.

3 Find the distance between two points.

An important characteristic of a line is its steepness, or the degree to which it slants. Mathematically, the concept of **slope** is used to measure the inclination of the line with respect to the horizontal axis. Two familiar concrete illustrations of the slope of a line are the grade of a roadway and the pitch of a roof. To introduce the definition of slope, we consider the line in Figure 2.63 that contains the arbitrary points (x_1, y_1) and (x_2, y_2). Notice how subscripts are used as a reminder that x_1 and y_1 are the coordinates of point 1, and that x_2 and y_2 are the coordinates of point 2. To find the slope, calculate the vertical change, $y_2 - y_1$, which is called the **rise**, and divide this number by the horizontal change, $x_2 - x_1$, which is called the **run**.

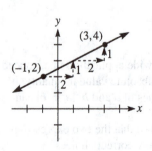
Courtesy of Digital Vision, Ltd.

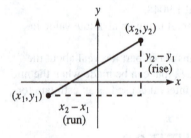
Figure 2.63

Slope of a Line

If (x_1, y_1) and (x_2, y_2) are any two distinct points on a line, with $x_1 \neq x_2$, then the slope m of the line is

$$m = \frac{\text{rise}}{\text{run}} = \frac{\text{change in } y}{\text{change in } x} = \frac{y_2 - y_1}{x_2 - x_1}.$$

EXAMPLE 1 Using the Definition of Slope

Find the slope of the line through the given points.
a. $(-1, 2)$ and $(3,4)$ b. $(-3, 3)$ and $(1,0)$

Solution

a. If we label $(-1, 2)$ as point 1, then $x_1 = -1$, $y_1 = 2$, $x_2 = 3$, and $y_2 = 4$. The slope formula now gives

$$m = \frac{\text{rise}}{\text{run}} = \frac{y_2 - y_1}{x_2 - x_1} = \frac{4 - 2}{3 - (-1)} = \frac{2}{4} = \frac{1}{2}.$$

The slope is $\frac{1}{2}$, which means that y increases 1 unit for each 2-unit increase in x, as shown in Figure 2.64.

Figure 2.64

Note The slope is not affected by the way in which the points are labeled. In this example, if we label (3,4) as point 1, then $x_1 = 3$, $y_1 = 4$, $x_2 = -1$, and $y_2 = 2$. So

$$m = \frac{y_2 - y_1}{x_2 - x_1} = \frac{2 - 4}{-1 - 3} = \frac{-2}{-4} = \frac{1}{2}.$$

b. We let $x_1 = -3$, $y_1 = 3$, $x_2 = 1$, and $y_2 = 0$ and substitute in the slope formula.

$$m = \frac{\text{rise}}{\text{run}} = \frac{y_2 - y_1}{x_2 - x_1} = \frac{0 - 3}{1 - (-3)} = \frac{-3}{4}$$

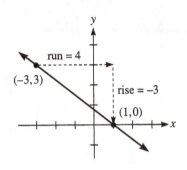

Figure 2.65

A slope of $-3/4$ indicates that as x increases 4 units, y *decreases* 3 units, as shown in Figure 2.65.

PROGRESS CHECK 1 Find the slope of the line through the given points.
a. $(1, -1)$ and $(5,3)$ **b.** $(1, -1)$ and $(-2, 3)$ ■

When the slope formula is applied to lines that are horizontal or vertical, then special cases occur, as shown next.

EXAMPLE 2 Finding the Slope of Horizontal or Vertical Lines
Find the slope of the line through the given points.

a. $(-1, 4)$ and $(2,4)$ **b.** $(3,5)$ and $(3,1)$

Solution

a. Because both points have the same y-coordinate, the line through them is horizontal. (See Figure 2.66.) Applying the slope formula gives

$$m = \frac{\text{rise}}{\text{run}} = \frac{y_2 - y_1}{x_2 - x_1} = \frac{4 - 4}{2 - (-1)} = \frac{0}{3} = 0.$$

The slope of every horizontal line is zero because the rise is always zero.

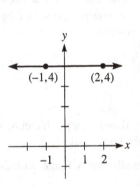

Figure 2.66

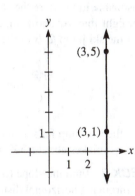

Figure 2.67

b. Because the two points have the same x-coordinate, the line through them is vertical. (See Figure 2.67.) As a consequence, the run will be zero, and the slope is not defined.

$$m = \frac{\text{rise}}{\text{run}} = \frac{y_2 - y_1}{x_2 - x_1} = \frac{1 - 5}{3 - 3} = \frac{-4}{0}$$

It follows that **the slope of every vertical line is undefined**.

PROGRESS CHECK 2 Find the slope of the line through the given points.

a. $(6,1)$ and $(0,1)$ **b.** $(-2, -3)$ and $(-2, 1)$ ■

Examples 1 and 2 have illustrated cases in which the slope of a line is positive, negative, zero, or undefined. These cases are summarized in Figure 2.68.

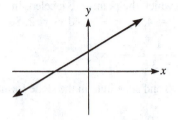

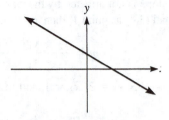

Slope is positive.
Line is higher on the right.
y increases as x increases.

Slope is negative.
Line is lower on the right.
y decreases as x increases.

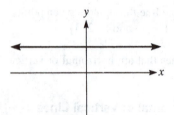

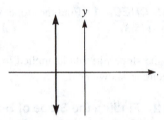

Slope is zero.
Line is horizontal.
y remains constant as x increases.

Slope is undefined.
Line is vertical.
x remains constant as y increases

Figure 2.68

The next two examples call for an interpretation of the slope in applied problems.

EXAMPLE 3 Interpreting Slope as Steepness or Pitch

Solve the problem in the section introduction on page 128.

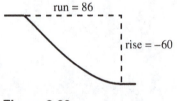

Figure 2.69

Solution It is reasonable to measure the steepness of this ski jump by slope because its shape is almost a straight line. As shown in Figure 2.69, the rise is represented by -60, because the height of the ski jump *falls* as the skier goes forward.

$$m = \frac{\text{rise}}{\text{run}} = \frac{-60}{86}$$

$$= -0.70$$

The slope shows that the ski jump falls about 0.7 m per horizontal meter. It can be shown that a line with this slope makes about a 35°; angle with the horizontal.

PROGRESS CHECK 3 Find the slope (pitch) of the wall of an A-frame ski lodge that rises 20 ft vertically through a horizontal distance of 15 ft. ■

In many applications, the slope of a line describes a *rate* relationship between two variables. This interpretation is illustrated in the next example.

EXAMPLE 4 Interpreting Slope as a Rate of Change

A printing shop charges $20 for 500 copies of a flyer and $25 for 750 copies. If the relation between the number of copies (x) and cost (y) graphs as a line, calculate and interpret the slope.

Solution Figure 2.70 shows the graph of the relation between x and y. We let $x_1 = 500$, $y_1 = 20$, $x_2 = 750$, and $y_2 = 25$ and substitute in the slope formula.

$$m = \frac{\text{change in } y}{\text{change in } x} = \frac{y_2 - y_1}{x_2 - x_1} = \frac{25 - 20}{750 - 500} = \frac{5}{250} = 0.02$$

In this problem, because the units for the numerator are dollars and the units for the denominator are numbers of copies, the slope describes the change in cost in *dollars per copy*. Therefore, a slope of 0.02 means that it costs 0.02 dollar (or 2 cents) for each additional copy. If the units for x and y had been reversed, so that x represented dollars and y represented copies, then the slope would have been 50 *copies per dollar*. The answers are equivalent, because 50 copies per dollar is the same as 2 cents per copy. In Figure 2.70 we see that the minimum charge for just setting up the job is $10, as given by the y-intercept.

PROGRESS CHECK 4   Redo the problem in Example 4, but assume that the cost is $50 for 500 copies and $58 for 700 copies.   ■

Slope is a convenient device for analyzing parallel and perpendicular lines. Two lines in a plane that never intersect are called **parallel.** Because they "go in the same direction," it is intuitively clear to say that lines are parallel if they have the *same* slope. Two lines in a plane are **perpendicular** if they meet at right angles. It can be shown mathematically that this happens when the product of their slopes is -1. These properties are summarized in the following box; but note that vertical lines are excluded, because the slope of vertical lines is undefined.

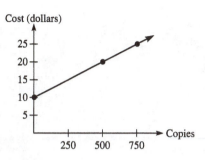

Figure 2.70

Parallel and Perpendicular Lines

1. Two nonvertical lines are parallel if and only if their slopes are equal.
2. Two nonvertical lines are perpendicular if and only if the product of their slopes is -1. The slope of one is the negative of the reciprocal of the slope of the other.

For the next example, recall that a **parallelogram** is a quadrilateral in which both pairs of opposite sides are parallel, while a **rectangle** is a parallelogram in which all four angles are right angles.

EXAMPLE 5   Using Slope to Analyze a Quadrilateral

A quadrilateral has vertices at $A(0,1)$, $B(6,3)$, $C(7,0)$, and $D(1, -2)$.
a. Show that quadrilateral $ABCD$ is a parallelogram.
b. Show that parallelogram $ABCD$ is a rectangle.

Solution   Quadrilateral $ABCD$ is shown in Figure 2.71.

a. First, compute the slope of each of the four sides.

$$m_{AB} = \frac{3 - 1}{6 - 0} = \frac{2}{6} = \frac{1}{3}$$

$$m_{BC} = \frac{0 - 3}{7 - 6} = \frac{-3}{1} = -3$$

$$m_{CD} = \frac{0 - (-2)}{7 - 1} = \frac{2}{6} = \frac{1}{3}$$

$$m_{AD} = \frac{-2 - 1}{1 - 0} = \frac{-3}{1} = -3$$

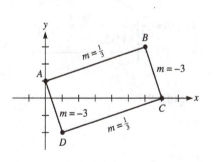

Figure 2.71

Each pair of opposite sides is parallel because $m_{AB} = m_{CD} = \frac{1}{3}$, and $m_{BC} = m_{AD}$ $= -3$. Thus, $ABCD$ is a parallelogram.

b. All four angles are right angles, because

$$m_{AB} \cdot m_{BC} = m_{AB} \cdot m_{AD} = m_{CD} \cdot m_{BC} = m_{CD} \cdot m_{AD} = \frac{1}{3}(-3) = -1.$$

Thus, parallelogram $ABCD$ is a rectangle.

PROGRESS CHECK 5 A quadrilateral has vertices at $A(0,1)$, $B(6,4)$, $C(7,2)$, and $D(1, -1)$.

a. Show that quadrilateral $ABCD$ is a parallelogram.
b. Show that quadrilateral $ABCD$ is a rectangle. ■

Besides the slope formula, another useful formula for analyzing line segments is the distance formula. If $P_1(x_1, y_1)$ and $P_2(x_2, y_2)$ are two points on a line, then the length of line segment P_1P_2 is defined as the distance between P_1 and P_2. It is easiest to find the distance between two points on a horizontal or vertical line. If the points lie on the same horizontal line, the distance between the points is given by the absolute value of the difference between their x-coordinates. If two points lie on the same vertical line, the distance between them is given by the absolute value of the difference between their y-coordinates.

EXAMPLE 6 Horizontal and Vertical Distance

Find the distance between the given points.

a. $(-4, -1)$ and $(-4, -3)$ **b.** $(-2, 2)$ and $(4, 2)$

Solution See Figure 2.72.

a. The points $(-4, -1)$ and $(-4, -3)$ have the same x-coordinate, so

$$d = |y_2 - y_1| = |-3 - (-1)| = |-2| = 2.$$

b. The points $(-2, 2)$ and $(4,2)$ have the same y-coordinate, so

$$d = |x_2 - x_1| = |4 - (-2)| = |6| = 6.$$

PROGRESS CHECK 6 Find the distance between the given points.

a. $(3,5)$ and $(3, -3)$ **b.** $(-7, -1)$ and $(0, -1)$ ■

To find the distance between two points that do not lie on the same horizontal or the same vertical line, we may construct a right triangle, as shown in Figure 2.73, and apply the Pythagorean theorem (which was discussed earlier in Section 1.4). Because the distance d is the length of the hypotenuse in the right triangle, we get

$$d^2 = |x_2 - x_1|^2 + |y_2 - y_1|^2$$
$$d = \sqrt{(x_2 - x_1)^2 + (y_2 - y_1)^2}.$$

This result gives the distance formula. Note that absolute value symbols are not needed in this formula because the square of any real number is never negative.

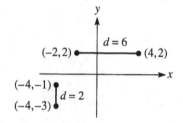

Figure 2.72

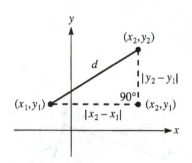

Figure 2.73

Distance Formula

The distance d between (x_1, y_1) and (x_2, y_2) is
$$d = \sqrt{(x_2 - x_1)^2 + (y_2 - y_1)^2}.$$

EXAMPLE 7   Using the Distance Formula

Find the distance between $(-2, 1)$ and $(5, -3)$.

Solution Let $x_1 = -2$, $y_1 = 1$, $x_2 = 5$, and $y_2 = -3$, and use the distance formula.

$$
\begin{aligned}
d &= \sqrt{(x_2 - x_1)^2 + (y_2 - y_1)^2} \\
&= \sqrt{[5 - (-2)]^2 + (-3 - 1)^2} \\
&= \sqrt{7^2 + (-4)^2} \\
&= \sqrt{49 + 16} \\
&= \sqrt{65}
\end{aligned}
$$

See Figure 2.74.

PROGRESS CHECK 7   Find the distance between $(-3, 2)$ and $(-4, -2)$.   ■

EXAMPLE 8   Proving a Triangle is a Right Triangle

Show that $(-5, -3)$, $(-4, 1)$ and $(0,0)$ are vertices of a right triangle using (a) the distance formula and (b) the slope formula.

Solution   Label $(-5, -3)$ as point A, $(-4, 1)$ as point B, and $(0,0)$ as point C, as shown in Figure 2.75.

a. By the distance formula,

$$
\begin{aligned}
d_{AB} &= \sqrt{[-5 - (-4)]^2 + (-3 - 1)^2} = \sqrt{17}, \\
d_{BC} &= \sqrt{(-4 - 0)^2 + (1 - 0)^2} = \sqrt{17}, \\
d_{AC} &= \sqrt{(-5 - 0)^2 + (-3 - 0)^2} = \sqrt{34}.
\end{aligned}
$$

Because $\left(\sqrt{34}\right)^2 = \left(\sqrt{17}\right)^2 + \left(\sqrt{17}\right)^2$, the Pythagorean theorem holds; so ABC is a right triangle with angle B as the right angle.

b. By the slope formula,

$$
m_{AB} = \frac{-3 - 1}{-5 - (-4)} = \frac{-4}{-1} = 4,
$$

$$
m_{BC} = \frac{1 - 0}{-4 - 0} = \frac{1}{-4} = -\frac{1}{4},
$$

$$
m_{AC} = \frac{-3 - 0}{-5 - 0} = \frac{-3}{-5} = \frac{3}{5}.
$$

Because $m_{AB} \cdot m_{BC} = 4\left(-\frac{1}{4}\right) = -1$, angle B is a right angle, and so ABC is a right triangle.

PROGRESS CHECK 8   Show that $A(-2, 0)$, $B(3,5)$, and $C(4,2)$ are vertices of a right triangle using (a) the distance formula and (b) the slope formula.   ■

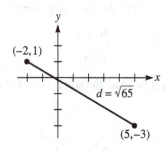

Figure 2.74

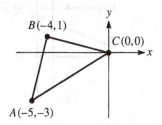

Figure 2.75

EXERCISES 2.7

In Exercises 1–10 find the slope of the line determined by each pair of points.

1. (1, 2) and (3, 4)   **2.** (3, −1) and (5, −7)
3. (5, 1) and (−2, −3)   **4.** (−1, 2) and (0, 0)
5. (4, −4) and (2, 7)   **6.** (−5, −1) and (−2, −4)
7. (−1, −3) and (2, −3)   **8.** (−2, 0) and (5, 0)
9. (1, 3) and (1, −1)   **10.** (−3, 2) and (−3, −2)

11. On a piece of graph paper, draw lines through the point (1, 2) with the following slopes:

    a. 2   **b.** −3   **c.** $-\dfrac{1}{4}$

    d. $\dfrac{2}{3}$ **e.** 0

12. Approximate the slope of each line in the figure below.

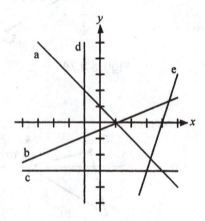

13. Find the slope of a mountain trail that rises 80 ft over a horizontal distance of 100 ft.

14. Find the slope of a segment of highway that falls 88 yards (yd) over a horizontal distance of 500 yd.

15. The world's steepest roller coaster drops a vertical distance of 192 ft over a horizontal distance of 110 ft. Find the slope of this portion of the coaster.

16. The Great Pyramid of Khufu, completed about 2700 B.C. at Giza, Egypt, is the tallest pyramid ever built. It has a square base 756 ft per side and rises to a height of about 480 ft. Thus, its sides rise 480 ft over a run of 378 ft. Find the slope.

17. The weekly cost y of renting a car is $100 if the weekly mileage x is 100 mi and $120 if the mileage is 200 mi. If the relationship between x and y graphs as a line, calculate and interpret the slope.

18. Redo the problem in Exercise 17, but assume that the weekly charge is $150 for 100 mi and $185 for 200 mi.

19. Shipping costs (c) within zone 1 charged by a delivery service have a linear relationship with the weight (w) of the parcel. The charge is $2.38 for a 10-oz parcel and $2.98 for a 20-oz parcel. Graph the line, and calculate and interpret the slope.

20. The company described in Exercise 19 has the following rates for zone 7: For 10 oz the charge is $7.79, and for 20 oz the charge is $11.49. Graph the line; then calculate and interpret the slope.

In Exercises 21–32 represent the ordered pairs as points in the Cartesian coordinate system and find the distance between them.

21. (−1, 3), (−1, 1)   **22.** (2, −4), (2, −1)
23. (4, 1), (0, 1)   **24.** (−3, −2), (2, −2)
25. (−12, 5), (0, 0)   **26.** (0, 0), (−4, 1)
27. (4, −1), (−2, −3)   **28.** (0, 2), (4, −3)
29. (−1, −1), (−2, −2)   **30.** (5, 2), (1, 3)
31. (−2, 5), (4, −3)   **32.** (6, −2), (−6, 3)

33. Three vertices of a square are (3, 3), (3, −1), and (−1, 3). Find the ordered pair corresponding to the fourth vertex. What is the perimeter of the square?

34. Three vertices of a rectangle are (4, 2), (−5, 2), and (−5, −4). Find the ordered pair corresponding to the fourth vertex. What is the perimeter of the rectangle?

35. Show that the points (3, 5), (−3, 7), and (−6, −2) are vertices of a right triangle.

36. Show that the points (−8, −2), (−11, 3) and (3, 8) are vertices of an isosceles triangle. Is this triangle a right triangle?

37. Find the radius of a circle whose diameter extends from (−2, 1) to (3, 4).

38. Find the radius of a circle with center at (0, 0) and which passes through the point (2, 3).

39. Find the area of a circle whose radius extends from (−1, 1) to (2, 1).

40. Find the area of a circle whose diameter extends from (−1, 3) to (3, 1).

41. A quadrilateral has vertices at $A(0,0)$, $B(4,1)$, $C(5, −3)$, and $D(1, −4)$.
    a. Show that $ABCD$ is a parallelogram.
    b. Show that $ABCD$ is a rectangle.
    c. Show that the lengths of both diagonals are equal.

42. A quadrilateral has vertices at $A(4, −1)$, $B(2, −4)$, $C(−4, 0)$, and $D(−2, 3)$.
    a. Show that $ABCD$ is a parallelogram.
    b. Show that $ABCD$ is a rectangle.
    c. Show that the lengths of both diagonals are equal.

43. Show that quadrilateral $ABCD$ is a parallelogram but *not* a rectangle. The vertices are $A(2,0)$, $B(3,3)$, $C(7,3)$, and $D(6,0)$. Confirm that the diagonals are unequal in length.

44. Show that quadrilateral *ABCD* is a parallelogram but *not* a rectangle. The vertices are $A(-2, 0)$, $B(2,0)$, $C(5, -2)$, and $D(1, -2)$. Confirm that the diagonals are unequal in length.

45. Two lines are perpendicular.
   a. If the slope of one is 5, then the slope of the other is _____.
   b. If the slope of one is 0, then the slope of the other is _____.
   c. If the slope of one is 0.7, then the slope of the other is _____.

46. Two lines are perpendicular.
   a. If the slope of one is $-\frac{1}{2}$, then the slope of the other is _____.
   b. If the slope of one is $\frac{2}{3}$, then the slope of the other is _____.
   c. If the slope of one is -0.23, then the slope of the other is _____.

For Exercises 47–50, use the fact that *A, B,* and *C* are on the same straight line (collinear), if the slope of *AB* equals the slope of *AC*.

47. Determine whether $A(-5, -2)$, $B(1, -1)$, and $C(13, 1)$ are collinear.

48. Determine whether $A(-4, 2)$, $B(-1, -1)$, and $C(2, -4)$ are collinear.

49. Determine whether $A(-3, -1)$, $B(1,0)$, and $C(9,1)$ are collinear.

50. Determine whether $A(-3, 2)$, $B(-2, -6)$, and $C(0, -23)$ are collinear.

THINK ABOUT IT 2.7

1. Give an example of two points that determine a line with the indicated slope.
   a. $m = 5/2$
   b. $m = -1/3$
   c. $m = 0$
   d. m is undefined

2. a. Since $\dfrac{-2}{3}$ is equal to $\dfrac{2}{-3}$, this means that a rise of -2 with a run of 3 describes the same slope as a rise of 2 and a run of -3. Show that this is correct by starting at the origin and drawing these rises and runs to find a second point.

b. Find two ordered pairs that satisfy $y = ax + b$ and use them to find the slope of the line determined by this equation.

3. Find a point (x, y) not on the *x*- or *y*-axis whose distance from the origin is 3 units. How many such points are there?

4. The world population in 1975 was 4 billion, and in 1990 it was 5.3 billion. If you graph these data as two points on a line, then the slope represents the average annual rate of population growth. Find the average annual growth rate (in millions per year) for the years 1975 to 1990.

5. This graph shows, in *millions*, the number of pieces of mail sent out by the U.S. House of Representatives over several years. [The graph is based on one in E. R. Tufte, *Visual Display of Quantitative Information* (Graphics Press, 1983).]
   a. The graph exhibits periodic behavior. When does it peak?
   b. Can you explain the behavior of the graph?
   c. In what months were more than 50 million pieces mailed?
   d. Interpret the slope of the segment between two consecutive months.
   e. What is the interpretation of the steep negative slope after October 1970?

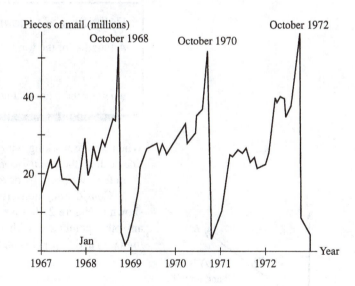

Courtesy of PhotoDisc/Getty Images.

2.8   Linear Functions

During exercise a person's maximum target heart rate is a function of age. This relation is specified by a linear function, and the recommended maximum number of beats per minute is 153 at age 40 and 136 at age 60.

a. Find the equation that defines this linear function.
b. What is the maximum target heart rate for an 18-year-old? (See Example 6.)

OBJECTIVES

1   Write an equation for a line, given its slope and a point on the line or given two points on the line.

2   Find the slope and *y*-intercept, given an equation for the line.

3   Graph and write an equation for a line, given the slope and y-intercept.

4   Find the equation of a linear function *f*, given two ordered pairs in *f*.

5   Solve applied problems involving linear functions

6   Solve problems involving the equations of parallel and perpendicular lines.

The formula for target heart rate that is considered in the section-opening problem involves a linear function, which is among the most widely applied functions in mathematics. Such functions are characterized by a rate of change that remains constant so that from a geometric viewpoint their graphs are straight lines. In algebraic terms, linear functions are first-degree equations in two variables, so the following definition applies.

Definition of Linear Function

A function of the form

$$y = ax + b$$

where a and b are real numbers with $a \neq 0$, is called a **linear function**.

When we are working with linear functions, two important formulas for an equation of a line, called the *point-slope equation* and the *slope-intercept equation* are often used. Therefore, we begin by developing these formulas.

Consider any nonvertical line L with slope m that passes through a point (x_1, y_1) as shown in Figure 2.76. (We eliminate vertical lines, since their slope is undefined.) Then, any other point (x, y) with $x \neq x_1$ is on L if and only if the slope of the line segment joining (x, y) and (x_1, y_1) is m, that is, if and only if

$$\frac{y - y_1}{x - x_1} = m.$$

If we write this equation in the form

$$y - y_1 = m(x - x_1),$$

then (x_1, y_1) also satisfies the equation, which means that the points on L match the solutions of $y - y_1 = m(x - x_1)$. We summarize this result as follows.

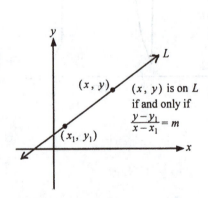

Figure 2.76

> ### Point-Slope Equation
>
> An equation of the line with slope m passing through (x_1, y_1) is
> $$y - y_1 = m(x - x_1).$$
> This equation is called the **point-slope** form of the equation of a line.

EXAMPLE 1   Writing an Equation Given the Slope and a Point

Find an equation for the line that contains the point $(1, 3)$ and whose slope is 2. Write the answer in the form $y = ax + b$.

Solution: We are given that $x_1 = 1$, $y_1 = 3$, and $m = 2$. Substituting these numbers in the point-slope equation, we have

$$y - 3 = 2(x - 1)$$
$$y - 3 = 2x - 2$$
$$y = 2x + 1.$$

PROGRESS CHECK 1 Find an equation of the line through $(-1, 0)$ with slope 3. Write the answer in the form $y = ax + b$.   ■

EXAMPLE 2   Writing an Equation Given Two Points

Find an equation for the line that contains the points $(1, -2)$ and $(4, 5)$. Write the answer in the form $y = ax + b$.

Solution   First, we find the slope

$$m = \frac{y_2 - y_1}{x_2 - x_1} = \frac{5 - (-2)}{4 - 1} = \frac{7}{3}$$

Now use the point-slope equation with $m = \frac{7}{3}$ and either $(1, -2)$ or $(4, 5)$ for (x_1, y_1). Using $x_1 = 4$ and $y_1 = 5$, we have

$$y - 5 = \frac{7}{3}(x - 4),$$

which is converted to the form requested as follows:

$$y - 5 = \frac{7}{3}x - \frac{28}{3}$$

$$y = \frac{7}{3}x - \frac{13}{3}.$$

PROGRESS CHECK 2   Find an equation for the line that contains the points $(-2, 2)$ and $(3, -2)$. Write the answer in the form $y = ax + b$.   ■

The point-slope equation is used extensively to find the equation of a line, but it is not very helpful for graphing lines or for interpreting linear relationships in applications. For these purposes it will often be more convenient to use the *slope-intercept form*, which we develop next. This form follows from the point-slope form by using the y-intercept as the point. Note that in Figure 2.77 we use the letter b to denote the y-coordinate of the

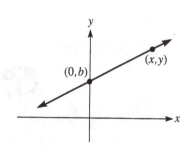

Figure 2.77

point where the graph crosses the y-axis, so the point $(0, b)$ is the y-intercept. Then we proceed using $(0, b)$ to replace (x_1, y_1).

$$y - y_1 = m(x - x_1) \qquad \text{Point-slope equation.}$$

$$y - b = m(x - 0) \qquad \text{Replace } y_1 \text{ by } b \text{ and } x_1 \text{ by 0.}$$

$$y - b = mx \qquad \text{Simplify.}$$

$$y = mx + b \qquad \text{Add } b \text{ to both sides.}$$

This result is called the *slope-intercept form* of the equation of a line. When an equation is written in this form, it is easy to find the slope and y-intercept.

Slope-Intercept Equation

The graph of the equation

$$y = mx + b$$

is a line with slope m and y-intercept $(0, b)$.

EXAMPLE 3   Finding the Slope and the y-Intercept
Find the slope and the y-intercept of the line defined by the following equations.
a. $y = 5x + 4$ **b.** $2x + 3y = 6$

Solution

a. The equation is given in the form $y = mx + b$, with $m = 5$ and $b = 4$. Thus,

the slope of the line is 5,

$$y = 5x + 4$$

and the y-intercept is $(0,4)$.

b. First, express the equation in the form $y = mx + b$.

$$2x + 3y = 6$$

$$3y = -2x + 6$$

$$y = -\frac{2}{3}x + 2$$

Matching this equation to the form $y = mx + b$, we conclude that

$$m = -\frac{2}{3} \qquad b = 2.$$

Thus, the slope is $-\frac{2}{3}$, and the y-intercept is $(0, 2)$.

Technology Link
To check these results on a grapher, we need to rewrite the equation $2x + 3y = 6$ so that y is expressed as a function of x. One possible equation is $y = -\frac{2}{3}x + 2$ (as shown above, while another is $y = \frac{(6 - 2x)}{3}$. Thus, Figure 2.78 shows a graph of either of these equations, and this graph is in agreement with the conclusion that the y-intercept is $(0, 2)$ and the slope is $-\frac{2}{3}$.

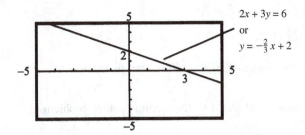

Figure 2.78

PROGRESS CHECK 3   Find the slope and the y-intercept of the line defined by the following equations.

a. $y = -2x + 3$ **b.** $4x - 3y = 12$ ■

    When the slope and the y-intercept of a line are known, its equation can be written directly and it can be graphed, as shown in Example 4.

EXAMPLE 4   Graphing Lines Using the Slope-Intercept Form

The slope of a line is $-\frac{1}{3}$ and the y-intercept is (0, 2).
a. Find the equation of the line in slope-intercept form.
b. Graph the line.

Solution

a. By substituting $m = -\frac{1}{3}$ and $b = 2$ in the slope-intercept equation $y = mx + b$, we determine that the equation is

$$y = -\tfrac{1}{3}x + 2.$$

b. The y-intercept (0, 2) is one point on the line. To find another point, interpret a slope of $-\frac{1}{3}$ to mean that when x increases 3 units, y decreases 1 unit. By starting at (0, 2) and going 3 units to the right and 1 unit down, we obtain (3, 1) as a second point on the line. Drawing a line through these two points produces the graph in Figure 2.79.

PROGRESS CHECK 4   The slope of a line is $-\frac{3}{4}$ and the y-intercept is 5.

a. Find the equation of the line in slope-intercept form.
b. Graph the line.   ■

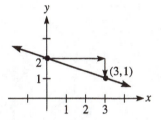

Figure 2.79

    Note that a linear function f may be defined by an equation of the form $y = f(x) = mx + b$ with $m \neq 0$. When two ordered pairs in f are known, then the equation for the linear function may be found as shown in Examples 5 and 6.

EXAMPLE 5   Defining a Linear Function f Using an Equation

Find the equation that defines the linear function f if $f(3) = 1$ and $f(5) = -3$.

Solution   If $f(3) = 1$, then when $x = 3$, $y = 1$. Similarly, if $f(5) = -3$, then when $x = 5$, $y = -3$. Thus, (3,1) and (5, −3) are points on the graph. First, calculate the slope.

$$m = \frac{y_2 - y_1}{x_2 - x_1} = \frac{-3 - 1}{5 - 3} = \frac{-4}{2} = -2$$

Now use the point-slope equation with one of the points, say (3,1), as follows.

$$
\begin{aligned}
y - y_1 &= m(x - x_1) \quad \text{Point-slope equation} \\
y - 1 &= -2(x - 3) \\
y - 1 &= -2x + 6 \\
y &= -2x + 7
\end{aligned}
$$

The equation that defines the function f is

$$f(x) = -2x + 7.$$

PROGRESS CHECK 5 Find the equation that defines the linear function f if $f(2) = 7$ and $f(4) = -1$. ■

An application of linear functions is illustrated by the section-opening problem.

Example 6   Maximum Target Heart Rate
Solve the problem in the section introduction on page 136.

Solution

a. Heart rate is a function of age, so let y represent the maximum target heart rate and x represent the person's age. Then we are asked to find the equation for the linear function f such that $(40,153)$ and $(60,136)$ belong to f. As in Example 5, first find the slope.

$$m = \frac{y_2 - y_1}{x_2 - x_1} = \frac{136 - 153}{60 - 40} = \frac{-17}{20} = -0.85$$

Now using one of the points, say $(40,153)$, and the point-slope equation gives

$$\begin{aligned} y - y_1 &= m(x - x_1) \qquad \text{Point-slope equation} \\ y - 153 &= -0.85(x - 40) \\ y - 153 &= -0.85x + 34 \\ y &= -0.85x + 187. \end{aligned}$$

The equation that defines the linear function f is

$$f(x) = -0.85x + 187.$$

b. When $x = 18$,

$$\begin{aligned} f(18) &= -0.85(18) + 187 \\ &= 171.7. \end{aligned}$$

Thus, the maximum target heart rate for an 18-year-old is about 172 beats per minute.

PROGRESS CHECK 6 During exercise a person's minimum target heart rate to have a training effect is a function of age. This relation is specified by a linear function, and the recommended minimum number of beats per minute is 126 at age 40 and 112 at age 60. (a) Find the equation that defines this linear function. (b) What is the minimum target heart rate for a 19-year-old? ■

In some applications it is important to be able to recognize a linear relationship from a table of data. Because a linear function is characterized by a rate of change that is constant, we can spot an exact linear relationship as follows: **In any table of a linear function $y = f(x)$, a fixed change in x produces a constant difference between the corresponding y-values**.

EXAMPLE 7   Recognizing a Linear Relation Numerically
The monthly cost y for x hours of usage of an "online" computer service company is shown in the following table.

Time (in hours) x	1	2	3	4	5
Cost (in dollars) y	14.75	19.55	24.35	29.15	33.95

Is y a linear function of x? If yes, find an equation that relates x and y.

Solution   As x increases by 1, observe that each y-value after the first may be found by adding 4.80 to the previous y-value, as shown below.

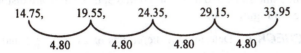

Therefore, a fixed change in x of 1 produces a constant difference of 4.80 between the corresponding y-values, so the relation is linear.

To find an equation for this relation, first observe that

$$\frac{\text{Change in } y}{\text{Change in } x} = \frac{4.80}{1} = 4.80,$$

so the slope is 4.8. Then, using the point-slope equation with one of the points, say $(1, 14.75)$, yields

$$y - y_1 = m(x - x_1)$$
$$y - 14.75 = 4.8(x - 1)$$
$$y - 14.75 = 4.8x - 4.8$$
$$y = 4.8x + 9.95$$

The relation is defined by $y = 4.8x + 9.95$, which means the company charges \$4.80 an hour on top of a \$9.95 monthly membership fee.

PROGRESS CHECK 7   An accountant creates a depreciation schedule for a purchase of office equipment, as shown below. Book values are in dollars and state the value at the beginning of the year given.

Year (x)	1	2	3	4	5
Book value (y)	20,000	12,000	7,200	4,320	2,592

Is y a linear function of x? If yes, find an equation that relates x and y.   ■

Parallel and Perpendicular Lines
The slope-intercept form of the equation of a line provides a technique for solving problems that deal with parallel and perpendicular lines. Several such problems are illustrated next.

EXAMPLE 8   Are Two Lines Parallel and Distinct?
Determine if the graphs of $x + 2y = 3$ and $2x + 4y = 5$ are distinct parallel lines.

Solution   Two distinct lines are parallel if they have the same slope but different y-intercepts. Therefore, we begin by expressing the equations in slope-intercept form in order to determine the slope and the y-intercept.

$$x + 2y = 1 \qquad\qquad 2x + 4y = 5$$
$$2y = -x + 1 \qquad\qquad 4y = -2x + 5$$
$$y = -\tfrac{1}{2}x + \tfrac{1}{2} \qquad\qquad y = -\tfrac{2}{4}x + \tfrac{5}{4}$$
$$\qquad\qquad\qquad\qquad y = -\tfrac{1}{2}x + \tfrac{5}{4}$$

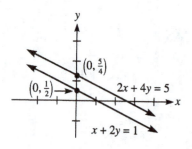

Figure 2.80

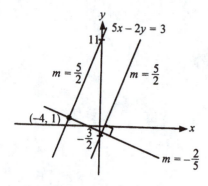

Figure 2.81

From these equations we get the following results.

Slope: $-\frac{1}{2}$ Slope: $-\frac{1}{2}$

y-intercept: $\left(0, \frac{1}{2}\right)$ y-intercept: $\left(0, \frac{5}{4}\right)$

The lines have the same slope and different y-intercepts, so they are distinct parallel lines. They are sketched in Figure 2.80.

PROGRESS CHECK 8   Determine if the graphs of $2x + y = 1$ and $2x + y = 3$ are distinct parallel lines.
■

EXAMPLE 9   Finding Equations of Parallel or Perpendicular Lines

Find an equation for the line passing through the point $(-4, 1)$ that is

a. parallel to $5x - 2y = 3$
b. perpendicular to $5x - 2y = 3$.

Solution   See Figure 2.81

a. First, find the slope of the given line by changing the equation to the form $y = mx + b$.

$$5x - 2y = 3$$
$$-2y = -5x + 3$$
$$y = \frac{5}{2}x - \frac{3}{2}$$

By inspection, the slope of this line is 5/2. Since the slopes of parallel lines are equal, we want an equation for the line through $(-4, 1)$ with slope 5/2. Using the point-slope equation, we have

$$y - 1 = \frac{5}{2}(x - (-4))$$

$$y = \frac{5}{2}x + 11.$$

b. As shown in part **a**, the slope of $5x - 2y = 3$ is 5/2. It follows from statement 2 that the slope m of every line perpendicular to the given line must satisfy $\left(5/2\right)m = -1$, so $m = -2/5$. Then we find an equation for the line through $(-4, 1)$ with slope $-2/5$ as follows:

$$y - y_1 = m(x - x_1)$$
$$y - 1 = -\frac{2}{5}(x - (-4))$$
$$y = -\frac{2}{5}x - \frac{3}{5}.$$

Technology Link
To check visually that lines are perpendicular on a grapher, it is necessary to use the Square Setting feature to correct the built-in angular distortion present in the standard display. For instance, Figure 2.82 shows a graphical check of the solution in part **b** using both Zoom Standard and Zoom Square. Observe that the lines appear to be perpendicular only when the Square Setting feature was used.

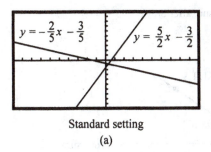
Standard setting
(a)

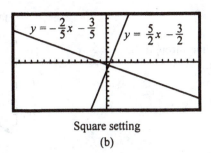
Square setting
(b)

Figure 2.82

PROGRESS CHECK 9   Find an equation for the line through the point $(3, 4)$ that is

a. parallel to $x - 2y = 1$ and
b. perpendicular to $x - 2y = 1$.   ■

EXERCISES 2.8

In Exercises 1–6 find an equation for the line that has the given slope m and passes through the given point.

1. $m = 5; (4, 3)$ **2.** $m = -4; (2, -1)$

3. $m = \dfrac{1}{2}; (-2, 0)$ **4.** $m = -\dfrac{3}{4}; (-5, 2)$

5. $m = -\dfrac{1}{2}; (0, 0)$ **6.** $m = 0; (1, 2)$

In Exercises 7–10 find an equation for the line that contains the given points.

7. $(3, 2)$ and $(4, 1)$ **8.** $(-4, 3)$ and $(-2, 5)$

9. $(-3, -3)$ and $(-4, -2)$ **10.** $(2, -3)$ and $(3, -3)$

In Exercises 11–20 find the slope and the y-intercept of the line determined by the following equations.

11. $y = x + 7$ **12.** $y = -\dfrac{2}{3}x - 5$

13. $y = 5x$ **14.** $y = -x$

15. $y = -2$ **16.** $y = 0$

17. $3y + 2x = -2$ **18.** $3x + 5y = 2$

19. $6x - y = -7$ **20.** $2x - 7y = -4$

In Exercises 21–26, (a) write the equation of the line in slope-intercept form, and (b) graph the line.

21. The slope is $-\frac{1}{2}$ and the y-intercept is $(0, 1)$.

22. The slope is $\frac{3}{4}$ and the y-intercept is $(0, -3)$.

23. The slope is 6 and the y-intercept is $\left(0, \frac{1}{2}\right)$.

24. The slope is -2 and the y-intercept is $\left(0, -\frac{3}{5}\right)$.

25. The slope is 0 and the y-intercept is $(0, -2)$.

26. The slope is 0 and the y-intercept is $\left(0, \frac{1}{3}\right)$.

In Exercises 27–30 find the equation that defines the function if f is a linear function

27. $f(3) = 0$ and $f(0) = -2$
28. $f(0) = -1$ and $f(2) = 0$
29. $f(-1) = -3$ and $f(2) = -7$
30. $f(-6) = -1$ and $f(-2) = -5$

In Exercises 31 and 32 determine the given function value; f is a linear function.

31. $f(3) = 1$ and $f(5) = -3$; find $f(4)$.
32. $f(-2) = 0$ and $f(1) = 6$; find $f(0)$.

In Exercises 33–38, determine if the two lines are distinct parallel lines.

33. $3x + y = -2; 6x + 2y = 4$
34. $2x - y = 1; 6x - 3y = -3$
35. $2x + 3y = 4; 4x + 6y = 8$
36. $x - 2y = 1; 2x - 4y = 2$

37. $x = 1; x = 4$
38. $y = -3; y = 2$

In Exercises 39–46, find an equation for the line through the given point which satisfies the stated condition.

39. Through (1, 2) parallel to $x + 3y = 4$
40. Through (3, 0) parallel to $2x - 3y = 1$
41. Through (3,2) parallel to $x = 1$
42. Through (5,3) parallel to $y = 0$
43. Through (1,3) perpendicular to $3x + 2y = 5$
44. Through $(-3, -2)$ perpendicular to $4x - y = 1$
45. Through (1,3) perpendicular to $y = 2$
46. Through $(-4, -2)$ perpendicular to $x = -3$

In Exercises 47–50 find an equation for the line passing through the given point that is
  a. parallel to the given line
  b. perpendicular to the given line

47. $y = x - 2$; (1,2)
48. $y = 3x + 1$; $(-2, -1)$
49. $x + 7y = 2$; (0, 0)
50. $3x - 2y = 5$; $(0, -5)$
51. As part of a 10-year medical research project, a statistician noted that the cholesterol level of subjects tended to go up over the 10-year period. Those who started with a level at about 180 went up to 251. Those who started at about 200 went up to 263.
  a. The relationship between the beginning level and the level 10 years later was graphed as a line, as shown in the figure. Write the equation of this line in the form $y = mx + b$.
  b. What level does this equation predict for someone whose original level is 220?

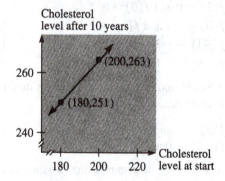

52. In a medical study a drug was found to lower patients' diastolic blood pressure in a way that could be graphed as a line. On average, the drug reduced a pressure of 96 to 87, and a pressure of 111 to 97, as shown in the figure.
  a. Write an equation in slope-intercept form for the line shown.
  b. Use the equation to predict, to the nearest unit, the diastolic blood pressure for someone whose pressure is 100 before using the drug.

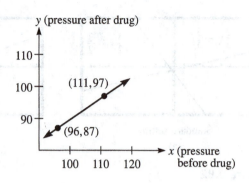

53. A moving company charges $46 to move a certain machine 10 mi, and $58 to move the same machine 30 mi.
  a. Find an equation that defines this relationship if it is linear.
  b. What will it cost to move the machine 25 mi?
  c. What is the minimum charge for moving the machine?
  d. What is the rate for each mile the machine is moved?
54. The total cost of producing a certain item consists of paying rent for the building and paying a fixed amount per unit for material. The total cost is $250 if 10 units are produced and $330 if 30 units are produced.
  a. Find an equation that defines this relationship if it is linear.
  b. What will it cost to produce 100 units?
  c. How much is paid in rent?
  d. What is the cost of the material for each unit?
55. A spring that is 24 in. long is compressed to 20 in. by a force of 16 lb and to 15 in. by a force of 36 lb.
  a. Find an equation that defines this relationship if it is linear.
  b. What is the length of the spring if a force of 28 lb is applied?
  c. How much force is needed to compress the spring to 10 in?
56. An office copier depreciates linearly in value from $11,000 to $1,000 in 8 years. Express this relationship with a function that expresses the value after t years have elapsed. To the nearest year, when does the value first fall below $5,000?

In Exercises 57–60 determine if the values shown in each table represent a linear relation. If so, express y as a function of x.

57.

x	1	2	3	4	5
y	12.1	12.8	13.5	14.2	14.9

58.

x	1	3	5	7	9
y	23	19	15	11	7

59.

x	0	6	9	14	15
y	6	18	24	34	36

60.

x	0	2	4	6	8
y	1	5	17	37	65

THINK ABOUT IT 2.8

1. Create a triangle from the intersection of three lines with positive slope such that the origin is inside the triangle. Write an equation for each of the three lines and display your solution graphically.
2. Suppose that the slope of a line equals the value where it crosses the y-axis. Find the x-intercept.
3. **a.** Find the slope of $3x + y = 1$.
   b. Find the slope of $3x + y = 2$.
   c. Find the slope of $3x + y = c$, where c is some real constant.
   d. Find the slope of $ax + by = c$.
   e. An equation is given that fits the form $ax + by = c$. True or false? If you change just the constant c, you get the equation of a line parallel to the original one.
4. If y is a linear function of x, is x also a linear function of y? Justify your conclusion algebraically.
5. The following figure shows five lines whose equations are as follows:
   a. $y = ax$
   b. $y = bx + c$
   c. $y = dx + e$
   d. $y = mx + k$
   e. $y = px + n$

If $d = n = 0, b = m,$ and $a < k < p$, then match each equation to the corresponding line.

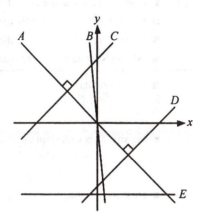

CHAPTER 2 OVERVIEW

Section	Key Concepts and Procedures to Review
2.1	■ Rule definitions of a function and its domain and range.
	■ Ordered-pair definitions of a relation and function and their domain and range.
2.2	■ Definition of the graph of a relation.
	■ General form of a linear equation in two variables: $Ax + By = C$
	■ Procedures for graphing a linear equation by plotting points and by using x- and y-intercepts
	■ The graph of $x = a$ is a vertical line containing $(a,0)$; the graph of $y = b$ is a horizontal line containing $(0,b)$.
	■ Graph of $y = mx + b$ is a straight line.
	■ Graph of $y = ax^2 + bx + c$ $(a \neq 0)$ is a parabola.
	■ Vertical line test
	■ Guidelines for graphing functions with a graphing calculator.
2.3	■ The statement "y varies directly as x" means that $y = kx$ (k is the variation constant).
	■ The statement "y varies inversely as x" means $xy = k$, or $y = k/x$.
2.4	■ The term $f(x)$ is read "f of x" or "f at x" and means the value of the function (the y value) corresponding to the value of x.
	■ If a is in the domain of f, then ordered pairs for the function defined by $y = f(x)$ all have the form $(a, f(a))$. **Note:** a is an x value and $f(a)$ is a y value.
	■ Definition of a piecewise function
	■ Methods to construct, evaluate, and graph a piecewise function
2.5	■ Graphs of the squaring function $(y = x^2)$, square root function $\left(y = \sqrt{x}\right)$, and absolute value function $(y = |x|)$
	■ Methods to graph variations of a familiar function by using vertical and horizontal translations, reflecting, stretching, and flattening

2.6
- ■ Definition of absolute value
- ■ Methods to solve absolute value equations and inequalities
  - ■ If $|ax + b| = c$ and $c > 0$, then $ax + b = c$ or $ax + b = -c$.
  - ■ If $|ax + b| < c$ and $c > 0$, then $-c < ax + b < c$
  - ■ If $|ax + b| > c$ and $c > 0$, then $ax + b < -c$ or $ax + b > c$.
- ■ Methods for translating between absolute value inequalities and interval notation.

2.7
- ■ Slope formula:

$$m = \frac{\text{rise}}{\text{run}} = \frac{\text{change in } y}{\text{change in } x} = \frac{y_2 - y_1}{x_2 - x_1} \quad (x_2 \neq x_1)$$

- ■ For two lines with slopes m_1 and m_2:

parallel lines: $m_1 = m_2$

perpendicular lines: $m_1 m_2 = -1$

- ■ Distance formula:

$$d = \sqrt{(x_2 - x_1)^2 + (y_2 - y_1)^2}$$

2.8
- ■ Definition of linear function
- ■ Point-slope equation: $y - y_1 = m(x - x_1)$
- ■ Slope-intercept equation: $y = mx + b$
- ■ For two lines with slopes m_1 and m_2:

parallel lines: $m_1 = m_2$

perpendicular lines: $m_1 \cdot m_2 = -1$

- ■ In a table of a linear function $y = f(x)$, a fixed change in x produces a constant difference between the corresponding y-value.

CHAPTER 2 REVIEW EXERCISES

1. Determine if the ordered pair $(2, -1)$ is a solution of the equation $-4x - y = -9$.
2. Graph the ordered pair $(1, -3)$, and indicate its quadrant location.
3. Graph the equation $y = 2x - 1$.
4. Graph $-x + y = -4$ by using the x- and y-intercepts.
5. Graph $x = 2$.
6. Find the slope of the line through the points $(-2, 1)$ and $(4, 5)$.
7. Shipping costs (c) charged by a delivery service have a linear relationship with the weight (w) of the parcel. The charge is $1.98 for a 5-oz parcel and $2.23 for a 10-oz parcel. Calculate and interpret the slope of the line.
8. A quadrilateral has vertices at $A(0,2)$, $B(1,0)$, $C(-1, -1)$, and $D(-2, 1)$. Show that quadrilateral $ABCD$ is a rectangle.
9. Solve $|3x - 4| = 11$.
10. Solve $|5 - x| = |4x - 5|$.
11. Find the domain and range of the relation $\{(2, 3), (10, 3), (21, 7), (70, 4)\}$.
12. Determine if the given relation is a function: $\{(2, 3), (10, 3), (21, 7), (70, 4)\}$.

13. Does the graph below represent a function?

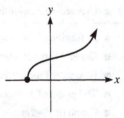

14. Determine the domain and range of the following function.

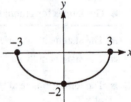

15. **a.** Write an equation to express the cost C before tax of n books if the books cost $35 each.
    b. What is the domain of the function?

16. If $f(x) = 2x^2 + 3x - 4$, find $f(0)$ and $f(-2)$.

17. If $g(x) = x^2 - 1$ and $h(x) = 2x$, find $2g(-1) - 3h(2)$.

18. If $f(x) = \begin{cases} -1 \text{ if } x < 1 \\ \ \ x \text{ if } x \geq 1, \end{cases}$ find the following.

    a. $f(3)$

    b. $f(1)$

    c. $f(-1)$

    d. Graph the function.

19. Consider the graph of $y = f(x)$ that is shown.

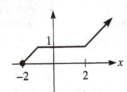

    a. What is the domain of f?

    b. What is the range of f?

    c. Determine $f(0)$.

    d. For what values of x does $f(x) = 0$?

    e. For what values of x is $f(x) < 0$?

    f. Solve $f(x) > 0$.

20. If $f(x) = 3x$, show that $f(a + b)$ does equal $f(a) + f(b)$ for all a and b.

21. Use the graph of $y = |x|$ to graph $y = |x| - 2$.

22. Use the graph of $y = x^2$ to graph $y = (x + 1)^2$.

23. Use the graph of $y = |x|$ to graph $y = -2|x|$.

24. Graph $y = 2 - \sqrt{x - 1}$ using the graph of $y = \sqrt{x}$.

25. If a stone is dropped from a bridge at a point that is 384 ft above water, then $y = -16t^2 + 384$ gives the height y above water in feet after t seconds have elapsed.

    a. To the nearest tenth of a second, when does the stone hit the water? Use a grapher.

    b. What is the domain of the function?

    c. Graph this function.

26. Graph $f(x) = -4$.

27. Graph $f(x) = \frac{3}{2}x - 1$ using the slope and y-intercept of the graph.

28. Find the equation that defines the linear function f if $f(2) = -1$ and $f(4) = -7$.

29. Consider the function defined by $f(x) = x^2 - 4x + 3$.

    a. Find the coordinates of the y-intercept.

    b. Graph the function and specify the range using this graph.

30. Find the distance between the points $(4,7)$ and $(3, -2)$

31. Find an equation in general form of the line through $(-1, 3)$ with slope 2.

32. Find an equation for the line through the points $(3,2)$ and $(-1, -1)$. Answer in the form $y = ax + b$.

33. Find the slope and y-intercept of the line defined by the equation $-2x - y = 1$.

34. Find the slope-intercept form of the equation of a line whose slope is -1 and whose y-intercept is $\frac{1}{2}$. Graph the line.

35. Find the equation of the line in slope-intercept form through $(0,5)$ that is parallel to $4x - 6y = 18$.

36. If y varies directly as x, and $y = 2$ when $x = 7$, find y when $x = -21$.

37. If y varies inversely as x, and $y = 4$ when $x = 50$, find y when $x = 5$.

38. Suppose that M varies jointly as a and b and inversely as c^2, and that $M = 20$ when $a = 5$, $b = 8$, and $c = 2$. Find M when $a = 4$, $b = 50$, and $c = 5$.

39. The weekly earnings of a part-time employee vary directly as the number of hours worked. For an employee who makes \$112.50 for 15 hours of work, what are the earnings for 19 hours of work?

40. Determine if $(-4, -5)$ is a solution of $y = -\frac{1}{2}x - 7$.

41. Are the lines $-2x - 3y = 4$ and $4x + 6y = -8$ parallel, perpendicular, or the same line?

42. If y varies inversely as x, and $x = 12$ when $y = 4$, find y when $x = 16$.

43. If y varies directly as x, and $y = \frac{1}{2}$ when $x = 3$, find y when $x = 24$.

44. Suppose that A varies directly as B^2 and inversely as C, and that $A = 2$ when $B = 1$ and $C = 3$. Find A when $B = 3$ and $C = 6$.

45. Find the slope and y-intercept of the line $x + 4y = 0$.

46. Show that the points $A(0,0)$, $B(2,3)$, and $C(6, -4)$ are the vertices of a right triangle.

47. A quadrilateral has vertices $A(0,2)$, $B(12,6)$, $C(14,0)$, and $D(2, -4)$. Show that quadrilateral $ABCD$ is a rectangle.

48. A car rents for \$70 a week plus 15¢ per mile.

    a. Write an equation for the weekly cost C. Let m represent the weekly mileage.

    b. Graph the equation.

49. A gasoline pump can fill a 15-gal tank in 3 minutes. Assume the relationship between gallons and time can be represented by a line through the origin. Calculate and interpret the slope of the line.

50. The weight (w) of a solid cube varies directly as the cube of an edge (e). If a cube with edge 8 in. weighs 10 lb, what will a cube with edge 7 in. made of the same material weigh? Round to the nearest tenth of a pound.

51. Solve $|x - 3| = 4$. Use both an algebraic and a geometric interpretation.

52. Solve $|x - 4| \leq 1$. Use both an algebraic and a geometric interpretation.

53. Solve $|2 + 3x| \geq 1$. Express the solution set graphically and in interval notation.

54. Fill in the missing component in each of the following ordered pairs so they are solutions of the equation $y = -2x + 4$: $(0, \ )$, $(\ , -1)$, $(-1, \ )$, $(\ , 0)$, $(3, \ )$.

Determine the domain and range of each function.

55. $\{(9, 95), (8, 85), (6, 65), (7, 75)\}$

56. $y = \sqrt{x + 6}$

57. $y = \dfrac{1}{x - 1}$

Find the equation of each line. Express it in slope-intercept form.

58. With slope $\frac{1}{2}$ and y-intercept 1

59. Through $(6,1)$ and $(0,2)$

60. Through $(4, -3)$ with slope 1

61. Through $(0,0)$, perpendicular to $4x - 4y = 7$

62. Through $(1,1)$, parallel to $4x - 4y = 7$

63. The relationship between the number of heating degree-days in a month and the average number of kilowatt-hours of electricity billed by a utility company for that month is approximately linear and is well illustrated by the line shown in the graph.

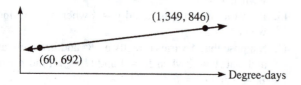

(1,349, 846)

(60, 692)

→ Degree-days

  a. Write the equation of this line in the form
  $y = mx + b$. To maintain accuracy over such a
  large domain, compute the slope to five decimal
  places, and round the intercept to two decimal
  places.

  b. To the nearest integer, what kilowatt-hour billing
  corresponds to 800 degree-days?

64. Write a formula that expresses the area of a square as a function of the diagonal. (*Hint*: Use the following drawing and the Pythagorean theorem.)

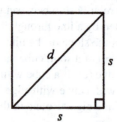

d

s

s

In Exercises 65–76 select the choice that answers the question or completes the statement.

65. The graph of $y = f(x) - 3$ is the graph of $y = f(x)$ shifted 3 units
  a. up   **b.** down
  c. left   **d.** right

66. If $f(x) = 5x^2$, then the difference quotient
$$\frac{f(x + h) - f(x)}{h}$$
with $h \neq 0$ in simplest form is
  a. $10x + 5h$ **b.** $5h$
  c. 1 **d.** $10xh + 5h$

67. The area of a circle whose radius extends from $(-2, 5)$ to $(5, 1)$ is
  a. 11π **b.** 25π
  c. 45π **d.** 65π

68. If y varies inversely with x, then when x is doubled y is
  a. decreased by 2   **b.** increased by 2
  c. multiplied by 2   **d.** divided by 2

69. If $(a, -1)$ is a solution of $y = -4x + 5$, then a equals
  a. 9   **b.** $\frac{3}{2}$
  c. $-\frac{2}{3}$ **d.** -1

70. If $f(1) = 6$ and $f(-1) = 2$, and f is a linear function, then $f(7)$ equals
  a. 11   **b.** 9
  c. 14   **d.** 18

71. If $f(x) = 2x$, then which one of the following is true?
  a. $f(-a) = -f(a)$ **b.** $f(-a) = f(a)$

  c. $f(ab) = f(a) \cdot f(b)$ **d.** $f\!\left(\dfrac{a}{b}\right) = \dfrac{f(a)}{f(b)}$

72. The equation of the line that passes through the point $(-3, 1)$ and is perpendicular to $y = \frac{1}{2}x + 4$ is
  a. $y = \frac{1}{2}x - \frac{1}{4}$ **b.** $y = \frac{1}{2}x + \frac{5}{2}$
  c. $y = 2x + 7$ **d.** $y = -2x - 5$

73. The slope of the line $3x - 2y = 6$ is
  a. 3   **b.** -3
  c. $\frac{3}{2}$ **d.** $-\frac{3}{2}$

74. Which number is not in the domain of $y = \dfrac{x + 2}{x + 3}$?
  a. 2   **b.** -2
  c. -3 **d.** 3

75. If $f(x) = 2x + b$ and $f(-2) = 3$, then b equals
  a. 7   **b.** -1
  c. 1   **d.** -8

76. If a square field is completely enclosed by x feet of fencing, then the area of the field as a function of x equals
  a. x^2 **b.** $\dfrac{x^2}{4}$

  c. $4x^2$ **d.** $\dfrac{x^2}{16}$

CHAPTER 2 TEST

1. Find the distance between the points $(-5, 1)$ and $(3, 7)$.
2. Write the equation of the line through $(2, 0)$ and $(0, -1)$ in slope-intercept form.
3. Find the slope and y-intercept of the line $-5x + 10y = 15$.
4. If y varies inversely as x, and $y = 12$ when $x = -2$, find y when $x = 6$.
5. A printing shop charges $25 for 100 invitations and $30 for 150. If the relation between the number of invitations (x) and the cost (y) graphs as a line, calculate and interpret the slope.
6. Determine whether the lines $4x + y = 1$ and $16x + 4y = -1$ are parallel, perpendicular, or the same line.
7. Graph $y = -2x - 1$
8. Graph $x - 2y = 3$
9. Determine if the given relation is a function: $\{(-3, 4), (-3, 5), (-2, 2)\}$.
10. Determine the domain and range of the function
$$y = \frac{2}{x + 4}$$
11. Express the length ℓ of a rectangle with width 6 cm as a function of its perimeter P.
12. If $f(x) = -x^2 + x - 1$ and $g(x) = x + 1$, find $3g(2) - f(-2)$.
13. If $y = f(x) = \begin{cases} -x & \text{if } x \le 0 \\ 2 & \text{if } x > 0, \end{cases}$ find the following.
    a. $f(-3)$
    b. $f(0)$
    c. $f(3)$
    d. Graph the function.

14. Consider the graph of $y = f(x)$ shown below.
    a. What is the domain of f?
    b. What is the range of f?
    c. For what values of x does $f(x) = 0$?
    d. For what values of x is $f(x) < 0$?
    e. Solve $f(x) > 0$.

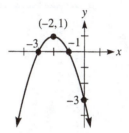

15. Use the graph of $y = x^2$ to graph $y = (x - 1)^2 + 2$. Identify the vertex and y-intercept of the graph.
16. Graph $y = 2 - \sqrt{x}$ using the graph of $y = \sqrt{x}$.
17. Solve $|-3x - 11| = 2$
18. Solve $|x + 6| < 9$. Express the solution set graphically and in interval notation.
19. A taxi ride costs $2 plus $0.50 per mile traveled.
    a. Write an equation for the cost C. Let n represent the number of miles.
    b. Graph the equation with n as the horizontal axis.
20. The distance d needed to stop a car after applying the brakes varies directly as the square of the speed r at which the car is traveling. If a car traveling 30 mi/hour needs 100 ft to stop, in how many feet will a car traveling 60 mi/hour be able to stop?

CHAPTER 3

Systems of Linear Equations

A company is trying to decide between two machines for packaging its new product. Machine A will cost $6,000 per year plus $2 to package each unit, so the total cost (y) of packaging x units annually is given by $y = 2x + 6{,}000$. Machine B will cost $4,000 per year plus $3 to package each unit, so $y = 3x + 4{,}000$ is the cost equation associated with this machine. How many units must be produced annually for the cost of the two machines to be the same? If the company plans to package more units than this, which machine should it purchase? (See Example 1 of Section 3.1.)

THE COMPANY described in the chapter-opening problem must take into account two linear equations in two variables to make its decision. The pair of equations in this problem,

$$y = 2x + 6{,}000 \quad \text{and} \quad y = 3x + 4{,}000,$$

is an example of a **linear system of equations**. Here are some other examples of linear systems.

$$\begin{array}{ccc} x + y = 9 & c = 1{,}000 + 5n & y = -3x + 1 \\ 5x - y = -3, & c = 4{,}000 + 3n, & x = 2. \end{array} \quad \text{and}$$

Note that the pair of equations in the system must contain the same variables and that an equation like $x = 2$ may be written as $x + 0y = 2$ when expressed as a linear equation in two variables. This chapter considers several methods for solving linear systems in two and in three variables and applies these methods to analyze a wide variety of problems.

3.1   Systems of Linear Equations in Two Variables

OBJECTIVES

1   Determine whether an ordered pair is a solution to a system of linear equations.

2   Solve a system of linear equations graphically.

3   Solve a system of linear equations by the addition-elimination method.

4   Solve a system of linear equations by the substitution method.

5   Use systems of linear equations to solve applied problems.

6   Solve linear equations and linear inequalities in one variable graphically.

To understand the meaning of the solution of a system of linear equations, we begin by analyzing the chapter-opening problem, using a graphing approach.

EXAMPLE 1   Comparing Two Cost Functions

Solve the problem in the chapter introduction on page 151.

Solution   A cost comparison between the two machines can be made by constructing the following tables and then graphing the two lines on the same coordinate system, as shown in Figure 3.1.

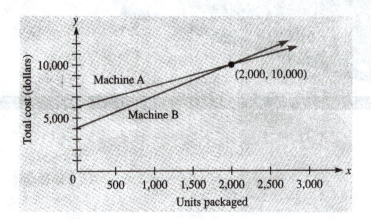

Figure 3.1

Machine A: $y = 2x + 6{,}000$		Machine B: $y = 3x + 4{,}000$	
Units Packaged x	Cost (Dollars) y	Units Packaged x	Cost (Dollars) y
500	7,000	500	5,500
1,000	8,000	1,000	7,000
1,500	9,000	1,500	8,500
2,000	10,000	2,000	10,000
2,500	11,000	2,500	11,500

From the graph and the table we see that if 2,000 units are packaged annually, then both machines A and B have the same cost, which is $10,000. If the company plans to package more than 2,000 units, the graph shows that it should purchase machine A, since the y values are lower on the line associated with A beyond the intersection point.

PROGRESS CHECK 1   Redo the problem in Example 1, but assume that machine B will cost \$7,000 per year plus \$1 to package each unit, so $y = x + 7,000$ is the cost associated with this machine.   ■

Note in Example 1 that there are many ordered pairs that satisfy $y = 2x + 6,000$ and many ordered pairs that satisfy $y = 3x + 4,000$, but there is only one ordered pair that satisfies both equations. In general, the **solution of a system of linear equations** consists of all ordered pairs that satisfy both equations at the same time (simultaneously).

The next example shows how to determine whether a given ordered pair is a solution of a system.

EXAMPLE 2   Testing for Ordered Pair Solutions

Determine if the given ordered pairs are solutions of the system

$$x + y = 25$$
$$6x - y = 3.$$

a. $(4,21)$ **b.** $(10,15)$

Solution

a. $(4,21)$ means $x = 4$, $y = 21$. Replace x by 4 and y by 21 in each equation.

$$
\begin{array}{ll}
x + y = 25 & 6x - y = 3 \\
4 + 21 \stackrel{?}{=} 25 & 6(4) - 21 \stackrel{?}{=} 3 \\
\quad 25 = 25 \;\; \text{True} & \quad 3 = 3 \;\; \text{True}
\end{array}
$$

$(4,21)$ is a solution of the system because it satisfies both equations.

b. To check $(10,15)$, replace x by 10 and y by 15 in each equation.

$$
\begin{array}{ll}
x + y = 25 & 6x - y = 3 \\
10 + 15 \stackrel{?}{=} 25 & 6(10) - 15 \stackrel{?}{=} 3 \\
\quad 25 = 25 \;\; \text{True} & \quad 45 = 3 \;\; \text{False}
\end{array}
$$

Because $(10,15)$ is not a solution of $6x - y = 3$, it is not a solution of the system.

PROGRESS CHECK 2   Determine if the given ordered pairs are solutions of the system

$$5x + 2y = 11$$
$$x + 2y = -1.$$

a. $(5,-7)$ **b.** $(3,-2)$ ■

Because the graph of a linear equation provides a picture of its solutions, we can find all common solutions to a pair of linear equations by drawing their graphs on the same coordinate system. The solution is given by all points where the lines intersect, and we specify the solution by giving the coordinates of such points.

There are three possible cases and they are represented in Figure 3.2.

Case 1   The equations represent two lines which intersect at one point and so have 1 point in common. This system is called **consistent**.

Case 2   The equations represent two distinct lines which are parallel and do not intersect at all and so have no points in common. This system is called **inconsistent**.

Consistent system

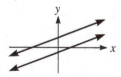

Inconsistent system

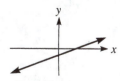

Dependent system

Figure 3.2

Case 3   Both equations represent the same line and so have all the points of that line in common. This system is called **dependent** (and consistent).

The most useful situation is usually when the graphs of the two equations intersect at exactly one point, as in our next example.

EXAMPLE 3   Solving a Linear System Graphically

Solve by graphing: $x + 2y = 4$
$$y = x + 5.$$

Solution $x + 2y = 4$ is a linear equation in general form that is easily graphed by finding intercepts. Letting $x = 0$ gives a y-intercept of $(0,2)$, and letting $y = 0$ gives an x-intercept of $(4,0)$. The equation $y = x + 5$ is in slope-intercept form and may be graphed by recognizing and using that the y-intercept is $(0,5)$ and the slope is 1.

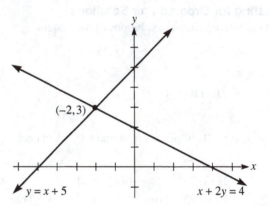

Figure 3.3

In Figure 3.3 we graph both of these equations on the same coordinate system, and it appears that the lines meet at $(-2,3)$. We check this apparent solution.

$$x + 2y = 4 \qquad\qquad y = x + 5$$
$$-2 + 2(3) \stackrel{?}{=} 4 \qquad\qquad 3 \stackrel{?}{=} -2 + 5$$
$$4 = 4 \quad \text{True} \qquad 3 = 3 \quad \text{True}$$

Thus, the solution is $(-2,3)$.

Technology Link

To obtain an approximate solution in this example using the graphing method and a graphing calculator, set $y1 = x + 5$ and $y2 = (4 - x)/2$. Then graph both equations in the standard viewing window and use the Trace feature to estimate the coordinates of the intersection point, as shown in Figure 3.4(a). Estimates obtained by this method may be improved as needed by repeated use of the Zoom and Trace features.

In addition, some calculators have a built-in operation that finds an intersection of two functions in an interval. For example, on one such calculator the Intersection operation may be utilized to display where two graphs intersect, as shown in Figure 3.4(b). We will use this feature throughout the text when simultaneous equations are displayed graphically, because this operation gives very accurate answers for x and y. But keep in mind that repeated use of Zoom and Trace is a workable alternative, if this special feature is not available on your calculator.

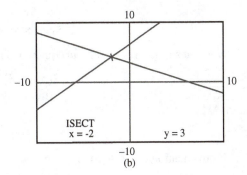

Figure 3.4

PROGRESS CHECK 3   Solve by graphing: $x + 2y = 6$
$$y = x + 6.$$ ■

The graphing method for solving simultaneous equations is good for illustrating the principle involved and for estimating the solution. However, for finding exact solutions, algebraic methods are usually preferable. When at least one equation in a linear system is solved for one of the variables, then the system may be solved efficiently by the **method of substitution**, as shown in the next example.

EXAMPLE 4   Solving a Linear System by Substitution
Solve by substitution: $y = 1,000 + 5x$
$$y = 4,000 + 3x.$$

Solution   Both equations are solved for y. We choose to substitute $1,000 + 5x$ for y in the bottom equation and solve for x.

$$1,000 + 5x = 4,000 + 3x$$
$$2x = 3,000$$
$$x = 1,500$$

Next, replace x by 1,500 in either equation that is solved for y.

$$y = 1,000 + 5x \qquad \text{or} \qquad y = 4,000 + 3x$$
$$y = 1,000 + 5(1,500) \qquad\qquad y = 4,000 + 3(1,500)$$
$$y = 8,500 \qquad\qquad\qquad y = 8,500$$

Thus, the solution is (1,500, 8,500).

PROGRESS CHECK 4   Solve by substitution: $y = 2,000 + 6x$
$$y = 9,000 + 2x.$$ ■

The substitution method also works well when at least one of the equations is easily solved for one of the variables. In this case, look to solve for a variable with a coefficient of 1 or -1.

EXAMPLE 5   Solving a Linear System by Substitution
Solve by substitution: $2x - 11y = 19$ (1)
$$5y = x - 8. \qquad (2)$$

Solution   We choose to solve for x in equation (2) because this choice leads to an equivalent equation that does not contain fractions.

$$5y = x - 8 \quad (2)$$
$$5y + 8 = x \quad (3)$$

Now substitute $5y + 8$ for x in equation (1) and solve for y.

$$2(5y + 8) - 11y = 19$$
$$10y + 16 - 11y = 19$$
$$-y = 3$$
$$y = -3$$

From equation (3), $x = 5y + 8$, so

$$x = 5(-3) + 8 = -7.$$

Use equations (1) and (2) to confirm that the solution is $(-7, -3)$.

PROGRESS CHECK 5   Solve by substitution: $4x = y - 21$
$$7x + 5y = -3.$$ ■

The substitution method of this section is summarized next.

Substitution Method Summary

To solve a linear system by substitution:

1. If necessary, solve for a variable in one of the equations. Avoid fractions if possible by solving for a variable with a coefficient of 1 or -1.
2. Use the result in step 1 to make a substitution in the *other* equation. The result is an equation with one unknown.
3. Solve the equation from step 2. A unique solution gives the value of one variable. If the equation is never true, the system is inconsistent. If the equation is always true, the system is dependent.
4. Use the known coordinate value to find the other coordinate value through substitution in the equation in step 1.
5. Check the solution in each of the original equations.

Another algebraic method for solving simultaneous equations is called the **addition-elimination method**. This method is based on the property that

$$\text{if } A = B$$
$$\text{and } C = D$$
$$\text{then } A + C = B + D$$

In words, adding equal quantities to equal quantities results in equal sums. For this method to result in the elimination of a variable, the coefficients of either x or y must be opposites, as in the system in Example 6.

EXAMPLE 6   Solving a Linear System by Addition-Elimination

Solve by addition-elimination: $5x + 2y = 4$
$$x - 2y = 8.$$

Solution   Because the coefficients of y are opposites, add the equations to eliminate this variable, and solve the resulting equation for x.

$$5x + 2y = 4$$
$$\underline{x - 2y = 8}$$
$$6x = 12 \quad \text{Add the equations.}$$
$$x = 2 \quad \text{Divide both sides by 6.}$$

The x-coordinate of the solution is 2. To find the y-coordinate, substitute 2 for x in either of the given equations.

$$
\begin{array}{ll}
5x + 2y = 4 \quad \text{or} & x - 2y = 8 \\
5(2) + 2y = 4 & 2 - 2y = 8 \\
2y = -6 & -2y = 6 \\
y = -3 & y = -3
\end{array}
$$

Thus, the solution is $(2, -3)$. Check this solution in the usual way.

Caution   When students solve a linear system of equations, a common error is to solve for only one variable and write answers like $x = 2$. Remember that it is important to find *both* coordinates of a solution.

PROGRESS CHECK 6   Solve by addition-elimination: $x - y = 6$
$2x + y = 9.$ ■

The equations in a linear system often need to be transformed using properties of equality so that adding on both sides will eliminate a variable. Such a solution is illustrated in Example 7.

EXAMPLE 7   Solving a Linear System by Addition-Elimination

Solve by addition-elimination: $6x + 10y = 7$ (1)
$15x - 4y = 3.$ (2)

Solution   If equivalent equations are formed by multiplying both sides of equation (1) by 5 and both sides of equation (2) by -2, then the x variable can be eliminated.

$$
\begin{array}{ll}
5(6x + 10y) = 5(7) \;\rightarrow\; 30x + 50y = 35 & (3) \\
-2(15x - 4y) = -2(3) \;\rightarrow\; \underline{-30x + 8y = -6} & (4) \\
\qquad\qquad\qquad\qquad\qquad 58y = 29 & \text{Add equations (3) and (4).} \\
\qquad\qquad\qquad\qquad\qquad y = \tfrac{29}{58}, \text{ or } \tfrac{1}{2} & \text{Divide both sides by 58.}
\end{array}
$$

To find x, replace y by $\tfrac{1}{2}$ in equation (1) or equation (2).

$$
\begin{array}{ll}
6x + 10y = 7 \quad \text{or} & 15x - 4y = 3 \\
6x + 10\left(\tfrac{1}{2}\right) = 7 & 15x - 4\left(\tfrac{1}{2}\right) = 3 \\
6x + 5 = 7 & 15x - 2 = 3 \\
6x = 2 & 15x = 5 \\
x = \tfrac{1}{3} & x = \tfrac{1}{3}
\end{array}
$$

The solution is $\left(\tfrac{1}{3}, \tfrac{1}{2}\right)$. Check it in the original equations (1) and (2).

Note   Sometimes the determined value for one of the solution coordinates is a fraction or a decimal that is awkward to use for finding the other coordinate. In such cases it may be easier to find the remaining coordinate value by returning to the original system of equations. For instance, in this example, after finding y, we may find x as follows.

$$2(6x + 10y) = 2(7) \rightarrow 12x + 20y = 14$$
$$5(15x - 4y) = 5(3) \rightarrow \underline{75x - 20y = 15}$$
$$87x \qquad = 29$$
$$x = \tfrac{29}{87}, \text{ or } \tfrac{1}{3}$$

PROGRESS CHECK 7   Solve by addition-elimination: $6x + 6y = 7$
$$8x - 9y = -2.$$ ■

Example 8 points out what happens when the addition-elimination method is applied to inconsistent systems and dependent systems.

EXAMPLE 8   An Inconsistent System and a Dependent System
Solve each system.

a. $2x + 4y = 3$ 　　　　　　　　　**b.** $\tfrac{1}{2}x - y = \tfrac{5}{2}$
　　$2x + 4y = 9$ 　　　　　　　　　　　　$-x + 2y = -5$

Solution

a. If the bottom equation is multiplied by -1 and added to the top equation, then both x and y are eliminated.

$$2x + 4y = 3$$
$$-1(2x + 4y) = 1(9) \rightarrow \underline{-2x - 4y = -9}$$
$$0 = -6 \quad \text{Add the equations.}$$

The false equation $0 = -6$ indicates that there is no solution and that the system is inconsistent. The solution set for every inconsistent system is $\emptyset$. Graphing these two equations as in Figure 3.5 reveals that they represent distinct parallel lines, which never intersect.

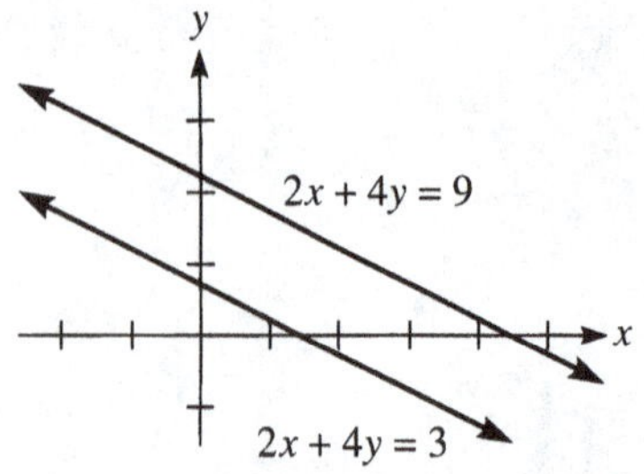

b. First, clear the top equation of fractions by multiplying both sides by 2. Then adding the equations in the resulting system eliminates both variables.

$$2\left(\tfrac{1}{2}x - y\right) = 2\left(\tfrac{5}{2}\right) \rightarrow \quad x - 2y = 5$$
$$\underline{-x + 2y = -5}$$
$$0 = 0 \quad \text{Add the equations.}$$

The equation $0 = 0$, which is always true, indicates that the system is dependent. Thus, the same line is the graph of both equations. Graphically, the solution set is the set of all points on that line, which may be specified by $\{(x, y): -x + 2y = -5\}$.

PROGRESS CHECK 8   Solve each system.

a. $-4x + y = -1$ 　　　　　　　**b.** $2x - 3y = 4$
　　$8x - 2y = 2$ 　　　　　　　　　　　$x - \tfrac{3}{2}y = 0$ ■

Use Examples 6–8 as a basis for understanding the summary that follows of the addition-elimination method of this section.

Figure 3.5

Addition-Elimination Method Summary

To solve a linear system by addition-elimination:
1. If necessary, write both equations in the form $ax + by = c$.
2. If necessary, multiply one or both equations by numbers that make the coefficients of either x or y opposites of each other. Add the two equations to eliminate a variable.
3. Solve the equation from step 2. A unique solution gives the value of one variable. If the equation is $0 = n$, where $n \neq 0$, the system is inconsistent. If the equation is $0 = 0$, the system is dependent.
4. Use the known coordinate value to find the other coordinate value through substitution in either of the original equations.
5. Check the solution in each of the original equations.

Many word problems that were solved in Chapter 1 using one variable are also readily solved using two variables and a system of linear equations. To illustrate, the next example reconsiders the problem in Example 4 of Section 1.6 and uses the addition-elimination method to solve the problem. Take the time to compare the solution methods in these two examples.

EXAMPLE 9   Managing Investments

How should a $160,000 investment be split so that the total annual earnings are $14,000 if one portion is invested at 6 percent annual interest and the rest at 11 percent?

Solution   To find the amount invested at each rate, let

$$x = \text{amount invested at 6 percent}$$

and

$$y = \text{amount invested at 11 percent.}$$

Use $I = Pr$ and analyze the investment in a chart format.

Investment	Principle	.	Rate	=	Interest
1st account	x		0.06		$0.06x$
2nd account	y		0.11		$0.11y$

The two principals add up to $160,000 and the sum of the interests is $14,000 so the required system is

$$x + y = 160{,}000 \qquad (1)$$
$$0.06x + 0.11y = 14{,}000 \qquad (2)$$

To solve this system, first multiply both sides of equation (2) by 100 to clear decimals.

$$x + y = 160{,}000 \qquad (1)$$
$$6x + 11y = 1{,}400{,}000 \qquad (3)$$

To eliminate x, we can multiply both sides of equation (1) by -6 and then add the result to equation (3).

$$-6x - 6y = -960,000$$
$$6x + 11y = 1,400,000$$
$$5y = 440,000 \quad \text{Add the equations.}$$
$$y = 88,000$$

To find x, substitute 88,000 for y in equation (1).

$$x + y = 160,000$$
$$x + 88,000 = 160,000$$
$$x = 72,000$$

Thus, the investment should be split so that $72,000 is invested at 6 percent and $88,000 is invested at 11 percent. Check this solution (as in Example 4 of Section 1.6).

PROGRESS CHECK 9 How should a $60,000 investment be split so that the total annual earnings are $6,000 if one portion is invested at 8.5 percent annual interest and the rest at 10.5 percent? ■

In the next problem two variables are defined in terms of each other. Thus, they have interlocking solutions that lead naturally to simultaneous equations.

EXAMPLE 10 Related Income Taxes

A corporation operates in a state that levies a 7 percent tax on the income that remains after paying the federal tax. Meanwhile, the federal tax is 28 percent of the income that remains after paying the state tax. If, during the current year, a corporation has $500,000 in taxable income, determine the state and federal income tax.

Solution Let s and f represent the state and federal income taxes, respectively, and write an equation for each in terms of the other.

State:	State tax	is	7 percent	of	income after federal deductions.	
	s	$=$	0.07	$\cdot$	$(500,000 - f)$	(1)
Federal:	Federal tax	is	28 percent	of	income after state deductions.	
	f	$=$	0.28	$\cdot$	$(500,000 - s)$	(2)

The resulting linear system with parentheses cleared is

$$s = 35,000 - 0.07f \quad (3)$$
$$f = 140,000 - 0.28s \quad (4)$$

Since the equations are solved for a variable, we choose to use the substitution method and replace f by $140,000 - 0.28s$ in equation (3).

$$s = 35,000 - 0.07(140,000 - 0.28s)$$
$$s = 35,000 - 9,800 + 0.0196s$$
$$0.9804s = 25,200$$
$$s = \frac{25,200}{0.9804} \approx 25,704$$

Then $f = 0.28(500,000 - s)$, so
$$f = 0.28(500,000 - 25,704) \approx 132,803.$$

Thus, to the nearest dollar, the state tax is $25,704 and the federal tax is $132,803.

Check $0.28(500,000 - 25,704) \approx 132,803$ and $0.07(500,000 - 132,803) \approx 25,704,$ so the solution checks.

PROGRESS CHECK 10   Redo the problem in Example 10, but assume that the state and federal income tax rates are 5 percent and 32 percent, respectively, and the corporation has \$800,000 in taxable income.   ■

The methods of this section may be used together with a graphing calculator to estimate solutions to linear equations and inequalities. This approach has the advantage of transforming questions about equations or inequalities to questions about graphs, which can then be answered (if only approximately) by looking at the calculator screen.

EXAMPLE 11   Solving Linear Equations and Inequalities Graphically

Solve each equation or inequality graphically. Approximate the solution to the nearest tenth.

a. $2(4 - x) = 3x - 6$ **b.** $2(4 - x) < 3x - 6$

Solution

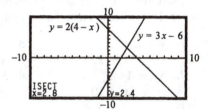

Figure 3.6

a. Solving $2(4 - x) = 3x - 6$ is equivalent to finding the x-coordinate of the point where the graphs of $y = 2(4 - x)$ and $y = 3x - 6$ intersect. We therefore begin by displaying the graphical solution of the system defined by these equations, as shown in Figure 3.6. We see "$x = 2.8$," and an algebraic check confirms that 2.8 is an exact solution. Thus, the solution set is $\{2.8\}$.
b. The graph of $y = 2(4 - x)$ lies **below** the graph of $y = 3x - 6$, to the right of the point of intersection. Thus, $2(4 - x) < 3x - 6$ is true provided $x > 2.8$. In interval notation the solution set is $(2.8, \infty)$.

PROGRESS CHECK 11   Solve each equation or inequality graphically. Approximate the solution to the nearest tenth.

a. $2x - 1 = -3(x + 1)$ **b.** $2x - 1 < -3(x + 1)$ ■

In this section we have shown several different methods for solving a linear system of equations. Keep in mind the following guidelines concerning the efficient use of each method.

Graphing   The graphing method is useful for *estimating* the solution and for *comparing* visually the linear equations in a system. When solving systems, we usually use it in conjunction with one of the algebraic methods.

Substitution   The substitution method is most efficient when at least one equation is solved for one of the variables. It is also a good choice when the system contains a variable with a coefficient of 1 or -1. We avoid this method when it leads to significant work with fractions.

Addition-Elimination   The addition-elimination method is usually the easiest when neither equation is solved for one of the variables. If you have trouble choosing, select this method.

EXERCISES 3.1

In Exercises 1–6, determine if the given ordered pairs are solutions of the system.

1. $x + y = 10$
$3x - 2y = 20$
a. $(8,2)$ **b.** $(7,3)$

2. $2x + 3y = 6$
$x - y = 3$
a. $(0,72)$ **b.** $(3,0)$

3. $\dfrac{x}{2} - \dfrac{y}{3} = 4$
$\dfrac{x}{3} + \dfrac{y}{3} = 1$
a. $(8,0)$ **b.** $(6, -3)$

4. $\dfrac{x}{4} + \dfrac{y}{6} = 1$
$3x = 2y$
a. $(2,3)$ **b.** $(4,0)$

5. $y = 3x + 1$
$y = -3x + 1$
a. $(1,4)$ **b.** $(0,1)$

6. $y = -x + 2$
$y = x - 2$
a. $(2,0)$ **b.** $(-2, 4)$

In Exercises 7–18, solve by graphing. Indicate whether the system is consistent, inconsistent, or dependent.

7. $y = x + 2$
$y = -x + 2$

8. $y = x + 3$
$y = -x + 3$

9. $5x = 4y$
$2y = 5x - 10$

10. $3y = x$
$y = x - 2$

11. $y = x + 2$
$2x + 3y = 1$

12. $x + 2y = 2$
$2x + y = -2$

13. $x = 5$
$y = -2$

14. $y = 2$
$x = -3$

15. $x + y = 3$
$x + y = 5$

16. $y = 3x + 2$
$y = 3x - 2$

17. $y = 2x + 1$
$2y - 4x = 2$

18. $2x + y = 5$
$2y = -4x + 10$

19. Which one of the figures would be used to graphically solve the system

$$2x + y = 4$$
$$3x - 5y = 45?$$

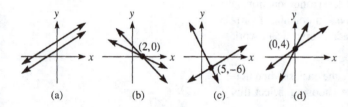

(a)   (b)   (c)   (d)

20. Describe the graph and the solution set of a system of linear equations in two variables for each type of system.
a. inconsistent system   **b.** dependent system

In Exercises 21–32, solve each system by the method of substitution.

21. $y = 500 + 2x$
$y = 600 + x$

22. $y = -1{,}000 + 10x$
$y = -2{,}000 + 15x$

23. $y = 30 - 5x$
$y = 50 + 20x$

24. $y = 100 - 5x$
$y = 10 + 20x$

25. $3x - 9y = 15$
$5y = x + 1$

26. $3x + 7y = 21$
$3y = x - 15$

27. $2y - x = 7$
$y + 3x = 10$

28. $3y + x = 4$
$y - 2x = 1$

29. $y = 2x - 1$
$y = 2x - 2$

30. $2y + x = 6$
$2y + x = 0$

31. $x = 3y - 1$
$6y - 2x = 2$

32. $6x + y = 8$
$3x = 4 - \frac{1}{2}y$

In Exercises 33–58, solve the system by using the addition-elimination method.

33. $4x + 3y = 7$
$x - 3y = 3$

34. $x - 2y = 1$
$x + 2y = 3$

35. $3x - 2y = 1$
$-3x + y = 3$

36. $2x - 2y = 1$
$-2x + y = 3$

37. $y = 3x + 5$
$y = 5 - 3x$

38. $y = 2x - 4$
$y = 4 - 2x$

39. $3x + 2y = 10$
$3x - 4y = 1$

40. $2x - 5y = 7$
$2x + 2y = 5$

41. $2x - 3y = 5$
$3x - 3y = 1$

42. $3x - 4y = 7$
$2x - 4y = -2$

43. $3x + 5y = 4$
$x - y = 1$

44. $5x + 2y = 3$
$2x - y = 1$

45. $x + 3y = 1$
$3x - 2y = 1$

46. $x - 4y = 4$
$2x - 2y = 1$

47. $2x + 3y = 5$
$3x + 2y = 5$

48. $3x - 4y = 1$
$4x - 3y = 1$

49. $2x + 3y = 5$
$3x + 5y = 7$

50. $3x + 4y = 10$
$4x + 4y = 9$

51. $2x + 5y = 3$
$5x + 7y = 11$

52. $2x - 3y = 4$
$5x + 2y = 1$

53. $3x + 2y = 1$
$-4x - 3y = 2$

54. $-2x + 5y = 3$
$3x - 7y = 4$

55. $2x + 5y = 7$
$4x + 10y = 6$

56. $-6x + 3y = 2$
$2x - y = 1$

57. $4x - 6y = 10$
$2x - 3y = 5$

58. $3x - 4y = 1$
$9x - 12y = 3$

In Exercises 59–64 solve each equation or inequality graphically. If necessary, approximate the solution to the nearest tenth.

59. a. $2x - 4 = 5x + 1$ **b.** $2x - 4 < 5x + 1$
60. a. $x = 1 - x$ **b.** $x > 1 - x$
61. a. $2(3 + x) = 6 + x$ **b.** $2(3 + x) \geq 6 + x$
62. a. $1 - 2x = 3 - 2x$ **b.** $1 - 2x \leq 3 - 2x$
63. a. $x = x + 2$ **b.** $x > x + 2$
64. a. $x + 1 = \dfrac{6x}{4} - \dfrac{x - 2}{2}$ **b.** $x + 1 < \dfrac{6x}{4} - \dfrac{x - 2}{2}$

In Exercises 65–100, solve the problem by setting up a system of two linear equations in two variables. Note carefully what each variable represents, and check that the solutions make sense. It may be helpful to refer to Section 1.6 for models of problems involving geometric figures, annual interest, uniform motion and liquid mixtures.

65. A $200,000 retirement fund was split into two investments, one portion (x) at 10 percent annual interest and the rest (y) at 6 percent. If the total annual interest is $18,000, how much was invested at each rate?

66. How should a $50,000 investment be split so that the total annual earnings are $5,000 if one portion is invested at 8.5 percent annual interest and the rest at 10.5 percent?

67. One year a couple had total income equal to $60,000 and their total tax bill came to $14,850. If the income from their salaries was taxed at 28 percent and the income from their investments was taxed at 15 percent, how much income did they have in each category?

68. A student borrowed a total of $6,200 one year to pay for tuition and other expenses. The tuition loan had an annual interest rate of 8 percent, and the other loan had an annual interest rate of 10 percent. The combined interest payments for the year came to $520. Find the amount of each loan.

69. A company gives a bonus to a division manager based on this principle: The bonus rate is 15 percent of the division's after-tax income. The tax meanwhile is 28 percent of the division's income after the bonus is paid. If the division's income is $400,000, to the nearest dollar what is the manager's bonus?

70. Redo Exercise 69, but assume that the income is cut in half to $200,000. Is the bonus half that found in Exercise 69?

71. A corporation operates in a state that levies a 4 percent tax on the income that remains after paying the federal tax. Meanwhile, the federal tax is 30 percent of the income that remains after paying the state tax. If, during the current year, a corporation has $1 million in taxable income, determine (to the nearest dollar) the state and federal income tax.

72. Redo Exercise 71, but assume that the state tax rate is 8 percent instead of 4. If, during the current year, a corporation has $1 million in taxable income, determine the state and federal income tax. Is the amount of the state tax double that found in Exercise 71?

73. On their joint income tax return, A's income was $\frac{1}{4}$ of B's income, and their total income was $47,500. Find each person's individual income.

74. Together, a newspaper and a magazine cost $5, and the magazine costs $2 more than the newspaper. What is the price of each? (Try guessing the answer first. Most people guess wrong.)

75. On a video display an air traffic controller notices two planes 90 mi apart and flying toward each other on a collision course. One plane is flying 500 mi/hour, and the other is flying 400 mi/hour. How much time is there for the controller to prevent a crash?

76. Two turtles are crawling toward each other in a straight line at constant speed. One goes at the rate of 2 ft in 10 minutes. The other moves 2.5 ft in 10 minutes. If they start 9 ft apart, how long will it take them to meet?

77. A machine shop has two large containers that are each filled with a mixture of oil and gasoline. Container A contains 2 percent oil (and 98 percent gasoline). Container B contains 5 percent oil (and 95 percent gasoline). How much of each should be used to obtain 6 gal of a new mixture that contains 3 percent oil?

78. A chemist has two acid solutions, one 30 percent acid and the other 20 percent acid. How much of each must be used to obtain 10 liters of a solution that is 22 percent acid?

79. A small company is trying to decide between two copy machines for the office. Machine A will cost $1,000 plus $0.04 per copy, while machine B will cost $4,000 plus $0.01 per copy. How many copies must be made for the cost to be the same? If they make 60,000 copies per year, about how long will it take before the costs are the same?

80. You are trying to decide between two positions as a salesperson. The first offer is a straight 15 percent commission, while the second offer pays a salary of $60 per week plus a 10 percent commission.
  a. Write a formula for each offer that expresses pay (y) as a function of sales (x).
  b. Sketch graphs of both functions on the same axes.
  c. How should you decide which offer is better financially?

81. Economists have made mathematical models which project production of various resources over time. For country A, the production index is given by $I = 1,000 + 60.5x$, where x is the number of years elapsed from the present. For country B, the index is given by $I = 1,120 + 58.1x$. According to these indexes, how many years will it take for country A to catch up to country B?

82. Refer to Exercise 81. Country C has a production index given by $I = 880 + 65.6x$. How long will it take country C to catch up to country B?

83. Find two numbers whose sum is 10 and whose difference is 15.

84. Find two numbers whose sum is $\frac{5}{8}$ and whose difference is $\frac{8}{5}$.

For Exercises 85–88, recall that the sum of two complementary angles is 90° and the sum of two supplementary angles is 180°.

85. Two angles are complementary. If the difference between the angle measures is 24°, find the angle measures.

86. Two angles are supplementary. If the difference between the angle measures is 54°, find the angle measures.

87. Two angles are complementary, and one is 4 times as large as the other. Find the smaller angle.

88. Two angles are supplementary, and one is $\frac{3}{5}$ the size of the other. Find the larger angle.

89. The length of a rectangle is 3 times the width, and the perimeter is 12 cm. Find the area.

90. The length of a rectangle is 4 times the width, and the perimeter is 12 cm. Find the area.

91. The perimeter of a rectangle is 22 in. and the length is 6 in. more than the width. Find the dimensions of the rectangle.

92. The perimeter of a rectangle is 22 in. and the width is $\frac{2}{3}$ the length. How much longer is the length than the width?

93. The total bill for a shopper who bought clothes and tools at a department store consisted of $180 in purchases and $9.20 in tax. The clothes were taxed at 4 percent and the tools at 6 percent. How much was spent on clothes (including tax)?

94. The total bill at a restaurant was $164.78, of which $7.78 was tax. The food was taxed at a 4 percent rate and the beverages at 10 percent. How much (including tax) was spent on food?

95. A shopper was offered a 20 percent discount on hardback books and a 10 percent discount on paperbacks. The regular price for the purchase was $254.70, on which the total discount was $40.44. How much did the shopper spend on each kind of book?

96. A ski shop discounts red-tag items by 30 percent and yellow-tag items by 20 percent. A shopper who bought only red- and yellow-tagged items got a total discount of $120 on a purchase, bringing the bill down to $305. After the discount, how much did the shopper spend in each category?

97. An airplane flying with the wind takes 48 minutes to fly 360 mi but 54 minutes to fly this distance against this wind. Find the wind speed and the speed of the plane with no wind. (*Hint:* 48 minutes = $\frac{48}{60}$ hour.)

98. Two friends paddle a canoe downstream a distance of 12 mi in 2 hours. Returning upstream, although they paddle at the same rate, takes them 3 hours. Find the speed of the current.

99. A child runs at her top speed for 0.1 mi the "wrong" way along a moving sidewalk in an airport. This takes 3 minutes. When she runs (also at top speed) the "right" way, it takes 1 minute. How fast is the sidewalk moving?

100. Redo Exercise 99 but with the speed of the sidewalk changed. It now takes the child 1.2 minutes running the right way and 2 minutes the wrong way. What is the speed of the moving sidewalk?

THINK ABOUT IT 3.1

1. **a.** When the equations in a system of two nonvertical lines are written in slope-intercept form, it is not difficult to classify the system as having exactly one solution, no solutions, or infinitely many solutions. How is this done?
   b. Find the number of solutions without solving the system.

$$4x - 2y = 5$$
$$y = 2x - 7$$

2. Find the forces F_1 and F_1 that achieve equilibrium for the beam in the following diagram.

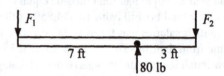

3. Create equations for a linear system in two variables that has a unique solution at (5,70) for each of the following cases:
   a. One line is horizontal and the other is vertical.
   b. One line is horizontal and the other is slanted.
   c. Both lines are slanted.

4. Create a verbal problem not considered in this section that may be solved by a system of linear equations in two variables. What is the solution to the problem you created?

5. In economics an analysis of the law of supply and demand involves the intersection of two curves. Basically, as the price for an item increases, the quantity of the product that is supplied increases while the quantity that is demanded decreases. The point at which the supply and demand curves intersect is called the **point of market equilibrium**. This principle is shown in the figure below where, for illustrative purposes, we assume the supply and demand equations to be linear.

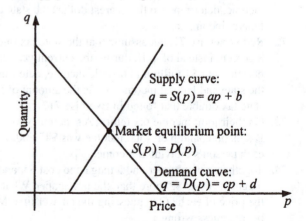

The equilibrium price is the value for p at which supply equals demand. Using the figure above, determine the equilibrium price (p) in terms of the constants a, b, c, and d.

3.2 Systems of Linear Equations in Three Variables

In electronics, applying Kirchhoff's laws to the circuit shown in the diagram yields the following system of equations.

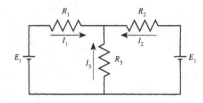

$$I_1 + I_2 + I_3 = 0$$
$$R_1 I_1 - R_3 I_3 = E_1$$
$$R_2 I_2 - R_3 I_3 = E_2$$

If $E_1 = 7$ volts, $E_2 = 2$ volts, $R_1 = 5$ ohms, $R_2 = 4$ ohms, and $R_3 = 9$ ohms, find values of currents I_1, I_2, and I_3, which are measured in amperes. (See Example 4.)

OBJECTIVES

1 Determine whether an ordered triple is a solution of a system of linear equations.

2 Solve linear systems in three variables with exactly one solution.

3 Solve linear systems in three variables that are inconsistent or dependent.

Often, problems involve many variables and many relationships among the variables, so it is useful to extend the methods of Section 3.1 beyond linear systems in two variables. In this section we deal with **linear (first-degree) equations in three variables**, which are equations of the form

$$ax + by + cz = d,$$

where a, b, c, and d are real numbers and x, y, and z are variables. A solution of such an equation is an **ordered triple** of numbers of the form (x,y,z) that satisfies the equation. Furthermore, the solution set of a system of three linear equations in three variables consists of all ordered triples that satisfy all the equations at the same time (simultaneously).

EXAMPLE 1   Testing for a Solution
Determine if $(-3,-1,6)$ is a solution of the system.

$$2x - 3y + z = 3 \quad (1)$$
$$5x - 4y + 2z = 1 \quad (2)$$
$$7x - 2y + 3z = 2 \quad (3)$$

Solution $(-3,-1,6)$ means $x = -3$, $y = -1$, and $z = 6$. Substitute and check to see if true statements result in all three equations.

$$2x - 3y + z = 3 \quad (1)$$
$$2(-3) - 3(-1) + 6 \stackrel{?}{=} 3$$
$$3 = 3 \quad \text{True}$$
$$5x - 4y + 2z = 1 \quad (2)$$
$$5(-3) - 4(-1) + 2(6) \stackrel{?}{=} 1$$
$$1 = 1 \quad \text{True}$$
$$7x - 2y + 3z = 2 \quad (3)$$
$$7(-3) - 2(-1) + 3(6) \stackrel{?}{=} 2$$
$$-1 = 2 \quad \text{False}$$

Thus, $(-3,-1,6)$ is a solution of equations (1) and (2) but not of equation (3). Because this ordered triple is not a solution of all three equations, it is not a solution of this system.

PROGRESS CHECK 1 Determine if $\left(\frac{1}{2}, 1, -2\right)$ is a solution of the system.

$$8x - 3y - 3z = 7$$
$$6x + y + 2z = 0$$
$$-2x + 4y + 3z = -3$$

The next example discusses how the addition-elimination method of the previous section may be extended to solve a linear system in three variables.

EXAMPLE 2 Solving a Linear System by Addition-Elimination

Solve the system.

$$2x - y + z = 7 \quad (1)$$
$$-x + 2y - z = 6 \quad (2)$$
$$2x - 3y - 2z = 9 \quad (3)$$

Solution The initial goal is to obtain two equations in two variables which may be solved as in Section 3.1. To obtain a first equation, select any pair of equations in the system and use the addition method to eliminate one of the variables. For the given system, z is eliminated simply by adding equations (1) and (2).

$$
\begin{array}{rcl}
2x - y + z & = & 7 \quad (1) \\
-x + 2y - z & = & 6 \quad (2) \\
\hline
x + y \phantom{{}+z} & = & 13 \quad (4)
\end{array}
$$

To obtain a second equation, select a different pair of equations in this system and eliminate the *same* variable z. We choose equations (1) and (3) and eliminate z by multiplying both sides of equation (1) by 2 and adding the result to equation (3).

$$
\begin{array}{rcl}
2(2x - y + z) = 2(7) \rightarrow 4x - 2y + 2z & = & 14 \\
2x - 3y - 2z & = & 9 \\
\hline
6x - 5y \phantom{{}-2z} & = & 23 \quad (5)
\end{array}
$$

Equations (4) and (5) can now be used to obtain a linear system in two variables (our initial goal).

$$
\begin{array}{rcl}
x + y & = & 13 \quad (4) \\
6x - 5y & = & 23 \quad (5)
\end{array}
$$

To solve this system, we choose to eliminate y and solve for x, as shown next.

$$
\begin{array}{rcl}
5(x + y) = 5(13) \rightarrow 5x + 5y & = & 65 \\
6x - 5y & = & 23 \\
\hline
11x \phantom{{}+5y} & = & 88 \\
x & = & 8
\end{array}
$$

Then substituting 8 for x in equation (4) gives

$$8 + y = 13$$
$$y = 5.$$

Finally, by replacing x by 8 and y by 5 in equation (1), we have

$$2(8) - 5 + z = 7$$
$$z = -4.$$

Thus, the solution is $(8, 5, -4)$. Check it in the original equations (1), (2), and (3).

PROGRESS CHECK 2   Solve the system.

$$3x + 2y + z = -3$$
$$2x + 3y + 2z = 5$$
$$-2x + y - z = 3$$

■

The methods of Example 2 illustrate a general procedure for solving a linear system in three variables, which is summarized next.

To Solve a Linear System in Three Variables

1. Select any pair of equations in the system and use the addition method to eliminate one of the variables.
2. Choose a different pair of equations in the system and eliminate the *same* variable by using the addition method again.
3. Use the results of steps 1 and 2 to obtain a linear system in two variables, and solve this system by the methods of Section 3.1.
4. Substitute the values of the two variables obtained in step 3 into one of the original equations to find the value of the third variable.
5. Check the solution in all three of the original equations.

The next example shows how a linear system in three variables may be used to determine the equation of a parabola that passes through three points (not all in a straight line).

EXAMPLE 3   Fitting an Equation to a Parabola

The points $(1,2)$, $(2,7)$, and $(-1,4)$ lie on the parabola given by $y = ax^2 + bx + c$. Find a, b, and c, and write an equation for the parabola. Check your result with a grapher.

Solution   Substituting the values $x = 1$ and $y = 2$, $x = 2$ and $y = 7$, and $x = -1$ and $y = 4$, respectively, into the equation $y = ax^2 + bx + c$ gives the following system of equations.

$$
\begin{array}{llll}
2 = a(1)^2 + b(1) + c & \text{or} & a + b + c = 2 & (1) \\
7 = a(2)^2 + b(2) + c & & 4a + 2b + c = 7 & (2) \\
4 = a(-1)^2 + b(-1) + c & & a - b + c = 4 & (3)
\end{array}
$$

To solve this system we follow the steps of the general procedure and choose to eliminate b.

Step 1   Eliminate b using equations (1) and (3)

$$
\begin{array}{ll}
a + b + c = 2 & (1) \\
\underline{a - b + c = 4} & (3) \\
2a \quad\;\; + 2c = 6 & \\
a + \;\; c = 3 & (4)
\end{array}
$$

Step 2   Eliminate b again using a different pair of equations, say (2) and (3).

$$
\begin{array}{rl}
 & 4a + 2b + \;\; c = \;\; 7 \\
2(a - b + c) = 2(4) \rightarrow & \underline{2a - 2b + 2c = \;\; 8} \\
 & 6a \qquad\; + 3c = 15 \\
 & 2a + \;\; c = \;\; 5
\end{array}
$$

Step 3   Solve the linear system in two variables resulting from steps 1 and 2.

$$-1(a + c) = -1(3) \rightarrow -a - c = -3$$
$$\underline{2a + c = 5}$$
$$a = 2$$

Then substituting 2 for a in equation (4) yields $c = 1$.

Step 4   Replacing a by 2 and c by 1 in equation (1) gives

$$2 + b + 1 = 2$$
$$b = -1.$$

Step 5   The solution to the linear system is $a = 2$, $b = -1$, and $c = 1$. Check it in the original equations (1), (2), and (3).

The solution to the linear system reveals that the equation of the parabola passing through the given points is $y = 2x^2 - x + 1$. Check this result numerically by substituting the coordinates of the three given points in this equation. Figure 3.7 shows a graphical check that confirms this solution.

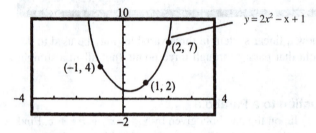

Figure 3.7

 Technology Link
Some graphing calculators have a built-in feature for solving linear systems (or simultaneous equations), and you should learn to use this feature if it is available. When this special feature is not available, then most graphing calculators have the ability to solve linear systems by using matrices, and this approach is discussed in Section 3.3.

PROGRESS CHECK 3   The points $(1,-2)$, $(2,-3)$, and $(3,-6)$ lie on the parabola given by $y = ax^2 + bx + c$. Find a, b, and c and write an equation for the parabola. Check your result with a grapher.   ■

The next example illustrates that the general procedure just given may be shortened when at least one equation in a linear system in three variables has a missing term.

EXAMPLE 4   Finding Currents in a Circuit
Solve the problem in the section introduction on page 165.

Solution   Using the equations and substitutions given in the question leads to the system

$$I_1 + I_2 + I_3 = 0 \quad (1)$$
$$5I_1 - 9I_3 = 7 \quad (2)$$
$$4I_2 - 9I_3 = 2. \quad (3)$$

Equation (2) is missing an I_2 term, and equation (3) has no I_1 term. Select one of these variables, say I_1, for further elimination. Multiplying both sides of equation (1) by -5 and adding the result to equation (2) gives

$$-5(I_1 + I_2 + I_3) = -5(0) \rightarrow -5I_1 - 5I_2 - 5I_3 = 0$$
$$\underline{5I_1 \qquad\quad - 9I_3 = 7}$$
$$-5I_2 - 14I_3 = 7. \quad (4)$$

Equations (3) and (4) now form a linear system in two variables, and I_3 may be found as follows.

$$5(4I_2 - 9I_3) = 5(2) \rightarrow \quad 20I_2 - 45I_3 = 10$$
$$4(-5I_2 - 14I_3) = 4(7) \rightarrow \underline{-20I_2 - 56I_3 = 28}$$
$$-101I_3 = 38$$
$$I_3 = -\tfrac{38}{101}$$

Because finding I_2 using I_3 involves a lot of work with fractions, we choose to find I_2 by again using equations (3) and (4).

$$14(4I_2 - 9I_3) = 14(2) \rightarrow \quad 56I_2 - 126I_3 = 28$$
$$-9(-5I_2 - 14I_3) = -9(7) \rightarrow \underline{45I_2 + 126I_3 = -63}$$
$$101I_2 \qquad\quad = -35$$
$$I_2 = -\tfrac{35}{101}$$

Finally, replacing I_2 by $-\tfrac{35}{101}$ and I_3 by $-\tfrac{38}{101}$ in equation (1) gives

$$I_1 - \tfrac{35}{101} - \tfrac{38}{101} = 0$$
$$I_1 - \tfrac{73}{101} = 0$$
$$I_1 = \tfrac{73}{101}.$$

Thus, $I_1 = \tfrac{73}{101}$ ampere, $I_2 = -\tfrac{35}{101}$ ampere, and $I_3 = -\tfrac{38}{101}$ ampere. Check this solution in all three of the original equations.

PROGRESS CHECK 4   Use the equations given in Example 4 and find I_1, I_2, and I_3 if $E_1 = 3$ volts, $E_2 = 10$ volts, $R_1 = 2$ ohms, $R_2 = 9$ ohms, and $R_3 = 5$ ohms. ■

When the application of our current methods for solving a linear system in three variables results in a false equation *at any step,* then the system is inconsistent and has no solution. Example 5 illustrates this case.

EXAMPLE 5   An Inconsistent System
Solve the system.

$$2x + y - z = 2 \qquad (1)$$
$$x + 2y + z = 5 \qquad (2)$$
$$x - y - 2z = -2 \qquad (3)$$

Solution   We follow the steps of the general procedure and choose to eliminate z.

Step 1 Eliminate z using equations (1) and (2).

$$2x + \quad y - z = 2 \qquad (1)$$
$$\underline{x + 2y + z = 5} \qquad (2)$$
$$3x + 3y \qquad = 7 \qquad (4)$$

Step 2 Eliminate z again using a different pair of equations, say (2) and (3).

$$2(x + 2y + z) = 2(5) \rightarrow \begin{array}{r} 2x + 4y + 2z = 10 \\ \underline{x - y - 2z = -2} \\ 3x + 3y \quad\quad = 8 \quad (5) \end{array}$$

Step 3 Solve the linear system in two variables resulting from steps 1 and 2.

$$-1(3x + 3y) = -1(8) \rightarrow \begin{array}{r} 3x + 3y = 7 \\ \underline{-3x - 3y = -8} \\ 0 = -1 \end{array}$$

The false equation $0 = -1$ indicates that the system is inconsistent and has no solution. The solution set for every inconsistent system is $\emptyset$.

Note At any step a false equation implies an inconsistent system. Therefore, if step 1 results in a false equation, then conclude without further work that the system is inconsistent.

PROGRESS CHECK 5 Solve the system.

$$\begin{array}{r} x - y - z = 5 \\ 4x + y + 3z = 8 \\ -2x + 2y + 2z = 7 \end{array}$$

■

A linear system in three variables may also be a dependent system, and the next example illustrates this case.

EXAMPLE 6   A Dependent System

Solve the system.

$$\begin{array}{rl} x - y + 2z = 0 & (1) \\ -x + 4y + z = 0 & (2) \\ -x + 2y - z = 0 & (3) \end{array}$$

Solution   We follow steps of the general procedure and choose to eliminate x.

Step 1 Eliminate x using equations (1) and (2).

$$\begin{array}{rl} x - y + 2z = 0 & (1) \\ \underline{-x + 4y + z = 0} & (2) \\ 3y + 3z = 0 & (4) \end{array}$$

Step 2 Eliminate x again using a different pair of equations.

$$\begin{array}{rl} x - y + 2z = 0 & (1) \\ \underline{-x + 2y - z = 0} & (3) \\ y + z = 0 & (5) \end{array}$$

Step 3 Solve the system comprised of equations (4) and (5).

$$-3(y + z) = -3(0) \rightarrow \begin{array}{r} 3y + 3z = 0 \\ \underline{-3y - 3z = 0} \\ 0 = 0 \end{array}$$

The identity $0 = 0$ indicates that the system is dependent and that the number of solutions is infinite. In higher mathematics, specifying the solution set for the system in this example is considered.

Note   It is also common to conclude that a system is dependent if *both* step 1 and step 2 in our current methods produce identities. In this case all the equations are equivalent, and the solution set is the set of all ordered triples satisfying any equation in the system. However, if one step produces an identity and the other step produces a false equation, then the system is inconsistent. Remember that a false equation *at any step* implies an inconsistent system.

PROGRESS CHECK 6   Solve the system.

$$3x + 2y - z = 3$$
$$x - y + z = 1$$
$$5x + z = 5$$
■

As with linear equations in two variables, it is possible to interpret geometrically a linear system in three variables. However, an equation that may be written in the form $ax + by + cz = d$ graphs as a plane in a three-dimensional space. Consider carefully Figure 3.8, which summarizes the geometric solution: either exactly one point, no point, infinitely many points on a line, or infinitely many points in a plane.

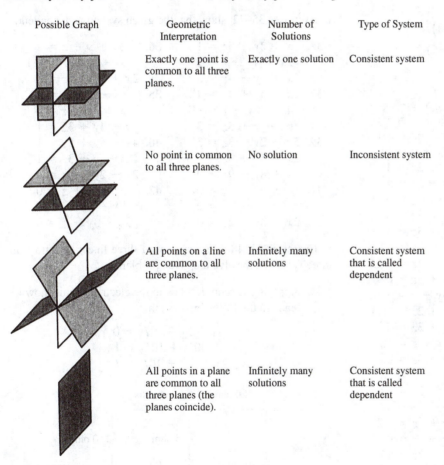

Possible Graph	Geometric Interpretation	Number of Solutions	Type of System
	Exactly one point is common to all three planes.	Exactly one solution	Consistent system
	No point in common to all three planes.	No solution	Inconsistent system
	All points on a line are common to all three planes.	Infinitely many solutions	Consistent system that is called dependent
	All points in a plane are common to all three planes (the planes coincide).	Infinitely many solutions	Consistent system that is called dependent

Figure 3.8

EXERCISES 3.2

In Exercises 1–6, determine if the given ordered triples are solutions of the system.

1. $x + y + z = 3$
$3x - 2y + z = 2$
$x + y - z = 1$
a. $(1,1,1)$
b. $(4, 3, -4)$

2. $2x + 3y - z = 1$
$2x - 3y - z = -5$
$2x + y + z = -1$
a. $(-1, 1, 0)$
b. $(2,1,6)$

3. $x - y + z = 6$
$2x - y + z = 7$
$2x - 2y + 2z = 12$
a. $(1,2,7)$
b. $(1,1,6)$

4. $x + y + z = 6$
$x - y + z = 4$
$2x + 2y + 2z = 12$
a. $(2,1,3)$
b. $(3,1,2)$

5. $4x - 3y + 5z = 7$
$5x - 3y + 4z = 5$
$3x - 4y + 5z = 6$
a. $(0,1,2)$
b. $\left(-\frac{1}{3}, 0, \frac{15}{9}\right)$

6. $4x - 2y + z = 1$
$2x + 4y + z = 3$
$x + y - z = 1$
a. $\left(\frac{1}{2}, \frac{1}{2}, 0\right)$
b. $(2,1,-5)$

In Exercises 7–26, solve the given system.

7. $x + y + z = 6$
$2x + y - z = 1$
$3x + 2y + z = 10$

8. $2x - y + z = 2$
$3x - 2y - z = -1$
$x - 3y + 6z = -1$

9. $3x - 2y + z = -3$
$3x + 2y + 3z = 5$
$x - y - 2z = -6$

10. $2x - 3y + z = 11$
$x + 3y + 2z = 4$
$3x - y - 3z = 4$

11. $x - y + 3z = 4$
$2x + 3y - 3z = -10$
$3x - 2y + z = -4$

12. $4x - 2y - z = -15$
$-4x - y - 2z = 6$
$2x - 3y + 3z = 3$

13. $x + 3y - 4z = 0$
$x - y + 2z = 4$
$x + 2y - z = 4$

14. $2x - y + 5z = 18$
$2x - 3y - 4z = -15$
$x - 4y + 3z = 0$

15. $x + 2y + 3z = 4$
$2x + 2y + 4z = 6$
$3x + 3y + 5z = 6$

16. $5x - 3y + z = -16$
$4x - 3y + 2z = -11$
$3x - 2y + 3z = 5$

17. $x + y + z = 9$
$2x + 3y + 4z = 23$
$4x - 6y - 2z = 0$

18. $x + y + z = 12$
$3x - 2y + 5z = 20$
$6x + 4y - 2z = 48$

19. $3x - 2y + 4z = 9$
$2x - \quad z = 1$
$\quad y + 2z = 1$

20. $2x - 4y + 3z = 18$
$3x + y \quad = 4$
$\quad 2y + z = -2$

21. $x + 2y = -1$
$2x + 3z = 9$
$3y + 4z = -2$

22. $2x - y = 0$
$2y - 3z = 13$
$3x - 4z = 15$

23. $2x + 3y + 4z = 3$
$4x + 3y - 4z = 2$
$6x - 6y + 8z = 3$

24. $3x - 4y + 3z = 2$
$3x + 4y + 3z = 4$
$4x + 4y + z = 3$

25. $x + y + z = 0$
$-x + y - z = 0$
$-x - y + z = 0$

26. $2x - y - z = 0$
$x - 2y - z = 0$
$x - y - 2z = 0$

In Exercises 27–34, show that the given system is inconsistent.

27. $x + y + z = 1$
$x + y + z = 2$
$x + y + z = 3$

28. $x + 2y + 3z = 0$
$2x + 4y - z = 2$
$3x + 6y - 4z = 3$

29. $x - 2y - z = 0$
$2x + y + 2z = 1$
$3x - y + z = 2$

30. $3x + 2y - 4z = 2$
$x - y + 2z = 1$
$2x + 3y - 6z = 3$

31. $2x - 3y + 4z = 2$
$-x - y + z = 1$
$3x - 2y + 3z = 4$

32. $2x - y + 2z = 3$
$2x - y - 3z = 1$
$2x - y + 4z = 3$

33. $x + y - z = 3$
$-x - y + z = -3$
$2x + 2y - 2z = 5$

34. $3x - y - z = 1$
$6x - 2y - 2z = 2$
$9x - 3y - 3z = 0$

In Exercises 35–42, show that the given system is dependent.

35. $x + 2y + 3z = 1$
$2x + 4y - z = 2$
$3x + 6y - 4z = 3$

36. $3x + y - z = 1$
$x - y + 2z = -1$
$2x + 2y - 3z = 2$

37. $2x - 3y + 4z = 4$
$4x + 2y - z = -1$
$6x - y + 3z = 3$

38. $x - y + z = 1$
$x + 2y - z = 1$
$x - 4y + 3z = 1$

39. $5x - 2y - 3z = 3$
$2x - 5y + 3z = -3$
$x + 8y - 9z = 9$

40. $4x - 3y + 5z = 1$
$2x - y - 3z = 1$
$2x - 2y + 8z = 0$

41. $x + y + z = 0$
$x - y - z = 0$
$2x - 2y - 2z = 0$

42. $-x + y + z = 0$
$x - y + z = 0$
$3x - 3y - z = 0$

In Exercises 43–48, use a system of three linear equations in three variables to solve the given problem.

43. Applying Kirchhoff's law to the electric circuit shown leads to the following system.

$$I_1 + I_2 - \quad I_3 = 0$$
$$30I_2 + 10I_3 = 4$$
$$25I_1 \quad + 10I_3 = 6$$

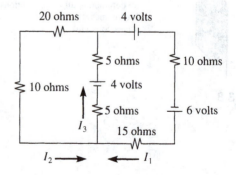

Find the values of currents I_1, I_2, and I_3, in amperes.

44. In the circuit of Exercise 43, if all the resistances are doubled, the resulting system is

$$I_1 + I_2 - \quad I_3 = 0$$
$$60I_2 + 20I_3 = 4$$
$$50I_1 \quad + 20I_3 = 6.$$

Solve the system for the three new currents. How do they compare with the answers in Exercise 43?

45. The points $(0,8)$, $(1,5)$, and $(2,4)$ lie on the parabola given by $y = ax^2 + bx + c$. Find a, b, and c, and write an equation for the parabola. Check your result with a grapher.

46. The points $(-5,-2)$, $(-2,1)$, and $(-1,-2)$ lie on the parabola given by $y = ax^2 + bx + c$. Find a, b, and c, and write an equation for the parabola. Check your result with a grapher.

47. The following problem is typical of those from algebra textbooks of 100 years ago. (It is from William J. Milne's *High School Algebra,* published by the American Book Company in 1892). Divide 125 into four parts such that, if the first be increased by 4, the second diminished by 4, the third multiplied by 4, and the fourth divided by 4, all these results will be equal. (*Hint:* Call the 4 parts a, b, c, and $125 - a - b - c$. The first equation is then $a + 4 = b - 4$.)

48. Divide 180 into four parts such that if the first be increased by 5, the second diminished by 5, the third multiplied by 5, and the fourth divided by 5, all these results will be equal.

THINK ABOUT IT 3.2

1. The following linear system in three variables is in **triangular form**.

$$3x + 2y - \quad z = 11 \quad (1)$$
$$5y + 3z = 1 \quad (2)$$
$$4z = 8 \quad (3)$$

Solve this system. Describe a general procedure for solving this type of system.

2. Extend the methods of this section to solve this system of four linear equations in four variables. (*Hint:* First eliminate one variable to get a new system of three linear equations in three variables.)

$$w - \quad x + \quad y + \quad z = -4$$
$$2w - 3x + \quad y - \quad z = -3$$
$$w + 2x - 2y + 3z = 1$$
$$3w + \quad x + 2y - 3z = 9$$

3. Recall that a system of three linear equations in three variables is inconsistent if there is no point which is simultaneously in all three planes (as shown in Figure 3.8). Draw and describe two other possible graphs of inconsistent systems.

4. Solve for x, y, and z in terms of a, b, and c.

$$x + z = a$$
$$x + y = b$$
$$y + z = c$$

5. In Exercises 35–42 the systems are dependent and therefore have infinitely many solutions. For Exercises 35 and 42, find three of the solutions.

3.3   Triangular Form and Matrices

A 4,000-seat theater was sold out for a weekend concert. Total receipts on Friday night were $53,200 when seats in the orchestra, mezzanine, and balcony sold for $16, $12, and $8, respectively. On Saturday, prices were raised to $20, $15, and $8, and total receipts increased to $65,300. How many seats of each type are in the theater? (See Example 4.)

OBJECTIVES

1 Solve a linear system by transforming the system to triangular form.

2 Solve a linear system using matrices.

Gaussian elimination is a systematic method that is commonly used by computers to analyze linear systems. To understand this method, first consider the following linear system in three variables.

$$3x - 5y + z = 3 \quad (1)$$
$$7y + 2z = 1 \quad (2)$$
$$3z = 12 \quad (3)$$

This system is said to be in **triangular form** and is easy to solve. Equation (3), $3z = 12$, quickly gives $z = 4$. Then replacing z by 4 in equation (2) yields

$$7y + 2(4) = 1$$
$$7y = -7$$
$$y = -1,$$

and replacing z by 4 and y by -1 in equation (1) gives

$$3x - 5(-1) + 4 = 3$$
$$3x = -6$$
$$x = -2.$$

Thus, the solution is $(-2, -1, 4)$.

The idea in Gaussian elimination is to transform any given system to triangular form by producing **equivalent systems** (ones with the same solution) using the operations that follow.

Operations that Produce Equivalent Systems

1. Interchange the order in which two equations are listed.
2. Multiply both sides of an equation by a nonzero number.
3. Add a multiple of one equation to another equation.

The three operations that produce equivalent systems are called the **elementary operations**. Note that the first operation clearly affects only the form of the system, and the other two operations were often used in the addition-elimination method of Section 3.1.

EXAMPLE 1 Using Elementary Operations on Equations

Solve by transforming to triangular form.

$$2x - 3y - 2z = 9$$
$$x - y + z = -1$$
$$-x + 2y + z = -2$$

Solution In triangular form x must be eliminated in all equations after the first one. This is usually easier to do when the coefficient of x in the first equation is 1, so begin by interchanging the order of the first two equations to obtain

$$x - y + z = -1$$
$$2x - 3y - 2z = 9$$
$$-x + 2y + z = -2.$$

Now adding -2 times the first equation to the second equation gives

$$x - y + z = -1$$
$$- y - 4z = 11$$
$$-x + 2y + z = -2.$$

And adding the first equation to the third equation gives

$$\begin{aligned} x - y + z &= -1 \\ -y - 4z &= 11 \\ y + 2z &= -3. \end{aligned}$$

In triangular form y must be eliminated in all equations after the second one. For this system adding the second equation to the third equation eliminates y in the third equation.

$$\begin{aligned} x - y + z &= -1 \\ -y - 4z &= 11 \\ -2z &= 8 \end{aligned}$$

The system is now in triangular form. Using $-2z = 8$, we have $z = -4$, and back substitution gives

$$\begin{aligned} -y - 4(-4) &= 11 & & & x - 5 + (-4) &= -1 \\ -y &= -5 & &\text{and} & x &= 8. \\ y &= 5 \end{aligned}$$

Thus, the solution is $(8, 5, -4)$. Check this solution in the original equations.

PROGRESS CHECK 1   Solve the system by transforming to triangular form.

$$\begin{aligned} 2x - 3y - z &= -9 \\ 3x - y + 6z &= 1 \\ x + 2y - 3z &= 0 \end{aligned}$$

■

Our current method may be shortened by writing down only the constants in the equations and leaving out all the x's, y's, and z's. The standard notation for such an abbreviation utilizes matrices. A **matrix** is a rectangular array of numbers that is enclosed in brackets (or parentheses). Each number in the matrix is called an **entry** or **element** of the matrix. A system like

$$\begin{aligned} a_1 x + b_1 y + c_1 z &= d_1 \\ a_2 x + b_2 y + c_2 z &= d_2 \\ a_3 x + b_3 y + c_3 z &= d_3 \end{aligned}$$

is abbreviated by the matrix

$$\left[\begin{array}{ccc|c} a_1 & b_1 & c_1 & d_1 \\ a_2 & b_2 & c_2 & d_2 \\ a_3 & b_3 & c_3 & d_3 \end{array} \right]$$

This matrix is called the **augmented matrix** of the system. Note that it consists of the coefficients of the variables and an additional column (separated by an optional dashed line) that contains the constants on the right side of the equals sign. When the elementary operations that produce equivalent systems of equations are restated in the language of matrices, we obtain operations, called **elementary row operations,** which are stated next.

Corresponding Operations for Solving a Linear System

Elementary Operations on Equations	Elementary Row Operations on Matrices
1. Interchange two equations.	1. Interchange two rows
2. Multiply both sides of an equation by a nonzero number.	2. Multiply each entry in a row by a nonzero number.
3. Add a multiple of one equation to another	3. Add a multiple of the entries in one row to another row.

A linear system may now be solved in matrix form by using elementary row operations to obtain matrices of equivalent systems until a system in triangular form is reached. In the next example both the matrix form and the equation form of the system will be displayed to reinforce the similarities in the methods.

EXAMPLE 2   Corresponding Operations for Solving a Linear System

Solve the system.

$$2x + 2y - z = -3$$
$$3x + y + z = 1$$
$$x - y + z = 3$$

Show both the matrix form of the system and the corresponding equations.

Solution   We use the operations above and proceed as follows.

Equation Form	Matrix Form

$2x + 2y - z = -3$
$3x + y + z = 1$
$x - y + z = 3$

$$\begin{bmatrix} 2 & 2 & -1 & -3 \\ 3 & 1 & 1 & 1 \\ 1 & -1 & 1 & 3 \end{bmatrix}$$

↓ Interchange equations 1 and 3.   ↓ Interchange rows 1 and 3.

$x - y + z = 3$
$3x + y + z = 1$
$2x + 2y - z = -3$

$$\begin{bmatrix} 1 & -1 & 1 & 3 \\ 3 & 1 & 1 & 1 \\ 2 & 2 & -1 & -3 \end{bmatrix}$$

↓ Add -3 times the first equation to the second equation.

↓ Add -3 times each entry in row 1 to the corresponding entry in row 2.

$x - y + z = 3$
$4y - 2z = -8$
$2x + 2y - z = -3$

$$\begin{bmatrix} 1 & -1 & 1 & 3 \\ 0 & 4 & -2 & -8 \\ 2 & 2 & -1 & -3 \end{bmatrix}$$

↓ Add -2 times the first equation to the third equation.

↓ Add -2 times each entry in row 1 to the corresponding entry in row 3.

$x - y + z = 3$
$4y - 2z = -8$
$4y - 3z = -9$

$$\begin{bmatrix} 1 & -1 & 1 & 3 \\ 0 & 4 & -2 & -8 \\ 0 & 4 & -3 & -9 \end{bmatrix}$$

↓ Add -1 times the second equation to the third equation.

↓ Add -1 times each entry in row 2 to the corresponding entry in row 3.

$x - y + z = 3$
$4y - 2z = -8$
$- z = -1$

$$\begin{bmatrix} 1 & -1 & 1 & 3 \\ 0 & 4 & -2 & -8 \\ 0 & 0 & -1 & -1 \end{bmatrix}$$

The last row or last equation tells us $-z = -1$, so $z = 1$. Then

$$4y - 1(1) = -8 \qquad x - \left(-\tfrac{3}{2}\right) + 1 = 3$$
$$4y = -6 \qquad x + \tfrac{5}{2} = 3$$
$$y = -\tfrac{3}{2} \qquad x = \tfrac{1}{2}$$

Confirm in the original equations that the solution is $\left(\tfrac{1}{2}, -\tfrac{3}{2}, 1\right)$.

PROGRESS CHECK 2   Solve the system.

$$5x + 4y + 3z = 0$$
$$x + y + z = 0$$
$$6x + 3y + 2z = 1$$

Show both the matrix form of the system and the corresponding equations.

■

   Gaussian elimination may lead to considerable work with fractions even in simple linear systems, as shown in the next example.

EXAMPLE 3   Using Elementary Row Operations on Matrices

Use matrix form to solve the system

$$2x + 5y - 1 = 0$$
$$3x - 2y - 11 = 0.$$

Solution   Both equations must be written in the form $ax + by = c$, so begin by transforming the system to

$$2x + 5y = 1$$
$$3x - 2y = 11.$$

The augmented matrix for the system is

$$\begin{bmatrix} 2 & 5 & | & 1 \\ 3 & -2 & | & 11 \end{bmatrix}.$$

For this system we first multiply each entry in row 1 by $\frac{1}{2}$. This choice results in a matrix with a 1 as the first entry in column 1.

$$\begin{bmatrix} 1 & \frac{5}{2} & | & \frac{1}{2} \\ 3 & -2 & | & 11 \end{bmatrix}$$

Now add -3 times row 1 to row 2.

$$\begin{bmatrix} 1 & \frac{5}{2} & | & \frac{1}{2} \\ 0 & -\frac{19}{2} & | & \frac{19}{2} \end{bmatrix}$$

The last row corresponds to $-\frac{19}{2}y = \frac{19}{2}$, so $y = -1$. Then replacing y by -1 in the equation corresponding to row 1 gives

$$x + \tfrac{5}{2}(-1) = \tfrac{1}{2}$$
$$x = \tfrac{1}{2} + \tfrac{5}{2}$$
$$x = 3$$

Thus, the solution is $(3, -1)$. Check this solution in the two original equations.

PROGRESS CHECK 3   Use matrix form to solve the system.

$$2x - 3y - 13 = 0$$
$$5x + 4y + 2 = 0$$ ■

EXAMPLE 4   Finding Seating from Total Receipts

Solve the problem in the section introduction on page 173.

Solution   Let x, y, and z represent the number of seats in the orchestra, mezzanine, and balcony, respectively. Because the theater has 4,000 seats,

$$x + y + z = 4,000. \qquad (1)$$

On Friday all seats were sold, with orchestra, mezzanine, and balcony seats producing $16x$, $12y$, and $8z$ dollars in revenue, respectively. Total receipts were $53,200, so

$$16x + 12y + 8z = 53,200. \qquad (2)$$

Similarly, using the higher ticket prices and total receipts from Saturday gives

$$20x + 15y + 8z = 65,300. \qquad (3)$$

The augmented matrix for the system of equations (1), (2), and (3) is

$$\begin{bmatrix} 1 & 1 & 1 & | & 4,000 \\ 16 & 12 & 8 & | & 53,200 \\ 20 & 15 & 8 & | & 65,300 \end{bmatrix}.$$

To obtain 0's in the first column after row 1, we add -16 times the first row to the second row, and -20 times the first row to the third row.

$$\begin{bmatrix} 1 & 1 & 1 & | & 4,000 \\ 0 & -4 & -8 & | & -10,800 \\ 0 & -5 & -12 & | & -14,700 \end{bmatrix}$$

To obtain 0 in the second column after row 2, we first multiply each entry in row 2 by $-\frac{1}{4}$ to make the coefficient of y in the second equation a 1.

$$\begin{bmatrix} 1 & 1 & 1 & | & 4,000 \\ 0 & 1 & 2 & | & 2,700 \\ 0 & -5 & -12 & | & -14,700 \end{bmatrix}$$

Now add 5 times the second row to the third row.

$$\begin{bmatrix} 1 & 1 & 1 & | & 4,000 \\ 0 & 1 & 2 & | & 2,700 \\ 0 & 0 & -2 & | & -1,200 \end{bmatrix}$$

The third row tells us $-2z = -1,200$, so $z = 600$. Then, back substitution into the equations corresponding to row 2 and row 1 gives

$$y + 2z = 2,700 \qquad\qquad x + y + z = 4,000$$
$$y + 2(600) = 2,700 \qquad \text{and} \qquad x + 1,500 + 600 = 4,000$$
$$y = 1,500 \qquad\qquad x = 1,900.$$

Thus, the theater has 1,900 orchestra seats, 1,500 mezzanine seats, and 600 balcony seats. Confirm that this solution checks in the context of this application.

PROGRESS CHECK 4   A 2,000-seat theater was sold out for a weekend concert. Total receipts on Friday night were \$31,500 when seats in the orchestra, mezzanine, and balcony sold for \$20, \$15, and \$10, respectively. On Saturday prices were raised to \$25, \$20, and \$10, and total receipts increased to \$39,000. How many seats of each type are in the theater?   ▪

There are two additional ideas to consider about solving linear systems using row operations. First, if a row of zeros results in the coefficient portion in any matrix, then there is no unique solution to the problem. Such systems are either dependent (if the last column entry is also zero) or inconsistent (if the last column entry is not zero). Second, in our example problems to this point, we stopped when we reached triangular form and completed the solution by back substitution. An alternative method, called **Gauss-Jordan elimination**, is to continue to produce equivalent matrices until we reach a form like

$$\begin{bmatrix} 1 & 0 & 0 & | & a \\ 0 & 1 & 0 & | & b \\ 0 & 0 & 1 & | & c \end{bmatrix}.$$

From this final form of the matrix, we directly read that the solution is $x = a$, $y = b$, and $z = c$. The matrix above is an example of a **reduced row echelon matrix,** which is defined as follows.

Reduced Row-Echelon Matrix

Matrix A is a reduced row-echelon matrix if and only if
1. Rows containing all 0's (if any exist) occur at the bottom of A.
2. The first nonzero entry in each nonzero row is 1, called a **leading 1**.
3. These leading 1's are positioned further to the right in succeeding lower rows of A.
4. Every column that contains a leading 1 has all 0's above and below that leading 1.

Matrices may be entered and utilized on most graphing calculators. Among the available operations is usually a command to return the reduced row-echelon form of a matrix. This command is commonly abbreviated as **rref** and this function provides a powerful method for finding the solution of a linear system of equations.

EXERCISES 3.3

In Exercises 1–10, solve the system. If necessary, transform to triangular form.

1. $3x - 4y - 5z = 6$
   $5y + 6z = -4$
   $7z = 7$

2. $2x + 3y - 4z = -9$
   $3y + z = 5$
   $3z = 6$

3. $x + 4y - z = 1$
   $3x + 2y = 6$
   $5x = 10$

4. $x - 4y - 2z = 7$
   $2x - 7y = 3$
   $3x = 15$

5. $x - 3y + 4z = 11$
   $2x + y + 3z = 3$
   $3x - 2y - 4z = 3$

6. $x + y + z = 1$
   $3x - 4y + z = 6$
   $2x + y + 3z = 5$

7. $2x - 3y + 2z = 5$
   $4x - y - 2z = -7$
   $x + y - z = 1$

8. $6x - 4y + z = 2$
   $x + y - z = 0$
   $3x + y - z = 4$

9. $x - 4y = -7$
   $2x + 3y = -3$

10. $x + 3y = 1$
    $-2x - 5y = -4$

In Exercises 11–16, solve the given system. Show both the matrix form of the system and the corresponding equations.

11. $3x + 3y = -9$
    $x + 2y = -5$

12. $2x + 3y = 2$
    $x - y = -1$

13. $x - 3y + 3z = 1$
    $2x + y + z = 1$
    $3x + 2y - z = 0$

14. $x + y + 2z = 2$
    $5x + y - 3z = 1$
    $3x - y + z = -3$

15. $2x + 3y - 4z = -2$
    $2x + y + 4z = 4$
    $x - 2y + 2z = 2$

16. $3x + y + 2z = 2$
    $x + 3y - z = 3$
    $x - y - 3z = -5$

In Exercises 17–24, solve the system using just the matrix form.

17. $4x - 8y - 3 = 0$
    $-2x + 2y + 1 = 0$

18. $6x + 15y = 8$
    $-3x + 6y = 5$

19. $3x - 5y - 14 = 0$
    $2x + 3y - 3 = 0$

20. $5x + 2y + 1 = 0$
    $3x - 4y + 11 = 0$

21. $x - y + z = 3$
    $2x - y - z = -1$
    $3x + 2y - 3z = 1$

22. $x - y + z = 2$
    $3x - y - z = 4$
    $2x + 3y - 2z = -1$

23. $2x - 3y - 2z = 1$
    $2x + 3y + 3z = 5$
    $3x - 2y - 4z = -3$

24. $2x + 5y - 3z = -6$
    $-3x + 2y - 5z = -10$
    $5x - 3y + 2z = -2$

In Exercises 25–28 the problems can be solved by setting up appropriate systems. Solve the system by using matrix form.

25. A 1,000-seat theater was sold out for two concerts by a performer. Total receipts for the first concert were $9,900 when seats in the orchestra, mezzanine, and balcony sold for $15, $10, and $6, respectively. For the second concert, total receipts were $12,200 when prices were $18, $12, and $8. How many seats of each type are in the theater?

26. A ballpark has three prices of tickets for the bleachers and the upper and lower stands. For a series of three baseball games the sales were as follows: On day 1, they sold 10,000 of each price and took in $900,000. On day 2, the number of middle-priced tickets increased by 5,000, while the others remained the same as on the previous day. Receipts were $1,025,000. On day 3, the number of high-priced tickets increased by 5,000, while the others remained the same as on the previous day. Receipts were $1,275,000. What prices were charged for each type of ticket?

27. A used-records shop sells records, CDs, and cassettes. The CDs sell for $8, while the records and cassettes sell for $4. One week the sales totaled $1,000. During the week they sold 10 more cassettes than records, and they sold twice as many CDs as records and cassettes combined. How many of each were sold?

28. A gas station sells three grades of gasoline, regular, plus, and super, for $2.10, $2.15, and $2.25 per gallon, respectively. One day sales were $5,160. On this day it sold as much regular as the other two combined, and the amount of plus sold was the same as the amount of super. How many gallons of each were sold?

THINK ABOUT IT 3.3

1. Use Gaussian elimination to solve for x, y, and z in terms of a, b, and c.

$$x + z = a$$
$$x + y = b$$
$$y + z = c$$

2. Let $f(x) = ax^2 + bx + c$. Find values of a, b, and c such that $f(1) = 0$, $f(2) = 8$ and $f(3) = 22$.

3. If the graph of $y = ax^3 + bx^2 + cx + d$ passes through the points $(1, 1)$, $(2, 1)$, $(3, -11)$, and $(-1, -11)$ find a, b, c, and d.

4. Refer to the discussion of a reduced row-echelon matrix that follows Example 4, and use Gauss-Jordan elimination to solve

$$
\begin{aligned}
x + y + z &= 6 \\
x - y - z &= -4 \\
-x + y - z &= -2.
\end{aligned}
$$

5. Solve this system of four linear equations in four variables. Use Gaussian elimination.

$$
\begin{aligned}
u + v + w + x &= 0 \\
u + v \quad\;\; + x &= -2 \\
v + w + x &= -3 \\
u + v + w \quad\;\; &= 2
\end{aligned}
$$

3.4   Determinants and Cramer's Rule

One perfume contains 1 percent essence of rose, while a second contains 1.8 percent essence of rose. How much of each should be combined to make 24 oz of perfume that contains 1.5 percent essence of rose? (See Example 4.)

OBJECTIVES

1 Evaluate the determinant of a 2-by-2 matrix.

2 Solve a linear system in two variables using Cramer's rule.

3 Evaluate the determinant of a 3-by-3 matrix.

4 Solve a linear system in three variables using Cramer's rule.

A linear system in two variables with exactly one solution may be solved by formulas using a method called Cramer's rule. To see how these formulas originate, we now find the general solution of the system.

$$
\begin{aligned}
a_1 x + b_1 y &= c_1 \quad (1) \\
a_2 x + b_2 y &= c_2 \quad (2)
\end{aligned}
$$

If equivalent equations are formed by multiplying both sides of equation (1) by b_2 and both sides of equation (2) by $-b_1$, then x may be found as follows.

$$
\begin{array}{lll}
a_1 b_2 x + b_1 b_2 y = c_1 b_2 & & (3) \\
\underline{-b_1 a_2 x - b_1 b_2 y = -b_1 c_2} & & (4) \\
a_1 b_2 x - b_1 a_2 x = c_1 b_2 - b_1 c_2 & & \text{Add equations (3) and (4).} \\
x(a_1 b_2 - b_1 a_2) = c_1 b_2 - b_1 c_2 & & \text{Factor out } x. \\
x = \dfrac{c_1 b_2 - b_1 c_2}{a_1 b_2 - b_1 a_2} & & \text{Divide by } a_1 b_2 - b_1 a_2, \\
& & \text{with } a_1 b_2 - b_1 a_2 \neq 0.
\end{array}
$$

Similarly, multiplying both sides of equation (1) by $-a_2$ and both sides of equation (2) by a_1, and then adding, leads to

$$
y = \frac{a_1 c_2 - c_1 a_2}{a_1 b_2 - b_1 a_2}.
$$

These formulas may now be used to find x and y whenever $a_1b_2 - b_1a_2 \neq 0$. If $a_1b_2 - b_1a_2 = 0$ there is no unique solution for x and y, and the system is either dependent or inconsistent.

We do not memorize the formulas in this form, since they may be obtained by defining what is called a determinant. Consider the expression $a_1b_2 - b_1a_2$, which is the denominator in the formulas for both x and y, and note that the coefficient matrix of the linear system is

$$A = \begin{bmatrix} a_1 & b_1 \\ a_2 & b_2 \end{bmatrix}.$$

This matrix is an example of a square matrix, which is a matrix having the same number of rows as columns. To each square matrix A there is assigned a unique real number called its determinant and denoted by $|A|$. As suggested above, when A has two rows and two columns, called a 2-by-2 matrix, then we define the value of $|A|$ to be $a_1b_2 - b_1a_2$.

Determinant of a 2-by-2 Matrix

If $A = \begin{bmatrix} a_1 & b_1 \\ a_2 & b_2 \end{bmatrix}$, then the determinant of A is given by

$$|A| = \begin{vmatrix} a_1 & b_1 \\ a_2 & b_2 \end{vmatrix} = a_1b_2 - b_1a_2.$$

The numbers a_1 and b_2 are elements of the principal diagonal, and the numbers b_1 and a_2 are elements of the secondary diagonal. Note in Figure 3.9 that the value of the determinant is the product of the elements of the principal diagonal minus the product of the elements of the secondary diagonal.

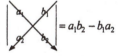

Figure 3.9

EXAMPLE 1   Determinant of a 2-by-2 Matrix
Find the value of each determinant.

a. $\begin{vmatrix} 5 & 6 \\ 2 & 3 \end{vmatrix}$ **b.** $\begin{vmatrix} -9 & -2 \\ 11 & 7 \end{vmatrix}$ **c.** $\begin{vmatrix} a_1 & c_1 \\ a_2 & c_2 \end{vmatrix}$

Solution

a. $\begin{vmatrix} 5 & 6 \\ 2 & 3 \end{vmatrix} = 5(3) - 6(2) = 15 - 12 = 3$

b. $\begin{vmatrix} -9 & -2 \\ 11 & 7 \end{vmatrix} = -9(7) - (-2)(11) = -63 + 22 = -41$

c. $\begin{vmatrix} a_1 & c_1 \\ a_2 & c_2 \end{vmatrix} = a_1c_2 - c_1a_2$

Technology Link
The determinant of a matrix A may be denoted by $|A|$ or det A. The latter notation is commonly used on calculators with a matrix capability, to offer a function DET that will evaluate the determinant of a matrix. If your calculator has a Determinant function, then you should evaluate the determinants shown in parts a and b of Example 1 using this function and compare your results to the text's answers.

PROGRESS CHECK 1   Find the value of each determinant.

a. $\begin{vmatrix} 6 & 8 \\ 5 & 7 \end{vmatrix}$
b. $\begin{vmatrix} 12 & -5 \\ 15 & -7 \end{vmatrix}$
c. $\begin{vmatrix} c_1 & b_1 \\ c_2 & b_2 \end{vmatrix}$ ▪

The formulas for the general solution of a linear system in two variables may now be stated efficiently in determinant form, as specified in Cramer's rule.

Cramer's Rule for 2 by 2 Systems

The solution to the system

$$a_1 x + b_1 y = c_1$$

$$a_2 x + b_2 y = c_2,$$

with $a_1 b_2 - b_1 a_2 \neq 0$, is

$$x = \frac{D_x}{D} = \frac{\begin{vmatrix} c_1 & b_1 \\ c_2 & b_2 \end{vmatrix}}{\begin{vmatrix} a_1 & b_1 \\ a_2 & b_2 \end{vmatrix}} = \frac{c_1 b_2 - b_1 c_2}{a_1 b_2 - b_1 a_2}$$

$$y = \frac{D_y}{D} = \frac{\begin{vmatrix} a_1 & c_1 \\ a_2 & c_2 \end{vmatrix}}{\begin{vmatrix} a_1 & b_1 \\ a_2 & b_2 \end{vmatrix}} = \frac{a_1 c_2 - c_1 a_2}{a_1 b_2 - b_1 a_2}.$$

Note how the determinants in the formulas for x and y are formed. The determinant in both denominators is denoted by D and is formed from the coefficients of x and y. In the determinants in the numerators, the column containing the constants on the right side of the equations first replaces in D the coefficients of x to form D_x and then the coefficients of y to form D_y.

Example 2   Using Cramer's Rule with a 2-by-2 System

Use Cramer's rule to solve the system of equations.

$$2x + 5y = 3$$
$$6x - 10y = -9$$

Solution   First, evaluate D, which is the determinant formed from the coefficients of x and y.

$$D = \begin{vmatrix} 2 & 5 \\ 6 & -10 \end{vmatrix} = 2(-10) - 5(6) = -50$$

Second, evaluate D_x. To form this determinant, replace the column in D containing the *coefficients of x* by the column with the constants on the right side of the equations.

$$D_x = \begin{vmatrix} 3 & 5 \\ -9 & -10 \end{vmatrix} = 3(-10) - 5(-9) = 15$$

Third, evaluate D_y. To form this determinant, replace the column in D containing the *coefficients of y* by the column with the constants on the right side of the equations.

$$D_y = \begin{vmatrix} 2 & 3 \\ 6 & -9 \end{vmatrix} = 2(-9) - 3(6) = -36$$

Fourth, use Cramer's rule.

$$x = \frac{D_x}{D} = \frac{15}{-50} = -\frac{3}{10}$$

and

$$y = \frac{D_y}{D} = \frac{-36}{-50} = \frac{18}{25}$$

Thus, the solution is $\left(-\frac{3}{10}, \frac{18}{25}\right)$. Check this solution in the given system.

PROGRESS CHECK 2   Solve by Cramer's rule: $2x - 7y = 4$
$6x + 14y = -3.$ ■

Cramer's rule may be used to find x and y whenever $D \neq 0$. If $D = 0$, then the system is either inconsistent or dependent and Cramer's rule does not apply.

EXAMPLE 3   Inconsistent or Dependent Systems

Determine whether Cramer's rule applies to the following system. If it does, find the solution.

$$x - 1 = 3y$$
$$6y + 2 = 2x$$

Solution   A condition in Cramer's rule is that both equations be written in the form $ax + by = c$, so we begin by transforming the given system to

$$x - 3y = 1$$
$$-2x + 6y = -2.$$

Now we find D.

$$D = \begin{vmatrix} 1 & -3 \\ -2 & 6 \end{vmatrix} = 1(6) - (-3)(-2) = 0$$

Because $D = 0$, Cramer's rule does not apply to the given system.

Note   When Cramer's rule does not apply, then elimination methods as considered in Sections 3.1 to 3.3 are usually used to analyze the system. In the system in this example, multiplying both sides of $x - 3y = 1$ by -2 results in $-2x + 6y = -2$, so this system is dependent.

PROGRESS CHECK 3   Determine whether Cramer's rule applies to the following system. If it does, find the solution.

$$3y = 4x - 7$$
$$3x = 4y$$ ■

To solve the section-opening problem, we recall from Section 1.6 that liquid mixture problems are analyzed using

$$\begin{pmatrix} \text{percent of} \\ \text{an ingredient} \end{pmatrix} \cdot \begin{pmatrix} \text{amount of} \\ \text{solution} \end{pmatrix} = \begin{pmatrix} \text{amount of} \\ \text{ingredient} \end{pmatrix}.$$

EXAMPLE 4   Determining a Perfume Mixture

Solve the problem in the section introduction on page 180.

Solution   Let x = amount used in ounces of 1 percent essence of rose

y = amount used in ounces of 1.8 percent essence of rose

and organize the key components in the problem in a chart format.

Solution	Percent of Essence of Rose	·	Amount of Solution (Ounces)	=	Amount of Essence of Rose (Ounces)
First perfume	1		x		$0.01x$
Second perfume	1.8		y		$0.018y$
New perfume	1.5		24		$0.015(24)$, or 0.36

Because x ounces of the first perfume are combined with y ounces of the second perfume to form 24 ounces of the new perfume,

$$x + y = 24. \quad (1)$$

Also, the amount of essence of rose in the new perfume is the sum of the amounts contributed by the two concentrations of perfume, so

$$0.01x + 0.018y = 0.36 \quad (2)$$

To solve the resulting system, we choose to first multiply both sides of equation (2) by 1000 to clear decimals, and then we apply Cramer's rule to the system.

$$x + \quad y = \quad 24$$
$$10x + 18y = 360$$

The three determinants defined in Cramer's rule are

$$D = \begin{vmatrix} 1 & 1 \\ 10 & 18 \end{vmatrix} = 1(18) - 1(10) = 8,$$

$$D_x = \begin{vmatrix} 24 & 1 \\ 360 & 18 \end{vmatrix} = 24(18) - 1(360) = 72,$$

$$D_y = \begin{vmatrix} 1 & 24 \\ 10 & 360 \end{vmatrix} = 1(360) - 24(10) = 120,$$

so

$$x = \frac{D_x}{D} = \frac{72}{8} = 9 \quad \text{and} \quad y = \frac{D_y}{D} = \frac{120}{8} = 15.$$

Thus, the desired perfume is obtained by mixing 9 oz of 1 percent essence of rose with 15 oz of 1.8 percent essence of rose.

PROGRESS CHECK 4   Jewelers often use alloys to add strength, color, or other properties to the metals in jewelry. If a jeweler has two alloys, one 35 percent gold and one 25 percent gold, to be combined by melting them down, how much of each should be used to produce 0.45 oz of 31 percent gold alloy?   ■

Cramer's rule may be extended to solve linear systems in three variables; but to apply it, we must learn to evaluate third-order determinants. We first define the **minor** of an element to be the determinant formed by deleting the row and column containing the given element. For example,

$$\text{minor of } a_1 = \begin{vmatrix} a_1 & b_1 & c_1 \\ a_2 & b_2 & c_2 \\ a_3 & b_3 & c_3 \end{vmatrix} = \begin{vmatrix} b_2 & c_2 \\ b_3 & c_3 \end{vmatrix}$$

$$\text{minor of } a_2 = \begin{vmatrix} a_1 & b_1 & c_1 \\ a_2 & b_2 & c_2 \\ a_3 & b_3 & c_3 \end{vmatrix} = \begin{vmatrix} b_1 & c_1 \\ b_3 & c_3 \end{vmatrix}$$

We can now show how to evaluate a third-order determinant using the first-column elements together with their respective minors.

Third-Order Determinant

A square array of numbers with three rows and three columns that is enclosed by vertical bars is called a **third-order determinant**. The value of a third-order determinant is given by

$$\begin{vmatrix} a_1 & b_1 & c_1 \\ a_2 & b_2 & c_2 \\ a_3 & b_3 & c_3 \end{vmatrix} = a_1 \begin{vmatrix} b_2 & c_2 \\ b_3 & c_3 \end{vmatrix} - a_2 \begin{vmatrix} b_1 & c_1 \\ b_3 & c_3 \end{vmatrix} + a_3 \begin{vmatrix} b_1 & c_1 \\ b_2 & c_2 \end{vmatrix}.$$

The method in this box is called the **expansion of the determinant by minors about the first column**.

EXAMPLE 5 Determinant of a 3-by-3 Matrix

Evaluate the determinant by expansion by minors about the first column.

$$\begin{vmatrix} 2 & -2 & 3 \\ 4 & 0 & 7 \\ 3 & 1 & -1 \end{vmatrix}$$

Solution

$$\begin{vmatrix} 2 & -2 & 3 \\ 4 & 0 & 7 \\ 3 & 1 & -1 \end{vmatrix}$$

$$= 2 \begin{vmatrix} 2 & -2 & 3 \\ 4 & 0 & 7 \\ 3 & 1 & -1 \end{vmatrix} - 4 \begin{vmatrix} 2 & -2 & 3 \\ 4 & 0 & 7 \\ 3 & 1 & -1 \end{vmatrix} + 3 \begin{vmatrix} 2 & -2 & 3 \\ 4 & 0 & 7 \\ 3 & 1 & -1 \end{vmatrix}$$

$$= 2 \begin{vmatrix} 0 & 7 \\ 1 & -1 \end{vmatrix} - 4 \begin{vmatrix} -2 & 3 \\ 1 & -1 \end{vmatrix} + 3 \begin{vmatrix} -2 & 3 \\ 0 & 7 \end{vmatrix}$$

$$= 2[0(-1) - 7(1)] - 4[-2(-1) - 3(1)] + 3[-2(7) - 3(0)]$$

$$= 2(-7) - 4(-1) + 3(-14)$$

$$= -14 + 4 - 42$$

$$= -52$$

PROGRESS CHECK 5 Evaluate the determinant by expansion by minors about the first column.

$$\begin{vmatrix} 1 & 1 & 2 \\ -5 & 2 & 2 \\ 2 & 0 & 3 \end{vmatrix}$$

■

```
+   −   +
−   +   −
+   −   +
```

Figure 3.10

A third-order determinant may be evaluated by expanding the determinant by minors about *any* row or column. However, when an element is multiplied by its minor, the resulting product must be added or subtracted according to the sign pattern in Figure 3.10. That is, we add the products associated with elements in positions labeled +, and we subtract the products associated with elements in positions labeled −. To illustrate, the next example evaluates once again the determinant in Example 5. But this time we choose to expand by minors about the second column, because it is usually easier to expand about columns or rows that contain the most zero elements.

EXAMPLE 6 Determinant of a 3-by-3 System

Evaluate the determinant by expansion by minors about the second column.

$$\begin{vmatrix} 2 & -2 & 3 \\ 4 & 0 & 7 \\ 3 & 1 & -1 \end{vmatrix}$$

Solution   The sign pattern in Figure 3.10 for column 2 is −, +, −. Therefore, expansion by minors about the second column is as follows.

$$\begin{vmatrix} 2 & -2 & 3 \\ 4 & 0 & 7 \\ 3 & 1 & -1 \end{vmatrix} = -(-2)\begin{vmatrix} 4 & 7 \\ 3 & -1 \end{vmatrix} + 0\begin{vmatrix} 2 & 3 \\ 3 & -1 \end{vmatrix} - 1\begin{vmatrix} 2 & 3 \\ 4 & 7 \end{vmatrix}$$

$$= 2(-25) + 0(\text{not needed}) - 1(2)$$

$$= -50 - 2$$

$$= -52$$

PROGRESS CHECK 6   Evaluate the determinant by expansion by minors about the second column.

$$\begin{vmatrix} 1 & 1 & 2 \\ -5 & 2 & 2 \\ 2 & 0 & 3 \end{vmatrix}$$

In Cramer's rule for linear systems in three variables, consider how the formulas for x, y, and z follow an arrangement similar to that for 2 by 2 systems.

Cramer's Rule for 3 by 3 Systems

The solution to the system

$$\begin{aligned} a_1x + b_1y + c_1z &= d_1 \\ a_2x + b_2y + c_2z &= d_2 \\ a_3x + b_3y + c_3z &= d_3 \end{aligned} \quad \text{with} \quad D = \begin{vmatrix} a_1 & b_1 & c_1 \\ a_2 & b_2 & c_2 \\ a_3 & b_3 & c_3 \end{vmatrix} \neq 0$$

is $x = D_x/D$, $y = D_y/D$, and $z = D_z/D$, where

$$D_x = \begin{vmatrix} d_1 & b_1 & c_1 \\ d_2 & b_2 & c_2 \\ d_3 & b_3 & c_3 \end{vmatrix}, \quad D_y = \begin{vmatrix} a_1 & d_1 & c_1 \\ a_2 & d_2 & c_2 \\ a_3 & d_3 & c_3 \end{vmatrix}, \quad \text{and} \quad D_z = \begin{vmatrix} a_1 & b_1 & d_1 \\ a_2 & b_2 & d_2 \\ a_3 & b_3 & d_3 \end{vmatrix}$$

The determinant in all denominators is denoted by D and is formed from the coefficients of x, y, and z. When solving for x, the determinant D_x is obtained from D by using

d_1, d_2, and d_3 as replacements for the corresponding a's (the coefficients of x). Similarly, the d's replace the coefficients of y to form D_y and replace the coefficients of z to form D_z.

EXAMPLE 7   Using Cramer's Rule with a 3-by-3 System

Use Cramer's rule to solve this system of equations.

$$\begin{aligned} -2x + y - z &= 3 \\ 2x + 3y + 2z &= 5 \\ 3x + 2y + z &= -3 \end{aligned}$$

Solution   The four determinants defined in Cramer's rule are

$$D = \begin{vmatrix} -2 & 1 & -1 \\ 2 & 3 & 2 \\ 3 & 2 & 1 \end{vmatrix} = 11, \qquad D_x = \begin{vmatrix} 3 & 1 & -1 \\ 5 & 3 & 2 \\ -3 & 2 & 1 \end{vmatrix} = -33,$$

$$D_y = \begin{vmatrix} -2 & 3 & -1 \\ 2 & 5 & 2 \\ 3 & -3 & 1 \end{vmatrix} = 11, \qquad D_z = \begin{vmatrix} -2 & 1 & 3 \\ 2 & 3 & 5 \\ 3 & 2 & -3 \end{vmatrix} = 44.$$

Then

$$x = \frac{D_x}{D} = \frac{-33}{11} = -3, \qquad y = \frac{D_y}{D} = \frac{11}{11} = 1, \qquad \text{and} \qquad z = \frac{D_z}{D} = \frac{44}{11} = 4.$$

Thus, the solution is $(-3, 1, 4)$. Check this solution in all three equations in the given system.

Note   For the purposes of Cramer's rule, zero elements are positioned in determinants to correspond to any missing terms, since a system like

$$\begin{aligned} 2x + 3y &= 10 \\ 3x + 2z &= 2 \\ 4y + z &= 6 \end{aligned} \quad \text{is equivalent to} \quad \begin{aligned} 2x + 3y + 0z &= 10 \\ 3x + 0y + 2z &= 2 \\ 0x + 4y + z &= 6. \end{aligned}$$

PROGRESS CHECK 7   Solve by Cramer's rule.

$$\begin{aligned} 3x + y + z &= 1 \\ x - y + z &= 3 \\ -2x - 2y + z &= 3 \end{aligned}$$ ■

EXERCISES 3.4

In Exercises 1–16, find the value of each determinant.

1. $\begin{vmatrix} 1 & 2 \\ 3 & 4 \end{vmatrix}$ **2.** $\begin{vmatrix} 3 & 4 \\ 1 & 2 \end{vmatrix}$

3. $\begin{vmatrix} 3 & -2 \\ 2 & -3 \end{vmatrix}$ **4.** $\begin{vmatrix} 4 & -1 \\ 1 & -4 \end{vmatrix}$

5. $\begin{vmatrix} 2 & 1 \\ 4 & 2 \end{vmatrix}$ **6.** $\begin{vmatrix} 1 & -2 \\ 3 & -6 \end{vmatrix}$

7. $\begin{vmatrix} a & b \\ c & d \end{vmatrix}$ **8.** $\begin{vmatrix} a & -b \\ c & -d \end{vmatrix}$

9. $\begin{vmatrix} a & 2a \\ b & 2b \end{vmatrix}$ **10.** $\begin{vmatrix} x & y \\ 3x & 3y \end{vmatrix}$

11. $\begin{vmatrix} 1 & 0 \\ 0 & 1 \end{vmatrix}$ **12.** $\begin{vmatrix} -1 & 0 \\ 0 & -1 \end{vmatrix}$

13. $\begin{vmatrix} a & 0 \\ 0 & a \end{vmatrix}$ **14.** $\begin{vmatrix} 0 & b \\ b & 0 \end{vmatrix}$

15. $\begin{vmatrix} \frac{3}{2} & \frac{1}{2} \\ \frac{1}{3} & 2 \end{vmatrix}$ **16.** $\begin{vmatrix} \frac{2}{3} & \frac{1}{4} \\ \frac{3}{4} & \frac{1}{3} \end{vmatrix}$

In Exercises 17–30, use Cramer's rule to solve the given system of equations. If Cramer's rule does not apply because $D = 0$, determine if the system is inconsistent or dependent.

17. $x + y = 1$
$x + 2y = 2$

18. $3x + y = 3$
$2x - y = 2$

19. $x + y = 0$
$x - y = 0$

20. $3x + y = 0$
$5x + 2y = 0$

21. $3x + 2y = 7$
$4x - y = 2$

22. $2x - 3y = -6$
$4x + y = 16$

23. $3x - 4y = 2$
$4y + 3x = -3$

24. $2x + 3y = 1$
$6y + 3x = 5$

25. $y = 2x + 1$
$y = 3x + 2$

26. $y = 3x - 2$
$y = 2x + 5$

27. $2x + 3y = 1$
$4x + 6y = 3$

28. $x - 2y = 0$
$-3x + 6y = 1$

29. $x - y = 4$
$-2x + 2y = -8$

30. $-3x + 2y = 6$
$6x - 4y = -12$

In Exercises 31–40, evaluate the determinant.

31. $\begin{vmatrix} 1 & 1 & 1 \\ 2 & 2 & 2 \\ 3 & 3 & 3 \end{vmatrix}$ **32.** $\begin{vmatrix} 1 & 2 & 3 \\ 2 & 4 & 6 \\ 3 & 6 & 9 \end{vmatrix}$

33. $\begin{vmatrix} 1 & 0 & 0 \\ 0 & 1 & 0 \\ 0 & 0 & 1 \end{vmatrix}$ **34.** $\begin{vmatrix} 2 & 0 & 0 \\ 0 & 2 & 0 \\ 0 & 0 & 2 \end{vmatrix}$

35. $\begin{vmatrix} 1 & 2 & 4 \\ 2 & 4 & 1 \\ 4 & 1 & 2 \end{vmatrix}$ **36.** $\begin{vmatrix} 1 & 3 & 9 \\ 3 & 9 & 1 \\ 9 & 1 & 3 \end{vmatrix}$

37. $\begin{vmatrix} a & a & a \\ a & a & a \\ a & a & a \end{vmatrix}$ **38.** $\begin{vmatrix} 1 & a & a^2 \\ a & a^2 & 1 \\ a^2 & 1 & a \end{vmatrix}$

39. $\begin{vmatrix} 0 & 1 & 2 \\ 1 & 0 & 2 \\ 2 & 1 & 0 \end{vmatrix}$ **40.** $\begin{vmatrix} 0 & 0 & 3 \\ 4 & 5 & 6 \\ 7 & 8 & 9 \end{vmatrix}$

In Exercises 41–44, evaluate first by expansion about the first column and then by expansion about the first row. Both computations should give the same result.

41. $\begin{vmatrix} 1 & -1 & 1 \\ 2 & 0 & 2 \\ 3 & 1 & 2 \end{vmatrix}$ **42.** $\begin{vmatrix} 2 & 5 & -1 \\ 0 & 1 & 4 \\ 3 & -2 & 6 \end{vmatrix}$

43. $\begin{vmatrix} 1 & -2 & 1 \\ -2 & 1 & -2 \\ 1 & -1 & 1 \end{vmatrix}$ **44.** $\begin{vmatrix} 3 & -2 & 1 \\ -2 & 0 & -2 \\ 1 & -2 & 1 \end{vmatrix}$

In Exercises 45–56, solve the given system using Cramer's rule.

45. $5x - y + z = 2$
$-x + 2y + 5z = 3$
$2x - 3y - 4z = 1$

46. $3x + y - 2z = 2$
$4x - 2y + z = 0$
$-x + 3y - 5z = -2$

47. $2x + 3y - 4z = -1$
$3x - 3y + 6z = -1$
$6x + 9y - 4z = -1$

48. $-x + 2y - 4z = -1$
$x + 2y + 4z = 3$
$3x + y + 2z = -1$

49. $x + y - 5z = 4$
$x - y + 5z = -4$
$2x + 2y - 5z = 9$

50. $x + y - 2z = 2$
$x - y + 2z = 0$
$-x + 3y + 4z = -3$

51. $2x + 2y = 1$
$y + z = 1$
$x + z = 1$

52. $2x + y = 1$
$y + z = 1$
$-x + 2z = 1$

53. $2x - 3y + z = 0$
$4x - 6y + 2z = 1$
$x - 2y + z = 2$

54. $x - 2y + 3z = 2$
$-2x + 3y + z = 1$
$6x - 9y - 3z = 3$

55. $x + y + z = 1$
$2x + 2y + 2z = 2$
$3x + 3y + 3z = 3$

56. $x + y + z = 0$
$3x + 3y + 3z = 0$
$5x + 5y + 5z = 0$

In Exercises 57–70 each problem can be solved by a system of equations. Solve the appropriate system by using Cramer's rule.

57. A certain kind of cleaning solution consists of bleach and water. One batch is 25 percent bleach, while a second is 35 percent bleach. How much of each should be mixed to get 3 quarts (qt) of a solution which is one-third bleach?

58. One perfume contains 1 percent essence of rose, while a second contains 1.8 percent essence of rose. How much of each should be combined to make 24 oz of perfume which contains 1.5 percent essence of rose?

59. A $250,000 retirement fund was split into two investments, one portion (x) at 12.5 percent annual interest and the rest (y) at 8.5 percent. If the total annual interest is $26,050, how much was invested at each rate?

60. How should a $50,000 investment be split so that the total annual earnings are $2,205 if one portion is invested at 6.25 percent annual interest and the rest at 3.75 percent?

61. The sum of two numbers is -1, and the larger minus the smaller is 8. Find both numbers.

62. The reciprocals of two numbers m and n have a sum of 2 and a difference of 1. Find the numbers.

$$\left(Hint: \text{let } x = \frac{1}{m} \text{ and let } y = \frac{1}{n}.\right)$$

63. A strand of barbed wire is 750 yards (yd) long. You wish to use it to make a rectangular enclosure that is twice as long as it is wide. What are the dimensions of the enclosure?

64. A strand of barbed wire is 750 yd long. You wish to use it to make a rectangular enclosure that is 4 times as long as it is wide. What are the dimensions of the enclosure?

65. A comparison is made between two liquids. In one container a liquid is evaporating at 1 liter per day. There are 300 liters of it to start with. The second is evaporating at 1.5 liters per day. There are 350 liters of it to start with.

  a. At what point do the two containers contain the same amount of liquid?

  b. At that time, what is the total amount of liquid left in both containers?

66. Starting at $0°$ C, one piece of metal is being heated at the rate of $2.5°$ C per minute. At the same time another piece, started at $20°$ C, is being heated at the rate of $1°$ C per minute.

  a. After what amount of time will they be the same temperature?

  b. At what temperature will they be the same temperature?

67. A silversmith has three alloys, each containing some gold, some silver, and some copper. Alloy 1 contains 40 percent gold, 40 percent silver, and 20 percent copper. Alloy 2 contains 60 percent gold, 10 percent silver, and 30 percent copper. Alloy 3 contains 80 percent gold, 15 percent silver, and 5 percent copper. Can these alloys be melted and remixed to make 100 oz of an alloy with 58 percent gold, 20 percent silver, and 22 percent copper? Use the table to derive a system of three equations in three variables.

Alloy	Amount of alloy	Amount of gold	Amount of silver
1	x	$0.40x$	$0.40x$
2	y	$0.60y$	$0.10y$
3	z	$0.80z$	$0.15z$
New	100	$0.58(100)$	$0.20(100)$

68. A silversmith has three alloys, each containing some gold, some silver, and some copper. Alloy 1 contains 45 percent gold, 45 percent silver, and 10 percent copper. Alloy 2 contains 60 percent gold, 10 percent silver, and 30 percent copper. Alloy 3 contains 80 percent gold, 15 percent silver, and 5 percent copper. Can these alloys be melted and remixed to make 100 oz of an alloy with 50 percent gold, 25 percent silver, and 25 percent copper? Make a table like the one in Exercise 67, and derive a system of three equations in three variables.

69. In triangle ABC angle A is $20°$ less than the sum of B and C; angle B is $40°$ less than the sum of A and C; and angle C is $120°$ less than the sum of A and B. Find the measure of each angle.

70. In a triangle with sides a, b, and c, side a is one-third the sum of the other two sides; side b is one-half the sum of the other two sides; and side c is 2 less than the sum of the other two sides. Find the length of each side.

THINK ABOUT IT 3.4

1. a. Explain why the value of a determinant which has integer elements must be an integer.

  b. Why does it follow from part **a** that the solution to the system

$$ax + by = c$$
$$dx + ey = f,$$

  where all coefficients are integers, must be a pair of *rational* numbers? (Assume $D \neq 0$.)

  c. Why does it follow from part **b** that the graphs of two lines given by $ax + by = c$ and $dx + ey = f$ can never intersect at $\left(\sqrt{2}, \sqrt{3}\right)$ no matter what integers are chosen for the coefficients?

2. For what value(s) of a does the following system have exactly one solution? What is this solution in terms of a?

$$2x + 3y = 5$$
$$ax + y = 1$$

3. a. Show that $\begin{vmatrix} 3 & 5 \\ 6 & 10 \end{vmatrix} = 0.$

  b. Show that if the second row of a 2 by 2 determinant is a multiple of the first row, then the value of the determinant is zero.

$$\left(Hint: \text{Evaluate } \begin{vmatrix} a & b \\ ka & kb \end{vmatrix}.\right)$$

  c. Find values for x and y which make the value of the determinant $\begin{vmatrix} 2 & 7 \\ x & y \end{vmatrix}$ equal to zero.

4. a. Fill in the blank with "rows" or "columns." In a determinant the _____ go vertically and the _____ go horizontally.

b. Evaluate $\begin{vmatrix} 3 & 1 \\ 5 & 7 \end{vmatrix}$.

c. Switch the columns in part **b** and evaluate again.

d. Verify that, in general, $\begin{vmatrix} a & b \\ c & d \end{vmatrix}$ and $\begin{vmatrix} b & a \\ d & c \end{vmatrix}$ are opposites.

e. Is it true that if you switch the *rows* in $\begin{vmatrix} a & b \\ c & d \end{vmatrix}$ you also get a sign change?

5. The evaluation of a determinant using expansion by minors can be extended to larger determinants. The pattern of signs shown in Figure 3.10 becomes

$$
\begin{matrix}
+ & - & + & - \\
- & + & - & + \\
+ & - & + & - \\
- & + & - & +
\end{matrix}
$$

in the 4 by 4 case. Evaluate $\begin{vmatrix} 3 & 2 & 4 & 1 \\ 1 & 0 & 1 & 0 \\ 2 & 0 & 3 & 2 \\ 4 & 0 & 2 & 3 \end{vmatrix}$ using expansion by minors along the second column. Why is this the easiest column to use?

CHAPTER 3 OVERVIEW

Section	Key Concepts or Procedures to Review
3.1	▪ The solution set of a system of linear equations consists of all pairs that satisfy both equations at the same time. Graphically, this is equivalent to finding all points the two lines have in common. ▪ Methods to solve a linear system by the addition-elimination method and by the substitution method
3.2	▪ The solution set of a system of three linear equations in three variables consists of all ordered triples that satisfy all the equations at the same time. ▪ Addition-elimination method of solving a linear system in three variables ▪ Geometric interpretations of consistent, inconsistent, and dependent linear systems in three variables

3.3 ▪ The following operations are used in Gaussian elimination to solve a linear system by transforming it to triangular form.

Elementary Operations on Equations	Elementary Row Operations on Matrices
1. Interchange two equations.	**1.** Interchange two rows.
2. Multiply both sides of an equation by a nonzero number.	**2.** Multiply each entry in a row by a nonzero number.
3. Add a multiple of one equation to another.	**3.** Add a multiple of the entries in one row to another row.

3.4 ▪ The value of a second-order determinant is given by

$$\begin{vmatrix} a_1 & b_1 \\ a_2 & b_2 \end{vmatrix} = a_1 b_2 - b_1 a_2.$$

▪ The value of a third-order determinant is given by

$$\begin{vmatrix} a_1 & b_1 & c_1 \\ a_2 & b_2 & c_2 \\ a_3 & b_3 & c_3 \end{vmatrix} = a_1 \begin{vmatrix} b_2 & c_2 \\ b_3 & c_3 \end{vmatrix} - a_2 \begin{vmatrix} b_1 & c_1 \\ b_3 & c_3 \end{vmatrix} + a_3 \begin{vmatrix} b_1 & c_1 \\ b_2 & c_2 \end{vmatrix}.$$

▪ Method to evaluate a third-order determinant by expansion by minors

▪ Cramer's rule for 2 by 2 and 3 by 3 systems

CHAPTER 3 REVIEW EXERCISES

1. Determine if $(5,-2)$ is a solution of the system.

$$x - y = 7$$
$$2x + 3y = 4$$

2. Solve by graphing: $2x + y = 5$
$$y = x + 2.$$

3. Solve by addition-elimination: $5x - 3y = 1$
$$-2x + 2y = -2.$$

4. Solve by substitution: $3x + 4y = -1$
$$-5x = y + 13.$$

5. How should a $40,000 investment be split so that the total annual earnings are $2,700 if one portion is invested at 7 percent annual interest and the rest at 5 percent?

6. Determine whether $(3,-2,4)$ is a solution of the system.

$$2x - y - z = 4$$
$$-3x + 2y + 3z = 1$$
$$5x + 3y - 2z = 1$$

7. Solve the system.

$$2x + y + 3z = 5$$
$$-x - 2y + z = -8$$
$$-3x + 3y - z = -2$$

8. Solve the system.

$$2B - 3C = 21$$
$$A + B + C = 0$$
$$5A - 3C = -6$$

9. Solve the system.

$$-x + 2y - z = 5$$
$$3x - y + 2z = -8$$
$$-2x - y - z = 3$$

10. Solve the system.

$$5x + 6y + 3z = 6$$
$$x + y + z = 6$$
$$x + 2y - z = 0$$

11. Find the value of $\begin{vmatrix} -4 & 5 \\ -8 & 3 \end{vmatrix}$.

12. Use Cramer's rule to solve the system.

$$3x + 7y = -1$$
$$-4x - 9y = 2$$

13. Solve by Cramer's rule.

$$-8y - 3 = -5x$$
$$10x - 1 = -24y$$

14. Evaluate the determinant by expansion by minors about the first column.

$$\begin{vmatrix} 2 & -3 & 4 \\ 1 & 0 & -2 \\ 2 & 1 & -1 \end{vmatrix}$$

15. Solve by Cramer's rule.

$$2x + 3y + 2z = 7$$
$$-2x + y - z = -5$$
$$3x + 2y + z = 12$$

16. Solve by transforming to triangular form.

$$3x + y + z = 0$$
$$x + 3y - z = -4$$
$$x - 4y + 4z = 5$$

17. Use matrix form (Gaussian elimination) to solve the system.

$$3x + 4y - 4 = 0$$
$$-2x - 5y - 2 = 0$$

18. Use matrix form (Gaussian elimination) to solve the system.

$$x - y + z = 2$$
$$2x - 3y + 2z = 6$$
$$3x + y + z = 2$$

19. The sum of two numbers is 70, and their difference is 22. What are the numbers?

20. Find two supplementary angles whose difference is $100°$.

21. A piece of lumber is 120 in. long. Where must it be cut for one piece to be four times longer than the other piece?

22. A container holding a liquid weighs 500 g. If one-half the liquid is poured out, the weight is 350 g. What is the weight of the empty container?

Evaluate.

23. $\begin{vmatrix} -6 & -5 \\ 1 & 0 \end{vmatrix}$

24. $\begin{vmatrix} 2 & -1 & 4 \\ 1 & 0 & 2 \\ 0 & 3 & -1 \end{vmatrix}$

Determine if the given ordered pair or triple is a solution of the system.

25. $(4,-3);$ $\begin{aligned} 2x - 5 &= y \\ x + y &= 1 \end{aligned}$

26. $(8,0,-2);$ $\begin{aligned} x - 2y + z &= 6 \\ -x + y - 3z &= -2 \\ -2x - 3y + 4z &= -24 \end{aligned}$

Solve. Use the indicated method.

27. $\begin{aligned} 4x - y &= -2 \\ 2x - y &= -5 \end{aligned}$ (substitution)

28. $\begin{aligned} 3x + 2y &= 4 \\ -4x - y &= 3 \end{aligned}$ (addition-elimination)

29. $\begin{aligned} 5x + 2y &= 1 \\ 4x + 3y &= 5 \end{aligned}$ (addition-elimination)

30. $\begin{aligned} y &= x + 7 \\ y &= 2x + 6 \end{aligned}$ (graphing)

31. $\begin{aligned} 4x - 3y &= -26 \\ -5x + 3y &= 7 \end{aligned}$ (Cramer's rule)

32. $\begin{aligned} x + y - 2z &= 0 \\ 2x + 2y - z &= 1 \\ 3x + 2y - 3z &= 3 \end{aligned}$ (Cramer's rule)

33. $\begin{aligned} 3a - 7b &= -2 \\ 5a + 2b &= -17 \end{aligned}$ (matrix form)

34. $\begin{aligned} -x - y + 2z &= 7 \\ x + 2y - 2z &= -7 \\ 2x - y + z &= -4 \end{aligned}$ (matrix form)

35. $\begin{aligned} -5x - 2y - 1 &= 0 \\ 8x + 4y + 4 &= 0 \end{aligned}$ (any method)

36. $\begin{aligned} x + y + 3z &= 1 \\ 2x + 5y + 2z &= 0 \\ 3x - 2y - z &= 3 \end{aligned}$ (triangular form)

37. $\begin{aligned} 2x - y + 3z &= 1 \\ -x + y - z &= -1 \\ 3x - 2y + 4z &= 2 \end{aligned}$ (any method)

38. One video store rents tapes for an annual membership of $12 plus $2.75 per rental. For nonmembers the cost is $3.15 per tape. How many tapes must be rented annually for the cost to be the same for members and nonmembers?

39. Admission to a concert was $5 for students and $7 for nonstudents. There were 525 paid admissions, and total receipts were $3,053. How many students attended the concert?

40. The points $(1,-1)$, $(2,3)$ and $(-1,9)$ lie on the parabola given by $y = ax^2 + bx + c$. Find a, b, and c.

41. Find the intersection point of the line $y = \dfrac{3}{4}x - \dfrac{1}{4}$ and the line whose x- and y-intercepts are $(6, 0)$ and $(0, 4)$.

42. A student took out three loans at different rates: a car loan at 8 percent annual interest, a tuition loan at 6 percent, and a loan for travel expenses at 10 percent. The total interest due in one year was $960. The car loan was $1000 less than the tuition loan. The car and travel loans combined were $1000 more than the tuition loan. Find the size of each loan.

CHAPTER 3 TEST

1. Evaluate $\begin{vmatrix} -2 & -1 \\ 5 & 1 \end{vmatrix}$.

2. Evaluate $\begin{vmatrix} 1 & 2 & 0 \\ 1 & 0 & 3 \\ 0 & 1 & -1 \end{vmatrix}$. Expand by minors around the first column.

3. The ordered pair $(-5, -2)$ is a solution of which of the following systems?

　a. $\begin{aligned} -x + 2y &= -1 \\ 2x + y &= 8 \end{aligned}$　**b.** $\begin{aligned} x + y + 7 &= 0 \\ -x + 2y - 1 &= 0 \end{aligned}$

　c. $\begin{aligned} x &= y - 3 \\ 2x &= y + 8 \end{aligned}$

4. Which of the following is a solution of the system?

$$\begin{aligned} -4x + y + 2z &= 3 \\ x + 2y - z &= -7 \\ 2x - y + 3z &= -4 \end{aligned}$$

　a. $(-2,-3,-1)$　**b.** $(0,1,1)$　**c.** $(2,-1,-5)$

In Questions 5–15, solve the given system using the method indicated.

5. $\begin{aligned} 2x + 3y &= 0 \\ 4x + 9y &= 1 \end{aligned}$ (addition-elimination)

6. $\begin{aligned} y &= -3x + 4 \\ y &= 2x - 6 \end{aligned}$ (substitution)

7. $\begin{aligned} x - y + z &= 5 \\ -x + 2y - 2z &= -5 \\ 2x - 2y + 3z &= 9 \end{aligned}$ (triangular form)

8. $\begin{aligned} 3x + y &= 2 \\ -3x + y &= -2 \end{aligned}$ (Cramer's rule)

9. $\begin{aligned} x + z &= 10 \\ y + 2z &= 3 \\ -x + y &= -2 \end{aligned}$ (Cramer's rule)

10. $\begin{aligned} 5x + 3y &= 1 \\ 3x + 2y &= 0 \end{aligned}$ (matrix form)

11. $\begin{aligned} -x + 3y - 5 &= 0 \\ 4x - y - 2 &= 0 \end{aligned}$ (matrix form)

12. $5x - 4y = -3$
    $2x + 7y = -27$ (addition-elimination)

13. $x + 3y + 3z = 5$
    $x + 4y + 3z = 2$
    $x + 3y + 4z = 8$ (matrix form)

14. $\ x + y - \ z = 2$
    $2x - y + 5z = 3$
    $-x - y + \ z = -1$ (addition-elimination)

15. $x + y = 6$
    $\quad\quad y = 2x$ (graphing)

16. Find two complementary angles whose difference is $20°$.

17. Find a, b, and c so that the parabola $y = ax^2 + bx + c$ passes through the points $(1, 3)$ $(-1, 9)$ and $(2, 6)$.

18. The total cost of producing necklaces consists of $300 per month for rent plus $4 per unit for material. If the selling price for the necklaces is $9, how many units must be made and sold per month for the company to break even?

19. A manager invests a total of $150,000. The investment is split between a bank CD yielding 6 percent interest and a stock that pays a 9 percent dividend. If the total annual income from the investment is $12,300, how much is invested in the bank CD?

20. A 3,000-seat theater was sold out for a weekend concert. Total receipts on Friday night were $45,300 when seats in the orchestra, mezzanine, and balcony sold for $18, $15, and $12, respectively. On Saturday, prices were raised to $25, $20, and $14, and total receipts increased to $59,800. How many seats are in the balcony?

Introduction to Trigonometry

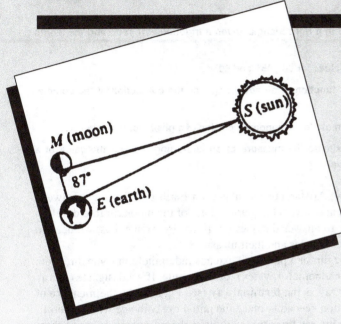

The first major attempt to measure the relative distances of the sun and the moon from Earth was made in about 280 B.C. by the Alexandrian astronomer Aristarchus. Basically, he reasoned that the moon has no light of its own since we do not always see a "full moon." Therefore, the moon, like Earth, must receive its light from the sun and then reflect this light toward Earth. As illustrated in the figure, he also correctly reasoned that at a quarter phase of the moon, when it is half light and half dark, angle *EMS* is a right angle. Using primitive instruments, Aristarchus measured angle *SEM* to be 29/30 of a right angle (or 87°). About how many times more distant is the sun than the moon in Aristarchus' estimate?

(See Example 7 of Section 4.1.)

In this chapter and in Chapter 9, we turn to trigonometry. This topic can be approached from different viewpoints, and in these chapters we provide three definitions of the trigonometric functions. These definitions are presented in order of abstraction and sophistication. In this section we begin with the rather concrete study of right-triangle trigonometry, and we follow this in Section 4.3 with a general angle approach. Finally, in Section 9.2 we discuss the modern concept of the trigonometric functions of real numbers which is the approach most useful in calculus. In the end, you must merge these definitions for a thorough understanding of trigonometry.

Historically, trigonometry involved the study of triangles for the purpose of measuring angles and distances in astronomy (as illustrated above). In early times this science was the primary concern of scholars who sought to understand God's design of the universe, aesthetically and, practically, sought to obtain a more accurate system of navigation. As is often the case in mathematics, the ideas developed in this study later proved useful in analyzing a wide variety of situations.

4.1 Trigonometric Functions of Acute Angles

OBJECTIVES

1. Find the six trigonometric functions of an acute angle in a right triangle, when given at least two side lengths.

2. Find the values of the five remaining trigonometric functions of an acute angle, given one function value.

3. Find the length of any side in a right triangle, given a trigonometric ratio and the length of one side.

4. State exact trigonometric values for 30°, 45°, and 60°.

5. Express any trigonometric function of an acute angle as the cofunction of the complementary angle.

6. Use a calculator to approximate the trigonometric value of a given acute angle.

7. Use a calculator to approximate the measure of an acute angle, given the value of a trigonometric function of that angle.

In the chapter-opening problem, Aristarchus calculated on Earth that the angle between the sun and the moon measures about 87° at a quarter phase of the moon. Before developing the trigonometry necessary to answer the question posed by Aristarchus, we need to review some basic concepts about angles and their measures.

A ray is a half-line that begins at a point and extends indefinitely in some direction. Two rays that share a common endpoint (or vertex) form an angle. If we designate one ray as the **initial ray** and the other ray as the **terminal ray** (see Figure 4.1), the **measure of the angle** is the amount of rotation needed to make the initial ray coincide with the terminal ray. Notice that there are many rotations that will make the rays coincide, since there is no limitation on the number of revolutions made by the initial ray. In fact, it is useful to allow the initial ray to rotate through many revolutions, since the rotating initial ray will demonstrate cyclic behavior that can serve as a model to simulate physical phenomena that occur in cycles. Also, the initial ray can rotate in two possible directions, as shown in Figure 4.1. To show the direction of the rotation, we define the measure of an angle to be positive if the rotation is counterclockwise, and negative if the rotation is clockwise.

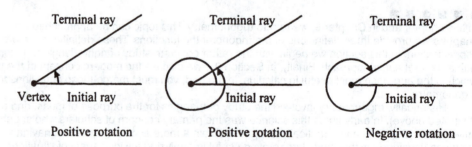

Figure 4.1

A common unit of the measure of an angle is a degree. We define **one degree (1°)** to be 1/360 of a complete counterclockwise rotation. Equivalently, this means that there are 360° in a complete counterclockwise rotation. Figure 4.2 illustrates this case, a straight angle, and a right angle using the Greek letter θ (theta) to represent the angle measure. An angle is **acute** if it measures between 0° and 90°, and **obtuse** if it measures between 90° and 180°.

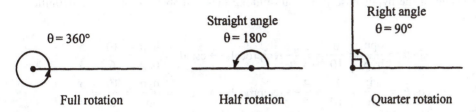

Figure 4.2

Because precise measurements are often needed, the degree is subdivided into 60 smaller units called minutes, with each minute being subdivided into 60 seconds. Thus, **one minute,** written 1′, equals 1/60 of one degree, and **one second,** written 1″, equals 1/60 of one minute—or 1/3600 of one degree. One degree may also be subdivided by using decimal degrees such as 18.5°, which is a unit more convenient for calculator evaluation.

To define the trigonometric functions with respect to a triangle, we start with a right triangle. A **right triangle** is a triangle that contains a 90° (or right) angle. The two other angles in the triangle are acute angles and the side opposite the right angle is called the **hypotenuse.** In a right triangle, six different ratios can be formed using the measures of the three sides of the triangle, and these ratios are related to the measure of an acute angle in the following definitions.

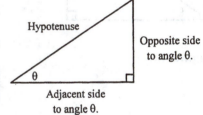

Figure 4.3

Definition of the Trigonometric Functions

If θ (theta) is an acute angle in a right triangle, as shown in Figure 4.3, then

Name of Function	Abbreviation	Ratio	
sine of angle θ	sin θ	$= \dfrac{\text{opposite}}{\text{hypotenuse}}$	reciprocal functions
cosecant of angle θ	csc θ	$= \dfrac{\text{hypotenuse}}{\text{opposite}}$	
cosine of angle θ	cos θ	$= \dfrac{\text{adjacent}}{\text{hypotenuse}}$	reciprocal functions
secant of angle θ	sec θ	$= \dfrac{\text{hypotenuse}}{\text{adjacent}}$	
tangent of angle θ	tan θ	$= \dfrac{\text{opposite}}{\text{adjacent}}$	reciprocal functions
cotangent of angle θ	cot θ	$= \dfrac{\text{adjacent}}{\text{opposite}}$	

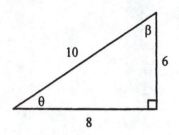

Figure 4.4

EXAMPLE 1   Finding Trigonometric Functions When Given Side Lengths

Find the values of the six trigonometric functions of angle θ in Figure 4.4.

Solution   The length of the side opposite angle θ is 6, the adjacent side length is 8, and the length of the hypotenuse is 10. Substituting these numbers in the above definitions gives

$$\sin \theta = \frac{\text{opp}}{\text{hyp}} = \frac{6}{10} = \frac{3}{5} \leftarrow \text{reciprocals} \rightarrow \csc \theta = \frac{\text{hyp}}{\text{opp}} = \frac{10}{6} = \frac{5}{3}$$

$$\cos \theta = \frac{\text{adj}}{\text{hyp}} = \frac{8}{10} = \frac{4}{5} \leftarrow \text{reciprocals} \rightarrow \sec \theta = \frac{\text{hyp}}{\text{adj}} = \frac{10}{8} = \frac{5}{4}$$

$$\tan \theta = \frac{\text{opp}}{\text{adj}} = \frac{6}{8} = \frac{3}{4} \leftarrow \text{reciprocals} \rightarrow \cot \theta = \frac{\text{adj}}{\text{opp}} = \frac{8}{6} = \frac{4}{3}.$$

Note that if we say $\tan \theta = 3/4$, we do not necessarily mean that the opposite side length is 3 and the adjacent side length is 4, but that their lengths are in the ratio of 3 to 4.

PROGRESS CHECK 1   Find the values of the six trigonometric functions of angle β (beta) in Figure 4.4.   ■

EXAMPLE 2   Finding Trigonometric Functions Given One Function Value

Find the values of the remaining trigonometric functions of acute angle θ if $\tan \theta = \frac{2}{5}$.

Solution   First, draw a right triangle, as in Figure 4.5, and label one acute angle θ. Since $\tan \theta = 2/5$, the ratio of the opposite side length to the adjacent side length is 2:5. Although many choices are possible, it is easiest to label the opposite side 2 and the adjacent side 5. The hypotenuse in the triangle is found by Pythagorean relationship,

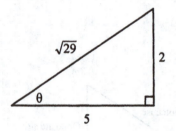

Figure 4.5

$$(\text{hypotenuse})^2 = 2^2 + 5^2 = 29$$
$$\text{hypotenuse} = \sqrt{29}.$$

Then

$$\sin \theta = \frac{2}{\sqrt{29}} \leftarrow \text{reciprocals} \rightarrow \csc \theta = \frac{\sqrt{29}}{2}$$

$$\cos \theta = \frac{5}{\sqrt{29}} \leftarrow \text{reciprocals} \rightarrow \sec \theta = \frac{\sqrt{29}}{5}$$

$$\cot \theta = \frac{5}{2}.$$

Note that $\cot \theta = 5/2$ can be determined from its reciprocal relation to $\tan \theta = 2/5$ without constructing the triangle.

PROGRESS CHECK 2   Find the values of the remaining trigonometric functions of acute angle θ if $\cos \theta = \frac{2}{5}$.   ■

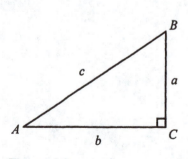

Figure 4.6

It is common notation to label a right triangle as in Figure 4.6. Capital letters such as A, B, and C denote angles, while the lengths of the sides opposite these angles are labeled with the corresponding lowercase letters, a, b, and c. The next example illustrates this notation.

EXAMPLE 3   Using a Trigonometric Ratio to Find a Side Length

In the right triangle ABC with $C = 90°$, if $\cos B = \dfrac{5}{13}$ and $c = 39$, find a.

Solution   From Figure 4.6 we have

$$\cos B = \frac{\text{adj}}{\text{hyp}} = \frac{a}{c} = \frac{5}{13}.$$

Substituting $c = 39$ gives

$$\frac{a}{39} = \frac{5}{13}.$$

Then

$$a = 39\left(\frac{5}{13}\right)$$

$$= 15.$$

PROGRESS CHECK 3   In triangle ABC with $C = 90°$, if $\sin A = \dfrac{8}{17}$ and $a = 40$, find c.   ■

   To demonstrate why the trigonometric relationships define functions, consider Figure 4.7. Right triangles ABC and $AB'C'$ contain the same angle measures. Two triangles with the same angle measures are called **similar triangles,** and one of the properties of similar triangles is that the lengths of corresponding sides are proportional. Therefore,

$$\frac{a}{c} = \frac{a'}{c'}, \quad \frac{b}{c} = \frac{b'}{c'}, \quad \frac{a}{b} = \frac{a'}{b'}, \quad \text{and so on.}$$

This means that the six trigonometric ratios depend only on angle A, and not on the size of the right triangle that contains A. Since there is exactly one number associated with a particular trigonometric ratio of angle A, the term *function* applies.

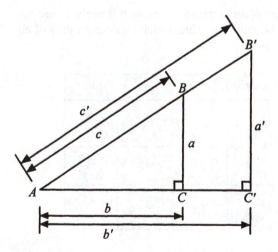

Figure 4.7

So far we have determined the values of the trigonometric functions by applying their definitions to triangles whose side measures were known. A common problem is determining these values if we know the measure of angle θ. First, let us consider the special angles whose trigonometric values are known exactly. Figure 4.8 shows the acute angles 30°, 45°, and 60° contained in two right triangles. The diagonal in a square with a side length of 1 unit forms the right triangle with a 45° angle; the altitude in an equilateral triangle with a side length of 2 units forms the right triangle with angles of 30° and 60°. Using these two triangles, we may determine the value of any of their trigonometric functions.

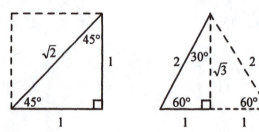

Figure 4.8

EXAMPLE 4   Exact Trigonometric Values for 30°, 45°, and 60°

Use Figure 4.8 to find the exact values of sin 30°, cos 45°, sec 45°, and tan 60°.

Solution   Applying the definitions of the trigonometric functions to the appropriate triangle in Figure 4.8 gives

$$\sin 30° = \frac{\text{opp}}{\text{hyp}} = \frac{1}{2}, \qquad \cos 45° = \frac{\text{adj}}{\text{hyp}} = \frac{1}{\sqrt{2}},$$

$$\sec 45° = \frac{\text{hyp}}{\text{adj}} = \sqrt{2}, \quad \text{and} \quad \tan 60° = \frac{\text{opp}}{\text{adj}} = \sqrt{3}.$$

PROGRESS CHECK 4   Use Figure 4.8 to find the exact values of sin 60°, cot 30°, csc 30°, and tan 45°.   ■

The angles 30°, 45°, and 60° appear often in trigonometry, so it is useful to use the methods shown in Example 4 to create the following table, which lists exact values of all trigonometric functions of these special angles.

θ	$\sin \theta$	$\csc \theta$	$\cos \theta$	$\sec \theta$	$\tan \theta$	$\cot \theta$
30°	$\dfrac{1}{2}$	2	$\dfrac{\sqrt{3}}{2}$	$\dfrac{2}{\sqrt{3}}$	$\dfrac{1}{\sqrt{3}}$	$\sqrt{3}$
60°	$\dfrac{\sqrt{3}}{2}$	$\dfrac{2}{\sqrt{3}}$	$\dfrac{1}{2}$	2	$\sqrt{3}$	$\dfrac{1}{\sqrt{3}}$
45°	$\dfrac{1}{\sqrt{2}}$	$\sqrt{2}$	$\dfrac{1}{\sqrt{2}}$	$\sqrt{2}$	1	1

This table may be used to provide numerical evidence for an important relation in trigonometry by noting the similarity between the values of the trigonometric functions for 30° and 60°. For example:

$$\sin 30° = \frac{1}{2} \quad \text{and} \quad \cos 60° = \frac{1}{2}$$

$$\tan 30° = \frac{1}{\sqrt{3}} \quad \text{and} \quad \cot 60° = \frac{1}{\sqrt{3}}$$

$$\sec 30° = \frac{2}{\sqrt{3}} \quad \text{and} \quad \csc 60° = \frac{2}{\sqrt{3}}.$$

This similarity results from the fact that in the right triangle, the side opposite the 30° angle is adjacent to the 60° angle. Thus,

$$\sin 30° = \frac{\text{side opposite 30° angle}}{\text{hypotenuse}} = \frac{1}{2}$$

$$= \frac{\text{side adjacent to 60° angle}}{\text{hypotenuse}} = \cos 60°$$

$$\tan 30° = \frac{\text{side opposite 30° angle}}{\text{side adjacent to 30° angle}} = \frac{1}{\sqrt{3}}$$

$$= \frac{\text{side adjacent to 60° angle}}{\text{side opposite 60° angle}} = \cot 60°$$

$$\sec 30° = \frac{\text{hypotenuse}}{\text{side adjacent to 30° angle}} = \frac{2}{\sqrt{3}}$$

$$= \frac{\text{hypotenuse}}{\text{side opposite 60° angle}} = \csc 60°.$$

Observe that in each case a trigonometric function of 30° is equal to the corresponding cofunction of 60°. The corresponding cofunction is easy to remember since the *co*function of the sine is the *co*sine, the cofunction of the tangent is the *co*tangent, and the cofunction of the secant is the *co*secant. We can generalize from these examples concerning 30° and 60° to any two angles A and B that are **complementary** (that is, $A + B = 90°$), since in any right triangle the side opposite angle A is adjacent to angle B. Thus, a trigonometric function of any acute angle is equal to the corresponding cofunction of the complementary angle. This result may be stated as follows.

Cofunction Properties

For any acute angle θ,

$$\sin(90° - \theta) = \cos \theta \qquad \cos(90° - \theta) = \sin \theta$$
$$\tan(90° - \theta) = \cot \theta \qquad \cot(90° - \theta) = \tan \theta$$
$$\sec(90° - \theta) = \csc \theta \qquad \csc(90° - \theta) = \sec \theta.$$

EXAMPLE 5   Equating Cofunctions of Complementary Angles

Express $\tan 75°$ as a function of the angle complementary to 75°.

Solution   Using $\cot(90° - \theta) = \tan \theta$ with $\theta = 75°$ yields

$$\tan 75° = \cot(90° - 75°)$$
$$= \cot 15°.$$

In other words, $\tan 75° = \cot 15°$, since 75° and 15° are complementary angles and the cofunction of the tangent is the cotangent.

PROGRESS CHECK 5 Express cos 34° as a function of the angle complementary to 34°.   ■

A fast and accurate method for evaluating trigonometric functions of acute angles is to use a calculator. Because calculators may be set in different modes for measuring angles, you must first consult the owner's manual to your calculator and learn the procedure for operating in Degree mode (instead of Radian mode, which is considered in Section 9.1). Then, the keys Sin, Cos, or Tan may be used to evaluate sine, cosine, or tangent expressions, while the reciprocals of these functions may be evaluated by using

$$\csc \theta = \frac{1}{\sin \theta}, \sec \theta = \frac{1}{\cos \theta}, \text{ or } \cot \theta = \frac{1}{\tan \theta}.$$

EXAMPLE 6   Evaluating Trigonometric Functions by Calculator

Evaluate each expression by calculator to four decimal places.

a. sin 18°   **b.** cos 52°20′   **c.** cot 35.6°

Solution See Figure 4.9.

a. sin 18° ≈ 0.3090
b. cos 52°20′ ≈ 0.6111. Note that 20 minutes may be entered as 20/60 because one minute is 1/60 of one degree.
c. Using cot 35.6° = 1/tan 35.6° yields cot 35.6° ≈ 1.3968.

Note Many calculators have special features for entering angles in degree-minute-second format and for displaying the degree symbol so that the calculator computes in Degree mode regardless of the current angular mode setting. You should learn how to use these features on your calculator if they are available.

PROGRESS CHECK 6 Evaluate each expression by calculator to four decimal places.

a. tan 62°   **b.** sec 16.7°   **c.** sin 81°50′   ■

EXAMPLE 7   Relative Distances of the Sun and the Moon

Solve the problem in the chapter introduction on page 195.

Solution Consider Figure 4.10. The length of the hypotenuse $(\overline{ES})$ represents the distance from the Earth to the sun, while the length of the adjacent side $(\overline{EM})$ represents the distance from Earth to the moon. The ratio $\overline{ES}/\overline{EM}$ represents how many times more distant is the sun than the moon from Earth. Then

$$\frac{\overline{ES}}{\overline{EM}} = \frac{\text{hypotenuse}}{\text{adjacent}} = \sec 87° \approx 19.11.$$

Thus, Aristarchus estimated that the sun is about 19 times farther away than the moon.

```
sin 18
              .309016994375
cos (52 + 20/60)
              .61106662153
1/tan 35.6
             1.39678522019
```

Figure 4.9

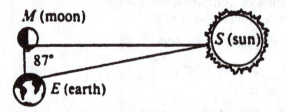

Figure 4.10

PROGRESS CHECK 7   In reality, Aristarchus' estimate is not close to the true ratio. The error is caused by his measurement for angle *SEM,* which should be about 89°50′. On the basis of this measurement for angle *SEM,* about how many times farther away is the sun than the moon?   ■

An important theme in problem solving is the notion that certain problems may be viewed as inverse problems. In the context of trigonometry, the following problems state the basic inverse problems with respect to the sine function.

Inverse   ┌──▶ Problem   Given θ, find $\sin \theta$.
problems └──▶ Problem   Given $\sin \theta$, find θ.

On the basis of this perspective, the function that reverses the assignments of the sine function is called the **inverse sine function.** On most calculators this function is labeled $\sin^{-1}$. Similar notation is used for the other inverse trigonometric functions, and the following table illustrates comparable information using a trigonometric function and its corresponding inverse trigonometric function.

Trigonometric relation	Relation in inverse notation
$\sin 30° = \dfrac{1}{2}$	$\sin^{-1}\dfrac{1}{2} = 30°$
$\tan 45° = 1$	$\tan^{-1} 1 = 45°$
$\cot 60° = \dfrac{1}{\sqrt{3}}$	$\cot^{-1}\left(\dfrac{1}{\sqrt{3}}\right) = 60°$

Most calculators have keys for $\sin^{-1}$, $\cos^{-1}$, and $\tan^{-1}$ that may be used to find an acute angle when one of the trigonometric functions is known, as illustrated in the next example. For such problems, it is important to recognize that a superscript -1 is used to denote an inverse function. Do *not* interpret the -1 in this notation as an exponent.

EXAMPLE 8   Using an Inverse Key on a Calculator

Use a calculator to approximate the acute angle θ that satisfies the given equation. Write solutions to the nearest tenth of a degree and to the nearest 10 minutes.

a. $\sin \theta = 0.7957$ **b.** $\cot \theta = 2.583$

Solution

a. If $\sin \theta = 0.7957$ and θ is an acute angle, then

$$\theta = \sin^{-1} 0.7957 \approx 52.7°,$$

as shown in Figure 4.11. To convert to degree-minute format, multiply the decimal portion of this answer by 60 minutes, as shown in the last four lines of Figure 4.11. To the nearest 10 minutes, the decimal portion rounds to 40 minutes, so $\sin^{-1} 0.7957 \approx 52°40′$.

b. Calculators do not have keys for inverse cotangent, secant, or cosecant functions, so first observe that $\cot \theta = 2.583$ is equivalent to $\tan \theta = 1/2.583$. The display in Figure 4.12 then shows that acute angle θ is given by

$$\theta = \tan^{-1}(1/2.583) \approx 21.2°.$$

By the methods discussed in part **a,** the decimal portion of this result rounds to 10 minutes, so we also have $\theta \approx 21°10′$. Many calculators have a special feature for converting from decimal degrees to degree-minute-second format, and the last two lines in Figure 4.12 display such a conversion that supports our result in this example.

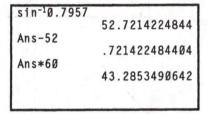

Figure 4.11

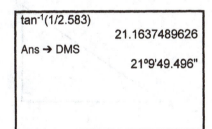

Figure 4.12

PROGRESS CHECK 8 Use a calculator to approximate the acute angle θ that satisfies the given equation. Write solutions to the nearest tenth of a degree and to the nearest 10 minutes.

a. $\cos \theta = 0.2728$ **b.** $\csc \theta = 1.448$ ■

Note For correct calculator evaluation of trigonometric expressions, the calculator Mode must be set properly. At this point in the course, the calculator should be set in Degree mode. Later you may want to switch to Radian mode. Another approach, which allows you to ignore the mode setting, is to always insert the degree symbol, but this is less convenient.

EXERCISES 4.1

In Exercises 1–4 find the six trigonometric functions of the acute angles in the right triangle.

1.

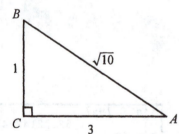

2.

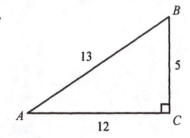

3.

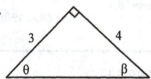

4.

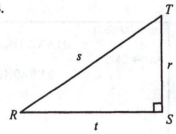

In Exercises 5–12 use these two triangles

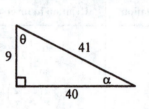
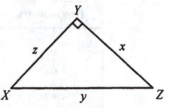

5. Find $\cos Z$. **6.** Find $\sec \theta$.
7. Find $\cot \alpha$. **8.** Find $\sin \alpha$.
9. Find $\csc X$. **10.** Find $\tan \theta$.

11. Represent the ratio $\dfrac{y}{z}$ as a trigonometric function of an acute angle.

12. Represent the ratio $\dfrac{9}{40}$ as a trigonometric function of an acute angle.

In Exercises 13–18 use the reciprocal relations between the functions.

13. If $\sin \theta = \dfrac{1}{3}$, find $\csc \theta$.

14. If $\cos \theta = \dfrac{3}{4}$, find $\sec \theta$.

15. If $\sec \theta = 1.4$, find $\cos \theta$.
16. If $\tan \theta = 0.7$, find $\cot \theta$.
17. What is the value of $\sin \theta \cdot \csc \theta$ for all acute angles θ?
18. What is the value of $3 \tan \theta \cdot \cot \theta$ for all acute angles θ?

In Exercises 19–24 use the given trigonometric ratio to find the other trigonometric functions of acute angle θ. Use the definitions of the functions, not a calculator.

19. $\sin \theta = \dfrac{1}{2}$ **20.** $\csc \theta = 2$

21. $\cot \theta = \dfrac{3}{5}$ **22.** $\cos \theta = \dfrac{8}{17}$

23. $\tan \theta = 2$ **24.** $\sec \theta = 5$

In Exercises 25–30 refer to this triangle

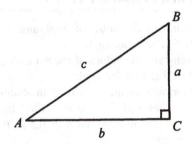

25. If $\cos B = \dfrac{4}{5}$ and $a = 16$, find c.

26. If $\sin A = \dfrac{12}{13}$ and $c = 39$, find a.

27. If $\tan A = \dfrac{7}{12}$ and $a = 21$, find b.

28. If $\csc B = 2$ and $c = 8$, find a

29. If $a = 5$, $b = 12$, and $c = 13$, find the cosine of the smaller acute angle.

30. If $c = 17$ and $a = 8$, find the tangent of the larger acute angle.

In Exercises 31–36 express each term as a function of the angle complementary to the given angle.

31. $\sin 17°$ **32.** $\cos 64°$

33. $\tan 81°30'$ **34.** $\sec 33°58'$

35. $\csc 68.1°$ **36.** $\cot 0.5°$

In Exercises 37–44 use the exact trigonometric values of 30°, 45°, or 60°.

37. Does $2 \sin 30° = \sin 60°$?

38. Does $\sin 60° \csc 30° = \tan 60°$?

39. Does $\sin 45° \cos 45° = 1$?

40. Does $\sin 30° = \sqrt{\dfrac{1 - \cos 60°}{2}}$?

41. Does $(\tan 45°)^2 + 1 = (\sec 45°)^2$?

42. Does $\cos 60° = 1 - 2(\sin 30°)^2$?

43. If the length of the short leg of a 30–60–90 triangle is 2, determine the lengths of the other two sides of the triangle.

44. If the length of a leg of a 45–45–90 triangle is 5, determine the length of the hypotenuse of the triangle.

In Exercises 45–52 use the given figures to find the exact values of the given expression

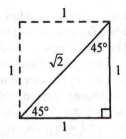 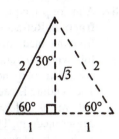

45. $\cos 30°$ **46.** $\sin 45°$

47. $\sec 30°$ **48.** $\csc 45°$

49. $\cot 60°$ **50.** $\tan 30°$

51. $\sin 45°$ **52.** $\cos 60°$

In Exercises 53–66 approximate each using a calculator.

53. $\cos 7°$ **54.** $\sin 42°$

55. $\cot 83°$ **56.** $\csc 54°$

57. $\tan 79°30'$ **58.** $\sec 65°10'$

59. $\csc 51°00'$ **60.** $\cot 16°40'$

61. $\sin 12.3°$ **62.** $\tan 47.6°$

63. $\cot 89.9°$ **64.** $\csc 0.1°$

65. $\cot 2°07'$ **66.** $\cos 19°19'$

For Exercises 67–72 use the figure given with Exercises 45–52 to find the acute angle given.

67. $\cos^{-1} \dfrac{1}{2}$ **68.** $\sec^{-1} \sqrt{2}$

69. $\sin^{-1} \dfrac{\sqrt{3}}{2}$ **70.** $\csc^{-1} \dfrac{2}{\sqrt{3}}$

71. $\tan^{-1} 1$ **72.** $\cot^{-1} \sqrt{3}$

In Exercises 73–84 approximate the measure of angle θ. Write solutions to the nearest 10 minutes and to the nearest tenth of a degree by calculator.

73. $\sin \theta = 0.7071$ **74.** $\cos \theta = 0.8660$

75. $\tan \theta = 0.7907$ **76.** $\cot \theta = 2.699$

77. $\sec \theta = 1.781$ **78.** $\csc \theta = 49.11$

79. $\cot \theta = 0.7651$ **80.** $\tan \theta = 0.0402$

81. $\csc \theta = 16.00$ **82.** $\sec \theta = 1.549$

83. $\sin \theta = 0.9973$ **84.** $\cos \theta = 0.9513$

85. The formula for the horizontal distance traveled by a projectile, neglecting air resistance, is

$$d = V^2 \frac{\sin A \sin B}{16}$$

where V is the initial velocity, A the angle of elevation, and $B = 90° - A$. In the 16-lb shot-putting event, an athlete releases the ball at an angle of elevation of 42°, with an initial velocity of 47 ft/second. Determine the distance of the throw. (The maximum distance is attained when the release angle is 45°.)

86. Answer the question posed in Exercise 85 if the ball is released at an angle of elevation of 48° with an initial velocity of 47 ft/second.

87. A major principle in the theory of light is the **law of refraction.** Refraction is the bending of light as it passes from one medium to another. For example, consider the following diagram, which shows a ray of light bending toward the perpendicular as it passes from air to water. The bending is caused by the change in speed of the light ray as it slows down in the water, which is the denser medium. The mathematical relation between the angle of incidence (*i*) and the angle of refraction (*r*) is a trigonometric ratio called **Snell's law.** The law is

$$\frac{\sin i}{\sin r} = \frac{v_i}{v_r},$$

where $\frac{v_i}{v_r}$ is the ratio between the velocities of light in the two media.

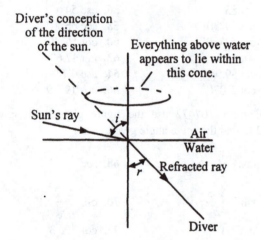

a. As light passes from air to water, $\frac{v_i}{v_r}$ is about $\frac{4}{3}$. Find the angle of refraction if $i = 68.5°$.

b. When the sun is near the horizon, the angle of incidence approaches 90° and the angle at which the sun's rays penetrate the water approaches a limiting value. Determine this value of *r*. It is interesting to note that this restriction on the angle of refraction causes an optical illusion for a diver under water, as shown in the diagram. As she looks up, the world above the surface appears to be in the shape of a cone. This distorted perspective is called the "fish-eye view of the world."

88. The ratio $\frac{v_i}{v_r}$ given in Exercise 87 is called the Index of Refraction when one medium is air. Most ordinary glass has a refraction index of about 1.5. Refer to the figure in Exercise 87, but assume that instead of water, the bottom medium is glass.

a. Find the angle of refraction if $i = 50°$.

b. Find *r*, the angle of refraction, when $i = 90°$.

THINK ABOUT IT 4.1

1. Explain why the values of $\sin \theta$ range between 0 and 1 when θ is an acute angle.

2. Explain why the values of $\csc \theta$ are always greater than 1 when θ is an acute angle.

3. The formula for the volume of an oblique cylinder (see diagram below) is $V = \pi R^2 H$. Find the volume of an oblique cylinder in which $R = 0.5$ m, $\theta = 75°$, and the slant height is 2.1 m.

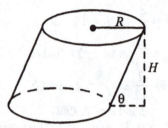

4. In the figure below find the exact values for *m*, *n*, *p*, and *q*.

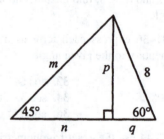

5. In the figure below find θ_1, θ_2, θ_3, θ_4 and θ_5. Which measures are exact and which are approximations?

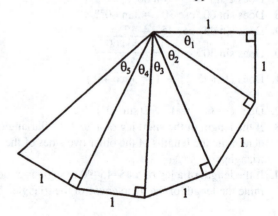

4.2 Right Triangle Applications

For maximum safety the distance between the base of a ladder and a building should be one-fourth of the length of the ladder. Find the angle that the ladder makes with the ground when it is set up in the safest position. (See Example 6.)

Courtesy of Prentice-Hall, Inc.

O B J E C T I V E S

1 Solve a right triangle, given one side and one acute angle.

2 Solve a right triangle, given two sides.

3 Solve applied problems involving right triangles.

Solving triangles is a basic goal in trigonometry. To solve a right triangle means to find the measures of the two acute angles and the lengths of the three sides of the triangle. To accomplish this, at least two of these five values must be known, and one or more must be a side length. In this section we follow the standard practice of simplifying the notation by always labeling the angles of the triangle as A, B, and C, with C designating the right angle.

EXAMPLE 1   Solving a Right Triangle: Angle-Side Case

Solve the right triangle ABC in which $A = 30°$ and $c = 100$ ft.

Solution   First, sketch Figure 4.13. We find angle B, since angles A and B are complementary.

$$A + B = 90°$$
$$30° + B = 90°$$
$$B = 60°$$

Second, we can find side length a by using the sine function.

$$\sin A = \frac{a}{c}$$

$$\sin 30° = \frac{a}{100}$$

$$100(\sin 30°) = a$$

$$50 \text{ ft} = a \quad \text{(two significant digits)}$$

Third, we can find b by using the cosine function.

$$\cos A = \frac{b}{c}$$

$$\cos 30° = \frac{b}{100}$$

$$100(\cos 30°) = b$$

$$87 \text{ ft} = b \quad \text{(two significant digits)}$$

To summarize, we found that $B = 60°$, $a = 50$ ft, and $b = 87$ ft.

PROGRESS CHECK 1   Solve the right triangle ABC in which $B = 58°$ and $a = 35$ ft.   ■

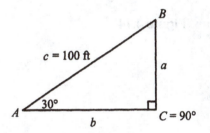

Figure 4.13

In applications of trigonometry our values are only as accurate as the devices we use to measure the data. However, although our answers are approximations, the symbol for equality ($=$) is generally used instead of the more precise symbol for approximation ($\approx$). Computed results should not be used to determine other parts of a triangle, since the given data produce more accurate answers. The results are usually rounded off as follows:

Accuracy of Sides	Accuracy of Angle
Two significant digits	Nearest degree
Three significant digits	Nearest 10 minutes or tenth of a degree
Four significant digits	Nearest minute or hundredth of a degree

EXAMPLE 2   Solving a Right Triangle: Angle-Side Case

Solve the right triangle ABC in which $B = 47°10'$ and $a = 45.6$ ft.

Solution   First, sketch Figure 4.14. Now find A.

$$A + B = 90°$$
$$A + 47°10' = 90°$$
$$A = 42°50'$$

Figure 4.14

Second, we can find the length of the hypotenuse c by using the secant function.

$$\sec B = \frac{c}{a}$$

$$\sec 47°10' = \frac{c}{45.6}$$

$$45.6(\sec 47°10') = c$$

$$67.1 \text{ ft} = c \quad \text{(three significant digits)}$$

Third, we can find b by using the tangent function.

$$\tan B = \frac{b}{a}$$

$$\tan 47°10' = \frac{b}{45.6}$$

$$45.6(\tan 47°10') = b$$

$$45.6(1.079) = b$$

$$49.2 \text{ ft} = b \quad \text{(three significant digits)}$$

To summarize, we determined that $A = 42°50'$, $c = 67.1$ ft, and $b = 49.2$ ft.

PROGRESS CHECK 2   Solve the right triangle ABC in which $A = 9°40'$ and $c = 7.52$ ft.   ▪

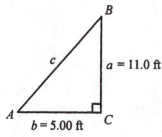

Figure 4.15

EXAMPLE 3   Solving a Right Triangle: Two Sides Case

Solve the right triangle ABC in which $a = 11.0$ ft and $b = 5.00$ ft.

Solution   First, sketch Figure 4.15. Now find the length of the hypotenuse by the Pythagorean theorem.

$$c^2 = a^2 + b^2$$
$$= 11^2 + 5^2$$
$$= 146$$
$$c = \sqrt{146}$$
$$= 12.1 \text{ ft} \quad \text{(three significant digits)}$$

Second, we can find angle A by using the tangent function.

$$\tan A = \frac{a}{b}$$
$$= \frac{11}{5}$$
$$A = \tan^{-1}\frac{11}{5} = 65°30' \quad \text{(nearest 10 minutes)}$$

Third, we can find angle B, since angle A and angle B are complementary.

$$A + B = 90°$$
$$65°30' + B = 90°$$
$$B = 24°30'$$

To summarize, we found that $c = 12.1$ ft, $A = 65°30'$, and $B = 24°30'$.

PROGRESS CHECK 3   Solve the right triangle ABC in which $b = 12.0$ ft and $c = 19.0$ ft. ■

In many practical applications of right triangles, an angle is measured with respect to a horizontal line. This measurement is often accomplished by means of a transit. (By centering a bubble of air in a water chamber, the table of this instrument may be horizontally leveled.) The sighting tube of the transit is then tilted upward or downward until the desired object is sighted. This measuring technique will result in an angle that is described as either an angle of elevation or an angle of depression (see Figure 4.16). The measurement results in an **angle of elevation** if the object being sighted is above the observer, and the measurement results in an **angle of depression** if the object being sighted is below the observer.

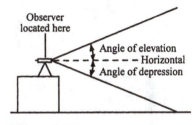

Figure 4.16

EXAMPLE 4   Height of a Smokestack

It is necessary to determine the height of a smokestack to estimate the cost of painting it. At a point 225 ft from the base of the stack, the angle of elevation is 33.0°. How high is the smokestack?

Solution   First, sketch Figure 4.17. In right triangle ABC we can find x, the height of the smokestack, by using the tangent function.

$$\tan A = \frac{\text{opposite}}{\text{adjacent}}$$
$$\tan 33.0° = \frac{x}{225}$$
$$225(\tan 33.0°) = x$$
$$146 \text{ ft} = x \quad \text{(three significant digits)}$$

PROGRESS CHECK 4   A ladder leans against the side of a building and makes an angle of 72.0° with the ground. If the ladder is 25.0 ft long, then find the height the ladder reaches on the building. ■

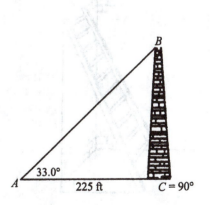

Figure 4.17

EXAMPLE 5 Distance to a Buoy

The measure of the angle of depression of a buoy from the platform of a radar tower that is 85 ft above the ocean is 15°. Find the distance of the buoy from the base of the tower. (See Figure 4.18.)

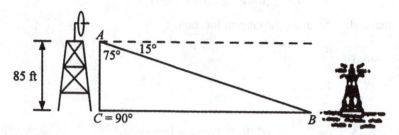

Figure 4.18

Solution In right triangle *ABC* we can find the measure of angle *A*, since angle *A* and the angle of depression are complementary.

$$A + 15° = 90°$$
$$A = 75°$$

We know the side length adjacent to angle *A* and we need to find *x*, which is the opposite side length. Thus

$$\tan 75° = \frac{x}{85}$$
$$85(\tan 75°) = x$$
$$320 \text{ ft} = x \quad (\text{two significant digits}).$$

PROGRESS CHECK 5 A surveyor stands on a cliff 175 ft above a river. If the angle of depression to the water's edge on the opposite bank is 8.4°, how wide is the river at this point? ■

EXAMPLE 6 Setting Up a Ladder in the Safest Position

Solve the problem in the section introduction on page 207.

Solution First, sketch Figure 4.19. The length of the hypotenuse is *x*, while the length of the side adjacent to θ is (1/4)*x*. Thus,

$$\cos \theta = \frac{(1/4)x}{x} = \frac{1}{4}$$

so,

$$\theta = \cos^{-1}\frac{1}{4} \approx 75.5°.$$

For maximum safety, a ladder should make an angle of 75.5° with the ground.

PROGRESS CHECK 6 A ladder is set up so that the distance between the base of the ladder and the building against which it leans is one-fifth the length of the ladder. Find the angle the ladder makes with the ground. ■

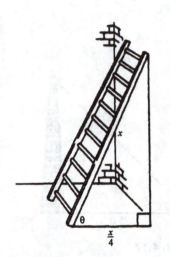

Figure 4.19

EXERCISES 4.2

In Exercises 1–20 solve each right triangle ABC ($C = 90°$) for the given data. Round off answers using the guidelines given in this section.

1. $A = 30°$, $a = 50$ ft
2. $B = 45°$, $a = 85$ ft
3. $A = 60°$, $c = 15$ ft
4. $A = 22°$, $b = 62$ ft
5. $B = 71°$, $c = 25$ ft
6. $A = 19°$, $a = 17$ ft
7. $A = 55°$, $c = 25$ ft
8. $B = 10.3°$, $a = 24.5$ ft
9. $A = 45.5°$, $a = 86.6$ ft
10. $A = 84°50'$, $c = 12.4$ ft
11. $B = 52°40'$, $c = 625$ ft
12. $A = 31.5°$, $b = 29.7$ ft
13. $B = 88°10'$, $a = 31.2$ ft
14. $A = 10.8°$, $a = 49.2$ ft
15. $a = 6.0$ ft, $c = 15$ ft
16. $b = 1.0$ ft, $c = 2.0$ ft
17. $a = 1.0$ ft, $b = 1.0$ ft
18. $a = 7.00$ ft, $c = 11.0$ ft
19. $b = 12.0$ ft, $c = 26.0$ ft
20. $a = 5.00$ ft, $b = 4.00$ ft

In Exercises 21–44 solve each problem by making a careful diagram and using right triangles.

21. An escalator from the first floor to the second floor of a building is 50 ft long and makes an angle of 30° with the floor. Find the vertical distance between the floors.
22. A ladder leans against the side of a building and makes an angle of 60° with the ground. If the foot of the ladder is 10 ft from the building, find the height the ladder reaches on the building.
23. A road has a uniform elevation of 6°. Find the increase in elevation in driving 500 yd along the road.
24. If the angle of elevation of the sun at a certain time is 40°, find the height of a tree that casts a shadow of 45 ft.
25. To find the width of a river, a surveyor sets up her transit at C and sights across the river to point B (both B and C are at the water's edge, as shown below). She then measures off 200 ft from C to A such that C is a right angle. If she determines that angle A is 24°, how wide is the river?

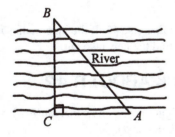

26. The distance from ground level to the underside of a cloud is called the "ceiling." At an airport, a ceiling light projector throws a spotlight vertically on the underside of a cloud. At a distance of 600 ft from the projector, the angle of elevation of the spot of light on the cloud is 58°. What is the ceiling?
27. A lighthouse built at sea level is 180 ft high. From its top, the angle of depression of a buoy is 24°. Find the distance from the buoy to the foot of the lighthouse.

28. A pilot in an airplane at an altitude of 4,000 ft observes the angle of depression of an airport to be 12°. How far is the airport from the point on the ground directly below the plane?
29. A surveyor stands on a cliff 50 ft above the water of the river below. If the angle of depression to the water's edge on the opposite bank is 10°, how wide is the river at this point?
30. A person looks down from the edge of the roof of a skyscraper to the nearest edge of the roof of another building. If the angle of depression is 15.6°, and the distance between the buildings is 205 yd, how much taller is the skyscraper than the other building?
31. At an airport, cars drive down a ramp 85 ft long to reach the lower baggage claim area 15 ft below the main level. What angle does the ramp make with the ground at the lower level?
32. Suppose the distance between the base of a ladder and a building is one-third of the length of the ladder. Find the angle that the ladder makes with the ground when it is set up in this position.
33. In building a warehouse, a carpenter checks the drawings and finds the roof span to be 40 ft, as shown in the sketch below. If the slope of the roof is 17°, what length of 2-by 6-in. stock will he need to make rafters if a 12-in. overhang is desired?

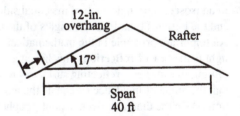

34. A welder is to weld vertical supports for a 25-ft conveyor so that it will operate at a 14° angle with respect to the horizontal. What is the length of the supports?
35. A carpenter is to build a concrete ramp with an 18° slope leading up to a platform. If the platform is 38 in. above the ground, how far from the base of the platform should she start to lay the concrete forms?
36. A tinsmith forms an angle of 120° for a 10-in flashing, as shown. Give the height of the bend in inches.

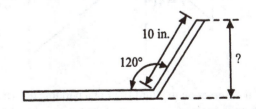

37. A right triangle, called an **impedance triangle,** is used to analyze alternating-current (a.c.) circuits. Consider diagram (a), which shows a resistor and an inductor in series. As current flows through these components, it encounters some resistance, and the total effective resistance is called the **impedance.** We determine the impedance by making the resistances of the two circuit components the measures of the legs of a right triangle. As shown in diagram (b), the hypotenuse of the triangle then represents the impedance. The degree to which the voltage and current are in phase is given by angle θ, which is called the **phase angle.** From the data in this figure, determine the impedance and the phase angle.

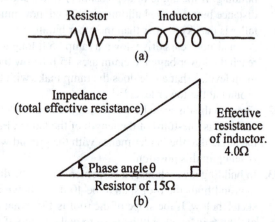

38. The sides of a rectangle are 18 and 31 ft. Find the angle that the diagonal makes with the shorter side.

39. In an isosceles triangle each of the equal sides is 70 in., and the base is 80 in. Find the angles of the triangle.

40. An important principle in the mathematical analysis of light is the **law of reflection.** This law states that a ray of light that strikes a reflecting surface is reflected so that the angle of incidence (i) equals the angle of reflection (r). In the diagram given, a photographer positions his flash at A. For a better lighting effect he aims this flash at position P on a reflecting surface to take a picture of a subject at B. If $\overline{AC} = 4.0$ ft, $\overline{CD} = 12$ ft and $i = 41°$, find the length of BD.

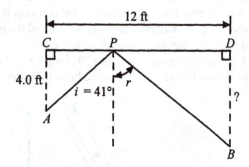

41. An observer on the third floor of a building determines that the angle of depression of the foot of a building across the street is 28°, and the angle of elevation of the top of the same building is 51°. If the distance between the two buildings is 50 ft, find the height of the observed building.

42. An observer on the top of a hill 350 ft above the level of a road spots two cars due east of her. Find the distance between the cars if the angles of depression noted by the observer were 16° and 27°.

43. An artillery spotter in a plane at an altitude of 950 m observes two tanks in a line due east of the plane. If the angles of depressions of the two tanks measures 62° and 44°, then find the distance between the tanks.

44. A circular disc 24.0 in diameter is to have five equally spaced holes as shown. Determine the correct setting (x) for the dividers to space these holes.

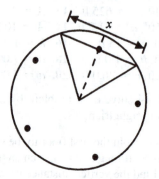

45. In pipe fitting there is a measure called the Take Out of an elbow. See the figure below, which shows the case of a 50° elbow. If the inner radius of the elbow shown is 2.0 in. and the outer radius is 4.0 in., find the take out. (Idea for this exercise was taken from Pipe Fitter's Math Guide by J.E. Hamilton, Construction Trades Press).

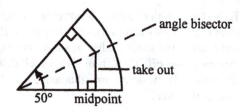

46. Refer to Exercise 45. If the inner radius is changed to 3.0 in., find the new take out.

THINK ABOUT IT 4.2

1. In the figure below show that $\tan(\theta/2) = \sin\theta/(1 + \cos\theta)$.

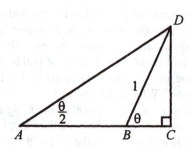

2. A machinist is given a 5.00-in.-diameter steel rod with instructions to make a tapered pin 12.0 in. long. The pin must have diameters of 4.00 and 2.00 in. What angle of taper should be used to obtain the right dimensions? (**Hint:** Make use of the dashed line parallel to the center axis in the diagram.)

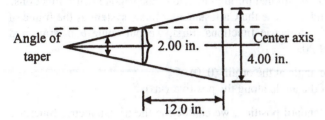

12.0 in.

3. Consider the diagram given, which illustrates that twilight lasts until the sun is 18° below the horizon. From this, estimate the height (h) of the atmosphere.

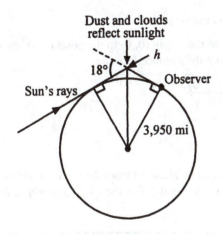

4. In the figure below, derive a formula for h in terms of d, $\cot \theta$, and $\cot \alpha$.

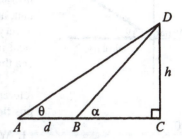

5. Create a word problem that may be solved by using the diagram and formula from Question 4. Then, find the solution to the problem you created.

4.3   Trigonometric Functions of General Angles

Two fire towers, A and B, are located 14 mi apart. A fire is sighted at point C, and observers in towers A and B measure angles A and B to be 108° and 33°, as illustrated. In accordance with the law of sines (see Section 9.7), the distance a between tower B and the fire is given by

$$a = \frac{c \sin A}{\sin C}$$

To the nearest mile, find a. (See Example 9.)

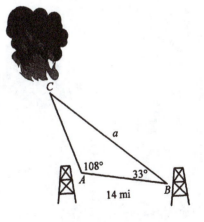

OBJECTIVES

1 Find the values of the six trigonometric functions of an angle, given the terminal ray of the angle.

2 Find the values of the five remaining trigonometric functions of θ, given one function value and the quadrant containing the terminal ray of θ.

3 Determine the exact value of any trigonometric function of a quadrantal angle.

4 Determine the exact value of any trigonometric function of angles with reference angles of 30°, 45°, or 60°.

5 Use a calculator to approximate the trigonometric value of a given angle.

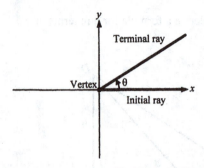

Figure 4.20

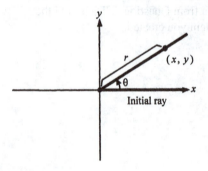

Figure 4.21

Right-triangle trigonometry is useful but limited. To solve triangles that might not contain a right angle, we need trigonometric functions that are defined for $0° < \theta < 180°$ as illustrated in the section-opening problem. Also, although triangle trigonometry is important, an approach emphasizing the repetitive characteristics of the trigonometric functions is very useful today. The rhythmic motion of the heart, the sound waves produced by musical instruments, and alternating electric current are only a few of the physical phenomena that occur in cycles and can be studied through the aid of the trigonometric functions.

To begin this general study, we use the Cartesian coordinate system as the frame of reference for defining the trigonometric functions. First, we put angle θ in **standard position,** as shown in Figure 4.20.

1. We place the vertex of the angle at the origin $(0, 0)$.
2. We place the initial ray of the angle along the positive x-axis.

When we have the angle in standard position, we can define the trigonometric functions of an angle by considering any point on the terminal ray of θ [except $(0, 0)$]. Three numbers can be associated with the location of this point (see Figure 4.21):

1. The x-coordinate of the point
2. The y-coordinate of the point
3. The distance r between the point and the origin

Since r represents the distance from the origin $(0, 0)$ to the point (x, y), we can find the relationship among x, y, and r by using the distance formula.

$$r = \sqrt{(x - 0)^2 + (y - 0)^2}$$
$$r = \sqrt{x^2 + y^2}$$

or

$$r^2 = x^2 + y^2$$

If we consider the number of ratios that can be obtained from the three variables x, y, and r, we find that there are six. It is these six ratios that define the six *trigonometric functions.*

Definition of the Trigonometric Functions

If θ is an angle in standard position, and if (x, y) is any point on the terminal ray of θ [except $(0, 0)$], then

Name of Function	Abbreviation	Ratio	
sine of angle θ	sin θ	$= \dfrac{y}{r}$	reciprocal functions
cosecant of angle θ	csc θ	$= \dfrac{r}{y}(y \neq 0)$	
cosine of angle θ	cos θ	$= \dfrac{x}{r}$	reciprocal functions
secant of angle θ	sec θ	$= \dfrac{r}{x}(x \neq 0)$	
tangent of angle θ	tan θ	$= \dfrac{y}{x}(x \neq 0)$	reciprocal functions
cotangent of angle θ	cot θ	$= \dfrac{x}{y}(y \neq 0)$	

EXAMPLE 1   Finding Trigonometric Functions Using Their Definition

Find the value of the six trigonometric functions of an angle θ if $(2, -5)$ is a point on the terminal ray of θ.

Solution   Figure 4.22 illustrates that the terminal ray of θ lies in quadrant 4, and that $x = 2$ and $y = -5$. Then

$$r = \sqrt{x^2 + y^2} = \sqrt{2^2 + (-5)^2} = \sqrt{29},$$

so by definition

$$\sin \theta = \frac{y}{r} = \frac{-5}{\sqrt{29}} \leftarrow \text{reciprocals} \rightarrow \csc \theta = \frac{r}{y} = \frac{\sqrt{29}}{-5}$$

$$\cos \theta = \frac{x}{r} = \frac{2}{\sqrt{29}} \leftarrow \text{reciprocals} \rightarrow \sec \theta = \frac{r}{x} = \frac{\sqrt{29}}{2}$$

$$\tan \theta = \frac{y}{x} = \frac{-5}{2} \leftarrow \text{reciprocals} \rightarrow \cot \theta = \frac{x}{y} = \frac{2}{-5}.$$

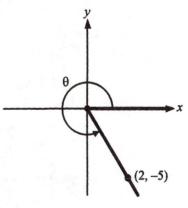

Figure 4.22

PROGRESS CHECK 1   Find the value of the six trigonometric functions of angle θ if $(-3, -1)$ is a point on the terminal ray of θ.   ■

Note two important features of the definition above. First, (x, y) may be any point (except the origin) on the terminal ray of θ. Figure 4.23 shows that if we pick different points on the terminal ray of θ, say (x_1, y_1) and (x_2, y_2), they determine similar triangles. It follows, as in Section 4.1, that corresponding side lengths are proportional, so the trigonometric ratios are uniquely determined by the terminal ray of θ. This means that in addition to picking any point on the terminal ray of θ, we may also choose any of the angle measures associated with the angle.

Second, note in Figure 4.24 that if θ is a positive acute angle in standard position with the point (x, y) on its terminal ray, then a right triangle may be formed with opposite side of length y, adjacent side of length x, and hypotenuse of length r. Thus, right triangle trigonometry is a special case of the more general definition of the trigonometric functions, for it arises when we are dealing with an acute angle whose terminal ray lies in the first quadrant.

By considering the definition of the trigonometric functions and the signs of x and y in the various quadrants, we can construct a chart of the signs of the trigonometric ratios, as shown in Figure 4.25. To illustrate, because $\cos \theta = x/r$ with $r > 0$, the sign in the cosine ratio depends on the sign of x. Thus, $\cos \theta$ is positive in Q_1 and Q_4 and negative in Q_2 and Q_3. As a memory aid, the underlined first letters in the chart in Figure 4.25 correspond to the first letters in the mnemonic "*A*ll *S*tudents *T*ake *C*alculus." One use for this chart is shown in the next example.

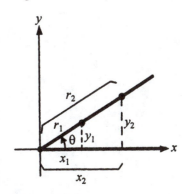

Figure 4.23

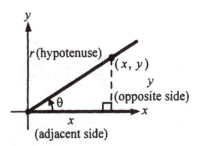

Figure 4.24

EXAMPLE 2   Finding Trigonometric Functions Given One Function Value

Find the value of the remaining trigonometric functions if $\tan \theta = \dfrac{2}{3}$ and $\sec \theta < 0$.

Solution   First, determine the quadrant that contains the terminal ray of θ. $\tan \theta = 2/3$, which is positive. Therefore, θ is in Q_1 or Q_3; $\sec \theta < 0$ means that $\sec \theta$ is negative and θ is in Q_2 or Q_3. Only Q_3 satisfies both conditions. Therefore, the terminal ray of θ is in Q_3, where x is negative and y is negative.

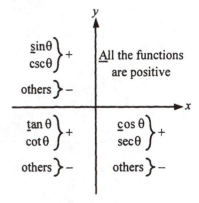

Figure 4.25

Second, determine appropriate values for x, y, and r:

$$\tan \theta = \frac{y}{x} = \frac{2}{3}$$

Since both x and y are negative in Q_3, let $x = -3$ and $y = -2$; then find r.

$$\begin{aligned}
r &= \sqrt{x^2 + y^2} \\
&= \sqrt{(-3)^2 + (-2)^2} \\
&= \sqrt{9 + 4} \\
&= \sqrt{13}
\end{aligned}$$

Third, calculate the values of the different trigonometric functions. If $x = -3$, $y = -2$, and $r = \sqrt{13}$, then

$$\sin \theta = \frac{y}{r} = \frac{-2}{\sqrt{13}} \leftarrow \text{reciprocals} \rightarrow \csc \theta = \frac{r}{y} = \frac{\sqrt{13}}{-2}$$

$$\cos \theta = \frac{x}{r} = \frac{-3}{\sqrt{13}} \leftarrow \text{reciprocals} \rightarrow \sec \theta = \frac{r}{x} = \frac{\sqrt{13}}{-3}$$

$$\tan \theta = \frac{y}{x} = \frac{-2}{-3} = \frac{2}{3} \leftarrow \text{reciprocals} \rightarrow \cot \theta = \frac{x}{y} = \frac{-3}{-2} = \frac{3}{2}.$$

Note once again that the value of a trigonometric function is a ratio. $\tan \theta = 2/3$ did not mean that $y = 2$ and $x = 3$. Also, in the second step we could have proceeded by drawing a right triangle with opposite side 2 and adjacent side 3. With this method we then determine the hypotenuse, set up the trigonometric ratios, and affix the correct sign depending on the function value in Q_3.

PROGRESS CHECK 2 Find the value of the remaining trigonometric functions if $\sin \theta = -3/4$ and $\tan \theta > 0$. ▪

We now consider the problem of evaluating a trigonometric function for any angle. It is easy to use a calculator for such evaluations, since we merely need to extend the methods shown in Section 4.1 for evaluating trigonometric functions of acute angles. Although most calculators limit the size of the angle you can enter, you will rarely exceed this input range. In case you do, we will discuss how to reduce large angles later in this section. Thus, a calculator should easily give you a number associated with a trigonometric evaluation.

What is missing in this simple calculator method, however, is an understanding of some important concepts in trigonometry. Reference and coterminal angles, the signs of the functions in the various quadrants, and special angles with exact trigonometric values that are easily found and often used are just some of the ideas associated with a noncalculator approach. So keep in mind that a final numerical answer is only part of the objective of this section. We begin by using the definition of the trigonometric functions in the following example to evaluate functions for a special angle.

EXAMPLE 3   Evaluating Trigonometric Functions by Definition
Find the six trigonometric functions of 90° using the definition of the trigonometric function.

Solution   We have shown that we may pick any point on the terminal ray of the angle when applying the definition. The terminal ray of a 90° angle is the positive y-axis, and a choice of $r = 1$ determines the point $(0, 1)$, as shown in Figure 4.26. Then, since $x = 0$, $y = 1$, and $r = 1$, we have

$$\sin 90° = \frac{y}{r} = \frac{1}{1} = 1 \leftarrow \text{reciprocals} \rightarrow \csc 90° = \frac{r}{y} = \frac{1}{1} = 1$$

$$\cos 90° = \frac{x}{r} = \frac{0}{1} = 0 \leftarrow \text{reciprocals} \rightarrow \sec 90° = \frac{r}{x} = \frac{1}{0} \text{ undefined}$$

$$\tan 90° = \frac{y}{x} = \frac{1}{0} \text{ undefined} \leftarrow \text{reciprocals} \rightarrow \cot 90° = \frac{x}{y} = \frac{0}{1} = 0.$$

You should check these results by calculator and note the cases in which the calculator is unable to produce an answer.

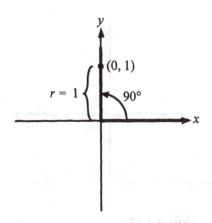

Figure 4.26

PROGRESS CHECK 3   Find the six trigonometric functions of 180°, using the definition of the trigonometric functions.   ■

An angle of 90° is "special" because its terminal ray coincides with one of the axes. Such angles are called **quadrantal angles,** and any quadrantal angle can be expressed as the product of 90° and some integer. For example, $270° = 90° \cdot 3$ and $-180° = 90° \cdot (-2)$. We can repeat the procedure from Example 3 when evaluating functions for any quadrantal angle, and Figure 4.27 shows the four possible positions for the terminal ray of such angles. There are other quadrantal angles besides 0°, 90°, 180°, and 270° (which are shown in the figure), but their trigonometric values must be the same as one of the four listed. For example, the trigonometric values for 360° will be the same as the trigonometric values for 0°, since the terminal ray for both angles is the same (positive x-axis). In general, if two angles have the same terminal ray, they are called **coterminal,** and the trigonometric functions of coterminal angles are equal. The following table summarizes the values of the trigonometric functions for quadrantal angles.

θ	$\sin \theta$	$\csc \theta$	$\cos \theta$	$\sec \theta$	$\tan \theta$	$\cot \theta$
0°	0	undefined	1	1	0	undefined
90°	1	1	0	undefined	undefined	0
180°	0	undefined	−1	−1	0	undefined
270°	−1	−1	0	undefined	undefined	0

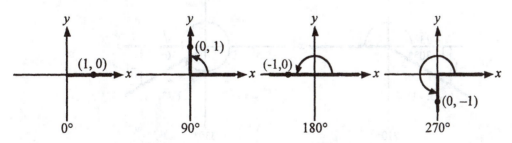

Figure 4.27

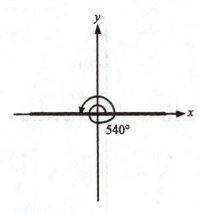

Figure 4.28

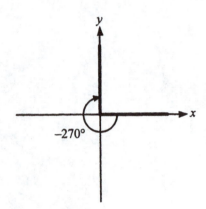

Figure 4.29

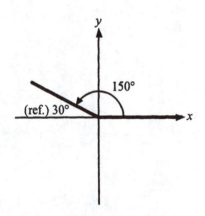

Figure 4.30

EXAMPLE 4 Finding Trigonometric Functions of Quadrantal Angles

Find the exact value of each expression.

a. sin 540°   **b.** cos(−270°)

Solution

a. 540° is a quadrantal angle that is coterminal with 180°, as shown in Figure 4.28. Therefore, sin 540° = sin 180° = 0.

b. Recall that a negative angle measure indicates a rotation in a clockwise direction. So −270° is a quadrantal angle that is coterminal with 90°, as shown in Figure 4.29. Thus, cos(−270°) = cos 90° = 0.

PROGRESS CHECK 4 Find the exact value of each expression.

a. cos 720°   **b.** cot(−90°)   ■

To evaluate trigonometric functions for angles that are not quadrantal angles, we introduce the concept of a **reference angle.** The reference angle for an angle θ is defined to be the positive acute angle formed by the terminal ray of θ and the horizontal axis. For example, the reference angle for 150° is 30°, since the closest segment of the horizontal axis (negative x-axis) may correspond to a rotation of 180° and |180° − 150°| = 30°, as shown in Figure 4.30.

Now consider the angles 30°, 150°, 210°, and 330°, where the reference angle for each of these angles is 30°. Note that the points on the terminal ray for each of these angles differ only in the sign of the x-coordinate or the y-coordinate. Therefore, the values of the trigonometric functions (which are ratios among, x, y, and r) of these angles can differ only in their sign. For instance, by considering the appropriate points in Figure 4.31, we

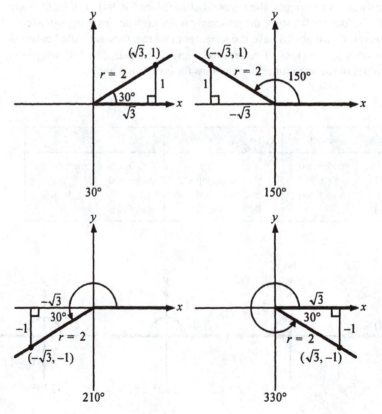

Figure 4.31

can determine $\sin 30° = 1/2$, $\sin 150° = 1/2$, $\sin 210° = -1/2$, and $\sin 330° = -1/2$. Thus, the reference angle provides us with a method for relating an angle in any quadrant to some acute angle.

Although the trigonometric values of an angle and its reference angle may differ in sign, we can determine the correct sign using the chart for the signs of the trigonometric ratios that was given in Figure 4.25. A systematic method for using this chart and the concept of a reference angle to evaluate trigonometric functions for nonquadrantal angles is shown in the next example.

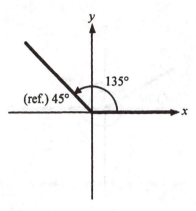

Figure 4.32

EXAMPLE 5 Evaluations Involving 30°, 45°, or 60° Reference Angles

Find the exact value of tan 135°.

Solution First, determine the reference angle.

$$|180° - 135°| = 45° \quad \text{(See Figure 4.32)}$$

Second, determine tan 45°.

$$\tan 45° = 1 \quad \text{(See Figure 4.33)}$$

Third, determine the correct sign.

135° is in Q_2, where the value of the tangent function is negative. Therefore, $\tan 135° = -1$. Check this result by calculator.

PROGRESS CHECK 5 Find the exact value of sin 300°. ■

In general, we can find the trigonometric value of nonquadrantal angles by doing the following.

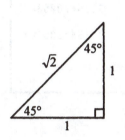

Figure 4.33

To Evaluate Trigonometric Functions

For nonquadrantal angles
1. Find the reference angle for the given angle.
2. Find the trigonometric value of the reference angle using the appropriate function. If the reference angle is 30°, 45°, or 60°, the exact answer is preferable.
3. Determine the correct sign according to the terminal ray of the angle and the chart in Figure 4.25.

EXAMPLE 6 Evaluations Involving 30°, 45°, or 60° Reference Angles

Find the exact value of cos 300°.

Solution First, determine the reference angle.

$$|360° - 300°| = 60° \quad \text{(See Figure 4.34)}$$

Second, determine cos 60°.

$$\cos 60° = \frac{1}{2} \quad \text{(See Figure 4.35)}$$

Third, determine the correct sign.

300° is in Q_4, where the cosine function is positive.

Therefore, $\cos 300° = \cos 60° = 1/2$. Check this result by calculator.

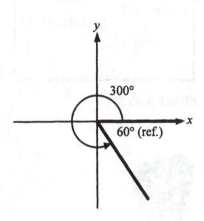

Figure 4.34

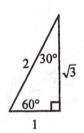

Figure 4.35

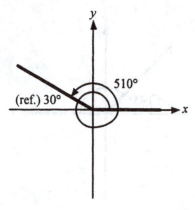

Figure 4.36

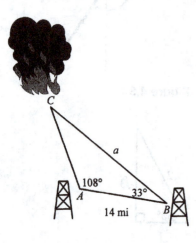

```
1/cos510
          -1.15470053838
-2/√3
          -1.15470053838
```

Figure 4.37

```
cos(227 + 20/60)
          -.677731999146
1/sin(-412)
          -1.26901821507
```

Figure 4.38

Figure 4.39

PROGRESS CHECK 6 Find the exact value of sin 315°. ■

EXAMPLE 7 Evaluations Involving 30°, 45°, or 60° Reference Angles
Find the exact value of sec 510°.

Solution First, determine the reference angle.

$$|540° - 510°| = 30° \quad \text{(See Figure 4.36)}$$

Second, determine sec 30°.

$$\sec 30° = \frac{2}{\sqrt{3}} \quad \text{(See Figure 4.35)}$$

Third, determine the correct sign.

510° is in Q_2, where the secant function is negative.

Therefore, $\sec 510° = -\sec 30° = -2/\sqrt{3}$.

A calculator check that supports this result, using $\sec\theta = 1/\cos\theta$, is shown in Figure 4.37.

PROGRESS CHECK 7 Find the exact value of cot 660°. ■

Quadrantal angles and angles with reference angles of 30°, 45°, or 60° may be considered special cases because exact values may be found for trigonometric functions of these angles. For other angles, we can easily approximate their function values by using a calculator, as shown in the next two examples.

EXAMPLE 8 Approximating Trigonometric Values by Calculator
Find the approximate value of each expression. Round off answers to four decimal places.

a. cos 227°20′ **b.** csc(−412°)

Solution See Figure 4.38.

a. cos 227°20′ ≈ −0.6777. Note that 20 minutes may be entered as 20/60 because one minute is 1/60 of one degree.
b. Using $\csc(-412°) = 1/\sin(-412°)$ yields $\csc(-412°) \approx -1.2690$.

PROGRESS CHECK 8 Find the approximate value of each expression. Round off answers to four decimal places.

a. sin 96°40′ **b.** sec(−518°) ■

EXAMPLE 9 Distance to a Forest Fire
Solve the problem in the section introduction on page 213.

Solution Consider the sketch of the problem in Figure 4.39. The angle measures sum to 180° in a triangle, so

$$\begin{aligned} A + B + C &= 180° \\ 108° + 33° + C &= 180° \\ C &= 39°. \end{aligned}$$

Then replacing c by 14, A by 108°, and C by 39° in $a = c \sin A/\sin C$ yields

$$a = \frac{14 \sin 108°}{\sin 39°} \approx 21.1574 \quad \text{(by calculator).}$$

To the nearest mile, the fire is 21 miles from tower B.

PROGRESS CHECK 9 Redo the problem in Example 9 assuming that $A = 97°$, $B = 29°$, and $\overline{AB} = 12$ mi. ■

EXERCISES 4.3

In Exercises 1–10 find the values of the six trigonometric functions of the angle θ that is in standard position and satisfies the given condition.

1. $(3, -4)$ is on the terminal ray of θ.
2. $(-1, -1)$ is on the terminal ray of θ.
3. $(-12, 5)$ is on the terminal ray of θ.
4. $(2, 4)$ is on the terminal ray of θ.
5. $(9, -12)$ is on the terminal ray of θ.
6. $(-7, -13)$ is on the terminal ray of θ.
7. The terminal ray of θ lies in Q_1 on the line $y = x$.
8. The terminal ray of θ lies in Q_3 on the line $y = x$.
9. The terminal ray of θ lies on the line $y = -2x$, and θ is in Q_2.
10. The terminal ray of θ lies on the line $y = -2x$, and θ is in Q_4.

In Exercises 11–16 determine in which quadrant the terminal ray of θ lies.

11. $\sin \theta$ is negative, $\cos \theta$ is positive.
12. $\cot \theta$ is positive, $\csc \theta$ is positive.
13. $\tan \theta$ is positive, $\sec \theta$ is negative.
14. $\sec \theta > 0$, $\csc \theta < 0$.
15. $\tan \theta < 0$, $\sin \theta > 0$.
16. $\cos \theta < 0$, $\cot \theta < 0$.

In Exercises 17–24 find the values of the remaining trigonometric functions of θ.

17. $\sin \theta = -\dfrac{3}{5}$, terminal ray of θ is in Q_3.
18. $\sec \theta = \dfrac{13}{12}$, terminal ray of θ is in Q_4.
19. $\cos \theta = \dfrac{1}{2}$, $\tan \theta$ is negative.
20. $\tan \theta = \dfrac{2}{3}$, $\sin \theta$ is negative.
21. $\csc \theta = -\dfrac{4}{3}$, $\cot \theta$ is positive.
22. $\cot \theta = 1$, $\csc \theta < 0$.
23. $\sin \theta = \dfrac{1}{3}$, $\sec \theta > 0$.
24. $\csc \theta = 2$, $\cos \theta < 0$.

In Exercises 25–30 find the six trigonometric functions of the given angle by using the definitions of the trigonometric functions

25. $-90°$
26. $-180°$
27. $360°$
28. $270°$
29. $-540°$
30. $450°$

In Exercises 31–36 find the exact value of the given expression.

31. $\sin(450°)$
32. $\cos(630°)$
33. $\sec(720°)$
34. $\csc(-450°)$
35. $\cot(990°)$
36. $\tan(-900°)$

In Exercises 37–64 find the *exact* value of each expression.

37. $\sin 210°$
38. $\tan 225°$
39. $\sec 330°$
40. $\cos 135°$
41. $\cot 315°$
42. $\csc 120°$
43. $\sin 150°$
44. $\tan 300°$
45. $\cos 225°$
46. $\cot 240°$
47. $\sec 390°$
48. $\tan 420°$
49. $\cot 690°$
50. $\cos 840°$
51. $\sin 1,035°$
52. $\csc 675°$
53. $\cos 495°$
54. $\sin 570°$
55. $\sin(-60°)$
56. $\cos(-45°)$
57. $\tan(-120°)$
58. $\sec(-225°)$
59. $\cot(-315°)$
60. $\csc(-210°)$
61. $\sec(-330°)$
62. $\cos(-480°)$
63. $\cot(-495°)$
64. $\sin(-1,050°)$

In Exercises 65–94 find the approximate value of each expression. Use a calculator, and round off answers to four decimal places.

65. $\sin 212°$
66. $\cos 307°$
67. $\tan 254°$
68. $\cot 115°$
69. $\sec 301°20'$
70. $\csc 163.4°$
71. $\cos 148°50'$
72. $\sin 354.5°$
73. $\cot 298°10'$
74. $\tan 190°40'$
75. $\sin 177°10'$
76. $\cos 252°20'$
77. $\csc 672°40'$
78. $\cot 392.1°$
79. $\sin 626°40'$
80. $\sin 531.5°$
81. $\cos 952°20'$
82. $\sec 452°20'$
83. $\tan 738°30'$
84. $\sin 521°50'$
85. $\cos(-81°)$
86. $\sin(-25°)$

87. $\tan(-131°)$

88. $\csc(-322°40')$

89. $\cos(-61°)$

90. $\sin(-251.5°)$

91. $\tan(-214°10')$

92. $\sec(-400°)$

93. $\cot(-512°)$

94. $\csc(-938°20')$

95. The cross-section of a teepee is shown in the figure. If the base angles are each 70.0° and the diameter of the floor is 16.0 ft, determine the minimum pole length needed for the side if the pole is to extend at least 1 ft beyond the peak. Solve this problem in two ways.

  a. Use the law of sines (discussed in Section 9.7), which states that $a = \dfrac{b \sin A}{\sin B}$.

  b. Split the given triangle into two right triangles, and apply right triangle trigonometry.

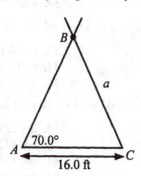

96. Refer to the figure in Exercise 95. Solve the problem again, but assume that the base angles are reduced to 65.0°.

97. A straight tunnel is to be cut through a mountain as indicated in the figure. Sighting from point A shows that angle A is 115.2°, the distance from A to B is 1.4 miles, and the distance from point A to point C is 2.1 miles. According to the law of cosines (discussed in Section 9.8),

$$a^2 = b^2 + c^2 - 2bc \cos A.$$

Use this relationship to determine the distance from B to C to the nearest tenth of a mile.

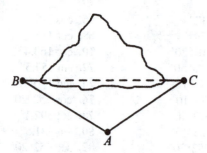

98. Refer to the figure in Exercise 97. Solve the problem again, but assume that angle A is 98.6°.

99. A formula for the horizontal distance traveled by a projectile, neglecting air resistance, is $d = \dfrac{1}{32}V^2 \sin 2\theta$.

If a ball is kicked with an initial velocity V of 76 ft/second, when θ is 35°, how far will it go? When V is given in ft/second, then d is in feet. Determine the answer to the nearest foot.

100. Refer to Exercise 99. If the angle θ is changed to 40°, how far will the ball go?

THINK ABOUT IT 4.3

1. a. Give two examples of specific values for θ_1 and θ_2 so that $\sin(\theta_1 + \theta_2)$ does not equal $\sin \theta_1 + \sin \theta_2$. Verify your answers without using a calculator.

  b. Give two examples of specific values for θ_1 and θ_2 so that $\sin(\theta_1 + \theta_2)$ does equal $\sin \theta_1 + \sin \theta_2$. Verify your answers without using a calculator.

2. Evaluate $\sin 1° + \sin 2° + \cdots + \sin 360°$.

3. If $\cos \theta = a$ and $270° < \theta < 360°$, express the values of the other trigonometric functions in terms of a.

4. Consider the unit circle in the accompanying figure, in which each of the six trigonometric functions can be represented as a line segment. For example, since $\overline{OC} = 1$ in right triangle OAC, we have

$$\sin \theta = \overline{AC}/\overline{OC} = \overline{AC}/1 = \overline{AC}.$$

Notice that we obtained the desired line segment by selecting a right triangle where the denominator in the defining ratio is 1. Determine the line segments representing the five remaining trigonometric functions in the figure.

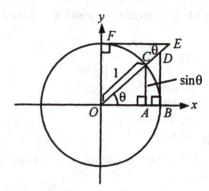

5. A simple method to obtain a rough estimate of the values of the trigonometric functions is to use construction. Start by using a compass to draw a circle with a radius of 20 spaces on a piece of graph paper. (**Note:** Do not be concerned if the circle goes slightly off the paper.) Label the graph so that a distance of 2 spaces corresponds to one-tenth of a unit, and the radius of 20 spaces corresponds to 1 unit (so $r = 1$). Now use a protractor to find the point on the circle that corresponds to the following rotations, and on the basis of your estimate for their x or y components, approximate to two significant digits the value of the given trigonometric functions.

  a. $\sin 30°$, $\sin 150°$, $\sin 210°$, $\sin 330°$

  b. $\cos 30°$, $\cos 150°$, $\cos 210°$, $\cos 330°$

  c. $\cos 45°$, $\cos 135°$, $\cos 225°$, $\cos 315°$

  d. $\sin 45°$, $\sin 135°$, $\sin 225°$, $\sin 315°$

  e. $\sin 62°$, $\sin 118°$, $\sin 242°$, $\sin 298°$

  f. $\cos 62°$, $\cos 118°$, $\cos 242°$, $\cos 298°$

  g. $\sec 15°$, $\sec 165°$, $\sec 195°$, $\sec 345°$

  h. $\csc 15°$, $\csc 165°$, $\csc 195°$, $\csc 345°$

4.4 Introduction to Trigonometric Equations

A formula for the horizontal distance traveled by a projectile, neglecting air resistance, is

$$d = \frac{1}{32} V^2 \sin 2\theta$$

where θ and V measure the angle of elevation and the initial velocity in ft/second of the projectile, respectively. If a professional field-goal kicker boots a football with an initial velocity of 76 ft/second, and the ball travels 180 ft, find θ to the nearest degree. (See Example 6.)

OBJECTIVES

1   Find the exact solution to certain trigonometric equations for $0° \leq \theta < 360°$.

2   Find the approximate solution to a trigonometric equation for $0° \leq \theta < 360°$.

3   Find all solutions to a trigonometric equation, specifying exact solutions where possible.

4   Solve applied problems involving trigonometric equations.

Equations that involve trigonometric expressions commonly appear in two types: identities and conditional equations. An identity is an equation such as

$$\csc \theta = \frac{1}{\sin \theta}$$

that is true for all values of θ for which the expressions are defined (this topic is discussed in detail in Section 9.4). Conditional trigonometric equations differ from identities in that they are true only for certain values of θ. For instance, in the section-opening problem we need to find all meaningful values for θ that satisfy

$$180 = \frac{1}{32}(76)^2 \sin 2\theta,$$

and we will find that there are just two possible solutions. Before we attempt to find a procedure for writing all the solutions to a particular equation, it is helpful to first establish a method for finding solutions where $0° \leq \theta < 360°$. A method for finding such solutions is shown in Examples 1–4.

EXAMPLE 1   Finding Exact Solutions Where $0° \leq \theta < 360°$

Find the exact values of $\theta(0° \leq \theta < 360°)$ for which the equation $\sin \theta = 1/2$ is a true statement.

Solution   First, determine the quadrant that contains the terminal ray of θ.

$$\sin \theta = \frac{1}{2}, \text{ which is a positive number.}$$

The terminal ray of θ could be in either quadrant 1 or 2, since the sine function is positive in both quadrants.
Second, determine the reference angle. Using Figure 4.40 we see that

$$\sin^{-1}\frac{1}{2} = 30°.$$

Third, determine the appropriate values of θ (see Figure 4.41).

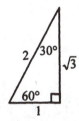

Figure 4.40

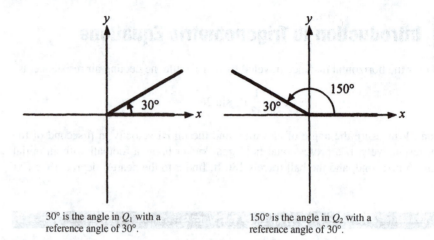

30° is the angle in Q_1 with a
reference angle of 30°.

150° is the angle in Q_2 with a
reference angle of 30°.

Figure 4.41

Therefore, 30° and 150° make the equation a true statement, and the solution set in the interval [0°, 360°) is {30°, 150°}.

Technology Link
Although formal coverage of the graphs of the trigonometric functions is presented in Chapter 9, you should find that it is easy to use a grapher to create a picture of the solution in this example, as shown in Figure 4.42. To obtain this display a grapher was first set to Degree mode. Then, the equations $y1 = \sin x$ and $y2 = 1/2$ were graphed in the viewing window shown, and the Intersection operation on a grapher was used to estimate the points of intersection. (If your calculator does not have this feature, then the Zoom and Trace features may be used to estimate these points.) Observe that the x-coordinates of the intersection points are in agreement with the solution set {30°, 150°}.

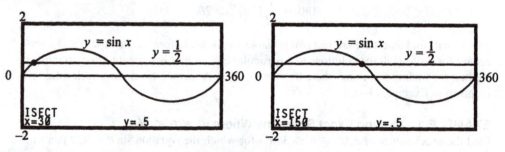

Figure 4.42

PROGRESS CHECK 1 Find the exact value of $\theta(0° \leq \theta < 360°)$ for which the equation $\cos \theta = \sqrt{3}/2$ is a true statement. ■

EXAMPLE 2 Finding Exact Solutions Where $0° \leq \theta < 360°$
Find the exact values of $\theta(0° \leq \theta < 360°)$ for which the equation $2 \sin \theta + \sqrt{3} = 0$ is a true statement.

Solution First, solve the equation for $\sin \theta$.

$$2 \sin \theta + \sqrt{3} = 0$$
$$2 \sin \theta = -\sqrt{3}$$
$$\sin \theta = \frac{-\sqrt{3}}{2}$$

Second, determine the quadrant that contains the terminal ray of θ.

$$\sin\theta = \frac{-\sqrt{3}}{2}, \text{ which is a negative number.}$$

The terminal ray of θ could be in either Q_3 or Q_4 since the sine function is negative in both quadrants.

Third, determine the reference angle. Discard the sign on the trigonometric ratio and use Figure 4.40 once again to determine that

$$\sin^{-1}\frac{\sqrt{3}}{2} = 60°.$$

Therefore, $60°$ is the reference angle.

Fourth, determine the appropriate values of θ (see Figure 4.43).

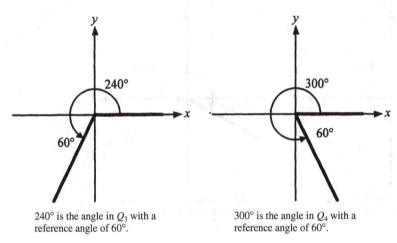

240° is the angle in Q_3 with a reference angle of 60°.

300° is the angle in Q_4 with a reference angle of 60°.

Figure 4.43

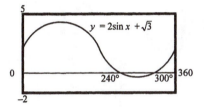

Figure 4.44

Therefore, $240°$ and $300°$ make the equation a true statement, and the solution set in the interval $[0°, 360°)$ is $\{240°, 300°\}$.

Figure 4.44 provides graphical evidence that supports this result.

PROGRESS CHECK 2   Find the exact values of $\theta(0° \le \theta < 360°)$ for which the equation $2\cos\theta + 1 = 0$ is a true statement.   ■

A solution in each of the four quadrants was illustrated in Examples 1 and 2. Observe that solutions in each of the quadrants are determined as follows:

Quadrant	Solution
1	reference angle
2	180° − reference angle
3	180° + reference angle
4	360° − reference angle

By using the inverse trigonometric function keys on a calculator, reference angles may be found exactly in the cases of $30°$, $45°$, and $60°$, and approximately in other cases. The use of a calculator to determine the approximate value of a reference angle is illustrated in the next three examples.

EXAMPLE 3   Finding Approximate Solutions Where $0° \le \theta < 360°$

To the nearest 10 minutes, approximate the values of $\theta(0° \le \theta < 360°)$ for which the equation $\cos\theta = -0.7969$ is a true statement.

Solution   First, determine the quadrant that contains the terminal ray of θ.

$$\cos \theta = -0.7969, \text{ which is a negative number.}$$

The terminal ray of θ could be in either quadrant 2 or 3, since the cosine function is negative in both quadrants.

Second, determine the reference angle. Discard the sign on the trigonometric ratio and use a calculator to determine that

$$\cos^{-1} 0.7969 \approx 37.165° \approx 37°10'.$$

To the nearest 10 minutes, the reference angle is $37°10'$.

Third, determine the appropriate values of θ (see Figure 4.45).

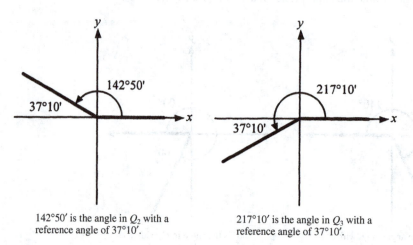

142°50′ is the angle in Q_2 with a reference angle of 37°10′.

217°10′ is the angle in Q_3 with a reference angle of 37°10′.

Figure 4.45

Therefore, $\{142°50', 217°10'\}$ is the solution set for $\theta(0° \leq \theta < 360°)$. A graphical check that supports this result is shown in Figure 4.46.

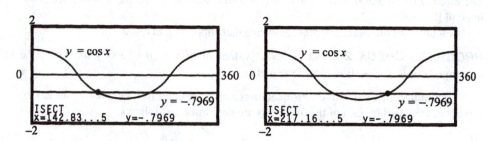

Figure 4.46

PROGRESS CHECK 3   To the nearest 10 minutes, approximate the values of $\theta(0° \leq \theta < 360°)$ for which the equation $\sin \theta = -0.4928$ is a true statement.   ■

EXAMPLE 4   Finding Approximate Solutions Where $0° \leq \theta < 360°$

Solve $4 \tan \theta = 1$ for $0° \leq \theta < 360°$. Round off answers to the nearest tenth of a degree.

Solution   The graphical solution to this equation necessitates a small adjustment in our methods, so we will deal with this issue first. The difficulty arises because the tangent function is not defined in the interval $[0°, 360°)$ at $90°$ and $270°$, so it is recommended that the calculator be set in Dot mode, not Connected mode, when drawing graphs involving $\tan \theta$. The Dot mode prevents the calculator from connecting points that are in separate pieces of the graph (as discussed in Section 2.4). Figure 4.47 shows graphs drawn in this mode that indicate that the solution set is $\{14.0°, 194.0°\}$ for $0° \leq \theta < 360°$.

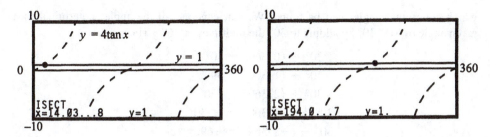

Figure 4.47

To confirm this result analytically, first solve the equation for $\tan \theta$.

$$4 \tan \theta = 1$$

$$\tan \theta = \frac{1}{4}$$

Second, determine the quadrant that contains the terminal ray of θ.

$$\tan \theta = \frac{1}{4}, \text{ which is a positive number.}$$

The terminal ray of θ could be in either Q_1 or Q_3, since the tangent function is positive in both quadrants.

Third, determine the reference angle.

$$\tan^{-1} \frac{1}{4} = 14.0°$$

Therefore, $14.0°$ is the reference angle.

Fourth, determine the appropriate values of θ (see Figure 4.48).

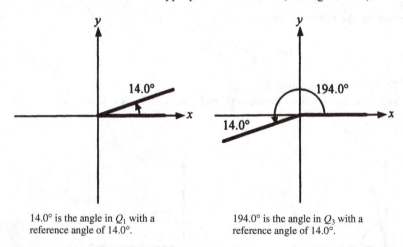

14.0° is the angle in Q_1 with a reference angle of 14.0°.

194.0° is the angle in Q_3 with a reference angle of 14.0°.

Figure 4.48

Therefore, $\{14.0°, 194.0°\}$ is the solution set for $0° \leq \theta < 360°$, which confirms the results we obtained initially through graphical analysis.

PROGRESS CHECK 4   Solve $3 \tan \theta = -5$ for $0° \leq \theta < 360°$. Round off answers to the nearest tenth of a degree.   ■

Once we are able to find the solutions of a trigonometric equation that are between $0°$ and $360°$, we can determine *all* the solutions by finding the angles that are coterminal with our results. That is, we wish to find all the angles that have the same terminal ray as the solutions that are between $0°$ and $360°$. The problem arises that we cannot possibly list all the angles that are coterminal with a given angle. Therefore, we indicate some rule by which coterminal angles can be found. We can generate all the angles coterminal to a given angle of, say, 30° by adding to 30° the multiples of 360°. Thus,

$$30° + (0)360° = 30°$$
$$30° + (1)360° = 390°$$
$$30° + (2)360° = 750°$$
$$30° + (-1)360° = -330°$$
$$30° + (-2)360° = -690° \quad \text{etc.}$$

In general, $\theta + k360°$, where k is an integer, will generate all the angles that have the same terminal ray as θ.

EXAMPLE 5   Approximating All Solutions to a Trigonometric Equation

Approximate all the solutions to $10 \cot \theta = 3$, to the nearest 10 minutes.

Solution   First solve the equation for $\cot \theta$. Then, for calculator purposes, use the reciprocal relation between the tangent and cotangent functions to rewrite the equation in terms of $\tan \theta$.

$$10 \cot \theta = 3$$
$$\cot \theta = \frac{3}{10}$$
$$\tan \theta = \frac{10}{3}$$

Second, determine which quadrant contains the terminal ray of θ.

$$\tan \theta \text{ is a positive number.}$$

The terminal ray of θ could be in either Q_1 or Q_3, since the tangent function is positive in both quadrants.

Third, determine the reference angle.

$$\tan^{-1}\frac{10}{3} \approx 73°20'$$

Therefore, $73°20'$ is the reference angle.

Fourth, determine the solutions between 0° and 360° (see Figure 4.49).

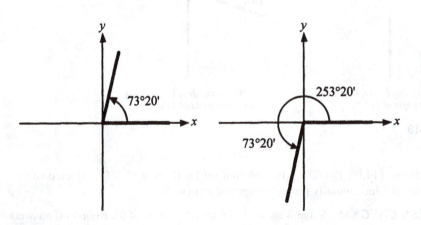

73°20' is the angle in Q_1 with a reference angle of 73°20'.   253°20' is the angle in Q_3 with a reference angle of 73°20'.

Figure 4.49

Therefore, $73°20'$ and $253°20'$ make the equation a true statement.

Fifth, indicate how angles coterminal to the above angles may be generated.

$$\left.\begin{array}{r} 73°20' + k360° \\ 253°20' + k360° \end{array}\right\} \text{ or equivalently } 73°20' + k180°,$$

where k is an integer, generates all the solutions to the equation. Thus, the solution set is $\{\theta: \theta = 73°20' + k180°, k \text{ any integer}\}$.

A graphical check that supports this result for $0° \le \theta < 360°$ is shown in Figure 4.50. Note that we use $\cot \theta = 1/\tan \theta$ to obtain this display, since $y = 10 \cot x$ is graphed by entering the equation $y = 10(1/\tan x)$.

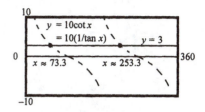

Figure 4.50

PROGRESS CHECK 5   Approximate all the solutions to $2 \sec \theta + 7 = 1$, to the nearest 10 minutes.   ▪

Applications in trigonometry sometimes involve functions of multiple angles such as 2θ or $\pi\theta/6$. We illustrate how to solve equations involving such angles in the next example.

EXAMPLE 6   Projectile Motion
Solve the problem in the section introduction on page 223.

Solution   Consider carefully how this problem may be solved using either a graphical approach or an analytic approach.

Graphic Approach   We will first try to obtain a picture of the solution through graphical analysis. Using

$$d = \frac{1}{32}V^2 \sin 2\theta$$

we replace d by 180 (since the ball traveled 180 ft) and V by 76 (since the initial velocity is 76 ft/second) to obtain

$$180 = \frac{1}{32}(76)^2 \sin 2\theta$$

Given the context of the problem, θ is meaningful for $0° < \theta < 90°$, so we choose a viewing window of $[0, 90]$ by $[0, 200]$ to obtain a picture of the situation in the problem, as shown in Figure 4.51. Then, zooming in on the maximum point in the graph and finding the intersection point shown in Figure 4.52 indicates that one solution (to the nearest degree) is 43°. Repeating the intersection process to the right of the maximum point yields a second solution at 47°. Thus, the angle of elevation of the kick was either 43° or 47°.

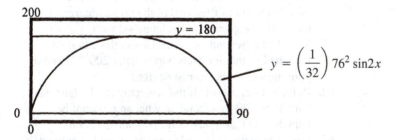

Figure 4.51

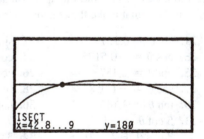

Figure 4.52

Analytic Approach   To obtain the solution analytically, follow these steps, as outlined in the previous examples.

1. $180 = \frac{1}{32}(76)^2 \sin 2\theta$ implies $\sin 2\theta = \frac{5760}{5776}$.
2. The sine function is positive in quadrants 1 and 2.

3. The reference angle is 86° since $\sin^{-1}\dfrac{5760}{5776} \approx 86°$.

4. Q_1 solution: $2\theta =$ reference angle $= 86°$
   Q_2 solution: $2\theta = 180° -$ reference angle $= 180° - 86° = 94°$

Finally, θ may now be found since

$$2\theta = 86° \text{ implies } \theta = 43°$$

and

$$2\theta = 94° \text{ implies } \theta = 47°$$

Thus, we have confirmed analytically that the angle of elevation of the kick was either 43° or 47°.

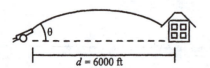

Figure 4.53

PROGRESS CHECK 6   A projectile is to be shot at an initial velocity of 450 ft/second at a target 6000 ft away, as shown in Figure 4.53. Use the formula in Example 6 to find all settings for θ, to the nearest tenth of a degree, such that the projectile hits the target.   ■

EXERCISES 4.4

In Exercises 1–20 find the exact values of θ between 0° and 360° that make the equation a true statement.

1. $\cos\theta = \dfrac{1}{2}$
2. $\cos\theta = -\dfrac{1}{2}$
3. $\tan\theta = -1$
4. $\tan\theta = 1$
5. $\sin\theta = \dfrac{1}{\sqrt{2}}$
6. $\sin\theta = \dfrac{-1}{\sqrt{2}}$
7. $\sec\theta = \dfrac{-2}{\sqrt{3}}$
8. $\sec\theta = \dfrac{2}{\sqrt{3}}$
9. $\cot\theta = \sqrt{3}$
10. $\cot\theta = -\sqrt{3}$
11. $\csc\theta = -\sqrt{2}$
12. $\csc\theta = \sqrt{2}$
13. $2\tan\theta = 2\sqrt{3}$
14. $-2\cos\theta = \sqrt{3}$
15. $2\sin\theta + \sqrt{3} = 0$
16. $\csc\theta - 2 = 0$
17. $4\sin\theta + 3 = 1$
18. $3\sec\theta - 7 = -1$
19. $2\tan\theta + 5 = 7$
20. $3\cot\theta + 4 = 1$

In Exercises 21–40 find the approximate values of θ between 0° and 360° that make the equation a true statement.

21. $\sin\theta = 0.1219$
22. $\sin\theta = -0.1219$
23. $\cos\theta = -0.5125$
24. $\cos\theta = 0.5125$
25. $\cot\theta = 2.457$
26. $\cot\theta = -2.457$
27. $\sec\theta = -1.058$
28. $\sec\theta = 1.058$
29. $\tan\theta = 3.145$
30. $\tan\theta = -3.145$
31. $5\cot\theta = -1$
32. $7\sin\theta = 2$
33. $3\cos\theta + 2 = 0$
34. $3\tan\theta - 1 = 0$
35. $2\tan\theta - 7 = 0$
36. $5\sin\theta + 2 = 0$
37. $4\csc\theta + 9 = 0$
38. $\cos\theta - 3 = 0$
39. $\sin\theta + 2 = 0$
40. $3\sec\theta - 1 = 1$

In Exercises 41–50 find five angles that are coterminal with the given angle.

41. 45°
42. 90°
43. 22°10′
44. 84.4°
45. 120°
46. 215°
47. −30°
48. −60°
49. −100°50′
50. −312°20′

In Exercises 51–60 find all the values of θ for which the given trigonometric equation is a true statement. Where possible, find exact solutions.

51. $\sqrt{2}\sin\theta = 1$
52. $\sqrt{3}\csc\theta = 2$
53. $3\sin\theta + 2 = 1$
54. $5\tan\theta + 2 = -3$
55. $10\cos\theta + 7 = 3$
56. $2\cot\theta - 3 = 0$
57. $5\sec\theta + 1 = 3$
58. $\sin\theta = 1$
59. $\cos\theta = -1$
60. $\cos\theta = 2$

61. A formula for the horizontal distance traveled by a projectile, neglecting air resistance, is

$$d = \frac{1}{32}V^2\sin 2\theta$$

where θ and V measure the angle of elevation and the initial velocity in ft/second of the projectile, respectively. If a projectile can be launched with $V = 100$ ft/second, at which two angles can it be launched so that it travels horizontally 200 ft? Round your answer to the nearest degree.

62. Refer to Exercise 61. If the projectile can be launched with $V = 100$ ft/ second, at what angle can it be launched so that it travels horizontally 312.5 ft?

63. For a projectile launched from the ground at angle θ, its height above the ground (in feet) at time t (seconds) is given by

$$h = V(\sin\theta)t - 16t^2.$$

Suppose a projectile is launched at 1000 ft/second. To the nearest degree, what angle of elevation should be used so that it achieves a height of 1500 feet when 3 seconds have elapsed?

64. Refer to Exercise 63. Suppose the projectile must be 1500 feet above the ground when 2 seconds have elapsed. What value of θ will achieve this result?

THINK ABOUT IT 4.4

1. Explain in terms of the general definition of the trigonometric functions why the solution set of the equation $\sin \theta = 2$ is $\emptyset$.
2. If the point $\left(-\sqrt{3}, -1\right)$ is on the terminal ray of θ, give one possible measure of θ.

3. Solve each equation for $0° < \theta < 180°$.
  a. $\dfrac{\sin 36.5°}{11.4} = \dfrac{\sin \theta}{19.7}$
  b. $(9.6)^2 = (4.2)^2 + (6.1)^2 - 2(4.2)(6.1)\cos \theta$

4. Solve $\cos 2\theta = -\frac{1}{2}$ for $0° \le \theta < 360°$.
5. Find all angles θ between $0°$ and $360°$ for which the absolute value of $\sin \theta$ equals the absolute value of $\sin(2\theta)$.

4.5 Vectors

A ship is headed due east at 20 knots (nautical miles per hour) while the current carries the ship due south at 5.0 knots. Find

a. the speed of the ship and
b. the direction (course) of the ship. (See Example 2.)

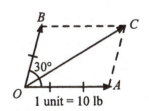

Courtesy of PhotoDisc/Getty Images.

OBJECTIVES

1 Find the resultant, or vector sum, of two vectors, using right-triangle trigonometry.

2 Resolve a vector into components.

3 Find the resultant, or vector sum, of two or more vectors, using components.

4 Solve applied problems using vectors.

An application of trigonometry occurs with the study of physical quantities that act in a definite direction. For example, when meteorologists describe wind, they mention both the speed of the wind and the direction from which the wind is blowing. Similarly, quantities such as forces, weights, and velocities must be described in such a way that both the strength (magnitude) and the direction of the quantity can be determined. Mathematically, we represent such a quantity by a line segment with an arrowhead at one end. This directed line segment is called a **vector.** The direction in which the arrowhead is pointing represents the direction in which the quantity is acting, while the length of the line segment is proportional to the magnitude of the quantity.

For instance, Figure 4.54 illustrates how to use a vector to represent graphically wind that is blowing due north at a speed of 40 mi/hour. Note that a vector that starts at **O** and ends at **A** is labeled **OA,** while a vector that starts at **A** and ends at **O** is a different vector and is labeled **AO.** In handwritten work, a vector such as **OA** is written $\vec{OA}$.

Frequently, there are two (or more) forces acting on a body from different directions, and their net effect is a third force with a new direction. This new force is called the **resultant,** or **vector sum,** of the given forces. For example, in Figure 4.55 two forces of 20 lb and 30 lb are both acting on a body with an angle of 30° between the two forces. It can be shown that the resultant of vectors **OA** and **OB** is vector **OC,** which is the diagonal of a parallelogram formed from the given vectors. The magnitude of the resultant **OC** can be determined by the length of the line segment from O to C. The direction of the resultant is the same as the direction of the arrowhead on vector **OC** and is described in terms of the original vectors by finding either angle AOC or angle BOC. The next two examples illustrate this procedure for finding the resultant of two forces in cases that involve only right-triangle trigonometry.

Figure 4.54

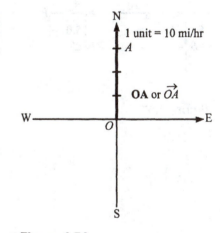

Figure 4.55

EXAMPLE 1   Vector Analysis Involving a Right Triangle

A force of 3.0 lb and a force of 4.0 lb are acting on a body with an angle of 90° between the two forces. Find

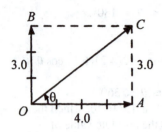

Figure 4.56

a. the magnitude of the resultant and
b. the angle between the resultant and the larger force.

Solution   Let **OA** represent the 4.0-lb force and **OB** the 3.0-lb force. Then vector **OC** represents the resultant (see Figure 4.56).

a. We can find the length of **OC** by using the Pythagorean theorem in right triangle *OAC*. Notice that line segments *OB* and *AC* have the same length.

$$(\overline{OC})^2 = (4)^2 + (3)^2$$
$$= 25$$
$$\overline{OC} = 5.0$$

Thus, the magnitude of the resultant is 5.0 lb.

b. We can find the angle between the resultant and the 4.0-lb force by using the tangent function in right triangle *OAC*.

$$\tan \theta = \frac{3}{4}$$
$$\theta = 37° \quad \text{(to the nearest degree)}$$

Thus, the angle between the resultant and the larger force is 37°.

PROGRESS CHECK 1   Two forces one 45 lb and the other 24 lb, act on the same object at right angles to each other. Find

a. the magnitude of the resultant and
b. the angle between the resultant and the smaller force.   ■

EXAMPLE 2   Speed and Course of a Ship

Solve the problem in the section introduction on page 231.

Solution   Let vector **OA** represent the velocity of the ship in the easterly direction Let vector **OB** represent the velocity of the ship in the southerly direction due to the current. Let vector **OC** represent the actual velocity of the ship. (See Figure 4.57.)

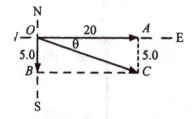

Figure 4.57

a. We can find the length of **OC** by using the Pythagorean theorem in right triangle *OAC*.

$$(\overline{OC})^2 = (20)^2 + (5)^2$$
$$= 425$$
$$\overline{OC} = \sqrt{425} \approx 21$$

Thus, the speed of the ship is 21 knots.

b. We can find the angle between the resultant and vector **OA,** which is due east, by using the tangent function in right triangle *OAC*.

$$\tan \theta = \frac{5}{20}$$
$$\theta = 14° \quad \text{(to the nearest degree)}$$

Thus, the ship is heading in a direction that is 14° south of east.

PROGRESS CHECK 2   An airplane can fly 560 mi/hour in still air. If it is heading due south in a wind that is blowing due east at a rate of 75.0 mi/hour, find

a. the distance the plane can fly in 1 hour and
b. the angle that the resultant force will make with respect to due east.   ■

In the previous examples we considered how the net effect of having two forces acting on a body produced a third force, the resultant. However, the reverse situation often arises, where we are given a single force that we think of as the resultant, and we need to calculate two forces, which are called **components,** that produce the resultant. This process of expressing a single force in terms of two components, which are usually at right angles to each other, is called **resolving a vector.** The following examples illustrate the usefulness of resolving a vector into components.

EXAMPLE 3   Effective Force Lowering a Window

A man pulls with a force of 40 lb on a window pole, in an effort to lower a window. What part of the man's force lowers the window if the pole makes an angle of 20° with the window?

Solution   Let vector **OA** represent the pull on the window pole of 40 lb. The resolution of vector **OA** results in the vertical component vector **OC** (the force lowering the window) and the horizontal component vector **OB** (wasted force) (see Figure 4.58).

We can find the magnitude of vector **OC** by using the cosine function in the right triangle *ACO*.

$$\cos 20° = \frac{\overline{OC}}{40}$$
$$40(\cos 20°) = \overline{OC}$$
$$38 = \overline{OC} \quad \text{(two significant digits)}$$

Thus, a force of 38 lb is lowering the window.

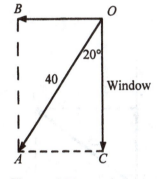

Figure 4.58

PROGRESS CHECK 3   A woman pulls with a force of 55 lb on a window pole, in an effort to lower a window. How much force is wasted if the pole makes an angle of 16° with the window?   ■

EXAMPLE 4   Component Forces Affecting a Plane's Velocity

An airplane, pointed due west, is traveling 10.0° north of west at a rate of 400 mi/hour. This resultant course is due to a wind blowing north. Find

a. the velocity of the plane if there were no wind (that is, the vector pointing due west) and

b. the velocity of the wind (that is, the vector pointing due north).

Solution   Let vector **OC** represent the resultant velocity of the plane. The resolution of vector **OC** results in a westerly component vector **OA** (the velocity of the plane if there were no wind) and northerly component vector **OB** (the velocity of the wind) (see Figure 4.59).

a. We can find the velocity of the plane if there were no wind by using the cosine function in right triangle *OAC*.

$$\cos 10.0° = \frac{x}{400}$$
$$400(\cos 10.0°) = x$$
$$394 = x \quad \text{(three significant digits)}$$

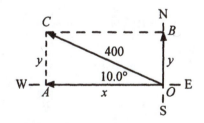

Figure 4.59

Thus, the velocity of the plane if there were no wind would be 394 mi/hour due west.

b. We can find the velocity of the wind by using the sine function in right triangle *OAC*.

$$\sin 10.0° = \frac{y}{400}$$

$$400(\sin 10.0°) = y$$

$$69.5 = y \quad \text{(three significant digits)}$$

Thus, the velocity of the wind would be 69.5 mi/hour due north.

PROGRESS CHECK 4   An airplane, pointed due east, is traveling 6.0° south of east at a rate of 460 mi/hour. The resultant course is due to a wind blowing south. Find

a. the velocity of the plane if there were no wind and
b. the velocity of the wind. ▪

EXAMPLE 5   Resolving a Vector Into Components

Find the horizontal and vertical components of a vector that has a magnitude of 25 lb and makes an angle of 40° with the positive x-axis.

Solution   Let vector **OA** be the given vector. The resolution of vector **OA** results in the horizontal component, vector **OB,** and the vertical component, vector **OC** (see Figure 4.60).

We can find the magnitude of the horizontal component, vector **OB,** by using the cosine function in right triangle *OBA.*

$$\cos 40° = \frac{x}{25}$$

$$25(\cos 40°) = x$$

$$19 = x \quad \text{(two significant digits)}$$

We can find the magnitude of the vertical component, vector **OC,** by using the sine function in right triangle *OBA.*

$$\sin 40° = \frac{y}{25}$$

$$25(\sin 40°) = y$$

$$16 = y \quad \text{(two significant digits)}$$

Thus, the magnitude of the horizontal component is 19 lb, and the magnitude of the vertical component is 16 lb.

PROGRESS CHECK 5   Find the horizontal and vertical components of a vector that has a magnitude of 42 lb and makes an angle of 28° with the positive x-axis. ▪

Example 5 shows how to resolve a vector into horizontal (or *x*) and vertical (or *y*) components. This breakdown can be very useful if we want to add two (or more) vectors. That is because the resultant of two (or more) vectors may be found by breaking each vector into its *x* and *y* components. The sum of the *x* components of each vector is the *x* component of the resultant (labeled R_x). Similarly, the sum of the *y* components of each vector is the *y* component of the resultant (labeled R_y). By the Pythagorean theorem, the magnitude of the resultant is then

$$R = \sqrt{(R_x)^2 + (R_y)^2},$$

and the angle the resultant makes with the positive x-axis (labeled θ_R) is determined from the equation

$$\tan \theta_R = \frac{R_y}{R_x}.$$

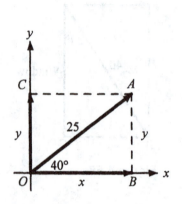

Figure 4.60

Example 6 illustrates this approach to vector addition.

EXAMPLE 6   Finding the Resultant Using Components

Vector **A** has a magnitude of 5.0 lb and makes an angle of 35° with the positive *x*-axis. Vector **B** has a magnitude of 9.0 lb and makes an angle of 160° with the positive *x*-axis. Find the resultant (or vector sum) of **A** and **B**.

Solution   We organize the procedure described above with the following table.

Vector	Magnitude	Direction	*x* Component	*y* Component
A	5.0	35°	$5.0 \cos 35° = 4.096$	$5.0 \sin 35° = 2.868$
B	9.0	160°	$9.0 \cos 160° = \underline{-8.457}$	$9.0 \sin 160° = \underline{3.078}$
R			$R_x = -4.361$	$R_y = 5.946$

The magnitude of the resultant is

$$R = \sqrt{(R_x)^2 + (R_y)^2}$$
$$= \sqrt{(-4.361)^2 + (5.946)^2}$$
$$= \sqrt{54.37}$$
$$= 7.4.$$

The angle the resultant makes with the positive *x*-axis is found by solving

$$\tan \theta_R = \frac{R_y}{R_x} = \frac{5.946}{-4.361} = -1.363.$$

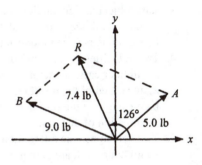

Figure 4.61

Since the *y* component is positive and the *x* component is negative, θ_R is in Q_2. By calculator we determine that the reference angle is 54°. Then

$$\theta_R = 180° - 54°$$
$$= 126°.$$

Thus, the resultant has magnitude 7.4 lb and makes an angle of 126° with the positive *x*-axis. (See Figure 4.61.)

Technology Link

Some calculators have the capability to find a vector sum in both rectangular form and polar form, which are often displayed as [*x y*] and [*r* ∠ *θ*], respectively. To illustrate, Figure 4.62 shows a display on one such calculator that indicates the solution to the problem in Example 6. You should learn to use this feature if it is available on your calculator.

PROGRESS CHECK 6   Vector **A** has a magnitude of 7.0 lb and makes an angle of 62° with the positive x-axis. Vector **B** has a magnitude of 4.0 lb and makes an angle of 175° with the positive x-axis. Find the resultant (or vector sum) of **A** and **B**.   ■

```
[5 ∠ 35] + [9 ∠ 160]
[-4.36147336563    5.94...
Ans ▶ Pol
[7.37415220404 ∠ 126.2...
```

Figure 4.62

EXERCISES 4.5

In Exercises 1–10 find the magnitude of all forces to two significant digits and all angles to the nearest degree.

1. A force of 5.0 lb and a force of 12 lb are acting on a body with an angle of 90° between the two forces. Find
   a. the magnitude of the resultant
   b. the angle between the resultant and the larger force

2. A force of 12 lb and a force of 16 lb are acting on a body with an angle of 90° between the two forces. Find.
   a. the magnitude of the resultant
   b. the angle between the resultant and the smaller force

3. Two forces, one 10 lb and the other 15 lb, act on the same object at right angles to each other. Find
   a. the magnitude of the resultant
   b. the angle between the resultant and the larger force

4. Two velocities, one 20 mi/hour north and the other 30 mi/hour east, are acting on the same body. Find
   a. the speed of the resultant velocity
   b. the angle of the resultant velocity with respect to a direction of due east

5. Two velocities, one 5.0 mi/hour south and the other 15 mi/hour west, are acting on the same body. Find
   a. the speed of the resultant velocity
   b. the angle of the resultant velocity with respect to a direction of due west

6. A ship is headed due south at 18 knots (nautical miles per hour) while the current carries the ship due west at 5.0 knots. Find
   a. the speed of the ship
   b. the direction (course) of the ship

7. An airplane can fly 500 mi/hour in still air. If it is heading due north in a wind that is blowing due east at a rate of 80.0 mi/hour, find
   a. the distance the plane can fly in 1 hour
   b. the angle that the resultant velocity will make with respect to due east

8. An object is dropped from a plane that is moving horizontally at a speed of 300 ft/second. If the vertical velocity of the object in terms of time is given by the formula $v = 32t$, 5 seconds later:
   a. What is the speed of the object?
   b. What angle does the direction of the object make with the horizontal?

9. A pilot wishes to fly due east at 300 mi/hour when a 70.0 mi/hour wind is blowing due north.
   a. How many degrees south of east should the pilot point the plane to attain the desired course?
   b. What airspeed should the pilot maintain?

10. A ship wishes to travel due south at 25 knots in an easterly current of 7.0 knots.
    a. How many degrees west of south should the navigator direct the ship?
    b. What speed must the ship maintain?

11. An airplane pointed due east is traveling 7.0° north of east at a rate of 350 mi/hour. The resultant course is due to a wind blowing north. Find
    a. the velocity of the plane if there were no wind (that is, the vector pointing due east)
    b. the velocity of the wind (that is, the vector pointing due north)

12. Answer the questions posed in Exercise 11 if the plane is traveling 14.0° north of east at 358 mi/hour.

13. A woman pushes with a force of 40 lb on the handle of a lawn mower that makes an angle of 33° with the ground. How much force pushes the lawn mower forward?

14. A man pulls with a force of 25 lb on a window pole, in an effort to lower a window. How much force is wasted if the pole makes an angle of 15° with the window?

15. A car weighing 3,500 lb is parked in a driveway that makes an angle of 10° with the horizontal. Find the minimum brake force that is needed to keep the car from rolling down the driveway. (Use the illustration below and assume no friction.)

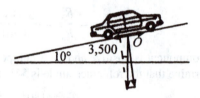

16. The answer to Exercise 15 is 608 pounds. If the driveway angle is cut in half to 5°, then what will the minimum brake force be?

17. Find the force needed to keep a barrel weighing 100 lb from rolling down a ramp that makes an angle of 15° with the horizontal (assume no friction).

18. A box is resting on a ramp that makes an angle of 18° with the horizontal. What is the force of friction between the box and the ramp if the box weights 80 lb?

19. A body is acted on by two forces with magnitudes of 16 lb and 25 lb, which act at an angle of 30° with each other. Find
    a. the magnitude of the resultant
    b. the angle between the resultant and the larger force

20. Two forces with magnitudes of 45 lb and 90 lb are applied to the same point. If the angle between them measures 72°, find
    a. the magnitude of the resultant
    b. the angle between the resultant and the smaller force

21. Forces with magnitudes of 126 lb and 198 lb act simultaneously on a body in such a way that the angle between the forces is 14°50′. Find
    a. the magnitude of the resultant
    b. the angle between the resultant and the larger force

22. Two forces with magnitudes of 15 lb and 20 lb act on a body in such a way that the magnitude of the resultant is 28 lb. Find the angles that the three forces make with each other.

23. Two forces act on a body to produce a resultant of 75 lb. If the angle between the two forces is 56° and one of the forces is 60 lb, find the magnitude of the other force.

24. City B is located 50° north of east of city A. There is a 30 mi/hour wind from the west and a pilot wishes to maintain an airspeed of 450 mi/hour. How many degrees north of east should the pilot head the plane to arrive directly at city B from city A?

25. Two forces with magnitudes of 42 lb and 71 lb are applied to the same object. If the magnitude of the resultant is 85 lb, find the angles that the three forces make with each other.

26. A force **A** of 400 lb and a force **B** of 600 lb act at a point. Their resultant, **R**, makes an angle of 42° with **A**. Find the magnitude of **R**.

In Exercises 27–30 find the horizontal and vertical component of each vector.

27. A magnitude of 100 lb; makes an angle of 30° with the positive x-axis.

28. A magnitude of 75 lb; makes an angle of 45° with the positive x-axis.

29. A magnitude of 18 lb; makes an angle of 27° with the positive x-axis.

30. A magnitude of 125 lb; makes an angle of 72° with the positive x-axis.

In Exercises 31–36 find the resultant (or vector sum) of the given vectors by resolving each vector into its x and y components.

	Vector	Magnitude	Direction (with respect to positive x-axis)
31.	A	5.0 lb	26°
	B	3.0 lb	84°
32.	C	6.0 lb	95°
	D	9.0 lb	15°
33.	C	12 lb	110°
	D	15 lb	180°

	Vector	Magnitude	Direction (with respect to positive x-axis)
34.	A	4.0 lb	90°
	B	3.0 lb	190°
35.	A	10 lb	42°
	B	20 lb	140°
	C	30 lb	240°
36.	A	5.0 lb	60°
	B	2.0 lb	210°
	C	1.0 lb	270°

THINK ABOUT IT 4.5

1. Two vectors **AB** and **CD** are said to be equal, and we write **AB** = **CD** if and only if they have the same length and direction. Use this definition to explain why the two methods shown below give the same result for the vector sum **A** + **B**.

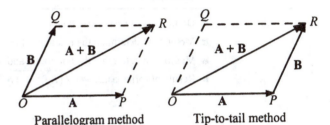

Parallelogram method   Tip-to-tail method

2. Use the tip-to-tail method of vector addition and show in a diagram that

   A + **B** = **B** + **A**   (commutative property)

3. Use the tip-to-tail method of vector addition and show in a diagram that

   (**A** + **B**) + **C** = **A** + (**B** + **C**)   (associate property)

4. If the magnitude of vector **A** is 6.0 lb and the magnitude of vector **B** is 8.0 lb, then show in a diagram how the vectors may be combined so that the vector sum has the given magnitude.
   a. 14 lb   **b.** 2.0 lb.   **c.** 10 lb   **d.** 7.2 lb

CHAPTER 4 OVERVIEW

Section	Key Concepts and Procedures to Review
4.1	■ Definitions of right triangle, acute angle, hypotenuse, similar triangles, cofunctions, complementary angles, one degree, one minute (written 1′), and reciprocal functions
	■ Definition of the trigonometric functions of an acute angle θ of a right triangle
	■ The side lengths in a 30–60–90 triangle are in the ratio of $1 : \sqrt{3} : 2$
	■ The side lengths in a 45–45–90 triangle are in the ratio of $1 : 1 : \sqrt{2}$
	■ A trigonometric function of any acute angle is equal to the corresponding cofunction of the complementary angle.
	■ Guidelines for using a calculator to evaluate a trigonometric function of an acute angle and to evaluate an inverse trigonometric function
4.2	■ Definitions of angle of elevation and of angle of depression
	■ Methods to solve a right triangle
	■ Guidelines for accuracy in computed results

4.3
■ Definitions of standard position of angle θ, quadrantal angle, coterminal angle, and reference angle
■ Definition of the trigonometric functions of an angle in standard position
■ Chart summarizing the signs of the trigonometric ratios
■ Methods to determine (if defined) approximate trigonometric values for any angle and exact values in special cases

4.4
■ Methods to solve trigonometric equations. Reference numbers and graphical calculator methods may be used.
■ Determine solutions between $0°$ and $360°$ as follows:

Quadrant	Solution
1	reference angle
2	$180°$ − reference angle
3	$180°$ + reference angle
4	$360°$ − reference angle

■ If θ is a solution of a trigonometric equation, then $\theta + k360°$ (where k is any integer) is also a solution of the equation.

4.5
■ Definitions of vector, resultant of two (or more) vectors, and components of a vector
■ Methods to determine the resultant of two (or more) vectors
■ Methods to determine the horizontal and vertical components of a vector
■ Resultant formulas: $R = \sqrt{(R_x)^2 + (R_y)^2}$ and $\tan \theta = R_y/R_x$

CHAPTER 4 REVIEW EXERCISES

1. Give five angles that are coterminal with $100°$. Include at least two negative angles.
2. Determine the exact value of sec $135°$.
3. If $\sin \theta = a$, find $\csc \theta$.
4. If $\tan \theta = \dfrac{3}{4}$ and $\cos \theta < 0$, find $\sin \theta$.
5. Express $\tan 22°$ as a function of the angle complementary to $22°$.
6. Determine an acute angle θ for which $\sin \theta = \cos 56°40'$.
7. Find the sine of the acute angle whose cosine is $\dfrac{2}{5}$.
8. What is the reference angle for $261°$?
9. If the point $(1, -1)$ is on the terminal ray of θ, find $\cos \theta$.
10. If the point $(-1, 1)$ is on the terminal ray of θ, give one possible measure of angle θ.

In Exercises 11–16 answer true or false.

11. $\sin 30° + \sin 60° = \sin 90°$
12. $\sin(30° + 60°) = \sin 30° + \sin 60°$
13. $\sin 45° = \cos 45°$
14. $\sin 30° = \dfrac{1}{2} \sin 60°$
15. $(\sin 30°)^2 = 2$
16. $\sin 30° \cdot \csc 30° = 1$

In Exercises 17–20 evaluate the given expression.

17. $\sin(-210°)$
18. $\cos 626°40'$
19. $3 \cos 720° + \tan(-540°)$
20. $\sin 2\theta$ if $\theta = 45°$

In Exercises 21–24 solve each equation for the given interval.

21. $3 \cot \theta - 1 = 0$; all solutions
22. $3 \csc \theta - 7 = -13$; $0° \le \theta < 360°$
23. $2 \sin \theta = -3$; all solutions
24. $2 \sin \theta = -2$; $0° \le \theta < 720°$
25. In a $30°$, $60°$, $90°$ triangle, the shortest side is 1 cm long. Find the lengths of the other two sides.
26. In right triangle ABC, $C = 90°$. If $\sin A = .8021$, find $\cos B$.
27. Solve the triangle ABC, if $C = 90°$, $B = 47°$, and $a = 45$ ft.
28. In right triangle ABC with $C = 90°$, if $b = 5.00$ and $c = 8.00$, determine B.
29. If $\cos \theta > 0$ and $\sin \theta < 0$, then in which quadrant is the terminal ray of θ?
30. What is the minimum value of $3 - \cos x$?
31. What is the maximum value of $2 + \sin x$?
32. True or False? In any triangle ABC,
$$\sin \frac{1}{2} A = \cos \frac{1}{2}(B + C).$$
33. Find the area of triangle ABC if $C = 90°$, $A = 40°$, and $b = 3.0$ ft.
34. If $\sin \theta = 0.7$ and θ is an acute angle, then find θ to the nearest tenth of a degree.
35. Consider Snell's law (see Exercise 87 in Section 4.1). As light passes from air to water, v_i/v_r is about 4/3. Find the angle of incidence of a ray of light if the angle of refraction is $25°40'$.

36. A carpenter has to build a stairway. The total rise is 8 ft 6 in. and the angle of rise is 30°, as shown in the illustration. What is the shortest piece of 2- × 12-in. stock that can be used to make the stringer?

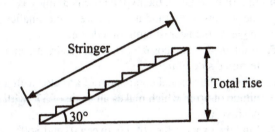

37. Two points, A and B, are 100 yd apart. Point C across a canyon is located so that angle CAB is 90° and angle CBA is 50°. Compute the distance $\overline{BC}$ across the canyon.

38. What is the vertical component of a vector with a magnitude of 50 lb which makes an angle of 25° with the positive x-axis?

39. A road rises 25 ft in a horizontal distance of 400 ft. Find the angle that the road makes with the horizontal.

40. A force of 12 lb and a force of 15 lb are acting on a body with an angle of 90° between the two forces. Find the magnitude of the resultant and the angle between the resultant and the larger force.

41. From the top of a building 30 ft tall, the angle of depression to the foot of a building across the street is 60° and the angle of elevation to the top of the same building is 70°. How tall is the building?

42. In a 3–4–5 right triangle find the smaller acute angle. Round to the nearest tenth of a degree.

43. A force of 40 lb and a force of 30 lb act on a body so that their resultant is a force of 38 lb. Find the angle between the two original forces.

44. To determine the radius of the sun, an observer on Earth at point O measures angle θ to be 16′, as illustrated by the diagram. If the distance from Earth to the sun is about 93,000,000 mi, what is the radius of the sun?

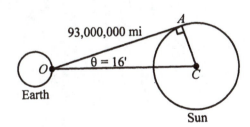

45. Vector **A** has a magnitude of 6.0 lb and makes an angle of 55° with the positive x-axis. Vector **B** has a magnitude of 2.0 lb and makes an angle of 110° with the positive x-axis. Find the resultant (or vector sum) of **A** and **B**.

46. The area of an equilateral triangle is $\sqrt{3}$. What are the lengths of the sides?

In Exercises 47–56 select the choice that completes the statement or answers the question.

47. The value of sin 100° is equal to
  a. sin 10°   **b.** sin 80°
  c. −sin 80°   **d.** −sin 10°

48. Which angle is a solution of $\tan \theta = -\sqrt{3}$?
  a. 120°   **b.** 150°
  c. 210°   **d.** 240°

49. The x component of a vector with a magnitude of 25 lb which makes an angle of 67° with the x-axis is
  a. 9.8 lb   **b.** 12 lb
  c. 17 lb   **d.** 23 lb

50. If the terminal ray of θ lies on the line $y = 2x$ and θ is in Q_3 then one angle measure for θ is
  a. 225°   **b.** 210°
  c. 207°   **d.** 243°

51. Find sec R in the following right triangle.

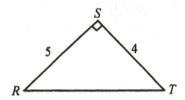

  a. $\dfrac{3}{5}$ **b.** $\dfrac{4}{3}$ **c.** $\dfrac{\sqrt{41}}{5}$ **d.** $\dfrac{\sqrt{41}}{4}$

52. Solve $\dfrac{\sin A}{a} = \dfrac{\sin B}{b}$ for a.
  a. $a = \dfrac{\sin A}{\sin B}$ **b.** $a = b \sin A - \sin B$
  c. $a = b$ **d.** $a = \dfrac{b \sin A}{\sin B}$

53. In a right triangle, the length of the hypotenuse is 17 and the longer side length is 15. The sine of the smaller acute angle is
  a. $\dfrac{15}{17}$ **b.** $\dfrac{8}{17}$ **c.** $\dfrac{15}{8}$ **d.** $\dfrac{17}{15}$

54. As angle θ increases from 180° to 360°, the sine of that angle
  a. increases
  b. decreases
  c. increases, then decreases
  d. decreases, then increases

55. Which of the following is an identity?
  a. $\sin \theta \cdot \cos \theta = 1$ **b.** $\sec \theta \cdot \csc \theta = 1$
  c. $\cos \theta \cdot \csc \theta = 1$ **d.** $\tan \theta \cdot \cot \theta = 1$

56. For $0° < \theta < 45°$ which statement must be true?
  a. $\sin \theta = \cos \theta$ **b.** $\sin \theta < \cos \theta$
  c. $\sin \theta > \cos \theta$ **d.** $\tan \theta < \sin \theta$

CHAPTER 4 TEST

1. Find the exact value of sin 60°.
2. In right triangle ABC with $C = 90°$, if $c = 17$ and $a = 15$, find the tangent of the smaller acute angle.
3. If $\cot \theta = \dfrac{4}{5}$ and θ is an acute angle, find $\cos \theta$.
4. Find the exact value of cos 225°.
5. Evaluate sec 132°50′ to four significant digits.
6. Find three angles coterminal to 150°. Include at least one negative angle measure.
7. If $\csc \theta = 3.85$ and θ is an acute angle, find θ to the nearest degree.
8. Solve $4 \cos \theta + 3 = 0$ for $0° \leq \theta < 360°$ to the nearest degree.
9. Find all solutions to $\tan \theta + 1 = 0$.
10. If $(3, -2)$ is a point on the terminal ray of θ, find sin θ.
11. True or False: In triangle ABC if $\cot A = 0$, then ABC is a right triangle.
12. In right triangle ABC with $C = 90°$, $\sin A = \dfrac{1}{2}$. Find $(\sin A)^2 + (\cos A)^2$.

13. Find the hypotenuse of right triangle ABC with $C = 90°$ if $A = 45°$ and $a = 55$ ft.
14. In a right triangle, the hypotenuse is 3 times as long as the shortest side. Find the measure of the smaller acute angle, to the nearest tenth of a degree.
15. If $\tan \theta > 0$ and $\cos \theta < 0$, what quadrant contains the terminal side of θ?
16. What is the vertical component of a vector with a magnitude of 56 lb which makes an angle of 37° with the positive x-axis?
17. Find the exact values of θ between 0° and 360° that make $\cos \theta = -\dfrac{1}{2}$ a true statement.
18. In right triangle ABC with $C = 90°$, $b = 35$ ft and $c = 45$ ft. Solve the triangle.
19. A road has a uniform elevation of 4.0°. Find the increase in elevation in driving 95 m along this road.
20. A force of 28 lb and a force of 12 lb are acting on a body with an angle of 28° between the two forces. Find the magnitude of the resultant force.

5

Further Algebraic Techniques

If a storekeeper raises a price 20 percent and then the following week reduces this new price by 20 percent, the final price can be represented as $(x + 0.20x) - 0.20(x + 0.20x)$, where x is the original price. Factor out the greatest common factor, $x + 0.20x$; then simplify and interpret the result. Is the final price more or less than the original price? (See Example 2 of Section 5.1.)

In Chapter 1 we discussed some essential topics in algebra that have served our purposes to this point. However, to continue our study of trigonometric and other functions, we need more algebraic techniques. In this chapter we will learn to factor expressions, perform the basic operations with algebraic fractions, and solve equations using factoring and fraction principles. Since factoring is a key technique in many algebraic manipulations, we begin with this topic.

Courtesy of Robert Brenner/PhotoEdit, Inc.

5.1 Factoring Polynomial and Trigonometric Expressions

OBJECTIVES

1 Factor out the greatest common factor (GCF).

2 Factor by grouping.

3 Factor trinomials of the form $ax^2 + bx + c$.

4 Factor out the GCF and then factor trinomials.

5 Use $b^2 - 4ac$ to determine if $ax^2 + bx + c$ can be factored.

The process of factoring undoes the process of multiplication, as shown below.

If we change a product into a sum, we are multiplying.

$$(x + 5)(x + 1) \xrightarrow{\text{multiplying}} x^2 + 6x + 5$$

If we change a sum into a product, we are factoring.

$$(x + 5)(x + 1) \xleftarrow{\text{factoring}} x^2 + 6x + 5$$

Both processes are important because in different situations one form may be more useful than the other. In general, the procedures for factoring are not as straightforward as those for multiplication, and we limit our discussion of factoring primarily to algebraic expressions called polynomials. Examples of polynomials are

$$64x^6 - y^6, 9x^2 + 24x + 16, \text{ and } 12ct^2 + 9c^2t,$$

and a **polynomial** is defined as an algebraic expression that may be written as a finite sum of terms that contain only nonnegative integer exponents on the variables. Thus, algebraic expressions such as

$$4x^{-2}, \sqrt{x} - 1, \text{ and } 5x^{1/3} + 5$$

are not polynomials. A polynomial with just one term is called a **monomial**; one that contains exactly two terms is a **binomial**; and one with exactly three terms is a **trinomial**. The **degree of a monomial** is the sum of the exponents on the variables in the term. The **degree of a polynomial** is the same as the degree of its highest monomial term. Thus, the degree of $5x^4y^2$ is 6, the degree of $2xy^2$ is 3, and the degree of $5x^4y^2 + 2xy^2$ is 6, since $5x^4y^2$ is the highest-degree term.

There are several techniques that enable us to factor certain polynomials, and you need to consider carefully each of the factoring methods that follow in this section and in Section 5.2.

Common Factors

The first method that should be employed in factoring a polynomial is to attempt to find a factor that is common to each of the terms. For example:

Polynomial	Common Factor
$9s + 6t$	3
$15x^2 + (-5x)$ (or $15x^2 - 5x$)	$5x$
$2a^2b + 8ab^2$	$2ab$

In each case we attempt to pick the greatest common factor (**GCF**) that divides into each term of the polynomial. Therefore, although 2 is a common factor of $2a^2b + 8ab^2$, a preferable common factor is $2ab$, since $2ab$ is the largest factor that divides both terms. With respect to variables, the GCF is the product of all common variable factors, with each variable appearing the fewest number of times it appears in any one of the terms. After we determine the greatest common factor, we use the distributive property to factor it out. For instance, the GCF of the terms in $3x^2 + 6x$ is $3x$, and we factor it out as follows.

$$3x^2 + 6x = 3x \cdot x + 3x \cdot 2 \quad \textit{Think:} \frac{3x^2}{3x} = x, \frac{6x}{3x} = 2$$

$$= 3x(x + 2) \qquad \text{Distributive property}$$

Thus, the factored form of $3x^2 + 6x$ is $3x(x + 2)$. Because factoring undoes multiplying, you should check factoring answers by multiplication. For this example,

$$3x(x + 2) = 3x \cdot x + 3x \cdot 2 = 3x^2 + 6x.$$

which checks. Use this example to clarify the following factoring procedure.

To Factor Out the GCF

1. Find the GCF of the terms in the polynomial.
2. Express each term in the polynomial as a product with the GCF as one factor.
3. Factor out the GCF using the distributive property.
4. Check the answer through multiplication.

You will notice that the directions in factoring problems use the phrase "factor completely." This expression directs us to continue factoring until the polynomial contains no factors of two or more terms that can be factored again. The restrictions we place on the form of the factors will determine whether a polynomial is factorable, so it is important to note that, unless otherwise specified, we are interested only in polynomial factors with integer coefficients.

EXAMPLE 1   Factoring Out the GCF
Factor completely.

a. $21x^2 - 7x$ **b.** $s(c + 2) - t(c + 2)$

Solution

a. The GCF of $21x^2$ and $7x$ is $7x$.

$$21x^2 - 7x = 7x \cdot 3x - 7x \cdot 1$$
$$= 7x(3x - 1) \quad \text{Distributive property}$$

b. The greatest common factor is the binomial $c + 2$. Factoring out the GCF using the distributive property gives

$$s(c + 2) - t(c + 2) = (c + 2)(s - t).$$

PROGRESS CHECK 1 Factor completely.

a. $8y^3 + 4y^2$ **b.** $2x(x + 3) + 5(x + 3)$ ■

EXAMPLE 2   Multiple Markups and Markdowns

Solve the problem in the chapter introduction on page 241.

Solution   We will factor out the GCF, which is $(x + 0.20x)$, and then simplify.

$$(x + 0.20x) - 0.20(x + 0.20x)$$

$= 1(x + 0.20x) - 0.20(x + 0.20x)$	GCF $= 1 \cdot$ GCF.
$= (x + 0.20x)(1 - 0.20)$	Factor out the GCF.
$= (1.20x)(0.80)$	Combine like terms.
$= 0.96x$	Simplify.

The final price is 96 percent of the original price. So, the final price is lower.

PROGRESS CHECK 2   If a storekeeper reduces a price by 50 percent and then increases this new price the following month by 50 percent, the final price can be represented as $(x - 0.50x) + 0.50(x - 0.50x)$, where x is the original price. Factor out the GCF, $x - 0.50x$; then simplify and interpret the result. Is the final price more or less than the original price?   ■

Trigonometric expressions are factored in the same manner as algebraic expressions. Throughout the chapter, we will often present problems in two parallel forms: the algebraic form in part **a** and a similar trigonometric expression in part **b**. The techniques for both problems are the same since a symbol in algebra, such as s, represents a real number; while an expression in trigonometry, such as $\sin \theta$, represents a ratio that is also a real number. Thus, the rules that govern both algebraic and trigonometric expressions are the rules that govern the real numbers. When using exponents with functions, it is common notation to avoid parentheses and to put the exponent between the name of the function and the symbol for the independent variable. For example, $(\sin \theta)^3$, which means $(\sin \theta)(\sin \theta)(\sin \theta)$, is written as $\sin^3 \theta$.

EXAMPLE 3   Contrasting Factorizations of Algebraic and Trigonometric Expressions

Factor completely.

a. $12ct^2 + 9c^2t$ 　　　**b.** $12 \cos \theta \tan^2 \theta + 9 \cos^2 \theta \tan \theta$

Solution

a. The GCF of $12ct^2$ and $9c^2t$ is $3ct$.

$$12ct^2 + 9c^2t = 3ct \cdot 4t + 3ct \cdot 3c$$
$$= 3ct(4t + 3c)$$

b. The GCF of $12 \cos \theta \tan^2 \theta$ and $9 \cos^2 \theta \tan \theta$ is $3 \cos \theta \tan \theta$.

$$12 \cos \theta \tan^2 \theta + 9 \cos^2 \theta \tan \theta = 3 \cos \theta \tan \theta \cdot 4 \tan \theta + 3 \cos \theta \tan \theta \cdot 3 \cos \theta$$
$$= 3 \cos \theta \tan \theta(4 \tan \theta + 3 \cos \theta)$$

PROGRESS CHECK 3   Factor completely.

a. $6s^2 - 9s$ 　　　**b.** $6 \sin^2 \theta - 9 \sin \theta$ ■

Factoring by Grouping

In Example 1b we factored out a common factor that was a binomial. This situation often occurs when factoring a polynomial with four terms by a method called **factoring by grouping**. For example,

$$3xy + 2y + 3xz + 2z$$

can be factored by rewriting the expression as

$$(3xy + 2y) + (3xz + 2z).$$

If we factor out the common factor in each group, we have

$$y(3x + 2) + z(3x + 2).$$

Now $3x + 2$ is a common factor, and the final result is

$$(3x + 2)(y + z).$$

You should check here that an alternate grouping of the original expression, such as

$$(3xy + 3xz) + (2y + 2z),$$

also achieves the same result.

EXAMPLE 4   Factoring by Grouping

Factor by grouping.

a. $3x^2 + 6x + 4x + 8$ **b.** $x^3 - 5x^2 - 3x + 15$

Solution

a. $3x^2 + 6x + 4x + 8$

$$
\begin{array}{ll}
\overset{\text{common factor}}{\overbrace{3x}} \quad \overset{\text{common factor}}{\overbrace{4}} \\
= (3x^2 + 6x) + (4x + 8) & \text{Group terms with common factors.} \\
= 3x(x + 2) + 4(x + 2) & \text{Factor in each group.} \\
= (x + 2)(3x + 4) & \text{Factor out the common binomial factor.}
\end{array}
$$

b. Note in the following solution that we factor out -3 instead of 3 from the grouping on the right to reach the goal of obtaining a common binomial factor.
$x^3 - 5x^2 - 3x + 15$

$$
\begin{array}{ll}
\overset{\text{common factor}}{\overbrace{x^2}} \quad \overset{\text{common factor}}{\overbrace{-3}} \\
= (x^3 - 5x^2) + (-3x + 15) & \text{Group terms with common factors.} \\
= x^2(x - 5) - 3(x - 5) & \text{Factor in each group.} \\
= (x - 5)(x^2 - 3) & \text{Factor out the common binomial factor.}
\end{array}
$$

PROGRESS CHECK 4   Factor by grouping.

a. $2x^2 + 4x + 3x + 6$ **b.** $x^3 - 6x^2 - 6x + 36$ ■

Factoring Trinomials (Leading Coefficient 1)

In some cases trinomials of the form $ax^2 + bx + c$ can be factored (with integer coefficients) by reversing the FOIL multiplication process shown earlier. Example 5 discusses this factoring procedure in the simplest case when the leading coefficient a equals 1.

EXAMPLE 5   Factoring $ax^2 + bx + c$ with $a = 1$

Factor completely $x^2 - 5x - 6$.

Solution   The first term, x^2, is the result of multiplying the first terms in the FOIL method. Thus,

$$x^2 - 5x - 6 = (x + ?)(x + ?).$$

The last term, -6, is the result of multiplying the last terms in the FOIL method. Since -6 equals $(-6)(1)$, $(6)(-1)$, $(-3)(2)$ and $(3)(-2)$, we have four possibilities. We want the pair whose sum is -5, which is the coefficient of the middle term. The combination of -6 and 1 satisfies this condition and produces the middle term of $-5x$.

$$(x - 6)(x + 1)$$

$$x + (-6x) = -5x$$

Thus, $x^2 - 5x - 6 = (x - 6)(x + 1)$. We summarize our method in this example with the factoring formula

$$x^2 + (m + n)x + mn = (x + m)(x + n),$$

which you can use as a model for factoring such expressions.

Technology Link

A graphing calculator can often be useful when factoring a polynomial in one variable. To see how, consider Figure 5.1, which shows a graph of the function associated with the polynomial in this example. Do you see a relation between the factors of the polynomial and the points where the graph crosses the x-axis?

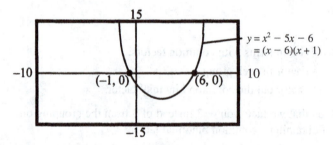

Figure 5.1

Observe that the graph crosses the x-axis at $x = 6$ and at $x = -1$, while $x - 6$ and $x + 1$ are factors of the polynomial. This result illustrates the general principle that if the graph of $y = f(x)$ intersects the x-axis at $x = a$, then $x - a$ is a factor of $f(x)$. Try to use this principle to factor the polynomial in the Progress Check exercise that follows.

PROGRESS CHECK 5   Factor completely $x^2 - x - 20$.   ■

Factoring Trinomials (General Case)

When the coefficient of the squared term is not 1, the trinomial is harder to factor. The reason for this difficulty can be seen in the following product.

$$(px + m)(qx + n) = (pq)x^2 + (pn + qm)x + mn$$

In factoring these more complicated trinomials, if you keep in mind that the middle term is the sum of the inside product and the outside product, then a little trial and error will eventually produce the answer. Although there are often many combinations to consider, experience and practice will help you *mentally* eliminate many of the possibilities.

EXAMPLE 6   Factoring $ax^2 + bx + c$ with $a \neq 1$
Factor completely.

a. $4c^2 - 12c + 5$ **b.** $4\cos^2\theta - 12\cos\theta + 5$

Solution

a. The first term, $4c^2$, is the result of multiplying the first terms in the FOIL method. Thus,

$$4c^2 - 12c + 5 \overset{?}{=} \quad \begin{matrix} (4c + ?)(c + ?) \\ \text{or} \\ (2c + ?)(2c + ?) \end{matrix}$$

The last term, 5, is the result of multiplying the last terms in the FOIL method. There is only one possibility for 5, $(-5)(-1)$, since we can eliminate $(5)(1)$ because the middle term in negative.

$$4c^2 - 12c + 5 \overset{?}{=} \begin{matrix} (4c - 5)(c - 1) \\ (4c - 1)(c - 5) \\ (2c - 5)(2c - 1) \end{matrix}$$

The middle term, $-12c$, is the sum of the inner and the outer terms.

$$(4c - 5)(c - 1) \qquad (2c - 5)(2c - 1) \qquad (4c - 1)(c - 5)$$

$$-4c - 5c = -9c \qquad -2c - 10c = -12c \qquad -20c - c = -21c$$

Thus, $4c^2 - 12c + 5 = (2c - 5)(2c - 1)$ is the correct choice.

b. In a similar way, $4 \cos^2 \theta - 12 \cos \theta + 5 = (2 \cos \theta - 5)(2 \cos \theta - 1)$.

PROGRESS CHECK 6 Factor completely.

a. $4t^2 - 4t - 15$ **b.** $4 \tan^2 \theta - 4 \tan \theta - 15$ ■

EXAMPLE 7 Factoring $ax^2 + bx + c$ with $a \neq 1$
Factor completely.

a. $9 \sin^2 \theta + 12 \sin \theta + 4$ **b.** $9s^2 + 12s + 4$

Solution

a. The first term, $9 \sin^2 \theta$, is the result of multiplying the first terms in the FOIL method.

$$9 \sin^2 \theta + 12 \sin \theta + 4 \overset{?}{=} \quad \begin{matrix} (9 \sin \theta + ?)(\sin \theta + ?) \\ \text{or} \\ (3 \sin \theta + ?)(3 \sin \theta + ?) \end{matrix}$$

The last term, 4, is the result of multiplying the last terms in the FOIL method. Since 4 equals $(4)(1)$ and $(2)(2)$, we have two possibilities. We eliminate negative factors of 4 since the middle term is positive.

$$9 \sin^2 \theta + 12 \sin \theta + 4 \overset{?}{=} \begin{matrix} (9 \sin \theta + 1)(\sin \theta + 4) \\ (9 \sin \theta + 4)(\sin \theta + 1) \\ (9 \sin \theta + 2)(\sin \theta + 2) \\ (3 \sin \theta + 4)(3 \sin \theta + 1) \\ (3 \sin \theta + 2)(3 \sin \theta + 2) \end{matrix}$$

The middle term, $12 \sin \theta$, is the sum of the inner and the outer terms.

$$(3 \sin \theta + 2)(3 \sin \theta + 2)$$

$$6 \sin \theta + 6 \sin \theta = 12 \sin \theta$$

Thus, $9 \sin^2 \theta + 12 \sin \theta + 4 = (3 \sin \theta + 2)^2$.

b. In a similar way, $9s^2 + 12s + 4 = (3s + 2)(3s + 2)$ or $(3s + 2)^2$.

Note   Very often when the first term and the last term of the trinomial to be factored are perfect squares, the factored form is also a perfect square. Try this possibility first. The factoring models in such cases (called perfect square trinomials) are

$$a^2 + 2ab + b^2 = (a + b)^2$$
$$a^2 - 2ab + b^2 = (a - b)^2.$$

You can spot a perfect square trinomial in one variable on a graphing calculator by looking for a graph that intersects the x-axis in exactly one point. For instance, Figure 5.2 shows that the graph of $y = 9x^2 + 12x + 4$ intersects the x-axis only at $x = -2/3$, so only $3x + 2$ is a factor of $9x^2 + 12x + 4$ (if integer coefficients are required).

PROGRESS CHECK 7   Factor completely.

a. $4 \cos^2 \theta - 4 \cos \theta + 1$ **b.** $4c^2 - 4c + 1$.   ■

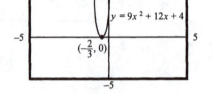

Figure 5.2

Factoring by grouping is a key step in the **ac method** for factoring the trinomial $ax^2 + bx + c$. Example 8 explains in detail the steps for this method, which is especially useful if our previous method of reversing FOIL results in many possible factorizations to consider.

EXAMPLE 8   Using the *ac* method

Factor completely $12x^2 - x - 20$.

Solution   Follow the steps below.

Step 1: Find two integers whose product is *ac* and whose sum is *b*. In the trinomial $a = 12$, $b = -1$, and $c = -20$. Thus $ac = 12(-20) = -240$, and we look for two integers whose product is -240 and whose sum is -1. With a little trial and error we find that

$$-16(15) = -240 \text{ and } -16 + 15 = -1,$$

so the required integers are -16 and 15.

Step 2: Replace *b* by the sum of the two integers from step 1 and then distribute *x*.

$$12x^2 - x - 20 = 12x^2 + (-16 + 15)x - 20$$
$$= 12x^2 - 16x + 15x - 20$$

Step 3: Factor by grouping.

$$(12x^2 - 16x) + (15x - 20) = 4x(3x - 4) + 5(3x - 4)$$
$$= (3x - 4)(4x + 5)$$

Thus, $12x^2 - x - 20 = (3x - 4)(4x + 5)$.

PROGRESS CHECK 8   Factor completely $12x^2 + 19x - 18$.   ■

In the next example more than one factoring method is required. As a general strategy, it is recommended that you factor out any common factors as your first factoring procedure.

EXAMPLE 9   Combining Factoring Methods

Factor completely $18x^3 + 15x^2 - 12x$.

Solution   First look for common factors. The GCF is $3x$, so factor it out.

$$18x^3 + 15x^2 - 12x = 3x(6x^2 + 5x - 4)$$

Now suppose we try to factor $6x^2 + 5x - 4$ as $(2x + 1)(3x - 4)$.

$$(2x + 1)(3x - 4)$$

$$-8x + 3x = -5x$$

This result is the opposite of the middle term we want, so we switch signs on the factors of -4, from $(1)(-4)$ to $(-1)(4)$.

$$(2x - 1)(3x + 4)$$

$$8x - 3x = 5x$$

Thus, $6x^2 + 5x - 4 = (2x - 1)(3x + 4)$, and so the complete factorization is

$$18x^3 + 15x^2 - 12x = 3x(2x - 1)(3x + 4)$$

PROGRESS CHECK 9   Factor completely $6y^4 - 15y^3 - 9y^2$.   ■

It should be noted that many trinomials cannot be factored with integer coefficients, and if you suspect that you are trying to find a factorization that may not exist, then apply the following test.

Factoring Test for Trinomials

A trinomial of the form $ax^2 + bx + c$, where a, b, and c are integers, is factorable into binomial factors with integer coefficients if and only if $b^2 - 4ac$ is a perfect square.

The expression $b^2 - 4ac$ is called the **discriminant**, and when we derive the discriminant in Section 7.2, the rationale for this test will be easy to understand.

EXAMPLE 10   Using a Factoring Test for Trinomials
Calculate $b^2 - 4ac$ and determine if $x^2 - 10x - 30$ can be factored into binomial factors with integer coefficients.

Solution   In this trinomial $a = 1$, $b = -10$, and $c = -30$. Therefore,

$$b^2 - 4ac = (-10)^2 - 4(1)(-30)$$
$$= 220.$$

Since 220 is not a perfect square, $x^2 - 10x - 30$ cannot be factored into binomial factors with integer coefficients.

PROGRESS CHECK 10   Calculate $b^2 - 4ac$ and determine if $9x^2 - 9x - 4$ can be factored into binomial factors with integer coefficients.   ■

A polynomial is said to be **irreducible** over the set of integers if it cannot be written as the product of two polynomials of positive degree with integer coefficients. Thus, we say $x^2 - 10x - 30$ is irreducible over the set of *integers*. Note, however, that $x^2 - 10x - 30$ is not irreducible over the set of *real numbers*, since we can show that

$$x^2 - 10x - 30 = \left[x - \left(5 + \sqrt{55}\right)\right]\left[x - \left(5 - \sqrt{55}\right)\right]$$

by using techniques that we will develop. Thus, whether or not a polynomial is irreducible depends on the number system from which the coefficients may be selected.

EXERCISES 5.1

In Exercises 1–20, factor out the greatest common factor.

1. $yx + yz$
2. $ab - ac$
3. $8x - 12$
4. $9y + 15$
5. $b - b^2$
6. $x^2 + x$
7. $5x^3y - 10x^2y^2$
8. $12ct^2 - 21c^2t$
9. $9a^2x^2 + 3ax$
10. $22x^3y^3 - 2x^2y^2$
11. $2x^2z^2 + 4xy - 5x^2y^2$
12. $3a^{10}x^6 - 9a^7x^7 + 6a^9x^4$
13. $x(x + 1) + 2(x + 1)$
14. $x(x - 2) - 3(x - 2)$
15. $7t(t - 4) - (t - 4)$
16. $(1 - y) - y(1 - y)$
17. $b(a - c) + d(a - c)$
18. $2x(y + z) - 5y(y + z)$
19. $(x - 5)^2 + 7(x - 5)$
20. $(x + 3)^2 - (x + 3)$

In Exercises 21–32 factor by grouping.

21. $ax + ay + 5x + 5y$
22. $2a + 2b + ka + kb$
23. $3xy + 6x + y + 2$
24. $1 + x + c + cx$
25. $4x^2 - 8x + 3x - 6$
26. $12y^2 - 18y + 8y - 12$
27. $a^2 - 3a - 3a + 9$
28. $4t^2 - 6t - 6t + 9$
29. $x^5 + x^3 + 5x^2 + 5$
30. $y^4 - 5y^3 + 2y - 10$
31. $x^3 + 7x^2 - 7x - 49$
32. $x^3 - 3x^2 - x + 3$

In Exercises 33–60 factor each polynomial.

33. $a^2 + 5a + 4$
34. $y^2 + 7y + 10$
35. $x^2 - 9x + 14$
36. $r^2 - 13r + 12$
37. $y^2 + 13y - 30$
38. $p^2 - 3p - 18$
39. $c^2 - 3c - 10$
40. $x^2 - x - 6$
41. $x^2 - 6x + 9$
42. $y^2 + 2y + 1$
43. $t^2 + 10t + 25$
44. $c^2 - 8c + 16$
45. $x^2 + 8xy + 15y^2$
46. $y^2 - 10ay + 16a^2$
47. $a^2 + 3ab - 4b^2$
48. $x^2 - bx - 20b^2$
49. $7y^2 - 13y + 6$
50. $2x^2 + 9x + 10$
51. $3x^2 - 5x - 2$
52. $5r^2 - 4r - 12$
53. $6k^2 - 7k + 2$
54. $4a^2 + 13a - 12$
55. $9a^2 - 12a + 4$
56. $4x^2 - 12x + 9$
57. $9b^2 - 25b - 6$
58. $12x^2 + 19x - 18$
59. $12x^2 - 29xy + 10y^2$
60. $18t^2 - 3kt - 10k^2$

In Exercises 61–70 factor each expression completely.

61. $3k^2 - 6k - 24$
62. $5y^2 - 15y - 50$
63. $6t^2 + 12t - 48$
64. $4x^2 - 12x + 8$
65. $3x^3 - 12x^2 + 9x$
66. $2k^3 - 18k^2 + 40k$
67. $9y^3 - 21y^2 + 10y$
68. $16a^3 - 4a^2 - 6a$
69. $24x^3y + 40x^2y^2 + 16xy^3$
70. $72a^3b - 12a^2b^2 - 60ab^3$

In Exercises 71–92 factor each expression completely.

71. $7 \sin \theta + 7 \cos \theta$
72. $3 \tan \theta - 3 \sin \theta$
73. $21 \sin^2 \theta - 14 \sin \theta$
74. $7 \tan \theta - 35 \tan^3 \theta$
75. $15 \cos \theta \tan^2 \theta - 21 \cos^2 \theta \tan \theta$
76. $20 \tan^2 \theta - 15 \tan \theta \sin \theta$
77. $\cos \theta (\sin \theta - 5) + \tan \theta (\sin \theta - 5)$
78. $\sin \theta (2 \tan \theta + 1) - \cos \theta (2 \tan \theta + 1)$
79. $\tan^2 \theta - 3 \tan \theta + 2$
80. $\tan^2 \theta - 8 \tan \theta + 12$
81. $\tan^2 \theta - 9 \tan \theta + 20$
82. $\sin^2 \theta - 8 \sin \theta - 20$
83. $3 \sin^2 \theta - 8 \sin \theta - 3$
84. $2 \tan^2 \theta - 7 \tan \theta + 6$
85. $6 \sin^2 \theta + 7 \sin \theta + 2$
86. $4 \cos^2 \theta - 13 \cos \theta + 3$
87. $20 \sin^2 \theta - 43 \sin \theta - 12$
88. $18 \cos^2 \theta - 57 \cos \theta + 24$
89. $4 \cos^2 \theta - 9 \cos \theta \tan \theta + 2 \tan^2 \theta$
90. $2 \sin^2 \theta + 5 \sin \theta \cos \theta - 7 \cos^2 \theta$
91. $4 \sin^2 \theta - 4 \sin \theta + 1$
92. $4 \tan^2 \theta + 20 \tan \theta + 25$

In Exercises 93–100 determine whether or not each expression can be factored into binomial factors with integer coefficients by calculating $b^2 - 4ac$.

93. $6s^2 + 7s + 2$
94. $3 \sin^2 \theta + \sin \theta - 1$
95. $t^2 - 5t + 3$
96. $2 \tan^2 \theta - \tan \theta - 3$
97. $2 \cos^2 \theta - 5 \cos \theta - 7$
98. $18x^2 + 19x - 12$
99. $12x^2 - 11x - 18$
100. $12s^2 - s + 1$

In Exercises 101–104 write an alternative formula by factoring the right side of the equation.

101. The surface area of the rectangular solid shown.
$$S = 2b^2 + 4ab$$

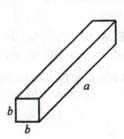

102. The total surface area of the metal gutter shown (not including edges) $S = 4ac + 2bc$.

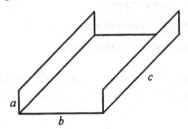

103. The area of a ring where the small radius is half the large radius, R. $A = \pi R^2 - \pi \left(\dfrac{R}{2}\right)^2$

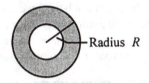

Radius R

104. The shaded area given that the small radii are half the large radius, R. $A = \pi R^2 - \pi \left(\dfrac{R}{2}\right)^2 - \pi \left(\dfrac{R}{2}\right)^2$

R

105. If a storekeeper raises a price 30 percent and one week later cuts this new price by 30 percent, the final price can be represented as $(x + 0.30x) - 0.30(x + 0.30x)$, where x is the original price. Factor out $x + 0.30x$; then simplify and interpret the result. Is the final price more or less than the original price?

106. If a storekeeper raises a price 70 percent and one week later cuts this new price by 70 percent, the final price can be represented as $(x + 0.70x) -$

$0.70(x + 0.70x)$, where x is the original price. Factor out $x + 0.70x$; then simplify and interpret the result. Is the final price more or less than the original price?

107. What is the overall result of raising a price by 10 percent and then raising the resulting price by 20 percent? Factor out $x + 0.10x$ in $(x + 0.10x) + 0.20(x + 0.10x)$ and simplify to find out.

108. What is the overall result of raising a price by 20 percent and then raising the resulting price by 10 percent? Factor out $x + 0.20x$ in $(x + 0.20x) + 0.10(x + 0.20x)$ and simplify to find out.

109. There are two numbers for which the number plus twice its square equals 55. They can be found by solving $x + 2x^2 - 55 = 0$. Factor the left side of this equation.

110. A ball is thrown down from a roof 160 feet high with an initial velocity of 48 ft/sec. To find the number of seconds it takes to hit the ground you can solve $16t^2 + 48t - 160 = 0$. Factor the left side of this equation.

THINK ABOUT IT 5.1

1. a. What does the word *common* mean in *greatest common factor*?
  b. Look up *factor* in the dictionary. What does it have to do with *factory*? English use of this word in algebra dates back to the seventeenth century.
2. If c is a prime number and $x^2 + bx + c$ is factorable, express b in terms of c.
3. Factor each expression completely. Assume that variables as exponents denote integers.
  a. $x^{n+1} + x^n$ **b.** $y^{2n} - y^n$
  c. $x^{2m} + 6x^m + 9$ **d.** $10x^{2n} - 9x^n + 2$
  e. $y^{2n+1} + y^{n+1} - 20y$ **f.** $x^{2m+2} + x^{m+2} - 30x^2$
4. Find two expressions whose greatest common factor is the following.
  a. $5x^2$ **b.** $3x - 1$
5. An odd number is a positive integer that can be written in the form $2k + 1$ where k is an integer. Show that the product of two odd numbers is an odd number.

5.2 Special Factoring Models and a Factoring Strategy

A formula for the height (y) above ground of an object dropped d ft above the earth's surface is $y = d - 16t^2$, where t is the elapsed time in seconds.

a. What is the formula for an object dropped from 625 ft?
b. Express the result from part **a** in factored form.
c. Show that the object hits the ground in 6.25 seconds. (See Example 3.)

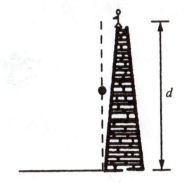

OBJECTIVES

1 Factor an expression that is the difference of squares.

2 Factor an expression that is the sum or difference of cubes.

3 Apply a general strategy to factor expressions systematically.

In this section we rely on certain models to factor three special types of binomials. All of these models may be verified through multiplication and they should all be memorized.

Difference of Squares

An important method of factoring comes from reversing the following special product that was considered in Section 1.4.

$$(a + b)(a - b) = a^2 - b^2$$

Note that the factors on the left differ only in the operation between a and b, while the result of the multiplication is two perfect squares with a minus sign between them. Thus, in factoring two perfect squares with a minus sign between them, we obtain two factors that consist of the sum and the difference of the square roots of each of the squared terms.

Factoring Model for a Difference of Squares

$$a^2 - b^2 = (a + b)(a - b)$$

Keep in mind that even powers of variables such as x^2, t^4, y^6, and so on are perfect squares.

EXAMPLE 1   Factoring a Difference of Squares

Factor completely.

a. $x^2 - 81$ **b.** $25y^6 - 49n^4$

Solution

a. Substitute x for a and 9 for b in the given model.

$$a^2 - b^2 = (a + b)(a - b)$$
$$x^2 - 81 = x^2 - 9^2 = (x + 9)(x - 9)$$

b. Because $25y^6 = (5y^3)^2$ and $49n^4 = (7n^2)^2$, replace a by $5y^3$ and b by $7n^2$ in the factoring formula for a difference of squares.

$$a^2 \quad - \quad b^2 = \quad (a + \quad b) \quad (a - \quad b)$$
$$25y^6 - 49n^4 = (5y^3)^2 - (7n^2)^2 = (5y^3 + 7n^2)(5y^3 - 7n^2)$$

Technology Link

Two expressions that are equivalent will produce the same graph. Therefore, one way to test for equivalent expressions on a graphing calculator is to set $y1$ equal to one of the expressions, $y2$ equal to the other, and then draw complete graphs of both functions in the same display. If you see two distinct graphs, then the expressions are not equivalent. Two graphs that appear to be the same will support the conclusion that the expressions are equivalent. To illustrate, visual support for the factorization in Example 1a may be obtained by letting

$$y1 = x^2 - 81$$
$$y2 = (x + 9)(x - 9)$$

and then graphing both functions as shown in Figure 5.3.

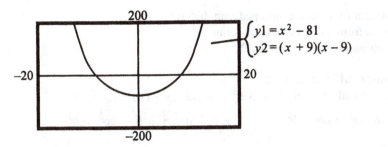

$$\begin{cases} y1 = x^2 - 81 \\ y2 = (x + 9)(x - 9) \end{cases}$$

Figure 5.3

PROGRESS CHECK 1   Factor completely.

a. $n^2 - 16$ **b.** $100x^2y^2 - 49z^2$ ▪

**EXAMPLE 2   Contrasting Factorizations of Algebraic
                    and Trigonometric Expressions**

Factor completely.

a. $16 - 9\tan^2\theta$ **b.** $16 - 9t^2$

Solution

a. Note that $16 - 9\tan^2\theta = 4^2 - (3\tan\theta)^2$ and apply the factoring formula with $a = 4$ and $b = 3\tan\theta$.

$$16 - 9\tan^2\theta = 4^2 - (3\tan\theta)^2$$
$$= (4 + 3\tan\theta)(4 - 3\tan\theta)$$

b. In a similar way, $16 - 9t^2 = (4 + 3t)(4 - 3t)$.

PROGRESS CHECK 2   Factor completely.

a. $1 - 4\sin^2\theta$ **b.** $1 - 4s^2$ ▪

EXAMPLE 3   Using Factoring to Rewrite a Formula

Solve the problem in the section introduction on page 251.

Solution

a. Replacing d by 625 in the formula $y = d - 16t^2$ yields

$$y = 625 - 16t^2.$$

b. The right side of the equation above factors as a difference of squares.

$$625 - 16t^2 = (25 + 4t)(25 - 4t)$$

Thus, $y = (25 + 4t)(25 - 4t)$ expresses the result from part **a** in factored form.

c. To show the object hits the ground in 6.25 seconds, we show that when $t = 6.25$, $y = 0$. Choosing the factored version of the formula we get

$$y = (25 + 4t)(25 - 4t)$$
$$= [25 + 4(6.25)][25 - 4(6.25)]$$
$$= (50)(0)$$
$$= 0.$$

Note that an expression in factored form has a value of 0 if and only if at least one of the factors has a value of 0.

PROGRESS CHECK 3   Because the moon is less massive than the earth, the pull of gravity at its surface is weaker, and so objects fall more slowly on the moon. The formula for the height (y) above ground of an object dropped d ft above the moon's surface is roughly $y = d - 4t^2$, where t is the elapsed time in seconds.

a. What is the formula for an object dropped from 625 ft?

b. Express the result from part **a** in factored form.

c. Show that the object hits the ground in 12.5 seconds.

Sum or Difference of Two Cubes

The product of $a + b$ and $a^2 - ab + b^2$ is $a^3 + b^3$, as shown below.

$$(a + b)(a^2 - ab + b^2) = a^3 - a^2b + ab^2 + a^2b - ab^2 + b^3$$
$$= a^3 + b^3$$

Similarly,

$$(a - b)(a^2 + ab + b^2) = a^3 + a^2b + ab^2 - a^2b - ab^2 - b^3$$
$$= a^3 - b^3.$$

By reversing these special products, we obtain factoring models for the sum and the difference of two cubes.

Factoring Models for Sums and Differences of Cubes

$$a^3 + b^3 = (a + b)(a^2 - ab + b^2)$$
$$a^3 - b^3 = (a - b)(a^2 + ab + b^2)$$

To use these models, we identify appropriate replacements for a and b in the expression to be factored and then substitute in these formulas.

EXAMPLE 4   Factoring a Sum or Difference of Cubes

Factor completely.

a. $8x^3 + 27$ **b.** $y^6 - 125$

Solution

a. Here we use the formula for the sum of two cubes. Since $8x^3 = (2x)^3$ and $27 = (3)^3$, we replace a with $2x$ and b with 3. The result is

$$a^3 + \quad b^3 = (a + \ b) \quad (a^2 - a \ b + \ b^2)$$

$$8x^3 + 27 = (2x)^3 + \quad 3^3 = (2x + 3)[(2x)^2 - (2x)(3) + (3)^2]$$
$$= (2x + 3)(4x^2 - 6x + 9)$$

b. To factor $y^6 - 125$, use the formula for the difference of two cubes. Because $y^6 = (y^2)^3$ and $125 = 5^3$, replace a with y^2 and b with 5.

$$a^3 - \quad b^3 = (a - b)(a^2 + \quad a \ b + \ b^2)$$

$$y^6 - 125 = (y^2)^3 - 5^3 = (y^2 - 5)[(y^2)^2 + (y^2)(5) + (5)^2]$$
$$= (y^2 - 5)(y^4 + 5y^2 + 25)$$

PROGRESS CHECK 4   Factor completely.

a. $8y^3 - 1$ **b.** $x^9 + 27y^3$

The next example points out that we often need to apply more than one factoring procedure to factor completely.

EXAMPLE 5   Combining Factoring Methods

Factor completely.

a. $10x^4 + 10x$ **b.** $y^4 - x^4$

Solution

a. First, factor out the common factor, $10x$; then apply the factoring model for the sum of two cubes.

$$10x^4 + 10x = 10x(x^3 + 1) \qquad\qquad \text{Factor out } 10x.$$
$$= 10x(x + 1)(x^2 - x + 1) \quad \text{Sum of cubes.}$$

b. First, factor $y^4 - x^4$ as the difference of squares.

$$y^4 - x^4 = (y^2 + x^2)(y^2 - x^2)$$

Then, $y^2 + x^2$ does not factor, but $y^2 - x^2$ is a difference of squares, so

$$y^4 - x^4 = (y^2 + x^2)(y + x)(y - x)$$

represents the complete factorization.

PROGRESS CHECK 5   Factor completely.

a. $5x^3 - 40$ **b.** $16m^4 - 81n^4$ ■

At this point it is useful to summarize all of our factoring models and to state a general strategy to help you to systematically factor a variety of expressions.

Summary of Factoring Models

1. Common factor: $ab + ac = a(b + c)$
2. Trinomial $(a = 1)$: $x^2 + (m + n)x + mn = (x + m)(x + n)$
3. General trinomial: $(pq)x^2 + (pn + qm)x + mn = (px + m)(qx + n)$
4. Perfect square trinomial: $a^2 + 2ab + b^2 = (a + b)^2$
5. Perfect square trinomial: $a^2 - 2ab + b^2 = (a - b)^2$
6. Difference of squares: $a^2 - b^2 = (a + b)(a - b)$
7. Sum of cubes: $a^3 + b^3 = (a + b)(a^2 - ab + b^2)$
8. Difference of cubes: $a^3 - b^3 = (a - b)(a^2 + ab + b^2)$

With the aid of these models you may use the following steps as a guideline for factoring polynomials.

Guidelines to Factoring a Polynomial

1. Factor out any common factors (if present) as the first factoring procedure.
2. Check for factorizations according to the number of terms in the polynomial.
   Two terms: Look for a difference of squares or cubes, or a sum of cubes. Then apply models 6, 7, or 8, if applicable. Remember that $a^2 + b^2$ is irreducible.
   Three terms: If the coefficient of the squared term is 1, try to use model 2. If the coefficient of the squared term is not 1, use FOIL reversal or the ac method. Check for the special case of a perfect square trinomial in which models 4 and 5 apply.
   Four terms: Try factoring by grouping.
3. Make sure that no factors of two or more terms can be factored again.

Also remember that trigonometric expressions are factored in the same manner as polynomials and that you can always check your factoring by multiplying out your answer.

EXAMPLE 6   Factoring a Polynomial Systematically
Factor completely $144 - 16t^2$.

Solution   Although $144 - 16t^2$ is a difference of two squares, we will first factor out the GCF, 16, as recommended in the guidelines above.

$$144 - 16t^2 = 16(9 - t^2)$$

Now by the difference of squares model, $9 - t^2 = (3 + t)(3 - t)$, so

$$144 - 16t^2 = 16(3 + t)(3 - t).$$

PROGRESS CHECK 6   Factor completely $64 - 16t^2$.   ■

EXAMPLE 7   Factoring a Trigonometric Expression Systematically
Factor completely $6 \sin^2 \theta - 19 \sin \theta + 10$

Solution   There are no common factors to factor out and this expression matches the general trinomial model. Use FOIL reversal or the *ac* method to obtain

$$6 \sin^2 \theta - 19 \sin \theta + 10 = (3 \sin \theta - 2)(2 \sin \theta - 5).$$

PROGRESS CHECK 7   Factor completely $6 \cos^2 \theta - 48 \cos \theta + 72$.   ■

EXAMPLE 8   Factoring a Polynomial Systematically
Factor completely $x^6 - a^6$.

Solution   The polynomial contains two terms with no common factors, and we find that $x^6 - a^6$ is both a difference of squares and a difference of cubes. In such cases, apply the difference of squares model first.

$$x^6 - a^6 = (x^3)^2 - (a^3)^2$$
$$= (x^3 + a^3)(x^3 - a^3)$$

Now factor $x^3 + a^3$ by the sum of cubes model, and $x^3 - a^3$ by the difference of cubes model. The final factorization is

$$x^6 - a^6 = (x + a)(x^2 - ax + a^2)(x - a)(x^2 + ax + a^2).$$

PROGRESS CHECK 8   Factor completely $y^6 - 1$.   ■

EXAMPLE 9   Factoring a Polynomial Systematically
Factor completely $x^2 + y^2 - z^2 - 2xy$.

Solution   The polynomial contains four terms with no common factors, so try factoring by grouping. We need to recognize that if we group together $x^2 - 2xy + y^2$, it factors into the perfect square $(x - y)^2$. We then have $(x - y)^2 - z^2$, which factors as the difference of two squares. Thus,

$$x^2 + y^2 - z^2 - 2xy = (x^2 - 2xy + y^2) - z^2$$
$$= (x - y)^2 - z^2$$
$$= (x - y + z)(x - y - z).$$

PROGRESS CHECK 9   Factor completely $c^2 - d^2 + 4c + 4$.   ■

EXERCISES 5.2

In Exercises 1–10 factor each difference of squares.

1. $n^2 - 9$
2. $x^2 - 64$
3. $36x^2 - 1$
4. $100 - 81y^2$
5. $25p^2 - 49q^2$
6. $s^2t^2 - 9c^2$
7. $(x + y)^2 - 4$
8. $(x - y)^2 - 121$
9. $36r^6 - k^4$
10. $25x^{12} - 36a^{10}$

In Exercises 11–20 factor each sum or difference of cubes.

11. $y^3 + 27$
12. $x^3 + 64$
13. $x^3 - 1$
14. $t^3 - 125$
15. $a^3b^3 + c^3$
16. $8x^3 - 27y^3$
17. $x^6 + 64$
18. $216 - y^9$
19. $(x + 3)^3 - 8$
20. $(x - 2)^3 + 1$

In Exercises 21–50 factor each expression completely.

21. $x - xy^2$
22. $n^3 - n$
23. $16 - 16t^2$
24. $4 - 16t^2$
25. $1 - t^4$
26. $x^4 - 81$
27. $27(x - 1)^2 - 48x^2$
28. $5(k + 7)^2 - 45k^2$
29. $t^4 + t$
30. $n^4 - 27n$
31. $2y^5 - 16y^2$
32. $ax^5 + 8ax^2$
33. $\pi R^2 - \pi r^2$
34. $\frac{4}{3}\pi R^3 - \frac{4}{3}\pi r^3$
35. $9n^2 + 3n + 3$
36. $12a^2 + 10a - 12$
37. $6x^3 - 24x^2 + 18x$
38. $2x^3y - 18x^2y + 40xy$
39. $x^5 + x^3 + x^2 + 1$
40. $y^4 - y^3 - 8y + 8$
41. $4x^4 - 144x^2$
42. $2x^5 - 162x$
43. $x^6 - 1$
44. $y^6 - x^6$
45. $x^8 - y^8$
46. $1 - x^{12}$
47. $x^2 + 4x + 4 - y^2$
48. $a^2 + x^2 - 2ax - 1$
49. $x^2 - y^2 - z^2 - 2yz$
50. $4x^2 + y^2 + 4xy - 1$

In Exercises 51–62 factor each expression completely.

51. $\sin^2 \theta - 1$
52. $9 - \tan^2 \theta$
53. $4 \tan^2 \theta - 25 \sin^2 \theta$
54. $49 \sin^2 \theta - 16 \cos^2 \theta$
55. $7 \sin^2 \theta - 63$
56. $3 \tan^2 \theta - 75 \sin^2 \theta$
57. $\cos^3 \theta - \cos \theta$
58. $\sin^2 \theta - \sin^4 \theta$
59. $\tan^4 \theta - 1$
60. $\cos^4 \theta - \sin^4 \theta$
61. $\sin^3 \theta - 1$
62. $\tan^3 \theta + 1$
63. A hole is cut from a rectangular solid as shown in the figure. The volume of the remaining solid is given by $4a^3 - 4ab^2$. Factor this expression for the volume.

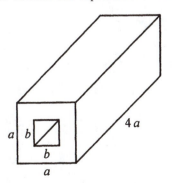

64. A rectangular solid with height h has a square cross-section of sides s. If a corner piece with two sides equal to x is removed, the volume of the solid that remains is $s^2h - x^2h$. Factor this to find another expression for the volume.

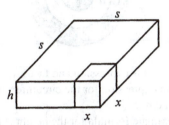

65. The sketch shown consists of three areas whose sum is $c^2 + 2cd + d^2$.
  a. Factor this polynomial to find another expression for this area.
  b. Show that the three pieces can be cut up and re-arranged to make a square whose dimensions correspond to the two factors from part **a.**

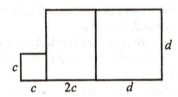

66. The sketch shown consists of three areas whose sum is $r^2 + 2r(2r + 1) + (2r + 1)^2$.

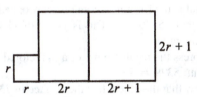

  a. Simplify and factor this polynomial to find another expression for this area.
  b. Show that the three pieces can be cut up and re-arranged to make a square whose dimensions correspond to the two factors from part **a.**

67. The area of a washer can be expressed as $\pi R^2 - \pi r^2$, where R is the radius of the larger circle and r is the radius of the smaller circle. (See the figure below.) A ring-shaped region of this type is called an **annulus**. Factor this polynomial to find another expression for the area.

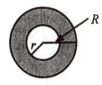

68. The total shaded area shown in the figure is given by
$$\underbrace{\pi(a + 2)^2 - \pi(a + 1)^2}_{\text{outside ring}} + \underbrace{\pi \cdot 1^2}_{\substack{\text{inside} \\ \text{circle}}}.$$

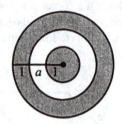

a. Simplify this expression and factor it.
b. Find an expression for the circumference of the largest circle.

69. An approximate formula for the height (y) above the sun's surface of an object dropped from a height of d feet is $y = d - 441t^2$, where t is the elapsed time in seconds, and y is given in feet.
a. What is the formula for an object dropped from a height of 5329 feet? This is a drop of a little more than a mile.
b. Express the result from part **a** in factored form. (Hint: $5329 = 73^2$, and $441 = 21^2$.)
c. Show that the object hits the surface in $\frac{73}{21}$ seconds. This is about 3.5 seconds.
d. What is the average speed (in feet per second, and in miles per hour) of the object while it falls this distance?

70. An approximate formula for the height (y) above Pluto's surface of an object dropped from a height of d feet is $y = d - t^2$, where t is the elapsed time in seconds, and y is given in feet.
a. What is the formula for an object dropped from a height of 5329 feet? This is a drop of a little more than a mile.
b. Express the result from part **a** in factored form. (Hint: $5329 = 73^2$.)
c. Show that the object hits the surface in 73 seconds.
d. What is the average speed (in feet per second, and in miles per hour) of the object while it falls this distance?

THINK ABOUT IT 5.2

1. Factor each expression completely. Assume that variables as exponents denote integers.
a. $x^{2n} - 16$ **b.** $y^{4n} - y^{2n}$
c. $y^{4n} - 49$ **d.** $x^{m+2} - x^m$
e. $1 - t^{3m}$ **f.** $x^{3n} + y^{3n}$

2. Consider the illustration below.
a. Explain why the shaded area is given by $a^2 - b^2$. Then, factor this polynomial to find an expression for this area in factored form.
b. Show that the shaded area can be cut up and re-arranged into a rectangle whose length and width are the two factors found in part **a.**

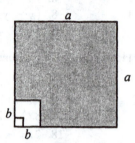

3. If the shaded region in Question 2 is divided into three regions as illustrated, find an expression for the shaded area by adding the areas of the three regions. Then, factor this sum to obtain the same result as in Question **2a.**

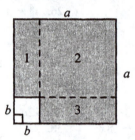

4. a. Multiply $(x - 1)(x + 1)$.
b. Multiply $(x - 1)(x^2 + x + 1)$.
c. Multiply $(x - 1)(x^3 + x^2 + x + 1)$.
d. Look at your results from parts **a–c.** Without multiplying, simplify the product $(x - 1)(x^7 + x^6 + x^5 + x^4 + x^3 + x^2 + x + 1)$.
e. What is a factoring model for $x^n - 1$?

5. Factor $x^6 - 64$ completely by the following methods.
Method 1 First, factor as a difference of squares, and then use the formulas for the sum and the difference of cubes.
Method 2 First, factor as a difference of cubes. Then, use the difference of squares formula on *both* factors and match the result from the first method. Applying the difference of squares formula to the trinomial factor requires some ingenuity.

5.3   Solving Equations by Factoring

The height (y) of a projectile that is shot directly up from the ground with an initial velocity of 80 ft/second is given by the formula

$$y = 80t - 16t^2,$$

where t is the elapsed time in seconds. For what value(s) of t is the projectile 96 ft off the ground? (See Example 6.)

Courtesy of Aneal Vohra/Unicorn Stock Photos.

OBJECTIVES

1   Solve certain quadratic equations using factoring.

2   Solve higher-degree equations using factoring.

3   Solve trigonometric equations using factoring.

4   Solve applied problems that lead to quadratic equations.

When we attempt to solve equations which contain polynomials that are higher than the first degree, we shall find factoring to be an extremely useful tool. We start by looking at polynomial equations of degree 2, which are also called quadratic equations.

Definition of Quadratic Equation

A **second-degree** or **quadratic equation** is an equation that can be written in the form

$$ax^2 + bx + c = 0,$$

where a, b, and c are real numbers, with $a \neq 0$.

Some examples of quadratic equations are

$$6x^2 - 5x + 1 = 0, \qquad y^2 = 4y, \qquad \text{and} \qquad (t - 2)^2 = 1.$$

A technique that can often be used to solve a quadratic equation relies on factoring. For example, the equation $x^2 + 5x + 4 = 0$ may be solved by first factoring on the left-hand side of this equation to obtain

$$(x + 4)(x + 1) = 0.$$

We now have the situation where the product of two factors is zero. In multiplication zero is a special number, as outlined in the following principle.

Zero Product Principle

For any numbers a and b,

$$ab = 0 \text{ if and only if } a = 0 \text{ or } b = 0.$$

By applying this principle, we know

$$(x + 4)(x + 1) = 0 \text{ if and only if } x + 4 = 0 \text{ or } x + 1 = 0.$$

Since $x + 4 = 0$ when $x = -4$ and $x + 1 = 0$ when $x = -1$, the solutions are -4 and -1, and the solution set is $\{-4, -1\}$. To catch any mistakes, it is recommended that solutions be checked in the original equation, so

$$x^2 + 5x + 4 = 0 \qquad\qquad x^2 + 5x + 4 = 0$$
$$(-4)^2 + 5(-4) + 4 \overset{?}{\underset{\checkmark}{=}} 0 \qquad (-1)^2 + 5(-1) + 40 \overset{?}{\underset{\checkmark}{=}} 0$$
$$0 = 0 \qquad\qquad\qquad 0 = 0$$

To summarize, quadratic equations that are factorable (with integer coefficients) are usually solved as follows.

Factoring Method for Solving Quadratic Equations

1. If necessary, change the form of the equation so one side is 0.
2. Factor the nonzero side of the equation.
3. Set each factor equal to zero and obtain the solution(s) by solving the resulting equations.
4. Check each solution by substituting it in the original equation.

EXAMPLE 1   Solving a Quadratic Equation by Factoring

Solve $4x^2 = 12x$ using the factoring method.

Solution   Rewrite the given equation so that one side is zero. Then, factor and apply the zero product principle.

$$4x^2 = 12x$$
$$4x^2 - 12x = 0 \qquad\qquad \text{Rewrite the equation so one side is 0.}$$
$$4x(x - 3) = 0 \qquad\qquad \text{Factor the nonzero side.}$$
$$4x = 0 \quad \text{or} \quad x - 3 = 0 \qquad \text{Set each factor equal to 0.}$$
$$x = \frac{0}{4} \qquad x = 3 \qquad\qquad \text{Solve each linear equation.}$$
$$x = 0$$

Check each possible solution by substituting it in the original equation

$$4x^2 = 12x \qquad\qquad 4x^2 = 12x$$
$$4(0)^2 \overset{?}{=} 12(0) \qquad 4(3)^2 \overset{?}{=} 12(3)$$
$$0 \overset{\checkmark}{=} 0 \qquad\qquad 36 \overset{\checkmark}{=} 36$$

Thus, the solution set is $\{0, 3\}$.

Technology Link

Figure 5.4 shows how a grapher may be used to display a picture of the solution in this example. To obtain this display the equations $y1 = 4x^2$ and $y2 = 12x$ were graphed in the viewing window shown, and the Intersection operation on a grapher was used to estimate the points of intersection. (If your calculator does not have this feature, then the Zoom and Trace features may be used to estimate these points.) Observe that the displayed x-coordinates of the intersection points are in agreement with the solution set $\{0, 3\}$.

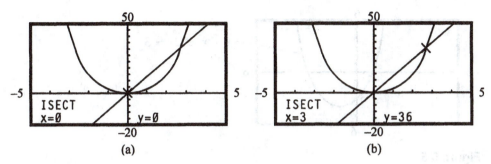

Figure 5.4

PROGRESS CHECK 1   Solve $3x^2 = -21x$ using the factoring method.   ■

The Technology Link in Example 1 showed how to picture the real number solutions of a quadratic equation in terms of simultaneous equations. To understand an alternative method that is often used when solving a wide variety of equations, recall that a point where a graph crosses the x-axis is called an **x-intercept**. Because an x-intercept lies on the x-axis, *its second component must be zero*. Similarly, a point where a graph crosses the y-axis is called a **y-intercept**, and *its first component must be zero*. This leads to a direct way to find intercepts.

To Find Intercepts

  1. To find x-intercepts, which have the form $(a, 0)$, let $y = 0$ and solve for x.
  2. To find y-intercepts, which have the form $(0, b)$, let $x = 0$ and solve for y.

EXAMPLE 2   Find x- and y-intercepts
Find the intercepts of the graph of $y = f(x) = x^2 - 2x - 3$.

Solution   To find y-intercepts, we let $x = 0$ and solve for y.

$$y = (0)^2 - 2(0) - 3$$
$$= -3$$

The y-intercept is the point $(0, -3)$.
     To find x-intercepts, let $y = 0$ and solve for x.

$$0 = x^2 - 2x - 3$$
$$0 = (x - 3)(x + 1)$$
$$x - 3 = 0 \quad \text{or} \quad x + 1 = 0$$
$$x = 3 \qquad\qquad x = -1$$

The x-intercepts are at $(3, 0)$ and $(-1, 0)$.
     To check these answers, use a grapher to graph f as shown in Figure 5.5. It appears that the graph crosses the y-axis when y is -3, and the graph crosses the x-axis when x is 3 and x is -1. So, our results check graphically.

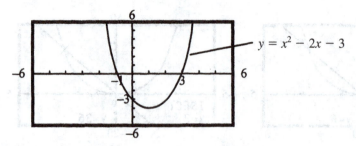

Figure 5.5

PROGRESS CHECK 2 Find the intercepts of the graph of $y = f(x) = x^2 + 2x - 8$. ■

In Example 2 observe that 3 and -1 are both the real-number roots of the equation $0 = x^2 - 2x - 3$ and the x-coordinates of the x-intercepts of the graph of $y = x^2 - 2x - 3$. This match illustrates an important connection between roots and x-intercepts.

Connection Between Roots and *x*-intercepts

The real-number roots of the equation $f(x) = 0$ are identical to the x-coordinates of the x-intercepts of the graph of $y = f(x)$.

Thus, for the remainder of the text, we can choose to display on a graphing calculator the real-number solutions of an equation by expressing the equation in the form $f(x) = 0$, graphing $y = f(x)$, and then estimating the x-coordinates of the x-intercepts. Note that this method will fail to reveal solutions that are not real numbers, because imaginary numbers are not represented on a number line.

Because a second-degree polynomial factors into *two* linear factors, quadratic equations usually have two solutions. But Example 3 shows that it is possible for a quadratic equation to have only one solution.

EXAMPLE 3   Solving a Quadratic Equation with One Root
Solve $y^2 + 9 = 6y$.

Solution   Follow the steps given.

$y^2 + 9 = 6y$	Original equation.
$y^2 - 6y + 9 = 0$	Rewrite the equation so one side is 0.
$(y - 3)(y - 3) = 0$	Factor the nonzero side.
$y - 3 = 0$ or $y - 3 = 0$	Set each factor equal to 0.
$y = 3$ $y = 3$	Solve each linear equation.

The solution, 3, checks, because $3^2 + 9 = 6(3)$ is a true statement, and the solution set is $\{3\}$.

Because of the relation between roots and x-intercepts, we anticipate a quadratic equation with only one real number solution will be associated with a parabola with exactly one x-intercept. In this case, we first express the equation in the form $f(x) = 0$ and graph $f(x) = x^2 - 6x + 9$ as shown in Figure 5.6. Observe that the parabola appears to have exactly one x-intercept at $(3, 0)$, so having only one root at 3 makes sense graphically.

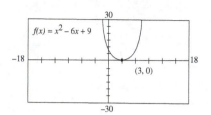

PROGRESS CHECK 3   Solve $y^2 + 4 = -4y$.   ■

The factoring method associated with the zero product principle may be applied to solve higher-degree equations provided we can factor the polynomial on the nonzero side of the equation.

Figure 5.6

EXAMPLE 4   Solving Higher-Degree Polynomial Equations

Solve each equation.

a. $(3x - 1)(x + 5)(x - 8) = 0$ **b.** $x^5 = 10x^3 - 9x$.

Solution

a. Because one side is already zero and the nonzero side is in factored form, we just set each factor equal to zero and solve each resulting equation.

$$(3x - 1)(x + 5)(x - 8) = 0 \qquad \text{Original equation.}$$
$$3x - 1 = 0 \quad \text{or} \quad x + 5 = 0 \quad \text{or} \quad x - 8 = 0 \qquad \text{Set each factor equal to 0.}$$
$$x = \tfrac{1}{3} \qquad\qquad x = -5 \qquad\qquad x = 8 \qquad \text{Solve each equation.}$$

You can verify that all three solutions check, and so the solution set is $\left\{\tfrac{1}{3}, -5, 8\right\}$.

b. First, rewrite the equation so that one side is zero.

$$x^5 = 10x^3 - 9x$$
$$x^5 - 10x^3 + 9x = 0$$

Now factor completely.

$$x(x^4 - 10x^2 + 9) = 0$$
$$x(x^2 - 9)(x^2 - 1) = 0$$
$$x(x + 3)(x - 3)(x + 1)(x - 1) = 0$$

Setting each factor equal to zero gives

$$x = 0 \quad \text{or} \quad x + 3 = 0 \quad \text{or} \quad x - 3 = 0 \quad \text{or} \quad x + 1 = 0 \quad \text{or} \quad x - 1 = 0$$
$$x = -3 \qquad\qquad x = 3 \qquad\qquad x = -1 \qquad\qquad x = 1.$$

Thus, the solution set is $\{0, -3, 3, -1, 1\}$.

Graphical support for this answer may be found by examining the x-intercepts in the graph of $y = x^5 - 10x^3 + 9x$ that is shown in Figure 5.7.

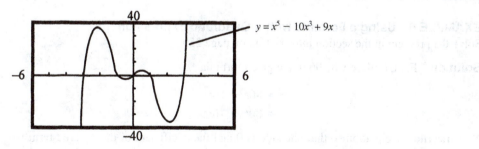

Figure 5.7

PROGRESS CHECK 4   Solve each equation.

a. $(3x + 2)(2x - 3)(x - 1) = 0$ **b.** $x^3 = 4x$ ■

Trigonometric equations were introduced in Section 4.4. The methods of that section combine with our current methods to expand the types of trigonometric equations that can be solved algebraically.

EXAMPLE 5   Solving a Trigonometric Equation by Factoring

For what values of θ $(0° \le \theta < 360°)$ will the equation $2 \sin^2 \theta - 5 \sin \theta = 3$ be a true statement?

Solution

$$2 \sin^2 \theta - 5 \sin \theta = 3$$
$$2 \sin^2 \theta - 5 \sin \theta - 3 = 0$$
$$(2 \sin \theta + 1)(\sin \theta - 3) = 0$$
$$2 \sin \theta + 1 = 0 \qquad \sin \theta - 3 = 0$$
$$\sin \theta = -\tfrac{1}{2} \qquad \sin \theta = 3$$

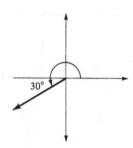

Figure 5.8

1. Since $\sin \theta$ is a negative number, θ could be in Q_3 or Q_4.
2. Since $\sin 30° = \tfrac{1}{2}$, the reference angle is 30°.
3. 210° is the angle in Q_3 with a reference angle of 30° (Figure 5.8). 330° is the angle in Q_4 with a reference angle of 30° (Figure 5.9).

Since the value of $\sin \theta$ never exceeds 1, there is no solution to this equation.

Thus, 210° and 330° are the solutions of the equation $(0° \le \theta < 360°)$.

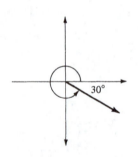

Figure 5.9

PROGRESS CHECK 5   For what values of θ $(0° \le \theta < 360°)$ will the equation $2 \cos^2 \theta - \cos \theta = 0$ be a true statement?   ■

Quadratic equations appear in many word problems. As a sample of this variety, we will discuss four situations which commonly involve quadratic equations:

1. Formulas which contain quadratic expressions
2. Number relations
3. Geometric figures
4. The Pythagorean theorem

The next example is a word problem in which a formula is given. Using this formula to solve the problem leads directly to a quadratic equation. Many applications from the physical sciences include such formulas.

EXAMPLE 6   Using a Formula with a Quadratic Expression

Solve the problem in the section introduction on page 259.

Solution   First, replace y by 96 in the given formula.

$$y = 80t - 16t^2$$
$$96 = 80t - 16t^2$$

Now, rewrite the equation so that one side is 0 and the coefficient of the squared term is positive. Then, factor the nonzero side.

$$16t^2 - 80t + 96 = 0$$
$$16(t^2 - 5t + 6) = 0$$
$$16(t - 3)(t - 2) = 0$$

Because the constant factor, 16, cannot be 0, we need only set equal to 0 the two factors that contain a variable.

$$t - 3 = 0 \quad \text{or} \quad t - 2 = 0$$
$$t = 3 \qquad\qquad t = 2$$

Both solutions check. The projectile attains a height of 96 ft after 2 seconds (on the way up) and again when 3 seconds have elapsed (on its way down).

Caution In this example both solutions of the quadratic equation lead to sensible answers in the application, but this is not always the case. In fact, it is common for one of the solutions to not make sense. Thus, it is especially important in applications to check that all solutions lead to reasonable answers to the original question.

PROGRESS CHECK 6 In Example 6, for what value(s) of t is the projectile 64 ft off the ground? ■

Problems about number relations often lead to quadratic equations, as shown in the next example. Such problems therefore often have two distinct solutions.

EXAMPLE 7 Solving a Number Relations Problem

The sum of the squares of two consecutive integers is 181. What are the integers?

Solution Using x to represent the smaller integer and $x + 1$ to represent the next consecutive integer, we can *set up an equation*.

The sum of the squares of two consecutive integers is 181.

$$x^2 + (x + 1)^2 = 181$$

Solve the Equation

$x^2 + x^2 + 2x + 1 = 181$	Expand $(x + 1)^2$.
$2x^2 + 2x + 1 = 181$	Combine like terms.
$2x^2 + 2x - 180 = 0$	Subtract 181 from both sides.
$2(x^2 + x - 90) = 0$	Factor out GCF.
$2(x - 9)(x + 10) = 0$	Factor the trinomial.
$x - 9 = 0 \quad \text{or} \quad x + 10 = 0$	Set each variable factor equal to 0.
$x = 9 \qquad\qquad x = -10$	Solve each linear equation.

Answer the Question There are two pairs of integers that answer the question. If x is 9, then $x + 1$ is 10; and if x is -10, then $x + 1$ is -9. One solution is 9 and 10, and the second solution is -10 and -9.

Check the Answer Both proposed solutions check, because both $9^2 + 10^2 = 181$ and $(-10)^2 + (-9)^2 = 181$ are true, and each answer is a pair of consecutive integers.

PROGRESS CHECK 7 The product of two consecutive integers is 132. Find the integers. ■

Word problems that involve areas of geometric figures often lead to quadratic equations. To solve them quickly, you should be familiar with the basic formulas for the area and perimeter of circles, triangles, and rectangles. As pointed out in the caution in Example 6, it is important to check that all solutions lead to sensible answers.

EXAMPLE 8   Solving an Area Problem

The area of a square is 5 more than the perimeter. Find the side length for the square measured in meters.

Solution   We represent the length of the side by s, as shown in Figure 5.10. It follows then that the area is s^2 and the perimeter is $4s$. Now *set up an equation.*

The area is 5 more than the perimeter.

$$s^2 = 4s + 5$$

Figure 5.10

Solve the Equation

$$s^2 - 4s - 5 = 0 \qquad \text{Rewrite so one side is 0.}$$
$$(s - 5)(s + 1) = 0 \qquad \text{Factor the nonzero side.}$$
$$s - 5 = 0 \quad \text{or} \quad s + 1 = 0 \qquad \text{Set each factor equal to 0.}$$
$$s = 5 \qquad\qquad s = -1 \qquad \text{Solve each linear equation.}$$

Answer the Question   The solution $s = -1$ does not make sense in this problem because a square cannot have a negative side length, so the only sensible solution is that the side length is 5 m.

Check the Answer   If $s = 5$, then the area is 25 and the perimeter is 20. Because 25 is 5 more than 20, the solution checks.

PROGRESS CHECK 8   The area of a square is 12 more than the perimeter. Find the side length of the square if the length is measured in feet.   ▪

Because the Pythagorean theorem states a relation among the *squares* of the side lengths in a right triangle, we often generate a quadratic equation when we apply this theorem.

EXAMPLE 9   Using the Pythagorean Theorem

The length of a rectangle is 3 more than the width, and a diagonal measures 15 m. Find the dimensions of the rectangle.

Solution   To find the dimensions, let

$$x = \text{width},$$
$$\text{so} \qquad x + 3 = \text{length}.$$

Now sketch the situation as in Figure 5.11 and note that the diagonal is the hypotenuse of a right triangle. We may then use the Pythagorean theorem to *set up an equation.*

$$c^2 = a^2 + b^2$$
$$15^2 = (x + 3)^2 + x^2 \qquad \text{Replace } c \text{ by 15, } a \text{ by } x + 3, \text{ and } b \text{ by } x.$$

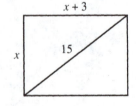

Figure 5.11

Solve the Equation

$$225 = x^2 + 6x + 9 + x^2 \qquad \text{Expand and evaluate powers.}$$
$$0 = 2x^2 + 6x - 216 \qquad \text{Rewrite so one side is 0.}$$
$$0 = 2(x^2 + 3x - 108) \qquad \text{Factor out 2.}$$
$$0 = 2(x - 9)(x + 12) \qquad \text{Factor } x^2 + 3x - 108.$$
$$x - 9 = 0 \quad \text{or} \quad x + 12 = 0 \qquad \text{Set each variable factor equal to 0.}$$
$$x = 9 \qquad\qquad x = -12 \qquad \text{Solve each linear equation.}$$

Answer the Question   Reject the negative solution. The width is 9 m and the length is $9 + 3 = 12$ m.

Check the Answer   Because 12 is 3 more than 9 and $15^2 = 9^2 + 12^2$ is a true statement, a rectangle that measures 9 m by 12 m satisfies the given conditions.

PROGRESS CHECK 9   The length of a rectangle is 2 more than the width, and a diagonal measures 10 ft. Find the dimensions of the rectangle.   ■

EXERCISES 5.3

In Exercises 1–40, solve each equation.

1. $5x^2 = 30x$ **2.** $7x^2 = 21x$

3. $4y^2 = -12y$ **4.** $3y^2 = -21y$

5. $5x^2 = 18x$ **6.** $2y^2 = -7y$

7. $x^2 - 49 = 0$ **8.** $x^2 = 1$

9. $3z^2 - 3 = 0$ **10.** $5z^2 - 45 = 0$

11. $y^2 + 10 = 7y$ **12.** $x^2 + 12 = 7x$

13. $x^2 + 7x = -6$ **14.** $y^2 + 2y = -1$

15. $z^2 = 2 - z$ **16.** $z^2 = 6 - z$

17. $2x^2 - 3x - 2 = 0$ **18.** $6x^2 - 13x + 6 = 0$

19. $12y^2 - 7y + 1 = 0$ **20.** $20y^2 + 9y + 1 = 0$

21. $2x^2 - 2x + 4 = x^2 + 2x$

22. $3x^2 - 4x + 4 = 2x^2 + 2x - 5$

23. $(4x)(3x - 1) = 0$ **24.** $2y(2y - 5) = 0$

25. $(y - 1)(y + 2) = 0$ **26.** $(x + 2)(x - 3) = 0$

27. $(x - 3)(x + 5) = 9$ **28.** $(y + 3)(y + 1) = 15$

29. $(3z + 1)(2z - 5) = -5$

30. $(2x - 1)(3x - 1) = 1$

31. $(x - 8)(x + 8) + 15 = 0$

32. $(x - 5)(x + 5) + 9 = 0$

33. $(x - 412)(x + 6.02)(x + \pi) = 0$

34. $(y - 87)(y + 64)(y - 1.6) = 0$

35. $(2y - 3)(3y - 4)(4y - 5) = 0$

36. $(3y - 2)(4y - 3)(5y - 4) = 0$

37. $x^3 = x$ **38.** $z^3 = 25z$

39. $x^3 - 3x^2 + 2x = 0$

40. $x^3 + 3x^2 + 2x = 0$

In Exercises 41–50 find the intercepts of the graph of the function.

41. $y = x^2 - 4x - 5$ **42.** $y = 6x^2 - x - 2$

43. $g(x) = x^2 - 4x + 4$

44. $g(x) = 25x^2 - 10x + 1$

45. $f(x) = 6x^2 + 5x - 6$ **46.** $y = 2x^2 + 3x - 2$

47. $y = x^3 - 4x$ **48.** $f(x) = x^3 + 3x^2$

49. $f(x) = (x + 4)(x - 1)(x - 5)$

50. $y = x^4 - 5x^2 + 4$

In Exercises 51–56 find the values of θ ($0° \le \theta < 360°$), to the nearest 10 minutes, which make the equation a true statement.

51. $\tan^2 \theta + 4 \tan \theta - 21 = 0$

52. $\sin^2 \theta = 4 \sin \theta + 5$

53. $6 \sin^2 \theta + \sin \theta - 2 = 0$

54. $2 \cos^2 \theta = 3 \cos \theta - 1$

55. $\cos^3 \theta = \cos \theta$ **56.** $\tan^3 \theta = \tan \theta$

In Exercises 57–60 find to the nearest 10 minutes all the values of θ that make the equation a true statement.

57. $\tan^2 \theta + 3 \tan \theta - 10 = 0$

58. $\cos^2 \theta = -4 \cos \theta - 3$

59. $\cos^2 \theta = \cos \theta$ **60.** $\sin^2 \theta = -\sin \theta$

61. The height (y) in feet of a baseball that is thrown straight up from the ground with an initial velocity of 33 mi/hour is given approximately by $y = 48t - 16t^2$, where t is elapsed time in seconds. (*Note*: 33 mi/hour is about 48 ft/second.) For what value(s) of t is the ball 36 ft off the ground?

62. For what value(s) of t is the ball described in Exercise 61, 32 ft off the ground?

63. The height (y) of a hammer dropped from the roof of the tallest building in Atlanta, the C & S Plaza, is given by the formula $y = 1,024 - 16t^2$. How long will it take the hammer to hit the ground?

64. The height (y) of a diver who steps off a cliff 64 ft above the water is given by $y = 64 - 16t^2$. To find how long it takes the diver to hit the water, set the height equal to zero and solve the resulting equation.

65. The sum of the squares of two consecutive integers is 113. Find the integers.

66. The product of two consecutive integers is zero. Find the integers.

67. The sum of two numbers is 3 and their product is -40. Find the numbers. (*Hint*: Let x represent one number and $-40/x$ represent the other.)

68. The sum of two numbers is one and their product is -30. Find the numbers. (*Hint*: Let x represent one number and $-30/x$ represent the other.)

69. The volume and the surface area of a cube are equal. Find the dimensions of the cube, and find the volume and area.

70. The volume of a cube is half the surface area. Find the dimensions of the cube, and find the volume and area.

71. The area of a square is 21 more than the perimeter. Find the area. The unit of length is feet.

72. The area of a square is equal to its perimeter. Find the area. The unit of length is centimeters.

73. The area of a rectangle is 24 in.^{2}. The perimeter is 28 in. Find its dimensions. (*Hint*: Let x represent the length and $24/x$ the width.)

74. The area of a rectangle is 60 m^2. The perimeter is 32 m. Find its dimensions. (*Hint*: Let x represent the length and $60/x$ the width.)

75. The length of a rectangle is 4 more than the width and the diagonal measures 20 yards (yd). Find the area of the rectangle.

76. The width of a rectangle is 9 ft. The diagonal is 9 less than twice the length. Find the area.

THINK ABOUT IT 5.3

1. Second-degree equations are called quadratic because *to quadrate* means "to make square," and any quadratic equation can be rewritten into the form $(x + a)^2 = b$, which is the square of a binomial equal to a constant.

a. Show that the equation $x^2 + 6x - 7 = 0$ is equivalent to $(x + 3)^2 = 16$ by solving the first equation and then showing that both of its solutions are also solutions of the second equation.

b. Show by expanding the left side of the second equation in part **a** and then simplifying that you get the first equation.

2. Why are both words *zero* and *product* crucial in the zero product principle?

3. Why is it not correct to solve $(x - 2)(x + 5) = 10$ by setting each factor equal to 10? Show that the results you get this way are wrong.

4. Use the zero product principle to make up a quadratic equation with solution set $\{7\}$.

5. Why can't a quadratic equation have three distinct solutions?

Courtesy of PhotoDisc/Getty Images.

5.4 Multiplication and Division of Fractions

A medical study is set up to compare the risk of illness for people who are exposed to a pollutant to the risk of illness for people who are not exposed. The quotient of these two risks is an important statistic called the **relative risk**. Suppose there are n people in each group. If s people get sick in the nonexposed group, and $s + x$ people get sick in the exposed group, then the relative risk is given by

$$\frac{s + x}{n} \div \frac{s}{n}.$$

Express this division in lowest terms. (See Example 7.)

OBJECTIVES

1 Express a fraction in simplest form.

2 Multiply fractions and simplify the product.

3 Divide fractions and simplify the quotient.

Algebraic fractions are the quotients of algebraic expressions, and the same principles that govern a fraction in arithmetic also apply when the numerator and the denominator contain algebraic expressions. Two fraction principles of particular importance follow.

> **Fraction Principles**
>
> Let a, b, c, d, and k be real numbers with b, d, and $k \neq 0$.
>
> **Equality of fractions** $\dfrac{a}{b} = \dfrac{c}{d}$ if and only if $ad = bc$
>
> **Fundamental principle** $\dfrac{ak}{bk} = \dfrac{a}{b}$

The fundamental principle can be established from the criterion for the equality of two fractions, since $(ak)b$ is equal to $(bk)a$. As its name suggests, the fundamental principle is applied often, and two common uses of this principle are shown below.

$$\text{Simplifying fractions } \frac{6}{8} = \frac{3 \cdot 2}{4 \cdot 2} = \frac{3}{4}$$

$$\uparrow \qquad \uparrow$$

fundamental principle

$$\downarrow \qquad \downarrow$$

$$\text{Adding fractions } \frac{1}{8} + \frac{3}{4} = \frac{1}{8} + \frac{3 \cdot 2}{4 \cdot 2} = \frac{1}{8} + \frac{6}{8} = \frac{7}{8}$$

When simplifying fractions by the fundamental principle, it is important to recognize that we may divide out only nonzero factors of the numerator and the denominator. Thus, we have a general procedure for expressing a fraction in simplest form.

To Simplify Fractions

1. Factor completely the numerator and the denominator of the fraction.
2. Divide out nonzero factors that are common to the numerator and the denominator according to the fundamental principle.

Example 1 illustrates this procedure on an algebraic expression and on a corresponding trigonometric expression.

EXAMPLE 1   Contrasting Simplifications of Algebraic and Trigonometric Expressions

Express in lowest terms.

a. $\dfrac{5s + 10}{s^2 - 4}$ **b.** $\dfrac{5 \sin \theta + 10}{\sin^2 \theta - 4}$

Solution   First, factor completely, then, divide out common nonzero factors.

a. $\dfrac{5s + 10}{s^2 - 4} = \dfrac{5(s + 2)}{(s + 2)(s - 2)}$

$$= \frac{5}{s - 2}, s \neq -2$$

b. $\dfrac{5 \sin \theta + 10}{\sin^2 \theta - 4} = \dfrac{5(\sin \theta + 2)}{(\sin \theta + 2)(\sin \theta - 2)}$

$$= \frac{5}{\sin \theta - 2}$$

$\sin \theta$ never equals -2, so no restriction is necessary.

PROGRESS CHECK 1   Express in lowest terms.

a. $\dfrac{c^2 - 8c + 16}{c^2 - 16}$ **b.** $\dfrac{\cos^2 \theta - 8 \cos \theta + 16}{\cos^2 \theta - 16}$ ■

EXAMPLE 2   Reducing Algebraic Fractions

Express in lowest terms.

a. $\dfrac{x^2 - 3x - 4}{x^2 - 2x - 8}$

b. $\dfrac{(x^2 + 2) - (a^2 + 2)}{x - a}$

Solution   Factor and use the fundamental principle.

a. $\dfrac{x^2 - 3x - 4}{x^2 - 2x - 8} = \dfrac{(x + 1)(x - 4)}{(x + 2)(x - 4)} = \dfrac{x + 1}{x + 2}, \ x \neq 4$

b. $\dfrac{(x^2 + 2) - (a^2 + 2)}{x - a} = \dfrac{x^2 - a^2}{x - a} = \dfrac{(x + a)(x - a)}{x - a} = x + a, \ x \neq a$

Technology Link

In the previous section we discussed a graphing calculator method to test for equivalent expressions, based on the fact that equivalent expressions produce the same graph. A disadvantage of this method is that it may be hard to interpret the resulting display if you are unfamiliar with the types of graphs that are associated with certain equations. One way to overcome this difficulty is to graph the quotient of the expressions in question. This quotient will be 1 for equivalent expressions throughout the domain of this quotient function. To illustrate, the simplification in Example 2 a may be checked by letting

$$y1 = \frac{x^2 - 3x - 4}{x^2 - 2x - 8}$$

$$y2 = \frac{x + 1}{x + 2}$$

$$y3 = \frac{y1}{y2}.$$

Then graph only $y3$ as shown in Figure 5.12.

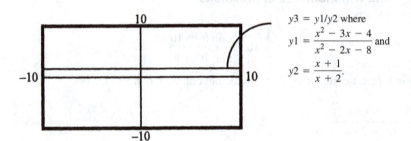

Figure 5.12

This graph, which is a horizontal line where y is fixed at 1, supports our results.

PROGRESS CHECK 2   Express in lowest terms.

a. $\dfrac{4x}{8x^2 - 4x}$

b. $\dfrac{(x^2 - 5) - (c^2 - 5)}{x - c}$

■

In Example 2 the restrictions $x \neq 4$ and $x \neq a$ are necessary because we may divide out only nonzero factors, since division by zero is undefined. With the understanding that such restrictions always apply, we will not continue to list them from this point on.

When working with fractions, it is important to keep in mind what happens in addition and subtraction if we change the order of the terms. In addition $a + b = b + a$. However, in subtraction $a - b = -(b - a)$. Thus,

$$\frac{a + b}{b + a} = 1, \text{ while } \frac{a - b}{b - a} = \frac{-(b - a)}{b - a} = -1.$$

Although $a - b$ does not equal $b - a$, the expressions differ only by a factor of -1 and can be simplified accordingly.

EXAMPLE 3   Simplification Involving Factors That Are Opposites

Express in lowest terms $\dfrac{x^2 - y^2}{y - x}$.

Solution   Since $y - x = -(x - y)$ we proceed as follows:

$$\frac{x^2 - y^2}{y - x} = \frac{(x + y)(x - y)}{(-1)(x - y)}$$
$$= \frac{x + y}{-1} \text{ or } -x - y.$$

PROGRESS CHECK 3   Express in lowest terms $\dfrac{2 - 3x}{9x^2 - 4}$.   ■

Multiplication

In arithmetic we know that the product of two or more fractions is the product of their numerators divided by the product of their denominators. In symbols, this principle is

$$\frac{a}{b} \cdot \frac{c}{d} = \frac{ac}{bd} \quad b, d \neq 0.$$

Similarly, we will use this procedure for multiplying algebraic and trigonometric fractions. To express products in simplest form, factoring and the fundamental principle are usually required.

EXAMPLE 4   Multiplying Contrasting Algebraic and Trigonometric Expressions

Express the following products in lowest terms.

a. $\dfrac{4c - 16}{9c} \cdot \dfrac{12c}{c^2 - 3c - 4}$

b. $\dfrac{4 \cos \theta - 16}{9 \cos \theta} \cdot \dfrac{12 \cos \theta}{\cos^2 \theta - 3 \cos \theta - 4}$

Solution   We factor, multiply, and then simplify as shown.

a. $\dfrac{4c - 16}{9c} \cdot \dfrac{12c}{c^2 - 3c - 4} = \dfrac{4(c - 4)}{9c} \cdot \dfrac{12c}{(c - 4)(c + 1)}$

$$= \frac{4 \cdot 12c \, (c - 4)}{9 \cdot c(c + 1)(c - 4)}$$

$$= \frac{16}{3(c + 1)}$$

b. $\dfrac{4\cos\theta - 16}{9\cos\theta} \cdot \dfrac{12\cos\theta}{\cos^2\theta - 3\cos\theta - 4}$

$= \dfrac{4(\cos\theta - 4)}{9\cos\theta} \cdot \dfrac{12\cos\theta}{(\cos\theta - 4)(\cos\theta + 1)}$

$= \dfrac{4 \cdot 12\cos\theta(\cos\theta - 4)}{9 \cdot \cos\theta(\cos\theta + 1)(\cos\theta - 4)}$

$= \dfrac{16}{3(\cos\theta + 1)}$

PROGRESS CHECK 4   Express in lowest terms the given products.

a. $\dfrac{3c + 6}{c^2 + 4c} \cdot \dfrac{c^2 + 2c}{3c^2 - 12}$ **b.** $\dfrac{3\cos\theta + 6}{\cos^2\theta + 4\cos\theta} \cdot \dfrac{\cos^2\theta + 2\cos\theta}{3\cos^2\theta - 12}$ ■

Example 5 shows how exponent properties and definitions may be used to express a product in lowest terms.

EXAMPLE 5   Using Exponent Properties to Simplify a Product

Multiply $\dfrac{(x + 4)^6}{a^8b^5} \cdot \dfrac{a^2b^5}{(x + 4)^3}$. Express the answer in lowest terms.

Solution   Recall that $a^m/a^n = a^{m-n}$, $a^{-n} = 1/a^n$, and $b^0 = 1$.

$\dfrac{(x + 4)^6}{a^8b^5} \cdot \dfrac{a^2b^5}{(x + 4)^3} = \dfrac{(x + 4)^6a^2b^5}{a^8b^5(x + 4)^3}$ Multiply fractions.

$= a^{2-8}b^{5-5}(x + 4)^{6-3}$ Quotient property of exponents.

$= a^{-6}b^0(x + 4)^3$ Simplify exponents.

$= \dfrac{(x + 4)^3}{a^6}$ Negative and zero exponent definitions.

PROGRESS CHECK 5   Multiply $\dfrac{(x - 5)^2}{a^3y^3} \cdot \dfrac{a^3y^9}{(x - 5)^6}$. Express the answer in lowest terms.   ■

Division

To divide two fractions, we must recall that division is defined in terms of multiplication. That is, to divide a by b, we multiply a by the reciprocal of b. Note that the reciprocal of a fraction can be found by inverting the fraction. For example, the reciprocal of $\frac{2}{7}$ is $\frac{7}{2}$. Thus, to divide two fractions, we invert the fraction by which we are dividing, to find its reciprocal, and then we multiply.

$$\frac{a}{b} \div \frac{c}{d} = \frac{a}{b} \cdot \frac{d}{c} \qquad b, d, \frac{c}{d} \neq 0$$

Example 6   Dividing Algebraic Fractions

Perform each division, and express the quotient in lowest terms.

a. $\dfrac{33}{x^2} \div \dfrac{3}{x}$ **b.** $\dfrac{(y - 2)^2}{5y} \div \dfrac{y^2 - 4}{15y}$ **c.** $\dfrac{3 - x}{y^2 - y} \div \dfrac{x^2 - 9}{y^2 - 2y + 1}$

Solution   In each case convert the division problem to multiplication.

a. $\dfrac{33}{x^2} \div \dfrac{3}{x} = \dfrac{33}{x^2} \cdot \dfrac{x}{3}$ Multiply $\dfrac{33}{x^2}$ by the reciprocal of $\dfrac{3}{x}$.

$= \dfrac{3 \cdot 11 \cdot x}{x \cdot x \cdot 3}$ Multiply and factor.

$= \dfrac{11}{x}$ Lowest terms.

b. $\dfrac{(y-2)^2}{5y} \div \dfrac{y^2 - 4}{15y} = \dfrac{(y-2)^2}{5y} \cdot \dfrac{15y}{y^2 - 4}$ Multiply by the reciprocal of the divisor.

$= \dfrac{(y-2)(y-2)}{5y} \cdot \dfrac{3 \cdot 5 \cdot y}{(y+2)(y-2)}$ Factor completely.

$= \dfrac{(y-2)(y-2) \cdot 3 \cdot 5 \cdot y}{5 \cdot y(y+2)(y-2)}$ Multiply fractions.

$= \dfrac{3(y-2)}{y+2}$ Lowest terms.

c. To obtain lowest terms in this example, recognize that $3 - x$ and $x - 3$ are opposites.

$\dfrac{3-x}{y^2 - y} \div \dfrac{x^2 - 9}{y^2 - 2y + 1} = \dfrac{3-x}{y^2 - y} \cdot \dfrac{y^2 - 2y + 1}{x^2 - 9}$ Multiply by the reciprocal.

$= \dfrac{3-x}{y(y-1)} \cdot \dfrac{(y-1)(y-1)}{(x+3)(x-3)}$ Factor completely.

$= \dfrac{(3-x)(y-1)(y-1)}{y(y-1)(x+3)(x-3)}$ Multiply fractions.

$= \dfrac{-1(x-3)(y-1)(y-1)}{y(y-1)(x+3)(x-3)}$ Replace $3 - x$ by $-1(x - 3)$.

$= \dfrac{-1(y-1)}{y(x+3)}$ or $\dfrac{1-y}{y(x+3)}$ Lowest terms.

PROGRESS CHECK 6   Do each division and express the answer in lowest terms.

a. $\dfrac{16}{x^4} \div \dfrac{12}{x^2}$ **b.** $\dfrac{(t+5)^2}{4t} \div \dfrac{t^2 - 25}{12t^2}$ **c.** $\dfrac{y-1}{x^2 + x} \div \dfrac{y - y^2}{x^2 + 4x + 3}$ ■

EXAMPLE 7   Finding an Expression for Relative Risk

Solve the problem in the section introduction on page 268.

Solution   By division we get a simpler expression for the relative risk.

$$\dfrac{s+x}{n} \div \dfrac{s}{n} = \dfrac{s+x}{n} \cdot \dfrac{n}{s}$$ Division definition.

$$= \dfrac{(s+x) \cdot n}{ns}$$ Multiply fractions.

$$= \dfrac{s+x}{s}$$ Lowest terms.

The relative risk is $\dfrac{s+x}{s}$.

PROGRESS CHECK 7   If r people in the exposed group get sick, and $r - x$ people in the nonexposed group get sick, the relative risk is $\dfrac{r}{n} \div \dfrac{r-x}{n}$. Do the division and get a simpler expression for the relative risk.   ■

EXERCISES 5.4

In Exercises 1–28 express each fraction in lowest terms.

1. $\dfrac{4x - 4}{11x - 11}$

2. $\dfrac{3a + 9}{15 + 5a}$

3. $\dfrac{y^2 + 2y}{y^2 + 3y}$

4. $\dfrac{2x + 4y}{2x - 4y}$

5. $\dfrac{4b}{12b^2 + 4b}$

6. $\dfrac{20z^2 - 5z}{10z}$

7. $\dfrac{y - x}{x - y}$

8. $\dfrac{(x - 4)^2}{4 - x}$

9. $\dfrac{x - a}{ax(a - x)}$

10. $\dfrac{-x + a}{x - a}$

11. $\dfrac{1 - x}{x^2 - 1}$

12. $\dfrac{i - I}{-(I^2 - i^2)}$

13. $\dfrac{a^2 - 3a - 4}{a^2 - 8a + 16}$

14. $\dfrac{(x^2 + 1) - (a^2 + 1)}{x - a}$

15. $\dfrac{49 - 14y + y^2}{49 - y^2}$

16. $\dfrac{2m^2 - 5m + 2}{4m - 2}$

17. $\dfrac{6x^3 - 3x^2 - 30x}{2x^2 - 4x - 16}$

18. $\dfrac{z^3 - z^2 - 6z}{z^3 + z^2 - 12z}$

19. $\dfrac{2(2 + h) - 3(2 + h)}{2h(2 + h)}$

20. $\dfrac{(2 + h)^2 - 4}{(2 + h) - 2}$

21. $\dfrac{x^2 - 1}{x^3 - 1}$

22. $\dfrac{y^3 + 8}{y^2 - 4}$

23. $\dfrac{a^3 + a^2}{a^3 + 1}$

24. $\dfrac{2b^3 - 4b^2}{b^3 - 8}$

25. $\dfrac{x^3 - a^3}{x - a}$

26. $\dfrac{x^4 - a^4}{x - a}$

27. $\dfrac{x + y - z}{y^2 - x^2 + xz - yz}$

28. $\dfrac{a^3 - 8}{a^3 - 2a^2 + 4a - 8}$

In Exercises 29–44 express each product or quotient in lowest terms.

29. $\dfrac{2x}{5y} \cdot \dfrac{5y^2}{8x^3}$

30. $\dfrac{14z}{10y} \cdot \dfrac{15y}{35z}$

31. $\dfrac{5a}{a^2 - 9} \cdot \dfrac{6a - 18}{15a^2}$

32. $\dfrac{n^2 - n - 12}{n^2} \cdot \dfrac{n}{n - 4}$

33. $\dfrac{(y - 1)^2}{(y + 2)^2} \cdot \dfrac{y^2 - 4}{y^2 - 1}$

34. $(x + 4)^2 \cdot \dfrac{x}{16 - x^2}$

35. $\dfrac{x^2 + 3x - 4}{x^2 - 3x - 4} \cdot \dfrac{x^2 - 5x + 4}{x^2 + 5x + 4}$

36. $\dfrac{2a^2 - 7a + 6}{a^2 - a - 6} \cdot \dfrac{5a - 15}{a^2 - 4}$

37. $\dfrac{xy}{z} \div \dfrac{x^2y}{z}$

38. $\dfrac{zy^2}{2x} \div \dfrac{yz^2}{x}$

39. $\dfrac{n^2 + n - 2}{n - 3} \div (n + 2)$

40. $\dfrac{4x^2 - 9}{4x - 9} \div (2x - 3)$

41. $\dfrac{x^4 - 1}{7x + 7} \div \dfrac{x^3 + x}{x^2 - 1}$

42. $\dfrac{3b^2 + 6b - 24}{b^2 - 7b + 10} \div \dfrac{3b^2 + 4b}{b^3 - 5b^2}$

43. $\dfrac{1 - a}{x^2 + x} \div \dfrac{a^2 - 1}{x^2 - 1}$

44. $\dfrac{x^2 - 7x + 10}{5x - 25} \div \dfrac{4 - 2x}{25 - x^2}$

In Exercises 45–52 express each fraction, product, or quotient in lowest terms.

45. $\dfrac{2(x + y)^2}{5(x + y)^5}$

46. $\dfrac{3z(x - y)^2}{4z^2(x - y)}$

47. $\dfrac{(x + 2)^3}{a^3b^3} \cdot \dfrac{ab}{(x + 2)^5}$

48. $\dfrac{(y - 5)^3}{ab^3} \cdot \dfrac{a^2b^4}{(y - 5)^2}$

49. $\dfrac{(y - 3)^2}{x^2} \div \dfrac{(y - 3)^4}{x^5}$

50. $\dfrac{5t}{(t + 5)^3} \div \dfrac{t^5}{(t + 5)^6}$

51. $\dfrac{x^2 + 2x + 1}{x^2 + 4x + 4} \cdot \dfrac{(x + 2)^3}{(x + 1)^3}$

52. $\dfrac{y^2 - 6y + 9}{(x + 4)^5} \cdot \dfrac{x^2 + 8x + 16}{(y - 3)^4}$

In Exercises 53–58 express each fraction in lowest terms.

53. a. $\dfrac{3s + 3c}{4s + 4c}$　**b.** $\dfrac{3 \sin \theta + 3 \cos \theta}{4 \sin \theta + 4 \cos \theta}$

54. a. $\dfrac{t^2 + tc}{t + c}$　**b.** $\dfrac{\tan^2 \theta + \tan \theta \cos \theta}{\tan \theta + \cos \theta}$

55. a. $\dfrac{64 - c^2}{2c + 16}$　**b.** $\dfrac{64 - \cos^2 \theta}{2 \cos \theta + 16}$

56. a. $\dfrac{6(s - c)^2}{9c - 9s}$　**b.** $\dfrac{6(\sin \theta - \cos \theta)^2}{9 \cos \theta - 9 \sin \theta}$

57. a. $\dfrac{5c^2 - 5}{2c^2 - 14c + 12}$

b. $\dfrac{5 \cos^2 \theta - 5}{2 \cos^2 \theta - 14 \cos \theta + 12}$

58. a. $\dfrac{3s^2 - 10s + 3}{s^2 + s - 12}$　**b.** $\dfrac{3 \sin^2 \theta - 10 \sin \theta + 3}{\sin^2 \theta + \sin \theta - 12}$

In Exercises 59–66 express each product or quotient in lowest terms.

59. a. $\dfrac{30s^2c^2}{7t} \cdot \dfrac{21t^3}{5sc}$ **b.** $\dfrac{30 \sin^2 \theta \cos^2 \theta}{7 \tan \theta} \cdot \dfrac{21 \tan^3 \theta}{5 \sin \theta \cos \theta}$

60. a. $\dfrac{24tc}{5s} \cdot \dfrac{10s^2}{c}$ **b.** $\dfrac{24 \tan \theta \cos \theta}{5 \sin \theta} \cdot \dfrac{10 \sin^2 \theta}{\cos \theta}$

61. a. $\dfrac{5}{s^2} \div \dfrac{5}{s}$ **b.** $\dfrac{5}{\sin^2 \theta} \div \dfrac{5}{\sin \theta}$

62. a. $\dfrac{21s}{20c} \div \dfrac{3s}{5c}$ **b.** $\dfrac{21 \sin \theta}{20 \cos \theta} \div \dfrac{3 \sin \theta}{5 \cos \theta}$

63. a. $\dfrac{4s - 6}{5} \div \dfrac{6s - 9}{25}$ **b.** $\dfrac{4 \sin \theta - 6}{5} \div \dfrac{6 \sin \theta - 9}{25}$

64. a. $\dfrac{t - 4}{t} \div \dfrac{t^2 - 16}{t^2}$ **b.** $\dfrac{\tan \theta - 4}{\tan \theta} \div \dfrac{\tan^2 \theta - 16}{\tan^2 \theta}$

65. a. $\dfrac{4}{7 - s} \cdot (s^2 - 5s - 14)$

 b. $\dfrac{4}{7 - \sin \theta} (\sin^2 \theta - 5 \sin \theta - 14)$

66. a. $\dfrac{4 - s^2}{s^2 - 9} \cdot \dfrac{9 + 3s}{8s - 16}$ **b.** $\dfrac{4 - \sin^2 \theta}{\sin^2 \theta - 9} \cdot \dfrac{9 + 3 \sin \theta}{8 \sin \theta - 16}$

In Exercises 67–70 for what value(s) of x or $\tan \theta$ is the fraction undefined?

67. $\dfrac{4x - 4}{11x - 11}$

68. $\dfrac{1 - \tan \theta}{\tan^2 \theta - 1}$

69. $\dfrac{4 \tan \theta}{12 \tan^2 \theta + 4 \tan \theta}$

70. $\dfrac{x^2 - 9}{6 - x - x^2}$

71. For what values of x does $\dfrac{3x + 9}{5x + 15} = \dfrac{3}{5}$?

72. For what values of x does $\dfrac{x^2 - 1}{x - 1} = x + 1$?

73. The percent change in the value of an investment in one year is given by $\dfrac{V_n - V_o}{V_o} \cdot 100$, where V_o is the original value and V_n is the value now.

 a. Find the percent change in an investment that grows from $1,200 to $1,500 in one year.

 b. For what value of V_o is the percent change undefined?

74. The width of a rectangle is 3 less than the length. The ratio of the area to the perimeter is given by $\dfrac{x(x - 3)}{2x + 2(x - 3)}.$

$\boxed{}^{\,x}$ $x - 3$

a. For what value of x is the ratio undefined? Why is this not a sensible value for x in the first place?

b. For what value of x is this ratio equal to 1? (Then the area and perimeter are equal.)

75. In the calculation of probabilities by a tree diagram, the probability that any particular sequence of events will occur is found by multiplying probabilities along the appropriate path in the tree. In the tree diagram shown, the fractions represent the probabilities. Use the given tree diagram to find the probability of (a) success at both stages and (b) failure at both stages.

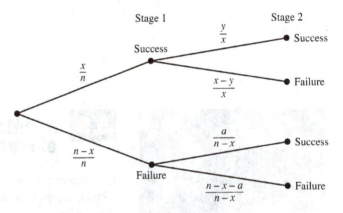

76. Use the tree diagram in Exercise 75 to find the probability of (a) success at stage 1 followed by failure at stage 2 and (b) failure at stage 1 followed by success at stage 2.

77. The odds *against* an event occurring equals the probability that it does *not* occur divided by the probability that it *does* occur. Find the odds against event A if the probability that A occurs is y/m and the probability that A does not occur is $1 - (y/m)$.

78. The odds *in favor* of an event equals the probability that it occurs divided by the probability that it does *not* occur. Find the odds in favor of event A if the probability that A occurs is a/n and the probability that A does *not* occur is $1 - (a/n)$.

THINK ABOUT IT 5.4

1. Some people say informally that you reduce $\dfrac{5x}{6x}$ to $\dfrac{5}{6}$ by "canceling" the x's. They also say that $5 + 2x - 2x$ equals 5 because $2x$ and $-2x$ "cancel out." Explain *in terms of arithmetic operations* why these two uses of the word *cancel* are not the same. (Consequently, many people prefer to avoid the word altogether.)

2. Explain why $\dfrac{x-2}{x^2+1}$ can never be undefined.

3. Make up a fractional expression that is undefined when $x = 2$ and equals 10 when $x = 3$.

4. Divide $\dfrac{(x-a)^n}{x^{-5}}$ by $\dfrac{(x-a)^{n-5}}{x^2}$.

5. Archimedes (287–212 B.C.) was one of the greatest mathematicians of all times. Among other things, he made a remarkable finding about a cylinder and its in-

scribed sphere (see the sketch). He proved that the ratio of the two volumes is the same as the ratio of the two surface areas. Use the given formulas to find out what he discovered. (*Hint:* Express h in terms of r, so that r is the only variable.)

Volume of a cylinder $= \pi r^2 h$

Volume of a sphere $= \frac{4}{3}\pi r^3$

Surface area of

cylinder $= 2\pi r h + 2\pi r^2$

Surface area of sphere $= 4\pi r^2$

Courtesy of PhotoDisc/Getty Images.

5.5   Addition and Subtraction of Fractions

In a certain game the player either wins d dollars or loses d dollars. If the probability of winning is s/n, then the average amount of money players can expect to win in this game is given by

$$\frac{sd}{n} - \frac{(n-s)d}{n},$$

which is called the "expected value" of the game. Express this difference as a single fraction. (See Example 3.)

OBJECTIVES

1   Add and subtract rational expressions with the same denominator.

2   Add and subtract rational expressions with opposite denominators.

3   Find the least common denominator (LCD).

4   Add and subtract rational expressions with unlike denominators.

The method for adding (or subtracting) rational expressions *which have the same denominator* is the same as the method for adding or subtracting such fractions in arithmetic. The sum (or difference) is equal to the sum (or difference) of the numerators divided by the common denominator. For example,

$$\frac{2}{7} + \frac{1}{7} = \frac{2+1}{7} = \frac{3}{7} \quad \text{and} \quad \frac{6}{5} - \frac{3}{5} = \frac{6-3}{5} = \frac{3}{5}.$$

We add or subtract fractions that contain algebraic or trigonometric expressions in a similar way. In symbols, the principle is

$$\frac{a}{b} \pm \frac{c}{b} = \frac{a \pm c}{b} \qquad b \neq 0$$

EXAMPLE 1   Adding Fractions with the Same Denominator

Write as a single fraction in lowest terms:

a. $\dfrac{2}{s} + \dfrac{5}{s}$

b. $\dfrac{2}{\sin\theta} + \dfrac{5}{\sin\theta}$

Solution   Add the numerators and divide by the common denominator.

a. $\dfrac{2}{s} + \dfrac{5}{s} = \dfrac{2+5}{s}$

$= \dfrac{7}{s}$

b. $\dfrac{2}{\sin\theta} + \dfrac{5}{\sin\theta} = \dfrac{2+5}{\sin\theta}$

$= \dfrac{7}{\sin\theta}$

PROGRESS CHECK 1   Write as a single fraction in lowest terms.

a. $\dfrac{6}{7t} + \dfrac{1}{7t}$

b. $\dfrac{6}{7\tan\theta} + \dfrac{1}{7\tan\theta}$

■

The next example, particularly the subtraction case, shows types that students commonly get wrong if they do not use parentheses in the numerators.

EXAMPLE 2   Combining Fractions and Simplifying

Write as a single fraction in lowest terms.

a. $\dfrac{x^2 + 2x}{x^2 + 1} + \dfrac{3x^2 - 4x}{x^2 + 1}$

b. $\dfrac{2x + 1}{3x - 5} - \dfrac{x + 4}{3x - 5}$

c. $\dfrac{4x + 1}{x^2 - 4} - \dfrac{3x - 1}{x^2 - 4}.$

Solution   Because the numerators contain more than one term, we enclose them in parentheses.

a. $\dfrac{x^2 + 2x}{x^2 + 1} + \dfrac{3x^2 - 4x}{x^2 + 1} = \dfrac{(x^2 + 2x) + (3x^2 - 4x)}{x^2 + 1}$ Add the fractions.

$= \dfrac{4x^2 - 2x}{x^2 + 1}$ Simplify in the numerator.

b. $\dfrac{2x + 1}{3x - 5} - \dfrac{x + 4}{3x - 5} = \dfrac{(2x + 1) - (x + 4)}{3x - 5}$ Subtract the fractions.

$= \dfrac{2x + 1 - x - 4}{3x - 5}$ Remove parentheses.

$= \dfrac{x - 3}{3x - 5}$ Combine like terms.

Caution   In this example, note that we insert and then remove parentheses to ensure that we subtract the entire numerator of the fraction on the right. A common error, when students do not use parentheses, is to subtract only the first term, as shown below.

$\dfrac{2x + 1}{3x - 5} - \dfrac{x + 4}{3x - 5} = \dfrac{2x + 1 - x + 4}{3x - 5}$ **Wrong**

c. $\dfrac{4x + 1}{x^2 - 4} - \dfrac{3x - 1}{x^2 - 4} = \dfrac{(4x + 1) - (3x - 1)}{x^2 - 4}$ Subtract the fractions.

$= \dfrac{4x + 1 - 3x + 1}{x^2 - 4}$ Remove parentheses.

$= \dfrac{x + 2}{x^2 - 4}$ Simplify in the numerator.

$$= \frac{x + 2}{(x + 2)(x - 2)} \qquad \text{Factor completely.}$$

$$= \frac{1}{x - 2} \qquad \text{Lowest terms.}$$

PROGRESS CHECK 2   Write as a single fraction in lowest terms.

a. $\dfrac{3x^2 - 6}{2x^2 + x} + \dfrac{3x^2 + 1}{2x^2 + x}$ **b.** $\dfrac{6x - 5}{x - 1} - \dfrac{6x - 1}{x - 1}$

c. $\dfrac{3x + 4}{x^2 - 1} + \dfrac{-2x - 5}{x^2 - 1}$

EXAMPLE 3   Expected Value of a Game

Solve the problem in the section introduction on page 276.

Solution   Simplify the expression given for the expected value.

$$\frac{sd}{n} - \frac{(n - s)d}{n} = \frac{sd - [(n - s)d]}{n} \qquad \text{Subtract the fractions.}$$

$$= \frac{sd - [nd - sd]}{n} \qquad \text{Distributive property.}$$

$$= \frac{sd - nd + sd}{n} \qquad \text{Remove parentheses.}$$

$$= \frac{2sd - nd}{n} \qquad \text{Simplify the numerator.}$$

The expected value is given in a single fraction as $\dfrac{2sd - nd}{n}$.

PROGRESS CHECK 3   In a certain game the player will either lose d dollars or win $2d$ dollars. If the probability of winning is s/n, then the expected value is given by

$$\frac{2sd}{n} - \frac{(n - s)d}{n}.$$

Express this difference as a single fraction.   ■

To add or subtract rational expressions when one denominator is the *opposite* of the other, choose either fraction and multiply both its numerator and denominator by -1. This will make both denominators the same.

EXAMPLE 4   Combining Fractions with Opposite Denominators

Write as a single fraction in lowest terms.

a. $\dfrac{2}{y} - \dfrac{7}{-y}$ **b.** $\dfrac{3x + 4}{4 - 3x} + \dfrac{1 - x}{3x - 4}$

Solution   For the common denominator we usually choose to make the coefficient of the highest power of the variable a positive number.

a. $\dfrac{2}{y} - \dfrac{7}{-y} = \dfrac{2}{y} - \dfrac{7(-1)}{-y(-1)}$ Fundamental principle.

$= \dfrac{2}{y} - \dfrac{-7}{y}$ Perform the -1 multiplications.

$= \dfrac{2 - (-7)}{y}$ Subtract the fractions.

$= \dfrac{9}{y}$ Simplify.

b. $\dfrac{3x + 4}{4 - 3x} + \dfrac{1 - x}{3x - 4} = \dfrac{(3x + 4)(-1)}{(4 - 3x)(-1)} + \dfrac{1 - x}{3x - 4}$ Fundamental principle.

$= \dfrac{-3x - 4}{3x - 4} + \dfrac{1 - x}{3x - 4}$ Perform the -1 multiplications.

$= \dfrac{(-3x - 4) + (1 - x)}{3x - 4}$ Add the fractions.

$= \dfrac{-4x - 3}{3x - 4}$ Simplify.

Note   This problem could also have been done by multiplying numerator and denominator in the right-hand fraction by -1. The answer would be $\dfrac{4x + 3}{4 - 3x}$, which is equivalent to the answer above.

PROGRESS CHECK 4   Write as a single fraction in lowest terms.

a. $\dfrac{2}{-x} - \dfrac{2}{x}$ **b.** $\dfrac{t + 3}{t - 3} + \dfrac{2 - 3t}{3 - t}$ ■

Working with rational expressions which have *different denominators* is often easier if they are first rewritten as equivalent expressions with the same denominator, usually the least common denominator, or LCD. Example 5 reviews the procedure for finding the LCD of fractions in arithmetic.

EXAMPLE 5   Finding the LCD in Numbers
Find the least common denominator for $\frac{5}{12}$ and $\frac{7}{100}$.

Solution   To find the LCD, first express 12 and 100 as products of prime factors.

$$12 = 2 \cdot 2 \cdot 3$$
$$100 = 2 \cdot 2 \cdot 5 \cdot 5$$

The LCD is the product of all the different prime factors, with each prime number appearing the most number of times it appears in any one factorization. Thus,

$$\text{LCD} = 2 \cdot 2 \cdot 3 \cdot 5 \cdot 5 = 300.$$

PROGRESS CHECK 5   Find the least common denominator for $\frac{1}{12}$ and $\frac{5}{30}$.   ■

To find the least common denominator for algebraic expressions, use a similar procedure.

> **To Find the LCD**
>
> 1. Factor each denominator completely.
> 2. The LCD is the product of all the different factors, with each factor appearing the most number of times it appears in any one factorization.

This procedure is illustrated in Example 6.

EXAMPLE 6 Finding the LCD in Algebraic Expressions

Find the least common denominator for the following.

a. $\dfrac{5}{12x^2y}$ and $\dfrac{4}{9xy^3}$

b. $\dfrac{x}{2x - 2}$ and $\dfrac{3}{x^2 - 1}$

Solution

a. First, factor each denominator completely.

$$12x^2y = 2 \cdot 2 \cdot 3 \cdot x \cdot x \cdot y$$
$$9xy^3 = 3 \cdot 3 \cdot x \cdot y \cdot y \cdot y$$

The LCD will contain the factors 2, 3, x, and y. In any factorization the greatest number of times that 2, 3, and x appear is twice, and that y appears is three times. Thus,

$$\text{LCD} = 2 \cdot 2 \cdot 3 \cdot 3 \cdot x \cdot x \cdot y \cdot y \cdot y = 36x^2y^3.$$

b. Factor each denominator completely.

$$2x - 2 = 2(x - 1)$$
$$x^2 - 1 = (x + 1)(x - 1)$$

The least common denominator will contain the factors 2, $x - 1$, and $x + 1$. The most number of times each factor appears in any one factorization is once. Thus,

$$\text{LCD} = 2(x + 1)(x - 1).$$

PROGRESS CHECK 6 Find the LCD for the following.

a. $\dfrac{1}{8xy^2}$ and $\dfrac{7}{6x^2y}$

b. $\dfrac{1}{x^2 + 5x}$ and $\dfrac{x}{3x + 15}$ ■

Example 7 reviews the arithmetic for adding fractions with different denominators. Then we present the equivalent procedure for algebraic and trigonometric expressions.

EXAMPLE 7 Adding Numerical Fractions with Unlike Denominators

Add $\frac{5}{12} + \frac{7}{100}$. Express the result in lowest terms.

Solution As shown in Example 5, the LCD is 300. We divide 300 by each denominator to find the factor to use in the fundamental principle. Because $\frac{300}{12} = 25$ and $\frac{300}{100} = 3$, we may add the fractions as shown below.

$$\frac{5}{12} + \frac{7}{100} = \frac{5 \cdot 25}{12 \cdot 25} + \frac{7 \cdot 3}{100 \cdot 3} \qquad \text{Fundamental principle.}$$

$$= \frac{125}{300} + \frac{21}{300} \qquad \text{Perform the multiplications.}$$

$$= \frac{146}{300} \qquad \text{Add the fractions.}$$

$$= \frac{73}{150} \qquad \text{Lowest terms.}$$

PROGRESS CHECK 7   Add $\frac{7}{18} + \frac{17}{30}$. Express the result in lowest terms.   ■

To Add or Subtract Algebraic and Trigonometric Expressions

1. Completely factor each denominator, and find the LCD.
2. For each fraction, obtain an equivalent fraction by applying the fundamental principle and multiplying the numerator and the denominator of the fraction by the factors of the LCD that are not contained in the denominator of that fraction.
3. Add or subtract the numerators, and divide this result by the common denominator.
4. Express the answer in lowest terms.

EXAMPLE 8   Combining with Unlike Denominators

Write as a single fraction in lowest terms.

a. $\dfrac{1}{6x} + \dfrac{5}{8}$
b. $\dfrac{5}{12x^2y} - \dfrac{4}{9xy^3}$

Solution

a. Since $6x$ factors as $2 \cdot 3 \cdot x$ and 8 factors as $2 \cdot 2 \cdot 2$, the most number of times that 2 appears is three, and that 3 and x appear is once. Thus, the LCD is $2 \cdot 2 \cdot 2 \cdot 3 \cdot x$, or $24x$. We divide the LCD by each denominator to get the factor to use in the fundamental principle step. Because $\dfrac{24x}{6x} = 4$ and $\dfrac{24x}{8} = 3x$, we have

$$\frac{1}{6x} + \frac{5}{8} = \frac{1 \cdot 4}{6x \cdot 4} + \frac{5 \cdot 3x}{8 \cdot 3x} \qquad \text{Fundamental principle.}$$

$$= \frac{1 \cdot 4 + 5 \cdot 3x}{24x} \qquad \text{Add the fractions.}$$

$$= \frac{4 + 15x}{24x} \quad \text{or} \quad \frac{15x + 4}{24x} \qquad \text{Simplify in the numerator.}$$

b. The LCD is $36x^2y^3$ (as explained in Example 6). Then,

$$\frac{5}{12x^2y} - \frac{4}{9xy^3} = \frac{5(3y^2)}{12x^2y(3y^2)} - \frac{4(4x)}{9xy^3(4x)} \qquad \text{Fundamental principle.}$$

$$= \frac{5(3y^2) - 4(4x)}{36x^2y^3} \qquad \text{Subtract the fractions.}$$

$$= \frac{15y^2 - 16x}{36x^2y^3}. \qquad \text{Simplify in the numerator.}$$

PROGRESS CHECK 8 Write as a single fraction in lowest terms.

a. $\dfrac{5}{6x} + \dfrac{2}{9}$

b. $\dfrac{3}{8xy^2} - \dfrac{7}{6x^2y}$

EXAMPLE 9 Contrasting Sums of Algebraic and Trigonometric Expressions

Write as a single fraction in simplest form:

a. $\dfrac{t}{t+1} + \dfrac{4}{t+2}$

b. $\dfrac{\tan\theta}{\tan\theta+1} + \dfrac{4}{\tan\theta+2}$

Solution None of the denominators factor, and the LCD is the product of the denominators.

a. $\dfrac{t}{t+1} + \dfrac{4}{t+2}$ [LCD: $(t+1)(t+2)$]

$$= \dfrac{t(t+2)}{(t+1)(t+2)} + \dfrac{4(t+1)}{(t+2)(t+1)} \qquad \text{Fundamental principle.}$$

$$= \dfrac{t(t+2) + 4(t+1)}{(t+2)(t+1)} \qquad \text{Add the fractions.}$$

$$= \dfrac{t^2 + 2t + 4t + 4}{(t+2)(t+1)} \qquad \text{Remove parentheses in the numerator.}$$

$$= \dfrac{t^2 + 6t + 4}{(t+2)(t+1)} \qquad \text{Simplify.}$$

b. $\dfrac{\tan\theta}{\tan\theta+1} + \dfrac{4}{\tan\theta+2}$ [LCD: $(\tan\theta+1)(\tan\theta+2)$]

$$= \dfrac{\tan\theta(\tan\theta+2)}{(\tan\theta+1)(\tan\theta+2)} + \dfrac{4(\tan\theta+1)}{(\tan\theta+2)(\tan\theta+1)} \qquad \text{Fundamental principle.}$$

$$= \dfrac{\tan\theta(\tan\theta+2) + 4(\tan\theta+1)}{(\tan\theta+2)(\tan\theta+1)} \qquad \text{Add the fractions.}$$

$$= \dfrac{\tan^2\theta + 2\tan\theta + 4\tan\theta + 4}{(\tan\theta+2)(\tan\theta+1)} \qquad \substack{\text{Remove parentheses} \\ \text{in the numerator.}}$$

$$= \dfrac{\tan^2\theta + 6\tan\theta + 4}{(\tan\theta+2)(\tan\theta+1)} \qquad \text{Simplify.}$$

PROGRESS CHECK 9 Write as a single fraction in lowest terms.

a. $\dfrac{4}{c-s} + \dfrac{4}{c+s}$

b. $\dfrac{4}{\cos\theta - \sin\theta} + \dfrac{4}{\cos\theta + \sin\theta}$

EXAMPLE 10 Combining with Unlike Denominators

Write as a single fraction in lowest terms.

a. $\dfrac{y}{y-3} + \dfrac{2}{y}$

b. $\dfrac{x}{x+3} - \dfrac{18}{x^2-9}$

c. $\dfrac{3x+1}{x^2+x-2} + \dfrac{x}{x^2-2x+1}$

Solution

a. Because neither denominator factors, the LCD is $y(y-3)$, which is the product of the denominators.

$$\frac{y}{y-3} + \frac{2}{y} = \frac{y(y)}{(y-3)(y)} + \frac{2(y-3)}{y(y-3)}$$ Fundamental principle.

$$= \frac{y(y) + 2(y-3)}{y(y-3)}$$ Add the fractions.

$$= \frac{y^2 + 2y - 6}{y(y-3)}$$ Simplify in the numerator.

The numerator does not factor, so we stop here.

b. Because $x^2 - 9$ factors as $(x+3)(x-3)$, the LCD is $(x+3)(x-3)$. Note that in this example an extra step is needed to reduce the answer to lowest terms.

$$\frac{x}{x+3} - \frac{18}{x^2-9}$$

$$= \frac{x}{x+3} - \frac{18}{(x+3)(x-3)}$$ Factor completely.

$$= \frac{x(x-3)}{(x+3)(x-3)} - \frac{18}{(x+3)(x-3)}$$ Fundamental principle.

$$= \frac{x(x-3) - 18}{(x+3)(x-3)}$$ Subtract the fractions.

$$= \frac{x^2 - 3x - 18}{(x+3)(x-3)}$$ Simplify in the numerator.

$$= \frac{(x+3)(x-6)}{(x+3)(x-3)}$$ Factor in the numerator.

$$= \frac{x-6}{x-3}$$ Lowest terms.

c. To find the LCD, we determine that $x^2 + x - 2$ factors as $(x+2)(x-1)$, while $x^2 - 2x + 1$ factors as $(x-1)(x-1)$. The most number of times that $x - 1$ appears is twice and that $x + 2$ appears is once. Thus, the LCD is $(x+2)(x-1)^2$.

$$\frac{3x+1}{x^2+x-2} + \frac{x}{x^2-2x+1}$$

$$= \frac{3x+1}{(x+2)(x-1)} + \frac{x}{(x-1)(x-1)}$$ Factor completely.

$$= \frac{(3x+1)(x-1)}{(x+2)(x-1)(x-1)} + \frac{x(x+2)}{(x-1)(x-1)(x+2)}$$ Fundamental principle.

$$= \frac{(3x+1)(x-1) + x(x+2)}{(x+2)(x-1)^2}$$ Add the fractions.

$$= \frac{3x^2 - 3x + x - 1 + x^2 + 2x}{(x+2)(x-1)^2}$$ Remove parentheses in the numerator.

$$= \frac{4x^2 - 1}{(x+2)(x-1)^2}$$ Simplify.

Although the numerator factors as $(2x+1)(2x-1)$, neither of these factors appear in the denominator, so the above result represents lowest terms.

PROGRESS CHECK 10   Write as a single fraction in lowest terms.

a. $\dfrac{t}{t-2} + \dfrac{3}{t}$ **b.** $\dfrac{2t}{t-1} - \dfrac{4}{t^2-1}$ **c.** $\dfrac{x-1}{x^2-x-6} + \dfrac{3x}{x^2-6x+9}$ ■

EXERCISES 5.5

In Exercises 1–12, rewrite the given expression as a single fraction; then express it in lowest terms.

1. $\dfrac{5x}{4} + \dfrac{3x}{4}$

2. $\dfrac{12y}{5} - \dfrac{7y}{5}$

3. $\dfrac{3}{8x} - \dfrac{1}{8x}$

4. $\dfrac{2}{15t} + \dfrac{8}{15t}$

5. $\dfrac{3y}{y+5} - \dfrac{2y-5}{y+5}$

6. $\dfrac{x-7}{2x-3} + \dfrac{x+4}{2x-3}$

7. $\dfrac{x^2+2x}{x+1} + \dfrac{x+2}{x+1}$

8. $\dfrac{y^2-y}{y+2} - \dfrac{y+8}{y+2}$

9. $\dfrac{2w+5}{w^2-9} - \dfrac{w+2}{w^2-9}$

10. $\dfrac{3z-2}{z^2-1} + \dfrac{1-2z}{z^2-1}$

11. $\dfrac{x^2+3x}{x^2+2x+1} + \dfrac{2}{x^2+2x+1}$

12. $\dfrac{x^2-x-8}{x^2-6x+9} - \dfrac{7-3x}{x^2-6x+9}$

In Exercises 13–20, write each expression as a single fraction; then express it in lowest terms.

13. $\dfrac{1}{x} + \dfrac{1}{-x}$

14. $\dfrac{2}{y} - \dfrac{3}{-y}$

15. $\dfrac{2}{x-4} - \dfrac{2}{4-x}$

16. $\dfrac{u}{2u-v} + \dfrac{v}{v-2u}$

17. $\dfrac{y+1}{2y-3} - \dfrac{y-1}{3-2y}$

18. $\dfrac{2x-4}{3x-1} + \dfrac{x-5}{1-3x}$

19. $\dfrac{t^2}{t-5} + \dfrac{25}{5-t}$

20. $\dfrac{t^2-7t}{t-5} - \dfrac{10}{5-t}$

In Exercises 21–32, find the lowest common denominator for the given fractions.

21. $\dfrac{3}{5xy^2}, \dfrac{4}{7x^2y}$

22. $\dfrac{1}{2x^3y^2}, \dfrac{1}{3xy}$

23. $\dfrac{5}{4x^3y^2z}, \dfrac{7}{6xy^2z^3}$

24. $\dfrac{3}{8x^4y^2}, \dfrac{5}{12y^2z}$

25. $\dfrac{3}{x^2+2x}, \dfrac{x}{x+2}$

26. $\dfrac{a}{x^2+x}, \dfrac{b}{x^2-x}$

27. $\dfrac{y+3}{y^2+2y+1}, \dfrac{y+2}{y^2-1}$

28. $\dfrac{y-3}{4y^2+12y+9}, \dfrac{y-1}{4y^2-9}$

29. $\dfrac{n}{2n+2}, \dfrac{n}{3n-3}$

30. $\dfrac{n+12}{6n+12}, \dfrac{n-16}{8n-16}$

31. $\dfrac{m+1}{3m-1}, \dfrac{3m-1}{6m}$

32. $\dfrac{m-3}{2m}, \dfrac{m}{2m+3}$

In Exercises 33–62, write the given expression as a single fraction in lowest terms.

33. $\dfrac{1}{2x} + \dfrac{1}{3}$

34. $\dfrac{5}{4x} + \dfrac{3}{8y}$

35. $\dfrac{3}{5y} - \dfrac{3}{10y^2}$

36. $\dfrac{y}{6x} - \dfrac{x}{7y}$

37. $\dfrac{a}{xy^2} + \dfrac{b}{x^2y}$

38. $\dfrac{1}{xyz} - \dfrac{1}{xy}$

39. $\dfrac{1}{x} - x$

40. $yz + \dfrac{y}{z}$

41. $\dfrac{x}{x-1} + \dfrac{1}{x}$

42. $\dfrac{2y}{y-5} + \dfrac{3}{y}$

43. $\dfrac{2}{x} - \dfrac{x}{x+3}$

44. $\dfrac{1}{u} - \dfrac{u}{2u-1}$

45. $\dfrac{1}{v+2} - \dfrac{1}{v^2-4}$

46. $\dfrac{1}{v+4} + \dfrac{v}{v^2-16}$

47. $\dfrac{-3}{2x-3} + \dfrac{6x}{4x^2-9}$

48. $\dfrac{2}{3x+1} - \dfrac{6x}{9x^2-1}$

49. $\dfrac{x}{x-2} - \dfrac{3x+2}{x^2-4}$

50. $\dfrac{x}{x+3} + \dfrac{5x-3}{x^2-9}$

51. $\dfrac{y}{y^2+3y+2} + \dfrac{1}{y^2+4y+3}$

52. $\dfrac{y+1}{y^2+5y+6} - \dfrac{y+3}{y^2+3y+2}$

53. $\dfrac{x}{x^2+3x+2} - \dfrac{1}{x^2+2x+1}$

54. $\dfrac{-1}{x^2-2x-8} + \dfrac{x-2}{x^2-8x+16}$

55. $\dfrac{4}{x+3} - \dfrac{16}{(x+3)^2}$

56. $\dfrac{x}{x-5} + \dfrac{4x^2}{(x-5)^2}$

57. $1 + \dfrac{2}{x+1} - \dfrac{8}{(x+1)^2}$

58. $1 - \dfrac{2}{x-2} + \dfrac{1}{(x-2)^2}$

59. $\dfrac{3}{t^2-t} + \dfrac{2}{t^2+t} + \dfrac{1}{t^2}$

60. $\dfrac{t+2}{t^2-2t} + \dfrac{t-2}{t^2+2t} + \dfrac{2}{t}$

61. $\dfrac{2b}{a^2-b^2} + \dfrac{1}{a-b} + \dfrac{1}{a+b}$

62. $\dfrac{6a+3b}{4a^2-9b^2} - \dfrac{1}{2a+3b} - \dfrac{1}{2a-3b}$

In Exercises 63–74 combine each expression into a single fraction in simplest form.

63. a. $\dfrac{5}{s} - \dfrac{11}{s}$ **b.** $\dfrac{5}{\sin\theta} - \dfrac{11}{\sin\theta}$

64. a. $\dfrac{2s-3}{4} - \dfrac{3s+2}{4}$ **b.** $\dfrac{2\sin\theta - 3}{4} - \dfrac{3\sin\theta + 2}{4}$

65. a. $\dfrac{1}{t-1} + \dfrac{2}{1-t}$ **b.** $\dfrac{1}{\tan\theta - 1} + \dfrac{2}{1 - \tan\theta}$

66. a. $\dfrac{2-t}{3-2t} - \dfrac{4}{2t-3}$ **b.** $\dfrac{2 - \tan\theta}{3 - 2\tan\theta} - \dfrac{4}{2\tan\theta - 3}$

67. a. $\dfrac{3t}{4} + \dfrac{7t}{8}$ **b.** $\dfrac{3\tan\theta}{4} + \dfrac{7\tan\theta}{8}$

68. a. $\dfrac{s}{12} - \dfrac{s}{15}$ **b.** $\dfrac{\sin\theta}{12} - \dfrac{\sin\theta}{15}$

69. a. $\dfrac{1}{t} - t$ **b.** $\dfrac{1}{\tan\theta} - \tan\theta$

70. a. $\dfrac{11}{3s} + \dfrac{2}{5}$ **b.** $\dfrac{11}{3\sin\theta} + \dfrac{2}{5}$

71. a. $\dfrac{t}{2t-6} + \dfrac{5t}{4t-12}$

 b. $\dfrac{\tan\theta}{2\tan\theta - 6} + \dfrac{5\tan\theta}{4\tan\theta - 12}$

72. a. $\dfrac{t}{t^2 - 4} + \dfrac{1}{t+2}$ **b.** $\dfrac{\tan\theta}{\tan^2\theta - 4} + \dfrac{1}{\tan\theta + 2}$

73. a. $\dfrac{1}{t+6} + \dfrac{1}{t+12}$ **b.** $\dfrac{1}{\tan\theta + 6} + \dfrac{1}{\tan\theta + 12}$

74. a. $s + t + \dfrac{t^2}{s-t}$

 b. $\sin\theta + \tan\theta + \dfrac{\tan^2\theta}{\sin\theta - \tan\theta}$

75. Find the perimeter of this rectangle.

76. Find the perimeter of this rectangle.

77. a. Show that $\dfrac{1}{n+1} + \dfrac{1}{n(n+1)} = \dfrac{1}{n}$.

This equation provides a way to find two fractions with 1 in the numerator which sum to another fraction with 1 in the numerator.

 b. Find two fractions whose sum is $\frac{1}{3}$ by letting $n = 3$ in the formula of part **a.**

78. If the chance of success in a business venture is s/n, then the chance of not obtaining success is $(n-s)/n$. Find the sum of these probabilities.

79. The weighted average of a and b is given by $\left(\dfrac{x}{n}\right)a + \left(\dfrac{n-x}{n}\right)b$. Express this as a single fraction.

80. When solving the formula $V = \frac{1}{2}hd(a+b)$ for a, a student gets $a = \dfrac{2V}{hd} - b$. The answer in the text is $a = \dfrac{2V - bhd}{hd}$. Perform the subtraction in $\dfrac{2V}{hd} - b$ to show that the student's answer is correct.

THINK ABOUT IT 5.5

1. Two expressions are negatives of each other if their sum is zero.
 a. What is the negative of $-3x$?
 b. What is the negative of $\dfrac{4}{x}$?
 c. What is the negative of $2x^2 - 3x + 1$?
 d. What is the negative of $\dfrac{x-1}{x+2}$?

2. If $g(x) = 1/x$ then write $g(cx) + cg(x)$ as a single fraction in simplest form.

3. Combine each expression into a single fraction in lowest terms.
 a. $\left(\dfrac{1}{x} + \dfrac{1}{y}\right) \div \left(\dfrac{x}{y} - \dfrac{y}{x}\right)$
 b. $\dfrac{1 + (1/\tan\theta)}{1 - (1/\tan\theta)}$

4. a. Show that the reciprocal of $\dfrac{1}{2}\left(\dfrac{1}{a} + \dfrac{1}{b}\right)$ is $\dfrac{2ab}{a+b}$.
 b. The expression $\dfrac{2ab}{a+b}$ is called the harmonic mean of a and b. Find the harmonic mean of 6 and 12.

5. The Egyptians in ancient times expressed most fractional quantities as sums of unit fractions, which are fractions with numerators equal to 1. For example, the answer given in the Rhind papyrus (1650 B.C.) to the question of how to divide 6 loaves among 10 men is $\frac{1}{2} + \frac{1}{10}$ (but we would write $\frac{6}{10}$ or $\frac{3}{5}$).
 a. Show that $\dfrac{x+y}{xy} = \dfrac{1}{x} + \dfrac{1}{y}$.
 b. For the equation in part **a**, let $x = 3$ and $y = 5$ to express $\frac{8}{15}$ as a sum of two unit fractions.
 c. Use the equality given in part **a** to find two unit fractions whose sum is $\frac{2}{7}$.

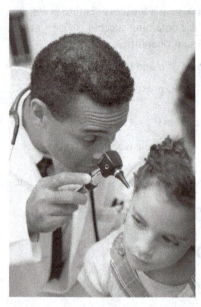

Courtesy of PhotoDisc/Getty Images.

5.6 Complex Fractions

In the determination of the reliability of medical screening tests a statistic called the **false positive rate**, which is a quotient of fractional expressions, is calculated. In one study the formula for the false positive rate was

$$F_+ = \frac{1 - \dfrac{1}{y}}{1 + \dfrac{10a - n}{ny}}.$$

Rewrite the formula by simplifying the right-hand side of the equation. (See Example 4.)

OBJECTIVES

1 Simplify complex fractions.

2 Simplify complex fractions arising from negative exponents.

A **complex fraction** is a fraction in which the numerator or the denominator or both involve fractions. In the diagram below, the complex fraction given in the section-opening problem is used to show the components of a complex fraction.

$$\left.\frac{1 - \dfrac{1}{y}}{1 + \dfrac{10a - n}{ny}}\right\}$$

⟵ Numerator of complex fraction
⟵ Primary fraction bar
⟵ Denominator of complex fraction

Every complex fraction can be rewritten as an equivalent fractional expression in which the numerator and denominator do *not* include fractions. This is called simplifying the complex fraction. Two methods for simplifying are illustrated in Example 1.

EXAMPLE 1   Contrasting Methods in a Numerical Complex Fraction

Simplify the complex fraction $\dfrac{3 - \dfrac{9}{10}}{\dfrac{2}{5} + 1}$.

Solution   Both methods show that the fraction simplifies to $\frac{3}{2}$.

Method 1   First, obtain a single fraction in the numerator and in the denominator of the complex fraction.

$$\frac{3 - \dfrac{9}{10}}{\dfrac{2}{5} + 1} = \frac{\dfrac{3 \cdot 10}{1 \cdot 10} - \dfrac{9}{10}}{\dfrac{2}{5} + \dfrac{1 \cdot 5}{1 \cdot 5}} = \frac{\dfrac{30}{10} - \dfrac{9}{10}}{\dfrac{2}{5} + \dfrac{5}{5}} = \frac{\dfrac{21}{10}}{\dfrac{7}{5}}$$

Then because a/b is equivalent to $a \div b$, we get

$$\frac{\dfrac{21}{10}}{\dfrac{7}{5}} = \frac{21}{10} \div \frac{7}{5} = \frac{21}{10} \cdot \frac{5}{7} = \frac{21 \cdot 5}{10 \cdot 7} = \frac{3}{2}.$$

Method 2   First, find the LCD of all the fractions in the numerator and the denominator of the complex fraction.

$$\text{LCD of } \frac{3}{1}, \frac{9}{10}, \frac{2}{5}, \text{ and } \frac{1}{1} \text{ is } 10.$$

Then multiply the numerator and the denominator of the complex fraction by this LCD and simplify the result.

$$\frac{3 - \dfrac{9}{10}}{\dfrac{2}{5} + 1} = \frac{10\left(3 - \dfrac{9}{10}\right)}{10\left(\dfrac{2}{5} + 1\right)} = \frac{10 \cdot 3 - 10 \cdot \dfrac{9}{10}}{10 \cdot \dfrac{2}{5} + 10 \cdot 1} = \frac{30 - 9}{4 + 10} = \frac{21}{14} = \frac{3}{2}$$

PROGRESS CHECK 1   Simplify $\dfrac{5 - \dfrac{1}{3}}{\dfrac{1}{6} + 3}$. Use both methods of Example 1.   ■

The two methods illustrated in Example 1 can also be used for simplifying complex fractions which contain algebraic and trigonometric expressions.

Methods to Simplify Complex Fractions

Method 1   (Obtain single fractions and divide): Obtain single fractions in both the numerator and the denominator of the complex fraction. Then divide by multiplying by the reciprocal of the denominator.

Method 2   (Multiply using the LCD): Find the LCD of all the fractions that appear in the numerator and the denominator of the complex fraction. Then multiply the numerator and the denominator of the complex fraction by the LCD, and simplify the results.

EXAMPLE 2   Contrasting Methods in an Algebraic Complex Fraction

Simplify the complex fraction $\dfrac{\dfrac{2}{x} - 5}{1 + \dfrac{1}{x}}$.

Solution   Consider carefully how both methods may be used to simplify the complex fraction to $\dfrac{2 - 5x}{x + 1}$.

Method 1   First, obtain single fractions in the numerator and denominator.

$$\frac{\dfrac{2}{x} - 5}{1 + \dfrac{1}{x}} = \frac{\dfrac{2}{x} - \dfrac{5x}{x}}{\dfrac{1x}{x} + \dfrac{1}{x}} = \frac{\dfrac{2 - 5x}{x}}{\dfrac{x + 1}{x}}$$

Then divide by multiplying by the reciprocal of the denominator.

$$\frac{2 - 5x}{x} \div \frac{x + 1}{x} = \frac{2 - 5x}{x} \cdot \frac{x}{x + 1} = \frac{2 - 5x}{x + 1}$$

Method 2 The LCD of $2/x$, $\frac{5}{1}$, $\frac{1}{1}$, and $1/x$ is x. Therefore, we multiply the numerator and the denominator of the complex fraction by x and then simplify.

$$\frac{\dfrac{2}{x} - 5}{1 + \dfrac{1}{x}} = \frac{x\left(\dfrac{2}{x} - 5\right)}{x\left(1 + \dfrac{1}{x}\right)} = \frac{x \cdot \dfrac{2}{x} - x \cdot 5}{x \cdot 1 + x \cdot \dfrac{1}{x}} = \frac{2 - 5x}{x + 1}$$

PROGRESS CHECK 2 Simplify the complex fraction $\dfrac{\dfrac{4}{y} + 1}{2 - \dfrac{3}{y}}$. ■

Whether to use method 1 or method 2 for simplifying complex fractions is a personal choice, but the next two examples include some guidelines that you should consider.

EXAMPLE 3 Simplifying by Converting to Division

Simplify the complex fraction $\dfrac{\dfrac{1}{a} + \dfrac{1}{b}}{\dfrac{2}{a + b}}$.

Solution The LCD, which is $ab(a + b)$, is relatively complex, and the denominator is already a single fraction. Therefore, we will choose method 1 and begin by adding in the numerator.

$$\frac{\dfrac{1}{a} + \dfrac{1}{b}}{\dfrac{2}{a + b}} = \frac{\dfrac{1b}{ab} + \dfrac{1a}{ba}}{\dfrac{2}{a + b}} = \frac{\dfrac{b + a}{ab}}{\dfrac{2}{a + b}}$$

Then divide by multiplying by the reciprocal of the denominator.

$$\frac{b + a}{ab} \div \frac{2}{a + b} = \frac{b + a}{ab} \cdot \frac{a + b}{2} = \frac{(a + b)^2}{2ab}$$

PROGRESS CHECK 3 Simplify the complex fraction $\dfrac{\dfrac{1}{y} + \dfrac{2}{x}}{\dfrac{3}{2y + x}}$. ■

EXAMPLE 4 Simplifying by Using the LCD

Solve the problem in the section introduction on page 286.

Solution The LCD of $\frac{1}{1}$, $1/y$, and $(10a - n)/ny$ is ny. The LCD is relatively simple, and method 1 would require us to obtain single fractions in both the numerator and the denominator. Therefore, we select method 2.

$$F_+ = \frac{1 - \dfrac{1}{y}}{1 + \dfrac{10a - n}{ny}}$$ Given formula.

$$= \frac{ny\left(1 - \dfrac{1}{y}\right)}{ny\left(1 + \dfrac{10a - n}{ny}\right)}$$ Multiply numerator and denominator by ny.

$$= \frac{ny \cdot 1 - ny \cdot \dfrac{1}{y}}{ny \cdot 1 + ny\dfrac{10a - n}{ny}}$$ Distributive property.

$$= \frac{ny - n}{ny + 10a - n}$$ Simplify.

PROGRESS CHECK 4   Medical screening tests also have false negative rates. A formula for one such rate is given next. Simplify the expression on the right side of the formula.

$$F_- = \frac{\dfrac{10 - an}{ny}}{9 - \dfrac{10a - 9n}{ny}}$$ ■

Example 5 points out that it is necessary to check to see that final results are expressed in lowest terms.

EXAMPLE 5   Simplifying and Then Reducing

Simplify the complex fraction $\dfrac{\dfrac{y}{x} - 2}{\dfrac{y^2}{x^2} - 4}$.

Solution   The LCD is x^2, and method 2 is a good choice.

$$\frac{\dfrac{y}{x} - 2}{\dfrac{y^2}{x^2} - 4} = \frac{x^2\left(\dfrac{y}{x} - 2\right)}{x^2\left(\dfrac{y^2}{x^2} - 4\right)}$$ Multiply in the numerator and denominator by x^2.

$$= \frac{xy - 2x^2}{y^2 - 4x^2}$$ Distributive property.

$$= \frac{x(y - 2x)}{(y + 2x)(y - 2x)}$$ Factor.

$$= \frac{x}{y + 2x}$$ Lowest terms.

PROGRESS CHECK 5   Simplify the complex fraction $\dfrac{\dfrac{1}{16} - \dfrac{1}{n^2}}{\dfrac{1}{4} + \dfrac{1}{n}}$.   ■

Problems involving negative exponents often lead to complex fractions, as shown in Example 6.

EXAMPLE 6   Simplifying a Fraction Involving Negative Exponents

Simplify $\dfrac{x^{-1} + 1}{1 - x^{-2}}$.

Solution   Begin by using the definition of a negative exponent to rewrite the expression with no negative exponents.

$$\frac{x^{-1} + 1}{1 - x^{-2}} = \frac{\dfrac{1}{x} + 1}{1 - \dfrac{1}{x^2}} \qquad \text{Definition of negative exponent.}$$

$$= \frac{x^2\left(\dfrac{1}{x} + 1\right)}{x^2\left(1 - \dfrac{1}{x^2}\right)} \qquad \text{Multiply numerator and denominator by the LCD, } x^2.$$

$$= \frac{x + x^2}{x^2 - 1} \qquad \text{Distributive property.}$$

$$= \frac{x(x + 1)}{(x + 1)(x - 1)} \qquad \text{Factor.}$$

$$= \frac{x}{x - 1} \qquad \text{Lowest terms.}$$

PROGRESS CHECK 6   Simplify $\dfrac{2x^{-1} - 1}{4x^{-2} - 1}$. ■

The trigonometric functions for tangent, cotangent, secant and cosecant can be defined by the following fractions that involve sine or cosine.

$$\tan \theta = \frac{\sin \theta}{\cos \theta}, \cot \theta = \frac{\cos \theta}{\sin \theta}, \sec \theta = \frac{1}{\cos \theta}, \csc \theta = \frac{1}{\sin \theta}$$

When an expression like $\csc \theta$ is replaced by $1/\sin \theta$ in a fractional expression, then the result is a complex fraction that can be simplified by the methods of this section. In Section 9.4 we will take particular advantage of this skill.

EXAMPLE 7   Contrasting Algebraic and Trigonometric Complex Fractions

Simplify:

a. $\dfrac{1 + (1/s)}{(1/s^2)}$ **b.** $\dfrac{1 + (1/\sin \theta)}{(1/\sin^2 \theta)}$

Solution

a. The LCD is s^2, and method 2 is a good choice.

$$\frac{1 + \dfrac{1}{s}}{\dfrac{1}{s^2}} = \frac{s^2\left(1 + \dfrac{1}{s}\right)}{s^2\left(\dfrac{1}{s^2}\right)} \qquad \text{Multiply numerator and denominator by } s^2$$

$$= \frac{s^2 + s}{1} \quad \text{or} \quad s^2 + s$$

b. The LCD is $\sin^2 \theta$.

$$\frac{1 + \dfrac{1}{\sin \theta}}{\dfrac{1}{\sin^2 \theta}} = \frac{\sin^2 \theta \left(1 + \dfrac{1}{\sin \theta} \right)}{\sin^2 \theta \left(\dfrac{1}{\sin^2 \theta} \right)}$$

Multiply numerator and denominator by $\sin^2 \theta$.

$$= \frac{\sin^2 \theta + \sin \theta}{1} \quad \text{or} \quad \sin^2 \theta + \sin \theta$$

PROGRESS CHECK 7   Simplify:

a. $\dfrac{4 + \dfrac{1}{c - 1}}{\dfrac{2}{c - 1} + 3}$

b. $\dfrac{4 + \dfrac{1}{\cos \theta - 1}}{\dfrac{2}{\cos \theta - 1} + 3}$

■

EXERCISES 5.6

In Exercises 1–30, simplify the complex fraction.

1. $\dfrac{1 - \dfrac{1}{3}}{\dfrac{5}{6} + 4}$

2. $\dfrac{2 + \dfrac{5}{8}}{\dfrac{1}{3} - \dfrac{1}{4}}$

3. $\dfrac{\dfrac{1}{x}}{\dfrac{2}{x^2}}$

4. $\dfrac{\dfrac{3}{x^2}}{\dfrac{4}{x}}$

5. $\dfrac{\dfrac{1}{n} + m}{\dfrac{1}{n} - m}$

6. $\dfrac{n + \dfrac{1}{m}}{n - \dfrac{1}{m}}$

7. $\dfrac{1 + \dfrac{1}{x}}{2 - \dfrac{1}{x}}$

8. $\dfrac{3 - \dfrac{2}{x^2}}{4 - \dfrac{3}{x^2}}$

9. $\dfrac{\dfrac{1}{a}}{\dfrac{2}{a} - \dfrac{3}{b}}$

10. $\dfrac{\dfrac{3}{a} - \dfrac{4}{b}}{\dfrac{5}{ab}}$

11. $\dfrac{\dfrac{1}{x + y}}{\dfrac{1}{x} - \dfrac{1}{y}}$

12. $\dfrac{\dfrac{x - y}{x + y}}{\dfrac{1}{y} - \dfrac{1}{x}}$

13. $\dfrac{\dfrac{3}{w} + w}{\dfrac{9}{w^2} - w^2}$

14. $\dfrac{\dfrac{16}{v^2} - \dfrac{9}{w^2}}{\dfrac{4}{v} - \dfrac{3}{w}}$

15. $\dfrac{a + \dfrac{1}{b} + \dfrac{1}{c}}{c + \dfrac{1}{b} + \dfrac{1}{a}}$

16. $\dfrac{1 - \dfrac{1}{a} - \dfrac{1}{b}}{b + \dfrac{1}{a} + 1}$

17. $\dfrac{\dfrac{x}{x + y}}{\dfrac{1}{x + y} + \dfrac{y}{x + y}}$

18. $\dfrac{\dfrac{m}{m - n}}{\dfrac{m}{m - n} + \dfrac{n}{m - n}}$

19. $\dfrac{\dfrac{4}{m - n}}{\dfrac{2}{n - m}}$

20. $\dfrac{\dfrac{x^2}{x - y}}{\dfrac{x}{y - x}}$

21. $\dfrac{3 + \dfrac{4}{h}}{2 - \dfrac{h + 6}{hk}}$

22. $\dfrac{\dfrac{1}{k} - \dfrac{h + k}{hk}}{\dfrac{2}{h} - \dfrac{h - k}{hk}}$

23. $\dfrac{\dfrac{x}{x + y} - \dfrac{y}{x - y}}{\dfrac{y}{x + y} - \dfrac{x}{x - y}}$

24. $\dfrac{\dfrac{a}{a + b} - \dfrac{b}{a - b}}{\dfrac{b}{a + b} + \dfrac{a}{a - b}}$

25. $\dfrac{\dfrac{1}{x} + \dfrac{x}{x + 2}}{\dfrac{3}{x^2 - 2x - 8}}$

26. $\dfrac{\dfrac{2x}{x^2 - 2x - 3}}{\dfrac{1}{x} + \dfrac{2}{x + 1}}$

27. $\dfrac{\dfrac{1}{x} + \dfrac{2}{x^2} + \dfrac{3}{x - 1}}{\dfrac{4}{(x - 1)^2}}$

28. $\dfrac{\dfrac{2}{x^2} + \dfrac{3}{x}}{\dfrac{1}{(x - 1)^2} + \dfrac{3}{x - 1}}$

29. $\dfrac{\dfrac{x}{y} - \dfrac{y}{x}}{\dfrac{x}{y^2} - \dfrac{y}{x^2}}$

30. $\dfrac{\dfrac{1}{j} + \dfrac{1}{k}}{\dfrac{k}{j^2} + \dfrac{j}{k^2}}$

In Exercises 31–36, simplify the complex fractions.

31. $\dfrac{x^{-2} - 1}{x^{-1} - 1}$

32. $\dfrac{x^{-2} - 2}{x^{-4} - 4}$

33. $\dfrac{n^{-1} + n^{-2}}{1 + n}$

34. $\dfrac{2n^{-2} - 3n^{-3}}{2n - 3}$

35. $\dfrac{y + 5 + 6y^{-1}}{y + 1 - 6y^{-1}}$

36. $\dfrac{2y - 5 - 3y^{-1}}{2y - 7 - 4y^{-1}}$

In Exercises 37–42 change the complex fraction to a fraction in lowest terms.

37. **a.** $\dfrac{s - (5/s)}{5}$ **b.** $\dfrac{\sin\theta - (5/\sin\theta)}{5}$

38. **a.** $\dfrac{t}{(1/t^2) + (2/t)}$ **b.** $\dfrac{\tan\theta}{(1/\tan^2\theta) + (2/\tan\theta)}$

39. **a.** $\dfrac{(s/c) - (c/s)}{(s/c) + (c/s)}$ **b.** $\dfrac{(\sin\theta/\cos\theta) - (\cos\theta/\sin\theta)}{(\sin\theta/\cos\theta) + (\cos\theta/\sin\theta)}$

40. **a.** $\dfrac{(1/c^2) + (1/t^2)}{(t/c) - (c/t)}$ **b.** $\dfrac{(1/\cos^2\theta) + (1/\tan^2\theta)}{(\tan\theta/\cos\theta) - (\cos\theta/\tan\theta)}$

41. **a.** $\dfrac{\dfrac{1}{s+1} + \dfrac{1}{s-1}}{\dfrac{1}{s-1} - \dfrac{1}{s+1}}$ **b.** $\dfrac{\dfrac{1}{\sin\theta+1} + \dfrac{1}{\sin\theta-1}}{\dfrac{1}{\sin\theta-1} - \dfrac{1}{\sin\theta+1}}$

42. **a.** $\dfrac{\dfrac{c+1}{c-1} - \dfrac{c-1}{c+1}}{\dfrac{c-1}{c+1} + \dfrac{c+1}{c-1}}$ **b.** $\dfrac{\dfrac{\cos\theta+1}{\cos\theta-1} - \dfrac{\cos\theta-1}{\cos\theta+1}}{\dfrac{\cos\theta-1}{\cos\theta+1} + \dfrac{\cos\theta+1}{\cos\theta-1}}$

43. Simplify this complex fraction, which approximates $\sqrt{28}$:

$$5 + \cfrac{1}{3 + \cfrac{1}{2}}.$$

44. A complex fraction which approximates π is

$$3 + \cfrac{1}{7 + \cfrac{1}{16}}.$$

a. Simplify this to one improper fraction.
b. Express the result of part a as a decimal, and compare it with π (which equals 3.14159265 to eight decimal places).

45. In photography the focal length of a lens is given by

$$f = \dfrac{1}{\dfrac{1}{d} + \dfrac{1}{a}}, \text{ where } d \text{ is the distance from some object}$$

to the lens and a is the distance of its image from the lens. Simplify the complex fraction in this equation.

46. When resistors R_1 and R_2 are connected in parallel, their combined resistance is given by

$$\dfrac{1}{\dfrac{1}{R_1} + \dfrac{1}{R_2}}.$$

Change this complex fraction to a fraction in simplest form.

47. **a.** Simplify the following formula for the weighted mean of a and b, where w_1 and w_2 are the weights.

$$m = \dfrac{a + \left(\dfrac{w_2}{w_1}\right)b}{1 + \dfrac{w_2}{w_1}}$$

b. Show that if w_1 and w_2 are equal, then this is just the ordinary mean (average) of a and b.

48. Simplify the following formula for the harmonic mean of three numbers a, b, and c.

$$M = \dfrac{3}{\dfrac{1}{a} + \dfrac{1}{b} + \dfrac{1}{c}}$$

THINK ABOUT IT 5.6

1. A person drives from home to work at an average speed of 30 mi/hour, and returns on the same route at an average speed of 20 mi/hour. What is the average speed for the whole trip? (Hint: average speed equals total distance divided by total time.)

2. Solve for d: $f = \dfrac{1}{\dfrac{1}{d} + \dfrac{1}{a}}.$

3. Simplify.

   a. $\dfrac{x^{-1}}{1 + \dfrac{1}{x^{-1}}}$ **b.** $\dfrac{x^{-2}}{1 + \dfrac{1}{x^{-2}}}$ **c.** $\dfrac{x^{-n}}{1 + \dfrac{1}{x^{-n}}}$

4. Simplify

$$\dfrac{\dfrac{(x+h)^2 + 1}{x+h} - \dfrac{x^2 + 1}{x}}{h}$$

5. **a.** The harmonic mean of two numbers a and b is given by

$$\dfrac{2}{\dfrac{1}{a} + \dfrac{1}{b}}.$$

Simplify this expression.
   b. Verify that the average speed in problem 1 is the harmonic mean of 30 and 20.
   c. A teacher invests \$6,000 in a growth-oriented mutual fund at \$10 a share. Six months later another \$6,000 is invested in the same fund at \$15 a share. Find the average per-share purchase price and verify that it is the harmonic mean of 10 and 15.

5.7   Division of Polynomials

When solving the formula $S = \frac{1}{2}n(a + \ell)$ for ℓ, a student obtains the answer $\ell = \frac{2S}{n} - a$. However, the answer given in the text is $\ell = \frac{2S - na}{n}$. Is the student's answer also correct? (See Example 3.)

Courtesy of PhotoDisc/Getty Images.

O B J E C T I V E S

1   Divide a polynomial by a monomial.

2   Divide a polynomial by a polynomial with at least two terms.

The simplest case of polynomial division is division of one monomial by another, by applying the quotient property of exponents, as shown in Section 1.3. This type of problem is reviewed briefly in Example 1. Because division by zero is undefined, assume throughout this section that we exclude any value for a variable that results in a zero denominator.

EXAMPLE 1   Dividing One Monomial by Another

Find each quotient. Write the result using only positive exponents.

a. $\dfrac{16x^6}{8x}$

b. $\dfrac{6y^2z^4}{-9y^3z^4}$

Solution   Divide the numerical coefficients and divide the variable factors.

a. $\dfrac{16x^6}{8x} = \dfrac{16}{8}x^{6-1} = 2x^5$

b. $\dfrac{6y^2z^4}{-9y^3z^4} = \dfrac{6}{-9}y^{2-3}z^{4-4} = -\dfrac{2}{3}y^{-1}z^0 = -\dfrac{2}{3}\cdot\dfrac{1}{y}\cdot 1 = -\dfrac{2}{3y}$

Note   The result of the addition, subtraction, or multiplication of two polynomials is always another polynomial. But as shown in Example 1b, the quotient of two polynomials is not necessarily a polynomial.

PROGRESS CHECK 1   Find each quotient. Write the result using only positive exponents.

a. $\dfrac{20y^5}{5y^3}$

b. $\dfrac{32xz^2}{-4x^4z^2}$ ■

The procedure for dividing a polynomial which has more than one term by a monomial follows from the distributive property, because every division problem can also be expressed as a multiplication problem, using the reciprocal of the divisor. Thus, we may divide $a + c$ by b as follows.

$$(a + c) \div b = (a + c) \cdot \frac{1}{b} \qquad \text{Rewrite as multiplication.}$$

$$= a \cdot \frac{1}{b} + c \cdot \frac{1}{b} \qquad \text{Distributive property.}$$

$$= \frac{a}{b} + \frac{c}{b} \qquad \text{Simplify.}$$

This result leads to the following efficient way to perform this type of division.

To Divide a Polynomial by a Monomial

To divide a polynomial by a monomial, divide each term of the polynomial by the monomial. In symbols

$$\frac{a + c}{b} = \frac{a}{b} + \frac{c}{b}, \qquad b \neq 0.$$

From a different viewpoint, this procedure can be thought of as the reverse of adding fractions with a common denominator, where we write

$$\frac{a}{b} + \frac{c}{b} = \frac{a + c}{b}, \qquad b \neq 0.$$

In addition we combine two or more fractions into one; in division by a monomial we split one fraction into two (or more) fractions.

EXAMPLE 2   Dividing a Polynomial by a Monomial

a. Divide $8x^3 - 4x^2 + 3x$ by $4x^2$ **b.** Divide $\dfrac{-15x^2y^2 - 2x^2y}{-5xy}$.

Solution

a. Divide each term of $8x^3 - 4x^2 + 3x$ by $4x^2$, and simplify.

$$\frac{8x^3 - 4x^2 + 3x}{4x^2} = \frac{8x^2}{4x^2} - \frac{4x^2}{4x^2} + \frac{3x}{4x^2}$$

$$= 2x - 1 + \frac{3}{4x}$$

Note   The answer to a division problem can be checked by multiplying the answer by the divisor. In this case $4x^2 \left(2x - 1 + \dfrac{3}{4x} \right) = 8x^3 - 4x^2 + 3x$, so the answer checks.

b. Because of the negative sign in the denominator, we choose to express the subtraction in the numerator as an addition expression, using the relationship $a - b = a + (-b)$.

$$\frac{-15x^2y^2 - 2x^2y}{-5xy} = \frac{-15x^2y^2}{-5xy} + \frac{-2x^2y}{-5xy}$$

$$= 3xy + \frac{2}{5}x$$

PROGRESS CHECK 2

a. Divide $10x^4 + 5x^2 - 4x$ by $5x^2$.   **b.** Divide $\dfrac{5x^2y - 8xy^2}{-2xy}$.   ■

EXAMPLE 3   Recognizing Equivalent Expressions

Solve the problem in the section introduction on page 293.

Solution   We may start from the answer given in the text and divide each term of $2S - na$ by n.

$$\ell = \frac{2S - na}{n}$$

$$= \frac{2S}{n} - \frac{na}{n} = \frac{2S}{n} - a$$

Thus, the student's answer is also correct.

Caution   Be sure to divide *all* terms of the numerator by the divisor. A common student error in Example 3 is to divide n only into na and incorrectly write $\ell = 2S - a$, forgetting that the $2S$ term must also be divided by n.

PROGRESS CHECK 3   When solving the formula $C = \frac{5}{9}(F - 32)$ for F, a student obtains the answer $F = \frac{9}{5}C + 32$. If the answer in the text key is $F = \dfrac{9C + 160}{5}$, is the student's answer also correct?   ■

Division of a polynomial by a polynomial with two or more terms is similar to long division in arithmetic. To illustrate, consider the division of 146 by 13 shown below, and note the names of the key components.

$$\text{Divisor} \longrightarrow 13\overline{)158} \quad\begin{array}{l}12 \longleftarrow \text{Quotient}\\ \longleftarrow \text{Dividend}\\ \underline{13}\\ 28\\ \underline{26}\\ 2 \longleftarrow \text{Remainder}\end{array}$$

The result may be expressed as

$$\frac{158}{13} = 12 + \frac{2}{13},$$

and in general,

$$\frac{\text{dividend}}{\text{divisor}} = \text{quotient} + \frac{\text{remainder}}{\text{divisor}}.$$

Dividing 13 into 158 is like dividing $x + 3$ into $x^2 + 5x + 8$, where x stands for 10. Note how the steps compare as we go through the problem.

The first step is to write both polynomials with descending powers.

$$x + 3\overline{)x^2 + 5x + 8}$$

Divide the first term of the dividend by the first term of the divisor to obtain the first term of the quotient.

$$x + 3\overline{)\begin{array}{l}x\\ x^2 + 5x + 8\end{array}} \qquad \textit{Think:} \frac{x^2}{x} = x.$$

Next, multiply the entire divisor by the first term of the quotient and subtract this product from the dividend.

$$\begin{array}{r}x\\ x + 3\overline{)x^2 + 5x + 8}\\ \text{Subtract:} \quad \underline{x^2 + 3x}\\ 2x + 8\end{array} \qquad \textit{Think:}\, x(x + 3) = x^2 + 3x.$$

Use the remainder as the new dividend and repeat the above procedure until the remainder is of lower degree than the divisor.

$$\begin{array}{r}x + 2\\ x + 3\overline{)x^2 + 5x + 8}\\ \text{Subtract:} \quad \underline{x^2 + 3x}\\ 2x + 8\\ \text{Subtract:} \quad \underline{2x + 6}\\ 2\end{array}$$

Thus, the quotient is $x + 2$, the remainder is 2, and the answer may be written as

$$\frac{x^2 + 5x + 8}{x + 3} = x + 2 + \frac{2}{x + 3}.$$

The procedure is summarized in the box below.

Long Division of Polynomials

1. Arrange the terms of the dividend and the divisor with descending powers. *If a lower power is absent in the dividend, write 0 as its coefficient.*
2. Divide the first term of the dividend by the first term of the divisor to obtain the first term of the quotient.
3. Multiply the entire divisor by the first term of the quotient, and subtract this result from the dividend.
4. Use the remainder as the new dividend and repeat the above procedure until the remainder is of lower degree than the divisor.

The next two examples illustrate the procedure.

EXAMPLE 4   Using Long Division
Divide $3x^2 - 7x - 5$ by $x - 3$.

Solution   As shown below, the key divisions are that $3x^2$ divided by x is $3x$, and $2x$ divided by x is 2.

$$\frac{3x^2}{x} = 3x \qquad \frac{2x}{x} = 2$$

$$
\begin{array}{r}
3x + 2 \\
x - 3 \overline{\smash{)}\, 3x^2 - 7x - 5}
\end{array}
$$

Subtract: $\underline{3x^2 - 9x}$ This line is $3x(x-3)$.

                $2x - 5$

    Subtract: $\underline{2x - 6}$ This line is $2(x - 3)$.

                    1

The quotient is $3x + 2$, the remainder is 1, and we may write

$$\frac{3x^2 - 7x - 5}{x - 3} = 3x + 2 + \frac{1}{x - 3}.$$

Note   Check that dividend = (divisor)(quotient) + remainder. In this example,

$$(x - 3)(3x + 2) + 1 = 3x^2 + 2x - 9x - 6 + 1$$
$$= 3x^2 - 7x - 5,$$

which is the correct dividend, so the answer checks.

PROGRESS CHECK 4   Divide $3x^2 - 2x + 6$ by $x + 2$, and check your answer.   ■

EXAMPLE 5   Adjusting for Missing Powers in the Dividend
Divide $\dfrac{y^3 + 1}{y + 1}$.

Solution The dividend is a polynomial of degree 3 with no second-degree or first-degree terms. Following step 1 of the procedure given in the box, $0y^2$ and $0y$ are inserted so that like terms align vertically.

$$
\begin{array}{r}
y^2 - y + 1 \\
y + 1\overline{)y^3 + 0y^2 + 0y + 1} \\
\end{array}
$$

Subtract: $\dfrac{y^3 + y^2}{}$

$-y^2 + 0y + 1$

Subtract: $\dfrac{-y^2 - y}{}$

$y + 1$

Subtract: $\dfrac{y + 1}{0}$

$\dfrac{y^3}{y} = y^2$, $-\dfrac{y^2}{y} = -y$, and $\dfrac{y}{y} = 1$.

This line is $y^2(y + 1)$.

This line is $-y(y + 1)$.

This line is $1(y + 1)$.

A zero remainder is not usually written in the answer, so

$$\frac{y^3 + 1}{y - 1} = y^2 - y + 1.$$

PROGRESS CHECK 5 Divide $\dfrac{x^3 - 1}{x - 1}$. ■

In the final example the divisor has degree 2. This focuses attention on step 4 of the procedure, which says to stop as soon as the remainder is of lower degree than the divisor.

EXAMPLE 6 Dividing by a Second Degree Polynomial

Divide $\dfrac{3x^4 - 9x^3 - x^2 + 7x - 10}{3x^2 + 2}$.

Solution Be careful to align like terms, as shown in the division below.

$$
\begin{array}{r}
x^2 - 3x - 1 \\
3x^2 + 2\overline{)3x^4 - 9x^3 - x^2 + 7x - 10} \\
\end{array}
$$

Subtract: $\dfrac{3x^4 + 2x^2}{}$

$-9x^3 - 3x^2 + 7x - 10$

Subtract: $\dfrac{-9x^3 - 6x}{}$

$-3x^2 + 13x - 10$

Subtract: $\dfrac{-3x^2 - 2}{13x - 8}$

$\dfrac{3x^4}{3x^2} = x^2$, $\dfrac{-9x^3}{3x^2} = -3x$ and $\dfrac{-3x^2}{3x^2} = -1$.

This line is $x^2(3x^2 + 2)$.

This line is $-3x(3x^2 + 2)$.

This line is $-1(3x^2 + 2)$.

Stop here, because the remainder is of lower degree than the divisor. The answer is

$$\frac{3x^4 - 9x^3 - x^2 + 7x - 10}{3x^2 + 2} = x^2 - 3x - 1 + \frac{13x - 8}{3x^2 + 2}.$$

PROGRESS CHECK 6 Divide $\dfrac{2x^4 - 6x^3 + 5x^2 + 5x - 3}{2x^2 + 3}$. ■

EXERCISES 5.7

In Exercises 1–40, find each quotient.

1. $\dfrac{24x^7}{6x}$

2. $\dfrac{30x^5}{5x^3}$

3. $\dfrac{4x^2y^2}{8xy^3}$

4. $\dfrac{2xy^4}{18x^3y^3}$

5. $\dfrac{-30x^{10}y^{10}z^{10}}{10x^{10}y^{12}z^8}$

6. $\dfrac{14xy^2z}{-4x^2yz}$

7. Divide $12n^3 - 4n^2 + n$ by $2n^2$.

8. Divide $15m^5 - 10m^3 + 5m$ by $5m^2$.

9. Divide $24xy - 18x^2y^2$ by $-6xy^2$.

10. Divide $-10x^2y + 12xy^2 - 14xy$ by $-2xy$.
11. Divide $-9rs^2t + 14rs$ by $12st^2$.
12. Divide $-6rs^2t^3 + 12r^3s^2t$ by $9r^2s^2t^2$.
13. $\dfrac{6x - 9y + 12}{-3xy}$
14. $\dfrac{8y^2 - 12x^2 + 16x^2y^2}{-4xy}$
15. $\dfrac{a^2 + 2ab + b^2}{ab}$
16. $\dfrac{a^3 + 3a^2b + 3ab^2 + b^3}{a^2b^2}$
17. Divide $3x^2 + 2x + 1$ by $x - 1$.
18. Divide $x^2 + 2x + 3$ by $x + 3$.
19. Divide $4y^2 - 2y - 1$ by $y + 2$.
20. Divide $-3y^2 + 13y + 12$ by $y - 3$.
21. Divide $3y^2 - 13y + 12$ by $y - 3$.
22. Divide $2y^2 + 5y - 12$ by $y + 4$.
23. Divide $\dfrac{6x^2 + 7x - 2}{2x + 3}$.
24. Divide $\dfrac{4x^2 - 4x - 17}{2x - 5}$.
25. Divide $\dfrac{x^3 + 8}{x + 2}$.
26. Divide $\dfrac{x^3 - 27}{x - 3}$.
27. Divide $\dfrac{n^3 - 1}{n + 1}$.
28. Divide $\dfrac{m^3 + 8}{m - 2}$.
29. Divide $4x^2 + 9$ by $2x + 3$.
30. Divide $x^2 + 16$ by $x + 4$.
31. Divide $9x^4 + 5x^2 + x + 3$ by $3x - 1$.
32. Divide $4x^4 + x^2 + x - 21$ by $2x + 3$.
33. Divide $\dfrac{2x^4 + 2x^3 + 3x^2 + 2x - 4}{2x^2 + 1}$.
34. Divide $\dfrac{6a^4 - 3a^3 - 11a^2 + 2a + 5}{3a^2 - 1}$.
35. Divide $2c^4 + c^3 - 5c^2 + 5c - 4$ by $c^2 - c + 1$.
36. Divide $3d^4 + 5d^3 + 2d^2 + 1$ by $3d^2 - d + 1$.
37. If $P(x) = x^4 + x^3 - x^2 + 2x + 3$ and $Q(x) = x + 1$, find $P(x) \div Q(x)$.
38. If $P(x) = x^5 - 2x^3 + 5x^2 - 10$ and $Q(x) = x^2 - 2$, find $P(x) \div Q(x)$.
39. Find $m^4 + 2m^3 + 3m^2 + 2m + 1$ divided by $m^2 + m + 1$.
40. Find $m^4 - 2m^3 + 3m^2 - 2m + 1$ divided by $m^2 - m + 1$.

In Exercises 41–44 we have given two solutions which resulted from two different ways of solving the given equation. Show that the two solutions are equivalent.

41. Solve $A = \dfrac{1}{2}(a + b)h$ for a: $a = \dfrac{2A - bh}{h}$;

$a = \dfrac{2A}{h} - b$.

42. Solve $x = \mu + z\sigma$ for σ: $\sigma = \dfrac{x - \mu}{z}$; $\sigma = \dfrac{x}{z} - \dfrac{\mu}{z}$.

43. Solve $y = \dfrac{a(x + b)}{c}$ for x: $x = \dfrac{cy - ab}{a}$;

$x = \dfrac{cy}{a} - b$.

44. Solve $\dfrac{1 + w}{-1} = \dfrac{p}{1 - p}$ for p: $p = \dfrac{1 + w}{w}$;

$p = \dfrac{1}{w} + 1$.

THINK ABOUT IT 5.7

1. If $y/x = 3$, evaluate $(2x + y)/3x$.
2. If the remainder is 6, the quotient is 4, and the divisor is 7, what is the dividend? What division problem is this?
3. If the dividend is $x^2 + 3x - 2$, the divisor is $x - 5$, and the remainder is 38, what is the quotient? What division problem is this?
4. In this section of the text all the problems were chosen to work out "nicely" with integers. Here's one that involves fractions. Divide $3x^2 - x + 4$ by $5x + 1$.
5. What happens if you use the long division procedure to divide a polynomial by one with a higher degree? We start such a problem for you. Divide 3 by $x + 2$.

$$\begin{array}{r} 3x^{-1} - 6x^{-2} \\ x + 2 \overline{)\,3} \\ \underline{3 + 6x^{-1}} \\ -6x^{-1} \\ \underline{-6x^{-1} - 12x^{-2}} \\ 12x^{-2} \end{array}$$

a. What is the next term in the quotient?
b. Will this procedure ever terminate?
c. Why do we stop long division when the degree of the remainder is smaller than the degree of the divisor?

5.8 Equations That Contain Fractions

A race car driver must average at least 100 mi/hour for two laps around a track to qualify for the finals. Because of mechanical trouble, the driver is only able to average 50 mi/hour for the first lap. What minimum speed must the driver average for the second lap to qualify for the finals? (See Example 9.)

OBJECTIVES

1 Solve fractional equations that lead to linear equations.

2 Solve fractional equations that lead to quadratic equations.

3 Solve formulas that contain fractions for a specified variable.

4 Solve applied problems involving fractional equations.

Courtesy of Corbis Images.

Many applications of algebra involve equations or formulas that contain fractions. The usual first step for solving such an equation is to multiply both sides of the equation by the least common denominator of all fractions that appear in it. This results in an equation that does not contain fractions and that may often be solved by methods we have already discussed. For instance, in Examples 1 to 3 this procedure will lead to a linear equation.

EXAMPLE 1   Solving a Fractional Equation with Constant Denominators

Solve $\dfrac{5x}{6} + \dfrac{1}{3} = \dfrac{x}{2}$.

Solution   Multiply both sides of the equation by the LCD, 6.

$$6\left(\frac{5x}{6} + \frac{1}{3}\right) = 6\left(\frac{x}{2}\right) \qquad \text{Multiply both sides by 6.}$$

$$6\left(\frac{5x}{6}\right) + 6\left(\frac{1}{3}\right) = 6\left(\frac{x}{2}\right) \qquad \text{Distributive property.}$$

$$5x + 2 = 3x \qquad \text{Simplify.}$$

$$2 = -2x \qquad \text{Subtract } 5x \text{ from both sides.}$$

$$-1 = x \qquad \text{Divide both sides by } -2.$$

To check this solution, replace x by -1 in the original equation.

$$\frac{5(-1)}{6} + \frac{1}{3} \stackrel{?}{=} \frac{-1}{2}$$

$$\frac{-5}{6} + \frac{1}{3} \stackrel{?}{=} \frac{-1}{2} \qquad \text{Simplify.}$$

$$\frac{-1}{2} \stackrel{\checkmark}{=} \frac{-1}{2} \qquad \text{Add fractions and simplify.}$$

Thus, the solution set is $\{-1\}$. This solution can be interpreted graphically as an intersection of two lines as shown in Figure 5.13.

PROGRESS CHECK 1   Solve $\dfrac{x}{5} + 1 = \dfrac{x + 2}{10}$.

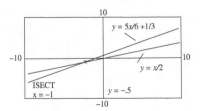

Figure 5.13

EXAMPLE 2 Solving a Fractional Equation with Variable Denominators

Solve $\dfrac{2}{3a} = \dfrac{3}{2a - 1}$.

Solution   We first remove the fractions by multiplying both sides of the equation by the LCD, which is $3a(2a - 1)$ in this equation. Note that this step requires the restrictions that $a \neq 0$ and $a \neq \frac{1}{2}$ to ensure that we are multiplying both sides of the equation by a nonzero number.

$$3a(2a - 1)\frac{2}{3a} = 3a(2a - 1)\frac{3}{2a - 1}$$ Multiply both sides by $3a(2a - 1)$.

$$2(2a - 1) = 9a$$ Simplify.

$$4a - 2 = 9a$$ Distributive property.

$$-2 = 5a$$ Subtract 4a from both sides.

$$\frac{-2}{5} = a$$ Divide both sides by 5.

The LCD is nonzero when $a = -\frac{2}{5}$; and the check of this solution is shown next.

$$\frac{2}{3\left(-\frac{2}{5}\right)} \overset{?}{=} \frac{3}{2\left(-\frac{2}{5}\right) - 1}$$

$$\frac{2}{-\frac{6}{5}} \overset{?}{=} \frac{3}{-\frac{9}{5}}$$

$$\frac{5}{-3} \overset{\checkmark}{=} \frac{5}{-3}$$

Thus the solution set is $\left\{-\frac{2}{5}\right\}$.

Technology Link

Graphical support for the solution of a fractional equation can be complicated because fractional expressions are undefined when the denominator is zero. Although a detailed discussion for graphing rational functions is given in Section 11.4, we can still use a calculator to draw such graphs at this time. First, it is recommended that the calculator be set in dot mode, not connected mode, when initially drawing such graphs. The dot mode prevents the calculator from connecting points that are in separate pieces of the graph (as discussed in Section 2.4). Figure 5.14 shows three graphs that are associated with the graphical solution of the equation in Example 2. Observe that the x-coordinate of the intersection point of the two graphs agrees with our finding that the root of the equation is $-\frac{2}{5}$.

PROGRESS CHECK 2   Solve $\dfrac{4 - 3x}{x} = \dfrac{5}{2x}$. ■

EXAMPLE 3 Finding the Tension in a String

In a physics experiment (illustrated in Figure 5.15) a block of mass m_1 on a smooth horizontal surface is pulled by a string which is attached to a block of mass m_2 hanging over a pulley. Ignoring friction and the mass of the pulley, the formula for the tension (T) in the string is

$$T = \frac{32m_1m_2}{m_1 + m_2}.$$

Find m_1 if $m_2 = 3$ units and $T = 60$ lb. The unit for mass in this notation is called a slug.

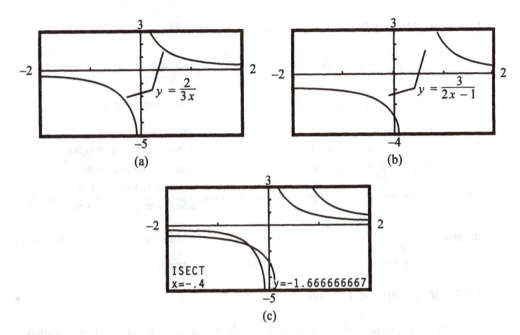

Figure 5.14

Solution   After replacing T and m_2 by their given values, multiply both sides of the equation by the LCD, which is $m_1 + 3$. (The denominator of the left-hand side is equal to 1.)

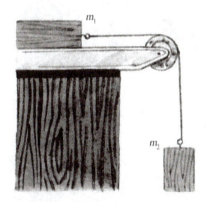

Figure 5.15

$$T = \frac{32m_1m_2}{m_1 + m_2} \qquad \text{Given formula.}$$

$$60 = \frac{32m_1(3)}{m_1 + 3} \qquad \text{Replace } T \text{ by 60 and } m_2 \text{ by 3.}$$

$$60 = \frac{96m_1}{m_1 + 3} \qquad \text{Simplify.}$$

$$60(m_1 + 3) = 96m_1 \qquad \text{Multiply both sides by } m_1 + 3.$$

$$60m_1 + 180 = 96m_1 \qquad \text{Distributive property.}$$

$$180 = 36m_1 \qquad \text{Subtract } 60m_1 \text{ from both sides.}$$

$$5 = m_1 \qquad \text{Divide both sides by 36.}$$

Because $60 = \dfrac{32(5)(3)}{5 + 3}$ is a true statement, 5 checks and m_1 is a mass of 5 slugs.

PROGRESS CHECK 3   Use the formula in Example 3 to find m_2 if $T = 48$ lb and $m_1 = 2$ slugs.   ■

Clearing fractions in the next two examples leads to quadratic equations that can be solved by the methods of Section 5.3.

**EXAMPLE 4   Solving a Fractional Equation that Leads
               to a Quadratic Equation**

Solve $x - \dfrac{10}{x} = 3$.

Solution   Multiply both sides of the equation by the LCD, x.

$$x\left(x - \frac{10}{x}\right) = x \cdot 3 \qquad \text{Multiply both sides by } x.$$

$$x \cdot x - x\left(\frac{10}{x}\right) = x \cdot 3 \qquad \text{Distributive property.}$$

$$x^2 - 10 = 3x \qquad \text{Simplify.}$$

$$x^2 - 3x - 10 = 0 \qquad \text{Subtract } 3x \text{ from both sides.}$$

$$(x - 5)(x + 2) = 0 \qquad \text{Factor the nonzero side.}$$

$$x - 5 = 0 \quad \text{or} \quad x + 2 = 0 \qquad \text{Set each factor equal to 0.}$$

$$x = 5 \qquad x = -2 \qquad \text{Solve each linear equation.}$$

Because $5 - \dfrac{10}{5}$ and $-2 - \dfrac{10}{-2}$ both simplify to 3, both solutions check. The solution set is $\{5, -2\}$. See Figure 5.16 for a graphical check of this result.

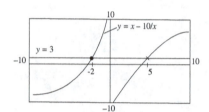

Figure 5.16

PROGRESS CHECK 4   Solve $y + \dfrac{6}{y} = 5$.   ■

The next example shows that the methods of this section may lead to **extraneous solutions**, which are apparent solutions that do not check in the original equation and are therefore not part of the solution set. When solving equations containing rational expressions, check for extraneous solutions at values for the variable that make the LCD zero.

EXAMPLE 5   Solving a Fractional Equation with an Extraneous Root

Solve $\dfrac{7}{t - 4} - \dfrac{56}{t^2 - 16} = 1$.

Solution   The LCD is or So, we begin by multiplying both sides of the equation by assuming $t \neq -4$ and $t \neq 4$.

$$(t^2 - 16)\left(\frac{7}{t - 4} - \frac{56}{t^2 - 16}\right) = (t^2 - 16) \cdot 1 \qquad \text{Multiply both sides by the LCD.}$$

$$7(t + 4) - 56 = t^2 - 16 \qquad \text{Distributive property.}$$

$$7t + 28 - 56 = t^2 - 16 \qquad \text{Distributive property.}$$

$$0 = t^2 - 7t + 12 \qquad \text{Rewrite so one side is 0.}$$

$$0 = (t - 3)(t - 4) \qquad \text{Factor.}$$

$$t - 3 = 0 \quad \text{or} \quad t - 4 = 0 \qquad \text{Set each factor equal to 0.}$$

$$t = 3 \qquad t = 4 \qquad \text{Solve each equation.}$$

The solution $t = 3$ does check, as shown next, but the restriction $t \neq 4$ means that 4 is an extraneous solution and should not be included in the solution set. Substitution of 4 for t shows that this extraneous solution leads to division by zero.

Check

$$\frac{7}{3 - 4} - \frac{56}{3^2 - 16} \overset{?}{=} 1 \qquad\qquad \frac{7}{4 - 4} - \frac{56}{4^2 - 16} \overset{?}{=} 1$$

$$-7 - (-8) \overset{?}{=} 1 \qquad\qquad\qquad \frac{7}{0} - \frac{56}{0} \neq 1$$

$$1 \overset{\checkmark}{=} 1 \qquad\qquad \text{4 is an extraneous solution.}$$

The solution set is {3}. The graph in Figure 5.17 may be used to reinforce this solution graphically.

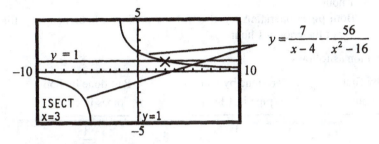

$$y = \frac{7}{x-4} - \frac{56}{x^2 - 16}$$

Figure 5.17

PROGRESS CHECK 5   Solve $1 = \dfrac{12}{x^2 - 4} - \dfrac{3}{x - 2}$.   ■

As mentioned in Section 1.5, it is sometimes necessary to convert a formula to a form that is more efficient for a particular problem. The methods of this section may be used to rearrange formulas that contain fractions.

EXAMPLE 6   Rearranging a Formula

Solve the formula $t = \dfrac{v - v_0}{v}$ for v.

Solution   The general approach is to first get rid of fractions and then isolate all terms containing the desired variable on one side of the equation, where it can be factored out.

$t = \dfrac{v - v_0}{v}$	Given formula.
$tv = v - v_0$	Multiply both sides by v.
$tv - v = -v_0$	Subtract v from both sides.
$v(t - 1) = -v_0$	Factor out v.
$v = \dfrac{-v_0}{t - 1}$	Divide both sides by $t - 1$.

PROGRESS CHECK 6   Solve the formula in Example 3 for m_1.   ■

One type of application that involves equations with fractions is called a **work problem**. The goal in such problems is to find the time needed to complete a job when two or more people or machines work together. The basis for analyzing work problems is to assume a *constant work rate*. **If a job requires t units of time to complete, then $1/t$ of the job is completed in one unit of time**. For example, if a pump can empty a storage tank in 4 hours, then (assuming a constant pumping rate) it empties $\frac{1}{4}$ of the tank for each hour of pumping.

EXAMPLE 7   Solving a Work Problem

One pipe can fill a swimming pool in 4 hours. A second pipe can fill the pool in 12 hours. How long will it take to fill the pool if both pipes operate together?

Solution   Let x represent the number of hours required to fill the pool if both pipes operate together. Then apply the basic principle outlined above.

First pipe: This pipe fills the pool in 4 hours, so it fills 1/4 of the pool in 1 hour.

Second pipe: This pipe fills the pool in 12 hours, so it fills 1/12 of the pool in 1 hour.

Together: Both pipes operating together fill the pool in x hours, so they fill $1/x$ of the pool in 1 hour.

Now set up an equation as follows.

$$\underbrace{\text{Part done by first pipe in 1 hour}} + \underbrace{\text{Part done by second pipe in 1 hour}} = \underbrace{\text{Part done by both pipes in 1 hour}}$$

$$\frac{1}{4} \quad + \quad \frac{1}{12} \quad = \quad \frac{1}{x}$$

To solve this equation multiply both sides by the LCD, $12x$.

$$12x\left(\frac{1}{4} + \frac{1}{12}\right) = 12x\left(\frac{1}{x}\right)$$

$$3x + x = 12 \qquad \text{Distributive property.}$$
$$4x = 12 \qquad \text{Add like terms.}$$
$$x = 3 \qquad \text{Divide both sides by 4.}$$

It takes the two pipes 3 hours to fill the pool when they are in operation simultaneously. To check this answer numerically, note that in 3 hours the first pipe does $3 \cdot \left(\frac{1}{4}\right)$ of the job, while the second pipe does $3 \cdot \left(\frac{1}{12}\right)$ of the job. Because $\frac{3}{4} + \frac{1}{4} = 1$, the whole pool is filled, and the solution checks. Figure 5.18 shows a graph that reaffirms that 3 is the solution of the equation that was set up to solve the problem.

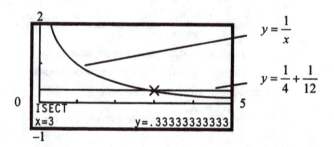

$$y = \frac{1}{x}$$

$$y = \frac{1}{4} + \frac{1}{12}$$

ISECT x=3   y=.33333333333

Figure 5.18

PROGRESS CHECK 7   A lawn can be mowed in 20 minutes with a ride-on mower and in 80 minutes with a self-propelled mower. How long will it take to mow the lawn using the two mowers together?   ■

In Section 1.6 we solved certain uniform motion problems using the formula

$$\text{distance} = \text{rate} \cdot \text{time} \qquad \text{or} \qquad d = rt.$$

But for uniform motion problems in which two events take the same time, it is more useful to rewrite the formula as

$$\text{time} = \frac{\text{distance}}{\text{rate}} \qquad \text{or} \qquad t = \frac{d}{r}.$$

This formula will lead to equations containing fractions.

EXAMPLE 8   Solving a Uniform Motion Problem

An experimental light plane, powered by the pilot's pedaling, flew a distance of $\frac{1}{2}$ mi against a 2-mi/hour wind. With that same wind behind it, it flew 1 mi in the same time. What is the speed of the plane in still air?

Solution   Let x represent the plane's rate in still air. Then,

$$x - 2 = \text{rate against the wind (subtract wind speed)}$$

and $$x + 2 = \text{rate with the wind (add wind speed).}$$

Now analyze the problem in a chart format using $t = d/r$.

Direction	Distance	÷	Rate	=	Time
Against wind	0.5		$x - 2$		$\dfrac{0.5}{x - 2}$
With the wind	1		$x + 2$		$\dfrac{1}{x + 2}$

To *set up an equation* use the given condition that both trips require the same amount of time.

Time against wind   equals   time with wind.

$$\frac{0.5}{x - 2} \qquad = \qquad \frac{1}{x + 2}$$

Solve the Equation

$0.5(x + 2) = 1(x - 2)$	Multiply both sides by $(x - 2)(x + 2)$.
$0.5x + 1 = x - 2$	Distributive property.
$1 = 0.5x - 2$	Subtract $0.5x$ from both sides.
$3 = 0.5x$	Add 2 to both sides.
$6 = x$	Divide both sides by 0.5.

Answer the Question   The plane's rate in still air is 6 mi/hour.

Check the Answer   If x is replaced by 6, then the flight against the wind takes $\dfrac{0.5}{6 - 2} = \dfrac{0.5}{4} = 0.125$ hour, and the trip with the wind takes $\dfrac{1}{6 + 2} = \dfrac{1}{8} = 0.125$ hour. The times are the same, so the solution checks.

PROGRESS CHECK 8   An improved version of the plane described in Example 8 flew 1 mi with a 3-mi/hour wind pushing it in the same amount of time it took to fly 0.6 mi against that wind. What is the speed of the plane in still air?   ■

EXAMPLE 9   Solving an Average Speed Problem

Solve the problem in the section introduction on page 299.

Solution   Let d represent the distance around the track and let x represent the minimum speed that the driver must average for the second lap to qualify. Since $t = d/r$, the times required for the first and second laps are denoted by $d / 50$ and d / x, respectively. Then,

$$\text{average speed} = \frac{\text{total distance}}{\text{total time}}$$

$$100 = \frac{2d}{\frac{d}{50} + \frac{d}{x}}$$

$$100\left(\frac{d}{50} + \frac{d}{x}\right) = 2d$$

$$2d + \frac{100d}{x} = 2d$$

$$\frac{100d}{x} = 0.$$

Since $100d$ cannot equal 0, the equation has no solution. This means that it is not possible to qualify, no matter how fast the driver goes on the second lap! To illustrate why this answer makes sense, note that the distance around the track divides out in the above equations, so let us suppose d equals 100 miles. Then the driver is required to travel 200 miles in 2 hours or less to qualify. However, the first lap took 2 hours to complete because the average speed was only 50 mi/hour, so the driver cannot qualify.

To view this solution graphically, let y represent the average speed and observe that

$$y = \frac{2d}{\frac{d}{50} + \frac{d}{x}} = \frac{100xd}{xd + 50d} = \frac{100x}{x + 50}.$$

Then Figure 5.19 illustrates that the graph of $y = 100x/(x + 50)$ approaches, but does not touch, the graph of $y = 100$.

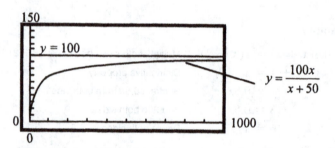

Figure 5.19

PROGRESS CHECK 9   A race car driver must average at least 120 mi/hour for two laps around a track, to qualify for the finals. Because of mechanical trouble the driver is only able to average 90 mi/hour for the first lap. What minimum speed must the driver average for the second lap, to qualify for the finals?   ▪

EXERCISES 5.8

In Exercises 1–42, solve the given equation.

1. $\dfrac{3x}{4} - \dfrac{1}{2} = \dfrac{x}{8}$

2. $\dfrac{1}{3} + \dfrac{x}{6} = \dfrac{x}{9}$

3. $\dfrac{y}{3} - 4 = \dfrac{y}{4}$

4. $\dfrac{2y}{3} - \dfrac{3y}{4} = 1$

5. $5 - \dfrac{u}{2} = u$

6. $1 + \dfrac{2v}{3} = \dfrac{3v}{2}$

7. $\dfrac{2x + 1}{2} = \dfrac{3x + 2}{3}$

8. $\dfrac{3x + 1}{2} = \dfrac{6x + 2}{4}$

9. $\dfrac{1}{x} + \dfrac{2}{x} = \dfrac{3}{x}$

10. $\dfrac{1}{x} - \dfrac{2}{x} = \dfrac{3}{x}$

11. $\dfrac{1}{n} + 2 = \dfrac{3}{2n}$

12. $\dfrac{3}{m} - 2 = \dfrac{1}{3m}$

13. $\dfrac{4}{a} + \dfrac{3}{2} + \dfrac{2}{3a} = 0$

14. $\dfrac{5}{2} - \dfrac{4}{3a} - \dfrac{3}{4a} = 0$

15. $\dfrac{x-1}{x+1} = \dfrac{x}{2x+2}$

16. $\dfrac{x}{x-1} = \dfrac{x+1}{3x-3}$

17. $\dfrac{4}{x} - \dfrac{1}{2x^2} = 0$

18. $\dfrac{5}{x^2} + \dfrac{1}{5x} = 0$

19. $\dfrac{6}{x+1} - \dfrac{4}{x-1} = \dfrac{10}{x^2-1}$

20. $\dfrac{1}{y-2} - \dfrac{2}{y^2-4} = \dfrac{3}{y+2}$

21. $\dfrac{5}{2m-3} - \dfrac{3m-1}{4m^2-9} = \dfrac{2}{2m+3}$

22. $\dfrac{2}{3m+1} + \dfrac{4}{3m-1} = \dfrac{6m+8}{9m^2-1}$

23. $\dfrac{6}{x+2} + \dfrac{4}{x-4} = \dfrac{5}{x^2-2x-8}$

24. $\dfrac{2}{x-3} - \dfrac{1}{x+5} = \dfrac{1}{x^2+2x-15}$

25. $\dfrac{1}{3x-1} - \dfrac{2}{x-2} = \dfrac{5x}{3x^2-7x+2}$

26. $\dfrac{5}{3x+2} + \dfrac{x+13}{6x^2+x-2} = \dfrac{4}{2x-1}$

27. $\dfrac{1}{s^2+3s} = \dfrac{2}{s^2+4s+3}$

28. $\dfrac{6}{s^2-s} = \dfrac{3}{s^2-3s+2}$

29. $x + \dfrac{1}{x} = \dfrac{5}{2}$

30. $y - \dfrac{1}{y} = \dfrac{8}{3}$

31. $3y - \dfrac{5}{2} - \dfrac{1}{2y} = 0$

32. $\dfrac{6}{5y} + \dfrac{4}{5} - 2y = 0$

33. $2 = \dfrac{x}{x^2-1} - \dfrac{2}{x-1}$

34. $3 = \dfrac{2x}{x^2-9} + \dfrac{x+9}{x+3}$

35. $1 = \dfrac{6}{x-1} - \dfrac{12}{x^2-1}$

36. $1 = \dfrac{7}{x-4} - \dfrac{56}{x^2-16}$

37. $\dfrac{2}{y^2-1} = 1 - \dfrac{1}{y+1}$

38. $\dfrac{5}{y+2} + \dfrac{20}{y^2-4} + 1 = 0$

39. $\dfrac{e+4}{e+2} - \dfrac{e-2}{e-4} = \dfrac{e^2-13}{e^2-2e-8}$

40. $\dfrac{e-3}{e-1} + \dfrac{e-1}{e+3} = \dfrac{22}{e^2+2e-3}$

41. $\dfrac{3}{x} + \dfrac{2}{x-1} = \dfrac{4x-12}{x^2-2x+1}$

42. $\dfrac{3}{2y} + \dfrac{3y+4}{y^2-8y+16} = \dfrac{4}{y-4}$

43. The harmonic mean H of two numbers a and b is given by $H = \dfrac{2ab}{a+b}$. If $H = 8$ and $a = 6$, find b.

44. Solve $\dfrac{1}{a} + \dfrac{1}{b} = \dfrac{1}{x}$ for x. Show that x is half the harmonic mean defined in Exercise 43.

45. If a resistor of R_1 ohms is connected in parallel to a resistor of R_2 ohms, then the total resistance R is given by the formula $\dfrac{1}{R} = \dfrac{1}{R_1} + \dfrac{1}{R_2}$. Find R_1 when $R = 6$ ohms and $R_2 = 10$ ohms.

46. Use the formula in Exercise 45 to find R_2 if $R = 4$ ohms and $R_1 = 12$ ohms.

47. If the total cost of producing n units of a product consists of \$1,000 in fixed costs and \$10 per unit, then the average cost per unit A is given by $A = \dfrac{10n + 1{,}000}{n}$. How many units should be produced for the average cost to be \$20 per unit?

48. In Exercise 47, how many units should be produced for the average cost to be \$15 per unit?

In Exercise 49–54, solve the given equation for the specified variable.

49. Solve $w = \dfrac{1-p}{p}$ for p.

50. Solve $p = \dfrac{1}{1+w}$ for w.

51. Solve $\dfrac{1}{f} = \dfrac{1}{d_1} + \dfrac{1}{d_2}$ for d_1.

52. Solve $\dfrac{1}{a} = \dfrac{1}{b} - \dfrac{1}{c}$ for c.

53. Solve $P = \dfrac{S}{1+ni}$ for i.

54. Solve $S = \dfrac{P}{1-nd}$ for d.

55. One person in an office can enter some data into a computer in 4 hours. Another person can do the job in 6 hours. If they work together from separate keyboards, how long will it take to enter the data?

56. One carpenter can install the plasterboard for a job in 20 hours, while another can install it in 16 hours. If they work together, will the job be done in less than 10 hours?

57. Coin sorter A can process a sack of coins in 20 minutes; sorter B can process the sack in 30 minutes. How long would it take the two machines working together to process the sack of coins?

58. A mail-processing machine can sort 50,000 pieces of mail in 1 hour. A newer one takes 40 minutes to do the same job.
   a. If they operate together, how long will it take them to sort 50,000 pieces of mail?
   b. If they operate together, how long will it take them to sort 80,000 pieces of mail?

59. A pump can empty a tank in 100 minutes. Show algebraically that two such pumps working together will cut the time in half.

60. One machine can complete a job in 2 hours. At what rate would a second machine need to operate so that together they could complete the job in $\frac{1}{2}$ hour?

61. A ferry can travel 20 mi downstream in the same time it can travel 10 mi upstream.
   a. If the current of the river is 2 mi/hour, what is the boat's rate in still water?
   b. How long would it take the boat to travel 16 mi upstream?
   c. About how long would it take to make a round-trip of 8 mi each way if it took 15 minutes to turn around?

62. A ferry can travel 12 mi downstream in the same time it can travel 8 mi upstream.
   a. If the current of the river is 1 mi/hour, what is the boat's rate in still water?
   b. How long would it take the boat to travel 15 mi downstream?
   c. About how long would it take to make a round-trip of 6 mi each way if it took half an hour to turn around?

63. A bicycle racer goes for a fixed time 10 mi along a level desert road moving the pedals at a constant rate against a 10 mi/hour head wind. Then the cyclist turns around and goes for that same time with the wind pushing. On the return trip the cyclist covers 30 mi. Cycling at this rate, how long would it take to cover 50 mi with a 5-mi/hour wind pushing from behind?

64. Two small children who run at the same speed are playing on a moving sidewalk in an airport. The sidewalk is $\frac{1}{4}$ mi long and moves at 1 mi/hour. One child starts at each end, and they run toward each other. They meet in 3 minutes. What is their running speed on regular ground?

65. A small group of hikers climbed a 1.5-mi trail up Mount Pisgah in 2 hours. How much time should they spend coming down the same trail so that their average rate of hiking for the entire hike is 1 mi/hour?

66. Two friends canoed downstream with a 2-mi/hour current and then canoed back paddling at the same rate. Their effective speed upstream was $\frac{1}{5}$ their downstream speed.
   a. What is their rate of speed in still water?
   b. If they paddled downstream for 1 hour, how long did the whole trip take?
   c. What is their average effective speed for the whole trip?

67. A driver drives 20 miles at 20 mi/hour. How fast must the driver go for the next 20 miles, to bring the average speed for the whole trip up to 30 mi/hour?

68. Because of an earlier accident on the autobahn, it takes a sports car driver 1 hour to travel the first 20 miles of a 40-mile trip. If the maximum possible speed of the car is 120 mi/hour, can the driver go fast enough over the next 20 miles to bring the average speed for the whole trip up to 35 mi/hour?

THINK ABOUT IT 5.8

1. People who do a lot of probability calculations often use shortcuts for solving some equations. For example, to solve the equation $\frac{1}{x-1} = \frac{2}{3}$ for x, they first notice that the top plus the bottom on the left equals x. To get a new simpler proportion, they say, "Replace each fraction by its (top plus its bottom) over its top." This would yield $x = \frac{5}{2}$ immediately.
   a. Check that $\frac{5}{2}$ is the solution to the original equation.
   b. Solve $\frac{3}{3-x} = \frac{4}{3}$ by first replacing each fraction by its "top minus bottom over top."
   c. Solve $\frac{p}{1+p} = \frac{1}{4}$ using "top over (bottom minus top)."

2. Explain why no real number is a solution to
$$\frac{5x^2}{6} + \frac{1}{3} = \frac{x^2}{2}.$$

3. Here are several versions of a classic puzzle.
   a. The weight of a brick is half a pound plus half the weight of a brick. How many pounds does the brick weigh?
   b. The weight of a brick is $\frac{1}{4}$ of a pound plus $\frac{1}{4}$ of a brick. How many pounds does the brick weigh?
   c. The brick weighs $\frac{4}{5}$ of a pound plus $\frac{4}{5}$ of a brick. How many pounds does the brick weigh?
   d. This is the problem stated in general. The weight w of brick is a certain fraction f of a pound plus that fraction of a brick. How many pounds does the brick weigh? (Solve for w in terms of f.)
   e. For which version of this problem is the answer that the brick weighs 10 lb?

4. A car travels at x mi/hour from A to B and returns on the same route at y mi/hour. Show that the average speed for the round-trip is the harmonic mean of x and y. (See Exercise 43.)

5. Show that in Exercise 59 the value 100 was not necessary to the problem. Show that two similar machines working together will cut the time in half regardless of how long they take working separately.

CHAPTER 5 OVERVIEW

Section	Key Concepts and Procedures to Review
5.1	■ Definitions of polynomial, monomial, binomial, trinomial, degree of a monomial, and degree of a polynomial.
	■ Methods to factor an expression by factoring out the greatest common factor, by factoring using grouping, or by factoring a trinomial using FOIL reversal or the ac method.
	■ Method to determine whether or not $ax^2 + bx + c$ can be factored into binomial factors with integer coefficients.
5.2	■ Methods to factor an expression that is a difference of squares, or that is a sum or difference of cubes.
	■ Summary of factoring models.
	■ Guidelines to factoring a polynomial.
5.3	■ Definition of quadratic equation
	■ Zero product principle: $a \cdot b = 0$ if and only if $a = 0$ or $b = 0$.
	■ Factoring method for solving quadratic equations
5.4	■ Methods to simplify, multiply, and divide fractions
	■ Equality principle: $\dfrac{a}{b} = \dfrac{c}{d}$ if and only if $ad = bc$ $(b, d \neq 0)$
	■ Fundamental principle: $\dfrac{ak}{bk} = \dfrac{a}{b}$ $(b, k \neq 0)$
	■ Multiplication principle: $\dfrac{a}{b} \cdot \dfrac{c}{d} = \dfrac{ac}{bd}$ $(b, d \neq 0)$
	■ Division principle: $\dfrac{a}{b} \div \dfrac{c}{d} = \dfrac{a}{b} \cdot \dfrac{d}{c}$ $\left(b, d, \dfrac{c}{d} \neq 0\right)$
5.5	■ Definition of least common denominator
	■ Methods to add and subtract fractions and to find the least common denominator
	■ Addition or subtraction principles $(b, d \neq 0)$:
	$\dfrac{a}{b} \pm \dfrac{c}{b} = \dfrac{a \pm c}{b}$ $\qquad \dfrac{a}{b} \pm \dfrac{c}{d} = \dfrac{ad \pm bc}{bd}$
5.6	■ Definition of a complex fraction
	■ Methods to simplify a complex fraction
5.7	■ Procedure for dividing a polynomial by a monomial: $\dfrac{a + c}{b} = \dfrac{a}{b} + \dfrac{c}{b}$ $\quad (b \neq 0)$
	■ Long division of polynomials
5.8	■ Methods to solve an equation containing fractional expressions
	■ When solving equations containing fractional expressions, check solutions in the original equation and reject extraneous solutions.
	■ Procedures for setting up and solving work problems and uniform motion problems

CHAPTER 5 REVIEW EXERCISES

1. Find the GCF of $40x^3y^3$ and $32xy^2$.
2. Factor out the GCF from $5x^3y + 4xy^3$.
3. Factor out the GCF from $7(y - 3) - y(y - 3)$.
4. Factor by grouping: $6x^2 + 3x + 8x + 4$.
5. What is the overall result of raising a price by 10 percent and then raising that price by 10 percent? Factor out $x + 0.10x$ from $(x + 0.10x) + 0.10(x + 0.10x)$ and simplify to find out.

Factor completely.

6. $x^2 - 7x + 10$　　　　7. $y^2 + 5y - 24$
8. $x^2 - 3ax + 2a^2$　　　9. $18x^4 + 3x^2 - 1$
10. Which of these are prime polynomials?
　　a. $x^2 + x + 1$　b. $x^2 + 2x + 1$　c. $x^2 + 4x + 3$

Factor completely.

11. $9x^2 - 24x + 16$　　　12. $9x^2 - 25y^2$
13. $6y^3 - 6y$　　　　　　14. $x^3y^3 + 27$
15. $c^2 - cd - 2d^2$　　　　16. $2x^3 - 18x^2 + 28x$
17. $abc + ac + 2bc + 2c$　18. $b^6 - c^6$
19. $x^4 - h^4$　　　　　　　20. $\cos^2\theta + 8\cos\theta + 16$
21. $2\sin^3\theta\cos\theta - 18\sin^2\theta\cos\theta$

Solve.

22. $x^2 + 12 = 7x$　　　　23. $8x^3 = 72x$
24. $9y^2 = 36y$　　　　　25. $(2y + 5)(y - 3) = 0$
26. $(x - 3)(x + 3) + 5 = 0$
27. $(2y - 1)(3y + 4)(4y + 1) = 0$
28. $x + 1 = \dfrac{42}{x}, x \neq 0$

29. If the area of a square is equal to twice its perimeter, find the area.
30. The height (y) of a projectile that is shot directly up from the ground with an initial velocity of 80 ft/second is given by the formula
$$y = 80t - 16t^2,$$
where t is the elapsed time in seconds. For what value(s) of t is the projectile 64 ft off the ground?
31. The product of two consecutive integers is 240. Find the integers.
32. The length of a rectangle is 5 more than the width and the diagonal measures 25 ft. Find the area of the rectangle.
33. Find all values of x which make the expression $\dfrac{x}{x^2 - 4}$ undefined.

34. Determine whether the fractions $\frac{4}{5}$ and $\frac{16}{25}$ are equivalent.
35. Express $\dfrac{-3x + 15}{x^3 - 5x^2}$ in lowest terms.

Multiply, and express each product in lowest terms.

36. $\dfrac{3x - 12}{5y + 15} \cdot \dfrac{y + 3}{4x - 16}$　　37. $x^4 \cdot \dfrac{5}{x^2} \cdot \dfrac{2y}{x^2}$

38. $\dfrac{(x - 2)^3}{3a^2b} \cdot \dfrac{3a^3b^4}{(x - 2)^2}$

Divide, and express the answer in lowest terms.

39. $\dfrac{50}{y} \div \dfrac{25}{y^6}$　　　　40. $\dfrac{(t + 2)^3}{t^3} \div \dfrac{(t + 2)}{t}$

41. Find the lowest common denominator for $\dfrac{7}{6x^3y^2z}$ and $\dfrac{5}{9x^2yz}$.

Write each expression as a single fraction in lowest terms.

42. $\dfrac{3w + 7}{w^2 - 4} - \dfrac{2w + 5}{w^2 - 4}$　43. $\dfrac{a}{3a - b} + \dfrac{b}{b - 3a}$

44. $\dfrac{2}{x} - \dfrac{x}{x + 5}$

45. $\dfrac{-1}{x^2 - x - 6} + \dfrac{x - 2}{x^2 - 6x + 9}$

Simplify the complex fraction.

46. $\dfrac{2 + \dfrac{1}{x}}{1 - \dfrac{1}{x}}$　　　　47. $\dfrac{\dfrac{25}{a^2} - \dfrac{4}{b^2}}{\dfrac{5}{a} - \dfrac{2}{b}}$

48. $\dfrac{\dfrac{1}{a} + \dfrac{a}{a + 3}}{\dfrac{2}{a^2 + a - 6}}$　　49. $\dfrac{3n^{-3} + 2n^{-2}}{2n + 3}$

Find each quotient.

50. $\dfrac{-9a^4b^2 - 2a^3b^2}{-3a^2b^2}$

51. $\dfrac{x^4 + 2x^3y^2 + 2x^2y^3 + y^4}{x^3y^3}$

52. $(x^2 - 2x + 3) \div (x - 3)$

53. $\dfrac{n^3 + 1}{n - 1}$

54. $(x^5 - 2x^3 + 5x^2 - 10) \div (x^3 + 5)$

Solve.

55. $\dfrac{3}{2y} - 1 = \dfrac{4}{y}$

56. $\dfrac{4}{x^2 + 3x + 2} = \dfrac{1}{x + 2} + \dfrac{3}{x + 1}$

57. $\dfrac{-x}{4} + \dfrac{3}{12} = \dfrac{3x}{8}$

58. $\dfrac{1}{x - 3} - \dfrac{6}{x^2 - 9} = 1$

59. $y + \dfrac{5}{y} = -6$

60. $a = \dfrac{b + c}{b}$, for b

61. $\dfrac{W_1}{W_2} = \dfrac{L_2}{L_1}$ for L_1

62. $I = \dfrac{E}{R + r}$ for r

63. $Z = \dfrac{Z_1 Z_2}{Z_1 + Z_2}$ for Z_2

64. $\dfrac{1}{f} = \dfrac{1}{a} + \dfrac{1}{b}$ for a

65. One man working alone can paint a room in 3 hours; another can paint it in 5 hours. How long will it take the two men working together to paint the room?

66. A lawn can be mowed in 30 minutes with a ride-on mower and in 1 hour with a self-propelled mower. How long will it take to mow the lawn using the two mowers together?

67. A boat can travel 3 mi downstream in the same time it can travel 1 mi upstream. If the current of the river is 3 mi/hour, what is the boat's rate in still water?

68. A bicyclist pedaled 2 mi against a 5-mi/hour wind. With the same wind at her back, she pedaled 4 mi in the same amount of time. At what speed would the bicyclist have been pedaling if there were no wind?

Perform the indicated operations and/or simplify.

69. $\dfrac{(\cos \theta - 1)^2}{\cos^2 \theta - 1}$

70. $\dfrac{\cos \theta}{(1/\cos^2 \theta) + (2/\cos \theta)}$

71. $\dfrac{1}{\tan \theta} - \dfrac{1}{\tan \theta + 1}$

72. $\dfrac{2 \sin \theta}{5} - \dfrac{7}{3 \sin \theta} + \dfrac{2}{\sin \theta}$

73. $\dfrac{\sin \theta \cos^3 \theta - 4 \sin^2 \theta \cos \theta}{\sin \theta \cos \theta}$

74. $\dfrac{\sin^2 \theta - 5 \sin \theta + 6}{\sin \theta + 6} \div (\sin \theta - 2)$

Perform the indicated operations and/or simplify.

75. $\dfrac{m}{m + 5} + \dfrac{4m}{m + 5}$

76. $\dfrac{2 - a}{b^2 + b} \div \dfrac{a^2 - 4}{b^2 - 3b - 4}$

77. $\dfrac{5}{6a^3 b^2} - \dfrac{1}{8ab^3}$

78. $\dfrac{16ab^4}{-2a^3 b^4}$ (use only positive exponents)

79. $\dfrac{3x - 9}{x^4} \cdot \dfrac{x^2}{4x - 12}$

80. $\dfrac{7a^3 b - 4ab^3}{-2ab}$

81. $\dfrac{5x + 4}{x^2 - 9} - \dfrac{3x - 2}{x^2 - 9}$

82. $(3x^2 + 7x + 4) \div (x + 2)$

83. $\dfrac{x^2}{x - 1} + \dfrac{x^2 + 4}{1 - x}$

84. $(2y^4 - 3y^3 - 2y^2 + 3y + 5) \div (y - 2)$

85. $\dfrac{(y - 2)^7}{x^9 w^3} \cdot \dfrac{x^4 w^3}{(y - 2)^5}$

86. $\dfrac{-3x + 6}{5x - 10}$

87. $\dfrac{x^2 - 5x + 4}{x^2 - 6x + 8}$

88. $\dfrac{3m + 3a}{a^2 + am}$

89. $\dfrac{6 - \dfrac{1}{2}}{\dfrac{1}{4} + 5}$

90. $\dfrac{\dfrac{3}{y} - 2}{3 + \dfrac{4}{y}}$

91. $\dfrac{4 - x}{x^2 - 16}$

92. $\dfrac{\dfrac{2}{a} + \dfrac{1}{b}}{\dfrac{3}{a + 2b}}$

93. $\dfrac{\dfrac{1}{25} - \dfrac{1}{x^2}}{\dfrac{1}{x} - \dfrac{1}{5}}$

94. $\dfrac{x^{-1} + x^{-2}}{1 + x}$

Solve to the nearest degree for $0° \leq \theta \leq 360°$:

95. $\tan^2 \theta - 3 \tan \theta - 4 = 0$ **96.** $2 \sin^2 \theta + \sin \theta = 0$

97. Find an expression for the perimeter of this rectangle, and write it in factored form.

$b^2 - ab$

$a^2 - ab$

98. Calculate $b^2 - 4ac$ for the expression $2c^2 - 3c + 7$. Can the expression be factored into binomial factors with integer coefficients?

99. a. Because of a company's financial crisis, all employees' weekly salaries are cut a fixed percent, p. What percent raise, x, is now needed to return the employees' weekly salaries to their original level. (*Hint:* Solve $S(1 - p)(1 + x) = S$ for x.)

   b. Use the answer to part a, and determine the raise needed when the pay cut is 20 percent.

100. The age at which Diophantus (the Greek father of algebra) died is preserved in the following riddle: "Diophantus's youth lasted $\frac{1}{6}$ of his life. He grew a beard after $\frac{1}{12}$ more. After $\frac{1}{7}$ more of his life Diophantus married; five years later he had a son. The son lived exactly $\frac{1}{2}$ as long as his father, and Diophantus died just four years after his son." At what age did Diophantus die?

In Exercises 101–106 select the choice that completes the statement or answers the question.

101. The fraction $\dfrac{x - y}{4}$ is *not* equal to

   a. $\dfrac{y - x}{-4}$

   b. $-\dfrac{x - y}{-4}$

   c. $\dfrac{-x + y}{-4}$

   d. $\dfrac{y - x}{4}$

102. $\left(1 + \dfrac{1}{n}\right)\left(\dfrac{1}{n+1} - 1\right)$ simplifies to

  a. -1 **b.** 1

  c. n **d.** $n+1$

103. $\left(1 - \dfrac{\sin x}{\cos x}\right) \div \left(\cos x - \dfrac{\sin^2 x}{\cos x}\right)$ simplifies to

  a. $\cos x - \sin x$ **b.** $\cos x + \sin x$

  c. $\dfrac{1}{\cos x + \sin x}$ **d.** $\dfrac{1}{\cos x - \sin x}$

104. The reciprocal of $3 + \dfrac{1}{n}$ is

  a. $\dfrac{3n+1}{3}$ **b.** $\dfrac{n}{3n+1}$

  c. $\dfrac{3n+1}{n}$ **d.** $3 + n$

105. If $\dfrac{1}{a} = \dfrac{1}{x} - \dfrac{1}{b}$ then x equals

  a. $\dfrac{ab}{a-b}$ **b.** $\dfrac{a+b}{ab}$

  c. $a + b$ **d.** $\dfrac{ab}{a+b}$

106. Which statement is an identity:

  a. $\dfrac{1}{n} - \dfrac{1}{n+1} = \dfrac{1}{n(n+1)}$

  b. $\dfrac{2x+y}{x+y} = 2$

  c. $\dfrac{1/a}{1/b} = \dfrac{1}{ab}$

  d. $\dfrac{1}{p} + \dfrac{1}{q} = \dfrac{2}{p+q}$

CHAPTER 5 TEST

For Questions 1–5, factor the given expression completely.

  1. $5x^2 + 10x$

  2. $4a^2 - 4a + 1$

  3. $16y^2 - 25$

  4. $n^3 + 1$

  5. $20 \sin^2 \theta + 2 \sin \theta - 6$

For Questions 6–10, perform the indicated operation and express the answer in lowest terms.

  6. $\dfrac{x^2 - 1}{4x - 12} \cdot \dfrac{x^2 - 6x + 9}{x^2 - 2x - 3}$

  7. $\dfrac{x^3 - 6x^2}{(x+2)^2} \div \dfrac{6 - x}{x^2 + 2x}$

  8. $\dfrac{x^2 + 2x - 3}{x^2 - 8x + 16} - \dfrac{1 + 5x}{x^2 - 8x + 16}$

  9. $\dfrac{4 \cos \theta - 6}{7} \div \dfrac{6 \cos \theta - 9}{35}$

  10. $\dfrac{\sin \theta}{\cos \theta} - \dfrac{\cos \theta}{\sin \theta}$

  11. Find all values of x for which $\dfrac{x+1}{x^2 - 4}$ is undefined.

  12. Simplify $\dfrac{1 + \dfrac{1}{xy}}{\dfrac{1}{x} + \dfrac{1}{y}}$.

  13. Simplify $\dfrac{3n^{-2} - 4n^{-3}}{3n - 4}$.

  14. Divide $\dfrac{-6x^2 + 8y^2 - 2x^2y^2}{-2xy}$.

  15. Divide $4x^2 - 4x + 3$ by $2x + 1$.

For Questions 16–18, solve the given equation.

  16. $(2x + 1)(3x - 5)x = 0$

  17. $x^2 + 4x = 60$

  18. Solve $\dfrac{8}{x+3} - \dfrac{6}{x-3} = \dfrac{14}{x^2 - 9}$.

  19. A mail-processing machine can sort 50,000 pieces of mail in 1 hour. An older machine takes $1\frac{1}{2}$ hours to do the same job. If they work together, how long will it take them to sort 50,000 pieces of mail?

  20. The area of a triangle is 30 in.^{2}, and the height is 4 in. less than the base. Find the height of the triangle.

Radicals and Complex Numbers

The **geometric mean** of n positive numbers is defined as the nth root of their product, so for positive numbers $a_1, a_2, \ldots, a_n$,

$$\text{geometric mean} = \sqrt[n]{(a_1)(a_2)\cdots(a_n)}.$$

a. Find the geometric mean of 2 and 18.

b. The geometric mean is used to average rates of change, ratios, or indexes. For instance, if sales at a biotechnology company over a three-year period had annual growth rates of 45 percent, 16 percent, and 73 percent, then annual sales increased by factors of 1.45, 1.16, and 1.73, respectively. Find the geometric mean of these three numbers, and interpret the result. (See Example 4 of Section 6.1.)

TO ANALYZE equations in one or two variables that extend beyond linear equations, we first need to develop some algebraic techniques for extracting roots. In this chapter we introduce radical notation and then establish some properties that enable us to simplify, add, subtract, multiply, and divide radicals. Methods for solving radical equations are then considered. The concluding sections of this chapter show how we may extend the number system beyond real numbers to the set of complex numbers. This coverage will include algebraic, geometric, and trigonometric representations of such numbers.

Courtesy of PhotoDisc/Getty Images.

6.1   Radicals and Rational Exponents

OBJECTIVES

1   Find square roots and principal square roots.

2   Find principal nth roots.

3   Evaluate expressions containing rational exponents.

4   Use exponent properties to simplify expressions with rational exponents.

In many applications we need to reverse the process of raising a number to a power, and we ask

$$\text{if } x^n = a, \text{ what is } x?$$

To answer this question when $n = 2$, it is useful to define a square root.

Definition of Square Root

The number b is a square root of a if $b^2 = a$.

When a is a positive number, then a always has two square roots, as illustrated next.

EXAMPLE 1   Finding Square Roots of a Positive Number

Find the square roots of 16.

Solution   Because $4^2 = 16$ and $(-4)^2 = 16$, the square roots of 16 are 4 and -4.

PROGRESS CHECK 1   Find the square roots of 49.   ■

To avoid ambiguity, we define the **principal square roots** of a positive number to be its *positive* square root, and we denote this root by using the symbol $\sqrt{}$. Thus,

$$\sqrt{16} = 4.$$

We write $-\sqrt{16}$ to symbolize the negative square root of 16, so

$$-\sqrt{16} = -4.$$

In general, note the following ideas concerning $\sqrt{a}$.

1. When $\sqrt{a}$ is a rational number, then a is called a **perfect square**.
2. When a is positive and not a perfect square, then $\sqrt{a}$ is an irrational number that may be approximated using the key $\boxed{\sqrt{}}$ on a calculator. Recall from Section 1.1 that irrational numbers are real numbers that are not rational.
3. When a is negative, then $\sqrt{a}$ is not a real number, because the product of two equal real numbers is never negative.
4. The number 0 has exactly one square root, and $\sqrt{0} = 0$.

EXAMPLE 2   Finding Principal Square Roots

Find each square root that is a real number. Approximate irrational numbers to the nearest hundredth, and identify all numbers that are not real numbers.

a. $\sqrt{144}$ **b.** $-\sqrt{144}$ **c.** $\sqrt{-144}$ **d.** $\sqrt{14}$

Solution

a. $\sqrt{144}$ denotes the positive square root of 144. Because $12^2 = 144$, $\sqrt{144} = 12$.

b. $-\sqrt{144}$ denotes the negative square root of 144, so $-\sqrt{144} = -12$.

c. Square roots of negative numbers are never real numbers, so $\sqrt{-144}$ is not a real number.

d. 14 is not a perfect square, so $\sqrt{14}$ is irrational. By calculator, an approximate value for $\sqrt{14}$ is 3.741657387. Rounding off to the nearest hundredth, $\sqrt{14} \approx 3.74$ where $\approx$ is read, "is approximately equal to."

PROGRESS CHECK 2 Find each square root that is a real number. Approximate irrational numbers to the nearest hundredth, and identify all numbers that are not real numbers.

a. $\sqrt{200}$ **b.** $\sqrt{225}$ **c.** $\sqrt{-225}$ **d.** $-\sqrt{225}$ ■

Our ideas to this point may be generalized with the following definition of an *n*th root. Note that square roots are specific cases of *n*th roots for the case when $n = 2$.

Definition of *n*th Root

For any positive integer n, the number b is an *n*th root of a if $b^n = a$.

The **principal *n*th root** of a is denoted $\sqrt[n]{a}$ and is defined by

$$\sqrt[n]{a} = b \quad \text{if and only if} \quad b^n = a \begin{cases} \text{for } a \geq 0, b \geq 0, \text{ if } n \text{ is even,} \\ \text{for any real number } a, \text{ if } n \text{ is odd.} \end{cases}$$

In the expression $\sqrt[n]{a}$, which is called a **radical,** we say $\sqrt{}$ is the **radical sign,** a is the **radicand,** and n is the **index.** The index is usually omitted for the square root radical, and $\sqrt[3]{a}$ is called the **cube root** of a.

EXAMPLE 3   Finding Roots of a Real Number

Find each root that is a real number.

a. $\sqrt[3]{8}$ **b.** $\sqrt[3]{-8}$ **c.** $\sqrt[4]{81}$ **d.** $\sqrt[4]{-81}$

Solution

a. $\sqrt[3]{8} = 2$, because $2^3 = 8$. Read $\sqrt[3]{8} = 2$ as "the cube root of 8 is 2."

b. $\sqrt[3]{-8} = -2$, because $(-2)^3 = -8$. Note that cube roots of negative numbers are negative numbers; and in general, odd roots of negative numbers are negative.

c. $\sqrt[4]{81}$ denotes the positive fourth root of 81. Since $3^4 = 81$, $\sqrt[4]{81} = 3$.

d. $\sqrt[4]{-81}$ is not a real number. In general, when n is even and a is negative, then $\sqrt[n]{a}$ is not a real number.

Technology Link

Graphing calculators routinely have a Square Root feature and an *n*th Root feature, and sometimes have a Cube Root feature. You should use these features to redo the problems in Example 3 and compare your results to the text's answers. In Example 3d a complex number result will appear, instead of an error message, if your calculator has a complex number capability. Such numbers will be discussed in detail in Sections 6.6 and 6.7.

PROGRESS CHECK 3   Find each root that is a real number.

a. $\sqrt[4]{16}$ b. $\sqrt[3]{-125}$ c. $\sqrt[4]{-16}$ d. $-\sqrt[3]{27}$ ▪

EXAMPLE 4   Finding and Interpreting a Geometric Mean

Solve the problem in the section introduction on page 313.

Solution   Use the definition of geometric mean given in the question.

a. The geometric mean of two numbers is the square root of their product. Therefore,

$$\text{geometric mean} = \sqrt{(2)(18)} = \sqrt{36} = 6.$$

The geometric mean of 2 and 18 is 6.

b. The geometric mean of *three* numbers is the *cube root* of their product. Thus,

$$\text{geometric mean} = \sqrt[3]{(1.45)(1.16)(1.73)}.$$
$$\approx 1.427657501. \text{ (by calculator)}$$

Over the three years, annual sales increased by an average factor of about 1.4276575, which translates to an average annual sales increase of about 42.77 percent.

PROGRESS CHECK 4   The geometric mean of *n* positive numbers is the *n*th root of their product.

a. Find the geometric mean of 3, 1, and 9.
b. If sales at a company over a two-year period had annual growth rates of 84 percent and 27 percent, then annual sales increased by factors of 1.84 and 1.27, respectively. Find the geometric mean of these two numbers, and interpret the result.   ▪

It is a goal of algebra to be able to use any real number as an exponent, and we can use our work with radicals to give meaning to expressions with rational number exponents such as

$$16^{1/2}, \ 16^{-3/4}, \text{ and } 8^{2/3}.$$

Recall that the power-to-a-power property for integral exponents is

$$(a^m)^n = a^{mn}.$$

If this law is to hold for rational exponents, then consider

$$(16^{1/2})^2 = 16^{(1/2)2} = 16^1 = 16.$$

We see that squaring $16^{1/2}$ results in 16, so $16^{1/2}$ is a square root of 16. We choose to define $16^{1/2}$ as the positive square root of 16, so

$$16^{1/2} = \sqrt{16} = 4.$$

In general, our previous laws of exponents may be extended by defining $a^{1/n}$ as the principal *n*th root of *a*.

Definition of $a^{1/n}$

If *n* is a positive integer and $\sqrt[n]{a}$ is a real number, then

$$a^{1/n} = \sqrt[n]{a}.$$

Visual support for this definition in the case when $n = 5$ is shown in Figure 6.1, where it appears that $y = x^{1/5}$ and $y = \sqrt[5]{x}$ have identical graphs.

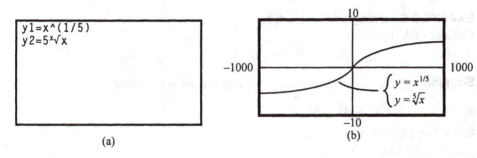

(a)

(b)

Figure 6.1

EXAMPLE 5   Using $a^{1/n} = \sqrt[n]{a}$

Evaluate each expression.

a. $8^{1/3}$ **b.** $81^{1/2}$ **c.** $81^{1/4}$ **d.** $(-8)^{1/3}$

Solution   Convert to radical form and then simplify.

a. $8^{1/3} = \sqrt[3]{8} = 2$
b. $81^{1/2} = \sqrt{81} = 9$
c. $81^{1/4} = \sqrt[4]{81} = 3$
d. $(-8)^{1/3} = \sqrt[3]{-8} = -2$

PROGRESS CHECK 5   Evaluate each expression.

a. $100^{1/2}$ **b.** $(-27)^{1/3}$ **c.** $32^{1/5}$ **d.** $625^{1/4}$ ■

The power-to-a-power property, $a^{mn} = (a^m)^n$, is the basis for extending the definition of rational exponent to the case when the numerator is not 1. For instance, to evaluate $8^{2/3}$, we reason that

$$8^{2/3} = (8^{1/3})^2 = \left(\sqrt[3]{8}\right)^2 = 2^2 = 4,$$

or

$$8^{2/3} = (8^2)^{1/3} = 64^{1/3} = \sqrt[3]{64} = 4.$$

By both methods $8^{2/3} = 4$, and this example suggests how a rational number exponent should be defined.

Rational Exponent

If m and n are integers with $n > 0$, and if m/n represents a reduced fraction such that $a^{1/n}$ is a real number, then

$$a^{m/n} = \left(\sqrt[n]{a}\right)^m = \sqrt[n]{a^m}.$$

When $a^{m/n}$ is a rational number, it is usually easier to find the root first by using $a^{m/n} = \left(\sqrt[n]{a}\right)^m$.

EXAMPLE 6 Using $a^{m/n} = \left(\sqrt[n]{a}\right)^m$

Evaluate each expression.

a. $27^{4/3}$ **b.** $16^{5/4}$ **c.** $9^{3/2}$ **d.** $9^{-1/2}$

Solution Use $a^{m/n} = \left(\sqrt[n]{a}\right)^m$, since each root is a rational number.

a. $27^{4/3} = \left(\sqrt[3]{27}\right)^4 = 3^4 = 81$

b. $16^{5/4} = \left(\sqrt[4]{16}\right)^5 = 2^5 = 32$

c. $9^{3/2} = \left(\sqrt{9}\right)^3 = 3^3 = 27$

d. $9^{-1/2} = \left(\sqrt{9}\right)^{-1} = 3^{-1} = \frac{1}{3}$

PROGRESS CHECK 6 Evaluate each expression.

a. $4^{5/2}$ **b.** $4^{-5/2}$ **c.** $(-27)^{2/3}$ **d.** $32^{4/5}$ ■

In this section the determining principle in our work is that properties that apply for integer exponents should continue to apply for rational number exponents. Therefore, an alternative method in Example 6d for evaluating $9^{-1/2}$ is

$$9^{-1/2} = \frac{1}{9^{1/2}} = \frac{1}{\sqrt{9}} = \frac{1}{3}.$$

And in general, if all powers are real numbers,

$$a^{-r} = \frac{1}{a^r}, \qquad \text{where } a \neq 0 \text{ and } r \text{ is a rational number.}$$

The simplifications in Example 7 also use this extended definition of negative exponent.

Example 7 Using $a^{-r} = 1/a^r$

Evaluate each expression.

a. $8^{-2/3}$ **b.** $(-32)^{-3/5}$ **c.** $\left(\dfrac{49}{4}\right)^{-1/2}$

Solution

a. $8^{-2/3} = \dfrac{1}{8^{2/3}} = \dfrac{1}{\left(\sqrt[3]{8}\right)^2} = \dfrac{1}{2^2} = \dfrac{1}{4}$

b. $(-32)^{-3/5} = \dfrac{1}{(-32)^{3/5}} = \dfrac{1}{\left(\sqrt[5]{-32}\right)^3} = \dfrac{1}{(-2)^3} = -\dfrac{1}{8}$

c. $\left(\dfrac{49}{4}\right)^{-1/2} = \dfrac{1}{\left(\frac{49}{4}\right)^{1/2}} = \dfrac{1}{\sqrt{\frac{49}{4}}} = \dfrac{1}{\frac{7}{2}} = \dfrac{2}{7}$

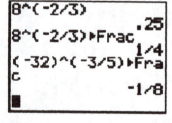

```
8^(-2/3)
                    .25
8^(-2/3)►Frac
                    1/4
(-32)^(-3/5)►Fra
c
                   -1/8
■
```

Figure 6.2

Technology Link

The screen in Figure 6.2 shows several illustrations of finding a rational power of a number. Note the importance of enclosing the exponent within parentheses. For negative exponents, be sure to use the negative sign key and not the subtraction key. Figure 6.2 also shows the use of the FRAC command from the MATH key to convert decimal notation to fractional notation.

PROGRESS CHECK 7   Evaluate each expression.

a. $25^{-3/2}$ **b.** $(-64)^{-2/3}$ **c.** $\left(\frac{27}{1,000}\right)^{-1/3}$ ■

Because all previous laws of exponents hold for rational number exponents, we may use these extended properties to simplify expressions with rational exponents.

EXAMPLE 8   Using Exponent Properties with Rational Exponents

Perform the indicated operations, and write the result with only positive exponents. Assume all variables represent positive real numbers.

a. $2^{1/2} \cdot 2^{3/2}$ **b.** $y^{2/3} \cdot y^{1/2}$ **c.** $(8x^9)^{1/3}$

d. $\dfrac{5}{5^{1/2}}$ **e.** $\dfrac{x^{4/5}y^{-3/2}}{x^{-1}y}$ **f.** $\left(\dfrac{4x^3}{100x^{-3}}\right)^{1/2}$

Solution

a. $2^{1/2} \cdot 2^{3/2} = 2^{1/2+3/2} = 2^2 = 4$

b. $y^{2/3} \cdot y^{1/2} = y^{2/3+1/2} = y^{4/6+3/6} = y^{7/6}$

c. $(8x^9)^{1/3} = 8^{(1)(1/3)}x^{(9)(1/3)} = 8^{1/3}x^3 = 2x^3$

d. $\dfrac{5}{5^{1/2}} = 5^{1-1/2} = 5^{1/2}$

e. $\dfrac{x^{4/5}y^{-3/2}}{x^{-1}y} = x^{4/5-(-1)}y^{-3/2-1} = x^{9/5}y^{-5/2} = \dfrac{x^{9/5}}{y^{5/2}}$

f. $\left(\dfrac{4x^3}{100x^{-3}}\right)^{1/2} = \left(\dfrac{x^{3-(-3)}}{25}\right)^{1/2} = \left(\dfrac{x^6}{25}\right)^{1/2} = \dfrac{x^{(6)(1/2)}}{25^{(1)(1/2)}} = \dfrac{x^3}{5}$

PROGRESS CHECK 8   Perform the indicated operations, and write the result with only positive exponents. Assume all variables represent positive real numbers.

a. $5^{1/2} \cdot 5^{1/2}$ **b.** $x^{3/2} \cdot x^{1/3}$ **c.** $(9y^6)^{1/2}$

d. $\dfrac{2^{1/3}}{2}$ **e.** $\dfrac{a^{1/4}b^{1/2}}{a^{3/4}b^{-1}}$ **f.** $\left(\dfrac{3y^2}{24y^{-4}}\right)^{2/3}$ ■

The definitions in this section give meaning to expressions with rational number exponents. This meaning is important when using functions of the form

$$y = f(x) = ax^b$$

where a and b are constants. This type of function is called a **power function** and such functions result when variable y is proportional to a constant power of variable x. For instance, the perimeter in a square is proportional to the side length, and when $P = 4s$ is matched to $y = ax^b$ we observe that this formula is a power function in which $a = 4$ and $b = 1$. The next example considers power functions with fractional powers.

EXAMPLE 9   Using a Power Function

Consider the power function $y = f(x) = ax^b$. Write out the specific formula for the function with the given values for a and b. Then, find $f(64)$.

a. $a = 2, b = 1/2$ **b.** $a = -2, b = -1/2$

Solution

a. Replacing a with 2 and b with 1/2 in $y = f(x) = ax^b$ gives

$$y = f(x) = 2x^{1/2}$$

Then

$$f(64) = 2(64)^{1/2} = 2(8) = 16.$$

b. In this case $a = -2$ and $b = -1/2$, so

$$y = f(x) = -2x^{-1/2}$$

and

$$f(64) = -2(64)^{-1/2} = -2(1/8) = -1/4.$$

PROGRESS CHECK 9   Find $f(27)$ for the power functions with the given values for a and b. In each case write out the formula for the function.

a. $a = 3, b = 1/3$ **b.** $a = -3, b = -1/3$

■

EXERCISES 6.1

In Exercises 1–6, find the square roots.

1. 121   **2.** 196
3. 361   **4.** 441
5. 576   **6.** 729

In Exercises 7–24, find each square root that is a real number. Approximate irrational numbers to the nearest hundredth, and identify all numbers that are *not* real numbers.

7. $\sqrt{289}$ **8.** $\sqrt{625}$
9. $\sqrt{12}$ **10.** $\sqrt{28}$
11. $-\sqrt{676}$ **12.** $-\sqrt{324}$
13. $\sqrt{-16}$ **14.** $\sqrt{-64}$
15. $\sqrt{34}$ **16.** $\sqrt{90}$
17. $-\sqrt{400}$ **18.** $-\sqrt{529}$
19. $\sqrt{-169}$ **20.** $\sqrt{-841}$
21. $-\sqrt{900}$ **22.** $-\sqrt{1,024}$
23. $\sqrt{-196}$ **24.** $\sqrt{-361}$

In Exercises 25–42, find each root that is a real number.

25. $\sqrt[3]{64}$ **26.** $\sqrt[3]{125}$
27. $-\sqrt[3]{216}$ **28.** $-\sqrt[3]{729}$
29. $\sqrt[3]{-27}$ **30.** $\sqrt[3]{-64}$
31. $\sqrt[4]{16}$ **32.** $\sqrt[4]{256}$
33. $-\sqrt[4]{16}$ **34.** $-\sqrt[4]{625}$
35. $\sqrt[4]{-64}$ **36.** $\sqrt[4]{-8}$
37. $\sqrt[3]{-512}$ **38.** $\sqrt[3]{-1,331}$
39. $\sqrt[4]{-225}$ **40.** $\sqrt[4]{-484}$
41. $\sqrt[5]{-32}$ **42.** $\sqrt[6]{64}$

In Exercises 43–66, evaluate each expression.

43. $49^{1/2}$ **44.** $256^{1/4}$
45. $(-216)^{1/3}$ **46.** $(-1,000)^{1/3}$
47. $27^{5/3}$ **48.** $16^{3/2}$
49. $16^{3/4}$ **50.** $81^{5/4}$
51. $81^{-1/4}$ **52.** $16^{-1/2}$
53. $4^{-3/2}$ **54.** $81^{-3/2}$
55. $-64^{4/3}$ **56.** $-125^{2/3}$
57. $(-216)^{-2/3}$ **58.** $(-343)^{-2/3}$
59. $(-32)^{-3/5}$ **60.** $(-243)^{-4/5}$
61. $\left(\frac{25}{16}\right)^{3/2}$ **62.** $\left(\frac{8}{27}\right)^{2/3}$
63. $\left(\frac{25}{16}\right)^{-1/2}$ **64.** $\left(\frac{8}{27}\right)^{-1/3}$
65. $\left(\frac{16}{81}\right)^{-1/4}$ **66.** $\left(\frac{32}{243}\right)^{-1/5}$

In Exercises 67–96, perform the indicated operations, and write the result with only positive exponents. Assume all variables represent positive real numbers.

67. $3^{1/4} \cdot 3^{3/2}$ **68.** $4^{1/3} \cdot 4^{1/2}$
69. $(3^{1/2})^6$ **70.** $(16^3)^{1/2}$
71. $\dfrac{7}{7^{1/3}}$ **72.** $\dfrac{3^{1/4}}{3^{3/4}}$
73. $a^{1/4} \cdot a^{7/4}$ **74.** $x^{2/3} \cdot x^{4/3}$
75. $b^{-1/2} \cdot b^{3/4}$ **76.** $y^{4/3} \cdot y^{-1/2}$
77. $(4b^8)^{1/2}$ **78.** $(27a^3)^{1/3}$
79. $(8x^6)^{2/3}$ **80.** $(27y^3)^{4/3}$
81. $\dfrac{a^{1/2}b^{3/8}}{a^{1/4}b^{1/8}}$ **82.** $\dfrac{x^{2/3}y^{5/6}}{x^{-1/3}y^{1/2}}$
83. $\dfrac{a^{1/2}b}{a^{3/2}b^{1/2}}$ **84.** $\dfrac{x^{-5/2}y^{3/4}}{xy^{-1/4}}$
85. $\dfrac{a^{3/4}b^{-4/3}}{a^{1/2}b^{1/3}}$ **86.** $\dfrac{x^{2/3}y^{7/3}}{x^{4/3}y^{-1/3}}$
87. $\left(\dfrac{81x^2}{9x^{-6}}\right)^{1/2}$ **88.** $\left(\dfrac{12y^5}{3y}\right)^{1/2}$
89. $\left(\dfrac{3a^6}{81a^{-6}}\right)^{1/3}$ **90.** $\left(\dfrac{2b^7}{128b^{-2}}\right)^{1/3}$
91. $\left(\dfrac{4a}{a^{-5}}\right)^{3/2}$ **92.** $\left(\dfrac{72b^6}{2b^{-2}}\right)^{3/2}$
93. $\left(\dfrac{32a^{-4}}{a^{-9}}\right)^{4/5}$ **94.** $\left(\dfrac{81b^{-1}}{b^7}\right)^{3/4}$
95. $\left(\dfrac{x^2}{64x^{-1/2}}\right)^{2/3}$ **96.** $\left(\dfrac{125y^{-3/4}}{y^{-3}}\right)^{2/3}$

In Exercises 97–100, refer to Example 4 of this section for the definition of the geometric mean of a set of positive numbers.

97. a. Find the geometric mean of 3 and 27.
   b. It can be shown that the geometric mean of two positive numbers can never be larger than their arithmetic mean (the ordinary average). Show that this is correct for 3 and 27.

98. a. Find the geometric mean of 1, 2, 8, and 16.
   b. Is the geometric mean smaller than the arithmetic mean?

99. If sales at a company over a two-year period had annual growth rates of 40 percent and 10 percent, then annual growth increased by factors of 1.40 and 1.10, respectively. Find and interpret the geometric mean of these two numbers. Give the answer to the nearest tenth of a percent.

100. The value of a house increased by factors of 1.10, 1.06, and 1.05 each year over a three-year period. Find and interpret the geometric mean of these three numbers. Give your answer to the nearest tenth of a percent.

101. a. A rectangle has length 16 in. and width 4 in. What size square has the same area?
   b. A rectangle has length a and width b. What size square has the same area?

102. a. A rectangular solid has length $= 12$, width $= 9$, and height $= 2$ cm. What size cube has the same volume?
   b. A rectangular solid has length $= a$, width $= b$, and height $= c$. What size cube has the same volume?

In Exercises 103–106 find the value of the power function $y = f(x) = ax^b$. Round decimal answers to two decimal places.

103. If $a = 2$ and $b = 3$, find
   a. f(1)   **b.** f(−1)   **c.** f(0)   **d.** f(2)   **e.** −f(−3)

104. If $a = 3$ and $b = 2$, find
   a. f(1)   **b.** f(−1)   **c.** f(0)   **d.** f(2)   **e.** −f(−3)

105. If $a = -2$ and $b = 1/4$, find
   a. f(1)   **b.** f(0)   **c.** f(1/16)   **d.** f(16)   **e.** −f(81)

106. If $a = -3$ and $b = 1/2$, find
   a. f(1)   **b.** f(0)   **c.** f(9)   **d.** f(2)   **e.** −f(1/9)

THINK ABOUT IT 6.1

1. In this section we defined rational exponents but not irrational exponents. For instance 2^π and $5^{\sqrt{2}}$ were not defined. We shall assume that it is possible to write irrational exponents and that the regular rules apply to them.
   a. Explain why $\left(5^{\sqrt{2}}\right)^{\sqrt{2}}$ must be equal to 25.
   b. Explain why 2^π should be between $2^{3.13}$ and $2^{3.15}$. Approximate π by 3.14159 and compute 2^π to three decimal places.

2. The Pythagoreans of ancient Greece studied many types of means. In general, a mean of a and b is some number between them. The three earliest recorded types are the arithmetic mean, $A = (a + b)/2$; the geometric mean, $G = \sqrt{ab}$; and the harmonic mean, $H = 2ab/(a + b)$. Compute each of these means when $a = 4$ and $b = 9$. Numerically, it is always true that A is largest and H is the smallest. Verify that this is true in this particular example.

3. Simplify. **a.** $3^{1/2}(3^{1/2} + 3^{1/2})$
                  b. $a^{1/2}(a^{1/2} + a^{1/2})$

4. Show that $a^{-1/n}$ and $a^{1/n}$ are reciprocals by showing that their product is 1. Use a calculator to find both $2^{-1/3}$ and its reciprocal to the nearest thousandth.

5. Use FOIL to multiply $(x^{1/2} + y^{1/2})(x^{1/2} - y^{1/2})$.

6.2 **Product and Quotient Properties of Radicals**

The period T of a pendulum is the time required for the pendulum to complete one round-trip of motion, that is, one complete cycle. When the period is measured in seconds, then a formula for the period is

$$T = 2\pi\sqrt{\frac{\ell}{32}},$$

where ℓ is the length in feet of the pendulum. In simplified radical form, what is the period for a pendulum that is 1 ft long? Approximate this number to the nearest hundredth of a second. (See Example 5.)

OBJECTIVES

1 Simplify radicals.

2 Multiply and divide radicals, and simplify where possible.

Properties of radicals are used often to simplify radicals and to operate on radicals. To illustrate two such properties, consider

$$\sqrt[3]{8 \cdot 27} = \sqrt[3]{216} = 6 \qquad \text{and} \qquad \sqrt[3]{8} \cdot \sqrt[3]{27} = 2 \cdot 3 = 6,$$

and

$$\sqrt{\frac{36}{4}} = \sqrt{9} = 3 \qquad \text{and} \qquad \frac{\sqrt{36}}{\sqrt{4}} = \frac{6}{2} = 3.$$

We see that $\sqrt[3]{8 \cdot 27} = \sqrt[3]{8} \cdot \sqrt[3]{27}$ and $\sqrt{36/4} = \sqrt{36}/\sqrt{4}$, which illustrates product and quotient properties of radicals, respectively.

Product and Quotient Properties of Radicals

For real numbers a, b, $\sqrt[n]{a}$, and $\sqrt[n]{b}$:

1. $\sqrt[n]{a \cdot b} = \sqrt[n]{a} \cdot \sqrt[n]{b}$
2. $\sqrt[n]{\dfrac{a}{b}} = \dfrac{\sqrt[n]{a}}{\sqrt[n]{b}} \ (b \neq 0)$

The product property may be proved by converting between radical form and exponential form and using the product-to-a-power property of exponents.

$$\sqrt[n]{ab} = (ab)^{1/n} = a^{1/n} \cdot b^{1/n} = \sqrt[n]{a} \cdot \sqrt[n]{b}$$

The quotient property is proved in a similar way, and this proof is requested in the exercises. The first application of these properties that we consider is their role in simplifying radicals.

Simplifying radicals

One condition that must be met for a radical to be expressed in simplified form is that we remove all factors of the radicand whose indicated root can be taken exactly.

EXAMPLE 1   Removing Constant Factors of the Radicand
Simplify each radical.

a. $\sqrt{45}$ **b.** $\sqrt{32}$ **c.** $\sqrt[3]{54}$ **d.** $\sqrt[4]{80}$

Solution

a. Rewrite 45 as the product of a perfect square and another factor and simplify.

$$\begin{aligned} \sqrt{45} &= \sqrt{9 \cdot 5} && \text{9 is a perfect square and } 45 = 9 \cdot 5. \\ &= \sqrt{9} \cdot \sqrt{5} && \text{Product property of radicals.} \\ &= 3\sqrt{5} && \text{Simplify.} \end{aligned}$$

b. Both 4 and 16 are perfect square factors of 32. Choosing the *larger* perfect square factor is more efficient, so

$$\sqrt{32} = \sqrt{16 \cdot 2} = \sqrt{16} \cdot \sqrt{2} = 4\sqrt{2}.$$

Check that using $\sqrt{32} = \sqrt{4 \cdot 8}$ leads to the same result but with more work.

c. To simplify cube roots, look for factors of the radicand from the perfect cubes 8, 27, 64, 125, and so on. Seeing $54 = 27 \cdot 2$ yields

$$\sqrt[3]{54} = \sqrt[3]{27 \cdot 2} = \sqrt[3]{27} \cdot \sqrt[3]{2} = 3\sqrt[3]{2}.$$

d. Consider fourth powers of 2, 3, 4, and so on, to simplify fourth roots. Since $2^4 = 16$, and 16 is a factor of 80, we have

$$\sqrt[4]{80} = \sqrt[4]{16 \cdot 5} = \sqrt[4]{16} \cdot \sqrt[4]{5} = 2\sqrt[4]{5}.$$

PROGRESS CHECK 1 Simplify each radical.

a. $\sqrt{75}$ **b.** $\sqrt{80}$ **c.** $\sqrt[3]{32}$ **d.** $\sqrt[4]{162}$ ▪

Example 2 discusses how to simplify $\sqrt[n]{a^m}$ when m and n have common factors (other than 1) and a is nonnegative. In parts **c** and **d,** note that the index for the radical has been reduced. A second consideration for expressing a radical in simplified form is that the index of the radical be as small as possible.

EXAMPLE 2 Using $\sqrt[n]{a^m} = a^{m/n}$ to Simplify Radicals

Simplify each radical. Assume $x \geq 0$, $y \geq 0$.

a. $\sqrt[3]{x^6}$ **b.** $\sqrt{7^4}$ **c.** $\sqrt[6]{5^3}$ **d.** $\sqrt[8]{y^6}$

Solution Use $\sqrt[n]{a^m} = a^{m/n}$ and reduce the rational exponent. Then convert back to radical form where necessary.

a. $\sqrt[3]{x^6} = x^{6/3} = x^2$
b. $\sqrt{7^4} = 7^{4/2} = 7^2 = 49$
c. $\sqrt[6]{5^3} = 5^{3/6} = 5^{1/2} = \sqrt{5}$
d. $\sqrt[8]{y^6} = y^{6/8} = y^{3/4} = \sqrt[4]{y^3}$

Note In this example we assumed $x \geq 0$ and $y \geq 0$ so that expressions like $\sqrt{x^2}$ simplify to x. Without this assumption it is necessary to use absolute value and write

$$\sqrt{x^2} = |x|.$$

For instance, $\sqrt{(-7)^2} \neq -7$. Instead, $\sqrt{(-7)^2} = \sqrt{49} = 7$, so $\sqrt{(-7)^2} = |-7| = 7$. The general rule is

$$\sqrt[n]{a^n} = \begin{cases} a, \text{ if } n \text{ is odd,} \\ |a|, \text{ if } n \text{ is even.} \end{cases}$$

Throughout this chapter we will restrict radicands involving variables to nonnegative real numbers so that simplifications involving absolute value will not be necessary.

PROGRESS CHECK 2 Simplify each radical. Assume $x \geq 0$, $y \geq 0$.

a. $\sqrt{11^2}$ **b.** $\sqrt[4]{y^{12}}$ **c.** $\sqrt[12]{5^4}$ **d.** $\sqrt[9]{x^6}$ ▪

Parts **a** and **b** in Example 2 showed how to simplify a radical when the radicand contains a power of a variable that is a multiple of the index. This method is also used in the simplifications in the next example.

EXAMPLE 3 Removing Constant and Variable Factors of the Radicand

Simplify each radical. Assume $x \geq 0$, $y \geq 0$.

a. $\sqrt{y^9}$ **b.** $\sqrt{24x^9y^6}$ **c.** $\sqrt[3]{x^5y^8}$

Solution

a. The largest power in which the exponent is a multiple of the index of 2 is y^8, so

$$\sqrt{y^9} = \sqrt{y^8 \cdot y} = \sqrt{y^8} \cdot \sqrt{y} = y^4\sqrt{y}.$$

b. Rewrite $24x^9y^6$ as a product of its largest perfect square factor and another factor, and simplify.

$$\sqrt{24x^9y^6} = \sqrt{(4x^8y^6)(6x)} = \sqrt{4x^8y^6} \cdot \sqrt{6x} = 2x^4y^3\sqrt{6x}$$

c. The largest powers in which exponents are multiples of the index of 3 are x^3 and y^6, so

$$\sqrt[3]{x^5y^8} = \sqrt[3]{(x^3y^6)(x^2y^2)} = \sqrt[3]{x^3y^6} \cdot \sqrt[3]{x^2y^2} = xy^2\sqrt[3]{x^2y^2}.$$

PROGRESS CHECK 3 Simplify each radical. Assume $x \geq 0$, $y \geq 0$.

a. $\sqrt{x^{11}}$ **b.** $\sqrt{125x^5y^8}$ **c.** $\sqrt[4]{x^7y^9}$ ▪

A third consideration for expressing a radical in simplified form is to eliminate any fractions in the radicand. The quotient property of radicals is used in such simplifications, as shown in Example 4.

EXAMPLE 4   Eliminating Fractions in the Radicand

Simplify each radical. Assume $x > 0$.

a. $\sqrt{\dfrac{9}{64}}$ **b.** $\sqrt{\dfrac{2}{5}}$ **c.** $\sqrt{\dfrac{25}{x}}$ **d.** $\sqrt[3]{\dfrac{2}{9x}}$

Solution

a. Both 9 and 64 are perfect squares, so

$$\sqrt{\frac{9}{64}} = \frac{\sqrt{9}}{\sqrt{64}} = \frac{3}{8}.$$

b. Rewrite $\frac{2}{5}$ as an equivalent fraction whose denominator is a perfect square, and simplify.

$$\sqrt{\frac{2}{5}} = \sqrt{\frac{2}{5} \cdot \frac{5}{5}} = \sqrt{\frac{10}{25}} = \frac{\sqrt{10}}{\sqrt{25}} = \frac{\sqrt{10}}{5}$$

c. Since $\sqrt{x^2} = x$ for $x > 0$,

$$\sqrt{\frac{25}{x}} = \sqrt{\frac{25}{x} \cdot \frac{x}{x}} = \sqrt{\frac{25x}{x^2}} = \frac{\sqrt{25}\sqrt{x}}{\sqrt{x^2}} = \frac{5\sqrt{x}}{x}.$$

d. Rewrite $\frac{2}{9x}$ as an equivalent fraction whose denominator is a perfect cube, and simplify.

$$\sqrt[3]{\frac{2}{9x}} = \sqrt[3]{\frac{2}{9x} \cdot \frac{3x^2}{3x^2}} = \sqrt[3]{\frac{6x^2}{27x^3}} = \frac{\sqrt[3]{6x^2}}{\sqrt[3]{27x^3}} = \frac{\sqrt[3]{6x^2}}{3x}$$

PROGRESS CHECK 4   Simplify each radical. Assume $y > 0$.

a. $\sqrt{\dfrac{4}{81}}$ **b.** $\sqrt{\dfrac{7}{11}}$ **c.** $\sqrt{\dfrac{8}{y}}$ **d.** $\sqrt[3]{\dfrac{5}{4y}}$ ■

EXAMPLE 5   Simplifying an Expression about the Period of a Pendulum

Solve the problem in the section introduction on page 321.

Solution   Replacing ℓ by 1 in

$$T = 2\pi\sqrt{\frac{\ell}{32}} \qquad \text{gives} \qquad T = 2\pi\sqrt{\frac{1}{32}}.$$

To express the period T in simplified radical form, rewrite $\frac{1}{32}$ as an equivalent fraction whose denominator is a perfect square, and then simplify.

$$T = 2\pi\sqrt{\frac{1}{32}} = 2\pi\sqrt{\frac{1}{32} \cdot \frac{2}{2}} = 2\pi\frac{\sqrt{2}}{\sqrt{64}} = 2\pi\frac{\sqrt{2}}{8} = \frac{\pi\sqrt{2}}{4}$$

The period is $\pi\sqrt{2}/4$ seconds. By calculator, this number is about 1.110720735. Thus, to the nearest hundredth of a second, the period is 1.11 seconds.

PROGRESS CHECK 5   In simplified radical form, what is the period of a pendulum that is 4 ft long? Approximate this answer to the nearest hundredth of a second.   ■

To multiply and divide expressions containing radicals, we use the product and quotient properties of radicals in the forms

$$\sqrt[n]{a} \cdot \sqrt[n]{b} = \sqrt[n]{ab},$$
$$\frac{\sqrt[n]{a}}{\sqrt[n]{b}} = \sqrt[n]{\frac{a}{b}}, \qquad b \neq 0.$$

Applying these properties sometimes results in expressions that can be simplified, and final answers must be stated in simplified radical form.

EXAMPLE 6   Multiplying Radical Expressions

Multiply and simplify where possible. Assume $x > 0$, $y > 0$.

a. $\sqrt{5} \cdot \sqrt{10}$ **b.** $5\sqrt[3]{7} \cdot 4\sqrt[3]{2}$ **c.** $\sqrt[4]{8x^3y^2} \cdot \sqrt[4]{4x^5y^5}$

Solution

a. First, multiply to get

$$\sqrt{5} \cdot \sqrt{10} = \sqrt{5 \cdot 10} = \sqrt{50}.$$

Now simplify.

$$\sqrt{50} = \sqrt{25 \cdot 2} = \sqrt{25} \cdot \sqrt{2} = 5\sqrt{2}$$

Thus, $\sqrt{5}\sqrt{10} = 5\sqrt{2}$.

b. Reorder and regroup as shown. Then multiply.

$$5\sqrt[3]{7} \cdot 4\sqrt[3]{2} = (5 \cdot 4)\left(\sqrt[3]{7} \cdot \sqrt[3]{2}\right) = 20\sqrt[3]{14}$$

No factor of 14 is a perfect cube, so the result does not simplify.

c. Multiply first.

$$\sqrt[4]{8x^3y^2} \cdot \sqrt[4]{4x^5y^5} = \sqrt[4]{8x^3y^2 \cdot 4x^5y^5} = \sqrt[4]{32x^8y^7}$$

Then simplify.

$$\sqrt[4]{32x^8y^7} = \sqrt[4]{16x^8y^4 \cdot 2y^3} = \sqrt[4]{16x^8y^4} \cdot \sqrt[4]{2y^3} = 2x^2y\sqrt[4]{2y^3}$$

Thus, $\sqrt[4]{8x^3y^2} \cdot \sqrt[4]{4x^5y^5} = 2x^2y\sqrt[4]{2y^3}$.

PROGRESS CHECK 6 Multiply and simplify where possible. Assume $x > 0$, $y > 0$.

a. $\sqrt{15} \cdot \sqrt{5}$ **b.** $8\sqrt[4]{9} \cdot 5\sqrt[4]{9}$ **c.** $\sqrt[3]{4x^2y} \cdot \sqrt[3]{6xy^7}$ ▪

EXAMPLE 7   Dividing Radical Expressions

Divide and simplify where possible. Assume $x > 0$, $y > 0$.

a. $\dfrac{\sqrt[3]{54}}{\sqrt[3]{2}}$ **b.** $\dfrac{\sqrt{3}}{\sqrt{10}}$ **c.** $\dfrac{\sqrt[3]{21x^2}}{\sqrt[3]{12x}}$

Solution

a. $\dfrac{\sqrt[3]{54}}{\sqrt[3]{2}} = \sqrt[3]{\dfrac{54}{2}}$ Quotient property of radicals.

$\phantom{\dfrac{\sqrt[3]{54}}{\sqrt[3]{2}}} = \sqrt[3]{27}$ Divide.

$\phantom{\dfrac{\sqrt[3]{54}}{\sqrt[3]{2}}} = 3$ Simplify.

b. Apply the quotient property and then simplify.

$$\frac{\sqrt{3}}{\sqrt{10}} = \sqrt{\frac{3}{10}} = \sqrt{\frac{3}{10} \cdot \frac{10}{10}} = \sqrt{\frac{30}{100}} = \frac{\sqrt{30}}{\sqrt{100}} = \frac{\sqrt{30}}{10}$$

c. Divide first.

$$\frac{\sqrt[3]{21x^2}}{\sqrt[3]{12x}} = \sqrt[3]{\frac{21x^2}{12x}} = \sqrt[3]{\frac{7x}{4}}$$

To simplify, we see that $4 \cdot 2$ gives the perfect cube 8, so

$$\sqrt[3]{\frac{7x}{4}} = \sqrt[3]{\frac{7x}{4} \cdot \frac{2}{2}} = \sqrt[3]{\frac{14x}{8}} = \frac{\sqrt[3]{14x}}{\sqrt[3]{8}} = \frac{\sqrt[3]{14x}}{2}.$$

Thus, $\sqrt[3]{21x^2}/\sqrt[3]{12x} = \sqrt[3]{14x}/2$.

PROGRESS CHECK 7   Divide and simplify where possible. Assume $x > 0$.

a. $\dfrac{\sqrt[4]{405}}{\sqrt[4]{5}}$ **b.** $\dfrac{\sqrt{2}}{\sqrt{7}}$ **c.** $\dfrac{\sqrt[3]{4y^7}}{\sqrt[3]{18y^5}}$ ▪

In Example 7b the quotient $\sqrt{3}/\sqrt{10}$ led to a division that did not reduce. In this case it is easier to obtain an equivalent fraction that eliminates the radical in the denominator by multiplying by 1 in the form $\sqrt{10}/\sqrt{10}$, as shown next.

$$\frac{\sqrt{3}}{\sqrt{10}} = \frac{\sqrt{3}}{\sqrt{10}} \cdot \frac{\sqrt{10}}{\sqrt{10}} = \frac{\sqrt{30}}{\sqrt{100}} = \frac{\sqrt{30}}{10}$$

The process of obtaining a radical-free denominator is called **rationalizing the denominator.** The method above is also used to rationalize the denominator when the numerator does not contain a radical. And as a final condition we adopt the requirement that a simplified radical expression cannot have radicals in the denominator.

EXAMPLE 8 Rationalizing the Denominator

Rationalize each denominator. Assume $x > 0$.

a. $\dfrac{5}{\sqrt{3}}$ 　　b. $\dfrac{6}{\sqrt{20}}$ 　　c. $\dfrac{\sqrt{6}}{\sqrt{7x}}$ 　　d. $\dfrac{2}{\sqrt[3]{3}}$

Solution

a. $\dfrac{5}{\sqrt{3}} = \dfrac{5}{\sqrt{3}} \cdot \dfrac{\sqrt{3}}{\sqrt{3}} = \dfrac{5\sqrt{3}}{\sqrt{9}} = \dfrac{5\sqrt{3}}{3}$

b. $\dfrac{6}{\sqrt{20}} = \dfrac{6}{\sqrt{20}} \cdot \dfrac{\sqrt{5}}{\sqrt{5}} = \dfrac{6\sqrt{5}}{\sqrt{100}} = \dfrac{6\sqrt{5}}{10} = \dfrac{3\sqrt{5}}{5}$

c. $\dfrac{\sqrt{6}}{\sqrt{7x}} = \dfrac{\sqrt{6}}{\sqrt{7x}} \cdot \dfrac{\sqrt{7x}}{\sqrt{7x}} = \dfrac{\sqrt{42x}}{\sqrt{49x^2}} = \dfrac{\sqrt{42x}}{7x}$

d. $\dfrac{2}{\sqrt[3]{3}} = \dfrac{2}{\sqrt[3]{3}} \cdot \dfrac{\sqrt[3]{9}}{\sqrt[3]{9}} = \dfrac{2\sqrt[3]{9}}{\sqrt[3]{27}} = \dfrac{2\sqrt[3]{9}}{3}$

PROGRESS CHECK 8 Rationalize each denominator. Assume $x > 0$, $y > 0$.

a. $\dfrac{1}{\sqrt{2}}$ 　　b. $\dfrac{\sqrt{x}}{\sqrt{y}}$ 　　c. $\dfrac{8}{\sqrt{12}}$ 　　d. $\dfrac{7}{\sqrt[3]{25}}$ 　　■

In summary, note that the following conditions have been given in this section for writing a simplified radical.

Simplified Radical

To write a radical in simplified form:
1. Remove all factors of the radicand whose indicated root can be taken exactly.
2. Write the radical so that the index is as small as possible.
3. Eliminate all fractions in the radicand and all radicals in the denominator (which is called rationalizing the denominator).

EXERCISES 6.2

In Exercises 1–62, simplify each radical. Assume $x > 0$, $y > 0$.

1. $\sqrt{28}$
2. $\sqrt{54}$
3. $\sqrt{147}$
4. $\sqrt{99}$
5. $\sqrt{72}$
6. $\sqrt{405}$
7. $\sqrt[3]{40}$
8. $\sqrt[3]{108}$
9. $\sqrt[3]{375}$
10. $\sqrt[3]{128}$
11. $\sqrt[4]{243}$
12. $\sqrt[4]{96}$
13. $\sqrt[4]{4^6}$
14. $\sqrt{5^4}$
15. $\sqrt{x^4}$
16. $\sqrt{y^8}$
17. $\sqrt[3]{9^6}$
18. $\sqrt[3]{2^9}$
19. $\sqrt[3]{14^3}$
20. $\sqrt[4]{13^4}$
21. $\sqrt[3]{y^9}$
22. $\sqrt[3]{x^{12}}$

23. $\sqrt[8]{x^2}$

24. $\sqrt[12]{y^2}$

25. $\sqrt[12]{y^{10}}$

26. $\sqrt[10]{x^4}$

27. $\sqrt{x^7}$

28. $\sqrt{y^5}$

29. $\sqrt{72y^3}$

30. $\sqrt{243x^{11}}$

31. $\sqrt[3]{y^{11}}$

32. $\sqrt[3]{x^{16}}$

33. $\sqrt{x^4y^9}$

34. $\sqrt{x^3y^6}$

35. $\sqrt{32x^2y^2}$

36. $\sqrt{147x^4y^6}$

37. $\sqrt{40x^5y^6}$

38. $\sqrt{48x^8y^9}$

39. $\sqrt{98x^3y^5}$

40. $\sqrt{162x^{11}y^9}$

41. $\sqrt[3]{24x^3y}$

42. $\sqrt[3]{108x^9y^7}$

43. $\sqrt[3]{81x^5y^4}$

44. $\sqrt[3]{125x^{11}y^7}$

45. $\sqrt[4]{x^{11}y^5}$

46. $\sqrt[5]{x^7y^{12}}$

47. $\sqrt{\dfrac{16}{121}}$

48. $\sqrt{\dfrac{36}{81}}$

49. $\sqrt{\dfrac{32}{49}}$

50. $\sqrt{\dfrac{147}{25}}$

51. $\sqrt{\dfrac{36}{7}}$

52. $\sqrt{\dfrac{9}{13}}$

53. $\sqrt[3]{\dfrac{2}{3}}$

54. $\sqrt[3]{\dfrac{3}{4}}$

55. $\sqrt{\dfrac{49}{y}}$

56. $\sqrt{\dfrac{121}{x}}$

57. $\sqrt{\dfrac{24}{x}}$

58. $\sqrt{\dfrac{50}{y}}$

59. $\sqrt[3]{\dfrac{3}{4y}}$

60. $\sqrt[3]{\dfrac{2}{25x^2}}$

61. $\sqrt[3]{\dfrac{7}{108y^2}}$

62. $\sqrt[3]{\dfrac{15}{32x}}$

63. In simplified radical form, what is the period of a pendulum that is 16 ft long? Approximate the answer to the nearest hundredth of a second. Use the formula from Example 5.

64. In simplified radical form, what is the period of a pendulum that is 9 ft long? Approximate the answer to the nearest hundredth of a second. Use the formula from Example 5.

65. When a piano string is struck, it vibrates at a certain frequency, which gives it its particular sound. Higher frequencies correspond to higher-pitched tones. The frequency f depends on the length of the string L, the tension in the string T, and the mass of the string m, as given by

$$f = \frac{1}{2L}\sqrt{\frac{T}{m}}.$$

Find the frequency when $L = 0.5$ m, $T = 400$ newtons, and $m = 10^{-6}$ kg. With these units the frequency is expressed in cycles per second.

66. Repeat Exercise 65, but change the length of the string to 2 m.

In Exercises 67–82, multiply and simplify where possible. Assume $x \geq 0$, $y \geq 0$.

67. $\sqrt{3} \cdot \sqrt{27}$

68. $\sqrt{20} \cdot \sqrt{5}$

69. $2\sqrt{3} \cdot 5\sqrt{2}$

70. $7\sqrt{2} \cdot 2\sqrt{5}$

71. $\sqrt{14} \cdot \sqrt{2}$

72. $\sqrt{6} \cdot \sqrt{30}$

73. $\sqrt{63} \cdot \sqrt{9}$

74. $\sqrt{8} \cdot \sqrt{24}$

75. $3\sqrt[3]{4} \cdot 2\sqrt[3]{6}$

76. $5\sqrt[3]{3} \cdot 6\sqrt[3]{18}$

77. $6\sqrt[4]{9} \cdot 4\sqrt[4]{27}$

78. $7\sqrt[4]{8} \cdot 3\sqrt[4]{4}$

79. $3\sqrt{8x^3y} \cdot 2\sqrt{5x^2y}$

80. $4\sqrt{2xy^3} \cdot \sqrt{8x^3y^4}$

81. $\sqrt[4]{6x^3y^2} \cdot \sqrt[4]{8x^2y^5}$

82. $\sqrt[3]{27x^3y} \cdot \sqrt[3]{9x^3y^4}$

In Exercises 83–102, divide and simplify where possible. Assume $x > 0$, $y > 0$.

83. $\dfrac{\sqrt{56}}{\sqrt{14}}$

84. $\dfrac{\sqrt{250}}{\sqrt{10}}$

85. $\dfrac{\sqrt[3]{88}}{\sqrt[3]{11}}$

86. $\dfrac{\sqrt[3]{135}}{\sqrt[3]{5}}$

87. $\dfrac{\sqrt[4]{192}}{\sqrt[4]{6}}$

88. $\dfrac{\sqrt[4]{256}}{\sqrt[4]{2}}$

89. $\dfrac{\sqrt{2}}{\sqrt{11}}$

90. $\dfrac{\sqrt{5}}{\sqrt{26}}$

91. $\dfrac{\sqrt[3]{32}}{\sqrt[3]{6}}$

92. $\dfrac{\sqrt[3]{108}}{\sqrt[3]{8}}$

93. $\dfrac{\sqrt{2x}}{\sqrt{5x}}$

94. $\dfrac{\sqrt{5x^3}}{\sqrt{2x}}$

95. $\dfrac{\sqrt{27y^2}}{\sqrt{6y}}$

96. $\dfrac{\sqrt{25y^5}}{\sqrt{15y^4}}$

97. $\dfrac{\sqrt[3]{3x^4}}{\sqrt[3]{4x^2}}$

98. $\dfrac{\sqrt[3]{6y^6}}{\sqrt[3]{49y^4}}$

99. $\dfrac{\sqrt{64x^2y^3}}{\sqrt{10x^2y^2}}$

100. $\dfrac{\sqrt{56x^8y^4}}{\sqrt{6x^7y^3}}$

101. $\dfrac{\sqrt[4]{45x^5}}{\sqrt[4]{8x^2}}$

102. $\dfrac{\sqrt[4]{7y^9}}{\sqrt[4]{125y^6}}$

In Exercises 103–122, rationalize each denominator. Assume $x > 0$, $y > 0$.

103. $\dfrac{7}{\sqrt{7}}$

104. $\dfrac{3}{\sqrt{3}}$

105. $\dfrac{12}{\sqrt{y}}$

106. $\dfrac{14}{\sqrt{x}}$

107. $\dfrac{\sqrt{3}}{\sqrt{2}}$

108. $\dfrac{\sqrt{5}}{\sqrt{3}}$

109. $\dfrac{4}{\sqrt{32}}$

110. $\dfrac{6}{\sqrt{27}}$

111. $\dfrac{\sqrt{3}}{\sqrt{2y}}$

112. $\dfrac{\sqrt{5}}{\sqrt{3x}}$

113. $\dfrac{\sqrt{10}}{\sqrt{5y}}$

114. $\dfrac{\sqrt{18}}{\sqrt{6x}}$

115. $\dfrac{\sqrt{2}}{\sqrt{98x}}$

116. $\dfrac{\sqrt{6}}{\sqrt{24y}}$

117. $\dfrac{3}{\sqrt[3]{49}}$

118. $\dfrac{4}{\sqrt[3]{9}}$

119. $\dfrac{5}{\sqrt[4]{4}}$

120. $\dfrac{6}{\sqrt[4]{9}}$

121. $\dfrac{6}{\sqrt{45y}}$ **122.** $\dfrac{4}{\sqrt{28x}}$

123. a. Find the solution set for $x = \sqrt{16}$.

    b. Find the solution set for $x^2 = 16$.

    c. Are your answers to parts **a** and **b** the same?

124. a. Find the solution set for $x = \sqrt[3]{8}$.

    b. Find the solution set for $x^3 = 8$.

    c. Are your answers to parts **a** and **b** the same?

125. Consider (i) $\sqrt{7^2}$ and (ii) $\left(\sqrt{7}\right)^2$.

    a. How do these two expressions compare in order of operations?

    b. How do these two expressions compare in value?

126. Compare (i) $\sqrt[3]{(-5)^3}$ and (ii) $\left(\sqrt[3]{-5}\right)^3$ in terms of value.

127. Prove $\sqrt[n]{\dfrac{a}{b}} = \dfrac{\sqrt[n]{a}}{\sqrt[n]{b}}\,(b \neq 0)$.

(*Hint:* The quotient property may be proved by converting between radical form and exponential form and using the quotient-to-a-power property of exponents.)

THINK ABOUT IT 6.2

1. It is easy to show that $\sqrt[3]{-8} \times \sqrt[3]{-8}$ equals $\sqrt[3]{(-8)(-8)}$. Do this. In contrast, it is not possible to show (unless you know about imaginary numbers) whether $\sqrt{-8} \times \sqrt{-8}$ is equal to $\sqrt{(-8)(-8)}$. What is the difficulty with the second problem?

2. The formula for the period of a pendulum as illustrated in Example 5 is $T = 2\pi\sqrt{\dfrac{\ell}{32}}$. The formula shows how the period depends on the length.

    a. Does the period increase or decrease if you make the pendulum longer?

b. Explain why the period does not double when you double the length.

c. The 32 in the formula represents the force of gravity near the surface of the earth. On the moon the force of gravity would be less than 32. If you moved a pendulum from the earth to the moon, would its period be longer or shorter there?

3. The length (L) of the edge of a regular hexagon can be found from the area (A) by $L = \sqrt{\dfrac{2A}{3\sqrt{3}}}$. Rewrite this formula by relationalizing the denominator, then find L when $A = 6\sqrt{3}$.

4. The length (L) of the edge of a regular pentagon can be found from the area (A) by $L = \dfrac{2\sqrt{A \tan 36°}}{\sqrt{5}}$. Rewrite this formula by relationalizing the denominator, then find L to the nearest hundredth when $A = 16$.

5. An important concept in statistics is that for a random survey the margin of error (e) is inversely proportional to the square root of the sample size (n).

    a. Write a variation equation for this relation.

    b. Rewrite this formula after rationalizing the denominator.

    c. If the error is 3% when $n = 900$, find k, then find the error when $n = 2500$.

6.3   Addition and Subtraction of Radicals

If a beam emerging from a laser travels as shown in the diagram, find the distance traveled by this beam in simplest radical form. (See Example 3.)

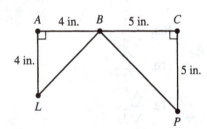

OBJECTIVES

1   Add and subtract radicals by using the distributive property.

2   Add and subtract radicals that involve rationalizing denominators.

We have seen that to add or subtract algebraic expressions, we combine like terms using the distributive property. For instance,

$$5x + 3x - x = (5 + 3 - 1)x = 7x.$$

Similarly, if x is replaced by $\sqrt{3}$,

$$5\sqrt{3} + 3\sqrt{3} - \sqrt{3} = (5 + 3 - 1)\sqrt{3} = 7\sqrt{3},$$

or if x is replaced by $\sqrt[3]{2x}$,

$$5\sqrt[3]{2x} + 3\sqrt[3]{2x} - \sqrt[3]{2x} = (5 + 3 - 1)\sqrt[3]{2x} = 7\sqrt[3]{2x}.$$

Thus, to add or subtract radicals, we combine like radicals using the distributive property. By definition, **like radicals** are radicals that have the same radicand and the same index. Note that only like radicals may be combined.

EXAMPLE 1   Adding and Subtracting Like Radicals

Simplify where possible. Assume $x > 0$, $y > 0$.

a. $\sqrt{11} + 14\sqrt{11}$ **b.** $\sqrt{7} + \sqrt{3}$ **c.** $4\sqrt[3]{5} - 6\sqrt[3]{5}$
d. $x\sqrt{xy} + 9\sqrt{xy}$ **e.** $\sqrt{3} + \sqrt[3]{3}$

Solution   Use the distribution property (where possible) and simplify.

a. $\sqrt{11} + 14\sqrt{11} = (1 + 14)\sqrt{11} = 15\sqrt{11}$

b. $\sqrt{7}$ and $\sqrt{3}$ are not like radicals, because the radicands are different, and $\sqrt{7} + \sqrt{3}$ does not simplify.

c. $4\sqrt[3]{5} - 6\sqrt[3]{5} = (4 - 6)\sqrt[3]{5} = -2\sqrt[3]{5}$

d. $x\sqrt{xy} + 9\sqrt{xy} = (x + 9)\sqrt{xy}$

e. $\sqrt{3}$ and $\sqrt[3]{3}$ are not like radicals, because the indexes are different, and $\sqrt{3} + \sqrt[3]{3}$ does not simplify.

Caution   Although $\sqrt[n]{a} \cdot \sqrt[n]{b} = \sqrt[n]{ab}$ and $\sqrt[n]{a}/\sqrt[n]{b} = \sqrt[n]{a/b}$ are properties of radicals, note that

$$\sqrt[n]{a} + \sqrt[n]{b} \qquad \text{does not equal} \qquad \sqrt[n]{a + b},$$

except for certain instances. For example,

$$\sqrt{16} + \sqrt{9} = 4 + 3 = 7, \qquad \text{while} \qquad \sqrt{16 + 9} = \sqrt{25} = 5,$$

so $\sqrt{16} + \sqrt{9} \neq \sqrt{16 + 9}$.

PROGRESS CHECK 1   Simplify where possible. Assume $x > 0$, $y > 0$.

a. $7\sqrt{5} - 19\sqrt{5}$ **b.** $8\sqrt[4]{2} + \sqrt[4]{2}$ **c.** $\sqrt[3]{x} + \sqrt[4]{x}$
d. $x\sqrt{y} + x\sqrt{y}$ **e.** $y\sqrt{x} + x\sqrt{y}$ ■

Sometimes, simplifying radicals in a sum or difference results in like radicals, which can then be combined.

EXAMPLE 2   Simplifying Radical Sums or Differences

Simplify where possible. Assume $x > 0$, $y > 0$.

a. $\sqrt{40} + \sqrt{90}$ **b.** $\sqrt[3]{-16} + \sqrt[3]{250}$ **c.** $2\sqrt{27x^2y} - 5\sqrt{12x^2y}$

Solution

a. First, simplify each square root.

$$\sqrt{40} = \sqrt{4 \cdot 10} = \sqrt{4} \cdot \sqrt{10} = 2\sqrt{10}$$
$$\sqrt{90} = \sqrt{9 \cdot 10} = \sqrt{9} \cdot \sqrt{10} = 3\sqrt{10}$$

Then, $\sqrt{40} + \sqrt{90} = 2\sqrt{10} + 3\sqrt{10} = (2 + 3)\sqrt{10} = 5\sqrt{10}.$

b. First, simplify each cube root.

$$\sqrt[3]{-16} = \sqrt[3]{-8 \cdot 2} = \sqrt[3]{-8} \cdot \sqrt[3]{2} = -2\sqrt[3]{2}$$
$$\sqrt[3]{250} = \sqrt[3]{125 \cdot 2} = \sqrt[3]{125} \cdot \sqrt[3]{2} = 5\sqrt[3]{2}$$

Then, $\sqrt[3]{-16} + \sqrt[3]{250} = -2\sqrt[3]{2} + 5\sqrt[3]{2} = (-2 + 5)\sqrt[3]{2} = 3\sqrt[3]{2}$.

c. Simplify each radical, and then combine like radicals.

$$2\sqrt{27x^2 y} - 5\sqrt{12x^2 y} = 2\sqrt{9x^2} \cdot \sqrt{3y} - 5\sqrt{4x^2} \cdot \sqrt{3y}$$
$$= 2 \cdot 3x\sqrt{3y} - 5 \cdot 2x\sqrt{3y}$$
$$= 6x\sqrt{3y} - 10x\sqrt{3y}$$
$$= (6x - 10x)\sqrt{3y}$$
$$= -4x\sqrt{3y}$$

PROGRESS CHECK 2   Simplify where possible. Assume $x > 0$, $y > 0$.

a. $\sqrt{80} + \sqrt{45}$ **b.** $\sqrt[3]{-54} - \sqrt[3]{128}$ **c.** $y\sqrt{63x^2 y} + x\sqrt{28y^3}$ ■

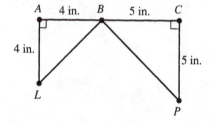

Figure 6.3

EXAMPLE 3   Distance Traveled by a Laser Beam

Solve the problem in the section introduction on page 328.

Solution   Consider the sketch of the problem in Figure 6.3. Using the Pythagorean relation in right triangles LAB and PCB gives

$$(LB)^2 = 4^2 + 4^2 \qquad \text{and} \qquad (PB)^2 = 5^2 + 5^2.$$
$$(LB)^2 = 32 \qquad\qquad\qquad\qquad (PB)^2 = 50$$
$$LB = \sqrt{32} \qquad\qquad\qquad\qquad PB = \sqrt{50}$$

The total distance $LB + PB$ is then

$$\sqrt{32} + \sqrt{50} = \sqrt{16}\sqrt{2} + \sqrt{25}\sqrt{2}$$
$$= 4\sqrt{2} + 5\sqrt{2}$$
$$= 9\sqrt{2}.$$

Thus, the beam from the laser travels $9\sqrt{2}$ in. Check by calculator that this distance is about 12.7 in.

PROGRESS CHECK 3   Redo Example 3 but assume that $LA = 10$, $AB = 5$, $CB = 4$, and $PC = 8$ cm.   ■

EXAMPLE 4   Testing for Identical Expressions with a Grapher

A common student error is to rewrite $\sqrt{x} + \sqrt{x}$ as $\sqrt{2x}$. Show that these two expressions are not identical by showing that the graphs of $y = \sqrt{x} + \sqrt{x}$ and $y = \sqrt{2x}$ are different. Use the graphs to find all values of x for which the expressions are equal.

Solution   The two functions are graphed in Figure 6.4 using a viewing window that takes into account that the domain for both functions is $x \geq 0$ and that the square root function grows slowly. It is apparent that the two graphs are different, so the expressions are not identical. We can also see that the two graphs intersect only at the origin, so that $\sqrt{x} + \sqrt{x} = \sqrt{2x}$ is true only when $x = 0$.

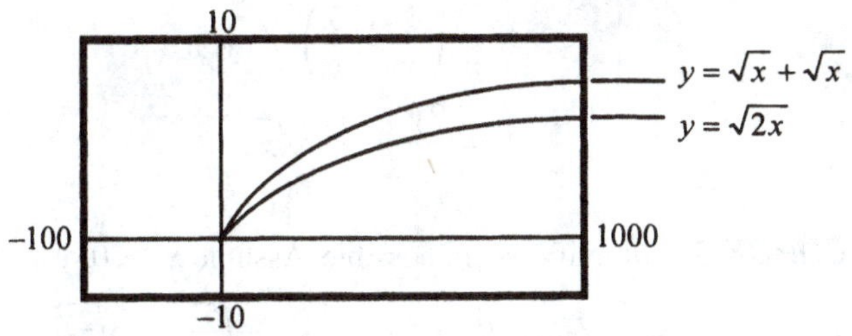

Figure 6.4

PROGRESS CHECK 4   A common student error is to rewrite $\sqrt{x^2 + 9}$ as $x + 3$. Show that these two expressions are not identical by showing that the graphs of $y = \sqrt{x^2 + 9}$ and $y = x + 3$ are different. Use the graphs to find all values of x for which the expressions are equal.   ■

Rationalizing denominators may also simplify radical expressions to a form that is more useful in addition and subtraction problems, as shown next.

EXAMPLE 5   Rationalizing Denominators to Obtain Like Radicals

Simplify where possible. Assume $x > 0$, $y > 0$.

a. $\sqrt{56} + \dfrac{1}{2}\sqrt{\dfrac{2}{7}}$ **b.** $\sqrt{3} + \dfrac{2}{\sqrt{3}}$ **c.** $2\sqrt{\dfrac{y}{x}} - 3\sqrt{\dfrac{x}{y}}$

Solution

a. First, simplify.

$$\sqrt{56} = \sqrt{4 \cdot 14} = \sqrt{4}\sqrt{14} = 2\sqrt{14}$$

$$\frac{1}{2}\sqrt{\frac{2}{7}} = \frac{1}{2}\sqrt{\frac{2 \cdot 7}{7 \cdot 7}} = \frac{1}{2}\frac{\sqrt{14}}{\sqrt{49}} = \frac{1}{2}\frac{\sqrt{14}}{7} = \frac{1}{14}\sqrt{14}$$

Then,

$$\sqrt{56} + \frac{1}{2}\sqrt{\frac{2}{7}} = 2\sqrt{14} + \frac{1}{14}\sqrt{14} = \left(2 + \frac{1}{14}\right)\sqrt{14} = \frac{29}{14}\sqrt{14}.$$

b. Rationalizing the denominator in $2/\sqrt{3}$ gives

$$\frac{2}{\sqrt{3}} = \frac{2}{\sqrt{3}} \cdot \frac{\sqrt{3}}{\sqrt{3}} = \frac{2\sqrt{3}}{3}.$$

Then,

$$\sqrt{3} + \frac{2}{\sqrt{3}} = \sqrt{3} + \frac{2\sqrt{3}}{3} = \left(1 + \frac{2}{3}\right)\sqrt{3} = \frac{5}{3}\sqrt{3}.$$

c. Simplify each radical, and then combine like radicals.

$$2\sqrt{\frac{y}{x}} - 3\sqrt{\frac{x}{y}} = 2\sqrt{\frac{y}{x} \cdot \frac{x}{x}} - 3\sqrt{\frac{x}{y} \cdot \frac{y}{y}}$$

$$= 2\sqrt{\frac{xy}{x^2}} - 3\sqrt{\frac{xy}{y^2}}$$

$$= 2\frac{\sqrt{xy}}{x} - 3\frac{\sqrt{xy}}{y}$$

$$= \left(\frac{2}{x} - \frac{3}{y}\right)\sqrt{xy}$$

$$= \frac{2y - 3x}{xy}\sqrt{xy}$$

PROGRESS CHECK 5   Simplify where possible. Assume $x > 0$, $y > 0$.

a. $\sqrt{75} - \dfrac{1}{5}\sqrt{\dfrac{1}{3}}$ **b.** $\sqrt{2} + \dfrac{1}{\sqrt{2}}$ **c.** $\sqrt{\dfrac{2x}{y}} - \sqrt{\dfrac{2y}{x}}$ ■

EXERCISES 6.3

In Exercises 1–32, simplify where possible. Assume $x > 0$, $y > 0$.

1. $2\sqrt{5} + 4\sqrt{5}$
2. $3\sqrt{7} + 8\sqrt{7}$
3. $6\sqrt[3]{17} + 3\sqrt[3]{17}$
4. $7\sqrt[3]{21} + 3\sqrt[3]{21}$
5. $\sqrt{6} + 8\sqrt{6}$
6. $\sqrt{15} + 7\sqrt{15}$
7. $9\sqrt{13} + \sqrt{13}$
8. $12\sqrt{2} + \sqrt{2}$
9. $6\sqrt{6} - 3\sqrt{6}$
10. $10\sqrt{19} - 4\sqrt{19}$
11. $12\sqrt{10} - 20\sqrt{10}$
12. $5\sqrt{23} - 72\sqrt{23}$
13. $\sqrt[4]{2} - 9\sqrt[4]{2}$
14. $12\sqrt[4]{6} - 18\sqrt[4]{6}$
15. $3\sqrt{2} + 2\sqrt{3}$
16. $5\sqrt{8} + 8\sqrt{5}$
17. $\sqrt{14} + \sqrt{15}$
18. $\sqrt{11} + \sqrt{17}$
19. $\sqrt{14} + \sqrt[3]{14}$
20. $\sqrt[4]{125} + \sqrt[3]{125}$
21. $4\sqrt{x} + y\sqrt{x}$
22. $x\sqrt{3} + 7\sqrt{3}$
23. $15\sqrt{13} - x\sqrt{13}$
24. $20\sqrt{10} - y\sqrt{10}$
25. $\sqrt[4]{7} + 5\sqrt[4]{7}$
26. $\sqrt[3]{12} + 7\sqrt[3]{12}$
27. $5\sqrt{x} + 5\sqrt{x}$
28. $6\sqrt{y} + 8\sqrt{y}$
29. $2y\sqrt{x} + y\sqrt{x}$
30. $23x\sqrt{y} + x\sqrt{y}$
31. $\sqrt[4]{3xy} + \sqrt[4]{3xy}$
32. $\sqrt{2y} - \sqrt{2y}$

In Exercises 33–54, simplify where possible. Assume $x > 0$, $y > 0$.

33. $3\sqrt{2} + \sqrt{8}$
34. $\sqrt{128} + 4\sqrt{2}$
35. $\sqrt{75} + \sqrt{12}$
36. $\sqrt{18} + \sqrt{50}$
37. $\sqrt{32} + \sqrt{98}$
38. $\sqrt{500} + \sqrt{180}$
39. $\sqrt{48} - \sqrt{27}$
40. $-\sqrt{108} + \sqrt{192}$
41. $-3\sqrt[3]{3} + \sqrt[3]{81}$
42. $-\sqrt[3]{3} + \sqrt[3]{24}$
43. $\sqrt[3]{-192} + 3\sqrt[3]{81}$
44. $\sqrt[3]{-375} + \sqrt[3]{81}$
45. $-\sqrt[3]{54} - 2\sqrt[3]{16}$
46. $-\sqrt[3]{128} - \sqrt[3]{432}$
47. $\sqrt{24xy^2} + y\sqrt{54x}$
48. $\sqrt{98xy^2} + \sqrt{50xy^2}$
49. $-\sqrt{49x^3y} + \sqrt{16x^3y}$
50. $-y\sqrt{75x} + \sqrt{12y^2x}$
51. $y\sqrt{27x^3} + x\sqrt{48y^2x}$
52. $\sqrt{40x^2y^3} + xy\sqrt{250y}$
53. $\sqrt{18x} - \sqrt{72xy^2}$
54. $\sqrt{180y} - \sqrt{80x^2y}$

In Exercises 55–60, give exact answers using radicals in simplest form.

55. If a beam emerging from a laser travels as shown in the diagram, find the distance traveled by the beam in simplified radical form.

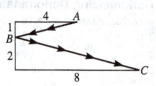

56. If a beam emerging from a laser travels as shown in the diagram, find the distance traveled by the beam in simplified radical form.

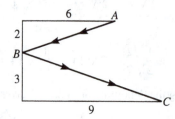

57. Square $ABCD$ is inscribed in a larger square as shown.
   a. Find the perimeter of $ABCD$.
   b. Find the area of $ABCD$.

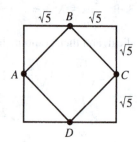

58. Square $ABCD$ is inscribed in a larger square as shown. The side of the large square is 4.

   a. Find the perimeter of $ABCD$.

   b. Find the area of $ABCD$.

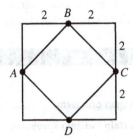

59. Use the triangle pictured.

   a. Find the hypotenuse of the small triangle.

   b. Find the hypotenuse of the large triangle.

   c. Find the length of the piece marked x.

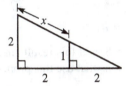

60. Use the triangle pictured.

   a. Find the hypotenuse of the small triangle.

   b. Find the hypotenuse of the large triangle.

   c. Find the length of the piece marked x.

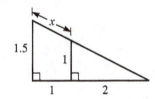

In Exercises 61–80, simplify when possible. Assume $x > 0, y > 0$.

61. $4\sqrt{50} + 6\sqrt{\frac{1}{2}}$

62. $\frac{1}{2}\sqrt{24} - \frac{12}{\sqrt{6}}$

63. $\frac{2}{3}\sqrt{6} - \frac{8}{\sqrt{6}}$

64. $5\sqrt{54} - \frac{6}{\sqrt{6}}$

65. $\frac{\sqrt{32}}{12} + \frac{2}{\sqrt{8}}$

66. $\frac{3}{\sqrt{5}} + 2\sqrt{45}$

67. $\sqrt{12} + \frac{1}{\sqrt{3}}$

68. $\frac{3}{2}\sqrt{80} + \frac{1}{\sqrt{5}}$

69. $\sqrt{\frac{5}{8}} + \sqrt{\frac{5}{2}}$

70. $\sqrt{\frac{4}{3}} + \sqrt{\frac{50}{6}}$

71. $\sqrt{\frac{2}{3}} - 3\sqrt{\frac{3}{2}}$

72. $\sqrt{\frac{3}{4}} - 3\sqrt{\frac{1}{3}}$

73. $-\frac{4}{\sqrt{3}} + \frac{2\sqrt{3}}{5}$

74. $4\sqrt{\frac{2}{3}} - \frac{3\sqrt{3}}{2\sqrt{2}}$

75. $3\sqrt{\frac{1}{6}} - \frac{\sqrt{150}}{2}$

76. $\frac{2}{3}\sqrt{108} - 4\sqrt{\frac{3}{4}}$

77. $x\sqrt{48x} - 12x\sqrt{\frac{x}{3}}$

78. $\sqrt{50y} - \sqrt{\frac{y}{2}}$

79. $3\sqrt{\frac{x}{y}} + 4\sqrt{\frac{y}{x}}$

80. $\sqrt{\frac{3x}{y}} - \sqrt{\frac{3y}{x}}$

81. If $f(x) = \sqrt{x + x^2}$ and $g(x) = \sqrt{x^2 - x}$ find $f(2) + g(3)$ and simplify.

82. If $f(x) = \sqrt{x + x^2}$ and $g(x) = \sqrt{x^2 - x}$ find $3f(2) - g(3)$ and simplify.

THINK ABOUT IT 6.3

1. Write each expression as a single fraction in simplest form.

   a. $600\sqrt{5} + \dfrac{360,000}{120\sqrt{5}}$

   b. $\dfrac{-b + \sqrt{b^2 - 4ac}}{2a} + \dfrac{-b - \sqrt{b^2 - 4ac}}{2a}$

2. By finding the lengths of AB, BC, and AC show that the points $A(-2, -6)$, $B(0, -2)$, and $C(1, 0)$ lie on a straight line.

3. If $\theta = 30°$, the value of $\tan 2\theta + \cot 2\theta$ is

   a. $2\sqrt{3}/3$ **b.** $(\sqrt{3} + 3)/3$

   c. $(1 + \sqrt{3})/3$ **d.** $4\sqrt{3}/3$

4. a. Using the figure, find the perimeter and area of the inscribed square.

   b. Find the area of the larger square, and then explain (using the result from part **a**) why $(a + b)^2$ does not equal $a^2 + b^2$.

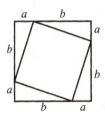

5. Write as a single fraction, and rationalize the denominator.

   a. $1 + \dfrac{1}{\sqrt{x}}$

   b. $1 + \dfrac{1}{\sqrt[3]{x}}$

   c. $1 + \dfrac{1}{\sqrt[n]{x}}$

Courtesy of PhotoDisc/Getty Images.

6.4 Further Radical Simplification

The design for a rectangular solar panel specifies that the area is to be 6 m^2 and the length is to be 2 m greater than the width. Verify that a rectangular panel that measures $\sqrt{7} + 1$ m by $\sqrt{7} - 1$ m satisfies these specifications. (See Example 4.)

OBJECTIVES

1. Use $(\sqrt[n]{a})^n = a$.

2. Multiply radical expressions involving more than one term.

3. Use a special product formula to multiply certain radical expressions.

4. Divide radical expressions involving more than one term in the numerator and a single term in the denominator.

5. Use a conjugate to rationalize a denominator.

A property that is used often when simplifying radicals stems from the definition of $\sqrt[n]{a}$ and states

$$(\sqrt[n]{a})^n = a$$

if $\sqrt[n]{a}$ is a real number. For instance, $(\sqrt[3]{8})^3 = 8$, and this result checks, since $\sqrt[3]{8} = 2$ and $2^3 = 8$. Example 1 shows some simplifications that use this property.

EXAMPLE 1   Using $(\sqrt[n]{a})^n = a$.
Simplify each radical.

a. $(7\sqrt{5})^2$ **b.** $\sqrt{41} \cdot \sqrt{41}$ **c.** $(\sqrt[3]{x^2 - 5})^3$ **d.** $(4\sqrt{3x})^2, x \geq 0$

Solution
a. $(7\sqrt{5})^2 = 7^2(\sqrt{5})^2 = 49 \cdot 5 = 245$
b. $\sqrt{41} \cdot \sqrt{41} = (\sqrt{41})^2 = 41$
c. $(\sqrt[3]{x^2 - 5})^3 = x^2 - 5$
d. $(4\sqrt{3x})^2 = 4^2(\sqrt{3x})^2 = 16 \cdot 3x = 48x$

PROGRESS CHECK 1   Simplify each radical.

a. $(-3\sqrt{2})^2$ **b.** $(\sqrt[3]{4x - 1})^3$ **c.** $2\sqrt{19} \cdot \sqrt{19}$ **d.** $(6\sqrt{10y})^2, y \geq 0$ ■

When a product involves a radical expression with more than one term, then we apply the distributive property, as shown in Example 2.

EXAMPLE 2   Multiplying Radical Expressions with More Than One Term
Simplify each expression.

a. $\sqrt{3}(\sqrt{6} - \sqrt{3})$ **b.** $(\sqrt{7} + \sqrt{2})(\sqrt{7} - \sqrt{2})$ **c.** $(\sqrt[3]{x} + 2)(\sqrt[3]{x} + 5)$

Solution
a. First, multiply.

$$\sqrt{3}(\sqrt{6} - \sqrt{3}) = \sqrt{3} \cdot \sqrt{6} - \sqrt{3} \cdot \sqrt{3} \qquad \text{Distributive property.}$$
$$= \sqrt{18} - 3$$

Now simplify. Since $\sqrt{18} = \sqrt{9} \cdot \sqrt{2} = 3\sqrt{2}$,

$$\sqrt{3}(\sqrt{6} - \sqrt{3}) = 3\sqrt{2} - 3.$$

b. Based on the distributive property, multiply each term of $\sqrt{7} + \sqrt{2}$ by each term of $\sqrt{7} - \sqrt{2}$, and then simplify.

$$(\sqrt{7} + \sqrt{2})(\sqrt{7} - \sqrt{2}) = \sqrt{7} \cdot \sqrt{7} + \sqrt{7}(-\sqrt{2}) + \sqrt{2} \cdot \sqrt{7} + \sqrt{2}(-\sqrt{2})$$
$$= 7 - \sqrt{14} + \sqrt{14} - 2$$
$$= 5$$

c. In this multiplication, note that $5\sqrt[3]{x}$ and $2\sqrt[3]{x}$ are like radicals that should be combined.

$$(\sqrt[3]{x} + 2)(\sqrt[3]{x} + 5) = \sqrt[3]{x}\sqrt[3]{x} + \sqrt[3]{x} \cdot 5 + 2 \cdot \sqrt[3]{x} + 2 \cdot 5$$
$$= \sqrt[3]{x^2} + 7\sqrt[3]{x} + 10$$

PROGRESS CHECK 2   Simplify each expression.

a. $\sqrt{5}(\sqrt{10} - \sqrt{5})$ **b.** $(\sqrt{10} - \sqrt{3})(\sqrt{10} + \sqrt{3})$ **c.** $(\sqrt[5]{y} + 3)(\sqrt[5]{y} + 1)$ ■

The special product formulas from Section 1.4 are often used to simplify certain products involving square roots. For instance, the product in Example 2b may be found more easily by using

$$(a + b)(a - b) = a^2 - b^2,$$

with a replaced by $\sqrt{7}$ and b replaced by $\sqrt{2}$, to obtain

$$(\sqrt{7} + \sqrt{2})(\sqrt{7} - \sqrt{2}) = (\sqrt{7})^2 - (\sqrt{2})^2$$
$$= 7 - 2 = 5.$$

Other useful special product formulas from Section 1.4 are

$$(a + b)^2 = a^2 + 2ab + b^2$$
$$(a - b)^2 = a^2 - 2ab + b^2.$$

EXAMPLE 3   Using Special Product Formulas

Simplify each expression. Assume $x \geq 0$.

a. $(3\sqrt{x} - 4)^2$ **b.** $(5 + 2\sqrt{3})(5 - 2\sqrt{3})$

Solution

a. Replace a with $3\sqrt{x}$ and b with 4 in the formula for $(a - b)^2$.

$$(a - b)^2 = \quad a^2 \quad - \quad 2ab \quad + \quad b^2$$
$$(3\sqrt{x} - 4)^2 = (3\sqrt{x})^2 - 2(3\sqrt{x})(4) + (4)^2$$
$$= 9x - 24\sqrt{x} + 16$$

b. Use $(a + b)(a - b) = a^2 - b^2$ with $a = 5$ and $b = 2\sqrt{3}$.

$$(5 + 2\sqrt{3})(5 - 2\sqrt{3}) = (5)^2 - (2\sqrt{3})^2$$
$$= 25 - 12$$
$$= 13$$

PROGRESS CHECK 3   Simplify each expression. Assume $x \geq 0$.

a. $(2\sqrt{3} + 5)^2$ **b.** $(4 + \sqrt{x})(4 - \sqrt{x})$ ■

EXAMPLE 4 Finding the Area of a Solar Panel

Solve the problem in the section introduction on page 334.

Solution If the length is $\sqrt{7} + 1$ m and the width is $\sqrt{7} - 1$ m, then the length is 2 m greater than the width, since

$$(\sqrt{7} + 1) - (\sqrt{7} - 1) = 2.$$

We verify the area is 6 m^2 for the rectangular solar panel next.

$$A = \ell w = (\sqrt{7} + 1)(\sqrt{7} - 1) = (\sqrt{7})^2 - (1)^2 = 7 - 1 = 6$$

Thus, a panel with the given measurement satisfies both specifications.

PROGRESS CHECK 4 The design for a rectangular computer chip specifies that the area is to be 18 mm^2 and the length is to be 4 mm greater than the width. Verify that a rectangular computer chip that measures $\sqrt{22} + 2$ mm by $\sqrt{22} - 2$ mm satisfies these specifications. ■

Methods for simplifying quotients involving radical expressions that have more than one term in the numerator and a single term in the denominator are shown in the next example.

EXAMPLE 5 Simplifying Quotients with One Term in the Denominator

Simplify each expression. Assume $r > 0$.

a. $\dfrac{3 - 9\sqrt{2}}{6}$ **b.** $\dfrac{2 + \sqrt{r}}{\sqrt{r}}$

Solution

a. Factor out the common factor 3 in the numerator, and then simplify.

$$\frac{3 - 9\sqrt{2}}{6} = \frac{3(1 - 3\sqrt{2})}{6}$$

$$= \frac{1 - 3\sqrt{2}}{2}$$

b. Since $\sqrt{r} \cdot \sqrt{r} = r$ if $r > 0$, multiply by $\sqrt{r}/\sqrt{r}$ to rationalize the denominator.

$$\frac{2 + \sqrt{r}}{\sqrt{r}} = \frac{2 + \sqrt{r}}{\sqrt{r}} \cdot \frac{\sqrt{r}}{\sqrt{r}}$$

$$= \frac{2\sqrt{r} + r}{r}$$

PROGRESS CHECK 5 Simplify each expression. Assume $x > 0$.

a. $\dfrac{8 + 4\sqrt{3}}{12}$ **b.** $\dfrac{\sqrt{x} - 3}{\sqrt{x}}$ ■

To eliminate radicals in denominators that contain square roots and two terms, consider that for nonnegative a and b

$$(\sqrt{a} + \sqrt{b})(\sqrt{a} - \sqrt{b}) = (\sqrt{a})^2 - (\sqrt{b})^2 = a - b.$$

In general, the sum and the difference of the same two terms are called **conjugates** of each other. Binomial denominators involving square roots are rationalized by multiplying the numerator and the denominator by the conjugate of the denominator.

EXAMPLE 6   Rationalizing a Binomial Denominator

Rationalize the denominator of $\dfrac{8}{3 - \sqrt{5}}$.

Solution   The conjugate of $3 - \sqrt{5}$ is $3 + \sqrt{5}$. Then,

$$\frac{8}{3 - \sqrt{5}} = \frac{8}{3 - \sqrt{5}} \cdot \frac{3 + \sqrt{5}}{3 + \sqrt{5}}$$ Multiply using the conjugate of the denominator.

$$= \frac{8(3 + \sqrt{5})}{(3)^2 - (\sqrt{5})^2}$$ Multiply fractions, and use $(a + b)(a - b) = a^2 - b^2$.

$$= \frac{8(3 + \sqrt{5})}{4}$$ Simplify the denominator.

$$= 2(3 + \sqrt{5})$$ Express in lowest terms.

$$= 6 + 2\sqrt{5}.$$ Remove parentheses.

Note   To express the result in lowest terms, it is recommended that fractions be simplified where possible before removing parentheses in the numerator, as was done in this example.

PROGRESS CHECK 6   Rationalize the denominator of $\dfrac{10}{3 + \sqrt{7}}$.   ■

EXAMPLE 7   Rationalizing a Binomial Denominator

Rationalize the denominator of $\dfrac{x\sqrt{2x}}{x + \sqrt{2x}}$. Assume $x > 0$.

Solution   Multiply the numerator and the denominator by $x - \sqrt{2x}$, which is the conjugate of the denominator.

$$\frac{x\sqrt{2x}}{x + \sqrt{2x}} = \frac{x\sqrt{2x}}{x + \sqrt{2x}} \cdot \frac{x - \sqrt{2x}}{x - \sqrt{2x}}$$ Multiply using the conjugate of the denominator.

$$= \frac{x\sqrt{2x}(x - \sqrt{2x})}{(x)^2 - (\sqrt{2x})^2}$$ Multiply fractions, and use $(a + b)(a - b) = a^2 - b^2$.

$$= \frac{x\sqrt{2x}(x - \sqrt{2x})}{x^2 - 2x}$$ Simplify the denominator.

$$= \frac{x\sqrt{2x}(x - \sqrt{2x})}{x(x - 2)}$$ Factor the denominator.

$$= \frac{\sqrt{2x}(x - \sqrt{2x})}{x - 2}$$ Divide out the common factor x.

$$= \frac{x\sqrt{2x} - 2x}{x - 2}$$ Remove parentheses.

PROGRESS CHECK 7   Rationalize the denominator of $\dfrac{y\sqrt{5y}}{y - \sqrt{5y}}$. Assume $y > 0$.   ■

EXERCISES 6.4

In Exercises 1–22, simplify each radical. Assume $x \geq 0$, $y \geq 0$.

1. $(3\sqrt{7})^2$
2. $(5\sqrt{3})^2$
3. $(8\sqrt{10})^2$
4. $(2\sqrt{15})^2$
5. $\sqrt{57} \cdot \sqrt{57}$
6. $\sqrt{29} \cdot \sqrt{29}$
7. $3\sqrt{21} \cdot \sqrt{21}$
8. $8\sqrt{2} \cdot \sqrt{2}$
9. $(-7\sqrt{6})^2$
10. $(-10\sqrt{5})^2$
11. $(-3\sqrt{17})^2$
12. $(-12\sqrt{2})^2$
13. $(\sqrt[3]{4 + 2x})^3$
14. $(\sqrt[3]{x^2 + 8})^3$
15. $(\sqrt[3]{3x^2 - 1})^3$
16. $(\sqrt[3]{5x - 3})^3$
17. $(3\sqrt{5x})^2$
18. $(6\sqrt{7y})^2$
19. $(7\sqrt{2y})^2$
20. $(10\sqrt{12x})^2$
21. $(-9\sqrt{11x})^2$
22. $(-3\sqrt{15y})^2$

In Exercises 23–44, simplify each expression.

23. $\sqrt{3}(\sqrt{6} + \sqrt{3})$
24. $\sqrt{7}(\sqrt{7} + \sqrt{14})$
25. $\sqrt{10}(\sqrt{20} - \sqrt{10})$
26. $\sqrt{11}(\sqrt{22} - \sqrt{11})$
27. $\sqrt{15}(\sqrt{5} - \sqrt{3})$
28. $\sqrt{21}(\sqrt{3} - \sqrt{7})$
29. $\sqrt{2}(\sqrt{3} + \sqrt{5})$
30. $\sqrt{7}(\sqrt{5} - \sqrt{11})$
31. $(\sqrt{12} + \sqrt{5})(\sqrt{12} - \sqrt{5})$
32. $(\sqrt{8} + \sqrt{6})(\sqrt{8} - \sqrt{6})$
33. $(\sqrt{40} - \sqrt{30})(\sqrt{40} + \sqrt{30})$
34. $(\sqrt{15} - \sqrt{11})(\sqrt{15} + \sqrt{11})$
35. $(\sqrt{5} + \sqrt{7})(\sqrt{5} - \sqrt{7})$
36. $(\sqrt{7} + \sqrt{8})(\sqrt{7} - \sqrt{8})$
37. $(\sqrt{15} - \sqrt{16})(\sqrt{15} + \sqrt{16})$
38. $(\sqrt{6} - \sqrt{12})(\sqrt{6} + \sqrt{12})$
39. $(\sqrt[3]{x} + 4)(\sqrt[3]{x} + 1)$
40. $(\sqrt[3]{y} + 1)(\sqrt[3]{y} + 3)$
41. $(\sqrt[3]{x} - 1)(\sqrt[3]{x} + 4)$
42. $(\sqrt[5]{y} + 7)(\sqrt[5]{y} - 3)$
43. $(\sqrt[5]{y} - 6)(\sqrt[5]{y} - 4)$
44. $(\sqrt[5]{y} - 4)(\sqrt[5]{y} - 5)$

In Exercises 45–62, simplify each expression. Assume $x \geq 0$.

45. $(2\sqrt{5} + 1)^2$
46. $(7\sqrt{6} + 5)^2$
47. $(3\sqrt{7} - 2)^2$
48. $(10\sqrt{3} - 4)^2$
49. $(3 + 4\sqrt{x})^2$
50. $(2 + 6\sqrt{4})^2$
51. $(5\sqrt{x} - 5)^2$
52. $(9\sqrt{x} - 7)^2$
53. $(3 + 2\sqrt{5})(3 - 2\sqrt{5})$
54. $(4 + 3\sqrt{2})(4 - 3\sqrt{2})$
55. $(7\sqrt{6} - 4)(7\sqrt{6} + 4)$
56. $(11\sqrt{7} - 3)(11\sqrt{7} + 3)$
57. $(5 + \sqrt{x})(5 - \sqrt{x})$
58. $(12 - \sqrt{x})(12 + \sqrt{x})$
59. $(\sqrt{x} + 3\sqrt{5})(\sqrt{x} - 3\sqrt{5})$
60. $(\sqrt{x} + 2\sqrt{7})(\sqrt{x} - 2\sqrt{7})$
61. $(2\sqrt{x} - 4\sqrt{3})(2\sqrt{x} + 4\sqrt{3})$
62. $(3\sqrt{x} - 5\sqrt{2})(3\sqrt{x} + 5\sqrt{2})$

63. Competitors in a contest were asked to find the dimensions of a rectangular plate where the length is 4 in. greater than the width and the area of the plate is 4 in.^{2}. Verify that $(2\sqrt{2} + 2)$ and $(2\sqrt{2} - 2)$ are the correct dimensions.

64. An architect requires the length and width of a rectangular shed to be such that the area of the shed floor is 12 ft^2 and the length of the shed is 6 ft longer than the width.
    a. Verify that the exact values of the length and width are $(\sqrt{21} + 3)$ and $(\sqrt{21} - 3)$, respectively.
    b. Give the dimensions to the nearest hundredth of a foot.

65. An important expression in statistics is $\sqrt{\dfrac{p(1 - p)}{n}}$, which is used in computing the margin of error for a survey of n people, where p is the proportion who agree on some opinion.
    a. Assume $p = 0.5$ and simplify the formula.
    b. Evaluate the formula to the nearest thousandth if $p = 0.5$ and $n = 1{,}000$.

66. Repeat Exercise 65, but take $p = 0.1$.

67. The harmonic mean of two numbers a and b is given by $\dfrac{2ab}{a + b}$.
    a. What is the harmonic mean of n and $\sqrt{n}$?
    b. Compute the harmonic mean of 3 and 9 by both formulas.

68. The contraharmonic mean of a and b is given by $\dfrac{a^2 + b^2}{a + b}$.
    a. What is the contraharmonic mean of n and $\sqrt{n}$?
    b. Compute the contraharmonic mean of 3 and 9 by both formulas.
    c. Show that the sum of the harmonic and contraharmonic means of a and b is $a + b$. See Exercise 67 for harmonic mean.

69. According to Ohm's law, if three resistors of R_1, R_2, and R_3 ohms are connected in parallel, then the total resistance of the circuit is given by

$$R = \frac{R_1 R_2 R_3}{R_1 R_2 + R_1 R_3 + R_2 R_3}.$$

Suppose $R_1 = c$ ohms while R_2 and R_3 equal $\sqrt{c}$ ohms. Find an expression for R in simplest radical form.

70. Repeat Exercise 69, but assume that R_1 and R_2 equal c ohms while $R_3 = \sqrt{c}$ ohms.

71. What is the volume of a cube with side length $\dfrac{1}{\sqrt{a}}$ cm?

72. What is the volume of a sphere with radius $\sqrt{3}$ ft? Give the answer in simplified radical form and also to the nearest hundredth.

In Exercises 73–84, simplify each expression. Assume $x > 0$.

73. $\dfrac{2 + 2\sqrt{3}}{12}$

74. $\dfrac{6 + 6\sqrt{6}}{36}$

75. $\dfrac{5 - 15\sqrt{15}}{10}$

76. $\dfrac{14 - 7\sqrt{5}}{21}$

77. $\dfrac{6 + 12\sqrt{7}}{18}$

78. $\dfrac{4 + 2\sqrt{3}}{8}$

79. $\dfrac{3 + \sqrt{5}}{\sqrt{5}}$

80. $\dfrac{7 - \sqrt{3}}{\sqrt{3}}$

81. $\dfrac{5 + \sqrt{x}}{\sqrt{x}}$

82. $\dfrac{\sqrt{x} + 4}{\sqrt{x}}$

83. $\dfrac{\sqrt{x} - 6}{\sqrt{x}}$

84. $\dfrac{7 - \sqrt{x}}{\sqrt{x}}$

In Exercises 85–94, rationalize the denominator. Assume $x > 0$, $y > 0$.

85. $\dfrac{4}{1 + \sqrt{3}}$

86. $\dfrac{20}{4 + \sqrt{6}}$

87. $\dfrac{2}{4 - \sqrt{2}}$

88. $\dfrac{5}{6 - \sqrt{6}}$

89. $\dfrac{9}{8 - \sqrt{10}}$

90. $\dfrac{10}{6 - \sqrt{11}}$

91. $\dfrac{x\sqrt{x}}{x + \sqrt{x}}$

92. $\dfrac{y\sqrt{3y}}{y + \sqrt{3y}}$

93. $\dfrac{y\sqrt{6y}}{y - \sqrt{6y}}$

94. $\dfrac{x\sqrt{7x}}{x + \sqrt{7x}}$

95. If $f(x) = \dfrac{x + 1}{1 + \sqrt{x}}$ find $f(3)$.

96. If $f(x) = \dfrac{3x + 2}{4 + \sqrt{x}}$, find $f(6)$

97. If $f(x) = x^2 - 4x - 3$, find $f\left(2 + \sqrt{7}\right)$.

98. If $f(x) = x^2 - 4x - 3$, find $f\left(2 - \sqrt{7}\right)$.

99. If $f(x) = x^2 - 2x + 5$, find $f\left(1 + \sqrt{2}\right)$.

100. If $f(x) = x^2 - 2x + 5$, find $f\left(1 - \sqrt{2}\right)$.

THINK ABOUT IT 6.4

1. For the rectangle shown, find the following.

$\sqrt{5} - 2$ ⎤ (height)
$\sqrt{5} + 2$ (width)

  a. The area
  b. The length of the diagonal

2. a. What is the volume of a cube with side length $\sqrt[3]{5}$ units?

  b. What is the volume of a cube with side length $\sqrt[3]{5} + 1$ units?

3. If $x_1 = \dfrac{-b + \sqrt{b^2 - 4ac}}{2a}$ and

$x_2 = \dfrac{-b - \sqrt{b^2 - 4ac}}{2a}$, find $x_1 \cdot x_2$.

4. In some cases, instead of rationalizing the denominator, it is useful to rationalize the numerator. For the following problem the method will be to multiply the numerator and the denominator by the conjugate of the numerator and then simplify.

  a. Rationalize the numerator of $\dfrac{\sqrt{x} - \sqrt{a}}{x - a}$.

  b. Replace x by a in the expression in the question in part **a**. What is the value of this expression?

  c. Replace x by a in the expression in the answer in part **a**. What is the value of this expression?

5. When drawing a rectangle what ratio of length to width should one use to achieve the most satisfying visual effect? The answer is obviously subjective but there is a common choice that is often used in art and architecture. This rectangle is called the **golden rectangle** and the ratio of the length to the width in this figure is called the **golden ratio.** The diagram below shows the simple geometric method used to construct a golden rectangle. We start with square $ABCD$ and extend this square to form golden rectangle $ABEF$ by drawing arc CF, which is centered at the midpoint M of AD.

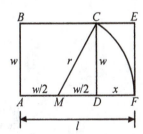

  a. Show in rectangle $ABEF$ that $l/w = \left(1 + \sqrt{5}\right)/2$, which is the exact value of the golden ratio. (*Hint*: Note that $l = (w/2) + r$.)

  b. Show that $w/x = \left(1 + \sqrt{5}\right)/2$, which means that rectangle $DCEF$ is also a golden rectangle.

  c. Subtracting 1 from the golden ratio yields its reciprocal. Verify this.

Courtesy of PhotoDisc/Getty Images.

6.5 Radical Equations

The formula $t = \sqrt{d}/4$ relates the distance d in feet traveled by a free-falling object to the time t of the fall in seconds, neglecting air resistance. If a stone is dropped from a bridge that spans a river and hits the water in 2.3 seconds, then to the nearest foot how far above the water is that particular point on the bridge? (See Example 1.)

OBJECTIVES

1   Solve radical equations using the principle of powers once.

2   Solve radical equations using the principle of powers twice.

To solve the problem that opens this section, we must solve an equation in which the unknown appears in a radicand. This type of equation is called a radical equation, and Example 1 shows how to solve a simple radical equation.

EXAMPLE 1   An Application Involving a Radical Equation

Solve the problem in the section introduction on this page.

Solution   Replacing t by 2.3 in

$$t = \frac{\sqrt{d}}{4} \text{gives } 2.3 = \frac{\sqrt{d}}{4}.$$

The resulting equation may be solved by squaring both sides of the equation and solving for d.

$$(2.3)^2 = \left(\frac{\sqrt{d}}{4}\right)^2 \qquad \text{Square both sides.}$$

$$(2.3)^2 = \frac{d}{16}$$

$$16(2.3)^2 = d$$

$$84.64 = d$$

To the nearest foot, the stone was dropped from a point on the bridge that is 85 ft above the water.

To check this answer, replace d by 85 in the given formula and determine that

$$t = \frac{\sqrt{85}}{4} \approx 2.3.$$

When $d \approx 85$ ft, $t \approx 2.3$ seconds as specified. Figure 6.5 shows a graphical check that confirms the solution in this example.

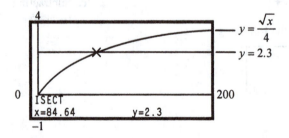

Figure 6.5

PROGRESS CHECK 1   A stone dropped from the recorded height of the Empire State Building in New York City takes about 9.592 seconds to hit the ground. To the nearest foot, what is this recorded height?   ■

Example 1 illustrates that the following steps may be used to solve a radical equation.

> ## To Solve Radical Equations
>
> 1. If necessary, isolate a radical term on one side of the equation.
> 2. Raise both sides of the equation to a power that matches the index of the isolated radical.
> 3. Solve the resulting equation, and check all solutions in the *original* equation.

This procedure is illustrated in Examples 2 and 3.

EXAMPLE 2   Solving an Equation Involving a Square Root
Solve $\sqrt{2x + 3} - 5 = 0$.

Solution   First, isolate the radical on one side of the equation.

$$\sqrt{2x + 3} - 5 = 0$$
$$\sqrt{2x + 3} = 5$$

Now, square both sides of the equation and solve for x.

$$\left(\sqrt{2x + 3}\right)^2 = 5^2 \qquad \text{Square both sides.}$$
$$2x + 3 = 25$$
$$2x = 22$$
$$x = 11$$

To check, replace x by 11 in the original equation.

$$\sqrt{2x + 3} - 5 = 0$$
$$\sqrt{2(11) + 3} - 5 \overset{?}{=} 0 \qquad \text{Replace } x \text{ by 11.}$$
$$0 \overset{\checkmark}{=} 0$$

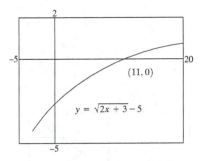

Figure 6.6

The proposed solution checks, and the solution set is $\{11\}$. Graphical support for this answer may be found by examining the *x*-intercept in the graph of $y = \sqrt{2x + 3} - 5$ that is shown in Figure 6.6.

PROGRESS CHECK 2   Solve $\sqrt{3x - 2} - 4 = 3$.   ■

EXAMPLE 3   Solving an Equation Involving Cube Roots
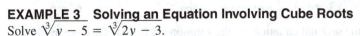
Solve $\sqrt[3]{y - 5} = \sqrt[3]{2y - 3}$.

Solution   A cube root term is isolated on each side of the equation, so begin by raising both sides to the third power, since the index of the radical is 3.

$$\sqrt[3]{y - 5} = \sqrt[3]{2y - 3}$$
$$\left(\sqrt[3]{y - 5}\right)^3 = \left(\sqrt[3]{2y - 3}\right)^3 \qquad \text{Cube both sides.}$$
$$y - 5 = 2y - 3$$
$$-2 = y$$

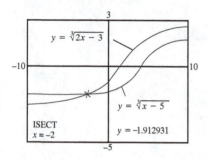

Figure 6.7

Check

$$\sqrt[3]{y - 5} = \sqrt[3]{2y - 3}$$
$$\sqrt[3]{(-2) - 5} \stackrel{?}{=} \sqrt[3]{2(-2) - 3} \qquad \text{Replace } y \text{ by } -2$$
$$\sqrt[3]{-t} \stackrel{\checkmark}{=} \sqrt[3]{-7}$$

Thus, the solution set is $\{-2\}$. Figure 6.7 shows a graphical check of this result.

PROGRESS CHECK 3 Solve $\sqrt[4]{3x + 3} = \sqrt[4]{5x - 35}$. ■

The check in step 3 of the procedure to solve radical equations is not optional, because this procedure is based on the following principle.

Principle of Powers

If P and Q are algebraic expressions, then the solution set of the equation $P = Q$ is a subset of the solution set of $P^n = Q^n$ for any positive integer n.

Thus, every solution of $P = Q$ is a solution of $P^n = Q^n$; but solutions of $P^n = Q^n$ may or may not be solutions of $P = Q$, so checking is necessary. Solutions of $P^n = Q^n$ that do not satisfy the original equation are called **extraneous solutions**, and Examples 4 and 5 illustrate this possibility.

EXAMPLE 4   Solving a Radical Equation with an Extraneous Root
Solve $\sqrt{3x + 18} = x$.

Solution   A radical is already isolated, so square both equation members and solve the resulting quadratic equation by the methods of Section 5.3.

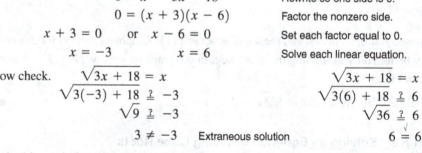

$$\sqrt{3x + 18} = x$$
$$\left(\sqrt{3x + 18}\right)^2 = x^2 \qquad \text{Square both sides.}$$
$$3x + 18 = x^2 \qquad \text{Simplify.}$$
$$0 = x^2 - 3x - 18 \qquad \text{Rewrite so one side is 0.}$$
$$0 = (x + 3)(x - 6) \qquad \text{Factor the nonzero side.}$$
$$x + 3 = 0 \quad \text{or} \quad x - 6 = 0 \qquad \text{Set each factor equal to 0.}$$
$$x = -3 \qquad\qquad x = 6 \qquad \text{Solve each linear equation.}$$

Now check.

$$\sqrt{3x + 18} = x \qquad\qquad\qquad \sqrt{3x + 18} = x$$
$$\sqrt{3(-3) + 18} \stackrel{?}{=} -3 \qquad\qquad \sqrt{3(6) + 18} \stackrel{?}{=} 6$$
$$\sqrt{9} \stackrel{?}{=} -3 \qquad\qquad\qquad \sqrt{36} \stackrel{?}{=} 6$$
$$3 \neq -3 \quad \text{Extraneous solution} \qquad\qquad 6 \stackrel{\checkmark}{=} 6$$

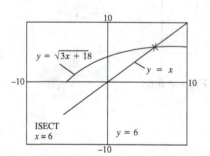

Figure 6.8

Only 6 is a solution of the original equation, so the solution set is $\{6\}$. Observe in Figure 6.8 that $y = \sqrt{3x + 18}$ and $y = x$ intersect only at $x = 6$.

PROGRESS CHECK 4   Solve $\sqrt{20 - 8x} = x$. ■

In the remaining examples it is necessary to square both sides of an equation where one side of the equation contains two terms. To square a binomial, use

$$(a + b)^2 = a^2 + 2ab + b^2 \qquad \text{or} \qquad (a - b)^2 = a^2 - 2ab + b^2.$$

EXAMPLE 5 Solving a Radical Equation with an Extraneous Root
Solve $x - \sqrt{x + 1} = 1$.

Solution We can first isolate the radical on one side of the equation.

$$x - \sqrt{x + 1} = 1$$
$$x - 1 = \sqrt{x + 1}$$

Then the intersection of the graphs of $y = x - 1$ and $y = \sqrt{x + 1}$, which is shown in Figure 6.9, indicates that $x - 1$ and $\sqrt{x + 1}$ have the same value only when $x = 3$. To confirm this result algebraically we square both sides of the equation $x - 1 = \sqrt{x + 1}$ and solve for x.

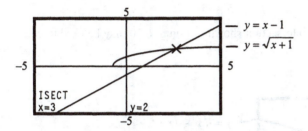

Figure 6.9

$$(x - 1)^2 = \left(\sqrt{x + 1}\right)^2$$
$$x^2 - 2x + 1 = x + 1$$
$$x^2 - 3x = 0$$
$$x(x - 3) = 0$$
$$x = 0 \quad \text{or} \quad x = 3$$

Check
$$x - \sqrt{x + 1} = 1 \qquad\qquad x - \sqrt{x + 1} = 1$$
$$0 - \sqrt{0 + 1} \stackrel{?}{=} 1 \qquad\qquad 3 - \sqrt{3 + 1} \stackrel{?}{=} 1$$
$$0 - 1 \stackrel{?}{=} 1 \qquad\qquad 3 - 2 \stackrel{?}{=} 1$$
$$-1 \neq 1 \quad \text{Extraneous solution} \qquad\qquad 1 \stackrel{\checkmark}{=} 1$$

Only 3 is a solution of the original equation, so the solution set is $\{3\}$.

PROGRESS CHECK 5 Solve $1 + \sqrt{x + 11} = x$. ■

In the next example we must square both sides of an equation twice in order to solve the equation.

EXAMPLE 4 Solving a Radical Equation with Two Radicals
Solve the equation $\sqrt{x} + \sqrt{x + 5} = 5$.

Solution We first isolate one of the radicals, and then square both sides of the resulting equation.

$$\sqrt{x} + \sqrt{x + 5} = 5$$
$$\sqrt{x + 5} = 5 - \sqrt{x}$$
$$\left(\sqrt{x + 5}\right)^2 = \left(5 - \sqrt{x}\right)^2 \qquad \text{Square both sides.}$$
$$x + 5 = 25 - 10\sqrt{x} + x$$

A radical remains, so isolate this radical term and square both sides again.

$$-20 = -10\sqrt{x}$$
$$2 = \sqrt{x}$$
$$(2)^2 = \left(\sqrt{x}\right)^2 \quad \text{Square both sides.}$$
$$4 = x$$

Check

$$\sqrt{x} + \sqrt{x + 5} = 5$$
$$\sqrt{4} + \sqrt{4 + 5} \overset{?}{=} 5$$
$$2 + 3 \overset{?}{=} 5$$
$$5 \overset{\checkmark}{=} 5$$

Thus, the solution set is {4}. The intersection shown in Figure 6.10 may be used to confirm this solution graphically.

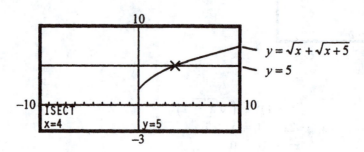

Figure 6.10

PROGRESS CHECK 6 Solve $\sqrt{4x + 1} - \sqrt{2x} = 1$. ■

EXERCISES 6.5

In Exercises 1–16, solve the given equation.

1. $\sqrt{3x - 9} - 6 = 0$
2. $\sqrt{4x + 9} - 5 = 0$
3. $\sqrt{2x - 4} - 2 = 4$
4. $\sqrt{5x + 14} + 6 = 13$
5. $\sqrt{6x - 2} + 6 = 10$
6. $\sqrt{3x - 5} + 15 = 22$
7. $10 - \sqrt{7x + 11} = 5$
8. $8 - \sqrt{2x + 18} = 2$
9. $\sqrt{x + 1} + 5 = 0$
10. $\sqrt{x - 3} + 4 = 0$
11. $\sqrt[3]{y + 10} = \sqrt[3]{6y - 20}$
12. $\sqrt[3]{2x + 3} = \sqrt[3]{5x - 18}$
13. $\sqrt[3]{6x + 10} = \sqrt[3]{3x + 1}$
14. $\sqrt[3]{9x - 3} = \sqrt[3]{5x - 27}$
15. $\sqrt[4]{12x + 3} = \sqrt[4]{9x + 9}$
16. $\sqrt[4]{9x + 13} = \sqrt[4]{5x + 9}$

The formula $t = \sqrt{d}/4$ relates the distance d in feet traveled by a free-falling object to the time t of the fall in seconds, neglecting air resistance. Use this relationship to solve Exercises 17 and 18.

17. As you travel along the rim of the Grand Canyon, you stop at a place called Mojave Cliffs. Using a stopwatch, you calculate the length of time it takes for a rock dropped off the edge to hit the bottom of the canyon as 13.7 seconds. Approximate, to the nearest foot, the depth of the Grand Canyon at this point.

18. On a farm there's an old well you'd like to use. You have a bucket, and you're going to buy some rope, but you don't know how much rope to get. You decide to measure the depth of the well by dropping a small stone. If it takes about 1.3 seconds for the stone to hit the water, how deep is the well (to the nearest foot)?

19. The period of a pendulum is the time required for the pendulum to complete one round-trip of motion, that is, one complete cycle. When the period is measured in seconds and the pendulum length ℓ is measured in feet, then a formula for the period is

$$T = 2\pi\sqrt{\frac{\ell}{32}}.$$

To the nearest hundredth of a foot, what is the length of a pendulum whose period is 1 second?

20. Using the formula from Exercise 19, find the length of a pendulum whose period is 2 seconds.

21. A kind of average called the **root-mean-square** is defined as the square root of the mean of a collection of squares. The formula $A = \sqrt{\dfrac{m^2 + n^2}{2}}$ gives the root-mean-square of two positive numbers, m and n. Find n if $m = 1$ and $A = 5$.

22. Use the formula from Exercise 21 and find n if $m = 2$ and $A = 2\sqrt{5}$.

In Exercises 23–50, solve the given equation.

23. $x = \sqrt{5x - 6}$ **24.** $x = \sqrt{6x - 5}$

25. $\sqrt{4x + 5} = x$ **26.** $\sqrt{3x + 10} = x$

27. $\sqrt{x + 6} = x$ **28.** $\sqrt{x + 42} = x$

29. $x = \sqrt{27 - 6x}$ **30.** $\sqrt{2x + 8} = x$

31. $\sqrt{x + 3} - 3 = x$ **32.** $\sqrt{x - 1} + 1 = x$

33. $3 + \sqrt{21 - 2x} = x$ **34.** $\sqrt{13 - 4x} - 2 = x$

35. $2\sqrt{12 - x} - 3 = x$ **36.** $5 + \sqrt{2x - 2} = x$

37. $\sqrt{2x + 3} - \sqrt{x - 2} = 2$

38. $\sqrt{2x - 1} - \sqrt{x - 4} = 2$

39. $1 = \sqrt{3x - 5} - \sqrt{2x - 5}$

40. $\sqrt{3x + 10} - \sqrt{2x + 6} = 1$

41. $\sqrt{3x - 11} - \sqrt{2x - 9} = 1$

42. $\sqrt{3x + 4} - \sqrt{2x + 1} = 1$

43. $\sqrt{2x + 3} + \sqrt{x - 2} = 2$

44. $\sqrt{3x - 6} + \sqrt{2x - 6} = 1$

45. $\sqrt{x + 4} = 2 - \sqrt{x + 16}$

46. $\sqrt{x - 5} + \sqrt{x + 10} = -3$

47. $3 = \sqrt{x + 11} - \sqrt{x - 4}$

48. $\sqrt{3x - 2} + \sqrt{2x - 2} = 1$

49. $\sqrt{x} = 3 - \sqrt{x - 5}$ **50.** $\sqrt{x} - \sqrt{x - 5} = 2$

51. Solve for s: $gt = \sqrt{2gs}$.   **52.** Solve for d: $r = \sqrt[3]{\dfrac{3a}{4\pi d}}$

53. Solve for y: $x = \sqrt[3]{y} + 2$.

54. Solve for g: $t = \pi\sqrt{\dfrac{L}{g}}$.

THINK ABOUT IT 6.5

1. Find all real numbers a for which the distance between $(-1, 1)$ and $(5, a)$ is 10.

2. Solve these equations.
   a. $\sqrt{(5x - 2)^2} = 5x - 2$
      (*Hint:* The solutions must satisfy the original equation.)
   b. $\dfrac{10}{\sqrt{x - 5}} = \sqrt{x - 5} - 3$
   c. $\dfrac{x}{\sqrt{x + 16}} - \dfrac{2}{\sqrt{3}} = 0$
   d. $\sqrt{1 + 4\sqrt{y}} = 1 + \sqrt{y}$

3. The perimeter of a right triangle is 3 in., and one of the legs is 1 in. Find the other leg and the hypotenuse.

4. Solve these equations by using the principle of powers.
   a. $\sqrt[3]{x} = x$ **b.** $\sqrt[3]{x^2} = x$
   c. $\sqrt[3]{x^3} = x$ **d.** $\sqrt[3]{x^4} = x$

5. Explain the apparent paradox.

$$\begin{aligned} a &= b \\ a^2 &= b^2 \\ a^2 - b^2 &= 0 \\ (a + b)(a - b) &= 0 \\ \frac{(a + b)(a - b)}{a - b} &= \frac{0}{a - b} \\ a + b &= 0 \\ a &= -b \end{aligned}$$

Thus, a equals both b and the negative of b!

6.6   Complex Numbers

Ohm's law for alternating current circuits states

$$V = IZ,$$

where V is the voltage in volts, I is the current in amperes, and Z is the impedance in ohms. If the voltage in a particular circuit is $18 - 21i$ volts, and the current is $3 - 6i$ amperes, find the complex number that measures the impedance. (See Example 6.)

Courtesy of PhotoDisc/Getty Images.

OBJECTIVES

1   Express square roots of negative numbers in terms of *i*.

2   Add, subtract, and multiply complex numbers.

3   Divide complex numbers.

4   Find powers of *i*.

In this section we extend the number system beyond real numbers to complex numbers which have significant applications in mathematics, physics, and engineering. For instance, in the section-opening problem complex numbers are used to describe voltage and other electrical quantities, because such a numerical representation indicates both the strength and time (or phase) relationships of the quantities.

To define a complex number, we first introduce a new set of numbers called **imaginary numbers** in which square roots of negative numbers are defined. The basic unit in imaginary numbers is $\sqrt{-1}$, and it is designated by *i*. Thus, by definition,

$$i = \sqrt{-1} \qquad \text{and} \qquad i^2 = -1.$$

Square roots of negative numbers may now be written in terms of *i* by defining the principal square root of a negative number as follows.

Principal Square Root of a Negative Number

If *a* is a positive number, then

$$\sqrt{-a} = i\sqrt{a}.$$

In this definition we choose to write *i* in front of any radicals so that expressions like $\sqrt{a}\, i$ are not confused with $\sqrt{ai}$.

EXAMPLE 1   Simplifying Square Roots of Negative Numbers

Express each number in terms of *i*.

a. $\sqrt{-3}$ **b.** $-\sqrt{-3}$ **c.** $\sqrt{-4}$ **d.** $\sqrt{-50}$

Solution

a. $\sqrt{-3} = i\sqrt{3}$ **b.** $-\sqrt{-3} = -i\sqrt{3}$

c. $\sqrt{-4} = i\sqrt{4} = 2i$ **d.** $\sqrt{-50} = i\sqrt{50} = i\sqrt{25}\sqrt{2} = 5i\sqrt{2}$

Technology Link

A graphing calculator may have a MODE choice to represent complex numbers in $a + bi$ form. Figure 6.11(a) shows such a choice in the next to the last line. Figure 6.11(b) shows the corresponding results of evaluating the square roots of negative numbers.

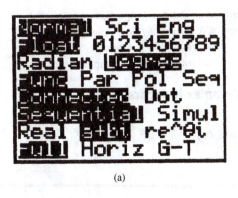
(a)

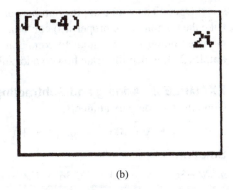
(b)

Figure 6.11

PROGRESS CHECK 1   Express each number in terms of i.

a. $\sqrt{-9}$ **b.** $-\sqrt{-9}$ **c.** $\sqrt{-7}$ **d.** $\sqrt{-8}$ ■

Using real numbers and imaginary numbers, we may extend the number system to include a number like $3 - 6i$ that was used to describe the current in the section-opening problem. This type of number is called a complex number.

Definition of Complex Number

A number of the form $a + bi$, where a and b are real numbers and $i = \sqrt{-1}$, is called a complex number.

The number a is called the **real part** of $a + bi$, and b is called the **imaginary part** of $a + bi$. Note that both the real part and the imaginary part of a complex number are real numbers. Two complex numbers are **equal** if and only if their real parts are equal and their imaginary parts are equal. That is,

$$a + bi = c + di \text{ if and only if } a = c \text{ and } b = d$$

If we let a and/or b equal zero, both real numbers and imaginary numbers may be expressed in $a + bi$ form. For instance:

Real number $\rightarrow 2 = 2 + 0i$ ↖

Complex number in $a + bi$ form

Imaginary number $\rightarrow 5i = 0 + 5i$ ↙

Thus, the complex numbers include the real numbers and the imaginary numbers. Figure 6.12 illustrates the relationship among the various sets of numbers.

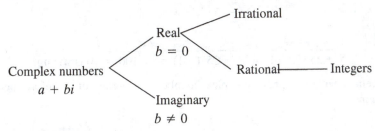

Figure 6.12

Operations with complex numbers are defined so that the properties of real numbers (like the commutative properties) continue to apply, and in many ways computations with complex numbers are similar to computations with polynomials. Consider carefully Examples 2–4, which illustrate how to add, subtract, and multiply with complex numbers.

EXAMPLE 2   Adding and Subtracting Complex Numbers

Combine the complex numbers.

a. $\sqrt{-36} + \sqrt{-100}$ **b.** $(7 - 3i) + (1 + 6i)$ **c.** $(5 + 4i) - (9 - i)$

Solution

a. $\sqrt{-36} + \sqrt{-100} = i\sqrt{36} + i\sqrt{100}$
$$= 6i + 10i$$
$$= 16i$$

b. $(7 - 3i) + (1 + 6i) = (7 + 1) + (-3 + 6)i$
$$= 8 + 3i$$

c. $(5 + 4i) - (9 - i) = 5 + 4i - 9 + i$
$$= (5 - 9) + (4 + 1)i$$
$$= -4 + 5i$$

PROGRESS CHECK 2   Combine the complex numbers.

a. $\sqrt{-9} - \sqrt{-25}$
b. $(-1 - 2i) + (8 + 5i)$
c. $(9 + 3i) - (16 - i)$

EXAMPLE 3   Multiplying Complex Numbers

Multiply the complex numbers.

a. $\sqrt{-25}\sqrt{-4}$ **b.** $(3 + 4i)(2 - 6i)$ **c.** $(5 + 2i)^2$

Solution

a. $\sqrt{-25}\sqrt{-4} = i\sqrt{25}i\sqrt{4}$
$$= 5i \cdot 2i$$
$$= 10i^2$$
$$= 10(-1) \qquad \text{Replace } i^2 \text{ by } -1.$$
$$= -10$$

b. $(3 + 4i)(2 - 6i)$
$$= 3(2) + 3(-6i) + 4i(2) + 4i(-6i) \qquad \text{Use FOIL.}$$
$$= 6 - 18i + 8i - 24i^2$$
$$= 6 - 18i + 8i - 24(-1) \qquad \text{Replace } i^2 \text{ by } -1.$$
$$= 30 - 10i$$

c. $(5 + 2i)^2 = 5^2 + 2(5)(2i) + (2i)^2 \qquad \text{Use } (a + b)^2 = a^2 + 2ab + b^2$
$$= 25 + 20i + 4i^2$$
$$= 25 + 20i + 4(-1) \qquad \text{Replace } i^2 \text{ by } -1.$$
$$= 21 + 20i$$

Caution   The property of radicals $\sqrt{a}\sqrt{b} = \sqrt{ab}$ does not hold when a and b are both negative. For instance, the solution in part **a** shows

$$\sqrt{-25} \cdot \sqrt{-4} = -10.$$

Therefore,

$$\sqrt{-25} \cdot \sqrt{-4} = \sqrt{(-25)(-4)} = \sqrt{100} = 10 \text{ is } \textbf{wrong.}$$

Always remember to express complex numbers in terms of i before performing computations.

Technology Link

A calculator with an $a + bi$ mode will also have a special key to represent i. Use of this key is illustrated in Figure 6.13.

PROGRESS CHECK 3   Multiply the complex numbers.

a. $\sqrt{-16}\sqrt{-9}$ **b.** $(2 + 3i)(10 - i)$ **c.** $(4 + 7i)^2$ ■

EXAMPLE 4   Evaluating Expressions Using Complex Numbers

Evaluate $x^2 + 2x + 3$ if $x = -1 - i\sqrt{2}$.

Solution   Substitute $-1 - i\sqrt{2}$ for x and simplify.

$$
\begin{aligned}
x^2 + 2x + 3 &= \left(-1 - i\sqrt{2}\right)^2 + 2\left(-1 - i\sqrt{2}\right) + 3 \\
&= (-1)^2 - 2(-1)\left(i\sqrt{2}\right) + \left(i\sqrt{2}\right)^2 - 2 - 2i\sqrt{2} + 3 \\
&= 1 + 2i\sqrt{2} + 2i^2 - 2 - 2i\sqrt{2} + 3 \\
&= 2i^2 + 2 \\
&= 0 \qquad (\text{since } i^2 = -1)
\end{aligned}
$$

```
(7-3i)+(1+6i)
            8+3i
(3+4i)(2-6i)
          30-10i
```

Figure 6.13

PROGRESS CHECK 4   Evaluate $x^2 + 2x + 3$ if $x = -1 + i\sqrt{2}$.   ■

Use Examples 2–4 as a basis for understanding the definitions of the following operations on complex numbers.

Addition, Subtraction, and Multiplication of Complex Numbers

Addition   Two complex numbers are added by adding separately their real parts and their imaginary parts.

$$(a + bi) + (c + di) = (a + c) + (b + d)i$$

Subtraction   Two complex numbers are subtracted by subtracting separately their real parts and their imaginary parts.

$$(a + bi) - (c + di) = (a - c) + (b - d)i$$

Multiplication   Two complex numbers are multiplied as two binomials are multiplied, with i^2 being replaced by -1.

$$
\begin{aligned}
(a + bi)(c + di) &= ac + adi + bci + bdi^2 \\
&= (ac - bd) + (ad + bc)i
\end{aligned}
$$

Conjugates and division

To understand the procedure for dividing two complex numbers, consider

$$
\begin{aligned}
(a + bi)(a - bi) &= a^2 - abi + abi - b^2i^2 \\
&= a^2 - b^2(-1) \\
&= a^2 + b^2.
\end{aligned}
$$

The complex numbers $a + bi$ and $a - bi$ are called **conjugates** of each other, and since a and b are real numbers, the above product shows that the product of a complex number and its conjugate is always a real number. Based on this property of conjugates, the quotient of two complex numbers can be written in the form $a + bi$ by multiplying both the numerator and the denominator by the conjugate of the denominator. Examples 5 and 6 illustrate this procedure.

EXAMPLE 5 Dividing Complex Numbers

Write the quotient $\dfrac{2 + i}{3 + i}$ in the form $a + bi$.

Solution As discussed, we divide two complex numbers by multiplying the numerator and the denominator by the conjugate of the denominator. The conjugate of $3 + i$ is $3 - i$, so

$$\frac{2 + i}{3 + i} = \frac{2 + i}{3 + i} \cdot \frac{3 - i}{3 - i}$$

$$= \frac{6 - 2i + 3i - i^2}{9 - 3i + 3i - i^2}$$

$$= \frac{6 + i - (-1)}{9 - (-1)}$$

$$= \frac{7 + i}{10} = \frac{7}{10} + \frac{1}{10}i.$$

PROGRESS CHECK 5 Write the quotient $\dfrac{2 + 5i}{4 + 2i}$ in the form $a + bi$. ■

EXAMPLE 6 Using Ohm's Law to Find Impedance

Solve the problem in the section introduction on page 345.

Solution To find the impedance, which is symbolized by Z, first solve $V = IZ$ for Z, to obtain

$$Z = \frac{V}{I}.$$

Now replace V by $18 - 21i$ and I by $3 - 6i$ and divide, using the conjugate of the denominator.

$$Z = \frac{18 - 21i}{3 - 6i} = \frac{18 - 21i}{3 - 6i} \cdot \frac{3 + 6i}{3 + 6i} = \frac{54 + 108i - 63i - 126i^2}{9 + 18i - 18i - 36i^2}$$

$$= \frac{54 + 45i - 126(-1)}{9 - 36(-1)} = \frac{180 + 45i}{45} = 4 + i$$

The impedance is therefore $4 + i$ ohms.

PROGRESS CHECK 6 Find the impedance in an alternating current circuit in which the voltage is $23 - 14i$ volts and the current is $3 - 4i$ amperes. ■

Powers of i

To simplify i^n, where n is a positive integer, consider the cyclic pattern contained in the following simplifications.

$$i^1 = i \qquad\qquad\qquad i^5 = i^4 i = 1i = i$$
$$i^2 = -1 \qquad\qquad\quad i^6 = i^4 i^2 = 1(-1) = -1$$
$$i^3 = i^2 i = (-1)i = -i \qquad i^7 = i^4 i^3 = 1(-i) = -i$$
$$i^4 = i^2 i^2 = (-1)(-1) = 1 \qquad i^8 = (i^4)^2 = 1^2 = 1$$

Continuing this pattern to higher powers of i gives the cyclic property shown in Figure 6.14. Note in particular that $i^n = 1$ if n is a multiple of 4, because we may use this property to simplify large powers of i, as shown in Example 7.

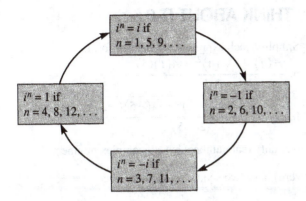

Figure 6.14

EXAMPLE 7   Simplifying Powers of *i*

Simplify each power of i.

a. i^{15} **b.** i^{50}

Solution

a. The largest multiple of 4 that is less than or equal to the exponent is 12. Therefore, rewrite i^{15} with i^{12} as one factor, and then simplify.

$$i^{15} = i^{12}i^3 = (i^4)^3 i^3 = (1)^3(-i) = -i$$

b. Because $i^{48} = (i^4)^{12} = 1$, we have

$$i^{50} = i^{48}i^2 = 1(-1) = -1.$$

PROGRESS CHECK 7   Simplify each power of i.

a. i^{18} **b.** i^{81} ■

EXERCISES 6.6

In Exercises 1–18, express each number in terms of i.

1. $\sqrt{-1}$ **2.** $\sqrt{-25}$
3. $\sqrt{-16}$ **4.** $\sqrt{-100}$
5. $-\sqrt{-4}$ **6.** $-\sqrt{-1}$
7. $-\sqrt{-49}$ **8.** $-\sqrt{-36}$
9. $\sqrt{-12}$ **10.** $\sqrt{-18}$
11. $\sqrt{-24}$ **12.** $\sqrt{-72}$
13. $\sqrt{-125}$ **14.** $\sqrt{-48}$
15. $-\sqrt{-27}$ **16.** $-\sqrt{-98}$
17. $-\sqrt{-75}$ **18.** $-\sqrt{-242}$

In Exercises 19–44, combine the complex numbers.

19. $\sqrt{-49} + \sqrt{-121}$ **20.** $\sqrt{-256} + \sqrt{-1}$
21. $\sqrt{-64} + \sqrt{-81}$ **22.** $\sqrt{-400} + \sqrt{-144}$
23. $\sqrt{-25} - \sqrt{-16}$ **24.** $\sqrt{-196} - \sqrt{-169}$
25. $\sqrt{-49} - \sqrt{-9}$ **26.** $\sqrt{-400} - \sqrt{-100}$
27. $(2 + i) + (3 + 2i)$ **28.** $(5 + 3i) + (7 + 4i)$

29. $(2 - 4i) + (5 + i)$ **30.** $(8 - 6i) + (4 + 5i)$
31. $(8 + 7i) + (8 - 3i)$ **32.** $(4 + 3i) + (9 - 7i)$
33. $(4 - 4i) + (6 + 4i)$ **34.** $(3 - 7i) + (7 + 7i)$
35. $(8 - i) + (7 - 2i)$ **36.** $(8 - 4i) + (3 - 8i)$
37. $(4 - 4i) - (6 + 4i)$ **38.** $(8 - 6i) - (4 + 5i)$
39. $(2 - 4i) - (5 - i)$ **40.** $(5 + 4i) - (7 + 3i)$
41. $(8 - 3i) - (8 + 7i)$ **42.** $(4 - 6i) - (4 + 4i)$
43. $(8 - i) - (-7 - i)$ **44.** $(-6 - 2i) - (4 - 2i)$

In Exercises 45–66, multiply the complex numbers.

45. $\sqrt{-64} \cdot \sqrt{-81}$ **46.** $\sqrt{-49} \cdot \sqrt{-121}$
47. $\sqrt{-36} \cdot \sqrt{-100}$ **48.** $\sqrt{-400} \cdot \sqrt{-144}$
49. $\sqrt{-25} \cdot \sqrt{-16}$ **50.** $\sqrt{-4} \cdot \sqrt{-196}$
51. $(2 + i)(3 + 2i)$ **52.** $(5 + 3i)(7 + 4i)$
53. $(2 - 4i)(5 + i)$ **54.** $(8 - 6i)(4 + 5i)$
55. $(8 + 7i)(8 - 3i)$ **56.** $(4 + 3i)(9 - 7i)$
57. $(2 - 4i)(5 - i)$ **58.** $(5 + 4i)(7 - 3i)$

59. $(3 + 4i)^2$

60. $(3 + 8i)^2$

61. $(2 + 6i)^2$

62. $(6 + 5i)^2$

63. $(5 - 2i)^2$

64. $(2 - 9i)^2$

65. $(7 - i)^2$

66. $(10 - 3i)^2$

In Exercises 67–72, evaluate the given polynomial.

67. Evaluate $x^2 + 4x + 5$ if $x = -2 + i$.

68. Evaluate $x^2 + 4x + 5$ if $x = -2 - i$.

69. Evaluate $x^2 + 6x + 12$ if $x = -3 - i\sqrt{3}$.

70. Evaluate $x^2 + 6x + 12$ if $x = -3 + i\sqrt{3}$.

71. Evaluate $x^2 + 2x + 9$ if $x = -1 + i\sqrt{5}$.

72. Evaluate $x^2 + 2x + 9$ if $x = -1 - i\sqrt{5}$.

In Exercises 73–78, write the indicated quotient in the form $a + bi$.

73. $\dfrac{1 + 2i}{1 + i}$

74. $\dfrac{1 + 3i}{2 + i}$

75. $\dfrac{6 + 2i}{7 + i}$

76. $\dfrac{1 + 5i}{4 + 3i}$

77. $\dfrac{7 + 2i}{6 - 2i}$

78. $\dfrac{5 - 4i}{3 - 5i}$

Ohm's law for alternating current circuits states that $V = IZ$, where V is the voltage in volts, I is the current in amperes, and Z is the impedance in ohms. Use this law to solve Exercises 79–84.

79. Find the complex number that represents the impedance in a particular circuit if the voltage is $14 + 8i$ volts and the current is $1 + 2i$ amperes.

80. Find the complex number that represents the impedance in a given circuit if the voltage is $12 - 5i$ volts and the current is $2 - 3i$ amperes.

81. Find the complex number that represents the voltage in a given circuit if the impedance is $240 - 50i$ ohms and the current is $0.4 + 0.3i$ amperes.

82. Find the complex number that represents the voltage in a given circuit if the impedance is $10 + i$ ohms and the current is $5 - 0.5i$ amperes.

83. Find the complex number that represents the current in a given circuit if the voltage is 12 volts and the impedance is $1 - i$ ohms.

84. Find the complex number that represents the current in a given circuit if the voltage is 120 volts and the impedance is $-3i$ amperes.

In Exercises 85–92, simplify each power of i.

85. i^5

86. i^7

87. i^8

88. i^{10}

89. i^{57}

90. i^{101}

91. i^{82}

92. $i^{1,002}$

THINK ABOUT IT 6.6

1. Simplify each expression to $a + bi$ form.

   a. $\dfrac{-(4) + \sqrt{(4)^2 - 4(1)(5)}}{2(1)}$

   b. $\dfrac{-(-2) + \sqrt{(-2)^2 - 4(-5)(-3)}}{2(-5)}$

2. Not only real numbers but *all* complex numbers (except zero) have two square roots. Show that $\dfrac{\sqrt{2}}{2} + \dfrac{\sqrt{2}}{2}i$ and $-\dfrac{\sqrt{2}}{2} - \dfrac{\sqrt{2}}{2}i$ are both square roots of i. To do this, show that the square of each number is i.

3. The complex numbers are said to be "closed" under the four basic arithmetic operations. That is, combining $a + bi$ and $c + di$ by any of the operations $+$, $-$, $\times$, $\div$ will always yield a number of that same form.

   a. Illustrate this by finding the sum, difference, product, and quotient of $1 + i$ and $2 - i$.

   b. Repeat part **a** in the general case for $a + bi$ and $c + di$.

4. Complex numbers are not ordered like real numbers. The relations "less than" and "greater than" do not apply to complex numbers. But they can be assigned a magnitude, similar to the concept of the absolute value of a real number. The **absolute value** of the complex number $a + bi$ is defined as $\sqrt{a^2 + b^2}$. Find the absolute value of these complex numbers.

   a. $1 + i$ **b.** $1 - i$ **c.** i **d.** $\dfrac{\sqrt{2}}{2} + \dfrac{\sqrt{2}}{2}i$

5. Just as a real number can be represented by a point on a line, a complex number can be represented by a point in a plane. The number $a + bi$ is represented by the point (a,b). Find the point represented by each of these. Verify that the absolute value of each number (see Exercise 4) equals its distance from the origin.

   a. $4 + i$ **b.** $3 - 2i$

   c. $(4 + i) + (3 - 2i)$ **d.** $(4 + i)(3 - 2i)$

6.7   Trigonometric Form of Complex Numbers

In an alternating current circuit, the total impedance Z for two impedances Z_1 and Z_2 that are connected in series and in parallel is given by

$$\text{Series} \qquad \text{Parallel}$$
$$Z = Z_1 + Z_2 \quad \text{and} \quad Z = \frac{Z_1 Z_2}{Z_1 + Z_2}.$$

Find the complex number in trigonometric form that measures the total impedance if

$$Z_1 = 2.81(\cos 11.7^\circ + i \sin 11.7^\circ) \text{ ohms,}$$
$$Z_2 = 3.54(\cos 57.2^\circ + i \sin 57.2^\circ) \text{ ohms,}$$

and the given impedances are connected
a. in series and
b. in parallel.
(See Example 5.)

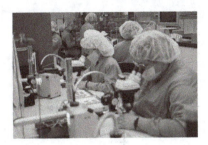

Courtesy of PhotoDisc/Getty Images.

OBJECTIVES

1 Graph a complex number $a + bi$ and find its absolute value.

2 Write a complex number $a + bi$ in trigonometric form.

3 Convert a complex number from trigonometric form to $a + bi$ form.

4 Find the product and quotient of complex numbers in trigonometric form.

5 Use De Moivre's theorem to find powers of complex numbers.

6 Use De Moivre's theorem to find roots of complex numbers and graph these roots.

Complex numbers were introduced in Section 6.6 from an algebraic perspective. We can now expand this coverage to include both geometric and trigonometric representations of such numbers. These representations will make more apparent why complex numbers can convey more information about a quantity. For example, a complex number is often used in physics to represent a vector, because this representation indicates both the magnitude and the direction of the vector. In electronics complex numbers are used extensively to represent voltage, current, and other electrical quantities, as illustrated in the section-opening problem. This representation is useful since it indicates both the strength and time (or phase) relationships of the quantities.

Each complex number $a + bi$ involves a pair of real numbers, a and b. Graphically, this means that we may represent a complex number as a point in a rectangular coordinate system. The values for a are plotted on the horizontal axis (x-axis) and the values for b are plotted on the vertical axis (y-axis). Thus, the complex number $a + bi$ is represented by the point (a, b) with x-value a and y value b. The plane on which complex numbers are graphed is called the **complex plane,** and in this context the horizontal axis is called the **real axis** and the vertical axis is called the **imaginary axis.** In Figure 6.15, the geometric representations of several complex numbers are shown.

The **absolute value** or **modulus** of a complex number $a + bi$, denoted $|a + bi|$, is interpreted geometrically as the distance from the origin to the point (a, b), as shown in Figure 6.16. Thus, algebraically $|a + bi|$ is defined by

$$|a + bi| = \sqrt{a^2 + b^2}.$$

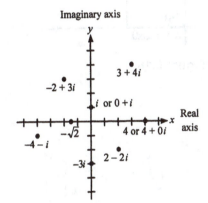

Figure 6.15

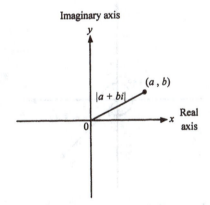

Figure 6.16

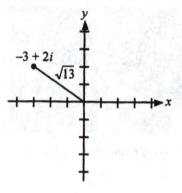

Figure 6.17

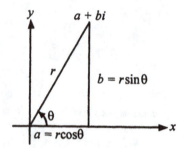

Figure 6.18

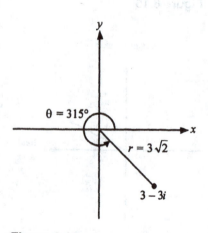

Figure 6.19

EXAMPLE 1   Graph and Absolute Value of a Complex Number

Graph $-3 + 2i$ and find $|-3 + 2i|$.

Solution   The complex number $-3 + 2i$, which is represented by the point $(-3, 2)$, is graphed in Figure 6.17. Since $a = -3$ and $b = 2$,

$$|-3 + 2i| = \sqrt{(-3)^2 + 2^2} = \sqrt{13}.$$

Thus, the absolute value of $-3 + 2i$ is $\sqrt{13}$.

PROGRESS CHECK 1   Graph $8 - 6i$ and find the absolute value of this number.   ■

A useful new way of writing a complex number is to interpret the position of its geometric representation in terms of the trigonometric functions. Consider the point corresponding to the nonzero complex number $a + bi$ in Figure 6.18. When we use trigonometry, we obtain the following relationships.

$$\sin \theta = \frac{b}{r} \text{ therefore } \boldsymbol{b = r \sin \theta}$$

$$\cos \theta = \frac{a}{r} \text{ therefore } \boldsymbol{a = r \cos \theta}$$

$$\boldsymbol{r = \sqrt{a^2 + b^2}}$$

$$\boldsymbol{\tan \theta = \frac{b}{a}}$$

Thus, we may change the form of the complex number as follows:

$$a + bi = r \cos \theta + (r \sin \theta)i = r(\cos \theta + i \sin \theta).$$

In this trigonometric form, r is the absolute value of $a + bi$, and θ is called the **argument** of the complex number. Note that the argument is not unique, since all angles of the form $\theta + k \cdot 360°$, where k is an integer, are coterminal to θ and serve as suitable choices for the argument. In most cases we use the **principal argument** of the complex number, which is the unique choice for θ that satisfies $0° \leq \theta < 360°$.

EXAMPLE 2   Expressing a Complex Number in Trigonometric Form

Write the number $3 - 3i$ in trigonometric form.

Solution   First, determine the absolute value, r. Since $a = 3$ and $b = -3$, we have

$$r = \sqrt{a^2 + b^2} = \sqrt{(3)^2 + (-3)^2} = \sqrt{18} \text{ or } 3\sqrt{2}.$$

Now determine the argument,

$$\tan \theta = \frac{b}{a} = \frac{-3}{3} = -1.$$

Since $(3, -3)$ is in Q_4 and the reference angle is $45°$, we conclude that

$$\theta = 315°.$$

The number is written in trigonometric form as

$$3\sqrt{2}(\cos 315° + i \sin 315°),$$

and this number is graphed in Figure 6.19. Observe that any angle coterminal with $315°$ may also be used. For instance, we may write $3\sqrt{2}[\cos(-45°) + i \sin(-45°)]$.

Note   In much of the literature dealing with complex numbers and their applications, the expression

$$r(\cos \theta + i \sin \theta)$$

is written as

$$r \text{ cis } \theta \text{ or } r \angle \theta.$$

These forms are merely convenient abbreviations, and the expressions are interchangeable.

Technology Link

Figure 6.20 indicates how two choices on the CPX menu of the MATH key of a graphing calculator produce the absolute value and a reference angle for a complex number you enter using $a + bi$ form. The calculator will give absolute value results in decimal form and not in a form using a square root symbol.

You can see that the absolute value of $3 - 3i$ is given as 4.242640687 instead of $3\sqrt{2}$, and that the angle is given as $-45°$ instead of $315°$.

PROGRESS CHECK 2   Write the number $-\sqrt{3} - i$ in trigonometric form.   ▪

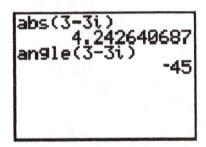

Figure 6.20

EXAMPLE 3   Converting a Complex Number to $a + bi$ Form

Write the number $2(\cos 150° + i \sin 150°)$ in the form $a + bi$.

Solution   Since $\cos 150° = -\sqrt{3}/2$ and $\sin 150° = 1/2$, we have

$$2(\cos 150° + i \sin 150°) = 2\left[\frac{-\sqrt{3}}{2} + i\left(\frac{1}{2}\right)\right]$$

$$= -\sqrt{3} + i.$$

PROGRESS CHECK 3   Write the number $6(\cos 225° + i \sin 225°)$ in the form $a + bi$.   ▪

Using trigonometric identities and $i^2 = -1$ it can be shown that the product and the quotient of two complex numbers in trigonometric form are given by the following two formulas.

Product Formula: $r_1(\cos \theta_1 + i \sin \theta_1) \cdot r_2(\cos \theta_2 + i \sin \theta_2)$
$$= r_1 r_2 [\cos(\theta_1 + \theta_2) + i \sin(\theta_1 + \theta_2)]$$

Quotient Formula: $\dfrac{r_1(\cos \theta_1 + i \sin \theta_1)}{r_2(\cos \theta_2 + i \sin \theta_2)} = \dfrac{r_1}{r_2}[\cos(\theta_1 - \theta_2) + i \sin(\theta_1 - \theta_2)],$
if $r_2 \neq 0$

In words, the product or quotient of two complex numbers is a third complex number. For the product the absolute value is the product of the absolute values of the given numbers, and the argument is the sum of the arguments of the given numbers.

For the quotient the absolute value is the quotient of the absolute values of the given numbers, and the argument is the difference of the arguments of the given numbers. In the quotient formula note that division by zero is not defined.

EXAMPLE 4   Multiplying and Dividing Complex Numbers

Determine

a. the product $z_1 \cdot z_2$ **b.** the quotient $\dfrac{z_1}{z_2}$ **c.** the quotient $\dfrac{z_2}{z_1}$

of the following complex numbers.

$$z_1 = 3(\cos 72° + i \sin 72°), z_2 = 5(\cos 43° + i \sin 43°)$$

Solution

a. $3(\cos 72° + i \sin 72°) \cdot 5(\cos 43° + i \sin 43°)$
$= 3 \cdot 5[\cos(72° + 43°) + i \sin(72° + 43°)]$
$= 15(\cos 115° + i \sin 115°)$

b. $\dfrac{3(\cos 72° + i \sin 72°)}{5(\cos 43° + i \sin 43°)} = \dfrac{3}{5}[\cos(72° - 43°) + i \sin(72° - 43°)]$

$= \dfrac{3}{5}(\cos 29° + i \sin 29°)$

c. $\dfrac{5(\cos 43° + i \sin 43°)}{3(\cos 72° + i \sin 72°)} = \dfrac{5}{3}[\cos(43° - 72°) + i \sin(43° - 72°)]$

$= \dfrac{5}{3}[\cos(-29°) + i \sin(-29°)]$

or

$= \dfrac{5}{3}(\cos 331° + i \sin 331°)$

PROGRESS CHECK 4   Find

a. the product $z_1 \cdot z_2$,   **b.** the quotient $\dfrac{z_1}{z_2}$, and

c. the quotient $\dfrac{z_2}{z_1}$ of the complex numbers given by

$$z_1 = 8(\cos 54° + i \sin 54°) \text{ and } z_2 = 4(\cos 90° + i \sin 90°).$$ ■

EXAMPLE 5   Total Impedance in Series and in Parallel

Solve the problem in the section introduction on page 353.

Solution

a. The total impedance in a series connection is given by

$$Z = Z_1 + Z_2.$$

The values for Z_1 and Z_2 are given in trigonometric form, and we cannot compute a sum in this form. So we first convert each number to $a + bi$ form.

$$Z_1 = 2.81(\cos 11.7° + i \sin 11.7°) \approx 2.7516 + 0.5698i$$
$$Z_2 = 3.54(\cos 57.2° + i \sin 57.2°) \approx 1.9176 + 2.9756i$$

Now we add.

$$Z = Z_1 + Z_2$$
$$= (2.7516 + 0.5698i) + (1.9176 + 2.9756i)$$
$$= 4.6692 + 3.5454i.$$

Finally, converting back to trigonometric form yields

$$Z = 5.86(\cos 37.2° + i \sin 37.2°) \text{ ohms}.$$

b. For a parallel connection, the total impedance is given by

$$Z = \dfrac{Z_1 Z_2}{Z_1 + Z_2}$$

The trigonometric form of complex numbers is ideal for finding products and quotients, and using the value for $Z_1 + Z_2$ that was determined in part **a** gives

$$Z = \frac{2.81(\cos 11.7° + i \sin 11.7°) \cdot 3.54(\cos 57.2° + i \sin 57.2°)}{5.86(\cos 37.2° + i \sin 37.2°)}$$

$$= \frac{2.81(3.54)}{5.86}[\cos(11.7° + 57.2° - 37.2°) + i \sin(11.7° + 57.2° - 37.2°)]$$

$$= 1.70(\cos 31.7° + i \sin 31.7°)\text{ohms}.$$

PROGRESS CHECK 5   Find the total impedance if impedances Z_1 and Z_2 are connected

a. in series and   **b.** in parallel, given that

$Z_1 = 4.09(\cos 24.5° + i \sin 24.5°)$ ohms and $Z_2 = 1.93(\cos 72.8° + i \sin 72.8°)$ ohms
■

The trigonometric form, $r[\cos(\theta) + i \sin(\theta)]$, is very useful when working with powers and roots of complex numbers. Consider the following statement, which is known as De Moivre's Theorem.

De Moivre's Theorem

If $r(\cos \theta + i \sin \theta)$ is any complex number and n is any real number, then

$$[r(\cos \theta + i \sin \theta)]^n = r^n(\cos n\theta + i \sin n\theta).$$

Although advanced mathematics is required to prove the above result, De Moivre's formula may be proved for every positive integer n by using mathematical induction and the result may be extended to all integral exponents.

EXAMPLE 6   Finding a Power of a Complex Number
Find $(1 + i)^{12}$.

Solution   First, write the number in trigonometric form.

$$r = \sqrt{a^2 + b^2} = \sqrt{(1)^2 + (1)^2} = \sqrt{2}$$

$$\tan \theta = \frac{b}{a} = \frac{1}{1} = 1 \qquad \theta = 45°$$

Thus, $1 + i = \sqrt{2}(\cos 45° + i \sin 45°)$. Now De Moivre's theorem tells us that

$$\left[\sqrt{2}(\cos 45° + i \sin 45°)\right]^{12} = \left(\sqrt{2}\right)^{12}[\cos(12 \cdot 45°) + i \sin(12 \cdot 45°)]$$

$$= (2^{1/2})^{12}[\cos 540° + i \sin 540°]$$

$$= 2^6[(-1) + i(0)]$$

$$= -64.$$

PROGRESS CHECK 6   Find $(1 - i)^8$.
■

Analogous to roots of real numbers, an **nth root of a complex number** z is a complex number w such that

$$w^n = z,$$

where n is a positive integer. Any complex number has two square roots, three cube roots, four fourth roots, and so on. To find these roots we use De Moivre's theorem. However, to find all of the roots, you must remember that there are many trigonometric representations for the same complex number. For example, since the angle $\theta + k \cdot 360°$ (k any integer) is coterminal to θ, we have

$$1 + i = \sqrt{2}(\cos 45° + i \sin 45°) = \sqrt{2}(\cos 405° + i \sin 405°)$$
$$= \sqrt{2}(\cos 765° + i \sin 765°), \text{ and so on.}$$

Thus, the method is to find one root, add $360°$ to θ, use the new trigonometric representation to find another root, and repeat this procedure until all n roots are found.

EXAMPLE 7   Find the nth Roots of a Number

Find and graph the five fifth roots of 32.

Solution   First, we write 32 in trigonometric form as

$$32(\cos 0° + i \sin 0°).$$

Now applying De Moivre's theorem, we have

$$[32(\cos 0° + i \sin 0°)]^{1/5} = 32^{1/5}\left(\cos\frac{0°}{5} + i \sin\frac{0°}{5}\right)$$
$$= 2(\cos 0° + i \sin 0°) = 2.$$

The first root is 2. To find another root, first add $360°$ to θ to obtain a different trigonometric representation for 32.

$$32 = 32[\cos(0° + 360°) + i \sin(0° + 360°)]$$

Then by De Moivre's theorem

$$\text{2nd root is } 32^{1/5}\left(\cos\frac{0° + 360°}{5} + i \sin\frac{0° + 360°}{5}\right) = 2(\cos 72° + i \sin 72°).$$

Repeating this procedure, we have

$$\text{3rd root is } 32^{1/5}\left(\cos\frac{0° + 2\cdot 360°}{5} + i \sin\frac{0° + 2\cdot 360°}{5}\right) = 2(\cos 144° + i \sin 144°)$$

$$\text{4th root is } 32^{1/5}\left(\cos\frac{0° + 3\cdot 360°}{5} + i \sin\frac{0° + 3\cdot 360°}{5}\right) = 2(\cos 216° + i \sin 216°)$$

$$\text{5th root is } 32^{1/5}\left(\cos\frac{0° + 4\cdot 360°}{5} + i \sin\frac{0° + 4\cdot 360°}{5}\right) = 2(\cos 288° + i \sin 288°).$$

The five roots are graphed in Figure 6.21, which illustrates that the roots all lie on a circle of radius 2 centered at O and that the arguments of consecutive roots differ by $72°$. We do not have to consider arguments outside of the interval $[0°, 360°)$ because the associated graphs will repeat points already obtained.

PROGRESS CHECK 7   Find and graph all the cube roots of -27.

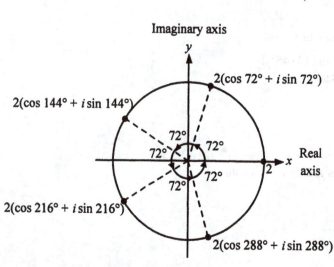

Imaginary axis

$2(\cos 72° + i \sin 72°)$

$2(\cos 144° + i \sin 144°)$

$2(\cos 216° + i \sin 216°)$

$2(\cos 288° + i \sin 288°)$

Real axis

Figure 6.21

EXERCISES 6.7

In Exercises 1–10 graph each complex number and find its absolute value.

1. $4 + 3i$
2. $5 - 12i$
3. $-1 + 2i$
4. $-2 - i$
5. $\sqrt{3} - i$
6. $\sqrt{2} + \sqrt{2}i$
7. -3
8. 1
9. $4i$
10. $-2i$

In Exercises 11–24 write the number in trigonometric form.

11. 3
12. i
13. $-2i$
14. -4
15. $1 - i$
16. $-1 + i$
17. $4 + 3i$
18. $-5 - 12i$
19. $-3 - 2i$
20. $7 - 4i$
21. $-1 + \sqrt{3}i$
22. $\sqrt{3} - i$
23. $\sqrt{2} - \sqrt{2}i$
24. $-2 - 2\sqrt{3}i$

In Exercises 25–34 write the number in the form $a + bi$.

25. $3(\cos 90° + i \sin 90°)$
26. $5(\cos 0° + i \sin 0°)$
27. $4(\cos 180° + i \sin 180°)$
28. $\sqrt{2}(\cos 270° + i \sin 270°)$
29. $\sqrt{3}(\cos 120° + i \sin 120°)$
30. $2(\cos 210° + i \sin 210°)$
31. $2(\cos 225° + i \sin 225°)$
32. $\sqrt{6}(\cos 315° + i \sin 315°)$
33. $\cos 52° + i \sin 52°$
34. $10(\cos 115° + i \sin 115°)$

In Exercises 35–44 find

a. the product $z_1 \cdot z_2$
b. the quotient $\dfrac{z_1}{z_2}$ and
c. the quotient $\dfrac{z_2}{z_1}$ of the given complex numbers.

35. $z_1 = 2(\cos 52° + i \sin 52°)$,
    $z_2 = 4(\cos 11° + i \sin 11°)$
36. $z_1 = 6(\cos 7° + i \sin 7°)$,
    $z_2 = 9(\cos 90° + i \sin 90°)$
37. $z_1 = \cos 90° + i \sin 90°$,
    $z_2 = \cos 180° + i \sin 180°$
38. $z_1 = \cos 33° + i \sin 33°$,
    $z_2 = 4(\cos 63° + i \sin 63°)$
39. $z_1 = 3(\cos 131° + i \sin 131°)$,
    $z_2 = 12(\cos 205° + i \sin 205°)$
40. $z_1 = \cos 270° + i \sin 270°$,
    $z_2 = 5(\cos 3° + i \sin 3°)$
41. $z_1 = 2(\cos 300° + i \sin 300°)$,
    $z_2 = \sqrt{2}(\cos 45° + i \sin 45°)$

42. $z_1 = 3\sqrt{2}(\cos 315° + i \sin 315°)$,
    $z_2 = \cos 0° + i \sin 0°$
43. $z_1 = \cos(-20°) + i \sin(-20°)$,
    $z_2 = \cos(-45°) + i \sin(-45°)$
44. $z_1 = 3(\cos 0° + i \sin 0°)$,
    $z_2 = 4[\cos(-90°) + i \sin(-90°)]$

In Exercises 45–58 use De Moivre's theorem and express the result in the form $a + bi$.

45. $[2(\cos 10° + i \sin 10°)]^3$
46. $[3(\cos 15° + i \sin 15°)]^4$
47. $[4(\cos 135° + i \sin 135°)]^5$
48. $[2(\cos 225° + i \sin 225°)]^6$
49. $(1 + i)^8$
50. $(-1 + i)^6$
51. $\left(1 - \sqrt{3}i\right)^5$
52. $\left(-\sqrt{3} - i\right)^7$
53. $\left(\dfrac{\sqrt{2}}{2} + \dfrac{\sqrt{2}}{2}i\right)^{16}$
54. $\left(\dfrac{\sqrt{2}}{2} - \dfrac{\sqrt{2}}{2}i\right)^{14}$
55. $\left(1 + \sqrt{3}i\right)^{-1}$
56. $(1 - i)^{-1}$
57. $\left(-\sqrt{2} + \sqrt{2}i\right)^{-3}$
58. $\left(-\sqrt{3} + i\right)^{-4}$

In Exercises 59–66 find all roots. Express the answers in both trigonometric form and in the form $a + bi$.

59. the square roots of $25(\cos 60° + i \sin 60°)$
60. the cube roots of $8(\cos 135° + i \sin 135°)$
61. the fourth roots of $16(\cos 80° + i \sin 80°)$
62. the square roots of $9(\cos 70° + i \sin 70°)$
63. the cube roots of 1
64. the fourth roots of -1
65. the square roots of $-i$
66. the square roots of i

For Exercises 67 and 68 refer to the formulas given in Example 5. Find the total impedance if impedances Z_1 and Z_2 are connected

a. in series and
b. in parallel, using the given values of Z_1 and Z_2.

67. $Z_1 = 3.14(\cos 12.5° + i \sin 12.5°)$ ohms
    $Z_2 = 3.14(\cos 77.5° + i \sin 77.5°)$ ohms
68. $Z_1 = 1.11(\cos 0.5° + i \sin 0.5°)$ ohms
    $Z_2 = 9.99(\cos 10.1° + i \sin 10.1°)$ ohms
69. In an electrical circuit, the admittance is the reciprocal of the impedance. If the impedance is $Z = 2.81(\cos 11.7° + i \sin 11.7°)$, what is the admittance?
70. Refer to Exercise 69. If the impedance is $Z = 3.54(\cos 57.2° + i \sin 57.2°)$, what is the admittance?

THINK ABOUT IT 6.7

1. Graph all complex numbers z that satisfy the given condition.
   a. $|z| = 1$ b. $z = \bar{z}$

2. Multiply $z = r(\cos \theta + i \sin \theta)$ by i in trigonometric form. Use the result and the diagram below to describe what happens geometrically when a complex number is multiplied by i.

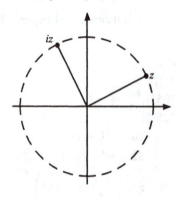

3. Find all solutions of the equation. Write answers in $a + bi$ form.
   a. $x^3 + 8 = 0$
   b. $x^3 - 27i = 0$

4. Let $z = r(\cos \theta + i \sin \theta)$ and establish each result.
   a. $z^2 = r^2(\cos 2\theta + i \sin 2\theta)$
   b. $-z = r[\cos(\theta + 180°) + i \sin(\theta + 180°)]$, where $-z = -1 \cdot z$
   c. $z^{-1} = r^{-1}[\cos(-\theta) + i \sin(-\theta)]$, where $z^{-1} = \dfrac{1}{z}$ and $z \neq 0$

5. a. Show that $\sin 2\theta = 2 \sin \theta \cos \theta$ by applying De Moivre's theorem to $(\cos \theta + i \sin \theta)^2$.
   b. Show that $\cos 2\theta = \cos^2 \theta - \sin^2 \theta$ by applying De Moivre's theorem to $(\cos \theta + i \sin \theta)^2$.

CHAPTER 6 OVERVIEW

Section	Key Concepts or Procedures to Review
6.1	■ Definitions of $a^{1/n}$, square root and nth root of a number ■ If m/n represents a reduced fraction such that $a^{1/n}$ is a real number, then $a^{m/n} = \left(\sqrt[n]{a}\right)^m = \sqrt[n]{a^m}$.
6.2	■ Product and quotient properties of radicals (a, b, $\sqrt[n]{a}$, $\sqrt[n]{b}$ denote real numbers) **1.** $\sqrt[n]{a \cdot b} = \sqrt[n]{a} \cdot \sqrt[n]{b}$ **2.** $\sqrt[n]{\dfrac{a}{b}} = \dfrac{\sqrt[n]{a}}{\sqrt[n]{b}}$ $(b \neq 0)$ ■ Methods to simplify a radical by removing any factor of the radicand whose indicated root can be taken exactly, by eliminating any fractions in the radicand, or by writing the radical so that the index is as small as possible ■ Methods to multiply and divide radicals ■ Methods to rationalize the denominator
6.3	■ Methods to add and subtract radicals
6.4	■ $\left(\sqrt[n]{a}\right)^n = a$ if $\sqrt[n]{a}$ is a real number. ■ Methods to multiply and divide radical expressions involving more than one term ■ Methods to rationalize a binomial denominator using conjugates
6.5	■ Methods to solve radical equations ■ Principle of powers
6.6	■ Definitions of principal square root of a negative number, imaginary number, complex number, and equality of complex numbers ■ $i = \sqrt{-1}$ and $i^2 = -1$ ■ Relationships among the various sets of numbers ■ Methods to add, subtract, multiply, and divide complex numbers ■ Property of conjugates: $(a + bi)(a - bi) = a^2 + b^2$ ■ Powers of i

6.7
- Definitions of complex plane, real axis, imaginary axis, and the argument and absolute value of a complex number
- Definitions of an nth root of a complex number
- Graph of a complex number
- In trigonometric form $a + bi$ is written as $r(\cos \theta + i \sin \theta)$
- The absolute value, r, is given by $r = |a + bi| = \sqrt{a^2 + b^2}$
- The argument, θ, is given by $\tan \theta = b/a$
- Methods to multiply and divide two complex numbers in trigonometric form
- De Moivre's theorem

CHAPTER 6 REVIEW EXERCISES

1. Find the square roots of 100.
2. Find $\sqrt[3]{-64}$.
3. Evaluate $16^{1/4}$.
4. Evaluate $(-27)^{-2/3}$.
5. Perform the indicated operation, and write the result using only positive exponents: $\left(\dfrac{3x^5}{12x^{-3}}\right)^{3/2}$.
6. Simplify $\sqrt{125x^7y^4}$.
7. Simplify $\sqrt[8]{x^4}$. Assume $x \geq 0$.
8. Simplify $\sqrt{\dfrac{12}{x}}$. Assume $x > 0$.
9. Multiply and simplify $6\sqrt[3]{16} \cdot 3\sqrt[3]{2}$.
10. Rationalize the denominator: $\dfrac{8}{\sqrt{12}}$.

Simplify where possible. Assume $x > 0$, $y > 0$.

11. $8\sqrt{7} - 12\sqrt{7}$.
12. $\sqrt[3]{-24} + 2\sqrt[3]{375}$.
13. $\sqrt{\dfrac{x}{y}} - \sqrt{\dfrac{y}{x}}$
14. $\sqrt{60} + \frac{1}{2}\sqrt{\frac{3}{5}}$.

Simplify. Assume $x > 0$, $y > 0$.

15. $\left(\sqrt[4]{x} + 7\right)^4$
16. $\sqrt{10}\left(\sqrt{5} - \sqrt{10}\right)$
17. $\left(2\sqrt{y} - 3\right)^2$
18. $\dfrac{4 - \sqrt{x}}{\sqrt{x}}$

19. Rationalize the denominator: $\dfrac{6}{1 + \sqrt{11}}$.

Solve each equation.

20. $\sqrt{3x + 1} - 4 = 0$
21. $\sqrt[3]{2x + 1} = \sqrt[3]{x - 2}$
22. $\sqrt{3x + 4} = x$
23. $\sqrt{3x + 16} - 6 = x$
24. $\sqrt{x + 1} - \sqrt{x - 4} = 1$
25. Combine $\sqrt{-16} + \sqrt{-100}$.
26. Multiply $(2 + 4i)(5 - 2i)$.
27. Evaluate $x^2 + 2x - 1$ if $x = 1 + i\sqrt{2}$.

28. Write the quotient $\dfrac{1 - 3i}{2 + 3i}$ in the form $a + bi$.
29. Simplify i^{23}.
30. Express $-\sqrt{-25}$ in terms of i.
31. Evaluate $x^2 + 3x + 1$ if $x = 1 + i\sqrt{3}$.
32. Express $\dfrac{4 + 5i}{3 + 2i}$ in the form $a + bi$.
33. Find the geometric mean of 60 and 15.
34. What is the period in simplified radical form of a pendulum that is 9 ft long? Use $T = 2\pi\sqrt{\dfrac{\ell}{32}}$.

Rationalize the denominator.

35. $\dfrac{8}{3 + \sqrt{5}}$
36. $\dfrac{5}{\sqrt{12x}}$
37. $\dfrac{x\sqrt{3x}}{x - \sqrt{3x}}$

Simplify where possible. Assume $x > 0$, $y > 0$.

38. $\sqrt[4]{48}$
39. $7\sqrt{20xy^2} - \sqrt{45xy^2}$
40. $\left(4\sqrt{5x}\right)^2$
41. $\left(8 + 2\sqrt{5}\right)\left(8 - 2\sqrt{5}\right)$
42. $\sqrt[4]{x^{12}}$
43. $5\sqrt{2xy} + y\sqrt{2xy}$
44. $\sqrt{-100}$
45. $(-32)^{-2/5}$
46. $\sqrt[3]{16x^7y^5}$
47. $3\sqrt{6} + \dfrac{9}{\sqrt{6}}$
48. $\left(\sqrt{3} + \sqrt{2}\right)\left(\sqrt{3} - \sqrt{2}\right)$
49. $\sqrt{\dfrac{5}{7}}$
50. $\dfrac{5 + 10\sqrt{3}}{10}$
51. i^{19}
52. $(-125)^{1/3}$
53. $\dfrac{5^{1/4}}{5}$
54. $\dfrac{x^{-3} \cdot x \cdot y^{3/4}}{x^{-2}y^{1/2}}$
55. $6\sqrt[3]{18} \cdot 3\sqrt[3]{4}$
56. $\dfrac{\sqrt[3]{15x^2}}{\sqrt[3]{10x}}$
57. $\sqrt{-16}\sqrt{-4}$
58. $(4 - 3i) - (2 + 6i)$

Solve.

59. $\sqrt{4x + 5} - 3 = 2$

60. $\sqrt[4]{2x - 6} = \sqrt[4]{3x - 24}$

61. $\sqrt{-4x - 3} = x$ **62.** $3 + \sqrt{-2x + 6} = x$

63. $\sqrt{8x + 1} - \sqrt{4x} = 1$

64. Express the number $-1 - i$ in trigonometric form.

Perform the indicated operations. Write the answers in the form $a + bi$ and in trigonometric form.

65. $8(\cos 90° + i \sin 90°) \div (\cos 0° + i \sin 0°)$

66. $2(\cos 73° + i \sin 73°) \cdot 3(\cos 107° + i \sin 107°)$

67. $\left(\dfrac{\sqrt{2}}{2} + \dfrac{\sqrt{2}}{2}i\right)^{10}$

68. $\sqrt[3]{-1}$ (all roots)

69. If $f(x) = x^2 - 5$, find $f\left(-\sqrt{5}\right)$.

70. If $f(x) = x^{3/2} + 2x^0$, find $f(4)$.

71. Verify that $1 + i$ is a solution of $x^2 - 2x + 2 = 0$.

72. Find the product of $3 + 2i$ and its conjugate.

73. $(1 + i)^6$ simplifies to

  a. 8

  b. -8

  c. $-8i$

  d. $8i$

74. The absolute value of the complex number $-2 + 2i$ is

  a. $2\sqrt{2}$

  b. 2

  c. 4

  d. $\sqrt{2}$

75. Write the number $4(\cos 300° + i \sin 300°)$ in the form $a + bi$.

76. An oil spill is dispersing such that the amount remaining after t hours is given approximately by $A = A_0 3^{-0.01t}$. What percent of the original amount is left after 24 hours? This percent is given by A/A_0.

77. The speed (v), in feet per second, that a dropped object acquires in falling d feet is given by $v = 8\sqrt{d}$.

  a. If a dropped object falls past a window at a rate of 75 ft/second, from what height above the window was it dropped? Answer to the nearest foot.

  b. If the window in part **a** is 56 feet above the ground, how fast will the object be going when it hits the ground? Answer to the nearest whole number.

78. Solve for L: $t = \pi\sqrt{\dfrac{L}{g}}$.

79. Ohm's law for alternating current states that $V = IZ$, where V is voltage in volts, I is current in amperes, and Z is impedance in ohms. Find the impedance in a particular circuit if the voltage is $10 + 6i$ volts, and the current is $2 + 3i$ amperes.

80. If the perimeter in the right triangle below is 12 ft, find x.

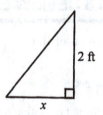

81. A classic geometry problem asks for the dimensions of a rectangle inscribed in a circle such that the rectangle has maximum possible area. If the radius is R and x is as shown, the problem leads to the equation

$$\sqrt{R^2 - x^2} - \dfrac{x^2}{\sqrt{R^2 - x^2}} = 0.$$

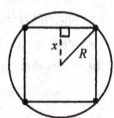

  a. Solve this equation for x in terms of R.

  b. Then find the area of the rectangle with maximum area.

82. Consider the following product:

$$\sqrt{-1} \cdot \sqrt{-1} = \sqrt{(-1)(-1)} = \sqrt{1} = 1 \text{ but}$$
$$\sqrt{-1} \cdot \sqrt{-1} = \left(\sqrt{-1}\right)^2 = -1$$

Therefore $1 = -1$! What is wrong?

CHAPTER 6 TEST

In Questions 1–7, simplify where possible. Assume $x > 0$, $y > 0$.

1. $\left(8\sqrt{6x}\right)^2$

2. $\dfrac{\sqrt[3]{6y^2}}{\sqrt[3]{2y}}$

3. $\left(\sqrt{5} + \sqrt{7}\right)\left(\sqrt{5} - \sqrt{7}\right)$

4. $8\sqrt{3xy} - 7\sqrt{27x^3y^3}$

5. $\sqrt{\dfrac{5}{3x}}$

6. $\sqrt[6]{x^8}$

7. $\left(6\sqrt{2x}\right)\left(3\sqrt{10x}\right)$

8. Evaluate $x^2 - 2x - 2$ for $x = 1 - i\sqrt{5}$.

9. Evaluate $(32)^{-1/5}$.

In Questions 10 and 11, solve each equation.

10. $\sqrt[3]{4x + 1} = \sqrt[3]{5x - 12}$

11. $\sqrt{2x + 3} = x$

12. If $f(x) = x^2 - 5$, find $f\left(\sqrt{8}\right)$.

13. Evaluate $(3 + 2i)(3 - 2i)$

14. Multiply $a^{1/2} \cdot a^{2/5}$ and write the result in radical form.

15. If complex numbers $z_1 = 6(\cos 44° + i \sin 44°)$ and $z_2 = 3(\cos 136° + i \sin 136°)$, write the product z_1z_2 in the form $a + bi$.

In Exercises 16–20 select the choice that completes the statement or answers the question.

16. We write $2(\cos 120° + i \sin 120°)$ in the form $a + bi$ as
    a. $1 - \sqrt{3}\,i$ b. $-\sqrt{3} + i$
    c. $\sqrt{3} - i$ d. $-1 + \sqrt{3}\,i$

17. The expression $\dfrac{\sqrt{2} + 1}{\sqrt{2} - 1}$ is equivalent to
    a. 3 b. -1
    c. $5 + \sqrt{2}$ d. $3 + 2\sqrt{2}$

18. The expression $x^{-1/3}$ is equivalent to
    a. $\sqrt[3]{x}$ b. $-\sqrt[3]{x}$
    c. $\dfrac{1}{\sqrt[3]{x}}$ d. $\dfrac{-1}{\sqrt[3]{x}}$

19. If $\sqrt{x^2 + 3} = 2x$, then x equals
    a. both 1 and -1 b. only 1
    c. only -1 d. no solution

20. Which statement is true for all values of x (for which it is defined)?
    a. $\left(\sqrt{x} + \sqrt{2}\right)^2 = x + 2$
    b. $\sqrt{x} + \sqrt{x} = \sqrt{2x}$
    c. $\left(\sqrt{x + 2}\right)^2 = x + 2$
    d. $\sqrt{x^2 + 1} = x + 1$

CHAPTER 7

Second-Degree Equations in One and Two Variables

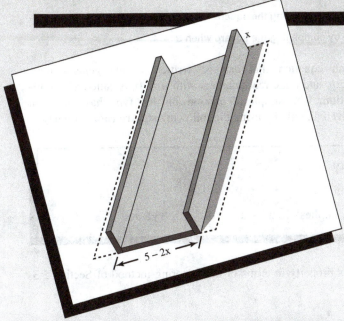

5 − 2x

For use in the construction of a computer case, a strip of metal 5 in. wide is to be shaped into an open channel with cross-sectional area of 1 in.^{2}. (See sketch.) For the channel to be useful, the height and the width must both be at least $\frac{1}{4}$ in. Find the height and width of the channel to the nearest hundredth of an inch. (See Example 5 of Section 7.1.)

FIRST-DEGREE (or linear) equations in one variable and in two variables were considered in Chapters 1 and 2, respectively. Moving up one degree, this chapter first shows how to solve any second-degree (or quadratic) equation and then considers second-degree equations in two variables. In this progression, the coverage of inequalities and systems of equations will be extended.

7.1 Solving Quadratic Equations by Completing the Square

OBJECTIVES

1 Solve quadratic equations using the square root property.

2 Complete the square for $x^2 + bx$, and express the resulting trinomial in factored form.

3 Solve $ax^2 + bx + c = 0$ by completing the square when $a = 1$.

4 Solve $ax^2 + bx + c = 0$ by completing the square when $a \neq 1$.

As stated in Chapter 5, an equation that can be written in the general form $ax^2 + bx + c = 0$, where a, b, and c are real numbers with $a \neq 0$, is called a **second-degree** or **quadratic equation.** The simplest equation of this type has the form $x^2 + c = 0$, and it can be solved directly by using the following **square root property.**

> ### Square Root Property
>
> If a is any real number, then
> $$x^2 = a \qquad \text{implies} \qquad x = 1\,\overline{a} \quad \text{or} \quad x = -1\,\overline{a}.$$

To see the origin of this property in terms of the factoring method of Section 5.3, consider the following steps.

$$x^2 = a$$
$$x^2 - a = 0$$
$$(x - \sqrt{a})(x + \sqrt{a}) = 0 \qquad \text{Factoring over the complex numbers}$$
$$x - \sqrt{a} = 0 \quad \text{or} \quad x + \sqrt{a} = 0 \qquad \text{Zero product principle}$$
$$x = \sqrt{a} \qquad\qquad x = -\sqrt{a}$$

Often, for convenience, the phrase "$x = \sqrt{a}$ or $x = -\sqrt{a}$" is abbreviated by writing $x = \pm\sqrt{a}$, which may be informally read as "plus or minus the square root of a."

Note that there are two real number solutions if $a > 0$, two (conjugate) complex number solutions if $a < 0$, and one solution (namely, 0) if $a = 0$.

EXAMPLE 1 Solving a Quadratic Equation by the Square Root Property

Solve each equation by using the square root property.

a. $x^2 = 27$ 　　　　　　　　　　　　**b.** $5(x - 3)^2 + 20 = 0$

Solution

a. $x^2 = 27$ implies $x = \pm\sqrt{27}$. Since $\sqrt{27} = \sqrt{9}\sqrt{3} = 3\sqrt{3}$, the solution set is $\{\pm 3\sqrt{3}\}$.

To check this answer graphically, we may look at the x-intercepts in the graph of $y = x^2 - 27$ that is shown in Figure 7.1. We see that the graph crosses the x-axis when x is a little to the right of 5 and when x is a little to the left of -5. Since $\pm 3\sqrt{3} \approx \pm 5.2$, this geometric result is in agreement with the solutions that were obtained algebraically.

b. First, transform the equation so $(x - 3)^2$ is on one side of the equation by itself.

$$5(x - 3)^2 + 20 = 0$$
$$5(x - 3)^2 = -20$$
$$(x - 3)^2 = -4$$

Now apply the square root property and simplify.

$$x - 3 = \pm\sqrt{-4}$$
$$x = 3 \pm 2i \quad \left(\text{since } \sqrt{-4} = 2i\right)$$

Thus, the solution set is $\{3 \pm 2i\}$.

Because the solutions to this equation are not real numbers, we cannot check the solution graphically. However, this type of solution does imply that the graph of $y = 5(x - 3)^2 + 20$ has no x-intercepts, and the graph in Figure 7.2 shows that this prediction is accurate.

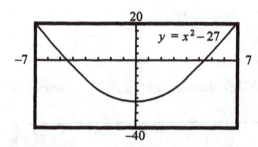

Figure 7.1

Figure 7.2

Technology Link
Some calculators have a built-in operation that finds an x-intercept of a graph in an interval. For example, on one such calculator the Root operation may be utilized to display the x-intercepts for the graph from part **a** of $y = x^2 - 27$, as shown in Figure 7.3. We will use this feature occasionally in the text to find x-intercepts because this operation gives very accurate answers. But keep in mind that repeated use of Zoom and Trace is a workable alternative, if the Root feature is not available on your calculator.

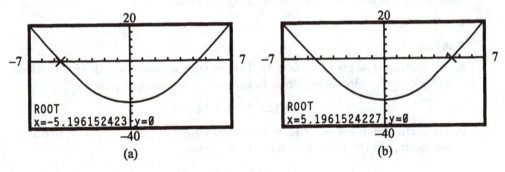

Figure 7.3

PROGRESS CHECK 1 Solve each equation, using the square root property.

a. $x^2 = 18$ **b.** $(x + 4)^2 + 7 = 0$ ■

Example 1b showed that the square root property can be used to solve quadratic equations of the form

$$(x + \text{constant})^2 = \text{constant}.$$

It is remarkable to note that by creative algebra it is possible to rewrite *any* quadratic equation in this desirable form. This ability means it is possible to derive a general method for solving all quadratic equations. As a first step, we develop a technique called **completing the square,** whose name dates back to the earliest Greek methods for solving quadratic equations geometrically. Consider an expression like

$$x^2 + 6x.$$

What constant needs to be added to make this expression a perfect square trinomial? Since the factoring model for a perfect square trinomial may be written as

$$x^2 + 2kx + k^2 = (x + k)^2,$$

we set $2k = 6$, so $k = 3$ and $k^2 = 9$. Thus, adding 9 gives

$$x^2 + 6x + 9 = (x + 3)^2.$$

More generally, to complete the square for

$$x^2 + bx,$$

we set $2k = b$, so $k = b/2$ and $k^2 = (b/2)^2$. Therefore, adding $(b/2)^2$ completes the square.

Completing the Square

To complete the square for $x^2 + bx$ with $b \neq 0$, add $(b/2)^2$, which is the square of one-half the coefficient of x.

In the diagram in Figure 7.4, note that the area of the figure is $x^2 + bx$ and that the area of the missing corner is $(b/2)^2$. This shows geometrically why adding $(b/2)^2$ turns the expression $x^2 + bx$ into a "complete" square.

EXAMPLE 2   Forming a Perfect Square Trinomial
Determine the number that should be added to make the given expression a perfect square. Then add this number, and factor the resulting trinomial.

a. $x^2 + 12x$ **b.** $y^2 - y$

Solution

a. The coefficient of x is 12, so $b = 12$. To complete the square, we add $(b/2)^2$, which is $(12/2)^2 = 6^2 = 36$. Adding 36 to the expression and factoring gives

$$x^2 + 12x + 36 = (x + 6)^2.$$

b. The coefficient of y is -1. Thus $b = -1$, and $(b/2)^2 = (-1/2)^2 = 1/4$. To complete the square, add 1/4. Doing this and factoring yields

$$y^2 - y + \tfrac{1}{4} = \left(y - \tfrac{1}{2}\right)^2.$$

PROGRESS CHECK 2   Determine the number that should be added to make the expression a perfect square. Then add this number, and factor the resulting trinomial.

a. $x^2 + x$ **b.** $y^2 - 10y$ ■

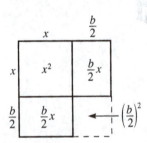

Figure 7.4

The next example shows how completing the square can be used to solve a quadratic equation.

EXAMPLE 3   Solving a Quadratic Equation by Completing the Square
Solve the equation $x^2 - 4x - 3 = 0$ by completing the square.

Solution   First, rearrange the equation with the x terms to the left of the equals sign and the constant to the right.

$$x^2 - 4x = 3$$

Now complete the square on the left. Half of -4 is -2, and $(-2)^2 = 4$. Add 4 to both sides of the equation and proceed as follows:

$$x^2 - 4x + 4 = 3 + 4 \qquad \text{Add 4 to both sides.}$$
$$(x - 2)^2 = 7 \qquad \text{Factor and simplify.}$$
$$x - 2 = \pm\sqrt{7} \qquad \text{Square root property.}$$
$$x = 2 \pm \sqrt{7}. \qquad \text{Add 2 to both sides.}$$

The solutions are $2 + \sqrt{7}$ and $2 - \sqrt{7}$, and the solution set is abbreviated $\{2 \pm \sqrt{7}\}$.

Figure 7.5 shows a graphical check and a numerical check that support this answer. Observe in the numerical check involving $2 - \sqrt{7}$ that our computed result is $-5E - 13$, which is scientific notation for -0.0000000000005. This discrepancy from 0 is due to round-off errors and should be ignored.

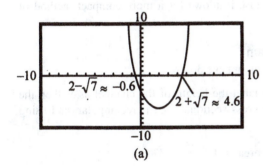

(a)

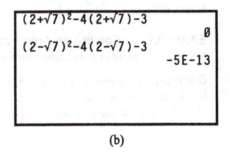

(b)

Figure 7.5

PROGRESS CHECK 3   Solve $x^2 + 6x - 1 = 0$.   ■

The procedure for completing the square requires that the coefficient of x^2 be one. When the coefficient is not one, then as a first step, divide both sides of the equation by the coefficient of x^2, as shown next.

EXAMPLE 4   Solving $ax^2 + bx + c = 0$ with $a \neq 1$
Solve $3x^2 - 2x - 3 = 0$.

Solution   First, divide both sides of the equation by 3. Then write the x terms to the left of the equal sign and the constant term to the right.

$$3x^2 - 2x - 3 = 0$$
$$x^2 - \tfrac{2}{3}x - 1 = 0$$
$$x^2 - \tfrac{2}{3}x = 1$$

Now complete the square. Half of $-\frac{2}{3}$ is $-\frac{1}{3}$, and $\left(-\frac{1}{3}\right)^2 = \frac{1}{9}$. Add $\frac{1}{9}$ to both sides of the equation and simplify.

$$x^2 - \frac{2}{3}x + \frac{1}{9} = 1 + \frac{1}{9}$$
$$\left(x - \frac{1}{3}\right)^2 = \frac{10}{9}$$

By the square root property,

$$x - \frac{1}{3} = \sqrt{\frac{10}{9}} \quad \text{or} \quad x - \frac{1}{3} = -\sqrt{\frac{10}{9}}.$$

Finally, simplify $\sqrt{10/9}$ to $\sqrt{10}/3$, and solve both equations.

$$x - \frac{1}{3} = \frac{\sqrt{10}}{3} \quad \text{or} \quad x - \frac{1}{3} = -\frac{\sqrt{10}}{3}$$
$$x = \frac{1}{3} + \frac{\sqrt{10}}{3} \qquad\qquad x = \frac{1}{3} - \frac{\sqrt{10}}{3}$$
$$x = \frac{1 + \sqrt{10}}{3} \qquad\qquad x = \frac{1 - \sqrt{10}}{3}$$

Check to confirm that the solution set is $\left\{\dfrac{1 + \sqrt{10}}{3}, \dfrac{1 - \sqrt{10}}{3}\right\}$.

PROGRESS CHECK 4   Solve $3x^2 - x - 5 = 0$.   ■

Recall that $x = \pm\sqrt{a}$ is the abbreviation for "$x = \sqrt{a}$ or $x = -\sqrt{a}$." In the next example we use such an abbreviation because it allows for a more compact method of solution.

EXAMPLE 5   Solving an Area Problem

Solve the problem in the chapter introduction on page 365.

Solution   Referring to Figure 7.6, if we label the height of the channel as x, then the width can be represented by $5 - 2x$. The cross-sectional area is rectangular, and using $A = \ell w$ leads to the equation

$$\text{area} = 1$$
$$x(5 - 2x) = 1.$$

Figure 7.7 indicates the graphs of

$$y = x(5 - 2x) \quad \text{and} \quad y = 1$$

intersect at two points where $x \approx 0.22$ or $x \approx 2.28$. So we can anticipate these two numbers are approximate solutions for the equation in question. To find the exact values of these roots by algebraic methods we now apply the method of completing the square.

$$5x - 2x^2 = 1 \qquad\qquad \text{Remove parentheses.}$$
$$-2x^2 + 5x = 1 \qquad\qquad \text{Reorder terms.}$$
$$x^2 - \frac{5}{2}x = -\frac{1}{2} \qquad\qquad \text{Divide both sides by } -2.$$
$$x^2 - \frac{5}{2}x + \frac{25}{16} = -\frac{1}{2} + \frac{25}{16} \qquad \text{Add } \left[\frac{1}{2}\left(-\frac{5}{2}\right)\right]^2 \text{ to both sides.}$$
$$\left(x - \frac{5}{4}\right)^2 = \frac{17}{16} \qquad\qquad \text{Factor and simplify.}$$

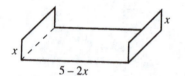

Figure 7.6

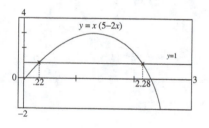

Figure 7.7

$$x - \frac{5}{4} = \pm\sqrt{\frac{17}{16}} \qquad \text{Square root property.}$$

$$x - \frac{5}{4} = \pm\frac{\sqrt{17}}{4} \qquad \text{Simplify the radical.}$$

$$x = \frac{5}{4} \pm \frac{\sqrt{17}}{4} \qquad \text{Add } \frac{5}{4} \text{ to both sides.}$$

$$x = \frac{5 \pm \sqrt{17}}{4} \qquad \text{Combine fractions.}$$

The solution set for the equation is $\left\{\dfrac{5 + \sqrt{17}}{4}, \dfrac{5 - \sqrt{17}}{4}\right\}$.

Finally, we check to see if both solutions meet the requirements of the problem that the height and width of the channel measure at least $\frac{1}{4}$ in. By calculator (to the nearest hundredth),

$$\frac{5 + \sqrt{17}}{4} = 2.28 \qquad \text{and} \qquad \frac{5 - \sqrt{17}}{4} = 0.22.$$

Therefore, only the first answer is useful, and the approximate dimensions of the channel are a height equal to 2.28 in. and a width equal to $5 - 2(2.28) = 0.44$ in.

PROGRESS CHECK 5   The design for a rectangular solar panel specifies that the area is to be 18 m^2 and the length is to be 4 m greater than the width. To the nearest hundredth of a meter, find the length and the width of this panel. ■

EXERCISES 7.1

In Exercises 1–34, solve using the square root property.

1. $x^2 = 4$
2. $x^2 = 9$
3. $3x^2 = 48$
4. $2x^2 = 72$
5. $y^2 = 12$
6. $y^2 = 20$
7. $x^2 + 4 = 0$
8. $x^2 + 9 = 0$
9. $y^2 + 28 = 0$
10. $y^2 + 50 = 0$
11. $(x + 2)^2 = 16$
12. $(x + 1)^2 = 25$
13. $(x + 3)^2 = -16$
14. $(y + 4)^2 = -27$
15. $(x + 2)^2 - 6 = 0$
16. $(x + 4)^2 - 12 = 0$
17. $(y + 5)^2 + 5 = 0$
18. $(y + 2)^2 + 20 = 0$
19. $(x - 3)^2 = -25$
20. $(x - 5)^2 = -36$
21. $(y - 4)^2 = -45$
22. $(y - 7)^2 = -50$
23. $(x - 5)^2 - 36 = 0$
24. $(x - 2)^2 - 60 = 0$
25. $(y - 3)^2 + 7 = 0$
26. $(y - 4)^2 + 6 = 0$
27. $(3x + 2)^2 = 9$
28. $(2x - 3)^2 = 4$
29. $(5x - 2)^2 = 10$
30. $(4x + 1)^2 = 7$
31. $(3x - 1)^2 + 4 = 0$
32. $(2x + 3)^2 + 1 = 0$
33. $(2x + 3)^2 = -12$
34. $(3x - 4)^2 = -18$

In Exercises 35–46, determine the number that should be added to make the given expression a perfect square. Then add this number, and factor the resulting trinomial.

35. $x^2 + 10x$
36. $x^2 - 20x$
37. $y^2 - 8y$
38. $y^2 + 14y$
39. $x^2 - 5x$
40. $x^2 + 7x$
41. $y^2 - \frac{1}{4}y$
42. $y^2 + \frac{1}{3}y$
43. $x^2 - \frac{2}{3}x$
44. $x^2 + \frac{2}{5}x$
45. $y^2 + \frac{3}{5}y$
46. $y^2 - \frac{5}{6}y$

In Exercises 47–76, solve the given quadratic equations by completing the square.

47. $x^2 + 6x = 0$ **48.** $x^2 - 10x = 0$
49. $x^2 - 2x - 2 = 0$ **50.** $x^2 + 2x - 4 = 0$
51. $y^2 - 12y + 6 = 0$ **52.** $y^2 + 14y - 6 = 0$
53. $x^2 + 10x - 4 = 0$ **54.** $x^2 - 16x + 8 = 0$
55. $x^2 + 2x + 2 = 0$ **56.** $x^2 + 2x + 4 = 0$
57. $x^2 + 4x = -2$ **58.** $x^2 - 10x = 4$
59. $y^2 - 8y = 2$ **60.** $y^2 + 12y = -6$
61. $y^2 - y = -4$ **62.** $y^2 + y = -6$
63. $x^2 + 6 = -2x$ **64.** $x^2 - 8 = 8x$
65. $y^2 - 12 = -6y$ **66.** $y^2 + 4 = -6y$
67. $2y^2 - y - 4 = 0$ **68.** $3x^2 + 4x - 6 = 0$
69. $2y^2 - 4y - 5 = 0$ **70.** $4y^2 - 2y - 5 = 0$
71. $3x^2 + 9x - 1 = 0$ **72.** $5x^2 - x - 1 = 0$
73. $2x^2 + 2x + 1 = 0$ **74.** $3x^2 + 3x + 2 = 0$
75. $3y^2 - 5y - 2 = 0$ **76.** $-2y^2 + 5y + 3 = 0$

In Exercises 77–84, solve the equation by completing the square or by using the square root property. Give solutions to the nearest hundredth.

77. A 14-in. piece of wire must be bent as shown in the figure to make a three-sided frame. The area is to be 10 in.^{2}. Show that there are two different solutions to the problem.

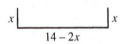

$14 - 2x$

78. Refer to Exercise 77. A student claims that she can achieve the required area of 10 in.^{2} using a shorter piece of wire (just 10 in. long). What are her two solutions?

79. Find the length of the side of the regular octagon that will fit between two studs set 30 in. apart. (See sketch.) Note that the corner right triangles have sides x, $\dfrac{30 - x}{2}$, and $\dfrac{30 - x}{2}$; and use the Pythagorean theorem to get a quadratic equation that you can solve for x.

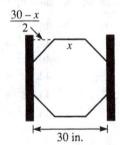

30 in.

80. Refer to Exercise 79. Find the length of the sides of the octagon if the studs are 18 in. apart.

81. On a sailboat the wind causes a wind pressure gauge to register 4.2 lb/ft^2. If the pressure p in pounds per square foot of a wind blowing at v mi/hour is given by

$$p = 0.003v^2,$$

find the wind speed at that moment. (Round to the nearest tenth.)

82. The scientist Galileo (1564–1642) discovered, when he rolled balls down an inclined plane (see figure), that the equation $v^2 = 64h$ relates the velocity of the ball and the *vertical* distance it has covered. Starting from rest, a ball which has dropped h ft has a velocity of v ft/second. It is remarkable that this velocity has nothing to do with the steepness of the plane. Use the given equation to find the velocity of a rolling ball when its vertical height is 2 ft below its starting height.

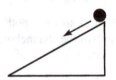

83. When P dollars is invested at an annual compound interest rate r for 2 years, then the compounded amount A is given by

$$A = P(1 + r)^2.$$

To the nearest hundredth of a percent, what compounded annual interest rate is needed for an investment to grow from $1,000 to $1,200 in 2 years?

84. Refer to Exercise 83. To the nearest hundredth of a percent, what compounded interest rate is needed for an investment to grow from $5,000 to $5,200 in 2 years?

THINK ABOUT IT 7.1

1. By analogy to the square root property, you can construct a "cube root property," useful in solving equations with the form $x^3 = a$. It would look like this: If a is any real number, then $x^3 = a$ implies $x = \sqrt[3]{a}$.
a. Use this property to solve $x^3 = -27$.
b. In more advanced work it is shown that every nonzero real number has three distinct cube roots, one real and two which have an imaginary component. Thus the cube root property in part **a** does not find *all* the solutions of $x^3 = -27$. Confirm that the other two solutions are $\dfrac{3 \pm 3i\sqrt{3}}{2}$ by showing that cubing each yields -27.
2. a. As in Exercise 1, write and use a "fourth root property" to solve $x^4 = 81$.
b. Confirm that there are four distinct fourth roots of 81 by showing that 3, -3, $3i$, and $-3i$ are all solutions to $x^4 = 81$.
3. Some quadratic equations of the form $P(x) = 0$ can be solved by factoring $P(x)$ into a product of the form $(x - a)(x - b)$, thus showing that a and b are the solutions. You can reverse this process to find a quadratic equation when you are given its solutions: Just set

$(x - \text{solution}_1)(x - \text{solution}_2)$ equal to zero. Use this approach to find equations with these given solution sets.

a. $\left\{ \pm\sqrt{7} \right\}$ **b.** $\left\{ \pm 2i \right\}$

c. $\left\{ 5 \pm \sqrt{7} \right\}$ **d.** $\left\{ -3 \pm i \right\}$

4. In Example 4 of this section completing the square gave $\dfrac{1 + \sqrt{10}}{3}$ and $\dfrac{1 - \sqrt{10}}{3}$ as the exact solutions of the equation $3x^2 - 2x - 3 = 0$.

   a. By substitution, show that both solutions check in the original equation.

b. By substitution, show that $\dfrac{1 \pm \sqrt{61}}{6}$ both check as solutions to "Progress Check" Exercise 4:

$$3x^2 - x - 5 = 0.$$

5. From a square sheet of metal an open box is made by cutting 2-in. squares from the four corners and folding up the ends. To the nearest tenth of an inch, how large a piece of metal should be used if the box is to have a volume of 100 in.^{3}?

7.2   The Quadratic Formula

A motorist sees a dangerous situation straight ahead and immediately applies the brakes. Under certain conditions, a formula that approximates the braking distance of a car is

$$d = 0.045s^2 + 1.1s,$$

where d is the distance in feet and s is the speed in miles per hour. If these conditions apply and the braking distance cannot exceed 200 ft, what is the highest (integer) speed at which this car can be traveling to stop in time? (See Example 6.)

Courtesy of Stone+/Getty Images.

OBJECTIVES

1   Solve quadratic equations using the quadratic formula.

2   Use the discriminant to determine the nature of the solutions of a quadratic equation.

3   Solve quadratic equations after choosing an efficient method.

The key feature of solving quadratic equations by completing the square is that this method applies to *all* quadratic equations. Therefore, if we apply this method to the general quadratic equation $ax^2 + bx + c = 0$ with $a \neq 0$, then we obtain a formula for solving quadratic equations that always works. In the following derivation of this formula, we also display the corresponding steps to solve the particular equation $2x^2 + 5x + 1 = 0$ to illustrate in specific terms what is happening.

General Equation	Particular Equation	Comment
$ax^2 + bx + c = 0,\ a \neq 0$	$2x^2 + 5x + 1 = 0$	Given equation.
$x^2 + \dfrac{b}{a}x + \dfrac{c}{a} = 0$	$x^2 + \dfrac{5}{2}x + \dfrac{1}{2} = 0$	Divide on both sides by the coefficient of x^2.
$x^2 + \dfrac{b}{a}x = -\dfrac{c}{a}$	$x^2 + \dfrac{5}{2}x = -\dfrac{1}{2}$	Subtract the constant term from both sides.
$x^2 + \dfrac{b}{a}x + \dfrac{b^2}{4a^2} = -\dfrac{c}{a} + \dfrac{b^2}{4a^2}$	$x^2 + \dfrac{5}{2}x + \dfrac{25}{16} = -\dfrac{1}{2} + \dfrac{25}{16}$	Add the square of one-half of the coefficient of x to both sides.
$\left(x + \dfrac{b}{2a} \right)^2 = \dfrac{b^2 - 4ac}{4a^2}$	$\left(x + \dfrac{5}{4} \right)^2 = \dfrac{17}{16}$	Factor on the left and add fractions on the right.

General Equation	Particular Equation	Comment
$x + \dfrac{b}{2a} = \pm\sqrt{\dfrac{b^2 - 4ac}{4a^2}}$	$x + \dfrac{5}{4} = \pm\sqrt{\dfrac{17}{16}}$	Apply the square root property.
$x + \dfrac{b}{2a} = \pm\dfrac{\sqrt{b^2 - 4ac}}{2a}$	$x + \dfrac{5}{4} = \dfrac{\pm\sqrt{17}}{4}$	Simplify the radical.
$x = \dfrac{-b}{2a} + \dfrac{\pm\sqrt{b^2 - 4ac}}{2a}$	$x = \dfrac{-5}{4} + \dfrac{\pm\sqrt{17}}{4}$	Isolate x on the left.
$x = \dfrac{-b \pm \sqrt{b^2 - 4ac}}{2a}$	$x = \dfrac{-5 \pm \sqrt{17}}{4}$	Combine fractions on the right.

In the particular equation, the two solutions are

$$x = \frac{-5 + \sqrt{17}}{4} \quad \text{and} \quad x = \frac{-5 - \sqrt{17}}{4},$$

and in the general equation, the two solutions are

$$x = \frac{-b + \sqrt{b^2 - 4ac}}{2a} \quad \text{and} \quad x = \frac{-b - \sqrt{b^2 - 4ac}}{2a}.$$

The work with the general equation results in the quadratic formula.

Quadratic Formula

If $ax^2 + bx + c = 0$, and $a \neq 0$, then

$$x = \frac{-b \pm \sqrt{b^2 - 4ac}}{2a}.$$

Any quadratic equation may be solved with this formula. The idea is to substitute appropriate values for a, b, and c in the formula and then simplify.

To illustrate the use of this formula, we next resolve the equation in Example 3 of Section 7.1, to show that the same result is obtained by both methods.

EXAMPLE 1   Quadratic Formula: Two Real Roots

Solve the equation $x^2 - 4x - 3 = 0$, using the quadratic formula.

Solution   In this equation $a = 1$, $b = -4$, and $c = -3$. Therefore,

$$
\begin{aligned}
x &= \frac{-b \pm \sqrt{b^2 - 4ac}}{2a} = \frac{-(-4) \pm \sqrt{(-4)^2 - 4(1)(-3)}}{2(1)} \\
&= \frac{4 \pm \sqrt{16 + 12}}{2} \\
&= \frac{4 \pm \sqrt{28}}{2} \\
&= \frac{4 \pm 2\sqrt{7}}{2} \qquad \text{Simplify the radical.} \\
&= 2 \pm \sqrt{7}. \qquad \text{Divide out 2.}
\end{aligned}
$$

Thus, $x_1 = 2 + \sqrt{7}$, $x_2 = 2 - \sqrt{7}$, and the solution set is $\{2 \pm \sqrt{7}\}$.

Once again, Figure 7.5 on page 369 shows a graphical check and a numerical check that support this answer.

Caution   A common student error is to interpret the quadratic formula as

Wrong		**Wrong**

$$x = -b \pm \frac{\sqrt{b^2 - 4ac}}{2a} \quad \text{or as} \quad x = \frac{-b}{2a} \pm \sqrt{b^2 - 4ac}.$$

Remember to divide the *entire* expression $-b \pm \sqrt{b^2 - 4ac}$ by $2a$.

PROGRESS CHECK 1   Solve $x^2 - 2x - 1 = 0$ using the quadratic formula.   ■

EXAMPLE 2   Quadratic Formula: One Repeated Root

Solve the equation $4x^2 = 20x - 25$ using the quadratic formula.

Solution   First, express the equation in the form $ax^2 + bx + c = 0$.

$$4x^2 - 20x + 25 = 0$$

In this equation $a = 4$, $b = -20$, and $c = 25$. Therefore,

$$x = \frac{-b \pm \sqrt{b^2 - 4ac}}{2a} = \frac{-(-20) \pm \sqrt{(-20)^2 - 4(4)(25)}}{2(4)}$$

$$= \frac{20 \pm \sqrt{400 - 400}}{8}$$

$$= \frac{20 \pm \sqrt{0}}{8}.$$

$$x_1 = \frac{20 + 0}{8} = \frac{20}{8} = \frac{5}{2} \qquad x_2 = \frac{20 - 0}{8} = \frac{20}{8} = \frac{5}{2}$$

The roots x_1 and x_2 both equal 5/2 so the solution set is $\{5/2\}$.

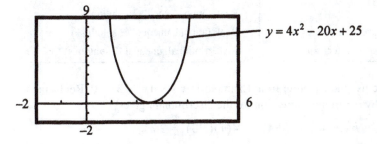
$y = 4x^2 - 20x + 25$

Figure 7.8

Since this equation has exactly one real solution 5/2, we anticipate the graph of $y = 4x^2 - 20x + 25$ should have exactly one x-intercept at $(5/2, 0)$. Figure 7.8 shows a graph that helps to confirm this observation.

PROGRESS CHECK 2   Solve $25x^2 + 16 = 40x$ by means of the quadratic formula.■

EXAMPLE 3   Quadratic Formula: No Real Roots

Solve the equation $2x^2 - x + 3 = 0$ using the quadratic formula.

Solution   In this equation $a = 2$, $b = -1$, and $c = 3$. Therefore,

$$x = \frac{-b \pm \sqrt{b^2 - 4ac}}{2a} = \frac{-(-1) \pm \sqrt{(-1)^2 - 4(2)(3)}}{2(2)}$$

$$= \frac{1 \pm \sqrt{1 - 24}}{4}$$

$$= \frac{1 \pm \sqrt{-23}}{4}$$

$$= \frac{1 \pm i\sqrt{23}}{4}.$$

$$x_1 = \frac{1 + i\sqrt{23}}{4} \qquad x_2 = \frac{1 - i\sqrt{23}}{4}$$

The solutions of this equation are (conjugate) complex numbers, and the solution set is $\{(1 \pm i\sqrt{23})/4\}$. A calculator with a key for i or with a complex number capability can be used to check that

$$2\big((1 + i\sqrt{23})/4\big)^2 - (1 + i\sqrt{23})/4 + 3$$

simplifies to 0 to confirm the answer. It is not necessary to also check $(1 - i\sqrt{23})/4$. Because the solutions must come in conjugate pairs, it is sufficient to check just one of them.

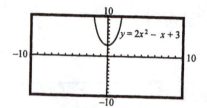

Figure 7.9

Figure 7.9 shows that the graph of $y = 2x^2 - x + 3$ has no x-intercepts, and this result is in agreement with the conclusion that $2x^2 - x + 3 = 0$ has no real roots.

PROGRESS CHECK 3 Solve $2x^2 + 3 = x$. ■

Examples 1–3 have illustrated quadratic equations with solutions that are irrational numbers, rational numbers, and complex conjugate numbers, respectively. Based on the quadratic formula, note that the nature of the solutions depends on the value of $b^2 - 4ac$, which is called the **discriminant.** This expression appears under the radical in the quadratic formula and reveals the following about the solutions of $ax^2 + bx + c = 0$.

When a, b, c Are Rational and	The Solutions Are
$b^2 - 4ac < 0$	Conjugate complex numbers
$b^2 - 4ac = 0$	Real, rational, equal (1 solution)
$b^2 - 4ac > 0$ and a perfect square	Real, rational, unequal (2 solutions)
$b^2 - 4ac > 0$ but not a perfect square	Real, irrational, unequal (2 solutions)

To illustrate, we use the equation from Example 1: $x^2 - 4x - 3 = 0$. Replacing a by 1, b by -4, and c by -3 in the expression for the discriminant gives

$$b^2 - 4ac = (-4)^2 - 4(1)(-3) = 28.$$

Because 28 is greater than 0 and is not a perfect square, we know (without solving the equation) that there are two different real number solutions that are irrational.

EXAMPLE 4 Using the Discriminant

Use the discriminant to determine the nature of the solutions of the equation $2x^2 + 5 = 4x$.

Solution This equation is equivalent to $2x^2 - 4x + 5 = 0$, in which $a = 2$, $b = -4$, and $c = 5$. The discriminant is

$$b^2 - 4ac = (-4)^2 - 4(2)(5) = -24.$$

Since -24 is less than 0, the solutions are a pair of complex conjugate numbers.

PROGRESS CHECK 4 Use the discriminant to determine the nature of the solutions of the equation $25y^2 + 16 = 40y$. ■

In this chapter we have shown several additional methods besides the factoring method of Section 5.3 for solving quadratic equations. Selecting an efficient method depends on the particular equation to be solved, and the following guidelines will help in your choice of methods.

Guidelines to Solve a Quadratic Equation

Equation Type	Recommended Method
$ax^2 + c = 0$	Use the square root property. If $ax^2 + c$ is a difference of squares, consider the factoring method.
$ax^2 + bx = 0$	Use the factoring method.
$(px + q)^2 = k$	Use the square root property.
$ax^2 + bx + c = 0$	First, try the factoring method, which applies when the discriminant reveals rational number solutions. If $ax^2 + bx + c$ does not factor or is hard to factor, use the quadratic formula.

Note that solving by completing the square is not recommended as an efficient method. Instead, this method is important because it is the basis for the quadratic formula and because in other problem-solving situations, completing the square is used to convert an expression to a standard form that is easier to analyze.

EXAMPLE 5   Solving a Quadratic Equation Efficiently

Solve the equation $80 = 96t - 16t^2$. Choose an efficient method.

Solution   This equation is equivalent to $16t^2 - 96t + 80 = 0$, in which $a = 16$, $b = -96$, and $c = 80$. First, we try the factoring method, and we find it can be used.

$$16t^2 - 96t + 80 = 0$$
$$16(t^2 - 6t + 5) = 0$$
$$16(t - 5)(t - 1) = 0$$
$$t - 5 = 0 \quad \text{or} \quad t - 1 = 0$$
$$t = 5 \qquad\qquad t = 1$$

Thus, there are two real roots, and the solution set is $\{5, 1\}$.

If the factoring step in this solution seemed hard, then an alternate solution method is to use the quadratic formula.

$$t = \frac{-b \pm \sqrt{b^2 - 4ac}}{2a} = \frac{-(-96) \pm \sqrt{(-96)^2 - 4(16)(80)}}{2(16)} = \frac{96 \pm \sqrt{4096}}{32}$$
$$= \frac{96 \pm 64}{32}$$

Then simplifying each solution separately gives

$$t_1 = \frac{96 + 64}{32} = 5 \text{ or } t_2 = \frac{96 - 64}{32} = 1.$$

By either method, the solution set is $\{5, 1\}$. These two roots can be seen in the graph of $y = 16x^2 - 96x + 80$ that is shown in Figure 7.10.

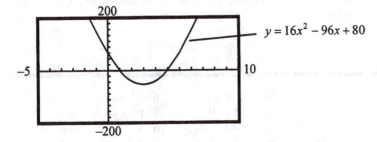

Figure 7.10

Technology Link

A quadratic equation may be viewed in a broader sense as a polynomial equation of degree or order 2. Some calculators have a built-in feature that may be used to solve polynomial equations. For instance, Figure 7.11 shows the coefficient entry screen and the solution screen associated with solving $16x^2 - 96x + 80 = 0$ on a particular calculator with a polynomial root finding feature.

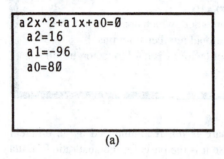
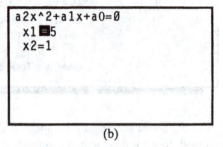

     (a)   (b)

Figure 7.11

PROGRESS CHECK 5   Solve $9x^2 = 100$. Choose an efficient method.   ■

EXAMPLE 6   Solve the problem in the section introduction on page 373.

Solution   Replacing d by 200 in the given formula leads to

$$200 = 0.045s^2 + 1.1s$$
$$0 = 0.045s^2 + 1.1s - 200.$$

Then applying the quadratic formula to the resulting equation in which $a = 0.045$, $b = 1.1$, and $c = -200$ gives

$$s = \frac{-1.1 \pm \sqrt{1.1^2 - 4(0.045)(-200)}}{2(0.045)} = \frac{-1.1 \pm \sqrt{1.21 + 36}}{0.09}$$
$$= \frac{-1.1 \pm \sqrt{37.21}}{0.09} = \frac{-1.1 \pm 6.1}{0.09}.$$

Because the speed cannot be negative, reject $s = (-1.1 - 6.1)/0.09$, which leaves

$$s = \frac{-1.1 + 6.1}{0.09} = \frac{5}{0.09} \approx 55.555556 \quad \text{(by calculator)}.$$

To the nearest integer, $s = 56$. But the braking distance is over 200 ft in this case, and the required value for s is 55, as confirmed in the following check.

$$s = 56: \quad d = 0.045(56)^2 + 1.1(56) = 202.72$$
$$s = 55: \quad d = 0.045(55)^2 + 1.1(55) = 196.625$$

Thus, if the car is to stop in time, the highest (integer) speed at which it can be traveling is 55 mi/hour. The intersection shown in Figure 7.12 agrees with this result.

PROGRESS CHECK 6   Redo the problem in Example 6, but assume that the braking distance cannot exceed 100 ft.   ■

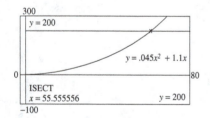

Figure 7.12

EXERCISES 7.2

In Exercises 1–16, solve the given equations using the quadratic formula.

1. $x^2 - 2x - 3 = 0$

2. $y^2 + 3y - 4 = 0$

3. $y^2 - 4y + 4 = 0$

4. $x^2 - 4x + 3 = 0$

5. $t^2 + 5t - 4 = 0$

6. $x^2 + 3x - 2 = 0$

7. $y^2 - 4y - 3 = 0$

8. $t^2 + 4t = -3$

9. $x^2 + 5x = -4$

10. $y^2 - 2y = -5$

11. $x^2 + 2x + 3 = 0$

12. $4x^2 - 4x - 15 = 0$

13. $2x^2 - 5x - 3 = 0$ **14.** $5t^2 + 33t = 14$
15. $6x^2 - 13x = -6$ **16.** $4x^2 - 25 = 0$

In Exercises 17–36, use the discriminant to determine the nature of the solutions.

17. $x^2 - 3x + 2 = 0$ **18.** $x^2 + x - 12 = 0$
19. $x^2 + 8x + 16 = 0$ **20.** $y^2 + 12y + 36 = 0$
21. $t^2 - 3t + 7 = 0$ **22.** $t^2 - 7t + 14 = 0$
23. $y^2 - 3y = 0$ **24.** $x^2 + 4x = 0$
25. $x^2 - 2 = -3x$ **26.** $x^2 - 3 = 5x$
27. $3t^2 - 7t + 4 = 0$ **28.** $2t^2 - 5t - 3 = 0$
29. $y^2 - 9 = 0$ **30.** $y^2 - 16 = 0$
31. $x^2 + 49 = 0$ **32.** $x^2 + 64 = 0$
33. $5y^2 - 3y + 4 = 0$ **34.** $2y^2 + 5y - 3 = 0$
35. $\frac{1}{2}t^2 - \frac{3}{8}t + \frac{1}{4} = 0$ **36.** $\frac{1}{8}t^2 + \frac{3}{2}t - \frac{1}{4} = 0$

In Exercises 37–60, solve the quadratic equations after choosing an efficient method.

37. $(x - 2)^2 = 16$ **38.** $(x + 3)^2 = 9$
39. $x^2 = 9$ **40.** $x^2 = 36$
41. $x^2 + 5x = 0$ **42.** $x^2 - 6x = 0$
43. $2t^2 - 5t - 3 = 0$ **44.** $5t^2 - 14 = -33t$
45. $y^2 - 2y - 15 = 0$ **46.** $y^2 + 7y + 12 = 0$
47. $t^2 - 16 = 0$ **48.** $t^2 - 121 = 0$
49. $x^2 + 5x - 4 = 0$ **50.** $x^2 + 3x - 1 = 0$
51. $9t^2 - 25 = 0$ **52.** $4t^2 - 1 = 0$
53. $2y^2 - 9y = 0$ **54.** $3y^2 + 7y = 0$
55. $3x^2 - 7x + 4 = 0$ **56.** $2t^2 - 5t - 3 = 0$
57. $x^2 + 64 = 0$ **58.** $x^2 = -25$
59. $5y^2 - 3y + 4 = 0$ **60.** $7y^2 - 3y + 5 = 0$

61. A rectangular plate is to have an area of 30 in.^{2} and the sides of the plate are to differ in length by 4 in. To the nearest tenth of an inch, find the dimensions of the plate.

62. The perimeter of a rectangle is 100 ft and the area is 400 ft^2. Find the dimensions of the rectangle.

63. The total cost of manufacturing x units of a certain product is given by $C = 0.1x^2 + 0.7x + 3$. How many units can be made for a total cost of $20?

64. A manufacturer sells a product for $10 per unit. The cost of manufacturing x units is estimated by the formula $C = 200 + x + 0.01x^2$. How many units must be manufactured and sold to earn a profit of $1,200? (**Hint:** profit = income − cost.)

65. Two adjacent building lots are each square with a total area of 14,600 ft^2. The total street frontage for the two lots is 160 ft. (See the figure.) Find the dimensions of each square lot.

66. Refer to the figure for Exercise 65. Two adjacent building lots have a total area of 10,952 ft^2. The total street frontage is 148 ft. Find the dimensions of each square lot.

67. An ancient problem leading to a quadratic equation is given on an Egyptian papyrus from about 2000 B.C. The problem is as follows: Divide 100 square units into two squares such that the side of one of the squares is three-fourths the side of the other.

68. Divide 10 square units into two squares such that the side of one of the squares is half the side of the other.

69. An object is thrown upward from a platform 20 ft above the ground with an initial velocity of 40 ft/second. The formula $y = 20 + 40t - 16t^2$ gives its height above the ground (y) t seconds after it is released. After how many seconds will the object be 40 ft above the ground? Why are there two answers? (Round to the nearest hundredth of a second.)

70. Refer to Exercise 69. After how many seconds will the object be 10 ft above the ground? Why is there only one answer? (Round to the nearest hundredth of a second.)

71. Babylonian mathematics texts from about 3000 B.C. contain problems asking for a number which added to its reciprocal gives a specified sum. They worked out a general procedure for such problems. Try this one. What number when added to its reciprocal equals 5? Give the answers in radical form and in decimal approximation.

72. What number when added to its reciprocal equals 6? Give the answer in radical form and in decimal approximation.

THINK ABOUT IT 7.2

1. The great equation solver of the sixteenth century, Gerolamo Cardano, perhaps the most bizarre character in the whole history of mathematics, used a technique called "depressing" to put equations in simpler form. When you "depress" an equation, you get rid of the term which has the next to the highest power of the variable. Through this technique Cardano was able to solve cubic equations. You can use it to solve quadratic equations.

a. Given the equation $ax^2 + bx + c = 0$, rewrite it by replacing each occurrence of x by $y - b/2a$. This will give you a simpler (depressed) equation in y which you can solve by the square root property. You will see that this is another way to arrive at the quadratic formula. [For more on Cardano see *Journey Through Genius* by William Dunham (Wiley, 1990) or any history of mathematics text.]

b. Solve the equation $x^2 + 4x + 1 = 0$ by the method of depression.

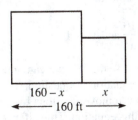

$160 - x$ x

← 160 ft →

2. a. Show that the sum of the solutions of
$ax^2 + bx + c = 0$ with $a \neq 0$ is $-b/a$.

b. Find a simple expression for the product of the solutions.

c. For the equation $3x^2 + 2x - 4 = 0$, find the sum and product of the solutions.

3. In general, there are n solutions (including all complex solutions) to $x^n = 1$; they are called the nth roots of 1. Find the six solutions of $x^6 = 1$. Rewrite as $x^6 - 1 = 0$; then use the zero product principle and the quadratic formula.

4. A fascinating number which appears in many areas of mathematics is called the golden ratio. For example, in an isosceles triangle where the base angles are double the vertex angle, it is the ratio of the side to the base. An early appearance is in Euclid's *Elements,* where an exercise says: "Divide a line segment such that the ratio of the large part to the whole is equal to the ratio of the small part to the large." Refer to the sketch, from which

we derive golden ratio $= \dfrac{\ell}{\ell + s} = \dfrac{s}{\ell}$. If you set $s = 1$ and solve the resulting quadratic equation, you will determine the exact value of the golden ratio.

5. In Example 4 of Section 7.2 the discriminant was used to determine the nature of the solutions of the equation $2x^2 - 4x + 5 = 0$.

a. Show that the discriminant is not changed if the equation is rewritten as $-2x^2 + 4x - 5 = 0$, which results when both sides are multiplied by -1.

b. Show that, in general, the discriminant $b^2 - 4ac$ is not changed if a, b, and c are replaced by their opposites.

c. Show that in the quadratic formula if a, b, and c are replaced by their opposites, then the solutions do not change.

Courtesy of PhotoDisc/Getty Images.

7.3   Other Equations Which Lead to Quadratic Equations

The cost C of producing x units of a product is often approximated by formulas of the form

$$C = px^2 + qx + r.$$

Solve this formula for x in terms of p, q, r, and C. (See Example 6.)

OBJECTIVES

1 Solve fractional equations and radical equations that lead to quadratic equations.

2 Solve equations with quadratic form.

3 Solve literal equations for a variable with highest power 2.

Equations containing fractional expressions and equations containing radicals may lead to quadratic equations, as was shown in Sections 5.8 and 6.5, respectively. With the aid of the additional methods of this chapter, we can now solve a wider variety of such equations.

EXAMPLE 1   Solving a Fractional Equation That Leads to a Quadratic Equation

Solve $\dfrac{2}{x} + \dfrac{10}{x^2} = 1$.

Solution   Figure 7.13 indicates that the graphs of

$$y = \frac{2}{x} + \frac{10}{x^2} \text{ and } y = 1$$

intersect at two points where $x \approx -2.3$ or $x \approx 4.3$. So we can anticipate that these two numbers are approximate solutions for the equation in question. To find the exact values of these roots by algebraic methods, we first remove fractions by multiplying both sides of the equation by the LCD, which is x^2 in this equation. Thus, if $x \neq 0$,

$$x^2\left(\frac{2}{x} + \frac{10}{x^2}\right) = x^2 \cdot 1$$
$$2x + 10 = x^2$$
$$0 = x^2 - 2x - 10.$$

Then, by the quadratic formula

$$x = \frac{-(-2) \pm \sqrt{(-2)^2 - 4(1)(-10)}}{2(1)} = \frac{2 \pm \sqrt{44}}{2} = \frac{2 \pm 2\sqrt{11}}{2} = 1 \pm \sqrt{11}.$$

The restriction $x \neq 0$ does not affect the proposed solution, and both numbers check in the original equation. Thus, the solution set is $\{1 \pm \sqrt{11}\}$. Observe that $1 + \sqrt{11} \approx 4.3$ and $1 - \sqrt{11} \approx -2.3$, so these roots are in agreement with the approximate solutions that we obtained graphically using Figure 7.13.

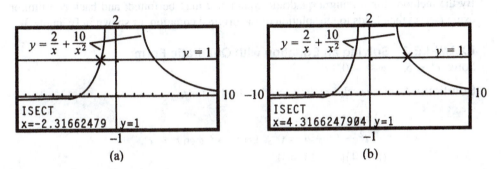

Figure 7.13

PROGRESS CHECK 1   Solve $1 - \frac{2}{x} = \frac{17}{x^2}$. ■

EXAMPLE 2   Solving a Radical Equation That Leads to a Quadratic Equation

Solve $x + \sqrt{14 - x^2} = 0$.

Solution   First, isolate the square root term.

$$x + \sqrt{14 - x^2} = 0$$
$$\sqrt{14 - x^2} = -x$$

Then square both sides of the equation and solve for x.

$$\left(\sqrt{14 - x^2}\right)^2 = (-x)^2 \quad \text{Square both sides.}$$
$$14 - x^2 = x^2$$
$$14 = 2x^2$$
$$7 = x^2$$
$$\pm\sqrt{7} = x \quad \text{Square root property.}$$

Now check both solutions in the original equation.

$$x + \sqrt{14 - x^2} = 0 \qquad\qquad x + \sqrt{14 - x^2} = 0$$
$$\sqrt{7} + \sqrt{14 - \left(\sqrt{7}\right)^2} \stackrel{?}{=} 0 \qquad -\sqrt{7} + \sqrt{14 - \left(-\sqrt{7}\right)^2} \stackrel{?}{=} 0$$
$$\sqrt{7} + \sqrt{7} \stackrel{?}{=} 0 \qquad\qquad -\sqrt{7} + \sqrt{7} \stackrel{?}{=} 0$$
$$2\sqrt{7} \neq 0 \quad \text{Extraneous} \qquad\qquad 0 = 0$$

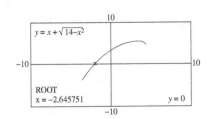

Figure 7.14

The check shows that $-\sqrt{7}$ is a solution, while $\sqrt{7}$ is extraneous. Thus, the solution set is $\{-\sqrt{7}\}$. The x-intercept for $y = x + \sqrt{14 - x^2}$ shown in Figure 7.14 is consistent with this result since $-\sqrt{7} \approx -2.6$.

PROGRESS CHECK 2 Solve $\sqrt{16 - x^2} - x = 0$. ▪

By a well-chosen substitution, it is sometimes possible to convert equations that are not originally quadratic into the form

$$at^2 + bt + c = 0 \qquad (a \neq 0),$$

where t is some variable expression. Such equations are called **equations with quadratic form.** For example, the fourth-degree equation

$$x^4 - 5x^2 + 4 = 0$$

is not a quadratic (or second-degree) equation. But if we let $t = x^2$, then $t^2 = x^4$; and this equation becomes

$$t^2 - 5t + 4 = 0.$$

By the methods for solving a quadratic equation, t may be found; and back substitution using $t = x^2$ then leads to the solution of the original equation, as shown in Example 3.

EXAMPLE 3   Solving an Equation with Quadratic Form
Solve $x^4 - 5x^2 + 4 = 0$.

Solution   As discussed, first let $t = x^2$ and solve for t.

$$x^4 - 5x^2 + 4 = 0$$
$$t^2 - 5t + 4 = 0 \qquad \text{Let } t = x^2; \text{ then } t^2 = x^4.$$
$$(t - 4)(t - 1) = 0$$
$$t - 4 = 0 \quad \text{or} \quad t - 1 = 0 \qquad \text{Use the factoring method.}$$
$$t = 4 \qquad\qquad t = 1$$

Now resubstitute x^2 for t and solve for x.

$$x^2 = 4 \quad \text{or} \quad x^2 = 1$$
$$x = \pm 2 \qquad x = \pm 1 \qquad \text{Square root property.}$$

Check all four solutions in the original equation to confirm that the solution set is $\{2, -2, 1, -1\}$. A graph of $y = x^4 - 5x^2 + 4$ is shown in Figure 7.15. Observe that the four x-intercepts in the graph appear to coincide with the four numbers in the solution set.

Note   The equation in this example is intended as a simple illustration of the substitution technique associated with equations that are quadratic in form. This equation is also easily solved without substitution, as follows.

$$x^4 - 5x^2 + 4 = 0$$
$$(x^2 - 4)(x^2 - 1) = 0 \qquad \text{Factor.}$$
$$x^2 - 4 = 0 \quad \text{or} \quad x^2 - 1 = 0 \qquad \text{Zero product principle.}$$
$$x^2 = 4 \qquad\qquad x^2 = 1 \qquad \text{Isolate } x^2.$$
$$x = \pm 2 \qquad\qquad x = \pm 1 \qquad \text{Square root property.}$$

However, the substitution method will be easier in some cases and required in others. For instance, try solving $x^4 - 4x^2 + 1 = 0$ (as requested in "Think About It" Exercise 2).

PROGRESS CHECK 3   Solve $x^4 - 11x^2 + 18 = 0$. ▪

To spot equations with quadratic form, look for the exponent in one term to be double the exponent in another term.

EXAMPLE 4   Solving an Equation with Quadratic Form
Solve $5x^{2/3} - 8x^{1/3} - 4 = 0$.

Solution   In the exponents in the variable terms, note that $\frac{2}{3}$ is double $\frac{1}{3}$. If we let $t = x^{1/3}$, then $t^2 = x^{2/3}$; and this substitution reveals an equation with quadratic form that we can solve for t.

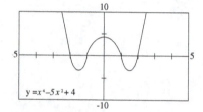

$y = x^4 - 5x^2 + 4$

Figure 7.15

$$5x^{2/3} - 8x^{1/3} - 4 = 0$$

$$5t^2 - 8t - 4 = 0 \qquad \text{Let } t = x^{1/3}; \text{ then } t^2 = x^{2/3}.$$

$$(5t + 2)(t - 2) = 0$$

$$5t + 2 = 0 \quad \text{or} \quad t - 2 = 0 \quad \text{Use the factoring method.}$$

$$t = -\tfrac{2}{5} \qquad\qquad t = 2$$

Now replace t by $x^{1/3}$ and solve for x.

$$x^{1/3} = -\tfrac{2}{5} \quad \text{or} \quad x^{1/3} = 2$$

$$x = -\tfrac{8}{125} \qquad\quad x = 8 \qquad \text{Cube both sides.}$$

Both solutions check, and the solution set is $\left\{-\tfrac{8}{125}, 8\right\}$. These two roots can be seen in the graph of $y = 5x^{2/3} - 8x^{1/3} - 4$ that is shown in Figure 7.16. Check that $-\tfrac{8}{125}$ and $-.064$ are equivalent.

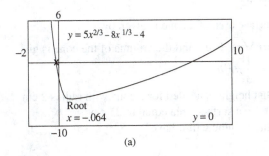
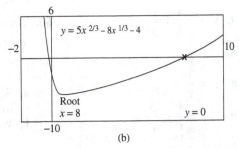

(a)   (b)

Figure 7.16

PROGRESS CHECK 4   Solve $x + 2x^{1/2} - 3 = 0$.   ■

The methods for solving quadratic equations may be applied to solve a literal equation or a formula for a variable with highest power 2.

EXAMPLE 5   Rewriting an Equation for a Relation

Solve $x = y^2 - 4$ for y.

Solution   Isolate y^2 and then solve for y using the square root property.

$$x = y^2 - 4$$

$$x + 4 = y^2 \qquad \text{Add 4 to both sides.}$$

$$\pm\sqrt{x + 4} = y \qquad \text{Square root property.}$$

Note   To graph an equation on a graphing calculator, you must enter an expression that is solved for y. Using the result in this example, $x = y^2 - 4$ may be graphed by displaying the graphs of $y = \sqrt{x + 4}$ and $y = -\sqrt{x + 4}$ in the same calculator screen.

PROGRESS CHECK 5   Solve $x^2 + y^2 = 1$ for y.   ■

EXAMPLE 6   Rewriting a Formula for Cost

Solve the problem in the section introduction on page 380.

Solution   We use the quadratic formula to solve the equation

$$C = px^2 + qx + r$$

for x. To match the form $0 = ax^2 + bx + c$, subtract C on both sides to obtain

$$0 = px^2 + qx + (r - C).$$

In this form the coefficient of x^2 represents a, the coefficient of x represents b, and the remaining expression represents c. Replacing a by p, b by q, and c by $r - C$ in the quadratic formula gives

$$x = \frac{-q \pm \sqrt{q^2 - 4p(r - C)}}{2p} \quad \text{or} \quad x = \frac{-q \pm \sqrt{q^2 - 4pr + 4pC}}{2p}.$$

PROGRESS CHECK 6 Solve $y = -16t^2 + v_0 t + y_0$ for t. ▪

EXERCISES 7.3

In Exercises 1–30, solve the given equation.

1. $\frac{4}{x} + \frac{12}{x^2} = 1$

2. $\frac{8}{x} - \frac{15}{x^2} = 1$

3. $-\frac{13}{x} - \frac{7}{x^2} = -2$

4. $3 = -\frac{4}{x} + \frac{15}{x^2}$

5. $\frac{1}{x} - \frac{12}{x^2} = -1$

6. $1 = \frac{5}{x} + \frac{6}{x^2}$

7. $3 = \frac{-2}{x} + \frac{2}{x^2}$

8. $2 = \frac{3}{x} + \frac{1}{x^2}$

9. $1 = \frac{2}{x} - \frac{2}{x^2}$

10. $1 = -\frac{4}{x} - \frac{5}{x^2}$

11. $1 = \frac{-9}{x^2}$

12. $1 = \frac{-16}{x^2}$

13. $2 + \frac{5}{x^2} = \frac{6}{x}$

14. $9 + \frac{5}{x^2} = \frac{12}{x}$

15. $2x - \frac{20}{x} = 0$

16. $2 = \frac{60}{x^2}$

17. $x + \sqrt{12 - x^2} = 0$

18. $x - \sqrt{12 - x^2} = 0$

19. $\sqrt{24 - x^2} = x$

20. $\sqrt{10 - x^2} = x$

21. $x + \sqrt{4 - x^2} = 0$

22. $\sqrt{6 - x^2} = -x$

23. $x - \sqrt{x^2 - 8} = 0$

24. $x - \sqrt{x^2 - 9} = 0$

25. $x = \sqrt{x^2}$

26. $x + \sqrt{x^2} = 0$

27. $\sqrt{14 - 3x^2} = 2x$

28. $\sqrt{45 - 6x^2} = 3x$

29. $\sqrt{1 + x + x^2} = 3x + 1$

30. $\sqrt{9 - x - x^2} = 2x + 3$

In Exercises 31–48, solve the given equations, which all have quadratic form.

31. $y^4 + 3y^2 - 4 = 0$

32. $y^4 - 4y^2 + 3 = 0$

33. $x^4 - 11x^2 + 30 = 0$

34. $6x^4 - 13x^2 + 6 = 0$

35. $y^4 - 2y^2 - 3 = 0$

36. $y^4 - 2y^2 - 8 = 0$

37. $x^4 - 25x^2 + 144 = 0$

38. $x^4 - 26x^2 + 25 = 0$

39. $x^4 - 3x^2 - 4 = 0$

40. $x^4 + 8x^2 - 9 = 0$

41. $y^4 - y^2 - 6 = 0$

42. $y^4 + y^2 - 6 = 0$

43. $x^{2/3} - 2x^{1/3} - 3 = 0$

44. $x^{2/3} + 3x^{1/3} - 4 = 0$

45. $x + 4x^{1/2} + 3 = 0$

46. $x + 5x^{1/2} + 4 = 0$

47. $x^{1/2} - 2x^{1/4} - 8 = 0$

48. $x^{1/2} - 4x^{1/4} + 3 = 0$

In Exercises 49–58, solve for x.

49. $x^2 = y + 3$

50. $x^2 = y - 7$

51. $y = x^2 - 8$

52. $y = x^2 + 7$

53. $y^2 = x^2 + 6$

54. $y^2 = x^2 - 8$

55. $t = a_1 x^2 + a_2 x + a_3$

56. $y = -16x^2 - 5x + y_0$

57. $t = dx^2 + rx$

58. $y = -16x^2 + 16x$

59. The perimeter of an isosceles right triangle is 12 inches. Find its area.

60. The surface area of a cone is given by

$S = \pi r \sqrt{r^2 + h^2}$, and the volume of the cone is given by $V = \frac{1}{3}\pi r^2 h$.

a. What height is needed for a cone with radius 2 cm to have a surface area equal to 25 cm²?

b. What volume will it have?

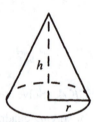

Exercises 61–64 are based on those found in American algebra texts of 100 years ago. The wording is quite dated, but you can still solve them by using quadratic equations, as algebra students did then.

61. A gentleman has two square rooms whose sides are to each other as 2 to 3. He finds that it will require 20 yd² more of carpeting to cover the floor of the larger than of the smaller room. What is the length of one side of each room? (*Hint:* The side of the smaller square is $\frac{2}{3}$ the size of the larger one.)

62. A man purchased a rectangular field whose length was $\frac{10}{9}$ times its breadth. It contained 9 acres. What was the length in rods of each side? (*Note:* 1 acre is 160 square rods, so 9 acres is 1,440 square rods. You don't need it for this exercise, but a rod is 6.5 yd, and an acre originally was supposed to indicate the size of a field that a team of oxen could plow in one day.)

63. An orchard containing 2,000 trees had 10 rows more than it had trees in a row. How many rows were there? How many trees were there in each row?

64. A person purchased a flock of sheep for $100. If he had purchased 5 more for the same sum, they would have cost $1 less per head. How many did he buy? [*Hint:* If

he bought x sheep, then each one cost $100/x$ dollars. If he bought $x + 5$ sheep, then each cost $100/(x + 5)$ dollars.]

THINK ABOUT IT 7.3

1. Give three examples of equations with quadratic form.
2. Solve $x^4 - 4x^2 + 1 = 0$.
3. If the perimeter and the area of a rectangle are given by p and a, respectively, then show that the length ℓ is given by
$$\ell = \frac{p \pm \sqrt{p^2 - 16a}}{4}.$$

Note that since $a = \ell\omega$, you can use a/ℓ in place of w.

4. **a.** Solve $x^{-2} - 4x^{-1} - 3 = 0$ by letting $t = x^{-1}$.
   b. Solve the same equation by multiplying both sides by x^2.
5. The formula $t = \sqrt{d}/4$ relates the distance d in feet traveled by a free-falling object to the time t of the fall in seconds, disregarding air resistance. If you drop a stone from a bridge that spans a river, and you hear the sound of the splash 3.7 seconds later, then to the nearest foot how far above the water is that particular point on the bridge? The sound created by the splash travels at a speed of about 1100 ft/second. (*Hint:* The total elapsed time equals the time for the stone to reach the water plus the time for the sound to reach you.)

7.4 Solving Inequalities Involving Polynomials

A long strip of galvanized sheet metal 9 in. wide is to be shaped into an open gutter by bending up the edges, as shown in the figure, to form a gutter with a rectangular cross-sectional area. If the area must be at least 9 in.^{2} for the gutter to be useful, then find all possible heights (x) of the gutter. (Ignore the thickness of the metal.) (See Example 4.)

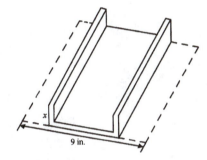

OBJECTIVES

1 Solve quadratic inequalities.

2 Solve polynomial inequalities of degree higher than 2.

3 Solve inequalities involving quotients of polynomials.

Quadratic inequalities are inequalities that may be expressed in the standard forms

$$ax^2 + bx + c > 0, \qquad ax^2 + bx + c \geq 0,$$
$$ax^2 + bx + c < 0, \quad \text{or} \quad ax^2 + bx + c \leq 0,$$

where a, b, and c are real numbers with $a \neq 0$. There are several methods for solving such inequalities, and Example 1 shows a method that is based on the ability to read a graph.

EXAMPLE 1   Using a Graphical Method

Figure 7.17 shows the graph of $f(x) = x^2 + 2x - 3$. Use this graph to solve each equation or inequality.

a. $x^2 + 2x - 3 = 0$ **b.** $x^2 + 2x - 3 < 0$

c. $x^2 + 2x - 3 > 0$ **d.** $x^2 + 2x - 3 \leq 0$

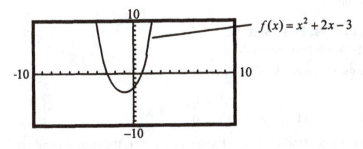

Figure 7.17

Solution

a. The real number roots of the equation $x^2 + 2x - 3 = 0$ are identical to the x-coordinates of the x-intercepts of the graph of $f(x) = x^2 + 2x - 3$. In Figure 7.17 it appears that the graph is *on the x-axis* when and so we check these numbers in the original equation.

$$\text{For } x = -3: \quad (-3)^2 + 2(-3) - 3 = 9 - 6 - 3 = 0$$
$$\text{For } x = 1: \quad (1)^2 + 2(1) - 3 = 1 + 2 - 3 = 0$$

Both apparent solutions check, and the solution set is $\{-3, 1\}$.

b. The y-values are less than zero when the graph is *below the x-axis.* Thus, $x^2 + 2x - 3 < 0$ for $-3 < x < 1$, so the solution set is the interval $(-3, 1)$.

c. The y-values are greater than zero when the graph is *above the x-axis.* Thus, $x^2 + 2x - 3 > 0$ when $x < -3$ or $x > 1$, so the solution set in interval notation is $(-\infty, -3) \cup (1, \infty)$.

d. They y-values are less than or equal to zero when the graph is *on or below the x-axis.* Thus, we need to modify the answer from part **b** to include -3 and 1 in the solution set. So $x^2 + 2x - 3 \leq 0$ for $-3 \leq x \leq 1$, and the solution set is the interval $[-3, 1]$.

PROGRESS CHECK 1   Figure 7.18 shows the graph of $f(x) = x^2 - x - 2$. Use this graph to solve each equation or inequality.

a. $x^2 - x - 2 = 0$ **b.** $x^2 - x - 2 > 0$
c. $x^2 - x - 2 < 0$ **d.** $x^2 - x - 2 \geq 0$ ■

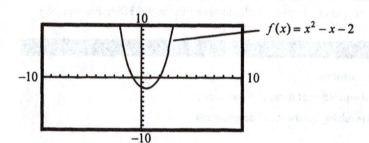

Figure 7.18

When solving quadratic equations or inequalities by the method shown in Example 1, note that the solution set is determined using the criteria described in Figure 7.19.

The graphing method just described can be used to formulate an algebraic method for solving quadratic inequalities that is also easy to use in practice. First, real numbers that make $ax^2 + bx + c$ equal to zero are called **critical numbers.** Note in Example 1 that the critical numbers are -3 and 1 and that these two critical numbers separate the number line into three intervals, namely, $(-\infty, -3)$, $(-3, 1)$, and $(1, \infty)$. Also, observe that throughout each interval the sign of $x^2 + 2x - 3$ remains the same. Thus an efficient method, called the **test point method,** for solving quadratic inequalities is to find the sign of a convenient number in each of the intervals determined by the critical numbers. By comparing the resulting sign with the inequality in question, we may determine the solution set, as shown in Example 2.

EXAMPLE 2   Using the Test Point Method
Solve $1 - x^2 \geq 0$ using the test point method.

Solution   First, factor the nonzero side of the inequality.

$$1 - x^2 \geq 0$$
$$(1 + x)(1 - x) \geq 0$$

Because $(1 + x)(1 - x)$ equals 0 when $x = -1$ and when $x = 1$, the critical numbers are -1 and 1. These numbers separate the number line into the intervals $(-\infty, -1)$, $(-1, 1)$, and $(1, \infty)$, and Figure 7.20 shows whether a true statement results when a specific number in each of these intervals is tested.

Quadratic Equation or Inequality	Possible Graph of $y = f(x)$	Interpretation of Solution Set
$ax^2 + bx + c = 0$	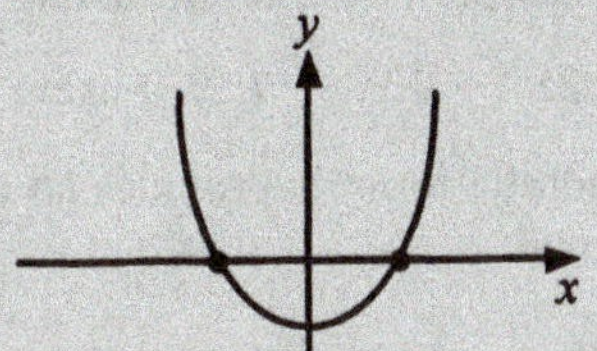	$f(x) = 0$ for all x-values where the graph is *on* the x-axis.
$ax^2 + bx + c < 0$	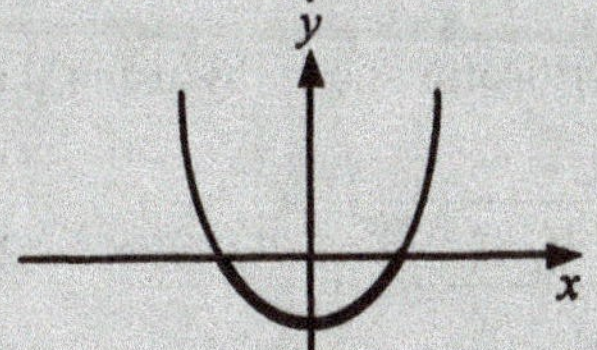	$f(x) < 0$ for all x-values where the graph is *below* the x-axis.
$ax^2 + bx + c > 0$	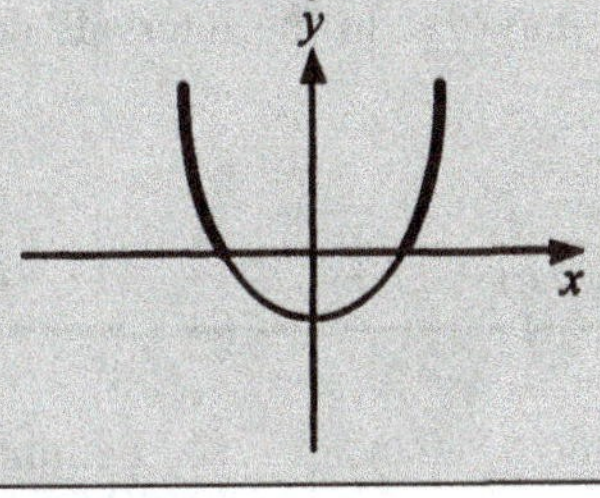	$f(x) > 0$ for all x-values where the graph is *above* the x-axis.

Figure 7.19

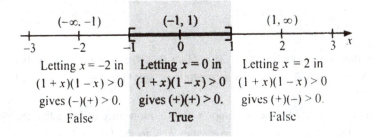

Figure 7.20

All numbers in each interval lead to the same result as the specific number tested, so $(1 + x)(1 - x) > 0$ is a true statement on the interval $(-1, 1)$. Because the inequality in question is greater than or equal to zero, -1 and 1 are also solutions, and the solution set is the interval $[-1, 1]$.

This answer may be checked using the graph in Figure 7.21, which shows that the graph of $f(x) = 1 - x^2$ is on or above the x axis for $-1 \leq x \leq 1$.

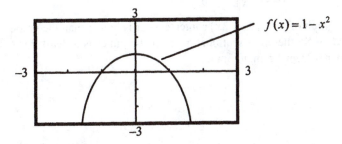

Figure 7.21

Note In this example specific numbers may be tested in $1 - x^2 \geq 0$ or in the equivalent inequality $(1 + x)(1 - x) \geq 0$. Although it is necessary to determine only the sign that results from the substitution, you may prefer to find the actual number.

PROGRESS CHECK 2 Solve $2x^2 - 13x - 7 \geq 0$ using the test point method. ■

In the next example the quadratic formula provides an efficient method for finding the critical numbers that are irrational.

EXAMPLE 3 Using the Test Point Method and the Quadratic Formula
Solve $x^2 - 2x - 1 > 0$.

Solution First, determine the critical numbers by using the quadratic formula to find when $x^2 - 2x - 1$ equals zero.

$$x = \frac{-(-2) \pm \sqrt{(-2)^2 - 4(1)(-1)}}{2(1)} = \frac{2 \pm \sqrt{8}}{2} = \frac{2 \pm 2\sqrt{2}}{2} = 1 \pm \sqrt{2}$$

The critical numbers are $1 + \sqrt{2}$ and $1 - \sqrt{2}$, which are approximately equal to 2.4 and -0.4, respectively. Now we may test in the intervals determined by these critical numbers, as shown in Figure 7.22.

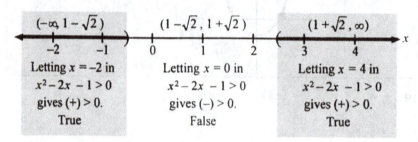

$(-\infty, 1 - \sqrt{2})$	$(1 - \sqrt{2}, 1 + \sqrt{2})$	$(1 + \sqrt{2}, \infty)$
Letting $x = -2$ in	Letting $x = 0$ in	Letting $x = 4$ in
$x^2 - 2x - 1 > 0$	$x^2 - 2x - 1 > 0$	$x^2 - 2x - 1 > 0$
gives $(+) > 0$.	gives $(-) > 0$.	gives $(+) > 0$.
True	False	True

Figure 7.22

The tests show that the inequality $x^2 - 2x - 1 > 0$ is true for all x such that $x < 1 - \sqrt{2}$ or $x > 1 + \sqrt{2}$. Thus the solution set is $\left(-\infty, 1 - \sqrt{2}\right) \cup (1 + \sqrt{2}, \infty)$.

The graph in Figure 7.23 may be used to support this solution since it shows that the graph of $f(x) = x^2 - 2x - 1$ is above the x-axis when x is to the left of $1 - \sqrt{2}$ or when x is to the right of $1 + \sqrt{2}$.

PROGRESS CHECK 3 Solve $x^2 - 6x + 4 < 0$. ■

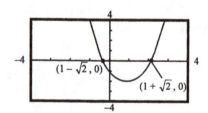

Figure 7.23

EXAMPLE 4 Finding a Useful Height for a Gutter
Solve the problem in the section introduction on page 385.

Solution The sheet metal is 9 in. wide, so bending up edges of length x on each side converts the sheet metal to a gutter with dimensions as shown in Figure 7.24. The rectangular cross-sectional area must be at least 9 in.^{2}, and using $A = lw$ leads to the inequality

$$(9 - 2x)x \geq 9.$$

Figure 7.25 shows that the graph of $y = (9 - 2x)x$ intersects or is higher than the graph of $y = 9$ when $1.5 \leq x \leq 3$. So the cross-sectional area for the gutter is at least 9 in.^{2} when the height of the gutter is from 1.5 in. to 3. in.

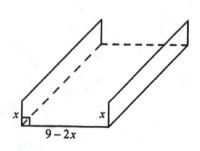

Figure 7.24

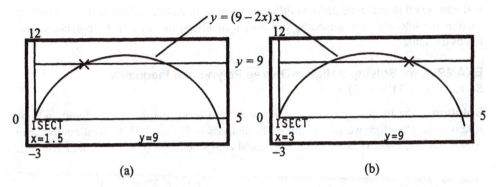

Figure 7.25

An algebraic verification of the proposed solution may be obtained by first converting the derived inequality to the form $ax^2 + bx + c \geq 0$.

$$(9 - 2x)x \geq 9$$
$$(9 - 2x)x - 9 \geq 0$$
$$-2x^2 + 9x - 9 \geq 0$$

Now determine the critical numbers by using the quadratic formula (or the factoring method) to determine when $-2x^2 + 9x - 9$ equals 0.

$$x = \frac{-9 \pm \sqrt{9^2 - 4(-2)(-9)}}{2(-2)} = \frac{-9 \pm \sqrt{9}}{-4} = \frac{-9 \pm 3}{-4}$$

Since

$$\frac{-9 + 3}{-4} = \frac{-6}{-4} = 1.5 \text{ and } \frac{-9 - 3}{-4} = \frac{-12}{-4} = 3$$

the critical numbers are 1.5 and 3, and we test in the intervals determined by the critical numbers, as shown in Figure 7.26.

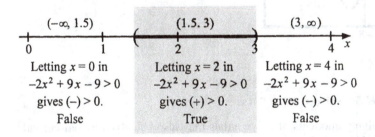

Figure 7.26

The tests show $-2x^2 + 9x - 9 > 0$ if $1.5 < x < 3$. Because the inequality in question is $\geq$, the possible heights for the gutter are from 1.5 in. to 3 in., and the solution set is the interval [1.5 in., 3 in.].

PROGRESS CHECK 4 Redo the problem in Example 4, but assume that the cross-sectional area of the gutter must be at least 7 in.^{2}. ■

The methods for solving quadratic inequalities may be applied to higher-degree polynomial inequalities. This extension is based on the definition that critical numbers are real numbers that make the *polynomial* in question zero, and the principle that throughout each of the intervals determined by the critical numbers, the sign of the polynomial remains the same.

EXAMPLE 5   Solving a Higher-Degree Polynomial Inequality

Solve $x(2x - 3)(x + 2) < 0$.

Solution   The inequality is already in a workable form; that is, it is factored and one side is zero. Therefore we go straight to the analysis in Figure 7.27. Critical numbers are 0, 3/2, and −2, since $x(2x - 3)(x + 2)$ equal zero when $x = 0$, $x = 3/2$, and $x = -2$.

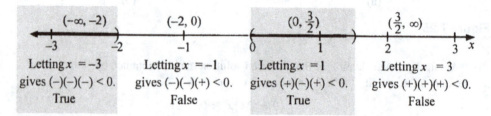

Figure 7.27

Thus, $x(2x - 3)(x + 2) < 0$ is true if $x < -2$ or $0 < x < 3/2$, and the solution set is $(-\infty, -2) \cup (0, 3/2)$.

We can see using Figure 7.28 that this solution checks, since the graph of $y = x(2x - 3)(x + 2)$ appears to be below the *x*-axis when *x* is to the left of −2 and when *x* is between 0 and 3/2.

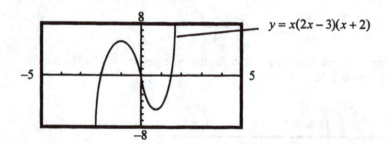

Figure 7.28

PROGRESS CHECK 5   Solve $x(3x + 2)(x - 2) > 0$.   ■

Inequalities involving quotients of polynomials may also be solved by our current methods if we define critical numbers in such problems to be real numbers that make either the numerator zero or the denominator zero. When analyzing quotients, it is important to remember that division by zero is undefined, so critical numbers that make the denominator zero are never included in the solution set.

EXAMPLE 6   Solving a Rational Inequality

For what value of x will $\sqrt{\dfrac{3x - 1}{x + 1}}$ be a real number?

Solution   For the square root to be a real number, the expression under the radical must be greater than or equal to 0. Thus, we need to solve

$$\frac{3x - 1}{x + 1} \geq 0.$$

The numerator is zero when $x = 1/3$, and the denominator is zero when $x = -1$. So 1/3 and -1 are critical numbers, and we may test in the intervals determined by these two numbers, as shown in Figure 7.29.

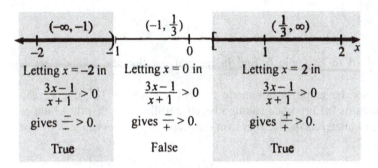

Figure 7.29

See in Figure 7.29 that $(3x - 1)/(x + 1) > 0$ is true if $x < -1$ or $x > 1/3$. The inequality in question is $\geq$, so we also determine that 1/3 is included and -1 is excluded from the solution set, because the quotient is 0 when $x = 1/3$ and undefined when $x = -1$. Thus, the solution set is $(-\infty, -1) \cup [1/3, \infty)$.

The graph of $y = \sqrt{(3x - 1)/(x + 1)}$, which is shown in Figure 7.30, may be used to support this solution because it shows that admissible values for x occur when x is to the left of -1 and when x is to the right of 1/3. The decision on whether to include the interval endpoints at -1 or 1/3 in the solution set is made more easily based on the algebraic conditions described above.

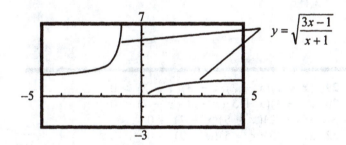

$$y = \sqrt{\frac{3x - 1}{x + 1}}$$

Figure 7.30

PROGRESS CHECK 6   For what values of x will $\sqrt{\dfrac{2x + 1}{x - 3}}$ be a real number?   ■

EXAMPLE 7   Solving a Rational Inequality

Solve $\dfrac{5x + 1}{x + 1} \geq 2$.

Solution   First, rewrite the inequality so the right side is zero. Then simplify the resulting expression on the left side into a single fraction.

$$\frac{5x + 1}{x + 1} \ge 2$$

$$\frac{5x + 1}{x + 1} - 2 \ge 0$$

$$\frac{5x + 1 - 2(x + 1)}{x + 1} \ge 0$$

$$\frac{3x - 1}{x + 1} \ge 0$$

This inequality is solved in Example 6, and in interval notation the solution set is $(-\infty, -1) \cup [1/3, \infty)$.

Figure 7.31 shows the graph in dot mode of both $y = (5x + 1)/(x + 1)$ and $y = 2$. This figure supports the proposed solution because it illustrates that the graph of $y = (5x + 1)/(x + 1)$ intersects or is higher than the graph of $y = 2$ when $x < -1$ or $x \ge 1/3$.

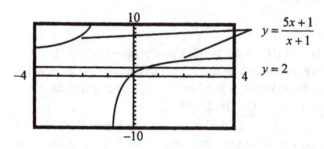

Figure 7.31

PROGRESS CHECK 7 Solve $\dfrac{2x + 3}{3x + 2} \le 1$. ■

EXERCISES 7.4

In Exercises 1–20, solve the quadratic inequality.

1. $x^2 - 2x - 8 \le 0$ **2.** $x^2 + x - 12 > 0$
3. $y^2 - 5y - 6 \le 0$ **4.** $x^2 - x - 20 < 0$
5. $2x^2 - 13x - 7 > 0$ **6.** $3x^2 + 4x - 15 \ge 0$
7. $9x^2 + 15x - 14 < 0$ **8.** $5x^2 - 9x - 2 \ge 0$
9. $3x^2 + 2x - 2 \le 0$ **10.** $2x^2 - 3x - 1 \ge 0$

(Give the endpoints to the nearest hundredth.)   (Give the endpoints to the nearest hundredth.)

11. $x^2 + 9 < 0$ **12.** $y^2 + 16 \le 0$
13. $(x - 5)^2 \le 0$ **14.** $(y + 8)^2 \le 0$
15. $x^2 \ge -1$ **16.** $y^2 + 3 \ge 0$
17. $y^2 - 25 < 0$ **18.** $t^2 - 36 \ge 0$
19. $2x^2 + 3x \le 7$ **20.** $5x^2 + 4 > 3x$

In Exercises 21–44, solve the given inequality.

21. $x(x + 2)(x - 3) < 0$ **22.** $x(x - 4)(x - 6) \le 0$
23. $x(x + 3)(x - 5) \ge 0$ **24.** $x(x + 7)(x - 4) > 0$
25. $x(x + 3)(x - 1) \le 0$
26. $(x + 3)(x - 2)(x - 5) \le 0$
27. $(2x + 1)(x - 1)(x + 4) < 0$
28. $(3x - 1)(x + 4)(2x + 3) \ge 0$

29. $(x + 1)(x + 2)(x - 3)(x - 5) > 0$
30. $(x + 3)(x + 5)(x - 4)(x - 7) < 0$
31. $x(x + 2)(x + 5)(x + 7) \le 0$
32. $x(x - 3)(x - 5)(x - 9) \ge 0$

33. $\dfrac{x + 2}{x - 1} < 0$ **34.** $\dfrac{x + 3}{x - 2} \ge 0$

35. $\dfrac{x - 3}{x + 4} \le 0$ **36.** $\dfrac{x - 5}{x - 2} > 0$

37. $\dfrac{x - 6}{x} \le 0$ **38.** $\dfrac{x + 7}{x} < 0$

39. $\dfrac{2x - 1}{x + 4} > 0$ **40.** $\dfrac{3x - 2}{x - 3} < 0$

41. $\dfrac{5}{x} < 2$ **42.** $\dfrac{4}{x} > 6$

43. $\dfrac{x}{5} < 2$ **44.** $\dfrac{x}{7} > -5$

45. The height of a projectile that is shot directly up from the ground with an initial velocity of 144 ft/second is given by

$$y = -16t^2 + 144t,$$

where y is measured in feet and t is the elapsed time in seconds. To the nearest hundredth of a second, for what values of t is the projectile more than 250 ft off the ground?

46. Refer to Exercise 45. To the nearest hundredth of a second, for what values of t is the projectile more than 304 ft off the ground?

47. A rectangle has perimeter 16 in. If the length is denoted by x, then the width is denoted by $8 - x$. (See the figure.) Assume that the length is not shorter than the width.

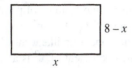

a. For what lengths is the area of the rectangle greater than 10 in.^{2}? (Give the answer exactly using radical notation and also as a decimal to the nearest hundredth.)

b. What length yields the maximum area?

48. Repeat Exercise 47, but use a perimeter equal to 20 in.

49. For what values of x will $\sqrt{4 - x^2}$ be a real number?

50. For what values of t will $\sqrt{1.44 - t^2}$ be a real number?

51. What is the domain of the function $y = \sqrt{x^2 - 4}$?

52. What is the domain of the function $y = \sqrt{\dfrac{x + 1}{x - 2}}$?

53. For a square metal plate to be useful in the design of a video component, its area must be between 1.08 and 1.12 square inches. If the side length is given by x, this condition gives $1.08 < x^2 < 1.12$. What are the permissible values of x? State answers in simplified radical form.

54. Under certain conditions the formula $d = 0.045s^2 + 1.1s$ gives the approximate distance in feet that it takes to stop a car that is going s mile per hour. Suppose that because of visibility and road conditions, the safe stopping distance one day is 150 feet. Use a grapher to determine safe speeds under these conditions.

THINK ABOUT IT 7.4

1. Create a quadratic inequality with the given solution set.

  a. $[1,3]$ b. $(-\infty, -1) \cup (2, \infty)$

  c. $\left(-\sqrt{2}, \sqrt{2}\right)$ d. $(-\infty, \infty)$

  e. $\{0\}$ f. $\varnothing$

2. Create an inequality involving a quotient of two polynomials that is greater than or equal to zero with the given solution set.

  a. $(-\infty, 0] \cup (3, \infty)$ b. $(0,3]$

3. Examine the following line of reasoning.

$$\frac{3}{x} > 1$$

$3 > x$ Multiply both sides by x.

$x < 3$ $a > b$ is equivalent to $b < a$.

The end result suggests that the solution set is $(-\infty, 3)$, but this answer is incorrect. What is wrong?

4. If $x^2 + 9 = kx$, what values for k lead to roots that are not real numbers?

5. What set of real numbers satisfies the following condition? When the number and its square are added together, the sum is between 6 and 42.

7.5   **Quadratic Functions and Parabolas**

The height (y) of a projectile shot vertically up from the ground with an initial velocity of 144 ft/second is given by the formula $y = 144t - 16t^2$. Graph the function defined by this formula and indicate

a. when the projectile will strike the ground

b. when the projectile attains its maximum height

c. the maximum height (see Example 5)

Courtesy of Aneal Vohra/Unicorn Stock Photos.

OBJECTIVES

1   Graph quadratic functions, indicating the vertex and intercepts of the graph.

2   Find the number of x-intercepts in the graph of $y = ax^2 + bx + c$ by using the discriminant.

3   Graph $x = ay^2 + by + c$ by using the vertex and intercepts of the graph.

4   Solve applied problems involving parabolas.

In the section-opening problem, the formula $y = 144t - 16t^2$ is based on a second-degree polynomial expression. This type of function is called a quadratic function.

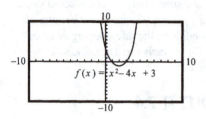

Figure 7.32

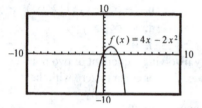

Figure 7.33

Quadratic Functions

A function of the form

$$f(x) = ax^2 + bx + c,$$

where a, b, and c are real numbers with $a \neq 0$, is called a **quadratic function.**

To see the essential properties of a quadratic function, consider the graphs of $f(x) = x^2 - 4x + 3$ (Figure 7.32) and $f(x) = 4x - 2x^2$ (Figure 7.33), which were obtained on a grapher.

The graphs in both instances are **parabolas.** It can be shown that the graph of every quadratic function is a parabola, and we may use some features of parabolas to graph quadratic functions efficiently. First, note in the graph of $f(x) = x^2 - 4x + 3$ in Figure 7.32 that the parabola has a minimum turning point and opens up like a cup. This occurs whenever the coefficient of x^2 is a positive number. If the coefficient of x^2 is a negative number, then the graph turns at the highest point on the graph, as shown in the graph of $f(x) = 4x - 2x^2$ in Figure 7.33. We now know some important facts about the graph of a quadratic function.

Graph of a Quadratic Function

For the function defined by $y = ax^2 + bx + c$ with $a \neq 0$

1. The graph is a parabola.
2. If $a > 0$, the parabola opens upward and turns at the lowest point on the graph.
3. If $a < 0$, the parabola opens downward and turns at the highest point on the graph.

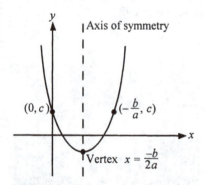

Figure 7.34

For both graphing and applications purposes, it is important to develop a way to locate the turning point of the parabola, which is called the **vertex.** Consider Figure 7.34, which illustrates that the vertex in the graph of a quadratic function is located on a vertical line called the **axis of symmetry** of the parabola. This line divides the parabola into two segments such that if we make a fold on the line, the two halves will coincide.

To find the equation of the axis of symmetry, note that this line is halfway between any pair of points on the parabola that have the same y-coordinate. The easiest pair of points to analyze is the pair of points on the graph of $y = ax^2 + bx + c$ whose y-coordinate is c. Therefore, we replace y by c in this equation and solve for x.

$$y = ax^2 + bx + c$$
$$c = ax^2 + bx + c \qquad \text{Replace } y \text{ by } c.$$
$$0 = ax^2 + bx \qquad \text{Subtract } c \text{ from both sides.}$$
$$0 = x(ax + b) \qquad \text{Factor the nonzero side.}$$
$$x = 0 \quad \text{or} \quad ax + b = 0 \qquad \text{Set each factor equal to 0.}$$
$$ax = -b$$
$$x = \frac{-b}{a}$$

The x-coordinate halfway between 0 and $-b/a$ is given by

$$x = \frac{0 + (-b/a)}{2},$$

so the equation of the axis of symmetry is

$$x = \frac{-b}{2a}.$$

Because the vertex lies on the axis of symmetry, the x-coordinate of the vertex is $-b/2a$. We may find the y-coordinate of the vertex by finding $f(-b/2a)$, which is the y value when $x = -b/2a$, and we have established the following formula.

> ### Vertex Formula
> The vertex of the graph of $y = f(x) = ax^2 + bx + c$, with $a \neq 0$, is located at
> $$\left(\frac{-b}{2a}, f\left(\frac{-b}{2a}\right)\right).$$

The last important feature of the graph of a quadratic function that we consider is the coordinates of the points where the curve crosses the axes. The point where the parabola crosses the y-axis (that is, the y-intercept) can be found by substituting 0 for x in the equation $y = ax^2 + bx + c$.

$$y = a(0)^2 + b(0) + c$$
$$= c$$

Thus the y-intercept is always $(0, c)$.

To find the points where the parabola crosses the x-axis (that is, the x-intercepts), we substitute 0 for y in the equation $y = ax^2 + bx + c$. Thus, the x-coordinates of the x-intercepts are found by solving the equation $ax^2 + bx + c = 0$.

EXAMPLE 1 Graphing a Quadratic Function
Graph the function defined by $f(x) = x^2 - 7x + 6$ and indicate

a. the coordinates of the x- and y-intercepts
b. the equation of the axis of symmetry
c. the coordinates of the maximum or minimum point

Solution   The graph is the parabola shown in Figure 7.35.

a. To find the x-intercepts, set $f(x) = 0$ and solve the resulting equation.

$$x^2 - 7x + 6 = 0$$
$$(x - 6)(x - 1) = 0$$
$$x - 6 = 0 \quad \text{or} \quad x - 1 = 0$$
$$x = 6 \qquad\qquad x = 1$$

x-intercepts: $(1,0)$ and $(6,0)$; y-intercept: $(0,6)$ since $c = 6$

b. Axis of symmetry:

$$x = \frac{-b}{2a} = \frac{-(-7)}{2(1)} = \frac{7}{2}.$$

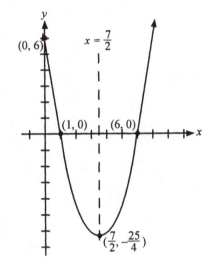

Figure 7.35

c. Since $a > 0$, we have a minimum point. The x-coordinate of the minimum point is 7/2, since the minimum point lies on the axis of symmetry. We find the y-coordinate of the minimum point by finding the y value when $x = 7/2$.

$$f(x) = x^2 - 7x + 6$$
$$f\left(\frac{7}{2}\right) = \left(\frac{7}{2}\right)^2 - 7\left(\frac{7}{2}\right) + 6$$
$$= \frac{49}{4} - \frac{49}{2} + 6$$
$$= \frac{49}{4} - \frac{98}{4} + \frac{24}{4}$$
$$= -\frac{25}{4}$$

Minimum point: $\left(\frac{7}{2}, -\frac{25}{4}\right)$

Technology Link

The results in this example are not difficult to check with a grapher. For instance, if we graph the given function as shown in Figure 7.36 and utilize the Trace feature, we can obtain approximations for the intercepts and vertex that support the exact answers we determined algebraically. In addition, many calculators have built-in operations for estimating an x-intercept, a maximum point, or a minimum point. You should learn to use these features, if they are available.

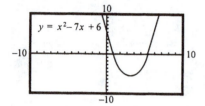

Figure 7.36

PROGRESS CHECK 1   Redo the problems in Example 1 for the function defined by $y = x^2 + 2x - 8$.   ■

EXAMPLE 2   Graphing a Quadratic Function

Graph the function defined by $f(x) = 3 - x - x^2$ and indicate

a. the coordinates of the x- and y-intercepts
b. the equation of the axis of symmetry
c. the coordinates of the maximum or minimum point
d. the range of the function

Solution

a. To find the x-intercepts, set $y = 0$ and solve the resulting equation:

$$3 - x - x^2 = 0$$

By the quadratic formula (with $a = -1$, $b = -1$, and $c = 3$) we have

$$x = \frac{-(-1) \pm \sqrt{(-1)^2 - 4(-1)(3)}}{2(-1)}$$

$$= \frac{1 \pm \sqrt{13}}{-2}.$$

x-intercepts: $\left((1 + \sqrt{13})/-2, 0\right)$ and $\left((1 - \sqrt{13})/-2, 0\right)$, which are about $(-2.3, 0)$ and $(1.3, 0)$ y-intercept: $(0,3)$, since $c = 3$.

b. Axis of symmetry:

$$x = \frac{-b}{2a} = \frac{-(-1)}{2(-1)} = -\frac{1}{2}$$

c. Since $a < 0$, we have a maximum point. The x-coordinate of the maximum point is $-1/2$, since the maximum point lies on the axis of symmetry. We find the y-coordinate of the maximum point by finding $f(-1/2)$, the value of the function when $x = -1/2$.

$$f(x) = 3 - x - x^2$$

$$f\left(-\frac{1}{2}\right) = 3 - \left(-\frac{1}{2}\right) - \left(-\frac{1}{2}\right)^2$$

$$= 3 + \frac{1}{2} - \frac{1}{4}$$

$$= \frac{13}{4}$$

Maximum point: $\left(-1/2, 13/4\right)$

d. By drawing a parabola through the vertex and the intercepts, we obtain the graph of f in Figure 7.37. From the graph, we read that the range is the interval $(-\infty, 13/4]$. Figure 7.38 shows a graph of $y = 3 - x - x^2$ from a grapher. Check that this graph is in agreement with our results in this example.

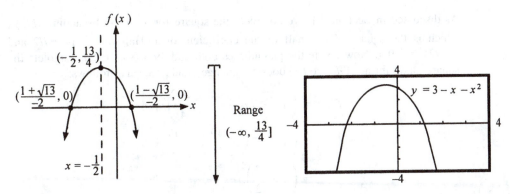

Figure 7.37

Figure 7.38

PROGRESS CHECK 2 Redo the problems in Example 2 for the function defined by $y = -x^2 + 5x - 7$. ■

The vertex of a parabola can be found more efficiently in some cases by employing the graphing techniques discussed in Section 2.5. For instance, in Example 4, of that section we graphed $y = (x + 2)^2 - 3$ by moving the graph of $y = x^2$, 2 units to the left and 3 units down, which placed the vertex of the parabola at $(-2, -3)$. More generally, any quadratic function may be placed in the standard form.

$$f(x) = a(x - h)^2 + k \quad (\text{with } a \neq 0)$$

by completing the square, and in this form our graphing techniques tell us that the graph of f is the graph of $y = ax^2$ (a parabola) shifted so the vertex is the point (h, k) and the axis of symmetry is the vertical line $x = h$ (see Figure 7.39). Example 3 illustrates this result using the functions analyzed in Examples 1 and 2.

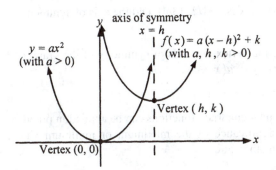

Figure 7.39

EXAMPLE 3 Writing a Quadratic Function in Standard Form
Determine the vertex and axis of symmetry of the graph of f by matching the function to the form $f(x) = a(x - h)^2 + k$.

a. $f(x) = x^2 - 7x + 6$ **b.** $f(x) = 3 - x - x^2$

Solution
a. First, write the equation as

$$f(x) = (x^2 - 7x) + 6.$$

As discussed in Section 7.1, we complete the square for $x^2 + bx$ by adding $(b/2)^2$, which is the square of one-half of the coefficient of x. Half of -7 is $-7/2$ and $(-7/2)^2 = 49/4$. Now inside the parentheses both add $49/4$ (so we can complete the square) and subtract $49/4$ [so $f(x)$ does not change], and proceed as follows:

$$f(x) = \left(x^2 - 7x + \frac{49}{4} - \frac{49}{4} \right) + 6$$

$$= \left(x^2 - 7x + \frac{49}{4} \right) - \frac{49}{4} + 6$$

$$= \left(x - \frac{7}{2} \right)^2 - \frac{25}{4}.$$

Matching this result to the form $f(x) = a(x - h)^2 + k$, we determine $h = 7/2$ and $k = -25/4$, so the vertex of the parabola is $(7/2, -25/4)$, and the axis of symmetry is $x = 7/2$.

b. To complete the square, the coefficient of x^2 must be 1, so first factor out -1 from the x terms and then proceed as in part **a.**

$$f(x) = 3 - x - x^2$$

$$= -1(x^2 + x) + 3$$

$$= -1\left(x^2 + x + \frac{1}{4} - \frac{1}{4} \right) + 3$$

$$= -1\left(x^2 + x + \frac{1}{4} \right) + (-1)\left(-\frac{1}{4} \right) + 3$$

$$= -1\left(x + \frac{1}{2} \right)^2 + \frac{13}{4}$$

Once again, we match this equation to the form $f(x) = a(x - h)^2 + k$, which gives $h = -1/2$ and $k = 13/4$. Thus, the vertex is $(-1/2, 13/4)$, and the axis of symmetry is $x = -1/2$.

PROGRESS CHECK 3   Determine the vertex and axis of symmetry of the graph of f by matching the equation to the form $f(x) = a(x - h)^2 + k$.

a. $f(x) = x^2 + 6x + 8$ **b.** $f(x) = 1 + x - x^2$ ■

The next two examples illustrate how quadratic functions can be applied in practical situations. Notice, in particular, the significance of the maximum or minimum value, which is an important topic in applied mathematics.

EXAMPLE 4   Finding a Maximum Area

A manager wants to fence in a parking lot of which one side is bounded by a building, but because of budget constraints, only a total of 300 ft of fencing is available. What are the dimensions of the largest rectangular parking lot that can be enclosed with the available fencing?

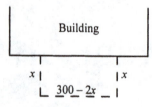

Figure 7.40

Solution   First, draw a sketch of the situation (Figure 7.40). If we let x represent the length of one side of the lot, the opposite side also has length x. The length of the side opposite of the building is then $300 - 2x$. We wish to maximize the area of this rectangular region, which is given by the following quadratic function.

$$\text{Area} = x(300 - 2x)$$

$$A = 300x - 2x^2$$

Since $a < 0$, we have a maximum point. Axis of symmetry:

$$x = \frac{-b}{2a} = \frac{-300}{2(-2)} = \frac{-300}{-4} = 75.$$

Length of the side opposite the building:

$$300 - 2x = 300 - 2(75) = 300 - 150 = 150.$$

The area is a maximum when the dimensions are 75 ft by 150 ft.

Technology Link

As mentioned in Example 1, some calculators have a built-in operation that finds a highest point of a graph in an interval. For example, on one such calculator the Function Maximum operation may be utilized to display the highest point for a graph of the equation in this example, as shown in Figure 7.41. This display is further evidence that the maximum area is attained when $x = 75$.

We will use the Function Maximum or Minimum feature occasionally in the text because this operation gives very accurate answers. But keep in mind that repeated use of Zoom and Trace is a workable alternative, if this special feature is not available on your calculator.

PROGRESS CHECK 4   A rectangular field is adjacent to a river and is to have fencing on three sides because the side on the river requires no fencing. If 500 yd of fencing are available, what are the dimensions of the rectangular section with largest area that can be enclosed with the available fencing?   ■

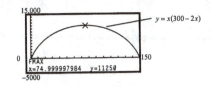

Figure 7.41

EXAMPLE 5   A Projectile with Up-Down Motion

Solve the problem in the section introduction on page 393.

Solution

a. When the projectile hits the grounds, the height (y) of the projectile is 0. Thus, we want to find the values of t for which $144t - 16t^2$ equals 0.

$$144t - 16t^2 = 0$$
$$16t(9 - t) = 0$$
$$16t = 0 \quad \text{or} \quad 9 - t = 0$$
$$t = 0 \qquad\qquad t = 9$$

The projectile will hit the ground 9 seconds later.

b. Since $a < 0$, we have a maximum point. Axis of symmetry:

$$t = \frac{-b}{2a} = \frac{-(144)}{2(-16)} = \frac{-144}{-32} = 4.5$$

The projectile reaches its highest point when $t = 4.5$ seconds.

c. We can find the maximum height by finding the value of y when $t = 4.5$ (or $t = \frac{9}{2}$) seconds.

$$y = f(t) = 144t - 16t^2$$
$$f\left(\frac{9}{2}\right) = 144\left(\frac{9}{2}\right) - 16\left(\frac{9}{2}\right)^2$$
$$= 72 \cdot 9 - 16\left(\frac{81}{4}\right)$$
$$= 324$$

Thus, the projectile reaches a maximum height of 324 ft, and Figure 7.42 shows the graph of this function.

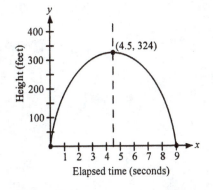

Figure 7.42

PROGRESS CHECK 5   The height (y) in feet of a projectile shot vertically up from the ground with an initial velocity of 128 ft/second is given by $y = 128t - 16t^2$. Answer the questions in Example 5 with respect to this formula.   ■

Equations of the form $y = ax^2 + bx + c$ have exactly one y-intercept at $(0,c)$, but the number of x-intercepts may vary. We can predict the number of x-intercepts by recalling from Section 7.2 that the discriminant $b^2 - 4ac$ tells us the nature of the solutions of the equation $ax^2 + bx + c = 0$ with $a \neq 0$. For instance, when the discriminant indicates real and unequal solutions, then there are two x-intercepts. One x-intercept results when the solutions are real and equal, and there are no x-intercepts when the solutions are not real numbers. Figure 7.43 summarizes these three cases.

Discriminant	Number of x-intercepts	Possible Graph	
$b^2 - 4ac > 0$	Two		
$b^2 - 4ac = 0$	One		
$b^2 - 4ac < 0$	None		

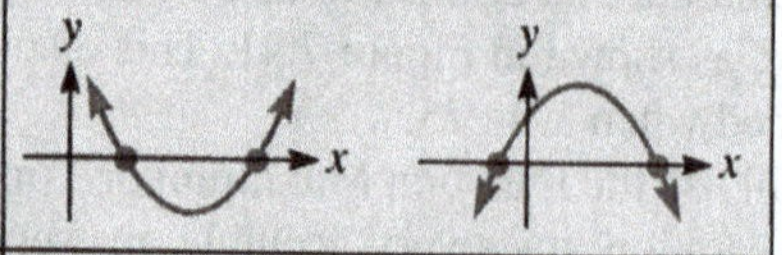

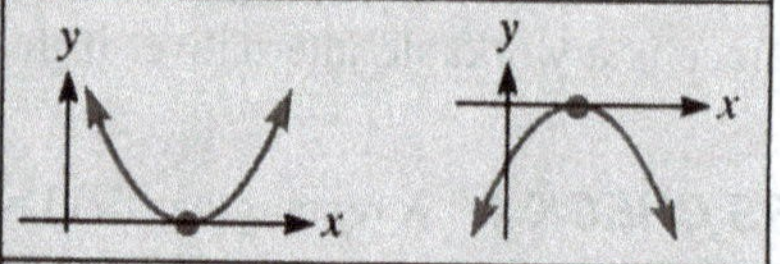

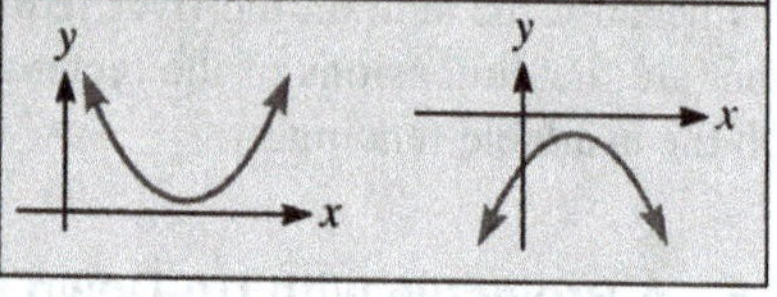

Figure 7.43

Example 6   Using the Discriminant

Use the discriminant to determine the number of x-intercepts of the graph of $y = 4x^2 - 4x + 1$.

Solution   In the given equation $a = 4$, $b = -4$, and $c = 1$, so

$$b^2 - 4ac = (-4)^2 - 4(4)(1) = 0.$$

Since the discriminant is 0, the graph has one x-intercept.

PROGRESS CHECK 6   Use the discriminant to determine the number of x-intercepts of the graph of $y = x^2 + 2x + 3$.   ■

Reversing the roles of x and y in the equation $y = ax^2 + bx + c$ produces a second-degree equation of the form

$$x = ay^2 + by + c.$$

Every equation of this form also graphs as a parabola. However, the parabola in such graphs will open to the right (if $a > 0$) or the left (if $a < 0$), instead of opening up or down. Because the equation of the axis of symmetry in this case is the horizontal line $y = -b/(2a)$, we refer to such parabolas as **horizontal parabolas.**

EXAMPLE 7   Analyzing a Horizontal Parabola

Consider the equation $x = y^2 + 4y$.

a. Find the equation of the axis of symmetry.
b. Find the coordinates of the vertex.
c. Find the coordinates of any x- and y-intercepts.
d. Graph the equation.

Solution

a. In the given equation $a = 1$ and $b = 4$, so

$$y = \frac{-b}{2a} = \frac{-4}{2(1)} = -2.$$

The equation of the axis of symmetry is $y = -2$.

b. The y-coordinate of the vertex is -2 since the vertex lies on the axis of symmetry. To
find the x-coordinate, replace y by -2 in the given equation.

$$x = y^2 + 4y$$
$$x = (-2)^2 + 4(-2) \qquad \text{Replace } y \text{ by } -2.$$
$$= -4$$

The vertex is located at $(-4, -2)$.

c. To find y-intercepts, let $x = 0$ and solve the resulting equation for y.

$$y^2 + 4y = 0$$
$$y(y + 4) = 0$$
$$y = 0 \qquad \text{or} \qquad y + 4 = 0$$
$$y = 0 \qquad\qquad\qquad y = -4$$

The y-intercepts are $(0,0)$ and $(0, -4)$. Letting $y = 0$ in the equation to be graphed
shows that $(0,0)$ is also an x-intercept.

d. By drawing a parabola through the vertex and the intercepts, we obtain the graph of
$x = y^2 + 4y$, which is shown in Figure 7.44. Notice that this graph is in agreement
with the general principle that a horizontal parabola opens to the right when $a > 0$.

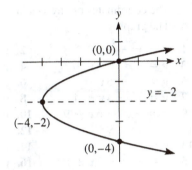

Figure 7.44

PROGRESS CHECK 7 Answer the questions in Example 7 for the equation
$x = 3y^2 - 6y$. ■

The equations $y = ax^2 + bx + c$ and $x = ay^2 + by + c$ can be viewed as particular cases of second-degree equations in two variables with general form

$$Ax^2 + Bxy + Cy^2 + Dx + Ey + F = 0$$

where A, B, and C are not all zero. The next two sections extend coverage of graphing of
such equations to include circles, ellipses, and hyperbolas. Overall, the four curves that
we analyze are called **conic sections.** This name was first used by Greek mathematicians
who discovered that these curves result from the intersection of a cone with an appropriate
plane, as shown in Figure 7.45.

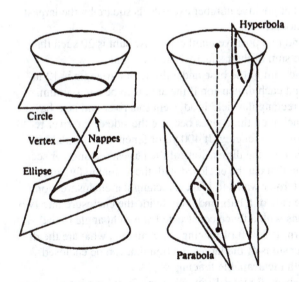

Figure 7.45

EXERCISES 7.5

In Exercises 1–44 for each equation, find the following:
a. The equation of the axis of symmetry
b. The coordinates of the vertex
c. The coordinates of any x- and y-intercepts
d. The graph

1. $y = x^2 + 2x$
2. $y = x^2 + 9x$
3. $y = -x^2 + 3x$
4. $y = -x^2 + 5x$
5. $y = x^2 - 5x$
6. $y = x^2 - 7x$
7. $y = x^2 - 4x + 4$
8. $y = x^2 + 6x + 9$
9. $y = -x^2 - 6x - 9$
10. $y = -x^2 + 4x - 4$
11. $y = x^2 + 9$
12. $y = -x^2 - 5$
13. $y = x^2 - 2x - 8$
14. $y = x^2 + x - 6$
15. $y = -x^2 + 2x + 8$
16. $y = -x^2 - x + 6$
17. $y = x^2 + x - 20$
18. $y = x^2 - 3x - 28$
19. $y = -x^2 + x + 20$
20. $y = -x^2 + 3x + 28$
21. $y = -x^2 - 9x - 18$
22. $y = -x^2 - 12x - 35$
23. $y = x^2 + 9x + 18$
24. $y = x^2 + 12x + 35$
25. $y = -6x^2 + x + 2$
26. $y = 12x^2 + 5x - 3$
27. $y = 6x^2 - x - 2$
28. $y = -12x^2 - 5x + 3$
29. $y = x^2 - 20$
30. $y = x^2 - 27$
31. $y = x^2 - 4x - 3$
32. $y = x^2 - 8x + 12$
33. $y = x^2 - 2x + 5$
34. $y = x^2 + 2x + 3$
35. $y = -x^2 + 2x - 5$
36. $y = -x^2 - 2x - 3$
37. $x = y^2 + 5y$
38. $x = y^2 + 9y$
39. $x = -y^2 + 3y$
40. $x = y^2 - 5y$
41. $x = -y^2 - 4y$
42. $x = y^2 - 2y - 8$
43. $x = -y^2 + 2y + 8$
44. $x = y^2 - 20$

In Exercises 45–50 for the given function, find the following.
a. The equation of the axis of symmetry
b. The coordinates of the vertex
c. The coordinates of the y-intercept
d. Then graph the function and specify the range using the graph.

45. $f(x) = 2x^2 - 4x + 5$
46. $f(x) = x^2 - 4x + 8$
47. $f(x) = x^2 + 2x + 3$
48. $f(x) = x^2 + 6x + 10$
49. $f(x) = -x^2 + 6x - 14$
50. $f(x) = -x^2 - 4x - 9$

In Exercises 51–60 for the given quadratic function, find the equation of the axis of symmetry and the vertex by matching the equation to the form $f(x) = a(x - h)^2 + k$.

51. $y = x^2 - 2x - 3$
52. $y = x^2 - 4x + 4$
53. $y = -x^2 - 6x - 14$
54. $y = -x^2 + 4x - 1$
55. $y = -x^2 + 3x + 4$
56. $y = -x^2 - 3x - 4$
57. $y = 2x^2 - 4x + 5$
58. $y = 2x^2 - 4x + 6$
59. $y = 2x^2 - 6x - 3$
60. $y = 2x^2 - 6x + 8$

In Exercises 61–70, use the discriminant to determine the number of x-intercepts.

61. $y = x^2 - 7x$
62. $y = -x^2 - 4x$
63. $y = -x^2 + 25$
64. $y = x^2 - 2x - 8$
65. $y = x^2$
66. $y = -x^2$
67. $y = x^2 - 2x + 5$
68. $y = x^2 + 2x + 3$
69. $y = x^2 - 2x + 1$
70. $y = 9x^2 - 12x + 4$

71. The height of a projectile shot directly from the ground with an initial velocity of 32 ft/second is given by $y = -16t^2 + 32t$.
a. Graph the equation.
b. When does the projectile attain its maximum height?
c. What is the maximum height?
d. When does it hit the ground?

72. The projectile of Exercise 71 is now launched with twice the old initial velocity, so that the equation becomes $y = -16t^2 + 64t$. Does it now go twice as high? Is it now in the air twice as long before hitting the ground? Answer all the questions from Exercise 71 for this new equation.

73. An object (like a ball or an apple) thrown from a height of 10 ft straight up into the air with an initial velocity of 78 ft/second has a distance (in feet) above the ground after t seconds given by the formula $y = 10 + 78t - 16t^2$.
a. Graph the equation.
b. When does the object attain its maximum height?
c. What is the maximum height?
d. When does it hit the ground?

74. If the object of Exercise 73 is thrown straight up from a height of 108 ft, then the equation becomes $y = 108 + 78t - 16t^2$. Answer the questions given in Exercise 73.

75. Find two positive numbers whose sum is 20 and whose product is a maximum.

76. What positive number exceeds its square by the largest amount?

77. Find two positive numbers whose sum is 20 such that the sum of their squares is a minimum.

78. The sum of the base and altitude of a triangle is 12 in. Find each dimension if the area is to be a maximum.

79. A rectangular field is adjacent to a river and is to have fencing on three sides because the side of the river requires no fencing. If 400 yd of fencing are available, what are the dimensions of the largest rectangular section that can be enclosed with the available fencing?

80. A farmer wants to make a rectangular enclosure along the side of a barn and then divide the enclosure into two pens with a fence constructed at a right angle to the barn. If 300 ft of fencing are available, what are the dimensions of the largest section that can be enclosed with the available fencing?

81. A sheet of metal 12 in. wide and 20 ft long is to be made into a gutter by turning up the same amount of material on each edge at right angles to the base. Determine the amount of material that should be turned up to maximize the volume that the gutter can carry.

82. Find the maximum possible area of a rectangle with a perimeter of 100 ft.

83. In estimating the margin of error for a statistical survey, one must find the value of x which maximizes the value

of the expression $x(1 - x)$. Solve this problem by analyzing the graph of $y = x(1 - x)$. What is the maximum value?

THINK ABOUT IT 7.5

1. This section of the text showed that the x-coordinate of the vertex of the graph of $y = ax^2 + bx + c$ is given by $-b/(2a)$. Find a general expression for the y-coordinate of the vertex.
2. Find an equation that defines the quadratic function f with the given properties.
   a. The graph of f passes through the origin and has its vertex at $(1, -4)$.
   b. The intercepts of the graph of f are $(1, 0)$, $(3, 0)$, and $(0, -2)$.
3. A bus tour charges a fare of \$10 per person and carries 200 people per day. The manager estimates that she will lose 10 passengers for each \$1 increase in fare. Find the most profitable fare for her to charge.
4. The great Greek mathematician Archimedes (225 B.C.) showed that the area inside a parabola (see the figure) equals $\frac{4}{3}$ the area of the triangle. Use his discovery to find the area enclosed by the parabola $y = x^2$ and the line $y = 4$.

5. If you draw a line and a point not on the line, and then you mark all other points that are equidistant from the original line and point, these new points will form a parabola. For example, if you draw the point $(0, 1)$ and the line $y = -1$, then the collection of points equidistant from them forms the parabola whose equation is $y = \frac{1}{4}x^2$.
   a. Draw the point $(0,1)$ and the line $y = -1$ on the same set of axes.
   b. Now add the graph of $y = \frac{1}{4}x^2$ to the picture.
   c. The point $(2,1)$ is on the parabola. Show that its distance from $(0,1)$ is the same as its distance from the line $y = -1$.
   d. The point $(4,4)$ is on the parabola. Show that its distance from $(0,1)$ is the same as its distance from the line $y = -1$.

7.6   The Circle

In addition to its great practical value, the circle is also an aesthetically pleasing figure. For instance, in architecture, circles are basic to the construction of many beautiful designs. If the diameter in a bridge is 100 m, how high above the water is the bridge 30 m on each side of the center? (See Example 6.)

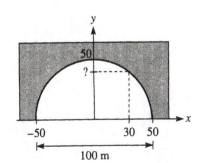

OBJECTIVES

1 Find the equation in standard form of a circle given its center and either the radius of the circle or a point on the circle.

2 Find the center and radius of a circle given its equation, and then graph it.

3 Graph and write equations for circles and semicircles with centers at the origin.

A **circle** is the set of all points in a plane at a given distance from a fixed point. To derive an equation for a circle, we recall from Section 2.7 that the distance between any two points (x_1, y_1) and (x_2, y_2) is given by the formula

$$d = \sqrt{(x_2 - x_1)^2 + (y_2 - y_1)^2}.$$

If we let (h, k) be the fixed point (the center of the circle), r be the given distance (the radius of the circle), and (x, y) be any point on the circle, as shown in Figure 7.46, then by the distance formula,

$$\sqrt{(x - h)^2 + (y - k)^2} = r.$$

Squaring both sides produces an equation for a circle that is called the standard form.

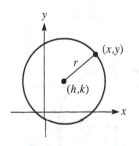

Figure 7.46

Equation of a Circle

The standard form of the equation of a circle of radius r with center (h, k) is

$$(x - h)^2 + (y - k)^2 = r^2.$$

EXAMPLE 1   Finding the Standard Equation of a Circle

Find the equation in standard form of the circle with center at $(5, -2)$ and radius 3.

Solution   Replacing h by 5, k by -2, and r by 3 in the equation

$$(x - h)^2 + (y - k)^2 = r^2$$

yields

$$(x - 5)^2 + [y - (-2)]^2 = (3)^2$$
$$(x - 5)^2 + (y + 2)^2 = 9.$$

PROGRESS CHECK 1   Find the equation in standard form of the circle with center at $(-1, 6)$ and radius 4.   ▪

EXAMPLE 2   Finding the Standard Equation of a Circle

Find the equation in standard form of the circle with center at $(-3, 0)$ that passes through $(-5, 2)$.

Solution   Substituting $h = -3$ and $k = 0$ into $(x - h)^2 + (y - k)^2 = r^2$ gives

$$[x - (-3)]^2 + (y - 0)^2 = r^2$$
$$(x + 3)^2 + y^2 = r^2.$$

Since the circle passes through $(-5, 2)$, we find r^2 by substituting the coordinates of this point in the equation.

$$(-5 + 3)^2 + 2^2 = r^2$$
$$8 = r^2$$

The standard form of the equation of this circle is then

$$(x + 3)^2 + y^2 = 8.$$

PROGRESS CHECK 2   Find the equation in standard form of the circle with center at $(2, -5)$ that passes through $(1, 0)$.   ▪

Expressing an equation for a circle in standard form is beneficial because the center and the radius of the circle can be identified by inspection of the equation. It is then easy to graph the circle once these features are known.

EXAMPLE 3   Finding the Center and the Radius

Find the center and the radius of the circle given by

$$x^2 + (y + 2)^2 = 9.$$

Also, sketch the circle.

Solution   To match standard form, view the given equation as

$$(x - 0)^2 + [y - (-2)]^2 = (3)^2.$$

Then $h = 0$, $k = -2$, and $r = 3$, so the center is $(0, -2)$ and the radius is 3. Figure 7.47 shows the graph of this circle.

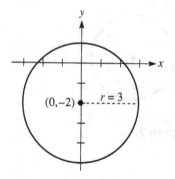

Figure 7.47

PROGRESS CHECK 3 Find the center and radius of the circle given by $(x + 3)^2 + y^2 = 4$. Also, sketch the circle. ■

EXAMPLE 4   Converting to Standard Form

Find the center and the radius of the circle given by

$$x^2 + y^2 - 10x + 6y - 15 = 0.$$

Solution   The initial objective is to transform the given equation to the standard form

$$(x - h)^2 + (y - k)^2 = r^2.$$

To obtain this form, we complete the square in the x terms and the y terms by first rewriting the given equation as

$$(x^2 - 10x) + (y^2 + 6y) = 15.$$

Recall from Section 7.1 that we complete the square for $x^2 + bx$ by adding $(b/2)^2$. So we complete the square for $x^2 - 10x$ by adding $(-10/2)^2$, which is 25, and this number must be added on both sides of the equation to preserve equality. Similarly, one-half of the coefficient of y is 3 and $3^2 = 9$, so we complete the square on the y terms by adding 9, and this number is added on both sides of the equation. Thus, we have

$$(x^2 - 10x + 25) + (y^2 + 6y + 9) = 15 + 25 + 9$$
$$(x - 5)^2 + (y + 3)^2 = 49.$$

By comparing this equation with the standard form, we determine that the center of the circle is at $(5, -3)$, and the radius is $\sqrt{49}$, or 7.

PROGRESS CHECK 4 Find the center and radius of the circle given by $x^2 + y^2 + 4x - 6y - 12 = 0$. ■

For circles centered at (0,0) the standard equation becomes

$$(x - 0)^2 + (y - 0)^2 = r^2,$$

so the standard equation of a circle with center at the origin and radius r is

$$x^2 + y^2 = r^2.$$

This result is used to graph the type of equations given in the next example.

EXAMPLE 5   Graphing Circles and Semicircles Centered at the Origin

Graph each equation.

a. $x^2 + y^2 = 4$ **b.** $y = \sqrt{4 - x^2}$ **c.** $y = -\sqrt{4 - x^2}$

Solution

a. The equation $x^2 + y^2 = 4$ fits the form $x^2 + y^2 = r^2$, so the graph is a circle centered at the origin. Because $r^2 = 4$, the radius is $\sqrt{4}$, or 2. This circle is graphed in Figure 7.48(a).

b. Squaring both sides of $y = \sqrt{4 - x^2}$ gives

$$y^2 = 4 - x^2$$
$$x^2 + y^2 = 4,$$

which is the equation from part **a.** However, because y represents a principal square root, y is restricted to positive numbers or zero in the equation $y = \sqrt{4 - x^2}$, so the graph is the semicircle shown in Figure 7.48(b).

c. As in part **b,** the graph of $y = -\sqrt{4 - x^2}$ is a semicircle. However, y is restricted to negative numbers or zero in this equation, so the graph is the semicircle in Figure 7.48(c).

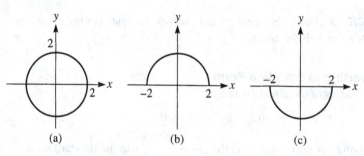

Figure 7.48

Note To graph $x^2 + y^2 = 4$ on a graphing calculator, we graph $y = \sqrt{4 - x^2}$ and $y = -\sqrt{4 - x^2}$ in the same calculator screen. This method is required because it is necessary to enter an expression that is solved for y on graphing calculators.

PROGRESS CHECK 6 Graph each equation.

a. $x^2 + y^2 = 1$ **b.** $y = -2\sqrt{1 - x^2}$ **c.** $y = 2\sqrt{1 - x^2}$ ■

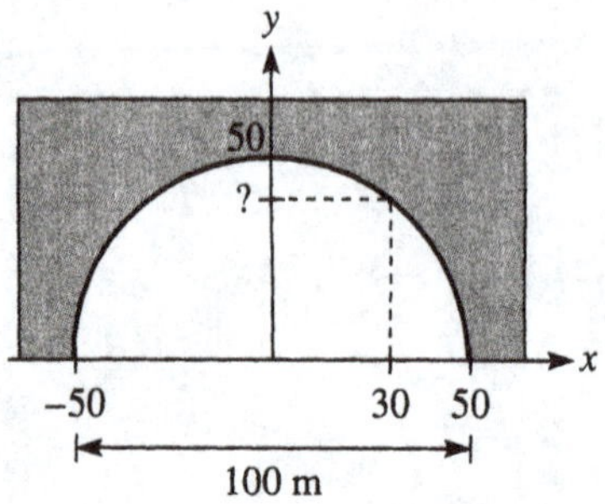

EXAMPLE 6 Height Above Water in a Bridge

Solve the problem in the section introduction on page 403.

Solution We are free to place the specific figure in any convenient position in a coordinate system, so we start by diagraming the problem as shown in Figure 7.49.

The equation for the entire circle is

$$x^2 + y^2 = (50)^2,$$

so

$$y^2 = 2{,}500 - x^2$$
$$y = \pm\sqrt{2{,}500 - x^2},$$

and the equation for the semicircle in the diagram is

$$y = \sqrt{2{,}500 - x^2}.$$

Now we find y when $x = 30$ to determine the requested height.

$$y = \sqrt{2{,}500 - (30)^2} = \sqrt{1{,}600} = 40$$

The bridge is 40 m above the water at the specified point.

PROGRESS CHECK 6 If the diameter of a bridge as described in Example 6 is 200 ft, how high above the water is the bridge 80 ft on each side of the center? ■

Figure 7.49

(Figure 7.49 labels: 50, ?, −50, 30, 50, 100 m)

EXERCISES 7.6

In Exercises 1–24, find the equation in standard form of a circle given its center and either its radius or a point on the circle.

1. Center $(0,0)$, radius 5
2. Center $(0,0)$, radius 4
3. Center $(0,0)$, point $(-3, 0)$
4. Center $(0,0)$, point $(0, -2)$
5. Center $(-2, 3)$, radius 7
6. Center $(4, -7)$, radius 9
7. Center $(-5, -8)$, radius 3
8. Center $(-3, -2)$, radius 2

9. Center $(4,4)$, radius 5   **10.** Center $(7,7)$, radius 12
11. Center $(0, -5)$, radius 6   **12.** Center $(-4, 0)$, radius 9
13. Center $(-5, 0)$, point $(4,0)$
14. Center $(0, -2)$, point $(0,6)$
15. Center $(2,3)$, point $(5,3)$
16. Center $(-5,2)$, point $(-5,7)$
17. Center $(6,3)$, point $(10,6)$
18. Center $(-5,12)$, point $(-8,16)$
19. Center $(-3,-5)$, point $(-7,-1)$
20. Center $(-2,-1)$, point $(3,11)$
21. Center $(3,2)$, point $\left(3\frac{5}{8}, 2\right)$

22. Center $(-3,7)$, point $\left(-3, 8\frac{1}{6}\right)$

23. Center $(2,-3)$, radius $\frac{2}{3}$

24. Center $(-5,-4)$, radius $\frac{3}{4}$

In Exercises 25–40, find the center and radius of a circle given its equation. Then graph it.

25. $(x - 5)^2 + (y - 3)^2 = 16$
26. $(x + 3)^2 + (y - 6)^2 = 25$
27. $(x + 4)^2 + (y + 3)^2 = 36$
28. $(x - 6)^2 + (y - 3)^2 = 9$
29. $x^2 + y^2 = 81$ **30.** $x^2 + y^2 = 49$
31. $x^2 + (y - 5)^2 = 4$ **32.** $(x + 4)^2 + y^2 = 12$
33. $(x - 2)^2 + (y + 1)^2 = 20$
34. $(x + 3)^2 + (y - 1)^2 = 32$
35. $x^2 + 4x + y^2 = 5$ **36.** $x^2 + y^2 + 10y = 11$
37. $x^2 + 12x + y^2 - 6y = 4$
38. $x^2 - 8x + y^2 - 4y = 5$
39. $x^2 - 14x + y^2 - 10y = 6$
40. $x^2 - x + y^2 + 2y = \frac{3}{4}$

In Exercises 41–48, graph the given equations.

41. a. $x^2 + y^2 = 9$ **b.** $y = \sqrt{9 - x^2}$
   c. $y = -\sqrt{9 - x^2}$
42. a. $x^2 + y^2 = 16$ **b.** $y = \sqrt{16 - x^2}$
   c. $y = -\sqrt{16 - x^2}$
43. a. $x^2 + y^2 = 25$ **b.** $y = \sqrt{25 - x^2}$
   c. $y = -\sqrt{25 - x^2}$
44. a. $x^2 + y^2 = 49$ **b.** $y = \sqrt{49 - x^2}$
   c. $y = -\sqrt{49 - x^2}$
45. a. $x^2 + y^2 = 20$ **b.** $y = \sqrt{20 - x^2}$
   c. $y = -\sqrt{20 - x^2}$
46. a. $x^2 + y^2 = 50$ **b.** $y = \sqrt{50 - x^2}$
   c. $y = -\sqrt{50 - x^2}$
47. a. $x^2 + y^2 = 13$ **b.** $y = \sqrt{13 - x^2}$
   c. $y = -\sqrt{13 - x^2}$
48. a. $x^2 + y^2 = 17$ **b.** $y = \sqrt{17 - x^2}$
   c. $y = -\sqrt{17 - x^2}$

49. The cross section of a tunnel is the semicircle shown in the figure. How high above the road is the tunnel ceiling 30 ft on each side of the center?

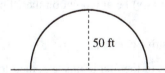

50 ft

50. Refer to the figure in Exercise 49. How high above the road is the tunnel 25 ft on each side of the center? Give the answer in exact radical form and also approximated to the nearest tenth of a foot.

51. The figure for this exercise shows two circles. Point A is on the larger circle and it is directly above C, the center of the smaller circle.

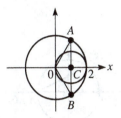

a. Find the coordinates of point C.
b. Find the equation of the larger circle.
c. Find the coordinates of point A.
d. Find the distance between A and B.
e. Find the area of triangle ABO.

52. For the given figure, answer the questions in Exercise 51.

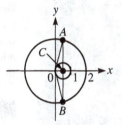

53. The circle shown has equation $x^2 + y^2 = 2$. Find the area of the shaded square.

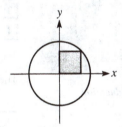

54. The circle shown has equation $x^2 + y^2 = 1$. Find the area of the shaded square.

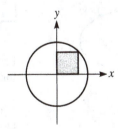

THINK ABOUT IT 7.6

1. Find the equation in standard form of the circle with $P(-4, 5)$ and $Q(4,5)$ at endpoints of a diameter.
2. If the line $y = mx$ passes through the center of the circle $4x^2 + 4y^2 - 4x + 12y - 1 = 0$, find the value of m.

3. Use the given figure and the concept of slope to show that if a triangle is inscribed in a circle with the diameter as one of its sides, then the triangle is a right triangle.

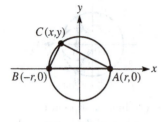

4. Do the circles given by $(x - 5)^2 + (y - 12)^2 = 121$ and $x^2 + y^2 = 4$ intersect? Explain in terms of the centers and radii of the circles.

5. Write each equation in standard form for the equation of a circle. Then describe its graph.
   a. $x^2 + y^2 + 4x - 6y + 13 = 0$
   b. $x^2 + y^2 + 4x - 6y + 14 = 0$

Courtesy of Pearson Education.

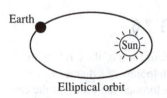

Elliptical orbit

Figure 7.51

7.7 The Ellipse and the Hyperbola

Because of uncertainties in world events, an investor decides to take a position in precious metals and buy $10,000 worth of gold. The amount (A) of gold in troy ounces that can be bought with $10,000 varies inversely as the price (P) per troy ounce of gold. Write a variation equation that expresses the relationship between A and P, and then graph the equation. (See Example 6.)

OBJECTIVES

1 Graph an ellipse.

2 Graph a hyperbola.

3 Graph $xy = c$.

4 Classify certain equations as defining either a circle, an ellipse, a hyperbola, or a parabola.

The ellipse, which is an oval-shaped curve, is defined geometrically as follows.

Definition of an Ellipse

An **ellipse** is the set of all points in a plane the sum of whose distances from two fixed points is a constant.

Each fixed point is called a **focus** of the ellipse, and the two fixed points are called the **foci.**

To understand this definition, consider Figure 7.50, which shows an ellipse centered at the origin with foci on the x-axis. If we let (x, y) be any point on the ellipse as shown, then by definition,

$$d_1 + d_2 = \text{positive constant.}$$

Although we do not determine the coordinates of the foci in this text, their location is important in many applications of the ellipse. For instance, one of the well-known applications of the ellipse is that the earth moves in an elliptical orbit with the sun at one focus, as shown in Figure 7.51.

From the given definition it can be shown that an ellipse with intercepts as shown in Figure 7.50 has the following equation.

Figure 7.50

Equation of an Ellipse

The **standard form** of the equation of an ellipse centered at the origin with x-intercepts $(a,0)$ and $(-a, 0)$ and y-intercepts $(0,b)$ and $(0, -b)$ is

$$\frac{x^2}{a^2} + \frac{y^2}{b^2} = 1.$$

where a and b are positive numbers.

When an equation for an ellipse is given in this standard form, then the equation may be graphed by drawing an ellipse through the four intercepts after determining the values of a and b.

EXAMPLE 1 Graphing an Ellipse in Standard Form

Graph $\dfrac{x^2}{16} + \dfrac{y^2}{9} = 1$.

Solution The equation fits the form for an ellipse, where

$$a^2 = 16, \quad \text{so} \quad a = 4; \quad \text{and} \quad b^2 = 9, \quad \text{so} \quad b = 3.$$

Thus the x-intercepts are $(4,0)$ and $(-4, 0)$, while the y-intercepts are $(0,3)$ and $(0, -3)$. Drawing an ellipse through these four intercepts gives the graph in Figure 7.52.

PROGRESS CHECK 1 Graph $\dfrac{x^2}{4} + \dfrac{y^2}{25} = 1$. ▪

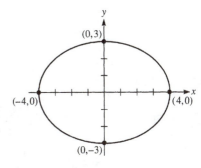

Figure 7.52

EXAMPLE 2 Converting to Standard Form and Then Graphing

Graph $4x^2 + y^2 = 4$.

Solution First, put the equation in standard form by dividing both sides of the equation by 4.

$$4x^2 + y^2 = 4$$
$$\frac{4x^2}{4} + \frac{y^2}{4} = \frac{4}{4}$$
$$\frac{x^2}{1} + \frac{y^2}{4} = 1$$

The rewritten equation fits the form for an ellipse, where

$$a^2 = 1, \quad \text{so} \quad a = 1; \quad \text{and} \quad b^2 = 4, \quad \text{so} \quad b = 2.$$

Drawing an ellipse through the intercepts, which are $(1,0)$, $(-1, 0)$, $(0,2)$, and $(0, -2)$, gives the graph of the equation in Figure 7.53.

PROGRESS CHECK 2 Graph $x^2 + 9y^2 = 36$. ▪

The next conic section we consider is the hyperbola, and its geometric definition resembles the definition of the ellipse.

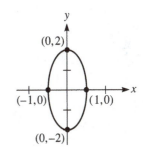

Figure 7.53

Definition of a Hyperbola

A **hyperbola** is the set of all points in a plane the difference of whose distances from two fixed points (foci) is a constant.

Note that the distances between the foci and a point in the figure maintain a *constant difference* for a hyperbola and a *constant sum* for an ellipse. Equations in standard forms for hyperbolas may be derived from the geometric definition, and the standard forms for the hyperbolas shown in Figure 7.54 are stated next.

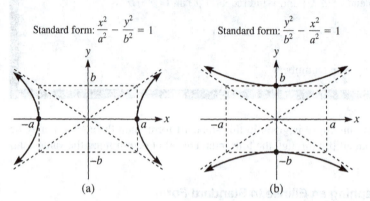

Standard form: $\dfrac{x^2}{a^2} - \dfrac{y^2}{b^2} = 1$ Standard form: $\dfrac{y^2}{b^2} - \dfrac{x^2}{a^2} = 1$

(a)   (b)

Figure 7.54

Equations of a Hyperbola

The **standard form** of the hyperbola centered at the origin with x-intercepts at $(a,0)$ and $(-a, 0)$ and no y-intercepts is

$$\frac{x^2}{a^2} - \frac{y^2}{b^2} = 1.$$

The **standard form** of the hyperbola centered at the origin with y-intercepts at $(0,b)$ and $(0, -b)$ and no x-intercepts is

$$\frac{y^2}{b^2} - \frac{x^2}{a^2} = 1.$$

In Figure 7.54, observe that a hyperbola consists of two disconnected curves, known as **branches.** In this figure note also the dashed lines that are the extended diagonals of a rectangle, called the **fundamental rectangle,** with corners at (a,b), $(a,-b)$, $(-a,b)$ and $(-a, -b)$. These diagonal lines are called the **asymptotes of the hyperbola.** They are a great aid in sketching the curve because the hyperbola approaches these lines as x increases in absolute value. In the next two examples we graph hyperbolas by drawing curves that pass through the intercepts on one of the axes and then approach asymptotes as the graph moves further from the origin in both the positive and the negative direction.

EXAMPLE 3   Graphing a Hyperbola in Standard Form

Graph $\dfrac{x^2}{9} - \dfrac{y^2}{4} = 1$.

Solution   The equation fits the form for a hyperbola, where

$$a^2 = 9, \quad \text{so} \quad a = 3; \quad \text{and} \quad b^2 = 4, \quad \text{so} \quad b = 2.$$

The graph has x-intercepts because the x^2 term is positive, and these intercepts are $(3,0)$ and $(-3, 0)$, since $a = 3$. Now we graph the hyperbola, as shown in Figure 7.55 by drawing branches that pass through the intercepts and approach the asymptotes that are the extended diagonals of the rectangle with corners $(3,2)$, $(3, -2)$, $(-3, 2)$, and $(-3, -2)$.

Note   The fundamental rectangle and the dashed lines associated with it are not part of the hyperbola but, rather, are graphing aids for sketching the hyperbola.

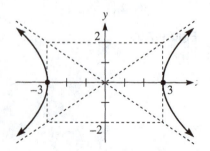

Figure 7.55

PROGRESS CHECK 3   Graph $\dfrac{x^2}{4} - \dfrac{y^2}{25} = 1$.   ■

EXAMPLE 4   Converting to Standard Form and then Graphing
Graph $4y^2 - 9x^2 = 144$.

Solution   Divide both sides of the given equation by 144 to obtain the standard form

$$\frac{y^2}{36} - \frac{x^2}{16} = 1.$$

This equation fits the form $(y^2/b^2) - (x^2/a^2) = 1$, with

$$b^2 = 36, \quad \text{so} \quad b = 6; \quad \text{and} \quad a^2 = 16, \quad \text{so} \quad a = 4.$$

Thus, the graph is a hyperbola with y-intercepts at $(0,6)$ and $(0,-6)$ and no x-intercepts. We graph the hyperbola as shown in Figure 7.56, using the fundamental rectangle with corners at $(4,6)$, $(4,-6)$, $(-4,6)$, and $(-4,-6)$.

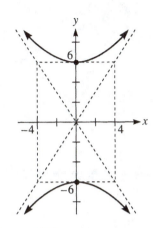

Figure 7.56

PROGRESS CHECK 4   Graph $y^2 - x^2 = 9$.   ■

An equation of the form

$$xy = c,$$

where c is a nonzero constant, is an important case of another type of second-degree equation that graphs as a hyperbola. The asymptotes in these graphs are the x-axis and the y-axis, and knowing these asymptotes along with some points on each branch enables us to draw these hyperbolas.

EXAMPLE 5   Graphing a Hyperbola with Axes as Asymptotes
Graph $xy = 2$.

Solution   The equation $xy = 2$, or $y = 2/x$, graphs as a hyperbola with both axes as asymptotes. Using these facts and plotting a few points, say $(1,2)$, $(-1,-2)$, $\left(4,\frac{1}{2}\right)$, and $\left(-4,-\frac{1}{2}\right)$, gives the graph in Figure 7.57.

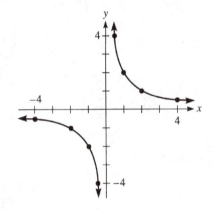

PROGRESS CHECK 5   Graph $xy = -2$.   ■

To solve the section-opening problem, you may need to review the concept of inverse variation considered in Section 2.3.

Figure 7.57

EXAMPLE 6   Graphing a Hyperbola in an Inverse Variation Problem
Solve the problem in the section introduction on page 408.

Solution   Since the amount (A) of gold in troy ounces that may be bought varies inversely with the price (P) per troy ounce of gold,

$$AP = k, \quad \text{or} \quad A = \frac{k}{P}.$$

Because $\$10,000$ is to be invested, the variation constant k is 10,000, and A and P are related by

$$A = \frac{10,000}{P}.$$

This equation graphs as a hyperbola with both axes as asymptotes. However, the graph is limited to the branch in quadrant 1, since both A and P must be positive. With the aid of the points specified by the following table, we can draw the graph as shown in Figure 7.58.

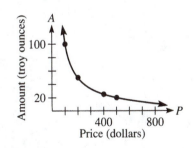

Figure 7.58

Price (in dollars), P	100	200	400	500
Amount (in troy ounces), A	100	50	25	20

PROGRESS CHECK 6 If a car travels at a constant rate r, then the time t required to drive 60 mi varies inversely with r. Write an equation that expresses the relationship between r and t, and then graph this equation. ■

With the exception of the equation $xy = c$, the equations considered in Sections 7.5–7.7 have all been of the general form

$$Ax^2 + Cy^2 + Dx + Ey + F = 0,$$

where A and C are not both zero. If a graph is a circle, an ellipse, a hyperbola, or a parabola, then A and C must satisfy certain conditions that follow from the forms given for each conic section.

Conditions on A and C	Conic Section	Degenerate Possibilities
$A = C \neq 0$	Circle	A point or no graph at all
$A \neq C$; A and C have the same sign	Ellipse	A point or no graph at all
A and C have opposite signs	Hyperbola	Two intersecting straight lines
$A = 0$ or $C = 0$ (but not both)	Parabola	A line, a pair of parallel lines, or no graph at all

In this text we do not consider equations that lead to the degenerate possibilities (but see "Think About It" Exercise 3). However, it is interesting to note that many of these cases also result from the intersection of a cone with an appropriate plane, and the degenerate possibilities are called **degenerate conic sections.** It can be shown that the graph of every second-degree equation in two variables is a conic section or a degenerate conic section.

EXAMPLE 7 Identifying a Conic Section

Identify the graph of each equation as a circle, an ellipse, a hyperbola, or a parabola.

a. $2x^2 + 2y^2 - 10x - 2y - 31 = 0$
b. $2x^2 - y + 5 = 0$
c. $4x^2 = 9y^2 + 36$

Solution Since the degenerate possibilities have been eliminated, we proceed as follows.

a. The given equation is in general form with $A = 2$ and $C = 2$. Since A and C are nonzero and equal, the graph is a circle.
b. In this equation $A = 2$ and there is no y^2 term, so $C = 0$. Because one (but not both) of these values is zero, the graph is a parabola.
c. Rewrite $4x^2 = 9y^2 + 36$ in general form as

$$4x^2 - 9y^2 - 36 = 0.$$

Then $A = 4$ and $C = -9$. Since A and C have opposite signs, the graph is a hyperbola.

PROGRESS CHECK 7 Identify the graph of each equation as a circle, an ellipse, a hyperbola, or a parabola.

a. $y^2 + 4y + 3x - 8 = 0$
b. $4y^2 - x^2 = 36$
c. $9y^2 = 36 - 4x^2$ ■

EXERCISES 7.7

In Exercises 1–10, graph the given ellipse.

1. $\dfrac{x^2}{9} + \dfrac{y^2}{16} = 1$ **2.** $\dfrac{x^2}{4} + \dfrac{y^2}{1} = 1$

3. $\dfrac{x^2}{4} + \dfrac{y^2}{25} = 1$ **4.** $\dfrac{x^2}{36} + \dfrac{y^2}{9} = 1$

5. $4x^2 + y^2 = 4$ **6.** $x^2 + 5y^2 = 20$

7. $9x^2 + 16y^2 = 144$ **8.** $4x^2 + 9y^2 = 36$

9. $100x^2 + 9y^2 = 900$ **10.** $64x^2 + 8y^2 = 16$

In Exercises 11–30, graph the given hyperbolas.

11. $\dfrac{x^2}{36} - \dfrac{y^2}{9} = 1$ **12.** $\dfrac{x^2}{4} - \dfrac{y^2}{25} = 1$

13. $\dfrac{x^2}{4} - y^2 = 1$ **14.** $\dfrac{x^2}{9} - \dfrac{y^2}{16} = 1$

15. $\dfrac{y^2}{9} - \dfrac{x^2}{25} = 1$ **16.** $\dfrac{y^2}{36} - \dfrac{x^2}{4} = 1$

17. $y^2 - \dfrac{x^2}{9} = 1$ **18.** $\dfrac{y^2}{16} - \dfrac{x^2}{4} = 1$

19. $4y^2 - x^2 = 4$ **20.** $y^2 - 5x^2 = 20$

21. $9y^2 - 16x^2 = 144$ **22.** $4y^2 - 9x^2 = 36$

23. $64y^2 - 8x^2 = 16$ **24.** $4x^2 - y^2 = 4$

25. $100x^2 - 9y^2 = 900$ **26.** $x^2 - 5y^2 = 20$

27. $xy = 3$ **28.** $xy = 9$

29. $xy = -5$ **30.** $xy = -7$

In Exercises 31–46, identify the graph of each equation as a circle, an ellipse, a hyperbola, or a parabola.

31. $-4x^2 - y + 3 = 0$

32. $9x^2 + 9y^2 - 81 = 0$

33. $9x^2 = 9y^2 + 81$

34. $2y^2 - x + 6 = 0$

35. $3x^2 + 3y^2 - 6x + 30y + 30 = 0$

36. $5x^2 - 4y^2 + 6x - 3y + 10 = 0$

37. $5x^2 + 9y^2 - 45 = 0$

38. $y^2 + 4 = x$

39. $6x^2 - 7y^2 - 42 = 0$

40. $4x^2 + 4y^2 + x - 4y + 1 = 0$

41. $5x^2 + 3y^2 + 10x - 9y - 3 = 0$

42. $9x^2 - 3y - 3 = 0$

43. $3x^2 + 7y^2 - 2x + y + 5 = 0$

44. $9x^2 - 4y^2 - 6x + 5y + 2 = 0$

45. $3x^2 + 3y^2 + 12x - 18y + 4 = 0$

46. $10x^2 + 7y^2 - 100x + 28y + 8 = 0$

47. a. Given that y varies inversely as x, and $y = 5$ when $x = 3$, find the variation constant, and write an equation which shows y in terms of x.

b. Graph the equation from part **a.**

48. a. Given that y varies inversely as x, and $y = 1$ when $x = -1$, find the variation constant, and write an equation which shows y in terms of x.

b. Graph the equation from part **a.**

In Exercises 49–50, use the relationship that for something traveling a fixed distance, the time elapsed varies inversely with the average speed.

49. a. Write an equation showing that the time t to get from A to B varies inversely with speed s.

b. Use the fact that a car averaging 55 mi/hour along an interstate highway takes 2 hours to get from point A to point B to find the variation constant for the equation in part **a.**

c. Graph this relation, with time on the vertical axis and speed on the horizontal axis. Indicate the appropriate units.

d. About how long will it take to get from A to B if the speed is reduced to 45 mi/hour?

50. a. Use the fact that a car averaging 55 mi/hour along an interstate highway takes 3 hours to get from point A to point C to find an equation expressing the time needed to get from A to C in terms of the average speed of the car.

b. Graph this relation, with time on the vertical axis and speed on the horizontal axis. Indicate the appropriate units.

c. About how long will it take to get from A to C if the speed is reduced to 45 mi/hour?

THINK ABOUT IT 7.7

1. An ellipse may be drawn using pencil, string, and tacks, as shown here. Explain the mathematical basis for this method, referring to the definition of the ellipse.

2. a. Find the equations of the asymptotes of the hyperbola in Example 3.

b. In general form, what are the equations of the asymptotes of $(x^2/a^2) - (y^2/b^2) = 1$ or $(y^2/b^2) - (x^2/a^2) = 1$?

3. Match each graph with the equation that illustrates that case.

Graph	Equation
1. Two distinct parallel lines	a. $y^2 = 0$
2. One line through the origin	b. $y^2 = 1$
3. Two distinct lines through the origin	c. $x^2 + y^2 = -1$
	d. $x^2 + y^2 = 0$
4. No graph	e. $x^2 - y^2 = 0$
5. A point	

4. The names *ellipse, parabola,* and *hyperbola* were given to the conic sections by the Greek mathematician Apollonius (c. 262–190 B.C.). His work was entirely geometric but is equivalent to algebraically noting three types of equations for conics.

$$y^2 = px - \frac{px^2}{d}$$ The case of "ellipsis," which means to fall short

$$y^2 = px$$ The case of "parabole," which means to coincide

$$y^2 = px + \frac{px^2}{d}$$ The case of "hyperbole," which means to exceed

The letters p and d refer to lengths of line segments used in the geometric construction of these shapes.

a. Let $p = 4$ and $d = 1$; then by plotting points, draw each of the resulting graphs and confirm that they do give the "correct" shape.

b. Let $p = 1$ and $d = 4$, and repeat part **a.**

c. What values for p and d will make the "ellipse" into a circle?

5. Refer to the given figure of an ellipse. It can be shown that $a^2 = b^2 + c^2$ (the Pythagorean relationship). The ratio c/a is called the *eccentricity* of the ellipse. Eccentricity means "out of roundness." If $c = 0$, then the focus is at the center, a equals b, the eccentricity is 0, and the figure is a circle. Recall that the orbits of the planets around the sun are ellipses with the sun at one focus. For instance, the orbit of Venus has eccentricity 0.0068, while earth's eccentricity is 0.0168 and Mercury's is 0.206.

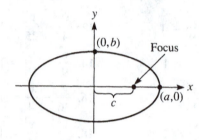

a. Use the Pythagorean relationship above to find the eccentricity of the ellipse whose x-intercepts are $(2,0)$ and $(-2,0)$ and whose y-intercepts are $(0,1)$ and $(0,-1)$.

b. If the x-intercepts are twice as far from the origin as the y-intercepts, will the eccentricity be the same as that in part **a?**

7.8 Nonlinear Systems of Equations

Courtesy of Prentice-Hall, Inc.

In economics an analysis of the law of supply and demand involves the intersection of two graphs. Basically, as the price for an item increases, the quantity of the product that is supplied increases while the quantity that is demanded decreases. The point at which the supply and demand graphs intersect is called the **point of market equilibrium.**

a. The supply and demand equations in a certain location for a model of sandal priced at p dollars are given by

$$\text{Supply: } q = p^2 + 4p - 60$$
$$\text{Demand: } q = 240 - p$$

Estimate the equilibrium price and the corresponding number of units supplied and demanded by finding the intersection of the graphs of these equations for $p > 0$ on a grapher.

b. Confirm your solution from part **a** by algebraic methods. (See Example 2.)

OBJECTIVES

1 Solve a nonlinear system of equations by the graphing method, the substitution method, or the addition-elimination method.

2 Solve applied problems involving a nonlinear system of equations.

Systems of linear equations in two variables were solved algebraically and graphically in Chapter 3. On the basis of the work with second-degree equations in this chapter, we can now solve certain **nonlinear systems of equations,** which are systems with at least one equation that is not linear. Graphically, solving most of the systems considered in this section will require finding all intersection points of one of the conic sections (parabola, circle, ellipse, hyperbola) with a line or another conic section. The algebraic approach for finding such solutions will rely once again on either the substitution method or the addition-elimination method. As with linear systems, when at least one equation in the system is solved for one of the variables, the substitution method is easy to apply, as illustrated in Example 1.

EXAMPLE 1   Solving a Nonlinear System Graphically and Algebraically

Solve the system:

$$y = x^2 - 6x + 8 \quad (1)$$
$$y = x + 2 \qquad\quad (2)$$

Use graphical and algebraic methods.

Solution   The solutions to this system are easy to picture on a grapher. Equation (1) graphs as a parabola, equation (2) graphs as a line, and these two graphs intersect at (1,3) and (6,8), as shown in Figure 7.59.

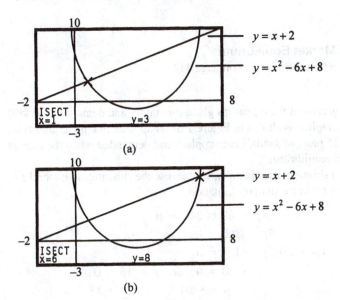

Figure 7.59

To confirm these solutions algebraically, we choose the substitution method and replace y by $x^2 - 6x + 8$ in equation (2) and solve for x.

$$x^2 - 6x + 8 = x + 2$$
$$x^2 - 7x + 6 = 0$$
$$(x - 6)(x - 1) = 0$$
$$x - 6 = 0 \quad \text{or} \quad x - 1 = 0$$
$$x = 6 \qquad\qquad\quad x = 1$$

Thus, the parabola and the line intersect at $x = 1$ and $x = 6$. To find the y coordinates, substitute these numbers in the simpler equation $y = x + 2$.

$$
\begin{array}{ll}
y = x + 2 & y = x + 2 \\
\ = (1) + 2 \quad \text{or} & \ = (6) + 2 \\
\ = 3 & \ = 8
\end{array}
$$

The solutions, (1,3) and (6,8), should be checked in both original equations (1) and (2).
Note   A line and a conic section may intersect in two, one, or no points, as illustrated in
Figure 7.60. Therefore, we can anticipate that a system with one first-degree equation and
one second-degree equation will have two, one, or no real solutions.

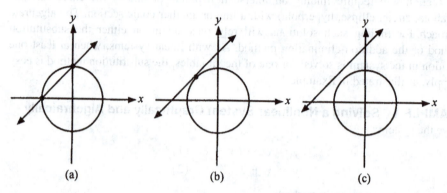

(a)   (b)   (c)

Figure 7.60

PROGRESS CHECK 1   Solve the system: $\begin{array}{l} x^2 + y^2 = 25 \\ y = x - 1. \end{array}$ Use graphical and alge-

braic methods.   ■

EXAMPLE 2   Point of Market Equilibrium

Solve the problem in the section introduction on page 414.

Solution

a. The intersection of the graphs of the equations given for supply and demand for $p > 0$
may be displayed on a grapher as shown in Figure 7.61. It appears that the equilibrium
price is \$15, and that 225 pairs of sandals are supplied and demanded when the market
for this commodity is in equilibrium.

b. To confirm the proposed solution algebraically, we can use the substitution method and
replace q by $p^2 + 4p - 60$ in the demand equation.

$$p^2 + 4p - 60 = 240 - p$$
$$p^2 + 5p - 300 = 0$$
$$(p + 20)(p - 15) = 0$$
$$p + 20 = 0 \quad \text{or} \quad p - 15 = 0$$
$$p = -20 \qquad\qquad p = 15$$

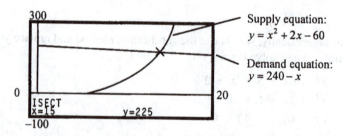

Supply equation:
$y = x^2 + 2x - 60$

Demand equation:
$y = 240 - x$

Figure 7.61

In the context of the problem only $p = 15$ is meaningful, so the equilibrium price is
\$15. To find q, replace p by 15 in the demand equation, which is the simpler equation.

$$q = 240 - p$$
$$= 240 - 15$$
$$= 225$$

When this market is in equilibrium, manufacturers will supply 225 pairs of sandals, and consumers will demand 225 pairs of sandals. Thus, we have algebraic confirmation of the results from part **a.**

PROGRESS CHECK 2   Redo the problems in Example 2, assuming that the supply equation is $q = p^2 + 3p - 70$, and the demand equation is $q = 410 - p$.   ■

The substitution method is also a useful method when one equation in a system is linear or one equation in a system is of the form $xy = c$, as shown in Example 3.

EXAMPLE 3   Solving a System Involving *xy = c*

The design for a rectangular component in an industrial robot specifies that the area must measure 120 cm^2 and the diagonal must measure 17 cm. Find the dimensions of the component.

Solution   Let x represent the width and y represent the length, and sketch the problem situation as in Figure 7.62. Then set up a system of equations.

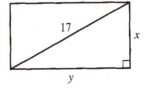

By the area formula: $xy = 120$ (1)
By the Pythagorean theorem: $x^2 + y^2 = 289$ (2)

Start with the equation of the form $xy = c$ and solve for one of the variables. Solving for y in equation (1) gives

Figure 7.62

$$xy = 120$$

$$y = \frac{120}{x}.$$ (3)

Now substitute $120/x$ for y in equation (2) and solve. (The solution will involve the methods of Section 7.3 for solving an equation in quadratic form.)

$$x^2 + \left(\frac{120}{x}\right)^2 = 289$$

$$x^2 + \frac{14{,}400}{x^2} = 289$$

$$x^4 + 14{,}400 = 289x^2$$

$$x^4 - 289x^2 + 14{,}400 = 0$$

$$t^2 - 289t + 14{,}400 = 0 \qquad \text{Let } t = x^2; \text{ then } t^2 = x^4.$$

$$t = 225 \quad \text{or} \quad t = 64 \qquad \text{By the quadratic formula.}$$

Then, since $t = x^2$,

$$x^2 = 225 \quad \text{or} \quad x^2 = 64$$

$$x = \pm 15 \qquad\qquad x = \pm 8.$$

In the context of the problem, negative solutions are rejected. Substituting the two positive solutions into equation (3) yields

$$y = 8 \qquad \text{when} \qquad x = 15$$

$$\text{and} \quad y = 15 \qquad \text{when} \qquad x = 8.$$

Because x represents the width (which must be smaller than the length), we conclude that the rectangular component must be 8 cm wide and 15 cm long.

PROGRESS CHECK 3   If the area of a rectangular component must measure 60 cm^2 and the diagonal must measure 13 cm, find the dimensions of the component.   ■

When the two equations in a system both contain an x^2 term and a y^2 term, then the addition-elimination method is often useful, as shown next.

EXAMPLE 4   Using the Addition-Elimination Method

Find all intersection points of the ellipse $3x^2 + y^2 = 35$ and the hyperbola $5y^2 - 2x^2 = 2$.

Solution   The system we need to solve is

$$3x^2 + 2y^2 = 35 \qquad (1)$$
$$-2x^2 + 5y^2 = 2. \qquad (2)$$

If equivalent equations are formed by multiplying both sides of equation (1) by 2, and both sides of equation (2) by 3, then the x variable can be eliminated.

$$6x^2 + 4y^2 = 70 \qquad (3)$$
$$\underline{-6x^2 + 15y^2 = 6} \qquad (4)$$
$$19y^2 = 76 \qquad \text{Add equations (3) and (4).}$$
$$y^2 = 4$$
$$y = \pm 2$$

Then substitute $y = \pm 2$ into equation (1) to find x. Because 2^2 and $(-2)^2$ are both 4, the solution may be continued in consolidated form.

$$3x^2 + 2(\pm 2)^2 = 35$$
$$3x^2 + 8 = 35$$
$$3x^2 = 27$$
$$x^2 = 9$$
$$x = \pm 3$$

Associating each solution for y with each solution for x gives the solution set $\{(3,2), (3,-2), (-3,2), (-3,-2)\}$. Figure 7.63 shows the ellipse and the hyperbola of this system intersecting at these points.

PROGRESS CHECK 4   Find all intersection points of the ellipse $2x^2 + 3y^2 = 5$ and the hyperbola $4y^2 - 3x^2 = 1$.   ■

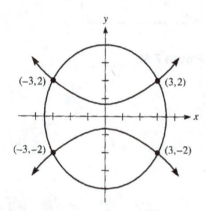

Figure 7.63

EXERCISES 7.8

In Exercises 1–14, solve the given system by the substitution method.

1. $y = x^2 - x + 2$
$y = 2x + 2$

2. $y = x^2 - 4x + 3$
$y = -5x + 9$

3. $y = -x^2 - x + 13$
$y = -4x + 3$

4. $y = -x^2 - 2x + 20$
$y = 2x - 1$

5. $y = x^2 - 4x + 12$
$y = 2x + 3$

6. $y = -x^2 + 3x - 1$
$y = -x + 3$

7. $y = x^2 + 6$
$y = x - 3$

8. $y = -3x^2 - 5$
$y = x + 3$

9. $x^2 + y^2 = 36$
$y = x - 6$

10. $x^2 + y^2 = 9$
$y = x + 3$

11. $x^2 + y^2 = 9$
$y = 2x - 3$

12. $x^2 + y^2 = 16$
$y = -3x + 4$

13. $x^2 + y^2 = 25$
$y = -x + 8$

14. $x^2 + y^2 = 1$
$y = x + 2$

In Exercises 15–20, find all the intersection points of the given ellipses and hyperbolas. Use the elimination method.

15. $2x^2 + 3y^2 = 93$
$2y^2 - x^2 = 41$

16. $3x^2 + 4y^2 = 19$
$-2x^2 + 5y^2 = 18$

17. $6x^2 + 7y^2 = 159$
$-3x^2 + y^2 = -39$

18. $x^2 + 2y^2 = 57$
$-x^2 + 3y^2 = 23$

19. $x^2 + 2y^2 = 33$
$2y^2 - x^2 = 3$

20. $3x^2 + 4y^2 = 34$
$2y^2 - x^2 = 2$

21. The area of a rectangle is 48 cm^2, and the diagonal is 10 cm. Find the dimensions of the rectangle.

22. The area of a right triangle is 120 in.^{2} and the hypotenuse is 26 in. Find the lengths of both legs.

23. To the nearest thousandth, find the dimensions of a rectangle whose diagonal is 10 in. and whose area is 10 in.^{2}.

24. To the nearest thousandth, find the dimensions of a rectangle whose diagonal is 10 cm and whose area is 1 cm^3.

25. a. Find the equations of the line and the circle in the figure.

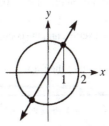

   b. Find both points of intersection.

26. Find all points on the ellipse $\dfrac{x^2}{9} + \dfrac{y^2}{25} = 1$ that are at a distance of 4 units from the origin.

THINK ABOUT IT 7.8

1. Show in a series of sketches that an ellipse and a hyperbola may intersect in four or less points. What does this say about the solution of a system that contains an equation for an ellipse and an equation for a hyperbola?

2. Create specific systems by writing equations that illustrate the given case.

   a. A circle and a line that do not intersect
   b. An ellipse and a hyperbola that intersect in two points
   c. Any two conic sections that intersect in one point

3. Greek legend has it that Apollo was responsible for a plague in Delos. The oracle there said that Apollo would be appeased if the people would double the size of the altar, keeping its shape the same. The shape was cubical. The mathematical question then is, "How much longer should each side of the new cube be so that its volume is double the original volume?" This was a difficult problem for Greek geometry. One solution, often attributed to Menaechmus (c. 350 B.C.), depended on finding the intersection of a parabola and a hyperbola. The side of the new altar is given by the x-coordinate of the intersection of the graphs of $y = x^2$ and $xy = 2$. Solve this system and show that multiplying the side (s) of a cube by this solution gives a new cube with double the volume of the old one.

4. When two resistors are connected in series, their combined resistance is given by $R = R_1 + R_2$. If the resistors are connected in parallel, their combined resistance is given by $R = R_1R_2/(R_1 + R_2)$. Find the value of resistors R_1 and R_2 if their combined resistance is 32 ohms when connected in series and 6 ohms when connected in parallel.

5. Find the radius of each circle in the illustration if their combined area is 68π cm^2.

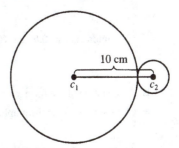

CHAPTER 7 OVERVIEW

Section	Key Concepts or Procedures to Review
7.1	■ Methods to solve a quadratic equation by using the square root property and by completing the square
7.2	■ Quadratic formula: If $ax^2 + bx + c = 0$ and $a \neq 0$, then $$x = \frac{-b \pm 2\sqrt{b^2 - 4ac}}{2a}.$$ ■ Methods to solve quadratic equations by using the quadratic formula ■ Methods to determine the nature of the solutions to a quadratic equation from the discriminant ($b^2 - 4ac$) ■ Guidelines for selecting an efficient method for solving a quadratic equation
7.3	■ Methods to solve fractional equations and radical equations that lead to quadratic equations and to solve equations with quadratic form ■ Methods to solve literal equations for a variable with highest power 2

7.4 ■ Methods to solve quadratic inequalities, polynomial inequalities of degree higher than 2, and inequalities involving quotients of polynomials

7.5 ■ The graph of an equation of the form $y = ax^2 + bx + c$ with $a \neq 0$ is a parabola. If $a > 0$, the parabola opens upward. If $a < 0$, the parabola opens downward.

■ The graph of an equation of the form $x = ay^2 + by + c$ with $a \neq 0$ is a parabola. If $a > 0$, the parabola opens to the right. If $a < 0$, the parabola opens to the left.

■ Procedure for graphing a parabola by determining the axis of symmetry, the vertex, and the coordinates of any x-and y-intercepts

■ Methods to determine the number of x-intercepts of the graph of an equation of the form $y = ax^2 + bx + c$ from the discriminant $(b^2 - 4ac)$

7.6 ■ Standard form of the equation of a circle of radius r with center (h, k): $(x - h)^2 + (y - k)^2 = r^2$

■ Standard equation of a circle with center at the origin and radius r: $x^2 + y^2 = r^2$

■ The graph of an equation of the form $y = 2\sqrt{r^2 - x^2}$ or $y = -2\sqrt{r^2 - x^2}$ is a semicircle.

7.7 ■ Definitions of an ellipse and a hyperbola

■ Standard form of the equation of an ellipse centered at the origin with x-intercepts $(a,0)$ and $(-a,0)$ and y-intercepts $(0,b)$ and $(0,-b)$:

$$\frac{x^2}{a^2} + \frac{y^2}{b^2} = 1, \quad \text{where} \quad a > 0, b > 0.$$

■ Standard form of the hyperbola centered at the origin, with

(1) x-intercepts at $(a,0)$ and $(-a,0)$ and no y-intercepts:

$$\frac{x^2}{a^2} - \frac{y^2}{b^2} = 1$$

(2) y-intercepts at $(0,b)$ and $(0,-b)$ and no x-intercepts:

$$\frac{y^2}{b^2} - \frac{x^2}{a^2} = 1$$

■ An equation of the form $xy = c$, with $c \neq 0$, graphs as a hyperbola with both axes as asymptotes.

■ Chart summarizing the graphing possibilities for

$$Ax^2 + Cy^2 + Dx + Ey + F = 0,$$

where A and C are not both zero

7.8 ■ Methods to solve a nonlinear system of equations by the substitution method and by the addition-elimination method

CHAPTER 7 REVIEW EXERCISES

1. Solve $x^2 = -3$ using the square root property.
2. Solve $(x - 2)^2 - 9 = 0$.
3. Determine the number that should be added to make the expression $x^2 + 8x$ a perfect square. Then add this number and factor the resulting trinomial.
4. Solve $x^2 + 4x - 15 = 0$ by completing the square.
5. Solve $3x^2 - x - 3 = 0$ by completing the square.
6. Solve $x^2 + 5x + 3 = 0$ using the quadratic formula.
7. Solve $4x^2 + 5x - 6 = 0$ using the quadratic formula.
8. Solve $x^2 + 5 = 2x$ using the quadratic formula.
9. Use the discriminant to determine the nature of the solutions of the equation $3x^2 - 4 = 5x$.
10. Solve the equation $4x^2 - 16 = -7$. Choose an efficient method.
11. Solve $\dfrac{5}{x} - \dfrac{6}{x^2} = 1$.

12. Solve $x + \sqrt{6 - x^2} = 0$.
13. Solve $x^4 - 10x^2 + 9 = 0$.
14. Solve $3x^{1/2} - 7x^{1/4} + 2 = 0$.
15. Solve $x^2 = 9 - y^2$ for y.
16. Solve $2x^2 + x - 3 \leq 0$.
17. Solve $(x - 1)^2 > -3$.
18. Solve $x(2x + 7)(x - 2) < 0$.
19. Solve $\dfrac{5}{x} > 3$.
20. The height of a projectile that is shot directly up from the ground with an initial velocity of 128 ft/second is given by $y = -16t^2 + 128t$, where y is measured in feet and t is the elapsed time in seconds. To the nearest hundredth of a second, for what values of t is the projectile more than 96 ft off the ground?

21. Graph $y = x^2 + 4$ by finding ordered-pair solutions.
22. Use the discriminant to determine the number of x-intercepts of the graph of $y = 2x^2 - 3x + 2$.

In Exercises 23 and 24 for the given equation, do the following:
   a. Find the equation of the axis of symmetry.
   b. Find the coordinates of the vertex.
   c. Find the coordinates of any x- and y-intercepts.
   d. Graph the equation.
23. $y = x^2 - x - 6$
24. $x = 2y^2 - 4y$
25. The height (y) of a projectile that is shot directly up from the ground with an initial velocity of 144 ft/second is given by $y = -16t^2 + 144t$, where y is measured in feet and t is the elapsed time in seconds.
   a. When does the projectile attain its maximum height?
   b. What is the maximum height?
   c. When does the projectile hit the ground?
26. Find the equation in standard form of the circle with center at $(2,-5)$ and radius 6.
27. Find the equation in standard form of the circle with center at $(-2,6)$ that passes through $(1,3)$.
28. Find the center and radius of the circle given by $(x - 1)^2 + y^2 = 16$.
29. Find the center and radius of the circle given by $x^2 - 6x + y^2 - 4y + 2 = 0$.
30. Graph the equation $y = \sqrt{9 - x^2}$.
31. Graph $\dfrac{x^2}{25} + \dfrac{y^2}{9} = 1$.
32. Graph $\dfrac{x^2}{16} - \dfrac{y^2}{4} = 1$.
33. Graph $9y^2 - 16x^2 = 144$.
34. If a car travels at a constant rate r, then the time t required to travel 40 mi varies inversely with r. Write an equation that expresses the relationship between r and t, and graph this equation.
35. Identify the graph of the equation $4y^2 = -25x^2 + 16$ as a circle, an ellipse, a hyperbola or a parabola.
36. Solve the system. $y = x^2 + x - 4$
                          $y = 3x - 1$
37. Solve the system. $x^2 + y^2 = 4$
                          $-3x + y = -6$
38. Find all intersection points of the ellipse $2x^2 + y^2 = 31$ and the hyperbola $3x^2 - 2y^2 = 1$.
39. Solve the system. $xy = 80$
                          $x^2 + y^2 = 281$
40. If the area of a rectangle measures 108 cm^2 and the diagonal measures 15 cm, find the dimensions of the rectangle.
41. Find all intersection points of the ellipse $3x^2 + 2y^2 = 5$ and the hyperbola $4x^2 - 3y^2 = 1$.
42. Find the center and radius of the circle given by $x^2 + y^2 - 4x - 2y + 1 = 0$.
43. Find the center and radius of the circle given by $(x + 1)^2 + y^2 = 6$.

44. Use the discriminant to determine the number of x-intercepts of the graph of $y = x^2 - 8x + 10$.
45. Find the equation in standard form of the circle with center at $(-1,4)$ and the radius 7.
46. Find the equation in standard form of the circle with center at $(-2,8)$ that passes through $(-1,-2)$.
47. Complete the square for $y^2 + 10y$, and express the resulting trinomial in factored form.
48. Use the discriminant to determine the nature of the solutions of the equation $3x^2 + 6 = 2x$.
49. The amount (A) of silver in troy ounces that can be bought with $500 varies inversely as the price (p) per troy ounce of silver. Write a variation equation that expresses the relationship between A and p, and then graph the equation.
50. The area of a rectangle measures 240 cm^2 and the diagonal measures 26 cm. Find the dimensions of the rectangle.
51. The length of a rectangle is 5 in. greater than its width, and its area is 22 in.^{2}. To the nearest thousandth of an inch, find the length and width of the rectangle.
52. The height (y) in feet of a projectile shot vertically up from the ground with an initial velocity of 32 ft/second is given by $y = -16t^2 + 32t$, where t is the elapsed time in seconds.
   a. When does the projectile attain its maximum height?
   b. What is the maximum height?
   c. When does the projectile hit the ground?
   d. Graph the equation.

In Exercises 53–55 for the given equation, do the following.
   a. Find the equation of the axis of symmetry.
   b. Find the coordinates of the vertex.
   c. Find the coordinates of the x- and y-intercepts.
   d. Graph the equation.

53. $y = x^2 - 4x + 4$
54. $y = -x^2 + 2x - 4$
55. $x = y^2 + 8y$
56. Solve for y: $x = y^2 + 6$.
57. Solve for t: $y = -32t^2 + pt + q$.

Solve each system.

58. $y = x^2 + 2x - 4$
    $y = x - 4$
59. $x^2 + y^2 = 34$
    $y - x = 2$

Solve using the indicated method.

60. $x^2 - 20 = 0$ (square root property)
61. $x^2 - 3x - 5 = 0$ (quadratic formula)
62. $x^2 - 10x + 16 = 0$ (completing the square)
63. $3x^2 + 7x = 6$ (quadratic formula)
64. $2x^2 + x - 2 = 0$ (completing the square)

Solve using any efficient method.

65. $x^2 + 5 = 4x$

66. $x - \sqrt{8 - x^2} = 0$

67. $9y^2 - 6y + 1 = 0$

68. $y^4 - 6y^2 = -5$

69. $y^2 + 25 = 0$

70. $3x^{2/3} - 2x^{1/3} - 1 = 0$

71. $(y - 4)^2 = 5$

72. $1 - \dfrac{3}{x} = \dfrac{10}{x^2}$

73. $\dfrac{x - 3}{x} \leq 0$

74. $2x^2 - x - 10 < 0$

75. $x(x + 1)(2x - 1) > 0$

Classify each equation as determining either a circle, a semicircle, an ellipse, a hyperbola, or a parabola. Graph the equation.

76. $y = 6x - 3x^2$

77. $x^2 + y^2 = 9$

78. $\dfrac{x^2}{4} - \dfrac{y^2}{9} = 1$

79. $y = x^2 - 25$

80. $xy = 10$

81. $\dfrac{x^2}{100} + \dfrac{y^2}{25} = 1$

82. $x^2 + 4y^2 = 36$

83. $x + 2y^2 + 4y = 0$

84. $y = \sqrt{16 - x^2}$

85. $y^2 - x^2 = 16$

CHAPTER 7 TEST

1. Complete the square for $x^2 - 8x$, and express the resulting trinomial in factored form.

2. Use the discriminant to determine the nature of the solutions of the equation $16x^2 + 16 = 32x$.

3. Find the center and radius of the circle given by $x^2 + y^2 + 2x - 2y - 3 = 0$.

4. Find the equation in standard form of the circle with center at $(5,1)$ that passes through $(2,-3)$.

5. Consider the equation $y = x^2 - 4x + 3$.
   a. Find the equation of the axis of symmetry.
   b. Find the coordinates of the vertex.
   c. Find the coordinates of any x- and y-intercepts.
   d. Graph the equation.

6. Solve $x^2 = y^2 + 7$ for y.

7. Solve the system. $\quad y = 2x + 1$
$\qquad\qquad\qquad\quad y = x^2 + 3x - 1$

8. Graph $\dfrac{x^2}{4} - \dfrac{y^2}{16} = 1$.

9. Graph $9x^2 + 4y^2 = 36$.

In Questions 10–19, solve the given equation or inequality. Use the method indicated, if any.

10. $x^2 - 4x - 1 = 0$ (quadratic formula)

11. $2y^2 + y - 4 = 0$ (completing the square)

12. $(x - 6)^2 + 4 = 0$ (square root property)

13. $1 - \dfrac{3}{x} = \dfrac{4}{x^2}$

14. $3y^2 + 4y - 4 = 0$

15. $\sqrt{4 - x^2} - x = 0$

16. $y^4 - 8y^2 + 12 = 0$

17. $x^2 + 6x > 7$

18. $x(x + 4)(3x - 1) < 0$

19. $\dfrac{x + 5}{x - 6} \leq 0$

20. The height (y) of a projectile that is shot directly up from the ground with an initial velocity of 112 ft/second is given by $y = -16t^2 + 112t$, where y is measured in feet and t is the elapsed time in seconds.
   a. When does the projectile attain its maximum height?
   b. What is the maximum height?
   c. When does the projectile hit the ground?

Exponential and Logarithmic Functions

If you win the state lottery and are offered $1 million or a penny that doubles in value on each day in the month of November, which option should you accept? Answer the following questions to find out.

a. Write a formula that gives the value (in cents) of the penny at the end of *x* days.

b. What is the value of the penny by the end of the month? Which offer is better?

(See Example 1 of Section 8.1.)

Exponential functions and their inverses, the logarithmic functions, are important rules for analyzing a wide variety of relationships. Compound interest, population growth, radioactive decay, pH, decibels, and heat loss (from a home or a murder victim) are but some of the applications we consider in this chapter. Whereas a typical polynomial function looks like $y = x^2$, a typical exponential function looks like $y = 2^x$. The explosive growth of exponential functions like $y = 2^x$ can be quite amazing, and the introductory problem given above addresses this issue. Throughout this chapter, you will find that a graphing calculator is particularly useful, while a knowledge of exponents is indispensible.

Courtesy of Brand X Pictures/Getty Images.

8.1   Exponential Functions

1. Determine function values for an exponential function.
2. Graph an exponential function.
3. Solve exponential equations using $b^x = b^y$ implies $x = y$.
4. Find the base in the exponential function $y = b^x$ given an ordered pair in the function.
5. Solve applied problems involving exponential functions.

The chapter-opening problem, with slight variations in wording, often appears in puzzle sections of newspapers and magazines. We begin by solving this problem because it provides an interesting and revealing introduction to the concept of an exponential function.

EXAMPLE 1   Finding a Formula for an Exponential Function

Solve the problem in the section introduction on page 423.

Solution

a. Let y represent the value (in cents) of the penny. Then

$$y = 1 \qquad\qquad \text{when } x = 0 \text{ days}$$
$$y = 1 \cdot 2 = 2 \qquad\qquad \text{when } x = 1 \text{ day}$$
$$y = 2 \cdot 2 = 2^2 = 4 \qquad \text{when } x = 2 \text{ days}$$
$$y = 2^2 \cdot 2 = 2^3 = 8 \qquad \text{when } x = 3 \text{ days}$$
$$y = 2^3 \cdot 2 = 2^4 = 16 \qquad \text{when } x = 4 \text{ days}$$

and in general

$$y = 2^x,$$

where x represents the number of complete days that have elapsed.

b. By the end of November, when $x = 30$ days,

$$y = 2^{30} = 1{,}073{,}741{,}824 \text{ cents}$$
$$= \$10{,}737{,}418.24.$$

Thus the penny is worth more than \$10 million by the end of the month, and the penny option is the better offer.

Note Often the results of calculations involving exponential expressions result in extremely large (or small) numbers that are displayed in scientific notation format. For instance, on some calculators 2^{30} is given as 1.073742×10^9.

PROGRESS CHECK 1 A scientist has 1 g of a radioactive element which is disappearing through radioactive decay. Careful observations reveal that for every hour that passes, the quantity of this element that still remains is one-half the amount that was present at the beginning of that hour. (Scientists say the "half-life" of the element is 1 hour.)

a. Find a formula showing the amount of the element present in x hours.
b. Approximately how much of this element is left at the end of 1 day?   ■

Example 1 requires that 2^x have meaning only for nonnegative integer values of x because no change is considered to have occurred until an entire time period has elapsed. However, for the exponential function defined by $y = 2^x$, we wish 2^x to be meaningful for *all* real values of x. Up to this point in the text, there is no difficulty interpreting 2^x where x is a rational number. For instance,

$$2^4 = 16,$$
$$2^0 = 1,$$
$$2^{-3} = \frac{1}{2^3} = \frac{1}{8},$$
$$2^{2/3} = \sqrt[3]{2^2} = \sqrt[3]{4} \approx 1.59.$$

A precise definition for 2^x, where x is irrational, is given in higher mathematics, and the Power key on a calculator may be used to approximate such expressions. For example, the display in Figure 8.1 shows $2^\pi \approx 8.82$ and $2^{\sqrt{2}} \approx 2.67$. Observe that a result like $2^\pi \approx 8.82$ is a sensible value, since $2^\pi \approx 2^{3.14}$, which is a little larger than 2^3, or 8. Thus, an expression like 2^x is meaningful for all real numbers x, and it can be shown that all previous laws of exponents (as first listed in Section 1.3) are valid for all real number exponents. An exponential function with a positive base other than 1 may now be defined.

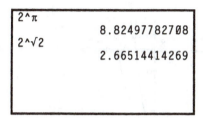

Figure 8.1

Exponential Function

The function f defined by

$$f(x) = b^x,$$

with $b > 0$ and $b \neq 1$, is called the **exponential function with base b**.

The restriction $b \neq 1$ is made because $1^x = 1$ for all values of x, so f is a constant function in this case. A nonpositive base is not used in the defining equation because expressions like $(-4)^{1/2}$ and 0^{-2} are not real numbers.

EXAMPLE 2   Evaluating an Exponential Function

If $f(x) = 4^x$, find $f(3)$, $f(-2)$, and $f\left(\frac{5}{2}\right)$. Also, approximate $f\left(\sqrt{2}\right)$ to the nearest hundredth.

Solution   Using $f(x) = 4^x$ gives

$$f(3) = 4^3 = 64,$$
$$f(-2) = 4^{-2} = \frac{1}{4^2} = \frac{1}{16},$$
$$f\left(\tfrac{5}{2}\right) = 4^{5/2} = \left(\sqrt{4}\right)^5 = 2^5 = 32.$$

By calculator,

$$f\left(\sqrt{2}\right) = 4^{\sqrt{2}} = 7.10 \text{ (to the nearest hundredth)}.$$

PROGRESS CHECK 2   If $f(x) = 8^x$, find $f(2)$, $f(-1)$, and $f\left(\frac{2}{3}\right)$. Also, approximate $f\left(\sqrt{3}\right)$ to the nearest hundredth.   ■

One method for graphing an exponential function is to generate a list of ordered-pair solutions and then draw a smooth curve through the points given by these solutions. The next example graphs two exponential functions where $b > 1$ to illustrate the case of exponential growth.

EXAMPLE 3 Graphing Exponential Functions with $b > 1$

Sketch the graphs of $g(x) = 2^x$ and $h(x) = 4^x$ on the same coordinate system.

Solution Generate a table of values by replacing x with integer values from, say, -3 to 3.

x	-3	-2	-1	0	1	2	3
2^x	$\frac{1}{8}$	$\frac{1}{4}$	$\frac{1}{2}$	1	2	4	8
4^x	$\frac{1}{64}$	$\frac{1}{16}$	$\frac{1}{4}$	1	4	16	64

By graphing these solutions and drawing a smooth curve through them, we sketch the graphs of g and h shown in Figure 8.2.

For each graph the domain is the set of all real numbers, and the range is the set of positive real numbers. Observe that both graphs are increasing over the whole domain, and that the graph with the larger value of b increases faster. The behavior of these functions is called exponential growth. Notice that in an exponential table, a fixed change in x produces a **constant ratio** between the corresponding y values. When the fixed change in x is 1, then the ratio of the y values is the base of the exponential function.

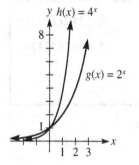

Figure 8.2

Technology Link

The appearance of an exponential graph on a grapher display is noticeably influenced by the choice of viewing window. In Figure 8.3 are displayed two different viewing window versions of the graphs in Figure 8.2.

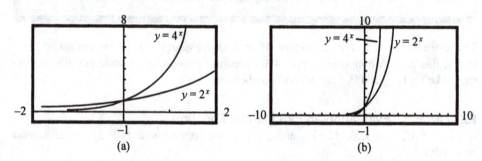

(a)	(b)

Figure 8.3

PROGRESS CHECK 3 Sketch the graphs of $g(x) = 3^x$ and $h(x) = 8^x$ on the same coordinate system. ■

When $0 < b < 1$, then the graph illustrates exponential decay. Comparison of the two graphs in the next example shows that the decay is faster when b is closer to zero.

EXAMPLE 4 Graphing Exponential Functions with $0 < b < 1$

Sketch the graphs of $g(x) = \left(\frac{1}{2}\right)^x$ and $h(x) = \left(\frac{1}{4}\right)^x$ on the same coordinate system.

Solution Construct a table of values, as follows, and then graph the equations, as shown in Figure 8.4.

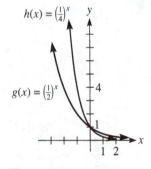

Figure 8.4

x	-3	-2	-1	0	1	2	3
$\left(\frac{1}{2}\right)^x$	8	4	2	1	$\frac{1}{2}$	$\frac{1}{4}$	$\frac{1}{8}$
$\left(\frac{1}{4}\right)^x$	64	16	4	1	$\frac{1}{4}$	$\frac{1}{16}$	$\frac{1}{64}$

Note   The equation $y = \left(\frac{1}{2}\right)^x$ is equivalent to $y = 2^{-x}$, since

$$\left(\frac{1}{2}\right)^x = \frac{1}{2^x} = 2^{-x}.$$

Therefore, exponential decay may also be described by equations of the form $y = b^{-x}$ with $b > 1$.

PROGRESS CHECK 4   Sketch the graphs of $g(x) = \left(\frac{1}{3}\right)^x$ and $h(x) = (0.8)^x$ on the same coordinate system.   ■

Important features of the exponential function with base b are illustrated in the graphs in Examples 3 and 4, and some of these properties are summarized next.

Properties of $f(x) = b^x$ (with $b > 0, b \neq 1$) and Its Graph

1. If $b > 1$, then as x increases, y increases; and a quantity is growing exponentially.
2. If $0 < b < 1$, then as x increases, y decreases; and a quantity is decaying exponentially.
3. The y-intercept is always $(0,1)$, and there are no x-intercepts.
4. The x-axis is a horizontal asymptote for the graph of f.
5. The domain of f is $(-\infty, \infty)$, and the range of f is $(0, \infty)$.

The graphing techniques of Section 2.5 may be used to graph certain variations of the function $y = b^x$, as discussed in Example 5.

EXAMPLE 5   Applying Graphing Techniques to Exponential Functions
Sketch the graph of each function.

a. $y = 4^x - 3$ **b.** $y = 1 - \left(\frac{1}{2}\right)^x$

Solution

a. The graph of $y = 4^x - 3$ is identical in shape to the graph of $y = 4^x$, shown in Figure 8.2. To position this curve correctly, observe that the constant 3 is subtracted after the exponential term, so the graph of $y = 4^x - 3$ is the graph of $y = 4^x$ shifted 3 units down, as shown in Figure 8.5.

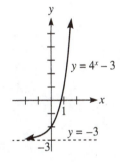

Figure 8.5

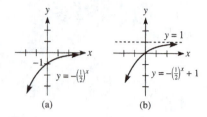

Figure 8.6

b. The equation $y = 1 - \left(\frac{1}{2}\right)^x$ is equivalent to $y = -\left(\frac{1}{2}\right)^x + 1$. To graph this function, first reflect the graph of $y = \left(\frac{1}{2}\right)^x$ about the x-axis to obtain the graph of $y = -\left(\frac{1}{2}\right)^x$, shown in Figure 8.6(a). Then raising the graph of $y = -\left(\frac{1}{2}\right)^x$ up 1 unit gives the graph of $y = -\left(\frac{1}{2}\right)^x + 1$, shown in Figure 8.6(b).

Note This example focused on sketching graphs using translations or reflection. Plotting convenient points on the graph as needed is also recommended in order to draw the graph accurately and to confirm that the graphing techniques are being applied correctly.

PROGRESS CHECK 5 Sketch the graph of each function.

a. $y = -4^x$ **b.** $y = \left(\frac{1}{2}\right)^x + 1$ ■

To analyze an exponential function, we often need to solve an **exponential equation,** which is an equation that has a variable in an exponent. In certain cases it is not difficult to write both sides of the equation in terms of the same base. Then because an exponential function takes on each value in its range exactly once, the following principle applies.

> ## Equation-Solving Principle
>
> If b is a positive number other than 1, then
>
> $$b^x = b^y \qquad \text{implies} \qquad x = y.$$

This principle indicates that when certain exponential expressions with the same base are equal, then the equation can be solved by equating exponents, as illustrated in Example 6.

EXAMPLE 6   Solving an Exponential Equation

Solve $8^x = 4$.

Solution Both sides of the equation can be written as powers of 2 by recognizing that $8 = 2^3$ and $4 = 2^2$.

$$8^x = 4$$
$$(2^3)^x = 2^2$$
$$2^{3x} = 2^2$$

Then $b^x = b^y$ implies $x = y$, so we equate exponents and solve.

$$3x = 2$$
$$x = \frac{2}{3}$$

Thus, the solution set is $\left\{\frac{2}{3}\right\}$.

Technology Link

Figure 8.7 shows how a grapher may be used to estimate the solution in this example. To obtain this display the equations $y1 = 8^x$ and $y2 = 4$ were graphed in the viewing window shown and the ISECT (intersection) operation was used to estimate the point of intersection. (If your calculator does not have this feature, then the Zoom and Trace features may be used to estimate this point). Observe that the displayed x-coordinate of the point of intersection is in agreement with the solution $x = 2/3$. On advantage of this method is that it may be applied to solve equations such as $8^x = 5$, in which it is difficult to rewrite expressions in terms of a common base. Algebraic methods for solving such equations involve logarithms, so this topic is not considered until Section 8.5.

Figure 8.7

PROGRESS CHECK 6 Solve $9^x = \frac{1}{27}$. ■

Another type of problem associated with analyzing exponential functions involves finding the base of an exponential function when given one ordered pair in the function.

EXAMPLE 7 Finding the Base of an Exponential Function

Find the base in the exponential function $y = b^x$ that contains the point (4,2).

Solution Replacing x by 4 and y by 2 in the equation $y = b^x$ gives

$$2 = b^4.$$

To find b, use an extension of the principle of powers and raise both sides of the equation to the reciprocal power of 4, which is $\frac{1}{4}$, and then simplify.

$$2^{1/4} = (b^4)^{1/4} \quad \text{Raise both sides to the reciprocal power.}$$
$$2^{1/4} = b$$

Thus, the base of the exponential function containing the given point is $2^{1/4}$, or $\sqrt[4]{2}$.

PROGRESS CHECK 7 Find the base of the exponential function $y = b^x$ that contains the point $\left(\frac{3}{2}, 27\right)$. ■

The next three examples illustrate applications of exponential functions. In particular, the examples focus on the topic of compound interest, where the growth of an investment can be seen as exponential growth.

EXAMPLE 8 Finding a Formula for Compound Interest

$5,000 is invested at 7 percent compounded annually.

a. Find a formula showing the value of the investment at the end of t years.
b. How much is the investment worth after 8 years?

Solution

a. Let A represent the compounded amount; then at the end of 1 year the $5,000 amounts to

$$A = \$5,000(1 + 0.07) \text{ or } \$5,350.$$

The principal during the second year is $5,000(1.07) and this principal grows by a factor of 1.07 by the end of the year. Thus, the amount at the end of 2 years is

$$A = \$5,000(1.07)(1.07) = \$5,000(1.07)^2 = \$5,724.50.$$

Continuing in this manner indicates that the value of the investment after t years is

$$A = \$5,000(1.07)^t.$$

b. When $t = 8$,

$$A = \$5,000(1.07)^8 = \$8,590.93.$$

PROGRESS CHECK 8 $9,000 is invested at 5 percent compounded annually.

a. Find a formula showing the value of this investment at the end of t years.
b. How much is the investment worth after 12 years? ■

The procedure from Example 8 can be generalized to obtain the following formula for the compounded amount A when an original principal P is compounded annually for t years at annual interest rate r:

$$A = P(1 + r)^t.$$

The next two examples make use of this formula.

EXAMPLE 9   Using a Compound Interest Formula

Financial planners advise that an individual retirement account (IRA) be started as early as possible, because the power of compounding an investment is realized over long periods of time. If just one $2,000 investment is made in an IRA by a college student on her 17th birthday and the account grows at 8.5 percent compounded annually, what will be the value of this account on her 65th birthday?

Solution   Observe that 48 years will elapse from the student's 17th birthday to her 65th birthday. Then substituting $P = 2,000$, $r = 0.085$, and $t = 48$ in the formula above gives

$$A = 2,000(1 + 0.085)^{48}$$
$$= \$100,382.37.$$

PROGRESS CHECK 9   If the student makes just one $2,000 deposit in an IRA and delays this deposit until her 27th birthday, then what will be the value of her account on her 65th birthday, assuming 8.5 percent compounded annually?   ■

EXAMPLE 10   Finding an Interest Rate

At what interest rate compounded annually must a sum of money be invested if it is to double in 5 years?

Solution   When an original principal P has doubled, then $A = 2P$. Replace A by $2P$ and t by 5 in the formula for interest compounded annually and solve for r.

$$2P = P(1 + r)^5$$
$$2 = (1 + r)^5$$
$$2^{1/5} = 1 + r \qquad \text{Raise both sides to the reciprocal power.}$$
$$2^{1/5} - 1 = r$$

By calculator, $2^{1/5} - 1 \approx 0.1486984$, so the required interest rate is about 14.87 percent.

PROGRESS CHECK 10   At what interest rate compounded annually must a sum of money be invested if it is to triple in 12 years?   ■

EXERCISES 8.1

In Exercises 1–20 for each of the given functions, find $f(0)$, $f(3)$, $f(-2)$, $f(\frac{1}{2})$, and $f(\sqrt{2})$. Approximate decimals to the nearest hundredth.

1. $f(x) = 5^x$
3. $f(x) = 3^x$
5. $f(x) = 4^{-x}$
7. $f(x) = 6^{-x}$
9. $f(x) = -9^x$
11. $f(x) = -5^x$
13. $f(x) = \left(\frac{1}{2}\right)^x$
15. $f(x) = \left(\frac{1}{4}\right)^x$
17. $f(x) = -\left(\frac{1}{2}\right)^x$
19. $f(x) = -\left(\frac{1}{4}\right)^x$

2. $f(x) = 7^x$
4. $f(x) = 9^x$
6. $f(x) = 9^{-x}$
8. $f(x) = 5^{-x}$
10. $f(x) = -9^{-x}$
12. $f(x) = -5^{-x}$
14. $f(x) = \left(\frac{1}{2}\right)^{-x}$
16. $f(x) = \left(\frac{1}{4}\right)^{-x}$
18. $f(x) = -\left(\frac{1}{2}\right)^{-x}$
20. $f(x) = -\left(\frac{1}{4}\right)^{-x}$

In Exercises 21–34, sketch the graphs of the given function.

21. $y = 5^x$
23. $y = 6^x$
25. $y = 5^{-x}$
27. $y = 6^{-x}$
29. $y = -5^x$
31. $y = \left(\frac{1}{2}\right)^x$
33. $y = -\left(\frac{1}{2}\right)^x$

22. $y = 3^x$
24. $y = 9^x$
26. $y = 3^{-x}$
28. $y = 9^{-x}$
30. $y = -3^{-x}$
32. $y = \left(\frac{1}{2}\right)^{-x}$
34. $y = -\left(\frac{1}{2}\right)^{-x}$

In Exercises 35–38, sketch the graph of f and g on the same coordinate system.

35. $f(x) = 3^x$, $g(x) = 5^x$
36. $f(x) = 3^{-x}$, $g(x) = 5^{-x}$

37. $f(x) = \left(\frac{1}{3}\right)^x$, $g(x) = \left(\frac{1}{5}\right)^x$

38. $f(x) = \left(\frac{1}{5}\right)^x$, $g(x) = \left(\frac{1}{5}\right)^{-x}$

In Exercises 39–48, solve for x.

39. $9^x = \frac{1}{27}$

40. $9^x = 27$

41. $16^x = 8$

42. $25^x = 125$

43. $36^x = \frac{1}{6}$

44. $8^x = \frac{1}{64}$

45. $\left(\frac{3}{4}\right)^x = \frac{16}{9}$

46. $\left(\frac{2}{3}\right)^x = \frac{27}{8}$

47. $3^{-x} = \frac{1}{81}$

48. $2^{3-x} = 1$

In Exercises 49–58, find the base b of the exponential function $y = b^x$ which contains the given point (x, y).

49. $(2, 9)$

50. $(3, 64)$

51. $\left(-2, \frac{1}{25}\right)$

52. $\left(-1, \frac{1}{7}\right)$

53. $(-2, 9)$

54. $(-5, 32)$

55. $(3, 2)$

56. $(2, 3)$

57. $\left(2, \sqrt[3]{5}\right)$

58. $\left(5, \sqrt[3]{2}\right)$

In Exercises 59–62, sketch the graph of f and g on the same coordinate system.

59. $f(x) = 5^x + 3$, $g(x) = 5^x - 2$

60. $f(x) = 3^x + 2$, $g(x) = 3^x - 1$

61. $f(x) = 5^{-x} + 3$, $g(x) = 5^{-x} - 2$

62. $f(x) = \left(\frac{1}{3}\right)^x - 2$, $g(x) = \left(\frac{1}{3}\right)^x + 2$

63. In 1990 the descendants of a man who lent the American government $450,000 at the time of the revolution asked to have the loan repaid. Suppose the loan is compounded annually at 6 percent. To the nearest thousand dollars, how much was the family owed if the loan was made in 1776 and repaid in 1990?

64. Which is worth more after compounding for 20 years: $10 at 5 percent, or $5 at 10 percent?

65. What is the value of a $10 investment after 10 years if it is compounded at an annual interest of 10 percent?

66. What is the value of an investment of $300 after 30 years if it is compounded at an annual interest rate of 6 percent?

67. The value of an investment which depreciates at a fixed rate every year can be evaluated by using negative values for r in the formula for compound interest. The value of a $10,000 investment which depreciates by 8 percent a year is given by $A = 10,000(1 - 0.08)^t$. What is its value after 4 years?

68. Use the definitions in Exercise 67 to find the value of a $1 million piece of machinery after 14 years of depreciation at the rate of 5 percent annually. Give the answer to the nearest dollar.

69. At what interest rate compounded annually must a sum of money be invested if it is to double in 10 years?

70. At what interest rate compounded annually must a sum of money be invested if it is to triple in 10 years?

71. What annual growth rate will cause a population to double in 50 years?

72. What annual growth rate will cause a population to double in 25 years?

THINK ABOUT IT 8.1

1. Solve $a^{x-4} = \left(\frac{1}{a}\right)^x$ for x if a is a positive real number other than 1.

2. The following table was generated using an exponential function.

x	0	1	2	3	4
y	10,000	8,000	6,400	5,120	4,096

a. For such a table a fixed change in x results in a constant ratio between the corresponding y values. What is that ratio when the change in x is 1?

b. Find an equation that will generate this table. (*Hint:* Think of it as the depreciating value of a $10,000 investment.)

3. There is often more than one equation whose graph will contain certain given points.

a. Given the points $(0, 1)$ and $(1, 4)$, find a linear function, a quadratic function, and an exponential function whose graphs contain both points. Sketch each graph.

b. For each function in part **a**, find y when $x = 2$.

4. Based on the graph of $y = 2^x$, place the following numbers in their correct numerical order:

$$2^{\sqrt{3}}, 2^{1/3}, 2^{\pi}, 2^{-\sqrt{2}}, 2^0.$$

Explain your method.

5. If $f(x) = b^x$ is the exponential function with base b, then show that $f(u + v) = f(u) \cdot f(v)$.

8.2 Inverse Functions

The function $y = f(x) = \frac{5}{9}(x - 32)$ converts degrees Fahrenheit (x) to degrees Celsius (y). Find an equation for the inverse function. What formula does the inverse function represent? (See Example 7.)

OBJECTIVES

1 Find the inverse of a function and its domain and range.

2 Determine if a function has an inverse function.

3 Graph $y = f^{-1}(x)$ from the graph of $y = f(x)$.

4 Find an equation that defines f^{-1}.

5 Determine whether two functions are inverses of each other.

6 Use inverse function concepts in applications.

Consider the following tables, which illustrate ordered pairs that belong to the function $f(x) = x^3$ and ordered pairs that belong to the function $g(x) = \sqrt[3]{x}$.

x	$f(x) = x^3$	Ordered Pairs in f
1	$1^3 = 1$	(1,1)
2	$2^3 = 8$	(2,8)
-2	$(-2)^3 = -8$	$(-2,-8)$
3	$3^3 = 27$	(3,27)
-3	$(-3)^3 = -27$	$(-3,-27)$

x	$g(x) = \sqrt[3]{x}$	Ordered Pairs in g
1	$\sqrt[3]{1} = 1$	(1,1)
8	$\sqrt[3]{8} = 2$	(8,2)
-8	$\sqrt[3]{-8} = -2$	$(-8,-2)$
27	$\sqrt[3]{27} = 3$	(27,3)
-27	$\sqrt[3]{-27} = 3$	$(-27,-3)$

Observe that functions f and g are related and have reverse assignments. For example, $f(3) = 27$ and $g(27) = 3$. Two functions with exactly reverse assignments are called **inverse functions** of each other, and $f(x) = x^3$ and $g(x) = \sqrt[3]{x}$ are examples of inverse functions. The special symbol f^{-1} is used to denote the inverse of function f, so

$$\text{if} \quad f(x) = x^3, \quad \text{then} \quad f^{-1}(x) = \sqrt[3]{x},$$
$$\text{and if} \quad f(x) = \sqrt[3]{x}, \quad \text{then} \quad f^{-1}(x) = x^3.$$

The reverse assignments of f and f^{-1} mean that when (a,b) belongs to a function, then (b,a) belongs to the inverse function. Because the components in the ordered pairs are reversed, the domain of f equals the range of f^{-1} and the range of f equals the domain of f^{-1}.

EXAMPLE 1   Finding an Inverse Function Numerically

If $f = \{(1, 5), (2, 6), (3, 7)\}$, find f^{-1}. Find and compare the domain and the range of the two functions.

Solution   Reversing assignments gives

$$f^{-1} = \{(5, 1), (6, 2), (7, 3)\}.$$

The set of all first components gives the domain of a function, and the set of all second components gives the range. Therefore,

$$\text{domain of } f = \text{range of } f^{-1} = \{1, 2, 3\},$$
$$\text{range of } f = \text{domain of } f^{-1} = \{5, 6, 7\}.$$

As expected, f and f^{-1} interchange their domain and range.

PROGRESS CHECK 1   If $f = \{(-1, 1), (-2, 2), (-3, 3)\}$, find f^{-1}. Find and compare the domain and the range of the two functions. ■

Not all functions have an inverse function. For instance, if a function f is given by

$$\{(1, 5), (2, 5), (3, 5)\}$$

then reversing assignments produces

$$\{(5, 1), (5, 2), (5, 3)\}.$$

The resulting relation is not a function because the number 5 is the first component in more than one ordered pair. Because the second component in f becomes the first component in the inverse relation, the following method may be used in determining whether f has an inverse function.

One-to-One Function

A function is **one-to-one** when each x value in the domain is assigned a different y value so that no two ordered pairs have the same second component. If f is one-to-one, then f has an inverse function; and if f is not one-to-one, then f does not have an inverse function.

EXAMPLE 2   Testing Numerically for an Inverse Function
If $f = \{(-5, 5), (0, 0), (5, 5)\}$, does f have an inverse function?

Solution   Because 5 appears as the second component in two ordered pairs, f is not a one-to-one function and f does not have an inverse function.

PROGRESS CHECK 2   If $f = \{(-3, 3), (0, 0), (3, -3)\}$, does f have an inverse function? ■

It is easy to recognize the graph of a one-to-one function because none of its points can have the same y-coordinate. Therefore, the graph of a one-to-one function cannot contain two or more points that lie on the same horizontal line. This feature is often summarized in the horizontal line test.

Horizontal Line Test

Imagine a horizontal line sweeping down the graph of a function f. If the horizontal line at any position intersects the graph in more than one point, then f is not a one-to-one function and f does not have an inverse function.

EXAMPLE 3   Testing Graphically for an Inverse Function
Which functions graphed in Figure 8.8 have an inverse function?

Solution

a. This function has an inverse function since no horizontal line intersects the graph at more than one point.
b. This function does not have an inverse function because a horizontal line may intersect the graph at two points.

PROGRESS CHECK 3   Which functions graphed in Figure 8.9 have an inverse function?

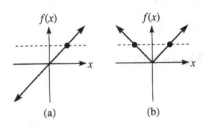

Figure 8.8

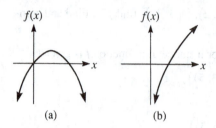

Figure 8.9

■

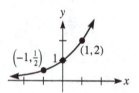

Figure 8.10

When the horizontal line test indicates that a function f has an inverse function, then there is a simple geometric method for drawing f^{-1}. Because the x- and y-coordinates change places in inverse functions, the graphs of f and f^{-1} are related in that each one is the reflection of the other about the line $y = x$. For instance, this relationship between the graphs of $f(x) = x^3$ and $f^{-1}(x) = \sqrt[3]{x}$ is shown in Figure 8.10. In the next example the graph of f^{-1} is obtained from the graph of f by using this reflection method.

EXAMPLE 4   Finding an Inverse Function Graphically
Use the graph of $y = f(x)$ in Figure 8.11 to graph $y = f^{-1}(x)$.

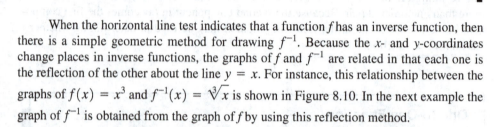

Figure 8.11

Solution   First, observe that f is a one-to-one function (by the horizontal line test), so f has an inverse function. To graph $y = f^{-1}(x)$, we reflect the graph of $y = f(x)$ about the line $y = x$. Note the ordered pairs $\left(-1, \frac{1}{2}\right)$, $(0,1)$, and $(1,2)$ from f become $\left(\frac{1}{2}, -1\right)$, $(1,0)$, and $(2,1)$ in f^{-1}. Both $y = f(x)$ and $y = f^{-1}(x)$ are graphed in Figure 8.12.

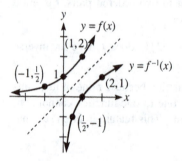

Figure 8.12

PROGRESS CHECK 4 Use the graph of $y = f(x)$ in Figure 8.13 to graph $y = f^{-1}(x)$.

■

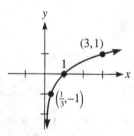

Figure 8.13

When f is a one-to-one function that is defined by an equation, then it is sometimes possible to find an equation that defines f^{-1}. The method is based on the fact that f and f^{-1} make reverse assignments, so we will reverse the roles of x and y in the equation that defines f and try to solve for y to obtain an equation that defines f^{-1}. For example, the inverse of the function defined by

$$y = x^3$$

is defined by

$$x = y^3.$$

Then taking the cube root of both sides of the resulting equation gives

$$y = \sqrt[3]{x}.$$

Thus, if $f(x) = x^3$, then $f^{-1}(x) = \sqrt[3]{x}$. The method just discussed is incorporated in the detailed procedure that follows for finding an equation that defines an inverse function.

To Find an Equation Defining f^{-1}

1. Start with a one-to-one function $y = f(x)$ and interchange x and y in this equation.
2. Solve the resulting equation for y, and then replace y by $f^{-1}(x)$.
3. Define the domain of f^{-1} to be equal to the range of f.

EXAMPLE 5   Finding an Inverse Function Algebraically

Find $f^{-1}(x)$ for each function. If the given function is not one-to-one, so that no inverse function exists, state this.

a. $f(x) = 4x - 1$
b. $f(x) = \sqrt{x + 1}$
c. $f(x) = x^2$

Solution   As a visual aid, the graphs of all functions considered in this example are shown in Figures 8.14–8.16.

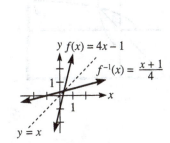

Figure 8.14

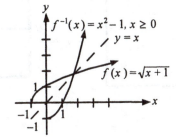

Figure 8.15

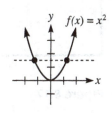

Figure 8.16

a. The function $f(x) = 4x - 1$ is a linear function. All such functions are one-to-one, so an inverse function exists. To find an equation defining f^{-1}, write the equation defining f as

$$y = 4x - 1$$

and then proceed as follows.

$$x = 4y - 1 \qquad \text{Interchange } x \text{ and } y.$$
$$\left.\begin{array}{c} x + 1 = 4y \\[4pt] \dfrac{x + 1}{4} = y \end{array}\right\} \qquad \text{Solve for } y.$$
$$\dfrac{x + 1}{4} = f^{-1}(x) \qquad \text{Replace } y \text{ by } f^{-1}(x).$$

Thus, if $f(x) = 4x - 1$, then $f^{-1}(x) = (x + 1)/4$. The domain of f^{-1} is equal to the range of f, which is the set of all real numbers. (See Figure 8.14.)

b. The square root function is a one-to-one function with range $[0, \infty)$, as can be seen in Figure 8.15. Thus, f has an inverse function whose equation is found as follows.

$$y = \sqrt{x + 1}. \qquad \text{Start with } y = f(x).$$
$$x = \sqrt{y + 1} \qquad \text{Interchange } x \text{ and } y.$$
$$\left.\begin{array}{c} x^2 = y + 1 \\[4pt] x^2 - 1 = y \end{array}\right\} \qquad \text{Solve for } y.$$
$$f^{-1}(x) = x^2 - 1. \qquad \text{Replace } y \text{ by } f^{-1}(x).$$

Finally, although $y = x^2 - 1$ is defined for any real number, we need to match the domain of f^{-1} to the range of f so that the functions will be inverses of each other. Thus, we restrict x as follows:

$$f^{-1}(x) = x^2 - 1, \quad x \geq 0.$$

c. The squaring function $f(x) = x^2$ is not a one-to-one function (as can be seen by applying the horizontal line test to its graph in Figure 8.16). Thus, f does not have an inverse function.

Caution   Remember that f^{-1} is the special symbol that denotes the inverse function of function f. Do *not* interpret the -1 in this symbol as an exponent.

Technology Link

If you have found a formula for the inverse of a function f, then it is straightforward to use a grapher to display the graphs of f, f^{-1}, and the line $y = x$ at the same time. This picture can serve as a visual check on the algebra, since the graphs of f and f^{-1} should appear as reflections about the line $y = x$. In Figure 8.17 we show a typical example using the functions from Example 5b. You should invoke the Zoom Square feature to correct the built-in angular distortion present in the standard display.

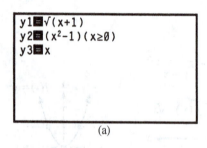

(a)

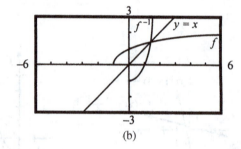

(b)

Figure 8.17

PROGRESS CHECK 5   Find $f^{-1}(x)$ for each function. If no inverse function exists, state this.

a. $f(x) = 3x + 2$ **b.** $f(x) = |x|$ **c.** $f(x) = \sqrt{x - 4}$ ■

An important concept associated with inverse functions is that each function "undoes" the other. Therefore, applying f and f^{-1}, one after the other, to a meaningful input x produces x as the output. For instance, if $f(x) = x^3$, then 2 is a meaningful input and $f^{-1}(x) = \sqrt[3]{x}$. Observe that

$$f(2) = 8 \quad \text{and} \quad f^{-1}(8) = 2, \quad \text{so} \quad f^{-1}[f(2)] = 2.$$

It is also true that $f[f^{-1}(8)] = f(2) = 8$, and these evaluations illustrate that inverse functions may be defined in terms of applying two functions in succession as follows.

Definition of Inverse Functions

Two functions f and g are said to be inverses of each other provided that

$$f[g(x)] = x \qquad \text{for all } x \text{ in the domain of } g$$

and

$$g[f(x)] = x \qquad \text{for all } x \text{ in the domain of } f.$$

This definition may be used to prove that two functions are inverse functions, as shown next.

EXAMPLE 6   Verifying Inverse Functions

Verify that $f(x) = \sqrt{x}$ and $g(x) = x^2$, $x \geq 0$, are inverses of each other.

Solution   First, show that $f[g(x)] = x$ for all nonnegative real numbers, which is the domain of g.

$$
\begin{aligned}
f[g(x)] &= f(x^2) \\
&= \sqrt{x^2} \\
&= x \quad \text{(since } x \geq 0\text{)}
\end{aligned}
$$

Next, show that $g[f(x)] = x$ for all nonnegative real numbers, which is the domain of f.

$$
\begin{aligned}
g[f(x)] &= g(\sqrt{x}) \\
&= (\sqrt{x})^2 \\
&= x \quad \text{(since } x \geq 0\text{)}
\end{aligned}
$$

Thus, f and g are inverses of each other.

PROGRESS CHECK 6   Verify that $f(x) = 4x - 1$ and $g(x) = \dfrac{x + 1}{4}$ are inverse functions.   ■

One type of application involving inverse functions is based on the fact that inverse functions contain the same information in different forms. Which function is more useful depends on what is given and what is to be found. In this context certain problems are viewed as inverse problems, as illustrated below.

Inverse problems

Problem: Find the Celsius temperature for a given Fahrenheit temperature.

Problem: Find the Fahrenheit temperature for a given Celsius temperature.

The inverse problems of converting between two temperature scales are analyzed further in the section-opening problem.

EXAMPLE 7   Using an Inverse with Temperature Scales

Solve the problem in the section introduction on page 432.

Solution   The equation $y = \frac{5}{9}(x - 32)$ defines a linear function, so an inverse function exists and an equation defining f^{-1} may be found as follows.

$$
\begin{aligned}
y &= \tfrac{5}{9}(x - 32) && \text{Start with } y = f(x). \\
x &= \tfrac{5}{9}(y - 32) && \text{Interchange } x \text{ and } y. \\
\left.\begin{aligned} \tfrac{9}{5}x &= y - 32 \\ \tfrac{9}{5}x + 32 &= y \end{aligned}\right\} && \text{Solve for } y. \\
\tfrac{9}{5}x + 32 &= f^{-1}(x) && \text{Replace } y \text{ by } f^{-1}(x).
\end{aligned}
$$

Thus, if $y = f(x) = \frac{5}{9}(x - 32)$, then $y = f^{-1}(x) = \frac{9}{5}x + 32$. In the context of the problem, it is stated that the formula given in function f converts degrees Fahrenheit (x) to degrees Celsius (y). Therefore, the formula in the inverse function converts degrees Celsius (x) to degrees Fahrenheit (y).

PROGRESS CHECK 7   The function $y = f(x) = x^2$, $x > 0$, gives the formula for the area (y) of a square in terms of the side length (x). Find an equation for the inverse function. What formula does the inverse function represent?   ■

The fact that inverse functions "undo" each other is the basis for another type of application considered in Example 8.

EXAMPLE 8   Using an Inverse to Undo a Function

Certain airline employees accept a 20 percent cut in hourly wage to avoid layoffs. What percent raise will then be needed to return these employees to their original hourly wage?

Solution   A 20 percent cut in hourly wage means the new wage is 80 percent of the original wage. Therefore, the reduced wage is given by

$$y = f(x) = 0.8x.$$

The rule for f^{-1} gives the formula to "undo f," and the inverse of the function defined by $y = 0.8x$ is defined by

$$x = 0.8y.$$

Solving this equation for y then yields

$$y = \frac{x}{0.8} \quad \text{or} \quad y = 1.25x.$$

The offsetting formula $y = f^{-1}(x) = 1.25x$ indicates that a 25 percent increase is needed to return the workers to their original hourly wage.

Note   To check this result, observe that

$$f^{-1}[f(x)] = f^{-1}(0.8x) = x.$$

Thus, f and f^{-1} undo each other to produce the original hourly wage.

PROGRESS CHECK 8   An investor's portfolio loses one-third of its value during the first year. For the following year, what percent increase is needed for the portfolio to return to its original value?   ▪

EXERCISES 8.2

In Exercises 1–8, find the inverse for each of the following functions, if it exists. Compare the domain and range of the two functions.

1. $\{(1, 2), (3, 4), (5, 6)\}$
2. $\{(-2, 1), (-3, 0), (5, 4)\}$
3. $\{(2, 1), (-3, 4), (5, 8)\}$
4. $\{(-3, 0), (0, -3), (7, 12)\}$
5. $\{(-2, -3), (-4, 2), (6, -3)\}$
6. $\{(5, 3), (2, 2), (-5, 3)\}$
7. $\{(3, 2), (4, 2), (5, 2)\}$
8. $\{(1, -4), (2, -4), (3, -4)\}$

In Exercises 9–20, determine if the function whose graph is shown has an inverse function.

9.
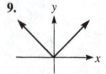

10.

11.

12.
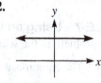

13.
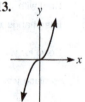

14.

15.

16.
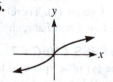

17.

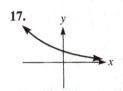

18.

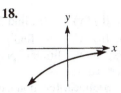

19.

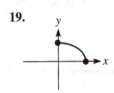

20.

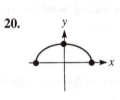

In Exercises 21–28, use the graph of f to graph f^{-1}.

21.

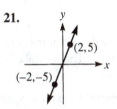

22.

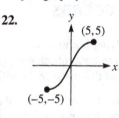

23.

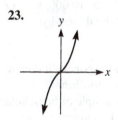

24.

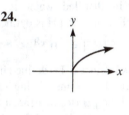

25.

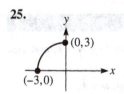

26.

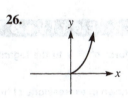

27.

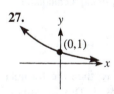

28.

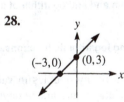

In Exercises 29–39, find $f^{-1}(x)$ for the given function. If the given function is not one-to-one, so that no inverse exists, state this.

29. $f(x) = x - 3$
30. $f(x) = x + 2$
31. $f(x) = 3x + 5$
32. $f(x) = -3x + 7$
33. $f(x) = -\sqrt{x}, x \geq 0$
34. $f(x) = -\sqrt{x + 2}, x \geq -2$
35. $f(x) = x^2 + 3$
36. $f(x) = -x^2 - 2$
37. $f(x) = |x + 3|$
38. $f(x) = x^3$
39. $f(x) = x^4, x \geq 0$

In Exercises 40–50, determine if f and g are inverses of each other.

40. $f(x) = x + 2, g(x) = x - 2$
41. $f(x) = \sqrt{x + 1}, g(x) = x^2 - 1, x \geq 0$
42. $f(x) = \sqrt[3]{x}, g(x) = x^3$
43. $f(x) = \dfrac{x - 5}{3}, g(x) = 3x + 5$
44. $f(x) = x^2 - 2, g(x) = x^2 + 2$
45. $f(x) = |x|, g(x) = |x|$
46. $f(x) = \dfrac{x}{3}, g(x) = 3x$
47. $f(x) = x^{1/4}, x \geq 0, g(x) = x^4, x \geq 0$
48. $f(x) = x, g(x) = x$
49. $f(x) = \dfrac{1}{x}, g(x) = \dfrac{1}{x}$
50. $f(x) = -\dfrac{1}{x}, g(x) = -\dfrac{1}{x}$

51. The function $y = f(x) = \frac{22}{15}x$ converts miles per hour (x) to feet per second (y). Find an equation for the inverse function. What formula does the inverse function represent?

52. The function $y = f(x) = 1.609x$ converts miles per hour (x) to kilometers per hour (y). Find an equation for the inverse function. What formula does the inverse function represent?

53. A music store manager marks up his purchase price on guitars by 100 percent to determine his usual selling price. Thus $y = f(x) = 2x$ gives the usual selling price (y) as a function of the purchase price (x). How much of a discount could he offer before he loses money on the sale?

54. If an investment portfolio loses 25 percent of its value during its first year, what percent increase is needed the next year to return it to its original value?

55. Mountain campers can use the formula $y = f(a)$ which gives the temperature in degrees Fahrenheit (y) at which water boils as a function of altitude in feet (a) above sea level.
  a. What is the meaning of $f(1,000) = 200$?
  b. What is the meaning of $f^{-1}(190) = 2,000$?
  c. What is the meaning of $f^{-1}(j) = k$?

56. The cost in dollars for a printing job is given by the formula $C = f(x) = 20 + 0.04x$, where x is the number of copies printed.
  a. What is the meaning of $f(1,000) = 60$?
  b. What is the meaning of $f^{-1}(100) = 2,000$?
  c. What is the meaning of $f^{-1}(m) = n$?
  d. Find an equation for $f^{-1}(x)$.

THINK ABOUT IT 8.2

1. It is possible for the inverse of a function to be the same as the function. One such example is $f(x) = x$. Find two other such functions, and draw their graphs.
2. **a.** Graph the function $f(x) = 2^x$ and use the graph to explain why the inverse of f is a function.
   b. Use the graph in part **a** to graph $y = f^{-1}(x)$.
   c. Find the domain and range of f.
   d. Find the domain and range of f^{-1}.

3. **a.** If $f(x) = 10^x$, find $f^{-1}(100)$.
   b. If $f(x) = 8^x$, find $f^{-1}(4)$.
4. Explain the different purposes of the horizontal and vertical line tests.
5. Every linear function has an inverse function. What is the inverse of the function $f(x) = mx + b, m \neq 0$?

Courtesy of PhotoDisc/Getty Images.

8.3 Logarithmic Functions

To analyze chemical reactions involving liquids, one often must know the pH of the solution, which measures its hydrogen ion concentration (symbolized [H⁺]). The formula for pH involves a logarithmic function, as discussed in the following problem.

a. Because hydrogen ion concentrations are small numbers, it is useful to express such concentrations in exponential form. For instance, the concentration (measured in moles per liter) of hydrogen ions in distilled water is 1 part H^+ in 10,000,000, or 1/10,000,000, or 10^{-7}. To simplify further, pH is defined in exponential form by

$$[H^+] = 10^{-pH}.$$

Thus, the pH of distilled water is 7. Since pH is defined in terms of an exponent, it is more convenient to write a formula for pH in terms of a logarithm. What is this formula?
b. Use the answer in part **a** to find the pH (to the nearest tenth) of a sample of household ammonia whose hydrogen ion concentration is 5.2×10^{-12}. (See Example 9.)

OBJECTIVES

1	Convert from the exponential form $b^L = N$ to the logarithmic form $\log_b N = L$, and vice versa.
2	Determine the value of the unknown in expressions of the form $\log_b N = L$.
3	Determine the common logarithm and antilogarithm of a number by using a calculator.
4	Graph logarithmic functions.
5	Solve applied problems involving logarithmic functions.

From Section 8.1 we know that if a penny doubles in value each day, then the formula $V = 2^t$ gives the value (in cents) of the penny after t days have elapsed. This formula is easy to apply to find V for a given value of t. However, to solve the inverse problem of finding how much time is required for V to grow to a given value, it is more useful to have a formula that gives t as a function of V. To write such a formula we must introduce the concept of a logarithm.

The **logarithm** (abbreviated **log**) of a number is the *exponent* to which a fixed base is raised to obtain the number. The exponential statement $2^3 = 8$ is written in logarithmic form as $\log_2 8 = 3$, and we say that 3 is the logarithm to the base 2 of 8. In general, the key relation between exponential form and logarithmic form is expressed in the following definition.

Definition of Logarithm

If b and N are positive numbers with $b \neq 1$, then

$$\log_b N = L \quad \text{is equivalent to} \quad b^L = N.$$

In this definition it is important to observe that a logarithm is an exponent, as the following diagram emphasizes.

$$\overbrace{\log_b N = L}^{\text{logarithm or exponent}} \quad \text{is equivalent to} \quad b^L = N$$

With the aid of this definition we may now solve $V = 2^t$ for t, since

$$2^t = V \text{ is equivalent to } \log_2 V = t.$$

Examples 1 and 2 give further illustrations of converting between exponential form and logarithmic form using this definition.

EXAMPLE 1   Converting from Exponential to Logarithmic Form

Write $10^2 = 100$ and $a^x = 4$ in logarithmic form.

Solution   Since $b^L = N$ implies $\log_b N = L$,

$$10^2 = 100 \text{ may be written as } \log_{10} 100 = 2,$$
$$a^x = 4 \text{ may be written as } \log_a 4 = x.$$

PROGRESS CHECK 1   Write $3^4 = 81$ and $b^0 = 1$ in logarithmic form.   ■

EXAMPLE 2   Converting from Logarithmic to Exponential Form

Write $\log_9 3 = \frac{1}{2}$ and $\log_b x = y$ in exponential form.

Solution   Since $\log_b N = L$ implies $b^L = N$,

$$\log_9 3 = \frac{1}{2} \text{ may be written as } 9^{1/2} = 3,$$
$$\log_b x = y \text{ may be written as } b^y = x.$$

PROGRESS CHECK 2   Write $\log_8 2 = \frac{1}{3}$ and $\log_a y = x$ in exponential form.   ■

The next example discusses how to find the value of an unknown in expressions of the form $\log_b N = L$.

EXAMPLE 3   Finding an Unknown in $\log_b N = L$

Determine the value of the unknown in each expression.

a. $\log_5 5 = y$ **b.** $\log_4 8 = x$
c. $\log_{10} x = -1$ **d.** $\log_b 4 = -2$

Solution   In each case it is helpful to first convert the expression from logarithmic form to exponential form.

a. $\log_5 5 = y$ is equivalent to $5^y = 5$. From the exponential form it is apparent that

$$y = \log_5 5 = 1.$$

b. $\log_4 8 = x$ is equivalent to $4^x = 8$. Recall from Section 8.1 that this type of exponential equation may be solved by writing both sides of the equation in terms of the same base, as shown below.

$$4^x = 8$$
$$(2^2)^x = 2^3$$
$$2^{2x} = 2^3$$
$$2x = 3 \quad \text{Since } b^x = b^y \text{ implies } x = y$$
$$x = \frac{3}{2}$$

Thus, $x = \log_4 8 = \frac{3}{2}$.

c. $\log_{10} x = -1$ is equivalent to $10^{-1} = x$. Thus,

$$x = 10^{-1} = \frac{1}{10}.$$

d. $\log_b 4 = -2$ is equivalent to $b^{-2} = 4$. To find b, raise both sides of the equation to the reciprocal power of -2 (which is $-1/2$) to get

$$(b^{-2})^{-1/2} = 4^{-1/2},$$

and then simplify to obtain

$$b = 4^{-1/2} = \frac{1}{4^{1/2}} = \frac{1}{\sqrt{4}} = \frac{1}{2}.$$

Thus, $b = \frac{1}{2}$.

PROGRESS CHECK 3   Determine the value of the unknown in each expression.

a. $\log_{10} 1 = y$ **b.** $\log_8 32 = x$
c. $\log_2 x = -4$ **d.** $\log_b 64 = -3$ ■

In applications of logarithms, two specific bases are most prevalent: base 10 or **common logarithms** and base e or **natural logarithms**. It is standard notation to write a common logarithm as log N (with base 10 being understood) and a natural logarithm as ln N (with base e being understood). Thus, a typical graphing calculator has two different logarithm keys that are labeled $\boxed{\text{LOG}}$ and $\boxed{\text{LN}}$. The next two examples show how to work with common logarithms on a calculator. Logarithms to the base e are used extensively in calculus and will not be considered until Section 8.6 where the irrational number e is developed.

EXAMPLE 4   Finding a Common Logarithm
Evaluate log 12.3 to four decimal places.

Solution   To approximate log 12.3 with a graphing calculator simply press

$$\boxed{\text{LOG}}\ 12.3\ \boxed{\text{ENTER}}.$$

The display that results in Figure 8.18 shows log 12.3 = 1.0899 to four decimal places.

PROGRESS CHECK 4   Evaluate log 325 to four decimal places.   ■

The next example asks that the answer be rounded off to a specified number of significant digits. Note that all digits, except the zeros that are used to indicate the position of the decimal point, are **significant digits**.

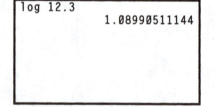

Figure 8.18

EXAMPLE 5   Finding an Antilogarithm
If log $N = -1.8$, find N to three significant digits.

Solution   log $N = -1.8$ is equivalent to $10^{-1.8} = N$. Thus, N may be found as shown in Figure 8.19 and we see that $N = 0.0158$ to three significant digits. Observe that the zeros in this answer are not significant digits, because the number is 158 ten-thousandths, and the zeros are written to indicate the correct position of the decimal point.

Note   In science it is common to refer to an inverse logarithm as an antilogarithm. In this convention,

$$\text{antilog } x = 10^x.$$

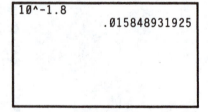

Figure 8.19

PROGRESS CHECK 5   If log $N = -2.3$, find N to three significant digits.   ■

Inverse functions for exponential functions may now be defined using logarithms. The exponential function defined by $f(x) = b^x$ (with $b > 0$, $b \neq 1$) is one-to-one, so f has an inverse, and an equation defining f^{-1} may be found as follows.

$$y = b^x \qquad \text{Start with } y = f(x).$$
$$x = b^y \qquad \text{Interchange } x \text{ and } y.$$
$$y = \log_b x \qquad \text{Solve for } y \text{ using the definition of logarithm.}$$
$$f^{-1}(x) = \log_b x \qquad \text{Replace } y \text{ by } f^{-1}(x).$$

Thus, $y = b^x$ and $y = \log_b x$ are inverse functions. Because the base in an exponential function must be a positive number other than 1, this same restriction applies to a logarithmic function.

To see another important restriction, consider that

$$y = \log_b x \qquad \text{is equivalent to} \qquad x = b^y.$$

Since a positive base raised to any power is positive, it is also necessary to require that x be positive. In other words, we must incorporate in the definition of a logarithmic function that we may only take the logarithms of positive numbers.

Logarithmic Function

If b and x are positive numbers with $b \neq 1$, then the function f defined by

$$f(x) = \log_b x$$

is called the **logarithmic function with base b**.

EXAMPLE 6   Graphing a Logarithmic Function and Its Inverse

Graph $y = \log_2 x$. Then sketch the graphs of $y = \log_2 x$ and $y = 2^x$ on the same coordinate system, and describe how the graphs are related.

Solution   To graph $y = \log_2 x$, first construct a table of values, as shown below. To generate this table, rewrite

$$y = \log_2 x \qquad \text{as} \qquad x = 2^y,$$

and then replace y with integer values from -3 to 3.

x	$\frac{1}{8}$	$\frac{1}{4}$	$\frac{1}{2}$	1	2	4	8
y	-3	-2	-1	0	1	2	3

By graphing these solutions and drawing a smooth curve through them, we obtain the graph of $y = \log_2 x$ shown in Figure 8.20.

To relate this graph to the graph of its inverse $y = 2^x$, sketch both graphs on the same coordinate system, as in Figure 8.21. As expected, the graphs are related in that each is the reflection of the other about the line $y = x$.

Technology Link
One way to obtain the graph of $f(x) = \log_2 x$ on a graphing calculator is to use the **change of base formula**

$$\log_b x = \frac{\log_a x}{\log_a b}$$

which will be proved in Section 8.5. Based on this formula,

$$f(x) = \log_2 x = \frac{\log x}{\log 2} \text{ or } f(x) = \log_2 x = \frac{\ln x}{\ln 2}.$$

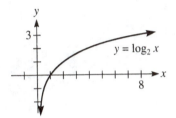

Figure 8.20

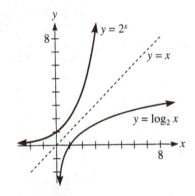

Figure 8.21

So Figure 8.22(a) shows an expression that may be entered to graph f. Figure 8.22(b) gives the graph that results in the viewing window $[-2, 8]$ by $[-4, 4]$.

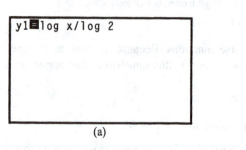

(a)

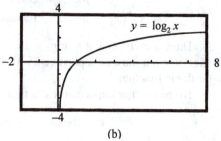

(b)

Figure 8.22

PROGRESS CHECK 6   Graph $y = \log_{1/2} x$. Then sketch the graphs of the functions $y = \log_{1/2} x$ and $y = \left(\frac{1}{2}\right)^x$ on the same coordinate system, and describe how the graphs are related.   ■

Two typical logarithmic functions were graphed in Example 6 and "Progress Check" Exercise 6:

$$y = \log_2 x \text{ in which } b > 1,$$
$$y = \log_{1/2} x \text{ in which } 0 < b < 1.$$

In general, the graphs of $y = \log_b x$ and $y = b^x$ for these two cases are as shown in Figure 8.23. From these graphs some properties of the logarithmic function with base b are apparent.

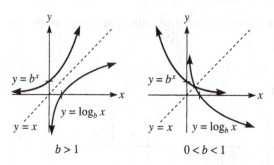

Figure 8.23

Properties of $f(x) = \log_b x$ (with $b > 0$, $b \neq 1$) and Its Graph

1. The domain of $y = \log_b x$ (which is the range of $y = b^x$) is $(0, \infty)$.
2. The range of $y = \log_b x$ (which is the domain of $y = b^x$) is $(-\infty, \infty)$.
3. The graph of $y = \log_b x$ has the x-intercept $(1, 0)$, and the y-axis is a vertical asymptote.
4. The graph of $y = \log_b x$ is the reflection of the graph of $y = b^x$ about the line $y = x$.
5. If $b > 1$, then as x increase, y increases. If $0 < b < 1$, then as x increases, y decreases.

Graphs of common logarithmic functions are easily shown by using the ⎡LOG⎤ key on a graphing calculator. An exploration involving such functions is discussed in Example 7.

EXAMPLE 7   Using a Grapher to Explore Common Logarithmic Functions
Graph the functions $y1 = f(x) = \log x$, $y2 = g(x) = 3 + \log x$, and $y3 = h(x) = \log(x + 3)$ on $[-3, 5]$ by $[-2, 4]$. Use the Trace feature and explain how the graph of g and the graph of h are related to the graph of f.

Solution   The appropriate calculator displays for defining and picturing the functions are given in Figure 8.24.

Use of the Trace feature suggests that the graph of g is the graph of f shifted 3 units up, while the graph of h is the graph of f shifted 3 units to the left. In fact these observations may be confirmed by the graphing techniques given in Section 2.5.

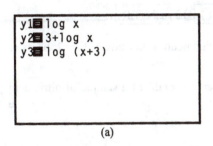
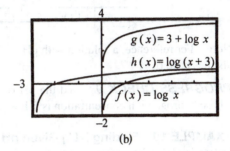

(a)   (b)

Figure 8.24

PROGRESS CHECK 7   Graph $y1 = f(x) = \log x$, $y2 = g(x) = -\log x$, and $y3 = h(x) = \log(x - 2)$ on $[-1, 7]$ by $[-3, 3]$. Use the Trace feature and explain how the graph of g and the graph of h are related to the graph of f.   ■

Example 7 illustrated that the graphing techniques of Section 2.5 may be used to graph certain variations of $y = \log x$. These techniques apply to any logarithmic function, and the next example illustrates the case of a horizontal shift of $y = \log_2 x$.

EXAMPLE 8   Applying Graphing Techniques to Logarithmic Functions
Graph $y = \log_2(x + 4)$.

Solution   The graph of the function $y = \log_2(x + 4)$ is identical in shape to the graph of $y = \log_2 x$. Since the constant 4 is added to x before the log rule is applied, shift the graph of $y = \log_2 x$ to the left 4 units to position this curve correctly. Convenient points to plot for the graph are $(-3, 0)$, $(0, 2)$, and $(4, 3)$. The completed graph is shown in Figure 8.25.

PROGRESS CHECK 8   Graph $y = -\log_2 x$.   ■

Calculators replace log *evaluations*, not log *functions*. To illustrate, we now solve the section-opening problem in which a relationship is analyzed by using a logarithmic function.

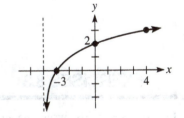

Figure 8.25

EXAMPLE 9   Finding pH given [H$^+$]
Solve the problem in the section introduction on page 440.

Solution

a. The problem states that pH is defined in exponential form by

$$[H^+] = 10^{-pH}.$$

Converting this expression to logarithmic form yields

$$-pH = \log_{10}[H^+],$$
$$pH = -\log[H^+].$$

Thus, pH is defined as the negative of the common logarithm of the hydrogen ion concentration.

b. For household ammonia, $[H^+] = 5.2 \times 10^{-12}$, so

$$pH = -\log[H^+]$$
$$= -\log(5.2 \times 10^{-12})$$
$$= 11.3 \quad \text{(to the nearest tenth)}.$$

Technology Link

Remember to take advantage of the scientific notation capabilities of a calculator when finding pH. For instance in part b the expression $-\log(5.2 \times 10^{-12})$ may be entered on a graphing calculator with the keystroke sequence

$\boxed{(-)}$ $\boxed{\text{LOG}}$ 5.2 $\boxed{\text{EE}}$ $\boxed{(-)}$ 12 $\boxed{\text{ENTER}}$.

Note   For reference, a solution with pH = 7 is called neutral. In acids, pH < 7; bases or alkalies have pH > 7.

PROGRESS CHECK 9   Find the pH (to the nearest tenth) of a sample of nitric acid whose hydrogen ion concentration is 5.1×10^{-4}. ■

EXAMPLE 10   Finding $[H^+]$ Given pH
Determine $[H^+]$ for a sample of tomato juice whose pH is 4.5.

Solution   From Example 9, the formula for pH is

$$pH = -\log[H^+].$$

To find $[H^+]$, first replace pH by 4.5 and solve for $\log[H^+]$.

$$4.5 = -\log[H^+]$$
$$-4.5 = \log[H^+]$$

Then $\log[H^+] = -4.5$ is equivalent to $10^{-4.5} = [H^+]$, so $[H^+]$ may be found by evaluating $10^{-4.5}$ on a calculator. The result for this calculation shows (to two significant digits).

PROGRESS CHECK 10   To two significant digits determine $[H^+]$ for a sample of sea-water whose pH is 8.9. ■

EXERCISES 8.3

In Exercises 1–16, write the given relation in logarithmic form.

1. $2^3 = 8$
2. $3^4 = 81$
3. $4^2 = 16$
4. $5^4 = 625$
5. $\left(\frac{1}{2}\right)^3 = \frac{1}{8}$
6. $\left(\frac{1}{3}\right)^4 = \frac{1}{81}$
7. $b^y = x$
8. $a^r = m$
9. $10^3 = 1,000$
10. $10^4 = 10,000$
11. $10^{-2} = \frac{1}{100}$
12. $10^{-5} = \frac{1}{100,000}$
13. $(0.2)^3 = 0.008$
14. $(0.1)^3 = 0.001$
15. $(0.1)^{-2} = 100$
16. $(0.5)^{-3} = 8$

In Exercises 17–30, write the given relation in exponential form.

17. $\log_4 64 = 3$
18. $\log_5 25 = 2$
19. $\log_4 2 = \frac{1}{2}$
20. $\log_{16} 2 = \frac{1}{4}$
21. $\log_{10} 1,000 = 3$
22. $\log_{10} 10,000 = 4$
23. $\log_8 \frac{1}{8} = -1$
24. $\log_6 \frac{1}{36} = -2$
25. $\log_2 \frac{1}{32} = -5$
26. $\log_3 \frac{1}{27} = -3$
27. $\log_b y = x$
28. $\log_{1/2} y = x$
29. $\log_{1/2} 8 = -3$
30. $\log_{1/3} 9 = -2$

In Exercises 31–50, determine the value of the unknown in each equation.

31. $\log_3 3 = y$
32. $\log_7 1 = y$
33. $\log_{1/2} 1 = y$
34. $\log_{1/2} 4 = y$
35. $\log_{1/2} \frac{1}{16} = y$
36. $\log_{1/3} 9 = y$
37. $\log_b 27 = 3$
38. $\log_b \frac{1}{4} = 2$
39. $\log_b \frac{1}{25} = -2$
40. $\log_b \frac{1}{729} = -3$
41. $\log_b 8 = -3$
42. $\log_b 81 = -4$
43. $\log_6 x = 2$
44. $\log_9 x = 3$
45. $\log_4 x = -2$
46. $\log_5 x = -3$
47. $\log_{1/5} x = -2$
48. $\log_{1/3} x = -3$
49. $\log_2 x = -3$
50. $\log_{1/2} x = 5$

In Exercises 51–58, graph the given logarithmic functions.

51. $y = \log_{10} x$ **52.** $y = \log_5 x$

53. $y = \log_3 x$ **54.** $y = \log_2 x$

55. $y = \log_{1/3} x$ **56.** $y = \log_{1/10} x$

57. $y = \log_b x, b > 1$ **58.** $y = \log_b x, 0 < b < 1$

In Exercises 59–64, graph the given pair of functions on the same coordinate system, and describe how the graphs are related.

59. $y = \log_{10} x, y = 10^x$ **60.** $y = \log_{1/3} x, y = \left(\frac{1}{3}\right)^x$

61. $y = \log_{1/4} x, y = \left(\frac{1}{4}\right)^x$

62. $y = \log_3 x, y = 3^x$

63. $y = \log_b x, b > 1; y = b^x, b > 1$

64. $y = \log_b x, 0 < b < 1; y = b^x, 0 < b < 1$

In Exercises 65–74, use graphing techniques for translation and reflection to graph the given function.

65. $y = \log_5(x + 4)$ **66.** $y = \log_3(x - 2)$

67. $y = \log_{1/2}(x + 4)$ **68.** $y = \log_{1/2}(x - 3)$

69. $y = -\log_3 x$ **70.** $y = -\log_5 x$

71. $y = -\log_{1/2} x$ **72.** $y = -\log_{1/3} x$

73. $y = -\log_5(x + 2)$ **74.** $y = -\log_5(x - 6)$

In Exercises 75–80, evaluate the given logarithms to four decimal places.

75. $\log 25$ **76.** $\log 75$

77. $\log 0.37$ **78.** $\log 0.54$

79. $\log 2.36$ **80.** $\log 0.004$

In Exercises 81–88, find N to three significant digits.

81. $\log N = 2.2$ **82.** $\log N = 1.7$

83. $\log N = 0.042$ **84.** $\log N = 0.057$

85. $\log N = -2.6$ **86.** $\log N = -1.41$

87. $\log N = -0.31$ **88.** $\log N = -0.46$

In Exercises 89–94, use the relationship between pH and $[H^+]$ given in Example 9.

89. The concentration of hydrogen ions in a solution is 4×10^{-5}. Find the pH to the nearest tenth. Is this an acid or a base?

90. The concentration of hydrogen ions in a solution is 1.8×10^{-9}. Find the pH to the nearest tenth. Is this an acid or a base?

91. Acid rain decreases the pH in rivers, which can endanger fish. For instance, salmon die when the pH falls to about 5.5. Determine the concentration of hydrogen ions $[H^+]$ for such river water.

92. Acid-base indicators are highly colored dyes which change color when the pH of a solution changes. One such indicator is red when the pH is above 7.5, yellow when the pH is below 6.5, and orange otherwise. Find the values of $[H^+]$ which correspond to these pH values.

93. A chemist must solve the equation $\dfrac{x^2}{0.05} = \dfrac{1 \times 10^{-14}}{1.8 \times 10^{-5}}$, where x gives the hydrogen ion concentration of a certain solution.

    a. Find $[H^+]$.

    b. Find the corresponding value for the pH.

94. A chemist must solve the equation $\dfrac{x^2}{0.15} = 2 \times 10^{-6}$, where x gives the hydrogen ion concentration of a certain solution.

    a. Find $[H^+]$.

    b. Find the corresponding value for the pH.

95. One version of the Richter scale for measuring the magnitude of earthquakes is given by

$$R = \tfrac{2}{3}(\log E - 4.4),$$

where E is the energy of the quake in joules and R is the Richter rating.

    a. Find the energy (E) released by an earthquake which measures 6 on the Richter scale.

    b. What is the energy released when R is 5?

    c. How many times more energy is released by a quake which measures 6 on the Richter scale than by one which measures 5?

96. Refer to Exercise 95. Compare the energy released by earthquakes which register 7.5 and 7 on the Richter scale. (Answer parts **a**, **b**, and **c** as in Exercise 95.)

THINK ABOUT IT 8.3

1. Recall that the equation $[H^+] = 10^{-pH}$ defines the pH of a solution.

    a. Show that when the pH is doubled, the hydrogen ion concentration is squared.

    b. In general, what happens to the hydrogen ion concentration when the pH is multiplied by n?

2. The logarithm function with $b > 1$ is one which increases very slowly. This is in marked contrast to the exponential function, which grows quickly. By making tables of ordered pairs for $x = 0, 1, 2, 4, 8, 16,$ and 32 and then drawing accurate graphs, compare the graphs of $y = \log_2 x$ and $y = x^{1/2}$, both of which grow slowly. Give function values to the nearest tenth. Where do the graphs intersect?

3. For the logarithmic function defined by $y = \log_b x$, explain why the restriction $b \neq 1$ is necessary for the equation to define a function.

4. Find the domain of $y = \log_2(x + 2)$. Use both a geometric and an algebraic approach.

5. **a.** If $\log_b 3 = m$ and $\log_b 4 = n$, find b^{m+n}.

    b. By calculator, find $10^{\log_{10} 3}$ and $10^{\log_{10} 5}$. Generalize to $b^{\log_b x}$, and explain why these answers make sense.

Courtesy of PhotoDisc/Getty Images.

8.4 Properties of Logarithms

An alternative formula for pH is

$$pH = \log\frac{1}{[H^+]}.$$

a. Show that the above formula is equivalent to the formula stated in the previous section. That is, show that

$$\log\frac{1}{[H^+]} = -\log[H^+].$$

b. Use the alternative formula above and find the pH (to the nearest tenth) of a sample of acid rain whose hydrogen ion concentration is 3.8×10^{-4}. (See Example 3.)

O B J E C T I V E S

1 Use properties of logarithms to express certain log statements in terms of simpler logarithms or expressions.

2 Use properties of logarithms to convert certain statements involving logarithms to a single logarithm with coefficient 1.

Because a logarithm is an exponent, properties of logarithms follow from exponent properties. Three key exponent properties from Section 1.3 that are the basis for the product, quotient, and power rules for logarithms may be stated as follows.

1. $b^m \cdot b^n = b^{m+n}$ **Product property**

2. $\dfrac{b^m}{b^n} = b^{m-n}$ **Quotient property**

3. $(b^m)^n = b^{mn}$ **Power-to-a-power property**

To each of these exponent properties, there corresponds a logarithm property, as stated next.

Product, Quotient, and Power Properties of Logarithms

If b, x, and y are positive numbers with $b \neq 1$, and k is any real number, then

1. $\log_b xy = \log_b x + \log_b y$ **Product property**

2. $\log_b \dfrac{x}{y} = \log_b x - \log_b y$ **Quotient property**

3. $\log_b x^k = k \log_b x,$ **Power property**

To use the product property of exponents to prove the product property of logarithms, let

$$x = b^m \quad \text{and} \quad y = b^n,$$

and observe that the respective logarithmic forms of these statements are

$$\log_b x = m \quad \text{and} \quad \log_b y = n.$$

By the product rule of exponents,

$$x \cdot y = b^m \cdot b^n = b^{m+n},$$

and converting $xy = b^{m+n}$ to logarithmic form gives

$$\log_b xy = m + n.$$

Finally, substituting $\log_b x$ for m and $\log_b y$ for n yields the property

$$\log_b xy = \log_b x + \log_b y.$$

The quotient and power properties of logarithms may be established in similar ways (and these proofs are requested in Exercises 75 and 76).

One use of these properties is to convert certain logarithms to a sum, difference, or product involving simpler logarithms, as illustrated in Example 1.

EXAMPLE 1 Converting to Expressions Involving Simpler Logarithms

Express each logarithm as a sum, difference, or product involving simpler logarithms.

a. $\log_b 5x$

b. $\log_4 \frac{3}{5}$

c. $\log_{10} x^4$

d. $\log_b \sqrt[3]{5}$

e. $\log_2 7x^2$

f. $\log_b \sqrt{\dfrac{x}{3y}}$

Solution In parts **d** and **f** note that radical expressions are converted to rational exponent form so that the power property can be applied.

a. $\log_b 5x = \log_b 5 + \log_b x$ Product property
b. $\log_4 \frac{3}{5} = \log_4 3 - \log_4 5$ Quotient property
c. $\log_{10} x^4 = 4 \log_{10} x$ Power property
d. $\log_b \sqrt[3]{5} = \log_b 5^{1/3}$ $\sqrt[3]{5} = 5^{1/3}$

$\qquad = \frac{1}{3}\log_b 5$ Power property

e. $\log_2 7x^2 = \log_2 7 + \log_2 x^2$ Product property

$\qquad = \log_2 7 + 2 \log_2 x$ Power property

f. $\log_b \sqrt{\dfrac{x}{3y}} = \log_b \left(\dfrac{x}{3y}\right)^{1/2}$ $\qquad \sqrt{\dfrac{x}{3y}} = \left(\dfrac{x}{3y}\right)^{1/2}$

$\qquad = \dfrac{1}{2}\log_b \dfrac{x}{3y}$ Power property

$\qquad = \frac{1}{2}(\log_b x - \log_b 3y)$ Quotient property

$\qquad = \frac{1}{2}[\log_b x - (\log_b 3 + \log_b y)]$ Product property

Caution Properties have been stated for the logarithm of a product, a quotient, and a power. Logarithms of a *sum* or *difference* may not be converted using logarithm properties. In particular,

$$\log_b(x + y) \text{ may } not \text{ be replaced by } \log_b x + \log_b y,$$
$$\text{and } \log_b(x - y) \text{ may } not \text{ be replaced by } \log_b x - \log_b y.$$

PROGRESS CHECK 1 Express each logarithm as a sum, difference, or product involving simpler logarithms.

a. $\log_b \left(\dfrac{x}{4}\right)$

b. $\log_2 10x$

c. $\log_{10} 4^x$

d. $\log_b \sqrt{7}$

e. $\log_b 5(x + 2)^3$

f. $\log_5 \sqrt[3]{\dfrac{2}{9N}}$ ■

Two additional properties that are often used to simplify logarithmic expressions are the direct result of the exponent laws $b^1 = b$ and $b^0 = 1$. Converting these expressions to logarithmic form gives the result that if b is a positive number other than 1, then

$$\log_b b = 1 \qquad \text{and} \qquad \log_b 1 = 0.$$

For instance, $\log_{10} 10 = 1$ and $\log_2 1 = 0$. In the remaining examples these two properties will be used to further simplify logarithmic expressions whenever applicable.

EXAMPLE 2   Simplifications Involving $\log_b b = 1$ and $\log_b 1 = 0$

Express each logarithm as a sum, difference, or product involving simpler logarithms.

a. $\log_{10} 10x$ **b.** $\log_4 4^5$ **c.** $\log_b \frac{1}{3}$

Solution

a. $\log_{10} 10x = \log_{10} 10 + \log_{10} x$ Product property
$\qquad\qquad = 1 + \log_{10} x$ $\log_b b = 1$

b. $\log_4 4^5 = 5 \log_4 4$ Power property
$\qquad\quad = 5(1)$ $\log_b b = 1$
$\qquad\quad = 5$

c. $\log_b \frac{1}{3} = \log_b 1 - \log_b 3$ Quotient property
$\qquad\quad = 0 - \log_b 3$ $\log_b 1 = 0$
$\qquad\quad = -\log_b 3$

PROGRESS CHECK 2 Express each logarithm as a sum, difference, or product involving simpler logarithms.

a. $\log_{10} 10^{-1}$ **b.** $\log_6 \frac{6}{5}$ **c.** $\log_6 \frac{1}{5}$ ■

EXAMPLE 3   Using Logarithm Properties to Establish Alternate Formulas

Solve the problem in the section introduction on page 448.

Solution

a. If the expression in the alternative formula for pH is viewed as the logarithm of a quotient, then we may show that the expressions in the formulas are equivalent, as follows.

$$\log \frac{1}{[H^+]} = \log 1 - \log[H^+] \quad \text{Quotient property}$$
$$= 0 - \log[H^+] \quad \log_b 1 = 0$$
$$= -\log[H^+]$$

b. For the sample of acid rain, $[H^+] = 3.8 \times 10^{-4}$, so

$$pH = \log \frac{1}{3.8 \times 10^{-4}}$$
$$= 3.4 \text{ (to the nearest tenth)}.$$

PROGRESS CHECK 3 The expression in the alternative formula for pH may also be viewed as the logarithm of the reciprocal of $[H^+]$.

a. Show that $\log \frac{1}{[H^+]} = -\log[H^+]$ by first rewriting $\frac{1}{[H^+]}$ as $[H^+]^{-1}$.

b. Use the alternative formula to find the pH (to the nearest tenth) of a sample of swimming pool water whose hydrogen ion concentration is 2.9×10^{-8}.   ■

EXAMPLE 4   Finding Relationships Among Logarithm Values

If $\log_b 2 = m$ and $\log_b 3 = n$, express each of the following in terms of m and / or n.

a. $\log_b \frac{1}{2}$ **b.** $\log_b 72$

Solution

a. By the quotient property,

$$\log_b \frac{1}{2} = \log_b 1 - \log_b 2.$$

Then $\log_b 1 = 0$ and $\log_b 2 = m$, so

$$\log_b \tfrac{1}{2} = 0 - m = -m.$$

b. Using factors of 2 and 3, we write 72 as $2^3 \cdot 3^2$. Then,

$$\log_b 72 = \log_b(2^3 \cdot 3^2) = \log_b 2^3 + \log_b 3^2 = 3 \log_b 2 + 2 \log_b 3.$$

Replacing $\log_b 2$ by m and $\log_b 3$ by n gives

$$\log_b 72 = 3m + 2n.$$

PROGRESS CHECK 4   If $\log_b 2 = m$ and $\log_b 3 = n$, express each of the following in terms of m and/or n.

a. $\log_b 24$ **b.** $\log_b \tfrac{1}{9}$ ■

Two other useful properties of logarithms are referred to as inverse properties because they are a direct consequence of the inverse relation between exponential and logarithmic functions. That is, since $y = b^x$ and $y = \log_b x$ "undo" each other, applying the two rules one after the other to a meaningful input x produces x as the output.

> **Inverse Properties**
>
> If b is a positive number with $b \neq 1$, then
> 1. $\log_b b^x = x$,
> 2. $b^{\log_b x} = x$, for $x > 0$.

From a different viewpoint, $\log_b b^x = x$ because $b^x = b^x$, and $b^{\log_b x} = x$ (for $x > 0$) because $\log_b x$ is the power of b that results in x.

EXAMPLE 5   Using Inverse Properties
Simplify each expression.
a. $\log_{10}(m \times 10^k)$ **b.** $10^{\log_{10} 100}$

Solution
a. By the product property,

$$\log_{10}(m \times 10^k) = \log_{10} m + \log_{10} 10^k.$$

Then the inverse property $\log_b b^x = x$ indicates that $\log_{10} 10^k = k$, so

$$\log_{10}(m \times 10^k) = \log_{10} m + k.$$

b. Using $b^{\log_b x} = x$ gives

$$10^{\log_{10} 100} = 100.$$

To confirm this answer, observe that $\log_{10} 100 = 2$, so

$$10^{\log_{10} 100} = 10^2 = 100.$$

PROGRESS CHECK 5   Simplify each expression.

a. $\log_{10}(a \times 10^3)$ **b.** $4^{\log_4 64}$ ■

To this point, logarithm properties have been used mainly to convert a simple log statement to a sum, difference, or product that involved simpler logarithms. Depending on the application, it may be more useful to convert sums and differences of logarithms to a single logarithm with coefficient 1. This type of conversion is considered in the next example.

EXAMPLE 6   Converting to a Single Logarithm

Express as a single logarithm with coefficient 1.

a. $\log_3 5 + \log_3 y$ **b.** $\log_{10} 2 - \log_{10} x$

c. $2 \log_b x + 3 \log_b y$ **d.** $\frac{1}{2}[\log_b(x + 1) - \log_b 3]$

Solution

a. $\log_3 5 + \log_3 y = \log_3 5y$ Product property

b. $\log_{10} 2 - \log_{10} x = \log_{10} \dfrac{2}{x}$ Quotient property

c. $2 \log_b x + 3 \log_b y = \log_b x^2 + \log_b y^3$ Power property
$= \log_b x^2 y^3$ Product property

d. $\dfrac{1}{2}[\log_b(x + 1) - \log_b 3] = \dfrac{1}{2} \log_b \dfrac{x + 1}{3}$ Quotient property

$= \log_b \left(\dfrac{x + 1}{3} \right)^{1/2}$ or $\log_b \sqrt{\dfrac{x + 1}{3}}$ Power property

PROGRESS CHECK 6   Express as a single logarithm with coefficient 1.

a. $\log_b 12 - \log_b 4$ **b.** $\log_2 x + \log_2(x - 1)$

c. $2 \log_{10} x + \frac{1}{2}\log_{10} 9$ **d.** $\frac{1}{2}[\log_{10} L - \log_{10} g]$

EXERCISES 8.4

In Exercises 1–36, express the given logarithm as a sum, difference, or product of simpler logarithms.

1. $\log_5 \frac{7}{9}$ **2.** $\log_8 \frac{2}{3}$

3. $\log_8 6x$ **4.** $\log_5 2x$

5. $\log_3 x^5$ **6.** $\log_5 x^4$

7. $\log_b \sqrt[3]{5}$ **8.** $\log_b \sqrt[3]{3}$

9. $\log_3 5x^3$ **10.** $\log_7 6x^4$

11. $\log_b \sqrt{\dfrac{x}{2y}}$ **12.** $\log_b \sqrt{\dfrac{3}{xy}}$

13. $\log_b \sqrt{\dfrac{xy}{z}}$ **14.** $\log_b \sqrt[3]{\dfrac{2x}{yz^2}}$

15. $\log_b \sqrt{\dfrac{x + 5}{y}}$ **16.** $\log_b \sqrt{\dfrac{x}{y - 3}}$

17. $\log_4 4$ **18.** $\log_9 9$

19. $\log_3 3^5$ **20.** $\log_5 5^9$

21. $\log_5 1$ **22.** $\log_6 1$

23. $\log_{10} \frac{1}{10}$ **24.** $\log_{10} \frac{1}{100}$

25. $\log_{10} 10^{-3}$ **26.** $\log_{10} 10^{-4}$

27. $\log_5 5^{-3}$ **28.** $\log_7 7^{-2}$

29. $\log_6 6^3$ **30.** $\log_8 8^5$

31. $\log_b \frac{1}{3}$ **32.** $\log_b \frac{1}{7}$

33. $\log_b \dfrac{b}{7}$ **34.** $\log_b \dfrac{b}{5}$

35. $\log_b \dfrac{3}{b^2}$ **36.** $\log_b \dfrac{5}{b^3}$

In Exercises 37–46, let $\log_b 2 = m$ and $\log_b 3 = n$. Express each of the following in terms of m and/or n.

37. $\log_b 108$ **38.** $\log_b 144$

39. $\log_b 48$ **40.** $\log_b 162$

41. $\log_b \frac{1}{27}$ **42.** $\log_b \frac{1}{64}$

43. $\log_b \frac{1}{32}$ **44.** $\log_b \frac{1}{81}$

45. $\log_b \frac{27}{64}$ **46.** $\log_b \frac{32}{81}$

In Exercises 47–54, simplify the given expression.

47. $\log_{10}(t \times 10^k)$ **48.** $\log_{10}(2y \times 10^k)$

49. $\log_{10}(y \times 100^k)$ **50.** $\log_{10}(y \times 1{,}000^k)$

51. $5^{\log_5 32}$ **52.** $5^{\log_5 64}$

53. $7^{\log_7 49}$ **54.** $8^{\log_8 23}$

In Exercises 55–66, express the given expression as a single log with coefficient 1.

55. $\log_2 8 + \log_2 y$ **56.** $\log_5 x + \log_5 y$

57. $\log_b 3 - \log_b y$ **58.** $\log_b 7 - \log_b y$

59. $3 \log_{10} y - 4 \log_{10} x$ **60.** $2 \log_{10} x - 9 \log_{10} y$

61. $\frac{1}{3}[\log_{10}(x + 3) - \log_{10}(y - 1)]$

62. $\frac{1}{2}[\log_{10}(x - 2) - \log_{10}(y + 5)]$

63. $\frac{1}{2}[\log_{10} x - (\log_{10} y + \log_{10} z)]$

64. $\frac{1}{3}\{\log_{10} y - [\log_{10}(x + 2) + \log_{10} z]\}$

65. $\frac{1}{2}(\log_{10} y - \log_{10} z - \log_{10} x)$

66. $\frac{1}{3}(\log_{10} x - \log_{10} y - \log_{10} z)$

67. Without using a calculator, fill in the missing entries. Make use of the properties of logarithms and the given entries.

(*Hint:* $\log 20 = \log(2 \times 10) = \log 2 + \log 10$.)

x	1	2	5	10	20	50	100
$y = \log x$	0	0.3010	0.6990	1			
$y = \log x^2$							
$y = \log \sqrt{x}$							

68. Without using a calculator, fill in the missing entries. Make use of the properties of logarithms and the given entries.

x	1	2	5	10	20	50	100
$y = \log_2 x$	0	1	2.3219				
$y = \log_2 x^2$	0	2					
$y = \log_2 \sqrt{x}$	0	0.5					

69. a. Assume that x is any positive real number. Use the graph of $y = \log x$ to draw the graph of $y = \log x^2$. Explain why each y value on the graph of $y = \log x^2$ is twice the corresponding value of y on the graph of $y = \log x$.

   b. Assume that x is any positive real number. Use the graph of $y = \log x$ to draw the graph of $y = \log \sqrt{x}$. Explain why each y value on the graph of $y = \log \sqrt{x}$ is half the corresponding value of y on the graph of $y = \log x$.

70. The graph of $y = \log x$ is shown. Use this graph and the properties of logarithms to sketch the graph of $y = \log(1/x)$.

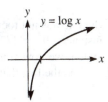

71. A useful equation in statistics is called the *log-linear model* because the logarithm of one variable is expressed as a linear function of the other variable. Such models are often used to investigate the effects of various health hazards on the survival time of patients. An example of a log-linear model is $\log y = ax + b$.

   a. Solve this equation for x.

   b. Find x when $a = 0.4$, $b = 0$, and $y = 16$.

   c. Solve the given equation for y.

   d. Find y when $a = 0.4$, $b = 0$, and $x = 3$.

72. In the statistical study of life expectancy, a simple but useful mathematical model is $\log p = -mt$, where p represents the fraction of some original population that is still alive after time t. The constant m is called the "hazard rate" or the "force of mortality."

   a. Solve this equation for p.

   b. Solve this equation for t.

   c. Assume that $m = 0.1$ and $t = 4$. Find p to the nearest hundredth.

   d. Assume that $m = 0.1$ and $p = 0.5$. Find t to the nearest hundredth.

73. In the scientific study of sound, several properties of sound are measured on the decibel scale. (Decibel $= \frac{1}{10}$ bel, a unit named after Alexander Graham Bell.) One such property is called sound intensity, and a formula for calculating the intensity level (L) in decibels (dB) is

$$L = 10 \log(I) + 90,$$

where I is the intensity measured in ergs per square centimeter per second.

   a. Show that the given formula is equivalent to

$$L = 10 \log\left(\frac{I}{10^{-9}}\right),$$

   which is another common version of this formula.

   b. Find L when $I = 100$.

   c. Find I when $L = 120$ decibels (this is the threshold of pain).

74. Another characteristic of sound is called the sound pressure. One formula for the pressure level is

$$L = 20 \log(p) + 74,$$

where p is measured in dynes per square centimeter.

   a. Show that the formula is equivalent to

$$L = 20 \log\left(\frac{p}{10^{-3.7}}\right).$$

   b. Find L when $p = 0.2$ dynes/cm^2.

   c. Find p when $L = 0$ decibels.

75. Prove the quotient property of logarithms in a way similar to that used in Section 8.4 to prove the product property.

76. Prove the power property of logarithms in a way similar to that used in Section 8.4 to prove the product property.

THINK ABOUT IT 8.4

1. In words, the product property of logarithms states that the logarithm of a product is equal to the sum of the logarithms of the factors. Give a verbal description for the quotient and power properties of logarithms.

2. Give some specific examples to *disprove* both of these statements.

   a. $\log_b(x + y) = \log_b x + \log_b y$

   b. $\dfrac{\log_b x}{\log_b y} = \log_b x - \log_b y$

3. If $\log_{10} 2 = m$ and $\log_{10} 3 = n$, express these logarithms in terms of m and/or n.

   a. $\log_{10} 5$

   b. $\log_{10} 15$

   c. $\log_{10} 6\frac{2}{3}$

4. Use the fact that $x = b^{\log_b x}$ and $y = b^{\log_b y}$ to prove the product property of logarithms.

5. Examine the following line of reasoning: $3 > 2$. If we multiply both sides of the inequality by $\log_{10}\left(\frac{1}{2}\right)$, we have

$$3 \log_{10}\left(\tfrac{1}{2}\right) > 2 \log_{10}\left(\tfrac{1}{2}\right)$$
$$\log_{10}\left(\tfrac{1}{2}\right)^3 > \log_{10}\left(\tfrac{1}{2}\right)^2$$
$$\log_{10}\left(\tfrac{1}{8}\right) > \log_{10}\left(\tfrac{1}{4}\right).$$

Thus,

$$\tfrac{1}{8} > \tfrac{1}{4}.$$

Our conclusion is incorrect. What went wrong?

Courtesy of Pearson Education.

8.5 Exponential and Logarithmic Equations

The doubling time of an exponentially increasing quantity is the time required for the quantity to double its size or value. Use the fact that the population of the United States is currently growing at a rate of about 0.71 percent per year to determine the current doubling time (to the nearest year) for the U.S. population. The required formula is

$$P = P_0(1 + r)^t$$

where P is the population t years from now, P_0 is the current U.S. population, and r is the annual growth rate. (See Example 3.)

OBJECTIVES

1 Solve exponential equations by using logarithms.

2 Apply the change of base formula.

3 Solve logarithmic equations.

In Section 8.1 we solved exponential equations in which it was not too hard to rewrite the expressions in terms of a common base. For instance, $9^x = 1/27$ was written as $3^{2x} = 3^{-3}$, so $x = -3/2$. Since this procedure is limited, we now consider a general approach that uses the following principle, which is based on the fact that a logarithmic correspondence is a one-to-one function.

Equation-Solving Principle

If x, y, and b are positive real numbers with $b \neq 1$, then

1. $x = y$ implies $\log_b x = \log_b y$, and conversely,
2. $\log_b x = \log_b y$ implies $x = y$.

We can therefore solve **exponential equations** (the unknown is in the exponent) by taking the logarithm of both sides of the equation, as shown in the following examples.

EXAMPLE 1   Solving an Exponential Equation

Solve for x: $3^x = 8$. Give the solution to four significant digits.

Solution   To obtain a picture of the solution to this equation, we can look for the intersection of the graphs of $y = 3^x$ and $y = 8$. As shown in Figure 8.26, $3^x = 8$ when $x \approx 1.893$. This solution can be confirmed algebraically by taking the common logarithm of both sides of $3^x = 8$ and applying the power property of logarithms.

$$3^x = 8$$
$$\log 3^x = \log 8 \qquad \text{Apply common logarithms to each side}$$
$$x \log 3 = \log 8 \qquad \text{Power property}$$
$$x = \frac{\log 8}{\log 3}$$
$$= 1.89278926\ldots \qquad \text{By calculator}$$

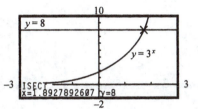

Figure 8.26

Thus, to four significant digits the solution set is $\{1.893\}$.

PROGRESS CHECK 1   Solve for t: $2^t = 9$. Give the solution to four significant digits.   ■

Example 1 illustrates a general approach for solving exponential equations.

To Solve Exponential Equations Using Logarithms

1. Take the logarithm to the same base of both sides of the equation.
2. Simplify by applying the property $\log_b x^k = k \log_b x$.
3. Solve the resulting equation using previous equation-solving methods.

EXAMPLE 2   Solving an Exponential Equation

Solve for x: $3^{x+2} = 5^{2x-1}$. Give the solution to four significant digits.

Solution   Figure 8.27 shows that 3^{x+2} and 5^{2x-1} have the same value when $x \approx 1.795$, and algebraic verification of this result is shown next.

$$3^{x+2} = 5^{2x-1}$$
$$\log 3^{x+2} = \log 5^{2x-1} \qquad \text{Apply common logarithms to each side}$$
$$(x + 2)\log 3 = (2x - 1)\log 5 \qquad \text{Power property}$$
$$x \log 3 + 2 \log 3 = 2x \log 5 - \log 5 \qquad \text{Distributive property}$$
$$x \log 3 - 2x \log 5 = -2 \log 3 - \log 5 \qquad \text{Equivalent equation grouping } x$$
$$x(\log 3 - 2 \log 5) = -2 \log 3 - \log 5 \qquad \text{Factoring}$$
$$x = \frac{-2 \log 3 - \log 5}{\log 3 - 2 \log 5} \approx 1.795$$

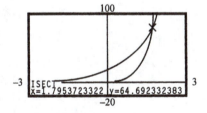

Figure 8.27

To four significant digits, the solution set is $\{1.795\}$.

PROGRESS CHECK 2   Solve for x: $5^x = 3^{x+1}$. Give the solution to four significant digits.   ■

EXAMPLE 3   Finding Doubling Time in Exponential Growth

Solve the problem in the section introduction on page 454.

Solution   When the current U.S. population has doubled, then $P = 2P_0$. Replace P by $2P_0$ and r by 0.71 percent (or 0.0071) in the given formula and solve for t.

$$P = P_0(1 + r)^t$$
$$2P_0 = P_0(1 + .0071)^t \qquad \text{Replace } P \text{ by } 2P_0 \text{ and } r \text{ by 0.0071}$$
$$2 = (1.0071)^t$$
$$\log 2 = \log(1.0071)^t \qquad \text{Apply common logarithms to each side}$$
$$\log 2 = t \log(1.0071) \qquad \text{Power property}$$
$$\frac{\log 2}{\log 1.0071} = t$$

By calculator, $t \approx 97.9725$, so the current doubling time for the U.S. population is about 98 years. Observe that the intersection of the graphs of $y = 1.0071^x$ and $y = 2$ that is shown in Figure 8.28 supports this estimate.

PROGRESS CHECK 3   What is the doubling time (to the nearest year) for the population of Greece given that the current annual growth rate is about 0.06 percent?   ■

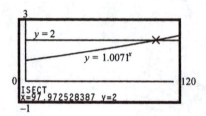

Figure 8.28

Depending on the application, it may be more convenient to write a logarithmic statement in a certain base, and the change-of-base formula that was given in Section 8.3 may be derived using our current methods for solving exponential equations. To express $\log_b x$ in terms of a different base, say a, first recall that

$$y = \log_b x \quad \text{is equivalent to} \quad b^y = x.$$

By taking the logarithm to the base a of both sides of $b^y = x$, we have

$$\log_a b^y = \log_a x$$
$$y \log_a b = \log_a x$$
$$y = \frac{\log_a x}{\log_a b}.$$

Then replacing y by $\log_b x$ yields the formula

$$\log_b x = \frac{\log_a x}{\log_a b}.$$

Because calculators have a Log key, converting to base 10 logarithms is often useful, as illustrated next.

EXAMPLE 4   Using the Change-of-Base Formula

Use logarithms to the base 10 to determine each logarithm to four significant digits.

a. $\log_2 7$  **b.** $\log_5 0.043$

Solution   Convert to common logarithms using the change-of-base formula.

a. $\log_2 7 = \dfrac{\log 7}{\log 2} \approx 2.807$ **b.** $\log_5 0.043 = \dfrac{\log 0.043}{\log 5} \approx -1.955$

Note   When solving equations such as $3^x = 8$, students sometimes begin by writing

$$x = \log_3 8$$

but then are stumped. The continuation of this line of reasoning uses the change-of-base formula, so

$$x = \log_3 8 = \frac{\log 8}{\log 3} \approx 1.893.$$

Compare this alternative method with the solution shown in Example 1.

PROGRESS CHECK 4   Evaluate each logarithm to four significant digits.

a. $\log_4 70$ **b.** $\log_{1/3} 0.45$ ■

The change-of-base formula was introduced in Section 8.3 so that a grapher could be used to quickly draw graphs for equations of the form $y = \log_b x$. The next example reviews this important use of the change-of-base formula.

EXAMPLE 5   Graphing $y = \log_b x$ by Calculator

Use a grapher to graph $f(x) = \log_2 x$ and $g(x) = \log_{1/3} x$.

Solution   Using the change-of-base formula to convert to common logarithms gives

$$f(x) = \log_2 x = \frac{\log x}{\log 2} \text{ and } g(x) = \log_{1/3} x = \frac{\log x}{\log(1/3)}$$

Figure 8.29 shows expressions that may be entered to graph f and g along with their graphs in the viewing window $[-1, 6]$ and $[-4, 4]$.

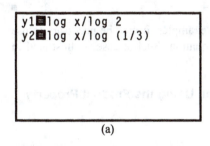

(a)

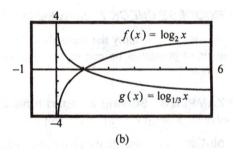

(b)

Figure 8.29

PROGRESS CHECK 5   Use a grapher to graph $f(x) = \log_3 x$ and $g(x) = \log_{1/2} x$. ■

A **logarithmic equation** is an equation that involves a logarithm of a variable expression. In some cases such equations may be solved by applying the principle that $\log_b x = \log_b y$ implies $x = y$. It is important to remember that logarithms are not defined for negative numbers or zero. Therefore, in the solution of logarithmic equations, it is necessary to check answers in the original equation and accept only solutions that result in the logarithms of positive numbers.

EXAMPLE 6   Using $\log_b x = \log_b y$ Implies $x = y$

Solve $\log x = \log(1 - x)$.

Solution

$$\log x = \log(1 - x)$$
$$x = 1 - x \qquad \log_b x = \log_b y \text{ implies } x = y.$$
$$2x = 1$$
$$x = \frac{1}{2}$$

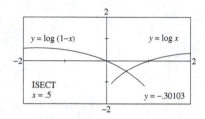

Figure 8.30

Replacing x by $\frac{1}{2}$ in the original equation leads to $\log \frac{1}{2} = \log \frac{1}{2}$, so the proposed solution checks, and the solution set is $\left\{\frac{1}{2}\right\}$. Figure 8.30 shows this solution in a graph.

PROGRESS CHECK 6   Solve $\log (2x - 7) = \log x$.   ■

When an equation contains only one log statement, then we may solve by converting the equation from logarithmic form to exponential form, as shown next.

EXAMPLE 7   Using $\log_b N = L$ Implies $N = b^L$
Solve $\log_5(3x - 8) = 2$.

Solution   We convert to exponential form and then solve for x.

$$\log_5(3x - 8) = 2$$
$$3x - 8 = 5^2 \qquad \log_b N = L \text{ implies } N = b^L.$$
$$3x = 33$$
$$x = 11$$

To check, replace x by 11 in the original equation.

$$\log_5[3(11) - 8] \overset{?}{=} 2$$
$$\log_5 25 \overset{?}{=} 2$$
$$2 \overset{\checkmark}{=} 2$$

The proposed solution checks, and the solution set is $\{11\}$.

PROGRESS CHECK 7   Solve $\log_2(5x + 1) = 4$.   ■

Before you apply the methods of the last two examples, it may be necessary to use logarithm properties on one or both sides of the equation. Such a case is illustrated in Example 8.

EXAMPLE 8   Solving a Logarithmic Equation Using the Product Property
Solve for x: $\log_2(x - 3) = 2 - \log_2 x$.

Solution   First rewrite the given equation as

$$\log_2 x + \log_2(x - 3) = 2$$

so that we may apply the product property of logarithms to obtain

$$\log_2[x(x - 3)] = 2.$$

Now change from logarithmic form to exponential form and solve

$$2^2 = x(x - 3)$$
$$4 = x^2 - 3x$$
$$0 = x^2 - 3x - 4$$
$$0 = (x - 4)(x + 1)$$
$$x - 4 = 0 \qquad x + 1 = 0$$
$$x = 4 \qquad\quad x = -1$$

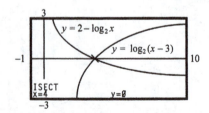

Figure 8.31

A check in the original equation shows that 4 is a solution, while -1 is extraneous, because the domain of $\log_2 x$ is the set of positive real numbers. Thus, the solution set is $\{4\}$. See Figure 8.31 for a graphical solution that supports this answer.

PROGRESS CHECK 8   Solve for x: $\log_3(x + 6) = 3 - \log_3 x$.   ■

EXERCISES 8.5

In Exercises 1–16, solve the given equation. Give solutions to four significant digits.

1. $2^x = 12$
2. $5^x = 75$
3. $7^x = 22$
4. $3^x = 19$
5. $4^x = 32$
6. $6^x = 23$
7. $\left(\frac{1}{2}\right)^x = 24$
8. $\left(\frac{1}{4}\right)^x = 9$
9. $6^x = 2^{x-2}$
10. $5^x = 3^{x+1}$
11. $7^x = 5^{x-1}$
12. $8^x = 2^{x+3}$
13. $3^x = 7^{x-2}$
14. $5^x = 3^{x+2}$
15. $4^x = 9^{x-4}$
16. $2^x = 7^{x+3}$

In Exercises 17–28, evaluate each logarithm to four significant digits.

17. $\log_2 7$
18. $\log_5 3$
19. $\log_4 12$
20. $\log_6 8$
21. $\log_2 7$
22. $\log_3 10$
23. $\log_{1/8} 12$
24. $\log_{1/5} 14$
25. $\log_{1/2} 21$
26. $\log_{3/5} 12$
27. $\log_{1/4} 14$
28. $\log_{3/8} 24$

In Exercises 29–50, solve the given equation for x.

29. $\log(3x - 2) = \log x$
30. $\log(5x - 8) = \log x$
31. $\log_3(x + 6) = \log_3(3x - 2)$
32. $\log_7(3x - 7) = \log_7(2x - 3)$
33. $\log_2(x - 5) = \log_2(7x + 7)$
34. $\log_5(3x + 4) = \log_5(6x + 5)$
35. $\log_3(1 - 2x) = 4$
36. $\log_5(3x + 2) = 3$
37. $\log_9(2x - 3) = 2$
38. $\log_2(11x - 1) = 5$
39. $\log_5(-2x + 5) = 3$
40. $\log_7(5x + 4) = 2$
41. $\log(3x + 100) = 5$
42. $\log(4x + 8) = 3$
43. $\log_2(x + 3) = 2 - \log_2 x$
44. $\log_2(x - 2) = 3 - \log_2 x$
45. $\log_3(x - 2) = 1 - \log_3 x$
46. $\log_3(x + 6) = 3 - \log_3 x$
47. $\log_2(x + 2) = 2 - \log_2(x - 1)$
48. $\log_6(x + 3) = 1 - \log_6(x - 2)$
49. $\log_2(x + 3) = 1 + \log_2(x + 2)$
50. $\log_3(x - 1) = 1 + \log_3(x - 3)$

In Exercises 51–56, use the formula for population growth given in Example 3.

51. Find the doubling time for a deer population with an annual growth rate of 10 percent. Round to the nearest year.
52. Find the doubling time for a mouse population with an annual growth rate of 20 percent. Round to the nearest year.

53. The U.S. population has been growing recently at about 1 percent annually. In 1990 the population was about 248.7 million.
   a. To the nearest year, when will the population reach 300 million?
   b. In about what year will the U.S. population be double the 1990 number?
54. The population of Canada has been growing recently at about 0.8 percent annually. In 1990 the population was about 26.6 million.
   a. To the nearest year, when will the population reach 30 million?
   b. In about what year will the Canadian population be double the 1990 number?
55. What annual growth rate (to the nearest tenth) will cause a population to double in 5 years?
56. What annual growth rate (to the nearest tenth) will cause a population to double in 25 years?
57. Some filters remove a fixed percentage of a substance each time a liquid is passed through the filter. For instance, if a filter removes 90 percent of some pollutant from a quantity of water each time the water goes through the filter, then the amount of pollutant remaining after n passes is given by $A = A_0(1 - 0.90)^n$, where A_0 is the original amount of pollutant.
   a. How many passes are needed to reduce the pollutant to 1 percent of its original value? (That is, A must equal $0.01A_0$.)
   b. How many passes are needed to reduce the pollutant to one-thousandth of its original value?
58. Suppose the filter described in Exercise 57 is only 60 percent effective.
   a. How many passes are needed to reduce the pollutant to below 1 percent of its original value?
   b. How many passes are needed to reduce the pollutant to below onethousandth of its original value?

THINK ABOUT IT 8.5

1. If $A = P(1 + r)^t$, express t in terms of the common logarithms of A, P, and $1 + r$.
2. If $\log_b x = a$, find $\log_{1/b} x$ in terms of a.
3. Solve each equation.
   a. $x^2 \, 10^x = 10^x$
   b. $\log(\log x) = 1$
   c. $2^{2x} - 20 = 2^x$

4. Just as squaring both sides of an equation can introduce extraneous roots, certain operations with logarithms can alter the solution set of an equation. Solve $\log_3(x - 5)^2 = 2$ by two methods and compare solution sets.

   Method 1: Use the definition of logarithm to get $3^2 = (x - 5)^2$. Then solve this quadratic equation.

   Method 2: Use the power property of logarithms to get $2 \log_3(x - 5) = 2$. Divide both sides by 2, and solve the resulting logarithmic equation.

Which method gives the correct solution set to the original equation?

5. In the equation for population growth, $P = P_0(1 + r)^t$ does doubling the annual growth rate (r) cut the doubling time in half?

   a. Compare the doubling time for $r = 5$ and $r = 10$ percent.

   b. Compare the doubling time for $r = 10$ and $r = 20$ percent.

   c. What value of r has exactly half the doubling time of $r = 5$ percent?

8.6   More Applications and the Number e

Newton's law of cooling states that when a warm body is placed in colder surroundings at temperature t_a, the temperature (T) of the body at time t is given by

$$T - t_a = D_0 e^{kt},$$

where D_0 is the initial difference in temperature and k is a constant. Because of an ice storm, there is a loss of power in a home heated to 68° F. If the outside temperature remains fixed at 28°F and the temperature in the house drops from 68 to 64°F in 1 hour, when will the temperature in the house be down to 50°F? (See Example 8.)

Courtesy of Library of Congress

OBJECTIVES

1   Use the compound-interest formula for an investment compounded n times per year.

2   Use the compound-interest formula for an investment compounded continuously.

3   Solve exponential and logarithmic equations involving the number e.

4   Solve applied problems involving continuous growth or decay.

The formula $A = P(1 + r)^t$ was used in Section 8.1 to analyze investments that are compounded once a year. However, if the interest is computed more frequently and added to the principal, then the amount grows at a faster rate as the additional interest earns interest. For instance, Example 8 of Section 8.1 showed that $5,000 amounts to $8,590.93 when compounded annually at 7 percent for 8 years. The effect of changing this investment to compounding twice per year is to increase the compounded amount by $79, as shown in Example 1.

EXAMPLE 1   Compounding n Times per Year

$5,000 is invested at 7 percent compounded semiannually.

a. Find a formula showing the value of the investment at the end of t years.

b. How much is the investment worth after 8 years?

Solution

a. Since the investment is compounded semiannually, the interest is determined two times per year, and the interest rate for each of these periods is 7 percent/2, or 0.035. Then,

$$A = 5,000(1.035) \qquad \text{when} \qquad t = \tfrac{1}{2}\text{year},$$
$$A = 5,000(1.035)^2 \qquad \text{when} \qquad t = 1 \text{ year},$$
$$A = 5,000(1.035)^4 \qquad \text{when} \qquad t = 2 \text{ years},$$

and in general, the compounded amount after *t* years is given by

$$A = 5,000(1.035)^{2t}.$$

b. When *t* = 8.

$$A = 5,000(1.035)^{2(8)}$$
$$= 5,000(1.035)^{16}$$
$$= \$8,669.93.$$

PROGRESS CHECK 1 $9,000 is invested at 5 percent compounded semiannually.

a. Find a formula showing the value of the investment at the end of *t* years.
b. How much is the investment worth after 12 years?   ■

The procedure for Example 1 can be generalized to obtain the following compound-interest formula.

Compound-Interest Formula

The compounded amount *A* when an original principal *P* is compounded *n* times per year for *t* years at annual interest rate *r* is given by

$$A = P\left(1 + \frac{r}{n}\right)^{nt}.$$

Observe that the above formula simplifies to $A = P(1 + r)^t$ for interest compounded annually, since *n* = 1 in this case.

EXAMPLE 2   Using a Compound Interest Formula

$2,000 is invested in an IRA account by a college student on her 17th birthday. If the account grows at 8.5 percent compounded daily, what will be the value of this account on her 65th birthday? Use *n* = 365, and round to the nearest dollar.

Solution   48 years will elapse from the student's 17th birthday to her 65th birthday. Then substituting *P* = 2,000, *r* = 0.085, *n* = 365, and *t* = 48 in the compound-interest formula gives

$$A = 2,000\left(1 + \frac{0.085}{365}\right)^{365(48)}$$
$$= 2,000\left(1 + \frac{0.085}{365}\right)^{17,520}$$

To evaluate the resulting expression, compute

2,000 $\boxed{\times}$ $\boxed{(}$ 1 $\boxed{+}$ 0.085 $\boxed{\div}$ 365 $\boxed{)}$ $\boxed{\wedge}$ 17,520 $\boxed{\text{ENTER}}$ $\boxed{118,234.76}$.

Thus, to the nearest dollar the compounded amount on her 65th birthday is $118,235.

Caution   In this example students sometimes introduce a large round-off error by approximating 1 + 0.085/365 with 1.0002 and computing

$$A = 2,000(1.0002)^{17,520} = \$66,473.06.$$

To avoid such errors, use a keystroke sequence (like the one displayed in Example 2) that allows intermediate computations to be carried forward with as much accuracy as possible.

PROGRESS CHECK 2 $1,500 is invested in an IRA account by a college student on her 27th birthday. If the account grows at 7.8 percent compounded daily, to the nearest dollar what will be the value of this account on her 65th birthday? Use $n = 365$.   ■

When an investment is compounded n times per year, then we have observed that the compounded amount increases as n increases. However, there is a limit to this growth. To illustrate, fix P, r, and t at 1 in the compound-interest formula to obtain

$$A = 1\left(1 + \frac{1}{n}\right)^{n(1)} = \left(1 + \frac{1}{n}\right)^{n}.$$

The result gives the compounded amount when $1 is invested at 100 percent interest for 1 year and is compounded n times. Now consider how A changes as the frequency of compounding is increased, as shown in the following table.

Type of Compounding	Number of Conversions (n)	Compounded Amount
Annually	1	$A = \left(1 + \frac{1}{1}\right)^{1} = 2$
Semiannually	2	$A = \left(1 + \frac{1}{2}\right)^{2} = 2.25$
Quarterly	4	$A = \left(1 + \frac{1}{4}\right)^{4} \approx 2.441\ldots$
Monthly	12	$A = \left(1 + \frac{1}{12}\right)^{12} \approx 2.613\ldots$
Daily	365	$A = \left(1 + \frac{1}{365}\right)^{365} \approx 2.714\ldots$
Hourly	8,760	$A = \left(1 + \frac{1}{8,760}\right)^{8,760} \approx 2.718\ldots$

Notice that A increases by a small amount as the conversion period changes from daily to hourly, and more frequent conversions lead to even smaller changes in A. In higher mathematics it is shown that as n gets larger, $(1 + 1/n)^{n}$ gets closer to an irrational number that is denoted by the letter e. To six significant digits,

$$e \approx 2.71828\ldots.$$

When n increases without bound, we say that the investment is **compounded continuously.** If the $1 investment analyzed above is compounded in this manner, then it grows to e by the end of the year. A base e exponential function therefore describes investments that are compounded continuously, and a general formula that allows for interest rates and principals that are more practical than 100 percent and $1 is stated next.

Continuous-Compounding Formula

The compounded amount A when an original principal P is compounded continuously for t years at annual interest rate r is given by

$$A = Pe^{rt}$$

EXAMPLE 3   Compounding Continuously

$2,000 is invested at 6 percent compounded continuously. How much will the investment be worth in 10 years?

Solution   Substituting $P = 2,000$, $r = 0.06$, and $t = 10$ in the formula $A = Pe^{rt}$ gives

$$A = 2,000e^{(0.06)(10)}$$
$$= 2,000e^{0.6}$$

To evaluate powers of e, most calculators make e^x the second function associated with the $\boxed{\text{LN}}$ key. So a typical keystroke sequence to evaluate $2,000e^{0.6}$ is

$$2,000 \boxed{\times} \boxed{\text{2nd}} \; [e^x] \, 0.6 \boxed{\text{ENTER}} .$$

The result of this computation shows that the compounded amount is $3,644.24.

PROGRESS CHECK 3 $2,000 is invested at 11 percent compounded continuously. How much is the investment worth in 10 years?   ■

For analysis of exponential growth or decay at a continuous rate for physical quantities, the formula $A = Pe^{rt}$ is expressed more generally as

$$A = A_0 e^{kt},$$

where A is the amount at time t, A_0 is the initial amount, and k is the growth or decay constant. The constant k is positive when describing growth and negative when describing decay. A specific formula that fits this form is used to date specimens in geology and archaeology as shown in Example 4.

EXAMPLE 4   Radiocarbon-Dating

In 1991 the oldest intact human body was discovered in an Alpine glacier. He became known as the Iceman, and radiocarbon-dating methods established his age at about 5,300 years. This dating method is based on the fact that there is a fixed ratio of radioactive carbon 14 to ordinary stable carbon in the cells of all living plants and animals. However, when the plant or animal dies, the carbon 14 decays exponentially according to the formula

$$A = A_0 e^{-0.000121t},$$

where A_0 is the initial amount present and A is the amount present after t years have elapsed. Use 5,300 years for the Iceman's age and find the percent of the initial carbon 14 that remains in a sample of bone from Iceman. Express the answer to the nearest percent.

Solution   The percent of the initial amount of carbon 14 remaining today is given by the current amount divided by the initial amount. Symbolically, this ratio is given by A/A_0, so begin by dividing both sides of the given formula by A_0.

$$A = A_0 e^{-0.000121t}$$
$$\frac{A}{A_0} = e^{-0.000121t}$$

Then replacing t by 5,300 yields

$$\frac{A}{A_0} = e^{-0.000121(5,300)}.$$
$$\frac{A}{A_0} \approx 0.5266073893$$

To the nearest percent, about 53 percent of the initial carbon 14 remains in the sample from Iceman.

PROGRESS CHECK 4   Egyptian mummies have been found that are older than Iceman, but their bodies were not fully intact because of embalming. What percent (to the

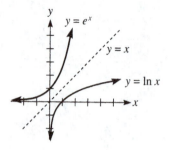

Figure 8.32

nearest percent) of the initial carbon 14 would be present in a sample from a mummy that is 5,900 years old? ■

The calculator evaluation of powers of e in Examples 3 and 4 once again suggests the inverse relation between exponential and logarithmic functions. The inverse of the function defined by $y = e^x$ is defined by $x = e^y$, which is equivalent to $y = \log_e x$. Logarithms to the base e are called **natural logarithms**, and $\log_e x$ is usually abbreviated as $\ln x$. Thus,

$$y = e^x \text{ and } y = \ln x \text{ are inverse functions.}$$

The graphs of $y = e^x$ and $y = \ln x$ are shown in Figure 8.32. Observe that the graphs are symmetric about the line $y = x$ (as are all pairs of inverse functions), and they behave as exponential and logarithmic functions with base b that satisfy $b > 1$ (since $e > 1$).

Properties of natural logarithms follow from the logarithm properties given in Section 8.4. For instance, stating the product, quotient, and power properties in terms of base e logarithms results in the following properties.

Properties of Natural Logarithms

If x and y are positive numbers and k is any real number, then

1. $\ln xy = \ln x + \ln y$ **Product property**
2. $\ln \dfrac{x}{y} = \ln x - \ln y$ **Quotient property**
3. $\ln x^k = k \ln x.$ **Power property**

Furthermore, the inverse properties $\log_b b^x = x$ and $b^{\log_b x} = x$ (if $x > 0$) become

$$\ln e^x = x \quad \text{and} \quad e^{\ln x} = x \quad (\text{if } x > 0)$$

when stated in terms of base e, while

$$\ln e = 1 \quad \text{and} \quad \ln 1 = 0.$$

In the remaining examples, properties of natural logarithms are used together with the equation-solving methods of Section 8.5 to solve exponential and logarithmic equations that involve the number e.

EXAMPLE 5 Solving an Exponential Equation Involving *e*

Solve $e^{-0.32t} = 0.5$. Give the solution to four significant digits.

Solution Because this equation involves e, we employ natural logarithms in the solution.

$$e^{-0.32t} = 0.5$$
$$\ln e^{-0.32t} = \ln 0.5 \qquad \text{Apply natural logarithms to each side.}$$
$$-0.32t = \ln 0.5 \qquad \text{Inverse property } \ln e^x = x.$$
$$t = \frac{\ln 0.5}{-0.32}$$
$$= 2.1660849\ldots$$

Thus, to four significant digits the solution set is $\{2.166\}$. See Figure 8.33 for a graphical solution that supports this answer.

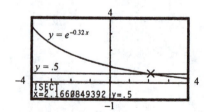

Figure 8.33

PROGRESS CHECK 5 Solve $e^{0.15t} = 2$. Give the solution to four significant digits. ■

EXAMPLE 6   Solving a Logarithmic Equation Involving e

Solve each equation. Give exact answers and also approximate the solution to four significant digits.

a. $\ln x = 1.9$

b. $\ln x = 1 - \ln 2$

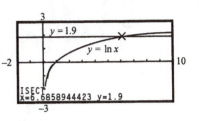

Figure 8.34

Solution

a. If $\ln x = 1.9$, then $x = e^{1.9}$, and the solution set is $\{e^{1.9}\}$. By calculator $e^{1.9} = 6.686$ to four significant digits, and this approximate answer is supported by the graphical solution shown in Figure 8.34.

b. First, rewrite the given equation as

$$\ln x + \ln 2 = 1$$

so that the product property of natural logarithms yields

$$\ln 2x = 1.$$

Then convert to exponential form and solve for x.

$$2x = e^1$$

$$x = \frac{e}{2}$$

Confirm next that the solution set is $\{e/2\}$ by substituting in the original equation. Using $\ln(x/y) = \ln x - \ln y$ and $\ln e = 1$ gives

$$\ln(e/2) = \ln e - \ln 2 = 1 - \ln 2.$$

The solution checks and to four significant digits, the solution set is $\{1.359\}$.

PROGRESS CHECK 6   Solve each equation. Give exact answers and also approximate solutions to four significant digits.

a. $\ln x = -1.8$

b. $\ln x = 2 + \ln 3$ ■

EXAMPLE 7   Finding Doubling Rate in Continuous Growth

At what rate of interest compounded continuously must money be deposited, if the amount is to double in 9 years? Answer to the nearest hundredth of a percent.

Solution   When the original principal P has doubled, then $A = 2P$. Substitute $2P$ for A and 9 for t in the formula $A = Pe^{rt}$ and solve for r.

$$A = Pe^{rt}$$
$$2P = Pe^{r(9)} \qquad \text{Replace } A \text{ by } 2P \text{ and then } t \text{ by 9.}$$
$$2 = e^{9r}$$
$$\ln 2 = \ln e^{9r} \qquad \text{Apply natural logarithms to each side.}$$
$$\ln 2 = 9r \qquad \text{Inverse property } \ln e^x = x.$$
$$\frac{\ln 2}{9} = r$$

By calculator, $r \approx 0.0770164$, so the required interest rate is 7.70 percent, to the nearest hundredth of a percent.

PROGRESS CHECK 7   At what rate of interest compounded continuously must money be deposited if the amount is to double in 6 years? Answer to the nearest hundredth of a percent.   ■

EXAMPLE 8   Newton's Law of Cooling

Solve the problem in the section introduction on page 460.

Solution   We know that $t_a = 28$ and $D_0 = 68 - 28 = 40$. Thus, or formula becomes

$$T - 28 = 40e^{kt}.$$

We can find k since we know that $T = 64$ when $t = 1$.

$$64 - 28 = 40e^{k(1)}$$
$$0.9 = e^k$$
$$\ln 0.9 = \ln e^k \qquad \text{Apply natural logarithms to both sides.}$$
$$\ln 0.9 = k \qquad \text{Inverse property } \ln e^x = x.$$
$$k \approx -0.105$$

(*Note:* k depends on the insulation in the house.) The formula is then

$$T - 28 = 40e^{-0.105t}.$$

To find the number of hours needed for the temperature to fall to 50°F, we let $T = 50$ and solve for t.

$$50 - 28 = 40e^{-0.105t}$$
$$0.55 = e^{-0.105t}$$
$$\ln 0.55 = \ln e^{-0.105t} \qquad \text{Apply natural logarithms to both sides.}$$
$$\ln 0.55 = -0.105t \qquad \text{Inverse property } \ln e^x = x$$
$$t = \frac{\ln 0.55}{-0.105}$$
$$t \approx 5.7 \text{ hours}$$

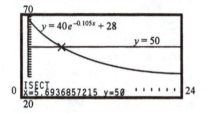

Figure 8.35

To check this answer graphically, it is instructive to first solve the formula in this example for T to obtain $T = 40e^{-0.105t} + 28$. The graph of this function then displays exponential decay where T is approaching the outside temperature of 28°F. Figure 8.35 shows that the intersection of this graph with the graph of $T = 50$ reaffirms that it takes about 5.7 hours for the temperature in the house to drop to 50°F.

PROGRESS CHECK 8 Redo the problem in Example 8 but assume that the temperature in the house drops from 68° to 62°F in 1 hour, and that the outside temperature remains fixed at 18°F. ■

EXERCISES 8.6

In Exercises 1–14, use the given amounts, rates, compounding periods, and years to find (a) a formula showing the value of the investment at the end of t years, and (b) how much the investment is worth at the end of the number of years given.

1. $10,000, 8 percent, quarterly, 5 years
2. $5,000, 12 percent, quarterly, 6 years
3. $20,000, 10 percent, semiannually, 8 years
4. $15,000, 6 percent, semiannually, 7 years
5. $8,000, 13 percent, annually, 10 years
6. $12,000, 16 percent, annually, 9 years
7. $30,000, 12 percent, monthly, 10 years
8. $6,000, 6 percent, monthly, 8 years
9. $10,000, 10 percent, daily, 7 years
10. $25,000, 5 percent, daily, 10 years
11. $15,000, 7 percent, continuously, 12 years
12. $8,000, 9 percent, continuously, 15 years
13. $10,000, 10 percent, continuously, 7 years
14. $25,000, 5 percent, continuously, 10 years

In Exercises 15–30, solve the given equation for t. Give the solution to four significant digits.

15. $e^{-0.21t} = 0.2231$
16. $e^{-0.36t} = 0.4628$
17. $e^{-0.14t} = 0.2134$
18. $e^{-0.43t} = 0.7341$
19. $e^{-3.52t} = 0.3753$
20. $e^{-4.71t} = 0.1246$
21. $e^{-1.26t} = 0.0315$
22. $e^{-2.34t} = 0.0684$
23. $e^{0.13t} = 1.364$
24. $e^{0.47t} = 3.413$
25. $e^{0.06t} = 2.175$
26. $e^{0.05t} = 1.831$
27. $e^{1.01t} = 0.821$
28. $e^{2.21t} = 0.532$
29. $e^{3.04t} = 0.041$
30. $e^{4.78t} = 0.035$

In Exercises 31–56, solve the given equation for x, and (a) give the exact value and (b) give the approximate value to four significant digits.

31. $\ln x = 7.4$
32. $\ln x = 2.8$
33. $\ln x = 0.21$
34. $\ln x = 0.56$
35. $\ln x = 5.2$
36. $\ln x = 6.4$
37. $\ln x = 0.02$
38. $\ln x = 0.05$

39. $\ln x = -3.8$

40. $\ln x = -6.2$

41. $\ln x = -0.2$

42. $\ln x = -0.4$

43. $\ln x + \ln 3 = 6$

44. $\ln x + \ln 5 = 8$

45. $\ln x + \ln 2 = 5$

46. $\ln x + \ln 8 = 3$

47. $\ln x = 1 - \ln 3$

48. $\ln x = 2 - \ln 5$

49. $\ln x = 4 - \ln 7$

50. $\ln x = 3 - \ln 4$

51. $\ln x = 2 + \ln 5$

52. $\ln x = 3 + \ln 2$

53. $\ln x = 5 + \ln 3$

54. $\ln x = 1 + \ln 7$

55. $2 \ln x = 3 + 2 \ln 5$

56. $3 \ln x = 2 + 3 \ln 2$

In Exercises 57–64, at what rate of interest compounded continuously must money be invested to grow as indicated? (Round to the nearest hundredth of a percent.)

57. Double in 15 years

58. Double in 5 years

59. Double in 7 years

60. Double in 10 years

61. Triple in 10 years

62. Triple in 7 years

63. Quadruple in 10 years

64. Quadruple in 7 years

65. Which becomes more valuable after 10 years, $1 invested continuously at 10 percent or $2 invested continuously at 5 percent?

66. Which becomes more valuable after 20 years, $1 invested continuously at 10 percent or $2 invested continuously at 5 percent?

67. About how long does it take an investment to double in value if it is invested at 5 percent interest compounded continuously?

68. About how long does it take an investment to double in value if it is invested at 4 percent interest compounded continuously?

69. In 1920 two scientists, Pearl and Reed, published a formula which described the growth of the U.S. population over the years 1790 to 1910. Their formula is $N = \dfrac{197{,}273{,}000}{1 + e^{-0.0314t}}$, where N is the population and t is the number of years elapsed since 1914 (t is negative for years before 1914). Their formula was almost exactly on target for the years 1790, 1850, and 1910. What population does their formula yield for each of these years? Round to the nearest thousand.

70. A formula published in 1922 by H. G. Thornton gives the area (A) in square centimeters of a growing colony of bacteria as a function of the number of days (x) elapsed. His formula was

$$A = \frac{0.2524}{0.005125 + e^{-2.13x}} \qquad (0 \le x \le 5).$$

What are the areas predicted by his formula after 1, 3, and 5 days?

71. The decay constant for carbon 14 is -0.000121. Approximately what percent of the initial carbon 14 remains in a fossil that is 10,000 years old?

72. The decay constant for carbon 14 is -0.000121. Approximately what percent of the initial carbon 14 remains in a fossil that is 100 years old?

73. The great physicist Ernest Rutherford was among the first to use radioactive decay to date the age of the earth. After analyzing the decay of radium and uranium in a pitchblende rock, he dramatically declared (about 100 years ago) to a geology professor at Cambridge University he was sure the rock in his hand was 700 million years old. The decay constant for uranium 238 is -1.55×10^{-10}. What percentage of an initial amount of uranium 238 remains after 700 million years?

74. The most widely used method for radiometric dating employed by geologists today involves the radioactive decay of potassium 40, which has a decay constant of -5.55×10^{-10}. What percentage of an initial amount of potassium 40 remains after 700 million years?

75. A nuclear accident at Chernobyl in Ukraine in 1986 released dangerous amounts of the radioactive isotope cesium 137, which has a decay constant -0.023. Approximately what percent of the cesium released in 1986 remains in the year 2000?

76. The Chernobyl accident in 1986 also released dangerous amounts of strontium 90, which has decay constant -0.024. Approximately what percent of the strontium released in 1986 remains in the year 2000?

77. A coroner examines the body of a murder victim at 9 A.M. and determines its temperature to be 88°F. An hour later the body temperature is down to 84°F. If the temperature of the room in which the body was found is 68°F, and if the victim's body temperature was 98°F at the time of death, approximate the time of the murder.

78. The temperature of a six-pack of beer (bought from a distributor on a hot summer day) is 90°F. The beer is placed in a refrigerator with a constant temperature of 40°F. If the beer cools to 60°F in 1 hour, when will the beer reach the more thirst-quenching temperature of 45°F?

79. A thermometer has been stored at 75°F. After 5 minutes outside it says 65°F. After another 5 minutes it says 60°F. What is the outside temperature?

80. A turkey which is at room temperature (68°F), is placed in a 350°F oven. After 10 minutes the temperature of the turkey is 90°F. About how long will it take the turkey to reach 300°F?

THINK ABOUT IT 8.6

1. From the following answers, identify *all* choices for k that result in the condition described.

  a. $0 < k < 1$

  b. $k > 1$

  c. $k = 0$

  d. $k = 1$

  e. $k < 0$

   (i) $A = A_0 e^{kt}$ describes growth

   (ii) $A = A_0(k)^t$ describes growth

   (iii) $A = A_0 e^{kt}$ describes decay.

2. If an amount is invested at p percent compounded continuously, then a convenient rule of thumb for estimating the number of years required for the amount to double is

$$\text{doubling time} \approx \frac{70}{p}.$$

For example, an amount will double in about 10 years at 7 percent, and in about 5 years at 14 percent. Explain the mathematical basis for this rule of thumb.

3. Given $A = A_0 e^{kt}$, find an equation that expresses half-life as a function of the decay constant, k.

4. After what amount of time are these two investments equally valuable, a $1 investment at 10 percent, compounded continuously, and a $2 investment at 5 percent, compounded continuously?

5. The analysis of growth given limited resources often involves equations containing e. A common form is called the **logistic growth function.** The equations given in Exercises 69 and 70 both can be written in one of the characteristic forms of a logistic growth function:

$$y = \frac{L}{1 + be^{-kt}}.$$

To see what a typical logistic growth curve looks like, assume that $L = 100$, $b = 99$, and $k = 2$, and plot the graph of y. Construct a table for $t = 0, 1, 2, 3, 4, 5, 6$. In the given equation y represents the size of the growing entity and t represents elapsed time.

CHAPTER 8 OVERVIEW

Section	Key Concepts or Procedures to Review
8.1	■ Definition of the exponential function with base b
	■ For $f(x) = b^x$ with $b > 0, b \neq 1$:
	Domain: $(-\infty,\infty)$ Horizontal asymptote: x-axis
	Range: $(0,\infty)$ y-intercept: $(0,1)$
	If $b > 1$, f represents exponential growth.
	If $0 < b < 1$, f represents exponential decay.
	■ Methods from Section 2.5 to graph variations of $f(x) = b^x$
	■ If $b > 0, b \neq 1$, then $b^x = b^y$ implies $x = y$.
	■ Formula for the compounded amount A when a principal P is compounded annually for t years at annual interest rate r:
	$$A = P(1 + r)^t$$
8.2	■ Definitions of one-to-one functions and inverse functions
	■ The special symbol f^{-1} is used to denote the inverse of function f.
	■ Methods to determine if the inverse of a function exists and to find f^{-1}, if it exists
	■ f and f^{-1} interchange their domain and range.
	■ f and f^{-1} are reflections of each other about the line $y = x$.
8.3	■ Definitions of logarithm and logarithmic function with base b
	■ $\log_b N = L$ is equivalent to $b^L = N$.
	■ The logarithmic function $y = \log_b x$ and the exponential function $y = b^x$ are inverse functions. Therefore:
	(a) their domain and range are interchanged;
	(b) their graphs are reflections of each other about the line $y = x$.
	■ For $f(x) = \log_b x$ (with $b > 0, b \neq 1$):
	Domain: $(0,\infty)$ Range: $(-\infty,\infty)$
	x-intercept: $(1,0)$ Vertical asymptote: y-axis
	If $b > 1$, then as x increases, y increases.
	If $0 < b < 1$, then as x increases, y decreases.
	■ Methods from Section 2.5 to graph variations of $y = \log_b x$.
	■ $\log_{10} N$ is usually abbreviated as $\log N$.

8.4   ■ Properties of logarithms (for $b, x, y > 0, b \neq 1$, and k any real number):

1. $\log_b xy = \log_b x + \log_b y$

2. $\log_b \dfrac{x}{y} = \log_b x - \log_b y$

3. $\log_b x^k = k \log_b x$

4. $\log_b b = 1$

5. $\log_b 1 = 0$

6. $\log_b b^x = x$

7. $b^{\log_b x} = x$

8.5   ■ If $x, y, b > 0$ with $b \neq 1$, then $x = y$ implies $\log_b x = \log_b y$; and $\log_b x = \log_b y$ implies $x = y$.

■ Change-of-base formula:

$$\log_b x = \frac{\log_a x}{\log_a b}$$

■ Methods to solve exponential and logarithmic equations

8.6   ■ Compound-interest formula:

$$A = P\left(1 + \frac{r}{n}\right)^{nt}$$

■ As n gets larger, $\left(1 + \dfrac{1}{n}\right)^n$ gets closer to an irrational number that is denoted by the letter e. To six significant digits, $e \approx 2.71828$.

■ Continuous-compounding formula: $A = Pe^{rt}$.

■ The general formula for continuous growth or decay is $A = A_0 e^{kt}$.

■ $\log_e x$ is usually abbreviated as $\ln x$.

■ $y = \ln x$ and $y = e^x$ are inverse functions.

■ Graphs of $y = \ln x$ and $y = e^x$

■ Properties of natural logarithms:

1. $\ln xy = \ln x + \ln y$

2. $\ln \dfrac{x}{y} = \ln x - \ln y$

3. $\ln x^k = k \ln x$

4. $\ln e^x = x$

5. $e^{\ln x} = x$, if $x > 0$

CHAPTER 8 REVIEW EXERCISES

1. If $f(x) = 9^x$, find $f(2), f(-3)$, and $f\left(\frac{3}{2}\right)$. Also, approximate $f\left(\sqrt{2}\right)$ to the nearest hundredth.

2. Sketch the graph of $f(x) = \left(\frac{1}{3}\right)^x$.

3. Solve $16^x = 64$.

4. Find the base of the exponential function $y = b^x$ that contains the point $\left(-\frac{1}{2}, \frac{1}{2}\right)$.

5. At what interest rate compounded annually must a sum of money be invested if it is to double in 6 years?

6. If $f = \{(-2, 3), (-1, 5), (0, 7)\}$, find f^{-1} and determine its domain and range.

7. Which functions graphed in this figure have inverse functions?

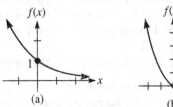

(a)

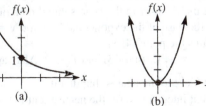

(b)

8. Use the graph of $y = f(x)$ in the figure to graph $y = f^{-1}(x)$.

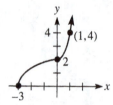

9. Find $f^{-1}(x)$ for the function $f(x) = -3x + 2$.

10. Verify that $f(x) = \sqrt{x - 1}$ and

$g(x) = x^2 + 1$, $x \geq 1$, are inverses of each other.

11. An inventor's portfolio loses one-sixth of its value during its first year. For the following year, what percent increase is needed for the portfolio to return to its original value?

12. Write $\log_b y = x$ in exponential form.

13. Determine the value of a: $\log_a \frac{1}{16} = -2$.

14. Graph $y = -\log_{1/2} x$.

15. Evaluate log 650 to four decimal places.

16. Determine [H$^+$] for a sample of unknown solution whose pH is 8.2.

17. Express as a sum, difference, or product involving simpler logarithms: $\log_b \sqrt{\dfrac{2x}{y}}$.

18. Simplify the expression $3^{\log_3 81}$.

19. Express as a single logarithm with coefficient 1: $5 \log_{10} x + \frac{1}{3} \log_{10} 8$.

20. If $\log_b 2 = m$ and $\log_b 3 = n$, then express $\log_b \frac{1}{27}$ in terms of m and/or n.

21. Solve $5^x = 18$. Give the solution to five significant digits.

22. Evaluate $\log_5 8$ to four significant digits.

23. Solve $\log(3x + 1) = \log x$.

24. Solve $\log_2(5x + 3) = 3$.

25. $8,000 is invested at 6 percent compounded monthly. How much is the investment worth in 10 years?

26. $8,000 is invested at 7 percent compounded continuously. How much is the investment worth in 15 years?

27. Solve $e^{0.12t} = 0.6$. Give the solution to four significant digits.

28. Solve $\ln 5 = 3 - \ln x$. Give the exact answer and also an approximate solution to four significant digits.

29. At what rate of interest compounded continuously must money be deposited if the amount is to double in 12 years? Answer to the nearest hundredth of a percent.

30. Find the base of the exponential function $y = b^x$ that contains the point $(4, 3)$.

31. If $f(x) = \left(\frac{1}{2}\right)^x$, find $f(3)$ and $f(-2)$. Also, approximate $f\sqrt{2}$ to the nearest hundredth.

32. At what interest rate (to the nearest tenth of a percent) compounded annually must a sum of money be invested to triple in 18 years?

33. $9,000 is invested at 5.5 percent compounded continuously. How much is the money worth in 8 years?

34. How long (to the nearest year) would it take the world's population to double if the annual growth rate was 2.65 percent?

35. Certain municipal workers accept a 15 percent cut in annual salary to avoid layoffs. What percent raise (to the nearest hundredth of a percent) will then be needed to return these employees to their original annual salary?

36. At what interest rate compounded continuously (to the nearest hundredth of a percent) must money be deposited if the amount is to double in 8 years?

37. $10,000 is invested at 6 percent compounded annually. How much is the investment worth after 7 years?

38. $1,000 is invested in an IRA account by a graduate student on her 25th birthday. If the account grows at 6.8 percent compounded daily, what will the value of the account be on her 65th birthday?

39. Find the pH (to the nearest tenth) of a solution whose hydrogen ion concentration [H$^+$] is 4.5×10^{-8}.

40. A scientist has 1 g of a radioactive element. This element is decaying to one-half its amount at a given time after 1 hour has elapsed. Approximately how much of this element is left at the end of 1 day?

Determine the value of the unknown in each expression.

41. $\log_4 32 = x$

42. $\log_6 1 = y$

43. $\log_{10} x = -2$

44. $\log_b 3 = \frac{1}{2}$

Express in logarithmic form.

45. $3^0 = 1$

46. $10^1 = 10$

47. $5^x = 125$

Express in exponential form.

48. $\log_{10} 1 = 0$

49. $\log_{10} 3 = x$

50. $\log_b 2 = -3$

Express as a sum, difference, or product involving simpler logarithms.

51. $\log_{10} x^6$

52. $\log_b \sqrt{7}$

53. $\log_b 8(x + 1)^3$

54. $\log_{10} \frac{1}{5}$

Express as a single logarithm with coefficient 1.

55. $\log_{10} x + \log_{10}(x + 2)$

56. $\frac{1}{3}[\log_2 3 - \log_2 x]$

57. $3 \log_b x + \frac{1}{2}\log_b 4$

Simplify.

58. $\log_6 6^{-2}$

59. $2^{\log_2 32}$

Solve. Give exact answers unless otherwise indicated.

60. $25^x = 125$

61. $\log N = -3.2$ (three significant digits)

62. $\log_4(2x - 10) = 3$
63. $\ln x = 2.5$ (four significant digits)
64. $e^{-0.05t} = 6$ (four significant digits)
65. $4^x = 3^{x+1}$ (four significant digits)
66. $\log x = \log(2 - x)$
67. $-\ln 2 + 4 = \ln x$
68. $\log 500 = x$ (four significant digits)
69. $6^x = 9$ (four significant digits)
70. $\log_2(x - 6) = 4 - \log_2 x$
71. $\log_{1/2} 0.6 = x$ (four significant digits)

Find the inverse of each function. If no inverse function exists, state this.

72. $f = \{(-2, 2), (-1, 3), (0, 4)\}$
73. $f = \{(3, 1), (0, 2), (-3, 1)\}$
74. $f = \{(-4, 4), (0, 0), (4, -4)\}$
75. $f(x) = 4x - 3$

76. $f(x) = 2x^2$

77. $f(x) = \dfrac{x - 1}{2}$

78. $f(x)$

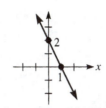

79. $f(x)$

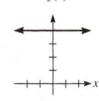

Sketch the graph.

80. $y = -\left(\frac{1}{3}\right)^x$
82. $y = \log_{1/3} x$

81. $y = 2^x - 3$
83. $y = \log_3(x + 5)$

CHAPTER 8 TEST

1. Express in logarithmic form: $b^3 = 8$.
2. Express in exponential form: $\ln x = \frac{1}{2}$.
3. Evaluate $\log_5 \frac{1}{125}$.
4. Simplify $7^{2 \log_7 6}$.
5. Find the base of the exponential function $y = b^x$ that contains the point $(-4, 16)$.
6. Express as a single logarithm with coefficient 1: $4 \log_2 x - \log_2 3$.
7. Express as a sum, difference, or product involving simpler logarithms: $\log_b 8\sqrt{x}$.
8. Evaluate $\log_6 11$ to four significant digits.
9. If $f(x) = \dfrac{5x - 6}{4}$, determine $f^{-1}(x)$.
10. Verify that $f(x) = x^2 - 2$ and $g(x) = \sqrt{x + 2}$, $x \geq 0$, are inverses of each other.
11. \$5,000 is invested at 7 percent compounded monthly. How much is the investment worth in 30 years?
12. At what rate of interest compounded continuously must money be deposited if the amount is to triple in 20 years? Answer to the nearest hundredth of a percent.

13. Solve $7^x = 0.9$. Give the solution to four significant digits.
14. If $\log N = -0.6$, find N to three significant digits.
15. Solve $2^{x-2} = 6^x$. Give the solution to four significant digits.
16. Solve $\log_4(10x + 4) = 3$.
17. Solve $e^{-0.8t} = 0.5$. Give the solution to four significant digits.
18. Graph $f(x) = -2^x$.
19. Graph $f(x) = \log_2 x + 1$.
20. Use the graph of $y = f(x)$ in the figure to graph $y = f^{-1}(x)$.

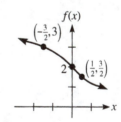

Topics in Trigonometry

The **latitude** of the location of a point on the Earth's surface specifies the angle north or south of the equator between the location and the plane of the Earth's equator. Find, to the nearest 10 minutes, the latitude of Chicago, Illinois, which is 2,890 mi north of the equator. Assume that the Earth is a sphere of radius 3,960 mi.
(See Example 4 of Section 9.1)

In Chapter 4 we initially viewed trigonometry in terms of right triangles, and then expanded our coverage to the general angle definitions of the trigonometric functions. We now consider the modern concept of the trigonometric functions of real numbers, which is the approach most useful when time is the independent variable. We begin by considering the radian measure of an angle. Radians are used extensively in calculus and are the link that makes a cohesive unit of trigonometry.

9.1   Radians

OBJECTIVES

1   Use $\theta = s/r$ to find either the central angle, the intercepted arc, or the radius, given measures for two variables in the relationship.

2   Convert from degree measure of an angle to radian measure, and vice versa.

3   Determine the area of a sector of a circle, given the radius and the central angle.

4   Find linear velocity, given an angular velocity and a radius.

5   Find angular velocity, given a linear velocity and a radius.

Up to now we have measured angles in degrees. However, in many applications of trigonometry, a different angle measure,—called a **radian,**—is more useful. We define the radian measure of an angle by first placing the vertex of the angle at the center of a circle. Let s be the length of the intercepted arc, and let r be the radius. Then

$$\theta = \frac{s}{r}$$

is the radian measure of the angle (see Figure 9.1). Equivalently, an angle measuring 1 radian intercepts an arc equal in length to the radius of the circle (see Figure 9.2). In plane geometry it is shown that *s varies directly as r,* so that we can find the radian measure of θ by using a circle of *any* radius.

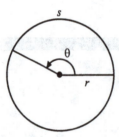

Figure 9.1

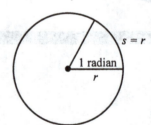

Figure 9.2

EXAMPLE 1   Finding the Radian Measure of an Angle

A central angle in a circle of radius 3 in. intercepts an arc of 12 in. Find the radian measure of the angle.

Solution   Substituting $r = 3$ in. and $s = 12$ in. in the formula

$$\theta = \frac{s}{r},$$

we have

$$\theta = \frac{12 \text{ in.}}{3 \text{ in.}} = 4.$$

Thus, the radian measure of the angle is 4. Note that r and s are measured in the same unit, which divides out in the ratio. Thus, the radian measure of an angle is a number without dimension. Although the word "radian" is often added, an angle measure with no units means radian measure.

PROGRESS CHECK 1 In a circle a central angle intercepts an arc equal in length to one-half the circumference of the circle. What is the measure of the central angle in radians? (**Hint:** Recall that $C = 2\pi r$.) ■

We may find the relation between degrees and radians by considering the measure of an angle that makes one complete rotation. In degrees, the measure of the angle is 360. Since the circumference of a circle is $2\pi r$, the radian measure is

$$\theta = \frac{s}{r} = \frac{2\pi r}{r} = 2\pi.$$

Thus,

$$360° = 2\pi \text{ radians.}$$

From this relation we derive the following conversion rules between degrees and radians.

Degree-Radian Conversion Rules

Degrees to radians formula:

$$1° = \frac{\pi}{180} \text{ radians} \approx 0.0175 \text{ radians}$$

Radians to degree formula:

$$1 \text{ radian} = \frac{180°}{\pi} \approx 57.3°.$$

EXAMPLE 2   Converting from Degrees to Radians
Express 30°, 45°, and 270°, in terms of radians.

Solution   Using the degrees to radians formulas, we have

$$30° = 30 \cdot 1° = 30 \cdot \frac{\pi}{180} = \frac{\pi}{6}$$

$$45° = 45 \cdot 1° = 45 \cdot \frac{\pi}{180} = \frac{\pi}{4}$$

$$270° = 270 \cdot 1° = 270 \cdot \frac{\pi}{180} = \frac{3\pi}{2}.$$

PROGRESS CHECK 2   Express 90°, 100°, and 315° in terms of radians. ■

EXAMPLE 3   Converting from Radians to Degrees
Express $\frac{\pi}{3}$, π, and $\frac{7\pi}{5}$ radians in terms of degrees.

Solution   Using the radians to degrees formula, we have

$$\frac{\pi}{3} = \frac{\pi}{3} \cdot 1 = \frac{\pi}{3} \cdot \frac{180°}{\pi} = 60°$$

$$\pi = \pi \cdot 1 = \pi \cdot \frac{180°}{\pi} = 180°$$

$$\frac{7\pi}{5} = \frac{7\pi}{5} \cdot 1 = \frac{7\pi}{5} \cdot \frac{180°}{\pi} = 252°.$$

PROGRESS CHECK 3   Express $\frac{\pi}{9}$, $\frac{2\pi}{5}$, and $\frac{5\pi}{2}$ radians in terms of degrees.   ■

EXAMPLE 4   Finding Latitude
Solve the problem in the chapter introduction on page 473.

Solution   A sketch of the situation in the problem is shown in Figure 9.3. Angle θ specifies the latitude for Chicago, and θ in radians is given by

$$\theta = \frac{s}{r} = \frac{2890 \text{ mi}}{3960 \text{ mi}} = \frac{289}{396}.$$

To convert this result to degrees, we multiply by $180°/\pi$ to obtain

$$\theta = \frac{289}{396} \cdot \frac{180°}{\pi} \approx 41.814°,$$

as shown in Figure 9.4. Finally, to convert to degree-minute format multiply the decimal portion of angle θ by 60 minutes, as shown in the last four lines of Figure 9.4. To the nearest 10 minutes, the decimal portion rounds to 50 minutes, so the latitude of Chicago is 41°50′ N.

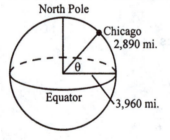

Figure 9.3

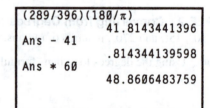

Figure 9.4

PROGRESS CHECK 4   Find, to the nearest 10 minutes, the latitude of Baltimore, Maryland, which is 2,720 mi north of the equator. Assume that the earth is a sphere of radius 3960 mi.   ■

To illustrate another application of radians, consider the problem of determining the area of the shaded section in Figure 9.5. If you do not remember from geometry, notice intuitively that the area (A) varies directly as the central angle (θ). That is,

$$A = k\theta, \text{ where } k \text{ is a constant.}$$

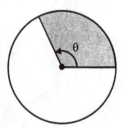

Figure 9.5

We may find k, since we know that $A = \pi r^2$ when the angle (θ) is a complete rotation of 2π radians. Thus,

$$\pi r^2 = k \cdot 2\pi$$
$$\tfrac{1}{2}r^2 = k.$$

The formula (when θ is expressed in radians) is then

$$A = \tfrac{1}{2}r^2\theta.$$

EXAMPLE 5   Finding the Area of a Sector of a Circle

In a circle of radius 12 in., find the area of a sector whose central angle is 120°.

Solution   To use the formula, we must first convert the angle to radians.

$$120° = 120 \cdot \frac{\pi}{180} = \frac{2\pi}{3}$$

Now, substituting $r = 12$ and $\theta = 2\pi/3$ in the formula

$$A = \tfrac{1}{2}r^2\theta,$$

we have

$$A = \tfrac{1}{2}(12)^2 \cdot \frac{2\pi}{3} = 48\pi \text{ in.}^2.$$

PROGRESS CHECK 5   Find the area of a sector of a circle whose central angle is 135° and whose radius is 8 ft.   ■

One of the important applications of radians concerns linear and angular velocity. If a point P moves along the circumference of a circle at a constant speed, then the linear velocity v is given by the formula

$$v = \frac{s}{t},$$

where s is the distance traveled by the point (or the length of the arc traversed), and t is the time required to travel this distance. During the same time interval, the radius of the circle connected to point P swings through θ angular units. Thus, the angular velocity ω (Greek lowercase omega) is given by

$$\omega = \frac{\theta}{t}.$$

We can relate linear and angular velocity through the familiar formula

$$s = \theta r.$$

Dividing both sides of this equation by t, we obtain

$$\frac{s}{t} = \frac{\theta}{t}r.$$

Substituting v for s/t and ω for θ/t yields

$$v = \omega r.$$

Thus, the linear velocity is equal to the product of the angular velocity and the radius.

Since $s = \theta r$ is valid only when θ is measured in radians, the angular velocity ω must be expressed in radians per unit of time when using the formula $v = \omega r$. However, in many common applications, the angular velocity is expressed in revolutions per minute. For these problems remember to convert ω to radians (rad) per unit of time through the relationship 1 rpm = 2π rad/minute, before using the formula.

EXAMPLE 6 Angular Velocity and Linear Velocity

A circular saw blade 12 in. in diameter rotates at 1,600 rpm. Find

a. the angular velocity in radians per second and
b. the linear velocity in inches per second at which the teeth would strike a piece of wood.

Solution

a. Since 1 rpm = 2π rad/minute, we have

$$\omega = 1{,}600 \text{ rpm} = 1{,}600\left(2\pi\frac{\text{rad}}{\text{minute}}\right) = 3{,}200\pi\frac{\text{rad}}{\text{minute}}.$$

To convert to rad/second, we use 1 minute = 60 seconds, as follows:

$$\omega = 3{,}200\pi\frac{\text{rad}}{\text{minute}}\frac{1 \text{ minute}}{60 \text{ seconds}} = \frac{160\pi}{3}\frac{\text{rad}}{\text{second}}.$$

b. Since ω is expressed in radians per unit of time, we find v by the formula $v = \omega r$, with $r = 6$ in.

$$v = \omega r$$
$$= \frac{160\pi}{3}\frac{\text{rad}}{\text{seconds}} \cdot 6 \text{ in.}$$
$$= 320\pi\frac{\text{in.}}{\text{second}}$$

Remember that the radian measure of an angle is a number without dimension, so the word *radian* does not appear in the units for linear velocity.

PROGRESS CHECK 6 A phonograph record 7 in. in diameter is being played at 45 rpm.

a. Find the angular velocity in radians per minute.
b. Find the linear velocity in inches per minute of a point on the circumference of the record.

■

EXERCISES 9.1

In Exercises 1–8 complete the table by replacing each question mark with the appropriate number.

The Radius Is	The Intercepted Arc Is	The Central Angle Is
1. 20 ft	100 ft	?
2. 8 in.	?	3
3. ?	56 yd	7
4. 5.2 m	5.2 m	?
5. ?	4.8 m	$\frac{1}{2}$
6. 11 ft	?	3.2
7. 1 unit	5 units	?
8. 1 unit	π units	?

In Exercises 9–28 express each angle in radian measure.

9. 30°   **10.** 45°
11. 60°   **12.** 90°
13. 120°   **14.** 135°
15. 150°   **16.** 180°
17. 210°   **18.** 225°
19. 240°   **20.** 270°

21. 300°

22. 315°

23. 330°

24. 360°

25. 200°

26. 75°

27. 20°

28. 162°

In Exercises 29–40 express each angle in degree measure.

29. $\dfrac{\pi}{3}$

30. $\dfrac{\pi}{4}$

31. $\dfrac{2\pi}{9}$

32. $\dfrac{\pi}{6}$

33. $\dfrac{2\pi}{3}$

34. $\dfrac{11\pi}{6}$

35. $\dfrac{7\pi}{9}$

36. $\dfrac{13\pi}{10}$

37. $\dfrac{12\pi}{5}$

38. $\dfrac{2\pi}{15}$

39. $\dfrac{7\pi}{18}$

40. $\dfrac{\pi}{12}$

In Exercises 41–46 find, to the nearest degree, the number of degrees in each angle. (**Note:** Use $\pi \approx 3.14$.)

41. 2

42. 1

43. 4

44. 6

45. 5.8

46. 3.5

47. Refer to Example 4 of Section 9.1. Find, to the nearest 10 minutes, the latitude of Miami, Florida, which is about 1,762 miles north of the equator.

48. Refer to Example 4 of Section 9.1. Find, to the nearest 10 minutes, the latitude of Bellingham, Washington, which is about 3,366 miles north of the equator.

49. a. Starting at the equator, if a ship sails north at 20 miles per hour, then to the nearest degree, what will its latitude be in 24 hours?

  b. Find the ship's average speed in degrees per hour.

50. a. Starting at the equator, if a ship sails south at 25 miles per hour, then to the nearest degree, what will its latitude be in 24 hours?

  b. Find the ship's average speed in degrees per hour.

51. If you consider Earth to be a sphere of radius 3,960 miles, then, to the nearest mile, how many miles north of the equator is latitude 1 degree?

52. If you consider Earth to be a sphere of radius 6,373 kilometers, then, to the nearest kilometer, how many kilometers north of the equator is latitude 1 degree?

For Exercises 53 and 54: When a ship travels at 4 **knots,** that means it travels 4 **nautical miles per hour.** The original idea of a nautical mile was 1 minute of arc along the equator. For ordinary calculations, the nautical mile can be considered equal to 1.15 mi.

53. If a ship travels due north from latitude 0° to latitude 2° in 12 hours, find its average speed in knots, to the nearest whole number.

54. If a ship travels from latitude 10° to latitude 15° in 24 hours, find its average speed in knots, to the nearest whole number.

55. Find the area of a sector of a circle whose central angle is $\dfrac{\pi}{4}$ and whose radius is 10 in.

56. Find the area of a sector of a circle whose central angle is 120° and whose radius is 5 in.

57. In a circle of radius 2 ft, the arc length of a sector is 8 ft. Find the area of the sector.

58. In a circle of radius 5 ft, the arc length of a sector is 3 ft. Find the area of the sector.

59. The radius of a wheel is 20 in. When the wheel moves 110 in., through how many radians does a point on the wheel turn? How many revolutions are made by the wheel?

60. The radius of a wheel is 16 in. Find the number of radians through which a point on the circumference turns when the wheel moves a distance of 2 ft. How many revolutions are made by the wheel?

61. What is the angular velocity in radians/second of an object that moves along the circumference of a circle of radius 9 in. with a linear velocity of 54 in./second?

62. What is the angular velocity in radians/second of the minute hand of a clock?

63. A phonograph record 12 in. in diameter is being played at $33\frac{1}{3}$ rpm.

  a. Find the angular velocity in radians/minute.

  b. Find the linear velocity in inches/minute of a point on the circumference of the record.

64. A pulley 20 in. in diameter makes 400 rpm.

  a. Find the angular velocity in radians/second.

  b. Find the speed in inches/minute of the belt that drives the pulley.

  (**Note:** The speed of a point on the circumference of the pulley is the same as the speed of the belt.)

65. In a dynamo, an armature 12 in. in diameter makes 1,500 rpm. Find the linear velocity in inches/second of the tip of the armature.

66. What is the linear velocity in inches/second of an object that moves along the circumference of a circle of radius 12 in. with an angular velocity of 7 rad/second?

67. A train is traveling at 120 mi/hr (176 ft/second) on wheels 40 in. in diameter. Find the angular velocity of the wheels in radians per minute.

68. A car is traveling at 60 mi/hr (88 ft/second) on tires 30 in. in diameter. Find the angular velocity of the tires in radians/second.

69. Arcs of circles are used in many styles of molding that can be found in homes. Consider the figure shown here. If $\overline{AB} = \overline{DE} = \frac{1}{2}\overline{BC} = \frac{1}{2}\overline{CD}$ and $\overline{AB} = \frac{1}{2}$ in., what is the length of the curved portion of the molding?

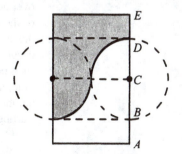

70. Refer to Exercise 69. If the length of $\overline{AB}$ is $\frac{3}{4}$ in., what is the length of the curved portion of the molding?

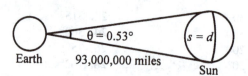

Earth   93,000,000 miles   Sun

$\theta = 0.53°$ $s = d$

THINK ABOUT IT 9.1

1. If a central angle of α radians intercepts an arc of length a in a circle of radius b, express b in terms of α and a.

2. In a circle a central angle intercepts an arc equal in length to $\frac{5}{8}$ of the diameter of the circle. What is the measure of the central angle in radians?

3. Express $74°25'12''$ in radian measure to four significant digits.

4. The formula $s = \theta r$ may be used to estimate certain distances when θ is a small angle (to about $10°$). For example, consider the given illustration. An observer measures the angle from Earth to opposite ends of the sun's diameter to be $0.53°$. Since θ is a small angle, the arc length s is a good approximation for the diameter d. If the distance from Earth to the sun is 93,000,000 mi, determine the diameter of the sun to two significant digits.

5. In architecture, arcs of circles are basic to the construction of many beautiful designs. For example, consider the quatrefoil in this illustration. If the side of the square measures 4 in., determine
a. the perimeter of the quatrefoil and
b. the area of the quatrefoil (the shaded portion of the figure).

Courtesy of Prentice-Hall, Inc.

9.2 Trigonometric Functions of Real Numbers

The monthly revenue R in dollars from sales of a sunscreen product in the New York region during a certain year is approximated by

$$R = 6{,}500 - 5{,}000 \cos(0.5236t),$$

where t is the number of months that have elapsed from February 1. Following this model, estimate the monthly revenue for this product for March and for August of the year in question. (See Example 8.)

OBJECTIVES

1 Determine the exact value of any trigonometric function of an arc length that terminates at one of the axes.

2 Determine the exact value of any trigonometric function of an arc length with a reference arc of $\pi/6$, $\pi/4$, or $\pi/3$.

3 Use a calculator to approximate a trigonometric value of a real number.

4 Solve applied problems involving the evaluating of a trigonometric function of a real number.

The revenue for a company from sales of a seasonal product, which is considered in the section-opening problem, provides one example of the many common events that repeat over definite periods of time. The waves broadcast by a radio station; the rhythmic motion of the heart; alternating electric current; weather-related issues such as air pollution; and the economic pattern of expansion, retrenchment, recession, and recovery—all these occur in cycles. The trigonometric functions, also repetitive, are very useful in analyzing such periodic phenomena. However, the independent variable in these applications is the time, not the angle. Thus, we need to define the trigonometric functions in terms of real numbers, not degrees. Since radians measure angles in terms of real numbers, they are the starting point for our discussion of the trigonometry of real numbers.

Consider Figure 9.6, in which the central angle θ is measured in radians. It is convenient to label the radius of the circle as 1 unit so that $r = 1$. Then

$$\theta = \frac{s}{r} = \frac{s}{1}$$

$$\theta = s.$$

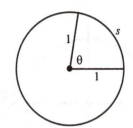

Figure 9.6

In a unit circle the same real number measures both the central angle θ and the intercepted arc s. Thus, we may base the definitions of the trigonometric functions on either an angle or an arc length. The results are valid for both interpretations. Since angles are less helpful in periodic phenomena, it is useful to emphasize the interpretation of a real number as the measure of an arc length s. We liberally interpret arc length as the distance traveled by a point as it moves around the unit circle, repeating its behavior every 2π units.

To illustrate more forcefully the correspondence between real numbers and arc lengths, consider a unit circle with its center at the origin of the Cartesian coordinate system. The equation of this circle is $x^2 + y^2 = 1$. Through the point $(1, 0)$ and parallel to the y-axis we draw a real number line, labeled s. The zero point of s coincides with the point $(1, 0)$ on the circle. Units are marked off in the same scale as the y-axis (see Figure 9.7).

If the positive half of s is wrapped around the circle counterclockwise, and the negative half of s is wrapped around the circle clockwise, we establish a one-to-one correspondence between real numbers and arc lengths of the circle (see Figure 9.8). Thus, each numbered point on s coincides with exactly one point on the circle, and the length of an arc may be read from this curved s-axis. We now relate this discussion to trigonometry.

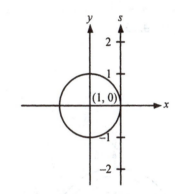

Figure 9.7

Definition of the Sine and Cosine Functions

Consider a point (x, y) on the unit circle $x^2 + y^2 = 1$ at arc length s from $(1, 0)$. We define the cosine of s to be the x-coordinate of the point, and the sine of s to be the y-coordinate.

$$\cos s = x$$
$$\sin s = y$$

Note in Figure 9.9 that our definitions are consistent with the definitions of sine and cosine in terms of the sides and hypotenuse of a right triangle. The domain of both the sine and cosine functions is the set of all real numbers, since the arc length s is determined by wrapping a real number line around the unit circle. The x- and y-coordinates in a unit circle vary between -1 and 1 (inclusive). Thus, for the range we have

$$-1 \leq \cos s \leq 1$$
$$-1 \leq \sin s \leq 1.$$

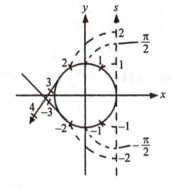

Figure 9.8

The remaining trigonometric functions are defined as follows:

Name of Function	Abbreviation	Ratio	
tangent of s	tan s	$y/x = \sin s/\cos s$	$(x \neq 0)$
cotangent of s	cot s	$x/y = 1/\tan s$	$(y \neq 0)$
secant of s	sec s	$1/x = 1/\cos s$	$(x \neq 0)$
cosecant of s	csc s	$1/y = 1/\sin s$	$(y \neq 0)$

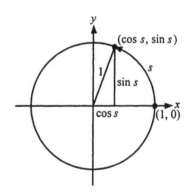

Figure 9.9

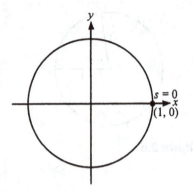

Figure 9.10

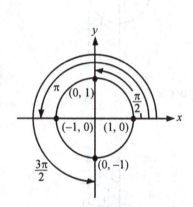

Figure 9.11

We evaluate trigonometric functions of real numbers by using these definitions or by using a calculator. Once again, the calculator method is most efficient for evaluating a trigonometric expression. Just set the calculator for Radian mode and use the appropriate function keys, as discussed in Section 4.1. However, this shortcut bypasses many important ideas in trigonometry. So let us consider how to evaluate the trigonometric functions from their definitions, as we did in Section 4.3.

Using the above definitions, we find the values of the trigonometric functions by determining the rectangular coordinates (x, y) of points on the unit circle. For certain real numbers these coordinates are easy to find. For example, let us determine the values of the trigonometric functions of zero. The coordinates for an arc length of zero are $(1, 0)$ (see Figure 9.10). Thus,

$$\sin 0 = y = 0 \quad \leftarrow \text{reciprocals} \rightarrow \quad \csc 0 = \frac{1}{y} = \frac{1}{0}\text{undefined}$$

$$\cos 0 = x = 1 \quad \leftarrow \text{reciprocals} \rightarrow \quad \sec 0 = \frac{1}{x} = \frac{1}{1} = 1$$

$$\tan 0 = \frac{x}{y} = \frac{0}{1} = 0 \quad \leftarrow \text{reciprocals} \rightarrow \quad \cot 0 = \frac{x}{y} = \frac{1}{0}\text{undefined.}$$

We can repeat this procedure for other arc lengths that terminate at one of the axes. Since the circumference of a circle of radius r is $2\pi r$, the circumference of a unit circle is 2π. The x- or y- axes may then intersect the unit circle at arc lengths of 0, $\pi/2$, π, $3\pi/2$, and so on. In the next example we consider how to find an exact trigonometric value when the arc length is $\pi/2$, π, or $3\pi/2$.

EXAMPLE 1   Evaluating Trigonometric Functions by Definition
Use the definition of the trigonometric functions to find each function value.

a. $\sin\dfrac{\pi}{2}$ **b.** $\cos \pi$ **c.** $\sec\dfrac{3\pi}{2}$

Solution Figure 9.11 shows the points on the unit circle that are assigned to $\pi/2$, π, and $3\pi/2$.
a. The point $(0, 1)$ is assigned to $\pi/2$, and $\sin s = y$, so $\sin(\pi/2) = 1$.
b. The point $(-1, 0)$ is assigned to π, and $\cos s = x$, so $\cos \pi = -1$.
c. The point $(0, -1)$ is assigned to $3\pi/2$, and $\sec s = 1/x$, so $\sec(3\pi/2) = 1/0$, which is undefined.

Technology Link
You should check these trigonometric evaluations by calculator, using the following guidelines on calculator usage.

1. Be sure to set the calculator for Radian mode.
2. Most calculators have a key labeled π that should be used to evaluate expressions involving π, as in this example.
3. You will often need to use parentheses around the argument of the trigonometric function. For instance,

$$\sin \pi/2 \text{ means } \frac{\sin \pi}{2},$$

while $\sin(\pi/2)$ means $\sin\dfrac{\pi}{2}$.

4. You may use

$$\csc s = \frac{1}{\sin s}, \ \sec s = \frac{1}{\cos s}, \ \text{or } \cot s = \frac{1}{\tan s}$$

to evaluate cosecant, secant, or cotangent expressions, respectively.

PROGRESS CHECK 1   Use the definition of the trigonometric functions to find each function value.

a. $\sin\dfrac{3\pi}{2}$ **b.** $\tan\pi$ **c.** $\csc\dfrac{\pi}{2}$ **d.** $\cot\dfrac{\pi}{2}$ ■

Trigonometric evaluations involving 0, $\pi/2$, π, and $3\pi/2$ appear often in trigonometry. It is, therefore, useful to use the methods shown in Example 1 to create the following table, which lists the exact values of all the trigonometric functions of these special numbers. Note that tabular values match our results for $0°$, $90°$, $180°$ and $270°$ from Section 4.3.

s	$\sin s$	$\csc s$	$\cos s$	$\sec s$	$\tan s$	$\cot s$
0	0	undefined	1	1	0	undefined
$\pi/2$	1	1	0	undefined	undefined	0
π	0	undefined	-1	-1	0	undefined
$3\pi/2$	-1	-1	0	undefined	undefined	0

Other numbers terminate at one of the axes, but their trigonometric values are the same as one of the four listed. For example, the trigonometric values of 2π are the same as the trigonometric values of 0, since both numbers are assigned the point $(1, 0)$ on the unit circle. The numbers $4\pi, 6\pi, -2\pi$, and -4π are also assigned this point. A basic fact in our development is that in laying off a length 2π, we pass around the circle and return to our original point. Thus, the x- and y-coordinates repeat themselves at intervals of length 2π, and for any trigonometric function f we have

$$f(s + 2\pi k) = f(s), \quad \text{where } k \text{ is an integer.}$$

For example,

$$f(4\pi) = f(0 + 2\pi(2)) = f(0)$$
$$f(-2\pi) = f(0 + 2\pi(-1)) = f(0).$$

This observation is very important because it means that if we determine the values of the trigonometric functions in the interval $[0, 2\pi)$, we know their values for all real s.

EXAMPLE 2   Using $f(s + 2\pi k) = f(s)$

Find $\sin 7\pi$, $\cos 12\pi$, $\tan\dfrac{11\pi}{2}$, $\cot\dfrac{17\pi}{2}$, and $\sec(-5\pi)$.

Solution   Since the values of the trigonometric functions repeat themselves at multiples of 2π, we have

$$\sin 7\pi = \sin(\pi + 6\pi) = \sin[\pi + 2\pi(3)] = \sin\pi = 0$$
$$\cos 12\pi = \cos(0 + 12\pi) = \cos[0 + 2\pi(6)] = \cos 0 = 1$$
$$\tan\frac{11\pi}{2} = \tan 5\tfrac{1}{2}\pi = \tan\left(\frac{3\pi}{2} + 4\pi\right) = \tan\left[\frac{3\pi}{2} + 2\pi(2)\right] = \tan\frac{3\pi}{2} \quad \text{undefined}$$
$$\cot\frac{17\pi}{2} = \cot 8\tfrac{1}{2}\pi = \cot\left(\frac{\pi}{2} + 8\pi\right) = \cot\left[\frac{\pi}{2} + 2\pi(4)\right] = \cot\frac{\pi}{2} = 0$$
$$\sec(-5\pi) = \sec[\pi + (-6\pi)] = \sec[\pi + 2\pi(-3)] = \sec\pi = -1$$

Check these results by calculator.

PROGRESS CHECK 2

Find $\sin\dfrac{7\pi}{2}$, $\cos 13\pi$, $\tan\dfrac{-5\pi}{2}$, $\sec 8\pi$, and $\csc\dfrac{15\pi}{2}$.   ■

A **trigonometric identity** is a statement that is true for all real numbers for which the expressions are defined. We simplify our work by developing identities that relate a trigonometric function of a negative number to the same function of a positive number. The symmetry of the unit circle makes these identities easy to derive. Consider Figures 9.12 and 9.13, which illustrate the symmetry for two possible values of s. Note that the numbers s and $-s$ are assigned the same x-coordinate, so

$$\cos(-s) = \cos s.$$

The y-coordinates differ only in their sign. Thus,

$$\sin(-s) = -\sin s.$$

The remaining functions are ratios of the sine and cosine, so it follows that

$$\tan(-s) = -\tan s$$
$$\cot(-s) = -\cot s$$
$$\sec(-s) = \sec s$$
$$\csc(-s) = -\csc s.$$

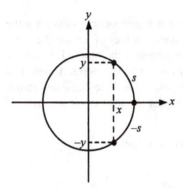

Figure 9.12   **Figure 9.13**

EXAMPLE 3   Using Negative Angle Identities

Find $\cos\dfrac{-3\pi}{2}$ and $\csc\dfrac{-5\pi}{2}$, using negative angle identities.

Solution $\cos(-s) = \cos s$ and $\csc(-s) = -\csc s$, so

$$\cos\left(\frac{-3\pi}{2}\right) = \cos\frac{3\pi}{2} = 0$$

$$\csc\left(\frac{-5\pi}{2}\right) = -\csc\frac{5\pi}{2} = -\csc 2\tfrac{1}{2}\pi = -\csc\left(\frac{\pi}{2} + 2\pi\right)$$

$$= -\csc\frac{\pi}{2} = -1.$$

You should confirm these results with a calculator.

PROGRESS CHECK 3 Find $\sin(-\pi/2)$ and $\sec(-3\pi)$, using negative angle identities. ■

Besides arc lengths that terminate at one of the axes, the numbers $\pi/4$, $\pi/3$, and $\pi/6$ are also considered special numbers. These numbers correspond to angles of $45°$, $60°$, and $30°$, respectively, and in Section 4.1 we derived their exact trigonometric values.

These results are given in the following table and repeated on the endpaper at the back of the book.

s	$\sin s$	$\csc s$	$\cos s$	$\sec s$	$\tan s$	$\cot s$
$\dfrac{\pi}{3}$	$\dfrac{\sqrt{3}}{2}$	$\dfrac{2}{\sqrt{3}}$	$\dfrac{1}{2}$	2	$\sqrt{3}$	$\dfrac{1}{\sqrt{3}}$
$\dfrac{\pi}{4}$	$\dfrac{1}{\sqrt{2}}$	$\sqrt{2}$	$\dfrac{1}{\sqrt{2}}$	$\sqrt{2}$	1	1
$\dfrac{\pi}{6}$	$\dfrac{1}{2}$	2	$\dfrac{\sqrt{3}}{2}$	$\dfrac{2}{\sqrt{3}}$	$\dfrac{1}{\sqrt{3}}$	$\sqrt{3}$

EXAMPLE 4   Evaluations Involving $\pi/3$, $\pi/4$ or $\pi/6$

Find the exact values of $\sin\dfrac{-\pi}{3}$, $\cos\dfrac{-\pi}{4}$, $\sin\dfrac{9\pi}{4}$, and $\tan\dfrac{13\pi}{3}$.

Solution   Using the table just developed and our previous procedure, we have

$$\sin\left(-\frac{\pi}{3}\right) = -\sin\frac{\pi}{3} = -\frac{\sqrt{3}}{2}$$

$$\cos\left(-\frac{\pi}{4}\right) = \cos\frac{\pi}{4} = \frac{1}{\sqrt{2}}$$

$$\sin\frac{9\pi}{4} = \sin 2\frac{1}{4}\pi = \sin\left(\frac{\pi}{4} + 2\pi\right) = \sin\frac{\pi}{4} = \frac{1}{\sqrt{2}}$$

$$\tan\frac{13\pi}{3} = \tan 4\frac{1}{3}\pi = \tan\left(\frac{\pi}{3} + 4\pi\right) = \tan\frac{\pi}{3} = \sqrt{3}.$$

To check these results by calculator, compare the decimal approximation from the calculator for a particular trigonometric evaluation to the approximation for the corresponding radical value. Such a check is shown in Figure 9.14 for the evaluation of $\sin(9\pi/4)$.

PROGRESS CHECK 4   Find the exact values of $\tan\dfrac{-\pi}{6}$ and $\sin\dfrac{7\pi}{3}$.   ■

A basic fact in our development has been that in laying off a length 2π, we pass around the unit circle and return to our original point. Thus, if we determine the values of the trigonometric functions in the interval $[0, 2\pi)$, we know their values for all real s. Consider Figure 9.15, which illustrates how the symmetry of the circle may be used to further simplify the evaluation.

Note that the coordinates of the point assigned to $\pi/6$ differ only in sign from the coordinates assigned to $\pi - \pi/6 = 5\pi/6$, $\pi + \pi/6 = 7\pi/6$, and $2\pi - \pi/6 = 11\pi/6$. Thus, for a specific trigonometric function, say sine, we have

$$\sin\frac{\pi}{6} = \left|\sin\frac{5\pi}{6}\right| = \left|\sin\frac{7\pi}{6}\right| = \left|\sin\frac{11\pi}{6}\right| = \frac{1}{2}.$$

The number $\pi/6$ is called the **reference number** for $5\pi/6$, $7\pi/6$, and $11\pi/6$. In general, we determine the reference number for s (denoted by s_R) by finding the shortest positive arc length between the point on the circle assigned to s and the x-axis. This discussion indicates that the trigonometric values of s and s_R are related as follows:

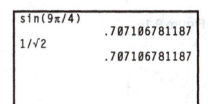

Figure 9.14

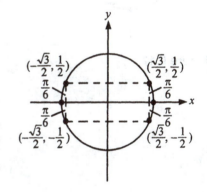

Figure 9.15

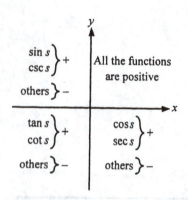

Figure 9.16

Trigonometric Values of s and s_R

Any trigonometric function of s is equal in absolute value to the same named function of its reference number s_R.

We determine the correct sign by considering the function definitions together with the sign of x and y in the four quadrants. The chart in Figure 9.16 indicates the signs of the functions in the various quadrants (and this diagram corresponds to our previous chart in Figure 4.25).

EXAMPLE 5   Evaluations Involving $\pi/3$, $\pi/4$ or $\pi/6$ Reference Numbers

Find the exact value of $\sin \dfrac{7\pi}{4}$.

Solution   First, determine the reference number.

$$s_R = 2\pi - \frac{7\pi}{4} = \frac{\pi}{4}\quad \text{(See Figure 9.17.)}$$

Second, determine $\sin(\pi/4)$.

$$\sin \frac{\pi}{4} = \frac{1}{\sqrt{2}}$$

Third, determine the correct sign. The point assigned to $7\pi/4$ is in Q_4, where the value of the sine function is negative. Therefore,

$$\sin \frac{7\pi}{4} = -\frac{1}{\sqrt{2}}.$$

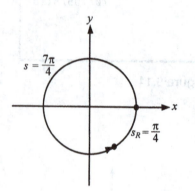

Figure 9.17

You should check this result by calculator.

PROGRESS CHECK 5   Find the exact value of $\cos \dfrac{11\pi}{6}$.   ■

EXAMPLE 6   Evaluations Involving $\pi/3$, $\pi/4$ or $\pi/6$ Reference Numbers

Find the exact value of $\cos \dfrac{-10\pi}{3}$.

Solution   First, simplify the expression to the form $\cos s$, where $0 \le s < 2\pi$.

$$\cos\left(\frac{-10\pi}{3}\right) = \cos \frac{10\pi}{3} = \cos 3\tfrac{1}{3}\pi = \cos\left(\frac{4\pi}{3} + 2\pi\right) = \cos \frac{4\pi}{3}$$

Second, determine s_R.

$$s_R = \frac{4\pi}{3} - \pi = \frac{\pi}{3}\ \text{(See Figure 9.18.)}$$

Third, determine $\cos(\pi/3)$.

$$\cos \frac{\pi}{3} = \tfrac{1}{2}$$

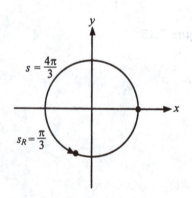

Figure 9.18

Fourth, determine the correct sign. The point assigned to $4\pi/3$ is in Q_3, where the value of the cosine function is negative. Therefore,

$$\cos\left(\frac{-10\pi}{3}\right) = -\frac{1}{2}.$$

Check this result by calculator.

PROGRESS CHECK 6 Find the exact value of $\sin\dfrac{-17\pi}{3}$. ■

Arc lengths that terminate on an axis or that have reference numbers of $\pi/3$, $\pi/4$, or $\pi/6$ may be considered special cases because exact values may be found for trigonometric functions of these numbers. For other numbers, we can easily approximate their function values by using a calculator, as shown in the next two examples.

EXAMPLE 7 Approximating Trigonometric Values by Calculator

Find the approximate value of each expression. Round off answers to four decimal places.

a. $\sin 2$ **b.** $\sec\dfrac{8\pi}{5}$

Solution See Figure 9.19.

a. $\sin 2 \approx 0.9093$. Note that a calculator interprets $\sin 2$ to mean the sine of 2 radians or the sine of 2 degrees, depending on the mode setting for the unit of angle measure.

b. Using $\sec(8\pi/5) = 1/\cos(8\pi/5)$ yields $\sec(8\pi/5) \approx 3.2361$,

PROGRESS CHECK 7 Find the approximate value of each expression. Round off answers to four decimal places.

a. $\cos 5$ **b.** $\cot\dfrac{9\pi}{7}$ ■

EXAMPLE 8 Revenue from Sales of a Seasonal Product

Solve the problem in the section introduction on page 480.

Solution By the end of March, 2 months have elapsed from February 1, and replacing t by 2 in the given formula yields

$$R = 6{,}500 - 5{,}000\cos(0.5236 \cdot 2) \approx \$4{,}000.$$

In a similar way, 7 months elapse from February 1 to the end of August, and replacing t by 7 gives

$$R = 6{,}500 - 5{,}000\cos(0.5236 \cdot 7) \approx \$10{,}830.$$

Thus, the estimates from the formula are that monthly revenue for March was \$4,000, and the monthly revenue for August was \$10,830.

PROGRESS CHECK 8 On May 2, the tide in a certain harbor is described by $y = 12 + 5.3\cos(0.5067t)$, where y is the height of the water in feet and t is the time in hours that has elapsed from 12 midnight on May 1. To one decimal place, estimate the water level in this harbor on May 2 at 7 a.m. and at 11 p.m. ■

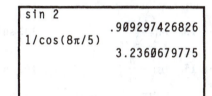

```
sin 2
            .909297426826
1/cos(8π/5)
            3.2360679775
```

Figure 9.19

EXERCISES 9.2

In Exercises 1–30, find the *exact* function value.

1. $\cos 4\pi$

2. $\sin 100\pi$

3. $\sin 5\pi$

4. $\cos 11\pi$

5. $\tan(-2\pi)$

6. $\cot(-36\pi)$

7. $\cos\left(-\dfrac{\pi}{2}\right)$

8. $\sin\left(-\dfrac{3\pi}{2}\right)$

9. $\sec\dfrac{5\pi}{2}$

10. $\tan\dfrac{19\pi}{2}$

11. $\csc\left(\dfrac{-7\pi}{2}\right)$

12. $\cos\left(\dfrac{-9\pi}{2}\right)$

13. $\sin\left(\dfrac{11\pi}{2}\right)$

14. $\sin\left(\dfrac{-97\pi}{2}\right)$

15. $\cos\left(-\dfrac{\pi}{3}\right)$

16. $\sin\left(-\dfrac{\pi}{4}\right)$

17. $\tan\dfrac{9\pi}{4}$

18. $\cos\dfrac{9\pi}{4}$

19. $\sin\dfrac{13\pi}{6}$

20. $\sec\dfrac{17\pi}{4}$

21. $\cot\dfrac{7\pi}{3}$

22. $\sin\dfrac{19\pi}{3}$

23. $\cos\left(\dfrac{-13\pi}{6}\right)$

24. $\sin\left(\dfrac{-13\pi}{3}\right)$

25. $\csc\left(\dfrac{-31\pi}{3}\right)$

26. $\cos\left(\dfrac{-25\pi}{4}\right)$

27. $\cot\dfrac{55\pi}{3}$

28. $\tan\left(\dfrac{-73\pi}{6}\right)$

29. $\sin\left(\pi - \dfrac{4\pi}{3}\right)$

30. $\cos\left(2\pi - \dfrac{13\pi}{6}\right)$

In Exercises 31–50, find the *exact* function value. Use reference numbers.

31. $\cos\dfrac{7\pi}{6}$

32. $\sin\dfrac{5\pi}{3}$

33. $\tan\dfrac{4\pi}{3}$

34. $\sec\dfrac{11\pi}{6}$

35. $\sin\dfrac{7\pi}{4}$

36. $\cos\dfrac{2\pi}{3}$

37. $\csc\dfrac{5\pi}{6}$

38. $\sin\dfrac{3\pi}{4}$

39. $\cos\dfrac{5\pi}{3}$

40. $\cot\dfrac{5\pi}{4}$

41. $\sin\left(\dfrac{-7\pi}{6}\right)$

42. $\cos\left(\dfrac{-4\pi}{3}\right)$

43. $\sec\left(\dfrac{-2\pi}{3}\right)$

44. $\tan\left(\dfrac{-7\pi}{4}\right)$

45. $\cos\dfrac{11\pi}{4}$

46. $\sin\dfrac{8\pi}{3}$

47. $\cot\dfrac{23\pi}{6}$

48. $\csc\dfrac{15\pi}{4}$

49. $\sin\left(\dfrac{-20\pi}{3}\right)$

50. $\cos\left(\dfrac{-23\pi}{6}\right)$

In Exercises 51–70 find the approximate function value. Round off answers to four decimal places.

51. $\cos 2$

52. $\sin 3$

53. $\tan 4$

54. $\sec 5$

55. $\sin 5.41$

56. $\csc 2.23$

57. $\cot 3.71$

58. $\cos 1.84$

59. $\sin(-6.07)$

60. $\tan(-1.69)$

61. $\cos 11.73$

62. $\cot 9.61$

63. $\csc(-7.57)$

64. $\sin(-10.25)$

65. $\sin\dfrac{2\pi}{5}$

66. $\tan\dfrac{9\pi}{5}$

67. $\cos\dfrac{3\pi}{7}$

68. $\sin\dfrac{4\pi}{9}$

69. $\sec\left(\dfrac{-7\pi}{8}\right)$

70. $\cos\left(\dfrac{-7\pi}{10}\right)$

71. The monthly revenue R in dollars from sales of ice cream for a sweet shop in Montpelier, Vermont is approximated by

$$R = 4200 + 2100 \cos(0.5236t),$$

where t is the number of months that have elapsed from August 1. Use this model to estimate to the nearest hundred dollars, the total revenue for the two month period August and September, and the total revenue for the two-month period January and February.

72. The monthly number of kilowatt hours (E) of electricity sold by a particular utility company is approximated by

$$E = 384.5 + 89.5 \cos(.5236t),$$

where t is the number of months that have elapsed from January 1. Use this model to approximate the total number of kilowatt hours sold in the 2-month period March and April, and the total number of kilowatt hours sold in the 2-month period September and October.

73. The analysis of oscillations in physics may involve trigonometric equations. For instance, the motion of a swinging pendulum can be described by such equations. Suppose that a body oscillates according to the equation

$$x = 6.0 \cos\left(3\pi t + \dfrac{\pi}{3}\right),$$

where x represents the horizontal displacement from a reference point in meters, and t is the elapsed time in

seconds. Because the cosine function periodically decreases and increases, the moving body periodically gets closer to and farther away from the reference point.
a. Find the horizontal displacement of the body when $t = 0$ and when $t = 2$.
b. What is the maximum possible value of

$$\cos\left(3\pi t + \frac{\pi}{3}\right)?$$ What is the maximum possible

horizontal displacement of this body?

74. The average daily temperature T in degrees Fahrenheit at the surface of the ground in Athens, Georgia, over the course of a year is approximated fairly well by the equation

$$T = 61.3 + 17.9 \cos\left(\frac{2\pi}{365}t\right),$$

where t is in days, and $t = 0$ represents July 1. [Source: *Mathematical Modeling and Cool Buttermilk in the Summer,* Corbitt and Edwards, 1979 Yearbook, NCTM]
a. Estimate the average temperature (to the nearest degree) on July 1.
b. Estimate the average temperature (to the nearest degree) on January 1.

THINK ABOUT IT 9.2

1. Explain why there is no real number s such that $\sin s > 1$.
2. The following formulas (derived from calculus) may be used to compute the values of $\cos x$ and $\sin x$.

$$\cos x = 1 - \frac{x^2}{2!} + \frac{x^4}{4!} - \frac{x^6}{6!} + \cdots$$

$$\sin x = x - \frac{x^3}{3!} + \frac{x^5}{5!} - \frac{x^7}{7!} + \cdots,$$

where $n! = 1 \cdot 2 \cdots n$ (for example, $3! = 1 \cdot 2 \cdot 3$). Use the first three terms of these formulas to approximate the following expressions. Compare your results with the values given by calculator.
a. $\sin 1$　　　　**b.** $\cos 1$
c. $\cos 0$　　　　**d.** $\sin 0.5$
3. In the study of chaos theory you explore the behavior of functions in which you use the current "output" as the next "input." Some functions tend toward a single value, some fluctuate periodically among a limited set of values, and some wildly fluctuate with no apparent pattern. [Source: R. Devaney, *Chaos, Fractals, and Dynamics,* Addison-Wesley]

a. To examine the behavior of the function $y = \cos x$, pick any starting value for x, and get its cosine, then get the cosine of that result, and then the cosine of that result, etc. Keep doing this until you can describe what is happening. Does it matter if the calculator is in degree or radian mode?
b. Examine the behavior of the sine function and the tangent function.

4. Consider the unit circle in the accompanying figure, in which each of the six trigonometric functions can be represented as a line segment. For example, since $\overline{OC} = 1$ in right triangle OAC, we have

$$\sin \theta = \frac{\overline{AC}}{\overline{OC}} = \frac{\overline{AC}}{1} = \overline{AC}.$$

Notice that we obtained the desired line segment by selecting a right triangle where the denominator in the defining ratio is 1. Determine the line segments representing the five remaining trigonometric functions in the figure.

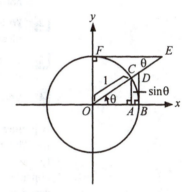

5. When you wiggle a rope to make a wave travel along it, you create what physicists call a **transverse wave.** If you look at a particular point along the rope, it will have different displacements at different times. For example, the equation

$$y = 10 \sin[\pi(0.01x - 2.00t)]$$

gives the displacement y (in centimeters) of a rope at a point x centimeters from the end at time t seconds.
a. Find the displacements of the rope 10 cm from the end when $t = 2, 2.25, 2.5,$ and 3.
b. What is the maximum possible value of $\sin[\pi(0.01x - 2.00t)]$? What is the maximum possible displacement of this rope?

Courtesy of PhotoDisc/Getty Images.

9.3 Graphs of Sine and Cosine Functions

Based on the orbit of Earth around the sun, the number of hours of daylight during each day in a specific location demonstrates cyclic behavior. This behavior may be modeled by a sine function whose specific equation depends on the latitude of the location. For the city of Houston, Texas, an equation that may be used to approximate the number of hours of daylight (y) during the xth day of the year is

$$y = 12 + 2.3 \sin\left[\frac{2\pi}{365}(x - 80)\right].$$

a. Graph this function over the interval from $x = 1$ (January 1) to $x = 365$ (December 31) with the aid of a grapher.
b. What are the amplitude and the period of the function?
c. According to your graph, which day of the year has the minimum number of hours of daylight in Houston? (See Example 10)

OBJECTIVES

1 Find the amplitude and period for functions of the form $y = a \sin bx$ and $y = a \cos bx$, and graph the function for a given interval.

2 Write the equation of the form $y = a \sin bx$ or $y = a \cos bx$ that corresponds to a given graph.

3 Graph sine and cosine functions that involve horizontal translations or vertical translations.

4 Solve applied problems involving the graph of a trigonometric function of a real number.

A picture or graph of the sine and cosine functions helps us understand their cyclic behavior. This insight is crucial because this behavior is the basis for the use of these functions to model periodic events (such as the number of hours of daylight in Houston, which is considered in the section-opening problem). In terms of notation we use the xy-plane and associate the arc length values with points on the horizontal or x-axis. This means that we are now using x, instead of s, to represent the independent variable, which is an arc length. The vertical axis, labeled the y-axis, is used to represent the function values.

We begin with a numeric approach, by considering the values of the sine function as we lay off on the x-axis a length 2π and pass around the unit circle. The following table indicates some values of the sine function on this typical interval.

$y = \sin x$ (for $0 \le x \le 2\pi$)												
x	0	$\frac{\pi}{6}$	$\frac{\pi}{3}$	$\frac{\pi}{2}$	$\frac{2\pi}{3}$	$\frac{5\pi}{6}$	π	$\frac{7\pi}{6}$	$\frac{4\pi}{3}$	$\frac{3\pi}{2}$	$\frac{5\pi}{3}$	$\frac{11\pi}{6}$	2π
y	0	0.5	0.87	1	0.87	0.5	0	-0.5	-0.87	-1	-0.87	-0.5	0

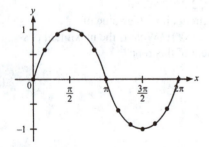

Figure 9.20

If we plot these points and join them with a smooth curve, we obtain the graph in Figure 9.20, which describes the essential characteristics of the sine function during one cycle. The plot of $y = \sin x$ starts at the origin, attains a maximum at one-fourth of the cycle length, returns to zero halfway through the cycle, attains a minimum at the three-quarter point, and returns to zero at the end of the cycle. Each time we lay off a length 2π, we pass around the circle and repeat this behavior. Thus, the graph of $y = \sin x$ weaves continuously through cycles in both directions, as illustrated in Figure 9.21.

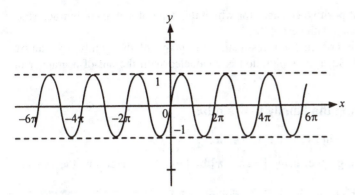

Figure 9.21

The graph in Figure 9.21 is easy to generate on a graphing utility. The main steps are to set the angle mode to *radian,* enter $y1 = \sin x$ in the equation editor, and use $[-6\pi, 6\pi]$ by $[-2, 2]$ to define a viewing window. To mimic Figure 9.21, set the x scale to π and the y scale to 1, and then graph the function as shown in Figure 9.22. Note that the standard viewing window $[-10, 10]$ by $[-10, 10]$ is not well suited for graphing $y = \sin x$. Therefore, many graphing calculators have a built-in feature that automatically sets a window that is suitable for many basic trigonometric graphs. For instance, Figure 9.23 shows the result of graphing $y = \sin x$ using the Zoom Trig feature on a particular Texas Instruments calculator. You should learn how to use this type of feature if it is available on your calculator.

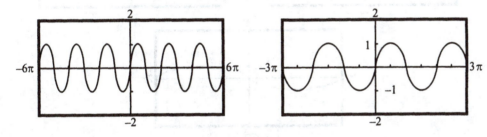

Figure 9.22   **Figure 9.23**

When we examine our graphs of the sine function we see that the function repeats its values on intervals of length 2π. For this reason, the sine function is said to be *periodic.* We define a periodic function as follows.

Periodic Function

A function f is periodic if

$$f(x) = f(x + p)$$

for all x in the domain of f. The smallest positive number p for which this is true is called the **period** of the function.

This definition applies to the sine function since

$$\sin x = \sin(x + 2\pi),$$

where 2π is the smallest positive constant for which this type of statement is true. Thus the sine function is periodic, with period 2π.

This information is critical for investigating the graph of the family $y = \sin bx$ as b changes for $b > 0$. Such an exploration is conducted with the aid of a grapher in Example 1.

EXAMPLE 1 Exploring the Family $y = \sin bx$

Let $f(x) = \sin x$, $g(x) = \sin 2x$, and $h(x) = \sin\frac{1}{2}x$.

a. Graph f, g, and h on a grapher using $[-2\pi, 2\pi]$ by $[-4, 4]$ to determine the viewing window.

b. Use the graphs in part **a** to determine the period of each function.

c. Describe how to obtain the period of g and the period of h by using the period of $f(x) = \sin x$.

Solution

a. The requested graphs are shown in Figure 9.24.

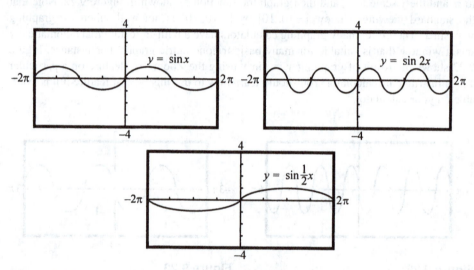

Figure 9.24

b. We read from the graphs that the smallest intervals on which the graphs complete one full cycle are 2π for $f(x) = \sin x$, π for $g(x) = \sin 2x$, and 4π for $h(x) = \sin\left(\frac{1}{2}x\right)$. Thus, the periods for f, g, and h are the 2π, π, and 4π, respectively.

c. The period of $g(x) = \sin 2x$ may be found by taking the period of $f(x) = \sin x$ and dividing it by 2. That is,

$$\text{period of } g = \frac{2\pi}{2} = \pi.$$

Similarly, taking the period of $f(x) = \sin x$ and dividing it by $\frac{1}{2}$ gives the period of $h(x) = \sin\left(\frac{1}{2}x\right)$. Thus,

$$\text{period of } h = \frac{2\pi}{1/2} = 4\pi.$$

PROGRESS CHECK 1 Let $g(x) = \sin 4x$ and $h(x) = \sin \pi x$.

a. Graph g and h using $[-2\pi, 2\pi]$ by $[-4, 4]$ to determine the viewing window.

b. Use the graphs in part **a** to determine the period of each function.

c. Describe how to obtain the period of g and the period of h by using the period of $f(x) = \sin x$.

■

The result in Example 1 suggests the period of $y = \sin bx$ for $b > 0$ is $2\pi/b$. This result makes sense analytically because $y = \sin bx$ completes one full cycle as bx ranges from 0 to 2π. Since

$$bx = 0 \text{ when } x = 0$$

and

$$bx = 2\pi \text{ when } x = \frac{2\pi}{b},$$

it follows that the period of $y = \sin bx$ for $b > 0$ is $2\pi/b$.

EXAMPLE 2   Graphing a Sine Function Using Its Period

State the period and graph $y = \sin\dfrac{x}{3}$ for $-p \le x \le p$, where p is the period of the function.

Solution   Since $\sin(x/3)$ is equivalent to $\sin\left(\frac{1}{3}x\right)$, we determine the period by substituting $\frac{1}{3}$ for b in the formula for the period.

$$\text{Period} = \frac{2\pi}{b} = \frac{2\pi}{1/3} = 6\pi$$

The length of one cycle is 6π, so we draw two cycles to graph the function on the interval $[-6\pi, 6\pi]$, as shown in Figure 9.25. You should confirm this result with a grapher.

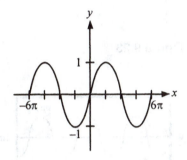

Figure 9.25

PROGRESS CHECK 2   State the period and graph $y = \sin\dfrac{x}{5}$ for $-p \le x \le p$, where p is the period of the function.   ■

Two other key characteristics of the graph of $y = \sin x$ are that the y values oscillate from -1 to 1, and that the x-axis serves as a *midline* that runs halfway between these minimum and maximum values. When the midline of the graph of a periodic function is the x-axis, then the maximum y value is called the *amplitude* of the function. Thus, the amplitude of $y = \sin x$ is 1.

We can use this information to sketch functions of the form $y = a \sin bx$, where a represents a real number. These functions are similar to $y = \sin bx$ in that they have the same basic shape and period, but they may differ by having different amplitudes. For example, to sketch the graph of $y = 3 \sin x$, we obtain values for $\sin x$ and multiply these values by 3. Since the greatest y value that $\sin x$ attains is 1, the greatest y value that $3 \sin x$ attains is 3. Thus, the amplitude of $y = 3 \sin x$ is 3.

In general, since the greatest value that $\sin x$ attains is 1, the greatest value that $a \sin x$ attains is $|a|$. Thus, the amplitude of $y = a \sin bx$ is $|a|$. Figure 9.26 compares the graphs of $y = \sin x$ and $y = 3 \sin x$ on $[0, 2\pi]$.

Note that we can anticipate the relation between these two graphs from our work with graphing techniques in Section 2.5, because the graph of $y = c \cdot f(x)$ with $c > 0$ is the graph of $y = f(x)$ stretched or flattened out by a factor of c.

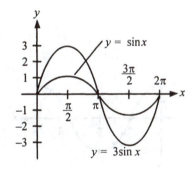

Figure 9.26

EXAMPLE 3   Graphing a Sine Function Using Its Amplitude and Period

State the amplitude and the period and sketch the graph of $y = 2 \sin 3x$ for $0 \le x \le 2\pi$.

Solution   First, determine the amplitude and period.

$$\text{Amplitude} = |a| = |2| = 2$$
$$\text{Period} = \frac{2\pi}{b} = \frac{2\pi}{3}$$

If the curve completes one cycle on the interval $[0, 2\pi/3]$, the curve completes three cycles on the given interval. Note that b gives the number of cycles on the interval $[0, 2\pi]$. Since the amplitude is 2, the curve oscillates between a maximum value of 2 and a minimum value of -2. The graph is sketched in Figure 9.27, and you should check this result with a grapher.

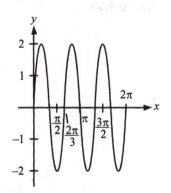

Figure 9.27

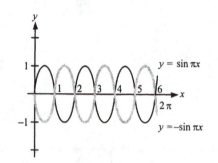

Figure 9.28

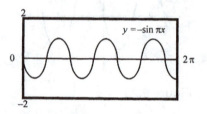

Figure 9.29

PROGRESS CHECK 3 State the amplitude and the period and sketch the graph of $y = 5 \sin 2x$ for $0 \leq x \leq 2\pi$. ■

EXAMPLE 4 Graphing *y* = *a* sin *bx* Where *a* < 0

State the amplitude and the period and sketch the graph of $y = -\sin \pi x$ for $0 \leq x \leq 2\pi$.

Solution First, determine the amplitude and period.

$$\text{Amplitude} = |a| = |-1| = 1$$

$$\text{Period} = \frac{2\pi}{b} = \frac{2\pi}{\pi} = 2$$

If the curve completes one cycle every 2 units, the curve completes slightly more than three cycles on the interval $[0, 2\pi]$. Since the amplitude is 1, the curve oscillates between a maximum value of 1 and a minimum value of -1. Because a is negative, we obtain the graph by reflecting the graph of $y = \sin \pi x$ about the x-axis, as shown in Figure 9.28.

Observe that this result is in agreement with the graph in Figure 9.29, which was obtained by graphing $y = -\sin \pi x$ on a grapher.

PROGRESS CHECK 4 State the amplitude and the period and sketch the graph of $y = -3 \sin 2\pi x$ for $0 \leq x \leq 2\pi$. ■

The graph of the cosine function has the same essential characteristics as the graph of the sine function. That is, the amplitude of the cosine function is 1 and the period is 2π. This is evidenced by the following table, which indicates some values of the cosine function on the interval $[0, 2\pi]$.

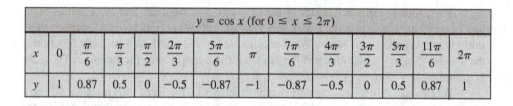

$y = \cos x$ (for $0 \leq x \leq 2\pi$)												
x	0	$\frac{\pi}{6}$	$\frac{\pi}{3}$	$\frac{\pi}{2}$	$\frac{2\pi}{3}$	$\frac{5\pi}{6}$	π	$\frac{7\pi}{6}$	$\frac{4\pi}{3}$	$\frac{3\pi}{2}$	$\frac{5\pi}{3}$	$\frac{11\pi}{6}$	2π
y	1	0.87	0.5	0	-0.5	-0.87	-1	-0.87	-0.5	0	0.5	0.87	1

If we plot these points and join them with a smooth curve, we obtain the graph shown in Figure 9.30. This graph demonstrates that the cosine function completes one cycle on the interval $[0, 2\pi]$ and attains a maximum value of 1. Like that of the sine function, this graph can be reproduced indefinitely in both directions to obtain as much of the graph of the cosine function as desired (see Figure 9.31).

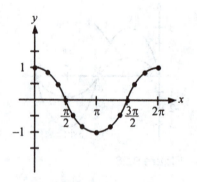

Figure 9.30

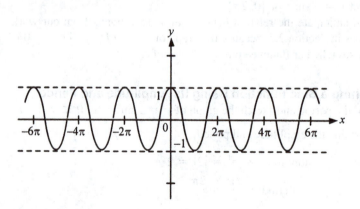

Figure 9.31

The great similarity between the graphs of the sine and cosine functions should be apparent. In fact, if we shift the graph of the cosine function $\pi/2$ units to the right, the resulting graph is the sine function. Thus, the only difference between the two graphs is that one curve leads the other by $\pi/2$. That is, $\cos(x - \pi/2) = \sin x$.

We graph functions of the form $y = a \cos bx$ in a manner similar to graphing $y = a \sin bx$; that is, we find the amplitude by computing $|a|$ and the period by using $2\pi/b$. The difference is that the graph of $y = a \cos bx$ attains a maximum or minimum height at $x = 0$.

EXAMPLE 5   Graphing y = a cos bx Where a > 0
State the amplitude and the period and sketch the graph of $y = \frac{1}{2}\cos 2x$ for $0 \le x \le 2\pi$.

Solution   First, determine the amplitude and period.

$$\text{Amplitude} = |a| = \left|\frac{1}{2}\right| = \frac{1}{2}$$

$$\text{Period} = \frac{2\pi}{b} = \frac{2\pi}{2} = \pi$$

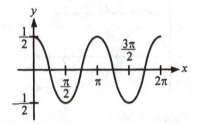

Figure 9.32

If the curve completes one cycle on $[0, \pi]$, the curve will complete two cycles on $[0, 2\pi]$. Since the amplitude is $1/2$, the curve oscillates between a maximum value of $1/2$, and a minimum value of $-1/2$, as shown in Figure 9.32. This result should be checked using a grapher.

PROGRESS CHECK 5   State the amplitude and the period and sketch the graph of $y = 10 \cos 4x$ for $0 \le x \le 2\pi$.   ■

EXAMPLE 6   Graphing y = a cos bx Where a < 0
State the amplitude and the period and sketch one cycle of the graph of $y = -4 \cos 10x$.

Solution   First, determine the amplitude and period.

$$\text{Amplitude} = |a| = |-4| = 4$$

$$\text{Period} = \frac{2\pi}{b} = \frac{2\pi}{10} = \frac{\pi}{5}$$

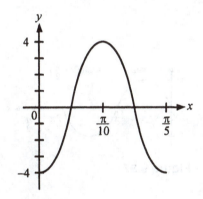

The curve completes one cycle on the interval $[0, \pi/5]$ and attains a maximum value of 4 and a minimum value of -4. Since a is a negative number, we obtain the graph shown in Figure 9.33 by starting and ending the graph at a minimum point. You should use a grapher to check this result.

Figure 9.33

PROGRESS CHECK 6   State the amplitude and the period and sketch one cycle of the graph of $y = -\frac{3}{2}\cos\frac{x}{4}$.   ■

EXAMPLE 7   Determining an Equation That Fits a Graph
Find an equation for the curve with the single cycle shown in Figure 9.34. The equation should be written in the form $y = a \sin bx$ or $y = a \cos bx$.

Solution   Since the cycle shown starts at a minimum y value, the form of the equation is $y = a \cos bx$ with $a < 0$. The amplitude is 30 and $a < 0$, so $a = -30$. Since the period is 5, we have

$$\frac{2\pi}{b} = 5 \text{ so } b = \frac{2\pi}{5}.$$

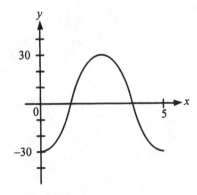

Thus, an equation for the graph is $y = -30 \cos\left(\frac{2\pi}{5} x\right)$. You should graph the equation on a grapher to check this result.

Figure 9.34

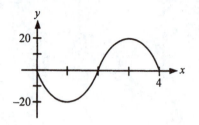

Figure 9.35

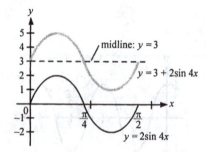

Figure 9.36

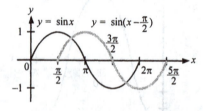

Figure 9.37

PROGRESS CHECK 7 Redo the question in Example 7 for the curve with the single cycle shown in Figure 9.35. ■

Vertical and Horizontal Shifts Involving Sine and Cosine

To model cyclic events in many applied problems, it is necessary to use vertical or horizontal translations of sine or cosine curves. To shift the midline of such curves off the x-axis, we use a vertical translation. Recall from Section 2.5 that if $d > 0$, then the graph of $y = f(x) + d$ is the graph of f raised d units, while the graph of $y = f(x) - d$ is the graph of f lowered d units. Thus, the midline of the functions $y = d + a \sin bx$ and $y = d + a \cos bx$ is the horizontal line $y = d$.

EXAMPLE 8 Using a Vertical Translation

Graph one cycle of the function $y = 3 + 2 \sin 4x$. Indicate the amplitude, period, and midline.

Solution First, observe that the amplitude and period of $y = 2 \sin 4x$ are 2 and $\pi/2$, respectively. So we graph one cycle of this function as shown in Figure 9.36. Then we graph $y = 3 + 2 \sin 4x$ by raising the graph of $y = 2 \sin 4x$ up 3 units where the graph oscillates about a midline of $y = 3$. Knowledge of the midline, the amplitude, and the period is crucial for setting an appropriate viewing window for such graphs, and you should try to use a grapher to duplicate the results in this example.

PROGRESS CHECK 8 Graph one cycle of the function $y = 800 - 400 \cos \dfrac{\pi}{6} x$. Indicate the amplitude, period, and midline. ■

A horizontal shift is created when the constant c is not zero in a function of the form $y = d + a \sin(bx + c)$. To illustrate, consider the equation $y = \sin(x - \pi/2)$. As $x - \pi/2$ ranges from 0 to 2π, the curve completes one sine wave.

$$x - \frac{\pi}{2} = 0 \text{ when } x = \frac{\pi}{2}$$

$$x - \frac{\pi}{2} = 2\pi \text{ when } x = \frac{5\pi}{2}$$

Thus, the function completes one cycle in the interval from $\pi/2$ to $5\pi/2$. The period of the function is 2π and the amplitude is 1. For comparison, one cycle of the graphs of $y = \sin x$ and $y = \sin(x - \pi/2)$ is given in Figure 9.37.

The complete graph of $y = \sin(x - \pi/2)$ is sketched by repeating the cycle shown in Figure 9.37 to the left and to the right. Notice that the graph of $y = \sin(x - \pi/2)$ may be obtained by shifting the graph of $y = \sin x$ to the right $\pi/2$ units. The sine wave then starts a cycle at $\pi/2$ instead of 0, and we call $\pi/2$ the **phase shift.** This horizontal shift can be anticipated from our work in Section 2.5, where we found that the graph of $y = f(x - c)$ with $c > 0$ is the graph of f shifted c units to the right.

In general, the constant c in the function $y = d + a \sin(bx + c)$ causes a shift of the graph of $y = d + a \sin bx$. The shift is of distance $|c/b|$ and is to the left if $c > 0$ and to the right if $c < 0$. The phase shift is given by $-c/b$. Similar remarks holds for functions of the form $y = d + a \cos(bx + c)$.

EXAMPLE 9 Using a Horizontal Translation

Graph one cycle of the function $y = 3 \cos\left(2x + \dfrac{\pi}{2}\right)$. Indicate the amplitude, period, and phase shift.

Solution Determine the amplitude and period.

$$\text{Amplitude} = |a| = |3| = 3$$

$$\text{Period} = \frac{2\pi}{b} = \frac{2\pi}{2} = \pi$$

The function completes one cosine cycle as $2x + \pi/2$ varies from 0 to 2π.

$$2x + \frac{\pi}{2} = 0 \text{ when } x = -\frac{\pi}{4}$$

$$2x + \frac{\pi}{2} = 2\pi \text{ when } x = \frac{3\pi}{4}$$

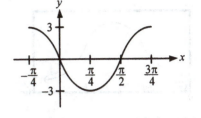

Figure 9.38

Thus, the function completes one cycle in the interval from $-\pi/4$ to $3\pi/4$ (see Figure 9.38). This interval checks with the computed period, since $3\pi/4 - (-\pi/4) = \pi$. A cycle starts at $-\pi/4$, so $-\pi/4$ is the phase shift. We may verify the phase shift, since

$$\frac{-c}{b} = \frac{-\pi/2}{2} = -\frac{\pi}{4}.$$

All of these results should be checked by graphing $y = 3\cos(2x + \pi/2)$ on a grapher.

PROGRESS CHECK 9 Graph one cycle of the function $y = 4\sin\left(\dfrac{x}{4} - \dfrac{\pi}{2}\right)$. Indicate the amplitude, period, and phase shift. ■

Before solving the section-opening problem, it is useful to consolidate our results about graphing sine and cosine curves.

Graphs of Sine and Cosine Functions

For the graphs of $y = d + a\sin(bx + c)$ and $y = d + a\cos(bx + c)$ where $a \neq 0$ and $b > 0$:

1. The **amplitude** is $|a|$.
2. The **period** is $2\pi/b$.
3. The **phase shift** is $-c/b$.
4. The **midline** is $y = d$.

EXAMPLE 10   Number of Hours of Daylight in a Day

Solve the problem in the section introduction on page 490.

Solution

a. For the given equation

$$y = 12 + 2.3 \sin\left[\frac{2\pi}{365}(x - 80)\right],$$

$a = 2.3$, $b = 2\pi/365$, $c = -80$, and $d = 12$. Because the curve oscillates 2.3 units about the midline $y = 12$, it is sensible to let $9 \leq y \leq 15$ when creating the viewing window for the graph. Given the context of the problem, it is also sensible to let $1 \leq x \leq 365$. Then, Figure 9.39 shows a graph of the given equation in the viewing window just described.

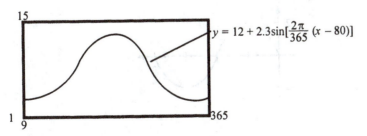

Figure 9.39

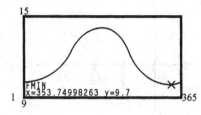

Figure 9.40

b. Since $a = 2.3$, and $b = 2\pi/365$,

$$\text{Amplitude} = |a| = |2.3| = 2.3$$

$$\text{Period} = \frac{2\pi}{b} = \frac{2\pi}{2\pi/365} = 365$$

Observe that the graph in Figure 9.39 supports these results.

c. Figure 9.40 shows that the given function has a minimum point at about $x = 354$, $y = 9.7$. (If your calculator does not have a Function Minimum feature, then you can use Zoom and Trace to determine this point.) Thus, the day of the year in Houston with the minimum number of hours of daylight is the 354th day, which is December 20.

PROGRESS CHECK 10   Based on the rhythmic motion of her heart, a certain woman's blood pressure y is given by $y = 105 + 20 \sin(140\pi t)$, where t is the elapsed time in minutes.

a. Graph this function on the interval [0 minutes, 0.1 minutes].
b. What are the maximum (systolic) and minimum (diastolic) readings for her blood pressure?
c. Find the woman's heart rate in beats per minute. ■

EXERCISES 9.3

In Exercises 1–12 indicate the amplitude, period, and midline, and sketch the curve for $-p \le x \le p$, where p is the period of the function.

1. $y = 2 \sin x$
2. $y = 3 \cos 2x$
3. $y = -3 \cos x$
4. $y = -4 \sin\frac{1}{3}x$
5. $y = 2 \sin 3x$
6. $y = \frac{1}{2}\cos 4x$
7. $y = -\cos 18x$
8. $y = -6 \sin\frac{x}{4}$
9. $y = 10 \cos(\pi x) + 4$
10. $y = 110 \sin(120\pi x) - 110$
11. $y = 5 + \sin 2x$
12. $y = 4 - 2 \sin x$

In Exercises 13–22 indicate the amplitude, period, and midline, and sketch the curve for $0 \le x \le 2\pi$.

13. $y = 3 \cos 4x$
14. $y = 2 \cos\frac{x}{4}$
15. $y = -\sin\frac{x}{2}$
16. $y = -3 \sin 2x$
17. $y = \frac{1}{2}\sin 3x$
18. $y = 1.5 \cos\frac{1}{3}x$
19. $y = \sin\frac{\pi}{2}x$
20. $y = 2 \cos \pi x$
21. $y = 100 + 2 \sin\frac{\pi}{4}x$
22. $y = -100 - 2 \sin\frac{\pi}{3}x$

In Exercises 23–32 indicate the amplitude, period, midline, and phase shift, and sketch one cycle of the function.

23. $y = \sin\left(x + \frac{\pi}{2}\right)$
24. $y = 2 \sin(x - \pi)$
25. $y = \cos\left(x - \frac{\pi}{4}\right)$
26. $y = 3 \cos\left(x + \frac{\pi}{3}\right)$

27. $y = \frac{1}{2}\cos\left(2x + \frac{\pi}{4}\right)$
28. $y = -\sin\left(\frac{x}{2} - \pi\right)$
29. $y = -\cos\left(\frac{x}{4} + \frac{\pi}{2}\right)$
30. $y = \sin(x - 1)$
31. $y = 30 + 30 \sin\left(\frac{\pi}{2}x - \frac{\pi}{2}\right)$
32. $y = -40 - 40 \cos\left(\frac{\pi}{3}x + \frac{\pi}{3}\right)$

In Exercises 33–40 find an equation for the curves with the given single cycle. The equations should be written in the form $y = a \sin bx$ or $y = a \cos bx$.

33.

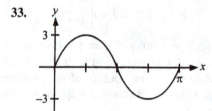

34.

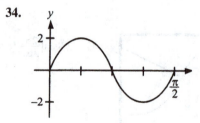

35.

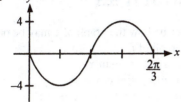

36.

37.

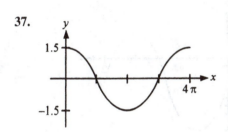

38.

39.

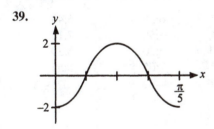

40.

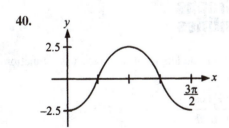

In Exercises 41–50 select the choice that answers the question or completes the statement.

41. The minimum value of $y = 2 \cos 3x$ is
  a. 0   **b.** -3
  c. 3   **d.** -2

42. The maximum value of $y = 2 + \sin x$ is
  a. 1   **b.** 2
  c. 3   **d.** 4

43. The expression $y = 3 \sin\frac{1}{2}x$ reaches its maximum value when x equals:
  a. 0   **b.** $\pi/2$
  c. π **d.** $3\pi/2$

44. The expression $y = 2 \cos 3x$ reaches its minimum value when x equals:
  a. 0   **b.** $\pi/3$
  c. $\pi/2$ **d.** $2\pi/3$

45. The period of the curve $y = 3 \cos 2x$ is:
  a. $\pi/2$ **b.** π
  c. 2π **d.** 4π

46. A function having a period of $\pi/2$ is:
  a. $y = \frac{1}{4}\sin x$ **b.** $y = 4 \sin 2x$
  c. $y = 2 \sin 4x$ **d.** $y = 4 \sin\frac{1}{4}x$

47. As x increases from $\pi/2$ to $3\pi/2$, then $y = \sin x$:
  a. increases   **b.** decreases
  c. increases, then decreases
  d. decreases, then increases

48. $y = \sin x$ and $y = \cos x$ both increase in:
  a. quadrant 1   **b.** quadrant 2
  c. quadrant 3   **d.** quadrant 4

49. Between $x = 0$ and $x = 2\pi$, the graphs of $y = \sin x$ and $y = \cos x$ have in common:
  a. no points   **b.** one point
  c. two points   **d.** four points

50. When graphs of $y = \sin x$ and $y = \cos x$ are drawn on the same axes, how many times do they intersect in the interval $\pi/2 \le x \le \pi$?
  a. 0   **b.** 1
  c. 2   **d.** 3

51. Refer to Example 10 of Section 9.3. For the city of Key West, Florida, an equation that may be used to approximate the length in hours (y) of the xth day is:

$$y = 12 + 1.65 \sin\left[\frac{2\pi}{365}(x - 80)\right].$$

  a. Graph this function over the interval from $x = 1$ (January 1) to $x = 365$ (December 31), with the aid of a grapher.
  b. What are the amplitude and period of the function?
  c. Find the day that has the maximum number of hours of daylight, and estimate the number of hours of daylight on that day.

52. Refer to Example 10 of Section 9.3. For the city of Nome, Alaska, an equation that may be used to approximate the length in hours (y) of the xth day is

$$y = 12.5 + 8.5 \sin\left[\frac{2\pi}{365}(x - 80)\right].$$

a. Graph this function over the interval from $x = 1$ (January 1) to $x = 365$ (December 31) with the aid of a grapher.

b. What are the amplitude and period of the function?

c. Find the day that has the maximum number of hours of daylight, and estimate the number of hours of daylight on that day.

53. The monthly revenue R in dollars from sales of ice cream for a sweet shop in Montpelier, Vermont is approximated by

$$R = 4,200 + 2,100 \cos\left(\frac{2\pi}{12}x\right),$$

where $x = 0$ represents July.

a. Graph this function over the interval from $x = 0$ to $x = 12$.

b. What are the amplitude and the period of the function?

c. According to this graph, which month has the minimum revenue?

54. The monthly number of kilowatt hours (E) of electricity sold by a particular utility company is approximated by

$$E = 384.5 + 89.5 \cos\left(\frac{2\pi}{12}x\right),$$

where $x = 0$ represents January.

a. Graph this function over the interval from $x = 0$ to $x = 12$.

b. What are the amplitude and the period of the function?

c. According to this graph, which month has the minimum usage?

THINK ABOUT IT 9.3

1. In each case describe how the graph of g may be obtained from the graph of f.
a. $f(x) = \sin x$, $g(x) = -\sin x$
b. $f(x) = \cos x$, $g(x) = 4 \cos x$
c. $f(x) = 4 \cos x$, $g(x) = 4 \cos(x + \pi)$
d. $f(x) = 3 \sin \pi x$, $g(x) = 3 \sin(\pi x - \pi)$

2. a. Give two examples of an equation of the form $y = \sin(bx + c)$ whose graph passes through $(\pi/4, 0)$.

b. Give two examples of an equation of the form $y = \cos(bx + c)$ whose graph passes through $(1, 0)$.

3. Find an equation for the curve with the given single cycle.

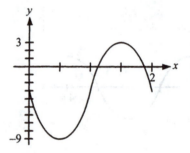

4. Find the smallest nonnegative value of a for which the graph of $y = \sin x$ is symmetric about the line $x = a$. Confirm your answer graphically.

5. Use this sunrise and sunset data for the city of Honolulu, Hawaii, to find a sine function that approximates the number of hours of daylight on the xth day of the year.

Day	Sunrise (a.m.)	Sunset (p.m.)
Mar. 21	6:35	6:43
June 21	5:50	7:16
Sept. 21	6:20	6:29
Dec. 21	7:05	5:55

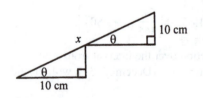

9.4   Other Trigonometric Graphs and Fundamental Identities

For the type of brace that is shown in the diagram, the length of the brace x is a function of θ. Show that

$$x = \frac{10(\sin \theta + \cos \theta)}{\sin \theta \cdot \cos \theta}.$$

(See Example 7.)

The objectives listed above indicate that in this section we will learn to sketch graphs of the trigonometric functions other than sine and cosine, and that identities will play a central role in the section. Recall that trigonometric identities are statements like

$$\csc x = \frac{1}{\sin x} \quad \text{and} \quad \sec x = \frac{1}{\cos x}$$

and such formulas are powerful because they are true for all values of *x* for which the expressions are defined. So the formulas above can be used to graph $y = \csc x$ and $y = \sec x$, respectively. They may also be used to derive the formula requested in the section-opening problem so that the length of the brace is stated in terms of $\sin \theta$ and $\cos \theta$. We begin by showing how to graph $y = \tan x$. Throughout this discussion it is helpful to keep in mind the identity that $\tan x = \sin x/\cos x$.

Although the tangent function is periodic, its behavior differs dramatically from that of the sine and cosine. To see this difference, compare the graph of $y = \tan x$ to the smooth, weaving curves of these functions. First, we use a numeric approach and construct the following table, which lists some values of the tangent function on the interval $[0, 2\pi]$.

$y = \tan x = \sin x/\cos x$ (for $0 \le x \le 2\pi$)												
x	0	$\frac{\pi}{6}$	$\frac{\pi}{3}$	$\frac{\pi}{2}$	$\frac{2\pi}{3}$	$\frac{5\pi}{6}$	π	$\frac{7\pi}{6}$	$\frac{4\pi}{3}$	$\frac{3\pi}{2}$	$\frac{5\pi}{3}$	$\frac{11\pi}{6}$	2π
y	0	0.6	1.7	und.	-1.7	-0.6	0	0.6	1.7	und.	-1.7	-0.6	0

Unlike the sine and cosine, the tangent function is not defined for all real numbers. That is, $y = \tan x = \sin x/\cos x$ is undefined when $\cos x = 0$. Thus, we must exclude from the domain of this function $\pi/2, 3\pi/2$, and any *x* for which $x = (\pi/2) + k\pi$ (*k* any integer). As *x* approaches $\pi/2$, $\sin x$ approaches 1, and $\cos x$ approaches 0. This means that $|\tan x|$ becomes very large as *x* gets close to $\pi/2$. On the basis of the preceding discussion and the fact that $\tan(-x) = -\tan x$, a portion of the graph $y = \tan x$ is presented in Figure 9.41.

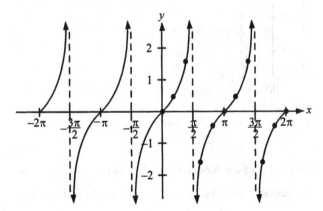

Figure 9.41

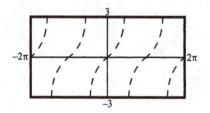

Figure 9.42

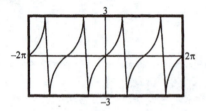

Figure 9.43

It is easy to use a grapher to check the result in Figure 9.41, and graphs for $y = \tan x$ are displayed in Dot mode and in Connected mode in Figures 9.42 and 9.43, respectively. Observe in Figure 9.43 that the calculator erroneously draws almost vertical lines near the vertical asymptotes because it is set to connect points that are in separate pieces of the graph. You should be prepared to experiment with different viewing windows and graphing modes, when graphing trigonometric functions with vertical asymptotes, until you obtain a picture you can interpret. However, under no circumstances should your hand-drawn graph show solid lines at vertical asymptotes like those that may appear on a calculator screen.

The graphs of $y = \tan x$ may be used to contrast the tangent function to the sine and cosine functions with regard to several basic features.

Comparison of the Sine, Cosine, and Tangent Functions

1. The domain of the sine and cosine functions is the set of all real numbers. The tangent function excludes $x = (\pi/2) + k\pi$ (k any integer).
2. The range of the sine and cosine functions is $[-1, 1]$. The range of the tangent function is the set of all real numbers.
3. The sine and cosine are periodic with period 2π. Careful consideration of Figure 9.41 shows that the tangent function repeats its value every π units. Thus, the period of the tangent function is π, and the period of $y = \tan bx$ ($b > 0$) is π/b.

EXAMPLE 1   Using a Reflection and a Translation

Graph one cycle of the function $y = -\tan x - 1$.

Solution   To graph $y = -\tan x - 1$, first reflect the graph of $y = \tan x$ about the x-axis to obtain the graph of $y = -\tan x$ [see Figure 9.44(a)]. Then we lower the graph in Figure 9.44(a) down 1 unit, because the constant 1 is subtracted from $-\tan x$. The completed graph is shown in Figure 9.44(b). You should use a grapher to check this result.

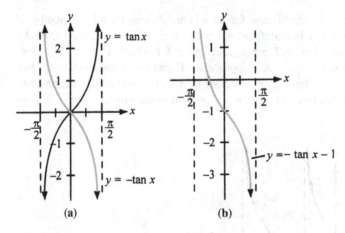

Figure 9.44

PROGRESS CHECK 1   Graph one cycle of the function $y = 2 - \tan x$.   ■

The other three trigonometric functions may be graphed as the reciprocals of the sine, cosine, or tangent. That is,

$$\csc x = \frac{1}{\sin x}, \quad \sec x = \frac{1}{\cos x}, \quad \cot x = \frac{1}{\tan x}.$$

In Figures 9.45–9.47 we first graph the sine, cosine, and tangent as black curves. After obtaining the reciprocals of various y values, we then graph the cosecant, secant, and cotangent. You should use a grapher to check each of the graphs by using the reciprocal identities and entering $1/\sin x$ for csc x, and so on. Observe from these graphs the following relations between a function and its reciprocal function.

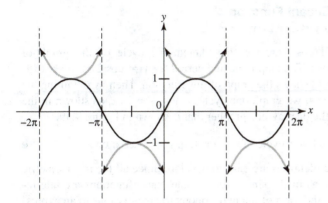

Figure 9.45
$y = \csc x$

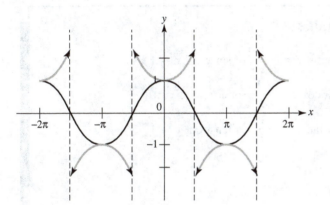

Figure 9.46
$y = \sec x$

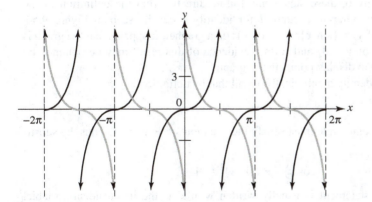

Figure 9.47
$y = \cot x$

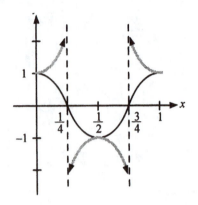

Figure 9.48

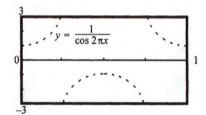

Figure 9.49

1. As one function increases, the other decreases, and vice versa.
2. The two functions always have the same sign.
3. When one function is zero, the other is undefined.
4. When the value of the function is 1 or -1, the reciprocal function has the same value.

EXAMPLE 2   Graphing a Secant Function

Graph one cycle of the function $y = \sec 2\pi x$.

Solution   Since $\sec 2\pi x = 1/\cos 2\pi x$, we first sketch one cycle of the graph of $y = \cos 2\pi x$ to use as a reference. The amplitude and period for $y = \cos 2\pi x$ are both 1, and the black curve in Figure 9.48 shows the graph of this function. Then by obtaining the reciprocals of the various y values, we graph one cycle of $y = \sec 2\pi x$, as shown in the figure. This result checks with the display in a grapher that is shown in Figure 9.49.

PROGRESS CHECK 2   Graph one cycle of the function $y = 2 \sec \pi x$. ■

Some basic trigonometric identities are easy to develop. Since all the trigonometric functions may be defined in terms of the sine and/or cosine, these functions are interrelated. This enables us to change the form of many trigonometric expressions to an expression that is either simpler or more useful for a particular problem. For convenience, we list next six fundamental identities that are used often.

Six Fundamental Identities

Identity 1 $\csc x = \dfrac{1}{\sin x}$ or $\sin x = \dfrac{1}{\csc x}$ or $\sin x \csc x = 1$

Identity 2 $\sec x = \dfrac{1}{\cos x}$ or $\cos x = \dfrac{1}{\sec x}$ or $\cos x \sec x = 1$

Identity 3 $\cot x = \dfrac{1}{\tan x}$ or $\tan x = \dfrac{1}{\cot x}$ or $\tan x \cot x = 1$

Identity 4 $\tan x = \dfrac{\sin x}{\cos x}$

Identity 5 $\cot x = \dfrac{\cos x}{\sin x}$

Identity 6 $\sin^2 x + \cos^2 x = 1$ or $\sin^2 x = 1 - \cos^2 x$ or $\cos^2 x = 1 - \sin^2 x$

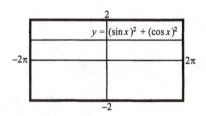

Figure 9.50

Except for identity 6, these statements follow directly from the definition of the trigonometric functions. Graphical support for identity 6 can be seen in Figure 9.50, which shows a graph of $y = (\sin x)^2 + (\cos x)^2$ on a grapher. It appears that the graph is the same as the graph of $y = 1$, and further evidence of this result may be obtained by using the Trace feature to display points in the graph.

To confirm this identity algebraically, recall that by definition

$$x = \cos s \text{ and } y = \sin s.$$

Any point (x, y) on the unit circle must satisfy the equation $x^2 + y^2 = 1$. Thus, by substitution we have

$$(\cos s)^2 + (\sin s)^2 = 1.$$

For convenience, this statement is usually written with x as the independent variable. Thus,

$$\sin^2 x + \cos^2 x = 1.$$

EXAMPLE 3   Verifying that Expressions Are Identical

Show that the expression $\sin x \cot x \sec x$ is identical to 1.

Solution

$$\sin x \cot x \sec x = \sin x \left(\frac{\cos x}{\sin x}\right)\sec x \qquad \text{Identity 5}$$

$$= \sin x \frac{\cos x}{\sin x} \frac{1}{\cos x} \qquad \text{Identity 2}$$

$$= 1 \qquad \text{Simplify}$$

Thus, $\sin x \cot x \sec x = 1$ for all values of x at which the expressions are defined. You can graph

$$y1 = (\sin x)\left(\frac{\cos x}{\sin x}\right)\left(\frac{1}{\cos x}\right)$$

and

$$y2 = 1$$

in the same display on a grapher to check this result. You should see that both equations graph as a horizontal line that is fixed at 1.

PROGRESS CHECK 3   Show that $\dfrac{\tan x}{\sin x}$ is identical to $\sec x$. ▪

EXAMPLE 4   Verifying an Identity

Prove the identity $\tan^2 x + 1 = \sec^2 x$.

Solution

$$\tan^2 x + 1 = \frac{\sin^2 x}{\cos^2 x} + 1 \qquad \text{Identity 4}$$

$$= \frac{\sin^2 x + \cos^2 x}{\cos^2 x}$$

$$= \frac{1}{\cos^2 x} \qquad \text{Identity 6}$$

$$= \sec^2 x \qquad \text{Identity 2}$$

Thus, $\tan^2 x + 1 = \sec^2 x$ is an identity. Graphical support for this identity may be seen in Figure 9.51, which shows that the graphs of $y1 = (\tan x)^2 + 1$ and $y2 = 1/(\cos x)^2$ are the same graph.

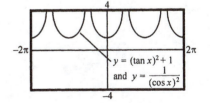

Figure 9.51

Note   Recall that you may also test for equivalent expressions on a grapher by graphing the quotient of the expressions in question. This quotient will be 1 for equivalent expressions throughout the domain of this quotient function. To illustrate, the identity in this example may be checked by defining $y1$ and $y2$ as stated above and then graphing only $y3 = y1/y2$, as shown in Figure 9.52.

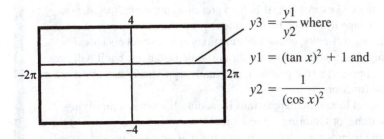

$$y3 = \frac{y1}{y2} \text{ where}$$

$$y1 = (\tan x)^2 + 1 \text{ and}$$

$$y2 = \frac{1}{(\cos x)^2}$$

Figure 9.52

This graph, which is a horizontal line where y is fixed at 1, supports our results. This method is recommended when you find it hard to interpret the display that results from graphing the expressions on both sides of the proposed identity.

PROGRESS CHECK 2   Prove the identity $\cot^2 x + 1 = \csc^2 x$.   ■

In Example 4 we established the identity $\tan^2 x + 1 = \sec^2 x$, and in the associated Progress Check exercise you were asked to confirm that $\cot^2 x + 1$ is identical to $\csc^2 x$. These two identities are used often, and we need to add them to our list of basic identities.

$$\textbf{Identity 7 } \tan^2 x + 1 = \sec^2 x$$
$$\textbf{Identity 8 } \cot^2 x + 1 = \csc^2 x$$

The eight identities listed are commonly referred to as the fundamental identities, and among these, identities 6, 7, and 8 are called the Pythagorean identities. In the next example we include an alternative solution that effectively employs identity 7.

EXAMPLE 5   Using Pythagorean Identities

Show that the equation $\cos^2 x(1 + \tan^2 x) = 1$ is an identity.

Solution

$$\cos^2 x(1 + \tan^2 x) = \cos^2 x\left(1 + \frac{\sin^2 x}{\cos^2 x}\right) \qquad \text{Identity 4}$$

$$= \cos^2 x \cdot 1 + \cos^2 x \cdot \frac{\sin^2 x}{\cos^2 x} \left.\rule{0pt}{40pt}\right\} $$

$$= \cos^2 x + \sin^2 x \qquad\qquad\qquad \text{Simplify}$$

$$= 1 \qquad\qquad\qquad\qquad\qquad \text{Identity 6}$$

Alternative Solution

$$\cos^2 x(1 + \tan^2 x) = \cos^2 x(\sec^2 x) \qquad \text{Identity 7}$$

$$= \cos^2 x\left(\frac{1}{\cos^2 x}\right) \qquad \text{Identity 2}$$

$$= 1$$

Thus, $\cos^2 x(1 + \tan^2 x) = 1$ is an identity.

PROGRESS CHECK 5

Verify the identity $\dfrac{\cot^2 x + 1}{\cot^2 x} = \sec^2 x$.   ■

In general, there is no standard procedure for working with identities. In fact, a given identity can usually be proved in several ways. However, these suggestions should be helpful.

Guidelines for Proving Identities

1. Change the more complicated expression in the identity to the same form as the less complicated expression. If both expressions are complicated, you might try to change them both to the same expression.
2. If you are having difficulty, change all functions to sines and cosines. This procedure might necessitate more algebra in some instances, but it will provide a direct approach to the problem. Gradually try to make use of the other trigonometric functions.
3. It is often helpful to rewrite expressions by adding fractions, simplifying complex fractions, or factoring expressions.
4. Do *not* attempt to prove an identity by treating it as an equation and using the associated techniques, for this involves assuming what you want to prove.

EXAMPLE 6   Using Factoring

Verify the identity $\sin x - \cos^2 x \sin x = \sin^3 x$.

Solution

$$
\begin{aligned}
\sin x - \cos^2 x \sin x &= \sin x(1 - \cos^2 x) \qquad \text{Factor} \\
&= \sin x(\sin^2 x) \qquad \quad \text{Identity 6} \\
&= \sin^3 x
\end{aligned}
$$

PROGRESS CHECK 6   Verify the identity $\dfrac{\sin^2 x}{1 + \cos x} = 1 - \cos x$. ■

Because calculators do not have keys for the cotangent, secant, and cosecant functions, it may be convenient to write certain formulas that arise in applied problems by using only the sine, cosine, or tangent functions. We will make such a conversion as we derive the formula that is required in the section-opening problem.

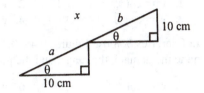

EXAMPLE 7   Using Identities to Derive a Formula

Solve the problem in the section introduction on page 500.

Figure 9.53

Solution   From the sketch of the brace that is shown in Figure 9.53, we see that

$$\sec \theta = \frac{a}{10}, \text{ so } a = 10 \sec \theta,$$

and

$$\csc \theta = \frac{b}{10}, \text{ so } b = 10 \csc \theta.$$

The length of the brace x is the sum of a and b. Thus,

$$x = 10 \sec \theta + 10 \csc \theta.$$

To convert to the requested formula, which involves only the sine and cosine functions, replace $\sec \theta$ with $1/\cos \theta$ and replace $\csc \theta$ with $1/\sin \theta$, to obtain

$$x = 10\left(\frac{1}{\cos \theta}\right) + 10\left(\frac{1}{\sin \theta}\right) = \frac{10 \sin \theta + 10 \cos \theta}{\sin \theta \cos \theta} = \frac{10(\sin \theta + \cos \theta)}{\sin \theta \cos \theta}.$$

PROGRESS CHECK 7   Show that the formula derived in Example 7 may also be written as $x = \dfrac{10(1 + \tan \theta)}{\sin \theta}$. ■

In Section 4.3 we considered a procedure for using a given trigonometric value to find other trigonometric values of that angle. We now show an alternative method for solving such problems that use identities.

EXAMPLE 8   Evaluating Functions Using Identities

If $\sin x = \dfrac{3}{5}$ and $\dfrac{\pi}{2} < x < \pi$, find

a. $\cos x$ **b.** $\tan x$ **c.** $\sec x$

Solution

a. Since $\pi/2 < x < \pi$, where $\cos x < 0$, the identity $\sin^2 x + \cos^2 x = 1$ when solved for $\cos x$ becomes

$$\cos x = -\sqrt{1 - \sin^2 x} = -\sqrt{1 - \left(\frac{3}{5}\right)^2} = -\sqrt{\frac{16}{25}} = -\frac{4}{5}.$$

b. $\tan x = \dfrac{\sin x}{\cos x} = \dfrac{3/5}{-4/5} = \dfrac{3}{-4}$ **c.** $\sec x = \dfrac{1}{\cos x} = \dfrac{1}{-4/5} = \dfrac{5}{-4}$

PROGRESS CHECK 8   If $\cos x = \dfrac{5}{13}$ and $\dfrac{3\pi}{2} < x < 2\pi$, find

a. $\sin x$ **b.** $\tan x$ **c.** $\csc x$ ■

EXERCISES 9.4

In Exercises 1–4 complete the table for the function and then sketch the curve from these points on the interval $[0, 2\pi]$. Confirm your result with a grapher.

x	0	$\frac{\pi}{6}$	$\frac{\pi}{3}$	$\frac{\pi}{2}$	$\frac{2\pi}{3}$	$\frac{5\pi}{6}$	π	$\frac{7\pi}{6}$	$\frac{4\pi}{3}$	$\frac{3\pi}{2}$	$\frac{5\pi}{3}$	$\frac{11\pi}{6}$	2π
y													

1. $y = \cot x$
3. $y = \csc x$
2. $y = \sec x$
4. $y = \cot 2x$

In Exercises 5–8 use Figures 9.45–9.47 or a grapher to determine the domain, the range, and the period of the function.

5. $y = \cot x$
7. $y = \csc x$
6. $y = \sec x$
8. $y = \cot 2x$

In Exercises 9–14 complete the table by determining if the function is increasing or decreasing in the interval. Use graphs to determine your answers.

		$\left(0, \frac{\pi}{2}\right)$	$\left(\frac{\pi}{2}, \pi\right)$	$\left(\pi, \frac{3\pi}{2}\right)$	$\left(\frac{3\pi}{2}, 2\pi\right)$
9.	$\sin x$				
10.	$\cos x$				
11.	$\tan x$				
12.	$\cot x$				
13.	$\sec x$				
14.	$\csc x$				

In Exercises 15–24 graph one cycle of the given functions. State the period.

15. $y = -\cot\left(x + \frac{\pi}{2}\right)$
16. $y = \tan\left(x - \frac{\pi}{4}\right)$

17. $y = \tan 2x$
18. $y = \cot\frac{1}{2}x$

19. $y = 3\csc\frac{x}{2}$
20. $y = \sec 2x$

21. $y = -\sec\left(x + \frac{\pi}{4}\right)$
22. $y = 2\csc \pi x$

23. $y = \csc(\pi x - \pi)$
24. $y = \sec\left(2\pi x - \frac{\pi}{2}\right)$

In Exercises 25–40 transform each first expression and show that it is identical to the second expression.

25. $\sin x \sec x$; $\tan x$
26. $\tan x \csc x$; $\sec x$
27. $\sin^2 x \csc x$; $\sin x$
28. $\tan x \cot^2 x$; $\cot x$
29. $\cos x \tan x \csc x$; 1
30. $\cot x \sec x \sin x$; 1
31. $\sin^2 x \cot^2 x$; $\cos^2 x$
32. $\tan^2 x \csc^2 x$; $\sec^2 x$
33. $\sin^2 x \sec^2 x$; $\tan^2 x$
34. $\dfrac{\cot x}{\csc x}$; $\cos x$
35. $\dfrac{\cos^2 x}{\cot^2 x}$; $\sin^2 x$
36. $\dfrac{\sin x \sec x}{\tan x}$; 1

37. $\dfrac{\cot x \tan x}{\sec x}$; $\cos x$
38. $1 + \cot^2 x$; $\csc^2 x$
39. $\dfrac{\cos^2 x}{1 + \sin x}$; $1 - \sin x$
40. $\sin^4 x - \cos^4 x$; $\sin^2 x - \cos^2 x$

In Exercises 41–50 prove that the equation is an identity.

41. $\dfrac{1 + \tan^2 x}{\csc^2 x} = \tan^2 x$
42. $\dfrac{1 + \tan^2 x}{\tan^2 x} = \csc^2 x$
43. $\sin x \tan x + \cos x = \sec x$
44. $\tan x \csc^2 x - \tan x = \cot x$
45. $\dfrac{\tan^2 x - \sin^2 x}{\tan^2 x} = \sin^2 x$
46. $\dfrac{\sec^2 x + \csc^2 x}{\sec^2 x} = \csc^2 x$
47. $\sin x \cos^3 x + \cos x \sin^3 x = \sin x \cos x$
48. $\cos^4 x + 2\cos^2 x \sin^2 x + \sin^4 x = 1$
49. $\dfrac{\sin x}{\csc x} + \dfrac{\cos x}{\sec x} = 1$
50. $\dfrac{\csc x}{\sin x} - \dfrac{\cot x}{\tan x} = 1$

In Exercises 51 and 52 use a grapher to graph the given expression, and make a conjecture about an identity involving $f(x)$. Then confirm the identity algebraically, if possible.

51. $f(x) = \dfrac{1 - \cos^2 x}{\cos x \tan x}$
52. $f(x) = \dfrac{1 - \sin^2 x}{\sin x \cos x}$

In Exercises 53–56 use identities to find the given function value if $\sin x = \dfrac{12}{13}$ and $\dfrac{\pi}{2} < x < \pi$.

53. $\csc x$
54. $\cos x$
55. $\tan x$
56. $\cot x$

In Exercises 57–60 use identities to find the given function value if $\cos x = a$ and $\pi < x < \dfrac{3\pi}{2}$.

57. $\sin x$
58. $\csc x$
59. $\sec x$
60. $\tan x$

61. In the study of polarized light, light is passed through two sheets of polarized material. As the top sheet is rotated through an angle θ, the intensity I of the light that is transmitted through both sheets changes. The relationship that describes this process was discovered in 1809 by Etienne Louis Malus, and is now called the Law of Malus. The Law is given by the trigonometric equation $I = M - M \tan^2 \theta \cos^2 \theta$, where M is the maximum intensity transmitted. Show that this law may also be expressed as $I = M \cos^2 \theta$.

62. Use the graph of $y = \tan^2 x$ that follows to graph $y = \sec^2 x$.

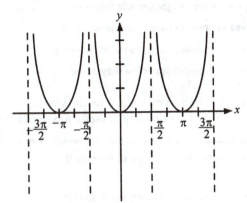

63. A major application of calculus is to describe the rate of change of functions. The following expression gives the rate of change of the function $y = \tan x$.

$$\text{rate of change of } \tan x = \frac{\cos x(\cos x) - \sin x(\sin x)}{(\cos x)^2}$$

Show that this expression simplifies to $\sec^2 x$.

64. The following expression gives the rate of change of the function $y = \cot x$.

$$\text{rate of change of } \cot x = \frac{-\sin x(\sin x) - \cos x(\cos x)}{(\sin x)^2}$$

Show that this expression simplifies to $-\csc^2 x$.

THINK ABOUT IT 9.4

1. a. Describe how we may translate the graph of $y = \csc x$ to obtain the graph of $y = \sec x$.
   b. What is the value of c closest to zero such that
   $$\csc(x + c) = \sec x$$
   for all values of x for which the expressions are defined?

2. Solve each inequality.
   a. $\tan x > 0$ **b.** $\cot x < 0$
3. Find all values of x in $[0, 2\pi)$ that make the given equation a true statement.
   a. $\sin x = \sqrt{1 - \cos^2 x}$ **b.** $\sin x = -\sqrt{1 - \cos^2 x}$
4. If $\log \sin a = b$, express $\log \csc a$ in terms of b.
5. The figure shown, called the **function hexagon,** arranges the six trigonometric functions of x so that many basic identities are easily generated, as shown in the following exercises.
   a. Describe in geometric terms how reciprocal functions are positioned in the hexagon.
   b. Any function of x is identical to the product of the two functions of x on either side of it. For example $\sin x = \cos x \tan x$ is an identity. Create another example of this type and verify that the equation is an identity.
   c. The identities $\tan x = \sin x/\cos x$ and $\tan x = \sec x/\csc x$ illustrate quotient identities that may be read from the arrangement. How is this done? State and prove two identities of this type for $\sin x$.
   d. Another type of identity involves the product of three functions of x in alternate positions around the hexagon. Give two specific examples and state the general rule for this type of identity.

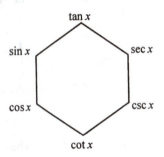

9.5   Inverse Trigonometric Functions

At an art gallery, a painting that is 3 ft high is mounted so that its base is 2 ft above the anticipated eye level of a viewer.

a. If a viewer is standing x ft from the wall, as shown in the diagram, then express the viewing angle θ in terms of x (**Hint:** θ may be expressed as the difference between two inverse trigonometric functions.)
b. Use a grapher to graph the relation in part **a.**
c. How far back should a viewer stand so that the picture appears to be the largest? In other words, what value for x produces the maximum value for θ? (See Example 3.)

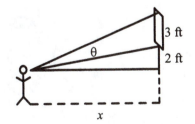

OBJECTIVES

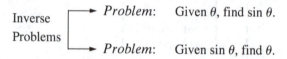

1 Evaluate expressions involving the inverse trigonometric functions.

2 Graph an expression that involves an inverse trigonometric function.

3 Simplify a trigonometric function of an inverse trigonometric function.

4 Use the inverse trigonometric function properties when they apply.

The problem in the section opener seeks to find an expression for the viewing angle θ. Recall from Section 4.1 that when the problem is to find θ, it is useful to view the following types of problems as inverse problems.

Inverse
Problems
$\left\{\begin{array}{l} \textit{Problem:} \quad \text{Given } \theta, \text{ find } \sin \theta. \\ \\ \textit{Problem:} \quad \text{Given } \sin \theta, \text{ find } \theta. \end{array}\right.$

Based on this perspective, the function that reverses the assignments of the sine function is called the **inverse sine function,** and, in general, the functions that reverse the assignments of the trigonometric functions are called the **inverse trigonometric functions.** Before we investigate these functions by introducing the inverse sine function, you should consider carefully four facts about any inverse functions that we learned in Section 8.2.

1. Two functions with exactly reverse assignments are inverse functions.
2. The domain of a function f is the range of its inverse function, and the range of f is the domain of its inverse.
3. A function is one-to-one when each x value in the domain is assigned a different y value so that no two ordered pairs have the same second component. We define the inverse of f, denoted f^{-1}, only when f is a one-to-one function.
4. The graphs of inverse functions are symmetric about the line $y = x$.

Now consider the graph of $y = \sin x$ in Figure 9.54. Because the sine function is periodic, many x values are assigned the same y value. For example,

$$\sin 0 = \sin \pi = \sin 2\pi = \sin(-\pi) = 0.$$

Thus, the inverse of the sine function is not a function. The so-called **inverse sine function** is defined by restricting the domain of $y = \sin x$ to the interval $[-\pi/2, \pi/2]$. Note in Figure 9.54 that each x value is assigned a different y value in this limited version of the sine function.

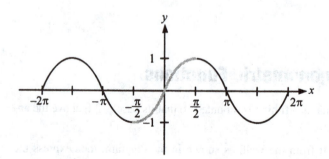

Figure 9.54

We find the rule for the inverse sine function by interchanging the x and y variables. Thus, the inverse of the function defined by

$$y = \sin x \qquad -\frac{\pi}{2} \le x \le \frac{\pi}{2}$$

is defined by

$$x = \sin y \qquad -\frac{\pi}{2} \le y \le \frac{\pi}{2},$$

which is written in inverse notation as

$$y = \arcsin x \text{ or } y = \sin^{-1} x.$$

For example, since $\sin(\pi/2) = 1$, we write

$$\frac{\pi}{2} = \arcsin 1 \text{ or} \frac{\pi}{2} = \sin^{-1} 1.$$

Both expressions are read "$\pi/2$ is the arc (or number) whose sine is 1," and note that the -1 in the function name $\sin^{-1}$ is not an exponent. Because a function and its inverse interchange their domain and range, for the inverse sine function the domain is the interval $[-1, 1]$ and the range is $[-\pi/2, \pi/2]$. The following definition sums up the key aspects of our discussion.

Inverse Sine Function

The inverse sine function, denoted by **arcsin** or **sin**$^{-1}$, is defined by

$$y = \arcsin x \text{ **if and only if** } x = \sin y,$$

where $-1 \le x \le 1$ and $-\pi/2 \le y \le \pi/2$.

Most graphing calculators have a key labeled $\sin^{-1}$ for the inverse sine function so it is easy to obtain a picture for $y = \sin^{-1} x$, as shown in Figure 9.55. To interpret this graph it is helpful to understand that the graph of $y = \sin^{-1} x$ may be obtained by reflecting the graph of $y = \sin x$ that is limited to $-\pi/2 \le x \le \pi/2$ about the line $y = x$, as shown in Figure 9.56. From this graph it is then apparent that the domain of $y = \sin^{-1} x$ is $[-1, 1]$, and the range is $[-\pi/2, \pi/2]$.

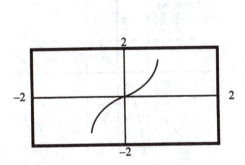

Figure 9.55

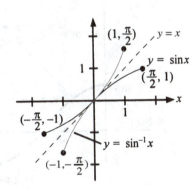

Figure 9.56

EXAMPLE 1   Evaluating the Inverse Sine Function

Evaluate each expression. Specify exact values, where possible.

a. $\arcsin\dfrac{1}{2}$ **b.** $\sin^{-1}(-0.5509)$ **c.** $\arcsin 2$

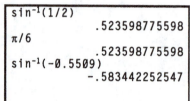

Figure 9.57

Solution   On the basis of our work in Section 9.2, it will be possible to specify exact values when answers involve 0, $\pi/6$, $\pi/4$, $\pi/3$, or $\pi/2$.

a. Let $\arcsin(1/2) = y$; then $1/2 = \sin y$. We solve this equation and find the number y in the interval $[-\pi/2, \pi/2]$ whose sine is $\frac{1}{2}$. Since $\sin(\pi/6) = 1/2$,

$$\arcsin\frac{1}{2} = \frac{\pi}{6}.$$

The first four lines in Figure 9.57 show a calculator check of this result.

b. We need to use a calculator to determine that

$$\sin^{-1}(-0.5509) \approx -0.58,$$

as shown in the last two lines in Figure 9.57.

c. The expression arcsin 2 has no value because $y = \arcsin 2$ implies $2 = \sin y$ and this equation has no solution. Check this result by calculator. You should obtain either an error message or a complex number result that has meaning only in advanced mathematics.

PROGRESS CHECK 1   Evaluate each expression. Specify exact values, where possible.

a. $\sin^{-1}\left(-\dfrac{\sqrt{3}}{2}\right)$ **b.** $\arcsin \pi$ **c.** $\sin^{-1}(0.8109)$ ■

Through similar considerations we may define inverses for the other five trigonometric functions. For example, Figure 9.58 shows that $y = \cos x$ is one-to-one and assumes all its range values for $0 \leq x \leq \pi$. Thus, we may define the inverse function, $y = \arccos x$, as graphed, with domain $[-1, 1]$ and range $[0, \pi]$ from this limited version of the cosine function. Similarly, Figure 9.59 shows that we use $y = \tan x$ for $-\pi/2 < x < \pi/2$ to define $y = \arctan x$ with the set of all real numbers for its domain and the interval $(-\pi/2, \pi/2)$ for its range. The remaining inverse functions are used less frequently, so we just list their respective domains and ranges in the following summary. A consideration of the graphs of $y = \cot x$, $y = \sec x$, and $y = \csc x$ would show the respective intervals to be suitable (though arbitrary) choices.

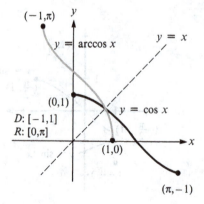

Figure 9.58

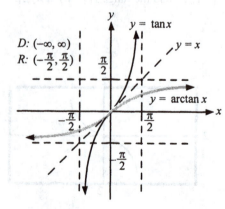

Figure 9.59

Inverse Trigonometric Functions

Function	Domain	Range
$y = \arcsin x$	$[-1, 1]$	$[-\pi/2, \pi/2]$
$y = \arccos x$	$[-1, 1]$	$[0, \pi]$
$y = \arctan x$	$(-\infty, \infty)$	$(-\pi/2, \pi/2)$
$y = \text{arccot } x$	$(-\infty, \infty)$	$(0, \pi)$
$y = \text{arcsec } x$	$(-\infty, -1] \cup [1, \infty)$	$[0, \pi], y \neq \pi/2$
$y = \text{arccsc } x$	$(-\infty, -1] \cup [1, \infty)$	$[-\pi/2, \pi/2], y \neq 0$

There are two areas concerning inverse trigonometric functions in which there is no general agreement, so take note.

1. In terms of notation, an inverse trig function is sometimes capitalized and written as Arcsin x or Sin^{-1} x. With this convention, arcsin x and sin^{-1} x do not represent functions but represent the set of all numbers whose sine is x with no restriction placed on the range values.
2. The inverse secant and cosecant functions are sometimes assigned different range intervals depending on the application of the functions. The intervals chosen above are usually selected in most precalculus texts.

EXAMPLE 2   Evaluating the Inverse Cosine or Tangent Function

Evaluate each expression. Specify exact answers, where possible.

a. $\arccos 0$ **b.** $\cos^{-1}\left(-\frac{1}{2}\right)$ **c.** $\arctan(-1)$ **d.** $\tan^{-1} 2$

Solution   On the basis of our work in Section 9.2, it is possible to specify exact values when answers involve $0, \pi/6, \pi/4, \pi/3, \pi/2$, or π. You should check each of the results that follow by using your calculator.

a. Let $y = \arccos 0$; then $0 = \cos y$. We seek the number y in the interval $[0, \pi]$ whose cosine is 0. Since $\cos \pi = 0$, $\arccos 0 = \pi$.
b. Let $y = \cos^{-1}(-1/2)$; then $-1/2 = \cos y$. We solve this equation and find the number y in the interval $[0, \pi]$ whose cosine is $-\frac{1}{2}$. Since $\cos(\pi/3) = 1/2$, we want the number in quadrant two with a reference arc of $\pi/3$.

$$\cos\left(\pi - \frac{\pi}{3}\right) = \cos\frac{2\pi}{3} = -\frac{1}{2}.$$

Thus, $\cos^{-1}(-1/2) = 2\pi/3$.
c. Let $y = \arctan(-1)$; then $-1 = \tan y$. We solve this equation and find the number y in the interval $(-\pi/2, \pi/2)$ whose tangent is -1. Since $\tan(-\pi/4) = -1$,

$$\arctan(-1) = -\frac{\pi}{4}.$$

d. By calculator, $\tan^{-1} 2 \approx 1.11$.

PROGRESS CHECK 2   Evaluate each expression. Specify exact answers, where possible.

a. $\arctan 0$ **b.** $\cos^{-1}\left(\frac{1}{\sqrt{2}}\right)$ **c.** $\cos^{-1}\left(-\frac{1}{\sqrt{2}}\right)$ **d.** $\tan^{-1}(-5)$ ■

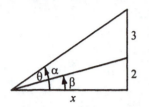

Figure 9.60

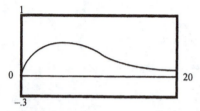

Figure 9.61

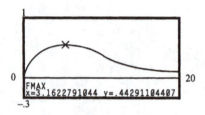

FMAX
x=3.1622791044 y=.44291104407

Figure 9.62

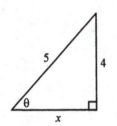

Figure 9.63
$\theta = \sin^{-1}\frac{4}{5}$

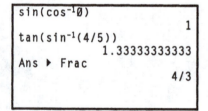

sin(cos⁻¹0)
                                1
tan(sin⁻¹(4/5))
                   1.33333333333
Ans ▶ Frac
                              4/3

Figure 9.64

EXAMPLE 3 Maximizing a Viewing Angle

Solve the problem in the section introduction on page 509.

Solution

a. Consider the simplified sketch of the problem in Figure 9.60. Observe that $\theta = \alpha - \beta$ where $\tan \alpha = 5/x$ and $\tan \beta = 2/x$. So

$$\alpha = \tan^{-1}\frac{5}{x}, \quad \beta = \tan^{-1}\frac{2}{x}, \quad \text{and } \theta = \tan^{-1}\frac{5}{x} - \tan^{-1}\frac{2}{x}.$$

b. The equation that defines θ in terms of x is graphed in Figure 9.61.

c. By using the Function Maximum feature (or Zoom and Trace), we can determine that the maximum point in the graph of this relation is reached at about (3.16, 0.44), as shown in Figure 9.62. Thus, when x is about 3.2 ft, the viewing angle reaches a maximum value of about 0.44 radians (or 25°).

PROGRESS CHECK 3 Redo the problem in Example 3, assuming that the painting is 5 ft high and its base is hung 3 ft above the anticipated eye level of a viewer. ■

EXAMPLE 4 Evaluating a Function of an Inverse Function

Evaluate each expression. Find exact answers where possible.

a. sin(arccos0)   **b.** $\tan\left(\sin^{-1}\frac{4}{5}\right)$

Solution

a. First, determine arccos 0. Since $\cos(\pi/2) = 0$, we have

$$\frac{\pi}{2} = \arccos 0.$$

Now replace arccos 0 by $\pi/2$ in the original expressions.

$$\sin(\arccos 0) = \sin\frac{\pi}{2} = 1$$

b. It is useful to interpret $\sin^{-1}(4/5)$ as the measure of an angle in a right triangle. Let $\theta = \sin^{-1}(4/5)$ and sketch the triangle in Figure 9.63. The length of the side opposite θ is 4 and the hypotenuse has length 5. The remaining side length is found by the Pythagorean relationship.

$$x = \sqrt{5^2 - 4^2} = 3$$

Thus,

$$\tan \theta = \tan\left(\sin^{-1}\frac{4}{5}\right) = \frac{4}{3}.$$

Note It is not difficult to evaluate functions in succession with a calculator, and Figure 9.64 shows a calculator display that confirms the results in this example.

PROGRESS CHECK 4 Evaluate each expression. Find exact answers where possible.

a. $\cos(\arcsin(-1))$ **b.** $\sin\left(\tan^{-1}\frac{15}{8}\right)$ ■

Inverse Properties

As discussed in Section 8.2, inverse functions offset each other; so that if f and g are inverses, then

$$f[g(x)] = x \text{ for all } x \text{ in the domain of } g$$

and

$$g[f(x)] = x \text{ for all } x \text{ in the domain of } f.$$

Applying this definition to the restricted sine, cosine, and tangent functions and their inverses yields the following properties.

$$\sin(\sin^{-1} x) = x \quad \text{for} \quad -1 \le x \le 1$$
$$\sin^{-1}(\sin x) = x \quad \text{for} \quad -\pi/2 \le x \le \pi/2$$
$$\cos(\cos^{-1} x) = x \quad \text{for} \quad -1 \le x \le 1$$
$$\cos^{-1}(\cos x) = x \quad \text{for} \quad 0 \le x \le \pi$$
$$\tan(\tan^{-1} x) = x \quad \text{for} \quad \text{all } x$$
$$\tan^{-1}(\tan x) = x \quad \text{for} \quad -\pi/2 < x < \pi/2$$

The next example shows that knowing the intervals for which these properties hold is essential to applying the properties.

EXAMPLE 5   Monitoring the Domain of the Inverse Properties

Evaluate each expression, if possible.

a. $\sin^{-1}\left[\sin\left(\dfrac{\pi}{4}\right)\right]$
b. $\cos^{-1}(\cos 2\pi)$
c. $\sin(\sin^{-1} 2)$

Solution

a. Because $\pi/4$ is in the interval $[-\pi/2, \pi/2]$, we use $\sin^{-1}(\sin x) = x$ to obtain $\sin^{-1}[\sin(\pi/4)] = \pi/4$. To check, note that $\sin(\pi/4) = 1/\sqrt{2}$ and $\sin^{-1}(1/\sqrt{2}) = \pi/4$.

b. Because 2π is not in the interval $[0, \pi]$, we cannot use $\cos^{-1}(\cos x) = x$. Instead, since $\cos 2\pi = 1$, we have

$$\cos^{-1}(\cos 2\pi) = \cos^{-1} 1 = 0.$$

c. Because 2 is not in the interval $[-1, 1]$, we cannot use $\sin(\sin^{-1} x) = x$. There is no value for $\sin(\sin^{-1} 2)$, since 2 is not in the domain of $y = \sin^{-1} x$.

PROGRESS CHECK 5   Evaluate each expression, if possible.

a. $\tan^{-1}\left[\tan\dfrac{\pi}{6}\right]$
b. $\cos(\cos^{-1} 2\pi)$
c. $\tan(\tan^{-1} 2)$ ■

EXERCISES 9.5

In Exercises 1–30 evaluate the expression. Specify exact values where possible.

1. $\arccos \dfrac{1}{2}$

2. $\arccos\left(-\dfrac{1}{2}\right)$

3. $\sin^{-1}\left(-\dfrac{\sqrt{3}}{2}\right)$

4. $\arcsin \dfrac{\sqrt{3}}{2}$

5. $\arctan 1$

6. $\arctan \pi$

7. $\arcsin(-1)$

8. $\arcsin\left(\dfrac{1}{\pi}\right)$

9. $\arcsin \dfrac{1}{\sqrt{2}}$

10. $\tan^{-1} \sqrt{3}$

11. $\tan^{-1}\left(-\sqrt{3}\right)$

12. $\arccos\left(-\dfrac{1}{\sqrt{2}}\right)$

13. $\arcsin 0.3124$

14. $\sin^{-1}(-0.3124)$

15. $\cos^{-1}(-0.5509)$

16. $\arccos 0.5509$

17. $\arctan 1.758$

18. $\tan^{-1}(-1.758)$

19. $\cos^{-1}\left(\dfrac{4}{5}\right)$

20. $\arctan \dfrac{3}{2}$

21. $\cos(\arcsin 0)$

22. $\sin(\arccos 1)$

23. $\sin\left(\cos^{-1} \dfrac{\sqrt{3}}{2}\right)$

24. $\cos\left[\sin^{-1}\left(-\dfrac{1}{2}\right)\right]$

25. $\cot(\arccos 0)$

26. $\tan^{-1}(\cos 0)$

27. $\arcsin(\tan 0)$

28. $\csc(\arcsin 1)$

29. $\tan[\arcsin(-0.5518)]$

30. $\csc(\arccos 0.0129)$

In Exercises 31–34 simplify the expression.

31. $\sin\left(\tan^{-1}\dfrac{3}{4}\right)$ **32.** $\cos\left[\arcsin\left(-\dfrac{1}{3}\right)\right]$

33. $\tan\left(\arcsin\dfrac{12}{13}\right)$ **34.** $\cot\left(\cos^{-1}\dfrac{8}{17}\right)$

In Exercises 35–44 evaluate each expression.

35. $\cos(\arccos 0)$ **36.** $\cos^{-1}(\cos 0)$
37. $\sin^{-1}[\sin(-1)]$ **38.** $\sin[\arcsin(-1)]$
39. $\cos^{-1}\left[\cos\left(\dfrac{3\pi}{2}\right)\right]$ **40.** $\sin^{-1}(\sin 2\pi)$
41. $\tan[\tan^{-1}(-1)]$ **42.** $\tan^{-1}[\tan(-\pi)]$
43. $\cos(\cos^{-1} 2)$ **44.** $\sin(\sin^{-1} 2\pi)$

In Exercises 45–48 solve the formula for θ.

45. $m\cdot\sin\theta = 1$, where $-\dfrac{\pi}{2} \le \theta \le \dfrac{\pi}{2}$

46. $\tan\theta = \dfrac{b}{a}$, where $-\dfrac{\pi}{2} < \theta < \dfrac{\pi}{2}$

47. $T = \dfrac{2V_0\sin\theta}{g}$, where $-\dfrac{\pi}{2} \le \theta \le \dfrac{\pi}{2}$

48. $V_x = V\cos\theta$, where $0 \le \theta \le \pi$
49. Consider the illustration below.
   a. Write θ as a function of a.
   b. Write θ as a function of b.

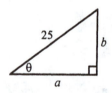

50. Consider the illustration below. Write θ as the difference between two inverse tangent expressions.

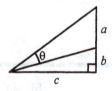

51. As shown in the figure, the length s of the shadow cast by a pole that is t feet tall depends on θ, the angle of inclination of the sun. Let the pole be 25 ft tall.
   a. Express s as a function of θ. State the domain and range of this function.
   b. Express θ as a function of s. State the domain and range of this function.

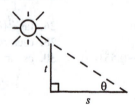

52. The height s of the right triangle shown in the figure depends on the acute angle θ.
   a. Express the height as a function of θ. Give the domain and range of this function.
   b. Express the area of the triangle as a function of θ. Give the domain and range of this function.
   c. Express θ as a function of the area. Give the domain and range of this function.

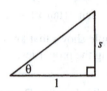

THINK ABOUT IT 9.5

1. Give an example of a value for x that shows that the given equation is *not true* for all values of x for which the expressions are defined.
   a. $\tan^{-1} x = (\sin^{-1} x)/(\cos^{-1} x)$
   b. $\sin^{-1} x = 1/(\sin x)$
   c. $\operatorname{arccot} x = 1/(\arctan x)$
   d. $\operatorname{arccot} x = \arctan(1/x)$
   e. $\arccos(\cos x) = x$
   f. $\cos(\cos^{-1} x) = x$

2. Explain why the calculator value for $\sin^{-1}(\sin 2) = 1.14159$, and not 2. What is the relationship between π and 1.14159?

3. Consider the illustration below. The area of the region enclosed by the graphs of $y = \dfrac{1}{x^2 + 1}$, $y = 0$, $x = -1$, and $x = 1$ is shown in calculus to be given by $\arctan 1 - \arctan(-1)$. Find this area.

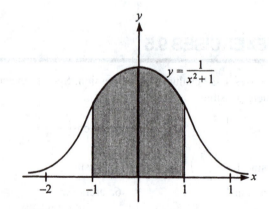

4. Simplify $\sin(\cos^{-1} x)$. Use the method in Example 4b.
5. a. Sketch the graph of $y = \arcsin(x - 1)$.
   b. Sketch the graph of $y = \arccos(x + 2)$.

9.6 Trigonometric Equations

On May 2 the tide in a certain harbor is described by

$$y = 12 + 5.3 \cos(0.5067t),$$

where y is the height of the water in feet and t is the time in hours that has elapsed from 12 midnight on May 1. To the nearest minute, find all times on May 2 when the water level is at a height of 14 ft. (See Examples 1 and 6.)

Courtesy of John Serafin.

O B J E C T I V E S

1 Find the approximate solution to trigonometric equations by using graphical methods.

2 Use reference numbers to solve trigonometric equations, specifying exact solutions where possible.

3 Use factoring or the square root property to solve certain trigonometric equations.

4 Solve trigonometric equations involving functions of multiple angles.

Recall from Section 4.4 that equations involving trigonometric expressions commonly appear in two types: identities and conditional equations. An identity is an equation such as

$$\tan \theta = \frac{\sin \theta}{\cos \theta}$$

that is true for all values of θ for which expressions are defined. Conditional trigonometric equations differ from identities in that they are true only for certain values of the unknown. For instance, in the section-opening problem we need to find all values of t in the interval $0 \le t \le 24$ that satisfy

$$14 = 12 + 5.3 \cos(0.5067t),$$

and we will find that there are just four such solutions. Now that we have discussed in detail how to graph trigonometric functions, it is instructive to first show how we can approximate these four solutions by using graphical methods.

EXAMPLE 1   Tidal Water Height—A Graphing Approach

Solve the problem in the above section introduction by using graphical methods.

Solution   To obtain a picture of the solution to the given equation, we first graph $y1 = 14$ and $y2 = 12 + 5.3 \cos(0.5067x)$ on a grapher that is set to Radian Mode, as shown in Figure 9.65. Observe that a viewing window of [0, 24], by [6, 18] was chosen because the problem requests all solutions for the 24-hour interval associated with May 2, and because this cosine graph oscillates about a midline of $y = 12$ with an amplitude of 5.3.

We see the two graphs intersect at four points, so there are four solutions in the interval shown. To estimate the earliest solution, we can use the Intersection operation (or Zoom and Trace) to find that $x \approx 2.3364$ for the intersection point shown in Figure 9.66. By the same method, you can determine that the x coordinates of the other three intersection points are 10.0638, 14.7366, and 22.4640. Thus, to the nearest minute, the water level in this harbor is at a height of 14 ft at 2:20 a.m., 10:04 a.m., 2:44 p.m. and 10:28 p.m.

PROGRESS CHECK 1   Use the formula from Example 1 and find all times on May 2 in this harbor when the water level is at a height of 11 ft. Use a graphical method.   ■

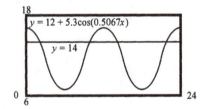

Figure 9.65

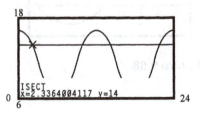

Figure 9.66

The solutions in Example 1 may be confirmed algebraically by extending the methods that were introduced in Section 4.4. Before considering the problem, it is helpful to first develop the necessary procedures using simpler equations. The next two examples illustrate how to find solutions for $0 \le x < 2\pi$ when exact solutions may be specified.

EXAMPLE 2   Finding Exact Solutions Where $0 \le x < 2\pi$

Solve $\sin x = -1/2$ for $0 \le x < 2\pi$. Specify exact solutions.

Solution   First, determine the quadrant that contains the point assigned to x.

$$\sin x = -\frac{1}{2}, \text{ which is a negative number.}$$

The point assigned to x could be in either Q_3 or Q_4, since the sine function is negative in both quadrants.

Second, determine the reference number. Discard the sign on the function value and use the inverse sine function to determine that

$$\sin^{-1}\frac{1}{2} = \frac{\pi}{6}.$$

Therefore, the reference number is $\pi/6$.

Third, determine the appropriate values of x (see Figure 9.67).

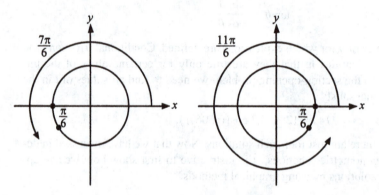

Figure 9.67
$\pi + \pi/6 = 7\pi/6$ is the number in Q_3 with a reference number of $\pi/6$.
$2\pi - \pi/6 = 11\pi/6$ is the number in Q_4 with a reference number of $\pi/6$.

Therefore, $7\pi/6$ and $11\pi/6$ make the equation a true statement, and the solution set in the interval $[0, 2\pi)$ is $\{7\pi/6, 11\pi/6\}$. Figure 9.68 provides graphical evidence that supports this result.

PROGRESS CHECK 2   Solve $\cos x = -1/\sqrt{2}$ for $0 \le x < 2\pi$. Specify exact solutions.   ■

When solving certain trigonometric equations, it may be necessary to first solve the equations for the functions of x in the problem. Factoring, the square root property, or identities may be needed in such cases. To illustrate, the next example shows a case in which factoring is useful.

EXAMPLE 3   Using Factoring

Solve the equation $2 \sin x \cos x - \sin x = 0$ in the interval $[0, 2\pi)$.

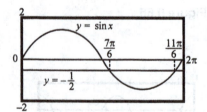

Figure 9.68

Solution   First, factor out the common factor sin x.

$$2 \sin x \cos x - \sin x = 0$$
$$\sin x (2 \cos x - 1) = 0$$

Note that we have found two factors whose product is zero. Hence, the original equation will be satisfied whenever either factor is zero, and we treat each factor separately from this point on.

First factor $\sin x = 0$ The sine function is 0 when $x = 0$ and $x = \pi$.
Second factor $2 \cos x - 1 = 0$
$$\cos x = 1/2$$

1. Since $\cos x$ is positive, the point assigned to x could be in Q_1 or Q_4.
2. Since $\cos^{-1}(1/2) = \pi/3$, the reference is $\pi/3$.
3. $\pi/3$ is the number in Q_1 with a reference number of $\pi/3$ (Figure 9.69). Meanwhile, $2\pi - \pi/3 = 5\pi/3$ is the number in Q_4 with a reference number of $\pi/3$ (Figure 9.70).

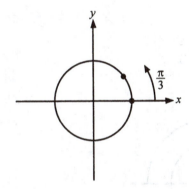

Figure 9.69

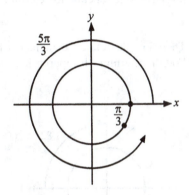

Figure 9.70

Thus, in the interval $[0, 2\pi)$ the solution set is $\{0, \pi/3, \pi, 5\pi/3\}$. Observe that the four x-intercepts in the graph in Figure 9.71 on $[0, 2\pi)$ are in agreement with these four solutions.

PROGRESS CHECK 3   Solve $2 \sin^2 x = \sin x$ for $0 \le x < 2\pi$.   ■

A solution in Q_1, Q_3 and Q_4 was illustrated in Examples 2 and 3. Observe that solutions in each of the quadrants are determined as follows:

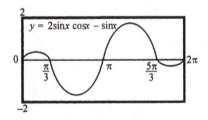

Figure 9.71

Quadrant	Solution
1	reference number
2	π − reference number
3	π + reference number
4	2π − reference number

Once we have the solutions of a trigonometric equation that are between 0 and 2π, we can determine all the solutions, since the trigonometric functions are periodic. In laying off a length 2π, we pass around the unit circle and return to our original point. Thus, we generate all the solutions to an equation by adding multiples of 2π to the solutions that are in the interval $[0, 2\pi)$.

EXAMPLE 4 Approximating All Solutions to a Trigonometric Equation

Approximate all the solutions to $4 \cos x + 1 = 0$.

Solution First, solve the equation for $\cos x$.

$$4 \cos x + 1 = 0$$

$$\cos x = -\frac{1}{4} = -0.2500$$

Second, determine the quadrant that contains the point assigned to x.

$$\cos x = -0.2500, \text{ which is a negative number.}$$

The point assigned to x could be in either Q_2 or Q_3, since the cosine function is negative in both quadrants.

Third, determine the reference number. Discard the sign on the function value and use the inverse cosine function to determine that

$$\cos^{-1} 0.25 \approx 1.32.$$

Therefore, the reference number is 1.32.

Fourth, determine the appropriate values of x (Figure 9.72).

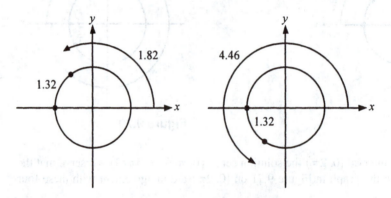

Figure 9.72

$3.14 - 1.32 = 1.82$ is the number in Q_2 with a reference number of 1.32.

$3.14 + 1.32 = 4.46$ is the number in Q_3 with a reference number of 1.32.

Thus, the formulas,

$$1.82 + k2\pi \text{ and } 4.46 + k2\pi,$$

where k is an integer, generate all the solutions to the equation, and the solution set is $\{x: x = 1.82 + k2\pi \text{ or } x = 4.46 + k2\pi, k \text{ any integer}\}$. A graphical check that supports this result for $-4\pi \le x \le 4\pi$ is shown in Figure 9.73.

PROGRESS CHECK 4 Approximate all the solutions to $5 \sin x + 2 = 0$. ■

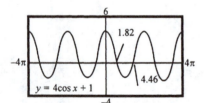

Figure 9.73

The last main idea we need to develop, in order to show an algebraic solution to the section-opening problem, is a method for solving trigonometric equations that involve multiple angles. Example 5 illustrates a basic procedure for solving an equation of this type.

EXAMPLE 5   Solving Equations Involving Functions of Multiple Angles

Solve $\sin 3x = \dfrac{1}{\sqrt{2}}$ for $0 \leq x < 2\pi$.

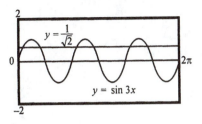

Solution   Since the function $y = \sin 3x$ completes three cycles for $0 \leq x < 2\pi$, we can anticipate that $\sin 3x = 1/\sqrt{2}$ has three times as many solutions as $\sin x = 1/\sqrt{2}$ for this interval. Figure 9.74 confirms this prediction since it shows that $\sin 3x = 1/\sqrt{2}$ has six solutions in the interval $[0, 2\pi)$.

Figure 9.74

   To solve this equation algebraically we initially solve the equation for $3x$. Then the formulas for $3x$ will imply formulas for x, as shown in Step 3 below.

1. Since $\sin 3x$ is positive, the point assigned to $3x$ could be in Q_1 or Q_2.
2. Since $\sin^{-1}\left(1/\sqrt{2}\right) = \pi/4$, the reference number is $\pi/4$.
3. Determine the appropriate values of $3x$ and then of x (Figure 9.75).

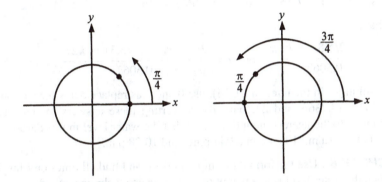

Figure 9.75
$\pi/4$ is the number in Q_1 with a reference number of $\pi/4$
$\pi - \pi/4 = 3\pi/4$ is the number in Q_2 with a reference number of $\pi/4$.

Thus,

$$3x = \frac{\pi}{4} + k2\pi \text{ or } 3x = \frac{3\pi}{4} + k2\pi,$$

from which we have

$$x = \frac{\pi}{12} + k\frac{2\pi}{3} \text{ or } x = \frac{\pi}{4} + k\frac{2\pi}{3}.$$

4. To obtain solutions in the interval $[0, 2\pi)$, use 0, 1, and 2 as replacements for k.

$$\frac{\pi}{12} + (0)\frac{2\pi}{3} = \frac{\pi}{12} \qquad \frac{\pi}{4} + (0)\frac{2\pi}{3} = \frac{\pi}{4}$$

$$\frac{\pi}{12} + (1)\frac{2\pi}{3} = \frac{3\pi}{4} \qquad \frac{\pi}{4} + (1)\frac{2\pi}{3} = \frac{11\pi}{12}$$

$$\frac{\pi}{12} + (2)\frac{2\pi}{3} = \frac{17\pi}{12} \qquad \frac{\pi}{4} + (2)\frac{2\pi}{3} = \frac{19\pi}{12}$$

Thus $\{\pi/12, \pi/4, 3\pi/4, 11\pi/12, 17\pi/12, 19\pi/12\}$ is the solution set in $[0, 2\pi)$.

PROGRESS CHECK 5 Solve $\cos 2x = -\dfrac{1}{2}$ for $0 \le x < 2\pi$. ■

EXAMPLE 6 Tidal Water Height—An Algebraic Approach

Solve the problem in the section introduction on page 517 by using algebraic methods.

Solution Replacing y by 14 in the given equation yields

$$14 = 12 + 5.3 \cos(0.5067t)$$

which is equivalent to

$$\cos(0.5067t) = \frac{2}{5.3}.$$

The cosine function is positive in Q_1 and Q_4, and the reference number is $\cos^{-1}(2/5.3)$. The numbers in Q_1 and Q_4 with this reference number are $\cos^{-1}(2/5.3)$ and $2\pi - \cos^{-1}(2/5.3)$, respectively. Thus,

$$0.5067t = \cos^{-1}(2/5.3) + k2\pi \qquad \text{or} \qquad 0.5067t = 2\pi - \cos^{-1}(2/5.3) + k2\pi$$

from which we have

$$t = \frac{\cos^{-1}(2/5.3) + k2\pi}{0.5067} \qquad \text{or} \qquad t = \frac{2\pi - \cos^{-1}(2/5.3) + k2\pi}{0.5067}.$$

Finally to obtain solutions in the interval $[0, 24)$, use 0 and 1 as replacements for k to obtain 2.3364, 10.0638, 14.7366, and 22.4640. By converting these answers to standard times that are rounded to the nearest minute, we find that the water level in this harbor is at a height of 14 ft at 2:20 a.m., 10:04 a.m., 2:44 p.m., and 10:28 p.m.

PROGRESS CHECK 6 Use the formula from Example 6 and find all times on May 2 in this harbor when the water level is at a height of 11 ft. Use an algebraic method. ■

EXERCISES 9.6

In Exercises 1–20 solve for x in the interval $[0, 2\pi)$. Specify exact solutions, where possible.

1. $\sin x = \dfrac{\sqrt{3}}{2}$ 2. $\sin x = -\dfrac{\sqrt{3}}{2}$

3. $\cos x = -\dfrac{1}{2}$ 4. $\tan x = 1$

5. $\tan x = -1$ 6. $\sec x = 2$

7. $\sin x = 0.1219$ 8. $\sin x = -0.1219$

9. $\tan x = -3.145$ 10. $\tan x = 3.145$

11. $\sqrt{2} \cos x = 1$ 12. $\csc x - \sqrt{2} = 0$

13. $\sin x + 2 = 0$ 14. $\cos x - 3 = 0$

15. $3 \tan x - 1 = 0$ 16. $2 \tan x + 7 = 0$

17. $2 \cot x + 3 = 0$ 18. $\dfrac{\cos x}{4} = \dfrac{1}{100}$

19. $\sec x = -5$ 20. $\dfrac{3 \sin x}{5} = \dfrac{3}{8}$

In Exercises 21–36 solve for x in the interval $[0, 2\pi)$. Specify exact solutions, where possible.

21. $2 \sin^2 x - 1 = 0$ 22. $3 \tan^2 x - 1 = 0$

23. $\cos^2 x = \cos x$ 24. $\sin^3 x = \sin x$

25. $2 \cos x \sin x = \cos x$ 26. $\tan x \cos x = \tan x$

27. $\tan^2 x + 4 \tan x - 21 = 0$

28. $2 \sin^2 x - 5 \sin x = 3$

29. $\cos 3x = 0$ 30. $\sin 4x = 1$

31. $\sin 2x = \dfrac{1}{2}$ 32. $\sin \frac{1}{2} x = \dfrac{1}{2}$

33. $\tan \frac{1}{3} x = 1$ 34. $\csc \frac{1}{4} x = 2$

In Exercises 35–40 find all solutions to the equation. Specify exact solutions, where possible.

35. $4 \sin x - 1 = 1$ 36. $10 \cos x - 2 = 0$

37. $4 \csc x + 9 = 0$ 38. $5 \cot x + 3 = 0$

39. $3 \tan x - 5 = 4$ 40. $5 \tan x - 3 = 4$

41. The average daily temperature T in degrees Fahrenheit at a certain location is approximated fairly well by the equation

$$T = 61.3 + 17.9 \cos\left(\frac{2\pi}{365} t\right),$$

where t is in days and $t = 0$ represents July 1. Find all days in the year (assume 365 days) for which the average daily temperature is between 70.5 and 71.5 degrees.

42. Suppose a pendulum oscillates according to the equation

$$x = 6.0 \cos\left(3\pi t + \frac{\pi}{3}\right),$$

where x represents the horizontal displacement from a reference point in meters, and t is the elapsed time in seconds. Use a grapher to find, to the nearest tenth of a second, the first time the displacement is 5 meters.

43. The monthly revenue R in dollars from sales of ice-cream for a sweet shop in Montpelier, Vermont is approximated by

$$R = 4,200 + 2,100 \cos(0.5236t)$$

where $t = 0$ represents August. Use a grapher to determine in which months the revenue is more than $5,000.

44. The monthly number of kilowatt hours (E) of electricity sold by a particular utility company is approximated by

$$E = 384.5 + 89.5 \cos(.5236t),$$

where $t = 0$ represents January. Use a grapher to determine in which months the utility sold at least 425 kilowatt hours.

THINK ABOUT IT 9.6

1. Explain in terms of the unit circle definitions of the trigonometric functions why the solution set of the equation $\sec t = -1/2$ is $\emptyset$.

2. Is $\sin(x - (\pi/2)) = \cos x$ a conditional equation or an identity? Explain why.

3. Solve for x in the interval $[0, 2\pi)$. Use the quadratic formula,

$$\cos^2 x + \cos x - 1 = 0.$$

4. Solve each equation for $0 \le x < 2\pi$ through the aid of the *fundamental identities*.
   a. $\sin x = \cos x$ **b.** $\sin x = \tan x$
   c. $1 - \cos^2 x = \sin x$

5. As the bottom of a ladder is pulled away from a wall, the top slides toward the floor with increasing speed. This means that the angle between the ladder and the floor shrinks with increasing speed. See the figure. The rate of speed at which the angle shrinks before the top loses contact with the wall is given in radians per second by

$$v = -\frac{k}{L \sin \theta},$$

where k is the speed in ft per second at which the bottom moves away from the wall, and L is the length of the ladder in feet.

Suppose for a particular 41-ft ladder, the bottom is being pulled away from the wall at 10 ft/second. At the moment the ladder loses contact with the wall, $v = -.6585$ radians per second. Find to the nearest hundredth, the angle θ at which the ladder loses contact with the wall. [Source: P. Scholten and A. Simpson, "The Falling Ladder Paradox," *The College Mathematics Journal*, Jan. 1996].

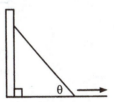

9.7 Law of Sines

Two observation towers, *A* and *B*, are located 10 mi apart. A fire is sighted at point *C*, and the observer in tower *A* measures angle *CAB* to be 80°. At the same time, the observer in tower *B* measures angle *CBA* to be 40°. How far is the fire from tower *A*? (See Example 1).

Courtesy of Prentice-Hall, Inc.

OBJECTIVES

1 Use the law of sines to solve a triangle, given two angles and one side of the triangle.

2 Determine exact solutions for unknowns associated with certain triangles, assuming exact numbers.

3 Use the law of sines to solve a triangle, given two sides of the triangle and the angle opposite one of them.

4 Determine how many triangles are described by certain conditions.

5 Solve applied problems using the law of sines.

In Section 4.2 we learned to solve right triangles. We now wish to extend our ability to solve triangles, by considering the solution of general triangles, which may or may not be right triangles. This generalization is useful because the analysis of a problem often leads to a triangle that does not contain a 90° angle. For instance, the angles in the triangle that is used to determine the distance to the fire in the section-opening problem measure 80°, 40°, and 60°, so right-triangle trigonometry is not useful in this case. Remember, we "solve" a triangle by finding the measures of its three angles and three sides. To accomplish this, at least three of these six values must be known, and one or more must be a side length.

The first technique that we use to solve general triangles is called the **law of sines.** We can derive this law by placing triangle *ABC* on a rectangular coordinate system so that angle *A* is in standard position. Figure 9.76 (a) and (b) show the result when A is an acute angle and an obtuse angle, respectively. In both cases we draw the altitude of the triangle, *CD*, and note that its length is *y*.

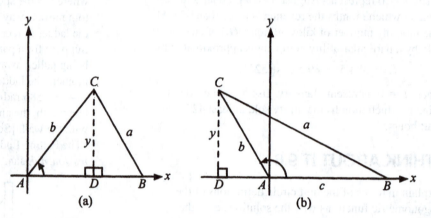

Figure 9.76

(a) *A* is an acute angle. (b) *A* is an obtuse angle.

Then by the general definition of the sine function,

$$\sin A = \frac{y}{b}, \text{ so } y = b \sin A.$$

Also, in the right triangle, *BDC,*

$$\sin B = \frac{y}{a}, \text{ so } y = a \sin B.$$

Setting these two expressions for *y* equal to each other, we have

$$b \sin A = a \sin B, \text{ so } \frac{\sin A}{a} = \frac{\sin B}{b}.$$

Similarly, by placing angle *C* in standard position, we can show that

$$\frac{\sin A}{a} = \frac{\sin C}{c}.$$

Combining these results, we have

$$\boxed{\frac{\sin A}{a} = \frac{\sin B}{b} = \frac{\sin C}{c}.}$$

This relationship, **the law of sines,** states the following.

Law of Sines

The sines of the angles in a triangle are proportional to the lengths of the opposite sides.

Note that if C is a right angle, $\sin C = \sin 90° = 1$, and the law of sines yields the right-triangle relationships

$$\sin A = \frac{a}{c} \quad \text{and} \quad \sin B = \frac{b}{c}.$$

With the assistance of the law of sines we can now solve the problem in the section introduction.

EXAMPLE 1   Distance to a Fire

Solve the problem in the section introduction on page 523.

Solution   First, draw a diagram picturing the data (Figure 9.77). Second, find angle C.

$$A + B + C = 180°$$
$$80° + 40° + C = 180°$$
$$C = 60°$$

Third, we find b by applying the law of sines.

$$\frac{\sin B}{b} = \frac{\sin C}{c}$$

$$\frac{\sin 40°}{b} = \frac{\sin 60°}{10}$$

$$b = \frac{10 \sin 40°}{\sin 60°}$$

$$= 7.4$$

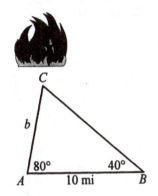

Figure 9.77

Thus, the fire is about 7.4 mi from station A.

Note   Remember that our computed results cannot be more accurate than the data that are given. Guidelines for the desired accuracy in a solution can be found in Section 4.2

PROGRESS CHECK 1   Two surveyors establish a baseline AB on a level field. The surveyor at point A is 375 ft from the surveyor at point B. Each one sights a stake at point C. The surveyor at A measures angle CAB to be 82.3°, while the surveyor at B measures angle CBA to be 65.4°. Find the distance from A to C.   ▪

The law of sines can be used to solve a triangle in the following two cases:

1. If we know the measures for two angles and one side of the triangle.
2. If we know the measures for two sides of the triangle and the angle opposite one of them.

The following example illustrates how the law of sines can be used to solve a triangle in the first case, in which the measures for two angles and one side of the triangle are known. Note that in computing results, the symbol for equality (=) is generally used, even though the symbol for approximation (≈) may be more appropriate.

EXAMPLE 2   Solving a Triangle: Angle-Angle-Side Case (AAS)

Approximate the missing parts of triangle ABC in which $A = 35°$, $B = 50°$ and $a = 12$ ft.

Solution   First, sketch Figure 9.78. We can find angle C, since the sum of the angles in a triangle is 180°.

$$A + B + C = 180°$$
$$35° + 50° + C = 180°$$
$$C = 95°$$

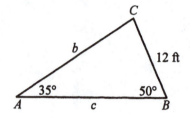

Figure 9.78

Second, we find side length b by applying the law of sines.

$$\frac{\sin A}{a} = \frac{\sin B}{b}$$

$$\frac{\sin 35°}{12} = \frac{\sin 50°}{b}$$

$$b = \frac{12 \sin 50°}{\sin 35°}$$

$$= 16 \text{ ft}$$

Third, we find c by applying the law of sines.

$$\frac{\sin A}{a} = \frac{\sin C}{c}$$

$$\frac{\sin 35°}{12} = \frac{\sin 95°}{c}$$

$$c = \frac{12 \sin 95°}{\sin 35°}$$

$$= 21 \text{ ft}$$

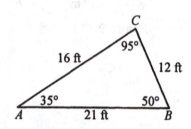

Figure 9.79

Thus, the solution to the triangle is as shown in Figure 9.79.

PROGRESS CHECK 2   Solve the triangle ABC in which $A = 30°$, $B = 40°$ and $a = 20$ ft.   ■

For the next example, we will assume that all numbers are exact numbers, and because the angles given measure 45° and 30°, we may determine an exact solution.

EXAMPLE 3   Using the Law of Sines, Assuming Exact Numbers

In triangle RST, $r = 8$, $R = 45°$ and $S = 30°$. Assume exact numbers and find s.

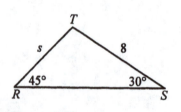

Figure 9.80

Solution   First, sketch Figure 9.80. Then relate r, s, $\sin R$, and $\sin S$ by the law of sines and solve for s.

$$\frac{\sin R}{r} = \frac{\sin S}{s}$$

$$\frac{\sin 45°}{8} = \frac{\sin 30°}{s}$$

$$s = \frac{8 \sin 30°}{\sin 45°}$$

$$s = \frac{8 \cdot 1/2}{\sqrt{2}/2}$$

$$s = 4\sqrt{2}$$

PROGRESS CHECK 3   In triangle PQR, $R = 120°$, $P = 30°$, and $p = 12$. Assume exact numbers and find r.   ■

The following examples illustrate how the law of sines can be used to solve a triangle in the second case, in which the measures for two sides of the triangle and the angle opposite one of them are known.

EXAMPLE 4   Solving a Triangle: Side-Side-Angle Case (SSA)

Solve the triangle ABC in which $B = 60°$, $b = 50$ ft, and $c = 30$ ft.

Solution   First, sketch Figure 9.81. We find angle C by applying the law of sines.

$$\frac{\sin B}{b} = \frac{\sin C}{c}$$

$$\frac{\sin 60°}{50} = \frac{\sin C}{30}$$

$$\frac{30(\sin 60°)}{50} = \sin C$$

$$0.5196 = \sin C$$

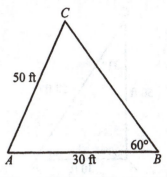

Figure 9.81

We now have two possibilities for angle C, since the sine of both first and second quadrant angles is positive.

Case 1   (acute angle in Q_1):   **Case 2**   (obtuse angle in Q_2):

$\sin C = 0.5196$ $\sin C = 0.5196$

reference angle $= \sin^{-1} 0.5196 = 31.3°$ (by calculator)

$31.3°$ is the angle in Q_1 with a reference angle of $31.3°$ [Figure 9.82(a)].
$148.7°$ is the angle in Q_2 with a reference angle of $31.3°$ [Figure 9.82(b)]

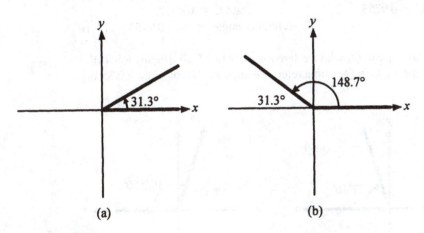

(a)   (b)

Figure 9.82

Therefore, $C = 31.3°$ or $C = 148.7°$.
Second, we find angle A in both of the above cases.

Case 1 $A + B + C = 180°$ Case 2 $A + B + C = 180°$
$A + 60° + 31.3° = 180°$ $B = 60°$ $C = 148.7°$
$A = 88.7°$

In Case 2 we find $B + C = 208.7°$, so regardless of the value of A, the sum of the angles of the triangle exceeds $180°$. Therefore, we reject $C = 148.7°$ as a solution.
Third, we find side length a by applying the law of sines.

$$\frac{\sin A}{a} = \frac{\sin B}{b}$$

$$\frac{\sin 88.7°}{a} = \frac{\sin 60°}{50}$$

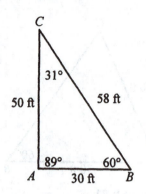

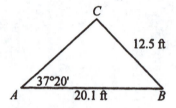

Figure 9.83

$$\frac{50(\sin 88.7°)}{\sin 60°} = a$$

$$58 \text{ ft} = a$$

When we round off the angle measures to the nearest degree, the solution to the triangle is as shown in Figure 9.83.

PROGRESS CHECK 4 Approximate the missing parts of the triangle ABC in which $A = 55°$, $a = 75$ ft, and $b = 42$ ft. ▪

EXAMPLE 5 Solving a Triangle: Side-Side-Angle Case (SSA)

Approximate the missing parts of triangle ABC in which $A = 37°20'$, $a = 12.5$ ft and $c = 20.1$ ft.

Solution First, sketch Figure 9.84. We find angle C by applying the law of sines.

$$\frac{\sin A}{a} = \frac{\sin C}{c}$$

$$\frac{\sin 37°20'}{12.5} = \frac{\sin C}{20.1}$$

$$\frac{20.1(\sin 37°20')}{12.5} = \sin C$$

$$0.9753 = \sin C$$

We now have two possibilities.

Case 1 (acute angle in Q_1):
$\sin C = 0.9753$

Case 2 (obtuse angle in Q_2):
$\sin C = 0.9753$
reference angle $= \sin^{-1} 0.9753 = 77°10'$

$77°10'$ is the angle in Q_1 with a reference angle of $77°10'$ [Figure 9.85(a)].
$102°50'$ is the angle in Q_2 with a reference angle of $77°10'$ [Figure 9.85(b)].

Figure 9.84

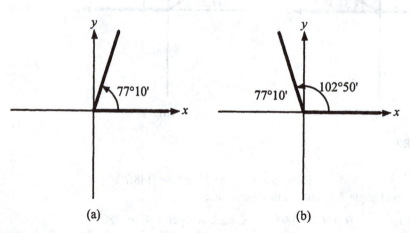

(a)   (b)

Figure 9.85

Therefore, $C = 77°10'$ or $C = 102°50'$.
Second, we find angle B in both of the above cases.

$$A + B + C = 180° \qquad\qquad A + B + C = 180°$$
$$37°20' + B + 77°10' = 180° \qquad 37°20' + B + 102°50' = 180°$$
$$B + 114°30' = 180° \qquad\qquad B + 140°10' = 180°$$
$$B = 65°30' \qquad\qquad\qquad B = 39°50'$$

Third, we find side length b by applying the law of sines.

$$\frac{\sin A}{a} = \frac{\sin B}{b}$$

$$\frac{\sin 37°20'}{12.5} = \frac{\sin 65°30'}{b}$$

$$b = \frac{12.5(\sin 65°30')}{\sin 37°20'}$$

$$= 18.8 \text{ ft}$$

$$\frac{\sin A}{a} = \frac{\sin B}{b}$$

$$\frac{\sin 37°20'}{12.5} = \frac{\sin 39°50'}{b}$$

$$b = \frac{12.5(\sin 39°50')}{\sin 37°20'}$$

$$= 13.2 \text{ ft}$$

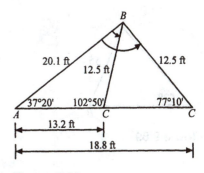

Figure 9.86

The two possible solutions from the given data are shown in Figure 9.86.

PROGRESS CHECK 5 Solve the triangle ABC in which $A = 28°40'$, $a = 162$ ft, and $b = 225$ ft.   ■

Note that when we attempt to solve a triangle in which the measures for two sides of the triangle and the angle opposite one of them are given, there may be one triangle that fits the data (as in Example 4), or there may be two triangles that fit the data (as in Example 5). Consequently, this case is called the **ambiguous case** of the law of sines. It is also possible in the ambiguous case that no triangle can be constructed from the data; then we say the data are inconsistent. Figure 9.87 shows conditions that determine the various cases when a, b, and acute angle A are given. In this diagram it is helpful to think that the side of length a can swing like a pendulum.

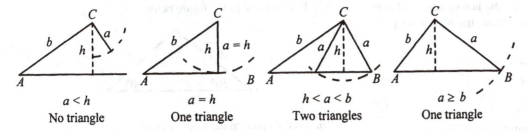

Figure 9.87

$\sin A = \dfrac{h}{b}$, so $h = b \sin A$.

If A is an obtuse angle, then the possibilities are more obvious, as shown in Figure 9.88.

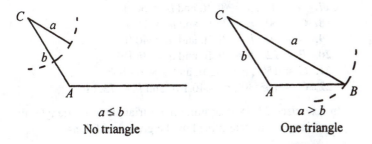

Figure 9.88

It is not recommended that the information in Figures 9.87 and 9.88 be memorized. Instead, in a given problem you should be aware of the various possibilities, make a careful sketch of the given information, and let an analysis based on the law of sines determine the case when the case is not obvious.

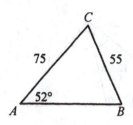

Figure 9.89

EXAMPLE 6 Finding the Number of Triangles in the SSA Case

Determine if no triangle, one triangle, or two triangles are determined by the conditions that $A = 52°$, $a = 55$, and $b = 75$.

Solution First, sketch Figure 9.89. Then relate a, b, $\sin A$ and $\sin B$ by the law of sines and solve for B using the given data.

$$\frac{\sin B}{b} = \frac{\sin A}{a}$$

$$\frac{\sin B}{75} = \frac{\sin 52°}{55}$$

$$\sin B = \frac{75 \sin 52°}{55} \approx 1.0746$$

Because the range of the sine function is $[-1, 1]$, $\sin B$ cannot equal 1.0746 so no triangle exists.

PROGRESS CHECK 6 Determine if no triangle, one triangle, or two triangles are determined by the conditions that $A = 52°$, $a = 45$ and $b = 55$. ■

EXERCISES 9.7

(**Note:** There are more problems on the law of sines in Exercises 9.8.) In Exercises 1–6 approximate the remaining parts of the triangle for the data given.

1. $A = 30°$, $a = 25$ ft, and $B = 45°$
2. $C = 60°$, $c = 40$ ft, and $A = 80°$
3. $B = 120°$, $C = 40°$, and $a = 55$ ft
4. $C = 135°$, $c = 98$ ft, and $B = 15°$
5. $A = 62°10'$, $a = 31.5$ ft, and $B = 76°30'$
6. $A = 98°30'$, $B = 6°10'$, and $a = 415$ ft

In Exercises 7–16 assume exact numbers and find exact answers.

7. In triangle ABC, $a = 8$, $b = 12$, and $A = 30°$. Find $\sin B$.
8. In triangle ABC, $b = 8$, $c = 10$, and $C = 150°$. Find $\sin B$.
9. In triangle PQR, $p = 9$, $\sin P = \frac{3}{4}$, and $\sin Q = \frac{1}{2}$. Find q.
10. In triangle PQR, $\sin R = 0.6$, $\sin Q = 0.4$, and $q = 14$. Find r.
11. In triangle RST, $\sin R = \frac{1}{4}$ and $\sin S = \frac{7}{8}$. Find $\frac{s}{r}$.
12. In triangle RST, $S = 30°$ and $T = 45°$. Find $\frac{s}{t}$.
13. In triangle ABC, $b = 20$, $B = 45°$, and $C = 30°$. Find c.
14. In triangle ABC, $a = 10$, $A = 30°$, and $B = 60°$. Find b.

15. Find b and c in the figure below.

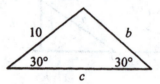

16. Find p and q in the figure below.

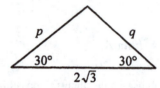

In Exercises 17–22 approximate the remaining parts of the triangle for the data given.

17. $A = 45°$, $a = 80$ ft, and $b = 50$ ft
18. $C = 60°$, $c = 75$ ft, and $a = 45$ ft
19. $B = 30°$, $b = 30$ ft, and $a = 40$ ft
20. $B = 22°$, $b = 78$ ft, and $a = 86$ ft
21. $C = 150°$, $c = 92$ ft, and $b = 69$ ft
22. $C = 105°30'$, $c = 46.1$ ft, and $b = 75.2$ ft

In Exercises 23–28 determine if no triangle, one triangle, or two triangles are determined by the given conditions.

23. $A = 18°$, $a = 15$, $b = 28$
24. $A = 65°$, $a = 18$, $b = 24$
25. $C = 30°$, $b = 16$, $c = 32$

26. $B = 45°, a = 26, b = 21$
27. $A = 130°, a = 14, b = 18$
28. $A = 96°, a = 15, b = 11$
29. Two surveyors establish a baseline AB on a level field. The surveyor at point A is 200 ft from the surveyor at point B. Each one sights a stake at point C. The surveyor at A measures angle CAB to be $72°30'$, while the surveyor at B measures angle CBA to be $81°20'$. Find the distance from B to C.
30. Engineers wish to build a bridge across a river to join point A on one side to either point B or point C on the other side. The distance from B to C is 400 ft, angle ABC is $67°20'$ and angle ACB is $84°30'$. By how many feet does the distance from A to B exceed the distance from A to C?
31. Airport A is 300 mi due north to airport B. Their radio stations receive a distress signal from a ship located at point C. It is determined that point C is located $54°$ south of east with respect to airport A, and $76°$ north of east from airport B. How far is the ship from airport A?
32. Two engineers are located at points A and B on the opposite sides of a hill. They are both able to see a stake at point C, which is at a distance of 800 ft from A and 700 ft from B. If angle ABC is $25°$, find the distance $\overline{AB}$ through the hill.
33. If ABC is a right triangle $(C = 90°)$, show that the law of sines simplifies to the right-triangle relationships $\sin A = a/c$ and $\sin B = b/c$.
34. In triangle RST express $\sin T$ in terms of r, t, and $\sin R$.

THINK ABOUT IT 9.7

1. In the given illustration find acute angles θ, α, and β to the nearest degree and x and y to two significant digits.

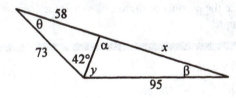

2. The following equations are equivalent forms of an equation that is one of the **Mollweide's check formulas.**

$$\frac{a - b}{c} = \frac{\sin\frac{1}{2}(A - B)}{\cos\frac{1}{2}C}; \quad \frac{b - a}{c} = \frac{\sin\frac{1}{2}(B - A)}{\cos\frac{1}{2}C}$$

These equations relate all the parts in a triangle and are therefore useful for checking solutions when solving triangles. Check the solution given in Example 2 of this section by using the form from above that produces positive results on both sides of the equation. If the same result is not obtained on both sides (with minor allowances for round-off error), then the solution is incorrect.
3. In a triangle if A, a, and b are given and $a = b \sin A$, then use the law of sines to show that the given conditions determine a right triangle.
4. Prove, using the law of sines, that if the measures of two angles of a triangle are equal, then the lengths of the sides opposite these angles are equal.
5. In the figure below use the law of sines to show that if line segments AB and DE are parallel, then $e/b = d/a$. (This problem shows that if a line is drawn parallel to a side of a triangle, then the other two sides are divided proportionately.)

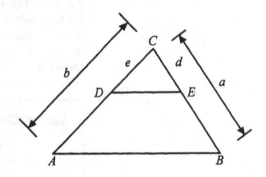

9.8   Law of Cosines and Area of Triangles

On a ground ball to the first base side, the pitcher is expected to cover first base and beat the batter to this bag. If a baseball diamond is a square that is 90.0 ft long on each side, and if the pitcher's mound is 60.5 ft from home plate on the diagonal from home to second base, then how far is the pitcher's mound from first base? (See Example 1.)

1   Use the law of cosines to solve a triangle, given two sides of the triangle and the angle between these two sides.

2   Use the law of cosines to solve a triangle, given the lengths of three sides of the triangle.

3   Solve applied problems using the law of cosines.

4   Solve a problem involving a triangle by determining whether the law of sines or the law of cosines is appropriate for the problem.

5   Find the area of a triangle, given two sides of the triangle and the angle between these two sides.

6   Find the area of a triangle, given the lengths of three sides.

In Section 9.7 we found that the law of sines can be used to solve a triangle in the following two cases:

1. If we know the measures for **two angles** and **one side** of the triangle
2. If we know the measures for **two sides** of the triangle and the **angle opposite** one of them

However, there exist two other cases for which the law of sines cannot be applied. They are:

3. If we know the measures for **two sides** of the triangle and the **angle between** these two sides
4. If we know the measures for the **three sides** of the triangle

An illustration of case 3 is readily available when we try to find the distance from the pitcher's mound to first base in the section-opening problem. Because the pitcher's mound is on the diagonal from home to second base, the angle from the pitcher's mound to home to first base measures one-half of 90°, which is 45°, and this angle is *between* the two known sides. To solve this type of problem and problems involving case 4, we use the law of cosines, which states the following.

Law of Cosines

In any triangle, the square of any side length equals the sum of the squares of the other two side lengths, minus twice the product of these other two side lengths and the cosine of their included angle.

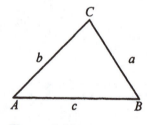

Figure 9.90

Thus, for triangle *ABC* in Figure 9.90 we have

$$a^2 = b^2 + c^2 - 2bc \cos A$$
$$b^2 = a^2 + c^2 - 2ac \cos B$$
$$c^2 = a^2 + b^2 - 2ab \cos C.$$

If we know the measures for two sides of the triangle and the included angle, we find the third side length by substituting in one of these formulas. After finding this part, we complete the solution by means of the law of sines. To obtain accuracy in the angle measures, the computed side length should be carried in the calculations to at least one more significant digit than stated in the solution.

If the three forms of the law of cosines are solved for the cosine of the angle, we have

$$\cos A = \frac{b^2 + c^2 - a^2}{2bc}$$

$$\cos B = \frac{a^2 + c^2 - b^2}{2ac}$$

$$\cos C = \frac{a^2 + b^2 - c^2}{2ab}.$$

These formulas are used to find the angle measures in a triangle when we know the three side lengths. In this case we do not use the law of sines to complete the solution because results are more accurate when they are computed from the data given.

Before starting the sample problems, let us first derive the law of cosines. Once again, we place triangle ABC on a rectangular coordinate system with angle A in standard position, and consider both an acute and obtuse possibility for angle A, as shown in Figure 9.91(a) and (b). In both cases vertex B obviously has coordinates $(c, 0)$. Also, in both cases the x-coordinate of vertex C is $b \cos A$, and the y-coordinate is $b \sin A$, because $\cos A = x/r$ and $\sin A = y/r$, where r is given by side length b in the triangles. If we now apply the distance formula to find the square of side length a, we have

$$a^2 = (c - b \cos A)^2 + (0 - b \sin A)^2$$
$$= c^2 - 2bc \cos A + b^2 \cos^2 A + b^2 \sin^2 A$$
$$= b^2(\sin^2 A + \cos^2 A) + c^2 - 2bc \cos A.$$

Since $\sin^2 A + \cos^2 A = 1$ is an identity, the equation becomes

$$a^2 = b^2 + c^2 - 2bc \cos A,$$

which is one form of the law of cosines. A similar procedure with angles B and C, respectively, placed in standard position yields the other two forms.

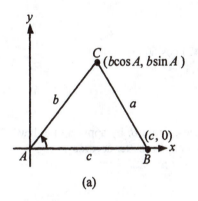

(a)   (b)

Figure 9.91

EXAMPLE 1   Distance Between the Pitcher's Mound and First Base

Solve the problem in the section introduction on page 531.

Solution   Consider the simplified sketch of the problem in Figure 9.92. Observe that the angle between the two known sides measures 45° because the pitcher's mound is on the diagonal from home to second base, and the diagonals in a square bisect the right angles in the square. We can now find x by applying the law of cosines, which says that the square of any side length in a triangle equals the sum of the squares of the other two side lengths, minus twice the product of these other two side lengths and the cosine of their included angle.

$$x^2 = (60.5)^2 + (90)^2 - 2(60.5)(90) \cos 45°$$
$$= 4{,}059.93$$
$$x = \sqrt{4{,}059.93} \approx 63.7$$

Thus, the pitcher's mound is about 63.7 ft from first base, which should give the pitcher an adequate head start in a race to the bag.

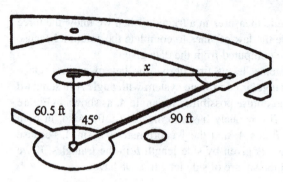

Figure 9.92

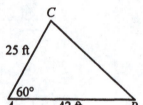

Figure 9.93

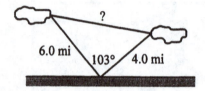

Figure 9.94

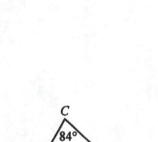

Figure 9.95

PROGRESS CHECK 1   What is the distance between the two islands shown in Figure 9.93?   ■

EXAMPLE 2   Solving a Triangle: Side-Angle-Side Case (SAS)

Approximate the missing parts of triangle ABC in which $A = 60°$, $b = 25$ ft, and $c = 42$ ft.

Solution   First, sketch Figure 9.94. We find side length a by applying the law of cosines.

$$a^2 = b^2 + c^2 - 2bc \cos A$$
$$= (25)^2 + (42)^2 - 2(25)(42) \cos 60°$$
$$= 1{,}339$$
$$a = \sqrt{1{,}339} \approx 36.6$$
$$a = 37 \text{ ft}$$

Second, we find the *smaller* of the remaining angles, angle B, by applying the law of sines. This angle must be acute. (Why?) We use 36.6 for a, for better accuracy.

$$\frac{\sin A}{a} = \frac{\sin B}{b}$$
$$\frac{\sin 60°}{36.6} = \frac{\sin B}{25}$$
$$\frac{25 \sin 60°}{36.6} = \sin B$$
$$0.5915 = \sin B$$
$$36° = B$$

(**Note:** $\sin B = 0.5915$ is true if $B = 36°$ or if $B = 144°$. We eliminate 144° as a possible solution, since we know that angle B must be acute.)

Third, we find angle C.

$$A + B + C = 180°$$
$$60° + 36° + C = 180°$$
$$C = 84°$$

Thus, the solution to the triangle is as shown in Figure 9.95.

PROGRESS CHECK 2   Solve the triangle ABC in which $B = 48°$, $a = 31$ ft, and $c = 55$ ft.   ■

EXAMPLE 3   Solving a Triangle: Side-Side-Side Case (SSS)

Approximate the missing parts of triangle ABC in which $a = 23.5$ ft, $b = 44.2$ ft, and $c = 30.1$ ft.

Solution   First, sketch Figure 9.96. We find angle A by applying the law of cosines.

$$\cos A = \frac{b^2 + c^2 - a^2}{2bc}$$

$$= \frac{(44.2)^2 + (30.1)^2 - (23.5)^2}{2(44.2)(30.1)}$$

$$= 0.8672$$

$$A = 29.9°$$

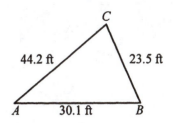

Figure 9.96

(**Note:** Remember that if the cosine of the angle is positive, the angle is acute; if the cosine of the angle is negative, the angle is in Q_2 and is obtuse.)

Second, we find the smaller of the remaining angles, acute angle C, by applying the law of cosines.

$$\cos C = \frac{a^2 + b^2 - c^2}{2ab}$$

$$= \frac{(23.5)^2 + (44.2)^2 - (30.1)^2}{2(23.5)(44.2)}$$

$$= 0.7701$$

$$C = 39.6°$$

Third, we find angle B.

$$A + B + C = 180°$$

$$29.9° + B + 39.6° = 180°$$

$$B = 110.5°$$

Thus, the solution to the triangle is as shown in Figure 9.97.

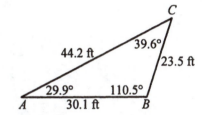

Figure 9.97

PROGRESS CHECK 3   Find the measures of the three angles in the triangle in which $a = 13$ ft, $b = 25$ ft, and $c = 22$ ft.   ■

We have now illustrated all four cases for solving a triangle by applying the law of sines or the law of cosines. At this point it is useful to consider problems in which it is necessary to determine which of these two laws is the appropriate law for the problem in question.

EXAMPLE 4   Choosing the Appropriate Law

In parallelogram $ABCD$ the lengths of sides AB and AD are 12 m and 19 m, respectively. If $A = 38°$, find the length of the longer diagonal of the parallelogram. Choose between the law of sines and the law of cosines to solve the problem.

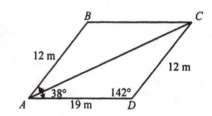

Figure 9.98

Solution   First, sketch Figure 9.98 and note that the longer diagonal is AC. In the parallelogram $\overline{AB} = \overline{DC} = 12$ and the sum of angles A and D is 180°. Thus,

$$A + D = 180°$$

$$38° + D = 180°$$

$$D = 142°.$$

We now know two side lengths of a triangle involving diagonal AC and the measure of the angle between these two sides. Therefore, we can find the length of the longer diagonal by applying the law of cosines.

$$(\overline{AC})^2 = (\overline{AD})^2 + (\overline{DC})^2 - 2(\overline{AD})(\overline{DC}) \cos D$$

$$(\overline{AC})^2 = (19)^2 + (12)^2 - 2(19)(12) \cos 142°$$

$$(\overline{AC})^2 = 864.3$$

$$\overline{AC} = 29$$

Thus, the longer diagonal is about 29 m.

PROGRESS CHECK 4 In a parallelogram the shorter diagonal makes angles of 36° and 68° with the sides. If the length of the longer side is 8.0 yd, what is the length of the shorter side? Choose between the law of sines and the law of cosines to solve the problem.   ■

Area of a Triangle

The area of a triangle is equal to one-half the product of its base and its altitude, which translates to the formula $A = (1/2) \, bh$. Because h is often unknown, it is useful to develop area formulas that do not require h. First, consider Figure 9.99 and note that in both cases by the general definition of the sine function

$$\sin A = \frac{h}{b}, \text{ so } h = b \sin A.$$

Thus, if we represent the area by K (to avoid ambiguity with angle A), then

$$K = \tfrac{1}{2}(base)(height)$$
$$K = \tfrac{1}{2}c(b \sin A)$$
$$K = \tfrac{1}{2}bc \sin A.$$

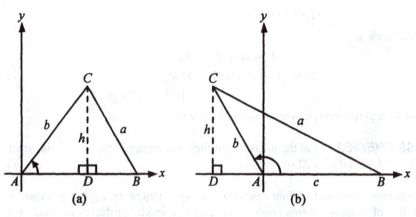

Figure 9.99
(a) A is an acute angle. (b) A is an obtuse angle.

Using similar reasoning with angle B and then angle C in standard position produces the formulas

$$K = \tfrac{1}{2}ac \sin B$$
$$K = \tfrac{1}{2}ab \sin C.$$

These formulas establish the following theorem.

Area of a Triangle

The area of a triangle is given by one-half the product of the lengths of two sides and the sine of the angle between these two sides.

EXAMPLE 5   Finding the Area of a Triangle

Find the area of triangle ABC if $a = 32.4$ cm, $b = 49.2$ cm, and $C = 18.5°$.

Solution   Using the formula containing a, b, and C, we have

$$K = \tfrac{1}{2}ab \sin C$$
$$= \tfrac{1}{2}(32.4)(49.2)\sin 18.5°$$
$$= 253 \text{ cm}^2 \qquad \text{(three significant digits).}$$

PROGRESS CHECK 5   Find the area of triangle ABC if $a = 14$ ft, $c = 11$ ft and $B = 37°$.   ■

When the three side measures of a triangle are known, then the area may be determined by using the following formula, which is named after the mathematician Heron of Alexandria.

Heron's Area Formula

The area K of the triangle with side lengths a, b, and c is

$$K = \sqrt{s(s - a)(s - b)(s - c)}$$

where s is the semiperimeter, which is given by $\frac{1}{2}(a + b + c)$.

EXAMPLE 6   Using Heron's Area Formula

Find the area of triangle ABC if $a = 3.0$ ft, $b = 4.0$ ft, and $c = 6.0$ ft.

Solution   First, find the semiperimeter s.

$$s = \tfrac{1}{2}(a + b + c) = \tfrac{1}{2}(3 + 4 + 6) = 6.5$$

Then, Heron's formula gives

$$
\begin{aligned}
K &= \sqrt{s(s - a)(s - b)(s - c)} \\
&= \sqrt{6.5(6.5 - 3)(6.5 - 4)(6.5 - 6)} \\
&= 5.3 \text{ ft}^2 \quad \text{(two significant digits).}
\end{aligned}
$$

PROGRESS CHECK 6   Find the area of triangle ABC if $a = 2.25$ km, $b = 3.07$ km, and $c = 2.08$ km.   ■

EXERCISES 9.8

In Exercises 1–6 use the law of cosines.

1. A surveyor at point C sights two points A and B on opposite sides of a lake. If C is 760 ft from A and 920 ft from B, and angle ACB is 96°, how wide is the lake?

2. What is the distance between the two islands in the illustration shown?

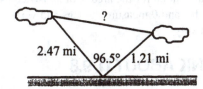

3. In parallelogram $ABCD$ the lengths of sides AB and AD are 21 m and 13 m, respectively. If $A = 52°$, find the length of the longer diagonal of the parallelogram.

4. In parallelogram $ABCD$ the length of sides AB and AD are 6.0 and 8.0 m, respectively. If the length of the shorter diagonal is 5.0 m, find angle A.

5. If the outfielders are positioned as shown below, then how far is each of them from third base in case they need to throw out a runner at that base?

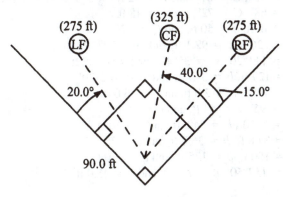

6. On a particular softball field the distance between the bases is 60 ft, and the pitcher's mound is 43 ft from home plate. Find the distance from the pitcher's mound to first base.

In Exercises 7–16 approximate the remaining parts of triangle ABC. The law of cosines will be needed in at least one of the steps.

7. $a = 12$ ft, $b = 15$ ft, and $C = 60°$
8. $a = 20$ ft, $c = 30$ ft, and $B = 30°$

9. $c = 19.2$ ft, $a = 46.1$ ft, and $B = 10°20'$
10. $b = 36$ ft, $c = 75$ ft, and $A = 98°$
11. $b = 11.1$ ft, $a = 19.2$ ft, and $C = 95°40'$
12. $a = 11$ ft, $b = 15$ ft, and $c = 19$ ft
13. $a = 12$ ft, $b = 5.2$ ft, $c = 8.1$ ft
14. $a = 4.9$ ft, $b = 5.3$ ft, and $c = 2.6$ ft
15. $a = 34.4$ ft, $b = 56.1$ ft, and $c = 42.3$ ft
16. $a = 45.0$ ft, $b = 108$ ft, and $c = 117$ ft

In Exercises 17–20 refer to the following triangle and complete each statement by using the law of cosines.

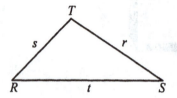

17. $r^2 =$ _____
18. $t =$ _____
19. $\cos T =$ _____
20. $\cos S =$ _____

In Exercises 21–24 assume exact numbers and find exact answers.

21. In triangle ABC, $a = 7$, $b = 5$, and $c = 6$. Find $\cos A$.
22. Find the cosine of the largest angle of the triangle whose sides measure 3, 5, and 6 units.
23. In triangle RST, $R = 60°$, $s = 7$ and $t = 4$. Find r.
24. Find the perimeter in triangle ABC if $A = 120°$, $b = 16$, and $c = 11$.

In Exercises 25–36 the problems are mixed; that is, some use the law of sines, some the law of cosines, and some use both. Solve each triangle.

25. $A = 15°$, $C = 87°$, and $b = 42$ ft
26. $B = 68°$, $C = 72°$, and $a = 18$ ft
27. $a = 40$ ft, $b = 50$ ft, and $C = 120°$
28. $b = 126$ ft, $c = 92.1$ ft, and $A = 72°50'$
29. $B = 111°20'$, $C = 35°40'$, and $a = 142$ ft
30. $c = 127$ ft, $b = 315$ ft, and $A = 162°30'$
31. $a = 4.0$ ft, $b = 2.0$ ft, and $c = 3.0$ ft
32. $A = 95°$, $a = 54$ ft, and $c = 38$ ft
33. $B = 7°10'$, $b = 74.8$ ft, and $c = 92.4$ ft
34. $a = 84.8$ ft, $b = 36.8$ ft, and $c = 76.5$ ft
35. $a = 150$ ft, $b = 175$ ft, and $c = 200$ ft
36. $B = 152°50'$, $b = 130$ ft, and $c = 45.0$ ft

In Exercises 37–40 the solution will require a decision as to whether the law of sines or the law of cosines is appropriate.

37. A ship sails due east for 40 mi and then changes direction and sails 20° north of east for 60 mi. How far is the ship from its starting point?

38. One gun is located at point A, while a second gun at point B is located 5.0 mi directly east of A. From point A the direction to the target is 27° north of east. From point B the direction to the target is 72° north of east. For what firing range should the guns be set?
39. In a parallelogram the shorter diagonal makes angles of 25° and 72° with the sides. If the length of the shorter side is 15 m, what is the length of the longer side?
40. A and B are two points located on opposite edges of a lake. A third point C is located so that $\overline{AC}$ is 421 ft and $\overline{BC}$ is 376 ft. Angle ABC is measured to be 65.5°. Compute the distance $\overline{AB}$ across the lake.

In Exercises 41–52 find the area of the triangle satisfied by the given conditions.

41. $a = 7.0$ ft, $b = 4.0$ ft, and $C = 30°$
42. $a = 6.0$ ft, $b = 8.0$ ft, and $C = 150°$
43. $a = 12$ m, $c = 14$ m, and $B = 110°$
44. $a = 25$ m, $c = 19$ m, and $B = 70°$
45. $b = 4.74$ km, $c = 3.42$ km, and $A = 21.5°$
46. $b = 51.7$ cm, $c = 55.9$ cm, and $A = 16°50'$
47. $a = 5.0$ ft, $b = 4.0$ ft, and $c = 7.0$ ft
48. $a = 3.0$ m, $b = 4.0$ m, and $c = 3.0$ m
49. $a = 23.0$ m, $b = 14.0$ m, and $c = 18.0$ m
50. $a = 538$ ft, $b = 726$ ft, and $c = 981$ ft
51. $a = 2.51$ km, $b = 1.95$ km, and $c = 2.14$ km
52. $a = 42.56$ cm, $b = 37.83$ cm, and $c = 53.17$ cm

In Exercises 53–56 assume exact numbers and find exact answers.

53. Find the area of triangle ABC if $A = 120°$, $b = 16$, and $c = 11$.
54. Find the area of an isosceles triangle in which the vertex angle measures 30° and each leg measures 8 units.
55. Find the area of an equilateral triangle in which each side measures 6 units by using $K = \frac{1}{2}ab \sin C$.
56. Find the area of an equilateral triangle in which each side measures 6 units by using Heron's formula.
57. If ABC is a right triangle ($C = 90°$), show that the law of cosines simplifies to the relationship $c^2 = a^2 + b^2$.
58. Write a formula for the area K of an isosceles triangle in which s and θ measure the legs and vertex angle, respectively.

THINK ABOUT IT 9.8

1. Discuss why it is important to know how the law of cosines is stated in words.
2. Use the law of cosines to show that if p, q, and r are the side lengths of a triangle and $r^2 = p^2 + q^2$, then triangle PQR is a right triangle.

3. Three circles are tangent externally, as shown in the diagram below. If the diameters of the circles are given by $d_1 = 32.0$ mm, $d_2 = 16.0$ mm, and $d_3 = 18.0$ mm, then find the area of the triangle joining their centers.

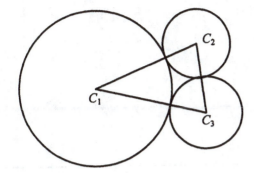

4. Show by using the law of sines that the area K of triangle ABC may be given by

$$K = \frac{a^2 \sin B \sin C}{2 \sin A}.$$

5. a. Find the perimeter of the regular pentagon in the given illustration.

   b. Find the area of the regular pentagon shown in the figure.

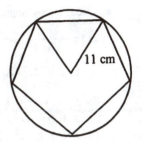

11 cm

CHAPTER 9 OVERVIEW

Section	Key Concepts and Procedures to Review
9.1	▪ Definition of 1 radian ▪ Radian measure formula: $\theta = s/r$ ▪ Degrees to radians formula: $1° = \pi/180$ radians ▪ Radians to degrees formula: 1 radian $= 180°/\pi$ ▪ Area formula: $A = \frac{1}{2}r^2\theta$ (θ in radians) ▪ Formula relating linear velocity (v) and angular velocity (ω): $v = \omega r$
9.2	▪ Definition of the trigonometric functions for a unit circle ▪ Definitions of trigonometric identity and reference number ▪ In a unit circle the same real number measures both the central angle θ and the intercepted arc s. (That is, $\theta = s$.) ▪ For the sine and cosine functions, the domain is the set of all real numbers, and the range is the set of real numbers between -1 and 1, inclusive. ▪ Methods to determine (if defined) approximate trigonometric values for any number and exact values in special cases ▪ For any trigonometric function f, we have $f(s + 2\pi k) = f(s)$, where k is an integer. ▪ Negative angle identities ▪ When using a calculator, be sure to set the calculator for radian mode. ▪ Any trigonometric function of s is equal in absolute value to the same named function of its reference number s_R.
9.3	▪ Definitions of periodic function, period, amplitude, phase shift, and midline ▪ For $y = d + a \sin(bx + c)$ and $y = d + a \cos(bx + c)$, with $b > 0$, amplitude $= |a|$, period $= 2\pi/b$, phase shift $= -c/b$, midline: $y = d$.

9.4
- Graphs of $y = \tan x$, $y = \cot x$, $y = \sec x$, and $y = \csc x$
- Domain, range, and period for $y = \tan x$, $y = \cot x$, $y = \sec x$, and $y = \csc x$
- Relations between a function and its reciprocal function
- Methods to graph trigonometric functions using horizontal shifting, vertical shifting, and reflection.
- Statements and applications of the **fundamental identities:**

$$\csc x = \frac{1}{\sin x} \qquad \sec x = \frac{1}{\cos x} \qquad \cot x = \frac{1}{\tan x}$$

$$\tan x = \frac{\sin x}{\cos x} \qquad \cot x = \frac{\cos x}{\sin x}$$

$$\left. \begin{array}{l} \sin^2 x + \cos^2 x = 1 \\ \tan^2 x + 1 = \sec^2 x \\ \cot^2 x + 1 = \csc^2 x \end{array} \right\} \begin{array}{l} \textbf{Pythagorean} \\ \textbf{Identities} \end{array}$$

- Guidelines for proving identities

9.5
- The inverse sine function is denoted by arcsin or $\sin^{-1}$. By definition, $y = \arcsin x$ if and only if $x = \sin y$, where $-1 \le x \le 1$ and $-\pi/2 \le y \le \pi/2$. Similar remarks hold for the other inverse trigonometric functions.
- Domain and range of the six inverse trigonometric functions
- Graphs of $y = \arcsin x$, $y = \arccos x$, and $y = \arctan x$
- Right triangle method to simplify a trigonometric function of an inverse trigonometric expression
- Inverse properties involving inverse trigonometric functions

9.6
- Methods to solve certain trigonometric equations (Reference numbers, factoring, and a graphing calculator may be involved.)
- Determine solutions between 0 and 2π as follows:

Quadrant	Solution
1	Reference number
2	$\pi -$ reference number
3	$\pi +$ reference number
4	$2\pi -$ reference number

- We generate all the solutions to a trigonometric equation by adding multiples of 2π to the solutions that are in the interval $[0, 2\pi)$.

9.7
- Law of sines: $\dfrac{\sin A}{a} = \dfrac{\sin B}{b} = \dfrac{\sin C}{c}$
- Guidelines on when to use the law of sines
- When given the measures for two sides of a triangle and the angle opposite one of them, there may be one triangle that fits the data (see Example 4) or there may be two triangles that fit the data (see Example 5). Sometimes no triangle can be constructed from the data; then we say the data are inconsistent.

9.8
- Law of cosines: $a^2 = b^2 + c^2 - 2bc \cos A$
$$b^2 = a^2 + c^2 - 2ac \cos B$$
$$c^2 = a^2 + b^2 - 2ab \cos C$$
- Guidelines on when to use the law of cosines
- The area of a triangle is given by one-half the product of the lengths of two sides and the sine of the angle between these two sides
- Heron's area formula: $K = \sqrt{s(s - a)(s - b)(s - c)}$ where $s = \frac{1}{2}(a + b + c)$

CHAPTER 9 REVIEW EXERCISES

In Exercises 1–10 find the *exact* value of the given expression.

1. $\sin\left(\dfrac{\pi}{3}\right)$ **2.** $\cos\left(-\dfrac{\pi}{4}\right)$

3. $\sin 99\pi$ **4.** $\tan\left(\dfrac{56\pi}{3}\right)$

5. $\cot\left(\dfrac{5\pi}{3}\right)$ **6.** $\cos\left(\dfrac{3\pi}{4}\right)$

7. $\arctan(-1)$ **8.** $\arccos\left(-\dfrac{\sqrt{3}}{2}\right)$

9. $\sin[\cos^{-1}(-1)]$ **10.** $\tan\left(\sin^{-1}\dfrac{2}{3}\right)$

In Exercises 11–20 use a calculator to find the value of the given expression to three significant digits.

11. $\sin 1$ **12.** $\sin 1°$

13. $\tan\left(\dfrac{8\pi}{5}\right)$ **14.** $\cot\left(\dfrac{\pi}{9}\right)$

15. $\sec 6$ **16.** $\csc(-4)$

17. $\arccos(-1.11)$ **18.** $\arcsin(-0.4439)$

19. $\cot(\operatorname{arcsec} 1.238)$ **20.** $\tan[\sin^{-1}(-0.9563)]$

In Exercises 21–24 sketch the graph for $0 \le x \le 2\pi$.

21. $y = -\cos x$ **22.** $y = \sin 2x$

23. $y = \cot x$ **24.** $y = \sec x$

In Exercises 25–30 state the amplitude, the period, the midline, and the phase shift, and sketch one cycle of the graph.

25. $y = \dfrac{1}{2}\cos 3x$ **26.** $y = 2 \sin \pi x$

27. $y = -\cos\left(2x + \dfrac{\pi}{2}\right)$ **28.** $y = \sin\left(\pi x - \dfrac{\pi}{4}\right)$

29. $y = 4 - 2\sin\left(\dfrac{1}{2}x\right)$ **30.** $y = -10 + 3\cos(2x)$

In Exercises 31–34 sketch one cycle of the function.

31. $y = 3\sec\left(\dfrac{x}{2}\right)$ **32.** $y = \csc 2x$

33. $y = 1 - \tan x$ **34.** $y = \cot\left(x + \dfrac{\pi}{4}\right)$

35. Graph $y = \sin^{-1} x$

36. Graph $y = \arccos(x - 1)$

In Exercises 37–42 state the domain and the range of the function.

37. $y = \tan x$ **38.** $y = \cos x$

39. $y = \csc x$ **40.** $y = \sec x$

41. $y = \arctan x$ **42.** $y = \arcsin x$

43. In which quadrant do $y = \sin x$ and $y = \cos x$ both decrease?

Find an equation for the curve in the following illustration. The equation should be written in the form $y = a \sin bx$ or $y = a \cos bx$.

44.

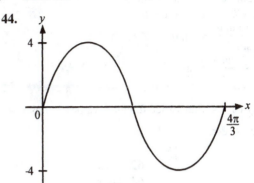

45. For the given diagram express θ as a function of x

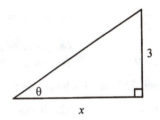

46. The diameter of a globe of the Earth is 12 in. A point on this globe is 4 in. north of the equator of the globe. To the nearest 10 minutes, find its latitude.

47. On June 15 the tide in a certain harbor is described by the equation $y = 20 + 8.2\cos(0.5067t)$, where y is the height of the water in feet and t is the time that has elapsed from 12 midnight on June 14. To one decimal place, estimate the water level in this harbor on June 15 at 2 p.m.

48. For the tide described in Exercise 47 find to the nearest minute all times on June 15 when the water level is 22 ft.

49. a. Change 210° to radians.
    b. Change $2\pi/5$ radians to degrees.

50. If $\tan \theta = \dfrac{1}{2}$ and $\cos \theta < 0$, find $\sin \theta$.

51. For what values of x is $\sin(\sin^{-1} x) = x$ a true statement?

52. Find the area of a sector of a circle of radius 10 in. that is subtended by a central angle of 60°.

53. In a circle a central angle intercepts an arc equal in length to the diameter of the circle. What is the measure of the central angle in radians?

54. A car is traveling at 60 mi/hour (88 ft/second) on tires 32 in. in diameter. Find the angular velocity of the tires in radians/second.

In Exercises 55–60 verify the given identity.

55. $\cot^2 x \sec^2 x = \csc^2 x$

56. $\dfrac{\sin^2 x}{1 + \cos x} = 1 - \cos x$

57. $\sin^2 x \tan^2 x = \tan^2 x - \sin^2 x$

58. $\sec \theta \csc \theta = \tan \theta + \cot \theta$

59. $\dfrac{\sin \theta + \tan \theta}{1 + \sec \theta} = \sin \theta$

60. $\dfrac{\sec x}{\cos x} - \dfrac{\tan x}{\cot x} = 1$

In Exercises 61–64 find exact function values if $\cos x = \dfrac{4}{5}$ and $\dfrac{3\pi}{2} < x < 2\pi$.

61. $\sin x$

62. $\csc x$

63. $\sec x$

64. $\tan x$

In Exercises 65–70 solve for x in the interval $[0, 2\pi)$.

65. $\sin x = -\dfrac{\sqrt{3}}{2}$

66. $\cos x = -\frac{1}{2}$

67. $\tan x = 1$

68. $\sec x = 2$

69. $\sin x = 0.1219$

70. $\sin x = -0.1219$

In Exercises 71 and 72 find all solutions to the equation.

71. $4 \sin x - 1 = 1$

72. $10 \cos x - 2 = 0$

In Exercises 73–80 solve for x in the interval $0 \le x < 2\pi$.

73. $2 \sin^2 x - 1 = 0$

74. $3 \tan^2 x - 1 = 0$

75. $\cos^2 x = \cos x$

76. $\sin^3 x = \sin x$

77. $\cos 3x = 0$

78. $\sin 4x = 1$

79. $\sin 2x = \frac{1}{2}$

80. $\sin \frac{1}{2} x = \frac{1}{2}$

In Exercises 81–86 find the indicated part in triangle ABC.

81. Determine B if $a = 5.0$, $b = 9.0$, and $c = 6.0$.

82. Determine C if $A = 81°$, $a = 11$, and $c = 35$.

83. Determine A if $C = 44°50'$, $B = 86°20'$, and $a = 62.7$.

84. Determine B if $C = 90°$, $b = 5.00$, and $c = 8.00$.

85. Determine c if $C = 120°$, $a = 3.0$, and $b = 4.0$.

86. Determine b if $A = 40°$, $B = 60°$, and $c = 6.0$.

87. Find the area of triangle ABC if $a = 16$ m, $c = 11$ m, and $B = 116°$.

88. In triangle ABC, $b = 5$, $c = 6$, and $\cos A = -\frac{1}{3}$. Find side length a.

89. A draftsman drew to scale $(1 \text{ in.} = 50 \text{ yd})$ a map of a development that includes a triangular recreation area with sides of lengths 75 yd, 125 yd, and 150 yd. What are the angles of the triangle representing the recreation area on the map?

90. Two points, A and B, are 100 yd apart. Point C across a canyon is located so that angle CAB is $70°$ and angle CBA is $80°$. Compute the distance $\overline{BC}$ across the canyon.

In Exercises 91–100 select the choice that completes the statement or answers the question.

91. The expression $\sin x + \dfrac{\cos^2 x}{\sin x}$ is identical to
   a. $\sec x$ **b.** $\csc x$
   c. $\cos x$ **d.** 1

92. If $x = \arccos\left(-\frac{1}{2}\right)$, then x equals
   a. $\dfrac{\pi}{3}$ **b.** $\dfrac{\pi}{6}$
   c. $\dfrac{5\pi}{6}$ **d.** $\dfrac{2\pi}{3}$

93. Which number is not in the range of $y = \sin x$?
   a. 1   **b.** $-\frac{1}{2}$
   c. 2   **d.** 0

94. If $\sin x < 0$ and $\tan x > 0$, then the point assigned to x lies in quadrant
   a. 1   **b.** 2
   c. 3   **d.** 4

95. The equation $\cos(-x) = -\cos x$ is true for
   a. all values of x
   b. only certain values of x
   c. no values of x

96. If $f(x) = \cos 3x + \tan 2x$, then $f\left(\dfrac{\pi}{6}\right)$ equals
   a. $\sqrt{3}$ **b.** $1 + \sqrt{3}$
   c. $\dfrac{\sqrt{3}}{3}$ **d.** $\dfrac{3 + \sqrt{3}}{3}$

97. If $\log \tan x = a$, then $\log \cot x$ equals
   a. $\dfrac{1}{a}$ **b.** $-a$
   c. $1 - a$ **d.** a

98. Which one of the following is an identity?
   a. $\sin x + \cos x = 1$ **b.** $\sec x \cdot \csc x = 1$
   c. $\sin \frac{1}{2} x = \frac{1}{2} \sin x$ **d.** $\cos^2 x = 1 - \sin^2 x$

99. The number of triangles satisfying the conditions that $B = 30°$, $a = 57$ ft, and $b = 39$ ft is
   a. two   **b.** one   **c.** none

100. In triangle ABC, if $\sin A = \frac{3}{4}$ and $\sin B = \frac{1}{2}$, then the ratio of side length a to side length b is
   a. 3:2   **b.** 8:3
   c. 3:1   **d.** 4:3

CHAPTER 9 TEST

1. What is the range of the function $y = \sin x$?

2. Find the exact value of $\tan\left(\dfrac{2\pi}{3}\right)$.

3. Sketch one cycle of the graph of $y = -3 \cos 4\pi x$.

4. Graph $y = \csc x$ for $0 \le x \le 2\pi$.

5. Find the amplitude, the period, and the phase shift for the graph of $y = -\sin\left(3x - \dfrac{\pi}{2}\right)$.

6. a. Change $270°$ to radians.
   b. Change $\dfrac{7\pi}{4}$ radians to degrees.

7. Find the arc length of a sector of a circle of radius 10 cm that is subtended by a central angle of $150°$.

8. Find the exact value of $\arcsin\left(-\dfrac{\sqrt{3}}{2}\right)$.

9. Simplify $\tan\left(\cos^{-1}\dfrac{1}{2}\right)$.

10. Simplify $\sec x \cos x - \dfrac{1}{\csc^2 x}$.

11. Find all real number solutions: $4 \sin x + 3 = 1$.

12. Solve for x in the interval $[0, 2\pi)$: $\tan x = -1$

13. Find $\tan x$ if $\cos x = \dfrac{5}{13}$ and $\dfrac{3\pi}{2} < x < 2\pi$.

14. Find the measure of the largest angle in a triangle with side measures of 18.5 m, 15.0 m, and 26.0 m.

15. Solve the triangle ABC in which $B = 76°$, $b = 45$ ft, and $c = 35$ ft.

16. Find the area of triangle PQR if $p = 5.6$ cm, $r = 4.1$ cm, and $Q = 48.0°$.

In Exercises 17–20 select the choice that completes the statement or answers the question.

17. A function having the period π is
    a. $y = 2 \sin x$ b. $y = \frac{1}{2}\sin x$
    c. $y = \sin\frac{1}{2}x$ d. $y = \sin 2x$

18. To convert from radians to degrees, we multiply the number of radians by
    a. $\dfrac{180°}{\pi}$ b. $\dfrac{\pi}{90°}$
    c. $\dfrac{90°}{\pi}$ d. $\dfrac{\pi}{180°}$

19. If a central angle of a radians intercepts an arc of length b in a circle of radius c, then
    a. $a = \dfrac{b}{c}$ b. $a = \dfrac{\pi}{b}$
    c. $a = \dfrac{c}{b}$ d. $a = bc$

20. To solve a triangle when we know the measures for two sides of the triangle and the angle between these two sides, we first apply the
    a. law of sines   b. law of cosines

CHAPTER 10

Sequences, Series, and the Binomial Theorem

Business equipment is often depreciated by using the **double-declining balance method.** Under this method, the value of the equipment at the beginning of each year (called the **book value**) is multiplied by a fixed percent to determine its value at the end of that year. When the estimated useful life for equipment is five years, then the equipment may be depreciated by this method at a rate of 40 percent each year. Use the double-declining balance method to find the depreciated book value at the end of five years for office equipment with a useful life of five years that is purchased for $20,000. (See Example 5 of Section 10.1.)

WHEN linear functions and exponential functions are restricted so that the independent variable is limited to positive integers, then the resulting functions are called arithmetic sequences and geometric sequences, respectively. This chapter focuses primarily on such sequences and the series (or sums of sequences) that are associated with them. Arithmetic and geometric series are just two examples of the many important types of series, and this chapter concludes by discussing the series contained in the binomial theorem.

Courtesy of PhotoDisc/Getty Images.

10.1 Sequences

1. Find any term in a sequence when given a formula for the *n*th term of the sequence.
2. Find a formula for the general term a_n in a given arithmetic sequence.
3. Find a formula for the general term a_n in a given geometric sequence.
4. Determine if a sequence is an arithmetic sequence, a geometric sequence, or neither.
5. Solve applied problems involving sequences.

A sequence of numbers is generated by listing numbers in a definite order. For example, the sequence of positive odd numbers is given by

$$1, 3, 5, 7, 9, \ldots.$$

Additionally, the sequence of year-end book values for the office equipment that is depreciating as described in the chapter-opening problem is given by

$$\$12,000, \$7,200, \$4,320, \$2,592, \$1,555.20$$

as shown in Example 5. Each number in a sequence is called a **term** of the sequence. A sequence with an infinite number of terms is called an **infinite sequence,** as illustrated by the sequence of positive odd numbers. When a sequence has a first and last term, like the sequence of book values above, then it is called a **finite sequence.**

In general form, we usually write a sequence as

$$a_1, a_2, a_3, \ldots, a_n, \ldots,$$

where the subscript gives the term number and a_n represents the general or *n*th term. The concept of a function applies to a sequence of numbers because a correspondence exists that assigns to each term number exactly one term, as illustrated in Figure 10.1.

Term Number	Term	Ordered Pair
1	a_1	$(1, a_1)$
2	a_2	$(2, a_2)$
.	.	.
.	.	.
.	.	.
n	a_n	(n, a_n)
.	.	.
.	.	.
.	.	.

Figure 10.1

To analyze a sequence, we usually work from a formula that defines the function. For example,

$$a(n) = 2n, \qquad n = 1, 2, 3, \ldots,$$

specifies the sequence of even positive integers. Note that a is a function name (just like f), and the domain of a is the set of positive integers. By substituting the positive integers for n in the given formula, we can generate the terms of the sequence, as shown in the following chart.

		Subscript Notation		Functional Notation			Terms of Sequence
1st term	=	a_1	=	$a(1)$	$= 2(1) =$		2
2nd term	=	a_2	=	$a(2)$	$= 2(2) =$		4
3rd term	=	a_3	=	$a(3)$	$= 2(3) =$		6
.		.		.	.		.
.		.		.	.		.
.		.		.	.		.
nth term	=	a_n	=	$a(n)$	$= 2(n) =$		$2n$
.		.		.	.		.
.		.		.	.		.
.		.		.	.		.

The discrete or unattached nature of a sequence is emphasized by the graph of function a shown in Figure 10.2. Observe that the graph consists of the isolated points

$$(1, 2), (2, 4), (3, 6), (4, 8), (5, 10), \ldots$$

and that only a portion of the graph may be drawn since only a finite number of points may be plotted. With the aid of the function concept we can now state more formally the definition of a sequence.

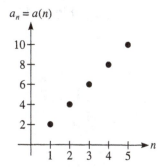

Figure 10.2

Definition of a Sequence

A **sequence** is a function whose domain is the set of positive integers 1, 2, 3, ... The functional values or range elements are called the **terms** of the sequence.

Note that this definition follows the standard practice of interpreting *sequence* to mean *infinite sequence*. It is also conventional to write a formula that defines a sequence in terms of subscript notation, and this practice will be used throughout this chapter.

EXAMPLE 1   Finding Terms in a Sequence

Write the first four terms of the sequence given by $a_n = 5n - 2$; also, find a_{50}.

Solution   Substituting $n = 1, 2, 3, 4$ in the formula for a_n gives

$$a_1 = 5(1) - 2 = 3, \qquad a_2 = 5(2) - 2 = 8,$$
$$a_3 = 5(3) - 2 = 13, \qquad a_4 = 5(4) - 2 = 18.$$

To find the 50th term a_{50}, replace n by 50 to obtain

$$a_{50} = 5(50) - 2 = 248.$$

Technology Link

A main theme when analyzing functions has been to express relations algebraically, numerically, and graphically. When the relation is a sequence, graphing calculators can usually be set in Sequence Mode and Dot mode to facilitate the analysis. Figures 10.3(a), (b), and (c) show typical calculator screens associated with these settings. The figures show the results from entering the sequence in Example 1 in the equation editor, generating a Table with the independent variable set in Ask Mode, and obtaining a graph with the window settings as shown.

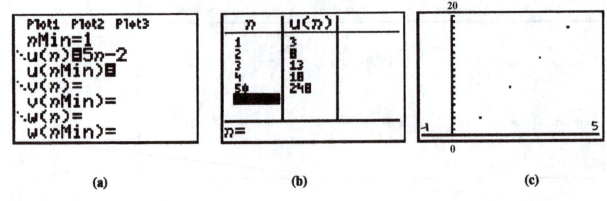

(a)   (b)   (c)

Figure 10.3

Note that in sequence mode the first function on the screen is labeled $u(n)$, so the function name is u and the independent variable is n. In previous work the calculator has usually been set in function mode, where the first function in the equation editor is $y1$ and the independent variable is x. If you wish to analyze up to three sequences at the same time, then the names of the second and third sequences are v and w.

PROGRESS CHECK 1   Write the first four terms of the sequence given by $a_n = 3n + 5$; also, find a_{75}.   ■

Two special types of sequences that have many applications are called arithmetic sequences and geometric sequences. To illustrate an arithmetic sequence, consider the sequence

$$4, 7, 10, 13, \ldots.$$

Observe that each term after the first may be found by adding 3 to the previous term, as shown below.

$$\underbrace{4, \quad 7,}_{3} \underbrace{\quad 10,}_{3} \underbrace{\quad 13,}_{3} \quad \ldots$$

Therefore, the sequence is called an arithmetic sequence, and the number 3 is called the common difference in this sequence, as specified in the following definitions.

Arithmetic Sequence

An **arithmetic sequence** is a sequence of numbers in which each number after the first is found by adding a constant to the preceding term. This constant is called the **common difference** and is symbolized by d.

A formula for the general term in an arithmetic sequence with first term a_1 and common difference d may be found by observing the following pattern in such a sequence.

1st term,   2nd term,   3rd term,   ..., nth term,   ...

$a_1,$ $a_1 + 1d,$ $a_1 + 2d,$ ..., $a_1 + (n - 1)d,$ ...

Thus, the nth term is given by $a_1 + (n - 1)d$, and we have the following formula for a_n.

Formula for *n*th Term of an Arithmetic Sequence

The nth term of an arithmetic sequence is given by

$$a_n = a_1 + (n - 1)d,$$

where a_1 is the first term and d is the common difference.

EXAMPLE 2   Finding the *n*th Term of an Arithmetic Sequence

Find a formula for the general term a_n in the arithmetic sequence

$$4, 7, 10, 13, \ldots.$$

What is the 28th term in the sequence?

Solution   The first term is 4, so $a_1 = 4$. By subtracting any term from the next term, say a_1 from a_2, we obtain the common difference.

$$d = 7 - 4 = 3$$

Then a formula for a_n may be found as follows.

$$
\begin{aligned}
a_n &= a_1 + (n - 1)d \\
&= 4 + (n - 1)3 \qquad \text{Replace } a_1 \text{ by 4 and } d \text{ by 3.} \\
&= 4 + 3n - 3 \\
&= 3n + 1
\end{aligned}
$$

To find the 28th term, substitute 28 for n in this formula.

$$
\begin{aligned}
a_n &= 3n + 1 \\
a_{28} &= 3(28) + 1 \qquad \text{Replace } n \text{ by 28.} \\
&= 85
\end{aligned}
$$

PROGRESS CHECK 2   Find a formula for the general term a_n in the arithmetic sequence 6, 13, 20, 27, ... What is the 45th term in this sequence?   ■

In an arithmetic sequence, the terms in the sequence maintain a *common difference.* When the terms in a sequence maintain a *common ratio,* then the sequence is called a geometric sequence, as given in the following definitions.

Geometric Sequence

A **geometric sequence** is a sequence of numbers in which each number after the first number is found by multiplying the preceding term by a constant. This constant is called the **common ratio** and is symbolized by r.

To illustrate, the following sequences are geometric sequences with common ratios r as shown.

$$3, 9, 27, 81, \ldots \qquad\qquad r = \tfrac{9}{3} = \tfrac{27}{9} = \tfrac{81}{27} = 3$$

$$1, 1.05, (1.05)^2, (1.05)^3, \ldots \qquad r = \frac{1.05}{1} = \frac{(1.05)^2}{1.05} = \frac{(1.05)^3}{(1.05)^2} = 1.05$$

A formula for the general term in a geometric sequence with first term a_1 and common ratio r may be found by observing the following pattern in such a sequence.

1st term,	2nd term,	3rd term,	$\ldots$,	nth term,	$\ldots$
a_1,	$a_1 r^1$,	$a_1 r^2$,	$\ldots$,	$a_1 r^{n-1}$	$\ldots$

Thus, $a_1 r^{n-1}$ specifies the general term, and we have the following formula for a_n in a geometric sequence.

Formula for nth Term in a Geometric Sequence

The nth term in a geometric sequence is given by

$$a_n = a_1 r^{n-1},$$

where a_1 is the first term and r is the common ratio.

EXAMPLE 3   Finding the nth Term of a Geometric Sequence

Find a formula for the general term a_n in the geometric sequence

$$2, -1, \tfrac{1}{2}, -\tfrac{1}{4}, \ldots.$$

What is the 10th term in the sequence?

Solution   The first term is 2, so $a_1 = 2$. By dividing any term into the next term, say a_2 into a_3, the common ratio is

$$r = \frac{\tfrac{1}{2}}{-1} = -\frac{1}{2}.$$

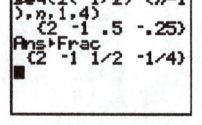

Then replacing a_1 by 2 and r by $-\tfrac{1}{2}$ in $a_n = a_1 r^{n-1}$ yields

$$a_n = 2\left(-\tfrac{1}{2}\right)^{n-1}.$$

To find the 10th term, substitute 10 for n in this formula to obtain

$$a_{10} = 2\left(-\tfrac{1}{2}\right)^{10-1} = 2\left(-\tfrac{1}{2}\right)^9 = 2\left(-\tfrac{1}{512}\right) = -\tfrac{1}{256}.$$

Note   In this example, to check that the 10th term is $-\tfrac{1}{256}$, just generate successive terms by multiplying by the common ratio of $-\tfrac{1}{2}$, to obtain

$$2, -1, \tfrac{1}{2}, -\tfrac{1}{4}, \tfrac{1}{8}, -\tfrac{1}{16}, \tfrac{1}{32}, -\tfrac{1}{64}, \tfrac{1}{128}, -\tfrac{1}{256}, \ldots.$$

Figure 10.4

Writing the sequence in this form confirms that the 10th term is $-\tfrac{1}{256}$.

Technology Link

Many graphing calculators have a special sequence generating command associated with List operations. We can then use this function to check that the formula $a_n = 2\left(-\tfrac{1}{2}\right)^{n-1}$ does, in fact, generate the 4 terms given in Example 3. The calculator screen in Figure 10.4 shows how this might appear.

The sequence command in Figure 10.4 consists of 4 expressions separated by commas. The 4 expressions are the formula for the sequence, the variable in the formula (n), and the starting and stopping values for n. Note that the answer first appears using decimal notation. We see .5 and $-.25$ instead of $\frac{1}{2}$ and $-\frac{1}{4}$. The second command on the screen uses the Frac function that converts decimals to fraction notation.

PROGRESS CHECK 3   Find a formula for the general term a_n in the geometric sequence $-9, 3, -1, \frac{1}{3}, \cdots$. What is the 8th term in the sequence?   ■

When given a sequence of numbers, we must be able to classify the sequence as arithmetic, geometric, or neither, as considered in the next example.

EXAMPLE 4   Classifying Sequences
State whether the sequence is an arithmetic sequence, a geometric sequence, or neither. For any arithmetic sequence, state the common difference and write the next two terms. For any geometric sequence, state the common ratio and write the next two terms.

a. 2, 6, 18, 54, ...
b. 1, 8, 15, 22, ...
c. 1, 4, 9, 16, ...

Solution

a. Each term after the first is found by multiplying the preceding term by 3, as illustrated below.

$$2, \qquad 6, \qquad 18, \qquad 54, \ldots$$

$$2 \cdot 3 = 6 \quad 6 \cdot 3 = 18 \quad 18 \cdot 3 = 54$$

Therefore, the sequence is geometric with common ratio 3. The next two terms in the sequence are 162 and 486.

b. Each term after the first is found by adding 7 to the preceding term, as shown next.

$$1, \qquad 8, \qquad 15, \qquad 22, \ldots$$

$$1 + 7 = 8 \quad 8 + 7 = 15 \quad 15 + 7 = 22$$

Therefore, the sequence is arithmetic with common difference 7. The next two terms in the sequence are 29 and 36.

c. The terms in this sequence do not have a common difference and they do not have a common ratio. Therefore, the sequence is neither arithmetic nor geometric.

PROGRESS CHECK 4   Answer the questions in Example 4 for each sequence.

a. 1.125, 1.25, 1.375, 1.5, ...
b. $1, \frac{1}{2}, \frac{1}{3}, \frac{1}{4}, \cdots$
c. 27, 9, 3, 1, ...   ■

The mathematics of finance contains many applications of sequences. One such application is considered in the chapter-opening problem.

EXAMPLE 5   Depreciation by the Double-declining Method
Solve the problem in the chapter introduction on page 545.

Solution   If the office equipment depreciates 40 percent each year, at the end of the year this equipment is worth 60 percent of the book value at which it began the year.

Thus, the sequence of year-end book values forms a geometric sequence with common ratio 0.6, and the terms in this sequence are computed as shown in the following table.

Year	Book Value at Beginning of Year	Book Value at End of Year
1	20,000	$20,000(0.6) = 12,000$
2	12,000	$12,000(0.6) = 7,200$
3	7,200	$7,200(0.6) = 4,320$
4	4,320	$4,320(0.6) = 2,592$
5	2,592	$2,592(0.6) = 1,555.20$

This depreciation schedule shows that the book value of the equipment at the end of five years is $1,555.20.

Note The book value at the end of five years may also be found using $a_n = a_1 r^{n-1}$. Substituting $a_1 = 12,000$, $r = 0.6$, and $n = 5$ in this formula gives

$$a_5 = 12,000(0.6)^{5-1} = 1,555.20.$$

PROGRESS CHECK 5 Use the double-declining balance method to find the depreciated book value at the end of 10 years for property with a useful life of 10 years that is purchased for $100,000. The allowable depreciation rate in this case is 20 percent each year. ■

EXERCISES 10.1

In Exercises 1–8, use the formula for the nth term to write the first four terms of the given arithmetic sequence; also, find the term indicated.

1. $a_n = 2n - 5$; a_{10} **2.** $a_n = 3n + 2$; a_{20}
3. $a_n = 6n + 8$; a_{15} **4.** $a_n = 7n - 3$; a_{25}
5. $a_n = \frac{1}{2}n + 2$; a_7 **6.** $a_n = \frac{2}{3}n - 5$; a_{12}
7. $a_n = \frac{3}{5}n - \frac{2}{5}$; a_{25} **8.** $a_n = \frac{2}{3}n - \frac{1}{6}$; a_{18}

In Exercises 9–18, find a formula for the general term a_n in each of the following arithmetic sequences. Also, find the indicated term for each sequence.

9. $1, 5, 9, 13, \ldots$; a_{12} **10.** $1, 6, 11, 16, \ldots$; a_{15}
11. $2, 8, 14, 20, \ldots$; a_{20} **12.** $3, 7, 11, 15, \ldots$; a_{17}
13. $5, 12, 19, 26, \ldots$; a_{27} **14.** $3, 13, 23, 33, \ldots$; a_{16}
15. $4, 13, 22, 31, \ldots$; a_{40} **16.** $8, 9\frac{1}{2}, 11, 12\frac{1}{2}, \ldots$; a_{11}
17. $12, 13\frac{1}{3}, 14\frac{2}{3}, 16, \ldots$; a_{16} **18.** $6, 17, 28, 39, \ldots$; a_{20}

In Exercises 19–28, find a formula for the general term a_n in the given geometric sequence. Also, find the indicated term in each sequence.

19. $2, 4, 8, 16, \ldots$; a_{10} **20.** $5, 10, 20, 40, \ldots$; a_{10}
21. $3, 15, 75, 375, \ldots$; a_7 **22.** $2, 8, 32, 128, \ldots$; a_8
23. $7, 21, 63, 189, \ldots$; a_9 **24.** $3, -1, \frac{1}{3}, -\frac{1}{9}, \ldots$; a_{10}

25. $5, -1, \frac{1}{5}, -\frac{1}{25}, \ldots$; a_7 **26.** $\frac{1}{3}, \frac{1}{9}, \frac{1}{27}, \frac{1}{81}, \ldots$; a_8
27. $\frac{1}{2}, -\frac{1}{4}, \frac{1}{8}, -\frac{1}{16}, \ldots$; a_{10} **28.** $\frac{1}{5}, -\frac{2}{15}, \frac{4}{45}, -\frac{8}{135}, \ldots$; a_6

In Exercises 29–38, state whether the sequence is an arithmetic sequence, a geometric sequence, or neither. For any arithmetic sequence, state the common difference and write the next two terms. For any geometric sequence, state the common ratio and write the next two terms.

29. $1, 4, 16, 64, \ldots$ **30.** $2, 7, 12, 17, \ldots$
31. $3, 5, 8, 11, \ldots$ **32.** $3, 12, 48, 192, \ldots$
33. $5, 15, 45, 135, \ldots$ **34.** $7, 21, 28, 35, \ldots$
35. $7, 13, 19, 25, \ldots$ **36.** $2, \frac{2}{3}, \frac{2}{9}, \frac{2}{27}, \ldots$
37. $\frac{1}{5}, \frac{1}{10}, \frac{1}{15}, \frac{1}{20}, \ldots$ **38.** $\frac{2}{3}, \frac{5}{3}, \frac{8}{3}, \frac{11}{3}, \ldots$

In Exercises 39–40, use the double-declining balance method from the problem which opens the chapter.

39. Find the depreciated book value at the end of five years for office equipment with a useful life of five years that is purchased originally for $8,000. It depreciates 40 percent per year. What kind of sequence is the yearly book value?

40. Find the depreciated book value at the end of 10 years for office equipment with a useful life of 10 years that is purchased originally for \$60,000. It depreciates 20 percent per year. What kind of sequence is the yearly book value?

41. An amount of \$1,000 is invested at 8 percent annual interest, payable on the anniversary of the deposit. The formula $a_n = 1{,}000(1.08)^n$ gives the value of the deposit after n complete years. Find the value of a_n for each of years 1, 2, 3, 4, 5. What kind of sequence is this?

42. An amount of \$2,000 is invested at 6 percent annual interest, payable on the anniversary of the deposit. The formula $a_n = 2{,}000(1.06)^n$ gives the value of the deposit after n complete years. Find the value of a_n for each of years 1, 2, 3, 4, 5. What kind of sequence is this?

43. Sequences are important in the theory of limits in calculus, where the object is to see if the terms of a sequence are approaching some fixed value. When this happens, that value is called the *limit* of the sequence. In these examples, write the first five terms of the given sequence, and guess the limit.

   a. $a_n = \dfrac{n}{n+1}$ **b.** $a_n = \dfrac{1}{n}$

   c. $a_n = \dfrac{1}{n^3 - 5n^2 + 11n - 6}$

   d. $a_n = \dfrac{1}{n^2}$

   e. $a_n = 2 - \dfrac{1}{3^n}$ **f.** $a_n = 1 - 0.6^n$

44. Here is a sequence, called the Galileo sequence, with a clear pattern.

$$\frac{1}{3}, \frac{1+3}{5+7}, \frac{1+3+5}{7+9+11}, \ldots$$

   a. Follow the given pattern and write the next term.
   b. Simplify each term as much as possible to notice a remarkable result.

45. Some sequences are clearly defined even though there is no obvious formula. For instance, what are the first five terms of the sequence of prime numbers? That is, $a_n = n$th prime number. Is this sequence arithmetic, geometric, or neither?

46. Prime numbers are positive integers that have exactly two factors. Thus, 3 is prime because it has exactly two factors, namely, 3 and 1. In a similar way, we can construct a sequence of positive integers that have exactly three factors.

Factors

$$a_1 = 4 \qquad 1, 2, 4$$
$$a_2 = 9 \qquad 1, 3, 9$$
$$a_3 = 25 \qquad 1, 5, 25$$

What is the next number in this sequence? Is this sequence arithmetic, geometric, or neither?

47. A sequence whose next term is found by adding the two preceding terms is called a Fibonacci sequence. For instance, if $a_1 = 1$ and $a_2 = 1$, then $a_3 = 2$ and $a_4 = 3$. Find a_5 and a_6. Is this sequence arithmetic, geometric, or neither?

48. Find the next two terms of this sequence of logarithms. Is the sequence arithmetic, geometric, or neither?
$a_1 = \log_2 2$, $a_2 = \log_2 4$, $a_3 = \log_2 8$, $a_4 = \log_2 16$

THINK ABOUT IT 10.1

1. Many sequences have been discovered whose terms approach irrational numbers. Here are two which you can investigate. For each sequence, (a) write out the fourth term, and (b) find the decimal value of the fourth term to the nearest thousandth, and compare it with the value of the irrational number as approximated by your calculator.

$$\pi: \qquad 4 \cdot 1, \, 4 \cdot \left(1 - \tfrac{1}{3}\right), \, 4 \cdot \left(1 - \tfrac{1}{3} + \tfrac{1}{5}\right), \ldots$$

$$\sqrt{2}: \qquad 1 + \tfrac{1}{2}, \, 1 + \frac{1}{2 + \tfrac{1}{2}}, \, 1 + \frac{1}{2 + \dfrac{1}{2 + \tfrac{1}{2}}}$$

2. If the first three terms in a geometric sequence are b^2, b^x, and b^8, find x.

3. Is 4,000 a term in the arithmetic sequence 2, 5, 8, … ? Explain your answer.

4. **a.** If a, b, and c are the first three terms in an arithmetic sequence, express b in terms of a and c.
   b. If a, b, and c are the first three terms in a geometric sequence, express c in terms of a and b.

5. In an arithmetic sequence $a_6 = 15$ and $a_{12} = 24$. Find a_1 and d.

*Courtesy of Pearson Education/
Prentice-Hall, Inc.*

10.2   Series

A free-falling body that starts from rest drops about 16 ft the first second, 48 ft the second second, 80 ft the third second, and so on. About how many feet does a parachutist drop during the first 10 seconds of free-fall? (See Example 7.)

OBJECTIVES

1   Find the sum of an indicated number of terms in an arithmetic sequence.

2   Find the sum of an indicated number of terms in a geometric sequence.

3   Write a series given in sigma notation in its expanded form, and determine the sum.

4   Write a series given in expanded form using sigma notation.

5   Solve applied problems involving series.

Associated with any sequence

$$a_1, a_2, \ldots, a_n, \ldots$$

is a series

$$a_1 + a_2 + \cdots + a_n + \cdots,$$

which is the sum of all the terms in the sequence. In this section we consider only series that are associated with finite sequences. In Section 10.3 a special type of infinite series will be discussed.

The series associated with an arithmetic sequence is called an **arithmetic series.** To illustrate a method for finding such a sum, consider the problem of finding the sum of the first 100 positive integers. This series can be written as

$$S = 1 + 2 + 3 + \cdots + 98 + 99 + 100.$$

By reversing the order of the terms, we can also write this series as

$$S = 100 + 99 + 98 + \cdots + 3 + 2 + 1.$$

If we now add, term by term, the two equivalent expressions for S, we have 100 pairs, which all add up to 101. So

$$2S = 100(101) \quad \text{and} \quad S = \frac{100(101)}{2} = 5{,}050.$$

Thus, the sum of the first 100 positive integers is 5,050.

By applying the above method to an arithmetic series in general form, we can derive a formula for the sum of an arithmetic series. The sum of the first n terms in an arithmetic sequence can be written as

$$S_n = a_1 + (a_1 + d) + (a_1 + 2d) + \cdots + (a_n - 2d) + (a_n - d) + a_n.$$

By reversing the order of the terms, we can also write this series as

$$S_n = a_n + (a_n - d) + (a_n - 2d) + \cdots + (a_1 + 2d) + (a_1 + d) + a_1.$$

Adding term by term the two equivalent expressions for S_n gives n pairs, which all add up to $a_1 + a_n$. So

$$2S_n = n(a_1 + a_n) \quad \text{and} \quad S_n = \frac{n}{2}(a_1 + a_n).$$

This formula is used when n, a_1, and a_n are known. However, d is often known in place of a_n. To derive an alternative formula, replace a_n in the above formula by $a_1 + (n - 1)d$ to get

$$S_n = \frac{n}{2}\{a_1 + [a_1 + (n - 1)d]\}$$

$$= \frac{n}{2}[2a_1 + (n - 1)d].$$

In summary, the following formulas have been derived.

Arithmetic Series Formulas

The sum of the first n terms of an arithmetic sequence is given by

$$S_n = \frac{n}{2}(a_1 + a_n)$$

or

$$S_n = \frac{n}{2}[2a_1 + (n - 1)d].$$

EXAMPLE 1   Finding the Sum of an Arithmetic Sequence

Find the sum of the first 250 positive integers.

Solution   The problem is to evaluate

$$S_{250} = 1 + 2 + 3 + \cdots + 250.$$

Because a_1, a_n, and n are known, use the top formula in the box above.

$$S_n = \frac{n}{2}(a_1 + a_n)$$

$$S_{250} = \frac{250}{2}(1 + 250) \qquad \text{Let } n = 250, a_1 = 1, \text{ and } a_n = 250.$$

$$= 31,375$$

The sum of the first 250 positive integers is 31,375.

PROGRESS CHECK 1   Find the sum of the first 180 positive integers.   ■

EXAMPLE 2   Finding the Sum of the First n Terms
of an Arithmetic Sequence

Find the sum of the first 25 terms of the arithmetic sequence 6, 13, 20, ...

Solution   For the given arithmetic sequence, $a_1 = 6$ and $d = 7$. To find the sum of the first 25 terms, let $n = 25$ and use the second formula in the box above.

$$S_n = \frac{n}{2}[2a_1 + (n - 1)d]$$

$$S_{25} = \frac{25}{2}[2(6) + (25 - 1)7] \qquad \text{Let } n = 25, a_1 = 6, \text{ and } d = 7.$$

$$= \frac{25}{2}(180) = 2,250$$

PROGRESS CHECK 2 Find the sum of the first 35 terms of the arithmetic sequence 4, 7, 10, ... ▪

The series associated with a geometric sequence is called a **geometric series,** and in general form, a geometric series with n terms can be written as

$$S_n = a_1 + a_1 r + a_1 r^2 + \cdots + a_1 r^{n-1}. \tag{1}$$

To derive a formula for the sum in a geometric series, first multiply both sides of equation (1) by r to obtain

$$r S_n = a_1 r + a_1 r^2 + \cdots + a_1 r^{n-1} + a_1 r^n. \tag{2}$$

Then subtracting equation (2) from equation (1) yields

$$S_n - r S_n = a_1 - a_1 r^n$$
$$S_n(1 - r) = a_1(1 - r^n)$$
$$S_n = \frac{a_1(1 - r^n)}{1 - r}, \quad \text{for} \quad r \neq 1.$$

The result is a formula for S_n when a_1, r, and n are known.

Geometric Series Formula

The sum of the first n terms of a geometric sequence with $r \neq 1$ is given by

$$S_n = \frac{a_1(1 - r^n)}{1 - r}.$$

EXAMPLE 3 Finding the Sum of a Geometric Sequence

Find the sum of the first eight terms of the geometric sequence 2, 6, 18, ...

Solution Here $a_1 = 2$, $r = 3$, and $n = 8$. Then,

$$S_n = \frac{a_1(1 - r^n)}{1 - r}$$

$$S_8 = \frac{2(1 - 3^8)}{1 - 3} \qquad \text{Let } a_1 = 2, r = 3, \text{ and } n = 8.$$

$$= \frac{2(1 - 6{,}561)}{-2}$$

$$= 6{,}560.$$

PROGRESS CHECK 3 Find the sum of the first seven terms of the geometric sequence 3, 6, 12, ... ▪

The Greek letter Σ, read "sigma," is commonly used to write a series in compact form. By this convention, called **sigma notation,**

$$S_n = a_1 + a_2 + \cdots + a_n$$

is abbreviated as

$$S_n = \sum_{i=1}^{n} a_i,$$

so that $\sum_{i=1}^{n} a_i$ means to add the terms that result from replacing i by 1, then 2, ..., then n. The letter i in this notation is called the **index of summation,** and the choice of this letter is arbitrary. For instance,

$$\sum_{i=1}^{n} a_i, \quad \sum_{j=1}^{n} a_j, \quad \sum_{k=1}^{n} a_k$$

all represent the same series.

EXAMPLE 4 Simplifying a Series in Sigma Notation

Write the series $\sum_{i=1}^{4} (i^2 - 1)$ in expanded form, and determine the sum.

Solution

$$\sum_{i=1}^{4} (i^2 - 1) = (1^2 - 1) + (2^2 - 1) + (3^2 - 1) + (4^2 - 1)$$
$$= 0 + 3 + 8 + 15$$
$$= 26$$

Technology Link

With a calculator set in sequence mode a combination of the sequence and sum commands can be used as shown in Figure 10.5 to find the sum of the first n terms of a series.

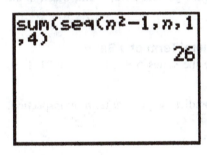

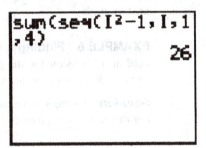

(a) (b)

Figure 10.5

Figure 10.5(a) shows the calculation of the sum of the first 4 terms of the series $\sum_{i=1}^{4} (i^2 - 1)$. In sequence mode, the default variable is n, rather than i, but you can use any letter you choose, as shown in Figure 10.5(b). The sequence and sum functions are both usually associated with the List key.

PROGRESS CHECK 4 Write the series $\sum_{i=1}^{5} (3i + 2)$ in expanded form, and determine the sum. ■

EXAMPLE 5 Simplifying a Geometric Series in Sigma Notation

Write the series $\sum_{i=1}^{5} 4\left(\frac{1}{2}\right)^i$ in expanded form, and determine the sum.

Solution   In expanded form the series is

$$\sum_{i=1}^{5} 4\left(\tfrac{1}{2}\right)^i = 4\left(\tfrac{1}{2}\right)^1 + 4\left(\tfrac{1}{2}\right)^2 + 4\left(\tfrac{1}{2}\right)^3 + 4\left(\tfrac{1}{2}\right)^4 + 4\left(\tfrac{1}{2}\right)^5.$$

This series is a geometric series with $a_1 = 4\left(\tfrac{1}{2}\right) = 2$, $r = \tfrac{1}{2}$, and $n = 5$. So

$$S_n = \frac{a_1(1 - r^n)}{1 - r}$$

$$S_5 = \frac{2\left[1 - \left(\tfrac{1}{2}\right)^5\right]}{1 - \tfrac{1}{2}} \qquad \text{Let } a_1 = 2, r = \tfrac{1}{2}, \text{ and } n = 5.$$

$$= \frac{2\left[1 - \tfrac{1}{32}\right]}{\tfrac{1}{2}} = \frac{\tfrac{31}{16}}{\tfrac{1}{2}} = \frac{31}{8}.$$

Therefore, $\displaystyle\sum_{i=1}^{5} 4\left(\tfrac{1}{2}\right)^i = \tfrac{31}{8}$.

PROGRESS CHECK 5   Write the series $\displaystyle\sum_{i=1}^{4} 6\left(\tfrac{1}{2}\right)^i$ in expanded form, and determine the sum. ■

When we need to convert a series from expanded form to compact form using sigma notation, the main obstacle is finding a formula for the general term, as illustrated in the next example.

EXAMPLE 6   Finding a Formula for the General Term of a Series

Find an expression for the general term and write the series $6 + 11 + 16 + 21 + 26 + 31 + 36$ in sigma notation.

Solution   In many cases we hope to be able to predict the general term by inspection. For this series a_i is given by

$$5i + 1$$

and since there are seven terms, we have

$$\sum_{i=1}^{7} (5i + 1) = 6 + 11 + 16 + 21 + 26 + 31 + 36.$$

If you had difficulty predicting the general term, you could note in this case that the series is arithmetic with $a_1 = 6$ and $d = 5$ so that

$$a_n = a_1 + (n - 1)d$$
$$= 6 + (n - 1)5$$
$$= 5n + 1.$$

Note   In sigma notation it is sometimes convenient to begin the index of summation at a number other than 1. For instance, the series in this example can also be represented by

$$\sum_{i=0}^{6} (5i + 6).$$

Keep in mind that a series can be represented in sigma notation in more than one way.

PROGRESS CHECK 6   Find an expression for the general term and write the series $7 + 13 + 19 + \cdots + 49$ in sigma notation.   ■

The problem that opens this section illustrates an application of an arithmetic series.

EXAMPLE 7   Distance Traveled by a Free-Falling Object
Solve the problem in the section introduction on page 554.

Solution   The drop in feet for the parachutist during the first 10 seconds of the free-fall is given by the sum of the first 10 terms of the sequence

$$16, 48, 80, \ldots.$$

This sequence is arithmetic with $a_1 = 16$ and $d = 32$. Let $n = 10$ and use the formula that gives S_n in terms of a_1, d, and n.

$$S_n = \frac{n}{2}[2a_1 + (n-1)d]$$

$$= \frac{10}{2}[2(16) + (10-1)32] \quad \text{Let } n = 10, a_1 = 16, \text{ and } d = 32.$$

$$= \frac{10}{2}(320) = 1{,}600$$

Thus, a parachutist drops about 1,600 ft during the first 10 seconds of free-fall.

PROGRESS CHECK 7   From the sequence given in Example 7, about how many feet does a parachutist drop during the first 15 seconds of free-fall?   ■

The next example shows an important type of application associated with geometric series.

EXAMPLE 8   Finding the Value of an Investment with Regular Deposits
To help finance their daughter's college education, a couple invests $4,000 on her birthday each year, starting with her 13th birthday. If the money is placed in an account that pays 8 percent interest compounded annually, how much is in this account on her 17th birthday? Assume that the last deposit is made on her 16th birthday.

Solution   Observe that four deposits will be made corresponding to the daughter's 13th, 14th, 15th, and 16th birthdays. Determine separately the compounded amount of each $4,000 deposit using the formula $A = P(1 + r)^t$ from Section 8.1.

Birthday	Deposit	Interest Period	Compounded Amount
13th	1st	4 years	$4{,}000(1 + 0.08)^4$
14th	2nd	3 years	$4{,}000(1 + 0.08)^3$
15th	3rd	2 years	$4{,}000(1 + 0.08)^2$
16th	4th	1 year	$4{,}000(1 + 0.08)^1$

The amount S in the account at the end of four years is the sum of the four compounded amounts, so

$$S = 4{,}000(1.08) + 4{,}000(1.08)^2 + 4{,}000(1.08)^3 + 4{,}000(1.08)^4.$$

This series is a geometric series with $a_1 = 4{,}000(1.08) = 4{,}320$, $r = 1.08$, and $n = 4$. Thus,

$$S_n = \frac{a_1(1 - r^n)}{1 - r}$$

$$S_4 = \frac{4{,}320(1 - 1.08^4)}{1 - 1.08} \approx 19{,}466.40 \text{ (by calculator).}$$

The daughter's college fund is worth $19,466.40 on her 17th birthday.

PROGRESS CHECK 8   Redo the problem in Example 8, but assume that $3,000 is deposited each year in an account that pays 7 percent interest compounded annually, and that deposits are started with the daughter's 7th birthday. ■

EXERCISES 10.2

In Exercises 1–10, find the sum of the first n positive integers.

1. $n = 6$
2. $n = 8$
3. $n = 12$
4. $n = 15$
5. $n = 18$
6. $n = 20$
7. $n = 125$
8. $n = 250$
9. $n = 300$
10. $n = 500$

In Exercises 11–20, find the sum of the first n terms of the given arithmetic sequence.

11. $n = 8; 1, 4, 7, \ldots$
12. $n = 12; 2, 6, 10, \ldots$
13. $n = 15; 5, 10, 15, \ldots$
14. $n = 20; 3, 9, 15, \ldots$
15. $n = 22; 1, 8, 15, \ldots$
16. $n = 37; 6, 9, 12, \ldots$
17. $n = 48; 14, 17, 20, \ldots$
18. $n = 78; 1, 5, 9, \ldots$
19. $n = 138; 2, 7, 12, \ldots$
20. $n = 537; 1, 3, 5, \ldots$

In Exercises 21–30, find the sum of the first n terms of the given geometric sequence.

21. $n = 5; 3, 9, 27$
22. $n = 6; 3, 15, 75$
23. $n = 10; 2, 8, 32$
24. $n = 9; 2, 10, 50$
25. $n = 7; 3, 6, 12$
26. $n = 8; 3, 12, 48$
27. $n = 11; 1, 3, 9$
28. $n = 12; 1, 5, 25$
29. $n = 15; 1, 2, 4$
30. $n = 17; 1, 4, 16$

In Exercises 31–42, write the given series in expanded form and determine the sum.

31. $\sum\limits_{i=1}^{5} 3i$
32. $\sum\limits_{i=1}^{9} 2i$

33. $\sum\limits_{i=0}^{4} (2i + 1)$
34. $\sum\limits_{i=0}^{3} (3i - 1)$

35. $\sum\limits_{i=1}^{6} (i^2 + 2)$
36. $\sum\limits_{i=1}^{5} (i^2 - 3)$

37. $\sum\limits_{i=2}^{4} 3^i$
38. $\sum\limits_{i=3}^{8} 2^i$

39. $\sum\limits_{i=1}^{4} 2^{i-2}$
40. $\sum\limits_{i=1}^{5} 3^{i+1}$

41. $\sum\limits_{i=1}^{4} \left(\tfrac{1}{3}\right)^i$
42. $\sum\limits_{i=1}^{5} 3\left(\tfrac{1}{2}\right)^i$

In Exercises 43–52, find an expression for the general term, and write the given series in sigma notation. (More than one form is possible.)

43. $6 + 12 + 18 + 24 + 30 + 36$
44. $4 + 8 + 12 + 16 + 20 + 24$
45. $1 + 4 + 7 + 10 + 13 + 16$
46. $-1 + 1 + 3 + 5 + 7$
47. $6 + 11 + 18 + 27 + 38$ (*Hint:* i^2 is needed.)
48. $6 + 13 + 22 + 33 + 46$ (*Hint:* i^2 is needed.)
49. $1 + 3 + 9 + 27 + 81$
50. $1 + 2 + 4 + 8$
51. $3 + \tfrac{3}{4} + \tfrac{3}{16} + \tfrac{3}{64} + \tfrac{3}{128}$
52. $\tfrac{2}{3} + \tfrac{2}{9} + \tfrac{2}{27} + \tfrac{2}{81} + \tfrac{2}{243}$

53. In many winter celebrations such as Kwanza or Hanukkah an increasing number of candles are burned each day for a period of time. For instance, over the 8 days of Hanukkah 2, 3, 4, 5, 6, 7, 8, and then 9 candles are used. Express the total number of candles as a series and find its sum. Is the series arithmetic, geometric, or neither?

54. In this famous riddle the correct answer is 1 (why?), but how many were coming *from* St. Ives? Express the answer as a series. Is it arithmetic, geometric, or neither?

As I was going to St. Ives,
I met a man with seven wives.
Each wife had seven sacks,
Each sack had seven cats,
Each cat had seven kits:
Kits, cats, sacks and wives,
How many were going to St. Ives?

55. A person makes a purchase for $6,000, paying $1,500 down and agreeing to pay at the end of each year 8 percent interest on the unpaid balance plus an additional $900 to reduce the principal.
   a. Show that the loan will be paid off after five years.
   b. Write out the five-term series which gives the total of the interest payments. What kind of series is this? What is the total amount of interest paid?

56. A person makes a purchase for $6,000, paying $1,200 down and agreeing to pay at the end of each year 8 percent interest on the unpaid balance plus an additional $800 to reduce the principal.

   a. Show that the loan will be paid off after six years.

   b. Write out the six-term series which gives the total of the interest payments. What kind of series is this? What is the total amount of interest paid?

57. Refer to the figure and express the total area as the sum of individual rectangular areas. Is this series arithmetic, geometric, or neither?

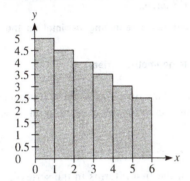

58. The area under the parabola $y = x^2$ may be estimated by the sum of the areas of the 10 rectangles shown in the figure. Write out the 10-term series which represents the sum of the areas of the rectangles and find the sum. (*Hint:* The base of each rectangle is 0.1; the height is given by x^2.) Is this series arithmetic, geometric, or neither?

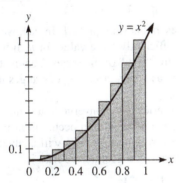

59. A young student is asked to memorize the "times" table for the digits from 0 to 9. How many products must be memorized? (Assume, for example, that 2×3 and 3×2 are just one item to be memorized.) Here is one way of listing the products. Write a series that gives the sum of the number of products in each row of the table.

$$0 \times 0, 0 \times 1, 0 \times 2, 0 \times 3, 0 \times 4, \ldots, 0 \times 9$$
$$1 \times 1, 1 \times 2, 1 \times 3, 1 \times 4, \ldots, 1 \times 9$$
$$2 \times 2, 2 \times 3, 2 \times 4, \ldots, 2 \times 9$$
$$3 \times 3, 3 \times 4, \ldots, 3 \times 9$$
$$\vdots$$
$$9 \times 9$$

60. In the familiar base 10 number system we use 10 symbols for digits from 0 to 9. In the base 12 number system 12 symbols are used for digits: 0, 1, 2, 3, 4, 5, 6, 7, 8, 9, *, #. How many products must be memorized for the base 12 times table? Model the solution after the one in Exercise 59.

61. A free-falling body that starts from rest drops about 16 ft the first second, 48 ft the second second, 80 ft the third second, and so on. About how many feet does an apple released from an airplane fall during the first 12 seconds of free-fall?

62. Redo Exercise 61, but assume that the apple falls for 16 seconds.

63. To help finance their son's college education, a couple invests $1,000 on his birthday each year starting with his 5th birthday. If the money is placed in an account that pays 6 percent interest compounded annually, how much is in the account on his 18th birthday? Assume that the last payment is made on his 17th birthday. How much of the total is interest?

64. Redo Exercise 63, but assume that they start investing on his first birthday.

THINK ABOUT IT 10.2

1. a. Show that the sum of the first n positive odd integers is n^2.

   b. What is the sum of the first n positive even integers?

2. a. Find the sum of the first 10 terms of the sequence 3, $3\sqrt{3}$, 9, ...

   b. Find the sum of the first 10 terms of the sequence $3^{-1}, 3^{-2}, 3^{-3}, \ldots$.

3. Show that $\displaystyle\sum_{i=1}^{n} c a_i = c \sum_{i=1}^{n} a_i$.

4. Start with the formula for the sum S_n of the first n terms of a geometric series given in this section and derive a formula for S_n in terms of a_1, a_n, and r.

5. The future value of an *ordinary annuity* is given by $S = p + p(1 + i) + p(1 + i)^2 + \cdots + p(1 + i)^{n-1}$. Find the sum of this series.

10.3 Infinite Geometric Series

In a certain filtration system wastewater is collected in a holding tank so that each time a liquid is passed through this system only 75 percent as much wastewater is collected as in the previous pass. If 12 gal of wastewater are collected the first time a liquid is passed through this system, how many gallons of wastewater must the holding tank be able to accommodate? (See Example 4.)

OBJECTIVES

1. Find the sum of certain infinite geometric series.

2. Use an infinite geometric series to express a repeating decimal as the ratio of two integers.

3. Solve applied problems involving infinite geometric series.

A question that intrigued mathematicians for some time was whether it was possible to assign a number as the sum of certain infinite series in some meaningful way. To explore this problem, consider the series

$$\frac{1}{2} + \frac{1}{4} + \frac{1}{8} + \frac{1}{16} + \cdots + \left(\frac{1}{2}\right)^n + \cdots$$

and examine the behavior of S_n (the sum of the first n terms in the series) as n increases from 1 to 6.

$$S_1 = \frac{1}{2}$$
$$S_2 = \frac{1}{2} + \frac{1}{4} = \frac{3}{4}$$
$$S_3 = \frac{1}{2} + \frac{1}{4} + \frac{1}{8} = \frac{7}{8}$$
$$S_4 = \frac{1}{2} + \frac{1}{4} + \frac{1}{8} + \frac{1}{16} = \frac{15}{16}$$
$$S_5 = \frac{1}{2} + \frac{1}{4} + \frac{1}{8} + \frac{1}{16} + \frac{1}{32} = \frac{31}{32}$$
$$S_6 = \frac{1}{2} + \frac{1}{4} + \frac{1}{8} + \frac{1}{16} + \frac{1}{32} + \frac{1}{64} = \frac{63}{64}$$

It appears that as n gets larger, S_n approaches, but never equals, 1. In fact, we can get S_n as close to 1 as we wish merely by taking a sufficiently large value for n. It is in this sense that we are going to assign the number 1 as the "sum" of the series. That is, to say 1 is the sum of the above infinite series is to say that as n gets larger, S_n converges to or closes in on 1.

On an intuitive level, observe that if a series is to converge to a sum, then the terms in the series must approach 0 as n gets larger. This condition occurs in infinite geometric series with $|r| < 1$ (or equivalently, with $-1 < r < 1$), so we will analyze this type of series. A formula for the sum of the first n terms of a geometric series is

$$S_n = \frac{a_1(1 - r^n)}{1 - r}.$$

Then if $|r| < 1$, r^n approaches 0 as n gets larger, so that

$$S_n \text{ converges to } \frac{a_1(1 - 0)}{1 - r} = \frac{a_1}{1 - r}.$$

This result establishes a useful formula.

Sum of an Infinite Geometric Series

An infinite geometric series with $|r| < 1$ converges to the value or sum

$$S = \frac{a_1}{1 - r}.$$

EXAMPLE 1   Finding the Sum of an Infinite Geometric Series

Find the sum of the infinite geometric series

$$5 + \frac{5}{3} + \frac{5}{9} + \frac{5}{27} + \cdots.$$

Solution   Here $a_1 = 5$ and $r = \frac{5}{3} \div 5 = \frac{1}{3}$. Since r is between -1 and 1, a sum can be assigned to this series. Substituting in the formula

$$S = \frac{a_1}{1 - r}$$

gives

$$S = \frac{5}{1 - \frac{1}{3}} = \frac{5}{\frac{2}{3}} = \frac{15}{2}.$$

PROGRESS CHECK 1 Find the sum of the infinite geometric series
$3 + \frac{3}{2} + \frac{3}{4} + \frac{3}{8} + \cdots.$ ■

EXAMPLE 2   Finding the Sum of an Infinite Geometric Series

Evaluate $\sum_{i=1}^{\infty} \left(-\frac{3}{4}\right)^{i-1}$.

Solution   In expanded form the series is

$$\sum_{i=1}^{\infty} \left(-\frac{3}{4}\right)^{i-1} = \left(-\frac{3}{4}\right)^0 + \left(-\frac{3}{4}\right)^1 + \left(-\frac{3}{4}\right)^2 + \left(-\frac{3}{4}\right)^3 + \cdots$$

$$= 1 - \frac{3}{4} + \frac{9}{16} - \frac{27}{64} + \cdots.$$

This series is an infinite geometric series with $a_1 = 1$ and $r = -\frac{3}{4}$. A sum S can be assigned to this series since $|r| < 1$, and

$$S = \frac{a_1}{1 - r} = \frac{1}{1 - \left(-\frac{3}{4}\right)} = \frac{1}{\frac{7}{4}} = \frac{4}{7}.$$

Technology Link

Some infinite series approach their sums more quickly than others. That is, you get closer to the infinite sum after adding fewer terms. You can use the calculator in sequence mode to approximate the sum of an infinite series one term at a time as shown in Figures 10.6 (a) and (b) for the series of Example 2. This will give you some impression of how quickly the sum converges to its final value. We know that this series converges to $\frac{4}{7}$, which is approximately .5714. You can see several intermediate sums in Figure 10.6 (b)

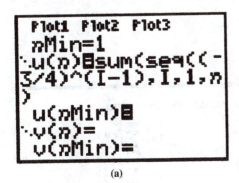

(a)   (b)

Figure 10.6

Note that we used I as the index for the summation and n to indicate the consecutive stopping values.

PROGRESS CHECK 2   Evaluate $\sum_{i=1}^{\infty} \left(-\frac{1}{2}\right)^{i-1}$. ■

Recall from Section 1.1 that every repeating decimal is a rational number and can be expressed as the quotient of two integers. One method for finding such a fraction is to use infinite geometric series, as illustrated next.

EXAMPLE 3   Expressing a Repeating Decimal as a Fraction

Express the repeating decimal $0.\overline{45}$ as the ratio of two integers.

Solution   When we write repeating decimals, a bar is placed above the portion of the decimal that repeats. Therefore $0.\overline{45}$ is equivalent to $0.454545\ldots$ and may be written as

$$0.45 + 0.0045 + 0.000045 + \cdots.$$

This series is an infinite geometric series with $a_1 = 0.45$ and $r = 0.01$. Since $|r| < 1$, a sum S can be determined for this series as follows.

$$S = \frac{a_1}{1 - r} = \frac{0.45}{1 - 0.01} = \frac{0.45}{0.99} = \frac{45}{99} = \frac{5}{11}$$

Thus, $0.\overline{45} = \frac{5}{11}$. Check this result using your calculator.

PROGRESS CHECK 3   Express the repeating decimal $0.\overline{4}$ as the ratio of two integers. ■

Using the concepts developed in this section enables us to solve the problem that opens the section.

EXAMPLE 4   Capacity of a Wastewater Tank

Solve the problem in the section introduction on page 562.

Solution   The amount S of wastewater being collected is given by

$$S = 12 + 12(0.75) + 12(0.75)^2 + \cdots.$$

This series is an infinite geometric series with $r = 0.75$, so S can be determined since $|r| < 1$. Replacing a_1 by 12 and r by 0.75 in the formula for S gives

$$S = \frac{a_1}{1 - r} = \frac{12}{1 - 0.75} = \frac{12}{0.25} = 48.$$

Thus, the holding tank must be able to accommodate 48 gal of wastewater.

PROGRESS CHECK 4   Redo the problem in Example 4, but assume that 18 gal of wastewater are collected on the first pass and that on each subsequent pass only 60 percent as much wastewater is collected as on the pass before. ■

EXERCISES 10.3

In Exercises 1–14, find the sum of the given infinite geometric series.

1. $1 + \frac{1}{10} + \frac{1}{100} + \cdots$

2. $1 + \frac{1}{5} + \frac{1}{25} + \cdots$

3. $3 + 1 + \frac{1}{3} + \cdots$

4. $3 + \frac{3}{7} + \frac{3}{49} + \cdots$

5. $6 + 3 + \frac{3}{2} + \cdots$

6. $6 + \frac{3}{2} + \frac{3}{8} + \cdots$

7. $\frac{1}{3} - \frac{1}{6} + \frac{1}{12} - \cdots$

8. $\frac{1}{3} - \frac{1}{9} + \frac{1}{27} - \cdots$

9. $\frac{1}{5} + \frac{2}{15} + \frac{4}{45} + \cdots$

10. $\frac{1}{5} + \frac{2}{25} + \frac{4}{125} + \cdots$

11. $3 + 0.3 + 0.03 + \cdots$

12. $2 + 0.4 + 0.08 + \cdots$

13. $2 + 0.6 + 0.18 + \cdots$

14. $3 + 1.5 + 0.75 + \cdots$

In Exercises 15–30, evaluate the given sum.

15. $\sum_{i=1}^{\infty} \left(\frac{2}{3}\right)^i$

16. $\sum_{i=1}^{\infty} \left(\frac{1}{5}\right)^i$

17. $\sum_{i=1}^{\infty} \left(-\frac{2}{5}\right)^i$

18. $\sum_{i=1}^{\infty} \left(-\frac{1}{3}\right)^i$

19. $\sum_{i=1}^{\infty} \left(\frac{1}{4}\right)^{i-1}$

20. $\sum_{i=1}^{\infty} \left(\frac{2}{5}\right)^{i-1}$

21. $\sum_{i=1}^{\infty} \left(\frac{1}{8}\right)^{i+1}$

22. $\sum_{i=1}^{\infty} \left(\frac{1}{7}\right)^{i+1}$

23. $\displaystyle\sum_{i=1}^{\infty} (-0.1)^{i-1}$

24. $\displaystyle\sum_{i=1}^{\infty} (-0.3)^{i-1}$

25. $\displaystyle\sum_{i=1}^{\infty} (0.5)^{i+1}$

26. $\displaystyle\sum_{i=1}^{\infty} (0.2)^{i+1}$

27. $\displaystyle\sum_{i=1}^{\infty} \left(-\tfrac{1}{5}\right)^{i+2}$

28. $\displaystyle\sum_{i=1}^{\infty} \left(-\tfrac{1}{9}\right)^{i-2}$

29. $\displaystyle\sum_{i=1}^{\infty} (-0.6)^{i-2}$

30. $\displaystyle\sum_{i=1}^{\infty} (-0.7)^{i+3}$

In Exercises 31–40, write the given repeating decimal as an infinite series (first three terms) and then as the quotient of two integers.

31. $0.\overline{2}$

32. $0.\overline{3}$

33. $0.\overline{7}$

34. $0.\overline{6}$

35. $0.\overline{13}$

36. $0.5\overline{6}$

37. $0.\overline{375}$

38. $0.\overline{241}$

39. $0.0\overline{7}$

40. $0.00\overline{5}$

41. A system for removing pollutants from kerosene involves passing the kerosene repeatedly through a filtering system. Suppose that each time the kerosene passes through the filters some waste is removed and stored in a special tank. In a certain application each pass through the filters removes 10 percent as much waste as the previous pass. Suppose the first pass produces 18 gal of waste. What size holding tank is large enough to hold all the waste this application will produce?

42. Redo Exercise 41, but assume that each pass through the filters removes 20 percent as much waste as the previous pass.

43. A game consists of tossing a coin until you get heads. The appearance of a head (H) is called a success (S). The appearance of a tail (T) is called a failure (F). Here are all the possible outcomes and their probabilities.

Outcome	Probability
Heads first appears on 1st toss: H	$\dfrac{1}{2}$
Heads first appears on 2nd toss: TH	$\dfrac{1}{2} \cdot \dfrac{1}{2} = \dfrac{1}{2^2}$
Heads first appears on 3rd toss: TTH	$\dfrac{1}{2} \cdot \dfrac{1}{2} \cdot \dfrac{1}{2} = \dfrac{1}{2^3}$
$\vdots$	$\vdots$
Heads first appears on nth toss: $\underbrace{\text{TTT}\dots\text{TH}}_{n-1 \text{ T's}}$	$\dfrac{1}{2^n}$

Show that the sum of the probabilities of all the possible outcomes is a geometric series whose sum is 1. (*Note:* In probability theory the sum of the probabilities of all possible outcomes of an experiment is always 1.)

44. A game consists of rolling a die until you get a 6. The appearance of a 6 is called a success (S). The appearance of any other number is called a failure (F). Here are all the possible outcomes for such a game.

Outcome	Probability
6 first appears on 1st roll: S	$\dfrac{1}{6}$
6 first appears on 2nd roll: FS	$\dfrac{5}{6} \cdot \dfrac{1}{6} = \dfrac{5}{6^2}$
6 first appears on 3rd roll: FFS	$\dfrac{5}{6} \cdot \dfrac{5}{6} \cdot \dfrac{1}{6} = \dfrac{5^2}{6^3}$
$\vdots$	$\vdots$
6 first appears on nth roll: $\underbrace{FFF\dots FS}_{n-1 \, F's}$	$\dfrac{5^{n-1}}{6^n}$

Show that the sum of the probabilities of all the possible outcomes is a geometric series whose sum is 1.

45. The curve drawn in the figure is a segment of a parabola. The largest triangle has the same base and vertex as the curve. Each smaller triangle is constructed in the same way, resulting in a sequence of polygons with more and more sides, whose perimeter approaches the shape of the parabola. Archimedes showed that the areas of the successive polygons are given by this sequence, where A represents the area of the largest triangle.

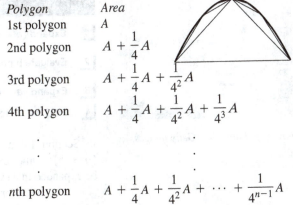

Polygon	Area
1st polygon	A
2nd polygon	$A + \dfrac{1}{4}A$
3rd polygon	$A + \dfrac{1}{4}A + \dfrac{1}{4^2}A$
4th polygon	$A + \dfrac{1}{4}A + \dfrac{1}{4^2}A + \dfrac{1}{4^3}A$
$\vdots$	
nth polygon	$A + \dfrac{1}{4}A + \dfrac{1}{4^2}A + \cdots + \dfrac{1}{4^{n-1}}A$

Archimedes argued that the sum of the infinite series gives the area of the parabola in terms of the area (A) of the largest triangle. Discover Archimedes' formula by finding the sum of this geometric series. This is the earliest recorded example of the summation of an infinite series. (*Hint:* Factor out A from the series before finding the sum.)

46. Here is a classic problem as discussed in W. W. Sawyer's *Mathematician's Delight* (Penguin Books, 1943): "If a ton of seed potatoes will produce a crop of 3 tons, which can either be consumed or used again as seed, how much must a gardener buy, if his family want to consume a ton of potatoes every year forever?" [*Hint:* For the first year's harvest $\frac{1}{3}$ ton of seed planted now will be enough. For the second year's harvest $\frac{1}{9}$ ton planted now will be enough. (Why?)]

    a. Write a geometric series for the total amount of seed potatoes needed.

    b. Find the sum of the series to answer the question.

47. A pendulum is swinging back and forth, but each diminishing swing takes 0.999 times as long as the previous one. If the first swing takes 2 seconds, what is the total time elapsed before the pendulum stops? Approximate this time as the sum of an infinite geometric series.

48. A certain ball always rebounds $\frac{2}{3}$ as far as it falls. If the ball is dropped from a height of 9 ft, how far up and down has it traveled before it comes to rest? Approximate this distance as the sum of an infinite geometric series.

THINK ABOUT IT 10.3

1. In the formula for the sum of an infinite geometric series $|r|$ is required to be less than 1. Try using the formula for the series $2 + 2^2 + 2^3 \cdots$ to see that nonsense results.

2. What is the common ratio in an infinite series whose first term is 4 and whose sum is $4\frac{1}{4}$?

3. Explain in terms of infinite geometric series why
$$\sum_{i=1}^{\infty} x^{i-1}$$
converges to a sum if $|x| < 1$. What is this sum?

4. For what values of x does the series
$$(x + 1) + 2(x + 1)^2 + 4(x + 1)^3 + \cdots$$
converge to a sum? What is the sum?

5. Express the repeating decimal $2.1\overline{43}$ as the ratio of two integers.

Courtesy of PhotoDisc/Getty Images.

10.4 Binomial Theorem

A student guesses randomly at six multiple-choice questions. If each question has four possible choices, then the probability that the student gets exactly three correct is given by the fourth term in the expansion of $\left(\frac{1}{4} + \frac{3}{4}\right)^6$. Find the probability. (See Example 7.)

OBJECTIVES

1   Expand $(a + b)^n$ using Pascal's triangle.

2   Evaluate binomial coefficients in the form $\binom{n}{r}$ for given values of *n* and *r*.

3   Expand $(a + b)^n$ using the binomial theorem.

4   Find the *r*th term in the expansion of $(a + b)^n$.

In Section 1.4 a special product formula was used to square a binomial and expand $(a + b)^2$. Other expressions of the form $(a + b)^n$, where *n* is a positive integer, may also be expanded in a systematic way, and we now discuss a method for finding such expansions.

    Consider carefully the following expansions of the powers of $a + b$ and try to find some patterns. Note that direct multiplication can be used to verify these results.

$$(a + b)^1 = a + b \qquad \qquad \text{(2 terms)}$$
$$(a + b)^2 = a^2 + 2ab + b^2 \qquad \text{(3 terms)}$$
$$(a + b)^3 = a^3 + 3a^2b + 3ab^2 + b^3 \qquad \text{(4 terms)}$$
$$(a + b)^4 = a^4 + 4a^3b + 6a^2b^2 + 4ab^3 + b^4 \qquad \text{(5 terms)}$$
$$(a + b)^5 = a^5 + 5a^4b + 10a^3b^2 + 10a^2b^3 + 5ab^4 + b^5 \qquad \text{(6 terms)}$$

In each case, observe that the expansion of $(a + b)^n$ behaved as follows:

1. The number of terms in the expansion is $n + 1$.

2. The first term is a^n and the last term is b^n.

3. The second term is $na^{n-1}b$ and the nth term is nab^{n-1}.

4. The exponent of a decreases by 1 in each successive term, while the exponent of b increases by 1.

5. The sum of the exponents of a and b in any term is n.

   It can be proved that the above patterns continue to hold if n is a positive integer greater than 5, so we now need only determine a method for finding the constant coefficients when we expand such expressions. For this purpose, we have arranged the constant coefficients in the above expansions of $(a + b)^n$ for $n \leq 5$ in the triangular array shown in the following chart.

Powers of $a + b$	Constant Coefficients (Pascal's Triangle)
$(a + b)^0$	Row 0
$(a + b)^1$	Row 1
$(a + b)^2$	Row 2
$(a + b)^3$	Row 3
$(a + b)^4$	Row 4
$(a + b)^5$	Row 5

The triangular array of numbers that specifies the constant coefficients in the expansions of $(a + b)^n$ for $n = 0, 1, 2, \ldots$ is called **Pascal's triangle.** Observe that except for the 1's, each entry in Pascal's triangle is the sum of the two numbers on either side of it in the preceding row, as diagramed in the chart. Based on our observations to this point, we can now expand positive integral powers of $a + b$ using

$$(a + b)^n = a^n + na^{n-1}b + (\text{constant})a^{n-2}b^2$$
$$+ (\text{constant})a^{n-3}b^3 + \cdots + nab^{n-1} + b^n,$$

where Pascal's triangle may be used to find the constant coefficients.

EXAMPLE 1   Expanding a Binomial Using Pascal's Triangle

Expand $(2x + y)^4$ using Pascal's triangle.

Solution   Use the expansion formula above with $a = 2x$, $b = y$, and $n = 4$. From Pascal's triangle we find the coefficients of the five terms in the expansion are 1, 4, 6, 4, and 1, respectively. Therefore,

$$(2x + y)^4 = (2x)^4 + 4(2x)^3y + 6(2x)^2y^2 + 4(2x)y^3 + y^4$$
$$= 16x^4 + 32x^3y + 24x^2y^2 + 8xy^3 + y^4.$$

PROGRESS CHECK 1   Expand $(x + 4y)^3$ using Pascal's triangle.   ■

EXAMPLE 2   Expanding a Binomial Using Pascal's Triangle

Expand $(y - 5)^3$ using Pascal's triangle.

Solution   First, rewrite $(y - 5)^3$ as $[y + (-5)]^3$. We now substitute y for a, -5 for b, and 3 for n in our expansion formula. The coefficients of the four terms in the expansion are determined from Pascal's triangle to be 1, 3, 3, and 1, respectively. Therefore,

$$(y - 5)^3 = y^3 + 3y^2(-5) + 3y(-5)^2 + (-5)^3$$
$$= y^3 - 15y^2 + 75y - 125.$$

Note   The terms in the expansion alternate in sign when the binomial is the difference of two terms, as illustrated by this example.

PROGRESS CHECK 2   Expand $(x - 3)^5$ using Pascal's triangle.   ■

EXAMPLE 3   Expanding a Binomial Using Pascal's Triangle

Expand $(x + h)^6$ using Pascal's triangle.

Solution   We substitute x for a, h for b, and 6 for n in our expansion formula. To determine the constant coefficients using Pascal's triangle, we must continue the pattern in the previous chart to specify the entries in row 6. Starting from row 5, the next row is obtained as follows:

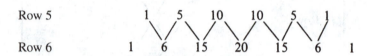

Row 5   1   5   10   10   5   1

Row 6   1   6   15   20   15   6   1

Thus, the expansion of $(x + h)^6$ is

$$(x + h)^6 = x^6 + 6x^5h + 15x^4h^2 + 20x^3h^3 + 15x^2h^4 + 6xh^5 + h^6.$$

PROGRESS CHECK 3   Expand $(y - m)^7$ using Pascal's triangle.   ■

Using Pascal's triangle to determine the constant coefficients in a binomial expansion is sometimes impractical, since constructing the table can be time-consuming, particularly for large values of n. Therefore, it is useful to have a formula for these constant coefficients. Before such a formula can be stated, it is helpful to first introduce **factorial notation.**

---

n Factorial

For any positive integer n, the symbol $n!$ (read "n factorial") is defined by

$$n! = n(n - 1)(n - 2)\cdots(2)(1).$$

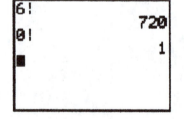

Figure 10.7

For example,

$$3! = 3\cdot2\cdot1 = 6 \quad \text{and} \quad 7! = 7\cdot6\cdot5\cdot4\cdot3\cdot2\cdot1 = 5,040.$$

As a special case, it is also useful to define 0! so that

$$0! = 1.$$

Technology Link

A graphing calculator will have a built-in factorial command, usually associated with the key marked MATH. Figure 10.7 shows the calculation of 6! And 0!. Note that the calculator produces 1 as the value of 0!.

Using factorials, we can now write a formula that determines a constant coefficient in a binomial expansion. Such numbers are called binomial coefficients.

Binomial Coefficient

Let r and n be nonnegative integers with $r \leq n$. Then the symbol $\binom{n}{r}$ is defined by

$$\binom{n}{r} = \frac{n!}{r!(n-r)!}.$$

Each of the numbers $\binom{n}{r}$ is called a **binomial coefficient.**

As you might expect, binomial coefficients are entries in Pascal's triangle, and the next example illustrates this point.

EXAMPLE 4   Comparing Binomial Coefficients to Entries in Pascal's Triangle

Evaluate the following binomial coefficients and compare the results with the entries in Pascal's triangle.

$$\binom{4}{0}, \binom{4}{1}, \binom{4}{2}, \binom{4}{3}, \binom{4}{4}$$

Solution   By applying the formula in the definition, we have

$$\binom{4}{0} = \frac{4!}{0!(4-0)!} = \frac{4!}{0!4!} = \frac{4 \cdot 3 \cdot 2 \cdot 1}{1 \cdot (4 \cdot 3 \cdot 2 \cdot 1)} = 1$$

$$\binom{4}{1} = \frac{4!}{1!(4-1)!} = \frac{4!}{1!3!} = \frac{4 \cdot 3 \cdot 2 \cdot 1}{1 \cdot (3 \cdot 2 \cdot 1)} = 4$$

$$\binom{4}{2} = \frac{4!}{2!(4-2)!} = \frac{4!}{2!2!} = \frac{4 \cdot 3 \cdot 2 \cdot 1}{(2 \cdot 1)(2 \cdot 1)} = 6$$

$$\binom{4}{3} = \frac{4!}{3!(4-3)!} = \frac{4!}{3!1!} = \frac{4 \cdot 3 \cdot 2 \cdot 1}{(3 \cdot 2 \cdot 1) \cdot 1} = 4$$

$$\binom{4}{4} = \frac{4!}{4!(4-4)!} = \frac{4!}{4!0!} = \frac{4 \cdot 3 \cdot 2 \cdot 1}{(4 \cdot 3 \cdot 2 \cdot 1) \cdot 1} = 1.$$

By direct comparison, observe that the binomial coefficients 1, 4, 6, 4, and 1 match the entries in row 4 of Pascal's triangle.

Note   This example illustrates the general result that the binomial coefficients

$$\binom{n}{0}, \binom{n}{1}, \binom{n}{2}, \dots, \binom{n}{n}$$

are precisely the numbers in the nth row of Pascal's triangle.

Technology Link

Graphing calculators have special commands to compute binomial coefficients. The menu choice for the command is usually symbolized nCr. This notation is chosen because of the applicability of these values in probability calculations where the "C" represents

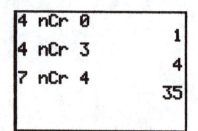

Figure 10.8

"combinations." This command is usually associated with a probability menu within a math menu. Figure 10.8 shows the computation of $\binom{4}{0}$, $\binom{4}{3}$, and $\binom{7}{4}$.

PROGRESS CHECK 4 Evaluate the following binomial coefficients and compare the results with the entries in Pascal's triangle.

$$\binom{5}{0}, \binom{5}{1}, \binom{5}{2}, \binom{5}{3}, \binom{5}{4}, \binom{5}{5}$$

A formula for expanding $(a + b)^n$ can be stated very efficiently by using binomial coefficients and sigma notation. This expansion formula is called the **binomial theorem.**

Binomial Theorem

For any positive integer n,

$$(a + b)^n = \sum_{r=0}^{n} \binom{n}{r} a^{n-r} b^r$$

$$= \binom{n}{0} a^n + \binom{n}{1} a^{n-1} b + \binom{n}{2} a^{n-2} b^2 + \cdots + \binom{n}{n} b^n.$$

EXAMPLE 5   Using the Binomial Theorem to Expand a Binomial
Expand $(y + d)^7$ using the binomial theorem.

Solution   Applying the binomial theorem with $y = a$, $d = b$, and $n = 7$ yields

$$(y + d)^7 = \binom{7}{0} y^7 + \binom{7}{1} y^6 d + \binom{7}{2} y^5 d^2 + \binom{7}{3} y^4 d^3$$

$$+ \binom{7}{4} y^3 d^4 + \binom{7}{5} y^2 d^5 + \binom{7}{6} y d^6 + \binom{7}{7} d^7.$$

Now evaluate the binomial coefficients. Use the symmetry in the coefficients and the binomial coefficient formula to obtain

$$\binom{7}{0} = \binom{7}{7} = \frac{7!}{0!7!} = 1, \qquad \binom{7}{1} = \binom{7}{6} = \frac{7!}{1!6!} = 7,$$

$$\binom{7}{2} = \binom{7}{5} = \frac{7!}{2!5!} = 21, \qquad \binom{7}{3} = \binom{7}{4} = \frac{7!}{3!4!} = 35.$$

Then, the desired expansion is

$$(y + d)^7 = y^7 + 7y^6 d + 21y^5 d^2 + 35y^4 d^3 + 35y^3 d^4 + 21y^2 d^5 + 7y d^6 + d^7.$$

PROGRESS CHECK 5   Expand $(x + c)^8$ using the binomial theorem.   ■

It is sometimes important to know only a single term in a binomial expansion, and this term may be found without producing the rest of the terms. Observe in the binomial theorem that the exponent of b is 1 in the second term, 2 in the third term, and in general, $r - 1$ in the rth term. Because the sum of the exponents of a and b is always n, the exponent above a in the rth term must be $n - (r - 1)$. Finally, the binomial coefficient of the term containing b^{r-1} is $\binom{n}{r-1}$. These observations lead to the following formula.

rth Term of the Binomial Expansion

The rth term of the binomial expansion of $(a + b)^n$ is

$$\binom{n}{r - 1} a^{n-(r-1)} b^{r-1}.$$

EXAMPLE 6   Finding a Specific Term in a Binomial Expansion

Find the seventh term in the expansion of $(2x - y)^{10}$.

Solution   Here $a = 2x$, $b = -y$, and $n = 10$. To find the seventh term, let $r = 7$, so $r - 1 = 6$. Then applying the above formula gives the seventh term as

$$\binom{10}{6} (2x)^4 (-y)^6 = 210(16x^4)(y^6)$$

$$= 3{,}360 x^4 y^6.$$

PROGRESS CHECK 6   Find the sixth term in the expansion of $(3x - y)^8$. ■

EXAMPLE 7   Multiple Choice Test

Solve the problem in the section introduction on page 566.

Solution   The requested probability is the fourth term in the expansion of $\left(\frac{1}{4} + \frac{3}{4}\right)^6$. In this case, $a = \frac{1}{4}$, $b = \frac{3}{4}$, $n = 6$, and $r = 4$ (so $r - 1 = 3$). By the above formula, the fourth term is

$$\binom{6}{3} \left(\frac{1}{4}\right)^3 \left(\frac{3}{4}\right)^3 = 20 \left(\frac{1}{4}\right)^3 \left(\frac{3}{4}\right)^3$$

$$= \frac{540}{4{,}096} = \frac{135}{1{,}024}.$$

The probability that this student gets exactly three correct is $\frac{135}{1{,}024} \approx 13.18$ percent.

PROGRESS CHECK 7   The probability that the student described in Example 7 gets exactly four correct is given by the third term in the expansion of $\left(\frac{1}{4} + \frac{3}{4}\right)^6$. Find this probability. ■

EXERCISES 10.4

In Exercises 1–12, use Pascal's triangle to expand the given expression.

1. $(x + y)^3$
2. $(x + y)^4$
3. $(x - y)^3$
4. $(x - y)^4$
5. $(x - 3)^5$
6. $(x + 2)^6$
7. $(x + 4)^3$
8. $(x - 5)^4$
9. $(2x - n)^6$
10. $(x + 3y)^5$
11. $(2x + 5y)^6$
12. $(3x - 2y)^4$

In Exercises 13 and 14, evaluate the given list of binomial coefficients, and match the list to a row in Pascal's triangle.

13. $\binom{7}{0}, \binom{7}{1}, \binom{7}{2}, \binom{7}{3}, \binom{7}{4}, \binom{7}{5}, \binom{7}{6}, \binom{7}{7}$

14. $\binom{8}{0}, \binom{8}{1}, \binom{8}{2}, \binom{8}{3}, \binom{8}{4}, \binom{8}{5}, \binom{8}{6}, \binom{8}{7}, \binom{8}{8}$

In Exercises 15–22, evaluate the given binomial coefficients.

15. $\dbinom{5}{2}$

16. $\dbinom{12}{4}$

17. $\dbinom{10}{6}$

18. $\dbinom{6}{1}$

19. $\dbinom{88}{0}$

20. $\dbinom{55}{0}$

21. $\dbinom{66}{66}$

22. $\dbinom{957}{957}$

In Exercises 23–30, expand the given expression using the binomial theorem. Do not refer to Pascal's triangle.

23. $(x + h)^4$

24. $(x + h)^5$

25. $(x - y)^7$

26. $(x - y)^{10}$

27. $(x + 3)^6$

28. $(x + 5)^8$

29. $(3x - 1)^3$

30. $(2x - 4)^5$

In Exercises 31–38, find the desired term in the given expansion.

31. $(x + y)^9$, sixth term

32. $(x + y)^{12}$, seventh term

33. $(x - y)^{10}$, eighth term

34. $(x - y)^7$, fourth term

35. $(x - 3)^8$, sixth term

36. $(x - 4)^{10}$, seventh term

37. $(2x - 1)^7$, fifth term

38. $(3x + 2)^6$, fifth term

39. A student guesses randomly at 10 multiple-choice questions. If each question has 5 possible choices, then the probability that the student gets exactly three correct is given by the eighth term in the expansion of $\left(\frac{1}{5} + \frac{4}{5}\right)^{10}$. Find this probability.

40. Refer to Exercise 39. The probability that the student gets no answers correct is given by the last term in the expansion of $\left(\frac{1}{5} + \frac{4}{5}\right)^{10}$. Find this probability.

41. If you guess randomly at five questions on a multiple-choice test, where each question has three possible choices, then the probability that you get *at least* four answers correct is the sum of the first and second terms in the expansion of $\left(\frac{1}{3} + \frac{2}{3}\right)^5$. Find this probability.

42. If you guess randomly at six questions on a multiple-choice test, where each question has three possible choices, then the probability that you get *at least* four answers correct is the sum of the first, second, and third terms in the expansion of $\left(\frac{1}{3} + \frac{2}{3}\right)^6$. Find this probability.

43. A seminar has six students from which a committee of two will be chosen to report to the dean about the conditions in the classroom. How many different combinations of students are possible for the makeup of this committee? Answer this question two ways.

    a. Call the students A, B, C, D, E, F; then write down all the distinct pairs you can find (AB, AC, and so on) and count them.

    b. Evaluate $\dbinom{6}{2}$ to get the correct answer directly.

44. Redo Exercise 43, but now suppose that the committee consists of three members of the class. For part **b**, evaluate $\dbinom{6}{3}$.

THINK ABOUT IT 10.4

1. Expand $\left(\sqrt{x} + \sqrt{y}\right)^4$. Assume $x, y \geq 0$.

2. Expand $(x + y + 1)^3$ by using the binomial theorem. [*Hint:* Treat $(x + y)$ as the first term.]

3. Simplify $\dfrac{(n + 1)!}{(n - 1)!}$.

4. A great early contribution by Isaac Newton was the extension of the binomial theorem to fractional and negative exponents.

    a. Note that the binomial coefficient $\dbinom{5}{2} = \dfrac{5!}{2!3!}$ reduces to $\dfrac{5 \cdot 4}{1 \cdot 2}$ because $3!$ divides out in the numerator and denominator. In general, $\dfrac{n!}{r!(n - r)!}$ reduces to $\dfrac{n \cdot (n - 1) \cdot (n - 2) \cdots (n - r + 1)}{r!}$ because $(n - r)!$ divides out in the numerator and denominator. Using this approach, show that $\dbinom{7}{3} = \dfrac{7 \cdot 6 \cdot 5}{1 \cdot 2 \cdot 3}$.

    b. Newton decided that he could follow the pattern in part **a** even with fractional and negative values in the binomial coefficients. For example,
$$\binom{\frac{1}{2}}{3} = \frac{\frac{1}{2}\left(\frac{1}{2} - 1\right)\left(\frac{1}{2} - 2\right)}{1 \cdot 2 \cdot 3} = \frac{\left(\frac{1}{2}\right)\left(-\frac{1}{2}\right)\left(-\frac{3}{2}\right)}{6} = \frac{3}{48}$$
$$= \frac{1}{16}, \quad \binom{-1}{3} = \frac{-1(-1 - 1)(-1 - 2)}{1 \cdot 2 \cdot 3}$$
$$= \frac{-1(-2)(-3)}{6} = \frac{-6}{6} = -1.$$

Use this technique to evaluate $\dbinom{\frac{1}{2}}{2}$ and $\dbinom{-2}{3}$.

5. a. Newton applied the method of Exercise 4 to the expansion of $(1 + x)^{1/2}$, producing a nonending expansion which he used to approximate irrational numbers. Write out the first four terms of this expansion; then let $x = 1$ to get an approximation for $\sqrt{2}$. Compare this with the calculator approximation for $\sqrt{2}$. The expansion is started below.

$$(1 + x)^{1/2} = \binom{\frac{1}{2}}{0}1^{1/2} + \binom{\frac{1}{2}}{1}1^{-1/2}x + \binom{\frac{1}{2}}{2}1^{-3/2}x^2 + \cdots$$

CHAPTER 10 OVERVIEW

Section	Key Concepts or Procedures to Review

10.1
- Definition of sequence, arithmetic sequence, and geometric sequence
- Formulas for the nth term of a sequence:

    Arithmetic sequence: $a_n = a_1 + (n - 1)d$

    Geometric sequence: $a_n = a_1 r^{n-1}$

10.2
- Formulas for the sum of the first n terms of a series:

    Arithmetic series: $S_n = \dfrac{n}{2}(a_1 + a_n)$

    or

    $\qquad\qquad S_n = \dfrac{n}{2}[2a_1 + (n - 1)d]$

    Geometric series: $S_n = \dfrac{a_1(1 - r^n)}{1 - r}$

- The Greek letter Σ, read "sigma," is used to write a series in compact form. In sigma notation,

$$\sum_{i=1}^{n} a_i = a_1 + a_2 + \cdots + a_n.$$

10.3
- An infinite geometric series with $|r| < 1$ converges to the value or sum $S = \dfrac{a_1}{1 - r}$.

10.4
- Pascal's triangle
- Method to expand $(a + b)^n$ using Pascal's triangle
- The symbol $n!$ (read "n factorial") means the product $n(n - 1)(n - 2)\cdots(2)(1)$.
- The binomial coefficient $\dbinom{n}{r}$ is defined by

$$\binom{n}{r} = \frac{n!}{r!(n - r)!}.$$

- The binomial coefficients $\dbinom{n}{0}, \dbinom{n}{1}, \dbinom{n}{2}, \ldots, \dbinom{n}{n}$ are the numbers in the nth row of Pascal's triangle.
- Binomial theorem: For any positive integer n,

$$(a + b)^n = \sum_{r=0}^{n} \binom{n}{r} a^{n-r} b^r$$

$$= \binom{n}{0} a^n + \binom{n}{1} a^{n-1}b + \binom{n}{2} a^{n-2}b^2 + \cdots + \binom{n}{n} b^n.$$

- The rth term of the binomial expansion of $(a + b)^n$ is

$$\binom{n}{r - 1} a^{n-(r-1)} b^{r-1}.$$

CHAPTER 10 REVIEW EXERCISES

1. Write the first four terms of the sequence given by $a_n = 3n + 2$; also, find a_{60}.
2. Find a formula for the general term a_n in the arithmetic sequence 5, 11, 17, 23, ... What is the tenth term in the sequence?
3. Find a formula for the general term in the geometric sequence 3, -6, 12, -24, ... What is the tenth term in the sequence?
4. State whether the following sequence is an arithmetic sequence, a geometric sequence, or neither. If the sequence is arithmetic, find the common difference; if it is geometric, find the common ratio.

$$2, -2, -6, -10, \ldots.$$

5. Use the double-declining balance method to find the depreciated book value at the end of 10 years for property with a useful life of 10 years that is purchased for $80,000. The allowable depreciation rate in this case is 20 percent each year.
6. Find the sum of the first 30 terms of the arithmetic sequence 5, 9, 13, 17, ...
7. Find the sum of the first 12 terms of the geometric sequence 2, 8, 32, 128, ...
8. Write the series $\sum_{i=1}^{5}(i^2 + 2)$ in expanded form, and determine the sum.
9. Find an expression for the general term and write the series $7 + 11 + 15 + 19 + 23 + 27$ in sigma notation.
10. A free-falling body that starts from rest drops about 16 ft the first second, 48 ft the second second, 80 ft the third second, and so on. About how many feet does a parachutist drop during the first 9 seconds of free-fall?
11. Find the sum of the infinite geometric series $3 + \frac{3}{4} + \frac{3}{16} + \frac{3}{64} + \cdots$.
12. Evaluate $\sum_{i=1}^{\infty}\left(-\frac{2}{3}\right)^{i-1}$.
13. Express the repeating decimal $0.\overline{63}$ as the ratio of two integers.
14. In a certain filtration system wastewater is collected in a holding tank so that each time a liquid is passed through the system only 80 percent as much wastewater is collected as on the pass before. If 20 gal of wastewater are collected on the first pass, how many gallons of wastewater must the holding tank be able to accommodate?
15. Expand $(x + 2y)^3$ using Pascal's triangle.
16. Expand $(y - a)^8$ using Pascal's triangle.
17. Evaluate $\binom{8}{6}$.
18. Expand $(x + m)^6$ using the binomial theorem.
19. Find the seventh term in the expansion of $(4x + y)^9$.

State whether each of the following sequences is arithmetic, geometric, or neither. If it is an arithmetic sequence, find the common difference. If it is a geometric sequence, find the common ratio.

20. $6, 1, \frac{1}{6}, \frac{1}{36}, \ldots$
21. $15, 18, 21, 24, \ldots$
22. $1, 2, 4, 7, 11, \ldots$
23. $1, -3, -7, -11, \ldots$

Find an expression for the general term a_n in each of the following sequences. What is the tenth term in the sequence?

24. $8, 11, 14, 17, \ldots$
25. $-5, -11, -17, -23, \ldots$
26. $-3, -\frac{3}{2}, -\frac{3}{4}, -\frac{3}{8}, \ldots$

Write the series in expanded form, and determine the sum.

27. $\sum_{i=1}^{6} 8\left(\frac{1}{2}\right)^i$
28. $\sum_{i=1}^{5}(3i - 1)$

Expand using Pascal's triangle.

29. $(4x + y)^3$
30. $(y - 6)^4$
31. $(x + h)^5$
32. Evaluate $\binom{9}{3}$.
33. Find the fifth term in the expansion of $(2x + y)^8$.
34. Find the sum of the first 20 terms of the arithmetic sequence 4, 10, 16, ...
35. Find the sum of the first nine terms of the geometric sequence 4, 12, 36, ...
36. Find the sum of the infinite geometric series $5 + \frac{5}{2} + \frac{5}{4} + \frac{5}{8} + \cdots$.
37. Find the sum of the first 200 positive integers.
38. Express $0.\overline{23}$ as the ratio of two integers.
39. Find an expression for the general term and write the series $6 + 10 + 14 + \cdots + 42$ in sigma notation.
40. Evaluate $\sum_{i=1}^{\infty}\left(-\frac{1}{3}\right)^{i-1}$.
41. A student guesses randomly at four multiple-choice questions. If each question has five possible choices, then the probability that the student gets exactly three correct is given by the second term in the expansion of $\left(\frac{1}{5} + \frac{4}{5}\right)^4$. Find this probability.
42. A free-falling body that starts from rest drops about 16 ft the first second, 48 ft the second second, 80 ft the third second, and so on. If a ball is dropped off the roof of an office building, how far will it drop during the first 6 seconds of free-fall?
43. Suppose that you place $200 in a savings account each year beginning with your 21st birthday. If the account pays 5 percent interest compounded annually, how much will the account be worth on your 26th birthday? (Assume that no deposit is made on your 26th birthday.)

CHAPTER 10 TEST

State whether the sequence is an arithmetic sequence, a geometric sequence, or neither. For any arithmetic or geometric sequence, write the next two terms.

1. $125, 25, 5, 1, \ldots$
2. $0.0001, 0.001, 0.01, 0.1, \ldots$
3. $1, 5, 9, 13, \ldots$
4. Find a formula for the general term a_n in the arithmetic sequence $-3, -2, -1, 0, \ldots$, and find a_{25}.
5. Find a formula for the general term a_n in the geometric sequence $-2, 1, -\frac{1}{2}, \frac{1}{4}, \ldots$, and find a_8.
6. Find the sum of the first 20 terms of the arithmetic sequence $-3, -1, 1, 3, \ldots$.
7. Find the sum of the first eight terms of the geometric sequence $2, 20, 200, \ldots$.
8. Find an expression for the general term and write the series $5 + 9 + 13 + \cdots + 41$ in sigma notation.

Determine the sum of each series.

9. $\displaystyle\sum_{i=1}^{4}(1 - i^2)$

10. $\displaystyle\sum_{i=1}^{5}9\left(\frac{1}{3}\right)^i$

11. $3 + \frac{3}{5} + \frac{3}{25} + \frac{3}{125} + \cdots$

12. $\displaystyle\sum_{i=1}^{\infty}\left(\frac{1}{2}\right)^{i-1}$

13. Express the repeating decimal $0.\overline{5}$ as the ratio of two integers.

14. Determine the entries in the fifth row of Pascal's triangle.

15. Expand $(x + 3y)^4$ using Pascal's triangle.

16. Evaluate $\dbinom{9}{3}$.

17. Expand $(x + y)^7$ using the binomial theorem.

18. Find the eighth term in the expansion of $(2x + y)^{10}$.

19. A couple invests $2,000 each year on their son's birthday, starting with his 12th birthday and stopping with his 18th birthday (when no investment is made). If the money is placed in an account that pays 6 percent interest compounded annually, how much is in the account on the son's 18th birthday?

20. A free-falling body that starts from rest drops about 4.9 m the first second, 14.6 m the second second, 24.3 m the third second, and so on. About how many meters does a parachutist drop during the first 7 seconds of free-fall?

11 Polynomial and Rational Functions

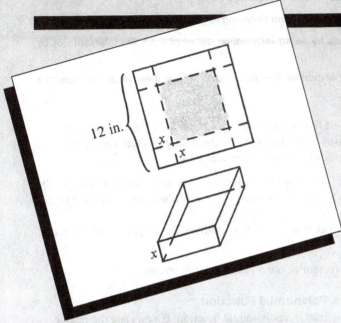

A manufacturer wants to convert a square piece of cardboard with side length 12 in. into an uncovered box, by cutting a small square of cardboard from each corner and bending up the sides as shown.
a. Find a formula for the volume V of the box in terms of the length (x) of the side of the square that is cut from each corner.
b. What is the domain of this volume function?
c. Use a grapher to graph this volume function and to estimate to two decimal places the length of the corner to cut out to obtain the box with maximum volume.
(See Example 9 of Section 11.1.)

In this chapter we continue with the theme of a function and discuss many ideas associated with a large and important class of functions called polynomial functions. Basically, a polynomial function is characterized by terms of the form:

$$(\text{real number})x^{\text{nonnegative integer}}$$

so that a polynomial function may contain terms such as 4, $2x$, $-3x^2$, $\sqrt{5}x^3$ and so on. More technically, a **polynomial function of degree n** is a function of the form

$$y = P(x) = a_n x^n + a_{n-1} x^{n-1} + \ldots + a_1 x + a_0 \quad (a_n \neq 0),$$

where n is a nonnegative integer and a_n, a_{n-1}, $\ldots$, a_1, and a_0 are real-number constants. For example, the function defined by $P(x) = 5x^3 + 2x^2 - 1$ is a polynomial function of degree 3 in which $a_3 = 5$, $a_2 = 2$, $a_1 = 0$, and $a_0 = -1$. Since n must be a nonnegative integer, note that functions with terms such as $x^{1/2}$ (or $\sqrt{x}$) and x^{-2} (or $1/x^2$) are not polynomial functions. Although $y = 1/x^2$ is not a polynomial function, it can be expressed as a quotient of two polynomials and is called a **rational function.** This chapter concludes by showing how to graph rational functions.

11.1   Zeros and Graphs of Polynomial Functions

OBJECTIVES

1 Determine if a function is a polynomial function.

2 Write a polynomial function, given its degree and zeros.

3 Find the zeros of a polynomial function in factored form.

4 Use translation, reflection, stretching, and shrinking to graph certain variations of $y = x^n$.

5 Graph a polynomial function, by using information obtained from the intercepts or by using a grapher.

6 Write an equation for a polynomial function, using information obtained from the intercepts.

The most widely applied family of functions is the polynomial functions. From the definition of a polynomial function given in the chapter introduction, you should recognize that we have already discussed the following polynomial functions.

1. The constant function $y = P(x) = c$ (with $c \neq 0$) is a polynomial function of degree 0.
2. The linear function $y = P(x) = mx + b$ (with $m \neq 0$) is a polynomial function of degree 1.
3. The quadratic function $y = P(x) = ax^2 + bx + c$ (with $a \neq 0$) is a polynomial function of degree 2.

The next example will help you recognize other polynomial functions.

EXAMPLE 1   Recognizing a Polynomial Function

Determine whether or not the function is a polynomial function. If yes, state the degree.

a. $f(x) = 4x^5 - 2x^{1/2} - 3$ **b.** $f(x) = 4x^5 - \dfrac{1}{2}x^2 - 3$

Solution

a. Every term in a polynomial in a single variable, say x, may be written in the form ax^n, where $n = 0, 1, 2, 3, 4, 5, \ldots$, and a is a real number constant. Thus, the function $f(x) = 4x^5 - 2x^{1/2} - 3$ is not a polynomial function because of the term $-2x^{1/2}$.

b. $f(x) = 4x^5 - (1/2)x^2 - 3$ is a polynomial function. The degree of this polynomial function is 5, because the highest-degree term $4x^5$ has degree 5. Observe that $-3 = -3x^0$, so this constant term has degree 0.

PROGRESS CHECK 1   Determine whether or not the function is a polynomial function. If yes, state the degree.

a. $f(x) = 50 - x^6$ **b.** $f(x) = 50 + x^{2.5}$ ■

In this section we are mainly concerned with graphing polynomial functions and finding their zeros. A **zero** of a function f is a value of x for which $f(x) = 0$. For example, the zeros of the function $f(x) = x^2 - 5x + 4$ are 1 and 4, since

$$f(1) = (1)^2 - 5(1) + 4 = 0$$

and

$$f(4) = (4)^2 - 5(4) + 4 = 0$$

Zeros is merely a new name applied to a familiar concept. Depending on the frame of reference, consider three closely related names applied to the preceding example.

1. The **solutions** or **roots** of the **equation** $x^2 - 5x + 4 = 0$ are 1 and 4.
2. The **zeros** of the **function** $f(x) = x^2 - 5x + 4$ are 1 and 4.
3. The **x-intercepts** of the **graph** of the function $y = x^2 - 5x + 4$ are $(1, 0)$ and $(4, 0)$ as shown in Figure 11.1.

Finding zeros for polynomial functions of degrees greater than 2 using algebraic methods is often difficult. There is no easy formula (like the quadratic formula) that can be used to produce them, and numerical methods that require a grapher or a computer are frequently used to approximate such zeros. Nevertheless, there are some theorems you should be aware of concerning zeros of polynomial functions. The first one we consider is called the *factor theorem*.

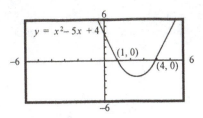

Figure 11.1

Factor Theorem

If b is a zero of the polynomial function $y = P(x)$, then $x - b$ is a factor of $P(x)$; conversely, if $x - b$ is a factor of $P(x)$, then b is as zero of $y = P(x)$.

We can illustrate this theorem using $P(x) = x^2 - 5x + 4$. Observe that the zeroes of this function are 1 and 4, as shown above, while $x^2 - 5x + 4$ factors as $(x - 1)(x - 4)$. The factor theorem indicates that if 1 and 4 are zeroes of $y = P(x)$, then $x - 1$ and $x - 4$ are factors of $P(x)$; conversely, if $x - 1$ and $x - 4$ are factors of $P(x)$, then 1 and 4 are zeros of $y = P(x)$. The following two examples illustrate the usefulness of the factor theorem (which will be proven formally in the next section).

EXAMPLE 2   Using the Factor Theorem
Write a polynomial function (in factored form) of degree 3 with zeros of 2, –4, and 3.

Solution   If 2, –4, and 3 are zeros of a polynomial function $y = P(x)$, then by the factor theorem, $x - 2$, $x - (-4)$, and $x - 3$ are factors of $P(x)$. Thus, a possible polynomial function is $P(x) = (x - 2)(x + 4)(x - 3)$.

PROGRESS CHECK 2   Write a polynomial function (in factored form) of degree 3 with zeros of –5, 0, and 1.   ■

EXAMPLE 3   Using the Factor Theorem
If $P(x) = x(x + 2)(x - 5)^2$, what are the zeros of the function?

Solution   Since x, $x + 2$, and $x - 5$ are factors of $P(x)$, we conclude by the factor theorem that 0, –2, and 5 are zeros of the function. Remember that from a slightly different viewpoint we can also conclude that 0, –2, and 5 are roots or solutions of the equation $x(x + 2)(x - 5)^2 = 0$, and that the graph of $P(x) = x(x + 2)(x - 5)^2$ intersects the x-axis at 0, –2, and 5, as shown with the aid of a grapher in Figure 11.2.

PROGRESS CHECK 3   If $P(x) = 4x^2(x - 1)(x + 3)$, what are the zeros of the function?   ■

Note in Example 3 that the function defined by $P(x) = x(x + 2)(x - 5)^2$ is shorthand for $P(x) = x(x + 2)(x - 5)(x - 5)$. In this case we have four factors but only three zeros, with the zero of 5 being repeated from two different factors. It is useful to adopt a convention that indicates how many factors of $P(x)$ result in the same zero. Using this convention in this example, we say 5 is a **zero of multiplicity** 2, since there are two factors of $x - 5$.

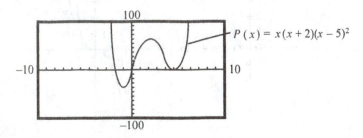

Figure 11.2

Similarly, for $P(x) = (x - 3)^4$ we say 3 is a zero of multiplicity 4. In general, the multiplicity of zero b is given by the highest power of $x - b$ that is a factor of $P(x)$.

EXAMPLE 4   Finding the Multiplicity of a Zero

If $P(x) = x^4(x - 2)(x + 7)^3$, find the zeros of the function as well as the multiplicity of each zero. What is the degree of the polynomial function?

Solution $P(x)$ contains only three different factors: x, $x - 2$, and $x + 7$. Thus, 0, 2, and −7 are the three distinct zeros of the function. However, since x appears as a factor four times, 0 is a zero of multiplicity 4. Similarly, $(x + 7)^3$ means −7 is a zero of multiplicity 3, while $(x - 2)^1$ means 2 is a zero of multiplicity 1 (called a **simple zero**). The degree of the polynomial function is given by the sum of the multiplicities of the zeros. Thus, the polynomial function is of degree 8.

PROGRESS CHECK 4   If $P(x) = (x - 4)^2(x + 1)$, find the zeros of the function as well as the multiplicity of each zero. What is the degree of the polynomial function?   ■

Knowing the multiplicity of a real-number zero is useful when graphing polynomial functions. Before we see how, let us first consider the graphs of polynomial functions of the form

$$y = x^n$$

in which y equals a power of x. We have already graphed such functions for $n = 1, 2,$ and 3, and the graphs of $y = x$, $y = x^2$, and $y = x^3$ are shown in Figure 11.3 for reference purposes.

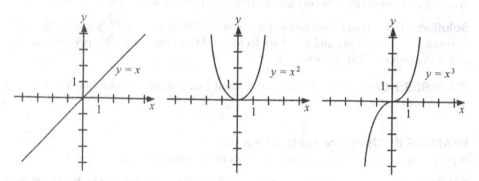

Figure 11.3

For larger values of n, the graph of $y = x^n$ is similar to the graph of $y = x^2$ if n is even, and it is similar to the graph of $y = x^3$ is n is odd. To see this, consider Figure 11.4. Note that when n is even, the graph is symmetric with respect of the y-axis and passes through $(-1, 1)$, $(0, 0)$, and $(1, 1)$. When n is odd, the graph is symmetric with respect to the origin and passes through $(-1, -1)$, $(0, 0)$, and $(1, 1)$. In both cases as the exponent increases, the graph becomes flatter on the interval $[-1, 1]$ and rises or falls more quickly for $|x| > 1$. To graph certain variations of $y = x^n$, we may use the graphing techniques discussed in Section 2.5 as shown in the next example.

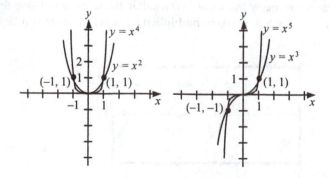

Figure 11.4

EXAMPLE 5   Graphing Variations of $y = x^4$

Use the graph of $f(x) = x^4$ to graph each function.

a. $y = -x^4$ **b.** $y = 3x^4$ **c.** $y = (x + 1)^4 - 2$

Solution

a. The graph of $y = -f(x)$ is the graph of $y = f(x)$ reflected about the x-axis. In Figure 11.5(a) the graph of $y = x^4$ has been reflected about the x-axis to obtain the graph of $y = -x^4$.

b. If $f(x) = x^4$, then $y = 3x^4 = 3f(x)$. To graph $y = 3f(x)$, we triple each y value in f and stretch the graph of f by a factor of 3. Thus, the graph in Figure 11.5(b) is the graph of $y = 3x^4$.

c. The graphs of $y = f(x + c)$ and $y = f(x) + c$ are horizontal and vertical translations of the graph of f, respectively. To graph $y = (x + 1)^4 - 2$, we translate the graph of $y = x^4$, 1 unit to the left and 2 units down, to obtain the graph in Figure 11.5(c).

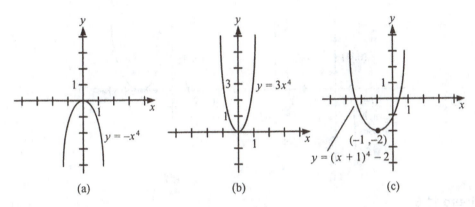

(a)   (b)   (c)

Figure 11.5

PROGRESS CHECK 5   Use the graph of $f(x) = x^4$ to graph each function.

a. $y = -\dfrac{1}{4}x^4$ **b.** $y = (x - 2)^4 - 10$ ■

We have already indicated that the real-number zeros of $y = P(x)$ also give the x-intercepts in the graph of $y = P(x)$. In the case of $y = ax^n$, note that the only real-number zero is 0; and that when n is odd, the graph crosses the x-axis at $x = 0$, while the graph turns around and stays on the same side of the x-axis if n is even. This behavior occurs because x values change sign as x passes through 0, so y changes sign when n is odd, and y keeps the same sign when n is even. This type of analysis is applicable to all x-intercepts and indicates that the multiplicity of each real-number zero reveals whether or not the graph crosses the x-axis at such intercepts, according to the following theorem.

Graph of $y = P(x)$ near x-intercepts

If b is a real-number zero with multiplicity n of $y = P(x)$, then the graph of $y = P(x)$ crosses the x-axis at $x = b$ if n is odd, while the graph turns around and stays on the same side of the x-axis at $x = b$ if n is even.

To use this theorem, we need to express $P(x)$ in factored form. Then the x-intercepts (or real-number zeros) can be obtained from the factor theorem, while the behavior of the graph at an x-intercept, say $(b, 0)$, can be determined from the multiplicity of zero b [or the highest power of $x = b$ that is a factor of $P(x)$]. We illustrate this theorem in the next three examples. The smooth, unbroken types of curves shown in the examples are characteristic of the graphs of polynomial functions.

EXAMPLE 6 Using Intercepts to Graph a Polynomial Function

Graph $y = (x + 1)(x - 2)^2$ on the basis of information obtained from the intercepts.

Solution By setting $x = 0$, we determine that the y-intercept is $(0, 4)$. Since $x + 1$ is a factor with an odd exponent, we conclude that $(-1, 0)$ is an x-intercept at which the graph crosses the x-axis. Since $(x - 2)^2$ is a factor with an even exponent, we conclude that $(2, 0)$ is an x-intercept at which the graph touches the x-axis and then turns around. We also note that as x gets very large, so does y; while as x increases in magnitude in the negative direction, y becomes very small. Figure 11.6(a) illustrates our results so far. Finally, since the function is a polynomial function, we draw a smooth, unbroken curve that satisfies the conditions in Figure 11.6(a), and we obtain the graph in Figure 11.6(b).

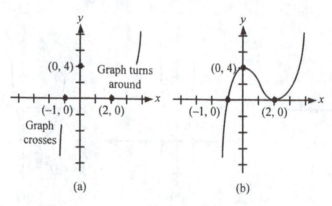

(a) (b)

Figure 11.6

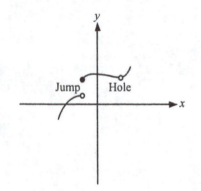

Figure 11.7

PROGRESS CHECK 6 Graph $y = (x - 1)^2(x + 2)$ on the basis of information obtained from the intercepts. ■

With the aid of the polynomial graphs drawn to this point, we now discuss some important properties of the graphs of polynomial functions.

Continuity

The graph of a polynomial function is a continuous curve. This property guarantees that polynomial graphs cannot have breaks such as those illustrated in Figure 11.7.

Turning Points

Points at which the graph changes from rising to falling, or vice versa, are called **turning points,** and it can be shown that a polynomial function of degree n has at most $n - 1$ turning points. For example, Figure 11.8 shows the two turning points for the third-degree polynomial graphed in Example 6. Note that it is possible for a polynomial function of degree n to have fewer than $n - 1$ turning points. For instance, $y = x^3$ is a polynomial function of degree 3 with no turning points. All turns in polynomial graphs are rounded turns, so a sharp turn (or corner), as illustrated in Figure 11.9, cannot occur in these graphs.

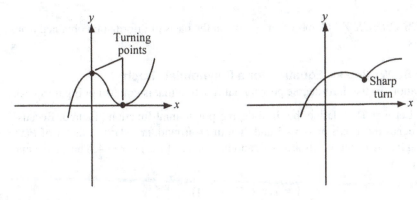

Figure 11.8   **Figure 11.9**

Behavior for Large $|x|$

The graph of the nth-degree polynomial function

$$y = a_n x^n + . . . + a_1 x + a_0$$

resembles the graph of $y = a_n x^n$ when $|x|$ is large. This behavior occurs because for x values far from the origin, the leading term $a_n x^n$ is much larger than the sum of all other terms in the polynomial. Thus, the behavior of a polynomial graph for large $|x|$ depends on whether n is even or odd, and on the sign of a_n, as specified in Figure 11.10.

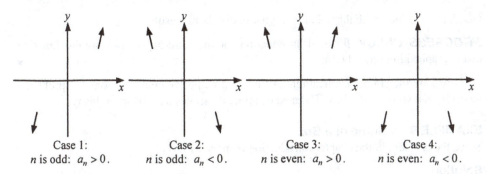

Case 1:
n is odd: $a_n > 0$.

Case 2:
n is odd: $a_n < 0$.

Case 3:
n is even: $a_n > 0$.

Case 4:
n is even: $a_n < 0$.

Figure 11.10

EXAMPLE 7   Using Intercepts to Graph a Polynomial Function

Graph $y = x^5 - 4x^3$ on the basis of information obtained from the intercepts.

Solution   By setting $x = 0$, we determine that $(0, 0)$ is a y- (and x-) intercept. To find x-intercepts, we next factor the polynomial as follows:

$$y = x^5 - 4x^3 = x^3(x^2 - 4) = x^3 (x + 2)(x - 2).$$

Since x^3, $x + 2$, and $x - 2$ are factors, we conclude that the x-intercepts are $(0, 0)$, $(-2, 0)$, and $(2, 0)$. All of these intercepts are derived from factors with odd exponents, so the graph crosses the x-axis at each of these points. By using this information and observing that the graph behaves like $y = x^5$ (or case 1 in Figure 11.10) for large values of $|x|$, we draw the graph in Figure 11.11. Keep in mind that our current methods produce only a rough sketch of the graph. A more detailed graph of $y = x^5 - 4x^3$ that is obtained on a grapher is given in Figure 11.12. Note that the graph indicates turning points when $x \approx \pm 1.55$ and an unanticipated wavy pattern between the turning points. Determining such subtleties is best left to displaying functions on a grapher or to analysis in a calculus course.

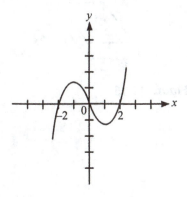

Figure 11.11

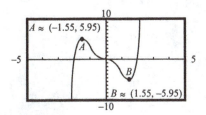

Figure 11.12

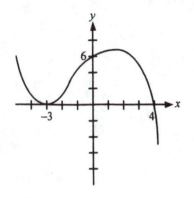

Figure 11.13

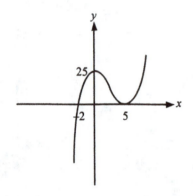

Figure 11.14

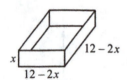

Figure 11.15

PROGRESS CHECK 7   Graph $y = x^4 - 9x^2$ on the basis of information obtained from the intercepts.   ■

EXAMPLE 8   Writing an Equation for a Polynomial Graph

Find an equation for the third-degree polynomial function that is graphed in Figure 11.13.

Solution   Let $y = P(x)$ define the third-degree polynomial function pictured. Because the graph touches the x-axis at $x = -3$ and then turns around, $(x + 3)^2$ is a factor of $P(x)$. Since the graph crosses the x-axis at $x = 4$, another factor of $P(x)$ is $x - 4$. Thus, the equation fits the form

$$y = k(x + 3)^2(x - 4).$$

To find k, observe that the y-intercept is $(0, 6)$ so

$$6 = k(0 + 3)^2(0 - 4)$$
$$6 = -36k$$
$$-\frac{1}{6} = k.$$

So, an equation for the function is

$$y = -\frac{1}{6}(x + 3)^2(x - 4).$$

Graph this function with the aid of a grapher to check this result.

PROGRESS CHECK 8   Find an equation for the third-degree polynomial function that is graphed in Figure 11.14.   ■

Among the simple applications of third-degree polynomial functions are problems involving the volume of a box. The next example illustrates a problem of this type.

EXAMPLE 9   Volume of a Box

Solve the problem in the chapter introduction on page 577.

Solution

a. When a square of side length x is cut from each corner, then x is the height of the box, and $12 - 2x$ is both the length and the width of the box, as shown in Figure 11.15. Using $V = lwh$, the volume of the box is given by

$$V = (12 - 2x)(12 - 2x)x,$$

or

$$V = x(12 - 2x)^2.$$

b. In the context of the problem, both x and $12 - 2x$ must be positive, so the domain is the set of real numbers between 0 and 6, which is (0 in., 6 in.) in interval notation.

c. Figure 11.16 shows a complete graph of $y = x(12 - 2x)^2$. However, the given formula is meaningful only for $0 < x < 6$, so we regraph the equation using this domain restriction, as shown in Figure 11.17. To find the value of x that yields the maximum volume, you may use the Zoom and Trace features (or a Function Maximum feature, if available) to determine that $x \approx 2.00$ and $y \approx 128$ at the highest point on the graph. So the maximum volume is obtained when a 2.00 in. square is cut from each corner.

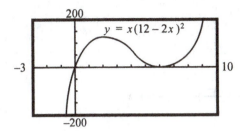

Figure 11.16

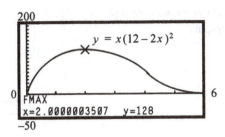

Figure 11.17

Note: To graph $y = x(12 - 2x)^2$ using the theorems in this section, it is useful to factor out -2 from each factor of $12 - 2x$, and then rewrite the equation as $y = 4x(x - 6)^2$. In this form it is apparent that the graph crosses the x-axis at $x = 0$ and that the graph turns when it intersects the x-axis at $x = 6$.

PROGRESS CHECK 9   Redo the questions in Example 9 assuming that the manufacturer starts with a rectangular piece of cardboard that measures 18 in. by 12 in.   ■

EXERCISES 11.1

In Exercises 1–10 is the function a polynomial function? If yes, state the degree.

1. $f(x) = x^3 + \sqrt{5}x - 3$ **2.** $f(x) = x^3 + 5\sqrt{x} - 3$
3. $f(x) = 4x - 3$ **4.** $f(x) = 7 + 4x - x^2$
5. $f(x) = x^2 + x^{1/2} - 1$ **6.** $f(x) = x^{-3} + 2x^2 - x + 3$
7. $f(x) = \dfrac{1}{x}$ **8.** $f(x) = 3^{-1}$
9. $f(x) = \pi$ **10.** $f(x) = x^{100} - 1$

In Exercises 11–16 write a polynomial function (in factored form) with the given degree and zeros.

11. degree 3; zeros are 1, 2 and 3
12. degree 3, zeros are $\sqrt{2}, -\sqrt{2}$, and 0
13. degree 4; zeros are $-4, 0, i$, and $-i$
14. degree 5; zeros are $5, 2 \pm i$, and $1 \pm \sqrt{3}$
15. degree 4; 1 and 5 are both zeros of multiplicity 2
16. degree 6; -2 is a zero of multiplicity 1; 0 is a zero of multiplicity 2; and 5 is a zero of multiplicity 3

In Exercises 17–24 find the zeros of each polynomial function. In each case state the degree of the polynomial function and the multiplicity of each zero.

17. $P(x) = (x + 3)^2$ **18.** $P(x) = x(x - 2)^3$
19. $P(x) = (x + 4)(x + \sqrt{2})(x - \sqrt{2})$
20. $P(x) = 4x^3(x - 1)^5(x + 6)$
21. $P(x) = 3x^2(2 - x)$ **22.** $P(x) = (x - 4)(2x - 1)$
23. $P(x) = \dfrac{1}{2}x^4$
24. $P(x) = -x(x - 1)^2\left(x + \dfrac{1}{3}\right)^3$

In Exercises 25–28 use the graph of $y = x^3$ to graph the given functions.

25. $y = x^3 - 1$ **26.** $y = 1 - x^3$
27. $y = (x - 2)^3$ **28.** $y = (x + 2)^3 - 5$

In Exercises 29–32 use the graph of $y = x^4$ to graph the given functions.

29. $y = (x + 2)^4$ **30.** $y = x^4 - 4$
31. $y = 2 - (x - 1)^4$ **32.** $y = -\dfrac{1}{2}x^4$

In Exercises 33–36 use the graph of $y = x^5$ to graph the given functions.

33. $y = -x^5$ **34.** $y = 2x^5$
35. $y = (x + 1)^5 + 4$ **36.** $y = 1 - (x - 1)^5$

In Exercises 37–40 use the graph of $y = x^6$ to graph the given functions.

37. $y = \dfrac{1}{4}x^6$ **38.** $y = -x^6$
39. $y = 2 - x^6$ **40.** $y = (x + 1)^6 + 3$

In Exercises 41–50 graph the functions on the basis of information obtained from the intercepts.

41. $y = (x - 2)(x + 1)$ **42.** $y = (x - 2)(x + 1)^2$
43. $y = (x - 2)^2(x + 1)$ **44.** $y = (x - 2)^2(x + 1)^2$
45. $y = (x^2 - 1)(x^2 - 4)$ **46.** $y = x^4 - 3x^2 + 2$
47. $y = x^3 - 2x^2 - 3x$ **48.** $y = x^3 - 4x$
49. $y = x^2 - x^3$ **50.** $y = x^3 + x^2$

In Exercises 51–56 find an equation of the lowest possible degree for the polynomial function that is graphed.

51.

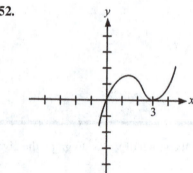

52.

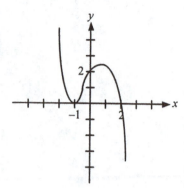

53.

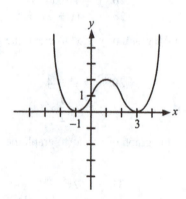

54.

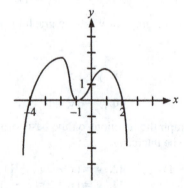

55.

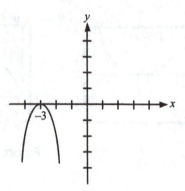

56.

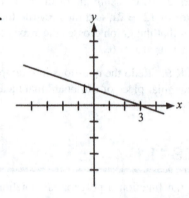

57. A square piece of cardboard with side length 10 in. is to be converted into an uncovered box, as described in Example 9.
   a. Find a formula for the volume V of the box in terms of the length (x) of the side of the square that is cut from each corner.
   b. What is the domain of this volume function?
   c. Use a grapher to graph this volume function and to estimate to two decimal places the length of the corner to cut out to obtain the box with maximum volume. What fraction of the side length is cut out to create the box with maximum volume?

58. Redo Exercise 57, but assume that the original piece of cardboard is square with a side length of 8 in.

59. The volume of a cube is supposed to be 125 cm^3. If there is an error of x cm in each side, then the volume is $(5 + x)^3$. For what values of x will the volume be between 120 and 130 cm^3?

60. Redo Exercise 59, if the volume must be less than 1 cm^3 in error from 125 cm^3.

THINK ABOUT IT 11.1

1. Since polynomial functions have smooth continuous graphs, there are no sharp turns or corners. In contrast, the graph of the absolute value function does change direction abruptly. Some interesting graphs therefore result from applying absolute value to polynomial functions. Graph each of these pairs of functions, and describe how the second is related to the first. Zoom in on any turning points of these graphs and describe the behavior of the graph there.

a. $y = x^2 - 3$; $y = |x^2 - 3|$
b. $y = x^3 + 3x^2 - x - 3$; $y = |x^3 + 3x^2 - x - 3|$

2. Create a third-degree polynomial inequality with the given solution set.

a. $(-\infty, -2] \cup [1, 5]$ **b.** $(-2, 3) \cup (3, \infty)$

3. What can't a cubic polynomial have exactly 1 turning point? Hint: consider the end behavior. Why can't a fourth-degree polynomial have exactly two turning points? What seems to be the relation between the degree of the polynomial and the possible numbers of turning points?

4. Here are three different boxes that can be constructed from cardboard.

a. In each case find the value of x that gives the box with maximum volume, and calculate the maximum value. Assume that the dimensions are in inches.

1. Open box: $V(x) = (24 - 2x)(12 - 2x)x$

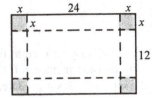
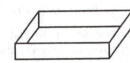

2. Reinforced end: $V(x) = (24 - 4x)(12 - 2x)x$

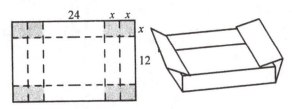

3. With top: $V(x) = (12 - x)(12 - 2x)x$

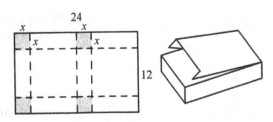

b. Are there any values of x for which two of the boxes have the same volume?

5. A square piece of tin, 12 inches on each side, is to be bent into a 3-edged pan, as shown, after square corners of side x are cut out. What size corner should be cut out so that the pan has maximum volume?

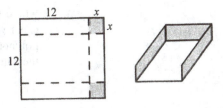

11.2   Synthetic Division and Theorems About Zeros

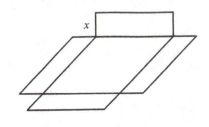

A rectangular piece of cardboard 18 in. by 12 in. is to be used to make an open-top box with a volume of 160 in.³, by cutting a small square from each corner and bending up the sides as shown. As determined in Progress Check 9 of Section 11.1, the volume of the box is given by $V = (18 - 2x)(12 - 2x)x$. So the side length x for each square cutout may be found by solving $160 = (18 - 2x)(12 - 2x)x$, which is equivalent to

$$x^3 - 15x^2 + 54x - 40 = 0.$$

It is apparent that 1 in. is a solution, since replacing x by 1 yields $1 - 15 + 54 - 40 = 0$, and $x = 1$ in. is meaningful in the context of the problem. Find all other possible side lengths for the cutout.

(See Example 6.)

OBJECTIVES

1   Divide one polynomial by another using long division.

2   Divide a polynomial by a polynomial of the form $x - b$, using synthetic division.

3   Evaluate a polynomial using the remainder theorem.

4   Find all zeros of a third-degree or fourth-degree polynomial function when one or two zeros, respectively, are apparent.

5   Use the conjugate-pair theorems to find zeros or write equations for polynomial functions.

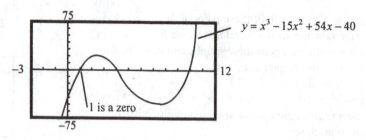

Figure 11.18

When we attempt to find exact values for the zeros of polynomial functions, we can sometimes spot some simple answers. For instance, in the section-opening problem we need to find the zeros for

$$P(x) = x^3 - 15x^2 + 54x - 40.$$

You may be able to spot a zero in this case because one of the zeros is a simple number, namely 1. Alternately, a graph of $y = P(x)$ on a grapher will reveal that 1 is a zero, because the graph has an x-intercept at $x = 1$ (along with other integer values), as shown in Figure 11.18.

Once it is known that 1 is a zero of a polynomial function $y = P(x)$, then the factor theorem indicates that $x - 1$ is a factor of $P(x)$. Therefore, $P(x) = x^3 - 15x^2 + 54x - 40$ may be written as

$$P(x) = (x - 1)Q(x),$$

where $Q(x)$ is a second-degree polynomial. To find $Q(x)$, which may be used to find the exact values of the remaining zeros, we may use the long-division method for dividing polynomials from Section 5.7 that is illustrated below. As you study this procedure, recall the names of the key components in such a division.

$$
\begin{array}{r}
x^2 - 14x + 40 \quad \leftarrow \text{Quotient} \\
\text{Divisor} \rightarrow x - 1 \overline{) x^3 - 15x^2 + 54x - 40} \quad \leftarrow \text{Dividend} \\
\text{Subtract: } x^3 - x^2 \\
\hline
-14x^2 + 54x - 40 \\
\text{Subtract: } -14x^2 + 14x \\
\hline
40x - 40 \\
\text{Subtract: } 40x - 40 \\
\hline
0 \quad \leftarrow \text{Remainder}
\end{array}
$$

Then, dividend = (divisor)(quotient) + remainder, so

$$x^3 - 15x^2 + 54x - 40 = (x - 1)(x^2 - 14x + 40).$$

From this result, it follows that

$$P(x) = (x - 1)(x - 4)(x - 10),$$

which implies that 1, 4, and 10 are the zeros of the function. Observe that the graph in Figure 11.18 supports this conclusion, because the graph appears to have x-intercepts when $x = 1$, $x = 4$, and $x = 10$.

The long-division method for dividing polynomials is useful in situations other than finding zeros of polynomial functions algebraically. Therefore, another example of this procedure is given in Example 1 and additional examples may be found in Section 5.7.

EXAMPLE 1   Using Long Division
Divide $2x^4 + 6x^3 - 5x^2 - 1$ by $2x^2 - 3$. Express the answer in the form

$$\frac{\text{dividend}}{\text{divisor}} = \text{quotient} + \frac{\text{remainder}}{\text{divisor}}.$$

Solution   The division is performed below. Note that $0x$ is inserted to help align like terms vertically, and that the division process stopped when the remainder $9x - 4$ was of lower degree than the divisor $2x^3 - 3$.

$$2x^4/2x^2 = x^2,\ 6x^3/2x^2 = 3x.$$
and $-2x^2/2x^2 = -1$

$$
\begin{array}{r}
x^2 + 3x - 1 \\
2x^2 - 3 \overline{)\ 2x^4 + 6x^3 - 5x^2 + 0x - 1}
\end{array}
$$

subtract $\underline{2x^4 \qquad\quad - 3x^2}$ This line is $x^2(2x^2 - 3)$.

$\qquad\qquad\qquad 6x^3 - 2x^2 + 0x - 1$

subtract $\qquad \underline{6x^3 \qquad\quad - 9x}$ This line is $3x(2x^2 - 3)$.

$\qquad\qquad\qquad\qquad -2x^2 + 9x - 1$

subtract $\qquad\qquad \underline{-2x^2 \qquad + 3}$ This line is $-1(2x^2 - 3)$.

$\qquad\qquad\qquad\qquad\qquad 9x - 4$

The answer in the form requested is

$$\frac{2x^4 + 6x^3 - 5x^2 - 1}{2x^2 - 3} = x^2 + 3x - 1 + \frac{9x - 4}{2x^2 - 3}.$$

Technology Link

One way to check this answer on a grapher is to let

$$y1 = \frac{2x^4 + 6x^3 - 5x^2 - 1}{2x^2 - 3}$$

$$y2 = x^2 + 3x - 1 + \frac{9x - 4}{2x^2 - 3}$$

$$y3 = \frac{y1}{y2}.$$

Then graph only $y3$. The quotient of identical expressions is 1, so check for a graph that is a horizontal line where y is fixed at 1.

PROGRESS CHECK 1   Divide $9x^4 + 5x^2 + x + 3$ by $3x - 1$. Answer in the form requested in Example 1.   ∎

The division of any polynomial by a polynomial of the form $x - b$ is of theoretical and practical importance. This division may be performed by a shorthand method called **synthetic division.** Consider the arrangement for dividing $2x^3 + 5x^2 - 1$ by $x - 2$.

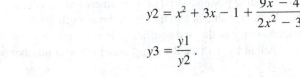

When the polynomials are written with terms in descending powers of x, there is no need to write all the x's. Only the coefficients are needed. Also, notice that the encircled coefficients entailed needless writing. Using only the necessary coefficients, we may abbreviate this division as follows:

$$
\begin{array}{r}
2 \quad\ 9 \quad\ 18 \\
-2\,\overline{)\ 2 \quad\ 5 \quad\ 0 \quad -1} \\
\underline{-4 \ -18 \ -36} \\
9 \quad 18 \quad 35.
\end{array}
$$

If we bring down 2 as the first entry in the bottom row, all the coefficients of the quotient appear. The arrangement may then be shorted to

$$
\begin{array}{r|rrrr}
-2| & 2 & 5 & 0 & -1 \\
 & & -4 & -18 & -36 \\
\hline
 & 2 & 9 & 18 & 35
\end{array}
$$

coefficients of dividend (row 1)

(row 2)

coefficients of quotient — remainder (row 3)

Finally, if we replace −2 by 2, which is the value of *b*, we may change the sign of each number in row 2 and add at each step instead of subtracting. The final arrangement for synthetic division is then as follows:

$$
\begin{array}{r|rrrr}
2| & 2 & 5 & 0 & -1 \\
 & & 4 & 18 & 36 \\
\hline
 & 2 & 9 & 18 & 35
\end{array}
$$

(row 1)

(row 2)

remainder (row 3)

quotient ⟶ $2x^2 + 9x + 18$

Use this example as a basis for understanding the synthetic division procedure outlined next.

Synthetic Division

To divide a polynomial $P(x)$ by $x - b$:

1. Form row 1 by writing the coefficients of the terms in the dividend $P(x)$. The dividend must be written in descending powers, and 0 must be entered as the coefficient of any missing term. Write the value of b to the left of these coefficients.
2. Bring down the first dividend entry as the first coefficient in the quotient.
3. Multiply this quotient coefficient by b. Place the result under the next number in row 1, and then add.
4. Repeat the procedure in step 3 until all entries in row 1 have been used.
5. The last number in the bottom row is the remainder. The other numbers in the bottom row are, from left to right, the coefficients of descending powers of the quotient.

It is important to remember that synthetic division applies only to division by a polynomial of the form $x - b$. Because this divisor is a first-degree polynomial, the degree of the polynomial in the quotient is always one less than the degree of the polynomial in the dividend.

EXAMPLE 2   Using Synthetic Division

Use synthetic division to divide $x^5 - 1$ by $x - 1$. Express the result in the form

$$\text{dividend} = (\text{divisor})(\text{quotient}) + \text{remainder}.$$

Solution   We use 0's as the coefficients of the missing x^4, x^3, x^2, and x terms. We divide by $x - 1$ so that $b = 1$ (not −1). The arrangement is as follows:

$$
\begin{array}{r|rrrrrr}
1| & 1 & 0 & 0 & 0 & 0 & -1 \\
 & & 1 & 1 & 1 & 1 & 1 \\
\hline
 & 1 & 1 & 1 & 1 & 1 & 0
\end{array}
$$

remainder

quotient ⟶ $x^4 + x^3 + x^2 + x + 1.$

The answer in the form requested is

$$x^5 - 1 = (x - 1)(x^4 + x^3 + x^2 + x + 1) + 0.$$

PROGRESS CHECK 2   Use synthetic division to divide $4x^3 - 2x^2 + 3x - 1$ by $x - 2$. Express the result in the form requested in Example 2.   ■

EXAMPLE 3   Using Synthetic Division

Use synthetic division to divide $4x^3 - x^2 + 2$ by $x + 3$. Express the result in the form

$$\text{dividend} = (\text{divisor})(\text{quotient}) + \text{remainder}.$$

Solution   We use 0 as the coefficient of the missing first degree term. We divide by $x + 3$ or $x - (-3)$, so that $b = -3$ (not 3). The arrangement is as follows:

$$
\begin{array}{r|rrrr}
-3 & 4 & -1 & 0 & 2 \\
   &   & -12 & 39 & -117 \\
\hline
   & 4 & -13 & 39 & -115 \quad\longleftarrow \text{ remainder} \\
\end{array}
$$

$$\text{quotient} \longrightarrow 4x^2 - 13x + 39.$$

The answer in the form requested is

$$4x^3 - x^2 + 2 = (x + 3)(4x^2 - 13x + 39) - 115.$$

PROGRESS CHECK 3   Use synthetic division to divide $3x^3 + 10x^2 - 6x + 8$ by $x + 4$. Express the result in the form requested in Example 3.   ■

In Example 3 we found that the function

$$P(x) = 4x^3 - x^2 + 2$$

may be written as

$$P(x) = (x + 3)(4x^2 - 13x + 39) - 115.$$

When $x = -3$, the factor $x + 3$ equals 0; thus,

$$P(-3) = 0 - 115$$
$$= -115.$$

The value of the function when $x = -3$ is the same as the remainder obtained when $P(x)$ is divided by $x - (-3)$. This discussion suggests the following theorem.

Remainder Theorem

If a polynomial $P(x)$ is divided by $x - b$, the remainder is $P(b)$.

To prove this theorem, let $Q(x)$ and r represent the quotient and remainder when $P(x)$ is divided by $x - b$. Then

$$\text{dividend} = (\text{divisor})(\text{quotient}) + \text{remainder}$$
$$P(x) = (x - b)Q(x) + r.$$

This statement is true for all values of x. If $x = b$, then

$$P(b) = (b - b)Q(b) + r$$
$$= 0 \cdot Q(b) + r.$$

Thus,

$$P(b) = r.$$

We know that $P(b)$ may be found by substituting b for x in the function. The remainder theorem provides an alternative method. That is, we find $P(b)$ by determining the remainder when $P(x)$ is divided by $x - b$. Since this remainder may be obtained by synthetic division, this approach is often simpler than direct substitution. Later in this section, other advantages of the remainder theorem will be discussed.

EXAMPLE 4   Using the Remainder Theorem

If $P(x) = 3x^5 + 5x^4 + 7x^3 - 4x^2 + x - 24$, find $P(-2)$ by

a. direct substitution and   **b.** the remainder theorem.

Solution

a. By direct substitution, we have

$$P(-2) = 3(-2)^5 + 5(-2)^4 + 7(-2)^3 - 4(-2)^2 + (-2) - 24$$
$$= -96 + 80 - 56 - 16 - 2 - 24$$
$$= -114.$$

b. By the remainder theorem, we have

$$
\begin{array}{r|rrrrrr}
-2 & 3 & 5 & 7 & -4 & 1 & -24 \\
   &   & -6 & 2 & -18 & 44 & -90 \\
\hline
   & 3 & -1 & 9 & -22 & 45 & -114.
\end{array}
$$

Since the remainder is -114, $P(-2) = -114$.

PROGRESS CHECK 4   If $P(x) = 2x^4 - 5x^3 + 11x^2 - 3x - 5$, find $P(-1/2)$ by

a. direct substitution and   **b.** the remainder theorem.   ■

In the previous section, the factor theorem was introduced. We restate this theorem next for reference purposes, and then prove it with the aid of the remainder theorem. Example 5 will then show an advantage of using the remainder theorem method to find $P(b)$.

Factor Theorem

If b is a zero of the polynomial function $y = P(x)$, then $x - b$ is a factor of $P(x)$; conversely, if $x - b$ is a factor of $P(x)$, then b is a zero of $y = P(x)$.

We now prove the first part of this theorem. As in the proof of the remainder theorem, let $Q(x)$ and r represent the quotient and remainder when $P(x)$ is divided by $x - b$. Then

$$P(x) = (x - b)Q(x) + r.$$

By the remainder theorem, $r = P(b)$, so we have

$$P(x) = (x - b)Q(x) + P(b).$$

If b is a zero of $y = P(x)$, then $P(b) = 0$. Thus,

$$P(x) = (x - b)Q(x) + 0,$$

and $x - b$ is a factor of $P(x)$. The proof of the second part of this theorem is left as Exercise 69.

EXAMPLE 5   Using the Factor and Remainder Theorems

If $P(x) = x^3 - 2x^2 - 5x + 6$, then is $x - 1$ a factor of $P(x)$? If yes, then factor $P(x)$ completely.

Solution   By the factor theorem, $x - 1$ is a factor of $P(x)$ if and only if $P(1) = 0$. We may find $P(1)$ by using direct substitution or by using the remainder theorem.

Direct substitution method: $P(1) = 1^3 - 2(1)^2 - 5(1) + 6 = 0$

Remainder theorem method:

$$\begin{array}{r|rrrr}
\underline{1} & 1 & -2 & -5 & 6 \\
& & 1 & -1 & -6 \\
\hline
& 1 & -1 & -6 & 0 \end{array} \longleftarrow P(1)$$

Both methods show $P(1) = 0$, so $x - 1$ is a factor of $P(x)$. However, observe that the remainder theorem method is especially helpful here because it also reveals that the quotient is $x^2 - x - 6$. Thus, $P(x)$ factors as

$$P(x) = (x - 1)(x^2 - x - 6).$$

For this polynomial we can factor further, since $x^2 - x - 6$ factors as $(x - 3)(x + 2)$. So the complete factorization is

$$P(x) = (x - 1)(x - 3)(x + 2).$$

To check this result on a grapher, note that applying the factor theorem to this factorization gives that 1, 3, and –2 are zeros of $y = P(x)$, so the graph of $y = P(x)$ should intersect the x-axis at these numbers. These intersections are apparent in the graph of $y = P(x)$ shown in Figure 11.19.

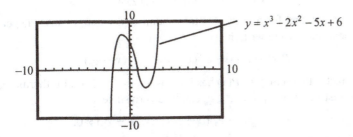

Figure 11.19

PROGRESS CHECK 5   If $P(x) = x^3 + 3x^2 - 10x - 24$, then is $x + 2$ a factor of $P(x)$? If yes, then factor $P(x)$ completely. ■

Now that we have developed methods for dividing polynomials and established the remainder and factor theorems, we can return to the main topic of finding zeros for polynomial functions. In this section we present three theorems that are fundamental to the theory of finding such zeros. You need a good grasp of number systems to understand these statements thoroughly and it may be helpful if you review the relationships among the various sets of numbers, which are given in Sections 1.1 and 6.6.

Fundamental Theorem of Algebra

Every polynomial function of degree $n \geq 1$ with complex number coefficients has at least one complex zero.

Although the proof of this theorem is beyond the scope of this book, we can prove an important corollary of this theorem that answers a basic question: How many zeros are there for a polynomial function of degree n?

Number of Zeros Theorem

Every polynomial function of degree $n \geq 1$ has exactly n complex zeros, where zeros of multiplicity k are counted k times.

For instance, we have seen that $P(x) = x^4(x - 2)(x + 7)^3$ is a polynomial function of degree 8 with distinct zeros of 0, 2 and −7 (see Example 4 of Section 11.1). However, the multiplicities of these zeros are 4, 1, and 3, respectively, so that if we take into account the idea of multiplicity, then this 8th-degree polynomial function has exactly eight zeros. More generally, we can prove the above theorem by first noting that if $y = P(x)$ is a polynomial function of degree $n \geq 1$ with leading coefficient a_n, then the fundamental theorem of algebra guarantees that $y = P(x)$ has at least one complex zero, say c_1. By the factor theorem, since c_1 is a zero, $x - c_1$ is a factor of $P(x)$, so

$$P(x) = (x - c_1)Q_1(x),$$

where polynomial $Q_1(x)$ has degree $n - 1$ and leading coefficient a_n. If the degree of $Q_1(x)$ is at least 1, then once again the fundamental theorem of algebra guarantees that $y = Q_1(x)$ has at least one zero, say c_2, so as above,

$$Q_1(x) = (x - c_2)Q_2(x),$$

where polynomial $Q_2(x)$ has degree $n - 2$ and leading coefficient a_n. Then combining results, we have

$$P(x) = (x - c_1)(x - c_2)Q_2(x).$$

This process is continued for a total of n times until $Q_n(x) = a_n$. Thus, $P(x)$ can be factored into n linear factors and written as

$$P(x) = a_n(x - c_1)(x - c_2) \ldots (x - c_n)$$

so that, by the factor theorem, $y = P(x)$ has n zeros: $c_1, c_2, \ldots, c_n$. Furthermore, no other number, say c, distinct from $c_1, c_2, \ldots, c_n$ can be a zero since

$$P(c) = a_n(c - c_1)(c - c_2) \ldots (c - c_n) \neq 0,$$

because none of the factors is zero. Thus, every polynomial function of degree $n \geq 1$ has exactly n (not necessarily distinct) complex zeros.

EXAMPLE 6   Using a Known Root to Find All Roots

Solve the problem in the section introduction on page 587.

Solution   We need to find all roots of the equation

$$x^3 - 15x^2 + 54x - 40 = 0,$$

given that 1 is a solution. Observe that this equation is a third-degree polynomial equation, so there are three (not necessarily distinct) roots. If we let $P(x)$ equal the polynomial on the left side of the equal sign, the solution at $x = 1$ implies that $x - 1$ is a factor of $P(x)$. We can then use synthetic division to find another factor of $P(x)$ as follows:

$$
\begin{array}{r|rrrr}
\underline{1} & 1 & -15 & 54 & -40 \\
  &   & 1 & -14 & 40 \\
\hline
  & 1 & -14 & 40 & 0.
\end{array}
$$

As expected, the remainder is 0, so $P(1) = 0$, and 1 is a solution. Because the remainder is 0, the division above indicates that $P(x)$ factors as

$$x^3 - 15x^2 + 54x - 40 = (x - 1)(x^2 - 14x + 40)$$

so we get

$$x^3 - 15x^2 + 54x - 40 = 0$$
$$(x - 1)(x^2 - 14x + 40) = 0.$$

The remaining roots are the solutions of $x^2 - 14x + 40 = 0$, and for this equation the factoring method applies.

$$x^2 - 14x + 40 = 0$$
$$(x - 4)(x - 10) = 0$$
$$x - 4 = 0 \quad \text{or} \quad x - 10 = 0$$
$$x = 4 \qquad\qquad x = 10$$

Thus, the three roots are 1, 4, and 10 (check Figure 11.18 again). In the context of the problem, 1 and 4 are meaningful answers, but it is not possible to cut out a square with side length 10 in. from each corner. Thus, the only other possible side length for the cutout is 4 in.

PROGRESS CHECK 6 If the box described in Example 6 is to have a volume of 224 in.^{3}, then the side length x for each square cutout may be found by solving the equation $(18 - 2x)(12 - 2x)x = 224$, which is equivalent to

$$x^3 - 15x^2 + 54x - 56 = 0.$$

One solution to this problem is $x = 2$ in. Find all other possible side lengths for the cutout. ▪

EXAMPLE 7 Using a Known Zero to Find All Zeros

If 2 is a zero of $P(x) = x^3 - 2x^2 + 3x - 6$, find the other zeros.

Solution Since $y = P(x)$ is a polynomial function of degree 3, there are exactly three (not necessarily distinct) zeros. We are given that 2 is one of these zeros, and if 2 is a zero of $y = P(x)$, then by the factor theorem, $x - 2$ is a factor of the polynomial. We can then use synthetic division to find another factor of $P(x)$ as follows:

$$
\begin{array}{r|rrrr}
2 & 1 & -2 & 3 & -6 \\
  &   & 2 & 0 & 6 \\
\hline
  & 1 & 0 & 3 & 0.
\end{array}
$$

The coefficients of another factor of $P(x)$ are given in the bottom row of this synthetic division. Thus,

$$P(x) = (x - 2)(x^2 + 3).$$

The remaining zeros of $y = P(x)$ are the solutions of $x^2 + 3 = 0$.

$$x^2 + 3 = 0$$
$$x^2 = -3$$
$$x = \pm i\sqrt{3}$$

Thus, the other two zeros are $i\sqrt{3}$ and $-i\sqrt{3}$. Figure 11.20 helps to confirm that the only real zero of this function is at $x = 2$.

PROGRESS CHECK 7 If 1 is a zero of $P(x) = x^3 - x^2 - 15x + 15$, find the other zeros. ▪

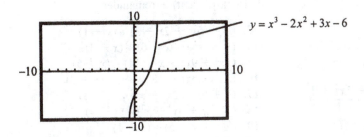

Figure 11.20

Note in Example 7 that the zeros $i\sqrt{3}$ and $-i\sqrt{3}$ are conjugates of each other. In general, the following theorems show that when certain restrictions are placed on the coefficients of a polynomial, then zeros of polynomial functions always occur in conjugate pairs.

Conjugate-Pair Theorems

1. If a complex number $a + bi$ is a zero of a polynomial function of degree $n \geq 1$ with *real*-number coefficients, then its conjugate $a - bi$ is also a zero.
2. Let a, b, and c be rational numbers. If an irrational number $a + b\sqrt{c}$ is a zero of a polynomial function of degree $n \geq 1$ with *rational*-number coefficients, then $a - b\sqrt{c}$ is also a zero.

The restrictions on the coefficients of the polynomial are crucial conditions in these theorems. For example $P(x) = x - \sqrt{2}$ has only one zero, namely $\sqrt{2}$. Note that the conjugate $-\sqrt{2}$ is not also a zero, and that the second conjugate-pair theorem does not apply to $P(x) = x - \sqrt{2}$, because the polynomial does not have rational-number coefficients.

EXAMPLE 8   Using the Conjugate-Pair Theorems

If $-2i$ and $2 + \sqrt{7}$ are zeros of the function $P(x) = x^4 - 4x^3 + x^2 - 16x - 12$, find the other zeros.

Solution $P(x)$ has a rational-number coefficient. Thus, both conjugate-pair theorems apply, and if $-2i$ and $2 + \sqrt{7}$ are zeros, then $2i$ and $2 - \sqrt{7}$ are also zeros. There are no other zeros, since the polynomial has degree 4.

PROGRESS CHECK 8   If $4 - 2i$ and $\sqrt{3}$ are zeros of the polynomial function $P(x) = x^4 - 8x^3 + 17x^2 + 24x - 60$ find the other zeros.   ■

EXAMPLE 9   Using the Conjugate-Pair Theorems

Write a polynomial function (in factored form) of the lowest possible degree that has rational coefficients and zeros of 0, $1 - i$, and $\sqrt{2}$.

Solution   Since the polynomial has rational coefficients, we utilize both conjugate-pair theorems. Thus, in addition to the three zeros given, $1 + i$ and $-\sqrt{2}$ are also zeros. The lowest possible degree for the polynomial is then degree 5, and in factored form one possibility is

$$P(x) = x(x - \sqrt{2})(x + \sqrt{2})(x - (1 + i))(x - (1 - i)).$$

PROGRESS CHECK 9   Write a polynomial function (in factored form) of the lowest possible degree that has rational coefficients and zeros of 2, $\sqrt{2}$, and $2i$.   ■

EXERCISES 11.2

In Exercises 1–6 perform the indicated divisions by using long division. Express the answer in the form

$$\frac{\text{dividend}}{\text{divisor}} = \text{quotient} + \frac{\text{remainder}}{\text{divisor}}.$$

1. $\dfrac{x^2 - 5}{x + 1}$ 2. $\dfrac{x^2 + 3x - 4}{x - 3}$

3. $\dfrac{3x^4 - 5x^2 + 7}{x^2 + 2x + 1}$ 4. $\dfrac{2x^4 - 8x^3 - 7x^2 + 1}{2x^2 - 5}$

5. $\dfrac{x^3 + 1}{x(x - 1)}$ 6. $\dfrac{x^3 - 5}{(x - 1)^2}$

In Exercises 7–12 perform the indicated divisions by using long division. Express the result in the form dividend = (divisor)(quotient) + remainder.

7. $(x^2 + 7x - 2) \div (x + 5)$ 8. $(x^2 - 4) \div (x - 1)$
9. $(6x^3 - 3x^2 + 14x - 7) \div (2x - 1)$
10. $(4x^3 + 5x^2 - 10x + 4) \div (4x - 3)$
11. $(3x^4 + x - 2) \div (x^2 - 1)$
12. $(2x^3 - 3x^2 + 10x - 5) \div (x^2 + 5)$

In Exercises 13–22 perform the indicated division by using synthetic division. Express the result in the form dividend = (divisor)(quotient) + remainder.

13. $(x^3 - 5x^2 + 2x - 3) \div (x - 1)$
14. $(x^3 + x^2 - 9x - 6) \div (x - 3)$
15. $(2x^3 + 9x^2 - x + 14) \div (x + 5)$
16. $(3x^3 - 5x^2 - 18x + 9) \div (x + 2)$
17. $(7 + 6x - 2x^2 - x^3) \div (x + 3)$
18. $(4 - x + 3x^2 - x^3) \div (x - 4)$
19. $(2x^3 + x - 5) \div (x + 1)$
20. $(3x^4 - x^2 + 7) \div (x + 3)$
21. $(x^4 - 16) \div (x - 2)$ 22. $(x^3 + 27) \div (x - 3)$

In Exercises 23–30 find the given function value by
a. direct substitution and   b. the remainder theorem.

23. $P(x) = x^3 - 4x^2 + x + 6$; find $P(2)$ and $P(3)$.
24. $P(x) = 2x^3 + 5x^2 - x - 7$; find $P(4)$ and $P(-3)$.
25. $P(x) = 2x^4 - 7x^3 - x^2 + 4x + 11$; find $P(2)$ and $P(-2)$.
26. $P(x) = x^4 - 5x^3 - 4x^2 + 17x + 15$; find $P(-1)$ and $P(5)$.
27. $P(x) = 2x^4 + 5x^3 - 20x - 32$; find $P(-2)$ and $P(2)$.
28. $P(x) = 2x^4 - x^3 + 2x - 1$; find $P\left(\dfrac{1}{2}\right)$ and $P\left(-\dfrac{1}{2}\right)$.
29. $P(x) = 6x^4 + 2x^3 - 5x - 5$; find $P\left(\dfrac{1}{3}\right)$ and $P\left(-\dfrac{1}{3}\right)$.

30. $P(x) = 3x^4 + x^2 - 7x + 2$; find $P(0.1)$ and $P(-0.1)$.

31. If $P(x) = x^3 - 2x^2 + 2x + 5$, then is $x + 1$ a factor of $P(x)$? If yes, then factor $P(x)$ completely.

32. If $P(x) = x^3 - 3x^2 + 8x - 12$, then is $x - 2$ a factor of $P(x)$? If yes, then factor $P(x)$ completely.

33. If $P(x) = x^3 - 5x^2 + 2x + 8$, then is $x - 4$ a factor of $P(x)$? If yes, then factor $P(x)$ completely.

34. If $P(x) = x^3 + 9x^2 + 24x + 20$, then is $x + 5$ a factor of $P(x)$? If yes, then factor $P(x)$ completely.

35. If $P(x) = x^3 + 3x^2 + x + 6$, then is $x - 2$ a factor of $P(x)$? If yes, then factor $P(x)$ completely.

36. If $P(x) = x^3 + x^2 + 2x + 6$, then is $x + 3$ a factor of $P(x)$? If yes, then factor $P(x)$ completely.

37. A rectangular piece of paper 8 in. by 10 in. is to be used to make an open-top box with volume 48 in.³, as described in Example 6 of this section. If the side for each cutoff corner is given by x, then the volume is given by $V = (8 - 2x)(10 - 2x)x$. Check that $x = 1$ in. is one solution, then find all other possible solutions.

38. Redo Exercise 37 if the volume is 24 in.³, given that $x = 3$ in. is one solution.

39. The rectangular open metal figure shown is made from 12 rods. The total amount of wire used for the edges is 40 inches.
  a. Confirm that $a + b + c = 10$.
  b. Suppose that height (b) is 2 inches more than the length (a). Confirm that the volume is then given by
$$V = a(8 - 2a)(a + 2).$$
  c. If $a = 1$, then the volume of the figure is 18 in.³. Is there any other choice for a that also yields volume 18 in.³?

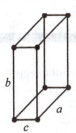

40. Redo Exercise 39 part **c,** assuming that $V = 32$ in.³. In this case $a = 2$ is one solution. Are there any others?

41. Given that -2 is a zero of $P(x) = x^3 + 2x^2 + x + 2$, find all other zeros.

42. Given that -3 is a zero of $P(x) = x^3 + 3x^2 - 5x - 15$, find all other zeros.

In Exercises 43–56 one or more zeros (is/are) given for each of the following polynomial functions. Find the other zeros.

43. $P(x) = x^2 - 4x - 3$; $2 + \sqrt{7}$

44. $P(x) = 3x^2 + 4x - 2$; $\dfrac{-2 - \sqrt{10}}{3}$

45. $P(x) = x^2 + 2$; $i\sqrt{2}$

46. $P(x) = 3x^2 - 2x + 1$; $\dfrac{1}{3} - \dfrac{i\sqrt{2}}{3}$

47. $P(x) = 2x^3 - 11x^2 + 28x - 24$; $\dfrac{3}{2}$ and $2 + 2i$

48. $P(x) = x^4 + 13x^2 - 48$; $\sqrt{3}$ and $-4i$

49. $P(x) = 2x^3 + 5x^2 + 4x + 1$; -1

50. $P(x) = 3x^3 - 2x^2 - 10x + 4$; 2

51. $P(x) = x^4 - 6x^3 + 7x^2 + 12x - 18$; 3 is a zero of multiplicity 2

52. $P(x) = 2x^4 - 5x^3 + 11x^2 - 3x - 5$; 1 and $-\dfrac{1}{2}$

53. $P(x) = x^4 - 4$; $\sqrt{2}$

54. $P(x) = x^4 - 14x^2 + 45$; $-\sqrt{5}$

55. $P(x) = x^4 - 1$; i **56.** $P(x) = x^4 - 16$; $2i$

In Exercises 57–62 write a polynomial function (in factored form) with rational coefficients of the lowest possible degree with the given zeros.

57. 2 and $\sqrt{3}$ **58.** i and 0

59. 0, $2 + 3i$, and $4 - \sqrt{3}$ **60.** -5, $-\sqrt{5}$, and $5i$

61. 3, -3 and $2i$ **62.** $3i$ and $1 + \sqrt{2}$

63. If -1 is a zero of $y = x^3 - x^2 - 10x - 8$, find all intercepts and then graph the function.

64. Graph the function in Exercise 51 on the basis of information obtained from the intercepts.

In Exercises 65–68 $y = P(x)$ is a polynomial function with real coefficients. Answer true or false.

65. Every polynomial function of degree 3 has at least one real zero.

66. Every polynomial function of degree 4 has at least one real zero.

67. Every polynomial function of degree $n \geq 1$ has exactly n (not necessarily different) real zeros.

68. Every polynomial function of degree $n \geq 1$ has exactly n (not necessarily different) complex zeros.

69. Show that if $x - b$ is a factor of the polynomial $P(x)$, then b is a zero of $y = P(x)$.

THINK ABOUT IT 11.2

1. The dividend is x^2, the quotient is $x - 4$, and the remainder is 16. What is the divisor?

2. For what value of k is $x - 2$ a factor of $2x^4 - 5x^3 + kx^2 - 5x + 2$?

3. Write a polynomial function (in factored form) with *real* coefficients of lowest possible degree with zeros of 0, $-\sqrt{3}$, and $3i$.

4. If $f(x) = ax^3 + bx^2 + cx + d$, where a, b, c, and d are real numbers with $a \neq 0$, then explain why the graph of f must have at least one x-intercept.

5. A polynomial function of degree n can't have more than n zeros. Thus its graph cannot hit the x-axis more than n times.
  a. Explain why the graph of a polynomial function of degree n cannot hit some other horizontal line more than n times. Hint: If $P(x)$ has degree n, what degree does $P(x) - c$ have, where c is a real constant?
  b. Explain why no section of a polynomial graph can be horizontal.

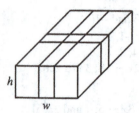

h

w

11.3 Additional Theorems About Zeros

The volume of a rectangular packaging carton is to be 30 ft^3. If the length and width are respectively 3 ft and 1 ft greater than the height, show that only one set of dimensions is possible for the given carton. What are these dimensions? (See Example 4.)

OBJECTIVES

1 List the possible rational zeros of a polynomial function with integer coefficients.

2 Determine the maximum number of positive and negative real zeros of a polynomial function.

3 Find all the zeros of a polynomial function, when given a function with a sufficient number of rational zeros to allow all zeros to be determined.

4 Use the location theorem to verify the existence of a zero of a function in a given interval.

5 Approximate a zero of a function in a given interval to the nearest tenth.

In the previous section we saw that we can find all the zeros of a third- or fourth-degree polynomial function when one or two zeros, respectively, are apparent. The following theorem can help us locate some apparent answers because it may be used to obtain a list of *possible* rational zeros of a polynomial function with integer coefficients. We emphasize the word *possible*. The zeros may all be either irrational or complex. This theorem states only that if there are rational zeros, they satisfy the requirement indicated.

Rational-Zero Theorem

If p/q, a rational number in lowest terms, is a zero of the polynomial function with integer coefficients

$$P(x) = a_n x^n + a_{n-1}x^{n-1} + \ldots + a_1 x + a_0 \quad (a_n \neq 0),$$

then p is an integral factor of the constant term a_0, and q is an integral factor of the leading coefficient a_n.

In practice, the rational-zero theorem is not difficult to apply.

EXAMPLE 1 Finding Possible Rational Zeros

List the possible rational zeros of the function $P(x) = 2x^3 - x^2 - 6x - 3$.

Solution The constant term a_0 is -3. The possibilities for p are the integers that are factors of 3. Thus,

$$p = \pm 3, \pm 1.$$

The leading coefficient a_n is 2. The possibilities for q are the integers that are factors of 2. Thus,

$$q = \pm 2, \pm 1.$$

The possible rational zeros p/q are then

$$3, \frac{3}{2}, 1, \frac{1}{2}, -\frac{1}{2}, -1, -\frac{3}{2}, -3.$$

PROGRESS CHECK 1 List the possible rational zeros of the polynomial function $P(x) = 5x^3 - 7x^2 - 8x + 4$.

Since we are often faced with a large list of possible rational zeros, we need some help in narrowing down the possibilities. Consider the theorem that follows, which helps us chip away at the problem. Note that it is a statement about real zeros. Thus, it applies to zeros that are rational or irrational.

Descartes' Rule of Signs

The maximum number of positive real zeros of the polynomial function $y = P(x)$ is the number of changes in sign of the coefficients in $P(x)$. The number of changes in sign of the coefficients in $P(-x)$ is the maximum number of negative real zeros. In both cases, if the number of zeros is not the maximum number, then it is less than this number by a multiple of 2.

We illustrate this theorem in the following example.

EXAMPLE 2   Finding Zeros of a Third-Degree Polynomial Function

Find the zeros of $P(x) = 2x^3 + 5x^2 + 4x + 1$.

Solution   Steps **a** to **d** outline a systematic approach to finding the zeros algebraically.

a. Use Descartes' rule of signs to determine the maximum number of positive and negative real zeros.

$$P(x) = 2x^3 + 5x^2 + 4x + 1.$$

All the coefficients in $P(x)$ are positive. There are no positive real zeros since there are no changes in sign.

$$P(-x) = 2(-x)^3 + 5(-x)^2 + 4(-x) + 1$$
$$= -2x^3 + 5x^2 - 4x + 1$$

There are three sign changes in $P(-x)$. At most, there may be three negative real zeros. By decreasing this number by 2, we determine that one negative real zero is the only other possibility.

b. Determine the possible rational zeros. The constant term a_0 is 1. The possibilities for p are the integers that are factors of 1. Thus,

$$p = \pm 1.$$

The leading coefficient a_n is 2. The integers that are factors of 2 give the possibilities for q. Thus,

$$q = \pm 2, \pm 1.$$

The possible rational zeros p/q are then

$$1, \frac{1}{2}, -\frac{1}{2}, -1.$$

From part **a** we eliminate the positive possibilities, leaving

$$-\frac{1}{2}, -1.$$

c. Use synthetic division to test whether one of the possibilities, say -1, is a zero.

$$
\begin{array}{r|rrrr}
-1 & 2 & 5 & 4 & 1 \\
   &   & -2 & -3 & -1 \\
\hline
   & 2 & 3 & 1 & 0 \\
\end{array}
$$

Since the remainder is zero, $P(-1) = 0$. Thus, -1 is a zero of the function.

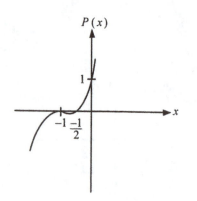

Figure 11.21

d. The factor theorem states that if -1 is a zero, $x - (-1)$ or $x + 1$ is a factor. The coefficients of the other factor are given in the bottom row of the synthetic division. That is,

$$2x^3 + 5x^2 + 4x + 1 = (x + 1)(2x^2 + 3x + 1).$$

We now find other zeros by setting the factor $2x^2 + 3x + 1$ equal to 0. The big advantage is that after finding a zero we may lower by 1 the degree of the equation we are solving. When we reach a second-degree equation, as in this case, we may apply the quadratic formula or (sometimes) the factoring method.

$$2x^2 + 3x + 1 = 0$$
$$(2x + 1)(x + 1) = 0$$
$$2x + 1 = 0 \qquad x + 1 = 0$$
$$x = -\frac{1}{2} \qquad x = -1$$

Thus the zeros are -1, -1, and $-1/2$. Remember that it is possible for a number to be counted as a zero more than once, and in this case we say -1 is a zero of multiplicity 2. Based on the x- and y-intercepts and the multiplicity of each zero, the function is graphed in Figure 11.21.

Technology Link

With a grapher it is possible to begin the analysis in this problem by first graphing the function in the standard viewing window, as shown in Figure 11.22, and then refining this graph so the x-intercepts are more apparent, as shown in Figure 11.23. This method will help you to locate quickly potential rational-number zeros.

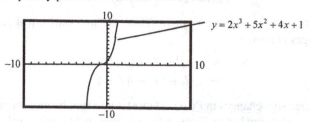

Figure 11.22

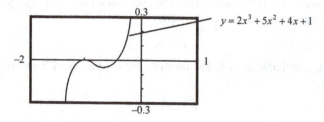

Figure 11.23

PROGRESS CHECK 2 Find the zeros of $P(x) = 2x^3 - 7x^2 + 8x - 3$. ■

For the next example we add another useful rule, which permits us to establish upper and lower bounds on the zeros of a polynomial function.

Upper and Lower Bounds Theorem

1. If we divide a polynomial $P(x)$ synthetically by $x - b$, where $b > 0$ and all the numbers in the bottom row have the same signs, then there is no zero greater than b. We say that b is an **upper bound** for the zeros of $y = P(x)$.

2. If we divide a polynomial $P(x)$ synthetically by $x - c$, where $c < 0$ and the numbers in the bottom row alternate in sign, then there is no zero less than c. We say that c is a **lower bound** for the zeros of $y = P(x)$.

For the purposes of these tests, zero may be denoted as $+0$ or -0.

A rationale for these tests is contained in the next example.

EXAMPLE 3   Finding Zeros of a Fourth-Degree Polynomial Function

Find the zeros of $P(x) = 2x^4 - 5x^3 + 11x^2 - 3x - 5$.

Solution   A systematic algebraic approach to obtaining the zeros is given in steps **a** to **e**.

a. Use Descartes' rule of signs to determine the maximum number of positive and negative real zeros.

$$P(x) = 2x^4 - 5x^3 + 11x^2 - 3x - 5$$

There are three sign changes in $P(x)$. Thus, the number of positive real zeros is three or one.

$$\begin{aligned} P(-x) &= 2(-x)^4 - 5(-x)^3 + 11(-x)^2 - 3(-x) - 5 \\ &= 2x^4 + 5x^3 + 11x^2 + 3x - 5 \end{aligned}$$

There is one sign change in $P(-x)$, so Descartes' rule of signs guarantees exactly one negative *real* zero in this case.

b. Determine the possible rational zeros. The constant term a_0 is -5. The possibilities for p are the integers that are factors of -5. Thus,

$$p = \pm 5, \pm 1.$$

The leading coefficient a_n is 2. The integral factors of 2 give the possibilities for q. Thus,

$$q = \pm 2, \pm 1.$$

The possible rational zeros are then

$$5, \frac{5}{2}, 1, \frac{1}{2}, -\frac{1}{2}, -1, -\frac{5}{2}, -5.$$

c. We test negative zeros first, because part **a** indicated that there is, at most, one negative zero. If we find a negative zero, we then switch to the positive possibilities. Pick -1, a number in the middle of the negative choices. If it is not a zero, it may be a lower bound that eliminates other possibilities.

$$\underline{-1|}\quad\begin{array}{rrrrr} 2 & -5 & 11 & -3 & -5 \\ & -2 & 7 & -18 & 21 \\ \hline 2 & -7 & 18 & -21 & 16 \end{array}$$

The remainder is 16, so -1 is not a zero. We tested a negative possibility, and the numbers in the bottom row alternate in sign. Thus, there is no zero less than -1, as specified in statement 2 of the above theorem. To see why, note that if we test a negative choice, say c, greater in absolute value than -1, then the numbers in the bottom row of the synthetic division will continue to alternate in sign with respective numbers of greater absolute value (after the first entry) than our previous bottom row $(2, -7, 18, -21, 16)$. Thus $P(c) > 16$ when $c < -1$, so -1 is a lower bound for the zeros of $y = P(x)$. This eliminates $-5/2$ and -5, so try $-1/2$.

$$\underline{-\tfrac{1}{2}|}\quad\begin{array}{rrrrr} 2 & -5 & 11 & -3 & -5 \\ & -1 & 3 & -7 & 5 \\ \hline 2 & -6 & 14 & -10 & 0 \end{array}$$

Since the remainder is zero, $P(-1/2) = 0$. Thus, $-1/2$ is a zero of the function.

d. Since $-1/2$ is a zero, $x - (-1/2)$ is a factor, and we write

$$2x^4 - 5x^3 + 11x^2 - 3x - 5 = \left(x + \frac{1}{2}\right)(2x^3 - 6x^2 + 14x - 10).$$

We now try to find the values of x for which $2x^3 - 6x^2 + 14x - 10$ equals 0. We found the one negative zero, so we switch to the positive possibilities. Pick 1. If it is not a zero, the numbers in the bottom row in the synthetic division may have the same sign. Such a result would establish 1 as an upper bound for the zeros (thereby eliminating 5/2 and 5), since any synthetic division by $x - b$, where $b > 1$, would continue to produce bottom-row entries that have the same sign and even larger absolute values (after the first entry) than those that result from the division involving $b = 1$.

$$\underline{1|}\quad \begin{array}{rrrr} 2 & -6 & 14 & -10 \\ & 2 & -4 & 10 \\ \hline 2 & -4 & 10 & 0 \end{array}$$

Therefore, 1 is a zero of the function.

e. We now use the quadratic formula to complete the solution.

$$2x^2 - 4x + 10 = 0$$
$$x^2 - 2x + 5 = 0$$
$$x = \frac{-(-2) \pm \sqrt{(-2)^2 - 4(1)(5)}}{2(1)} = \frac{2 \pm \sqrt{-16}}{2} = \frac{2 \pm 4i}{2} = 1 \pm 2i$$

The zeros are $-1/2$, 1, $1 + 2i$, and $1 - 2i$.

A graph of this function which illustrates the two real-number zeros, is shown in Figure 11.24.

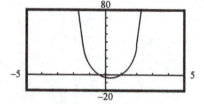

Figure 11.24

Technology Link

Some calculators have a built-in feature that may be used to solve polynomial equations. For instance, Figure 11.25 shows the coefficient entry screen and the solution screen associated with solving the equation in this example, on a particular calculator with a Polynomial Root-Finding feature. Observe that the calculator output displays the complex number $a + bi$ in the form (a, b).

PROGRESS CHECK 3   Find the zeros of $P(x) = 2x^4 - 9x^3 + 42x - 20$.   ■

```
a4X^4+...+a1X+a0=0
 a4=2
 a3=-5
 a2=11
 a1=-3
 a0=-5
```
(a)

```
a4X^4+...+a1X+a0=0
 x1■(1,2)
 x2=(1,-2)
 x3=(1,0)
 x4=(-.5,0)
```
(b)

Figure 11.25

EXAMPLE 4   Solving a Volume Problem

Solve the problem in the section introduction on page 598.

Solution   If x represents the height of the carton, then $x + 3$ and $x + 1$ represent the length and width, respectively. Since the formula for the volume is $V = lwh$ and the volume of the carton is 30 ft³, we have

$$(x + 3)(x + 1)x = 30$$
$$x^3 + 4x^2 + 3x = 30$$
$$x^3 + 4x^2 + 3x - 30 = 0$$

The possible rational zeros are then

$$30, 15, 10, 6, 5, 3, 2, 1.$$

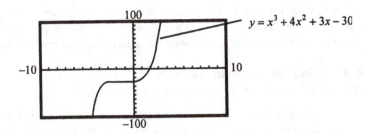

Figure 11.26

We can determine that 2 is a solution either by graphing the associated function, as shown in Figure 11.26, or by testing possibilities with the aid of the upper bound theorem. The synthetic division that confirms that 2 is a solution is shown next.

$$\underline{2\rfloor}\ \ \begin{array}{rrrr} 1 & 4 & 3 & -30 \\ & 2 & 12 & 30 \\ \hline 1 & 6 & 15 & 0 \end{array}$$

The two other roots are then determined by solving $x^2 + 6x + 15 = 0$. However, since the discriminant ($b^2 - 4ac$) is less than 0, these roots are not real numbers. Thus, the only real-number solution is 2, and the box has unique dimensions of 5 ft by 3 ft by 2 ft.

PROGRESS CHECK 4   The volume of a rectangular box is to be 350 in.^{3}. If the width is 2 in. greater than the height, and the length is twice the height, show that only one set of dimensions is possible for the given box. What are these dimensions?   ■

Up to this point we have limited our discussion to finding rational zeros of polynomial functions of degree greater than 2. Unfortunately, irrational zeros of higher-degree polynomial functions are usually very difficult to find algebraically. Complicated formulas are available for polynomial functions of degrees 3 and 4, and it can be shown that no formula exists for degree 5 and greater. In such cases, numerical methods that utilize a grapher or a computer are employed to approximate irrational zeros, and this topic is usually considered in detail in a course in numerical analysis. For our purposes, we need only illustrate the following two theorems which enable us to approximate zeros of polynomial functions.

Intermediate Value Theorem for Polynomials

Let $y = P(x)$ be a polynomial function. If a and b are real numbers with $a < b$, and if d is any number between $P(a)$ and $P(b)$, inclusive, then there is at least one number c in the interval $[a, b]$ such that $P(c) = d$.

This result is easy to see geometrically. Consider Figure 11.27 and keep in mind that the graph of a polynomial function is an unbroken curve. Through any number d between $P(a)$ and $P(b)$, inclusive, a horizontal line may be drawn that must intersect the graph of $y = P(x)$ at least once in the interval $[a, b]$. Then, the x-coordinate of an intersection point is a number c in the interval $[a, b]$ such that $P(c) = d$.

The intermediate value theorem is used in many ways when analyzing polynomial functions, and a special case of this theorem, called the *location theorem*, may be used to approximate zeros of such functions. When $P(a)$ and $P(b)$ are opposite in sign, then 0 is between $P(a)$ and $P(b)$ so the intermediate value theorem guarantees that there is at least one number c in the interval (a, b) such that $P(c) = 0$. Thus, $y = P(x)$ has at least one real zero between a and b, which leads to the following result.

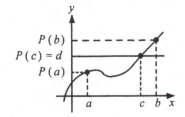

Figure 11.27

Location Theorem

Let $y = P(x)$ be a polynomial function. If $P(a)$ and $P(b)$ have opposite signs, then $y = P(x)$ has at least one real zero between a and b.

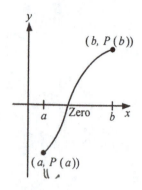

Figure 11.28

The geometric interpretation of this theorem is shown in Figure 11.28. Since the graph is on different sides of the x-axis at a and b, and no breaks are possible, the graph must cross the x-axis between a and b, guaranteeing at least one real zero in this interval.

EXAMPLE 5 Using the Location Theorem
Verify that $P(x) = 3x^3 + 16x^2 - 8$ has a zero between −5 and −6.

Solution By direct substitution or synthetic division, we determine that $P(-5) = 17$ and $P(-6) = -80$. Since $P(-5)$ and $P(-6)$ have opposite signs, the location theorem assures us of at least one real zero between −5 and −6. This zero can be seen in the graph of the function that is shown in Figure 11.29.

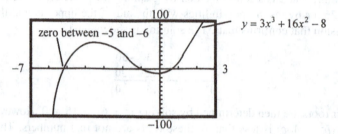

Figure 11.29

PROGRESS CHECK 5 Verify that $P(x) = 3x^3 + 16x^2 - 8$ has zero between 0 and 1. ■

Once we have determined an interval that contains a zero, the job is to keep narrowing the interval until we obtain a sufficient degree of accuracy. The most efficient methods for narrowing the interval are developed in calculus. A simple and relatively effective alternative is basically to halve the interval each time until we attain a specified accuracy.

EXAMPLE 6 Approximating a Zero of a Polynomial Function
To the nearest tenth, approximate the zero of the function $P(x) = 3x^3 + 16x^2 - 8$ that is between −5 and −6.

Solution By using the location theorem and a calculator, and by successively halving the intervals, we determine the following.

Calculation	Comment: A Zero is Between
$P(-5) = 17$	
$P(-6) = -80$	−5 and −6
$P(-5.5) \approx -23$	−5 and −5.5
$P(-5.25) \approx -1.1$	−5 and −5.25
$P(-5.13) \approx 8.1$	−5.13 and −5.25
$P(-5.19) \approx 3.6$	−5.19 and −5.25

Thus, to the nearest tenth, a zero is −5.2. Figure 11.30 shows a check of this answer on a grapher.

PROGRESS CHECK 6 To the nearest tenth, approximate the zero of the function $P(x) = 3x^3 + 16x^2 - 8$ that is between 0 and 1. ■

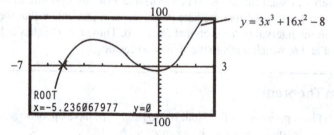

Figure 11.30

EXERCISES 11.3

In Exercises 1–4 list the possible rational zeros of the function.

1. $P(x) = x^3 + 8x^2 - 10x - 20$
2. $P(x) = x^4 - 3x^3 + x^2 - x - 6$
3. $P(x) = 4x^4 - 3x^3 + x^2 - x - 6$
4. $P(x) = 3x^3 + 7x^2 + 8$

In Exercises 5–8 use Descartes' rule of signs to determine the maximum number of positive and negative real zeros.

5. $P(x) = x^3 - 2x^2 + x - 3$
6. $P(x) = 5x^3 + x^2 + 4x + 1$
7. $P(x) = 2x^4 + 5x^3 - x^2 - 3x - 7$
8. $P(x) = x^8 + 1$

In Exercises 9–18 find the zeros of the function.

9. $P(x) = x^3 - x^2 - 10x - 8$
10. $P(x) = x^3 + 6x^2 + 11x + 6$
11. $P(x) = 3x^3 + x^2 + 15x + 5$
12. $P(x) = 4x^3 - x^2 - 28x + 7$
13. $P(x) = 8x^3 - 12x^2 + 6x - 1$
14. $P(x) = 3x^3 + 16x^2 - 8$
15. $P(x) = 4x^4 - 5x^3 - 2x^2 - 3x - 10$
16. $P(x) = x^4 - 6x^3 + 7x^2 + 12x - 18$
17. $P(x) = 2x^4 + 7x^3 + 25x^2 + 47x + 18$
18. $P(x) = 6x^4 + 11x^3 - 63x^2 - 7x + 5$

In Exercises 19–22 answer the following questions with respect to the given functions.

a. What are all the zeros of the function?
b. How many zeros are the rational numbers? Name them.
c. How many zeros are real numbers? Name them.
d. How many zeros are imaginary numbers? Name them.

19. $P(x) = x^3 - x^2 - 2x - 12$
20. $P(x) = x^3 + 7x^2 + 12x + 6$
21. $P(x) = 3x^4 + 5x^3 - 23x^2 - 35x + 14$
22. $P(x) = 10x^4 + 35x^3 - 73x^2 + 7x - 15$
23. The volume of a rectangular box is 105 in.³. If the width is 2 in. greater than the height, and the length is 1 in. greater than twice the height, show that only one set of dimensions is possible for the given box. What are these dimensions?
24. The volume of a rectangular box is 20 ft³. If the box has a square base and the height is 3 ft greater than the measure of the edges of the base, show that only one set of dimensions is possible for the given box. What are these dimensions?
25. A rectangular piece of cardboard 12 in. by 18 in. is to be used to make an open-top box, by cutting a small square from each corner and bending up the sides. If the volume of the box is to be 216 in.³, then find the length of the side of the square that is to be cut from each corner.

26. A rectangular sheet of tin 20 cm by 24 cm has identical squares cut out from each corner. The sides are then turned up to form an open box. Find the side length for each square cutout, given that the volume is to be 640 cm³.

In Exercises 27–30 use the location theorem and verify each statement.

27. $P(x) = 3x^3 + 16x^2 - 8$ has a zero between 0 and –1.
28. $P(x) = 4x^3 - x^2 - 28x + 7$ has a zero between 2 and 3.
29. $P(x) = x^4 - 6x^3 + 7x^2 + 12x - 18$ has a zero between 1 and 2 and another zero between –1 and –2.
30. $P(x) = 6x^4 + 11x^3 - 63x^2 - 7x + 5$ has a zero between 0 and 1 and another zero between –4 and –5.

In Exercises 31–36 approximate the zero of the function in the given interval to the nearest tenth.

31. $P(x) = x^3 + x - 1$; a zero is between 0.6 and 0.7.
32. $P(x) = x^3 + x^2 - 10x - 10$; a zero is between –3.1 and –3.2.
33. $P(x) = x^3 - 3x + 1$; a zero is between 0 and 1.
34. $P(x) = x^3 - 3x + 1$; a zero is between 1 and 2.
35. $P(x) = 2x^3 - 5x^2 - 3x + 9$; a zero is between –1 and –2.
36. $P(x) = 2x^3 - 5x^2 - 3x + 9$; a zero is between 2 and 3.

THINK ABOUT IT 11.3

1. Find a polynomial function that has 1 zero between 2 and 3. Find a polynomial function that has 2 zeros between 2 and 3. Find a polynomial function that has 4 zeros between 2 and 3. What is the minimum degree possible for a polynomial function that has 10 zeros between 2 and 3?
2. If $P(x) = x^3 + px + q$, determine the nature of the zeros when
   a. p and q are both positive and
   b. p is positive and q is negative.
3. Consider the function defined by $f(x) = x^n + a$.
   a. If n is a positive even integer and a is a negative real number, find in terms of n the number of zeros of f that are not real numbers.
   b. Find in terms of n the number of zeros of f that are not real numbers, if n is a positive odd integer and a is a positive real number.
4. Use the rational-zero theorem and the function $P(x) = x^2 - 2$ to show that $\sqrt{2}$ is not a rational number.
5. Show that $\sqrt[5]{7}$ is not a rational number, by using the rational-zero theorem.

Courtesy of Medioimages/Photodisc.

11.4 Rational Functions

A regional telephone company charges 25 cents per minute plus an 80-cent surcharge for a typical call made with its calling card. Therefore, the average cost (y) of a call per minute is given by

$$y = \frac{25x + 80}{x},$$

where x is the length of the call in minutes, and y is measured in cents.

a. What is the total cost for a 10-minute call? What is the average cost per minute for a 10-minute call?

b. Graph the function and describe how y changes as x increases for $x > 0$. What is the significance of the horizontal asymptote?

(See Example 4.)

OBJECTIVES

1 Determine any vertical and horizontal asymptotes for rational function and graph the function.

2 Determine any vertical and slant asymptotes for a rational function and graph the function.

3 Graph rational functions that involve common factors.

In the section-opening problem, the formula for the average cost per minute of a certain type of telephone call is

$$y = \frac{25x + 80}{x}.$$

This equation is an example of a formula that involves a quotient of two polynomials. In general, a function of the form

$$y = \frac{P(x)}{Q(x)},$$

where $P(x)$ and $Q(x)$ are polynomials with $Q(x) \neq 0$, is called a **rational function.** Some additional examples of rational functions are

$$y = \frac{1}{x}, \; y = \frac{2x^2 + x - 3}{x^2}, \text{ and } y = \frac{x^2 - 1}{x + 2}.$$

The behavior of a rational function often differs dramatically from that of a polynomial function. This difference may be seen easily by comparing the graph of a rational function to the smooth unbroken curves that characterize polynomial functions.

Consider the rational function $y = 1/x$. Since division by zero is undefined, x cannot equal zero. Thus, the graph of this function does not intersect the line $x = 0$ (the y-axis). We can, however, let x approach zero and consider x values as close to zero as we wish. From the following tables, note that as the x values squeeze in on zero, $|y|$ becomes larger.

x	1	0.5	0.1	0.01	0.001
$y = \dfrac{1}{x}$	1	2	10	100	1,000

x	−1	−0.5	−0.1	−0.01	−0.001
$y = \dfrac{1}{x}$	−1	−2	−10	−100	−1,000

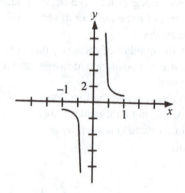

Figure 11.31

Figure 11.31 shows the behavior of $y = 1/x$ in the interval $-1 \leq x \leq 1$. The vertical line $x = 0$ that the curve approaches, but never touches, is called a **vertical asymptote.** We may use the following rule to determine if the graph of a rational function has any vertical asymptotes.

Vertical Asymptotes

If $P(x)$ and $Q(x)$ have no common factors, then the graph of the rational function $y = P(x)/Q(x)$ has as a vertical asymptote the line $x = a$ for each real number a at which $Q(a) = 0$.

Initially we will consider only functions where $P(x)$ and $Q(x)$ have no common factors, so the rational function is in lowest terms. In this case the rule above indicates that a vertical asymptote occurs whenever the denominator is zero.

EXAMPLE 1   Finding Vertical Asymptotes

Find any vertical asymptotes of the function

$$y = \frac{x + 1}{(x - 3)(x + 2)}.$$

Solution   The polynomial in the denominator

$$Q(x) = (x - 3)(x + 2)$$

equals 0 when x is 3 or –2. Thus, there are two vertical asymptotes: $x = 3$ and $x = -2$. **Note:** As a visual aid, the graph of this function is shown in Figure 11.32. By the end of this section, we will have developed sufficient techniques for you to be able to draw this graph.)

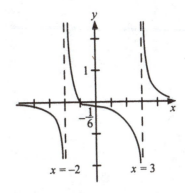

Figure 11.32

PROGRESS CHECK 1   Find any vertical asymptotes of $y = \dfrac{3x}{x^2 - 4}$.   ■

To complete the graph of $y = 1/x$, we must consider the behavior of the function as $|x|$ becomes larger (this is called the end behavior of the function). It is not difficult to see that $1/x$ squeezes in on zero from the positive side when x takes on larger positive values. Similarly, $1/x$ squeezes in on zero from the negative side when x increases in magnitude in the negative direction. Thus, the curve gets closer to the line $y = 0$, and the x-axis is a **horizontal asymptote.** Figure 11.33 shows a graph of $y = 1/x$.

Identifying any vertical and horizontal asymptotes is very important. These lines, together with plotting the intercepts and a few points, enable us to graph a rational function. A technique for determining horizontal asymptotes is included in the following examples.

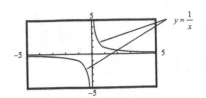

Figure 11.33

EXAMPLE 2   Graphing a Rational Function

If $y = \dfrac{x - 1}{x + 1}$, find any asymptotes and graph the function.

Solution   Steps **a** to **d** outline a systematic approach to graphing this function.

a. The polynomial in the denominator $x + 1$ equals zero when x is –1. Thus, $x = -1$ is a vertical asymptote.

b. To determine any horizontal asymptotes, we change the form of the function by dividing each term in the numerator and the denominator by the highest power of x in the expression.

$$y = \frac{x - 1}{x + 1} = \frac{\frac{x}{x} - \frac{1}{x}}{\frac{x}{x} + \frac{1}{x}} = \frac{1 - \frac{1}{x}}{1 + \frac{1}{x}} \quad \text{(assuming that } x \neq 0\text{)}$$

Now as $|x|$ gets larger, $1/x$ approaches zero. Thus, y approaches $(1 - 0)/(1 + 0)$, and $y = 1$ is a horizontal asymptote.

c. By setting $x = 0$, we determine that $(0, -1)$ is the y-intercept. Similarly, by setting $y = 0$, we determine that $(1, 0)$ is the x-intercept.

d. The vertical asymptote divides the x-axis into two regions. The intercepts are two points to the right of $x = -1$. If we plot a couple of points to the left of the vertical asymptote, say $(-2, 3)$ and $(-3, 2)$, we may complete the graph (see Figure 11.34).

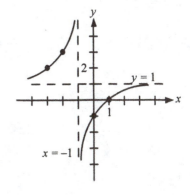

Figure 11.34

Technology Link

When graphing rational functions on a grapher, extra care is often needed to determine an appropriate viewing window and to decide whether Connected Mode or Dot Mode gives a more recognizable graph. For instance, Figure 11.35 shows a graph of the function in this example using the standard viewing window and Connected Mode. Note that the calculator erroneously draws an almost vertical line at about $x = -1$ because it is set to connect points that are in separate pieces of the graph.

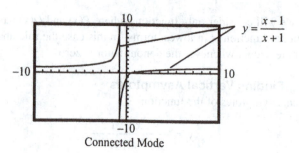

Connected Mode

Figure 11.35

One way to make the graph more readable may be to switch the calculator to Dot Mode and redraw the graph in the viewing window as shown in Figure 11.36. Now the graph is centered about the two asymptotes, and only the calculated points for the function are displayed. You should be prepared to experiment with different viewing windows and graphing modes when graphing a rational function, until you obtain a picture you can interpret. However, under no circumstances should your hand-drawn graph show solid lines at vertical asymptotes, like those that may appear on a calculator screen.

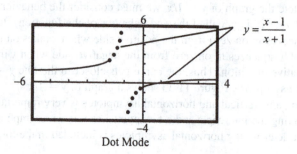

Dot Mode

Figure 11.36

PROGRESS CHECK 2   If $y = \dfrac{4x - 5}{2x + 6}$, find any asymptotes and graph the function. ■

In Example 2 an important question is unanswered. We know that as $|x|$ becomes large, y approaches, but never quite reaches, 1. How do we know that y is not 1 when $|x|$ is small? We answer this question by determining if there is any value of x for which

$$\frac{x - 1}{x + 1} = 1.$$

Solving this equation, we have

$$x - 1 = x + 1$$
$$-1 = 1 \quad \text{false.}$$

The equation has no solution, and we may conclude that the curve never crosses the horizontal asymptote. Example 3 illustrates why this possibility must be considered.

EXAMPLE 3   Graphing a Rational Function

If $y = \dfrac{2x^2 + x - 3}{x^2}$, find any asymptotes and graph the function.

Solution   A systematic algebraic approach to obtaining the graph is given in steps **a** to **e**.

a. The polynomial in the denominator equals zero when x is zero. Thus, $x = 0$ is a vertical asymptote.

b. To determine any horizontal asymptotes, we use the procedure from Example 2. Dividing each term in the numerator and the denominator by x^2 gives

$$y = \frac{\frac{2x^2}{x^2} + \frac{x}{x^2} - \frac{3}{x^2}}{\frac{x^2}{x^2}} = \frac{2 + \frac{1}{x} - \frac{3}{x^2}}{1} \quad (x \neq 0).$$

As $|x|$ gets larger, $1/x$ and $-3/x^2$ approach 0. Thus, y approaches 2, and $y = 2$ is a horizontal asymptote.

c. To determine if the curve ever crosses the horizontal asymptote, find out if there are any values of x for which

$$\frac{2x^2 + x - 3}{x^2} = 2.$$

Solving this equation for x, we have

$$2x^2 + x - 3 = 2x^2$$
$$x - 3 = 0$$
$$x = 3.$$

The curve crosses the asymptote at $(3, 2)$.

d. Since x cannot be zero, there is no y-intercept. After setting $y = 0$, we solve the equation $2x^2 + x - 3 = 0$ to find the x-intercepts $(1, 0)$ and $(-3/2, 0)$.

e. To determine the behavior of the curve before it drops and starts approaching 2, we plot a couple of points to the right of $x = 3$, say $(4, 33/16)$ and $(5, 52/25)$. Additional points may always be plotted. Figure 11.37 shows the graph of the function.

Figure 11.37

Technology Link

Figure 11.38 shows a complete graph of the function in this example on a grapher. Observe that it is not easy to recognize in this graph that the curve crosses the horizontal asymptote at $(3, 2)$ and then approaches $y = 2$ from above. However, this behavior is apparent if we adjust the viewing window and also graph $y = 2$ as shown in Figure 11.39.

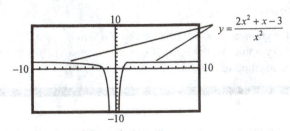

Figure 11.38

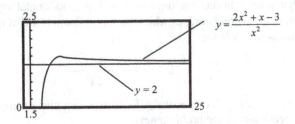

Figure 11.39

PROGRESS CHECK 3 If $y = \dfrac{2x^2 - 2}{x^3}$, find any asymptotes and graph the function. ■

There are two theorems about asymptotes that can simplify our work. The first theorem indicates the behavior of the graph near any vertical asymptote. It is based on the fact that even powers of positive and negative numbers have the same sign (positive), while odd powers of positive and negative numbers are opposite in sign.

Graph of $y = P(x)/Q(x)$ Near Vertical Asymptotes

If $P(x)$ and $Q(x)$ have no common factors, and if $(x - a)^n$ is a factor of $Q(x)$, where n is the largest positive integer for which this statement is true, then:

1. The graph of $y = P(x)/Q(x)$ goes in opposite directions about the vertical asymptote $x = a$ when n is odd.
2. The graph of $y = P(x)/Q(x)$ goes in the same direction about the vertical asymptote $x = a$ when n is even.

For instance, in Example 2 the graph goes to positive infinity on the left side of $x = -1$ and to negative infinity on the right side (see Figure 11.34). We can predict this type of behavior since $Q(x) = (x + 1)^1$, and the odd exponent indicates that the graph goes in opposite directions about the vertical asymptote. In Example 3, however, $Q(x) = x^2$, and the even exponent indicates that the graph goes in the same direction (to negative infinity) about the vertical asymptote ($x = 0$), as shown in Figure 11.37.

The second theorem about asymptotes enables us to pick out horizontal asymptotes almost by inspection. This theorem may be derived by using the procedure shown in Examples 2 and 3 for determining a horizontal asymptote, and applying it to the general form for a rational function given below.

Horizontal Asymptote Theorem

The graph of the rational function

$$y = \frac{P(x)}{Q(x)} = \frac{a_n x^n + a_{n-1} x^{n-1} + \cdots + a_0}{b_m x^m + b_{m-1} x^{m-1} + \cdots + b_0},$$

where $a_n, b_m \neq 0$, has

1. a horizontal asymptote at $y = 0$ (the x-axis) if $n < m$
2. a horizontal asymptote at $y = a_n/b_m$ if $n = m$
3. no horizontal asymptote if $n > m$

For instance, the graph of $y = 1/x$ satisfies the first case, since the numerator is a zero-degree polynomial while the denominator is a first-degree polynomial. Since the higher-degree polynomial is in the denominator, $y = 0$ is a horizontal asymptote. Examples 2 and 3 illustrate the second case, in which both polynomials are of the same degree. Thus, the horizontal asymptotes for

$$y = \frac{1x - 1}{1x + 1} \text{ and } y = \frac{2x^2 + x - 3}{1x^2}$$

are $y = 1/1 = 1$ and $y = 2/1 = 2$, respectively. To illustrate another example of the second case, we solve the section-opening problem next.

EXAMPLE 4   Average Cost of Using a Calling Card

Solve the problem in the section introduction on page 606.

Solution

a. The telephone company charges 25 cents per minute plus an 80-cent surcharge, so the total cost c of a 10-minute call is

$$c = 25(10) + 80 = 330 \text{ cents or } \$3.30.$$

The formula $y = (25x + 80)/x$ gives the average cost (y) of a call per minute. For a 10-minute call,

$$y = \frac{25(10) + 80}{10} = 33$$

Thus, the average cost per minute for a 10-minute call is 33 cents per minute.

b. To graph $y = (25x + 80)/x$ for $x > 0$, first determine any asymptotes.

Vertical asymptote: The polynomial in the denominator equals zero when x is zero. Thus, $x = 0$ is a vertical asymptote.

Horizontal asymptote: The polynomial in the numerator has the same degree (degree 1) as the polynomial in the denominator. So the horizontal asymptote for

$$y = \frac{25x + 80}{1x}$$

is $y = 25/1 = 25$. To determine if the curve ever crosses the horizontal asymptote, we set $y = 25$ and solve

$$25 = \frac{25x + 80}{x}.$$

This equation is equivalent to $25x = 25x + 80$, which is never true. Therefore the curve does not cross the horizontal asymptote.

Figure 11.40 gives a graph of this function that shows the curve approaching these asymptotes. Observe that as x increases for $x > 0$, the average cost per minute always decreases. However, y decreases rapidly at first, and then y levels off and approaches $y = 25$. Thus, the horizontal asymptote is significant because it reveals that as the length of the call increases, the average cost per minute approaches 25 cents, which is the charge per minute for the call.

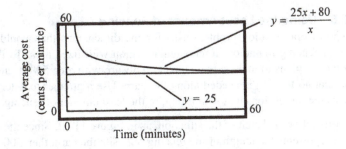

Figure 11.40

PROGRESS CHECK 4   Redo the problem in Example 4 given that the company charges 30 cents per minute plus a 50-cent surcharge. The average cost per minute is then given by $y = \dfrac{30x + 50}{x}$.   ■

When there are no horizontal asymptotes as described in the third case of the horizontal asymptote theorem, other techniques may be employed. In particular, if $n = m + 1$ (that is, if the degree of the numerator is one more than the degree of the denominator), then the graph has a slant or oblique asymptote, as discussed in the next example.

EXAMPLE 5　Graphing a Rational Function with a Slant Asymptote

If $f(x) = \dfrac{x^2 - 1}{x + 2}$ find any asymptotes and graph the function.

Solution　Steps **a** to **d** outline a systematic approach to graphing this function.

a. The polynomial in the denominator equals zero when x is -2. Thus, $x = -2$ is a vertical asymptote. Also, since $Q(x) = (x + 2)^1$, $Q(x)$ is an odd power of $x + 2$, so the graph of f goes in opposite directions about $x = -2$.

b. Because the higher-degree polynomial is in the numerator, there is no horizontal asymptote. However, we can change the form of the equation by dividing $x^2 - 1$ by $x + 2$ as follows:

$$
\begin{array}{r}
x - 2 \\
x + 2 \overline{)\,x^2 - 1} \\
\underline{x^2 + 2x } \\
-2x - 1 \\
\underline{-2x - 4} \\
3.
\end{array}
$$

Thus,

$$ f(x) = \frac{x^2 - 1}{x + 2} = x - 2 + \frac{3}{x + 2}. $$

Now as $|x|$ gets larger, $3/(x + 2)$ approaches 0, and y approaches $x - 2$. Thus, the graph of f approaches the oblique (neither horizontal nor vertical) line $y = x - 2$, and we call this line a **slant asymptote** of the graph of f.

c. By setting $x = 0$, we may determine that $(0, -1/2)$ is the y-intercept. Similarly, by setting $f(x) = 0$, we may determine that $(1, 0)$ and $(-1, 0)$ are x-intercepts.

d. Using the above information and plotting one point to the left of the vertical asymptote, say $(-3, -8)$, we draw the graph in Figure 11.41.

Use a grapher to check the results in this example.

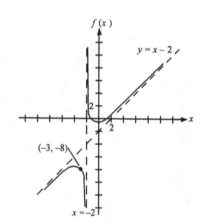

Figure 11.41

PROGRESS CHECK 5　If $f(x) = \dfrac{x^2 - 4}{x - 1}$, find any asymptotes and graph the function.

■

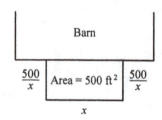

Figure 11.42

EXAMPLE 6　Using the Least Amount of Fencing

A classic type of optimization problem asks for the dimensions that would require the least amount of fencing to enclose a rectangular region with fixed area. To illustrate, assume that a farmer plans to make a rectangular enclosure with area 500 ft² along the side of a barn, so that no fencing is needed along the barn. Use a grapher to determine to two decimal places the dimensions that would require the least amount of fencing.

Solution　First, draw a sketch of the situation, as in Figure 11.42. Since the area is fixed at 500 ft², if x represents the length of the fencing opposite the barn, then $500/x$ represents the length of the fencing perpendicular to the barn. So the length y of the required fencing is given by

$$ y = x + 2\left(\frac{500}{x}\right) $$

$$ = x + \frac{1000}{x}. $$

From the form of the equation, it is apparent that the graph has a vertical asymptote at $x = 0$ and a slant asymptote at $y = x$. Figure 11.43 gives a graph of this function for $x > 0$ that

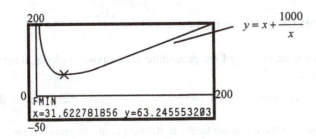

Figure 11.43

shows the curve approaching these asymptotes. To find the lowest point in the graph you may use the Zoom and Trace features (or a Function Minimum feature, if available) to determine that $x \approx 31.62$ at the minimum point. The other side dimension is given by $500/x$, so this side length is

$$\frac{500}{31.62} \approx 15.81.$$

Thus, the least amount of fencing is required when the length of the fencing opposite the barn is 31.62 ft, and the length of the fencing perpendicular to the barn is 15.81 ft.

Note: In a calculus course, algebraic methods are developed for finding the exact value of x that minimizes the amount of fencing. In this problem, that dimension is $x = \sqrt{1000}$ ft.

PROGRESS CHECK 6   Redo the problem in Example 6, but assume that fencing is needed on all four sides (including the side along the barn).   ■

In our statements about rational functions, we have assumed that $P(x)$ and $Q(x)$ had no common factors. If the same factor does appear in the numerator and the denominator, we can divide it out as long as we keep track of all values that make the factor zero. The next example illustrates such a case.

EXAMPLE 7   Graphing a Rational Function with Common Factors

Graph the function $f(x) = \dfrac{x^2 - 4}{x - 2}$.

Solution   By factoring the numerator, we rewrite the expression as

$$f(x) = \frac{x^2 - 4}{x - 2} = \frac{(x + 2)(x - 2)}{x - 2}.$$

If $x = 2$, the expression becomes $0/0$, which is undefined. If $x \neq 2$, we can divide out common factors and obtain $x + 2$. Thus, we can rewrite the expression as follows:

$$f(x) = \frac{x^2 - 4}{x - 2} = \frac{(x + 2)(x - 2)}{x - 2} = \begin{cases} x + 2 & \text{if} \quad x \neq 2 \\ \text{undefined} & \text{if} \quad x = 2. \end{cases}$$

As shown in Figure 11.44, the graph is the set of all points on the line $f(x) = x + 2$ except $(2, 4)$.

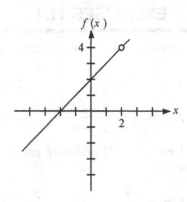

Figure 11.44

Technology Link

On a grapher the graph of $y = (x^2 - 4)/(x - 2)$ is indistinguishable from the graph of $y = x + 2$, unless a trace point coincides with $(2, 4)$. So be careful in your graph to account for all values that make the denominator zero.

PROGRESS CHECK 7   Graph the function $f(x) = \dfrac{x^2 - x}{x - 1}$.

Finally, here is an outline of the procedure for graphing rational functions with the form $y = P(x)/Q(x)$.

1. If $P(x)$ and $Q(x)$ have common factors, we can divide them out on the following conditions:
   a. If the degree of the common factor in the numerator is greater than or equal to the degree of the common factor in the denominator, then any value of x that makes the common factor zero produces a hole in the graph, as shown in Example 7.
   b. If the degree of the common factor in the numerator is less than the degree of the common factor in the denominator, then any value of x that makes the common factor zero produces a vertical asymptote.
2. If $P(x)$ and $Q(x)$ have no common factors, find any vertical asymptotes by solving $Q(x) = 0$. Determine the behavior of the graph near any vertical asymptote by using the theorem given in this section.
3. Find any horizontal asymptotes by using the horizontal asymptote theorem or by dividing each term by the highest power of x and determining the value approached by y as $|x|$ gets larger. If the degree of the numerator is one more than the degree of the denominator, then determine a slant asymptote by dividing $P(x)$ and $Q(x)$ and setting y equal to the quotient.
4. Check if the curve crosses the horizontal asymptote for small values of x by finding if there are any values of x for which $P(x)/Q(x)$ equals the value of the horizontal asymptote. There's no need to check for crossings of vertical asymptotes—they can't happen.
5. Find any x-intercepts by setting $y = 0$ and solving $P(x) = 0$. Find any y-intercepts by setting $x = 0$ and evaluating the expression.
6. Plot additional points as needed and draw the graph. Use a grapher to check all of your results.

EXERCISES 11.4

In Exercises 1–4 find any vertical asymptotes of the function.

1. $y = \dfrac{x + 7}{2x - 3}$

2. $y = \dfrac{x^2 + 1}{x(x + 4)}$

3. $y = \dfrac{2}{x^2 - 5x - 6}$

4. $y = \dfrac{x - 3}{x^2 + x}$

In Exercises 5–24 determine any asymptotes and graph the function.

5. $y = \dfrac{-1}{x}$

6. $y = \dfrac{3}{x^2}$

7. $y = \dfrac{2}{x + 1}$

8. $y = \dfrac{-5}{3x + 2}$

9. $y = \dfrac{x - 2}{x + 2}$

10. $y = \dfrac{x + 3}{x - 5}$

11. $y = \dfrac{2x - 5}{3x + 5}$

12. $y = \dfrac{4x + 1}{2x + 7}$

13. $y = \dfrac{2}{(x - 1)^2}$

14. $y = \dfrac{2}{x^2 - 1}$

15. $y = \dfrac{1}{(x + 1)(x - 4)}$

16. $y = \dfrac{x - 1}{x^2 - 4}$

17. $y = \dfrac{x^2 - 1}{x^3}$

18. $y = \dfrac{x}{x^2 + 1}$

19. $y = \dfrac{x^2 - x - 6}{x^2}$

20. $y = \dfrac{3x^2 + x - 2}{2x^2}$

21. $y = \dfrac{x^2 + 1}{x}$

22. $y = \dfrac{(x - 1)^2}{x}$

23. $y = \dfrac{x^2 - 9}{x + 2}$

24. $y = \dfrac{x^2 - 2x - 3}{x + 3}$

In Exercises 25–34 graph the given function, with particular emphasis on any value of x for which $P(x) = Q(x) = 0$.

25. $h(x) = \dfrac{x(x + 1)}{x}$

26. $y = x\dfrac{(x + 1)}{x + 1}$

27. $y = \dfrac{x^2 - 4}{x + 2}$

28. $y = \dfrac{x^2 - x}{x}$

29. $g(x) = \dfrac{(2x + 1)(x - 3)(x + 2)}{(x - 3)(x + 2)}$

30. $f(x) = \dfrac{(x - 1)(x - 2)(x - 3)}{(x - 1)(x - 2)}$

31. $f(x) = \dfrac{x}{x(x + 1)}$

32. $y = \dfrac{x}{x^2 - 2x}$

33. $y = \dfrac{x - 1}{(x - 1)^2}$

34. $y = \dfrac{x + 1}{(x + 1)^2}$

35. The cost to rent a recording studio is a flat fee of $100 plus $1 per minute. Thus the average cost per minute for x minutes use of the studio is given by $y = \dfrac{100 + x}{x}$.

    a. What is the total cost for a 3-hour recording session? What is the average cost per minute for a 3-hour session?

    b. Graph the function and describe how y changes as x increases for $x > 0$. What is the significance of the horizontal asymptote?

36. Redo Exercise 35 if the cost is a $75 flat fee plus $10 per hour.

37. Assume that a farmer plans to make a rectangular enclosure with area 900 ft^2 along the side of a barn, so that no fencing is needed along the barn. Use a grapher to determine to 2 decimal places the dimensions that would require the least amount of fencing.

38. Redo Exercise 37 but assume that fencing is needed on all four sides (including the side along the barn). Does your solution imply that the yard is square?

39. Some "pure" orange juice is diluted by adding water. At first, a 64-ounce jug contains just 32 ounces of pure juice.

    a. What percent of the solution is juice after 4 ounces of water have been added? After 8 ounces have been added?

    b. Write a formula that gives y the percent of juice in the solution after x ounces of water have been added. What is the domain of this function?

    c. Graph the formula from part **b** over the domain from part **b**.

    d. At what point is the solution 80% juice? 50%? 40%?

    e. Explain algebraically and realistically why the graph has a horizontal asymptote.

    f. How big a container is needed if the juice is diluted down to a 10% solution?

40. Redo Exercise 39, but assume that at the beginning the jug contains a mixture of 9 ounces of orange juice and 1 ounce of water.

THINK ABOUT IT 11.4

1. What is the difference between the graphs of $y = (x^2 - 1)/(x - 1)$ and $y = x + 1$?

2. If $f(x) = 4/(x^2 - 1)$, what is the range of f?

3. Give two examples of an equation that defines a rational function such that the vertical asymptote is $x = -3$ and the horizontal asymptote is $y = 5/2$.

4. **a.** Explain why the graph of a rational function cannot cross a vertical asymptote.

    b. We have seen that it is possible for the graph of a rational function to cross its horizontal asymptote. Do you think a graph may cross its oblique asymptote? Explain.

    c. Graph $y = x^3/(x^2 - 1)$ and check that your explanation in part **b** is in agreement with this graph.

5. In a math journal, Brian Bolt described the effect of some factors on the flight of a golf ball hit from a tee. He showed that the velocity U of the ball is roughly proportional to the velocity V of the clubhead at the moment the clubhead hits the ball. That is, $U = kV$. The constant of proportionality k was shown to be $M(1 + e)/(M + m)$, where M is the mass of the clubhead, e is a constant that depends mostly on the elastic quality of the ball, and m is the mass of the ball. The author analyzed the effect of the weight of the clubhead on the velocity of the ball. For this purpose he used 0.7 as a representative value of e, and 46g as a typical mass for a ball. This gives the equation $k = 0.7\,M/(M + 46)$.

    a. Graph this function, and describe what happens to k as the mass of the clubhead increases.

    b. A typical value for M is 200 g. What is the corresponding value of k?

    c. How much would k increase if the mass of the club were increased from 200 g to 1000 g? (Of course, it would be much harder to swing the club.)

[Source: *UMAP Journal*, vol. 4, no. 1, 1983]

CHAPTER 11 OVERVIEW

Section	Key Concepts or Procedures to Review
11.1	▪ Definition of a polynomial function of degree n
	▪ Definitions of a zero of a function and the multiplicity of a zero
	▪ Factor theorem
	▪ Theorem about graphing polynomial functions by knowing the multiplicity of real-number zeros
	▪ Properties of polynomial graphs concerning continuity, turning points, and behavior for large $\lvert x \rvert$
11.2	▪ Long-division procedure for the division of polynomials
	▪ Synthetic division procedure for the division of a polynomial by $x - b$
	▪ Remainder theorem
	▪ Fundamental theorem of algebra
	▪ Number of zeros theorem
	▪ Theorem about when complex zeros come in conjugate pairs
	▪ Theorem about when irrational zeros of the form $a \pm b\sqrt{c}$ come in conjugate pairs
11.3	▪ Rational-zero theorem
	▪ Descartes' rule of signs
	▪ Upper and lower bounds theorem
	▪ Intermediate value theorem
	▪ Location theorem
11.4	▪ Definition of a rational function
	▪ Methods to determine vertical, horizontal, or slant asymptotes
	▪ Horizontal asymptote theorem
	▪ Theorem about the behavior of a graph near any vertical asymptote(s)
	▪ Outline of the procedure for graphing rational functions

CHAPTER 11 REVIEW EXERCISES

In Exercises 1–6 indicate if the given function is a polynomial function

1. $f(x) = \dfrac{2x - 1}{3}$ **2.** $y = \dfrac{2x - 1}{x}$

3. $y = x^2 + x^{-1} + 2$ **4.** $y = x^2 + x + 2^{-1}$

5. $y = \sqrt{x}$ **6.** $y = \sqrt{2}$

In Exercises 7–12 find the zeros of the function.

7. $y = 2x^2 - 3x$ **8.** $f(x) = 3 - 5x$

9. $g(x) = x^3 - 2x^2 + x - 2$ **10.** $y = x^2(x + 7)(x - 4)$

11. $f(x) = \dfrac{2x^2 - 5x + 1}{x^3}$ **12.** $y = \dfrac{1}{x^2 - 1}$

In Exercises 13–22 graph each function.

13. $y = \dfrac{-2}{3x^2}$ **14.** $y = \dfrac{3}{2x - 3}$

15. $y = \dfrac{x + 1}{x}$ **16.** $y = \dfrac{x + 1}{2}$

17. $y = \dfrac{x^2 + 2x}{x}$ **18.** $y = \dfrac{5x^2 + 4}{4x^2 - 1}$

19. $y = (x + 2)(x - 1)^2$ **20.** $y = x^2(x + 7)(x - 4)$

21. $y = x^3 - 3x^2 - 4x$ **22.** $y = x^4 - x^2$

23. Determine the vertical asymptotes for the function
$y = \dfrac{3x + 1}{x^2 + 2x}$.

24. Determine the horizontal asymptote for the function
$y = \dfrac{2x^2 + 3}{3x^2 + x - 2}$. Does the graph cross the horizontal asymptote? If yes, find the point at which it crosses.

25. What is the difference between the graphs of
$y = \dfrac{x^2 - 4}{x - 2}$ and $y = x + 2$?

26. Write a polynomial function (in factored form) with rational coefficients of the lowest possible degree with zeros of $-i$, $\sqrt{2}$, and 0.

27. Write a polynomial function (in factored form) of degree 4 with zeros of 5, –2, 0, and 3.

28. If $f(x) = 2x^4 - x + 7$, find $f(-2)$ by
a. direct substitution and
b. the remainder theorem
29. Divide $2x^4 - x + 7$ by $x^2 + 2$. Express the result in the form dividend = (divisor)(quotient) + remainder.
30. The dividend is x^2, the quotient is $x + 3$, and the remainder is 9. What is the divisor?
31. List the possible rational zeros of the function $P(x) = 3x^3 - 7x^2 + x - 2$.
32. Use Descartes' rule of signs to determine the maximum number of
a. positive and
b. negative real zeros of $P(x) = x^4 - 3x^3 + x^2 - x + 1$.
33. If 2 is a zero of $P(x) = 2x^3 - 4x^2 - 6x + 12$, find the other zeros.
34. Describe how to graph $y = (x + 1)^4 - 3$ using the graph of $y = x^4$.
35. If $P(x) = 7x^3(x + 2)^2$, find the zeros of the function and state the multiplicity of each zero.
36. If 1 is a root of $x^3 - 2x^2 - 5x + 6 = 0$, what is the quadratic equation that can be used to find the other two roots?
37. If b is a zero of $P(x) = x^3 + ax^2 + ax + 1$, show that $1/b$ is also a zero.
38. Find an equation for the third degree polynomial shown.

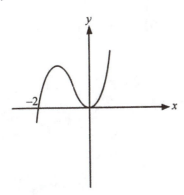

39. Verify that $P(x) = x^3 - 3x^2 - 1$ has a real zero between 3 and 4, by using the location theorem.

40. Approximate the zero of $P(x) = x^3 - 2x - 7$ that is between 2 and 3, to the nearest tenth.

In Exercises 41–50 select the choice that answers the question or completes the statement.

41. The degree of $P(x) = x^2(x + 3)(x - 3)^4$ is
a. 6 **b.** 7 **c.** 8 **d.** 16
42. If $P(x) = x^2(x + 3)(x - 3)^4$, what is the multiplicity of the zero of –3?
a. 1 **b.** 2 **c.** 4 **d.** 5
43. The graph of $y = \dfrac{x^2 + 1}{x^3}$ lies in quadrants
a. 1 and 2 **b.** 1 and 3
c. 2 and 4 **d.** 3 and 4
44. If $x^3 - 2x^2 + ax + 9$ is exactly divisible by $x + 3$ then a equals
a. –10 **b.** –12 **c.** 7 **d.** 16
45. The remainder when $2x^9 + 5x^4 + 3$ is divided by $x - 1$ is
a. 0 **b.** 6 **c.** –4 **d.** 10
46. The vertical asymptote for $y = \dfrac{x - 1}{x - 2}$ is
a. $x = 1$ **b.** $y = 1$ **c.** $y = 2$ **d.** $x = 2$
47. Which one of the following is a rational zero of $P(x) = 2x^3 + 19x^2 + 37x + 14$?
a. $-\dfrac{1}{2}$ **b.** $\dfrac{7}{2}$ **c.** $\dfrac{5}{2}$ **d.** $-\dfrac{3}{2}$
48. According to Descartes' rule of signs, the maximum number of negative real zeros for $P(x) = 3x^3 + x^2$ is
a. none **b.** one **c.** two **d.** three
49. If $\dfrac{2}{5}$ is a zero of $y = ax^3 + bx^2 + cx + d$, in which a, b, c, and d are integers with $a \neq 0$, then 5 must be a factor of
a. a **b.** b **c.** c **d.** d
50. The function $y = x^3 - 3x - 3$ has exactly one positive real zero in which one of the following intervals?
a. [0, 1] **b.** [1, 2] **c.** [2, 3] **d.** [3, 4]

CHAPTER 11 TEST

1. True or false: The function $y = 1 - x^3$ is a polynomial function.
2. What is the degree of $P(x) = 3x^2(x - 1)(x + 2)^4$?
3. Write a polynomial function of degree 3 with zeros of –2, –1, and 4.
4. Describe how to graph $y = (x - 3)^4 + 2$ using the graph of $y = x^4$.
5. Verify that $P(x) = x^3 - x^2 + 5$ has a real zero between –1 and –2 by using the location theorem.

6. True or false: The graph of $y = \dfrac{x^2 - 3x}{x}$ has a vertical asymptote at $x = 0$.
7. Divide $\dfrac{x^3 - 1}{x(x + 1)}$. Express the answer in the form
$$\dfrac{\text{dividend}}{\text{divisor}} = \text{quotient} + \dfrac{\text{remainder}}{\text{divisor}}.$$

8. What is the remainder when $5x^4 - 3x + 12$ is divided by $x^2 - 2$?

9. What is the quotient when $2x^4 - x^2 + 5$ is divided by $x + 3$?

10. If $P(x) = x^3 - 3x^2 + x + 9$, find $P(-2)$ by
   a. direct substitution and
   b. the remainder theorem.

11. If $P(x) = 4x^2(x + 1)^3$, find the zeros of the function and state the multiplicity of each zero.

12. Graph $y = x^4 - 4x^2$ based on information obtained from the intercepts.

13. If -5 is a zero of $P(x) = x^3 + 5x^2 - 6x - 30$, then find the other zeros for the function.

14. By the rational-zero theorem what are the possible rational zeros for $P(x) = 3x^3 + 2x^2 - 3x - 2$?

15. By Descartes' rule of signs what is the maximum number of negative real zeros of the function $P(x) = x^3 + 4x^2 - x + 5$?

16. Find the zeros of $P(x) = 2x^3 + 3x^2 + 6x + 9$.

17. Find any vertical asymptotes for the graph of
$$y = \frac{2x - 7}{x^2 - 6x}.$$

18. Find all points at which the graph of $y = \dfrac{x^2 - 4}{x^3}$ crosses its horizontal asymptote.

19. Find the slant asymptote for the graph of
$$y = \frac{x^2 - 4x - 5}{x - 2}.$$

20. Graph $y = \dfrac{2x - 5}{x + 3}$.

Answers to Progress Check Exercises

Progress Check 1.1   **1.** (number line from −4 to 8 with points marked)   **2.** (number line from −2 to 2 showing $-\frac{2}{3}$ and $\sqrt{2}$)

3. a. None of these   **b.** Irrational, real   **c.** Rational, real   **d.** Integer, rational, real   **4. a.** Multiplication inverse property
b. Commutative property of multiplication   **c.** Associative property of multiplication   **d.** Distributive property   **5. a.** $<$
b. $=$ **c.** $>$ **6. a.** $\sqrt{2}$ **b.** -5 **c.** 0 **7. a.** -44 **b.** $\frac{5}{9}$ **c.** -8 **8. a.** -4 **b.** $-\frac{76}{9}$ **c.** 3.6 **9. a.** -56 **b.** 14.1

c. 81 **10. a.** -125 **b.** -64 **c.** 64 **11. a.** Undefined   **b.** 0 **c.** Undefined   **d.** 0 **12. a.** 6 **b.** $-\frac{21}{11}$ **13.** -72

14. a. $-\frac{4}{7}$ **b.** 5 **15.** $\$235,488.15, \$557,222.03, \$1,287,203.63, \$2,906,651.72$

Progress Check 1.2   **1. a.** -17 **b.** 247 **2.** $-\frac{3}{2}$ **3. a.** $-4x^3, x^2, -3x, 7$ **b.** $-\frac{7x}{2}$ **4. a.** $-7x$ **b.** Cannot be simplified

c. $3p$ **d.** $5x^2 + 5x$ **5. a.** $2x - 4y$ **b.** $5x + 4$ **6.** 6π ft   **7. a.** $1,351$ ft^3 **b.** $10,133$ gal   **8. a.** $p + 5$ **b.** $0.08(ab)$
9. a. The sum of a times b and c **b.** The quotient of a and 5 more than a

Progress Check 1.3   **1. a.** $3^5 = 243$ **b.** $3^8 = 6,561$ **c.** $4^3 \cdot 2^3 = 512$ **d.** $3^2 = 9$ **e.** $\frac{1}{3^2} = \frac{1}{9}$ **2. a.** $144x^7$ **b.** $\frac{2y}{3x^3}$

3. a. -5 **b.** -1 **c.** 4.72 **4. a.** $\frac{1}{7}$ **b.** $\frac{1}{81}$ **c.** $\frac{125}{8}$ **5.** $\$365.36$ **6. a.** $\frac{1}{256}$ **b.** $\frac{3}{y}$ **c.** $\frac{125}{8x^3}$ **d.** $\frac{y^4}{6}$ **e.** $\frac{27}{x^8 y^2}$

7. a. 16 **b.** $\frac{27}{x^8 y^2}$ **8. a.** a^{2x} **b.** 3^{2n} **c.** x^n **9. a.** 6.15×10^8 **b.** -9×10^{-2} **10. a.** $9,200,000,000$ **b.** -0.0000027
11. 26.1%

Progress Check 1.4   **1. a.** $-6x^4 + 2x^3 - 18x^2$ **b.** $21y^2 - 3xy$ **2.** $-3nx + \frac{1}{2}x$ **3. a.** $21y^2 - 34y + 8$

b. $a^{2x} - 2a^x - 15$ **4.** $4x^3 + 15x^2 + 7x - 6$ **5.** $20y^2 - 31y + 12$ **6.** Revenue $=$ (number of units sold) $\cdot$ (price per unit),
where number of units sold $= 20,000 + 700x$, and price per unit $= 3,000 - 100x$; $60,000,000 + 100,000x - 70,000x^2$
7. a. $k^2 - 16k + 64$ **b.** $x^2 + 2xh + h^2$ **c.** $9y^2 - 25$ **8. a.** $4x^2 + 28x + 49$ **b.** $4x^2 - 49$ **c.** $9m^2 - 30mn + 25n^2$
9. $6x + 3h$

Progress Check 1.5   **1.** $\{-11\}$ **2.** $\left\{-\frac{9}{2}\right\}$ **3.** $\left\{\frac{3}{4}\right\}$ **4.** $\emptyset$ **5.** $r = 0.08$ **6.** 2.7 kg ≈ 5.9 lb   **7.** $y = mx + b$

8. $g = \frac{2t - 2S}{t^2}$ **9. a.** $x = \frac{2y + 30}{5}$ **b.** $y = \frac{5x - 30}{2}$

Progress Check 1.6   **1.** $\$1,056$ **2.** 73 and 74 **3.** $63°$ **4.** $\$150,000$ at 10%; $\$50,000$ at 6% **5.** $\frac{3}{20}$ hr or 9 minutes
6. 3.75 lb of 30%; 1.25 lb of 50% **7.** 183 minutes

Progress Check 1.7   **1. a.** $\left(-\infty, -\frac{1}{2}\right]$ (number line)   **b.** $(0, \infty)$ (number line)

2. $(-\infty, -4)$ (number line)   **3.** $(2, \infty)$ (number line)   **4.** $(-\infty, 2]$ (number line)   **5.** $\emptyset$

6. Revenue is greater than cost when more than $24,000$ CDs are sold.

Progress Check 1.8 **1. a.** $\{0, 1, 2, 3, 4, 5\}$ **b.** $\emptyset$ **c.** $\{0, 1\}$ **2. a.** $[3, \infty)$

b. $\emptyset$ **c.** $[1, 3]$ **d.** $[1, 3]$

3. $(-\infty, 4)$ **4.** $[1, 9]$ **5.** $[72, 92)$ **6.** $(-\infty, -1) \cup (2, \infty)$

7. a. $(-\infty, \infty)$ **b.** $(-\infty, -1] \cup [1, \infty)$

c. $(-\infty, 1)$

Progress Check 2.1 **1. a.** $C = 1.35x$; $[0, \infty)$ **b.** $s = \sqrt{A}$; $(0, \infty)$ **2. a.** $C = \dfrac{P^2}{4}$ **b.** \$36 **c.** $(0, \infty)$

3. $C = 9n + 2.95$; D: $\{1, 2, 3, \dots\}$; R: $\{\$11.95, \$20.95, \$29.95, \dots\}$ **4. a.** D: $\{x : x \neq -3\}$; R: $\{y : y \neq 0\}$

b. D: $[2, \infty)$; R: $[0, \infty)$ **5. a.** Yes **b.** No **6.** Domain $= \{65, 100, 43, 94\}$; range $= \{A, D, F\}$

7. Domain $= \{4, 9\}$; range $= \{1, 4\}$ **8. a.** Yes **b.** No

Progress Check 2.2 **1.**

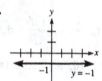

2.

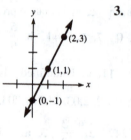

3.

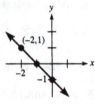

4.

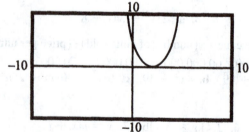

5.

6.

7.

8.

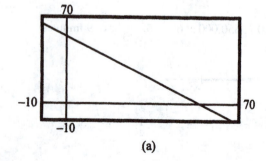

9. Figure (a) shows a complete graph.

(a)

(b)

10.

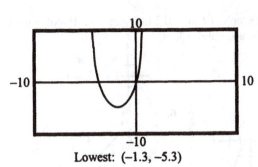

Lowest: $(-1.3, -5.3)$

11. Function: (a), (b); not a function: (c), (d)   **12.** Domain: $[-8, 8]$; range: $[-4, 4]$; no

13.

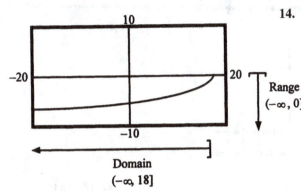

Domain
$(-\infty, 18]$

14. $A = 2x\sqrt{4 - x^2}$; $D{:}(0,2)$; $R{:}(0, 4]$

Progress Check 2.3   **1. a.** $C = kd$; $k = \pi$ **b.** $T = kv$; k depends on the tax rate of the particular tax district.

2. $y = \left(\dfrac{3}{4}\right)x$; 9 **3.** \$124   **4. a.** $W_m = \left(\dfrac{1}{6}\right)W_e$ **b.**

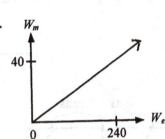

c. 23 lb   **5.** $y = \dfrac{65}{x}$; 65

6. 180 rpm   **7.** $\dfrac{15,625}{16}$ **8.** The gravitational attraction drops to $\dfrac{1}{16}$ of its original value.

Progress Check 2.4   **1.** $f(4) = 4$; $f(20) = -300$; $f(-5) = -50$ **2.** $f(6) = 75,036.52$; in six years the value of this art work will be about \$75,000.   **3.** -14 **4.** $f(a + b) = 3(a + b) = 3a + 3b$; $f(a) = 3a$; $f(b) = 3b$. Since $3a + 3b = 3a + 3b$, $f(a + b) = f(a) + f(b)$.   **5.** $2x + h + 3$ **6.** $e = \begin{cases} \$600 & \text{if } \$0 \le a \le \$10,000 \\ \$600 + 0.08(a - \$10,000) & \text{if } a > \$10,000 \end{cases}$

7. a. 2   **b.** Undefined   **c.** 0   **8.**

9. a. $(-\infty, \infty)$ **b.** $(-\infty, 4]$ **c.** 3   **d.** $\{-1, 3\}$
e. $(-\infty, -1) \cup (3, \infty)$ **f.** $(-1, 3)$

Progress Check 2.5   **1. a.**

b.

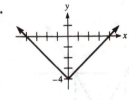

2. a.

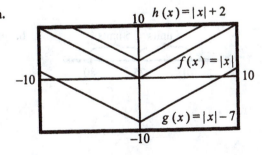

b. The graph of g is the graph of f shifted 7 units down; the graph of h is the graph of f shifted 2 units up. **c.** Possible trace points are $(0,0)$ in f, $(0, -7)$ in g, and $(0,2)$ in h. The descriptions appear to be accurate. **3. a.**

b.

4.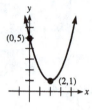

5. a.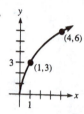

b.

6.

7.

8. Domain = [0 seconds, 3.5 seconds]

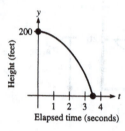

Progress Check 2.6 **1. a.**

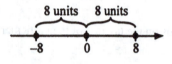

b. 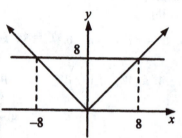 **c.** $\{8, -8\}$

2. $\{6, -3\}$ **3.** $\left\{-10, -\dfrac{1}{4}\right\}$ **4. a.**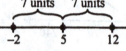

b. 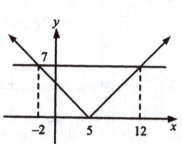 **c.** $\{-2, 12\}$

5. a.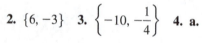

b. 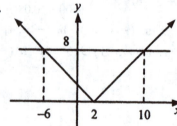 **c.** $[-6, 10]$ **6.** $\left(-\dfrac{19}{5}, 1\right)$

7. a.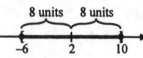

b. 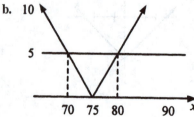 **c.** $(-\infty, 70) \cup (80, \infty)$

8. a.

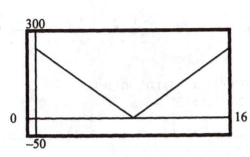

The speed decreases uniformly from 256 ft/second until it stops momentarily when $t = 8$ seconds; then the speed increases uniformly until it hits the ground at 216 ft/second when $t = 16$ seconds.

b. {6.5 seconds; 9.5 seconds}   **c.** [0 seconds, 6.5 seconds] $\cup$ [9.5 seconds, 16 seconds]   **9.** {$x: |x - 0.5| < 2.5$}

Progress Check 2.7   **1. a.** 1   **b.** $-\frac{4}{3}$ **2. a.** 0   **b.** Undefined   **3.** $\frac{4}{3}$ **4.** Slope $= 0.04$; cost is 4¢ per copy.

5. a. $m_{AB} = m_{CD} = \frac{1}{2}$; $m_{BC} = m_{AD} = -2$ **b.** $\frac{1}{2}(-2) = -1$ **6. a.** 8   **b.** 7   **7.** $\sqrt{17}$

8. a. $d_{AB} = \sqrt{50}$, $d_{BC} = \sqrt{10}$, $d_{AC} = \sqrt{40}$; $(\sqrt{10})^2 + (\sqrt{40})^2 = (\sqrt{50})^2$ **b.** $m_{AB} = 1$, $m_{BC} = -3$, $m_{AC} = \frac{1}{3}$; angle C is a right angle.

Progress Check 2.8   **1.** $y = 3x + 3$ **2.** $y = -\frac{4}{5}x + \frac{2}{5}$ **3. a.** -2, (0,3)   **b.** $\frac{4}{3}$, (0, -4)   **4.**

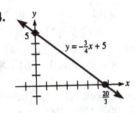

5. $f(x) = -4x + 15$ **6. a.** $f(x) = -0.7x + 154$ **b.** 141   **7.** No   **8.** Yes

9. a. $y = \frac{1}{2}x + \frac{5}{2}$ **b.** $y = -2x + 10$

Progress Check 3.1   **1.** At 1,000 units both machines have a cost of $8,000; machine B

2. a. No   **b.** Yes   **3.**

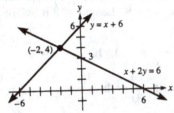

4. (1,750, 12,500)   **5.** $(-4, 5)$
6. $(5, -1)$ **7.** $\left(\frac{1}{2}, \frac{2}{3}\right)$
8. a. Dependent system; {$(x, y): -4x + y = -1$}
b. Inconsistent system; $\emptyset$ **9.** $15,000 at 8.5 percent; $45,000 at 10.5 percent   **10.** State tax: $27,642; federal tax: $247,155
11. a. {-0.4}   **b.** $(-\infty, -0.4)$

Progress Check 3.2   **1.** Solution   **2.** $(-3, 1, 4)$ **3.** $a = -1, b = 2, c = -3$; $y = -x^2 + 2x - 3$

4. $I_1 = -\frac{8}{73}$ ampere, $I_2 = \frac{55}{73}$ ampere, $I_3 = -\frac{47}{73}$ ampere   **5.** Inconsistent system; $\emptyset$ **6.** Dependent system; infinitely many solutions

Progress Check 3.3   **1.** $(-1, 2, 1)$ **2.** $\left(\frac{1}{2}, -1, \frac{1}{2}\right)$ **3.** $(2, -3)$ **4.** Orchestra: 800; mezzanine: 700; balcony: 500

Progress Check 3.4   **1. a.** 2   **b.** -9 **c.** $c_1b_2 - b_1c_2$ **2.** $\left(\frac{1}{2}, -\frac{3}{7}\right)$ **3.** Cramer's rule applies; (4, 3).   **4.** 0.27 oz of 35% gold, 0.18 oz of 25% gold   **5.** 17   **6.** 17   **7.** $\left(\frac{1}{2}, -\frac{3}{2}, 1\right)$

Progress Check 4.1   **1.** $\sin \beta = \dfrac{4}{5}$, $\cos \beta = \dfrac{3}{5}$, $\tan \beta = \dfrac{4}{3}$, $\cot \beta = \dfrac{3}{4}$, $\sec \beta = \dfrac{5}{3}$, $\csc \beta = \dfrac{5}{4}$

2. $\sin \theta = \dfrac{\sqrt{21}}{5}$, $\tan \theta = \dfrac{\sqrt{21}}{2}$, $\cot \theta = \dfrac{2}{\sqrt{21}}$, $\sec \theta = \dfrac{5}{2}$, $\csc \theta = \dfrac{5}{\sqrt{21}}$ **3.** 85

4. $\sin 60° = \dfrac{\sqrt{3}}{2}$, $\cot 30° = \sqrt{3}$, $\csc 30° = 2$, $\tan 45° = 1$ **5.** $\sin 56°$ **6. a.** 1.8807   **b.** 1.0440   **c.** 0.9899   **7.** 344

8. a. $74.2°, 74°10'$ **b.** $43.7°, 43°40'$

Progress Check 4.2   **1.** $A = 32°$, $b = 56$ ft, $c = 66$ ft   **2.** $B = 80°20'$, $a = 1.26$ ft, $b = 7.41$ ft
3. $a = 14.7$ ft, $A = 50°50'$, $B = 39°10'$ **4.** 23.8 ft   **5.** 1,190 ft   **6.** 78.5°

Progress Check 4.3   **1.** $\sin \theta = -\dfrac{1}{\sqrt{10}}$, $\csc \theta = -\sqrt{10}$, $\cos \theta = -\dfrac{3}{\sqrt{10}}$, $\sec \theta = -\dfrac{\sqrt{10}}{3}$, $\tan \theta = \dfrac{1}{3}$, $\cot \theta = 3$

2. $\csc \theta = -\dfrac{4}{3}$, $\cos \theta = -\dfrac{\sqrt{7}}{4}$, $\sec \theta = -\dfrac{4}{\sqrt{7}}$, $\tan \theta = \dfrac{3}{\sqrt{7}}$, $\cot \theta = \dfrac{\sqrt{7}}{3}$ **3.** $\sin 180° = 0$, $\csc 180°$ is undefined,

$\cos 180° = -1$, $\sec 180° = -1$, $\tan 180° = 0$, $\cot 180°$ is undefined   **4. a.** 1   **b.** 0   **5.** $-\dfrac{\sqrt{3}}{2}$ **6.** $-\dfrac{1}{\sqrt{2}}$ **7.** $-\dfrac{1}{\sqrt{3}}$
8. a. 0.9932   **b.** -1.0785 **9.** 15 mi

Progress Check 4.4   **1.** $\{30°, 330°\}$ **2.** $\{120°, 240°\}$ **3.** $\{209°30', 330°30'\}$ **4.** $\{121.0°, 301.0°\}$
5. $\{\theta : \theta = 109°30' + k360°$ or $\theta = 250°30' + k360°, k$ any integer$\}$ **6.** 35.7° or 54.3°

Progress Check 4.5   **1. a.** 51 lb   **b.** 62°   **2. a.** 565 mi   **b.** 82.4° south of east   **3.** 15 lb   **4. a.** 457 mi/hour due east
b. 48 mi/hour due south   **5.** v, 20 lb; h, 37 lb   **6.** $R = 6.6$ lb, $\theta = 96°$

Progress Check 5.1   **1. a.** $4y^2(2y + 1)$ **b.** $(x + 3)(2x + 5)$ **2.** $0.75x$; less   **3. a.** $3s(2s - 3)$ **b.** $3 \sin \theta (2 \sin \theta - 3)$
4. a. $(x + 2)(2x + 3)$ **b.** $(x - 6)(x^2 - 6)$ **5.** $(x - 5)(x + 4)$ **6. a.** $(2t + 3)(2t - 5)$
b. $(2 \tan \theta + 3)(2 \tan \theta - 5)$ **7. a.** $(2 \cos \theta - 1)^2$ **b.** $(2c - 1)^2$ **8.** $(4x + 9)(3x - 2)$ **9.** $3y^2(2y + 1)(y - 3)$
10. 225; factorable

Progress Check 5.2   **1. a.** $(n + 4)(n - 4)$ **b.** $(10xy + 7z)(10xy - 7z)$ **2. a.** $(1 + 2 \sin \theta)(1 - 2 \sin \theta)$
b. $(1 + 2s)(1 - 2s)$ **3. a.** $y = 625 - 4t^2$ **b.** $y = (25 + 2t)(25 - 2t)$ **c.** When $t = 12.5$,
$y = [25 + 2(12.5)][25 - 2(12.5)] = 50(0) = 0$ **4. a.** $(2y - 1)(4y^2 + 2y + 1)$ **b.** $(x^3 + 3y)(x^6 - 3x^3y + 9y^2)$
5. a. $5(x - 2)(x^2 + 2x + 4)$ **b.** $(4m^2 + 9n^2)(2m + 3n)(2m - 3n)$ **6.** $16(2 + t)(2 - t)$
7. $6(\cos \theta - 2)(\cos \theta - 6)$ **8.** $(y + 1)(y^2 - y + 1)(y - 1)(y^2 + y + 1)$ **9.** $(c + 2 + d)(c + 2 - d)$

Progress Check 5.3   **1.** $\{0, -7\}$ **2.** $(-4, 0), (2, 0), (0, -8)$ **3.** $\{-2\}$ **4. a.** $\left\{-\frac{2}{3}, \frac{3}{2}, 1\right\}$ **b.** $\{0, 2, -2\}$
5. $\{60°, 90°, 270°, 300°\}$ **6.** 2 seconds   **7.** 11, 12 and $-12, -11$ **8.** 6 ft   **9.** Length = 8 ft, width = 6 ft

Progress Check 5.4   **1. a.** $\dfrac{c - 4}{c + 4}, c \neq 4$ **b.** $\dfrac{\cos \theta - 4}{\cos \theta + 4}$ **2. a.** $\dfrac{1}{2x - 1}, x \neq 0$ **b.** $x + c, x \neq c$ **3.** $-\dfrac{1}{3x + 2}$
4. a. $\dfrac{c + 2}{(c + 4)(c - 2)}$ **b.** $\dfrac{\cos \theta + 2}{(\cos \theta + 4)(\cos \theta - 2)}$ **5.** $\dfrac{y^6}{(x - 5)^4}$ **6. a.** $\dfrac{4}{3x^2}$ **b.** $\dfrac{3(t + 5)}{t - 5}$ **c.** $\dfrac{-1(x + 3)}{xy}$ **7.** $\dfrac{r}{r - x}$

Progress Check 5.5   **1. a.** $\dfrac{1}{t}$ **b.** $\dfrac{1}{\tan \theta}$ **2. a.** $\dfrac{6x^2 - 5}{2x^2 + x}$ **b.** $\dfrac{-4}{x - 1}$ **c.** $\dfrac{1}{x + 1}$ **3.** $\dfrac{3sd - nd}{n}$ **4. a.** $-\dfrac{4}{x}$ **b.** $\dfrac{4t + 1}{t - 3}$
5. 60   **6. a.** $24x^2y^2$ **b.** $3x(x + 5)$ **7.** $\frac{43}{45}$ **8. a.** $\dfrac{15 + 4x}{18x}$ **b.** $\dfrac{9x - 28y}{24x^2y^2}$ **9. a.** $\dfrac{8c}{(c - s)(c + s)}$
b. $\dfrac{8 \cos \theta}{(\cos \theta - \sin \theta)(\cos \theta + \sin \theta)}$ **10. a.** $\dfrac{t^2 + 3t - 6}{t(t - 2)}$ **b.** $\dfrac{2(t + 2)}{t + 1}$ **c.** $\dfrac{4x^2 + 2x + 3}{(x - 3)^2(x + 2)}$

Progress Check 5.6   **1.** $\dfrac{28}{19}$ **2.** $\dfrac{4 + y}{2y - 3}$ **3.** $\dfrac{(x + 2y)^2}{3xy}$ **4.** $\dfrac{10 - an}{9ny - 10a + 9n}$ **5.** $\dfrac{n - 4}{4n}$ **6.** $\dfrac{x}{2 + x}$ **7. a.** $\dfrac{4c - 3}{3c - 1}$
b. $\dfrac{4 \cos \theta - 3}{3 \cos \theta - 1}$

Progress Check 5.7   **1. a.** $4y^2$ **b.** $-\dfrac{8}{x^3}$ **2. a.** $2x^2 + 1 - \dfrac{4}{5x}$ **b.** $-\frac{5}{2}x + 4y$ **3.** Yes   **4.** $3x - 8 + \dfrac{22}{x + 2}$
5. $x^2 + x + 1$ **6.** $x^2 - 3x + 1 + \dfrac{14x - 6}{2x^2 + 3}$

Progress Check 5.8   **1.** $\{-8\}$ **2.** $\left\{\dfrac{1}{2}\right\}$ **3.** 6 slugs   **4.** $\{2, 3\}$ **5.** $\{-5\}$ **6.** $m_1 = \dfrac{Tm_2}{T - 32m_2}$ **7.** 16 minutes
8. 12 mi/hour   **9.** 180 mi/hour

Progress Check 6.1   **1.** $7, -7$ **2. a.** 14.14   **b.** 15   **c.** Not real   **d.** -15 **3. a.** 2   **b.** -5 **c.** Not real   **d.** -3
4. a. 3   **b.** 1.5287; average annual increase in sales is about 52.9 percent.   **5. a.** 10   **b.** -3 **c.** 2   **d.** 5   **6. a.** 32   **b.** $\frac{1}{32}$
c. 9   **d.** 16   **7. a.** $\frac{1}{125}$ **b.** $\frac{1}{16}$ **c.** $\frac{10}{3}$ **8. a.** 5   **b.** $x^{11/6}$ **c.** $3y^3$ **d.** $\dfrac{1}{2^{2/3}}$ **e.** $\dfrac{b^{3/2}}{a^{1/2}}$ **f.** $\dfrac{y^4}{4}$ **9. a.** $y = f(x) = 3x^{1/3}$; 9
b. $y = f(x) = -3x^{-1/3}$; -1

Progress Check 6.2 **1. a.** $5\sqrt{3}$ **b.** $4\sqrt{5}$ **c.** $2\sqrt[3]{4}$ **d.** $3\sqrt[4]{2}$ **2. a.** 11 **b.** y^3 **c.** $\sqrt[3]{5}$ **d.** $\sqrt[3]{x^2}$ **3. a.** $x^5\sqrt{x}$

b. $5x^2y^4\sqrt{5x}$ **c.** $xy^2\sqrt[4]{x^3y}$ **4. a.** $\frac{2}{9}$ **b.** $\frac{\sqrt{77}}{11}$ **c.** $\frac{2\sqrt{2y}}{y}$ **d.** $\frac{\sqrt[3]{10y^2}}{2y}$ **5.** $\frac{\pi\sqrt{2}}{2}$ seconds; 2.22 seconds **6. a.** $5\sqrt{3}$

b. 120 **c.** $2xy^2\sqrt[3]{3y^2}$ **7. a.** 3 **b.** $\frac{\sqrt{14}}{7}$ **c.** $\frac{\sqrt[3]{6y^2}}{3}$ **8. a.** $\frac{\sqrt{2}}{2}$ **b.** $\frac{\sqrt{xy}}{y}$ **c.** $\frac{4\sqrt{3}}{3}$ **d.** $\frac{7\sqrt[3]{5}}{5}$

Progress Check 6.3 **1. a.** $-12\sqrt{5}$ **b.** $9\sqrt[4]{2}$ **c.** Does not simplify **d.** $2x\sqrt{y}$ **e.** Does not simplify **2. a.** $7\sqrt{5}$

b. $-7\sqrt[3]{2}$ **c.** $5xy\sqrt{7y}$ **3.** $9\sqrt{5}$ cm ≈ 20.12 cm **4.**

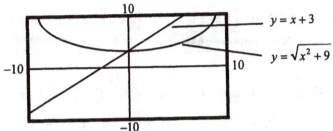

The graphs are different, so $\sqrt{x^2 + 9}$ is not identical to $x + 3$. These two expressions are equal only when $x = 0$.

5. a. $\frac{74\sqrt{3}}{15}$ **b.** $\frac{3\sqrt{2}}{2}$ **c.** $\frac{x - y}{xy}\sqrt{2xy}$

Progress Check 6.4 **1. a.** 18 **b.** $4x - 1$ **c.** 38 **d.** $360y$ **2. a.** $5\sqrt{2} - 5$ **b.** 7 **c.** $\sqrt[5]{y^2} + 4\sqrt[5]{y} + 3$

3. a. $37 + 20\sqrt{3}$ **b.** $16 - x$ **4.** $\left(\sqrt{22} + 2\right)\left(\sqrt{22} - 2\right) = 18$; $\left(\sqrt{22} + 2\right) - \left(\sqrt{22} - 2\right) = 4$ **5. a.** $\frac{2 + \sqrt{3}}{3}$

b. $\frac{x - 3\sqrt{x}}{x}$ **6.** $15 - 5\sqrt{7}$ **7.** $\frac{y\sqrt{5y} + 5y}{y - 5}$

Progress Check 6.5 **1.** 1472 ft **2.** $\{17\}$ **3.** $\{19\}$ **4.** $\{2\}$ **5.** $\{5\}$ **6.** $\{0, 2\}$

Progress Check 6.6 **1. a.** $3i$ **b.** $-3i$ **c.** $i\sqrt{7}$ **d.** $2i\sqrt{2}$ **2. a.** $-2i$ **b.** $7 + 3i$ **c.** $-7 + 4i$ **3. a.** -12

b. $23 + 28i$ **c.** $-33 + 56i$ **4.** 0 **5.** $\frac{9}{10} + \frac{4}{5}i$ **6.** $5 + 2i$ ohms **7. a.** -1 **b.** i

Progress Check 6.7 **1.**

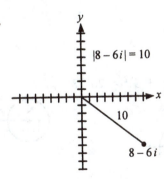

2. $2(\cos 210° + i \sin 210°)$ **3.** $-3\sqrt{2} - 3\sqrt{2}i$

4. a. $32(\cos 144° + i \sin 144°)$ **b.** $2[\cos(-36°) + i \sin(-36°)]$

c. $\frac{1}{2}(\cos 36° + i \sin 36°)$ **5. a.** $5.56(\cos 39.5° + i \sin 39.5°)$ ohms

b. $1.42(\cos 57.8° + i \sin 57.8°)$ ohms **6.** 16

7. $3(\cos 60° + i \sin 60°) = \frac{3}{2} + \frac{3\sqrt{3}}{2}i$;

$3(\cos 180° + i \sin 180°) = -3$;

$3(\cos 300° + i \sin 300°) = \frac{3}{2} - \frac{3\sqrt{3}}{2}i$

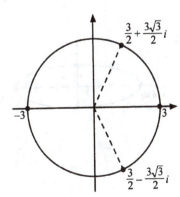

Progress Check 7.1 **1. a.** $\left\{\pm 3\sqrt{2}\right\}$ **b.** $\left\{-4 \pm i\sqrt{7}\right\}$ **2. a.** $x^2 + x + \frac{1}{4} = \left(x + \frac{1}{2}\right)^2$ **b.** $y^2 - 10y + 25 = (y - 5)^2$

3. $\left\{-3 + \sqrt{10}, -3 - \sqrt{10}\right\}$ **4.** $\left\{\dfrac{1 + \sqrt{61}}{6}, \dfrac{1 - \sqrt{61}}{6}\right\}$ **5.** Width = 2.69 m, length = 6.69 m

Progress Check 7.2 **1.** $\left\{1 \pm \sqrt{2}\right\}$ **2.** $\left\{\dfrac{4}{5}\right\}$ **3.** $\left\{\dfrac{1 + i\sqrt{23}}{4}, \dfrac{1 - i\sqrt{23}}{4}\right\}$ **4.** One real number that is rational
5. $\left\{\dfrac{10}{3}, -\dfrac{10}{3}\right\}$ **6.** 36 mi/hour

Progress Check 7.3 **1.** $\left\{1 \pm 3\sqrt{2}\right\}$ **2.** $\left\{2\sqrt{2}\right\}$ **3.** $\left\{\pm 3, \pm\sqrt{2}\right\}$ **4.** $\{1\}$; 9 is extraneous. **5.** $y = \pm\sqrt{1 - x^2}$
6. $t = \dfrac{-v_0 \pm \sqrt{v_0^2 + 64y_0 - 64y}}{-32}$

Progress Check 7.4 **1. a.** $\{-1, 2\}$ **b.** $(-\infty, -1) \cup (2, \infty)$ **c.** $(-1, 2)$ **d.** $(-\infty, -1] \cup [2, \infty)$
2. $\left(-\infty, -\dfrac{1}{2}\right] \cup [7, \infty)$ **3.** $\left(3 - \sqrt{5}, 3 + \sqrt{5}\right)$ **4.** $\left[1 \text{ in.}, \dfrac{7}{2}\text{in.}\right]$ **5.** $\left(-\dfrac{2}{3}, 0\right) \cup (2, \infty)$ **6.** $\left(-\infty, -\dfrac{1}{2}\right] \cup (3, \infty)$
7. $\left(-\infty, -\dfrac{2}{3}\right) \cup [1, \infty]$

Progress Check 7.5 **1.** 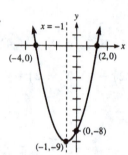 **2.** 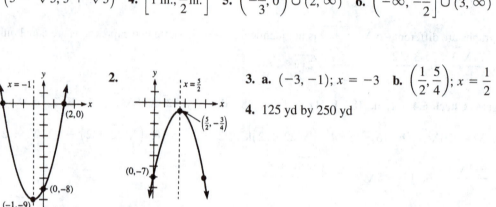 **3. a.** $(-3, -1)$; $x = -3$ **b.** $\left(\dfrac{1}{2}, \dfrac{5}{4}\right)$; $x = \dfrac{1}{2}$
4. 125 yd by 250 yd

5. 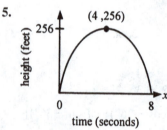 **a.** 8 seconds **b.** 4 seconds **c.** 256 ft **6.** No x-intercept **7.**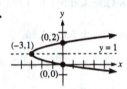

Progress Check 7.6 **1.** $(x + 1)^2 + (y - 6)^2 = 16$ **2.** $(x - 2)^2 + (y + 5)^2 = 26$ **3.**
4. $(-2, 3)$; 5 **5. a.** **b.** **c.**

6. 60 ft

Progress Check 7.7 **1.** 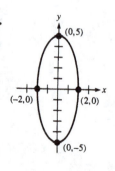 **2.** 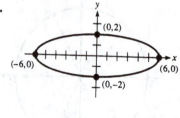 **3.**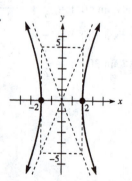

4.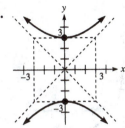

5.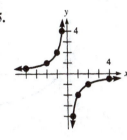

6. $rt = 60$, or $t = \dfrac{60}{r}$

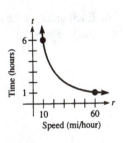

7. a. Parabola **b.** Hyperbola **c.** Ellipse

Progress Check 7.8 1.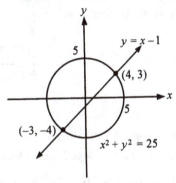

2. a.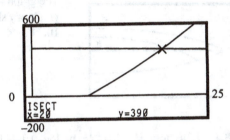

Equilibrium price: \$20; Quantity supplied and demanded: 390 pairs of sandals

b. $p^2 + 3p - 70 = 410 - p$ implies $p = 20$ if $p > 0$. Then, $q = 410 - 20 = 390$. **3.** 5 cm wide; 12 cm long
4. $(1, 1), (1, -1), (-1, 1), (-1, -1)$

Progress Check 8.1 1. a. $y = \left(\frac{1}{2}\right)^x$, x in hours **b.** 5.96×10^{-8} g **2.** $64, \frac{1}{8}, 4, 36.66$ **3.**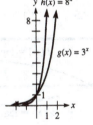

4. 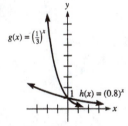 **5. a.** **b.**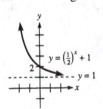

6. $\left\{-\frac{3}{2}\right\}$ **7.** 9 **8. a.** $A = 9{,}000(1.05)^t$ **b.** \$16,162.71 **9.** \$44,397.66 **10.** 9.59 percent

Progress Check 8.2 1. $f^{-1} = \{(1, -1), (2, -2), (3, -3)\}$; $D_f = R_{f^{-1}} = \{-1, -2, -3\}$; $R_f = D_{f^{-1}} = \{1, 2, 3\}$

2. Yes **3. a.** No **b.** Yes **4.** 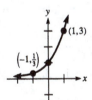 **5. a.** $f^{-1}(x) = \dfrac{x - 2}{3}$ **b.** No inverse function exists.

c. $f^{-1}(x) = x^2 + 4, x \geq 0$ **6.** $f[g(x)] = 4\left(\dfrac{x + 1}{4}\right) - 1 = x + 1 - 1 = x$; $g[f(x)] = \dfrac{(4x - 1) + 1}{4} = \dfrac{4x}{4} = x$

7. $y = f^{-1}(x) = \sqrt{x}, x > 0$; formula for the side length (y) of a square in terms of the area (x). **8.** 50 percent

Progress Check 8.3 1. $\log_3 81 = 4, \log_b 1 = 0$ **2.** $8^{1/3} = 2, a^x = y$ **3. a.** 0 **b.** $\frac{5}{3}$ **c.** $\frac{1}{16}$ **d.** $\frac{1}{4}$ **4.** 2.5119

5. 0.00501   **6.** Each graph is the reflection of the other about
the line $y = x$.

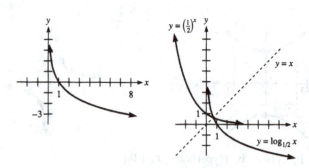

7.

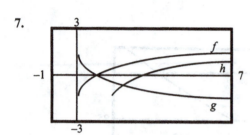

The graph of g is the graph of f reflected about the x-axis; the graph of h is the
graph of f shifted 2 units to the right.   **8.**   **9.** 3.3
10. 1.3×10^{-9}

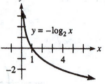

Progress Check 8.4   **1. a.** $\log_b x - \log_b 4$ **b.** $\log_2 10 + \log_2 x$ **c.** $x \log_{10} 4$ **d.** $\frac{1}{2}\log_b 7$
e. $\log_b 5 + 3 \log_b(x + 2)$ **f.** $\frac{1}{3}[\log_5 2 - (\log_5 9 + \log_5 N)]$ **2. a.** -1 **b.** $1 - \log_6 5$ **c.** $-\log_6 5$

3. a. $\log\dfrac{1}{[H^+]} = \log[H^+]^{-1} = -1 \log[H^+] = -\log[H^+]$ **b.** 7.5   **4. a.** $3m + n$ **b.** $-2n$ **5. a.** $\log_{10} a + 3$ **b.** 64

6. a. $\log_b 3$ **b.** $\log_2(x^2 - x)$ **c.** $\log_{10} 3x^2$ **d.** $\log_{10}\sqrt{\dfrac{L}{g}}$

Progress Check 8.5   **1.** $\{3.170\}$ **2.** $\{2.151\}$ **3.** 1,156 years   **4. a.** 3.065   **b.** 0.7268
5.   **6.** $\{7\}$ **7.** $\{3\}$ **8.** $\{3\}$

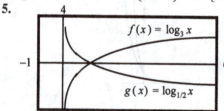

Progress Check 8.6   **1. a.** $A = 9,000(1.025)^{2t}$ **b.** \$16,278.53   **2.** \$29,054   **3.** \$6,008.33   **4.** 49 percent   **5.** $\{4.621\}$
6. a. $\{e^{-1.8}\}$; $\{0.1653\}$ **b.** $\{3e^2\}$; $\{22.17\}$ **7.** 11.55 percent   **8.** 3.5 hours

Progress Check 9.1   **1.** π **2.** $\dfrac{\pi}{2}, \dfrac{5\pi}{9}, \dfrac{7\pi}{4}$ **3.** $20°, 72°, 450°$ **4.** $39°20'$ N   **5.** 24π ft^2 **6. a.** 90π rad/minute
b. 315π in./minute

Progress Check 9.2   **1. a.** -1 **b.** 0   **c.** 1   **d.** 0   **2.** $-1, -1$, undefined, $1, -1$ **3.** $-1, -1$ **4.** $-\dfrac{1}{\sqrt{3}}, \dfrac{\sqrt{3}}{2}$
5. $\dfrac{\sqrt{3}}{2}$ **6.** $\dfrac{\sqrt{3}}{2}$ **7. a.** 0.2837   **b.** 0.7975   **8.** 7.1 ft at 7 AM; 15.2 ft at 11 PM

Progress Check 9.3   **1. a.**

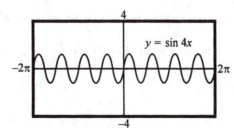

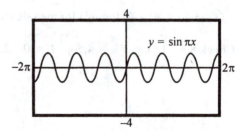

b. Period of $g = \dfrac{\pi}{2}$; period of $h = 2$ **c.** The period of $g(x) = \sin 4x$ is the period of $f(x) = \sin x$, which is 2π, divided by 4.

The period of $h(x) = \sin \pi x$ is the period of $f(x) = \sin x$ divided by π.   **2.**

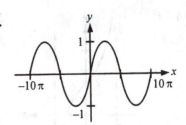

Period: 10π

3.

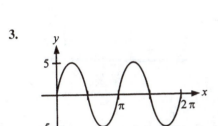

Amplitude: 5; Period: π **4.**

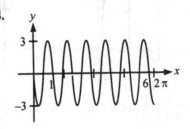

Amplitude: 3
Period: 1

5.

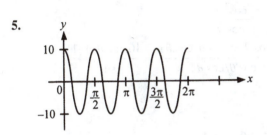

Amplitude: 10;
Period: $\dfrac{\pi}{2}$ **6.**

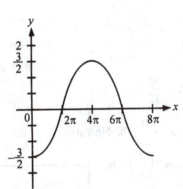

Amplitude: $\dfrac{3}{2}$;
Period: 8π

7. $y = -20 \sin \dfrac{\pi}{2} x$ **8.**

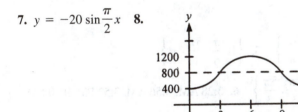

Amplitude: 400; Period: 12; Midline: $y = 800$

9.

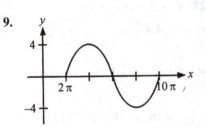

Amplitude: 4; Period: 8π; Phase shift: 2π

10. a.

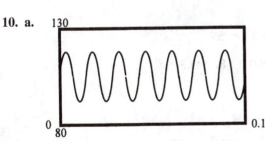

b. Maximum: 125; minimum 85   **c.** 70 beats/minute

Progress Check 9.4   1.

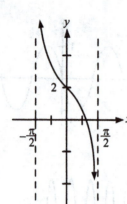

2.

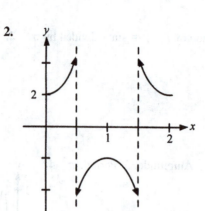

3. $\dfrac{\tan x}{\sin x} = \dfrac{\sin x/\cos x}{\sin x} = \dfrac{1}{\cos x} = \sec x$ **4.** $\cot^2 x + 1 = \dfrac{\cos^2 x}{\sin^2 x} + 1 = \dfrac{\cos^2 x + \sin^2 x}{\sin^2 x} = \dfrac{1}{\sin^2 x} = \csc^2 x$

5. $\dfrac{\cot^2 x + 1}{\cot^2 x} = \dfrac{\csc^2 x}{\cot^2 x} = \dfrac{1/\sin^2 x}{\cos^2 x/\sin^2 x} = \dfrac{1}{\cos^2 x} = \sec^2 x$ **6.** $\dfrac{\sin^2 x}{1 + \cos x} = \dfrac{1 - \cos^2 x}{1 + \cos x} =$

$\dfrac{(1 + \cos x)(1 - \cos x)}{1 + \cos x} = 1 - \cos x$ **7.** $x = \dfrac{10(\sin \theta + \cos \theta)}{\sin \theta \cos \theta} = \dfrac{10(\sin \theta/\cos \theta + \cos \theta/\cos \theta)}{\sin \theta \cos \theta/\cos \theta} = \dfrac{10(\tan \theta + 1)}{\sin \theta}$

8. a. $-\dfrac{12}{13}$ **b.** $-\dfrac{12}{5}$ **c.** $-\dfrac{13}{12}$

Progress Check 9.5   1. a. $-\dfrac{\pi}{3}$ **b.** No value   **c.** 0.95 **2. a.** 0 **b.** $\dfrac{\pi}{4}$ **c.** $\dfrac{3\pi}{4}$ **d.** -1.37

3. a. $\theta = \tan^{-1}\left(\dfrac{8}{x}\right) - \tan^{-1}\left(\dfrac{3}{x}\right)$ **b.**

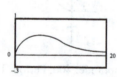

   c. 4.9 ft   **4. a.** 0 **b.** $\dfrac{15}{17}$ **5. a.** $\dfrac{\pi}{6}$ **b.** No value   **c.** 2

Progress Check 9.6   1. 3:28 AM, 8:56 AM, 3:52 PM, 9:20 PM   **2.** $\left\{\dfrac{3\pi}{4}, \dfrac{5\pi}{4}\right\}$ **3.** $\left\{0, \dfrac{\pi}{6}, \dfrac{5\pi}{6}, \pi\right\}$

4. $\{x: x = 3.55 + k2\pi$ or $x = 5.87 + k2\pi,\ k$ any integer$\}$ **5.** $\left\{\dfrac{\pi}{3}, \dfrac{2\pi}{3}, \dfrac{4\pi}{3}, \dfrac{5\pi}{3}\right\}$ **6.** 3:28 AM, 8:56 AM, 3:52 PM, 9:20 PM

Progress Check 9.7   1. 638 ft   **2.** $C = 110°, b = 26$ ft, $c = 38$ ft   **3.** $12\sqrt{3}$ **4.** $B = 27°, C = 98°, c = 91$ ft
5. $B = 41°50', C = 109°30', c = 318$ ft or $B = 138°10', C = 13°10', c = 76.6$ ft   **6.** Two triangles

Progress Check 9.8   1. 7.9 mi   **2.** $b = 41$ ft, $A = 34°, C = 98°$ **3.** $A = 31°, B = 87°, C = 62°$ **4** 5.4 yd
5. 46 ft^2 **6.** 2.34 km^2

Progress Check 10.1   1. 8, 11, 14, 17; 230   **2.** $a_n = 7n - 1$; 314   **3.** $a_n = -9\left(-\dfrac{1}{3}\right)^{n-1}; \dfrac{1}{243}$ **4. a.** Arithmetic; 0.125;
1.625, 1.75   **b.** Neither   **c.** Geometric; $\dfrac{1}{3}; \dfrac{1}{3}, \dfrac{1}{9}$ **5.** $10,737.42

Progress Check 10.2   1. 16,290   **2.** 1,925   **3.** 381   **4.** $5 + 8 + 11 + 14 + 17 = 55$

5. $6\left(\dfrac{1}{2}\right) + 6\left(\dfrac{1}{2}\right)^2 + 6\left(\dfrac{1}{2}\right)^3 + 6\left(\dfrac{1}{2}\right)^4 = \dfrac{45}{8}$ **6.** $a_i = 6i + 1$; $\displaystyle\sum_{i=1}^{8}(6i + 1)$ **7.** 3,600 ft   **8.** $44,350.80

Progress Check 10.3   1. 6   **2.** $\dfrac{2}{3}$ **3.** $\dfrac{4}{9}$ **4.** 45 gal

Progress Check 10.4   1. $x^3 + 12x^2y + 48xy^2 + 64y^3$ **2.** $x^5 - 15x^4 + 90x^3 - 270x^2 + 405x - 243$
3. $y^7 - 7y^6m + 21y^5m^2 - 35y^4m^3 + 35y^3m^4 - 21y^2m^5 + 7ym^6 - m^7$

4. $\binom{5}{0} = \binom{5}{5} = 1$, $\binom{5}{1} = \binom{5}{4} = 5$, $\binom{5}{2} = \binom{5}{3} = 10$; the binomial coefficients 1, 5, 10, 10, 5, 1 match the entries in row 5 of Pascal's triangle. **5.** $x^8 + 8x^7c + 28x^6c^2 + 56x^5c^3 + 70x^4c^4 + 56x^3c^5 + 28x^2c^6 + 8xc^7 + c^8$ **6.** $-1,512x^3y^5$

7. $\dfrac{135}{4,096} \approx 3.30$ percent

Progress Check 11.1 **1. a.** Yes; degree 6 **b.** No **2.** $P(x) = x(x + 5)(x - 1)$ **3.** 0, 1, -3 **4.** 4 is a zero of multiplicity 2, and -1 is a zero of multiplicity 1; degree 3

5. a.

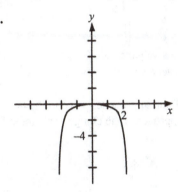

b.

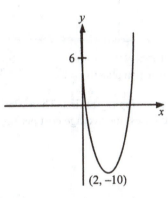

6.

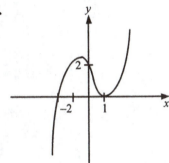

7.

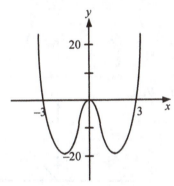

8. $y = \dfrac{1}{2}(x + 2)(x - 5)^2$

9. a. $V = (18 - 2x)(12 - 2x)x$ **b.** (0 in., 6 in.)
c. 2.35 in.

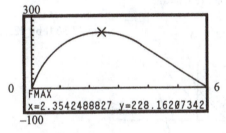

Progress Check 11.2 **1.** $\dfrac{9x^4 + 5x^2 + x + 3}{3x - 1} = 3x^3 + x^2 + 2x + 1 + \dfrac{4}{3x - 1}$

2. $4x^3 - 2x^2 + 3x - 1 = (x - 2)(4x^2 + 6x + 15) + 29$

3. $3x^3 + 10x^2 - 6x + 8 = (x + 4)(3x^2 - 2x + 2) + 0$ **4.** $P\left(-\dfrac{1}{2}\right) = 0$ **5.** Yes; $P(x) = (x + 2)(x - 3)(x + 4)$

6. $x \approx 2.73$ in. **7.** $\pm\sqrt{15}$ **8.** $4 + 2i$; $-\sqrt{3}$ **9.** $P(x) = (x - 2)(x - \sqrt{2})(x + \sqrt{2})(x - 2i)(x + 2i)$

Progress Check 11.3 **1.** $4, 2, 1, \dfrac{4}{5}, \dfrac{2}{5}, \dfrac{1}{5}, \dfrac{-1}{5}, \dfrac{-2}{5}, \dfrac{-4}{5}, -1, -2, -4$ **2.** $\dfrac{3}{2}, 1$ (multiplicity 2) **3.** $-2, \dfrac{1}{2}, 3 + i, 3 - i$

4. $2x(x + 2)x = 350$, so $2x^3 + 4x^2 - 350 = 0$. Then 5 is a root, while the reduced equation $2x^2 + 14x + 70 = 0$ has no real number solution. Unique dimensions: 10 in. by 7 in. by 5 in. **5.** $P(0) = -8, P(1) = 11$; since $P(0)$ and $P(1)$ have opposite signs, the location theorem guarantees at least one zero between 0 and 1. **6.** 0.7.

Progress Check 11.4   **1.** $x = 2, x = -2$ **2.**

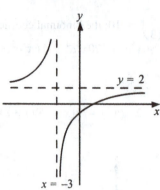

Vertical asymptote: $x = -3$
Horizontal asymptote: $y = 2$

3.

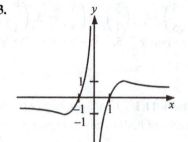

Vertical asymptote: $x = 0$
Horizontal asymptote: $y = 0$

4. a. $3.50; 35¢ per minute   **b.** As x increases, y decreases rapidly at first. Then y levels off and approaches $y = 30$. The horizontal asymptote reveals that as the length of the call increases, the average cost per minute approaches the charge per minute for the call.

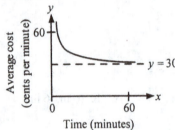

5.

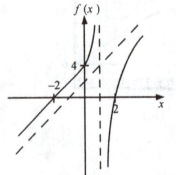

Vertical asymptote: $x = 1$
Slant asymptote: $y = x + 1$

6. 22.36 ft by 22.36 ft   **7.**

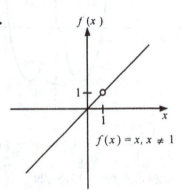

$f(x) = x, x \neq 1$

Answers to Odd-Numbered Problems

Chapter 1

Exercises 1.1 **1.** **3.** **5.**

7. **9.** **11.** Real number, rational number, integer **13.** None of these

15. Real number, rational number, integer **17.** Real number, rational number, integer **19.** Real number, irrational number
21. Real number, rational number **23. a.** $\sqrt{9}$ **b.** All **c.** None **d.** All **25. a.** $\sqrt{1}, \sqrt{4}$ **b.** $\sqrt{1}, \sqrt{4}$
c. $\sqrt{2}, \sqrt{3}, \sqrt{5}$ **d.** All **27.** False, $\frac{1}{2}$ **29.** False, 1 **31.** Commutative property of addition **33.** Associative property of
multiplication **35.** Multiplication identity property **37.** Commutative property of multiplication **39.** Distributive property
41. Associative property of multiplication **43.** Commutative property of addition **45.** Commutative property of multiplication
47. Multiplication inverse property **49.** Commutative property of addition **51.** $<$ **53.** $<$ **55.** $<$ **57.** $<$
59. $>$ **61.** 1.7 **63.** -4 **65.** -7 **67.** -2 **69.** $\frac{14}{5}$ **71.** -0.54 **73.** -4.1 **75.** -66 **77.** 2 **79.** $-\frac{1}{32}$ **81.** $\frac{20}{9}$
83. 0 **85.** -0.04 **87.** 10.8 **89.** -2 **91.** -14 **93.** 6 **95.** -27 **97.** -16 **99.** $-\frac{1}{16}$ **101.** -126 **103.** -40
105. -70 **107. a.** $\frac{5}{4}$ **b.** 3.74 **c.** $\frac{3}{5}$ **d.** 11 **109.** 2; 2.594; 2.705; 2.717; 2.718 **111.** \$3,720.59; \$6,799.13; \$12,217.62
113. 896.2; 413.1; 135.5; 89.2

Exercises 1.2 **1.** -3 **3.** -32 **5.** -2 **7.** 10 **9.** 64 **11.** -52 **13.** -30 **15.** -12 **17.** -15 **19.** 14 **21.** $\frac{1}{2}$ **23.** 1
25. $-\frac{1}{2}$ **27.** 2 terms: $2n, 4w$ **29.** 3 terms: $x^2, -3x, -2$ **31.** 1 term: $\frac{1}{2}bh$ **33.** $19a$ **35.** $14a - 8b$ **37.** $3xy + 5cd$
39. $-3x^3 + 8y^2$ **41.** $2x - 5y$ **43.** $-16a + 11b$ **45.** $10x - 7y$ **47.** $2x^3 + 13x^2y^2 + 9xy^3 - 3x^3y$
49. $7y^3 - 3y^2 + 4y + 6$ **51.** $b^3 - 3b^2 + b + 5$ **53.** $12a + 14$ **55.** $2a + 5b$ **57.** 8 **59.** $12.71x$
61. $3.14x^2 + 12x + 7.065$ **63. a.** 302 cubic feet **b.** 2,270 gals **65.** $0.045t$ **67.** $c + 1$
69. $p + 1 = p + 0.04p = 1.04p$ **71.** $a + mn$ **73.** The sum of x and the product of four and y **75.** The quotient of a and
the product of b and c

Exercises 1.3 **1.** $3^5 = 243$ **3.** 1 **5.** $\frac{1}{9}$ **7.** .00204 **9.** 576 **11.** $\frac{3}{4}$ **13.** $4^3 = 64$ **15.** $(-3)^5 = -243$ **17.** $\frac{1}{2^3} = \frac{1}{8}$
19. $2^3 = 8$ **21.** $\frac{1}{3^2} = \frac{1}{9}$ **23.** $\frac{3}{4}$ **25.** x^7 **27.** x^{12} **29.** $4p^2$ **31.** $-125y^{15}z^3$ **33.** c^6 **35.** $\frac{9}{x}$ **37.** $\frac{1}{(x+y)^3}$ **39.** $-27x^4$
41. x^2 **43.** $\frac{1}{t^2}$ **45.** $\frac{25}{y^2}$ **47.** $\frac{1}{x}$ **49.** $\frac{-8}{x^3}$ **51.** $\frac{9}{(x+h)^2}$ **53.** $\frac{a^2x^2}{4}$ **55.** $\frac{2}{a^2}$ **57.** $\frac{-x^4}{4y^5z^8}$ **59.** $\frac{x^4}{27}$ **61.** $\frac{xz^2}{y^2}$ **63.** $\frac{a^4}{8x^{10}}$ **65.** 2^{x+y}
67. 2^{1-n} or $\frac{1}{2^{n-1}}$ **69.** 5^{2x^2} **71.** y^{7a} **73.** $(a - b)^{x+y}$ **75.** 1 **77.** x^{1+x} **79.** y^{6x^2} **81.** $\frac{1}{y}$ **83.** x^{ap-1} **85.** $\frac{x^a}{y}$
87. $(1 - x)^{a+2}$ **89.** \$257.49 **91.** 4.2×10^1 **93.** 3.4251×10^4 **95.** 5.9×10^{12} **97.** 1.26×10^6 **99.** 5.3×10^{-23}
101. 92,000 **103.** 42.1 **105.** 580,000,000 **107.** 6,280,000,000,000,000,000 **109.** .0000000000000000000000003
111. 5.58×10^8 miles **113.** 3.6×10^{-25} grams **115.** 1 trillion $= 1 \times 10^{12}$; 1 million $= 1 \times 10^6$; 10^6 times
117. a. 3.35×10^{25} **b.** .0000002%

Exercises 1.4 **1.** $2x - 2y$ **3.** $-5x^4 + 5x^3 + 5x^2$ **5.** $-8x^2yz + 2xy^2z - 14xyz^2$ **7.** $p^4q^2 + p^2q^4$ **9.** $4n + 3x$
11. $2x + h$ **13.** $6x^3 + 8x^2 - 10x$ **15.** $a^2 + 7a + 12$ **17.** $x^2 + 2x - 35$ **19.** $x^2 - 16$ **21.** $6x^2 - 11x + 4$
23. $12t^2 + 28ct - 5c^2$ **25.** $k^2 - 4k + 4$ **27.** $4x^2 + 12xy + 9y^2$ **29.** $x^3 - 3x^2 + 3x - 1$ **31.** $y^3 + y^2 - 21y + 4$
33. $x^3 - y^3$ **35.** $-6y^3 + 5y^2 + 3y - 2$ **37.** $x^2 - 2xy + y^2 - 2x + 2y + 1$ **39.** $x^4 - 2x^2y^2 + y^4$ **41.** $y^2 - 9$
43. $25n^2 - 49$ **45.** $36x^2 - y^2$ **47.** $a^2 + 2a + 1$ **49.** $x^2 - 14x + 49$ **51.** $9c^2 + 30c + 25$ **53.** $4 - 28x + 49x^2$

55. $25x^2 + 40xy + 16y^2$ **57.** $100a^2 - 100ab + 25b^2$ **59.** $x^2 - 2xy + y^2 - 2x + 2y + 1$ **61.** $x^{2n} + 7x^n + 10$

63. $z^{2a} + 6z^a + 9$ **65.** $x^{2a} - y^{2b}$ **67.** $a^{2bx} + 2 + a^{-2bx}$ **69.** $x^{3n} + y^{3n}$

71. $\dfrac{x^2 + 2xh + h^2 + 1 - x^2 - 1}{h} = \dfrac{2xh + h^2}{h} = 2x + h$ **73.** $3x^2 + 3xh + h^2$ **75.** $2x + h + 2$ **77.** $810{,}000 - 2{,}500x^2$

The gross monthly income would constantly decrease, as seen by the second term. On the 18th cut, there would be no revenue.

79. a. $225 - x^2$ **b.** $x = 0$ **81.** $20x + 25$

Exercises 1.5   **1.** $\{3\}$ **3.** $\{6\}$ **5.** $\{-1\}$ **7.** $\{3\}$ **9.** $\{2\}$ **11.** $\{-6\}$ **13.** Set of all real numbers   **15.** $\varnothing$ **17.** $\{0\}$

19. $\{8\}$ **21.** $\{0\}$ **23.** $\{5\}$ **25.** $\{-5\}$ **27.** $\{3\}$ **29.** $\left\{\frac{36}{7}\right\}$ **31.** 32   **33.** 40   **35.** 8   **37.** 11   **39.** 6   **41.** $m = \frac{F}{a}$

43. $a = \frac{2d}{t^2}$ **45.** $m = \frac{P}{gh}$ **47.** $b = 3A - a - c$ **49.** $L = \frac{2s}{n} - a$ **51.** $t = \frac{a - p}{pr}$ **53.** $R^2 = \frac{A}{\pi} + r^2$ **55.** $r = \frac{a - S}{-S}$

57. $D = An - A$ **59.** $r = \frac{2E - IR}{2I}$ **61.** $x = \frac{a}{2}$ **63.** $x = 3az - 1 - t$ **65.** $x = \frac{c - b}{4}$ **67.** $x = \frac{a + 5b}{2}$

69. a. $x = 4 - 2y$ **b.** $y = \frac{4 - x}{2}$ **71. a.** $x = -y - 2$ **b.** $y = -x - 2$ **73. a.** $x = \frac{6 - 4y}{3}$ **b.** $y = \frac{6 - 3x}{4}$

75. a. $x = \frac{2y - 50}{3}$ **b.** $y = \frac{3x + 50}{2}$ **77. a.** $w = 5h - 200$ **b.** $w = 130$ pounds   **79.** 1.3 seconds   **81.** 61.75 in.^{2}

Exercises 1.6   **1.** 1,100 cans, 3,300 cans, 1,110 cans   **3.** \$8,500   **5.** \$5,450   **7.** \$1,200   **9.** 2   **11.** -5 **13.** 45

15. 40 degrees, 60 degrees, 80 degrees   **17.** 67.5 degrees   **19.** 35 degrees, 145 degrees   **21.** \$18,000 @12\%; \$36,000 @9\%

23. a. \$271,000 @5\%; \$104,000 @12\%   **b.** \$129,000 @5\%; \$246,000 @12\%   **25.** 4 hours   **27.** 21 miles   **29.** 6.5 hours

31. A: 4.5 quarts; B: 13.5 quarts   **33.** 38 lb @35\%; 57 lb @10\%   **35.** 20 quarts   **37.** 12.5 lb   **39.** 9 hours   **41.** 44 ft

43. 95   **45.** 324 gal   **47.** 92 mi   **49.** 25 qt   **51. a.** 15 ft   **b.** $\frac{12}{5}$ ft   **c.** $\frac{25}{4}$ mi

Exercises 1.7   **1.** $(-\infty, 4]$ **3.** $[-1, \infty)$ **5.** $(-\infty, 0)$

7. $\left[\frac{1}{2}, \infty\right)$ **9.** $(-\infty, 3)$ **11.** $[4, \infty)$

13. $\left[\frac{1}{2}, \infty\right)$ **15.** $(-14, \infty)$ **17.** $(-\infty, -9]$

19. $\left(-\infty, -\frac{3}{4}\right)$ **21.** $(-3, \infty)$ **23.** $(-\infty, 3)$

25. $[4, \infty)$ **27.** $(-\infty, -4]$ **29.** $(4, \infty)$

31. $(-5, \infty)$ **33.** $(-\infty, 9)$ **35.** $(-\infty, 2]$

37. $(-10, \infty)$ **39.** $[-2, \infty)$ **41.** $(-\infty, 1]$

43. $[1, \infty)$ **45.** $(-\infty, \infty)$ **47.** $\varnothing$ **49.** $(-\infty, \infty)$

51. More than 20   **53.** $k > 27.21$ **55.** $\{x: x > 11{,}500,$ where x is an integer$\}$

Exercises 1.8   **1.** $\{0\}$ **3.** $\{1\}$ **5.** False   **7.** $\{0, 1, 2, 3, 4, 8, 9\}$ **9.** $\{0, 2, 4, 8\}$ **11.** $(1, 3)$

13. $\varnothing$ **15.** $[-2, 5]$ **17.** $(-1, 4]$ **19.** $(-\infty, -5]$

21. $[-5, 3)$ **23.** $\varnothing$ **25.** $\left(-3, -\frac{3}{4}\right]$ **27.** $[-8, -2]$

29. $[-1, 9)$ **31.** $(-\infty, -5)$ **33.** $(-1, 2]$

35. $[-4, -1)$ **37.** $(2, 3)$ **39.** $(5, 31)$

41. $(2, 14]$ **43.** $[-14, 4]$ **45.** $[80, 100]$ **47.** $2.78 < C < 3.89$

49. $(-\infty, 5) \cup (7, \infty)$ **51.** $(-\infty, \infty)$ **53.** $(-\infty, 7)$

55. $(-\infty, -5) \cup (1, \infty)$ **57.** $(-\infty, \infty)$ **59.** $(-\infty, 8]$

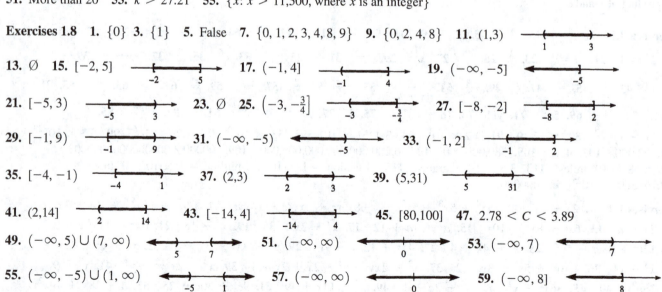

61. $(-\infty, 1)$ 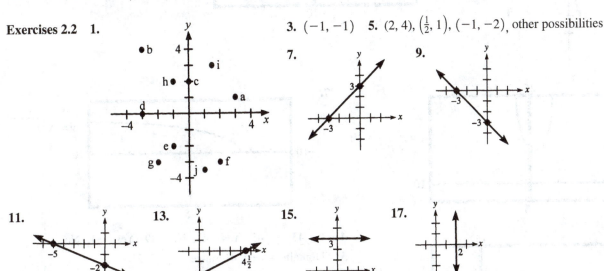   **63.** $(-\infty, -1) \cup [2, \infty)$ **65.** $(-\infty, \infty)$

67. $\varnothing$ **69.** $[-1, 2]$ **71.** $(-\infty, 7] \cup [12, \infty)$

Chapter 1 Review Exercises   **1. a.** 7   **b.** $\frac{1}{2}$ **3.** $-\frac{5}{7}$ **5.** 9   **7.** $3x - 3$ **9.** $1.\overline{18}$ **11.** $3x - 1$ **13. a.** Commutative property of addition   **b.** Distributive property   **15.** Real, rational   **17.** -2 **19.** 0.000040 **21.** $81x^6$ **23.** 2^{x+1} **25.** 3^{2x^2}
27. $\frac{1}{81}$ **29.** 3^{1-n} **31.** $\frac{27}{\frac{8}{x\,y}}$ **33.** $2x^3y - 3x^2y^2 + 4x^2y$ **35.** $s - 2c^2$ **37.** $1 - 2k + k^2$ **39.** $x^{2a} - 2x^a y^b + y^{2b}$
41. $a^3 + b^3$ **43.** $\{2\}$ **45.** $[0, \infty)$ **47.** $\{100\}$ **49.** $(1, \infty)$ **51.** $\varnothing$ **53.** $\frac{7}{2} > x > \frac{1}{2}$ **55.** $r = \frac{C}{2\pi}$ **57.** $x = \frac{n-b}{a}$
59. $y = x - z - 10P$ **61.** False, $\sqrt{2}$ **63.** False, 0   **65.** True   **67.** False, -1 **69.** True   **71.** 678.6 cubic inches   **73.** 82
75. \$522   **77.** $R = \frac{E}{I}$ **79.** 51.3 mi   **81.** \$85,106   **83.** a   **85.** d   **87.** a   **89.** c   **91.** a

Chapter 1 Test   **1.** Real number, rational number, integer   **2.** Distributive property   **3.** -220 **4.** $\frac{1}{81}$ **5.** $\frac{a^3 x^6}{1,000}$ **6.** $\frac{1}{x^2}$
7. $\{-6\}$ **8.** $\left(-\infty, \frac{2}{3}\right]$ **9.** $(-\infty, \infty)$ **10.** $\left\{\frac{10}{3}\right\}$ **11.** $15x^2 + 16x - 7$ **12.** $-11x + 2$ **13.** $-\frac{1}{2}$ **14.** 5
15. $[3, 8)$ **16.** $x = \frac{5 - 2y}{3}$ **17.** $c = \frac{2A - hb}{h}$ **18.** $2x + h$ **19.** 1.72×10^8 **20.** \$882

Chapter 2

Exercises 2.1 (There are many possibilities for 1–10)   **1.** $(-2, -2), (-1, -1), (0, 0), (1, 1), (2, 2)$ **3.** $(0, 2), (4, 0), (3, 1),$
$(-5, 3), \left(1, \sqrt{3}\right)$ **5.** $(-2, -1), (-1, -2), (0, -1), (1, 2), (2, 7)$ **7.** $(1, 60), (2, 120), (3, 180), (4, 240), \left(\frac{1}{2}, 30\right)$
9. $(32, 0), (41, 5), (50, 10), \left(0, -\frac{160}{9}\right), (-4, -20)$ **11.** $(-2, -5), (1, 4)$ **13.** $(1, 1), (-1, 1)$ **15.** Yes   **17.** No   **19.** Yes
21. $(0, 7), \left(\frac{7}{3}, 0\right), (-5, 22), \left(\frac{2}{3}, 5\right)$ **23.** 5   **25.** Domain $= \{80, 89, 85, 79, 78\}$; range $= \{B, C\}$ **27.** Domain $= \{1, 2\}$;
range $= \{2, 3, 4\}$ **29.** Domain $= \{-1, 0\}$; range $= \{0, 1\}$ **31.** Yes   **33.** No   **35.** Yes   **37.** No   **39.** Yes
41. Domain $= (-\infty, \infty)$; range $= (-\infty, \infty)$ **43.** Domain $= \{x: x \neq -4\}$; range $= \{y: y \neq 0\}$
45. Domain $= \{x: x \neq 0\}$; range $= (0, \infty)$ **47.** Domain $= [2, \infty)$; range $= [0, \infty)$ **49.** Domain $= (-\infty, 2]$;
range $= [0, \infty)$ **51.** $A = s^2: (0, \infty)$ **53.** $s = P/4; (0, \infty)$ **55.** $e = 48n; [0, \infty)$ **57.** $e = 0.08a + 600; [0, \infty)$
59. $c = 5x + 400; \{x: x \geq 0 \text{ where } x \text{ is an integer}\}$ **61.** $a = 10,000 - 50n; [0, 200]; [0, 10,000]$
63. $t = 31, 172 + .36(i - 115,000); [115,000, 250,000], [31,172, 79,772]$ **65.** $A = 3(8 - x); (0, 8), (0, 24)$

Exercises 2.2   **1.**   **3.** $(-1, -1)$ **5.** $(2, 4), \left(\frac{1}{2}, 1\right), (-1, -2)$, other possibilities

19.

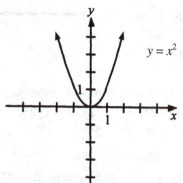

$y = x^2$

21.

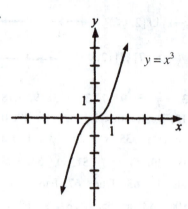

$y = x^3$

23.

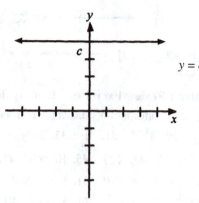

$y = c$

25.

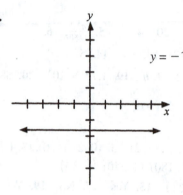

$y = -\sqrt{3}$

27.

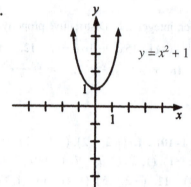

$y = x^2 + 1$

29.

$y = (x - 1)^2$

31.

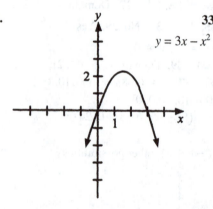

$y = 3x - x^2$

33.

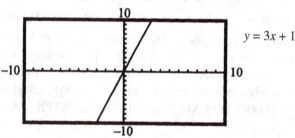

$y = 3x + 1$

35.

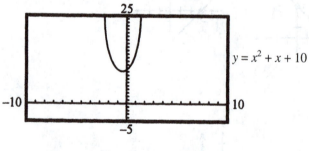

$y = x^2 + x + 10$

37.

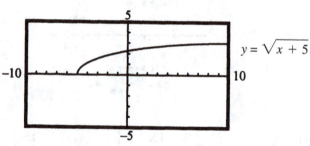

$y = \sqrt{x + 5}$

39.

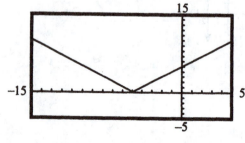

$y = |x + 5|$

41. b   **43.** a   **45.** Yes   **47.** No   **49.** Yes   **51.** No

53. Domain $= [-4, 4]$; range $= [-2, 2]$

55. Domain $= (0, \infty)$; range $= (0, \infty)$

57. Domain $= (-2, 2)$; range $= (0, 2]$

59. Domain $= [0, \infty)$; range $= \{4\}$

61. $[-6, \infty)$; $[0, \infty)$

63. $[3, \infty)$; $[5, \infty)$

65. $(-\infty, \infty)$; $[2, \infty)$ **67.** $(-\infty, \infty)$; $\{7\}$ **69.** $x \neq -1, y \neq 0$ **71.** $(2.5, 3.3)$ **73.** $(-0.2, -2.2)$

75. a. $C = 60 + 0.20m$ **b.**

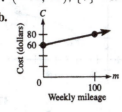

77.

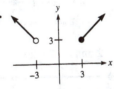

$D: [0, 8]$; $R: [0, 128]$

79. $A = 2x\sqrt{9 - x^2}$; $(0, 3), (0, 9]$

Exercises 2.3   **1.** $P = ks$; $k = 3$ **3.** $T = kp$ **5.** $V = \frac{k}{P}$ **7.** $y = \frac{7}{3}x$; $\frac{70}{3}$ **9.** $y = \frac{3}{4}x^2$; 12   **11.** $y = \frac{72}{x}$; 3   **13.** $y = \frac{24}{x^3}$; $\frac{8}{9}$
15. 60   **17.** 49   **19.** 4 in.   **21.** 2,000,000 tons   **23.** 3 in.   **25.** 600 rpm   **27.** $\frac{500\pi}{3}$ cubic units   **29.** 181 lb.
31. Exposure time is multiplied by 4.   **33.** $\frac{5}{3}$ atm   **35.** Force is multiplied by 24.   **37. a.**

	A	B	C
1.	385	692	923
2.	692	1246	1662

b. $A = \left(\frac{5}{26}\right)P$ $B = \left(\frac{9}{26}\right)P$; $C = \left(\frac{6}{13}\right)P$ **39.** $y = \frac{8}{x}$; $(1, 8)$; $(4, 2)$

Exercises 2.4   **1.** $2, -4$ **3.** $-1, 9$ **5.** $-2, -3, 2$ **7.** $11, 5, -3$ **9.** $19, 4, 7$ **11.** $\frac{2}{5}, -2$, undefined   **13.** $5, 5, 5$
15. $3a + 3$ **17. a.** 3   **b.** -1 **c.** No   **19.** $f(4) = 13{,}122$; in 4 years the value will be about \$13,100; $f(7) = 9{,}565.94$; in
7 years the value will be about \$9,600.   **21.** $f(50) = 48{,}764.58$; the current value is about \$48,800.   **23.** $f(1) = 5.1$; 1 second
after stepping off, the diver is 5.1 m above the water. $f(1.42) = 0.12$; 1.42 seconds after stepping off, the diver is 0.12 m above
the water (about to hit the water).   **25.** $f(20) = 170$; the recommended maximum heart rate for a 20-year-old is 170 beats per
minute; $f(40) = 153$; the recommended maximum heart rate for a 40-year-old is 153 beats per minute.   **27.** 10   **29.** -62
31. 25   **33.** 13   **35.** 82   **37.** $a - b - 3 \neq (a - 3) - (b - 3)$ **39.** $3(a - b) = 3a - 3b$ **41.** $(a + b)^2 \neq a^2 + b^2$
43. a. $2(x + h)^2 - 1$ **b.** $4xh + 2h^2$ **c.** $4x + 2h$ **45.** $1 + 2x + h$ **47.** 7   **49.** 0   **51.** $-2x - h$

53. $e = \begin{cases} 400 & \text{if } 0 \leq a \leq 5000 \\ 400 + 0.1(a - 5000) & \text{if } a > 5000 \end{cases}$ **55.** $c = \begin{cases} 5.25 & \text{if } 0 \leq n \leq 12 \\ 5.25 + 0.1282(n - 12) & \text{if } 12 < n \leq 48 \end{cases}$ **57. a.** -1 **b.** 6

c. 9   **d.**

59. a. 3   **b.** 3   **c.** -8 **d.**

61. a. 1   **b.** 2   **c.** 3   **d.**

63. a. 2

b. 1   **c.** 1   **d.**

65. a. 4   **b.** Undefined   **c.** 3   **d.** 4   **e.**

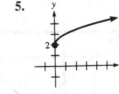

67. a. $(-\infty, \infty)$

b. $[-4, \infty)$ **c.** -3 **d.** $\{-1, 3\}$ **e.** $(-1, 3)$ **f.** $(-\infty, -1) \cup (3, \infty)$ **69. a.** $(-\infty, \infty)$ **b.** $[0, \infty)$ **c.** 0   **d.** $\{0\}$
e. $\emptyset$ **f.** $(-\infty, 0) \cup (0, \infty)$ **71. a.** $(-\infty, \infty)$ **b.** $(-\infty, 4]$ **c.** -5 **d.** $\{-5, -1\}$ **e.** $(-\infty, -5) \cup (-1, \infty)$
f. $(-5, -1)$ **73. a.** $(-\infty, \infty)$ **b.** $(-\infty, -1]$ **c.** -3 **d.** $\emptyset$ **e.** $(-\infty, \infty)$ **f.** $\emptyset$

Exercises 2.5   **1.**

3.

5.

7.

9.

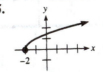

11.

13.

15.

17.

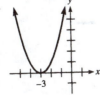

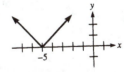

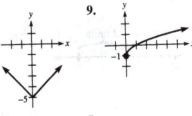

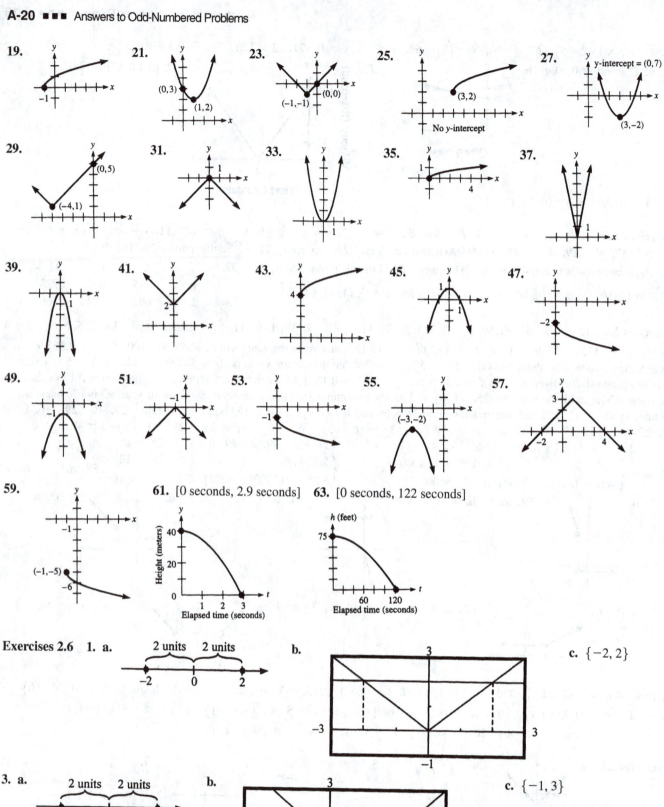

61. [0 seconds, 2.9 seconds]   **63.** [0 seconds, 122 seconds]

Exercises 2.6   1. a.

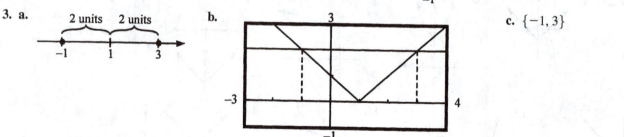

c. $\{-2, 2\}$

3. a.

c. $\{-1, 3\}$

5. a. 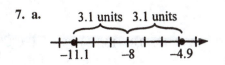   **b.** 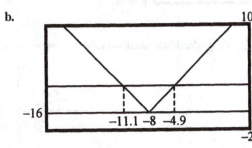   **c.** $\{-3, -1\}$

7. a. 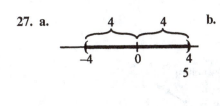   **b.**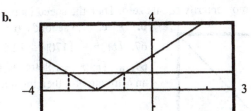
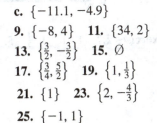

c. $\{-11.1, -4.9\}$
9. $\{-8, 4\}$ **11.** $\{34, 2\}$
13. $\left\{\frac{3}{2}, -\frac{3}{2}\right\}$ **15.** $\varnothing$
17. $\left\{\frac{3}{4}, \frac{5}{2}\right\}$ **19.** $\left\{1, \frac{1}{3}\right\}$
21. $\{1\}$ **23.** $\left\{2, -\frac{4}{3}\right\}$
25. $\{-1, 1\}$

27. a. 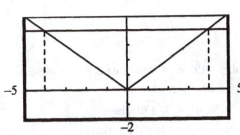   **b.** 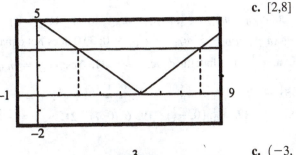   **c.** $(-4, 4)$

29. a. 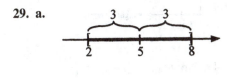   **b.** 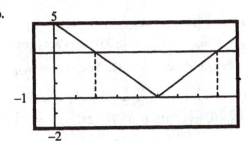 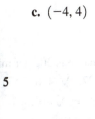 **c.** $[2, 8]$

31. a. 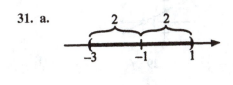   **b.** 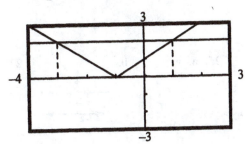   **c.** $(-3, 1)$

33. a. 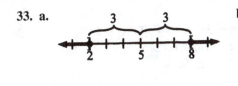   **b.** 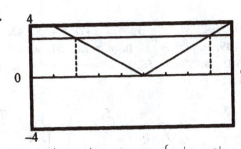   **c.** $(-\infty, 2] \cup [8, \infty)$
35. $(-\infty, -2) \cup (2, \infty)$
37. $\left(-\frac{13}{3}, 1\right)$ **39.** $[-6, 7]$
41. $(-\infty, -1) \cup (2, \infty)$
43. $\{x: |x| < 2\}$
45. $\{x: |x - 1.15| < 0.05\}$
47. $\{x: |x| > 2\}$

49. $\{x: |x - 3| > 3\}$ **51.** $\{x: |x| < 5\}$ **53.** $\{x: |x - 3| < 1\}$ **55.** $\{x: |x - 3| < \frac{1}{2}\}$ **57.** 5, 10 seconds   **59.** $\left\{-\frac{92}{3}, 36\right\}$
61. $(5, 10)$ 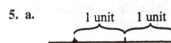   **63.** $(-\infty, -18.75) \cup (31.25, \infty)$ **65. a.** As t increases during the

first 4 seconds, the speed decreases and momentarily equals zero. Then the speed increases as t increases during the next four seconds.

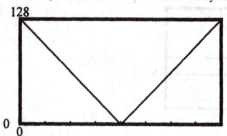

b. Ø   **c.** (1.5 seconds, 6.5 seconds)   **d.** 128 ft/second

67. $\{b: |b - 1170| \le 12.5\}$; [1157.5, 1182.5]

69. a. $\{r: |r - 1.8994| < 0.0054\}$ **b.** If $M = 1.8994$ is used as an estimate of r, then the maximum error is 0.0054.

Exercises 2.7   **1.** 1   **3.** $\frac{4}{7}$ **5.** $-\frac{11}{2}$ **7.** 0   **9.** Undefined   **11.**

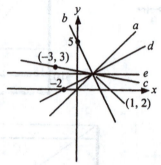

13. 0.8   **15.** -1.75

17. $m = 0.20$; mileage charge is 20¢ per mile.   **19.** $m = 0.06$; rate is 6¢ per ounce.

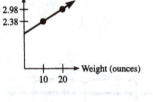

21. 2   **23.** 4   **25.** 13   **27.** $\sqrt{40}$ or $2\sqrt{10}$ **29.** $\sqrt{2}$ **31.** 10

33. $(-1, -1)$; 16   **35.** $d_1 = \sqrt{40}, d_2 = \sqrt{90}, d_3 = \sqrt{130}$; since $(d_3)^2 = (d_1)^2 + (d_2)^2$, the Pythagorean theorem ensures a right triangle.

37. $\frac{\sqrt{34}}{2}$ **39.** 9π **41. a.** $m_{AB} = m_{CD} = \frac{1}{4}$; $m_{AD} = m_{BC} = -4$ **b.** $\frac{1}{4}(-4) = -1$
c. $\sqrt{34} = \sqrt{34}$ **43.** $m_{AB} = m_{CD} = 3$; $m_{BC} = m_{AD} = 0$; $3 \cdot 0$ does not equal
-1; $\sqrt{34} \neq \sqrt{18}$ **45. a.** $-\frac{1}{5}$ **b.** Undefined   **c.** $-\frac{10}{7}$ **47.** Yes; $m_{AB} = m_{AC} = \frac{1}{6}$ **49.** No; $m_{AB} = \frac{1}{4}, m_{AC} = \frac{1}{6}$

Exercises 2.8   **1.** $y = 5x - 17$ **3.** $y = \frac{1}{2}x + 1$ **5.** $y = -\frac{1}{2}x$ **7.** $y = -x + 5$ **9.** $y = -x - 6$ **11.** 1; (0,7)
13. 5; (0, 0)   **15.** 0; (0, −2)   **17.** $-\frac{2}{3}$; $\left(0, -\frac{2}{3}\right)$ **19.** 6; (0, 7)   **21. a.** $y = -\frac{1}{2}x + 1$ **b.**

23. a. $y = 6x + \frac{1}{2}$ **b.**

25. a. $y = -2$ **b.**

27. $f(x) = \frac{2}{3}x - 2$ **29.** $f(x) = -\frac{4}{3}x - \frac{13}{3}$

31. -1 **33.** Yes   **35.** Same line   **37.** Yes   **39.** $x + 3y = 7$ **41.** $x = 3$ **43.** $2x - 3y = -7$ **45.** $x = 1$
47. a. $y = x + 1$ **b.** $y = -x + 3$ **49. a.** $y = -\frac{1}{7}x$ **b.** $y = 7x$ **51. a.** $y = \frac{3}{5}x + 143$ **b.** 275
53. a. $y = 0.6x + 40$ **b.** \$55   **c.** \$40   **d.** \$0.60   **55. a.** $y = -\frac{1}{4}x + 24$ **b.** 17 in.   **c.** 56 lb
57. linear; $y = 0.7x + 11.4$ **59.** linear; $y = 2x + 6$

Chapter 2 Review Exercises   **1.** No   **3.**

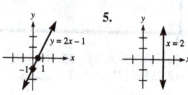

5.

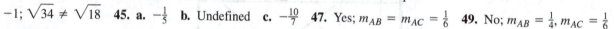

7. $m = 0.05$; rate is 5¢ per ounce.

9. $\left\{-\frac{7}{3}, 5\right\}$ **11.** Domain = $\{2, 10, 21, 70\}$; range = $\{3, 4, 7\}$ **13.** Yes **15. a.** $C = 35n$

b. Domain = $\{n: n \text{ is a nonnegative integer}\}$ **17.** -12 **19. a.** $[-2, \infty)$ **b.** $[0, \infty)$ **c.** 1 **d.** -2 **e.** None **f.** $(-2, \infty)$

21. 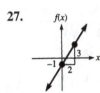 **23.**   **25. a.** 4.9 seconds **b.** [0 seconds, 4.9 seconds] **c.**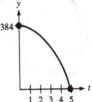

27.   **29. a.** $(0, 3)$ **b.**   **31.** $-2x + y = 5$ **33.** $m = -2, b = -1$ **35.** $y = \frac{2}{3}x + 5$

37. 40 **39.** $142.50 **41.** Same line **43.** 4 **45.** $-\frac{1}{4}$, $(0,0)$ **47.** $m_{AB} = m_{CD} = \frac{1}{3}; m_{BC} = m_{AD} = -3; \frac{1}{3}(-3) = -1$

49. $m = 5$; pump provides 5 gal/minute. **51.** $\{-1, 7\}$ **53.** $(-\infty, -1] \cup \left[-\frac{1}{3}, \infty\right)$

55. Domain = $\{6, 7, 8, 9\}$; range = $\{65, 75, 85, 95\}$ **57.** Domain = $\{x: x \neq 1\}$; range = $\{y: y \neq 0\}$ **59.** $y = -\frac{1}{6}x + 2$

61. $y = -x$ **63. a.** $y = 0.11947x + 684.83$ **b.** 780 kilowatt-hours **65.** b **67.** d **69.** b **71.** a **73.** c **75.** a

Chapter 2 Test **1.** 10 **2.** $y = \frac{1}{2}x - 1$ **3.** $m = \frac{1}{2}, b = \frac{3}{2}$ **4.** -4 **5.** $m = 0.10$; 10¢ per invitation **6.** Parallel

7. 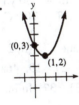 **8.**   **9.** No **10.** Domain = $\{x: x \neq -4\}$; range = $\{y: y \neq 0\}$ **11.** $\ell = \frac{P}{2} - 6$

12. 16 **13. a.** 3 **b.** 0 **c.** 2 **d.**   **14. a.** $(-\infty, \infty)$ **b.** $(-\infty, 1]$ **c.** $-3, -1$ **d.** $(-\infty, -3) \cup (-1, \infty)$

e. $(-3, -1)$ **15.**   **16.**   **17.** $\left\{-\frac{13}{3}, -3\right\}$ **18.** $(-15, 3)$

19. a. $C = 0.50n + 2$ **b.**   **20.** 400 ft

Chapter 3

Exercises 3.1 **1. a.** Yes **b.** No **3. a.** No **b.** Yes **5. a.** No **b.** Yes **7.**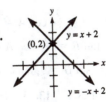

$(0,2)$; consistent

9.

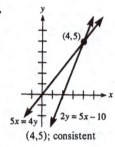

$5x = 4y$ $2y = 5x - 10$
(4,5); consistent

11.

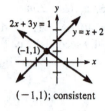

$2x + 3y = 1$ $y = x + 2$
$(-1,1)$
$(-1,1)$; consistent

13.

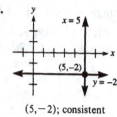

$x = 5$
$(5,-2)$
$y = -2$
$(5,-2)$; consistent

15.

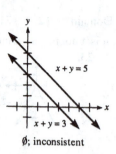

$x + y = 5$
$x + y = 3$
Ø; inconsistent

17.

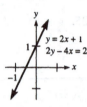

$y = 2x + 1$
$2y - 4x = 2$
Dependent

19. c **21.** $(100, 700)$ **23.** $\left(-\frac{4}{5}, 34\right)$ **25.** $(14, 3)$ **27.** $\left(\frac{13}{7}, \frac{31}{7}\right)$ **29.** Ø **31.** Dependent system; $\{(x, y): x = 3y - 1\}$ **33.** $\left(2, -\frac{1}{3}\right)$ **35.** $\left(-\frac{7}{3}, -4\right)$ **37.** $(0, 5)$ **39.** $\left(\frac{7}{3}, \frac{3}{2}\right)$ **41.** $\left(-4, -\frac{13}{3}\right)$ **43.** $\left(\frac{9}{8}, \frac{1}{8}\right)$ **45.** $\left(\frac{5}{11}, \frac{2}{11}\right)$ **47.** $(1, 1)$ **49.** $(4, -1)$ **51.** $\left(\frac{34}{11}, -\frac{7}{11}\right)$ **53.** $(7, -10)$ **55.** Ø **57.** Dependent system; $\{(x, y): 4x - 6y = 10\}$ **59. a.** $\{-1.7\}$ **b.** $(-1.7, \infty)$ **61. a.** $\{0\}$ **b.** $[0, \infty)$ **63. a.** Ø **b.** Ø **65.** $150,000 at 10 percent; $50,000 at 6 percent **67.** $45,000 salary; $15,000 investments **69.** $45,094 **71.** State tax: $28,340; federal tax: $291,498 **73.** A's income: $9,500; B's income: $38,000 **75.** 6 minutes **77.** 4 gal of 2 percent solution; 2 gal of 5 percent solution **79.** 100,000 copies; 20 months **81.** 50 years **83.** 12.5 and -2.5 **85.** $57°$ and $33°$ **87.** $18°$ **89.** 6.75 cm^2 **91.** 8.5 in. by 2.5 in. **93.** $83.20 **95.** $94.50 on paperbacks; $119.76 on hardbacks **97.** Plane speed $= 425$ mi/hour; wind speed $= 25$ mi/hour **99.** $\frac{1}{30}$ mi/minute, or 2 mi/hour

Exercises 3.2 **1. a.** Yes **b.** No **3. a.** Yes **b.** Yes **5. a.** Yes **b.** No **7.** $(1, 2, 3)$ **9.** $(-1, 1, 2)$ **11.** $(-2, 0, 2)$ **13.** $(2, 2, 2)$ **15.** $(-1, -2, 3)$ **17.** $(5, 3, 1)$ **19.** $(1, -1, 1)$ **21.** $(3, -2, 1)$ **23.** $\left(\frac{1}{2}, \frac{1}{3}, \frac{1}{4}\right)$ **25.** $(0, 0, 0)$ **27–33.** Answers will vary. Solutions lead to $0 = a, a \neq 0$. **35–41.** Answers will vary. Solutions lead to $0 = 0$. **43.** $I_1 = \frac{2}{13}$ ampere, $I_2 = \frac{4}{65}$ ampere, $I_3 = \frac{14}{65}$ ampere **45.** $a = 1, b = -4, c = 8, y = x^2 - 4x + 8$ **47.** 16, 24, 5, 80

Exercises 3.3 **1.** $(1, -2, 1)$ **3.** $(2, 0, 1)$ **5.** $(1, -2, 1)$ **7.** $(3, 5, 7)$ **9.** $(-3, 1)$ **11.** $(-1, -2)$ **13.** $\left(0, \frac{1}{3}, \frac{2}{3}\right)$ **15.** $\left(\frac{1}{2}, 0, \frac{3}{4}\right)$ **17.** $\left(\frac{1}{4}, -\frac{1}{4}\right)$ **19.** $(3, -1)$ **21.** $(2, 2, 3)$ **23.** $(1, -1, 2)$ **25.** 300 orchestra and mezzanine; 400 balcony **27.** 30 cassettes, 20 records, 100 CDs

Exercises 3.4 **1.** -2 **3.** -5 **5.** 0 **7.** $ad - bc$ **9.** 0 **11.** 1 **13.** a^2 **15.** $\frac{17}{6}$ **17.** $(0, 1)$ **19.** $(0, 0)$ **21.** $(1, 2)$ **23.** $\left(-\frac{1}{6}, -\frac{5}{8}\right)$ **25.** $(-1, -1)$ **27.** $D = 0$; inconsistent system; Ø. **29.** $D = 0$; dependent system; $\{(x, y): x - y = 4\}$ **31.** 0 **33.** 1 **35.** -49 **37.** 0 **39.** 6 **41.** -2 **43.** 0 **45.** $\left(-\frac{1}{2}, -\frac{20}{7}, \frac{23}{14}\right)$ **47.** $\left(-\frac{1}{2}, \frac{1}{3}, \frac{1}{4}\right)$ **49.** $\left(0, 5, \frac{1}{5}\right)$ **51.** $\left(\frac{1}{4}, \frac{1}{4}, \frac{3}{4}\right)$ **53.** Ø, inconsistent system **55.** Dependent system **57.** 80 oz of 35 percent solution; 16 oz of 25 percent solution **59.** $120,000 at 12.5 percent; $130,000 at 8.5 percent **61.** $-4.5, 3.5$ **63.** Width $= 125$ yd; length $= 250$ yd **65. a.** 100 days b. 200 liters **67.** Yes; 30 oz alloy 1, 50 oz alloy 2, 20 oz alloy 3 **69.** $A = 80°, B = 70°, C = 30°$

Chapter 3 Review Exercises **1.** Yes **3.** $(-1, -2)$ **5.** $35,000 at 7 percent; $5,000 at 5 percent **7.** $(3, 2, -1)$ **9.** Dependent system; infinitely many solutions **11.** 28 **13.** $\left(\frac{2}{5}, -\frac{1}{8}\right)$ **15.** $(4, 1, -2)$ **17.** $(4, -2)$ **19.** 46, 24 **21.** 24 in. or 96 in. **23.** 5 **25.** No **27.** $\left(\frac{3}{2}, 8\right)$ **29.** $(-1, 3)$ **31.** $(19, 34)$ **33.** $(-3, -1)$ **35.** $(1, -3)$ **37.** Infinitely many solutions **39.** 311 **41.** $(3, 2)$

Chapter 3 Test **1.** 3 **2.** -1 **3.** b **4.** a **5.** $\left(-\frac{1}{2}, \frac{1}{3}\right)$ **6.** $(2, -2)$ **7.** $(5, -1, 1)$ **8.** $\left(\frac{2}{3}, 0\right)$ **9.** $(15, 13, -5)$ **10.** $(2, -3)$ **11.** $(1, 2)$ **12.** $(-3, -3)$ **13.** $(5, -3, 3)$ **14.** Inconsistent system; Ø **15.**

$y = 2x$
$(2,4)$
$x + y = 6$

16. $55°$ and $35°$ **17.** $a = 2, b = -3, c = 4$ **18.** 60 **19.** $40,000 **20.** 700

Chapter 4

Exercises 4.1 **1.** $\sin A = \cos B = \frac{5}{13}, \cos A = \sin B = \frac{12}{13}$, $\tan A = \cot B = \frac{5}{12}, \cot A = \tan B = \frac{12}{5}, \sec A = \csc B = \frac{13}{12}, \csc A = \sec B = \frac{13}{5}$ **3.** $\sin \theta = \cos \beta = \frac{4}{5}, \cos \theta = \sin \beta = \frac{3}{5}, \tan \theta = \cot \beta = \frac{4}{3}, \cot \theta = \tan \beta = \frac{3}{4}, \sec \theta = \csc \beta = \frac{5}{3}, \csc \theta = \sec \beta = \frac{5}{4}$ **5.** $\frac{x}{y}$ **7.** $\frac{40}{9}$ **9.** $\frac{y}{x}$ **11.** $\sec X$ or $\csc Z$ **13.** 3 **15.** $\frac{5}{7}$ **17.** 1 **19.** $\csc \theta = 2, \cos \theta = \frac{\sqrt{3}}{2}, \sec \theta = \frac{2}{\sqrt{3}}, \tan \theta = \frac{1}{\sqrt{3}}$, cot $\theta = \sqrt{3}$ **21.** tan $\theta = \frac{5}{3}$, sin $\theta = \frac{5}{\sqrt{34}}$, csc $\theta = \frac{\sqrt{34}}{5}$, cos $\theta = \frac{3}{\sqrt{34}}$, sec $\theta = \frac{\sqrt{34}}{3}$

23. cot $\theta = \frac{1}{2}$, sin $\theta = \frac{2}{\sqrt{5}}$, csc $\theta = \frac{\sqrt{5}}{2}$, cos $\theta = \frac{1}{\sqrt{5}}$, sec $\theta = \sqrt{5}$ **25.** 20   **27.** 36   **29.** cos $A = \frac{12}{13}$ **31.** cos 73°

33. cot 8°30′   **35.** sec 21.9°   **37.** No   **39.** No   **41.** Yes   **43.** $2\sqrt{3}$, 4 (hypotenuse)   **45.** $\frac{\sqrt{3}}{2}$ **47.** $\frac{2}{\sqrt{3}} = \frac{2\sqrt{3}}{3}$

49. $\frac{1}{\sqrt{3}} = \frac{\sqrt{3}}{3}$ **51.** $\frac{1}{\sqrt{2}} = \frac{\sqrt{2}}{2}$ **53.** 0.9925   **55.** 0.1228   **57.** 5.396   **59.** 1.287   **61.** 0.2130   **63.** 0.0017   **65.** 27.06

67. 60°   **69.** 60°   **71.** 45°   **73.** 45°00′ or 45.0°   **75.** 38°20′ or 38.3°   **77.** 55°50′ or 55.8°   **79.** 52°30′ or 52.6°

81. 3°30′ or 3.6°   **83.** 85°50′ or 85.8°   **85.** 69 ft   **87. a.** 44.25°   **b.** 48.6°

Exercises 4.2   **1.** $b = 87$ ft, $c = 100$ ft, $B = 60°$ **3.** $a = 13$ ft, $b = 7.5$ ft, $B = 30°$ **5.** $a = 8.1$ ft, $b = 24$ ft, $A = 19°$
7. $a = 20$ ft, $b = 14$ ft, $B = 35°$ **9.** $b = 85.1$ ft, $c = 121$ ft, $B = 44.5°$ **11.** $a = 379$ ft, $b = 497$ ft, $A = 37°20′$
13. $b = 975$ ft, $c = 975$ ft, $A = 1°50′$ **15.** $b = 14$ ft, $A = 24°$, $B = 66°$ **17.** $c = 1.4$ ft, $A = 45°$, $B = 45°$
19. $a = 23.1$ ft, $A = 62°30′$, $B = 27°30′$ **21.** 25 ft   **23.** 52 yd   **25.** 89 ft   **27.** 400 ft   **29.** 280 ft   **31.** 10°   **33.** 22 ft
35. 120 in.   **37.** 16 ohms, 15°   **39.** 55°, 55°, 70°   **41.** 88 ft   **43.** 480 m   **45.** 1.4 in.

Exercises 4.3

	sin θ	csc θ	cos θ	sec θ	tan θ	cot θ
1.	$-\frac{4}{5}$	$-\frac{5}{4}$	$\frac{3}{5}$	$\frac{5}{3}$	$-\frac{4}{3}$	$-\frac{3}{4}$
3.	$\frac{5}{13}$	$\frac{13}{5}$	$-\frac{12}{13}$	$-\frac{13}{12}$	$-\frac{5}{12}$	$-\frac{12}{5}$
5.	$-\frac{4}{5}$	$-\frac{5}{4}$	$\frac{3}{5}$	$\frac{5}{3}$	$-\frac{4}{3}$	$-\frac{3}{4}$
7.	$\frac{1}{\sqrt{2}}$	$\sqrt{2}$	$\frac{1}{\sqrt{2}}$	$\sqrt{2}$	1	1
9.	$\frac{2}{\sqrt{5}}$	$\frac{\sqrt{5}}{2}$	$-\frac{1}{\sqrt{5}}$	$-\sqrt{5}$	-2	$-\frac{1}{2}$

11. Q_4 **13.** Q_3 **15.** Q_2

	sin θ	csc θ	cos θ	sec θ	tan θ	cot θ
17.	$-\frac{3}{5}$	$-\frac{5}{3}$	$-\frac{4}{5}$	$-\frac{5}{4}$	$\frac{3}{4}$	$\frac{4}{3}$
19.	$-\frac{\sqrt{3}}{2}$	$-\frac{2}{\sqrt{3}}$	$\frac{1}{2}$	2	$-\sqrt{3}$	$-\frac{1}{\sqrt{3}}$
21.	$-\frac{3}{4}$	$-\frac{4}{3}$	$-\frac{\sqrt{7}}{4}$	$-\frac{4}{\sqrt{7}}$	$\frac{3}{\sqrt{7}}$	$\frac{\sqrt{7}}{3}$
23.	$\frac{1}{3}$	3	$\frac{\sqrt{8}}{3}$	$\frac{3}{\sqrt{8}}$	$\frac{1}{\sqrt{8}}$	$\sqrt{8}$
25.	-1	-1	0	undef	undef	0
27.	0	undef	1	1	0	undef
29.	0	undef	-1	-1	0	undef

31. 1   **33.** 1   **35.** undefined   **37.** $-\frac{1}{2}$ **39.** $\frac{2}{\sqrt{3}}$ **41.** -1 **43.** $\frac{1}{2}$ **45.** $-\frac{1}{\sqrt{2}}$ **47.** $\frac{2}{\sqrt{3}}$ **49.** $-\sqrt{3}$ **51.** $-\frac{1}{\sqrt{2}}$ **53.** $-\frac{1}{\sqrt{2}}$

55. $-\frac{\sqrt{3}}{2}$ **57.** $\sqrt{3}$ **59.** 1   **61.** $\frac{2}{\sqrt{3}}$ **63.** 1   **65.** -0.5299 **67.** 3.487   **69.** 1.923   **71.** -0.8557 **73.** -0.5354

75. 0.0494   **77.** -1.360 **79.** -0.9983 **81.** -0.6111 **83.** 0.3346   **85.** 0.1564   **87.** 1.150   **89.** 0.4848   **91.** -0.6787

93. 1.881   **95. a.** $\frac{16 \sin 70°}{\sin 40°} = 24.39$ ft   **b.** $\frac{8}{\cos 70°} + 1 = 24.39$ ft   **97.** 8.9 mi   **99.** 165 ft

Exercises 4.4   **1.** $\{60°, 300°\}$ **3.** $\{135°, 315°\}$ **5.** $\{45°, 135°\}$ **7.** $\{150°, 210°\}$ **9.** $\{30°, 210°\}$ **11.** $\{225°, 315°\}$
13. $\{60°, 240°\}$ **15.** $\{240°, 300°\}$ **17.** $\{210°, 330°\}$ **19.** $\{45°, 225°\}$ **21.** $\{7°00′, 173°00′\}$ **23.** $\{120°50′, 239°10′\}$
25. $\{22°10′, 202°10′\}$ **27.** $\{161°00′, 199°00′\}$ **29.** $\{72°20′, 252°20′\}$ **31.** $\{101°20′, 281°20′\}$
33. $\{131°50′, 228°10′\}$ **35.** $\{74°00′, 254°00′\}$ **37.** $\{206°20′, 333°40′\}$ **39.** Ø   **41.** 405°, 765°, 1,125°, $-315°$, $-675°$
43. 382°10′, 742°10′, 1,102°10′, $-337°50′$, $-697°50′$ **45.** 480°, 840°, 1,200°, $-240°$, $-600°$ **47.** $-390°$, $-750°$, $-1,120°$,
330°, 690°   **49.** $-460°50′$, $-820°50′$, $-1,180°50′$, 259°10′, 619°10′   **51.** $\{\theta: \theta = 45° + k360°$ or $\theta = 135° + k360°\}$
53. $\{\theta: \theta = 199°30′ + k360°$ or $\theta = 340°30′ + k360°\}$ **55.** $\{\theta: \theta = 113°30′ + k360°$ or $\theta = 246°30′ + k360°\}$
57. Ø   **59.** $\{\theta: \theta = 180° + k360°\}$ **Note** In Exercises 41–50 other solutions are possible; in Exercises 51–60 k may be any
integer.   **61.** 20°, 70°   **63.** 33°

Exercises 4.5   **1. a.** 13 lb   **b.** 23°   **3. a.** 18 lb   **b.** 34°   **5. a.** 16 mi/hour   **b.** 18°   **7. a.** 510 mi   **b.** 81°   **9. a.** 13°
b. 310 mi/hour   **11. a.** 340 mi/hour   **b.** 91 mi/hour   **13.** 34 lb   **15.** 608 lb   **17.** 26 lb   **19. a.** 40 lb   **b.** 12°
21. a. 321 lb   **b.** 5°50′   **23.** 23 lb   **25.** 30°, 56°, 86°   **27.** v, 50 lb; h, 87 lb   **29.** v, 8.2 lb; h, 16 lb
31. $R = 7.1$ lb, $\theta = 47°$ **33.** $R = 22$ lb, $\theta = 149°$ **35.** $R = 24$ lb, $\theta = 196°$

Chapter 4 Review Exercises   **1.** 460°, 820°, 1,180°, $-260°$, $-620°$ **3.** $\frac{1}{a}$ **5.** cot 68°   **7.** $\frac{\sqrt{21}}{5}$ **9.** $\frac{1}{\sqrt{2}}$ **11.** False
13. True   **15.** False   **17.** $\frac{1}{2}$ **19.** 3   **21.** $\{\theta: \theta = 71°30′ + k360°$ or $\theta = 251°30′ + k360°\}$, k any integer   **23.** Ø
25. 2 and $\sqrt{3}$ cm.   **27.** $A = 43°$, $b = 48$ ft, $c = 66$ ft   **29.** Q_4 **31.** 3   **33.** 3.8 ft^2 **35.** 35°20′   **37.** 190 yd   **39.** 4°
41. 77 ft   **43.** 116°   **45.** $R = 7.3$ lb, $\theta = 68°$ **47.** b   **49.** a   **51.** c   **53.** b   **55.** d

Chapter 4 Test   1. $\frac{\sqrt{3}}{2}$ **2.** $\frac{8}{15}$ **3.** $\frac{4}{\sqrt{41}}$ **4.** $-\frac{1}{\sqrt{2}}$ **5.** -1.471 **6.** $510°, 870°, -210°$ **7.** $15°$ **8.** $\{139°, 221°\}$
9. $\{\theta: \theta = 135° + k360° \text{ or } \theta = 315° + k360°\}$, k any integer   **10.** $-\frac{2}{\sqrt{13}}$ **11.** True   **12.** 1   **13.** 78 ft   **14.** 19.5°
15. Q_3 **16.** 34 lb   **17.** $\{120°, 240°\}$ **18.** $A = 39°$, $B = 51°$, $a = 28$ ft   **19.** 6.6 m   **20.** 39 lb

Chapter 5

Exercises 5.1   1. $y(x + z)$ **3.** $4(2x - 3)$ **5.** $b(1 - b)$ **7.** $5x^2y(x - 2y)$ **9.** $3ax(3ax + 1)$ **11.** $x(2xz^2 + 4y - 5xy^2)$
13. $(x + 1)(x + 2)$ **15.** $(t - 4)(7t - 1)$ **17.** $(a - c)(b + d)$ **19.** $(x - 5)(x + 2)$ **21.** $(x + y)(a + 5)$
23. $(y + 2)(3x + 1)$ **25.** $(x - 2)(4x + 3)$ **27.** $(a - 3)^2$ **29.** $(x^2 + 1)(x^3 + 5)$ **31.** $(x + 7)(x^2 - 7)$
33. $(a + 4)(a + 1)$ **35.** $(x - 7)(x - 2)$ **37.** $(y + 15)(y - 2)$ **39.** $(c - 5)(c + 2)$ **41.** $(x - 3)^2$ **43.** $(t + 5)^2$
45. $(x + 5y)(x + 3y)$ **47.** $(a + 4b)(a - b)$ **49.** $(7y - 6)(y - 1)$ **51.** $(3x + 1)(x - 2)$ **53.** $(3k - 2)(2k - 1)$
55. $(3a - 2)^2$ **57.** $(9b + 2)(b - 3)$ **59.** $(12x - 5y)(x - 2y)$ **61.** $3(k - 4)(k + 2)$ **63.** $6(t + 4)(t - 2)$
65. $3x(x - 3)(x - 1)$ **67.** $y(3y - 5)(3y - 2)$ **69.** $8xy(3x + 2y)(x + y)$ **71.** $7(\sin \theta + \cos \theta)$
73. $7 \sin \theta(3 \sin \theta - 2)$ **75.** $3 \cos \theta \tan \theta(5 \tan \theta - 7 \cos \theta)$ **77.** $(\sin \theta - 5)(\cos \theta + \tan \theta)$
79. $(\tan \theta - 2)(\tan \theta - 1)$ **81.** $(\tan \theta - 5)(\tan \theta - 4)$ **83.** $(3 \sin \theta + 1)(\sin \theta - 3)$ **85.** $(3 \sin \theta + 2)(2 \sin \theta + 1)$
87. $(5 \sin \theta - 12)(4 \sin \theta + 1)$ **89.** $(4 \cos \theta - \tan \theta)(\cos \theta - 2 \tan \theta)$ **91.** $(2 \sin \theta - 1)^2$ **93.** 1, factorable
95. 13, not factorable   **97.** 81, factorable   **99.** 985, not factorable   **101.** $S = 2b(b + 2a)$ **103.** $A = \frac{3\pi R^2}{4}$ **105.** $0.91x$; less
107. $1.32x$; a 32 percent increase of the original price   **109.** $(2x + 11)(x - 5) = 0$

Exercises 5.2   1. $(n + 3)(n - 3)$ **3.** $(6x + 1)(6x - 1)$ **5.** $(5p + 7q)(5p - 7q)$ **7.** $(x + y + 2)(x + y - 2)$
9. $(6r^3 + k^2)(6r^3 - k^2)$ **11.** $(y + 3)(y^2 - 3y + 9)$ **13.** $(x - 1)(x^2 + x + 1)$ **15.** $(ab + c)(a^2b^2 - abc + c^2)$
17. $(x^2 + 4)(x^4 - 4x^2 + 16)$ **19.** $(x + 1)(x^2 + 8x + 19)$ **21.** $x(1 + y)(1 - y)$ **23.** $16(1 + t)(1 - t)$
25. $(1 + t^2)(1 + t)(1 - t)$ **27.** $3(7x - 3)(-x - 3)$ **29.** $t(t + 1)(t^2 - t + 1)$ **31.** $2y^2(y - 2)(y^2 + 2y + 4)$
33. $\pi(R + r)(R - r)$ **35.** $3(3n^2 + n + 1)$ **37.** $6x(x - 3)(x - 1)$ **39.** $(x^2 + 1)(x + 1)(x^2 - x + 1)$
41. $4x^2(x + 6)(x - 6)$ **43.** $(x + 1)(x^2 - x + 1)(x - 1)(x^2 + x + 1)$ **45.** $(x^4 + y^4)(x^2 + y^2)(x + y)(x - y)$
47. $(x + 2 + y)(x + 2 - y)$ **49.** $(x + y + z)(x - y - z)$ **51.** $(\sin \theta + 1)(\sin \theta - 1)$
53. $(2 \tan \theta + 5 \sin \theta)(2 \tan \theta - 5 \sin \theta)$ **55.** $7(\sin \theta + 3)(\sin \theta - 3)$ **57.** $\cos \theta(\cos \theta + 1)(\cos \theta - 1)$
59. $(\tan^2 \theta + 1)(\tan \theta + 1)(\tan \theta - 1)$ **61.** $(\sin \theta - 1)(\sin^2 \theta + \sin \theta + 1)$ **63.** $4a(a + b)(a - b)$ **65. a.** $(c + d)^2$
b.

67. $\pi(R + r)(R - r)$ **69. a.** $y = 5329 - 441t^2$ **b.** $y = (73 + 21t)(73 - 21t)$
c. $\left[73 + 21\left(\frac{73}{21}\right)\right]\left[73 - 21\left(\frac{73}{21}\right)\right] = 146(0) = 0$ **d.** 1533 ft/second $\approx$ 1045 mi/hour

Exercises 5.3   1. $\{0, 6\}$ **3.** $\{0, -3\}$ **5.** $\{0, \frac{18}{5}\}$ **7.** $\{7, -7\}$ **9.** $\{1, -1\}$ **11.** $\{2, 5\}$ **13.** $\{-1, -6\}$ **15.** $\{1, -2\}$
17. $\{-\frac{1}{2}, 2\}$ **19.** $\{\frac{1}{3}, \frac{1}{4}\}$ **21.** $\{2\}$ **23.** $\{0, \frac{1}{3}\}$ **25.** $\{1, -2\}$ **27.** $\{4, -6\}$ **29.** $\{0, \frac{13}{6}\}$ **31.** $\{7, -7\}$
33. $\{412, -6.02, -\pi\}$ **35.** $\{\frac{3}{2}, \frac{4}{3}, \frac{5}{4}\}$ **37.** $\{0, 1, -1\}$ **39.** $\{0, 1, 2\}$ **41.** $(5, 0), (-1, 0), (0, -5)$ **43.** $(2, 0), (0, 4)$
45. $(\frac{2}{3}, 0), (-\frac{3}{2}, 0), (0, -6)$ **47.** $(0, 0), (2, 0), (-2, 0)$ **49.** $(-4, 0), (1, 0), (5, 0), (0, 20)$
51. $\{71°30', 98°10', 251°30', 278°10'\}$ **53.** $\{30°, 150°, 221°50', 318°10'\}$ **55.** $\{0°, 90°, 180°, 270°\}$
57. $63°30' + k360°; 101°20' + k360°; 243°30' + k360°; 281°20' + k360°$ **59.** $0° + k360°; 90° + k360°; 270° + k360°$
61. $t = \frac{3}{2}$ seconds   **63.** 8 seconds   **65.** 7, 8 and $-7, -8$ **67.** 8 and -5 **69.** Side $= 6$; area $=$ volume $= 216$
71. 49 ft^2 **73.** Length $= 12$ in.; width $= 2$ in.   **75.** 192 yd^2

Exercises 5.4   1. $\frac{4}{11}$ **3.** $\frac{y + 2}{y + 3}$ **5.** $\frac{1}{3b + 1}$ **7.** -1 **9.** $\frac{-1}{ax}$ **11.** $\frac{-1}{x + 1}$ **13.** $\frac{a + 1}{a - 4}$ **15.** $\frac{7 - y}{7 + y}$ **17.** $\frac{3x(2x - 5)}{2(x - 4)}$ **19.** $\frac{-1}{2h}$
21. $\frac{x + 1}{x^2 + x + 1}$ **23.** $\frac{a^2}{a^2 - a + 1}$ **25.** $x^2 + ax + a^2$ **27.** $\frac{1}{y - x}$ **29.** $\frac{y}{4x^2}$ **31.** $\frac{2}{a(a + 3)}$ **33.** $\frac{(y - 1)(y - 2)}{(y + 2)(y + 1)}$ **35.** $\frac{(x - 1)^2}{(x + 1)^2}$

37. $\frac{1}{x}$ **39.** $\frac{n-1}{n-3}$ **41.** $\frac{(x+1)(x-1)^2}{7x}$ **43.** $\frac{1-x}{x(a+1)}$ **45.** $\frac{2}{5(x+y)^3}$ **47.** $\frac{1}{a^2b^2(x+2)^2}$ **49.** $\frac{x^3}{(y-3)^2}$ **51.** $\frac{x+2}{x+1}$

53. $\frac{3}{4}$ **55. a.** $\frac{8-c}{2}$ **b.** $\frac{8-\cos\theta}{2}$ **57. a.** $\frac{5(c+1)}{2(c-6)}$ **b.** $\frac{5(\cos\theta+1)}{2(\cos\theta-6)}$ **59. a.** $18sct^2$ **b.** $18\sin\theta\cos\theta\tan^2\theta$ **61. a.** $\frac{1}{s}$

b. $\frac{1}{\sin\theta}$ **63.** $\frac{10}{3}$ **65. a.** $-4(s+2)$ **b.** $-4(\sin\theta+2)$ **67.** 1   **69.** $0, -\frac{1}{3}$ **71.** All real numbers except -3

73. a. 25 percent   **b.** 0   **75. a.** $\frac{y}{n}$ **b.** $\frac{n-x-a}{n}$ **77.** $\frac{m-y}{y}$

Exercises 5.5   **1.** $2x$ **3.** $\frac{1}{4x}$ **5.** 1   **7.** $x+2$ **9.** $\frac{1}{w-3}$ **11.** $\frac{x+2}{x+1}$ **13.** 0   **15.** $\frac{4}{x-4}$ **17.** $\frac{2y}{2y-3}$ **19.** $t+5$

21. $35x^2y^2$ **23.** $12x^3y^2z^3$ **25.** $x(x+2)$ **27.** $(y+1)^2(y-1)$ **29.** $6(n+1)(n-1)$ **31.** $6m(3m-1)$ **33.** $\frac{3+2x}{6x}$

35. $\frac{6y-3}{10y^2}$ **37.** $\frac{ax+by}{x^2y}$ **39.** $\frac{1-x^2}{x}$ **41.** $\frac{x^2+x-1}{x(x-1)}$ **43.** $\frac{-x^2+2x+6}{x(x+3)}$ **45.** $\frac{y-3}{y^2-4}$ **47.** $\frac{-9}{4x^2-9}$ **49.** $\frac{x+1}{x+2}$

51. $\frac{y^2+4y+2}{(y+1)(y+2)(y+3)}$ **53.** $\frac{x^2-2}{(x+1)^2(x+2)}$ **55.** $\frac{4x-4}{(x+3)^2}$ **57.** $\frac{x^2+4x-5}{(x+1)^2}$ **59.** $\frac{t+5}{t^2-1}$ **61.** $\frac{2}{a-b}$ **63. a.** $\frac{-6}{s}$ **b.** $\frac{-6}{\sin\theta}$

65. a. $\frac{-1}{t-1}$ **b.** $\frac{-1}{\tan\theta-1}$ **67. a.** $\frac{13t}{8}$ **b.** $\frac{13\tan\theta}{8}$ **69. a.** $\frac{1-t^2}{t}$ **b.** $\frac{1-\tan^2\theta}{\tan\theta}$ **71. a.** $\frac{7t}{4(t-3)}$ **b.** $\frac{7\tan\theta}{4(\tan\theta-3)}$

73. a. $\frac{2t+18}{(t+6)(t+12)}$ **b.** $\frac{2\tan\theta+18}{(\tan\theta+6)(\tan\theta+12)}$ **75.** 2   **77. a.** $\frac{n}{n(n+1)}+\frac{1}{n(n+1)}=\frac{n+1}{n(n+1)}=\frac{1}{n}$ **b.** $\frac{1}{4}+\frac{1}{12}=\frac{1}{3}$

79. $\frac{ax-bx+bn}{n}$

Exercises 5.6   **1.** $\frac{4}{29}$ **3.** $\frac{x}{2}$ **5.** $\frac{1+mn}{1-mn}$ **7.** $\frac{x+1}{2x-1}$ **9.** $\frac{b}{2b-3a}$ **11.** $\frac{xy}{y^2-x^2}$ **13.** $\frac{w}{3-w^2}$ **15.** $\frac{a^2bc+ac+ab}{abc^2+ac+bc}$ **17.** $\frac{x}{1+y}$

19. -2 **21.** $\frac{3hk+4k}{2hk-h-6}$ **23.** $-\frac{x^2-2xy-y^2}{x^2+y^2}$ **25.** $\frac{x^3-3x^2-2x-8}{3x}$ **27.** $\frac{(x-1)(4x^2+x-2)}{4x^2}$ **29.** $\frac{(x+y)xy}{x^2+xy+y^2}$

31. $\frac{1+x}{x}$ **33.** $\frac{1}{n^2}$ **35.** $\frac{y+2}{y-2}$ **37. a.** $\frac{s^2-5}{5s}$ **b.** $\frac{\sin^2\theta-5}{5\sin\theta}$ **39. a.** $\frac{s^2-c^2}{s^2+c^2}$ **b.** $\frac{\sin^2\theta-\cos^2\theta}{\sin^2\theta+\cos^2\theta}$ **41. a.** s **b.** $\sin\theta$

43. $\frac{37}{7}$ **45.** $f=\frac{ad}{a+d}$ **47. a.** $m=\frac{w_1a+w_2b}{w_1+w_2}$ **b.** $m=\frac{a+b}{2}$

Exercises 5.7   **1.** $4x^6$ **3.** $\frac{x}{2y}$ **5.** $-\frac{3z^2}{y^2}$ **7.** $6n-2+\frac{1}{2n}$ **9.** $-\frac{4}{y}+3x$ **11.** $-\frac{3rs}{4t}+\frac{7r}{6t^2}$ **13.** $-\frac{2}{y}+\frac{3}{x}-\frac{4}{xy}$ **15.** $\frac{a}{b}+2+\frac{b}{a}$

17. $3x+5+\frac{6}{x-1}$ **19.** $4y-10+\frac{19}{y+2}$ **21.** $3y-4$ **23.** $3x-1+\frac{1}{2x+3}$ **25.** x^2-2x+4 **27.** $n^2-n+1-\frac{2}{n+1}$

29. $2x-3+\frac{18}{2x+3}$ **31.** $3x^3+x^2+2x+1+\frac{4}{3x-1}$ **33.** $x^2+x+1+\frac{x-5}{2x^2+1}$ **35.** $2c^2+3c-4-\frac{2c}{c^2-c+1}$

37. x^3-x+3 **39.** m^2+m+1 **41.** $\frac{2A-bh}{h}=\frac{2A}{h}-\frac{bh}{h}=\frac{2A}{h}-b$ **43.** $\frac{cy-ab}{a}=\frac{cy}{a}-\frac{ab}{a}=\frac{cy}{a}-b$

Exercises 5.8   **1.** $\left\{\frac{4}{5}\right\}$ **3.** $\{48\}$ **5.** $\left\{\frac{10}{3}\right\}$ **7.** No solution; false equation   **9.** Identity; all real numbers except 0   **11.** $\left\{\frac{1}{4}\right\}$

13. $\left\{-\frac{28}{9}\right\}$ **15.** $\{2\}$ **17.** $\left\{\frac{1}{8}\right\}$ **19.** $\{10\}$ **21.** $\left\{-\frac{22}{3}\right\}$ **23.** $\left\{\frac{21}{10}\right\}$ **25.** $\{0\}$ **27.** $\{1\}$ **29.** $\left\{\frac{1}{2},2\right\}$ **31.** $\left\{-\frac{1}{6},1\right\}$

33. $\left\{-\frac{1}{2},0\right\}$ **35.** $\{5\}$ **37.** $\{2\}$ **39.** $\{1,-1\}$ **41.** $\{-1,-3\}$ **43.** $b=12$ **45.** $R_1=15$ ohms   **47.** 100 units

49. $p=\frac{1}{1+w}$ **51.** $d_1=\frac{fd_2}{d_2-f}$ **53.** $i=\frac{S-P}{Pn}$ **55.** 2.4 hours   **57.** 12 minutes   **59.** $\frac{1}{100}+\frac{1}{100}=\frac{1}{x}$; $x=50$ minutes

61. a. 6 mi/hour   **b.** 4 hours   **c.** $3\frac{1}{4}$ hours   **63.** 2 hours   **65.** 1 hour   **67.** 60 mi/hour

Chapter 5 Review Exercises   **1.** $8xy^2$ **3.** $(y-3)(7-y)$ **5.** $1.21x$; the result is a 21 percent increase of the original price.

7. $(y+8)(y-3)$ **9.** $(6x^2-1)(3x^2+1)$ **11.** $(3x-4)^2$ **13.** $6y(y+1)(y-1)$ **15.** $(c+d)(c-2d)$

17. $c(a+2)(b+1)$ **19.** $(x^2+h^2)(x+h)(x-h)$ **21.** $2\sin^2\theta\cos\theta(\sin\theta-9)$ **23.** $\{-3,0,3\}$ **25.** $\left\{-\frac{5}{2},3\right\}$

27. $\left\{\frac{1}{2},-\frac{4}{3},-\frac{1}{4}\right\}$ **29.** 64 square units   **31.** -15 and -16; 15 and 16   **33.** $-2,2$ **35.** $\frac{-3}{x^2}$ **37.** $10y$ **39.** $2y^5$ **41.** $18x^3y^2z$

43. $\frac{a-b}{3a-b}$ **45.** $\frac{x^2-x-1}{(x-3)^2(x+2)}$ **47.** $\frac{5b+2a}{ab}$ **49.** $\frac{1}{n^3}$ **51.** $\frac{x}{y^3}+\frac{2}{y}+\frac{2}{x}+\frac{y^2}{x^3}$ **53.** $n^2+n+1+\frac{2}{n-1}$

55. $\left\{-\frac{5}{2}\right\}$ **57.** $\left\{\frac{2}{5}\right\}$ **59.** $\{-1,-5\}$ **61.** $L_1=\frac{L_2W_2}{W_1}$ **63.** $Z_2=\frac{ZZ_1}{Z_1-Z}$ **65.** $1\frac{7}{8}$ hours   **67.** 6 mi/hour   **69.** $\frac{\cos\theta-1}{\cos\theta+1}$

71. $\frac{1}{\tan\theta(\tan\theta+1)}$ **73.** $\cos^2\theta-4\sin\theta$ **75.** $\frac{5m}{m+5}$ **77.** $\frac{20b-3a^2}{24a^3b^3}$ **79.** $\frac{3}{4x^2}$ **81.** $\frac{2}{x-3}$ **83.** $\frac{-4}{x-1}$ **85.** $\frac{(y-2)^2}{x^5}$

87. $\frac{x-1}{x-2}$ **89.** $\frac{22}{21}$ **91.** $\frac{-1}{x+4}$ **93.** $\frac{-(x+5)}{5x}$ **95.** $\{76°,135°,256°,315°\}$ **97.** $2(a-b)^2$ **99. a.** $x=p/(1-p)$

b. 25 percent   **101.** d   **103.** c   **105.** d

Chapter 5 Test **1.** $5x(x + 2)$ **2.** $(2a - 1)^2$ **3.** $(4y + 5)(4y - 5)$ **4.** $(n + 1)(n^2 - n + 1)$

5. $2(5 \sin \theta + 3)(2 \sin \theta - 1)$ **6.** $\frac{x - 1}{4}$ **7.** $\frac{-x^3}{x + 2}$ **8.** $\frac{x + 1}{x - 4}$ **9.** $\frac{10}{3}$ **10.** $\frac{\sin^2 \theta - \cos^2 \theta}{\cos \theta \sin \theta}$ **11.** $2, -2$ **12.** $\frac{xy + 1}{y + x}$ **13.** $\frac{1}{n^3}$

14. $\frac{3x}{y} - \frac{4y}{x} + xy$ **15.** $2x - 3 + \frac{6}{2x + 1}$ **16.** $\left\{-\frac{1}{2}, \frac{5}{3}, 0\right\}$ **17.** $\{6, -10\}$ **18.** $\{28\}$ **19.** 36 minutes   **20.** 6 in.

Chapter 6

Exercises 6.1 **1.** $11, -11$ **3.** $19, -19$ **5.** $24, -24$ **7.** 17 **9.** 3.46 **11.** -26 **13.** Not real   **15.** 5.83 **17.** -20
19. Not real   **21.** -30 **23.** Not real   **25.** 4 **27.** -6 **29.** -3 **31.** 2 **33.** -2 **35.** Not real   **37.** -8 **39.** Not real
41. -2 **43.** 7 **45.** -6 **47.** 243 **49.** 8 **51.** $\frac{1}{3}$ **53.** $\frac{1}{8}$ **55.** -256 **57.** $\frac{1}{36}$ **59.** $-\frac{1}{8}$ **61.** $\frac{125}{64}$ **63.** $\frac{4}{5}$ **65.** $\frac{3}{2}$ **67.** $3^{7/4}$
69. 27 **71.** $7^{2/3}$ **73.** a^2 **75.** $b^{1/4}$ **77.** $2b^4$ **79.** $4x^4$ **81.** $a^{1/4}b^{1/4}$ **83.** $\frac{b^{1/2}}{a}$ **85.** $\frac{a^{1/4}}{b^{5/3}}$ **87.** $3x^4$ **89.** $\frac{a^4}{3}$ **91.** $8a^9$
93. $16a^4$ **95.** $\frac{x^{5/3}}{16}$ **97. a.** 9 **b.** $9 < 15$ **99.** Geometric mean $= 1.24097$; average annual increase in sales is about 24.1 percent.
101. a. Side $= 8$ in.   **b.** Side $= \sqrt{ab}$ **103. a.** 2 **b.** -2 **c.** 0 **d.** 16 **e.** 54 **105. a.** -2 **b.** 0 **c.** -1 **d.** -4 **e.** 6

Exercises 6.2 **1.** $2\sqrt{7}$ **3.** $7\sqrt{3}$ **5.** $6\sqrt{2}$ **7.** $2\sqrt[3]{5}$ **9.** $5\sqrt[3]{3}$ **11.** $3\sqrt[4]{3}$ **13.** 64 **15.** x^2 **17.** 81 **19.** 14 **21.** y^3
23. $\sqrt[4]{x}$ **25.** $\sqrt[6]{y^5}$ **27.** $x^3\sqrt{x}$ **29.** $6y\sqrt{2y}$ **31.** $y^3\sqrt[3]{y^2}$ **33.** $x^2y^4\sqrt{y}$ **35.** $4xy\sqrt{2}$ **37.** $2x^2y^3\sqrt{10x}$ **39.** $7xy^2\sqrt{2xy}$
41. $2x\sqrt[3]{3y}$ **43.** $3xy\sqrt[3]{3x^2y}$ **45.** $x^2y\sqrt[4]{x^3y}$ **47.** $\frac{4}{11}$ **49.** $\frac{4\sqrt{2}}{7}$ **51.** $\frac{6\sqrt{7}}{7}$ **53.** $\frac{\sqrt[3]{18}}{3}$ **55.** $\frac{7\sqrt{y}}{y}$ **57.** $\frac{2\sqrt{6x}}{x}$ **59.** $\frac{\sqrt[3]{6y^2}}{2y}$
61. $\frac{\sqrt[3]{14y}}{6y}$ **63.** $\pi\sqrt{2} \approx 4.44$ seconds   **65.** $20{,}000$ cycles/second   **67.** 9 **69.** $10\sqrt{6}$ **71.** $2\sqrt{7}$ **73.** $9\sqrt{7}$ **75.** $12\sqrt[3]{3}$
77. $72\sqrt[4]{3}$ **79.** $12x^2y\sqrt{10x}$ **81.** $2xy\sqrt[4]{3xy^3}$ **83.** 2 **85.** 2 **87.** $2\sqrt[4]{2}$ **89.** $\frac{\sqrt{22}}{11}$ **91.** $\frac{2\sqrt[3]{18}}{3}$ **93.** $\frac{\sqrt{10}}{5}$ **95.** $\frac{3\sqrt{2y}}{2}$
97. $\frac{\sqrt[3]{6x^2}}{2}$ **99.** $\frac{4\sqrt{10y}}{5}$ **101.** $\frac{\sqrt[4]{90x^3}}{2}$ **103.** $\sqrt{7}$ **105.** $\frac{12\sqrt{y}}{y}$ **107.** $\frac{\sqrt{6}}{2}$ **109.** $\frac{\sqrt{2}}{2}$ **111.** $\frac{\sqrt{6y}}{2y}$ **113.** $\frac{\sqrt{2y}}{y}$ **115.** $\frac{\sqrt{x}}{7x}$
117. $\frac{3\sqrt[3]{7}}{7}$ **119.** $\frac{5\sqrt[4]{4}}{2}$ **121.** $\frac{2\sqrt[4]{5y}}{5y}$ **123. a.** $\{4\}$; principal root only   **b.** $\{4, -4\}$; both square roots   **c.** No
125. a. (i) Square first; then extract square root. (ii) Get square root; then square.   **b.** Same value   **127.** $\sqrt[n]{\frac{a}{b}} = \left(\frac{a}{b}\right)^{1/n} = \frac{a^{1/n}}{b^{1/n}} = \frac{\sqrt[n]{a}}{\sqrt[n]{b}}$

Exercises 6.3 **1.** $6\sqrt{5}$ **3.** $9\sqrt[3]{17}$ **5.** $9\sqrt{6}$ **7.** $10\sqrt{13}$ **9.** $3\sqrt{6}$ **11.** $-8\sqrt{10}$ **13.** $-8\sqrt[4]{2}$ **15.** Does not simplify.
17. Does not simplify   **19.** Does not simplify   **21.** $(4 + y)\sqrt{x}$ **23.** $(15 - x)\sqrt{13}$ **25.** $6\sqrt[4]{7}$ **27.** $10\sqrt{x}$ **29.** $3y\sqrt{x}$
31. $2\sqrt[4]{3xy}$ **33.** $5\sqrt{2}$ **35.** $7\sqrt{3}$ **37.** $11\sqrt{2}$ **39.** $\sqrt{3}$ **41.** 0 **43.** $5\sqrt[3]{3}$ **45.** $-7\sqrt[3]{2}$ **47.** $5y\sqrt{6x}$ **49.** $-3x\sqrt{xy}$
51. $7xy\sqrt{3x}$ **53.** $(3 - 6y)\sqrt{2x}$ **55.** $3\sqrt{17}$ **57. a.** $4\sqrt{10}$ **b.** 10 **59. a.** $\sqrt{5}$ **b.** $2\sqrt{5}$ **c.** $\sqrt{5}$ **61.** $23\sqrt{2}$
63. $-\frac{2}{3}\sqrt{6}$ **65.** $\frac{5}{6}\sqrt{2}$ **67.** $\frac{7}{3}\sqrt{3}$ **69.** $\frac{3}{4}\sqrt{10}$ **71.** $-\frac{7}{6}\sqrt{6}$ **73.** $-\frac{14}{15}\sqrt{3}$ **75.** $-2\sqrt{6}$ **77.** 0 **79.** $\left(\frac{3x + 4y}{xy}\right)\sqrt{xy}$
81. $2\sqrt{6}$

Exercises 6.4 **1.** 63 **3.** 640 **5.** 57 **7.** 63 **9.** 294 **11.** 153 **13.** $4 + 2x$ **15.** $3x^2 - 1$ **17.** $45x$ **19.** $98y$ **21.** $891x$
23. $3\sqrt{2} + 3$ **25.** $10\sqrt{2} - 10$ **27.** $5\sqrt{3} - 3\sqrt{5}$ **29.** $\sqrt{6} + \sqrt{10}$ **31.** 7 **33.** 10 **35.** -2 **37.** -1
39. $\sqrt[3]{x^2} + 5\sqrt[3]{x} + 4$ **41.** $\sqrt[3]{x^2} + 3\sqrt[3]{x} - 4$ **43.** $\sqrt[5]{y^2} - 10\sqrt[5]{y} + 24$ **45.** $21 + 4\sqrt{5}$ **47.** $67 - 12\sqrt{7}$
49. $9 + 24\sqrt{x} + 16x$ **51.** $25x - 50\sqrt{x} + 25$ **53.** -11 **55.** 278 **57.** $25 - x$ **59.** $x - 45$ **61.** $4x - 48$
63. $\left(2\sqrt{2} + 2\right) - \left(2\sqrt{2} - 2\right) = 4$; $\left(2\sqrt{2} + 2\right)\left(2\sqrt{2} - 2\right) = 4$ **65. a.** $\frac{0.5\sqrt{n}}{n}$ **b.** 0.016 **67. a.** $\frac{2n(\sqrt{n} - 1)}{n - 1}$
b. 4.5 **69.** $R = \frac{c(2\sqrt{c} - 1)}{4c - 1}$ **71.** $\sqrt{a}/a^2$ cm^3 **73.** $\frac{1 + \sqrt{3}}{6}$ **75.** $\frac{1 - 3\sqrt{15}}{2}$ **77.** $\frac{1 + 2\sqrt{7}}{3}$ **79.** $\frac{3\sqrt{5} + 5}{5}$ **81.** $\frac{5\sqrt{x} + x}{x}$
83. $\frac{x - 6\sqrt{x}}{x}$ **85.** $2\sqrt{3} - 2$ **87.** $\frac{4 + \sqrt{2}}{7}$ **89.** $\frac{8 + \sqrt{10}}{6}$ **91.** $\frac{x\sqrt{x} - x}{x - 1}$ **93.** $\frac{y\sqrt{6y} + 6y}{y - 6}$ **95.** $2\sqrt{3} - 2$ **97.** 0 **99.** 6

Exercises 6.5 **1.** $\{15\}$ **3.** $\{20\}$ **5.** $\{3\}$ **7.** $\{2\}$ **9.** $\varnothing$ **11.** $\{6\}$ **13.** $\{-3\}$ **15.** $\{2\}$ **17.** $3{,}003$ ft   **19.** 0.81 ft
21. $n = 7$ **23.** $\{3, 2\}$ **25.** $\{5\}$ **27.** $\{3\}$ **29.** $\{3\}$ **31.** $\{-3, -2\}$ **33.** $\{6\}$ **35.** $\{3\}$ **37.** $\{3, 11\}$ **39.** $\{3, 7\}$
41. $\{5, 9\}$ **43.** $\varnothing$ **45.** $\varnothing$ **47.** $\{5\}$ **49.** $\left\{\frac{49}{9}\right\}$ **51.** $s = \frac{gt^2}{2}$ **53.** $y = x^3 - 2$

Exercises 6.6 **1.** i **3.** $4i$ **5.** $-2i$ **7.** $-7i$ **9.** $2i\sqrt{3}$ **11.** $2i\sqrt{6}$ **13.** $5i\sqrt{5}$ **15.** $-3i\sqrt{3}$ **17.** $-5i\sqrt{3}$ **19.** $18i$
21. $17i$ **23.** i **25.** $4i$ **27.** $5 + 3i$ **29.** $7 - 3i$ **31.** $16 + 4i$ **33.** 10 **35.** $15 - 3i$ **37.** $-2 - 8i$ **39.** $-3 - 3i$
41. $-10i$ **43.** 15 **45.** -72 **47.** -60 **49.** -20 **51.** $4 + 7i$ **53.** $14 - 18i$ **55.** $85 - 32i$ **57.** $6 - 22i$
59. $-7 + 24i$ **61.** $-32 + 24i$ **63.** $21 - 20i$ **65.** $48 - 14i$ **67.** 0 **69.** 0 **71.** 3 **73.** $\frac{3}{2} + \frac{1}{2}i$ **75.** $\frac{22}{25} + \frac{4}{25}i$

77. $\frac{19}{20} + \frac{13}{20}i$ **79.** $6 - 4i$ ohms **81.** $111 + 52i$ volts **83.** $6 + 6i$ amperes **85.** i **87.** 1 **89.** i **91.** -1

Exercises 6.7 **1.**

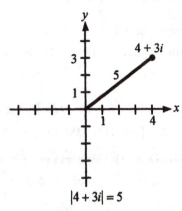

$|4 + 3i| = 5$

3.

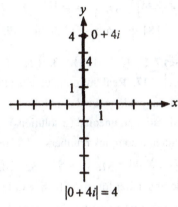

$|-1 + 2i| = \sqrt{5}$

5.

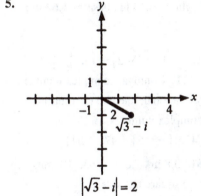

$|\sqrt{3} - i| = 2$

7.

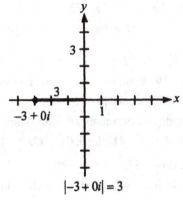

$|-3 + 0i| = 3$

9.

$|0 + 4i| = 4$

11. $3(\cos 0° + i \sin 0°)$ **13.** $2(\cos 270° + i \sin 270°)$ **15.** $\sqrt{5}(\cos 315° + i \sin 315°)$ **17.** $5(\cos 36°50' + i \sin 36°50')$

19. $\sqrt{13}(\cos 213°40' + i \sin 213°40')$ **21.** $2(\cos 120° + i \sin 120°)$ **23.** $2(\cos 315° + i \sin 315°)$ **25.** $0 + 3i$

27. $-4 + 0i$ **29.** $-\frac{\sqrt{3}}{2} + \frac{3}{2}i$ **31.** $-\sqrt{2} - \sqrt{2}i$ **33.** $0.6157 + 0.7880i$ **35. a.** $8(\cos 63° + i \sin 63°)$

b. $\frac{1}{2}(\cos 41° + i \sin 41°)$ **c.** $2[\cos(-41°) + i \sin(-41°)]$ **37. a.** $\cos 270° + i \sin 270°$ **b.** $\cos(-90°) + i \sin(-90°)$

c. $\cos 90° + i \sin 90°$ **39. a.** $36(\cos 336° + i \sin 336°)$ **b.** $\frac{1}{4}[\cos(-74°) + i \sin(-74°)]$ **c.** $4(\cos 74° + i \sin 74°)$

41. a. $2\sqrt{2}(\cos 345° + i \sin 345°)$ **b.** $\sqrt{2}(\cos 255° + i \sin 255°)$ **c.** $\frac{\sqrt{2}}{2}[\cos(-255°) + i \sin(-255°)]$

43. a. $\cos(-65°) + i \sin(-65°)$ **b.** $\cos 25° + i \sin 25°$ **c.** $\cos(-25°) + i \sin(-25°)$ **45.** $4\sqrt{3} + 4i$

47. $512\sqrt{2} - 512\sqrt{2}i$ **49.** $16 + 0i$ **51.** $16 + 16\sqrt{3}i$ **53.** $1 + 0i$ **55.** $\frac{1}{4} - \frac{\sqrt{3}}{4}i$ **57.** $\frac{\sqrt{2}}{16} - \frac{\sqrt{2}}{16}i$

59. $5(\cos 30° + i \sin 30°) = \frac{5\sqrt{3}}{2} + \frac{5}{2}i$, $5(\cos 210° + i \sin 210°) = -\frac{5\sqrt{3}}{2} - \frac{5}{2}i$

61. $2(\cos 20° + i \sin 20°) \approx 1.8794 + 0.6840i$, $2(\cos 110° + i \sin 110°) \approx -0.6840 + 1.8794i$,

$2(\cos 200° + i \sin 200°) \approx -1.8794 - 0.6840i$, $2(\cos 290° + i \sin 290°) \approx 0.6840 - 1.8794i$

63. $\cos 0° + i \sin 0° = 1 + 0i$, $\cos 120° + i \sin 120° = -\frac{1}{2} + \frac{\sqrt{3}}{2}i$, $\cos 240° + i \sin 240° = -\frac{1}{2} - \frac{\sqrt{3}}{2}i$

65. $\cos 135° + i \sin 135° = -\frac{\sqrt{2}}{2} + \frac{\sqrt{2}}{2}i$, $\cos 315° + i \sin 315° = \frac{\sqrt{2}}{2} - \frac{\sqrt{2}}{2}i$ **67. a.** $5.30(\cos 45° + i \sin 45°)$ ohms

b. $1.86(\cos 45° + i \sin 45°)$ ohms **69.** $0.36[\cos(-11.7°) + i \sin(-11.7°)]$ or $0.36(\cos 11.7° + i \sin 11.7°)$

Chapter 6 Review Exercises **1.** $-10, 10$ **3.** 2 **5.** $\frac{x^{12}}{8}$ **7.** $\sqrt{x}$ **9.** $36\sqrt[3]{4}$ **11.** $-4\sqrt{7}$ **13.** $\frac{x - y}{xy}\sqrt{xy}$ **15.** $x + 7$

17. $4y - 12\sqrt{y} + 9$ **19.** $\frac{-3 + 3\sqrt{11}}{5}$ **21.** -3 **23.** $\{-5, -4\}$ **25.** $14i$ **27.** $4i\sqrt{2}$ **29.** $-i$ **31.** $2 + 5i\sqrt{3}$

33. 30 **35.** $6 - 2\sqrt{5}$ **37.** $\frac{x\sqrt{3x} + 3x}{x - 3}$ **39.** $11y\sqrt{5x}$ **41.** 44 **43.** $(5 + y)\sqrt{2xy}$ **45.** $\frac{1}{4}$ **47.** $\frac{9\sqrt{6}}{2}$ **49.** $\frac{\sqrt{35}}{7}$ **51.** $-i$

53. $\frac{1}{5^{3/4}}$ **55.** $36\sqrt[3]{9}$ **57.** -8 **59.** $\{5\}$ **61.** $\varnothing$ **63.** $\{0, 1\}$ **65.** $8(\cos 90° + i \sin 90°)$; $0 + 8i$

67. $\cos 450° + i \sin 450°$; $0 + i$ **69.** 0 **71.** $(1 + i)^2 - 2(1 + i) + 2 = 1 + 2i + i^2 - 2 - 2i + 2 = 0$ **73.** c

75. $2 - 2\sqrt{3}i$ **77. a.** 88 ft **b.** 96 ft/second **79.** $\frac{38}{13} - \frac{18}{13}i$ **81. a.** $x = R\sqrt{2}/2$ **b.** $A = 2R^2$

Chapter 6 Test **1.** $384x$ **2.** $\sqrt[3]{3y}$ **3.** -2 **4.** $(8 - 21xy)\sqrt{3xy}$ **5.** $\frac{\sqrt{15x}}{3x}$ **6.** $x\sqrt[3]{x}$ **7.** $36x\sqrt{5}$ **8.** -8 **9.** $\frac{1}{2}$
10. $\{13\}$ **11.** $\{3\}$ **12.** 3 **13.** 13 **14.** $a^{9/10}, \sqrt[10]{a^9}$ **15.** $-18 + 0i$ **16.** d **17.** d **18.** c **19.** b **20.** c

Chapter 7

Exercises 7.1 **1.** $\{\pm 2\}$ **3.** $\{\pm 4\}$ **5.** $\{\pm 2\sqrt{3}\}$ **7.** $\{\pm 2i\}$ **9.** $\{\pm 2i\sqrt{7}\}$ **11.** $\{-6, 2\}$ **13.** $\{-3 \pm 4i\}$
15. $\{-2 \pm \sqrt{6}\}$ **17.** $\{-5 \pm i\sqrt{5}\}$ **19.** $\{3 \pm 5i\}$ **21.** $\{4 \pm 3i\sqrt{5}\}$ **23.** $\{-1, 11\}$ **25.** $\{3 \pm i\sqrt{7}\}$ **27.** $\{\frac{1}{3}, -\frac{5}{3}\}$
29. $\{\frac{2 \pm \sqrt{10}}{5}\}$ **31.** $\{\frac{1 \pm 2i}{3}\}$ **33.** $\{-\frac{3}{2} \pm i\sqrt{3}\}$ **35.** $25; (x + 5)^2$ **37.** $16; (x - 4)^2$ **39.** $\frac{25}{4}; (x - \frac{5}{2})^2$ **41.** $\frac{1}{64}; (x - \frac{1}{8})^2$
43. $\frac{1}{9}; (x - \frac{1}{3})^2$ **45.** $\frac{9}{100}; (x + \frac{3}{10})^2$ **47.** $\{0, -6\}$ **49.** $\{-1 \pm \sqrt{3}\}$ **51.** $\{6 \pm \sqrt{30}\}$ **53.** $\{-5 \pm \sqrt{29}\}$
55. $\{-1 \pm i\}$ **57.** $\{-2 \pm \sqrt{2}\}$ **59.** $\{4 \pm 3\sqrt{2}\}$ **61.** $\{\frac{1 \pm i\sqrt{15}}{2}\}$ **63.** $\{-1 \pm i\sqrt{5}\}$ **65.** $\{-3 \pm \sqrt{21}\}$
67. $\{\frac{1 \pm \sqrt{33}}{4}\}$ **69.** $\{\frac{2 \pm \sqrt{14}}{2}\}$ **71.** $\{\frac{-9 \pm \sqrt{93}}{6}\}$ **73.** $\{\frac{-1 \pm i}{2}\}$ **75.** $\{2, -\frac{1}{3}\}$ **77.** Height = 6.19 in., base = 1.62 in.;
height = 0.81 in., base = 12.38 in. **79.** 12.43 in. **81.** 37.42 mi/hour **83.** 9.54 percent

Exercises 7.2 **1.** $\{-1, 3\}$ **3.** $\{2\}$ **5.** $\{\frac{-5 \pm \sqrt{41}}{2}\}$ **7.** $\{2 \pm \sqrt{7}\}$ **9.** $\{-4, -1\}$ **11.** $\{-1 \pm i\sqrt{2}\}$ **13.** $\{-\frac{1}{2}, 3\}$
15. $\{\frac{2}{3}, \frac{3}{2}\}$ **17.** Real, rational, unequal (2 solutions) **19.** Real, rational, equal (1 solution) **21.** Conjugate complex numbers
23. Real, rational, unequal (2 solutions) **25.** Real, irrational, unequal (2 solutions) **27.** Real, rational, unequal (2 solutions)
29. Real, rational, unequal (2 solutions) **31.** Conjugate complex numbers **33.** Conjugate complex numbers
35. Conjugate complex numbers **37.** $\{-2, 6\}$ **39.** $\{\pm 3\}$ **41.** $\{-5, 0\}$ **43.** $\{-\frac{1}{2}, 3\}$ **45.** $\{-3, 5\}$ **47.** $\{\pm 4\}$
49. $\{\frac{-5 \pm \sqrt{41}}{2}\}$ **51.** $\{-\frac{5}{3}, \frac{5}{3}\}$ **53.** $\{0, \frac{9}{2}\}$ **55.** $\{\frac{4}{3}, 1\}$ **57.** $\{\pm 8i\}$ **59.** $\{\frac{3 \pm i\sqrt{71}}{10}\}$ **61.** 3.8 in., 7.8 in. **63.** 10 units
65. Side of smaller lot = 50 ft; side of larger lot = 110 feet **67.** Small square has side 6; large square has side 8.
69. 0.69 and 1.81 seconds; one is for the way up and one is for the way down. **71.** $\frac{5 \pm \sqrt{21}}{2}$; 4.791 and 0.209

Exercises 7.3 **1.** $\{-2, 6\}$ **3.** $\{-\frac{1}{2}, 7\}$ **5.** $\{-4, 3\}$ **7.** $\{\frac{-1 \pm \sqrt{7}}{3}\}$ **9.** $\{1 \pm i\}$ **11.** $\varnothing$ **13.** $\{\frac{3 \pm i}{2}\}$ **15.** $\{\pm \sqrt{10}\}$
17. $\{-\sqrt{6}\}$ **19.** $\{2\sqrt{3}\}$ **21.** $\{-\sqrt{2}\}$ **23.** $\varnothing$ **25.** $\{x: x \geq 0\}$ **27.** $\{\sqrt{2}\}$ **29.** $\{0\}$ **31.** $\{\pm 1, \pm 2i\}$
33. $\{\pm\sqrt{5}, \pm\sqrt{6}\}$ **35.** $\{\pm\sqrt{3}\}$ **37.** $\{\pm 3, \pm 4\}$ **39.** $\{\pm 2, \pm i\}$ **41.** $\{\pm\sqrt{3}, \pm i\sqrt{2}\}$ **43.** $\{-1, 27\}$ **45.** $\varnothing$
47. $\{256\}$ **49.** $x = \pm\sqrt{y + 3}$ **51.** $x = \pm\sqrt{y + 8}$ **53.** $x = \pm\sqrt{y^2 - 6}$ **55.** $x = \frac{-a_2 \pm \sqrt{a_2^2 - 4a_1(a_3 - t)}}{2a_1}$
57. $x = \frac{-r \pm \sqrt{r^2 + 4dt}}{2d}$ **59.** 6.18 in.^{2} **61.** 6 yd, 4 yd **63.** 50 rows of 40 trees each

Exercises 7.4 **1.** ────┼────┼──►x   **3.** ───┼────┼──►y   **5.** ◄──┼────┼──►x   **7.** ──┼────┼──►x
     −2 4   −1 6   −$\frac{1}{2}$ 7   −$\frac{7}{3}$ $\frac{2}{3}$

9. ────┼────┼──►x **11.** $\varnothing$ **13.** $\{5\}$ **15.** $(-\infty, \infty)$ **17.** ──┼────┼──►y **19.** ──┼────┼──►x
 −1.22 0.55   −5 5   −2.77 1.27

21. ◄─┼────┼──►x **23.** ──┼────┼──►x **25.** ◄─┼────┼──►x **27.** ◄───┼────┼──►x
 −2 0 3   −3 0 5   −3 0 1   −4 −$\frac{1}{2}$ 1

29. ◄─┼──┼──►x **31.** ──┼────┼──►x **33.** ──┼────┼──►x **35.** ──┼────┼──►x
 −2 −1 3 5 −7 −5 −2 0   −2 1   −4 3

37. ──┼────┼──►x **39.** ◄─┼────┼──►x **41.** ◄──┼────┼──►x **43.** ◄────────┼──►x **45.** $(2.35, 6.65)$
 0 6   −4 $\frac{1}{2}$ 0 $\frac{5}{2}$ 10

47. a. Lengths from 4 to $4 + \sqrt{6}$ in., or 4 to 6.45 in. **b.** 4 in. **49.** $[-2, 2]$ **51.** $(-\infty, -2] \cup [2, \infty)$ **53.** $\left(\frac{3\sqrt{3}}{5} \text{ in.}, \frac{2\sqrt{7}}{5} \text{ in.}\right)$

Exercises 7.5 **1. a.** $x = -1$ **b.** $(-1, -1)$ **c.** $(-2, 0), (0,0)$ **d.** **3. a.** $x = \frac{3}{2}$ **b.** $\left(\frac{3}{2}, \frac{9}{4}\right)$

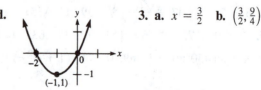

c. $(3,0), (0,0)$ **d.**

5. a. $x = \frac{5}{2}$ **b.** $\left(\frac{5}{2}, -\frac{25}{4}\right)$ **c.** $(0,0), (5,0)$ **d.**

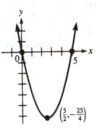

7. a. $x = 2$ **b.** $(2,0)$ **c.** $(2,0), (0,4)$ **d.**

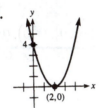

9. a. $x = -3$ **b.** $(-3,0)$ **c.** $(-3,0), (0,-9)$

d.

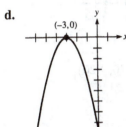

11. a. $x = 0$ **b.** $(0,9)$ **c.** $(0,9)$ **d.**

13. a. $x = 1$ **b.** $(1,-9)$

c. $(-2,0), (4,0), (0,-8)$ **d.**

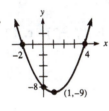

15. a. $x = 1$ **b.** $(1,9)$ **c.** $(-2,0), (4,0), (0,8)$

d.

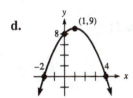

17. a. $x = -\frac{1}{2}$ **b.** $\left(\frac{1}{2}, \frac{81}{4}\right)$ **c.** $(4,0), (-5,0), (0,-20)$ **d.**

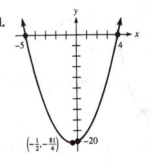

19. a. $x = \frac{1}{2}$ **b.** $\left(\frac{1}{2}, \frac{81}{4}\right)$ **c.** $(-4,0), (5,0), (0,20)$ **d.**

21. a. $x = -\frac{9}{2}$ **b.** $\left(-\frac{9}{2}, \frac{9}{4}\right)$

c. $(-6, 0), (-3, 0), (0, -18)$ **d.**

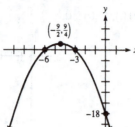

23. a. $x = -\frac{9}{2}$ **b.** $\left(-\frac{9}{2}, -\frac{9}{4}\right)$ **c.** $(-6, 0), (-3, 0), (0, 18)$

d.

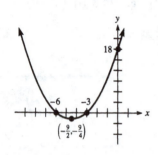

25. a. $x = \frac{1}{12}$ **b.** $\left(\frac{1}{12}, \frac{49}{24}\right)$ **c.** $\left(-\frac{1}{2}, 0\right), \left(\frac{2}{3}, 0\right), (0, 2)$ **d.**

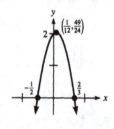

27. a. $x = \frac{1}{12}$ **b.** $\left(\frac{1}{12}, -\frac{49}{24}\right)$ **c.** $\left(-\frac{1}{2}, 0\right), \left(\frac{2}{3}, 0\right), (0, -2)$ **d.**

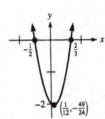

29. a. $x = 0$ **b.** $(0, -20)$

c. $\left(\pm 2\sqrt{5}, 0\right), (0, -20)$ **d.**

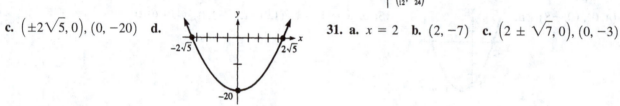

31. a. $x = 2$ **b.** $(2, -7)$ **c.** $\left(2 \pm \sqrt{7}, 0\right), (0, -3)$

d.

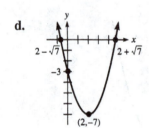

33. a. $x = 1$ **b.** $(1, 4)$ **c.** $(0, 5)$ **d.**

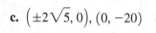

35. a. $x = 1$ **b.** $(1, -4)$

c. $(0, -5)$ **d.**

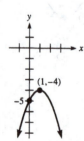

37. a. $y = -\frac{5}{2}$ **b.** $\left(-\frac{25}{4}, -\frac{5}{2}\right)$ **c.** $(0, 0), (0, -5)$ **d.**

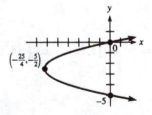

39. a. $y = \frac{3}{2}$ **b.** $\left(\frac{9}{4}, \frac{3}{2}\right)$ **c.** $(0, 0), (0, 3)$ **d.**

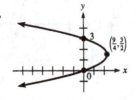

41. a. $y = -2$ **b.** $(4, -2)$ **c.** $(0, -4), (0, 0)$

d.

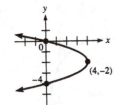

43. a. $y = 1$ **b.** $(9,1)$ **c.** $(0, -2), (0,4), (8,0)$ **d.**

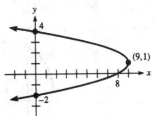

45. a. $x = 1$ **b.** $(1,3)$ **c.** $(0,5)$ **d.**

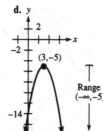

47. a. $x = -1$ **b.** $(-1, 2)$ **c.** $(0,3)$ **d.**

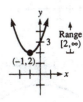

49. a. $x = 3$ **b.** $(3, -5)$ **c.** $(0, -14)$ **d.** **d.**

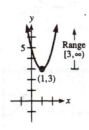

51. $x = 1; (1, -4)$ **53.** $x = -3; (-3, -5)$

55. $x = \frac{3}{2}; \left(\frac{3}{2}, \frac{25}{4}\right)$ **57.** $x = 1; (1,3)$ **59.** $x = \frac{3}{2}; \left(\frac{3}{2}, -\frac{15}{2}\right)$ **61.** 2 **63.** 2 **65.** 1 **67.** 0 **69.** 1 **71. a.**

b. 1 second **c.** 16 ft **d.** 2 seconds **73. a.**

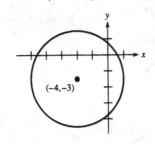

b. $\frac{78}{32} = 2.4375$ seconds **c.** $105\frac{1}{16} = 105.0625$ ft

d. 5 seconds **75.** 10, 10 **77.** 10, 10 **79.** 200 yd by 100 yd **81.** 3 in. **83.** $\frac{1}{2}$ exceeds $\left(\frac{1}{2}\right)^2$ by $\frac{1}{4}$.

Exercises 7.6 **1.** $x^2 + y^2 = 25$ **3.** $x^2 + y^2 = 9$ **5.** $(x + 2)^2 + (y - 3)^2 = 49$ **7.** $(x + 5)^2 + (y + 8)^2 = 9$
9. $(x - 4)^2 + (y - 4)^2 = 25$ **11.** $x^2 + (y + 5)^2 = 36$ **13.** $(x + 5)^2 + y^2 = 81$ **15.** $(x - 2)^2 + (y - 3)^2 = 9$
17. $(x - 6)^2 + (y - 3)^2 = 25$ **19.** $(x + 3)^2 + (y + 5)^2 = 32$ **21.** $(x - 3)^2 + (y - 2)^2 = \frac{25}{64}$
23. $(x - 2)^2 + (y + 3)^2 = \frac{4}{9}$ **25.** Center $(5,3)$; radius 4 **27.** Center $(-4, -3)$; radius 6 **29.** Center $(0,0)$; radius 9

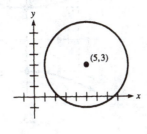

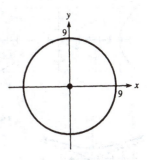

31. Center $(0,5)$; radius 2   **33.** Center $(2,-1)$; radius $2\sqrt{5}$ **35.** Center $(-2, 0)$; radius 3   **37.** Center $(-6, 3)$; radius 7

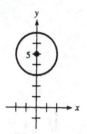

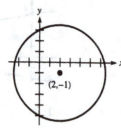

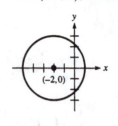

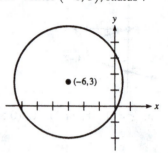

39. Center $(7, 5)$; radius $4\sqrt{5}$ **41. a.**

 **b.** **c.**

43. a.

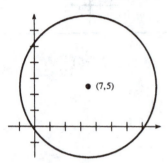

b.   **c.**

45. a. 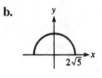   **b.**

c.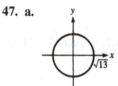

47. a.    **b.**   **c.**

49. 40 ft   **51. a.** $(1, 0)$

b. $x^2 + y^2 = 4$ **c.** $\left(1, \sqrt{3}\right)$ **d.** $2\sqrt{3}$ **e.** $\sqrt{3}$ **53.** 1

Exercises 7.7   1.

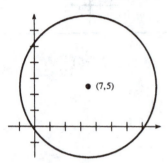

3. 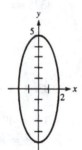 **5.** 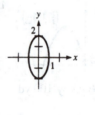 **7.** 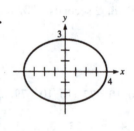 **9.**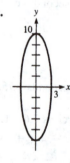

11.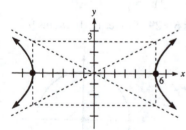

13.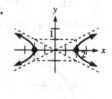

15.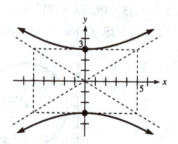

17.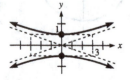

19.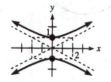

21.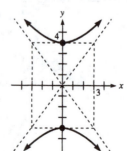

23.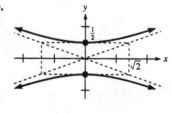

25.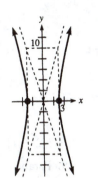

27.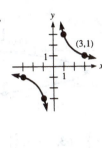

29.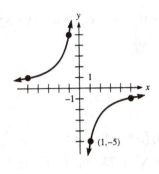

31. Parabola **33.** Hyperbola

35. Circle **37.** Ellipse **39.** Hyperbola **41.** Ellipse **43.** Ellipse **45.** Circle **47. a.** $k = 15$; $y = 15/x$
b. $xy = 15$

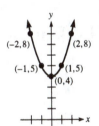

49. a. $t = k/s$ **b.** $k = 110$ **c.**

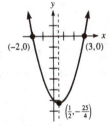

d. $t = 2.444$ hours
$= 2$ hours 27 minutes

Exercises 7.8 **1.** $\{(0, 2), (3, 8)\}$ **3.** $\{(-2, 11), (5, -17)\}$ **5.** $\{(3, 9)\}$ **7.** $\varnothing$ **9.** $\{(0, -6), (6, 0)\}$
11. $\left\{(0, -3), \left(\frac{12}{5}, \frac{9}{5}\right)\right\}$ **13.** $\varnothing$ **15.** $(3, 5), (3, -5), (-3, 5), (-3, -5)$ **17.** $(4, 3), (4, -3), (-4, 3), (-4, -3)$
19. $\left(\sqrt{15}, -3\right), \left(\sqrt{15}, 3\right), \left(-\sqrt{15}, 3\right), \left(-\sqrt{15}, -3\right)$ **21.** 6 by 8 cm **23.** 1.005 by 9.949 in.
25. a. $y = \sqrt{3}x$; $x^2 + y^2 = 4$ **b.** $\left(1, \sqrt{3}\right), \left(-1, -\sqrt{3}\right)$

Chapter 7 Review Exercises **1.** $\left\{i\sqrt{3}, -i\sqrt{3}\right\}$ **3.** $x^2 + 8x + 16 = (x + 4)^2$ **5.** $\left\{\frac{1 + \sqrt{37}}{6}, \frac{1 - \sqrt{37}}{6}\right\}$ **7.** $\left\{-2, \frac{3}{4}\right\}$
9. 2 solutions; real, irrational, unequal **11.** $\{2, 3\}$ **13.** $\{\pm 1, \pm 3\}$ **15.** $y = \pm\sqrt{9 - x^2}$ **17.** $(-\infty, \infty)$ **19.** $\left(0, \frac{5}{3}\right)$
21.

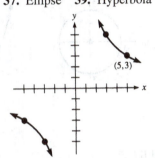

23. a. $x = \frac{1}{2}$ **b.** $\left(\frac{1}{2}, -\frac{25}{4}\right)$ **c.** $(-2, 0), (3, 0), (0, -6)$ **d.**

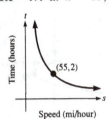

25. a. 4.5 seconds **b.** 324 ft **c.** 9 seconds **27.** $(x + 2)^2 + (y - 6)^2 = 18$ **29.** Center $(3, 2)$; radius $\sqrt{11}$
31.

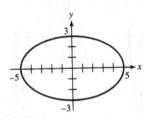

33.

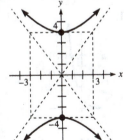

35. Ellipse **37.** $\left\{(2, 0), \left(\frac{8}{5}, -\frac{6}{5}\right)\right\}$

39. $\{(16, 5), (-16, -5), (5, 16), (-5, -16)\}$ **41.** $(1, 1), (1, -1), (-1, 1), (-1, -1)$ **43.** $(-1, 0)$; $r = \sqrt{6}$
45. $(x + 1)^2 + (y - 4)^2 = 49$ **47.** $y^2 + 10y + 25 = (y + 5)^2$ **49.** $Ap = 500$, or $A = \frac{500}{p}$
51. Width 2.815 in.; length 7.815 in.
53. a. $x = 2$ **b.** $(2, 0)$ **c.** $(2, 0), (0, 4)$

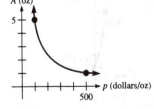

d.

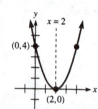

55. a. $y = -4$ **b.** $(-16, -4)$ **c.** $(0, 0), (0, -8)$ **d.**

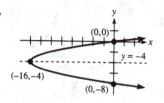

57. $t = \dfrac{-p \pm \sqrt{p^2 + 128q - 128y}}{-64}$ **59.** $\{(3, 5), (-5, -3)\}$ **61.** $\left\{\dfrac{3 - \sqrt{29}}{2}, \dfrac{3 + \sqrt{29}}{2}\right\}$ **63.** $\left\{-3, \dfrac{2}{3}\right\}$ **65.** $\{2 + i, 2 - i\}$

67. $\left\{\dfrac{1}{3}\right\}$ **69.** $\{5i, -5i\}$ **71.** $\left\{4 - \sqrt{5}, 4 + \sqrt{5}\right\}$ **73.** $(0, 3]$ **75.** $(-1, 0) \cup \left(\dfrac{1}{2}, \infty\right)$ **77.** Circle **79.** Parabola

81. Ellipse **83.** Parabola **85.** Hyperbola

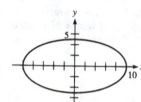
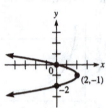
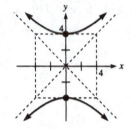
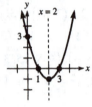
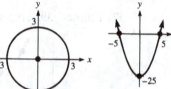

Chapter 7 Test **1.** $x^2 - 8x + 16 = (x - 4)^2$ **2.** One rational solution **3.** $(-1, 1); r = \sqrt{5}$
4. $(x - 5)^2 + (y - 1)^2 = 25$ **5. a.** $x = 2$ **b.** $(2, -1)$ **c.** $(1, 0), (3, 0), (0, 3)$ **d.** **6.** $y = \pm\sqrt{x^2 - 7}$
7. $\{(-2, -3), (1, 3)\}$ **8.** **9.**

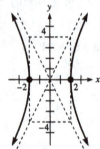
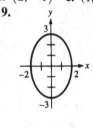
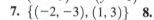

10. $\left\{2 + \sqrt{5}, 2 - \sqrt{5}\right\}$ **11.** $\left\{\dfrac{-1 + \sqrt{33}}{4}, \dfrac{-1 - \sqrt{33}}{4}\right\}$ **12.** $\{6 + 2i, 6 - 2i\}$ **13.** $\{-1, 4\}$ **14.** $\left\{\dfrac{2}{3}, -2\right\}$ **15.** $\left\{\sqrt{2}\right\}$
16. $\left\{\sqrt{6}, -\sqrt{6}, \sqrt{2}, -\sqrt{2}\right\}$ **17.** $(-\infty, -7) \cup (1, \infty)$ **18.** $(-\infty, -4) \cup \left(0, \dfrac{1}{3}\right)$ **19.** $[-5, 6)$
20. a. 3.5 seconds **b.** 196 ft **c.** 7 seconds

Chapter 8

Exercises 8.1 **1.** $1, 125, \dfrac{1}{25}, 2.24, 9.74$ **3.** $1, 27, \dfrac{1}{9}, 1.73, 4.73$ **5.** $1, \dfrac{1}{64}, 16, \dfrac{1}{2}, 0.14$ **7.** $1, \dfrac{1}{216}, 36, 0.41, 0.08$
9. $-1, -729, -\dfrac{1}{81}, -3, -22.36$ **11.** $-1, -125, -\dfrac{1}{25}, -2.24, -9.74$ **13.** $1, \dfrac{1}{8}, 4, 0.71, 0.38$ **15.** $1, \dfrac{1}{64}, 16, \dfrac{1}{2}, 0.14$
17. $-1, -\dfrac{1}{8}, -4, -0.71, -0.38$ **19.** $-1, -\dfrac{1}{64}, -16, -\dfrac{1}{2}, -0.14$ **21.** **23.** **25.**

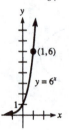
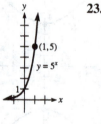
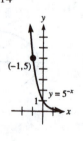

27. **29.** **31.** **33.** **35.**

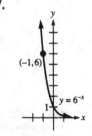
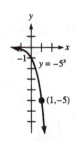
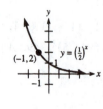
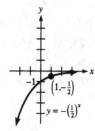
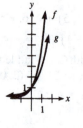

37.
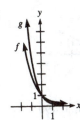

39. $-\frac{3}{2}$ **41.** $\frac{3}{4}$ **43.** $-\frac{1}{2}$ **45.** -2 **47.** 4 **49.** 3 **51.** 5 **53.** $\frac{1}{3}$ **55.** $\sqrt[3]{2}$ **57.** $\sqrt[6]{5}$ **59.**

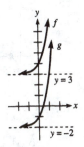

61.
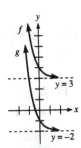

63. $117, 129, 875, 000$ **65.** $25.94 **67.** $7,163.93 **69.** 7.18 percent **71.** 1.40 percent

Exercises 8.2 **1.** $f^{-1} = \{(2, 1), (4, 3), (6, 5)\}; D_f = R_{f^{-1}} = \{1, 3, 5\}; R_f = D_{f^{-1}} = \{2, 4, 6\}$
3. $f^{-1} = \{(1, 2), (4, -3), (8, 5)\}; D_f = R_{f^{-1}} = \{-3, 2, 5\}; R_f = D_{f^{-1}} = \{1, 4, 8\}$ **5.** No inverse function
7. No inverse function **9.** No **11.** Yes **13.** Yes **15.** No **17.** Yes **19.** Yes **21.**

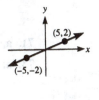

23.
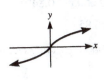

25.

27.

29. $f^{-1}(x) = x + 3$ **31.** $f^{-1}(x) = \frac{x - 5}{3}$ **33.** $f^{-1}(x) = x^2, x \leq 0$ **35.** No inverse function exists. **37.** No inverse function exists. **39.** $f^{-1}(x) = \sqrt[4]{x}$, or $x^{1/4}, x \geq 0$ **41.** Yes **43.** Yes **45.** No **47.** Yes **49.** Yes **51.** $f^{-1}(x) = \frac{15}{22}x$; this converts feet/second to miles/hour. **53.** $y = f^{-1}(x) = 0.50x$; 50 percent **55. a.** At 1,000 ft above sea level, water boils at 200° F. **b.** At 2,000 ft above sea level, water boils at 190° F. **c.** At k ft above sea level, water boils at j° F.

Exercises 8.3 **1.** $\log_2 8 = 3$ **3.** $\log_4 16 = 2$ **5.** $\log_{1/2} \frac{1}{8} = 3$ **7.** $\log_b x = y$ **9.** $\log_{10} 1,000 = 3$ **11.** $\log_{10} \frac{1}{100} = -2$
13. $\log_{0.2} 0.008 = 3$ **15.** $\log_{0.1} 100 = -2$ **17.** $4^3 = 64$ **19.** $4^{1/2} = 2$ **21.** $10^3 = 1,000$ **23.** $8^{-1} = \frac{1}{8}$ **25.** $2^{-5} = \frac{1}{32}$
27. $b^x = y$ **29.** $\left(\frac{1}{2}\right)^{-3} = 8$ **31.** 1 **33.** 0 **35.** 4 **37.** 3 **39.** 5 **41.** $\frac{1}{2}$ **43.** 36 **45.** $\frac{1}{16}$ **47.** 25 **49.** $\frac{1}{8}$

51.
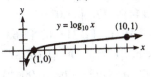

53.
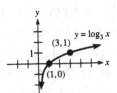

55.
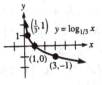

57.
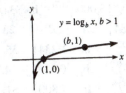

59–63. In each case one graph is the reflection of the other about the line $y = x$. **59.**

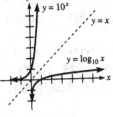

61.
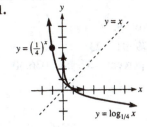

63.
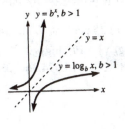

65.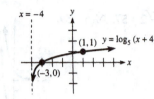

67.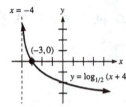

69.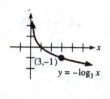

71.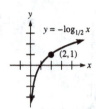

73.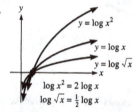

75. 1.3979   **77.** -0.4318 **79.** 0.3729   **81.** 158   **83.** 1.10   **85.** 0.00251   **87.** 0.490
89. 4.4; acid   **91.** 3.16×10^{-6} **93. a.** 5.27×10^{-6} **b.** 5.28   **95. a.** 2.51×10^{13} joules
b. 7.94×10^{11} joules   **c.** 31.6

Exercises 8.4   **1.** $\log_5 7 - \log_5 9$ **3.** $\log_8 6 + \log_8 x$ **5.** $5 \log_3 x$ **7.** $\frac{1}{3} \log_b 5$ **9.** $\log_3 5 + 3 \log_3 x$
11. $\frac{1}{2}[\log_b x - (\log_b 2 + \log_b y)]$ **13.** $\frac{1}{2}[\log_b x + \log_b y - \log_b z]$ **15.** $\frac{1}{2}[\log_b(x + 5) - \log_b y]$ **17.** 1   **19.** 5   **21.** 0
23. -1 **25.** -3 **27.** -3 **29.** 3   **31.** $-\log_b 3$ **33.** $1 - \log_b 7$ **35.** $\log_b 3 - 2$ **37.** $2m + 3n$ **39.** $4m + n$ **41.** $-3n$
43. $-5m$ **45.** $3n - 6m$ **47.** $\log_{10} t + k$ **49.** $\log_{10} y + 2k$ **51.** 32   **53.** 49   **55.** $\log_2 8y$ **57.** $\log_b \frac{3}{y}$ **59.** $\log_{10} \frac{y^3}{x}$
61. $\log_{10} \sqrt[3]{\frac{x + 3}{y - 1}}$ **63.** $\log_{10} \sqrt{\frac{x}{yz}}$ **65.** $\log_{10} \sqrt{\frac{y}{xz}}$ **67.**

x	1	2	5	10	20	50	100
$y = \log x$	0	0.3010	0.6990	1	1.3010	1.6990	2
$y = \log x^2$	0	0.6020	1.3980	2	2.6020	3.3980	4
$y = \log \sqrt{x}$	0	0.1505	0.3495	0.5	0.6505	0.8495	1

69.

71. a. $x = (\log y - b)/a$ **b.** $x = 3.0103$ **c.** $y = 10^{ax+b}$ **d.** $y = 15.85$
73. a. $L = \log(I) + 90 = 10[\log(I) + \log(10^9)]$ **b.** 110 dB   **c.** 1,000 ergs/cm^2/second
$\qquad = \log(I \cdot 10^9) = 10 \log \frac{I}{10^{-9}}$
75. Let $x = b^m$ and $y = b^n$. $\frac{x}{y} = \frac{b^m}{b^n} = b^{m-n}$
$\qquad \log_b \frac{x}{y} = m - n = \log_b x - \log_b y$

Exercises 8.5   **1.** {3.585}   **3.** {1.588}   **5.** {2.500}   **7.** {−4.585}   **9.** {−1.262}   **11.** {−4.783}   **13.** {4.593}
15. {10.84}   **17.** 2.807   **19.** 1.792   **21.** 2.807   **23.** −1.195   **25.** −4.392   **27.** −1.904   **29.** {1}   **31.** {4}   **33.** Ø
35. {−40}   **37.** {42}   **39.** {−60}   **41.** {33,300}   **43.** {1}   **45.** {3}   **47.** {2}   **49.** {−1}   **51.** 7 years   **53. a.** 2009
b. 2060   **55.** 14.9 percent   **57. a.** 2   **b.** 3

Exercises 8.6   **1. a.** $A = 10,000(1.02)^{4t}$ **b.** $14,859.47   **3. a.** $A = 20,000(1.05)^{2t}$ **b.** $43,657.49   **5. a.** $A = 8,000(1.13)^t$
b. $27,156.54   **7. a.** $A = 30,000(1.01)^{12t}$ **b.** $99,011.61   **9. a.** $A = 10,000\left(1 + \frac{0.1}{365}\right)^{365t}$ **b.** $20,135.60
11. a. $A = 15,000e^{0.07t}$ **b.** $34,745.50   **13. a.** $A = 10,000e^{0.10t}$ **b.** $20,137.53   **15.** {7.144}   **17.** {11.03}
19. {0.2784}   **21.** {2.744}   **23.** {2.388}   **25.** {12.95}   **27.** {−0.1953}   **29.** {−1.051}   **31. a.** $\{e^{7.4}\}$ **b.** {1,636}
33. a. $\{e^{0.21}\}$ **b.** {1.234}   **35. a.** $\{e^{5.2}\}$ **b.** {181.3}   **37. a.** $\{e^{0.02}\}$ **b.** {1.020}   **39. a.** $\{e^{-3.8}\}$ **b.** {0.02237}
41. a. $\{e^{-0.2}\}$ **b.** {0.8187}   **43. a.** $\{e^6/3\}$ **b.** {134.5}   **45. a.** $\{e^5/2\}$ **b.** {74.21}   **47. a.** $\{e/3\}$ **b.** {0.9061}
49. a. $\{e^4/7\}$ **b.** {7.800}   **51. a.** $\{5e^2\}$ **b.** {36.95}   **53. a.** $\{3e^5\}$ **b.** {445.2}   **55. a.** $\{5e^{3/2}\}$ **b.** {22.41}
57. 4.62 percent   **59.** 9.90 percent   **61.** 10.99 percent   **63.** 13.86 percent   **65.** $2 at 5 percent   **67.** 13.9 years
69. 3,939,000; 23,317,000; 92,450,000   **71.** 29.8 percent   **73.** 89.7 percent   **75.** 72.5 percent   **77.** 7:10 a.m.   **79.** 55 degrees

Chapter 8 Review Exercises   **1.** 81, $\frac{1}{729}$, 27, 22.36   **3.** $\left\{\frac{3}{2}\right\}$ **5.** 12.25 percent   **7. a.** Yes   **b.** No   **9.** $f^{-1}(x) = \frac{-x + 2}{3}$
11. 20 percent   **13.** 4   **15.** 2.8129   **17.** $\frac{1}{2}(\log_b 2 + \log_b x - \log_b y)$ **19.** $\log_{10} 2x^5$ **21.** {1.7959}   **23.** Ø
25. $14,555.17   **27.** {−4.257}   **29.** 5.78 percent   **31.** $\frac{1}{8}$, 4, 0.38   **33.** $13,974.36   **35.** 17.65 percent   **37.** $15,036.30

39. 7.3 **41.** $\frac{5}{2}$ **43.** $\frac{1}{100}$ **45.** $\log_3 1 = 0$ **47.** $\log_5 125 = x$ **49.** $10^x = 3$ **51.** $6 \log_{10} x$ **53.** $3[\log_b 8 + \log_b(x + 1)]$
55. $\log_{10}(x^2 + 2x)$ **57.** $\log_b 2x^3$ **59.** 32 **61.** $\{0.000631\}$ **63.** $\{12.18\}$ **65.** $\{3.819\}$ **67.** $\left\{\frac{e^4}{2}\right\}$ **69.** $\{1.226\}$
71. $\{0.7370\}$ **73.** f^{-1} does not exist. **75.** $f^{-1}(x) = \frac{x + 3}{4}$ **77.** $f^{-1}(x) = 2x + 1$ **79.** f^{-1} does not exist.

81. **83.**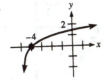

Chapter 8 Test **1.** $\log_b 8 = 3$ **2.** $e^{1/2} = x$ **3.** -3 **4.** 36 **5.** $\frac{1}{2}$ **6.** $\log_2 \frac{x^4}{3}$ **7.** $\log_b 8 + \frac{1}{2}\log_b x$ **8.** 1.338
9. $f^{-1}(x) = \frac{4x + 6}{5}$ **10.** $f[g(x)] = \left(\sqrt{x + 2}\right)^2 - 2 = x;\ g[f(x)] = \sqrt{(x^2 - 2) + 2} = x$ **11.** \$40,582.49
12. 5.49 percent **13.** $\{-0.05414\}$ **14.** 0.251 **15.** $\{-1.262\}$ **16.** $\{6\}$ **17.** $\{0.8664\}$ **18.**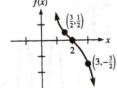

19. **20.**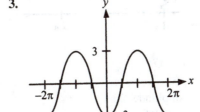

Chapter 9

Exercises 9.1 **1.** 5 **3.** 8 yd **5.** 9.6 m **7.** 5 **9.** $\frac{\pi}{6}$ **11.** $\frac{\pi}{3}$ **13.** $\frac{2\pi}{3}$ **15.** $\frac{5\pi}{6}$ **17.** $\frac{7\pi}{6}$ **19.** $\frac{4\pi}{3}$ **21.** $\frac{5\pi}{3}$ **23.** $\frac{11\pi}{6}$
25. $\frac{10\pi}{9}$ **27.** $\frac{\pi}{9}$ **29.** 60° **31.** 40° **33.** 120° **35.** 140° **37.** 432° **39.** 70° **41.** 115° **43.** 229° **45.** 332°
47. 25°30′N **49. a.** 7°N **b.** 0.3 deg/hr **51.** 69 mi **53.** 10 knots **55.** $\frac{25\pi}{2}$ in.² **57.** 8 ft² **59.** $\frac{11}{2}, \frac{11}{4\pi}$ **61.** 6 rad/second
63. a. $\frac{200\pi}{3}$ rad/minute **b.** 400π in./minute **65.** 300π in./second **67.** 6,336 rad/minute **69.** π in.

Exercises 9.2 **1.** 1 **3.** 0 **5.** 0 **7.** 0 **9.** Undefined **11.** 1 **13.** -1 **15.** $\frac{1}{2}$ **17.** 1 **19.** $\frac{1}{2}$ **21.** $\frac{1}{\sqrt{3}}$ **23.** $\frac{\sqrt{3}}{2}$
25. $-\frac{2}{\sqrt{3}}$ **27.** $\frac{1}{\sqrt{3}}$ **29.** $-\frac{\sqrt{3}}{2}$ **31.** $-\frac{\sqrt{3}}{2}$ **33.** $\sqrt{3}$ **35.** $-\frac{1}{\sqrt{2}}$ **37.** 2 **39.** $\frac{1}{2}$ **41.** $\frac{1}{2}$ **43.** -2 **45.** $-\frac{1}{\sqrt{2}}$ **47.** $-\sqrt{3}$
49. $-\frac{\sqrt{3}}{2}$ **51.** -0.4161 **53.** 1.158 **55.** -0.7664 **57.** 1.566 **59.** 0.2116 **61.** 0.6702 **63.** -1.042 **65.** 0.9511
67. 0.2225 **69.** -1.082 **71.** \$11,300; \$4,500 **73. a.** 3 meters; 3 meters **b.** 6; 6 meters

Exercises 9.3 **1.** **3.** **5.**

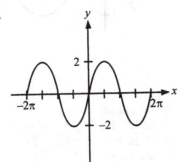 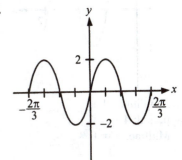

Amplitude: 2
period: 2π
Midline: $y = 0$

Amplitude: 3
period: 2π
Midline: $y = 0$

Amplitude: 2
period: $\frac{2\pi}{3}$
Midline: $y = 0$

7.

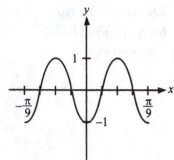

Amplitude: 1
period: $\frac{\pi}{9}$
Midline: $y = 0$

9.

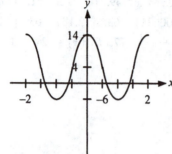

Amplitude: 10
period: 2
Midline: $y = 4$

11.

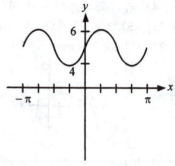

Amplitude: 1
period: π
Midline: $y = 5$

13.

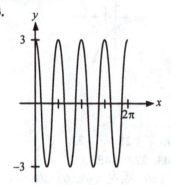

Amplitude: 3
period: $\frac{\pi}{2}$
Midline: $y = 0$

15.

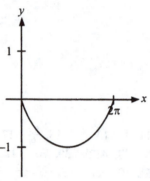

Amplitude: 1
period: 4π
Midline: $y = 0$

17.

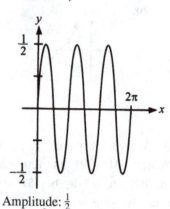

Amplitude: $\frac{1}{2}$
period: $\frac{2\pi}{3}$
Midline: $y = 0$

19.

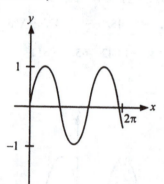

Amplitude: 1
period: 4
Midline: $y = 0$

21.

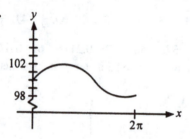

Amplitude: 2
period: 8
Midline: $y = 100$

23.

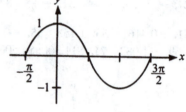

Amplitude: 1
period: 2π
Phase shift: $-\frac{\pi}{2}$
Midline: $y = 0$

25.

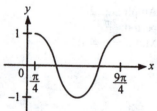

Amplitude: 1
period: 2π
Phase shift: $\frac{\pi}{4}$
Midline: $y = 0$

27.

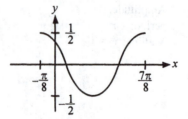

Amplitude: $\frac{1}{2}$
Period: π
Phase shift: $-\frac{\pi}{8}$
Midline: $y = 0$

29.

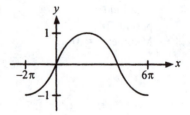

Amplitude: 1
Period: 8π
Phase shift: -2π
Midline: $y = 0$

31.

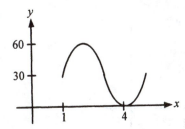

Amplitude: 30
Period: 4
Phase shift: 1
Midline: $y = 30$

33. $y = 3 \sin 2x$ **35.** $y = -4 \sin 3x$ **37.** $y = 1.5 \cos \frac{1}{2}x$ **39.** $y = -2 \cos 10x$

41. d **43.** c **45.** b **47.** b **49.** c **51. a.**

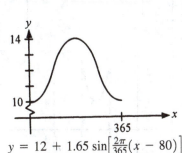

$y = 12 + 1.65 \sin\left[\frac{2\pi}{365}(x - 80)\right]$

b. Amplitude $= 1.65$; Period $= 365$ days
c. Days number 171 and 172 have about 13.65 hours of daylight. (About June 20 or June 21)

53. a.

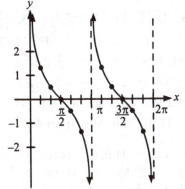

$y = 4200 + 2100 \cos\left(\frac{2\pi}{12}x\right)$

b. Amplitude $= 2,100$; Period $= 12$ months **c.** Month 6, (January)

Exercises 9.4 1.

x	0	$\frac{\pi}{6}$	$\frac{\pi}{3}$	$\frac{\pi}{2}$	$\frac{2\pi}{3}$	$\frac{5\pi}{6}$	π
$\cot x$	und.	1.7	0.6	0	−0.6	−1.7	und.

x	$\frac{7\pi}{6}$	$\frac{4\pi}{3}$	$\frac{3\pi}{2}$	$\frac{5\pi}{3}$	$\frac{11\pi}{6}$	2π
$\cot x$	1.7	0.6	0	−0.6	−1.7	und.

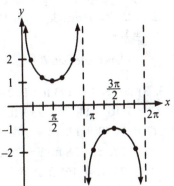

3.

x	0	$\frac{\pi}{6}$	$\frac{\pi}{3}$	$\frac{\pi}{2}$	$\frac{2\pi}{3}$	$\frac{5\pi}{6}$	π
$\csc x$	und.	2	1.2	1	1.2	2	und.

x	$\frac{7\pi}{6}$	$\frac{4\pi}{3}$	$\frac{3\pi}{2}$	$\frac{5\pi}{3}$	$\frac{11\pi}{6}$	2π
$\csc x$	−2	−1.2	−1	−1.2	−2	und.

5. *D:* set of all real numbers except $x = k\pi$ (*k* any integer); *R:* $(-\infty, \infty)$; period: π **7.** *D:* set of all real numbers except $x = k\pi$ (*k* any integer); *R:* $(-\infty, -1] \cup [1, \infty)$; period: 2π
9. Inc., dec., dec., inc. **11.** Always increasing
13. Inc., inc., dec., dec.

15.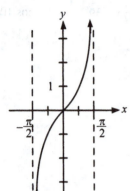

17.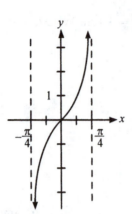

19.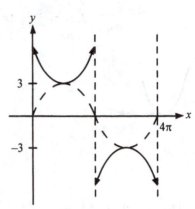

51. $f(x) = \sin x$ **53.** $\frac{13}{12}$ **55.** $-\frac{12}{5}$

57. $-\sqrt{1-a^2}$ **59.** $\frac{1}{a}$

21.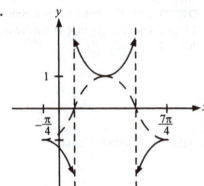

23.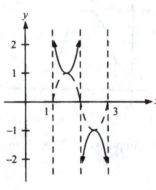

Exercises 9.5 **1.** $\frac{\pi}{3}$ **3.** $-\frac{\pi}{3}$ **5.** $\frac{\pi}{4}$ **7.** $-\frac{\pi}{2}$ **9.** $\frac{\pi}{4}$ **11.** $-\frac{\pi}{3}$ **13.** 0.32 **15.** 2.15 **17.** 1.05 **19.** 0.64 **21.** 1 **23.** $\frac{1}{2}$
25. 0 **27.** 0 **29.** -0.6616 **31** $\frac{3}{5}$ **33.** $\frac{12}{5}$ **35.** 0 **37.** -1 **39.** $\frac{\pi}{2}$ **41.** -1 **43.** No value **45.** $\theta = \arcsin\left(\frac{1}{m}\right)$
47. $\theta = \arcsin\left(\frac{Tg}{2v_0}\right)$ **49. a.** $\theta = \arccos\left(\frac{a}{25}\right)$ **b.** $\theta = \arcsin\left(\frac{b}{25}\right)$ **51. a.** $s = 25\cot\theta$, D: $(0°, 90°)$, R: $(0, \infty)$
b. $\theta = \operatorname{arccot}(s/25)$; D: $(0, \infty)$, R: $(0°, 90°)$

Exercises 9.6 **1.** $\left\{\frac{\pi}{3}, \frac{2\pi}{3}\right\}$ **3.** $\left\{\frac{2\pi}{3}, \frac{4\pi}{3}\right\}$ **5.** $\left\{\frac{3\pi}{4}, \frac{7\pi}{4}\right\}$ **7.** $\{0.12, 3.02\}$ **9.** $\{1.88, 5.02\}$ **11.** $\left\{\frac{\pi}{4}, \frac{7\pi}{4}\right\}$ **13.** $\varnothing$
15. $\{0.32, 3.46\}$ **17.** $\{2.55, 5.70\}$ **19.** $\{1.77, 4.51\}$ **21.** $\left\{\frac{\pi}{4}, \frac{3\pi}{4}, \frac{5\pi}{4}, \frac{7\pi}{4}\right\}$ **23.** $\left\{0, \frac{\pi}{2}, \frac{3\pi}{2}\right\}$ **25.** $\left\{\frac{\pi}{6}, \frac{\pi}{2}, \frac{5\pi}{6}, \frac{3\pi}{2}\right\}$
27. $\{1.25, 1.71, 4.39, 4.85\}$ **29.** $\left\{\frac{\pi}{6}, \frac{\pi}{2}, \frac{5\pi}{6}, \frac{7\pi}{6}, \frac{3\pi}{2}, \frac{11\pi}{6}\right\}$ **31.** $\left\{\frac{\pi}{12}, \frac{5\pi}{12}, \frac{13\pi}{12}, \frac{17\pi}{12}\right\}$ **33.** $\left\{\frac{3\pi}{4}\right\}$
35. $\left\{x: x = \frac{\pi}{6} + k2\pi \text{ or } x = \frac{5\pi}{6} + k2\pi, k \text{ any integer}\right\}$ **37.** $\{x: x = 3.60 + k2\pi \text{ or } x = 5.82 + k2\pi, k \text{ any integer}\}$
39. $\{x: x = 1.249 + k\pi, k \text{ any integer}\}$ **41.** Days 57, 58, 59 and 306, 307, 308; August 27, 28, 29 and May 2, 3, 4
43. 0, 1, 2, 10, 11, 12; May through October

Exercises 9.7 **1.** $b = 35$ ft, $c = 48$ ft, $C = 105°$ **3.** $b = 140$ ft, $c = 100$ ft, $A = 20°$
5. $b = 34.6$ ft, $c = 23.5$ ft, $C = 41°20'$ **7.** $\frac{3}{4}$ **9.** 6 **11.** $\frac{7}{2}$ **13.** $10\sqrt{2}$ **15.** $b = 10$, $c = 10\sqrt{3}$
17. $c = 110$ ft, $B = 26°$, $C = 109°$ **19.** $c = 57$ ft, $A = 42°$, $C = 108°$ or $c = 12$ ft, $A = 138°$, $C = 12°$
21. $a = 26$ ft, $A = 8°$, $B = 22°$ **23.** Two triangles **25.** One triangle **27.** No triangle **29.** 433 ft **31.** 95 mi
33. Since $\sin C = \sin 90° = 1$, $\frac{\sin A}{\sin 90°} = \frac{a}{c}$

   becomes $\sin A = \frac{a}{c}$ and $\frac{\sin B}{\sin 90°} = \frac{b}{c}$ becomes $\sin B = \frac{b}{c}$.

Exercises 9.8 **1.** 1,300 ft **3.** 31 m **5.** LF: 193 ft; CF: 276 ft; RF: 266 ft **7.** $c = 14$ ft, $A = 49°$, $B = 71°$
9. $b = 27.4$ ft, $A = 162°30'$, $C = 7°10'$ **11.** $c = 23.1$ ft, $A = 55°50'$, $B = 28°30'$ **13.** $A = 128°$, $B = 20°$, $C = 32°$
15. $A = 37°40'$, $B = 93°30'$, $C = 48°50'$ **17.** $r^2 = s^2 + t^2 - 2st\cos R$ **19.** $\cos T = \frac{r^2 + s^2 - t^2}{2rs}$ **21.** $\frac{1}{5}$ **23.** $\sqrt{37}$
25. $a = 11$ ft, $c = 43$ ft, $B = 78°$ **27.** $c = 78$ ft, $A = 26°$, $B = 34°$ **29.** $b = 243$ ft, $c = 152$ ft, $A = 33°00'$
31. $A = 104°$, $B = 29°$, $C = 47°$ **33.** $a = 165$ ft, $A = 164°00'$, $C = 8°50'$ or $a = 17.4$ ft, $A = 1°40'$, $C = 171°10'$
35. $A = 46°30'$, $B = 58°00'$, $C = 75°30'$ **37.** 99 mi **39.** 34 m **41.** 7.0 ft^2 **43.** 79 m^2 **45.** 2.97 km^2 **47.** 9.8 ft^2
49. 126 m^2 **51.** 2.02 km^2 **53.** $44\sqrt{3}$ square units **55.** $9\sqrt{3}$ square units
57. Since $\cos C = \cos 90° = 1$, $c^2 = a^2 + b^2 - 2ab\cos 90°$ becomes $c^2 = a^2 + b^2$.

Chapter 9 Review Exercises

1. $\frac{\sqrt{3}}{2}$ **3.** 0 **5.** $-\frac{\sqrt{3}}{3}$ **7.** $-\frac{\pi}{4}$ **9.** 0 **11.** 0.841 **13.** -3.08 **15.** 1.04 **17.** No value **19.** 1.37

21. 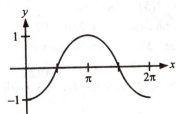 **23.** 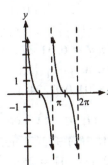 **25.**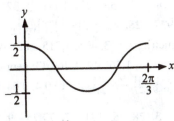

Amplitude: $\frac{1}{2}$
Period: $\frac{2\pi}{3}$
Phase shift: 0
Midline: $y = 0$

27. 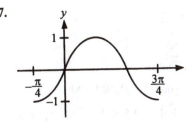 **29.** 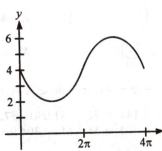 **31.**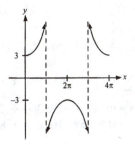

Amplitude: 1   Phase shift: $-\frac{\pi}{4}$ Amplitude: Phase shift: 0
Period: π Midline: $y = 0$ Period: 4π Midline: $y = 4$

33. 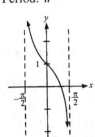 **35.**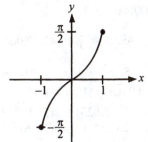

37. Domain: set of all real numbers except $x = \frac{\pi}{2} + k\pi$ (k any integer); range: $(-\infty, \infty)$ **39.** Domain: set of all real numbers except $x = k\pi$ (k any integer); range: $(-\infty, -1] \cup [1, \infty)$

41. Domain: $(-\infty, \infty)$; range: $\left(-\frac{\pi}{2}, \frac{\pi}{2}\right)$ **43.** Q_2 **45.** $\theta = \tan^{-1}\frac{3}{x}$

47. 25.7 ft **49. a.** $\frac{7\pi}{6}$ **b.** $72°$ **51.** $[-1, 1]$ **53.** 2 **61.** $-\frac{3}{5}$

63. $\frac{5}{4}$ **65.** $\left\{\frac{4\pi}{3}, \frac{5\pi}{3}\right\}$ **67.** $\left\{\frac{\pi}{4}, \frac{5\pi}{4}\right\}$ **69.** $\{0.12, 3.02\}$

71. $\left\{x: x = \frac{\pi}{6} + k2\pi \text{ or } x = \frac{5\pi}{6} + k2\pi, k \text{ any integer}\right\}$

73. $\left\{\frac{\pi}{4}, \frac{3\pi}{4}, \frac{5\pi}{4}, \frac{7\pi}{4}\right\}$ **75.** $\left\{0, \frac{\pi}{2}, \frac{3\pi}{2}\right\}$ **77.** $\left\{\frac{\pi}{6}, \frac{\pi}{2}, \frac{5\pi}{6}, \frac{7\pi}{6}, \frac{3\pi}{2}, \frac{11\pi}{6}\right\}$

79. $\left\{\frac{\pi}{12}, \frac{5\pi}{12}, \frac{13\pi}{12}, \frac{17\pi}{12}\right\}$ **81.** $109°$ **83.** $48°50'$ **85.** $\sqrt{37} \approx 6.1$ **87.** 79 m^2 **89.** $30°, 56°, 94°$ **91.** b **93.** c **95.** b

97. b **99.** a

Chapter 9 Test   **1.** $[-1, 1]$ **2.** $-\sqrt{3}$ **3.**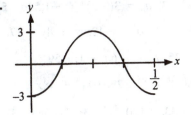

5. Amplitude: 1; period: $\frac{2\pi}{3}$; phase shift: $\frac{\pi}{6}$

6. a. $\frac{3\pi}{2}$ **b.** $315°$ **7.** $\frac{25\pi}{3}$ cm   **4.**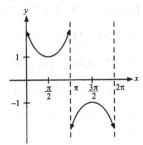

8. $-\frac{\pi}{3}$ **9.** $\sqrt{3}$ **10.** $\cos^2 x$

11. $\left\{x: x = \frac{7\pi}{6} + k2\pi \text{ or } x = \frac{11\pi}{6} + k2\pi, k \text{ any integer}\right\}$

12. $\left\{\frac{3\pi}{4}, \frac{7\pi}{4}\right\}$ **13.** $-\frac{12}{5}$ **14.** $101.3°$ **15.** $C = 49°, A = 55°, a = 38$ ft **16.** 8.5 cm^2 **17.** d **18.** a **19.** a **20.** b

Chapter 10

Exercises 10.1 **1.** $-3, -1, 1, 3; 15$ **3.** $14, 20, 26, 32; 98$ **5.** $\frac{5}{2}, 3, \frac{7}{2}, 4; \frac{11}{2}$ **7.** $\frac{1}{5}, \frac{4}{5}, \frac{7}{5}, 2; \frac{73}{5}$ **9.** $4n - 3; 4$ **11.** $6n - 4; 116$
13. $7n - 2; 187$ **15.** $9n - 5; 355$ **17.** $\frac{4}{3}n + \frac{32}{3}; 32$ **19.** $a_n = 2(2)^{n-1}; 1{,}024$ **21.** $a_n = 3(5)^{n-1}; 46{,}875$
23. $a_n = 7(3)^{n-1}; 45{,}927$ **25.** $a_n = 5\left(-\frac{1}{5}\right)^{n-1}; \frac{1}{3{,}125}$ **27.** $a_n = \frac{1}{2}\left(-\frac{1}{2}\right)^{n-1}; -\frac{1}{1{,}024}$ **29.** Geometric, $r = 4; 256, 1{,}024$
31. Neither **33.** Geometric, $r = 3; 405, 1{,}215$ **35.** Arithmetic, $d = 6; 31, 37$ **37.** Neither **39.** \$622.08; geometric
41. $1{,}080, 1{,}166.40, 1{,}259.71, 1{,}360.49, 1{,}469.33$; geometric **43. a.** $\frac{1}{2}, \frac{2}{3}, \frac{3}{4}, \frac{4}{5}, \frac{5}{6}; 1$ **b.** $1, \frac{1}{2}, \frac{1}{3}, \frac{1}{4}, \frac{1}{5}; 0$ **c.** $1, \frac{1}{4}, \frac{1}{9}, \frac{1}{22}, \frac{1}{49}; 0$
d. $1, \frac{1}{4}, \frac{1}{9}, \frac{1}{16}, \frac{1}{25}; 0$ **e.** $\frac{5}{3}, \frac{17}{9}, \frac{53}{27}, \frac{161}{81}, \frac{485}{243}; 2$ **f.** $0.4, 0.64, 0.784, 0.8704, 0.92224; 1$ **45.** $2, 3, 5, 7, 11$; neither **47.** $5, 8$; neither

Exercises 10.2 **1.** 21 **3.** 78 **5.** 171 **7.** $7{,}875$ **9.** $45{,}150$ **11.** 92 **13.** 600 **15.** $1{,}639$ **17.** $4{,}056$ **19.** $47{,}541$
21. 363 **23.** $699{,}050$ **25.** 381 **27.** $88{,}573$ **29.** $32{,}767$ **31.** $3(1) + 3(2) + 3(3) + 3(4) + 3(5) = 45$
33. $[2(0) + 1] + [2(1) + 1] + [2(2) + 1] + [2(3) + 1] + [2(4) + 1] = 25$
35. $(1^2 + 2) + (2^2 + 2) + (3^2 + 2) + (4^2 + 2) + (5^2 + 2) + (6^2 + 2) = 103$ **37.** $3^2 + 3^3 + 3^4 = 117$
39. $2^{1-2} + 2^{2-2} + 2^{3-2} + 2^{4-2} = 7\frac{1}{2}$ **41.** $\left(\frac{1}{3}\right)^1 + \left(\frac{1}{3}\right)^2 + \left(\frac{1}{3}\right)^3 + \left(\frac{1}{3}\right)^4 = \frac{40}{81}$ **43.** $a_i = 6i; \sum_{i=1}^{6} 6i$
45. $a_i = 3i - 2; \sum_{i=1}^{6}(3i - 2)$ **47.** $a_i = (i + 1)^2 + 2; \sum_{i=1}^{5}[(i + 1)^2 + 2]$ **49.** $a_i = 3^{i-1}; \sum_{i=1}^{5}3^{i-1}$
51. $a_i = 3\left(\frac{1}{4}\right)^{i-1}; \sum_{i=1}^{5}3\left(\frac{1}{4}\right)^{i-1}$ **53.** $2 + 3 + 4 + \cdots + 9 = 44$; arithmetic, $d = 1$ **55. a.** $(6{,}000 - 1{,}500)/900 = 5$ years
b. Arithmetic series with $d = -72; 360 + 288 + 216 + 144 + 72 = \$1{,}080$ **57.** $5 + 4.5 + 4 + 3.5 + 3 + 2.5 = 22.5$;
arithmetic with $d = -0.5$ **59.** $10 + 9 + 8 + 7 + \cdots + 1 = 55$ **61.** $2{,}304$ ft **63.** \$20,015.07; \$7,015.07

Exercises 10.3 **1.** $\frac{10}{9}$ **3.** $\frac{9}{2}$ **5.** 12 **7.** $\frac{2}{9}$ **9.** $\frac{3}{5}$ **11.** $\frac{10}{3}$ **13.** $\frac{20}{7}$ **15.** 2 **17.** $-\frac{2}{7}$ **19.** $\frac{4}{3}$ **21.** $\frac{1}{56}$ **23.** $\frac{10}{11}$ **25.** 0.5
27. $-\frac{1}{150}$ **29.** $-\frac{25}{24}$ **31.** $0.2 + 0.02 + 0.002 + \cdots; \frac{2}{9}$ **33.** $0.7 + 0.07 + 0.007 + \cdots; \frac{7}{9}$
35. $0.13 + 0.0013 + 0.000013 + \cdots; \frac{13}{99}$ **37.** $0.375 + 0.000375 + 0.000000375 + \cdots; \frac{375}{999}$
39. $0.07 + 0.007 + 0.0007 + \cdots; \frac{7}{90}$ **41.** 20 gal **43.** $S = \dfrac{\frac{1}{2}}{1 - \frac{1}{2}} = 1$ **45.** $S = \frac{4}{3}A$ **47.** $2{,}000$ seconds $= 33\frac{1}{3}$ minutes

Exercises 10.4 **1.** $x^3 + 3x^2y + 3xy^2 + y^3$ **3.** $x^3 - 3x^2y + 3xy^2 - y^3$ **5.** $x^5 - 15x^4 + 90x^3 - 270x^2 + 405x - 243$
7. $x^3 + 12x^2 + 48x + 64$ **9.** $64x^6 - 192x^5n + 240x^4n^2 - 160x^3n^3 + 60x^2n^4 - 12xn^5 + n^6$
11. $64x^6 + 960x^5y + 6{,}000x^4y^2 + 20{,}000x^3y^3 + 37{,}500x^2y^4 + 37{,}500xy^5 + 15{,}625y^6$ **13.** $1, 7, 21, 35, 35, 21, 7, 1$;
matches seventh row of Pascal's triangle **15.** 10 **17.** 210 **19.** 1 **21.** 1 **23.** $x^4 + 4x^3h + 6x^2h^2 + 4xh^3 + h^4$
25. $x^7 - 7x^6y + 21x^5y^2 - 35x^4y^3 + 35x^3y^4 - 21x^2y^5 + 7xy^6 - y^7$
27. $x^6 + 18x^5 + 135x^4 + 540x^3 + 1{,}215x^2 + 1{,}458x + 729$ **29.** $27x^3 - 27x^2 + 9x - 1$ **31.** $126x^4y^5$ **33.** $-120x^3y^7$
35. $-13{,}608x^3$ **37.** $280x^3$ **39.** $393{,}216/1{,}953{,}125 \approx 20.13$ percent **41.** $\frac{11}{243} = 4.53$ percent **43. a.** 15 **b.** 15

Chapter 10 Review Exercises **1.** $5, 8, 11, 14; 182$ **3.** $a_n = 3(-2)^{n-1}; -1{,}536$ **5.** \$8,589.93 **7.** $11{,}184{,}810$
9. $a_i = 4i + 3; \sum_{i=1}^{6}(4i + 3)$ **11.** 4 **13.** $\frac{7}{11}$ **15.** $x^3 + 6x^2y + 12xy^2 + 8y^3$ **17.** 28 **19.** $5{,}376x^3y^6$
21. Arithmetic; $d = 3$ **23.** Arithmetic; $d = -4$ **25.** $a_n = -6n + 1; -59$
27. $8\left(\frac{1}{2}\right)^1 + 8\left(\frac{1}{2}\right)^2 + 8\left(\frac{1}{2}\right)^3 + 8\left(\frac{1}{2}\right)^4 + 8\left(\frac{1}{2}\right)^5 + 8\left(\frac{1}{2}\right)^6 = \frac{63}{8}$ **29.** $64x^3 + 48x^2y + 12xy^2 + y^3$
31. $x^5 + 5x^4h + 10x^3h^2 + 10x^2h^3 + 5xh^4 + h^5$ **33.** $1{,}120x^4y^4$ **35.** $39{,}364$ **37.** $20{,}100$ **39.** $a_i = 4i + 2; \sum_{i=1}^{10}(4i + 2)$
41. $\frac{16}{625}$ **43.** \$1,160.38

Chapter 10 Test **1.** Geometric; $\frac{1}{5}, \frac{1}{25}$ **2.** Geometric; $1, 10$ **3.** Arithmetic; $17, 21$ **4.** $a_n = n - 4; 21$
5. $a_n = -2\left(-\frac{1}{2}\right)^{n-1}; \frac{1}{64}$ **6.** 320 **7.** $22{,}222{,}222$ **8.** $a_i = 4i + 1; \sum_{i=1}^{10}(4i + 1)$ **9.** -26 **10.** $\frac{121}{27}$ **11.** $\frac{15}{4}$ **12.** 2 **13.** $\frac{5}{9}$
14. $1, 5, 10, 10, 5, 1$ **15.** $x^4 + 12x^3y + 54x^2y^2 + 108xy^3 + 81y^4$ **16.** 84
17. $x^7 + 7x^6y + 21x^5y^2 + 35x^4y^3 + 35x^3y^4 + 21x^2y^5 + 7xy^6 + y^7$ **18.** $960x^3y^7$ **19.** \$14,787.68 **20.** 238 m

Chapter 11

Exercises 11.1 **1.** Yes; 3 **3.** Yes; 1 **5.** No **7.** No **9.** Yes; 0 **11.** $P(x) = (x - 1)(x - 2)(x - 3)$

13. $P(x) = x(x + 4)(x - i)(x + i)$ **15.** $P(x) = (x - 1)^2(x - 5)^2$ **17.** Degree 2; -3 is a zero of multiplicity 2

19. Degree 3; -4, $\sqrt{2}$, and $-\sqrt{2}$ are zeros of multiplicity 1. **21.** Degree 3; 0 is a zero of multiplicity 2; 2 is a zero of multiplicity 1. **23.** Degree 4; 0 is a zero of multiplicity 4 **25.**

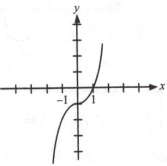

27.

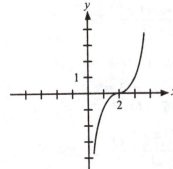

29.

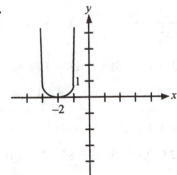

31.

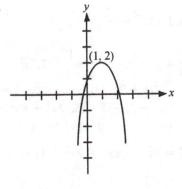

33.

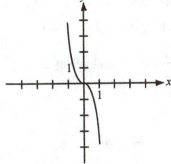

35.

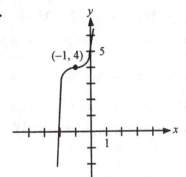

37.

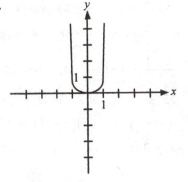

39.

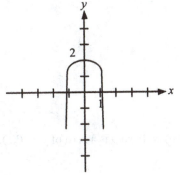

41.

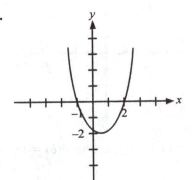

43.

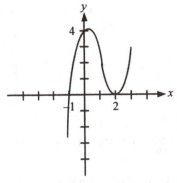

45.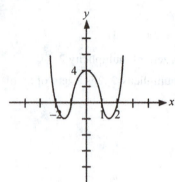

47.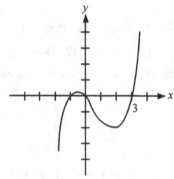

49.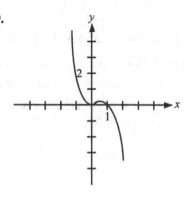

51. $y = -(x + 1)^2(x - 2)$ **53.** $y = \dfrac{1}{9}(x + 1)^2(x - 3)^2$ **55.** $y = -k(x + 3)^2$ where $k > 0$ **57. a.** $V = x(10 - 2x)^2$

b. Domain; $(0, 5)$ **c.** $\dfrac{5}{3}; \dfrac{1}{6}$ **59.** $-.068 < x < .006; \sqrt[3]{120} - 5 < x < \sqrt[3]{130} - 5$

Exercises 11.2   **1.** $\dfrac{x^2 - 5}{x + 1} = x - 1 + \dfrac{-4}{x + 1}$ **3.** $\dfrac{3x^4 - 5x^2 + 7}{x^2 + 2x + 1} = 3x^2 - 6x + 4 + \dfrac{-2x + 3}{x^2 + 2x + 1}$

5. $\dfrac{x^3 + 1}{x(x - 1)} = x + 1 + \dfrac{x + 1}{x(x - 1)}$ **7.** $x^2 + 7x - 2 = (x + 5)(x + 2) - 12$ **9.** $6x^3 - 3x^2 + 14x - 7 =$
$(2x - 1)(3x^2 + 7) + 0$ **11.** $3x^4 + x - 2 = (x^2 - 1)(3x^2 + 3) + x + 1$ **13.** $x^3 - 5x^2 + 2x - 3 =$
$(x - 1)(x^2 - 4x - 2) - 5$ **15.** $2x^3 + 9x^2 - x + 14 = (x + 5)(2x^2 - x + 4) - 6$ **17.** $7 + 6x - 2x^2 - x^3 =$
$(x + 3)(-x^2 + x + 3) - 2$ **19.** $2x^3 + x - 5 = (x + 1)(2x^2 - 2x + 3) - 8$

21. $x^4 - 16 = (x - 2)(x^3 + 2x^2 + 4x + 8) + 0$ **23.** $0, 0$ **25.** $-9, 87$ **27.** $0, 0$ **29.** $-\dfrac{176}{27}, -\dfrac{10}{3}$ **31.** Yes;

$P(x) = (x + 1)(x^2 - 3x + 5)$ **33.** Yes; $P(x) = (x - 4)(x + 1)(x - 2)$ **35.** Not factorable   **37.** $x = 2$ in.

39. a. perimeter $= 4a + 4b + 4c = 40$, so $a + b + c = 10$ **b.** $b = a + 2; c = 8 - 2a; V = a(a + 2)(8 - 2a)$

c. $a = \dfrac{1 + \sqrt{37}}{2} \approx 3.54$ in.   **41.** $i, -i$ **43.** $2 - \sqrt{7}$ **45.** $-i\sqrt{2}$ **47.** $2 - 2i$ **49.** $-\dfrac{1}{2}$ and -1 (multiplicity 2)

51. $\pm \sqrt{2}$ **53.** $\pm i\sqrt{2}, -\sqrt{2}$ **55.** $1, -1, -i$ **57.** $P(x) = (x - 2)\left(x - \sqrt{3}\right)\left(x + \sqrt{3}\right)$

59. $P(x) = x\left(x - \left(4 - \sqrt{3}\right)\right)\left(x - \left(4 + \sqrt{3}\right)\right)\left(x - \left(2 + 3i\right)\right)\left(x - \left(2 - 3i\right)\right)$

61. $P(x) = (x - 3)(x + 3)(x - 2i)(x + 2i)$ **63.**

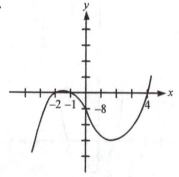

65. True   **67.** False

69. Since $x - b$ is a factor of $P(x)$, we know $P(x) = (x - b)Q(x)$. Then $P(b) = (b - b)Q(b) = 0$, so b is a zero of $y - P(x)$.

Exercises 11.3   **1.** $\pm 20, \pm 10, \pm 5, \pm 4, \pm 2, \pm 1$ **3.** $\pm 6, \pm 3, \pm 2, \pm \dfrac{3}{2}, \pm 1, \pm \dfrac{3}{4}, \pm \dfrac{1}{2}, \pm \dfrac{1}{4}$ **5.** Positive: 3; negative: 0   **7.** Positive: 1;

negative: 3   **9.** $4, -1, -2$ **11.** $-\dfrac{1}{3}, \pm i\sqrt{5}$ **13.** $\dfrac{1}{2}$ (multiplicity 3)   **15.** $-1, 2, \dfrac{1 \pm i\sqrt{79}}{8}$ **17.** $-2, -\dfrac{1}{2}, \dfrac{-1 \pm i\sqrt{35}}{2}$

19. a. $3, -1 \pm i\sqrt{3}$ **b.** One; 3   **c.** One; 3   **d.** Three; $3 + 0i, -1 + \sqrt{3}i, -1 - \sqrt{3}i$ **21. a.** $-2, \dfrac{1}{3}, \pm \sqrt{7}$

b. Two; $-2, \dfrac{1}{3}$ **c.** Four; $-2, \dfrac{1}{3}, \sqrt{7}, -\sqrt{7}$ **d.** Four; $-2 + 0i, \dfrac{1}{3} + 0i, \sqrt{7} + 0i, -\sqrt{7} + 0i$ **23.** $105 = x(x + 2)(2x + 1)$, so $2x^3 + 5x^2 + 2x - 105 = 0$. Then 3 is a root, while the reduced equation $2x^3 + 11x + 35 = 0$ has no real number solutions. Unique dimensions: 7 in. by 5 in. by 3 in.   **25.** 3 in. or $6 - 3\sqrt{2}$ in.   **27.** $P(0) = -8$, $P(-1) = 5$; since $P(0)$ and $P(-1)$ have

opposite signs, the location theorem guarantees at least one real zero between 0 and -1.   **29.** $P(1) = -4$; $P(2) = 2$; since $P(1)$ and $P(2)$ have opposite signs, the location theorem guarantees at least one real zero between 1 and 2. Similarly, since $P(-1) = -16$ and $P(-2) = 50$, there is at least one real zero between -1 and -2.   **31.** 0.7   **33.** 0.3   **35** -1.3

Exercises 11.4   **1.** $x = \dfrac{3}{2}$ **3.** $x = 6, x = -1$ **5.**

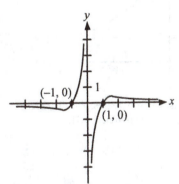

Vertical asymptote: $x = 0$
Horizontal asymptote: $y = 0$

7.

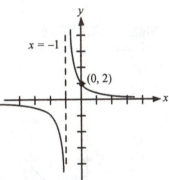

Vertical asymptote: $x = -1$
Horizontal asymptote: $y = 0$

9.

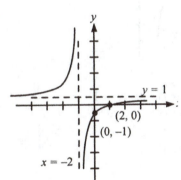

Vertical asymptote: $x = -2$
Horizontal asymptote: $y = 1$

11.

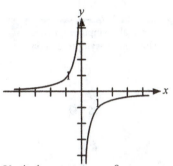

Vertical asymptote: $x = -\dfrac{5}{3}$

Horizontal asymptote: $y = \dfrac{2}{3}$

13.

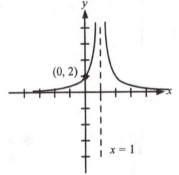

Vertical asymptote: $x = 1$
Horizontal asymptote: $y = 0$

15.

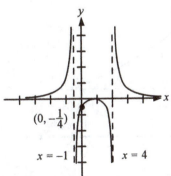

Vertical asymptotes: $x = -1$
      $x = 4$
Horizontal asymptote: $y = 0$

17.

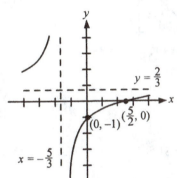

Vertical asymptote: $x = 0$
Horizontal asymptote: $y = 0$

19.

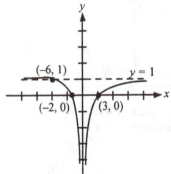

Vertical asymptote: $x = 0$
Horizontal asymptote: $y = 1$

21.

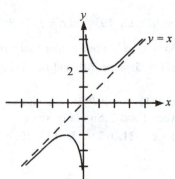

Vertical asymptote: $x = 0$
Horizontal asymptote: none

23.

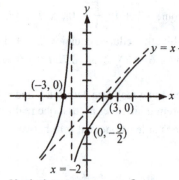

Vertical asymptote: $x = -2$
Horizontal asymptote: none

25.

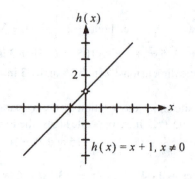

27.

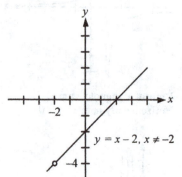

29.

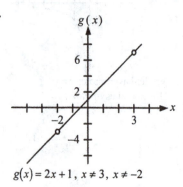

31.

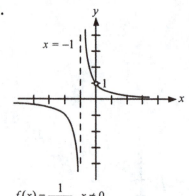

$f(x) = \dfrac{1}{x+1}$, $x \neq 0$
Vertical asymptote: $x = -1$
Horizontal asymptote: $y = 0$

33.

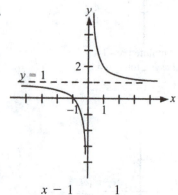

$y = \dfrac{x-1}{(x-1)^2} = \dfrac{1}{x-1}$
Vertical asymptote: $x = 1$
Horizontal asymptote: $y = 0$

35. a. $280; $1.56

b.

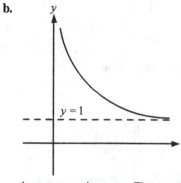

y decreases as x increases. The average cost per minute approaches $1.

37. 21.2 by 42.4

39. a. 88.89%; 80%

b. $y = \dfrac{32}{32 + x} \cdot 100$ D: [0, 32]

c.

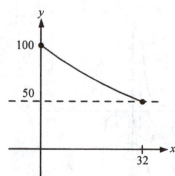

d. 8 oz. of water, 32 oz. of water; not possible in a 64 oz. jug

e. The percentage of juice can only approach zero because there is always some juice.

f. 320 ounce

Chapter 11 Review Exercises **1.** Yes **3.** No **5.** No **7.** $0, \dfrac{3}{2}$ **9.** $2, i, -i$ **11.** $\dfrac{5 \pm \sqrt{17}}{4}$

13.

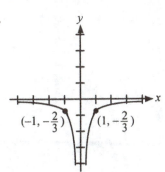

15.

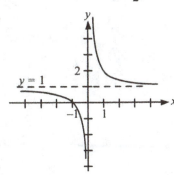

17.

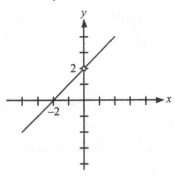

19.

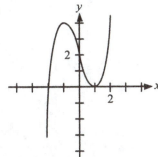

21.

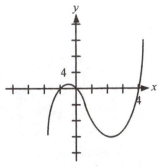

23. $x = 0, x = -2$ **25.** For $x \neq 2$, the same straight line is the graph for both functions. At $x = 2$ the graph of $y = x + 2$ contains the point $(2, 4)$. Since $\dfrac{x^2 - 4}{x - 2}$ is undefined at $x = 2$, the graph of this function shows an open circle at $(2, 4)$.

27. $P(x) = x(x - 5)(x + 2)(x - 3)$

29. $2x^4 - x + 7 = (x^2 + 2)(2x^2 - 4) + (-x + 15)$

31. $\pm 2, \pm 1, \pm \dfrac{2}{3}, \pm \dfrac{1}{3}$ **33.** $\pm \sqrt{3}$ **35.** 0 is a zero of multiplicity 3; -2 is a zero of multiplicity 2. **37.** Since b is a zero, $P(b) = b^3 + ab^2 + ab + 1 = 0$. Then, $P\left(\dfrac{1}{b}\right) = \dfrac{1}{b^3} + \dfrac{1}{b^2} + \dfrac{a}{b} + 1 = \dfrac{1 + ab + ab^2 + b^3}{b^3} = \dfrac{0}{b^3} = 0$

39. $P(3) = -1$ and $P(4) = 15$. Since $P(3)$ and $P(4)$ have opposite signs, the location theorem guarantees at least one real zero between 3 and 4. **41.** b **43.** b **45.** d **47.** a **49.** a

Chapter 11 Test **1.** True **2.** Degree 7 **3.** $P(x) = (x + 2)(x + 1)(x - 4)$ **4.** Translate the graph of $y = x^4$ right 3 units and up 2 units. **5.** $P(-1) = 3, P(-2) = -7$; since $P(-1)$ and $P(-2)$ have opposite signs, the location guarantees at least one real zero between -1 and -2. **6.** False **7.** $\dfrac{x^3 - 1}{x^2 + x} = x - 1 + \dfrac{x - 1}{x^2 + x}$ **8.** $-3x + 32$ **9.** $2x^3 - 6x^2 + 17x - 51$

10. a. -13 **b.** -13 **11.** 0 is a zero of multiplicity 2; -1 is a zero of multiplicity 3.

12.

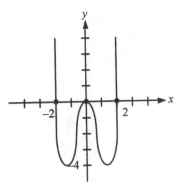

13. $\pm \sqrt{6}$ **14.** $\pm 2, \pm 1, \pm \dfrac{2}{3}, \pm \dfrac{1}{3}$ **15.** 1 **16.** $-\dfrac{3}{2}, \pm i\sqrt{3}$ **17.** $x = 0, x = 6$

18. $(2, 0), (-2, 0)$ **19.** $y = x - 2$ **20.**

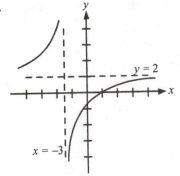

Index

Trigonometry

General Angle Definitions
If θ is an angle in standard position, and if (x, y) is any point on the terminal ray of θ [except $(0, 0)$], then

$$\sin\theta = \frac{y}{r} \leftarrow \text{reciprocals} \rightarrow \csc\theta = \frac{r}{y}$$

$$\cos\theta = \frac{x}{r} \leftarrow \text{reciprocals} \rightarrow \sec\theta = \frac{r}{x}$$

$$\tan\theta = \frac{y}{x} \leftarrow \text{reciprocals} \rightarrow \cot\theta = \frac{x}{y}.$$

Note: $r = \sqrt{x^2 + y^2}$

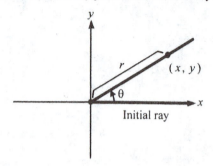

Initial ray

Unit Circle Definitions
Consider a point (x, y) on the unit circle $x^2 + y^2 = 1$ at arc length s from $(1, 0)$. Then

$$\sin s = y \leftarrow \text{reciprocals} \rightarrow \csc s = \frac{1}{y}$$

$$\cos s = x \leftarrow \text{reciprocals} \rightarrow \sec s = \frac{1}{x}$$

$$\tan s = \frac{y}{x} \leftarrow \text{reciprocals} \rightarrow \cot s = \frac{x}{y}.$$

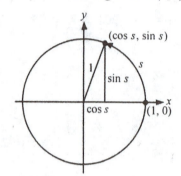

Right Triangle Definitions
If θ is an acute angle in a right triangle, as shown below, then

$$\sin\theta = \frac{\text{opposite}}{\text{hypotenuse}} \leftarrow \text{reciprocals} \rightarrow \csc\theta = \frac{\text{hypotenuse}}{\text{opposite}}$$

$$\cos\theta = \frac{\text{adjacent}}{\text{hypotenuse}} \leftarrow \text{reciprocals} \rightarrow \sec\theta = \frac{\text{hypotenuse}}{\text{adjacent}}$$

$$\tan\theta = \frac{\text{opposite}}{\text{adjacent}} \leftarrow \text{reciprocals} \rightarrow \cot\theta = \frac{\text{adjacent}}{\text{opposite}}.$$

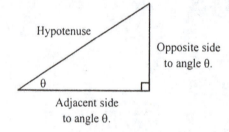

Hypotenuse

Opposite side to angle θ.

Adjacent side to angle θ.

Signs of the Trigonometric Ratios

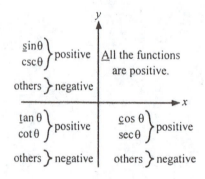